HISTORY & GEOGRAPHY 800
Teacher's Guide

Author:

Teresa Busky, B.A., J.D.

Editor:

Alan Christopherson, M.S.

804 N. 2nd Ave. E.
Rock Rapids, IA 51246-1759

HISTORY & GEOGRAPHY 800

LIFEPAC® Overview

HISTORY & GEOGRAPHY SCOPE & SEQUENCE

	Your World (Grade 1)	U.S. History (Grade 2)	U.S. Geography and History (Grade 3)
Unit 1	I AM A SPECIAL PERSON • God made me • You are God's child • All about you • Using proper manners	LOOKING BACK Remembering last year Learning about early times The trail of the Native Americans Symbols and historic places	U.S. GEOGRAPHY AND HISTORY STUDY SKILLS • Map skills • Resources • Community
Unit 2	LET'S COMMUNICATE • Sounds people make • Sounds that communicate • Communicating without sound • Communicating with God	SETTLING THE NEW WORLD The first settlers Colonies of the new world War for Independence Symbols and historical places	NEW ENGLAND STATES • ME, NH, VT, MA, RI, and CT • New England geography • New England resources • New England community
Unit 3	I HAVE FEELINGS • I feel sad • I feel afraid • I feel happy • I have other feelings	A NEW GOVERNMENT FOR A NEW COUNTRY A study of government Creating a government Our government Symbols and historical places	MID-ATLANTIC STATES • NY, PA, NJ, DE, MD, and DC • Mid-Atlantic geography • Mid-Atlantic resources • Mid-Atlantic community
Unit 4	I LIVE IN A FAMILY • My mother and father • My brothers and sisters • My grandparents • What my family does	GOVERNMENT UNDER THE CONSTITUTION Article One -- The Legislative Branch Article Two -- The Executive Branch Article Three -- The Judicial Branch The Bill of Rights -- Symbols and historical places	SOUTHERN-ATLANTIC STATES • WV, VA, NC, SC, GA, and FL • Southern Atlantic geography • Southern Atlantic resources • Southern Atlantic community
Unit 5	YOU BELONG TO FAMILIES • Getting ready in the morning • Walking to school • The school family • The church family	OUR GOVERNMENT CLOSE TO HOME Our state governments Our local governments Citizens of the United States Symbols and historical places	SOUTHERN STATES • KY, TN, MS, LA, AL, OK, TX, and AR • Southern geography • Southern resources • Southern community
Unit 6	PLACES PEOPLE LIVE • Life on the farm • Life in the city • Life by the sea	WESTWARD -- FROM THE ORIGINAL COLONIES The United States grows The Lewis and Clark Expedition The Old Southwest Symbols and historical places	GREAT LAKES STATES • OH, IN, IL, MI, WI, and MN • Great Lakes geography • Great Lakes resources • Great Lakes community
Unit 7	COMMUNITY HELPERS • Firefighters and police officers • Doctors • City workers • Teachers and ministers	SETTLING THE FRONTIER The Texas frontier Westward expansion Meet America's pioneers Symbols and historical places	MIDWESTERN STATES • ND, SD, NE, KS, MO, and IA • Midwestern geography • Midwestern resources • Midwestern community
Unit 8	I LOVE MY COUNTRY • America discovered • The Pilgrims • The United States begins • Respect for your country	EXPLORING AMERICA WITH MAPS Directions on a map Reading roads and symbols Natural features Symbols and historical places	MOUNTAIN STATES • MT, ID, WY, NV, UT, CO, AZ, and NM • Mountain geography • Mountain resources • Mountain community
Unit 9	I LIVE IN THE WORLD • The globe • Countries • Friends in Mexico • Friends in Japan	PAST, PRESENT, AND FUTURE MAPS City maps Building maps History of maps Symbols and historical places	PACIFIC STATES • WA, OR, CA, AK, and HI • Pacific geography • Pacific resources • Pacific community
Unit 10	THE WORLD AND YOU • You are special • Your family • Your school and church • Your world	REVIEW UNITED STATES HISTORY The United States begins Creating a government Mapping the United States	U.S. GEOGRAPHY AND HISTORY REVIEW • U.S. geographical features • Eastern U.S. review • Western U.S. review

HISTORY & GEOGRAPHY SCOPE & SEQUENCE

World Geography and Culture (Grade 4)	U.S. History (Grade 5)	Civilizations (Grade 6)	
OUR EARTH • The surface of the Earth • Early explorations of the Earth • Exploring from space • Exploring the oceans	**A NEW WORLD** • Exploration of America • The first colonies • Conflict with Britain • Birth of the United States	**WORLD GEOGRAPHY** • Latitude and longitude • Western and eastern hemispheres • The southern hemisphere • Political and cultural regions	Unit 1
SEAPORT CITIES • Sydney • Hong Kong • Istanbul • London	**A NEW NATION** • War for Independence • Life in America • A new form of government • The nation's early years	**THE CRADLE OF CIVILIZATION** • Mesopotamia • The land of Israel • The nation of Israel • Egypt	Unit 2
DESERT LANDS • What is a desert? • Where are the deserts? • How do people live in the desert?	**A TIME OF TESTING** • Louisiana Purchase • War of 1812 • Sectionalism • Improvements in trade and travel	**THE CIVILIZATIONS OF GREECE AND ROME** • Geography of the region • Beginning civilizations • Contributions to other civilizations • The influence of Christianity	Unit 3
GRASSLANDS • Grasslands of the world • Ukraine • Kenya • Argentina	**A GROWING NATION** • Andrew Jackson's influence • Texas and Oregon • Mexican War • The nation divides	**LIFE IN THE MIDDLE AGES** • The feudal system • Books and schools • The Crusades • Trade and architecture	Unit 4
TROPICAL RAINFORESTS • Facts about rainforests • Rainforests of the world • The Amazon rainforest • The Congo rainforest	**A DIVIDED NATION** • Civil War • Reconstruction • Gilded Age • The need for reform	**SIX SOUTH AMERICAN COUNTRIES** • Brazil • Colombia • Venezuela • Three Guianas	Unit 5
THE POLAR REGIONS • The polar regions: coldest places in the world • The Arctic polar region • The Antarctic polar region	**A CHANGING NATION** • Progressive reforms • Spanish-American War • World War I • Roaring Twenties	**OTHER SOUTH AMERICAN COUNTRIES** • Ecuador and Peru • Bolivia and Uruguay • Paraguay and Argentina • Chile	Unit 6
MOUNTAIN COUNTRIES • Peru — the Andes • The Incas and modern Peru • Nepal — the Himalayas • Switzerland — the Alps	**DEPRESSION AND WAR** • The Great Depression • War begins in Europe • War in Europe • War in the Pacific	**AFRICA** • Geography and cultures • Countries of northern Africa • Countries of central Africa • Countries of southern Africa	Unit 7
ISLAND COUNTRIES • Islands of the Earth • Cuba • Iceland • Japan	**COLD WAR** • Korean War and other crises • Vietnam War • Civil Rights movement • Upheaval in America	**MODERN WESTERN EUROPE** • The Renaissance • The Industrial Revolution • World War I • World War II	Unit 8
NORTH AMERICA • Geography • Lands, lakes, and rivers • Northern countries • Southern countries	**INTO THE NEW MILLENNIUM** • Watergate and détente • The fall of communism • The Persian Gulf • Issues of the new millennium	**MODERN EASTERN EUROPE** • Early government • Early churches • Early countries • Modern countries	Unit 9
OUR WORLD IN REVIEW • Europe and the explorers • Asia and Africa • Southern continents • North America and the North Pole	**THE UNITED STATES OF AMERICA** • Beginning America until 1830 • Stronger America 1830-1930 • 1930 to the end of the millennium • The new millennium	**DEVELOPMENT OF OUR WORLD** • Cradle of civilization • The Middle Ages • Modern Europe • South America and Africa	Unit 10

HISTORY & GEOGRAPHY SCOPE & SEQUENCE

Anthropology, Sociology, Economics, and State History (Grade 7)	U.S. History (Grade 8)	Civics and World Geography (Grade 9)
Unit 1 WHAT IS HISTORY? • Definition and significance of history • Historians and the historical method • Views of history	EUROPE COMES TO AMERICA • Voyages of Columbus • Spanish exploration • Other exploration • The first colonies	HERITAGE OF THE UNITED STATES • American colonies • Acquisitions and annexations • Backgrounds to freedom • Backgrounds to society
Unit 2 WHAT IS GEOGRAPHY? • Classes of geography • Geography and relief of the Earth • Maps and the study of our world • Time zones	BRITISH AMERICA • English colonies • Government • Lifestyle • Wars with France	OUR NATIONAL GOVERNMENT • Ideals of national government • National government developed • Legislative and executive branches • Judicial branch
Unit 3 U.S. HISTORY AND GEOGRAPHY • Geography of the United States • Early history of the United States • Physical regions of the United States • Cultural regions of the United States	THE AMERICAN REVOLUTION • British control • Rebellion of the colonies • War for independence • Constitution	STATE AND LOCAL GOVERNMENT • Powers of state government • County government • Township government • City government
Unit 4 ANTHROPOLOGY • Understanding anthropology • The unity of man • The diversity of man • The culture of man	A FIRM FOUNDATION • Washington's presidency • Adams' administration • Jeffersonian Democracy • War of 1812	PLANNING A CAREER • Definition of a career • God's will concerning a career • Selecting a career • Preparation for a career
Unit 5 SOCIOLOGY — MAN IN GROUPS • Sociology defined • Historical development • Importance to Christians • Method of sociology	A GROWING NATION • Jacksonian Era • Northern border • Southern border • Industrial Revolution	CITIZENSHIP • Citizenship defined • Gaining citizenship • Rights of citizenship • Responsibilities of citizenship
Unit 6 U.S. ANTHROPOLOGY AND SOCIOLOGY • Cultural background of the United States • Native American cultures • Cultures from distant lands • Cultural and social interaction	THE CIVIL WAR • Division and secession • Civil War • Death of Lincoln • Reconstruction	THE EARTH AND MAN • Man inhabits the Earth • Man's home on the Earth • Man develops the Earth • The future of the Earth
Unit 7 ECONOMICS — RESOURCES AND NEED • Economics defined • Methods of the economist • Tools of the economist • An experiment in economy	GILDED AGE TO PROGRESSIVE ERA • Rise of industry • Wild West • America as a world power • Progressive era	REGIONS OF THE WORLD • A region defined • Geographic and climate regions • Cultural and political regions • Economic regions of Europe
Unit 8 POLITICAL SCIENCE • Definition of political science • Roots of Western thought • Modern political thinkers • Political theory	A WORLD IN CONFLICT • World War I • Great Depression • New Deal • World War II	MAN AND HIS ENVIRONMENT • The physical environment • Drug abuse • The social environment • Man's responsibilities
Unit 9 STATE ECONOMICS AND POLITICS • Background of state government • State government • State finance • State politics	COLD WAR AMERICA • Origins of the Cold War • Vietnam • Truman to Nixon • Ending of the Cold War	TOOLS OF THE GEOGRAPHER • The globe • Types of maps • Reading maps • The Earth in symbol form
Unit 10 SOCIAL SCIENCES REVIEW • History and geography • Anthropology • Sociology • Economics and politics	RECENT AMERICA AND REVIEW • Europe to independence • Colonies to the Civil War • Civil War to World War II • World War II through the Cold War	MAN IN A CHANGING WORLD • Development of the nation • Development of government • Development of the Earth • Solving problems

HISTORY & GEOGRAPHY SCOPE & SEQUENCE

World History (Grade 10)	American History (Grade 11)	Government and Economics (Grade 12)	
ANCIENT CIVILIZATIONS 1 • Origin of civilization • Early Egypt • Assyria and Babylonia • Persian civilization	FOUNDATION OF THE REPUBLIC • Democracy develops • Virginia • New England colonies • Middle and southern colonies	INTERNATIONAL GOVERNMENTS • Why have governments? • Types of governments • Governments in our world • Political thinkers	Unit 1
ANCIENT CIVILIZATIONS 2 • India • China • Greek civilization • Roman Empire	DEVELOPMENT OF CONSTITUTIONAL GOVERNMENT • Relations with England • The Revolutionary War • Articles of Confederation • Constitution of the United States	UNITED STATES GOVERNMENT • U.S. Constitution • Bill of Rights • Three branches of government • Legislative process	Unit 2
THE MEDIEVAL WORLD • Early Middle Ages • Middle Ages in transition • High Middle Ages	NATIONAL EXPANSION • A strong federal government • Revolution of 1800 • War of 1812 • Nationalism and sectionalism	AMERICAN PARTY SYSTEM • American party system • Development of political parties • Functions of political parties • Voting	Unit 3
RENAISSANCE AND REFORMATION • Changes in government and art • Changes in literature and thought • Advances in science • Reform within the church	A NATION DIVIDED • Issues of division • Division of land and people • Economics of slavery • Politics of slavery	HISTORY OF GOVERNMENTS • Primitive governments • Beginnings of democracy • Feudalism, theocracy, and democracy • Fascism and Nazism	Unit 4
GROWTH OF WORLD EMPIRES • England and France • Portugal and Spain • Austria and Germany • Italy and the Ottoman Empire	A NATION DIVIDED AND UNITED • Regionalism • The division • The Civil War • Reconstruction	THE CHRISTIAN AND HIS GOVERNMENT • Discrimination and the Christian • Christian attitudes • Public opinion and truth in politics • Politics and propaganda	Unit 5
THE AGE OF REVOLUTION • Factors leading to revolution • The English Revolution • The American Revolution • The French Revolution	U.S. INVOLVEMENT AT HOME AND ABROAD • Surge of industry • The industrial lifestyle • Isolationism • Involvement in conflict	FREE ENTERPRISE • Economics • Competition • Money through history • International finance and currency	Unit 6
THE INDUSTRIAL REVOLUTION • Sparks of preparation • Industrial Revolution in England • Industrial Revolution in America • Social changes of the revolution	THE SEARCH FOR PEACE • World War I and its aftermath • The Golden Twenties • The Great Depression • The New Deal	BUSINESS AND YOU • Running a business • Government and business • Banks and mergers • Deregulation and bankruptcy	Unit 7
TWO WORLD WARS • Mounting tension • World War I • Peace and power quests • World War II	A NATION AT WAR • Causes of the war • World War II • Korean conflict • Vietnam conflict	THE STOCK MARKET • How it started and works • Selecting stocks • Types of stocks • Tracking stocks	Unit 8
THE 20TH CENTURY AFTER 1945 • The Cold War • Korean War and Vietnam War • Collapse of the Soviet Union • The 20th century closes	CONTEMPORARY AMERICA • America in the 1960s • America in the 1970s • America in the 1980s and 1990s • International scene of the 1980s and 1990s	BUDGET AND FINANCE • Cash, credit, and checking • Buying a car • Grants, loans, and IRAs • Savings and eCash	Unit 9
ANCIENT TIMES TO THE 21ST CENTURY • Ancient civilizations • Medieval times • Renaissance and Reformation • Revolutions and Globalization	UNITED STATES HISTORY • Basis of democracy • The 1800s • Industrialization • Current history	GEOGRAPHY • Euro and International finance • U.S. geography • The global traveler • Neighbors, heroes, and the Holy Land	Unit 10

STRUCTURE OF THE LIFEPAC CURRICULUM

The LIFEPAC curriculum is conveniently structured to provide one Teacher's Guide containing teacher support material with answer keys and ten student worktexts for each subject at grade levels 2 through 12. The worktext format of the LIFEPACs allows the student to read the textual information and complete workbook activities all in the same booklet. The easy-to-follow LIFEPAC numbering system lists the grade as the first number(s) and the last two digits as the number of the series. For example, the Language Arts LIFEPAC at the 6th grade level, 5th book in the series would be LAN0605.

Each LIFEPAC is divided into three to five sections and begins with an introduction or overview of the booklet as well as a series of specific learning objectives to give a purpose to the study of the LIFEPAC. The introduction and objectives are followed by a vocabulary section which may be found at the beginning of each section at the lower levels or in the glossary at the high school level. Vocabulary words are used to develop word recognition and should not be confused with the spelling words introduced later in the LIFEPAC. The student should learn all vocabulary words before working the LIFEPAC sections to improve comprehension, retention, and reading skills.

Each activity or written assignment in grades 2 through 12 has a number for easy identification, such as 1.1. The first number corresponds to the LIFEPAC section and the number to the right of the decimal is the number of the activity.

Teacher checkpoints, which are essential to maintain quality learning, are found at various locations throughout the LIFEPAC.

The teacher should check 1) neatness of work and penmanship, 2) quality of understanding (tested with a short oral quiz), 3) thoroughness of answers (complete sentences and paragraphs, correct spelling, etc.), 4) completion of activities (no blank spaces), and 5) accuracy of answers as compared to the answer key (all answers correct).

The self test questions in grades 2 through 12 are also number coded for easy reference. For example, 2.015 means that this is the 15th question in the self test of Section 2. The first number corresponds to the LIFEPAC section, the zero indicates that it is a self test question, and the number to the right of the zero the question number.

The LIFEPAC test is packaged at the center of each LIFEPAC. It should be removed and put aside before giving the booklet to the student for study.

Answer and test keys in grades 2 through 12 have the same numbering system as the LIFEPACs. The student may be given access to the answer keys (not the test keys) under teacher supervision so that they can score their own work.

A thorough study of the Scope & Sequence by the teacher before instruction begins is essential to the success of the student. The teacher should become familiar with expected skill mastery and understand how these grade-level skills fit into the overall skill development of the curriculum. The teacher should also preview the objectives that appear at the beginning of each LIFEPAC for additional preparation and planning.

TEST SCORING AND GRADING

Answer keys and test keys give examples of correct answers. They convey the idea, but the student may use many ways to express a correct answer. The teacher should check for the essence of the answer, not for the exact wording. Many questions are high level and require thinking and creativity on the part of the student. Each answer should be scored based on whether or not the main idea written by the student matches the model example. "Any Order" or "Either Order" in a key indicates that no particular order is necessary to be correct.

Most self tests and LIFEPAC tests at the lower elementary levels are scored at 1 point per answer; however, the upper levels may have a point system awarding 2 to 5 points for various answers or questions. Further, the total test points will vary; they may not always equal 100 points. They may be 78, 85, 100, 105, etc.

Example 1

Example 2

A score box similar to ex. 1 above is located at the end of each self test and on the front of the LIFEPAC test. The bottom score, 72, represents the total number of points possible on the test. The upper score, 58, represents the number of points your student will need to receive an 80% or passing grade. If you wish to establish the exact percentage that your student has achieved, find the total points of their correct answers and divide it by the bottom number (in this case 72). For example, if your student has a point total of 65, divide 65 by 72 for a grade of 90%. Referring to ex. 2, on a test with a total of 105 possible points, the student would have to receive a minimum of 84 correct points for an 80% or passing grade. If your student has received 93 points, simply divide the 93 by 105 for a percentage grade of 89%. Students who receive a score below 80% should review the LIFEPAC and retest using the appropriate Alternate Test found in the Teacher's Guide.

The following is a guideline to assign letter grades for completed LIFEPACs based on a maximum total score of 100 points.

Example:

LIFEPAC Test	=	60% of the Total Score (or percent grade)
Self Test	=	25% of the Total Score (average percent of self tests)
Reports	=	10% or 10* points per LIFEPAC
Oral Work	=	5% or 5* points per LIFEPAC

*Determined by the teacher's subjective evaluation of the student's daily work.

Example:

LIFEPAC Test Score	= 92%	92 × .60	=	55 points
Self Test Average	= 90%	90 × .25	=	23 points
Reports			=	8 points
Oral Work			=	4 points
TOTAL POINTS			=	90 points

Grade Scale based on point system:

100 – 94	=	A
93 – 86	=	B
85 – 77	=	C
76 – 70	=	D
Below 70	=	F

TEACHER GUIDANCE AND STUDYING TECHNIQUES

LIFEPAC activities are written to check the level of understanding of the preceding text. The student may look back to the text as necessary to complete these activities; however, a student should never attempt to do the activities without reading (studying) the text first. Self tests and LIFEPAC tests are never open book tests.

Language arts activities (skill integration) often appear within other subject curriculum. The purpose is to give the student an opportunity to test their skill mastery outside of the context in which it was presented.

Writing complete answers (paragraphs) to some questions is an integral part of the LIFEPAC curriculum in all subjects. This builds communication and organization skills, increases understanding and retention of ideas, and helps enforce good penmanship. Complete sentences should be encouraged for this type of activity. Obviously, single words or phrases do not meet the intent of the activity, since multiple lines are given for the response.

Review is essential to student success. Time invested in review where review is suggested will be time saved in correcting errors later. Self tests, unlike the section activities, are closed book. This procedure helps to identify weaknesses before they become too great to overcome. Certain objectives from self tests are cumulative and test previous sections; therefore, good preparation for a self test must include all material studied up to that testing point.

The following procedure checklist has been found to be successful in developing good study habits in the LIFEPAC curriculum.

1. Read the introduction and Table of Contents.
2. Read the objectives.
3. Recite and study the entire vocabulary (glossary) list.
4. Study each section as follows:
   a. Read the introduction and study the section objectives.
   b. Read all the text for the entire section, but answer none of the activities.
   c. Return to the beginning of the section and memorize each vocabulary word and definition.
   d. Reread the section, complete the activities, check the answers with the answer key, correct all errors, and have the teacher check.
   e. Read the self test but do not answer the questions.
   f. Go to the beginning of the first section and reread the text and answers to the activities up to the self test you have not yet done.
   g. Answer the questions to the self test without looking back.
   h. Have the self test checked by the teacher.
   i. Correct the self test and have the teacher check the corrections.
   j. Repeat steps a–i for each section.
5. Use the **SQ3R** method to prepare for the LIFEPAC test.
   Scan the whole LIFEPAC.
   Question yourself on the objectives.
   Read the whole LIFEPAC again.
   Recite through an oral examination.
   Review weak areas.
6. Take the LIFEPAC test as a closed book test.
7. LIFEPAC tests are administered and scored under direct teacher supervision. Students who receive scores below 80% should review the LIFEPAC using the **SQ3R** study method and take the Alternate Test located in the Teacher's Guide. The final test grade may be the grade on the Alternate Test or an average of the grades from the original LIFEPAC test and the Alternate Test.

GOAL SETTING AND SCHEDULES

Each school must develop its own schedule, because no single set of procedures will fit every situation. The following is an example of a daily schedule that includes the five LIFEPAC subjects as well as time slotted for special activities.

Possible Daily Schedule

8:15 – 8:25	Pledges, prayer, songs, devotions, etc.
8:25 – 9:10	Bible
9:10 – 9:55	Language Arts
9:55 – 10:15	Recess (juice break)
10:15 – 11:00	Math
11:00 – 11:45	History & Geography
11:45 – 12:30	Lunch, recess, quiet time
12:30 – 1:15	Science
1:15 –	Drill, remedial work, enrichment*

*Enrichment: *Computer time, physical education, field trips, fun reading, games and puzzles, family business, hobbies, resource persons, guests, crafts, creative work, electives, music appreciation, projects.*

Basically, two factors need to be considered when assigning work to a student in the LIFEPAC curriculum.

The first is time. An average of 45 minutes should be devoted to each subject, each day. Remember, this is only an average. Because of extenuating circumstances, a student may spend only 15 minutes on a subject one day and the next day spend 90 minutes on the same subject.

The second factor is the number of pages to be worked in each subject. A single LIFEPAC is designed to take three to four weeks to complete. Allowing about three to four days for LIFEPAC introduction, review, and tests, the student has approximately 15 days to complete the LIFEPAC pages. Simply take the number of pages in the LIFEPAC, divide it by 15 and you will have the number of pages that must be completed on a daily basis to keep the student on schedule. For example, a LIFEPAC containing 45 pages will require three completed pages per day. Again, this is only an average. While working a 45-page LIFEPAC, the student may complete only one page the first day if the text has a lot of activities or reports, but go on to complete five pages the next day.

Long-range planning requires some organization. Because the traditional school year originates in the early fall of one year and continues to late spring of the following year, a calendar should be devised that covers this period of time. Approximate beginning and completion dates can be noted on the calendar as well as special occasions such as holidays, vacations and birthdays. Since each LIFEPAC takes three to four weeks or 18 days to complete, it should take about 180 school days to finish a set of ten LIFEPACs. Starting at the beginning school date, mark off 18 school days on the calendar and that will become the targeted completion date for the first LIFEPAC. Continue marking the calendar until you have established dates for the remaining nine LIFEPACs making adjustments for previously noted holidays and vacations. If all five subjects are being used, the ten established target dates should be the same for the LIFEPACs in each subject.

TEACHING SUPPLEMENTS

The sample weekly lesson plan and student grading sheet forms are included in this section as teacher support materials and may be duplicated at the convenience of the teacher.

The student grading sheet is provided for those who desire to follow the suggested guidelines for assignment of letter grades as previously discussed. The student's self test scores should be posted as percentage grades. When the LIFEPAC is completed the teacher should average the self test grades, multiply the average by .25 and post the points in the box marked self test points. The LIFEPAC percentage grade should be multiplied by .60 and posted. Next, the teacher should award and post points for written reports and oral work. A report may be any type of written work assigned to the student whether it is a LIFEPAC or additional learning activity. Oral work includes the student's ability to respond orally to questions which may or may not be related to LIFEPAC activities or any type of oral report assigned by the teacher. The points may then be totaled and a final grade entered along with the date that the LIFEPAC was completed.

The Student Record Book, which was specifically designed for use with the Alpha Omega curriculum, provides space to record weekly progress for one student over a nine-week period as well as a place to post self test and LIFEPAC scores. The Student Record Books are available through the current Alpha Omega catalog; however, unlike the enclosed forms these books are not for duplication and should be purchased in sets of four to cover a full academic year.

WEEKLY LESSON PLANNER

Week of:

	Subject	Subject	Subject	Subject
Monday				
Tuesday				
	Subject	Subject	Subject	Subject
Wednesday				
	Subject	Subject	Subject	Subject
Thursday				
	Subject	Subject	Subject	Subject
Friday				

WEEKLY LESSON PLANNER

Week of:

	Subject	Subject	Subject	Subject
Monday				
Tuesday	Subject	Subject	Subject	Subject
Wednesday	Subject	Subject	Subject	Subject
Thursday	Subject	Subject	Subject	Subject
Friday	Subject	Subject	Subject	Subject

Student Name _____   Year _____

Bible

LP	Self Test Scores by Sections					Self Test Points	LIFEPAC Test	Oral Points	Report Points	Final Grade	Date
	1	2	3	4	5						
01											
02											
03											
04											
05											
06											
07											
08											
09											
10											

History & Geography

LP	Self Test Scores by Sections					Self Test Points	LIFEPAC Test	Oral Points	Report Points	Final Grade	Date
	1	2	3	4	5						
01											
02											
03											
04											
05											
06											
07											
08											
09											
10											

Language Arts

LP	Self Test Scores by Sections					Self Test Points	LIFEPAC Test	Oral Points	Report Points	Final Grade	Date
	1	2	3	4	5						
01											
02											
03											
04											
05											
06											
07											
08											
09											
10											

Student Name _____   Year _____

Math

LP	Self Test Scores by Sections 1	2	3	4	5	Self Test Points	LIFEPAC Test	Oral Points	Report Points	Final Grade	Date
01											
02											
03											
04											
05											
06											
07											
08											
09											
10											

Science

LP	Self Test Scores by Sections 1	2	3	4	5	Self Test Points	LIFEPAC Test	Oral Points	Report Points	Final Grade	Date
01											
02											
03											
04											
05											
06											
07											
08											
09											
10											

Spelling/Electives

LP	Self Test Scores by Sections 1	2	3	4	5	Self Test Points	LIFEPAC Test	Oral Points	Report Points	Final Grade	Date
01											
02											
03											
04											
05											
06											
07											
08											
09											
10											

INSTRUCTIONS FOR HISTORY & GEOGRAPHY

The LIFEPAC curriculum from grades 2 through 12 is structured so that the daily instructional material is written directly into the LIFEPACs. The student is encouraged to read and follow this instructional material in order to develop independent study habits. The teacher should introduce the LIFEPAC to the student, set a required completion schedule, complete teacher checks, be available for questions regarding both content and procedures, administer and grade tests, and develop additional learning activities as desired. Teachers working with several students may schedule their time so that students are assigned to a quiet work activity when it is necessary to spend instructional time with one particular student.

The Teacher Notes section of the Teacher's Guide lists the required or suggested materials for the LIFEPACs and provides additional learning activities for the students. The materials section refers only to LIFEPAC materials and does not include materials which may be needed for the additional activities. Additional learning activities provide a change from the daily school routine, encourage the student's interest in learning and may be used as a reward for good study habits.

HISTORY & GEOGRAPHY 801

Unit 1: Europe Comes to America

TEACHER NOTES

MATERIALS NEEDED FOR LIFEPAC	
Required	Suggested
None	• atlas • world globe • encyclopedia • reference books or online sources

ADDITIONAL LEARNING ACTIVITIES

Section 1: Quest and Conquest

1. Discuss these questions.

    a. What did Western Civilization get from Greece? from Rome? from Judaism? from Christianity?

    b. Why was Prince Henry's work so revolutionary?

    c. What kind of man was Columbus? a hero? an opportunist? a fool?

2. Assign a class or individual project on spices for students to find out which were important, where they came from, and how they were used. Have groups/individuals do a report.

3. Assign a research project and a report or paper on the Viking exploration of America.

4. Different students should read about the lives of different *conquistadors*. Each should make a brief report to the class. As a class, draw some conclusions. What kind of men were they?

5. As a class, map out Magellan's trip around the world. Discuss what the circumstances would be like for the sailors at different points on the journey.

6. Discuss this question: Could the Aztec and Inca Empires have defeated the Spanish? If so, how?

Section 2: The Chase

1. Discuss the circumstances in England that hindered exploration between 1490 and 1600.

2. Assign students to research and do a report or paper on the life of Francis Drake.

3. Ask students to research and do a report or paper on the Grand Banks.

4. Discuss what life would have been like on a ship exploring the New World in the late 1400s and early 1500s.

5. Have students create an ending for the story of Henry Hudson's life after he was marooned.

6. Discuss what drove the people of the 15th and 16th centuries to explore the earth, and compare it with space exploration (in the present and potential exploration in the future).

7. Different students should read about the lives of Cartier, Champlain, Jolliet, Marquette, and LaSalle. Have them give a brief report to the class. As a class, draw some conclusions. What kind of men were they?

8. Discuss the morality of the European custom of claiming for themselves any lands they "discovered."

Section 3: The First Colonies

1. Each student or group of students should assume the role of a person in a Spanish colony— enslaved person, member of the lower class, Spanish nobleman, etc. Have each student discuss what their 'role' is in society in the 1500s. Follow the same process for the French, Dutch, and English colonies.

2. As a class, discuss how life was different in Spanish, Dutch, French, and English colonies as well as how it was similar.

3. Every student should write their own story about what happened to the Lost Colony. Have students read them in class and discuss which is the most likely and the least likely.

4. As a class, discuss what life was like for the colonists in the early years of Jamestown.

5. Discuss what it must have been like for Pocahontas to go to England.

6. Discuss the long-term effects of the three major events of 1619 at Jamestown (the arrival of women and enslaved people, the founding of the House of Burgesses). Which was the most important event and why?

7. Discuss why the Native Americans would help the colonists and why they would fight them.

8. Discuss whether the Native Americans could have stopped European colonization of North America. If so, how?

Administer the LIFEPAC Test

The test is to be administered in one session. Give no help except with directions.
Evaluate the tests and review areas where the students have done poorly.
Review the pages and activities that stress the concepts tested.
If necessary, administer the Alternate LIFEPAC Test.

ANSWER KEYS

SECTION 1

1.1   Any order:
    a. Rome
    b. Greece
    c. Jews
    d. Christianity

1.2   Asia, across the Bering Strait

1.3   Either order:
    a. Crusades
    b. Marco Polo's book

1.4   Trade from the contact with Asia led to improved ships, education, larger cities, and stronger governments.

1.5   AD 476, Medieval

1.6   Roman Catholic Church

1.7   Seljuk Turks

1.8   China

1.9   Any order:
    a. long trade routes over land and sea
    b. land routes controlled by Muslims
    c. Italian monopoly on the trade

1.10   Either order:
    a. find the source of African gold
    b. find a route to Asia

1.11   false
    — change *Spain* to *Portugal*

1.12   true

1.13   false
    — change *alchemy* to *geography*

1.14   true

1.15   false
    — change *Bartholomeu Diaz* to *Vasco da Gama*

1.16   true

1.17   Genoa

1.18   west

1.19   half

1.20   Any order:
    Portugal, France, England

1.21   Any order:
    Ferdinand, Isabella

1.22   Muslim, Granada

1.23   Any order:
    Niña, *Pinta*, *Santa Maria*

1.24   He believed his own experts who said the earth was larger than Columbus' estimates and he did not want to grant the explorer's demands for himself.

1.25   Either order:
    a. on the island of Hispaniola
    b. Columbus

1.26   four

1.27   Yes, Central America is part of North America.

1.28   Amerigo Vespucci

1.29   that they were in or near Asia

1.30   Vikings under Leif Ericson

1.31   It established permanent contact between the Americas and Europe.

1.32   Ponce de León

1.33   Balboa

1.34   Ponce de León

1.35   Magellan

1.36   Coronado

1.37   Pizarro

1.38   Magellan

1.39   De Soto

1.40   Cortes

1.41   Coronado

1.42   De Soto

1.43   Spain and Portugal

1.44   to divide the non-Christian lands of the world "fairly" between the two

1.45   Line of Demarcation

1.46   They were soldiers and noblemen who came to get rich.
They explored, mapped, and conquered much of the Americas for Spain.

1.47   Any order:
    a. America was a long way from Asia
    b. the world is a sphere

1.48   Any order:
    a. Spain concentrated its attention on Mexico and South America
    b. the treasure excited the interest of the other nations of Europe

1.49   Teacher check

SELF TEST 1

1.01   d
1.02   e
1.03   j
1.04   f
1.05   c
1.06   g
1.07   i
1.08   h
1.09   b
1.010   a
1.011   The Treaty was an agreement between Spain and Portugal to divide the newly discovered non-Christian lands of the world between them.
1.012   The Crusades were a series of campaigns to capture the Holy Land from the Turks. They brought Europe into contact with the goods and science of Asia which increased trade and knowledge in Europe.
1.013   The long route on land and sea was controlled on land by the Muslims and in Europe monopolized by the Italian cities.
1.014   A Portuguese prince who increased Europe's knowledge of ship building, navigation, and geography while organizing a trade route around Africa to Asia.
1.015   Any order:
   a. Rome
   b. Greece
   c. Jews
   d. Christianity
1.016   X
1.017   X
1.018   ___
1.019   X
1.020   ___
1.021   ___
1.022   X
1.023   ___
1.024   X
1.025   ___
1.026   X
1.027   ___
1.028   ___
1.029   X
1.030   true
1.031   false
1.032   true
1.033   true

SECTION 2

2.1   Henry VII
2.2   John Cabot
2.3   Sir Francis Drake
2.4   Elizabeth I
2.5   Grand Banks
2.6   Invincible Armada
2.7   He gave England a claim to North America along Canada and the eastern United States as well as discovering the Grand Banks.
2.8   They kept the Spanish fleet busy, reduced Spain's profit, and gave Elizabeth income.
2.9   He attacked Spanish interests on the American west coast, explored the west coast of North America, and captured a great deal of treasure.
2.10   The defeat of the Invincible Armada, pirate attacks, rebellions in Spanish lands, bad management, and overspending.
2.11   false
   — change *Northeast* to *Northwest*
2.12   false
   — new wording: *three* times for England and *one* time for the Netherlands
2.13   true
2.14   false
   — change Hudson *Bay* to Hudson *River*
2.15   true
2.16   false
   — change the *United States* to *Canada*
2.17   They were fishermen who came to fish the Grand Banks and dry their catch on land.
2.18   the Gulf of St. Lawrence and the St. Lawrence River
2.19   St. Lawrence River, Great Lakes, the east coast south to Massachusetts, northern New York
2.20   The Iroquois became enemies of France, allies with England, and interfered with French settlements south of the Great Lakes
2.21   yes
2.22   no
2.23   no
2.24   no
2.25   no
2.26   *coureus de bois*
2.27   fur
2.28   Mississippi
2.29   Asia
2.30   landowner, fur
2.31   Louisiana

2.32 Down the Fox River from Lake Michigan to the Wisconsin River, south to the Mississippi until the Arkansas River, back up the Mississippi to the Illinois and Chicago River, and back to Lake Michigan

2.33 South of the Great Lakes around the Ohio River, the Mississippi River, and part of Texas on the Gulf of Mexico

2.34 All of the Mississippi Basin, from the Appalachians to the Rocky Mountains

SELF TEST 2

2.01 France
The Gulf of St. Lawrence and the St. Lawrence River

2.02 Netherlands
Hudson River and the east coast of the U.S.

2.03 England
Hudson Bay area, eastern Canada

2.04 France
St Lawrence River, Great Lakes, east coast south to Massachusetts

2.05 England
Newfoundland and U.S. east coast

2.06 France
Mississippi River and tributaries from Lake Michigan to the Arkansas River

2.07 France
Ohio River valley and Mississippi River

2.08 g

2.09 h

2.010 d

2.011 e

2.012 i

2.013 a

2.014 c

2.015 j

2.016 f

2.017 b

2.018 true

2.019 false

2.020 false

2.021 true

2.022 true

2.023 false

2.024 false

SECTION 3

3.1 false
— change *California* to *Florida*

3.2 false
— change *Santa Fe* to *St. Augustine*

3.3 true

3.4 true

3.5 false
— change *San Diego* to *Santa Fe*

3.6 false
— new wording: governor *appointed* by the
king

3.7 true

3.8 false
— change *America* to *Spain*

3.9 true

3.10 Dutch

3.11 French

3.12 French

3.13 Dutch

3.14 French

3.15 Strict government control of politics and
trade, land held by rich landowners, and
no religious freedom

3.16 The French needed the Native Americans to
trap furs and the small French population
was less of a threat to the Native Americans

3.17 The Dutch West India Company

3.18 Huge tracts of land were given to company
members who brought over fifty people to
settle on it.

3.19 They were ruled by a privileged land-owning
aristocracy and despotic governors who
were appointed by the West India Company
and were often poor administrators.

3.20 Any order:
Humphrey Gilbert, Walter Raleigh

3.21 Any order:
1585, 1587

3.22 Virginia Dare

3.23 king

3.24 John Smith

3.25 Algonquin, Powhatan

3.26 Pocahontas

3.27 It disappeared without a trace while the
leader was in England for three years.

3.28 Roanoke was sponsored by an individual
nobleman while Jamestown's sponsor was a
joint stock company.

3.29 It was chosen because it was an easily
defendable peninsula but it was swampy and
subjected the men to disease.

3.30 Any order:
a. lack of unity
b. inferior weapons
c. lack of immunity to European diseases
d. Europeans kept coming

3.31 Too many settlers arrived. They overwhelmed
the food and shelter resources of the colony.
Most of the people starved to death.

3.32 Every settler in Virginia was given 50 acres of
land if they stayed three years.

3.33 Any order:
a. House of Burgesses meets
b. boatload of women sent from England
c. first enslaved African people arrive

3.34 About three hundred and fifty colonists were
killed, the London Company lost its charter,
Virginia became a crown colony

3.35 Almost 500 colonists were killed, the
power of the Native Americans of Virginia
was broken and they were confined to
reservations

3.36 tobacco

3.37 An indentured servant is bound for a term of
seven years and is then free.
An enslaved person is bound for life unless
freed by their master.

3.38 Pocahontas

3.39 Any order:
a. Spain
Florida, Mexico, and the southwest U.S.
b. France
St. Lawrence, Great Lakes, and the
Mississippi Basin
c. England
U.S. east coast and the Hudson Bay area

SELF TEST 3

3.01 Netherlands
3.02 England
3.03 France
3.04 Spain
3.05 Netherlands
3.06 France
3.07 England
3.08 Spain
3.09 Spain
3.010 France
3.011 c
3.012 f
3.013 g
3.014 i
3.015 a
3.016 d
3.017 e
3.018 j
3.019 b
3.020 h
3.021 France
3.022 England
3.023 Spain
3.024 France
3.025 Spain
3.026 France
3.027 Spain
3.028 France
3.029 France
3.030 England
3.031 ___
3.032 _X_
3.033 ___
3.034 ___
3.035 _X_
3.036 _X_
3.037 _X_
3.038 ___
3.039 _X_
3.040 _X_
3.041 Any two:
lack of unity
inferior weapons
lack of immunity to European diseases
overwhelmed by the Europeans
3.042 Company members were given large tracts of land in exchange for bringing over 50 settlers.
3.043 Hudson River

3.044 Any two:
autocratic government
government control of trade
land owned by wealthy landlords
no religious freedom

LIFEPAC TEST

1. d
2. t
3. r
4. a
5. i
6. k
7. e
8. q
9. l
10. n
11. f
12. s
13. m
14. g
15. b
16. o
17. p
18. j
19. c
20. h
21. d
22. b
23. c
24. d
25. d
26. b
27. c
28. c
29. b
30. b
31. tobacco
32. Portugal
33. Henry the Navigator
34. Italy
35. sea dogs
36. Northwest Passage
37. Grand Banks
38. Huguenots
39. fur
40. St. Augustine
41. true
42. false
43. false
44. true
45. true
46. true
47. true
48. false
49. false
50. false

ALTERNATE LIFEPAC TEST

1. a
2. j
3. c
4. g
5. h
6. i
7. j
8. f
9. b
10. l
11. k
12. d
13. e
14. a
15. e
16. England
17. Spain
18. Portugal
19. France
20. Netherlands
21. Spain
22. Spain
23. Spain
24. France
25. France
26. England
27. Spain
28. England
29. Spain
30. France
31. Britain
32. Spain
33. France
34. Spain
35. Netherlands
36. Marco Polo
37. Crusades
38. tobacco
39. Any order:
    Rome, Greece, Jews, Christianity
40. Jamestown
41. Asia
42. Henry the Navigator

HISTORY & GEOGRAPHY 801

ALTERNATE LIFEPAC TEST

NAME _____

DATE _____

SCORE _____

80
100

Match these people with the best description of the land they explored. Some answers will be used more than once (each answer, 2 points).

1. _____ Marquette

2. _____ La Salle

3. _____ Columbus

4. _____ Balboa

5. _____ Magellan

6. _____ Drake

7. _____ Coronado

8. _____ Cartier

9. _____ Ponce de Leon

10. _____ Champlain

11. _____ De Soto

12. _____ Hudson

13. _____ Cabot

14. _____ Jolliet

15. _____ Ericson

a. the Mississippi River

b. Florida

c. the Caribbean, Central America, and northern South America

d. New York and northern Canada

e. Newfoundland

f. St. Lawrence River

g. Isthmus of Panama

h. coast of South America and the Pacific Ocean on the way to Asia

i. west coast of North America on the way to Asia

j. southwestern United States

k. Mississippi River, Georgia, Alabama, Mississippi, and Arkansas

l. St. Lawrence, Great Lakes, east coast south to Massachusetts

m. Ohio River Valley, Mississippi River

Name the European country that sponsored each item or person (each answer, 2 points).

16. _____ Jamestown

17. _____ Columbus

18. _____ opening the trade route around Africa

19. _____ claimed the Mississippi River basin by 1700

20. _____ Fort Orange; settlements on the Hudson River

21. _____ the first permanent European settlement in the United States

22. _____ Cortes and Pizarro

23. _____ Magellan

24. _____ persecuted Huguenots; encouraged *coureurs de bois*

25. _____ Detroit; New Orleans; Quebec

26. _____ Roanoke; John Cabot

27. _____ claimed Florida and southwestern U.S. by 1700

28. _____ claimed the U.S. east coast and Hudson Bay area by 1700

29. _____ divided up the non-Catholic world with Portugal with the Treaty of Tordesillas

30. _____ few settlers; mostly fur traders; no religious or political freedom; best relations with the Native Americans

31. _____ House of Burgesses; Elizabeth I; James I

32. _____ La Isabela; Santa Fe; San Diego

33. _____ Champlain; Cartier

34. _____ Invincible Armada; a tremendous wealth of gold and silver from Mexico and Peru

35. _____ West India Company; purchased Manhattan Island; *patroon* system

Identify each of the following items or persons (each answer, 3 points).

36. _____ traveled to China in the 1200s; wrote a book that interested Europe in the Far East

37. _____ two hundred year attempt to take the Holy Land from the Muslims; brought Europe into contact with Asian markets and science

38. _____ cash crop of Virginia

39. _____ the four cultural ancestors of Western Civilization

    _____

    _____

    _____

40. _____ settlement established by the London Company of Virginia in 1607 on a marshy peninsula

41. _____ the continent the very first American settlers came from

42. _____ prince who organized voyages around Africa to Asia

HISTORY & GEOGRAPHY 802

Unit 2: British America

TEACHER NOTES

MATERIALS NEEDED FOR LIFEPAC	
Required	Suggested
None	• atlas • globe • encyclopedia • reference books or online sources

ADDITIONAL LEARNING ACTIVITIES

Section 1: English Colonies

1. Assign students to report on the founding and growth of one of the thirteen colonies.

2. Have students find a sketch of the interior of the *Mayflower* and a description that lists its dimensions. With your permission, students can measure out how big it would be in an open field, marking its size with string or paint. As a class, discuss what it would be like to live in that area with 100 other people, in unsanitary conditions, for three months.

3. As a class, discuss what conditions would be awful enough for you to leave your home to live in an undeveloped wilderness.

4. As a group, agree on a government for yourselves and try it out.

5. Discuss why the Massachusetts Bay Colony was so strict in religion.

6. Let students plan their own colony, including the government, religious laws, and citizenship requirements.

7. As a class, read the Fundamental Orders of Connecticut and discuss it.

8. Assign students to research and write a paper on any one of the colonial founders.

9. Have students discuss which of the thirteen colonies they would prefer to live in and why.

Section 2: Colonial Growth

1. Discuss why proprietary and company colonies failed to make a profit. How could they have been profitable?

2. Set up a mock colonial government for a discussion of one or more of these issues:

    a. The governor wants a larger salary.

    b. The assembly wants a judge removed from office.

    c. The citizens are worried about the threat of Native American attacks.

    d. A merchant with a monopoly (granted by the governor) on the sale of sugar to the colony has been charging very high prices.

  e. The governor has borrowed money from several important citizens to entertain the elite of the colony and cannot repay it.

  f. Farmers are letting their animals run loose in the capital city.

  g. The Board of Trade instructed the governor to improve the dock facilities at the main port of the colony.

  h. The English navy needs to set up a supply depot in the colony's main port.

3. Set up three groups, each group assuming the role of colonists from one of the three sections of the English colonies. Have each group defend their lifestyle in a debate.

4. As a class, discuss the role of religion in the life of the colonists. How was it different from today? Are the changes good or bad?

5. Have students research and do a report or paper on Quakers, Puritans, or Deism.

6. Have students research the effects of the Great Awakening and discuss them in class.

7. Assign research and a report or paper on Jonathan Edwards or George Whitefield.

8. Assign research and a report or paper on the slave trade in the 1700s.

Section 3: Wars with France

1. Assign research and a report on the European part of one of the wars in this section.

2. Assign research and a report or paper on the Iroquois people.

3. Discuss these questions:

  a. Why were France and Britain fighting at this time?

  b. Why were the Iroquois people so important in the American conflicts?

  c. Why did Edward Braddock act so stupidly?

  d. How did his experience in the French and Indian War help George Washington later in his life?

  e. How would the Revolution have been different if the Albany Plan had been accepted?

  f. What could have been done to foster the good will between the colonies and Britain after the French and Indian War to prevent the Revolution?

4. Assign research and a report or paper on one of these people: William Pitt, Benjamin Franklin, Pontiac, James Wolfe, or the Marquis de Montcalm.

5. Have students make a model showing how Quebec was captured in the 1760s.

6. Set up two groups, colonists and the British government, and instruct them to debate the Proclamation of 1763.

Administer the LIFEPAC Test

  The test is to be administered in one session. Give no help except with directions.
  Evaluate the tests and review areas where the students have done poorly.
  Review the pages and activities that stress the concepts tested.
  If necessary, administer the Alternate LIFEPAC Test.

ANSWER KEYS

SECTION 1

1.1	Puritans wanted to stay in the Anglican church and purify it. Separatists wanted to leave it.	**1.36**	true
1.2	Separatists	**1.37**	true
1.3	They were arrested after having their goods stolen by a dishonest captain. On the second try, the women and children were arrested when the men were on the ship.	**1.38**	false; parliament
		1.39	true
		1.40	true
		1.41	false; Massachusetts
		1.42	New York
1.4	They did not want their children to become Dutch, and they feared a Dutch-Spanish war.	**1.43**	New York, New Jersey
		1.44	New Jersey, Delaware, Pennsylvania
1.5	It leaked.	**1.45**	New Jersey, Delaware, Pennsylvania
1.6	Overcrowding, foul conditions, lack of exercise, no fresh air	**1.46**	New York
		1.47	New Jersey
1.7	They were at Cape Cod, north of Virginia. They only had permission to settle in Virginia.	**1.48**	New Jersey
		1.49	New York
1.8	For the glory of God, to advance the Christian faith, to honor their king and country	**1.50**	New York
		1.51	New Jersey
1.9	God and each other	**1.52**	New Jersey
1.10	Ireland-18 years; Scotland-54 years	**1.53**	To settle a debt the king owed to Penn's father
1.11	They agreed to form a "Civil Body Politic"— a government; to establish laws which they promised to obey for the better ordering and preservation of the colony	**1.54**	Interference from the Duke of York and colonists who would not pay quit-rents
		1.55	Charles II gave the land to his brother, the Duke of York, who sent four ships to capture it. They did so without firing a shot.
1.12	b	**1.56**	A religious sect that were pacifists, emphasized an "inner light," did not take oaths, or pay taxes to the Anglican church
1.13	e		
1.14	d		
1.15	a		
1.16	c	**1.57**	Pennsylvania
1.17	false	**1.58**	Maryland
1.18	true	**1.59**	Georgia
1.19	false	**1.60**	Carolinas
1.20	false	**1.61**	Maryland
1.21	true	**1.62**	Georgia
1.22	true	**1.63**	South Carolina
1.23	Teacher check	**1.64**	North Carolina
1.24	Charles I	**1.65**	Georgia
1.25	William Laud	**1.66**	Carolinas
1.26	Massachusetts Bay	**1.67**	South Carolina
1.27	John Winthrop	**1.68**	Georgia
1.28	Puritan	**1.69**	Maryland
1.29	Anne Hutchinson	**1.70**	Maryland
1.30	The charter did not specify that the company must meet in England. So, the company moved to America—charter and all.	**1.71**	Georgia
		1.72	Maryland
		1.73	Georgia
1.31	The assembly was elected by the church members who owned property.	**1.74**	false; South Carolina
		1.75	true
1.32	false, Fundamental Orders of Connecticut	**1.76**	false; Catholics
1.33	true	**1.77**	true
1.34	false; Hartford	**1.78**	false; Spanish Florida
1.35	false; Native Americans, should not be	**1.79**	false; eight

SELF TEST 1

1.01 Plymouth (Massachusetts)
1.02 Rhode Island
1.03 Connecticut
1.04 Maryland
1.05 Massachusetts
1.06 Connecticut
1.07 Georgia
1.08 Georgia
1.09 Maryland
1.010 Massachusetts
1.011 Connecticut
1.012 Massachusetts
1.013 New York
1.014 New Jersey
1.015 Pennsylvania
1.016 Virginia
1.017 Delaware
1.018 Georgia
1.019 South Carolina
1.020 North Carolina
1.021 c
1.022 a
1.023 b
1.024 c
1.025 b
1.026 d
1.027 c
1.028 d
1.029 a
1.030 c
1.031 false
1.032 true
1.033 true
1.034 true
1.035 false
1.036 true
1.037 false
1.038 true
1.039 false
1.040 false

SECTION 2

2.1
  a. Massachusetts, Virginia
  b. Connecticut, Rhode Island
  c. Maryland, North and South Carolina, New Hampshire, New York, New Jersey, Georgia, Delaware, Pennsylvania

2.2
  a. none
  b. Connecticut, Rhode Island
  c. Pennsylvania, Delaware, Maryland
  d. North and South Carolina, New Hampshire, New York, New Jersey, Georgia, Virginia, Massachusetts

2.3 Land was owned by the nobles who rented it to farmers.

2.4 The farmers could get land elsewhere if they did not want to pay rent.

2.5
  a. Governor; veto laws, appoint officials, lead council, pardon criminals, control militia, handle both diplomatic and religious affairs
  b. council; highest court, approve laws, assist governor
  c. assembly; control finances, write laws

2.6
  a. supervision by Board of Trade
  b. most governors let assembly do the work
  c. assembly controlled the money

2.7 after the French and Indian War, 1760s
2.8 true
2.9 false
2.10 true
2.11 false
2.12 true
2.13 false
2.14 true

2.15
  a. fishing
  b. whaling
  c. shipbuilding

2.16
  a. so that people could learn to read the Bible and thwart Satan
  b. when it had fifty households
  c. all children that came

2.17 wheat
2.18 the West Indies
2.19 tobacco
2.20 Any order:
rice, indigo
2.21 indentured servants; enslaved Africans
2.22 Philadelphia
2.23 southern
2.24 trade; farming
2.25 Middle
2.26 high wages
2.27 Charleston

2.28	plantations
2.29	slave holding; plantation
2.30	Any order:
	Jonathan Edwards, George Whitefield
2.31	Any order:
	Congregationalists, Anglicans
2.32	Any order:
	Rhode Island, Pennsylvania, Delaware,
	New Jersey
2.33	Halfway
2.34	Salem witch
2.35	Deism
2.36	*Sinners in the Hands of an Angry God*
2.37	taxes
2.38	pastors
2.39	Teacher check
	(Does the student understand the event?)
2.40	c
2.41	b
2.42	b
2.43	a
2.44	d
2.45	e
2.46	e
2.47	a
2.48	e
2.49	c
2.50	a
2.51	d
2.52	d
2.53	e
2.54	c
2.55	b

SELF TEST 2

2.01	g
2.02	f
2.03	i
2.04	j
2.05	h
2.06	b
2.07	c
2.08	d
2.09	e
2.010	a
2.011	New England
2.012	Southern
2.013	All
2.014	None
2.015	Middle
2.016	Middle
2.017	Southern
2.018	New England
2.019	None
2.020	Southern
2.021	New England
2.022	Southern
2.023	Middle
2.024	New England
2.025	Middle
2.026	a. governor
	b. council
	c. assembly
2.027	Great Awakening
2.028	a. corporate
	b. proprietary
	c. self-governing
2.029	a. Congregationalists
	b. Anglican
2.030	New England Confederation
2.031	true
2.032	false
2.033	false
2.034	false
2.035	true

SECTION 3

3.1	a. King William's War;		**3.40**	false
	War of the Grand Alliance or		**3.41**	true
	War of the League of Augsburg		**3.42**	false
	b. Queen Anne's War;		**3.43**	false
	War of the Spanish Succession		**3.44**	true
	c. King George's War;		**3.45**	_X_
	War of the Austrian Succession		**3.46**	___
3.2	War of Jenkin's Ear		**3.47**	_X_
3.3	a		**3.48**	___
3.4	a		**3.49**	___
3.5	c		**3.50**	_X_
3.6	a, b		**3.51**	_X_
3.7	a, b		**3.52**	_X_
3.8	c		**3.53**	_X_
3.9	b		**3.54**	a. fur trade
3.10	d			b. farming
3.11	b		**3.55**	British took land for farming while the French only built forts and traded
3.12	b		**3.56**	To destroy the frontier forts and then attack the unprotected settlers
3.13	b		**3.57**	All along the British frontier
3.14	b		**3.58**	They began to run out of supplies.
3.15	British		**3.59**	No settlers west of the Appalachians, land there must be bought from the Native Americans or obtained by treaty
3.16	British		**3.60**	They ignored it.
3.17	British		**3.61**	Teacher check
3.18	French			
3.19	French			
3.20	French			
3.21	a			
3.22	b			
3.23	b			
3.24	c			
3.25	a			
3.26	b			
3.27	a			
3.28	b			
3.29	c			
3.30	c			
3.31	a			
3.32	b			
3.33	a			
3.34	a. Gave gifts to the Iroquois and encouraged them to be loyal to Britain			
	b. Put together a plan for a united colonial government			
3.35	a. Oswego			
	b. William Henry			
3.36	Seven Years'			
3.37	b			
3.38	c			
3.39	d			

SELF TEST 3

3.01   a. King William's War
             b. Queen Anne's War
             c. King George's War
             d. French and Indian War
3.02 Great Awakening
3.03 a. Puritans
             b. Quakers
             c. Catholics
             d. Separatists
             e. Quakers
3.04 c
3.05 h
3.06 a
3.07 i
3.08 f
3.09 e
3.010 b
3.011 j
3.012 d
3.013 g
3.014 New England Confederation
3.015 Mayflower Compact
3.016 Deism
3.017 Fort Necessity
3.018 Dominion of New England
3.019 Quebec
3.020 Treaty of Paris
3.021 Ohio Valley
3.022 Anglican
3.023 Proclamation of 1763
3.024 false
3.025 false
3.026 true
3.027 false
3.028 true
3.029 false
3.030 false
3.031 true
3.032 false
3.033 true

LIFEPAC TEST

1. f
2. g
3. m
4. i
5. o
6. n
7. j
8. h
9. k
10. c
11. l
12. d
13. a
14. b
15. e
16. fishing
17. wheat
18. rice
19. proprietary
20. Congregationalists
21. Mayflower Compact
22. Georgia
23. French and Indian War
24. Proclamation
25. Quaker
26. Massachusetts
27. Massachusetts
28. Maryland
29. Rhode Island
30. Connecticut
31. New York
32. New Jersey
33. Georgia
34. North Carolina
35. South Carolina
36. true
37. true
38. false
39. false
40. true
41. true
42. true
43. true
44. false
45. true

ALTERNATE LIFEPAC TEST

1. Pennsylvania
2. Rhode Island
3. New York
4. Virginia
5. Pennsylvania
6. Maryland
7. Connecticut
8. Delaware
9. Maryland
10. Georgia
11. North Carolina
12. Massachusetts
13. Georgia
14. New Jersey
15. South Carolina
16. French and Indian War
17. Pontiac's War
18. Glorious Revolution
19. King William's War
20. Bacon's Rebellion
21. King Phillip's War
22. French and Indian War
23. Queen Anne's War
24. French and Indian War
25. Pontiac's War
26. King George's War
27. French and Indian War
28. Great Awakening
29. Mayflower Compact
30. Dominion of New England
31. a. governor
    b. council
    c. assembly
32. Proclamation of 1763

HISTORY & GEOGRAPHY 802

ALTERNATE LIFEPAC TEST

NAME _____

DATE _____

SCORE _____

80 / 100

Name the colony associated with each item or person (each answer, 3 points).

1. _____ William Penn; received for a debt Charles II owed Penn's father

2. _____ Roger Williams

3. _____ founded by the Dutch West India Company

4. _____ first of the thirteen colonies

5. _____ had largest port city in the colonies at the Revolution

6. _____ Catholic haven

7. _____ the Fundamental Orders were the first constitution

8. _____ Pennsylvania's outlet to the sea

9. _____ Lord Baltimore

10. _____ James Oglethorpe

11. _____ settled by poor farmers from Virginia; lacked good ports

12. _____ Puritan colony; took its charter to America

13. _____ haven for debtors; buffer against Spanish America

14. _____ order of ownership: Duke of York; Berkeley and Carteret; Quakers; royal

15. _____ group of eight wealthy proprietors founded it; settled from the West Indies; established an aristocratic, slave holding economy

Choose the correct conflict for each item. Some answers will be used more than once (each answer, 3 points).

King William's War   Queen Anne's War   King Philip's War
King George's War   Pontiac's War   Bacon's Rebellion
French and Indian War   Glorious Revolution

16. _____ the one British-French conflict that brought numbers of British troops to the colonies

17. _____ largest Indian War of the colonial period

18. _____ James II left England; William and Mary became the rulers

19. _____ War of the Grand Alliance, or League of Augsburg, in Europe

20. _____ led by a popular western Virginia landowner against the governor

21. _____ Matacom; leader of the Wampanoag; tried to drive out the New England settlers

22. _____ cost the French almost all of their land in North America

23. _____ War of the Spanish Succession in Europe

24. _____ General Braddock ambushed and killed on the way to Fort Duquesne

25. _____ Native Americans attacked all along the British frontier, first at the forts

26. _____ War of the Austrian Succession in Europe; colonists captured Louisbourg

27. _____ Washington gained his military experience and reputation

Name each one (each answer, 3 points).

28. The American revival of the 1730s and 40s:

    _____

29. Plymouth colonists' agreement to form a government:

    _____

30. The union of New York, New England, and New Jersey created by James II:

    _____

31. The three parts of most colonial governments:

    a. _____

    b. _____

    c. _____

32. Decree that ordered the colonists not to settle west of the Appalachians:

    _____

HISTORY & GEOGRAPHY 803

Unit 3: The American Revolution (1763-1789)

TEACHER NOTES

MATERIALS NEEDED FOR LIFEPAC	
Required	Suggested
None	• atlas • encyclopedia • reference books or online sources

ADDITIONAL LEARNING ACTIVITIES

Section 1: Growing Conflict

1. Discuss these questions with your class.

    a. Prior to the American Revolution, people lived quietly and submissively under oppressive governments. What changed this pattern in the New World?

    b. Can you single out one factor that put the colonists on a "collision course" with the British?

    c. Can you see the hand of God in the series of incidents that led to war and independence from Europe?

    d. Analyze one incident leading the British and the colonists to war; e.g., the Boston Massacre or the Intolerable Acts, etc. Could it have been resolved better, in a way that would have reconciled the two sides?

2. Have the class act out a fireside chat between two colonial groups. The first group should argue that God requires us to obey the British government and honor the king. The other should argue that we have a God-given right to rebel. Use the Bible for reference. Encourage students to engage in a spirited conversation.

3. Isolate one cause of the American Revolution, and have students do an in-depth research of the personalities involved. They should emphasize the person's conviction and sincerity and the degree to which they appeared to be guided either by the spirit of the world or the Spirit which is from God.

4. Assign students to write a paper defending the British position that the colonists had a responsibility to alleviate the British war debts.

5. Tell students to pretend that they are the members of the Second Continental Congress debating the Declaration of Independence: Which parts would you keep, and which would you change? Then, as a wealthy member of colonial society, decide if you would sign the document or not. (If you sign and the cause fails, you will hang for treason.)

6. Have students make a list of the lesser known men who signed the Declaration of Independence, and assign each person research one of them. After students share information, have the class draw some conclusions about what kind of men they were.

Section 2: War

1. Debate this topic as a class: "Resolved: The French, not the Americans, won the Revolutionary War."

2. Have students choose a battle in the Revolution and do a model or diagram of it.

3. Assign a 250- or 500-word paper on any of these people: Thomas Paine, Benedict Arnold, Ethan Allen, George Rogers Clark, Nathanael Greene, Lafayette, Baron von Steuben, Horatio Gates, Daniel Morgan, John Paul Jones, Benjamin Lincoln, or Nathan Hale.

4. Have students discuss what they believe were the major mistakes made by the British.

5. Have students discuss what America would be like today if Washington had decided to make himself king. They can research Napoleon and the French Revolution for ideas.

Section 3: Constitution

1. Have students read a copy of the Articles of Confederation. (Check at your local library or on the internet.) As a class, discuss problems students find in it.

2. Discuss what the United States would be like today if the government did not allow territories to become states with equal rights.

3. Have the class assemble some statistics on the men at the Constitutional Convention: their ages, wealth, backgrounds, experience in the Revolution, etc. Discuss the results.

4. As a class, read and discuss all or parts of *The Federalist*.

5. Assign students to research one of these men, and report on what impact they had on the founding of the United States of America: Samuel Adams, John Adams, Thomas Jefferson, Benjamin Franklin, James Madison, Alexander Hamilton, John Marshall, or John Jay.

6. As a class, read and discuss the Constitution of the United States. Possible topics include (but are not limited to):

    a. Why has it lasted so long?

    b. Why did the compromises work?

    c. Do the checks and balances still work today?

    d. How does the elector system work to choose the president and what are the problems with that system?

    e. How would the government be limited if it could only do exactly what the Constitution stated and nothing else?

7. As a class, read the Bill of Rights and discuss:

    a. Why were these particular Amendments so important?

    b. Which do you consider to be the most important and why?

Administer the LIFEPAC Test

The test is to be administered in one session. Give no help except with directions.
Evaluate the tests and review areas where the students have done poorly.
Review the pages and activities that stress the concepts tested.
If necessary, administer the Alternate LIFEPAC Test.

ANSWER KEYS

SECTION 1

1.1 mercantilism

1.2 supply the mother country with raw materials and buy manufactured goods from her

1.3 Any order:
a. bring them under better control
b. have them pay some of the cost of running the colonies

1.4 Any order:
a. All trade on British or colonial ships
b. All trade must go through Britain
c. Certain goods could be sold only to Britain

1.5 The Molasses Act set a high tax on non-British molasses. It would have hurt New England because the British source for molasses (British West Indies) could not supply all that New England needed. It was avoided by smuggling.

1.6 The colonies were not allowed to mint coins nor could colonial goods be purchased with coins from Britain.

1.7 1763 - strict enforcement of the Navigation Acts
1764 - Sugar Act
1765 - Quartering Act

1.8 Grenville

1.9 Benjamin Franklin

1.10 Patrick Henry

1.11 Virginia Resolves

1.12 Any order:
a. Stamp Act Congress
b. boycotts
c. mob action

1.13 Sons of Liberty

1.14 "No taxation without representation."

1.15 Declaratory Act

1.16 A stamp had to be purchased for all legal and public papers: like wills, bills of sale, and even playing cards.

1.17 Any four:
first direct tax, tax fell on everyone,
it was not passed by the colonial assemblies,
violators would be tried in Admiralty Court,
and colonists were already short of money

1.18 Those men killed the tyrants they opposed. George III might face the same fate if he continued to act as a tyrant.

1.19 false
— change *France* to *England*

1.20 false
— change *Prime Minister* to *Chancellor of the Exchequer*

1.21 true

1.22 false
— change *Massachusetts* to *New York* and *Stamp* to *Quartering*

1.23 true

1.24 false
— change *colonial assemblies* to *Parliament*

1.25 true

1.26 false
— change *West* to *North* and *paint* to *tea*

1.27 true

1.28 true

1.29 Tax on goods from Britain like tea, lead, and paint; gave greater powers of enforcement to customs officials; revenue to be used to pay British officials

1.30 A mob threw snowballs and debris at soldiers. The soldiers fired and five people were killed.

1.31 British East India Company

1.32 Charleston

1.33 New York

1.34 Boston Port

1.35 Quebec

1.36 First Continental Congress

1.37 Boston Tea Party

1.38 The Boston harbor was closed, town meetings were forbidden, an important official was put under royal control, and Boston was put under military rule.

1.39 A group of colonists, disguised as Native Americans, took the tea off of ships in the harbor and dumped it into the ocean.

1.40 It passed a Declaration of Rights, declared several acts of Parliament illegal, formed an association to stop all trade, petitioned the king, and agreed to meet again if necessary.

1.41 It took away the Ohio land, spread Catholicism, and was a further attempt to contain their liberties.

1.42 b

1.43 a

1.44 c

1.45 b

1.46 c
1.47 a
1.48 a
1.49 b
1.50 c
1.51 c
1.52 a
1.53 b
1.54 c
1.55 Second Continental Congress
1.56 militia
1.57 George Washington
1.58 d
1.59 e
1.60 b
1.61 f
1.62 a
1.63 c
1.64 g
1.65 Olive Branch
1.66 Montreal
1.67 *Common Sense*
1.68 July 2, 1776
1.69 15
1.70 first two paragraphs
1.71 a. "He has refused ... "
       b. "... in Peace Friends."
1.72 last
1.73 Teacher check
1.74-1.84 (teacher may approve alternate answers)
1.74 "He has dissolved Representative Houses repeatedly"
1.75 "He has refused his Assent to Laws"
1.76 "He has made Judges dependent on his will alone"
1.77 "For imposing taxes on us without our consent"
1.78 "For depriving us ... of the benefits of Trial by Jury"
1.79 "For taking away our Charters ... and altering fundamentally the Forms of our Government"
1.80 "For cutting off our Trade with all parts of the world"
1.81 "has endeavoured to bring on the inhabitants of our frontiers, the merciless Indian Savages"
1.82 "transporting large armies of foreign Mercenaries to compleat the works of death"
1.83 "For Quartering large bodies of armed troops among us"
1.84 "to render the military independent of and superior to the Civil Power"
1.85 "For abolishing the free System of English Laws in a neighbouring Province ... and enlarging its Boundaries"

SELF TEST 1

1.01 f
1.02 i
1.03 h
1.04 a
1.05 j
1.06 d
1.07 c
1.08 e
1.09 g
1.010 b
1.011 A tax on all legal and public papers, must buy a stamp for them. It was the first direct tax on the colonies.
1.012 A tax on imports from Britain, revenue to be used to pay British officials, greater enforcement power given to customs officers, and threatened to dissolve New York assembly if it did not obey the Quartering Act.
1.013 Mob in Boston threw things at British soldiers who fired on the crowd. Five people were killed.
1.014 Colonists disguised as Native Americans took the tea off three ships in Boston harbor and threw it in the water.
1.015 Boston harbor was closed, Massachusetts charter was changed so the officials were responsible to the king, town meetings were restricted, Boston put under military rule
1.016 French laws and religion in Quebec were protected. The colony's boundaries were expanded south into the Ohio Valley.
1.017 Americans fortified Breeds Hill near Boston, British attacked straight up the hill, Americans drove them back with heavy losses until forced to retreat because they ran out of powder
1.018 Any order:
       a. Stamp Act Congress
       b. boycotts
       c. mob action
1.019 mercantilism
1.020 Navigation
1.021 Declaratory
1.022 Sons of Liberty
1.023 Quartering
1.024 Sugar
1.025 Intolerable
1.026 Lexington
1.027 Ticonderoga
1.028 *Common Sense*

1.029	true
1.030	false
1.031	false
1.032	false
1.033	true
1.034	false
1.035	true
1.036	false
1.037	true
1.038	true

SECTION 2

2.1 British
2.2 British
2.3 Americans
2.4 British
2.5 Americans
2.6 Americans
2.7 British
2.8 British
2.9 Americans
2.10 British
2.11 Keeping the army together
2.12 cannons from Ticonderoga
2.13 The British withdrew and had to start from Canada, not New York, in 1777.
2.14 It failed, and the South was left alone for awhile
2.15 They were attacked from the front and rear. They were defeated and fled to Brooklyn Heights.
2.16 An American officer who was collecting information, was caught, and hanged as a spy.
2.17 The British captured them.
2.18 Washington snuck away in small boats at night.
2.19 Very poor. They had little food or supplies.
2.20 It is not easily conquered.
2.21 God
2.22 summer soldiers and sunshine patriots
2.23 esteem it too lightly
2.24 b
2.25 c
2.26 e
2.27 e
2.28 a
2.29 b
2.30 a
2.31 f
2.32 e
2.33 f
2.34 a
2.35 d
2.36 e
2.37 a
2.38 f
2.39 c
2.40 Burgoyne, St. Leger, Howe
2.41 Fort Stanwix, Oriskany Creek
2.42 Ticonderoga, Defiance
2.43 30, cannons
2.44 Jane McCrea
2.45 Bennington

2.46	Freeman's Farm
2.47	Any order:
	Benedict Arnold, Daniel Morgan
2.48	Horatio Gates
2.49	Saratoga
2.50	Saratoga
2.51	Any order:
	Saratoga, Germantown
2.52	Marquis de Lafayette
2.53	Benjamin Franklin
2.54	Monmouth Courthouse
2.55	George Rogers Clark
2.56	Vincennes
2.57	Benedict Arnold, West Point
2.58	Charles Lee
2.59	John Paul Jones, *Bonhomme Richard, Serapis*
2.60	Major John André
2.61	d
2.62	b
2.63	c
2.64	a
2.65	g
2.66	e
2.67	f
2.68	Francis Marion
2.69	Daniel Morgan
2.70	Nathanael Greene
2.71	Horatio Gates
2.72	Lord Cornwallis
2.73	A French fleet cut off his supply and retreat route. A combined French and American army surrounded him by land.
2.74	Rochambeau
2.75	de Grasse
2.76	Ben Franklin, John Adams, John Jay
2.77	General Benjamin Lincoln
2.78	It prevented America from falling under a military dictatorship and gave the country a tremendous confidence in Washington that would be used later.
2.79	Any order:
	1. Independence for America
	2. America got all the land between Canada and Florida east of the Mississippi
	3. British troops to leave
	4. Americans could use the Mississippi
	5. Americans could fish in Newfoundland
	6. Spain got Florida back
	7. France got back its islands in the West Indies
	8. Congress recommended that Loyalists get their property back
	9. All debts to Britain were to be honored

SELF TEST 2

2.01	c
2.02	m
2.03	g
2.04	l
2.05	n
2.06	k
2.07	o
2.08	a
2.09	d
2.010	h
2.011	b
2.012	i
2.013	j
2.014	e
2.015	f
2.016	Monmouth Courthouse
2.017	Trenton
2.018	Saratoga
2.019	Oriskany
2.020	King's Mountain
2.021	Valley Forge
2.022	Yorktown
2.023	Long Island
2.024	Charleston
2.025	Camden
2.026	France
2.027	Fort Ticonderoga
2.028	Philadelphia
2.029	mercantilism
2.030	Quebec Act
2.031	Stamp Act
2.032	Boston Tea Party
2.033	Any three:
	large, professional army; control of the seas; loyalists; unified government; good supplies; money to hire mercenaries
2.034	true
2.035	false
2.036	true
2.037	false
2.038	true
2.039	true
2.040	false
2.041	true
2.042	true
2.043	true

SECTION 3

3.1   ___

3.2   _X_

3.3   _X_

3.4   ___

3.5   ___

3.6   ___

3.7   ___

3.8   _X_

3.9   ___

3.10   _X_

3.11   ___

3.12   ___

3.13   Northwest Ordinance

3.14   national government

3.15   national debt

3.16   six miles, six miles

3.17   36; 16

3.18   60,000

3.19   false

      — change *creditors* to *debtors*

3.20   false

      — change *state boundaries* to *commerce*

3.21   false

      — change *seven* to *five*

3.22   true

3.23   true

3.24   true

3.25   false

      — change *poor* to *rich*

3.26   false

      — change *good* to *bad*

3.27   true

3.28   false

      — change *same* to *different*

3.29   12

3.30   wealthy

3.31   Any order:

      a.   George Washington elected president

      b.   meeting would be secret

      c.   throw out the Articles of Confederation

3.32   Any order:

      a.   Virginia Plan —
      Congressional representation would be based on population

      b.   New Jersey Plan —
      Congressional representation would be a set number per state

3.33   Connecticut Plan

3.34   Congress would have two houses, the lower one with representation by population, the upper with representation by state and money bills would start in the lower house.

3.35   Each slave would be counted as three-fifths of a person for representation and taxation purposes.

3.36   Congress could not vote to outlaw it until 1807.

3.37   Any order:

      a.   executive

      b.   legislative

      c.   judicial

3.38   a.   veto laws

      b.   override veto, impeach

      c.   declare laws unconstitutional

      d.   appoints judges

      e.   approves judges

3.39   They kept it but gave up certain powers to the federal government.

3.40   no

3.41   nine

3.42   Federalists, Anti-Federalists

3.43   Bill of Rights

3.44   Delaware

3.45   New Hampshire

3.46   Any order:
      Virginia, New York

3.47   Any order:
      North Carolina, Rhode Island

3.48   Any order:

      1.   to form a more perfect union

      2.   establish justice

      3.   insure domestic tranquility

      4.   provide for the common defense

      5.   promote the general welfare

      6.   secure the blessings of liberty

SELF TEST 3

3.01	i
3.02	g
3.03	h
3.04	d
3.05	j
3.06	b
3.07	e
3.08	c
3.09	a
3.010	f
3.011	Benjamin Franklin
3.012	George Washington
3.013	Thomas Jefferson
3.014	James Madison
3.015	Benedict Arnold
3.016	Nathanael Greene
3.017	Lafayette
3.018	John Hancock
3.019	George Rogers Clark
3.020	Cornwallis
3.021	Saratoga
3.022	Any order:
	a. executive
	b. legislative
	c. judicial
3.023	veto laws
3.024	nine
3.025	mercantilism
3.026	Any order:
	a. Stamp Act Congress
	b. boycotts
	c. mob action
3.027	true
3.028	true
3.029	false
3.030	false
3.031	false
3.032	true
3.033	false
3.034	true
3.035	true
3.036	true

LIFEPAC TEST

1. g
2. c
3. d
4. j
5. a
6. b
7. i
8. e
9. f
10. h
11. Congress would be made of two houses: representation in the Senate would be by state and in the House by population
12. Cornwallis was trapped on Chesapeake Bay by the French navy and a combined America/French army. He was surrounded and surrendered his whole army.
13. Britain was arrogant after winning the Seven Years' War and deeply in debt. They wanted some revenue from the colonies and greater control over them.
14. Stamp Act: tax on legal and public documents by way of a stamp
Quebec Act: French kept their laws and expanded into the Ohio Valley
Quartering Act: troops kept at the expense of the colonists
Townshend Acts: tax on British imports
Intolerable Acts: close Boston harbor, change charter
15. A rebellion of debtors in Massachusetts. It scared many people into supporting a stronger government.
16. Lexington
17. Lafayette
18. Rochambeau
19. Monmouth
20. Cornwallis
21. Steuben
22. Ticonderoga
23. Camden
24. Saratoga
25. Trenton
26. Second Continental Congress
27. Stamp Act Congress
28. Articles of Confederation
29. Confederation Congress
30. Constitution of the U.S.
31. Second Continental Congress
32. First Continental Congress
33. Articles of Confederation
34. Constitution of the U.S.
35. Second Continental Congress

ALTERNATE LIFEPAC TEST

1. m
2. f
3. n
4. s
5. t
6. g
7. q
8. e
9. j
10. r
11. k
12. b
13. c
14. o
15. i
16. a
17. h
18. l
19. p
20. d
21. Any order:
   a. Stamp Act Congress
   b. boycotts
   c. mob action
22. Valley Forge
23. a. France
   b. Benjamin Franklin
24. Boston Tea Party
25. Any order:
   a. trial by jury
   b. presumed innocent
26. Olive Branch Petition
27. Britain was deeply in debt from the Seven Years' (French and Indian) War.
28. Any two:
   representation in Congress, counting slaves, the slave trade
29. Articles of Confederation
30. The Federalist
31. Any two:
   location; quality of commanders; soldiers' ability to shoot accurately; righteous cause; tough and capable people; wide spaces to withdraw; Britain had to defeat a large territory and uncooperative people; foreign allies
32. Any order:
   a. executive
   b. judicial
   c. legislative

HISTORY & GEOGRAPHY 803

ALTERNATE LIFEPAC TEST

NAME _____

DATE _____

SCORE _____

Match these names (each answer, 2 points).

1. _____ French admiral
2. _____ turning point of the war
3. _____ president; Second Continental Congress
4. _____ Act that closed Boston harbor
5. _____ German mercenaries
6. _____ author of *Common Sense*
7. _____ plan at Constitutional Convention to base representation on population
8. _____ final major battle of the war
9. _____ American general who lost at Guilford Courthouse and Eutaw Springs but freed most of the South
10. _____ Acts that restricted American trade
11. _____ surprise attack day after Christmas, 1776; revived the American cause
12. _____ author of Declaration of Independence
13. _____ French aristocrat; volunteer American officer
14. _____ hero of Saratoga and Ticonderoga; traitor
15. _____ Acts taxing tea, lead, glass and other British goods
16. _____ American commander at Yorktown
17. _____ Boston radical; Committees of Correspondence
18. _____ French army commander at Yorktown
19. _____ British commander at Saratoga
20. _____ British commander at Yorktown

a. Washington
b. Jefferson
c. Lafayette
d. Cornwallis
e. Yorktown
f. Saratoga
g. Paine
h. Adams
i. Townshend
j. Greene
k. Trenton
l. Rochambeau
m. de Grasse
n. Hancock
o. Arnold
p. Burgoyne
q. Virginia
r. Navigation
s. Intolerable
t. Hessians

Complete the following (each answer, 3 points).

21. What were the three reactions in America to the Stamp Act?

  a. _____

  b. _____

  c. _____

22. The American army spent the winter of 1777-78 drilling under harsh conditions at
  _____ near Philadelphia.

23. The Americans gained a valuable alliance in 1778.
  What nation was it and who was the American representative there?

  a. _____

  b. _____

24. The Intolerable Acts were a British reaction to what event?

  _____

25. What two English liberties were the American colonists denied in Admiralty Court?

  a. _____

  b. _____

26. Name the petition sent by the Second Continental Congress in 1775 asking the king
  to intervene on behalf of the colonies and avert further hostilities.

  _____

27. Why was Britain so in need of money after 1763?

  _____

  _____

  _____

28. Name two things that the Constitutional Convention delegates compromised about.

  a. _____

  b. _____

29. What was the first constitution for the United States?

  _____

30. Name the famous series of essays written in support of the Constitution by Madison, Hamilton, and Jay.

   _____

31. Name two advantages the Americans had in the Revolutionary War.

   a. _____

   b. _____

32. What were the three branches of government set up by the Constitution?

   a. _____

   b. _____

   c. _____

HISTORY & GEOGRAPHY 804

Unit 4: A Firm Foundation (1789-1820)

TEACHER NOTES

MATERIALS NEEDED FOR LIFEPAC	
Required	Suggested
None	• atlas • encyclopedia • reference books or online sources

ADDITIONAL LEARNING ACTIVITIES

Section 1: Federalist Era

1. Discuss these questions:

    a. Why was George Washington an obvious choice for the first president?

    b. Why was Alexander Hamilton's finance plan so controversial?

    c. Should political parties have been avoided?

    d. In what way was the Whiskey Rebellion like the revolt against the Stamp Act?

    e. Why was Washington's two term precedent important?

    f. Could the U.S. have done anything to stop impressment?

    g. Why was the first change of power in 1800 so important?

    h. Why did America avoid alliances after the Convention of 1800?

2. Assign students to research the French Revolution and discuss why Americans would or would not approve of it.

3. Debate this statement as a class: "Resolved: John Adams was an excellent president."

4. Have students research the Alien and Sedition Acts and write a 250-word paper on why these were dangerous precedents for American liberties.

Section 2: Jeffersonian Democracy

1. Have students research and write a 250-word paper on the Enlightenment describing how it agreed with or disagreed with Christian principles.

2. The modern Democratic Party sometimes claims Thomas Jefferson as its founder. As a class, discuss how its beliefs compare to those of Jefferson.

3. As a class, discuss the importance of *Marbury v. Madison*. What would American government be like without judicial power to invalidate laws—especially in reference to abortion?

4. Have students read about the Lewis and Clark Expedition. As a class, discuss what it would be like exploring such an unknown land.

5. Have students assume the roles of members of the Senate in 1807 (most senators would be Democratic-Republicans) to debate and vote on the Embargo Act.

6. Have students assume the roles of members of the House of Representatives in 1812 (some will have to be War Hawks) to debate and vote on the declaration of war with Britain.

7. Have students research the war by Tecumseh and do a paper or report on why it started and why it was dangerous to the new American republic.

8. Discuss why the U.S. went to war with so little practical preparation.

Section 3: War of 1812

1. Have students prepare a model or diagram of any of the battles of the war.

2. Assign students to research and do a report or paper on the *U.S.S. Constitution*.

3. Discuss why the Americans wanted to capture Canada and why the effort failed.

4. Have students research the Napoleonic Wars in Europe, and discuss why Britain was so desperate to defeat Napoleon.

5. Discuss what the long-term effects would have been in America if the United States had agreed to the harsh terms offered by the British in early 1814, before the victories at Baltimore and Plattsburgh Bay.

6. Debate this statement as a class: "Resolved: America won the War of 1812."

7. Have students prepare a map of the major hard-surface roads in 1820.

8. Tell students to assume the role of the House of Representatives in 1816 to debate and vote on the American System. (Be sure that someone takes the role of Henry Clay.)

9. Discuss what caused the "Era of Good Feelings."

10. Create a mock Supreme Court where students argue one of these cases after researching it:

    a. *Marbury v. Madison*

    b. *Fletcher v. Peck*

    c. *McCulloch v. Maryland*

    d. *Dartmouth College v. Woodard*

    e. *Cohens v. Virginia*

    f. *Gibbons v. Ogden*

11. Have students research the Monroe Doctrine. Assign them to do a report or write a paper to describe its impact on the Western Hemisphere.

Administer the LIFEPAC Test

The test is to be administered in one session. Give no help except with directions.
Evaluate the tests and review areas where the students have done poorly.
Review the pages and activities that stress the concepts tested.
If necessary, administer the Alternate LIFEPAC Test.

ANSWER KEYS

SECTION 1

1.1   c

1.2   d

1.3   e

1.4   f

1.5   b

1.6   a

1.7   Any order:
  a. pay debt at full value
  b. take over state debts
  c. National Bank

1.8   The national capital would be located in the South.

1.9   tariffs

1.10   Most of the original owners of the bonds had sold them at a small part of their value to rich people who could hold them until some payment was made on them.

1.11   H

1.12   H

1.13   J

1.14   J

1.15   J

1.16   J

1.17   H

1.18   H

1.19   Any order:
  a. stars
  b. stripes on shield
  c. olives
  d. arrows
  e. layers on pyramid

1.20   Any order:
  a. ring of golden light, obverse
  b. eye surrounded by light, reverse

1.21   The right is the more important side and it shows that America prefers peace.

1.22   "One out of many"

1.23   Neutrality Proclamation

1.24   Britain, Austria, Spain, Prussia

1.25   Citizen Edmond Genêt

1.26   Any order:
  a. commissioned privateers
  b. tried to organize expeditions against Spanish territory
  c. appealed to U.S. people to support France

1.27   Any order:
  a. holding forts in U.S. territory
  b. supporting the Native Americans
  c. seizing ships and cargo
  d. impressing sailors

1.28   Any order:
  a. leave the forts
  b. pay for some ships and cargo
  c. improve U.S. trading rights

1.29   It did not deal with the major issues, such as impressment; English support of the Native Americans or repayment for stolen slaves. It also restated the obligation of Americans to pay old debts to Britain.

1.30   It was a revolt in Pennsylvania against the excise tax. It collapsed when militia troops were sent in from out of state.

1.31   partisan politics and foreign alliances

1.32   two

1.33   Alien Act

1.34   Democratic-Republican

1.35   John Adams

1.36   Jay's Treaty

1.37   Virginia and Kentucky Resolves

1.38   Convention of 1800

1.39   XYZ Affair

1.40   Sedition Act

1.41   John Adams and Alexander Hamilton

1.42   not going to war with France

1.43   Democratic-Republican publishers

1.44   "Millions for defense but not one cent for tribute."

1.45   It was a tie between Jefferson and Burr

1.46   Jefferson, he was from a different political party.

1.47   Any order:
  a. basic structure of the government
  b. solid financial system
  c. protected the nation from early wars
  d. "loose construction" of Constitution

SELF TEST 1

1.01 e
1.02 c
1.03 b
1.04 g
1.05 h
1.06 f
1.07 j
1.08 a
1.09 d
1.010 i
1.011 Federalist
1.012 Democratic-Republican
1.013 pyramid
1.014 Whiskey Rebellion
1.015 none
1.016 XYZ Affair
1.017 Alien and Sedition Acts
1.018 Convention of 1800
1.019 "One out of many"
1.020 *Farewell Address*
1.021 Any order:
   a. pay debt at full value
   b. take over state debts
   c. National Bank
1.022 The Constitution did not specifically allow it.
1.023 Any three; any order:
   a. set up basic government structures
   b. kept the peace in early years
   c. set up a strong financial base
   or loose construction of Constitution
1.024 Any three; any order:
   a. giving aid to the Native Americans
   b. seizing U.S. ships and cargo
   c. impressing American sailors
   or holding forts in U.S. territory
1.025 false
1.026 false
1.027 false
1.028 true
1.029 false
1.030 true
1.031 true
1.032 true
1.033 false
1.034 false
1.035 true

SECTION 2

2.1 true
2.2 false
  — change *Marshall* to *Madison*
2.3 false
  — change *John Marshall* to *Samuel Chase*
2.4 true
2.5 false
  — change *unpopular* to *popular*
2.6 true
2.7 false
  — change *a year* to *two years*
2.8 false
  — change *Pocahontas* to *Sacajawea*
2.9 true
2.10 It was the first successful, peaceful change in power from one political party to another.
2.11 Nothing except to repeal the excise tax.
2.12 Spain was an aging power that was very little threat and had agreed to American use of the Mississippi. France was an expanding, dangerous power.
2.13 He let them expire or repealed them, freed the men convicted under them, and returned their fines.
2.14 They ran the government as cheaply as possible while reducing the debt.
2.15 A Constitutional Amendment.
2.16 Up the Missouri River, across the Rocky Mountains, and down the Columbia River
2.17 Alexander Hamilton
2.18 Austerlitz, Trafalgar
2.19 treason
2.20 *Leopard, Chesapeake*
2.21 Africa
2.22 Embargo
2.23 James Wilkinson
2.24 Orders in Council
2.25 impressment
2.26 repeal
2.27 No. It destroyed America's legitimate trade but did not seriously hurt Britain.
2.28 They demanded tribute to not capture trading ships. The pasha of Tripoli wanted a larger share and declared war.
2.29 They opposed it, calling it "O-grab-me." Illegal trade grew along the Canadian border and New England talked of leaving the Union.
2.30 A plot to separate New England, New York and New Jersey from the U.S.

2.31 James Madison
2.32 Henry Clay, John Calhoun
2.33 William Henry Harrison
2.34 Any order:
a. wanted Canada
b. wanted free trade
c. wanted to end Native American attacks
d. wanted to defend national honor
2.35 It was the 50th anniversary of the Declaration of Independence.
2.36 He formed an anti-American Confederacy among Native Americans all over the eastern Mississippi.
2.37 Any order:
a. small navy
b. small, disorganized army
c. militia would not leave the country
d. no National Bank
e. very little income from tariffs
or new taxes not raised before the war
2.38 mainly from the West, some from the South
2.39 They found British guns and powder in the Native American camp.
2.40 They had not fought in the Revolution and had no memory of the difficulties of war.
2.41 Canada
2.42 He said he had ended his trade restrictions when he had not. Madison believed him and restarted the embargo against Britain.
2.43 June 1812
2.44 Any order:
a. impressment
b. seizure of U.S. ships and cargoes
c. aid to Native Americans

SELF TEST 2

2.01 XYZ Affair
2.02 War Hawks
2.03 Whiskey Rebellion
2.04 Alien and Sedition Acts
2.05 Louisiana Purchase
2.06 Lewis and Clark
2.07 Federalist
2.08 Democratic-Republican
2.09 *Marbury v. Madison*
2.010 Embargo Act
2.011 Any order:
a. impress American sailors
b. aiding the Native Americans
c. seizing U.S. ships and cargoes
2.012 No
Any one of the following examples or others that the teacher approves:
– He kept the National Bank,
– made the Louisiana Purchase,
– passed and enforced the Embargo Act
2.013 The British ship *Leopard* fired on the *Chesapeake* killing several men and damaging the ship to recover four deserters.
2.014 Any three:
set up government structure,
kept peace,
set up strong financial base,
loose construction of Constitution
2.015 It was the first peaceful change of power between political parties.
2.016 against the Barbary pirates
2.017 g
2.018 a
2.019 f
2.020 c
2.021 b
2.022 j
2.023 h
2.024 i
2.025 e
2.026 d
2.027 a, b
2.028 a, d, e

SECTION 3

3.1 g

3.2 f

3.3 c

3.4 b

3.5 e

3.6 h

3.7 i

3.8 a

3.9 d

3.10 Mr. Madison's War

3.11 Michilimackinac

3.12 *Old Ironsides*

3.13 "We have met the enemy and they are ours."

3.14 privateers

3.15 Any order:
  a. They opposed Napoleon and did not want to help defeat Britain.
  b. The war cut off all trade with Britain.

3.16 Canada

3.17 The frigates were larger, with better guns. All of the American ships were manned by free patriots, not men forced into the job.

3.18 He built five ships on Lake Erie and had five more towed up the Niagara River by oxen.

3.19 Napoleon was defeated in Europe.

3.20 Native American Nation south of the Great Lakes, British control of the Lakes and British keep land in Maine.

3.21 They did not get the victories they expected.

3.22 To inflict several defeats on America and then make demands for land in exchange for peace.

3.23 A hastily assembled militia force.

3.24 John Quincy Adams

3.25 Maine

3.26 They blockaded the American coast; doubled up their ships—no more single sailing

3.27 Battle of Plattsburgh Bay; Thomas Macdonough

3.28 They burned most of the public buildings.

3.29 They attacked by land and sea.

3.30 Fort McHenry

3.31 Lundy's Lane and Chippewa

3.32 A return to the status quo.

3.33 Teacher check
  This is an example:
  Can you see when the sun rises or what we saw last evening? The flag that was flying over the fortifications through the dangerous night. The light from the bombs and rockets showed it was still there. Does that star-studded flag still wave over the land of the free and brave?

Thus it will always be when free men protect the homes they love from the ravages of war. Blessed with both peace and victory, may the land God rescued praise Him who made and preserved our nation. We will win when we fight for a just cause under the motto, "In God is our trust." Does that star-studded flag and still wave over the land of the free and brave?

3.34 Andrew Jackson

3.35 Hartford Convention

3.36 Creek

3.37 two weeks

3.38 Florida

3.39 Horseshoe Bend

3.40 Andrew Jackson, Seminole

3.41 Adams-Onis

3.42 manufacturing

3.43 arbitration

3.44 respect

3.45 They began to steadily improve. They did not fight any more wars, but settled problems by diplomacy.

3.46 The war had removed the major Native American and foreign powers there.

3.47 They made a frontal attack on a well- fortified position.

3.48 That America won the war.

3.49 To expand across the continent.

3.50 Any order:
  a. tariff to protect industry
  b. National Bank
  c. improve transportation

3.51 a. 640
  b. 320
  c. 160
  d. 80

3.52 Era of Good Feelings

3.53 a. *Dartmouth College v. Woodard*
  b. *McCulloch v. Maryland*
  c. *Gibbons v. Ogden*
  d. *Fletcher v. Peck*
  e. *Cohens v. Virginia*

3.54 Any order:
  a. America closed to more European colonies
  b. any European intervention in the Americas would be viewed as a hostile act against the U.S.
  c. U.S. would not intervene in Europe
  d. U.S. would not interfere with current European Colonies

3.55 Nationalism

3.56 Improvements within a state were opposed because they believed it was unconstitutional to use federal money for a project in just one state.

3.57 a. Nicholas Biddle
b. Panic of 1819

3.58 Eastern Mississippi

3.59 Great Britain

3.60 a. John Marshall
b. Hamilton's Federalists

3.61 Its tighter policies contributed to the Panic of 1819 and it foreclosed on many farms, especially in the west.

3.62 a. Cumberland Road
b. 1811
c. Cumberland, Maryland to Vandalia, Illinois

3.63 turnpikes

SELF TEST 3

3.01 capture Canada

3.02 Any two:
keep part of Maine,
Native Americans south of Great Lakes,
control of the Great Lakes

3.03 Any order:
a. tariffs to protect industries
b. National Bank
c. improvements in transportation

3.04 Any two:
impressment of sailors,
aid to the Native Americans,
seizure of ships and cargoes

3.05 Any two:
pay debt at full value,
take over state debts,
National Bank

3.06 Monroe Doctrine

3.07 Battle of New Orleans

3.08 Washington

3.09 Democratic-Republican

3.010 New England

3.011 Hartford Convention

3.012 Era of Good Feelings

3.013 Whiskey Rebellion

3.014 *U.S.S. Constitution*

3.015 Star-Spangled Banner

3.016 d

3.017 c

3.018 g

3.019 b

3.020 i

3.021 h

3.022 e

3.023 j

3.024 f

3.025 a

3.026 true

3.027 false

3.028 false

3.029 false

3.030 true

3.031 false

3.032 true

3.033 false

3.034 true

3.035 true

LIFEPAC TEST

1. P
2. C
3. R
4. R
5. C
6. P
7. C
8. R
9. R
10. C
11. Florida
12. XYZ Affair
13. Federalist
14. Great Seal
15. Louisiana Purchase
16. Alien and Sedition Acts
17. tariffs
18. Era of Good Feelings
19. McHenry
20. Hartford Convention
21. h
22. e
23. g
24. d
25. i
26. b
27. a
28. c
29. f
30. j
31. b
32. c
33. a
34. d
35. c
36. b
37. a
38. b
39. c
40. b

ALTERNATE LIFEPAC TEST

1. g
2. p
3. i
4. h
5. t
6. x
7. w
8. a
9. l
10. s
11. m
12. v
13. f
14. j
15. k
16. o
17. u
18. r
19. q
20. y
21. n
22. b
23. c
24. d
25. e
26. Thomas Jefferson
27. George Washington
28. James Monroe
29. Alexander Hamilton
30. Aaron Burr
31. John Marshall
32. Andrew Jackson
33. John Adams
34. Henry Clay
35. William Henry Harrison
36. true
37. true
38. false
39. false
40. true
41. false
42. false
43. false
44. true
45. true
46. true
47. true

48. true
49. true
50. false
51. false
52. true
53. false
54. false
55. false

HISTORY & GEOGRAPHY 804

ALTERNATE LIFEPAC TEST

NAME _____

DATE _____

SCORE _____

Match the following (each answer, 2 points).

1. _____ XYZ Affair
2. _____ War Hawks
3. _____ Whiskey Rebellion
4. _____ Federalists
5. _____ Democratic-Republican
6. _____ Alien and Sedition Acts
7. _____ Convention of 1800
8. _____ Citizen Genêt
9. _____ Battle of New Orleans
10. _____ Battle of Plattsburgh Bay
11. _____ Barbary pirates
12. _____ *Chesapeake-Leopard* Affair
13. _____ *U.S.S. Constitution*
14. _____ Louisiana Purchase
15. _____ Lewis and Clark
16. _____ Tecumseh
17. _____ *Marbury v. Madison*
18. _____ Embargo Act
19. _____ Jay's Treaty
20. _____ War of 1812
21. _____ Battle of Lake Erie
22. _____ Spain ceded Florida
23. _____ American System
24. _____ Nationalism
25. _____ Monroe Doctrine

a. French envoy who threatened U.S. neutrality by trying to get Americans into British-French war

b. after Andrew Jackson defeated the Seminoles

c. Henry Clay's proposal to use higher tariffs to aid transportation in the states

d. the nation's reaction after the War of 1812

e. Europe told to stay out of America

f. *Old Ironsides*, famous U.S. frigate

g. French try to get bribes to negotiate

h. political party of John Adams

i. revolt against the excise tax

j. land bought from France west of Mississippi

k. expedition that explored Louisiana Territory

l. American victory after war ended

m. Jefferson sent the navy against them

n. victory by Oliver Perry, "We have met the enemy and they are ours."

o. set up Native American confederacy against U.S.

p. young congressman from the west who wanted war with Britain

q. American-British agreement under Washington that held off war, but was very unpopular

r. Jefferson's attempt to avoid war by stopping trade

s. stopped the British from invading New York along Lake Champlain

t. political party that dominated early 1800s

u. Supreme Court claimed for itself the right to declare laws unconstitutional

v. British warship fires on American ship; seizes four seamen

w. French-American agreement that ended the Revolutionary alliance

x. Federalist laws to silence opposition

y. Second War for Independence

Name the person (each answer, 3 points).

26. _____ third president; first secretary of state

27. _____ only president to receive unanimous electoral vote

28. _____ president of the "Era of Good Feelings"

29. _____ first secretary of treasury; set the nation's finances up securely

30. _____ vice president under Jefferson; tried to start a conspiracy in the west, acquitted of treason

31. _____ Federalist chief justice of the Supreme Court; set up the court's power

32. _____ American general who defeated the Creek people and the British at New Orleans

33. _____ vice president under Washington; second president

34. _____ Speaker of the House; leader of War Hawks

35. _____ American victor at Tippecanoe and the Thames

Answer *true* **or** *false* (each answer, 1 point).

36. _____ One result of the War of 1812 was the beginning of manufacturing tradition in America.

37. _____ One result of the War of 1812 was the end of wars with Britain.

38. _____ One result of the War of 1812 was the end of the Democratic-Republican party.

39. _____ The Great Seal of the United States has an eagle on one side and the White House on the other.

40. _____ The southern states agreed to allow the Revolutionary war debts to be taken by the federal government in exchange for the capital being located in the South.

41. _____ Jefferson believed in "strict construction" of the Constitution and lived by that when he was in office.

42. _____ The lack of a national bank helped the nation during the War of 1812.

43. _____ The Federalist party left only a legacy of disunity and factionalism.

44. _____ Washington urged the nation to avoid permanent alliances in his *Farewell Address* and the nation followed that advice for years.

45. _____ The British were supporting the Native Americans harassing the American frontier before the War of 1812.

46. _____ Jefferson reduced the national debt and ran the government as cheaply as possible.

47. _____ The election of 1800 was important because it was the first peaceful change of political power from one party to another.

48. _____ British impressment of sailors on American ships was an issue under every president from Washington to Madison.

49. _____ John Adams lost his popularity because he refused to go to war with France.

50. _____ New Englanders heavily supported the War of 1812.

51. _____ George Washington served one term as president.

52. _____ John Adams and his vice president were from different parties.

53. _____ The Hartford Convention destroyed what was left of the popularity of the early Democratic Party.

54. _____ Tecumseh was killed at the Battle of Tippecanoe.

55. _____ America had an excellent, well-supplied navy and army ready by the time the War of 1812 started.

HISTORY & GEOGRAPHY 805

Unit 5: A Growing Nation (1820-1855)

TEACHER NOTES

MATERIALS NEEDED FOR LIFEPAC	
Required	Suggested
None	• atlas • encyclopedia • reference books or online sources

ADDITIONAL LEARNING ACTIVITIES

Section 1: Jacksonian Era

1. Have students write a 500-word biography of one of these men: Henry Clay, John C. Calhoun, or Daniel Webster.

2. Tell students to assume the role of the Senate in 1820 (half would be from slave states, half from free; a few would be strong unionist and a few strongly anti-slavery) in order to debate and vote on the Missouri Compromise.

3. Debate this statement as a class: "Resolved: Andrew Jackson was a poor president."

4. Discuss these questions:

    a. Would you vote for John Quincy Adams for president?

    b. Were tariffs good or bad for the nation?

    c. Was Andrew Jackson good or bad for the United States?

    d. Was the campaign of 1828 more or less civilized than the most recent presidential campaign?

5. Have students re-enact the Webster-Hayne Debate and evaluate the arguments.

6. Instruct students to research the National Bank issue under Andrew Jackson. Have them list the arguments that could be made for and against the Bank.

7. Assign students to research the Trail of Tears and do a report or write a paper about it.

8. As a class, debate the issue of nullification.

9. Have students research and discuss the causes of the Panics in early American history.

Section 2: Manifest Destiny

1. Have students debate the morality of Manifest Destiny.

2. Have students research the conflict between Britain and the U.S. over Maine and summarize it in one page (250 words).

3. Have students read the true story of one person who traveled the Oregon Trail.

4. Play a computer game that requires you to survive a trip down the Oregon Trail (an online game can be found on traveloregon.com/thegame).

5. Have students read a book on the Texas Revolution or the life of one of its heroes: Stephen Austin, Davy Crockett, Sam Houston, Jim Bowie, or William Travis.

6. Have students build a model or diagram of the battle for the Alamo or San Jacinto.

7. As a class, read a detailed description of one of the battles in the Mexican War.

8. Assign students to write a 500-word biography of one of these men: Santa Anna, Zachary Taylor, Winfield Scott, or John C. Fremont.

9. As a class, assemble a list of Civil War generals who served in the Mexican War. Have students write a brief statement of each person's rank and accomplishments in the earlier war.

10. As a class, discuss the Mexican War from the Mexican point of view.

11. Have students read the true story of one person who was in the California Gold Rush.

Section 3: Growth and Division

1. Have students research the conditions of the textile factories in the 1850s, and then write a report to the government, recommending laws to protect the workers.

2. Assign students to write a 250-word paper on the development and impact of one of these inventions: mechanical reaper, telegraph, cotton gin, steamboat, railroad engines, sewing machine, or spinning jenny.

3. Have students read a description of travel and transport on the Erie Canal.

4. Students can build a model of a canal barge.

5. As a class, read about the Irish Potato Famine, and have students discuss what they would have done if they were one of the farmers hit by it.

6. Have students research and discuss the American traditions that came from Germany.

7. Assign students to write a paper on one of the following: camp meetings, Charles Finney, Francis Asbury, Joseph Smith, Mormonism, Brigham Young, the settlement of Utah, the Seneca Falls Convention, William Wilberforce, or the temperance movement in the 1800s.

8. Have students assume the role of the Senate in 1850 (don't forget Webster, Calhoun, and Clay) to debate and vote on the Compromise of 1850. (Note: half the senators were from slave states and half were from free states).

9. Have students read a book about the Underground Railroad or a person who worked on it.

10. Have the class research and debate the morality of Perry's treaty with Japan.

11. Discuss why things became so out of control in "Bleeding Kansas."

12. Let students select reading material about slavery (fiction, nonfiction, or autobiography)

Administer the LIFEPAC Test

The test is to be administered in one session. Give no help except with directions.
Evaluate the tests and review areas where the students have done poorly.
Review the pages and activities that stress the concepts tested.
If necessary, administer the Alternate LIFEPAC Test.

ANSWER KEYS

SECTION 1

1.1	d		**1.40**	a
1.2	a, d		**1.41**	b
1.3	b		**1.42**	c
1.4	c		**1.43**	d
1.5	a		**1.44**	e
1.6	a		**1.45**	d
1.7	d		**1.46**	a
1.8	b		**1.47**	f
1.9	a, d		**1.48**	f
1.10	a		**1.49**	c
1.11	d		**1.50**	a
1.12	c		**1.51**	d
1.13	d		**1.52**	e
1.14	a		**1.53**	e
1.15	b		**1.54**	b

1.16 Any order:
   a. slavery
   b. tariff

1.17 Any order:
   a. Missouri admitted as slave state
   b. Maine admitted as free state
   c. no slavery north of 36° 30′ in the Louisiana Purchase

1.18 cotton gin
1.19 ___
1.20 ___
1.21 _X_
1.22 ___
1.23 _X_
1.24 ___
1.25 _X_
1.26 _X_
1.27 _X_
1.28 ___
1.29 _X_
1.30 _X_
1.31 ___
1.32 _X_
1.33 "Jackson and Reform."
1.34 Tariff of Abominations
1.35 Andrew Jackson
1.36 Old Man Eloquent
1.37 A series of resolutions that barred any petition on slavery from being heard in the House.
1.38 Henry Clay
1.39 adultery and bigamy

1.55 d
1.56 c
1.57 d
1.58 He was slashed with a sword across the face and hand for refusing to clean a British officer's boots.
1.59 duels
1.60 Any order:
   a. hatred of Native Americans
   b. distrust of banks
   c. determination to expand the nation
1.61 A state can nullify any federal law they believed was unconstitutional.
1.62 kitchen cabinet
1.63 John Calhoun
1.64 Martin Van Buren
1.65 He hoped to hurt Jackson's popularity in the election of 1832 by forcing him to charter a bank distrusted by the west or veto it when eastern businessmen wanted it.
1.66 Andrew Jackson
1.67 Trail of Tears
1.68 pet
1.69 tariff
1.70 Panic of 1837
1.71 censure
1.72 speculation
1.73 Seminole
1.74 Cherokee
1.75 Force
1.76 hang
1.77 Black Hawk

1.78   Martin Van Buren

1.79   Jackson

1.80   Martin Van Buren

1.81   A new tariff was passed that gradually reduced the tariff over a number of years.

1.82   That the Native Americans would be moved to lands where they would be forever free from white encroachment.

1.83   He moved federal money out of it and placed it into loyal state banks.

SELF TEST 1

1.01   j

1.02   d

1.03   b

1.04   g

1.05   f

1.06   i

1.07   e

1.08   c

1.09   a

1.010   h

1.011   Tariff of Abominations

1.012   Missouri Compromise

1.013   cotton gin

1.014   Democrats

1.015   National Republicans or Whigs

1.016   John Quincy Adams

1.017   Panic of 1837

1.018   Spoils System

1.019   Trail of Tears

1.020   *Specie Circular*

1.021   A state could nullify any federal law it believed was unconstitutional.

1.022   He was not popular and too honest to use government jobs to gain popularity.
He was opposed at every turn by the Democrats angry over the defeat of Andrew Jackson.

1.023   He was the son of poor immigrants in Tennessee, orphaned as a young man. Became a successful lawyer, politician, and land speculator. Defeated the Creek people as a militia general and the British at New Orleans as a U.S. army general.

1.024   He prepared troops and supplies.
He requested the Force Bill to authorize the army to collect the tariff in South Carolina.
It was resolved by a compromise tariff that lowered the rates over several years.

1.025   He wanted to force Jackson to veto or accept the charter believing that either one would hurt the president's popularity. Jackson did veto it and won the election anyway.

1.026   Hundreds of people crowded in, breaking and tearing things. The crush forced Jackson to leave. The crowds left when punch was served on the lawn.

1.027	false
1.028	true
1.029	true
1.030	true
1.031	true
1.032	false
1.033	false
1.034	false
1.035	false
1.036	false

SECTION 2

2.1 g
2.2 f
2.3 d
2.4 c
2.5 a
2.6 b
2.7 Log cabin; Hard Cider
2.8 Henry Clay
2.9 Democratic
2.10 Webster-Ashburton
2.11 Oregon Trail
2.12 Columbia River; 49th parallel
2.13 harbor
2.14 "Fifty-four Forty or Fight."
2.15 "Tippecanoe and Tyler, too."
2.16 His Accidency
2.17 Aroostook
2.18 American Desert
2.19 49th
2.20 Any order: a national bank, higher tariffs, internal improvements
2.21 Texas; Oregon
2.22 Marcus Whitman
2.23 Britain
2.24 2,000
2.25 false
— change *Moses* to *Stephen*
2.26 false
— change *Most* to *All*
2.27 true
2.28 false
— change *Goliad* to *San Jacinto*
2.29 true
2.30 true
2.31 false
— change *Webster-Ashburton* to *Adams-Onis*
2.32 false
— change *Henry Clay* to *James Polk*
2.33 true
2.34 true
2.35 Any order:
a. William Travis,
b. Jim Bowie,
c. Davy Crockett
2.36 Any order:
a. lower the tariff
b. create an independent treasury
c. settle border dispute in Oregon
d. add California to the U.S.
2.37 Gone to Texas
2.38 He sent Zachary Taylor into an area of South Texas claimed by Mexico hoping the Mexicans would attack and they did.

2.39 Santa Anna declared himself dictator and suspended the constitution.

2.40 "Remember the Alamo! Remember Goliad!"

2.41 He retreated in front of Santa Anna, gaining strength as Santa Anna lost his.

2.42 b

2.43 a

2.44 b

2.45 c

2.46 a

2.47 d

2.48 e

2.49 f

2.50 b

2.51 b

2.52 c

2.53 g

2.54 b

2.55 f

2.56 the Military Academy at West Point

2.57 Civil War

2.58 It was questionable whether it began with an attack on American soil. It was believed to be a conspiracy to add slave states. It was feared that fighting over the new territory might divide the nation.

2.59 He believed they were politically motivated.

2.60 artillery

2.61 Guadalupe-Hidalgo

2.62 slavery

2.63 Old Fuss and Feathers

2.64 gold

2.65 Zachary Taylor

2.66 Free Soil

2.67 Gadsden

2.68 Forty-niners

2.69 Mexico City

2.70 Nicholas Trist

2.71 Any order:
   a. overland via wagon trail
   b. by ship to the Isthmus of Panama, across, and north again by ship
   c. around South America by ship

2.72 fifteen million

2.73 Santa Anna

2.74 1849; territory

2.75 "Free soil, free speech, free labor, free men."

2.76 railroad

2.77 Cerro Gordo

2.78 Mexican Cession

2.79 Rio Grande

2.80 Wilmont

2.81 slavery

2.82 Millard Fillmore

2.83 Winfield Scott

SELF TEST 2

2.01 i

2.02 f

2.03 g

2.04 c

2.05 j

2.06 h

2.07 a

2.08 d

2.09 b

2.010 e

2.011 Any order:
   a. Daniel Webster
   b. Henry Clay
   c. John Calhoun

2.012 Mexican Cession

2.013 Fifty-four Forty or Fight

2.014 Remember the Alamo! *or* Remember Goliad!

2.015 Texas

2.016 California

2.017 Nullification

2.018 National Bank

2.019 Maine and Oregon

2.020 Taylor took a position in the disputed land north of the Rio Grande and was attacked by the Mexican army.

2.021 The campaign against Mexico City led by Winfield Scott

2.022 Santa Anna surrounded it. The defenders held him off for two weeks, then were all killed.

2.023 He was a popular military hero with no political experience.

2.024 U.S. received all of California and the land west of Texas, with borders set at the Rio Grande and Gila Rivers. U.S. paid $15 million to Mexico and took over Mexican debts to U.S. citizens.

2.025 Clay gave Adams the presidency in the House of Representatives vote in exchange for the position of Secretary of State.

2.026 They were split over the topic of slavery in the new lands.

2.027 The party could not agree on one of the major candidates and Jackson supported Polk.

2.028 It split into the Democrats and the Whigs (National Republicans).

2.029 j
2.030 g
2.031 i
2.032 d
2.033 a
2.034 h
2.035 f
2.036 b
2.037 e
2.038 c

SECTION 3

3.1 h
3.2 e
3.3 e
3.4 g
3.5 h
3.6 d
3.7 c
3.8 f
3.9 g
3.10 a
3.11 h
3.12 b
3.13 Britain
3.14 it became profitable
3.15 Any three:
water source, capital, population, poor soil, seaports
3.16 Any four:
long hours, low wages, use of children, unsafe working conditions, no job protection, law opposed unions
3.17 A change from farming and hand crafts to industry and machine manufacturing.
3.18 Cities devoted to manufacturing needed transport to get food from the farms and a way to ship finished goods.
3.19 There was a strong feeling against using federal money to benefit one state.
3.20 It connected the west with the cities of the east even when the Mississippi River was in Confederate hands.
3.21 States saw the success of the Erie Canal and wanted to copy it.
3.22 steamships
3.23 a
3.24 c
3.25 a
3.26 h
3.27 d
3.28 f
3.29 g
3.30 g
3.31 b
3.32 f
3.33 b
3.34 a
3.35 h
3.36 c
3.37 f
3.38 e
3.39 e
3.40 d

3.41 d

3.42 Second Great Awakening

3.43 Know-Nothing

3.44 Any order:
Ireland; Germany

3.45 polygamy

3.46 Potato Famine

3.47 camp meetings

3.48 Seneca Falls Convention

3.49 Unitarians

3.50 *The Liberator*

3.51 Temperance

3.52 Joseph Smith

3.53 William Wilberforce

3.54 Any order:
Baptists; Methodists

3.55 Brigham Young; Utah

3.56 Any six:
prisons, treatment of the insane, debt law, drinking, working conditions, punishments, women's rights, slavery

3.57 true

3.58 true

3.59 false

3.60 true

3.61 false

3.62 false

3.63 true

3.64 false

3.65 false

3.66 true

3.67 Any order:
a. California admitted as free state
b. Popular sovereignty in Mexican Cession
c. Texas border set as it is today
d. Texas given $10 million compensation
e. Slave trade ended in Washington D.C.
f. Fugitive Slave Law

3.68 Clay: proposed and supported it
Calhoun: opposed it
Webster: supported it

3.69 Taylor opposed the Compromise, but Fillmore supported it and signed it.

3.70 It had a slave-run plantation economy.

3.71 He used threats and tact to convince Japan to allow trade with the U.S.

3.72 A plan to take Cuba by force if Spain refused to sell. It embarrassed Pierce's administration and caused him to back away from Cuba.

3.73 A series of people and homes that hid and helped runaway slaves reach Canada.

3.74 ___

3.75 ___

3.76 _X_

3.77 _X_

3.78 _X_

3.79 ___

3.80 _X_

3.81 _X_

3.82 ___

3.83 *Uncle Tom's Cabin*

3.84 Stephen Douglas

3.85 Republican

3.86 Harriet Beecher Stowe

3.87 northern

3.88 _K_

3.89 ___

3.90 _K_

3.91 _K_

3.92 ___

3.93 ___

3.94 _K_

3.95 ___

3.96 ___

SELF TEST 3

3.01	h		**3.047**	false
3.02	d		**3.048**	false
3.03	b		**3.049**	true
3.04	i		**3.050**	true
3.05	o		**3.051**	false
3.06	p		**3.052**	false
3.07	m		**3.053**	false
3.08	f		**3.054**	true
3.09	g		**3.055**	true
3.010	k		**3.056**	false
3.011	b			
3.012	e			
3.013	l			
3.014	j			
3.015	f			
3.016	n			
3.017	c			
3.018	i			
3.019	a			
3.020	d			
3.021	f			
3.022	g			
3.023	e			
3.024	k			
3.025	d			
3.026	Industrial Revolution			
3.027	Know-Nothing			
3.028	Second Great Awakening			
3.029	Alamo			
3.030	Underground Railroad			
3.031	Kansas-Nebraska			
3.032	turnpikes			
3.033	Potato Famine			
3.034	Fugitive Slave Law			
3.035	Republican			
3.036	true			
3.037	true			
3.038	false			
3.039	false			
3.040	false			
3.041	false			
3.042	true			
3.043	true			
3.044	false			
3.045	false			
3.046	true			

LIFEPAC TEST

1. d
2. f
3. c
4. a
5. a
6. b
7. b
8. h
9. i
10. e
11. f
12. g
13. b
14. b
15. f
16. Missouri Compromise
17. Compromise of 1850
18. Trail of Tears
19. Manifest Destiny
20. "Fifty-four Forty or Fight"
21. Clipper Ships
22. Erie Canal
23. the tariff
24. Spoils system
25. Oregon Trail
26. e
27. o
28. j
29. f
30. m
31. b
32. a
33. l
34. n
35. c
36. k
37. g
38. i
39. d
40. h
41. true
42. false
43. true
44. false
45. true
46. true
47. false
48. false
49. true
50. false

ALTERNATE LIFEPAC TEST

1. r
2. h
3. n
4. s
5. d
6. i
7. o
8. q
9. k
10. t
11. c
12. b
13. a
14. p
15. g
16. f
17. m
18. j
19. e
20. l
21. e
22. m
23. r
24. c
25. n
26. p
27. l
28. a
29. j
30. t
31. s
32. q
33. f
34. i
35. b
36. h
37. d
38. o
39. k
40. g
41. Any three:
   treatment of the insane, women's rights, working conditions, education, slavery, temperance, prison and punishment, debt laws
42. Any order:
   a. Democratic
   b. Whig (National Republicans)
43. a. Kansas-Nebraska Act
   b. Stephen Douglas

44. Andrew Jackson
45. Any one:
land speculation,
credit from unstable banks,
Jackson's economic policies (close National
Bank, *Specie Circular*)
46. gold rush

HISTORY & GEOGRAPHY 805

ALTERNATE LIFEPAC TEST

NAME _____

DATE _____

SCORE _____

Match these people (each answer, 2 points).

1. _____ telegraph
2. _____ "His Accidency,"; Whig with Democrat ideas
3. _____ hero of northern Mexico campaign and later president
4. _____ Compromise of 1850 was the only major accomplishment of his accidental presidency
5. _____ added more land to the U.S. than any other president; first "dark horse" candidate
6. _____ sewing machine
7. _____ mechanical reaper
8. _____ hero of Mexico City
9. _____ pro-South northern president; wanted to add Cuba to the U.S.; embarrassed by the Osten Manifesto
10. _____ hero of Tippecanoe; shortest presidency in U.S. history
11. _____ steamboat
12. _____ fought against the National Bank and for Peggy Eaton as president
13. _____ the Great Compromiser; leader in Congress; never became president
14. _____ opened the first machine operated textile factory in America
15. _____ hand-chosen successor to Andrew Jackson; inherited the Panic of 1837
16. _____ leader of the South; favored nullification
17. _____ leader of the Texas Revolution; victor at San Jacinto
18. _____ interchangeable parts; cotton gin
19. _____ served with distinction as a representative in the House after being president; "Old Man Eloquent"
20. _____ northern orator; famous for debate with Haynes "Liberty and Union, now and forever, one and inseparable."

a. Henry Clay
b. Andrew Jackson
c. Robert Fulton
d. James K. Polk
e. John Quincy Adams
f. John Calhoun
g. Martin Van Buren
h. John Tyler
i. Elias Howe
j. Eli Whitney
k. Franklin Pierce
l. Daniel Webster
m. Sam Houston
n. Zachary Taylor
o. Cyrus McCormick
p. Samuel Slater
q. Winfield Scott
r. Samuel F. B. Morse
s. Millard Fillmore
t. William H. Harrison

Match these items (each answer, 2 points).

21. _____ the removal of the Native Americans of the southeast to land across the Mississippi

22. _____ secretive; anti-immigrant group

23. _____ California admitted as a free state; popular sovereignty in the Mexican Cession

24. _____ Polk's way of getting California

25. _____ revival

26. _____ popular anti-slavery novel

27. _____ the first workable steamboat

28. _____ attempt by South Carolina to void enforcement of the tariff in their state

29. _____ Treaty that ended the Mexican War and gave the U.S. the Mexican Cession

30. _____ punished people who aided runaway slaves and turned many Northerners against slavery

31. _____ replaced canals as the major carriers of bulk cargo in the U.S.

32. _____ religion started by Joseph Smith; practiced polygamy

33. _____ change from farming and hand crafts to industry and machines

34. _____ "Fifty-four Forty or Fight," never happened; British and U.S. agreed to extend the 49th parallel as the boundary

35. _____ Maine admitted as a free state; no slavery north of 36° 30′ in Louisiana Territory

36. _____ bought from Mexico for a southern railroad to California

37. _____ prevented any petition on slavery from being presented in Congress, John Quincy Adams successfully fought it

38. _____ a group that helped runaway slaves safely reach Canada

39. _____ early locomotive that lost a race with a horse

40. _____ America should expand all over the continent

a. Nullification Crisis
b. Missouri Compromise
c. Mexican War
d. Gag Rule
e. Trail of Tears
f. Industrial Revolution
g. Manifest Destiny
h. Gadsden Purchase
i. Oregon
j. Guadalupe Hidalgo
k. *Tom Thumb*
l. *Clermont*
m. Know-Nothing Party
n. Second Great Awakening
o. Underground Railroad
p. *Uncle Tom's Cabin*
q. Mormon
r. Compromise of 1850
s. railroad
t. Fugitive Slave Law

Complete these items (each answer, 2 points).

41. Name three areas in which reformers were active in the early 1800s.

    a. _____

    b. _____

    c. _____

42. What two parties did the Democratic-Republican Party split into?

    a. _____

    b. _____

43. Name the law that ended the era of compromise and the man who created it.

    a. _____

    b. _____

44. Who was the only president of this era to serve two terms?

    _____

45. Name one of the reasons for the Panic of 1837.

    _____

46. Why did California's population grow so quickly after 1848?

    _____

HISTORY & GEOGRAPHY 806

Unit 6: The Civil War (1855-1880)

TEACHER NOTES

MATERIALS NEEDED FOR LIFEPAC	
Required	Suggested
None	• atlas • encyclopedia • reference books or online sources

ADDITIONAL LEARNING ACTIVITIES

Section 1: Increasing Disunion

1. As a class, discuss the issues that divided the country prior to the Civil War and whether or not war could have been avoided.

2. Discuss the debate over slavery as viewed by the North and the South in 1860.

3. As a class, discuss the people's reactions to the Dred Scott decision, and prompt students to explain their own reaction.

4. Two students can pretend they are Lincoln and Douglas and debate the issues of 1860.

5. Assign students to write a report on John Brown's Raid, the election of 1860, the Dred Scott Decision, the Abolitionist movement, black soldiers in the Civil War, or Bleeding Kansas; and present it to the class.

6. Have students research and do a report or paper on any Civil War political or military leader, North or South.

Section 2: Civil War

1. Students can create a model or diagram of any battle.

2. Have students find and read personal stories of men and women (mainly nurses and spies) who served in the war.

3. Students or groups can construct models of the *Merrimac* and the *Monitor* and demonstrate why they could not harm each other.

4. The class can watch and discuss the movie *Gettysburg*.

5. Have the class do a dramatic reading of the Gettysburg Address.

6. Assign students to research and do a report or paper on medical science in the 1860s.

7. Have students read an account of Andersonville prison.

8. After research, students can do a re-enactment of Lee's surrender at Appomattox Courthouse.

9. Have students read an account of the conspiracy organized by John Wilkes Booth to assassinate Lincoln and other government leaders, and report to the class.

10. Have the class use the internet to find artifacts, memorabilia, documents, clothing and pictures from the Civil War.

Section 3: Reconstruction

1. Have students assume the role of the Senate in 1865 (only Union representatives) in order to debate the issue of what to do with the conquered Confederacy.

2. Discuss the impeachment of Andrew Johnson and why it happened.

3. Read and discuss the 13th, 14th, and 15th Amendments as a class. What were they intended to do and what did they actually accomplish?

4. Have students read different stories of life in the South during Reconstruction and discuss them in class.

5. Help students research the methods of the Ku Klux Klan and other redeemers (you may want to provide resources in advance). As a class, discuss why these groups thought they were right and how God viewed their actions. You can also tie in connections with modern times.

6. As a class, draw a map of Alaska, marking the locations of its many resources.

7. Have students read about Ulysses S. Grant's life and debate what kind of a man, general and president he was.

8. Have the class read about Boss Tweed and Tammany Hall.

9. Assign students to research and do a report or paper on the election of 1876 or how the Civil War changed the South.

10. Have the class read about Lucy Web Hayes and discuss the role of the First Lady.

Administer the LIFEPAC Test

The test is to be administered in one session. Give no help except with directions.
Evaluate the tests and review areas where the students have done poorly.
Review the pages and activities that stress the concepts tested.
If necessary, administer the Alternate LIFEPAC Test.

ANSWER KEYS

SECTION 1

1.1 Brooks; Sumner
1.2 Any order:
James Buchanan, John Fremont,
Millard Fillmore
1.3 Democratic
1.4 James Buchanan; Stephen Douglas
1.5 1830s
1.6 agriculture
1.7 South
1.8 Lawrence
1.9 anti-
1.10 The Crime Against Kansas
1.11 John Brown
1.12 Free soil, free men, and Fremont
1.13 The abolitionist movement along with the north's larger population, political power, and the growth of the anti-slavery Republican Party.
1.14 They ignored it as much as possible.
1.15 It protected slavery. The people could vote for the constitution only, with or without slavery. Thus, the anti-slavery voters could not stop slavery by voting against it.
1.16 The pro- and anti-slavery factions fought with each other.
1.17 He had been in Britain and had not been involved with the unpopular Kansas-Nebraska Act.
1.18 He had lived in free states for several years.
1.19 The arsenal at Harper's Ferry
1.20 Robert E. Lee
1.21 speculation in land and railroads
1.22 Lincoln-Douglas Debates
1.23 That Scott could not sue because he was not a citizen.
1.24 That he was property that was fully protected by the Constitution from seizure.
1.25 Slavery could only safely exist in a state if the local governments passed laws to protect it.
1.26 He was tried and hanged.
1.27 Any order:
a. Abraham Lincoln – Republican
b. Stephen Douglas – Democrat (North)
c. John Breckinridge – Democrat (South)
d. John Bell – Constitutional Union
1.28 Slavery was legal in all of the U.S.
1.29 It was morally wrong. It could not be ended where it already existed, but it must not spread.

1.30 He became an abolitionist martyr.
1.31 Any order:
a. no expansion of slavery
b. protective tariff
c. internal improvements
d. transcontinental railroad in North
e. protect rights of immigrants
f. free homesteads
1.32 a. The North refused to accept it and the South applauded it.
b. The South had little trouble with it and saw themselves as superior as a result.
c. The South saw the public support of Brown's violence as a threat.
1.33 Fort Sumter
1.34 Abraham Lincoln
1.35 4
1.36 Crittenden
1.37 James Buchanan
1.38 Any order:
Missouri, Kentucky, Delaware, Maryland
1.39 Honest Abe
1.40 South Carolina
1.41 Any order:
a. called for volunteers
b. suspended civil rights in border areas
c. ordered blockade of southern ports
d. ordered federal money to pay for the war effort
1.42 House of Representatives
1.43 provisions
1.44 Jefferson Davis
1.45 Montgomery, Alabama; Richmond, Virginia
1.46 West Virginia; 1863
1.47 S
1.48 N
1.49 N
1.50 S
1.51 S
1.52 N
1.53 N
1.54 S
1.55 N
1.56 N
1.57 S
1.58 N
1.59 N

1.60 It cut off incoming trade and stopped outgoing cotton which was the major source of southern income, creating shortages of money and supplies.

1.61 They did not favor the American democratic experiment, the South had a European-like aristocratic culture, and Confederacy would be an advantageous trading partner.

1.62 Corn, wheat, and the purchase of war material

1.63 An American warship arrested two Confederate diplomats on a British steamer. Britain threatened war. The men were released, and their capture disavowed.

1.64 Emancipation Proclamation

SELF TEST 1

1.01 b
1.02 g
1.03 i
1.04 j
1.05 c
1.06 f
1.07 a
1.08 h
1.09 e
1.010 d
1.011 Lecompton
1.012 Republican
1.013 Fort Sumter
1.014 Harper's Ferry
1.015 Lincoln-Douglas
1.016 Dred Scott
1.017 cotton
1.018 Kansas-Nebraska
1.019 South Carolina
1.020 Emancipation Proclamation
1.021 Any four:
farms, money, railroads, population, factories, resources, black soldiers, navy, government
1.022 Any two:
ideals, military leaders, defensive position
1.023 Any two:
to keep their supply of cotton, to divide the U.S. democracy, to have a non-manufacturing trading partner, to support the Confederate aristocracy
1.024 Any two:
Maryland, Delaware, Kentucky, Missouri
1.025 true
1.026 true
1.027 false
1.028 true
1.029 true
1.030 true
1.031 true
1.032 false
1.033 true
1.034 true

SECTION 2

2.1 Military tactics used mass attacks from the days when weapons were inaccurate and slow. The faster, more accurate Civil War weapons made such attacks slaughters.

2.2 He rebuilt, organized, and supplied a large, effective Union army.

2.3 He was hesitant to attack unless he was certain of superior numbers and position.

2.4 World War II

2.5 620,000

2.6 First Bull Run

2.7 Donelson

2.8 New Orleans

2.9 First Bull Run

2.10 First Bull Run

2.11 Fort Henry

2.12 Shiloh

2.13 First Bull Run

2.14 Henry and Donelson

2.15 Shiloh

2.16 Corinth

2.17 First Bull Run

2.18 First Bull Run

2.19 Emancipation Proclamation

2.20 Fair Oaks (Seven Pines)

2.21 *Monitor*

2.22 Seven Days

2.23 Antietam

2.24 Second Bull Run

2.25 Robert E. Lee

2.26 Antietam

2.27 Fredericksburg

2.28 Stonewall Jackson

2.29 Emancipation Proclamation

2.30 *Merrimac*

2.31 British West Indies

2.32 Fair Oaks (Seven Pines)

2.33 Seven Days

2.34 Antietam

2.35 Fredericksburg

2.36 McClellan

2.37 Gettysburg

2.38 Chancellorsville

2.39 Vicksburg

2.40 Murfreesboro

2.41 Vicksburg

2.42 Chancellorsville

2.43 Gettysburg

2.44 Gettysburg

2.45 Vicksburg

2.46 Gettysburg

2.47 Gettysburg

2.48 Chancellorsville

2.49 Chancellorsville

2.50 Gettysburg

2.51 eighty-seven years

2.52 It had already been dedicated by the men who had fought and died there. They could not add to that dedication.

2.53 to finishing the work (the war) those men had died for

2.54 these dead shall not have died in vain

2.55 He failed to pursue Lee who was allowed to escape.

2.56 William Rosencrans; Braxton Bragg

2.57 Confederate

2.58 200,000 – 300,000

2.59 George Thomas

2.60 Andersonville

2.61 Sanitary Commission

2.62 Any order:
paying a substitute; paying a $300 fee

2.63 Union

2.64 Chickamauga

2.65 Rock of

2.66 Battle above the Clouds

2.67 Ulysses S. Grant

2.68 amputation

2.69 the draft law

2.70 Chattanooga

2.71 Petersburg

2.72 Jubal Early

2.73 Cold Harbor

2.74 Wilderness

2.75 David Farragut

2.76 George McClellan

2.77 Andrew Johnson

2.78 William T. Sherman

2.79 Copperheads

2.80 Philip Sheridan

2.81 Mobile, Alabama

2.82 War Democrats

2.83 John Hood

2.84 lieutenant-general

2.85 When his army was mauled by Lee, he kept going.

2.86 The re-election of Abraham Lincoln

2.87 Attack, shift, attack, and keep at it until Lee gave out

2.88 Everything that might aid the enemy is destroyed. (farms, factories, crops, etc.)

2.89 false
— change *Nashville* to *Atlanta*

2.90 true

2.91 false
— change *January* to *April*

2.92 true

2.93 true

2.94 false
— change *Richmond* to *Appomattox Courthouse*

2.95 false
— change *Grant* to *Sheridan*

2.96 true

2.97 true

2.98 false
— change *was captured* to *fled*

2.99 true

2.100 true

2.101 false
— change *rifles* to *horses*

2.102 false
— change *hanged after a trial* to *shot by Union troops*

2.103 true

2.104 false
— change *Meade* to *Grant*

2.105 Teacher check

SELF TEST 2

2.01 m

2.02 h

2.03 i

2.04 a

2.05 k

2.06 c

2.07 j

2.08 b

2.09 k

2.010 b

2.011 d

2.012 f

2.013 l

2.014 g

2.015 e

2.016 C

2.017 U

2.018 U

2.019 C

2.020 C

2.021 U

2.022 U

2.023 C

2.024 U

2.025 C

2.026 Kansas-Nebraska

2.027 Dred Scott

2.028 Emancipation Proclamation

2.029 Gettysburg

2.030 James Buchanan

2.031 Andersonville

2.032 disease

2.033 Appomattox Courthouse

2.034 John Wilkes Booth

2.035 South Carolina

2.036 Any two:
military leaders, defensive position, ideals (early in the war)

2.037 He kept going after Lee hit him hard.

2.038 Any two:
a. Emancipation Proclamation
b. North sold them wheat and com; North bought military supplies

2.039 Slavery could not constitutionally be ended where it existed, but it should not be allowed to spread.

2.040 The pro- and anti-slavery forces fought with each other.

2.041 The North had more factories, farms, money, and better transportation to deliver what the army needed.

2.042 It was peaceful and reasonably normal in the midst of a civil war.

2.043 Older military tactics called for mass attacks which were mowed down by new rifles and artillery.

2.044 true

2.045 false

2.046 false

2.047 true

2.048 false

2.049 true

2.050 false

2.051 false

2.052 false

2.053 false

SECTION 3

3.1 ten percent

3.2 Any order:
   a. approve the 13th Amendment
   b. repudiate Confederate debts
   c. repeal secession

3.3 Radical Republicans

3.4 Thirteenth

3.5 tailor

3.6 Civil Rights Act

3.7 Freedmen's Bureau

3.8 overrode it

3.9 Any order:
   a. made Freedmen citizens
   b. cut Congressional representation if they were denied the right to vote
   c. barred certain Confederate leaders from office
   d. voided Confederate debts

3.10 He hoped to influence Congressional elections to get a body that favored his reconstruction plan.

3.11 He believed it interfered with the rights of southern states.

3.12 Any order:
   a. Homestead Act
   b. high tariff
   c. subsidy for northern transcontinental railroad

3.13 To keep the black people subjugated and as a cheap labor supply for the South.

3.14 Tennessee

3.15 National Union Party

3.16 He did not secede with his state.

3.17 Joint Committee on Reconstruction

3.18 Thaddeus Stevens

3.19 carpetbaggers

3.20 5

3.21 Seward's Folly or Icebox

3.22 share crop

3.23 Ku Klux Klan

3.24 Fifteenth

3.25 Seven

3.26 Ulysses S. Grant

3.27 7.2 million

3.28 Tenure of Office

3.29 Democratic

3.30 Scalawags

3.31 redeemed

3.32 Edwin Stanton

3.33 Any order:
   a. terrorized black people who voted
   b. literacy tests
   c. grandfather clauses
3.34 Any order:
   a. corruption
   b. tired of trying to control the South
   c. thought white people should control the government
3.35 They terrorized Republicans, black people, and others who supported Republican governments
3.36 Any order:
   a. set up public schools
   b. internal improvements
   c. modernized the tax system
3.37 a. Indebted landowners needed cash.
   b. It exhausted the soil.
3.38 They were separated from white people and supplied with less money.
3.39 The president could not successfully be thrown out of office for political reasons.
3.40 hard money
3.41 Horatio Seymour
3.42 Boss Tweed
3.43 Crédit Mobilier
3.44 Resumption Act
3.45 Whiskey Ring
3.46 Greenbacks
3.47 Treaty of Washington
3.48 civil service reform
3.49 Black Friday
3.50 Liberal Republicans
3.51 William Belknap
3.52 $15.5 million
3.53 Thomas Nast
3.54 false
3.55 true
3.56 false
3.57 false
3.58 true
3.59 false
3.60 true
3.61 Democrats and Republicans had different election results in four states.
3.62 He supported civil service reform and appointed men based on ability, not party loyalty.
3.63 secession and slavery
3.64 Hayes was awarded the election. In exchange, he agreed to withdraw the last occupation troops in the South and support a southern continental railroad.
3.65 When Hayes removed the federal troops on occupation duty in 1877.
3.66 The Republicans had 8 of the 15 votes on the committee making the decision.
3.67 She had a college degree, was active in social causes, and banned alcohol in the White House.
3.68 Samuel Tilden; governor of New York, helped put Boss Tweed in jail
3.69 none
3.70 U.S. Representative, governor of Ohio, Union veteran, honest and competent

SELF TEST 3

3.01 Andrew Johnson
3.02 Alaska
3.03 Thirteenth
3.04 Boss Tweed
3.05 Crédit Mobilier
3.06 Fifteenth
3.07 Radical Reconstruction
3.08 Black Codes
3.09 Emancipation Proclamation
3.010 Fourteenth
3.011 Compromise of 1877
3.012 South Carolina
3.013 Vicksburg
3.014 Carpetbaggers
3.015 Fort Sumter
3.016 Abraham Lincoln
3.017 Dred Scott
3.018 Jefferson Davis
3.019 Robert E. Lee
3.020 Thaddeus Stevens
3.021 Stephen Douglas
3.022 John Brown
3.023 Ulysses S. Grant
3.024 Stonewall Jackson
3.025 Rutherford B. Hayes
3.026 false
3.027 true
3.028 true
3.029 false
3.030 false
3.031 true
3.032 true
3.033 true
3.034 true
3.035 true
3.036 true
3.037 false
3.038 true
3.039 true
3.040 true
3.041 true
3.042 true
3.043 false
3.044 true
3.045 true

LIFEPAC TEST

1. b; the South had better generals and the South could not break the blockade because the North had more resources
2. b; corruption and share cropping had other causes beyond Reconstruction and it was white power that had the longest negative effect
3. c; disease killed more than bullets
4. a; without the issue of slavery the rest would not have mattered
5. c; this was the prime Republican issue
6. Appomattox Courthouse
7. Gettysburg
8. Emancipation Proclamation
9. Robert E. Lee
10. John Wilkes Booth
11. Thirteenth
12. Alaska
13. Gettysburg Address
14. Ulysses S. Grant
15. William T. Sherman
16. Black Codes
17. Bleeding Kansas
18. Dred Scott
19. Fourteenth
20. Crittenden Compromise
21. He kept going after Lee mauled his army.
22. He was acquitted by one vote.
23. It had more resources to get supplies and a better transportation system to deliver them.
24. It gave Lincoln a victory he needed to publish the Emancipation Proclamation.
25. The South passed Black Codes and elected Confederate leaders to Congress.
26. e
27. h
28. j
29. a
30. d
31. i
32. g
33. c
34. b
35. f

ALTERNATE LIFEPAC TEST

1. k
2. o
3. h
4. r
5. t
6. d
7. a
8. c
9. l
10. s
11. n
12. b
13. q
14. m
15. e
16. f
17. i
18. j
19. g
20. p
21. Abraham Lincoln
22. James Buchanan
23. Ulysses S. Grant
24. Andrew Johnson
25. Rutherford B. Hayes
26. Robert E. Lee
27. Jefferson Davis
28. David Farragut
29. Thadeus Stevens
30. Stonewall Jackson
31. Stephen Douglas
32. William T. Sherman
33. William Seward
34. Ulysses S. Grant
35. John Crittenden
36. The South thought Britain would need their cotton, but it needed northern wheat and corn more and found other sources for cotton.
37. Congress passed the Tenure of Office Act which forbade the president to dismiss cabinet members. The president would be impeached if they did so and acquitted by one vote.
38. Rifles and artillery had become more accurate but old military tactics called for mass attacks that were suicidal against the new weapons.
39. The South had better generals, fought for the ideal of independence and only had to fight a defensive war. A draw would be a southern victory.

40.   It is a policy that all money is gold, silver, or
      paper backed by a certain value of one of
      those. It shrinks the money supply which can
      make a depression worse.
41.   true
42.   true
43.   false
44.   false
45.   false

HISTORY & GEOGRAPHY 806

ALTERNATE LIFEPAC TEST

NAME _____

DATE _____

SCORE _____

Match these items (each answer, 2 points).

1. _____ almost started a war between the Union and Britain when Confederates taken off it
2. _____ "... government of the people, by the people, for the people shall not perish from this earth."
3. _____ South was divided into five military districts
4. _____ the worst effects of popular sovereignty
5. _____ almost cost Grant his military career
6. _____ ended the pre-Civil War era of compromise
7. _____ made slavery legal in all states
8. _____ beginning of the Civil War
9. _____ British raider with a Confederate flag
10. _____ John Brown's act of martyrdom
11. _____ end of Lee's army
12. _____ end of the last southern invasion of the North
13. _____ railroad construction scandal
14. _____ Confederate ironclad
15. _____ post-war laws to subjugate Freedmen
16. _____ ended slavery
17. _____ gave Republicans the presidency in exchange for the end of Reconstruction
18. _____ made former slaves citizens
19. _____ ensured that anti-slavery Britain would not aid the Confederacy
20. _____ bribery used to cheat government out of excise revenue

a. Dred Scott Decision
b. Battle of Gettysburg
c. Fort Sumter
d. Kansas-Nebraska Act
e. Black Codes
f. 13th Amendment
g. Emancipation Proclamation
h. Radical Reconstruction
i. Compromise of 1877
j. 14th Amendment
k. *Trent*
l. *Alabama*
m. *Merrimac*
n. Appomattox Courthouse
o. Gettysburg Address
p. Whiskey Ring
q. Crédit Mobilier
r. Bleeding Kansas
s. Harper's Ferry Raid
t. Shiloh

Name the president (each answer, 3 points).

21. _____ little formal education; excellent speaker; assassinated

22. _____ pro-South; did nothing to stop secession

23. _____ poor president; corrupt administration; Civil War memoirs provided for his family

24. _____ never elected president; former tailor; did not secede with his state

25. _____ governor of Ohio; favored civil service reform; election questionable

Name the person (each answer, 2 points).

Robert E. Lee   Stephen Douglas   John Crittenden
Ulysses S. Grant   William Seward   Jefferson Davis
David Farragut   Stonewall Jackson   Thaddeus Stevens
William T. Sherman

26. _____ most brilliant general in the Civil War

27. _____ president of the Confederacy

28. _____ admiral who captured Mobile and New Orleans

29. _____ leader of the Radical Republicans

30. _____ Lee's brilliant subordinate; killed at Chancellorsville

31. _____ Lincoln's Democratic opponent; favored popular sovereignty

32. _____ marched to the sea; Union general

33. _____ bought Alaska for the U.S.

34. _____ victor at Petersburg

35. _____ tried to compromise to save the Union after secession began

Answer these questions (each answer, 4 points).

36. Why did the South expect Britain to support them and why (outside of slavery) did they not do so?

_____

_____

_____

37. How did Congress arrange to impeach Johnson and what was the result?

_____

_____

_____

38. Why were the number of battle deaths so high in the Civil War?

_____

_____

_____

39. What were the South's main advantages in the Civil War?

_____

_____

_____

40. What is a hard money policy and how does it affect a depression?

_____

_____

_____

Answer *true* or *false* (each answer, 1 point).

41. _____ The North won the war largely because it had greater resources than the South.

42. _____ Antietam allowed Lincoln to issue the Emancipation Proclamation after a Union victory.

43. _____ First Bull Run, Chancellorsville, and Fredericksburg were Union victories.

44. _____ The election of 1864 was remarkable because Lincoln almost lost in spite of the war being very popular.

45. _____ The Civil War settled the issues of the civil right of black Americans and the power of industry in America.

HISTORY & GEOGRAPHY 807

Unit 7: Gilded Age to Progressive Era (1880-1915)

TEACHER NOTES

MATERIALS NEEDED FOR LIFEPAC	
Required	Suggested
None	• atlas • encyclopedia • reference books or online sources

ADDITIONAL LEARNING ACTIVITIES

Section 1: The Gilded Age

1. As a class, discuss why this era was called the Gilded Age and have students give specific examples. Then, students can choose an alternate name for the era.

2. Assign students to research and do a report or paper on the transcontinental railroad, the Homestead Act, Andrew Carnegie, John D. Rockefeller, J.P. Morgan, Immigration in the late 1800s, the Knights of Labor, the American Federation of Labor, High Society life in the late 1800s, the Grange, or Thomas Edison.

3. Students can choose the topic of either "Immigration to the U.S." or "Homesteading on the Great Plains." Different students should read the personal stories of people who emigrated or homesteaded. Have them tell the person's story to the class and discuss connections/reactions.

4. Debate as a class: "Social Darwinism is an unavoidable result if you believe in evolution."

5. Have students make a collage of pictures contrasting how the wealthy and the poor lived in the Gilded Age.

6. As a class, make a visual history of the circus in America.

7. Assign students to research and do a paper on one of the Native American Nations of the Great Plains.

8. Have students make a diagram or model of the Battle of Little Big Horn, and then discuss the mistakes made by Custer.

9. Have students read about how cowboys lived in the late 1800s. View a cowboy movie about a cattle drive. Have students write a short paper on how realistic the movie was.

10. As a class, discuss what it meant to the United States to no longer have a frontier.

Section 2: Gilded Politics

1. Assign research and a report on James Blaine, Roscoe Conkling, Chester A. Arthur, Grover Cleveland, William McKinley, William Jennings Bryan, Theodore Roosevelt, or George Dewey.

2. Discuss why civil service reform finally passed.

3. Have students research and discuss why silver coinage was such a hot issue.

4. Debate this topic as a class: "Resolved: American business owned the American government in the late 1800s before the Progressive reforms."

5. Have the class discuss the presidents between 1880 and 1900. Who was the least notable?

6. As a class, discuss whether or not the U.S. had strong reasons to get involved in the Spanish-American War.

7. Have the class read "yellow journalism" articles about Cuba and the Spanish-American War. Discuss them as journalism and propaganda. How do they compare to modem articles about sensational stories?

8. Assign students to research and do a report or paper on the annexation of Hawaii.

9. Have the class read a book on the Spanish-American War.

10. Students can make a model or diagram of the capture of Santiago.

11. Instruct students to assume the role of the House of Representatives in 1898 to debate and vote on what to do with the islands ceded by Spain.

12. Debate this issue as a class: "Resolved: America became an imperialist nation after 1898."

Section 3: The Progressive Era

1. Have students read a biography or book about any of the Progressive reformers.

2. As a class, discuss why reform was so badly needed in the U.S.

3. Have students read a muckraking book or article from this era. Discuss it in class.

4. Discuss the Roosevelt Administration as a class. Why was T.R. so popular and what did he actually accomplish?

5. Students can make a model or diagram of the Panama Canal.

6. Have students read about the Panama Canal and discuss whether or not the U.S. dealt fairly with the people of that nation.

7. Debate this issue as a class: "Resolved: Theodore Roosevelt was an arrogant bully."

8. Discuss these questions:
   a. Why was it so difficult for William Taft to be president after Theodore Roosevelt?
   b. Why was Dollar Diplomacy such a bad idea?
   c. Was Taft really a Progressive?
   d. Why was the Model T so successful?
   e. Why was Woodrow Wilson such an unusual president?
   f. What mistakes did Wilson make in regard to Mexico?

9. Have partners build a model of the Wright Brother's airplane.

10. Write a paper or work as a class to speculate how America would be different if the Progressive reformers had failed.

Administer the LIFEPAC Test

ANSWER KEYS

SECTION 1

1.1	stockholders	**1.36**	c
1.2	Union Pacific, Central Pacific	**1.37**	g
1.3	air brakes	**1.38**	f
1.4	Pullman sleeping cars and dining cars	**1.39**	e
1.5	Andrew Carnegie	**1.40**	d
1.6	Standard Oil, John D. Rockefeller	**1.41**	b
1.7	dividends	**1.42**	a

1.1 stockholders
1.2 Union Pacific, Central Pacific
1.3 air brakes
1.4 Pullman sleeping cars and dining cars
1.5 Andrew Carnegie
1.6 Standard Oil, John D. Rockefeller
1.7 dividends
1.8 created a national market
1.9 took stock from several companies and ran them together
1.10 a big, industry dominating corporation
1.11 Promontory Point, Utah; May 1869
1.12 They charged more for short hauls, which had no competition, than for long hauls that did. They gave rebates to big customers and divided up business using pools.
1.13 Bessemer
1.14 holding company
1.15 New Immigration
1.16 Samuel Gompers
1.17 depression (panic)
1.18 five million
1.19 Terrence Powderly
1.20 Chinese
1.21 strikes, Gould railroad
1.22 city political machine
1.23 Haymarket Riot
1.24 literacy test
1.25 They looked different, kept their old ways, took low paying jobs, and were often non-Protestant.
1.26 It organized a federation of craft unions, not all jobs in one union, and concentrated on job issues.
1.27 Their strikes halted commerce, were often violent, and unions had small numbers of active members who were anti-capitalism.
1.28 banned paupers, criminals, contract workers, anarchists, insane, polygamists, those with contagious diseases, and later the illiterate
1.29 f
1.30 b
1.31 e
1.32 c
1.33 g
1.34 a
1.35 d

1.36 c
1.37 g
1.38 f
1.39 e
1.40 d
1.41 b
1.42 a
1.43 Any five:
typewriter, cash register, adding machine, telephone, electric street cars, refrigeration, improved canning, Kodak camera
1.44 Any three:
phonograph, light bulb, storage battery, duplicating machine
1.45 Any three:
typewriter, stock ticker, motion pictures, electric generator, electric trains
1.46 Any order:
a. laissez-faire
b. Social Darwinism
c. admiration for the rich and successful
1.47 Chief Joseph
1.48 miners
1.49 *A Century of Dishonor*
1.50 160; 5
1.51 cowboy
1.52 Sioux
1.53 Any order:
Chisholm, Goodnight-Loving
1.54 drop; over-grazing
1.55 Grange
1.56 Any order:
a. repeating rifles
b. railroad
c. extermination of buffalo
d. European diseases
1.57 Geronimo
1.58 winter of 1886-87
1.59 1890
1.60 Colonel George Custer
1.61 Dawes
1.62 Any order:
wheat, com
1.63 debt; railroad
1.64 Any order:
railroad, Homestead Act

SELF TEST 1

1.01	g
1.02	e
1.03	a
1.04	d
1.05	i
1.06	j
1.07	h
1.08	c
1.09	b
1.010	f
1.011	trusts
1.012	railroad
1.013	Dawes Act
1.014	New Immigration
1.015	Haymarket Riot
1.016	Laissez-faire
1.017	Homestead Act
1.018	Social Darwinism
1.019	Gilded Age
1.020	frontier
1.021	The cattle were raised cheaply on government grassland. They were driven to railroad junctions and taken to the cities for sale.
1.022	stockholders own it, board of directors runs it
1.023	Union Pacific, Central Pacific
1.024	immigrants were hard to organize, accepted low wages, and were used as strikebreakers
1.025	It was a federation of craft unions that focused on job issues.
1.026	railroad, Homestead Act
1.027	They set rates high and often took the farmer's profit.
1.028	They were getting higher wages than in Europe, did not complain, and seldom organized.
1.029	with strikebreakers, police, the army, and injunctions
1.030	They were proof of the success of the American way of life.
1.031	g
1.032	c
1.033	i
1.034	j
1.035	h
1.036	a
1.037	e
1.038	b
1.039	d
1.040	f

SECTION 2

2.1	e
2.2	d
2.3	e
2.4	a
2.5	e
2.6	g
2.7	e
2.8	b
2.9	c
2.10	e
2.11	c
2.12	e
2.13	d
2.14	b
2.15	c
2.16	b
2.17	f
2.18	a
2.19	d
2.20	c
2.21	e
2.22	e
2.23	a
2.24	e
2.25	e
2.26	Mugwumps
2.27	none
2.28	Silver prices had dropped making the silver dollar less valuable than a gold one.
2.29	West and South
2.30	The treasury had to buy silver and mint it at a 16 to 1 ratio with gold.
2.31	Pendleton Act
2.32	10 percent
2.33	assassination of President Garfield
2.34	rate discrimination, rebates, pools, charging more for short hauls
2.35	Billion Dollar Congress
2.36	Democrat – Grover Cleveland Republican – Benjamin Harrison
2.37	Democrat – Grover Cleveland Republican – Benjamin Harrison Populist – James Weaver
2.38	Any order: Sherman Silver Purchase Act; McKinley Tariff
2.39	Farmer's Alliance
2.40	depression in 1893
2.41	the tariff
2.42	Sherman Anti-Trust Act
2.43	People's (Populist) Party
2.44	Sherman Silver Purchase Act
2.45	Pullman

2.46	William Jennings Bryan
2.47	Grover Cleveland
2.48	G.A.R. (Civil War veterans)
2.49	silver coinage
2.50	Wilson-Gorman Bill
2.51	selling bonds through J.P. Morgan
2.52	debt, low agriculture prices, railroads
2.53	Eugene Debs
2.54	strikes for better wages
2.55	the courts and government quickly aided the corporation owners
2.56	spent it
2.57	Any order:

a. free coinage of silver
b. new banking system
c. income tax
d. government ownership of railroads, telegraph, and telephone
e. eight-hour day
f. restrict immigration
g. direct election of senators

2.58	Gold Standard Act
2.59	*Cross of Gold*
2.60	silver coinage
2.61	William J. Bryan
2.62	Marcus Hanna
2.63	A full dinner pail
2.64	William J. Bryan
2.65	Dingley
2.66	William J. Bryan
2.67	William J. Bryan
2.68	Marcus Hanna
2.69	front porch
2.70	fifty cents
2.71	1897
2.72	e
2.73	c
2.74	h
2.75	f
2.76	d
2.77	i
2.78	a
2.79	b
2.80	g

2.81	yellow journalism
2.82	*Maine*
2.83	Open Door
2.84	Teller Amendment
2.85	Philippines
2.86	Spanish-American War
2.87	Rough Riders
2.88	Anti-Imperialist League
2.89	Hawaii
2.90	Boxer Rebellion
2.91	yellow fever
2.92	Platt Amendment
2.93	Kettle *or* San Juan
2.94	Puerto Rico
2.95	four months
2.96	Santiago

SELF TEST 2

2.01	e
2.02	e
2.03	d
2.04	g
2.05	h
2.06	c
2.07	h
2.08	a
2.09	c
2.010	d
2.011	f
2.012	d
2.013	h
2.014	f
2.015	c
2.016	a. silver coinage
	b. inflation and debt relief
2.017	fight Native Americans
2.018	laissez-faire
2.019	Cuba's
2.020	Spanish-American War
2.021	Populist
2.022	tariff
2.023	spent it
2.024	Knights of Labor
2.025	h
2.026	i
2.027	c
2.028	e
2.029	j
2.030	g
2.031	b
2.032	d
2.033	f
2.034	a
2.035	false
2.036	false
2.037	true
2.038	true
2.039	false
2.040	true
2.041	true
2.042	true
2.043	false
2.044	true
2.045	false
2.046	false

SECTION 3

3.1	muckrakers
3.2	city
3.3	Wisconsin
3.4	Elkins Act
3.5	Northern Securities Company
3.6	Teddy Bear
3.7	Ira Tarbell
3.8	Full dinner pail
3.9	Square Deal
3.10	Hepburn Act
3.11	Robert La Follette
3.12	Samuel Jones
3.13	Depression of 1893
3.14	Any order:
	Anti-Saloon League; Women's Christian Temperance Union
3.15	They wanted to use his popularity, but keep him out of power.
3.16	Any eight:
	secret ballot, primary elections, voter referendums, recall elections, tax reform, regulatory commissions, control of public utilities, civil service reform, open bidding for public contracts, professional city management as well as laws against corruption, prostitution, and unsafe housing
3.17	He revitalized it and made the president the national leader even in legislation.
3.18	Newlands
3.19	Alton Parker
3.20	*The Jungle*; Upton Sinclair
3.21	Colombia
3.22	Big Stick
3.23	Russo-Japanese War
3.24	Moroccan
3.25	1907
3.26	Commerce and Labor
3.27	Roosevelt Corollary
3.28	Port Arthur
3.29	Great White Fleet
3.30	George Goethals
3.31	$400 million; 1914
3.32	segregate Japanese children
3.33	Santo Domingo
3.34	Venezuela
3.35	William Gorgas
3.36	Meat Inspection
3.37	Pure Food and Drug
3.38	He offered to arbitrate and threatened to use the army to mine coal when the owners refused.

3.39 T.R. supported a revolution in Panama and signed a treaty with the new government.
3.40 The school board reversed the segregation order and Japan limited emigration to the U.S.
3.41 Taft
3.42 Roosevelt
3.43 Wilson
3.44 Bryan
3.45 Roosevelt
3.46 Orville and Wilbur Wright
3.47 Taft
3.48 Robert La Follette
3.49 Joseph Cannon
3.50 Henry Ford
3.51 Taft
3.52 Taft
3.53 Taft
3.54 Henry Ford
3.55 Richard Ballinger
3.56 Taft
3.57 Roosevelt
3.58 Gifford Pinchot
3.59 Any order:
  a. Payne-Aldrich Tariff
  b. Pinchot-Ballinger fight
  c. failed to support move against the power of Joseph Cannon
3.60 to use investment to spread U.S. influence abroad
3.61 Any four:
  a. women's suffrage
  b. minimum wage
  c. government pensions
  d. unemployment compensation;
  or control of stock market
3.62 He started almost twice as many suits as T.R. Standard Oil and the American Tobacco Company were dissolved when he was president.
3.63 Victoriano Huerta
3.64 John Pershing; Pancho Villa
3.65 World War I
3.66 Clayton
3.67 Thomas Jefferson
3.68 Federal Trade
3.69 Any order: tariff reduction, banking reform, anti-trust laws
3.70 Underwood Tariff
3.71 Federal Reserve Board
3.72 Any order:
  Nicaragua, Haiti, Santo Domingo
3.73 William J. Bryan
3.74 New Jersey; Princeton
3.75 Any order: Roosevelt, Taft, Wilson
3.76 Tampico; Any order: Argentina, Brazil, Chile

SELF TEST 3

3.01 Roosevelt
3.02 Taft
3.03 Roosevelt
3.04 Wilson
3.05 Taft
3.06 Roosevelt
3.07 Wilson
3.08 Wilson
3.09 Taft
3.010 Roosevelt
3.011 Roosevelt
3.012 Wilson
3.013 Roosevelt
3.014 Taft
3.015 Roosevelt
3.016 city
3.017 muckrakers
3.018 *Cross of Gold*
3.019 Spanish-American War
3.020 Square Deal
3.021 Social Darwinism
3.022 railroads
3.023 Knights of Labor
3.024 Populists
3.025 Plains Indians
3.026 i
3.027 h
3.028 j
3.029 a
3.030 e
3.031 g
3.032 b
3.033 c
3.034 f
3.035 d
3.036 i
3.037 h
3.038 c
3.039 j
3.040 e
3.041 g
3.042 b
3.043 a
3.044 f
3.045 d

LIFEPAC TEST

1. Gilded Age
2. silver coinage
3. Spanish-American War
4. Any order:
   a. Homestead Act
   b. railroad
5. Federal Reserve Act
6. railroads
7. He supported a revolution in Panama and signed a treaty with the new government.
8. Cattle was raised cheaply on government grassland then driven to railroad junctions and shipped to cities.
9. Forbid political "donations" from government employees, established Civil Service Commission to test people for certain government jobs
10. R, T, W
11. G, M
12. C, W
13. C
14. A
15. M
16. R
17. R, T
18. T
19. W
20. Big Stick
21. New Immigration
22. William J. Bryan
23. Billion Dollar Congress
24. Sherman Anti-Trust
25. Model T
26. Civil War veterans (G.A.R.)
27. 1890
28. *Maine*
29. Open Door
30. true
31. false
32. true
33. true
34. false
35. false
36. false
37. true
38. false
39. false
BONUS:
40. Grange, Farmer's Alliance, Populists

ALTERNATE LIFEPAC TEST

1. j
2. t
3. n
4. d
5. c
6. b
7. m
8. r
9. l
10. p
11. g
12. s
13. e
14. q
15. f
16. o
17. k
18. i
19. h
20. a
21. Corporate monopolies and abuse of power
22. Populist
23. He supported a revolution in Panama and signed the treaty with the new government.
24. city
25. It was a time of rapid industrialization, progress, wealth, and invention on the surface with exploitation, corruption, and social problems underneath.
26. Roosevelt and Taft split the Republican vote.
27. f
28. j
29. m
30. d
31. l
32. k
33. n
34. h
35. g
36. e
37. o
38. i
39. b
40. c
41. a
42. false
43. false
44. false
45. true
46. true
47. false
48. true

49.   false
50.   true
51.   false
52.   true
53.   true

HISTORY & GEOGRAPHY 807

ALTERNATE LIFEPAC TEST

NAME _____

DATE _____

SCORE _____

Match these people (each answer, 2 points).

1. _____ professional inventor: light bulb, phonograph

2. _____ Wilson would not recognize his government in Mexico

3. _____ first powered airplane flight

4. _____ Democratic leader; 3 time presidential candidate; Wilson's Secretary of State

5. _____ 1st Democratic president after Civil War; two non-consecutive terms

6. _____ his assassination encouraged civil service reform

7. _____ made the Model T cheap enough for most Americans

8. _____ famous American writer; author of *Gilded Age*

9. _____ Republican Half-Breed leader; presidential candidate

10. _____ union leader and organizer

11. _____ president; got tariff reduction and banking reform

12. _____ attacked town in New Mexico; pursued into Mexico

13. _____ chosen as Roosevelt's successor; preferred to be a judge

14. _____ president; Billion Dollar Congress; Sherman Anti-Trust

15. _____ worker in Roscoe Conkling's political machine; surprisingly pushed civil service reform as president

16. _____ Progressive leader; Wisconsin governor

17. _____ Standard Oil Trust; squashed competitors

18. _____ made fortune in steel, gave most of it away

19. _____ pro-business president; front porch campaign; tried to avoid war with Spain; assassinated

20. _____ first Progressive president; served in Spanish-American War; extremely popular

a. Theodore Roosevelt

b. James Garfield

c. Grover Cleveland

d. William J. Bryan

e. William H. Taft

f. Chester A. Arthur

g. Woodrow Wilson

h. William McKinley

i. Andrew Carnegie

j. Thomas Edison

k. John D. Rockefeller

l. James Blaine

m. Henry Ford

n. Wright brothers

o. Robert La Follette

p. Samuel Gompers

q. Benjamin Harrison

r. Mark Twain

s. Pancho Villa

t. Victoriano Huerta

Answer these questions (each answer, 3 points).

21. Why did America change its policy of no government interference in business?

_____

22. What was the reform party that proceeded the Progressives and nominated Byran?

_____

23. How did Theodore Roosevelt arrange for a canal treaty after Colombia refused it?

    _____

    _____

24. Progressive reforms began at what level of government? _____

25. Why was Gilded Age a good description of the period of 1865 to 1900?

    _____

    _____

    _____

26. Why did Woodrow Wilson win the 1912 election?

    _____

Match these item (each answer, 2 points).

27. _____ craft unions, pro-capitalist, pushed wages and conditions

28. _____ exposed unsanitary meat packing conditions

29. _____ poor are unfit and deserve poverty

30. _____ T.R.'s policy to accomplish results

31. _____ helped rapid settlement of Great Plains

32. _____ gave Native American families land

33. _____ U.S. intervened in Americas to stop Europe from intervening

34. _____ Bryan's famous convention speech, 1896

35. _____ sought debt relief and railroad regulation

36. _____ 1st major U.S. union movement; discredited by Haymarket Riot

37. _____ expanded American influence by investments abroad

38. _____ major political issue right after Spanish-American War

39. _____ government should interfere as little as possible with business

40. _____ federal civil service reform

41. _____ writers who exposed corruption or social problems

a. muckrakers

b. laissez-faire

c. Pendleton Act

d. Big Stick

e. Knights of Labor

f. AFL

g. Grange

h. *Cross of Gold*

i. imperialism

j. *The Jungle*

k. Dawes Act

l. Homestead Act

m. Social Darwinism

n. Roosevelt Corollary

o. Dollar Diplomacy

Answer *true* **or** *false* (each answer, 1 point).

42. _____ Theodore Roosevelt started more anti-trust suits than Taft.

43. _____ The New Immigration of the 1870s and 80s came from central Asia.

44. _____ The U.S. had a transcontinental railroad since before the Civil War.

45. _____ The Plains Indians put up stiff resistance to American settlers.

46. _____ Railroads, before regulation, had tremendous, arbitrary control over the profitability of businesses and farmers that depended on rail shipment.

47. _____ Immigrants were not hired as industrial workers because they did not understand American business practices.

48. _____ In the late 1800s, unions were opposed by owners, courts, and the government.

49. _____ Woodrow Wilson won the Nobel Peace Prize for his handling of the crisis with Mexico.

50. _____ The poorer working people hooked onto the issue of silver coinage as their issue in the late 1800s.

51. _____ Wilson sent the American navy, the Great White Fleet, on a tour of the world to showcase American strength.

52. _____ One problem of a gold standard was keeping enough gold reserves.

53. _____ Much of the 1888 budget surplus was given away in liberal pensions to Civil War veterans.

HISTORY & GEOGRAPHY 808

Unit 8: A World in Conflict (1915-1945)

TEACHER NOTES

MATERIALS NEEDED FOR LIFEPAC	
Required	Suggested
None	• atlas • encyclopedia • reference books or online sources

ADDITIONAL LEARNING ACTIVITIES

Section 1: World War I

1. As a class, discuss whether or not the U.S. could have or should have stayed out of World War I.

2. Have students build a model of a World War I trench system.

3. Have students read about conditions on a World War I U-boat.

4. Through discussion or a written assignment, have students give the German point of view on the U-boat issue.

5. As a class, assemble memorabilia, artifacts, documents, clothing and pictures from World War I (use online sources).

6. Have the class read about the Russian Revolution and discuss why it happened.

7. As a class, discuss why the Treaty of Versailles was a failure and what (if anything) could have been done to save it.

8. Assign students to research and do a report or paper on one of these topics: weapons of World War I; World War I from a German, French or British point of view; the League of Nations; or the influenza pandemic of 1918-19.

9. As a class, watch and discuss the movie *Sergeant York*, starring Gary Cooper.

10. Have students read personal accounts of soldiers in World War I and discuss them.

Section 2: The Great Depression

1. As a class, discuss how the "Roaring Twenties" are like and unlike society today.

2. Have students read a biography of Warren Harding, Calvin Coolidge, Herbert Hoover, Al Capone, Charles Lindbergh, Babe Ruth, or Franklin D. Roosevelt.

3. Tell students to collect personal accounts of life in the Great Depression by using online sources (interviews, written accounts). Students may also gather information from family members or family friends, if any people have any first-hand accounts. Have students present information in class.

4. Have students research and do a report or paper on one of these topics: the Scopes Monkey Trial, the Fundamentalists, flappers, Prohibition, the birth of the American auto industry, the Stock Market Crash of 1929, the activities of Ku Klux Klan in the 1920s, the kidnapping of Charles Lindbergh's son, and any one or more of the New Deal organizations.

5. Instruct students to research the basic facts of either the Sacco and Vanzetti trial or the Scopes Monkey Trial. Have them present the trial in class, complete with attorneys, judge, and jury.

6. Have students read or view an interview of someone who lived during the Great Depression. Assign them to write a paper on what they learn.

7. Assign students to research and report on the scandals of the Harding Administration.

8. Have a debate on this issue: "Resolved: Prohibition was good for the nation."

9. Instruct students to research the treatment of black Americans as soldiers during World War I and in the 1920s. Discuss as a class.

10. Have students research and do a paper or report on conditions in Germany between the World Wars.

Section 3: World War II

1. Assign students to read a biography of one of these people: Adolf Hitler, Benito Mussolini, Joseph Stalin, Winston Churchill, Bernard Montgomery, Edwin Rommel, Charles de Gaulle, George Marshall, Dwight Eisenhower, George Patton, Omar Bradley, Douglas MacArthur, or Chester Nimitz.

2. Have students bring in artifacts, memorabilia, documents, clothing, and pictures from World War II (check the internet).

3. Have students research the history of their family's connection with World War II (everyone was affected by the war in some way). Assign a paper or report on the results.

4. As a class, watch a movie about a specific incident or battle in World War II, like Iwo Jima or D-day. Have students read about the incident and discuss how realistic the movie was.

5. Discuss these questions:
   a. Would the U.S. have gotten into World War II without Pearl Harbor?
   b. Could the Allies have won without the United States?
   c. What would the world be like today if Hitler and the Japanese had been victorious?
   d. How did the war change America?
   e. Was the atomic bomb a moral weapon to use in battle?

6. Students can draw a diagram or make a model of any World War II battle.

7. Have the class watch or listen to a recorded interview of a World War II veteran. Discuss the impact the war had on the veterans life.

8. Teachers should use some caution on this assignment and consider previewing any reading assigned to the students. Read about Nazi atrocities and treatment of Japanese people (internment and racism). Discuss what these incidents tell us about human nature.

9. As a class, put together a Holocaust memorial using pictures, facts, and stories from survivor's accounts.

10. Debate one of these topics:

    a. "Resolved: Doolittle's Raid was an American victory."

    b. "Resolved: The Invasion of North Africa unnecessarily delayed the attack on Hitler's Europe."

    c. "Resolved: The Japanese military culture made the atomic bomb unavoidable."

11. Students can watch a documentary on any aspect of World War II that interests them.

12. Have the class make a collage of the damage caused by World War II in Europe.

13. Have the class do a dramatic reading of one of Winston Churchill's wartime speeches.

14. Assign students to research and report or do a paper on the effects of the atomic bomb on Hiroshima and Nagasaki.

Administer the LIFEPAC Test

The test is to be administered in one session. Give no help except with directions.
Evaluate the tests and review areas where the students have done poorly.
Review the pages and activities that stress the concepts tested.
If necessary, administer the Alternate LIFEPAC Test.

ANSWER KEYS

SECTION 1

1.1	Wilhelm II	**1.30**	German submarine attacks
1.2	Balkan Peninsula	**1.31**	Lenin; communists (Bolsheviks)
1.3	France	**1.32**	American Expeditionary Force; John Pershing
1.4	poison gas	**1.33**	influenza
1.5	Archduke Ferdinand	**1.34**	the world safe for democracy
1.6	1st Battle of the Marne	**1.35**	War Industries Board
1.7	ace	**1.36**	Doughboys; early 1918
1.8	Sir Edward Grey	**1.37**	Château-Thierry; Belleau
1.9	Alsace, Lorraine	**1.38**	Alvin York
1.10	Otto von Bismarck	**1.39**	Herbert Hoover
1.11	Belgium	**1.40**	Meuse-Argonne
1.12	Dardanelles	**1.41**	November 11, 1918; 11:00 A.M.
1.13	zeppelins		
1.14	No Man's Land		
1.15	Eddie Rickenbacker		
1.16	Balance of Power		

1.17
a. Sarajevo, Bosnia
b. Austria-Hungary; Serbia
c. Austria-Hungary; Serbia
d. Russia
e. Germany; Russia; France
f. Germany; Belgium
g. Britain; Germany

1.18 To attack and defeat France before Russia could get its huge army into battle

1.19 Alliances, national pride, and an arms race

1.20 The men charged across open ground into established fortifications protected by machine guns and artillery.

1.21 It offered Mexico an alliance with Germany in exchange for recovering the American southwest after a Central Powers victory.

1.22 They attacked without warning, destroyed the ships instead of seizing the cargo and often killed the crew.

1.23 The invasion of neutral Belgium

1.24 Stay neutral at all cost

1.25 "He Kept Us Out of War." It was ironic because he asked Congress to declare war a few months after the election.

1.26 The British had an effective blockade against the Central Powers who could not get loans to buy supplies.

1.27 Neutrality

1.28 It was sunk by a U-boat and 1,198 people died. Bryan resigned rather than sign a strong note of protest.

1.29 A revolution established a democratic government.

1.42 Men between 18 and 45 must register. No one could buy an exemption, but some were given to workers in key industries.

1.43 The communists took Russia out of the war, giving Germany a large chunk of east Europe and leaving them free to concentrate on the west.

1.44 America was repaying a debt it owed the America Revolutionary hero from France by defending his nation.

1.45 He wanted them to have control of a section of the front.

1.46	a
1.47	i
1.48	e
1.49	b
1.50	d
1.51	g
1.52	c
1.53	j
1.54	f
1.55	k
1.56	h
1.57	_X_
1.58	___
1.59	___
1.60	_X_
1.61	_X_
1.62	___
1.63	___
1.64	_X_
1.65	___
1.66	___
1.67	___
1.68	_X_
1.69	_X_

1.70 a. He went on a speaking tour to win the support of the American people.
b. He collapsed and suffered a stroke.

1.71 It forced Germany to pay large war damages, ruined their economy, created bitterness which led to the rise of Adolf Hitler.

1.72 To make Germany pay for the costs of the war and cripple it so it could never threaten France again.

1.73 They signed a separate peace treaty.

1.74 It included only one minor Republican and no senators.

1.75 The League of Nations

1.76 U.S., Britain, France, and Italy

1.77 Territory (the spoils of war)

1.78 the Saar region

1.79 Much of its richest land had been taken from it

1.80 It began to decline.

SELF TEST 1

1.01 e
1.02 f
1.03 g
1.04 j
1.05 b
1.06 a
1.07 h
1.08 c
1.09 d
1.010 i
1.011 alliances, arms race, national pride
1.012 Assassination of Archduke Ferdinand in Sarajevo, Bosnia
1.013 Both sides were protected in deep trenches and could rake unprotected attackers with machine gun and artillery fire.
1.014 submarine attacks
1.015 The invasion of neutral Belgium
1.016 A Communist Revolution
1.017 Influenza
1.018 Fourteen Points
1.019 Germany to pay the cost of the war and be crippled so as never to threaten France again
1.020 Any three:
Poland, Yugoslavia, Czechoslovakia, Turkey, Austria, Hungary
1.021 League of Nations
1.022 He went on a national speaking tour to win the support of the American people for the treaty.
1.023 U.S.
1.024 observation
1.025 stay neutral
1.026 The British effectively blockaded the Central Powers who also could not get loans to pay for supplies.
1.027 Austria-Hungary and Serbia
1.028 They always destroyed the ship with its cargo and often killed the crew/ passengers. Warships only seized cargo.
1.029 A note from the German Foreign Minister offering Mexico an alliance in exchange for recovering the American southwest.
1.030 Men
1.031 War Industries Board
1.032 Château-Thierry
1.033 zeppelins
1.034 Eddie Rickenbacker
1.035 Herbert Hoover
1.036 Meuse-Argonne
1.037 St. Mihiel
1.038 Dardanelles
1.039 Alvin York
1.040 *Lusitania*

SECTION 2

2.1	e	2.41	Any three: cars, refrigerators, radios, vacuum cleaners, electricity
2.2	i	2.42	Roaring Twenties
2.3	j	2.43	Stock market crash of 1929
2.4	f	2.44	agriculture
2.5	a	2.45	a New Deal
2.6	d	2.46	He provided money to buy surpluses and raised tariffs on food.
2.7	c	2.47	mining engineer
2.8	l	2.48	Take a loan to buy stock and use the stock itself as collateral for the loan.
2.9	h	2.49	Hawley-Smoot tariff
2.10	g	2.50	They wanted early payment of a bonus promised to World War I veterans. They were chased out of Washington by the army.
2.11	b		
2.12	k	2.51	After the crash people cut their spending as a precaution. Businesses cut back production, employment and wages as purchases fell. That meant people had even less money to spend and made fewer purchases.

2.13 selling supplies at cut rates; awarding construction contracts
2.14 police strike
2.15 blindly trusted his friends
2.16 Keep Cool with Coolidge
2.17 Treaty of Versailles
2.18 1920; Nineteenth
2.19 quotas; Northern Europe
2.20 Harry M. Daugherty
2.21 a. They should be repaid with interest.
b. Some should be forgiven as part of the American contribution to the war.
2.22 oil leases
2.23 b
2.24 h
2.25 g
2.26 d
2.27 c
2.28 f
2.29 e
2.30 a
2.31 A time when the sale of alcohol was illegal, 1919-1932
2.32 No. People just drank illegally.
2.33 They began to spend rather than save and used credit to increase their buying power.
2.34 A private saloon during Prohibition.
2.35 A free-living woman of the 1920s who drank, smoked, danced, dressed daringly and enjoyed life.
2.36 Any three:
illegal drinking, flappers, baseball, boxing, personal sports, movies, crossword puzzles, flagpole sitting, dance marathons
2.37 The rise of organized crime
2.38 A person who does not believe in miracles and sees Christianity as a set of ethics not a relationship with Jesus Christ.
2.39 Fundamentalists
2.40 The public believed Fundamentalists were bigoted fools who didn't accept science.

2.52 X
2.53 X
2.54 ___
2.55 X
2.56 X
2.57 X
2.58 ___
2.59 X
2.60 X
2.61 X
2.62 ___
2.63 He immediately declared a bank holiday, promising that only safe banks would reopen.
2.64 F.D.R. wanted to add a new justice for everyone over 70 years old because the court was throwing out New Deal laws.
2.65 Any two:
It increased the size and expense of the government, increased government regulation and set up the regular use of deficit spending.
2.66 Good Neighbor Policy
2.67 His legs were paralyzed, and his character strengthened.
2.68 k
2.69 h
2.70 l
2.71 i
2.72 c

2.73	o
2.74	n
2.75	d
2.76	m
2.77	j
2.78	a
2.79	g
2.80	b
2.81	e
2.82	f
2.83	1929; stock market; 1933; 25; New Deal; 1937; 1938; 1942; World War II

SELF TEST 2

2.01	Roaring Twenties
2.02	stock market crash, 1929
2.03	Fundamentalists
2.04	Prohibition
2.05	agriculture
2.06	submarine attacks
2.07	Bonus Army or Bonus Expeditionary Force
2.08	World War II
2.09	Hundred Days
2.010	trench
2.011	1933; 25
2.012	John Pershing
2.013	credit
2.014	Scopes Monkey
2.015	Archduke Ferdinand
2.016	bank holiday
2.017	organized crime
2.018	immigration
2.019	war
2.020	Teapot Dome
2.021	b
2.022	c
2.023	a
2.024	c
2.025	d
2.026	b
2.027	e
2.028	e
2.029	d
2.030	e
2.031	Any five:

	FERA:	gave money to the states for relief or jobs
	CWA:	temporary jobs
	HOLC:	low interest home loans
	WPA:	public works projects
	NRA:	set up codes to encourage production
	TVA:	built dams in Tennessee River Valley for electricity
	AAA:	paid farmers not to farm
	CCC:	low-paying conservation jobs for young men
	SEC:	monitor the stock market
	FDIC:	insure bank deposits

2.032	true
2.033	true
2.034	false
2.035	false
2.036	false
2.037	false
2.038	true
2.039	true
2.040	true
2.041	false

SECTION 3

3.1 appeasement

3.2 Miracle at Dunkirk

3.3 Maginot Line

3.4 Benito Mussolini

3.5 Berlin-Rome-Tokyo Axis

3.6 Phony War

3.7 Sudetenland

3.8 Neville Chamberlain

3.9 blitzkrieg

3.10 Battle of Britain

3.11 Spanish Civil War

3.12 Adolf Hitler

3.13 Any order:
Denmark, Norway

3.14 Neutrality Acts

3.15 Winston Churchill

3.16 Any order:
Belgium, Netherlands

3.17 Vichy France

3.18 the Blitz

3.19 Poland

3.20 Joseph Stalin

3.21 invasion of Poland

3.22 Francisco Franco

3.23 Manchukuo

3.24 Ethiopia

3.25 sue for peace

3.26 France, seas, oceans, air, beaches, landing grounds, hills, and Empire

3.27 In the same railroad car where Germany signed the armistice in 1918

3.28 Japanese; Pearl Harbor, Hawaii

3.29 Harry S. Truman

3.30 Atlantic

3.31 *U.S.S. Arizona*

3.32 Wendell Willkie; Thomas Dewey

3.33 that will live in infamy

3.34 a. Any order:
conscription law, traded destroyers for bases
b. Lend-lease approved
c. U.S. navy convoyed merchant ships to Iceland
d. Any order:
U.S. merchant ships armed and carried cargo all the way to Britain

3.35 They destroyed much of the Pacific fleet but they united America against them.

3.36 Japan captured southeast Asia, the main source of natural rubber. It was solved by creating a synthetic rubber industry.

3.37 Any four:
unity, rationing, scrap drives,
Victory gardens, full employment,
massive arms production, consumer goods
not available, price/production controls

3.38 They were forced into internment camps in the Midwest.

3.39 c

3.40 e

3.41 f

3.42 g

3.43 h

3.44 i

3.45 h

3.46 b

3.47 f

3.48 e

3.49 d

3.50 a

3.51 b

3.52 c

3.53 d

3.54 d

3.55 e

3.56 a

3.57 e

3.58 d

3.59 e

3.60 c

3.61 i

3.62 b

3.63 h

3.64 e

3.65 g

3.66 h

3.67 g

3.68 a

3.69 c

3.70 d

3.71 g

3.72 d

3.73 c

3.74 g

3.75 Edwin Rommel

3.76 Bernard Montgomery

3.77 Charles de Gaulle

3.78 George Marshall

3.79 George Patton

3.80 Adolf Hitler

3.81 Dwight Eisenhower

3.82 Zhukov

3.83 Admiral Karl Doenitz
3.84 Omar Bradley
3.85 Soviet
3.86 Tehran Conference
3.87 He did not want to come into conflict with the Red Army and he needed to send men south into the Alps.
3.88 the Allies
3.89 Guadalcanal
3.90 Battle of Leyte Gulf
3.91 island hopping
3.92 Midway
3.93 Chester Nimitz
3.94 Doolittle's Raid
3.95 Chiang Kai-shek
3.96 Iwo Jima
3.97 Manhattan Project
3.98 Douglas MacArthur
3.99 Bataan Death March
3.100 Himalaya Mountains
3.101 July 16, 1945
3.102 Battle of Philippine Sea
3.103 kamikaze
3.104 Battle of the Coral Sea
3.105 Potsdam
3.106 Marianas
3.107 Any order:
Hiroshima, Nagasaki
3.108 53 million
3.109 Corregidor
3.110 Seabees
3.111 Tarawa
3.112 Okinawa
3.113 Any five:
Guam, Wake, Philippines, Hong Kong, Singapore, Indochina, Thailand, Dutch East Indies, Malay Peninsula, most of New Guinea, Burma
3.114 The Japanese defenders would not surrender. Almost all had to be killed in hard fighting.
3.115 They committed suicide.
3.116 two days

SELF TEST 3

3.01 e
3.02 a
3.03 j
3.04 d
3.05 b
3.06 f
3.07 h
3.08 i
3.09 c
3.010 g
3.011 Adolf Hitler
3.012 Franklin D. Roosevelt
3.013 Winston Churchill
3.014 Pearl Harbor
3.015 appeasement
3.016 Britain
3.017 Japanese Americans
3.018 blitzkrieg
3.019 Stalingrad
3.020 Midway
3.021 trench
3.022 island hopping
3.023 Battle of the Bulge
3.024 Holocaust
3.025 Doolittle's Raid
3.026 stock market crash of 1929
3.027 German submarine attacks
3.028 North Africa; Italy; France (Normandy)
3.029 The assassination of Archduke Ferdinand, Austria-Hungarian heir
3.030 Nazi invasion of Poland
3.031 It supplied the Allies with huge amounts of arms and supplies.
3.032 the Roaring Twenties
3.033 He committed suicide.
3.034 Soviet Union
3.035 Atomic bombs dropped on Hiroshima and Nagasaki
3.036 false
3.037 false
3.038 false
3.039 true
3.040 false

LIFEPAC TEST

1. h
2. i
3. e
4. j
5. g
6. c
7. b
8. a
9. d
10. f
11. Nazi invasion of Poland
12. Atomic bomb
13. German submarine attacks
14. Fourteen Points
15. Communist Revolution
16. World War II
17. 25%
18. Treaty of Versailles
19. bank
20. Fundamentalists
21. false
    — change *Herbert Hoover* to *Woodrow Wilson*
22. false
    — change *kamikaze* to *blitzkrieg*
23. true
24. false
    — change *Mao Tse-tung* to *Chiang Kai-shek*
25. false
    — change *Great Britain* to *Pearl Harbor*
26. true
27. true
28. false
    — change *a depression* to *an arms race*
29. false
    — change *France* to *Belgium*
30. false
    — change *Pas-de-Calais* to *Normandy*
31. Their code of honor would not let them surrender so they often fought to the death.
32. They were New Deal agencies created to help Americans during the Great Depression.
33. Stock prices rose on speculation based on credit purchases.
34. He blindly trusted his friends who took advantage of their power in a series of scandals.
35. The British attacked from Egypt. Another American led force landed in Morocco, trapping them in the middle.
36. The death of about six million people in Nazi concentration camps.

ALTERNATE LIFEPAC TEST

1. s
2. q
3. g
4. m
5. d
6. c
7. o
8. w
9. p
10. y
11. i
12. x
13. j
14. v
15. t
16. e
17. u
18. f
19. b
20. r
21. a
22. h
23. k
24. l
25. n
26. Dwight D. Eisenhower
27. Woodrow Wilson
28. Douglas MacArthur
29. Adolf Hitler
30. Winston Churchill
31. John Pershing
32. Herbert Hoover
33. Benito Mussolini
34. Joseph Stalin
35. Archduke Ferdinand
36. false
    — change *blitzkrieg* to *trench*
37. false
    — change *50%* to *25%*
38. true
39. false
    — change *became a free and stable democracy* to *paid for the war and could never threaten France again*
40. false
    — change *the Soviet Union* to *Great Britain*
41. false
    — change *Japanese* to *Chinese*
42. true
43. true

44.   false
        — change *cigarettes* to *alcohol*
45.   false
        — change *Sicily* to *North Africa* or
        — change *first* to *second*

HISTORY & GEOGRAPHY 808

ALTERNATE LIFEPAC TEST

NAME _____

DATE _____

SCORE _____

Match these items "WWI" will be used as an abbreviation for World War I and "WWII" for World War II (each answer, 2 points).

1. _____ revolution in Russia; pulled it out of WWI
2. _____ island fortress; Manila Bay
3. _____ trial on evolution education, ridiculed Christianity
4. _____ volcanic island between Japan and Mariana Islands; taken by the Marines in 1944
5. _____ largest American attack of WWI
6. _____ Japanese navy's fighting effectiveness ended; WWII
7. _____ American strategy in Pacific; WWII
8. _____ Wilson's liberal peace plan
9. _____ WWI Veterans; needing money in 1932; marched on Washington
10. _____ turning point in Europe; WWII
11. _____ ended WWI; set up WWII
12. _____ gave Hitler the countries he wanted without a fight before WWII
13. _____ young men did conservation work for small wages
14. _____ killed more Americans than WWI did in 1918-19
15. _____ scandal under Warren G. Harding
16. _____ section of the economy in trouble in early 1920s
17. _____ declared by F.D.R. right after his inauguration
18. _____ triggered the Great Depression
19. _____ U.S. fought wolf packs to get supplies to Britain
20. _____ 6 million deaths in Nazi concentration camps
21. _____ Hitler's last major offensive
22. _____ destroyed Hiroshima and Nagasaki
23. _____ first British victory of WWII, North Africa
24. _____ location of Allied invasion of France, WWII
25. _____ F.D.R.'s plan to fight the Great Depression

a. Battle of the Bulge
b. Battle of the Atlantic
c. Battle of Leyte Gulf
d. Meuse-Argonne Offensive
e. agriculture
f. stock market crash
g. Scopes Monkey Trial
h. atomic bombs
i. Treaty of Versailles
j. CCC
k. El Alamein
l. Normandy
m. Iwo Jima
n. New Deal
o. island hopping
p. Bonus Army (Bonus Expeditionary Force)
q. Corregidor
r. Holocaust
s. communist
t. Tea Pot Dome
u. bank holiday
v. influenza
w. Fourteen Points
x. appeasement
y. Stalingrad

Name the person (each answer, 3 points).

26. _____ Supreme commander of Allied forces in Europe, WWII

27. _____ President of the U.S., WWI

28. _____ U.S. general who lost and recaptured the Philippines, WWII

29. _____ Dictator of Germany, WWII

30. _____ Prime Minister of Britain during most of WWII

31. _____ Commander American Expeditionary Force, WWI

32. _____ President who was blamed for the Great Depression

33. _____ Fascist dictator of Italy, WWII

34. _____ Communist dictator of the U.S.S.R., WWII

35. _____ Austrian heir; assassination began WWI

Answer *true* **or** *false.* **If the answer is false, change a word or phrase to make it true.**
Note: Putting the word "not" into the sentence is insufficient (each answer, 2 points).

36. _____ During World War I, the front was mainly a stalemate of blitzkrieg warfare.

37. _____ At the height of the Great Depression, 50% of all Americans were out of work.

38. _____ The Zimmerman note pushed America to get involved in World War I.

39. _____ After World War I, the main goal of France was to be sure Germany became a free and stable democracy.

40. _____ Immediately after the fall of France in World War II, only the Soviet Union was still fighting Germany.

41. _____ Charles de Gaulle was a Free French leader and Chiang Kai-shek was a Japanese leader.

42. _____ Charles Lindbergh was famous for being the first person to fly an airplane across the Atlantic alone.

43. _____ The Ku Klux Klan became popular during the years after World War I.

44. _____ Prohibition was an attempt from 1919 to 1932 to outlaw cigarettes. It failed.

45. _____ The first major military action by America in Europe during World War II was the invasion of Sicily.

HISTORY & GEOGRAPHY 809

Unit 9: Cold War America (1945-1990)

TEACHER NOTES

MATERIALS NEEDED FOR LIFEPAC	
Required	Suggested
None	• atlas • encyclopedia • reference books or online sources

ADDITIONAL LEARNING ACTIVITIES

Section 1: Hot or Cold?

1. Discuss these questions:

    a. Was containment a good policy?

    b. Who was right about how to proceed in the Korean War: Eisenhower or MacArthur?

    c. Why did the U.S. get so involved in Vietnam?

    d. Why was communism so frightening to Americans?

    e. Could the West have stopped the Berlin Wall from being built?

    f. Should America have tried to prevent the communist takeover of China?

    g. What would have happened after World War II if America had returned to its traditional isolation from foreign problems?

    h. Why didn't the Cold War ever become hot?

2. Assign students to research and do a report or paper on one of these topics: the Korean War, the Berlin Airlift, the Marshall Plan, NATO, the U-2 Affair, the Space Race, the Cuban Missile Crisis, the Bay of Pigs, the Berlin Wall, the Gulf of Tonkin Resolution, or the Anti-war protests of the 1960s and 70s.

3. Have students read personal accounts or view interviews of soldiers in the Korean or Vietnam War, and discuss them in class.

4. As a class, find memorabilia, artifacts, documents, clothing, and pictures from the Korean or Vietnam Wars (check the internet).

5. Have students read about life under communism in eastern Europe and discuss it in class.

6. Instruct students to talk to someone who was old enough to remember Kennedy's assassination, and ask about their reaction and memories of the investigation afterward. If this is not possible, students can view an interview.

7. Have students read about the Hungarian revolt in 1956, or the one in Czechoslovakia in 1968.

8. As a class, watch a documentary on the Korean or Vietnam War.

9. Have students assume the role of the Senate in 1964 (two-thirds of the people should be Democrats and one-third Republicans) to debate and vote on the Gulf of Tonkin Resolution.

10. Invite someone who participated in the Vietnam anti-war protests to talk to your class. Have the class prepare questions for them in advance. If someone cannot be located, view recorded interview found online.

Section 2: Between War and Watergate

1. Assign students to read a biography of one of these people: Harry Truman, John Kennedy, Lyndon B. Johnson, Richard Nixon, Joseph McCarthy, W.E.B. DuBois, Booker T. Washington, Martin Luther King, Jr., Robert Kennedy, Alger Hiss, or George McGovern.

2. As a class, discuss why the Civil Rights Movement succeeded.

3. Have students research the facts in the Alger Hiss perjury trial or the trial of the Rosenbergs. As a class, try one of the cases with your own attorneys, judge, and jury.

4. Have students research and create a chart showing the steps of the Watergate scandal.

5. Provide the following directions: Knowing that the police in Birmingham, Alabama were likely to attack civil rights protesters, write a one-page paper explaining why you would or would not have joined a march through that city in 1963.

6. Have the class do a dramatic reading of Martin Luther King's speech "I Have a Dream."

7. Have the class assume the role of the U.S. Senate in 1974 (Democrats controlled slightly more than half of the seats, 56 to 42 with 2 independents) in order to debate and vote on the impeachment of Richard Nixon.

8. Assign students to research and do a report or paper on one of these topics: the U.S. effort to land on the moon, hippies, abortion in America, busing in the 1970s, Détente, education for black students under "Separate but Equal" (before 1954), divorce in America, the election of 1948 (*Truman v. Dewey*), the hunt for communists in the 1950s, or the Peace Corps.

9. Do a class project to assemble a presentation on the Civil Rights Movement, using pictures, details, and personal stories.

10. Assign the following project: Pretend you are a journalist with Nixon in China in 1972. Do some research and write a one-page paper describing the visit and explaining its importance to your readers in the United States.

Section 3: Unexpected Victory

1. Assign students to write a two-page biography on one of these people: Gerald Ford, Jimmy Carter, Anwar Sadat, Menachem Begin, Ayatollah Khomeini, Ronald Reagan, George Bush, Mikhail Gorbachev, Norman Schwarzkopf, Colin Powell, Saddam Hussein, or Boris Yeltsin.

2. Discuss these questions:
    a. Should Gerald Ford have pardoned Richard Nixon?
    b. Could the Iran Hostage Crisis have been resolved quickly?
    c. Does the U.S. still have an energy crisis?
    d. Should the U.S. have interfered in Nicaragua, Grenada, or Panama?

   e. Is the world safer or more dangerous after the fall of communism?

3. Assign students to research the fall of communism in one nation in Eastern Europe, and then report to the class.

4. Ask a Persian Gulf War veteran to speak to your class. Prepare questions in advance.

5. Instruct students to survey their parents, teachers, and adult friends about the fall of communism. Did they expect it to happen? What did it mean to them?

6. Have the class read about the Persian Gulf War and the occupation of Kuwait.

7. Compare a 1988 map of Europe with a 1998 map as a class. What is different?

8. Assign students to research and do a report or paper on one of the nations of Eastern Europe or the former Soviet Union after the fall of communism.

9. Have students research and prepare a chart showing the development of the Iran-Contra Scandal.

Administer the LIFEPAC Test

The test is to be administered in one session. Give no help except with directions.
Evaluate the tests and review areas where the students have done poorly.
Review the pages and activities that stress the concepts tested.
If necessary, administer the Alternate LIFEPAC Test.

ANSWER KEYS

SECTION 1

1.1   Any order:
Democracy, communism

1.2   Security Council

1.3   containment

1.4   Berlin Airlift

1.5   NATO

1.6   Truman

1.7   Marshall Plan

1.8   Iron Curtain

1.9   Any order:
Turkey, Greece

1.10 United Nations

1.11 Baruch Plan

1.12 It was divided into four parts occupied by the Soviet Union, U.S., Britain, and France.

1.13 The Soviet Union refused to allow its section to rejoin the others and set up a communist government there.

1.14 The fall of the Czech Republic to communism

1.15 Any order:
Yugoslavia, Bulgaria, Romania, Poland, East Germany, Hungary and Albania, Czechoslovakia

1.16 They refused to remove their troops from Iran until threatened and refused to participate in a plan for international control of nuclear power.

1.17 a. Led by the U.S. – democracies, mainly in Europe
b. Led by the U.S.S.R. – communist nations
c. Poorer nations not part of the other two blocks

1.18 Communism would be contained where it already existed by aiding nations threatened by it.

1.19 Teacher check
— can include the differences in systems and ideas, Soviet aggression, fear and distrust

1.20 g

1.21 d

1.22 f

1.23 h

1.24 e

1.25 a

1.26 d

1.27 b

1.28 c

1.29 e

1.30 g

1.31 h

1.32 a

1.33 b

1.34 c

1.35 Any order:
Soviets set off their first atomic bomb, Communists won the civil war in China

1.36 They were boycotting the council over Taiwan

1.37 Pusan Perimeter

1.38 Austria

1.39 repatriation of prisoners

1.40 fall of the Dien Bien Phu fortress

1.41 The Soviet Union invaded, overthrew the new government and restored communism.

1.42 amphibious landing behind enemy lines at Inchon

1.43 38th Parallel

1.44 Any order:
France, Britain, Israel

1.45 Soviet Union occupied the North after World War II while the U.S. occupied the South. Each set up its own kind of government.

1.46 Warsaw Pact

1.47 a. The president could use armed force to protect any Middle East nation that asked for help against communism.
b. Lebanon

1.48 U-2 Affair

1.49 Berlin Wall

1.50 Cuban Missile Crisis

1.51 Bay of Pigs

1.52 Sputnik I

1.53 NASA

1.54 Fulgencio Batista

1.55 Fidel Castro

1.56 ICBM

1.57 U.S.S.R.

1.58 United States

1.59 Nikita Khrushchev

1.60 Cuba

1.61 Any order:
Kennedy, Khrushchev

1.62 Berlin

1.63 invade Cuba

1.64 Gulf of Tonkin Resolution

1.65 television

1.66 Tet Offensive

1.67 Ngo Dinh Diem

1.68 Viet Cong; Vietminh

1.69 Vietnamization
1.70 Pol Pot; Khmer Rouge
1.71 domino
1.72 destroy the communists; North Vietnam
1.73 Saigon
1.74 guerrilla
1.75 re-education; boat people
1.76 cease-fire; withdraw
1.77 protests
1.78 Any order:
Laos, Cambodia

SELF TEST 1

1.01 g
1.02 a
1.03 h
1.04 e
1.05 d
1.06 j
1.07 f
1.08 c
1.09 k
1.010 i
1.011 b
1.012 It was a conflict of ideas, economics, propaganda and intimidation between the U.S. and the Soviet Union that never became a hot war because of the fear of nuclear war.
1.013 Communism was to be contained, kept where it already existed by giving money, weapons and military assistance to stop communist aggression in free countries.
1.014 g
1.015 p
1.016 r
1.017 e
1.018 k
1.019 f
1.020 l
1.021 h
1.022 t
1.023 v
1.024 c
1.025 q
1.026 d
1.027 m
1.028 i
1.029 b
1.030 a
1.031 u
1.032 o
1.033 s
1.034 n
1.035 j
1.036 The North attacked driving the U.S. and the South back to the Pusan Perimeter. MacArthur landed at Inchon and drove the North back to near the Chinese border. Chinese soldiers then drove the U.S. back. The war stalemated at the 38th Parallel.
1.037 Repatriation, the communists wanted their prisoners of war returned by force. After Stalin's death, they agreed to voluntary repatriation with the right to visit those who refused to go.

1.038 It was a long, expensive war in favor of a corrupt government. Americans began to protest against it and many young men avoided the draft.

1.039 They set up communist regimes in their part of Europe and closed them off from the west. They also tried to gain control of Iran, Greece and Turkey.

1.040 The U.S.S.R. exploded an atomic bomb and the communists won the civil war in China.

SECTION 2

2.1 Fair Deal

2.2 Joseph McCarthy

2.3 Booker T. Washington

2.4 inflation

2.5 Alger Hiss

2.6 Dwight Eisenhower

2.7 Any order:
Democrat, Progressive, States' Rights (Dixiecrat)

2.8 Taft-Hartley

2.9 Federal Employee Loyalty Program

2.10 I like Ike

2.11 W.E.B. DuBois

2.12 Rosa Parks

2.13 Little Rock, Arkansas

2.14 G.I. Bill of Rights

2.15 Earl Warren

2.16 Any order:
interstate highway system, St. Lawrence Seaway

2.17 Richard Nixon

2.18 *Brown v. Board of Education*

2.19 Martin Luther King

2.20 Julius and Ethel Rosenberg

2.21 *Plessy v. Ferguson*

2.22 Thomas Dewey, the Republican, was expected to win because the Democrats were divided. He lost because Truman campaigned hard on specific issues. Dewey did not.

2.23 Any order:
civil rights, nationals health insurance, agricultural reform

2.24 By the content of their character

2.25 "My Country 'Tis of Thee"

2.26 Constitution and Declaration of Independence

2.27 sit down at a table of brotherhood

2.28 not to use physical violence or resort to wrongful deeds

2.29 Teacher check

2.30 Johnson

2.31 Profiles in Courage

2.32 the New Frontier; Great Society

2.33 televised debates

2.34 Vietnam War

2.35 nonviolent

2.36 Martin Luther King; James Earl Ray

2.37 John Kennedy; Harvey Oswald

2.38 Peace Corps

2.39 legislator

2.40 Alliance for Progress

2.41 "I Have a Dream"
2.42 PT Boat
2.43 attacks on peaceful protesters in Birmingham, Ala.; John Kennedy
2.44 the atmosphere, underwater and outer space; hot line
2.45 sit quietly at the table when they were refused service
2.46 Richard Nixon; Barry Goldwater
2.47 Watts, Los Angeles
2.48 balance of power
2.49 détente
2.50 Nixon Doctrine
2.51 Leonid Brezhnev
2.52 Vietnam
2.53 antiwar protesters
2.54 Richard Nixon
2.55 Watergate
2.56 Stagflation
2.57 Gerald Ford
2.58 Kent State University, Ohio
2.59 Busing
2.60 people 18 or older could vote
2.61 "bug" the Democratic headquarters
2.62 Spiro Agnew
2.63 Any order:
Archibald Cox, Leon Jaworski
2.64 Taiwan
2.65 Warren Burger
2.66 War Powers Act
2.67 Hubert Humphrey
2.68 George McGovern
2.69 Any order:
SALT; an agreement not to increase the number of missiles for five years
2.70 John Dean
2.71 tape recordings of all conversations
2.72 Robert Kennedy
2.73 the youth rebellions of the 1960s
2.74 Henry Kissinger
2.75 marriage, careers, morals, traditions
2.76 He was very anticommunist
2.77 Any two:
increased drug use, increased divorce, increased illegitimate children, falling moral standards
2.78 He tried to balance the budget but then tried a price freeze and price controls
2.79 Teacher check

SELF TEST 2

2.01 f
2.02 b
2.03 i
2.04 g
2.05 j
2.06 d
2.07 c
2.08 h
2.09 a
2.010 e
2.011 containment
2.012 Rosa Parks refused to sit in the back of the bus in Montgomery starting a bus boycott there.
2.013 Booker T. Washington
2.014 "I Have a Dream"
2.015 inflation
2.016 Peace Corps
2.017 Berlin Wall
2.018 détente
2.019 Dwight Eisenhower
2.020 Gulf of Tonkin Resolution
2.021 Sputnik I, U.S.S.R.
2.022 "I Like Ike."
2.023 Warsaw Pact
2.024 Alliance for Progress
2.025 Fair Deal
2.026 Spy planes showed missile bases being built in Cuba. Kennedy ordered the island blockaded to stop the missiles from being delivered. The Soviets did not challenge the blockade and agreed not to give Cuba missiles if the U.S. would not invade it.
2.027 Europe was not recovering from World War IL The U.S. offered aid to rebuild if Europe would draw up a plan. They did but the Iron Curtain nations were not allowed to participate. It was a great success.
2.028 The court ordered the school to integrate and nine black students registered. The governor tried to stop them with the National Guard and a mob. Eisenhower sent in soldiers to escort the students.
2.029 Burglars were captured trying to bug the Democratic headquarters, one worked for Nixon's campaign. Several Nixon aides were involved and tried to cover it up. Recordings of Nixon's conversations proved he knew about the cover up. He resigned.

2.030 They peacefully disobeyed the laws by sitting, wading, walking and praying where they were not allowed. They also staged peaceful marches, registered voters, and appealed to the courts.

2.031 A mass rebellion against traditional values like marriage and careers.
Protests of all kinds were common, especially against the Vietnam War.
Caused increases in divorce, drug use, and immorality.

2.032 *Plessy v. Ferguson* said that black and white people could have "separate but equal" facilities. *Brown v. Board* said separate was inherently unequal and schools must integrate "with all deliberate speed."

SECTION 3

3.1 human rights

3.2 invasion of Afghanistan

3.3 OPEC

3.4 Whip Inflation Now (WIN)

3.5 Iran Hostage Crisis

3.6 interest rates

3.7 honest outsider

3.8 *Mayaguez*

3.9 pardoned Nixon

3.10 Panama Canal; Panama

3.11 China

3.12 Camp David Accords

3.13 Nelson Rockefeller

3.14 boycotting; withdrawing

3.15 52; 444

3.16 Ayatollah Khomeini; Mohammad Reza Pahlavi

3.17 Iraq

3.18 Edward Kennedy

3.19 Ronald Reagan

3.20 He hoped to convince Iran to free American hostages in Beirut.

3.21 Weapons were sold to Iran, the profits were sent to the *Contras*, guerrillas who were fighting a pro-communist regime in Nicaragua.

3.22 Any order:
a. suicide bomb attack on military barracks in Lebanon, 1983
b. TWA jet hijacked, 1985
c. *Achille Lauro* hijacked, 1985
d. bomb in German disco, 1986
or hostages held in Lebanon

3.23 *perestroika* – restructuring of the economy
glasnost – openness, greater freedom of speech

3.24 It was an oppressive government supported by the U.S.S.R. and was sending weapons to rebel groups in nearby nations.

3.25 Any order:
a. reduced taxes
b. cut welfare
c. reduced the power of federal regulatory agencies
d. increased military spending

3.26 The U.S. invaded to overthrow a communist government that was building an airport for a possible Soviet base.

3.27 It was the first treaty to reduce, not just limit nuclear weapons.

3.28 four

3.29 Any three:
cost of paying for revolutions all over the world, out-of-date industries, slow to develop computer technology and people worked as little as possible

3.30 inflation

3.31 Sandra Day O'Connor

3.32 Strategic Defense Initiative – space based missile defense system

3.33 air traffic controllers

3.34 e

3.35 c

3.36 f

3.37 b

3.38 h

3.39 d

3.40 g

3.41 a

3.42 Savings and Loan Crisis

3.43 *Exxon Valdez*

3.44 Police officers who had been videotaped beating a black man were acquitted

3.45 1989

3.46 1991

3.47 Persian Gulf War

3.48 Norman Schwarzkopf

3.49 Manuel Noriega

3.50 Colin Powell

3.51 Saddam Hussein

3.52 They shifted their forces north to go into Iraq around the defenses on the border of Kuwait, trapping the Iraqi army.

3.53 U.S.S.R. had held elections that allowed communists to compete for seats, reformers won most of them.

3.54 Coalition missiles and bombs had destroyed all radar and air surveillance.

3.55 fifteen

SELF TEST 3

3.01 Watergate

3.02 inflation

3.03 Iran Hostage Crisis

3.04 Beirut, Lebanon

3.05 Iran-Contra Affair

3.06 communism collapsed in Europe

3.07 Persian Gulf War

3.08 pardoned Nixon

3.09 invasion of Afghanistan

3.010 Camp David Accords

3.011 Rosa Parks refused to sit in the back of the bus starting the Montgomery bus boycott

3.012 Cuban Missile Crisis

3.013 Marshall Plan

3.014 Western Bloc (Free or First World);
Eastern Bloc (Communist or Second World);
Third World

3.015 containment

3.016 j

3.017 o

3.018 c

3.019 g

3.020 i

3.021 k

3.022 l

3.023 b

3.024 m

3.025 n

3.026 a

3.027 e

3.028 d

3.029 f

3.030 h

3.031
a. X
b. ___
c. X
d. ___
e. X

3.032
a. X
b. ___
c. ___
d. X
e. X
f. X
g. ___
h. ___
i. X
j. ___

3.033
 a. <u> X </u>
 b. <u> X </u>
 c. <u> X </u>
 d. <u>___</u>
 e. <u>___</u>
 f. <u>___</u>
 g. <u>___</u>
 h. <u> X </u>
 i. <u> X </u>
 j. <u>___</u>

LIFEPAC TEST

1. Marshall Plan
2. Warsaw Pact
3. Persian Gulf War
4. Vietnam War
5. Cuban Missile Crisis
6. Iran Hostage Crisis
7. "I Have a Dream"
8. inflation
9. Gulf of Tonkin Resolution
10. Watergate
11. Korean War
12. Iran-Contra Affair
13. Berlin Wall
14. Peace Corps
15. NATO
16. U.S. policy during the Cold War—communism was to be contained where it already existed by fighting it in free nations.
17. A conflict of ideas, propaganda, economics and intimidation between the U.S. and Soviet Union from 1945 to 1991. The fear of nuclear destruction kept it from ever being a hot war.
18. A war fought during the Cold War to stop communism in one country. It was not allowed to spread any further than that nation or area.
19. Reforms by Gorbachev in the 1980s in the Soviet Union. Perestroika was economic reform while glasnost was greater freedom of speech.
20. A "thaw" in the Cold War in the 1970s. It included SALT I & II, Nixon's visit to the Soviet Union and greater trade.
21. Communism collapsed all over eastern Europe as people demonstrated for more freedom. The Berlin Wall was destroyed.
22. Black people would peacefully challenge the laws by going where they were not allowed to be and staying. They also marched, filed lawsuits and registered voters.
23. Americans lost confidence in their government, the military and themselves, particularly in their ability to defeat communism.
24. f
25. h
26. i
27. j
28. d
29. b
30. c
31. e
32. g
33. a

ALTERNATE LIFEPAC TEST

1. h; Ford
2. f; Truman
3. g; Nixon
4. o; Johnson
5. m; Bush
6. c; Kennedy
7. j; Bush
8. d; Johnson
9. k; Truman
10. a; Carter
11. e; (a) Truman   (b) Eisenhower
12. b; Eisenhower
13. n; Bush
14. i; Reagan
15. p; Kennedy
16. Cold War
17. Civil Rights Movement
18. Containment
19. Marshall Plan
20. inflation
21. Mikhail Gorbachev
22. *détente*
23. Peace Corps
24. separate but equal
25. Cambodia
26. communism
27. false
28. false
29. true
30. true
31. false

HISTORY & GEOGRAPHY 809

ALTERNATE LIFEPAC TEST

NAME _____

DATE _____

SCORE _____

Match each event, scandal, or crisis with its description. Then, on the line after the description, name the president(s) during the event. Some presidents will be used more than once. One matching answer will not be used. (each answer — matching and president's name — is worth 2 points)

1. _____ Navy task force sent in to rescue U.S. merchant ship seized by Cambodia _____

2. _____ Korean commander had public approval when he disagreed with his superiors _____

3. _____ attempt to "bug" the Democrats and a cover up of White House involvement _____

4. _____ attack by the North Vietnamese at New Year's that proved they were still strong _____

5. _____ The U.S.S.R. said it would no longer defend Iron Curtain governments, 1989 _____

6. _____ Cuban exiles failed to overthrow Castro in an attempt the U.S. did not fully support _____

7. _____ Iraqi army was driven out of Kuwait in a 100 hour ground war _____

8. _____ U.S. ship allegedly attacked; gave the president a free hand in Vietnam _____

9. _____ opened in San Francisco,1945; Security Council makes major decisions _____

10. _____ embassy staff held for 444 days; U.S. military rescue fails _____

11. _____ North attacked the South; drove them back to the Pusan Perimeter; conflict ended by a cease fire, not a treaty (a) _____ (b) _____

12. _____ U.S. spy plane shot down over the U.S.S.R.; pilot captured _____

13. _____ General Manuel Noriega invalidated an election; was indicted for drug trafficking; unrest endangered American soldiers _____

14. _____ weapons were sold to a terrorist nation to gain the release of hostages; profits from the sale were used to finance anti-communist rebels in Central America _____

15. _____ naval blockade set up to prevent the arrival of Soviet nuclear weapons; Soviets did not challenge it _____

a. Iran Hostage Crisis

b. U-2 Affair

c. Bay of Pigs

d. Gulf of Tonkin Resolution

e. Korean War

f. Firing of MacArthur

g. Watergate

h. *Mayaguez*

i. Iran-Contra Affair

j. Persian Gulf War

k. United Nations

l. Warsaw Pact

m. Fall of Communism in Europe

n. Invasion of Panama

o. Tet Offensive

p. Cuban Missile Crisis

Name the item, event, or person (each answer, 3 points).

16. Conflict of ideas, economics, propaganda and intimidation between the U.S. and the U.S.S.R. from 1945 to 1991

    _____

17. Reform movement that began with the Montgomery bus boycott led by Martin Luther King in 1955

    _____

18. The main policy of the U.S. toward communism from 1945 to 1991

    _____

19. American aid given to rebuild Europe after World War II

    _____

20. America's biggest economic problem after World War II until the early 1980s

    _____

21. Man who began *perestroika* and *glasnost* in the Soviet Union in the 1980s

    _____

22. Thaw in relations between America and the Soviet Union in the 1970s

    _____

23. Volunteer organization set up by Kennedy to aid Third World nations

    _____

24. Segregation policy ended by *Brown v. Board of Education of Topeka*

    _____

25. Nation in which Pol Pot and the Khmer Rouge killed over a million people

    _____

26. Joseph McCarthy accused many people of this

    _____

Answer *true* **or** *false* (each answer, 1 point).

27. _____ The Vietnam War helped America recover from the failure in Korea.

28. _____ Jimmy Carter was the first president to visit the U.S.S.R.

29. _____ The fear of nuclear weapons is one important reason why America and the Soviet Union never went to war with each other.

30. _____ The Soviet Union was the early leader in space exploration.

31. _____ Mao Zedong and Communist China became American allies right after World War II to counter Soviet influence in Korea.

HISTORY & GEOGRAPHY 810

Unit 10: Recent America and Review (1990-Present)

TEACHER NOTES

MATERIALS NEEDED FOR LIFEPAC	
Required	Suggested
None	• atlas • encyclopedia • reference books or online sources

ADDITIONAL LEARNING ACTIVITIES

Section 1: Recent America

1. Assign students to research and do a report or paper on one of these topics: NAFTA, the 1992 rescue mission in Somalia, the Tiananmen Square rebellion and massacre, contract with America with its results, Yugoslavia since the fall of communism, computers, medical technology, or the impeachment of William Clinton.

2. Have the class research and discuss U.S. relations with China, Cuba, or North Korea in the last year.

3. Make a chart of the U.S. national debt for as far back as you can find.

4. Have the class research and discuss this question: Did the U.S. interference in Haiti in 1994 help that nation?

5. Assign students to write a 250-word paper on the benefits and problems of the internet.

6. Provide the following directions for a research project: Choose a Christian organization that is fighting the decline in American morals. Do research and assemble a list of their efforts. Prepare to discuss in class whether you believe their efforts will be effective or not.

Sections 2 and 3: Reviews

1. As a class, discuss how the founding fathers interpreted the Constitution, and compare it with the politicians and judges of today.

2. Assign students to do a paper or report comparing life in Virginia (or any other colony/state) in 1650, 1750, 1820, 1880, and 1950.

3. Assign students to do a paper or report comparing life in any western state at the time it was first settled, at statehood, during the Great Depression, and in the 1960s.

4. In a class discussion or in a paper, have students compare and contrast the impeachments of Johnson and Clinton.

5. As a class, assemble a display that shows the battle uniforms of the U.S. army from the Revolution until the Persian Gulf War.

6. Assign students to research and do a paper or report that shows how firearms and artillery used by the U.S. armed forces have changed from the Revolution to the Persian Gulf War.

7. Have students assemble a display that shows changes in the architecture of American homes from 1607 to 2000.

8. Invite a Native American person to speak to your class about American history from their people's point of view. Have the class prepare questions in advance.

9. Debate as a class: "Resolved: The Monroe Doctrine is still an important part of American policy."

10. Have the class make a wall map for your classroom showing the outline of the growth of the United States (show the Louisiana Purchase, Mexican Cession and so forth), marking each state with the date it was admitted to the Union.

11. Have the class prepare a wall display of the presidents of the United States. The display should include a picture, dates in office, and a brief list of accomplishments.

12. Instruct students to rank the presidents of the United States from best to worst (opinion).

13. Assign students to write a 500-word paper on the subject "The most important event in American history was..." describing and defending their choice.

14. Provide these directions for a class project: Describe a journey between two cities that were important to your region at different times in American History. Each student should be assigned a different point in time. Share your reports with the class. For example: If you are in New York, you might pick a trip between Buffalo and New York City in 1700, 1800, 1830, 1880, 1920, 1950, and 1990. If you are in Missouri, you might pick a trip from St. Louis to any of the major pioneer destinations or to New Orleans. Use your imagination!

15. Tell students to record a history of your city or town as a part of American History.

16. Have students research and do a report or paper comparing Christian worship in your church today with worship in America's history (go back at least 100 years).

17. As a class, discuss how Democrats Andrew Jackson, Grover Cleveland, Harry Truman, and William Clinton would have gotten along together in politics.

18. As a class, discuss how Republicans, Abraham Lincoln, Benjamin Harrison, Theodore Roosevelt, and Ronald Reagan would have gotten along together in politics.

19. Discuss these questions:

    a. What was the biggest change in American life from 1776 to 1880? from 1880 to 2000?

    b. What was the biggest change in American government from 1776 to 1880? from 1880 to 2000?

    c. What would most Americans have thought about their homeland in 1750? in 1815? in 1860? in 1890? in 1916? in 1935? in 1945? in 1960?
        <u>Teachers, this is a good question to use for review because the students have to know what is happening on those dates to answer.</u>

    d. What made the United States the most powerful nation on earth?

    e. What is your favorite part of American history and why?

Administer the LIFEPAC Test

ANSWER KEYS

SECTION 1

1.1	North Korea, China, Cuba
1.2	Tiananmen Square
1.3	Timothy McVeigh
1.4	Republican
1.5	Somalia
1.6	NAFTA
1.7	Yugoslavia
1.8	Jean-Bertrand Aristide
1.9	Persian Gulf War
1.10	recession
1.11	Contract with America
1.12	Newt Gingrich
1.13	two charges of perjury
1.14	three witnesses testified by video tape
1.15	U.S. prepared to invade but Jimmy Carter convinced the military leaders to leave prior to invasion
1.16	$290 billion
1.17	Ross Perot
1.18	They were sent back to Cuba, not allowed to settle in the U.S.
1.19	He was acquitted, the impeachment did not even get a majority vote
1.20	$5.6 trillion
1.21	g
1.22	i
1.23	h
1.24	a
1.25	d
1.26	j
1.27	f
1.28	c
1.29	b
1.30	e
1.31	c
1.32	d
1.33	e
1.34	a
1.35	b
1.36	divorce
1.37	It is socially acceptable, and selfishness is encouraged by society.
1.38	a. Prison Fellowship
	b. Barney Clark
	c. Focus on the Family
	d. racist propaganda, altered history, and adult content
1.39	euthanasia and abortion

1.40	They can keep the body functioning after the person is dead.
1.41	gathering information, communication, navigation
1.42	a. vacuum tubes
	b. transistors
	c. integrated circuits
	d. microprocessors
1.43	as an interconnection of government and military computers
1.44	Teacher check
1.45	e
1.46	c
1.47	d
1.48	f
1.49	a
1.50	b
1.51	false
1.52	false
1.53	false
1.54	true
1.55	true
1.56	false

SELF TEST 1

1.01 h
1.02 b
1.03 f
1.04 g
1.05 d
1.06 e
1.07 j
1.08 a
1.09 i
1.010 c
1.011 Improvements led to advances in communications, satellite usage, and medicine.
1.012 Machines can keep a body functioning after a person is dead.
1.013 Students protesting for greater freedom were attacked by the army, but the government denied that it happened.
1.014 Using a computer to visit information sites on the internet.
1.015 People are encouraged to do what makes them happy (not what is right) and society does not condemn divorce.
1.016 e-mail
1.017 NAFTA
1.018 Contract with America
1.019 cell phone/pager
1.020 Apple II
1.021 Social Security tax
1.022 Haiti
1.023 fax/facsimile
1.024 satellite
1.025 ENIAC
1.026 North Korea, China, Cuba
1.027 vacuum tubes
1.028 abortion
1.029 true
1.030 false
1.031 false
1.032 true
1.033 false
1.034 true
1.035 true
1.036 false
1.037 true
1.038 true
1.039 true
1.040 false
1.041 true

SECTION 2

2.1 Any order:
    a. Crusades
    b. Marco Polo's travels
2.2 a. John Cabot
    b. Francis Drake
    c. London Company
    d. Sir Walter Raleigh
    e. Henry Hudson
2.3 Hudson R. area, Dutch West India Co.
2.4 The Great Lakes, St. Lawrence River, Mississippi River
2.5 Henry the Navigator; around Africa
2.6 Christopher Columbus
2.7 a. Jolliet and Marquette
    b. Jacques Cartier
    c. Samuel de Champlain
    d. La Salle
2.8 Any order:
    a. House of Burgesses established
    b. A shipload of women arrived
    c. 1st enslaved African people arrived
2.9 Either order:
    a. De Soto
    b. Balboa
    c. Ponce de Leon
    d. Magellan
    e. Coronado
2.10 Either order:
    a. underestimated the distance
    b. did not know America was there
2.11 Patroon
2.12 French
2.13 Jamestown
2.14 the headright
2.15 tobacco
2.16 conquest of wealthy empires (Aztec and Inca)
2.17 Any two:
European diseases, colonists had better weapons, Native American Nations did not work together and were overwhelmed by the number of colonists
2.18 furs
2.19 New York
2.20 Massachusetts (Bay)
2.21 Maryland
2.22 Roger Williams
2.23 Royal
2.24 William Penn
2.25 governor, council, assembly
2.26 Mayflower Compact
2.27 company, proprietary, self-governing
2.28 finances

2.29	North Carolina	2.74	Stamp Act
2.30	New York	2.75	New York City
2.31	Squanto	2.76	Intolerable Acts
2.32	South Carolina	2.77	Bunker Hill
2.33	Rhode Island	2.78	*Common Sense*
2.34	Fundamental Orders of Connecticut	2.79	Valley Forge
2.35	Thomas Hooker	2.80	mercantilism
2.36	Massachusetts (Bay)	2.81	Second Continental Congress
2.37	Pennsylvania, Delaware	2.82	America
2.38	Pennsylvania, Delaware, Maryland	2.83	Britain
2.39	Georgia	2.84	Philadelphia
2.40	Maine	2.85	Thomas Jefferson
2.41	settlers didn't pay their rent	2.86	Samuel Adams
2.42	Puritan church members	2.87	Fort Ticonderoga
2.43	George Washington	2.88	Any order: Ethan Allen, Benedict Arnold
2.44	Congregationalists	2.89	Either order: Gage, Howe, Cornwallis
2.45	Great Awakening		
2.46	King Philip's War	2.90	a. Never attempted b. Retreated after he was unable to take Fort Stanwix c. He captured Ticonderoga but his advance was slowed by the local militia. His entire army was defeated at Saratoga.
2.47	New England		
2.48	Anglican Church		
2.49	Any order: Fishing, whaling, ship building		
2.50	New England Confederation		
2.51	French and Indian		
2.52	Deism	2.91	He worked with guerrilla bands to draw out the British, inflict heavy losses and retreat. The losses eventually forced the British to withdraw.
2.53	The South		
2.54	William Pitt		
2.55	Edward Braddock		
2.56	George Whitefield; Jonathan Edwards	2.92	Benedict Arnold
2.57	King William's War-War of the League of Augsburg; Queen Anne's War-War of the Spanish Succession; King George's War-War of the Austrian Succession	2.93	The federal government had no executive, no power to tax, control commerce or provide justice.
		2.94	It was sold to pay off federal debts. The territories were allowed to organize into states with equal rights when they had enough people.
2.58	Middle colonies		
2.59	New England		
2.60	Dominion of New England		
2.61	Albany Congress	2.95	Shay's Rebellion
2.62	Middle Colonies	2.96	Saratoga
2.63	New England	2.97	Cornwallis was trapped by the French fleet and a combination American/French army and surrendered.
2.64	Proclamation of 1763		
2.65	Any four: Britain was the dominant world power and deeply in debt, colonists began to work together and gained military experience, Britain was angry over the lack of colonial support and unity	2.98	America was given independence and all the land east of the Mississippi
		2.99	a. It would be by state in the Senate and by population in the House b. they counted as three-fifths of a person c. George Washington d. to allow free debate & compromise e. It could not be outlawed until 1807
2.66	First Continental Congress		
2.67	Quebec Act		
2.68	Lexington		
2.69	Boston Massacre	2.100	executive, legislative, judicial
2.70	Navigation Acts	2.101	no Bill of Rights
2.71	Townshend Acts	2.102	Federalists
2.72	Boston Tea Party	2.103	First ten amendments to the Constitution
2.73	Trenton	2.104	essays in favor of the Constitution

2.105 Thomas Jefferson

2.106 XYZ Affair

2.107 1800

2.108 Whiskey Rebellion

2.109 Democratic-Republican

2.110 Louisiana Purchase

2.111 Lewis and Clark

2.112 Alexander Hamilton

2.113 Declaration of Neutrality

2.114 Federalist

2.115 Convention of 1800

2.116 Alien and Sedition Acts

2.117 *Marbury v. Madison*

2.118 Thomas Jefferson

2.119 John Adams

2.120 Federalist

2.121 Jay's Treaty

2.122 George Washington

2.123 They established our basic institutions, set up strong federal government and kept the new nation out of war

2.124 Tecumseh

2.125 *Constitution*

2.126 War Hawks

2.127 Barbary pirates

2.128 Canada

2.129 *Chesapeake-Leopard*

2.130 Embargo

2.131 Lake Erie

2.132 Democratic-Republican

2.133 Plattsburgh Bay

2.134 impressment

2.135 Washington; Baltimore

2.136 Ghent

2.137 Aaron Burr

2.138 decreased

2.139 John Marshall

2.140 American System

2.141 Monroe Doctrine

2.142 Andrew Jackson; New Orleans

2.143 Era of Good Feelings

2.144 Napoleon was defeated and exiled

2.145 _X_

2.146 ___

2.147 _X_

2.148 _X_

2.149 _X_

2.150 ___

2.151 ___

2.152 Government jobs were given to loyal supporters of the party regardless of qualifications. It led to corruption and poor quality work.

2.153 Adams won it in the House of Representatives because Henry Clay supported him. Then, Clay was made Secretary of State.

2.154 Missouri was admitted as a slave state, Maine as a free one, there was to be no more slavery north of 36° 30' boundary.

2.155 the cotton gin

2.156 South Carolina declared the tariff null and void in their state. Jackson threatened to use force. Clay arranged a compromise that lowered the tariff over ten years.

2.157 The Cherokee people were forced to move west, off of their land; many died on the journey.

2.158 It was closed when the president moved the federal funds out of it into "pet" banks.

2.159 A very high tariff proposed to embarrass Adams

2.160 He wanted all of it to 54° 40' but accepted a division with Britain at 49.0

2.161 A group of Texans held the fort for two weeks, inflicted heavy losses on the Mexicans and then were all killed.

2.162 Could states nullify federal laws

2.163 He sent soldiers south of the Nueces River into land claimed by Mexico, provoking a war.

2.164 d

2.165 g

2.166 c

2.167 a

2.168 f

2.169 e

2.170 b

2.171 Kansas-Nebraska Act

2.172 Compromise of 1850

2.173 Republican

2.174 steamboat

2.175 Zachary Taylor

2.176 railroads

2.177 Guadalupe Hidalgo

2.178 gold rush

2.179 Industrial Revolution

2.180 Second Great Awakening

2.181 Samuel Morse

2.182 shipping

2.183 Mormonism

2.184 mechanical reaper

2.185 abolitionist

2.186 Fugitive Slave Act

2.187 *Uncle Tom's Cabin*

2.188 Winfield Scott

2.189 Eli Whitney

2.190 Erie Canal
2.191 Irish
2.192 John Deere
2.193 Gadsden Purchase
2.194 Samuel Slater
2.195 hard surface roads
2.196 textile

SELF TEST 2

2.01 a
2.02 p
2.03 r
2.04 m
2.05 j
2.06 y
2.07 s
2.08 b
2.09 h
2.010 u
2.011 e
2.012 v
2.013 c
2.014 d
2.015 n
2.016 o
2.017 t
2.018 w
2.019 l
2.020 x
2.021 f
2.022 q
2.023 k
2.024 g
2.025 i
2.026 c
2.027 h
2.028 n
2.029 q
2.030 b
2.031 g
2.032 j
2.033 a
2.034 k
2.035 d
2.306 m
2.037 l
2.038 e
2.039 f
2.040 i
2.041 o
2.042 r
2.043 p
2.044 Massachusetts (Bay)
2.045 Georgia
2.046 France
2.047 Spain
2.048 France
2.049 Britain
2.050 Jamestown (Virginia)
2.051 New York
2.052 Rhode Island

2.053 Delaware and Pennsylvania
2.054 South
2.055 Maryland
2.056 Plymouth
2.057 It ended the era of compromise by allowing slavery north of the Missouri Compromise line.
2.058 Any two:
      generals, location, possible allies
2.059 A change from agriculture and handcrafts to industry and machine manufacturing.

SECTION 3

3.1 election of Abraham Lincoln
3.2 the beginning of the Civil War
3.3 10%
3.4 14th
3.5 Redeemers
3.6 Emancipation Proclamation
3.7 John Brown
3.8 Ulysses S. Grant
3.9 Dred Scott
3.10 Tenure in Office Act
3.11 14th
3.12 Lincoln-Douglas Debates
3.13 Alaska
3.14 Kansas
3.15 Carpetbaggers and Scalawags
3.16 Black Friday
3.17 13th
3.18 Hayes became president, Reconstruction was ended
3.19 hard money
3.20 Black Codes
3.21 15th
3.22 Whiskey Ring
3.23 Charles Sumner
3.24 hire a replacement
3.25 Ulysses S. Grant
3.26 sharecropping
3.27 abolitionist
3.28 N
3.29 S
3.30 N
3.31 S
3.32 S
3.33 N
3.34 N
3.35 N
3.36 S
3.37 S
3.38 N
3.39 S
3.40 S
3.41 S
3.42 N
3.43 N
3.44 S
3.45 S
3.46 S
3.47 N
3.48 N
3.49 N
3.50 N
3.51 N

3.52	N
3.53	N
3.54	i
3.55	m
3.56	g
3.57	a
3.58	j
3.59	o
3.60	n
3.61	f
3.62	b
3.63	d
3.64	k
3.65	c
3.66	e
3.67	h
3.68	l
3.69	q
3.70	j
3.71	v
3.72	s
3.73	z
3.74	f
3.75	p
3.76	a
3.77	t
3.78	b
3.79	k
3.80	n
3.81	w
3.82	o
3.83	g
3.84	e
3.85	d
3.86	x
3.87	h
3.88	i
3.89	l
3.90	u
3.91	c
3.92	y
3.93	m
3.94	r
3.95	Low pay, no job protection, squalid slums, cities run by corrupt bosses
3.96	rich on the surface, corrupt underneath
3.97	repeating rifles, diseases, mobile army units and the destruction of the buffalo
3.98	kept all of it except for Cuba
3.99	Woodrow Wilson
3.100	Island hopping
3.101	U-boats; Pearl Harbor

3.102	Any two: free spending, illegal drinking, fads, prosperity
3.103	Stock Market Crash
3.104	Hundred Days
3.105	Denmark, Norway, Belgium, Netherlands, France
3.106	Germany invaded Poland
3.107	New Deal
3.108	John Pershing
3.109	the heir to the Austrian throne was assassinated
3.110	Scopes Monkey
3.111	Great Depression
3.112	Dwight D. Eisenhower
3.113	appeasement
3.114	Treaty of Versailles
3.115	Communist Revolution
3.116	18th
3.117	Stalingrad; Midway
3.118	MacArthur
3.119	the U.S. dropped two atomic bombs on Japan
3.120	Harding
3.121	Harry Truman
3.122	arms race, national pride, alliances
3.123	Herbert Hoover
3.124	World War II
3.125	North Africa; Italy; France
3.126	Manhattan
3.127	trench; *Blitzkrieg*
3.128	Calvin Coolidge
3.129	Battle of the Bulge
3.130	Holocaust
3.131	A conflict of ideas, economics, propaganda and intimidation between the U.S. and U.S.S.R. (1945-91).
3.132	nonviolent protest
3.133	*Brown v. Board of Education*
3.134	Peace Corps, Alliance for Progress, Nuclear Test Ban Treaty
3.135	Gulf of Tonkin Resolution
3.136	He made accusations about communists in the government and business.
3.137	The North attacked the South driving them back to the Pusan Perimeter. MacArthur sent an amphibious assault that drove the North back to near the Chinese border. Chinese soldiers counter attacked and it stalemated near the old border.
3.138	China became communist and the U.S.S.R. exploded an atomic bomb
3.139	legal inequality for black Americans was finally ended

3.140 Missile sites were being built in Cuba. Kennedy blockaded the island to stop the delivery of missiles. The Soviets did not challenge the blockade and dismantled the sites.

3.141 James Earl Ray

3.142 Great Society

3.143 Civil Rights Act & Voting Rights Act

3.144 Berlin Wall

3.145 Fair Deal

3.146 U-2 Incident

3.147 Containment

3.148 Marshall Plan

3.149 NATO

3.150 Douglas MacArthur

3.151 Montgomery Bus Boycott

3.152 Dwight Eisenhower

3.153 "I Have a Dream"

3.154 Sputnik

3.155 Vietnam

3.156 Lee Harvey Oswald

3.157 communists

3.158 United Nations

3.159 Tet Offensive

3.160 NASA

3.161 b

3.162 c

3.163 d

3.164 e

3.165 a

3.166 f

3.167 c

3.168 b

3.169 a

3.170 f

3.171 b

3.172 c

3.173 d

3.174 a

3.175 e

3.176 d

3.177 f

3.178 c

3.179 f

3.180 inflation

3.181 Burglars who tried to bug the Democratic headquarters were connected to the White House staff. Nixon instructed them to hide their knowledge of the break-in. That was later proven using tapes he made in his office.

3.182 Revolts against communist rule occurred all over eastern Europe and all the governments eventually fell. Even the Berlin Wall was torn down.

3.183 Iraqi forces were driven out of Ku wait.

3.184 Fifty-two Americans from the Iran embassy staff were held for 444 days.

3.185 1991

3.186 the Soviet invasion of Afghanistan

3.187 racial balance in all the schools in a district

3.188 social revolts of the 1960s

SELF TEST 3

3.01 m
3.02 aa
3.03 g
3.04 f
3.05 p
3.06 o
3.07 d
3.08 dd
3.09 t
3.010 s
3.011 e
3.012 x
3.013 h
3.014 b
3.015 q
3.016 cc
3.017 j
3.018 a
3.019 v
3.020 u
3.021 c
3.022 z
3.023 l
3.024 r
3.025 k
3.026 n
3.027 w
3.028 bb
3.029 y
3.030 i
3.031 b
3.032 p
3.033 w
3.034 v
3.035 x
3.036 g
3.037 k
3.038 c
3.039 i
3.040 h
3.041 a
3.042 t
3.043 e
3.044 q
3.045 j
3.046 f
3.047 l
3.048 r
3.049 m
3.050 o
3.051 s

3.052 n
3.053 u
3.054 d
3.055 War of 1812
3.056 Civil War
3.057 World War I
3.058 Revolutionary War
3.059 French and Indian War (Seven Years' War)
3.060 Mexican War
3.061 Persian Gulf War
3.062 Korean War
3.063 Great Depression
3.064 Spanish-American War
3.065 World War II
3.066 Vietnam War
3.067 Take off 1 point for every 4 mistakes.
Grover Cleveland, 1885 -1889
Benjamin Harrison, 1889-1893
Grover Cleveland, 1893-1897
William McKinley, 1897-1901
Theodore Roosevelt, 1901-1909
William Howard Taft, 1909-1913
Woodrow Wilson, 1913-1921
Warren Gamaliel Harding, 1921-1923
Calvin Coolidge, 1923-1929
Herbert Clark Hoover, 1929-1933
Franklin Delano Roosevelt, 1933-1945
Harry S. Truman, 1945-1953
Dwight David Eisenhower, 1953-1961
John Fitzgerald Kennedy, 1961-1963
Lyndon Baines Johnson, 1963-1969
Richard Milhous Nixon, 1969-1974
Gerald Rudolph Ford, 1974-1977
James Earl Carter, Jr., 1977-1981
Ronald Wilson Reagan, 1981-1989
George Herbert Walker Bush, 1989-1993
William Jefferson Clinton, 1993-2001
George Walker Bush, 2001-2009
Barack Hussein Obama, 2009-2017
Donald J. Trump, 2017-

LIFEPAC TEST

1. 13
2. 4
3. 15
4. 12
5. 20
6. 14
7. 10
8. 8
9. 11
10. 18
11. 6
12. 19
13. 5
14. 16
15. 7
16. 9
17. 17
18. 3
19. 1
20. 2

21. f
22. e
23. i
24. p
25. r
26. a
27. j
28. n
29. q
30. g
31. b
32. o
33. t
34. c
35. l
36. k
37. d
38. h
39. m
40. s

41. ended the era of compromise before the Civil War
42. this harsh treaty set up World War II by its treatment of Germany
43. convinced many Americans to seek independence from Britain
44. last major battle of the Revolution, convinced the British to grant independence
45. a lot of activity that brought hope and confidence to a nation devastated by the Great Depression
46. book that portrayed the evils of slavery and turned the north against it
47. put Europe in permanent contact with the Americas
48. ended 100 years of legal inequality for black Americans after the Civil War
49. triggered the Great Depression
50. Congress gave the president free reign to act in Vietnam, Johnson used it to send in more and more soldiers, getting the nation deeper into that conflict
51. George Washington
52. Theodore Roosevelt
53. Lyndon Johnson
54. Andrew Jackson

55. Harry Truman
56. Abraham Lincoln
57. Jimmy Carter
58. Thomas Jefferson
59. Woodrow Wilson
60. John Adams
61. Andrew Johnson
62. Warren Harding
63. George Bush
64. John Kennedy
65. Franklin Roosevelt
66. i
67. h
68. a
69. g
70. j
71. f
72. b
73. d
74. c
75. e

BONUS: Take off 1 point for every 2 mistakes.
Grover Cleveland, 1885 -1889
Benjamin Harrison, 1889-1893
Grover Cleveland, 1893-1897
William McKinley, 1897-1901
Theodore Roosevelt, 1901-1909
William Howard Taft, 1909-1913
Woodrow Wilson, 1913-1921
Warren Gamaliel Harding, 1921-1923
Calvin Coolidge, 1923-1929
Herbert Clark Hoover, 1929-1933
Franklin Delano Roosevelt, 1933-1945
Harry S. Truman, 1945-1953
Dwight David Eisenhower, 1953-1961
John Fitzgerald Kennedy, 1961-1963
Lyndon Baines Johnson, 1963-1969
Richard Milhous Nixon, 1969-1974
Gerald Rudolph Ford, 1974-1977
James Earl Carter, Jr., 1977-1981
Ronald Wilson Reagan, 1981-1989
George Herbert Walker Bush, 1989-1993
William Jefferson Clinton, 1993-2001
George Walker Bush, 2001-2009
Barack Hussein Obama, 2009-2017
Donald J. Trump, 2017-

ALTERNATE LIFEPAC TEST

1. Congress could not tax or control commerce, no executive or federal courts
2. Many people left because of the strict religious control of the Puritans
3. An arms race, competing alliances and national pride
4. The U.S. could not win the war and were supporting a corrupt and unpopular government
5. They established our institutions, set up a strong government and kept the new nation out of war
6. Impressment of U.S. sailors, interference with trade and the desire to take Canada
7. A conflict of ideas, economics, intimidation and propaganda between the U.S. and U.S.S.R. (1945-91)
8. A change from agriculture and handcrafts to industry and machine manufacturing.
9. Overuse of credit, problems in the farm economy, bad distribution of wealth and stock market speculation
10. They were defending their homes, only had to survive to win, had better generals and hope of allies
11.-30. Subtract one point for a single item out of order, not for all that follow it.
11. 3
12. 20
13. 19
14. 2
15. 4
16. 6
17. 12
18. 18
19. 16
20. 11
21. 1
22. 14
23. 10
24. 5
25. 7
26. 9
27. 17
28. 8
29. 13
30. 15
31. l
32. r
33. c
34. i
35. a

36. q
37. u
38. v
39. h
40. e
41. n
42. x
43. b
44. f
45. s
46. g
47. t
48. w
49. j
50. d
51. p
52. k
53. m
54. y
55. o

BONUS: 10 points maximum
Grover Cleveland, 1885 -1889
Benjamin Harrison, 1889-1893
Grover Cleveland, 1893-1897
William McKinley, 1897-1901
Theodore Roosevelt, 1901-1909
William Howard Taft, 1909-1913
Woodrow Wilson, 1913-1921
Warren Gamaliel Harding, 1921-1923
Calvin Coolidge, 1923-1929
Herbert Clark Hoover, 1929-1933
Franklin Delano Roosevelt, 1933-1945
Harry S. Truman, 1945-1953
Dwight David Eisenhower, 1953-1961
John Fitzgerald Kennedy, 1961-1963
Lyndon Baines Johnson, 1963-1969
Richard Milhous Nixon, 1969-1974
Gerald Rudolph Ford, 1974-1977
James Earl Carter, Jr., 1977-1981
Ronald Wilson Reagan, 1981-1989
George Herbert Walker Bush, 1989-1993
William Jefferson Clinton, 1993-2001
George Walker Bush, 2001-2009
Barack Hussein Obama, 2009-2017
Donald J. Trump, 2017-

HISTORY & GEOGRAPHY 810

ALTERNATE LIFEPAC TEST

NAME _____

DATE _____

SCORE _____

Answer these questions (each answer, 3 points).

1. What were the weaknesses of the Articles of Confederation?
    _____
    _____

2. Why were so many colonies settled from Massachusetts?
    _____
    _____

3. What were the causes of World War I?
    _____
    _____

4. Why was the Vietnam War controversial?
    _____
    _____

5. What was the legacy of the Federalists?
    _____
    _____

6. What were the causes of the War of 1812?
    _____
    _____

7. What was the Cold War?
    _____
    _____

8. What was the Industrial Revolution?
    _____
    _____

9. What caused the Great Depression?
    _____
    _____

10. What advantages did the South have in the Civil War?
    _____
    _____

Put these events in chronological order (20 points, take off only one point for every event out of order).

11. _____ Founding of Virginia

12. _____ Impeachment of Clinton

13. _____ Vietnam War protests

14. _____ Exploration of Coronado

15. _____ Stamp Act

16. _____ Declaration of Independence

17. _____ Gettysburg Address

18. _____ Korean War

19. _____ Battle of the Bulge

20. _____ Attack on Fort Sumter

21. _____ The Crusades

22. _____ Impeachment of Johnson

23. _____ Kansas-Nebraska Act

24. _____ *Common Sense*

25. _____ Constitutional Convention

26. _____ Missouri Compromise

27. _____ Berlin Airlift

28. _____ Battle of New Orleans

29. _____ Appomattox Courthouse

30. _____ Fourteen Points

Match these items (each answer, 2 points).

31.	_____ largest American battle of WWI	a.	T. Roosevelt, Taft, Wilson
32.	_____ Civil War generals	b.	Saratoga
33.	_____ training ground for the Civil War; acquired California	c.	Mexican War
34.	_____ The Alamo; San Jacinto	d.	Persian Gulf War
35.	_____ Progressive presidents	e.	Great Compromiser
36.	_____ America's first permanent alliance since the Revolution	f.	Harding and Grant
37.	_____ area settled by Puritans; fishing and shipbuilding	g.	Erie Canal
38.	_____ first 10 amendments to the Constitution	h.	Garfield, McKinley, Kennedy
39.	_____ presidents who were assassinated	i.	Texas Revolution
40.	_____ Henry Clay	j.	Great Awakening
41.	_____ last, decisive battle of the Revolutionary War	k.	Truman, Johnson, Nixon
42.	_____ dominant power in North America after 1793	l.	Meuse-Argonne
43.	_____ turning point of the Revolutionary War	m.	Midway
44.	_____ poor presidents with corrupt administrations	n.	Yorktown
45.	_____ WWII generals	o.	Mercantilism
46.	_____ vastly reduced shipping costs from the Great Lakes to New York City	p.	Arthur, Cleveland, Hayes
47.	_____ had the best relations with the Native Americans in North America; America's ally in the revolution	q.	NATO
48.	_____ freed the slaves in the rebellious states, 1862	r.	Lee, Sherman, Grant
49.	_____ revival in colonial America	s.	MacArthur, Patton, Eisenhower
50.	_____ conflict to free Kuwait from Iraq	t.	France
51.	_____ Gilded Age presidents	u.	New England
52.	_____ Cold War presidents	v.	Bill of Rights
53.	_____ turning point of the Pacific War, WWII	w.	Emancipation Proclamation
54.	_____ scandal that forced President Nixon to resign	x.	Britain
55.	_____ economic theory of the 1700s; colonies should benefit the mother country	y.	Watergate

BONUS: On a separate piece of paper, list the last 23 presidents of the United States, following James Garfield and Chester A. Arthur. (10 points maximum)

HISTORY & GEOGRAPHY 803
The American Revolution (1763–1789)

LIFEPAC Test is located in the center of the booklet. Please remove before starting the unit.

Author:
Theresa Buskey, B.A., J.D.

Editor:
Alan Christopherson, M.S.

Westover Studios Design Team:
Phillip Pettet, Creative Lead
Teresa Davis, DTP Lead
Nick Castro
Andi Graham
Jerry Wingo

Alpha Omega
PUBLICATIONS

804 N. 2nd Ave. E.
Rock Rapids, IA 51246-1759

The American Revolution (1763–1789)

Introduction

The struggle for independence by the United States has often baffled historians. Raw courage and determination in many cases were the only resources the colonists had to depend upon. The American government during the war was ineffective and disorganized. The army lacked basic supplies and regular soldiers. Yet, these raw colonials defeated the greatest military power of their era, Great Britain.

Historians have also long debated the reasons for the war. At the end of the French and Indian War, the American colonies were joyfully, deeply British. No one dreamed in 1763 that there would be a war between the colonies and Britain just twelve years later. Those years were a litany of miscalculations on the part of Britain that drove the colonists further and further from the loyalty of 1763.

This LIFEPAC® will discuss the events that caused the Revolution. It will also present a history of the Revolution itself, the major battles, ideas, and events. Finally, this LIFEPAC will show how the colonists finally managed to create a stable government under the United States Constitution.

Objectives

Read these objectives. The objectives tell you what you will be able to do when you have successfully completed this LIFEPAC. When you have finished this LIFEPAC, you should be able to:

1. Identify the men who contributed to the Revolution.

2. Identify and describe the incidents and thinking which led to the Revolution.

3. Identify and describe the governing bodies that acted for the colonies/states.

4. Name the major battles of the war and tell their significances.

5. Outline the terms of the peace agreements that the United States signed with Great Britain.

6. Explain the Articles of Confederation and why they were replaced.

7. Describe the Constitutional Convention.

8. Describe the main features of the Constitution and the process by which it was approved.

Survey the LIFEPAC. Ask yourself some questions about this study and write your questions here.

1. GROWING CONFLICT

The American colonists were delighted with the outcome of the French and Indian War. The hated French had finally been driven out of their land. They were free to expand into the rich lands of the eastern Mississippi basin. They were proud to be British, part of the mighty British Empire.

But, even in the midst of the joy, the first signs of the difference between the colonists and the government in Britain appeared, the Proclamation of 1763. The king tried to block the colonists behind the Appalachian Mountains, but the colonists chose to ignore the order. Worse was to come.

In the years that followed, the British tried to tax and control the colonies for the first time in colonial history. The Sugar Act, the Stamp Act, the Townshend Acts, and the Intolerable Acts beat a steady path to rebellion in the colonies. The colonists saw a conspiracy to deprive them of their liberty and reacted with resistance. The British saw no valid reason for the increasing resistance to their "lawful" decrees and reacted with more force. Finally, the colonists gave up hope of a peaceful settlement and chose to fight rather than submit.

SECTION OBJECTIVES

Review these objectives. When you have completed this section, you should be able to:

1. Identify the men who contributed to the Revolution.
2. Identify and describe the incidents and thinking which led to the Revolution.
3. Identify and describe the governing bodies that acted for the colonies/states.

VOCABULARY

Study these words to enhance your learning success in this section.

arbitrary (är′ bi trer′ ē). Not going by any rule or law.

conservative (kon sėr′ va tiv). A person who is opposed to change.

militia (mu lish′ a). Army of citizens who are not regular soldiers.

moderate (mod′ er it). A person whose political views are not extreme in any way.

Prime Minister (prīm′ min′ i stir). The chief official in certain types of government.

propaganda (prop′ a gan′ da). Systematic efforts to spread opinions or beliefs.

protocol (prō′ tu kol). Rules (written or unwritten) for a procedure.

providential (prov′ u den′ shul). Good fortune happening by God's intervention (the Christian version of "good luck"-author).

radical (rad′ i kal). A person who favors extreme changes or reform.

Note: *All vocabulary words in this LIFEPAC appear in* **boldface** *print the first time they are used. If you are not sure of the meaning when you are reading, study the definitions given.*

Pronunciation Key: hat, āge, cãre, fär; let, ēqual, tėrm; it, īce; hot, ōpen, ôrder; oil; out; cup, pùt, rüle; child; long; thin; /ᴛH/ for then; /zh/ for measure; /u/ or /ə/ represents /a/ in about, /e/ in taken, /i/ in pencil, /o/ in lemon, and /u/ in circus.

Britain Flexes its Muscles

British attitudes. Britain was the greatest power on earth after the Seven Years (French and Indian) War. It had soundly defeated its great rival, France, and taken her North American empire. The British were proud and arrogant about their victory. They were confident of their own glory and were not in a mood to compromise with anyone, especially their backwoods colonies.

Moreover, the war had left Britain deeply in debt. The national debt had doubled and the new territory in America would be expensive to administer. Pontiac's War was launched by Native American tribes in the Great Lakes region, proving that the British needed to maintain troops in the colonies for their protection. That was expensive. The government felt it was high time the colonists bore some of the cost of their own defense.

Mercantilism. The popular economic theory of the 1700s was mercantilism. This theory held that only gold or silver was real wealth, and countries must work to obtain more of it. Colonies were used to doing this through trade. Colonies were to supply the mother country with raw materials such as wood, iron, and indigo. Then, the colonies would be a market for goods manufactured by the mother country, like cloth, hats, and tools. The colony was not to compete with the mother country by building its own manufacturing and industry. This theory held that the colony only existed to serve the mother country and should never be allowed to develop. It should be kept dependent on the mother country at all times.

British policy towards America was based on mercantilism. The Navigation Acts, which were passed mainly in the late 1600s, were intended to force the colonies to act in accord with this theory. One of the laws required that all trade with the colonies had to be on English or colonial ships.

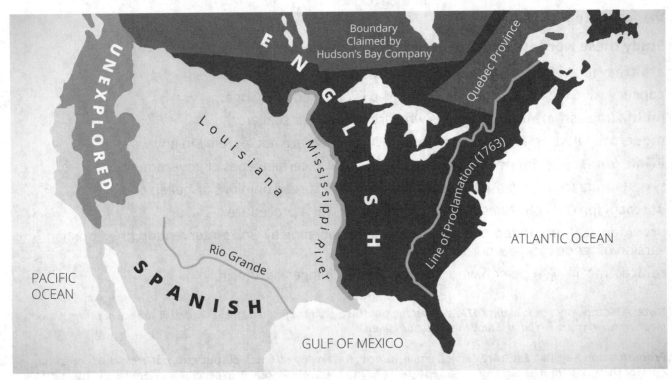

| The American British Empire in 1763

Another required all colonial trade to go through England to be taxed. That meant that goods going from the colonies to the French West Indies, just south of Florida, had to go to England, be unloaded, stored, and taxed before they could go to their destination. The same was true in reverse for goods coming from the West Indies or Europe to the colonies. This gave English merchants a virtual monopoly on colonial trade, because the cost of going through England made foreign trade too expensive. Other laws stated that certain important goods like tobacco and naval supplies could only be sold to Britain, even if Britain could not possibly buy all that the colonies could produce. These laws would have crippled colonial trade, but until 1763 they were rarely enforced, and the colonists traded with many nations by smuggling.

There were other laws on the books by 1763 that were intended to keep the colonies economically backward and dependent on Britain. The colonies were forbidden to export wool cloth, hats or tools. They were also forbidden to build iron mills to make tools. The Molasses Act of 1733 put a high tax on molasses, sugar, and rum imported from non-British sources, primarily the French West Indies. The problem was that the British West Indies could not supply half of the molasses needed by the distilleries in New England. (The molasses was made into rum for sale at home and abroad). So, the law was routinely and easily avoided by smuggling.

One of the more damaging laws forbade the colonies to mint coins. British merchants could not pay for colonial products in hard money (coins). That meant the colonies were always short of coins they needed to pay for British goods. It also made it difficult for colonists to collect enough money to start any large businesses. The colonists had to barter for most of their goods and try to get coins by trade with French and Spanish lands. These restrictions were very unpopular in the colonies, but, obviously, very popular in London.

| George III, King of England

Changes in policy. After the Seven Years War, Britain began to change her policy toward the colonies. The British government had been content for over a hundred and fifty years to let the colonies govern themselves. Now, flush with pride in their victory, they felt it was time for Parliament to establish better control over the empire. There was also a strong feeling that since the British had spent both blood and treasure to protect the colonies, the colonies owed them something in return. What the British expected to get was loyalty and some income to help defray the huge costs of stationing troops in America.

George Grenville became **Prime Minister** of Great Britain in 1763. He moved quickly to meet the new mood of the king, George III, and Parliament. He began in 1763 by ordering that the Navigation Acts be strictly enforced. He obtained the Sugar Act of 1764 from the Parliament that decreased the high tax on French molasses but kept high taxes on sugar and rum. He arranged for this act to actually be enforced by customs offices and an Admiralty Court.

That court did not use a jury and the defendant was assumed to be guilty, not innocent as in regular courts. The colonists saw this as a threat to their English liberties. The next law was a Quartering Act in 1765 that required colonists to provide food and lodging for British troops. These acts angered the Americans, but it was the next one that set fire to the dynamite, the Stamp Act.

| An early U.S. Flag

 Answer these questions.

1.1 What was the popular economic theory of the 1700s?

_____

1.2 According to that theory what should a colony do for a mother country?

_____

_____

1.3 What were the goals of the British government toward the colonies in 1763?

a. _____

b. _____

1.4 What were the major parts of the Navigation Acts?

a. _____

b. _____

c. _____

1.5 What was the Molasses Act of 1733? Why would it have hurt the New England colonies and why didn't it? _____

_____

_____

1.6 Why were the colonies short of hard money? _____

_____

1.7 What did George Grenville do to anger the colonies in

1763? _____

1764? _____

1765? _____

The Stamp Act. Grenville proposed to raise a substantial amount of money in the colonies by the Stamp Act, passed in 1765. The law required all legal documents and public papers, such as wills, playing cards, newspapers, and bills of sale, to be marked with a stamp purchased from the government. Grenville thought this was a reasonable way to raise money. The amount charged for the stamps would be less than a similar stamp in Britain and the money would be used to pay British troops in the colonies. Even Benjamin Franklin, the colonial representative in London, who disapproved of the law expected the colonists to accept it after a few protests.

However, the Stamp Act was seen as a threat in America. It was the first time Britain had tried to directly tax the colonists. Taxes before had been on imports and were intended mostly to control trade. Any other taxes had only come from the colonial assemblies elected by the colonists. The tax fell on everyone from the card playing sailors to wealthy merchants or lawyers whose trade depended on documents. Moreover, the colonists were constantly short of the money needed to buy the stamps. Even worse, people who violated the act were to be tried in Admiralty Courts! The colonists thought Britain was trying to reduce them to virtual slavery with all these new laws.

It was the very visible Stamp Act that drew the wrath of the colonists, who were united in their opposition to it. The Americans said Parliament could not tax them, since there were no American representatives in Parliament. The battle cry that would open the Revolution was: "No taxation without representation." But, more than shouting slogans, the Americans began to organize, unite, and resist. This was the real legacy of the Stamp Act.

The controversy was a repeat of the conflict between Parliament and the king in England. The Glorious Revolution (1688) had established that political power in England would be in the hands of an elected body, Parliament, not an

| Patrick Henry

autocratic king. The colonists felt that if they indeed had the rights of Englishmen, then the political power in their land should be in the hands of their representatives. The British Parliament could not step in as a new monarch to rob the colonists of their traditional English liberties. Parliament thought of the colonists as subjects who should obey, not as citizens who should participate. This arrogant attitude was intolerable.

The House of Burgesses in Virginia debated and passed the Virginia Resolves, which declared the act illegal, stating that only Virginians could tax Virginians. The debate over the Resolves included a famous speech by **radical** member Patrick Henry. He said, "Caesar had his Brutus–Charles the First, his Cromwell–and George the Third–may profit by their example." When the **conservative** members of the Burgesses began to whisper, "Treason," Henry replied, "If this be treason, make the most of it."

The reaction to the Stamp Act came in three major ways: the Stamp Act Congress, boycotts, and mob action. The Massachusetts assembly invited all the colonies to send delegates to New York to discuss the Stamp Act.

Nine of the colonies sent delegates to what became known as the Stamp Act Congress. The delegates were wealthy, distinguished men from the elite of the colonies. They passed a Declaration of Rights and Grievances stating that only the colonies could tax their own citizens. Britain ignored it. It was, however, a significant step in uniting the colonies, most of which thought of themselves almost as separate nations.

A much more effective message was sent to Parliament when the colonies began to boycott British goods. They were very successful in organizing agreements not to import British products. Colonists found other sources to meet their needs, or self-sufficiently went without them. The boycott began to threaten the prosperity of the English merchants who complained to Parliament. Parliament listened.

The last way that the colonists resisted the Stamp Act was by mob action, this was also very effective. The "Sons of Liberty," secret societies opposed to the act, took the law into their own hands. They attacked stamp sellers, royal officials, and people who violated the boycott. On the date the law was to take effect, November 1, 1765, there were no officials to sell the hated stamps. All had resigned in fear of the mobs.

Faced with an outcry in Britain and the colonies, and knowing they were not collecting any revenue, Parliament repealed the Stamp Act four months after it went into effect. At the same time they passed the face-saving Declaratory Act, stating that Parliament had the right to tax the colonies. The colonists rejoiced at their victory and, with a few exceptions, ignored the dark implications of the Declaratory Act. They had acted together, sometimes with violence, and accomplished what they wanted. The lesson would be remembered.

 Name the requested item or person.

1.8 British Prime Minister who passed the Stamp Act

_____

1.9 Colonial representative in London who thought the Act would be obeyed

_____

1.10 Radical in House of Burgesses who said, "If this be treason, make the most of it."

_____

1.11 Burgesses statement against the Stamp Act

_____

1.12 Three ways the colonies reacted to the Stamp Act

a. _____

b. _____

c. _____

1.13 Secret societies that led mob action against the Stamp Act

_____

1.14 The slogan against the tax

_____

1.15 Law stating that Parliament had a right to tax the colonies

_____

_____

Answer these questions.

1.16 What did the Stamp Act require?

_____

_____

_____

1.17 Why did the colonists object so much to it? (four reasons)

_____

_____

_____

1.18 What did Patrick Henry mean in his speech about Brutus and Cromwell? (Look up the named people if you need to.)

_____

_____

_____

Actions and Reactions

Townshend Acts. The failure of the Stamp Act did not help Britain's financial problems. The debt remained along with the huge expense of protecting North America. The king and the powerful people in Britain were furious. They wanted the rebellious colonies brought in line. Finally, Britain had another change in government (this happened frequently). The new Chancellor of the Exchequer (Treasury), Charles Townshend promised to pluck the colonial goose with a minimum of squawking.

Townshend succeeded in passing a series of laws through Parliament in 1767. Called the Townshend Acts, they were designed to increase revenue and control. The most important put a tax on a large number of goods such as paint, lead, glass, paper, and tea that the colonies imported from Britain. This was an indirect tax which Townshend thought the colonies would accept.

Another act greatly increased the power of customs officials to enforce the tax laws, including the use of writs of assistance which allowed **arbitrary** searches of homes and businesses. Another law threatened to shut down the New York assembly if it did not comply with the Quartering Act (it had refused up until that point). Moreover, the money raised was to be used to pay British officials, including governors, in the colonies. This meant the colonists could no longer hope to control royal officials by limiting their salary!

The colonists were alarmed. They had fought with royal governors often enough to know the loss of the power of the purse would leave them helpless against arbitrary rule. They also saw the strict enforcement procedures as a violation of the basic legal rights of all Englishmen. The threat to suspend the New York legislature threatened every assembly in the colonies.

The uneasy colonists began to believe there was a conspiracy afoot to take away their rights. The taxes themselves, however, did not create the unanimous outcry of the Stamp Act. They were subtle and indirect, but still not acceptable.

The colonists objected to the Townshend Acts, but the reactions were not as strong or as quick as under the Stamp Act. Radicals like Samuel Adams from Boston wrote pamphlets urging action. John Dickinson, a lawyer and legislator, wrote a series of widely read articles called *Letters from a Farmer in Pennsylvania,* which argued that the Parliament had no power over colonial affairs. Several colonial assemblies were dissolved for supporting that idea. A boycott was slowly pulled together. The colonists also engaged in widespread smuggling to bring in products and avoid paying the taxes.

Boston Massacre. Massachusetts, founded by independent-minded Puritans, had always been a restive colony. Boston quickly became a center for the opposition to Britain. The Sons of Liberty were especially active there, interfering with the British officials and creating public disturbances. Finally, the government sent in British soldiers to keep order. The presence of soldiers in the midst of an angry population was asking for trouble, and it came.

On the evening of March 5, 1770, a crowd decided to entertain themselves by throwing snowballs at a soldier guarding the Customs House. Troops were sent to his aid. The crowd threw snowballs and debris at them. Despite the efforts of Captain Preston, the commander, to prevent it, someone opened fire on the mob. Five people were killed. The colonial **propaganda** called the incident the Boston Massacre.

Radicals spread the news all through the colonies. The public story made martyrs out of the dead. The soldiers involved were tried for murder. John Adams, patriot and future president, took the unpopular job of defending them. He did so well that only two were convicted and those received light sentences. The results added to colonial distrust and anger.

| The Boston Massacre

Repeal. In Britain, the boycotts slowly began to have some effect on commerce. Thanks in part to colonial interference, the taxes were bringing in very little money. Moreover, the British government realized it was foolish to tax their own goods they were trying to sell in America. Lord North, who was now in control of the government, repealed the taxes in 1770, except for the tax on tea. The king and others insisted it must remain as a symbol of the government's right to tax.

The repeal calmed the **moderates** and relieved the conservatives, but radicals still looked for a confrontation with the British. Samuel Adams of Boston took the lead in organizing groups to communicate between the towns in Massachusetts. These *Committees of Correspondence* were set up to exchange information and the latest news. They also kept the rebellious spirit active. Eventually, they were set up by all the colonies to communicate with each other, laying the foundation for future cooperation.

Answer true or false.

If the statement is false, change some of the nouns or adjectives to make it true.

1.19 _____ The Townshend duties taxed goods imported from France.

1.20 _____ Charles Townshend was the Prime Minister.

1.21 _____ Money from the Townshend taxes was to be used to pay British officials in the colonies.

1.22 _____ The Townshend Acts threatened to dissolve the Massachusetts assembly if it did not comply with the Stamp Act.

1.23 _____ The colonists did not react as fiercely to the Townshend Acts as they had to the Stamp Act.

1.24 _____ *Letters from a Farmer in Pennsylvania* argued that colonial assemblies had no power over affairs in the colonies.

1.25 _____ The Townshend Acts were also met with a boycott.

1.26 _____ Lord West repealed all of the Townshend duties except the tax on paint.

1.27 _____ Committees of Correspondence encouraged communication and cooperation between the colonies.

1.28 _____ Britain was deeply in debt and was paying to protect America.

Describe the following.

1.29 The Townshend Acts

_____

_____

_____

_____

1.30 The Boston Massacre

_____

_____

_____

_____

Boston Tea Party. In 1773, the British East India Company was in serious financial trouble. Lord North decided to help it by giving it a monopoly on the sale of tea to the American colonies. The prices were set so that, even with the tax, it was cheaper than tea smuggled in from other sources. The colonists distrusted the monopoly and saw the lower price as a way to sneak the tax by them. They made sure that none of the tea was ever sold in America.

The colonies reacted differently to the tea when it arrived. Pennsylvania stuck it in a warehouse to rot. Charleston also stored it, and later sold it to support the Revolution. But, it was the reaction of the Sons of Liberty in Boston that gained the most fame. Three tea ships were floating in Boston harbor on the night of December 16, 1773. None had been able to unload their cargo. That evening a group of colonists, thinly disguised as Native American people, boarded the ships, took the tea, and dumped it into the harbor. The entire protest, known as the Boston Tea Party, was orderly and completely without violence. They simply refused to accept the tea. The tea party was repeated in New York harbor by a group of patriots there.

The Intolerable Acts. The reaction in London to the Tea Party was one of uncontrolled fury. The public destruction of valuable property in defiance of the king was the last straw. Public opinion was united behind Lord North and the king as they decided that Boston must be brought to heel. A series of laws called the Coercive Acts in Britain, and the Intolerable Acts in America were rapidly passed by Parliament.

The most important of the Intolerable Acts was the Boston Port Bill. It ordered the port of Boston blockaded and closed until the tea was paid for, with the tax. The implication of this was staggering. The closing of the harbor would mean the destruction of the city which depended on commerce for its supplies, jobs, and revenue. An entire city was being destroyed for the non-violent actions of a few individuals, clearly an excessive and dangerous use of force.

The other parts of the Intolerable Acts were equally as odious. The Massachusetts charter was changed so that all important officials were appointed and controlled by the Crown. Town meetings were forbidden without the express approval of the governor. A military governor was appointed for Boston and more troops were sent in, putting it under military rule.

The British government expected the other colonies to see this as a matter only involving Boston and stay out of it. They expected other port cities to jump at the chance to take over some of Boston's trade. In fact, the other colonies did not see it that way. They realized that if Britain could successfully use that kind of force against Boston, it would likely be used later against other colonies. They acted, therefore, in support of Boston, sending supplies to the city by land from as far away as South Carolina.

Quebec Act. Passed with the Intolerable Acts in Britain was a piece of legislation called the Quebec Act. It was not a part of the laws aimed at the colonies, but the touchy Americans assumed it was. The law confirmed the rights of the French in Quebec to follow their own customs (which did not include the usual traditions of English liberty) and protected the Catholic religion. Moreover, it extended the boundaries of Quebec down into the Ohio Valley south of the Great Lakes. That cut the Americans off from any possibility of controlling that coveted land, and put the land under a foreign system of government. The Quebec Act was a wise attempt by Parliament to win the support of the citizens in the former French lands. The Americans saw it as a spread of hated Catholicism, and a further attempt to contain their liberties.

The First Continental Congress. The primary response to the Intolerable Acts was the First Continental Congress. The colonies realized they needed to act together. Using the Committees of Correspondence, they set up a meeting for September 1774 in Philadelphia. Every colony except Georgia sent delegates. The fifty-four delegates included Samuel and John Adams from Massachusetts, John Jay from New York, as well as George Washington and Patrick Henry from Virginia.

The Congress accomplished several things during the seven weeks it met. They passed a Declaration of Rights that included life, liberty, property, the right to assemble and to tax themselves. Several acts of Parliament were declared to be illegal and an Association was formed to enforce a *full stoppage* of trade until the acts were repealed. A petition was sent to the king to address the colonial complaints.

| The First Continental Congress

The Congress further agreed to meet again in May of 1775 if their demands had not been met by then.

Choose the correct word(s) to complete these sentences.

1.31 Lord North gave the _____ a monopoly on the sale of tea to America to in 1773.

1.32 The tea that was shipped to the city of _____ was stored and later sold to support the Revolution.

1.33 A second tea party occurred in the city of _____ after the one at Boston.

1.34 The _____ Bill closed Boston harbor until the tea and tax were paid for.

1.35 The _____ Act protected the traditional customs of the French in Quebec and expanded their territory.

1.36 The primary colonial response to the Intolerable Acts was to organize the _____
_____ .

1.37 The Intolerable Acts were the British reaction to the _____ .

Describe the following.

1.38 The Intolerable Acts

_____

_____

_____

1.39 The Boston Tea Party

_____

_____

_____

1.40 The actions of the First Continental Congress

_____

_____

_____

1.41 The American view of the Quebec Act

_____

_____

_____

Rebellion

Lexington and Concord. All of the American colonies had **militias** in the 1700s. They had been been organized to protect the colonists from the Native Americans and the French. In the wake of the occupation of Boston, the militias began to drill and collect supplies to defend themselves against British troops. The Massachusetts assembly, which had been meeting illegally, chose the city of Concord as a major supply depot for the militia. The assembly also began meeting there to be out of the reach of General Gage, the military commander of Boston.

Gage found out about the supplies and decided to destroy them. He also hoped to arrest some of the colonial leaders such as Samuel Adams and John Hancock, who were staying in Lexington. In April of 1775, Gage sent over 700 men to Lexington during the night. Paul Revere, a Boston silversmith who had worked for many years as a courier for the Sons of Liberty, rode to warn the patriots. In accordance with plans laid in advance, two lights were put in the steeple of the Old North Church to let the patriots know that the soldiers were coming across the Charles River. Revere only made it as far as Lexington before he was captured by a British patrol. But, other riders brought word to Concord.

When the British arrived at Lexington on the morning of April 19th, they were met by two companies of militia drawn up in battle order.

Battle order in the 1700s was two lines of men, one behind the other, close together. This was the standard because of the type of weapon they used, muskets. Muskets were very inaccurate and could not be counted on to hit a target more than 100 yards away. The only way to be sure of hitting anything was to have a large mass of men, firing together at the target at close range. Military **protocol** required that this be done on an open field until one side withdrew leaving the victors in command of the field.

The American commander realized that he was heavily outnumbered. When he was ordered to disperse, he began to do so. As the Americans began to leave, someone fired a shot. That bullet has been called "The Shot Heard Around the World" because it started the Revolutionary War. When the British officers finally got their men back under control, eight Americans were dead.

The British went on to Concord where they destroyed some supplies. There, they confronted a larger militia force who forced them to retreat. The retreat quickly became dangerous. The Americans, contrary to all the rules of gentlemanly warfare, began firing at the soldiers from behind trees, rocks, and buildings as they withdrew. The arrival of reinforcements at Lexington kept the British from being destroyed. Even then, it was a long march back to Boston as the militia opened fire from any vantage point they could find all along the route back. In the end, about seventy British soldiers were killed. America was at war with Britain.

Capture of Lake Champlain. Roads in the colonies were terrible. The best and most reliable transportation was by water. In central New York, there was a key water route that almost bridged the gap between Canada and the Atlantic coast. The Riechelieu River connected the St. Lawrence with Lake Champlain. The southern end of the lake was only 23 miles from the Hudson River, which flowed through Albany to New York City. This key route was protected by two old forts, Ticonderoga and Crown Point. Both forts were taken by a New England force under Ethan Allen and Benedict Arnold in May of 1775, to protect New England from a Canadian-based invasion. The forts were in bad shape, but Ticonderoga had a large supply of good cannon, something the colonists needed. Henry Knox, who would eventually become the first Secretary of War, went to Ticonderoga to get them. In the dead of winter in 1775-76, he moved 59 cannons across miles of wilderness to give the British a nasty surprise.

Bunker Hill. Militia from all over New England began to gather around Boston after Lexington and Concord. The slowly assembling citizen's army was put under the command of Artemas Ward of Massachusetts. Ward decided to fortify Bunker Hill on the Charlestown Peninsula facing Boston. By mistake, his men put up their fortifications on nearby Breeds Hill, but the battle that followed was named for the place where it should have happened.

The British foolishly decided to make a frontal attack on the entrenched, protected Americans at the top of the hill. They probably believed that the amateurs would run at the first sight of a regular army. The Americans did not bring enough gunpowder with them for a long battle, but they were determined to stay.

On June 17, 1775, about 2,000 British soldiers in neat lines marched up the hill toward the Americans. The militia calmly waited and held their fire until they "could see the whites of their eyes." Then, the Americans opened fire, mowing down the unprotected "Redcoats." The British retreated and came again, with the same result. The Americans held until they ran out of gunpowder and then managed to retreat. The British had lost almost half of their men, dead or wounded. Even though the British took the hill, the heavy losses made it more of an American victory. One colonial leader commented that he would gladly sell the British another hill at the same price.

A Colonial army. The Second Continental Congress assembled in May of 1775 as they had arranged. This time all thirteen colonies were represented, and Benjamin Franklin, newly returned from London, was a Pennsylvania delegate. The Congress at that time still did not want independence, nor did most of the country. They saw the fighting more as a civil war in defense of their rights. Congress, however, agreed to take on the assembling forces around Boston as an *American* army and to appoint a commander-in-chief. They chose George Washington for the post. It was a **providential** choice.

Washington was the son of a wealthy Virginia planter and had increased his fortune by marrying a rich widow, Martha Custis. He had been a colonial officer in the French and Indian War. He was not a brilliant strategist, but he was very determined and faithful. He was able to win and hold the loyalty of the men who served under him. His religious beliefs were private, but appeared to follow traditional Christianity, not Deism. He believed deeply in the patriot cause and took a fearful chance when he agreed to lead the army. He would have been hanged as a traitor if the Americans had lost.

Washington did accept the commission from the Congress to lead the new "army." He refused to accept any pay, however, and asked only to be reimbursed for his expenses. He left at once for Boston and took command two weeks after Bunker Hill on July 2, 1775.

Choose the correct match for each item.

1.42 _____ Ethan Allen

1.43 _____ Shot Heard Around the World

1.44 _____ Artemas Ward

1.45 _____ valuable cannons captured

1.46 _____ fortified Breeds Hill

1.47 _____ militia fires along the road at British in retreat

1.48 _____ British destroy supplies, but are forced to retreat

1.49 _____ protects water route from Canada to New York

1.50 _____ Americans forced to quit when they run out of gunpowder

a. Lexington and Concord

b. Ticonderoga

c. Bunker Hill

1.51 _____ About half of the British forces are killed or wounded

1.52 _____ April 1775

1.53 _____ May 1775

1.54 _____ June 1775

Complete these sentences.

1.55 The assembled militia around Boston were taken as an American army by the _____

_____ .

1.56 After the occupation of Boston, the American _____ began to drill and gather supplies.

1.57 Congress appointed _____ as commander-in-chief of the colonial army.

Olive Branch Petition. Congress was still hoping that the British government would come to terms and they could end this revolt. The Americans blamed most of what had happened on Parliament. They still declared their loyalty to the king. In July of 1775, the Congress made one last attempt to stop the war. At the insistence of John Dickinson of Delaware, the colonists prepared a petition directed to the king in July of 1775. The "Olive Branch Petition" affirmed their loyalty to the crown and asked the king to intervene with Parliament on behalf of the colonists. The petition was sent to Britain in the hands of one of William Penn's descendants. The king refused to even receive him. Instead he declared the colonies to be in rebellion.

The king further alienated the colonists by hiring German soldiers to fight the Americans. This was a common practice among European powers. Germany was divided into many small states, each with their own army. The kings would hire out these well-disciplined men to raise money. The Americans were shocked by the involvement of the foreign "Hessians" (many of the mercenaries came from the German state of Hesse) and many who had favored the king now joined the patriots.

Invasion of Canada. The war continued even while Congress and the country debated what to do. Several of the colonial leaders thought that the French Canadians might be persuaded to join the rebellion. In any case, New England needed to be secure from invasion from the North. So, American Generals Richard Montgomery and Benedict Arnold led an assault on Canada in late 1775.

Montgomery led his forces up from Lake Champlain and successfully captured Montreal. He then met up with Arnold at Quebec. Arnold's men had been struck by disease and reduced to eating shoe leather on their long march through the wilds of Maine. Still, the commanders attempted an attack in December. It failed miserably. Montgomery was killed. Arnold was wounded in the leg and retreated after a siege failed. The French, who had been treated generously by the Quebec Act, did not join the Americans; they remained firmly on the British side.

Common sense. The double life most Americans were leading, fighting British soldiers while declaring loyalty to the British crown, was shattered in early 1776 by the publication of a pamphlet called *Common Sense*. *Common Sense* was written by Thomas Paine, a recently arrived English immigrant. It was one of the most influential pamphlets ever written. Paine argued that British control over America was a violation of common sense. Why should an island rule over a continent? The colonists had no reason to be loyal to a king who had treated them so harshly. The Americans had a clear choice between independence or tyranny.

Common Sense was a phenomenal best seller. The pamphlet sold hundreds of thousands of copies in a few months. Public opinion turned in favor of independence. The American people decided to cross the line from loyal subjects defending their rights to a free and independent nation. Delegates at the Second Continental Congress were instructed by their state governments to vote for independence.

Declaration of Independence. On June 7, 1776 Richard Henry Lee of Virginia proposed to the Second Continental Congress that "These United Colonies are, and of right ought to be, free and independent states..." Debate began on the proposal and, since it was expected to pass, a committee was appointed to write a document explaining their reasons. The committee included Thomas Jefferson, John Adams, and Benjamin Franklin. As the best writer in the group, Jefferson was elected to do the writing. The other members only made suggestions after they had seen his draft of the paper.

| The signing of the Declaration of Independence

Jefferson's document became one of the most famous in American history. It included a brilliant preamble which was accepted by Congress without any changes. The remainder, a list of the acts of tyranny committed by the king and the actual statement that the colonies were now independent, were accepted with some changes. The document was accepted by Congress on July 4, 1776. A perfect copy was written and signed later by fifty-six of the delegates, including the president of the congress, John Hancock, who deliberately signed in very large letters. That bold act was the origin of the American saying that a person's signature is their "John Hancock."

The Fourth of July is celebrated as Independence Day in the United States. Congress voted for independence, in favor of Lee's proposal, on July 2, 1776. The day the Declaration of Independence was accepted, July 4th, has become the holiday. That document is simply too vibrant and stirring to take a second place to anything. You will study why as you examine the document in the next few pages.

Match these items.

1.58 _____ American general killed; invasion of Canada

1.59 _____ Congressman who insisted on one more petition to the king in July of 1775

1.60 _____ author of *Common Sense*

1.61 _____ American general wounded in the invasion of Canada

1.62 _____ Congressman who proposed independence

1.63 _____ author of the Declaration of Independence

1.64 _____ president of the Second Continental Congress

a. Richard Henry Lee
b. Thomas Paine
c. Thomas Jefferson
d. Richard Montgomery
e. John Dickinson
f. Benedict Arnold
g. John Hancock

Complete these sentences.

1.65 The Second Continental Congress sent a petition called the _____ Petition to request the king's help in July of 1775.

1.66 Montgomery succeeded in capturing the Canadian city of _____.

1.67 American public opinion was turned in favor of independence by the popular pamphlet called _____.

1.68 Congress voted for independence on _____.

1.69 The American Revolution was fought for _____ months before independence was declared.

The unanimous Declaration of the thirteen united States of America,

When in the Course of human events, it becomes necessary for one people to dissolve the political bands which have connected them with another, and to assume among the powers of the earth, the separate and equal station to which the Laws of Nature and of Nature's God entitle them, a decent respect to the opinions of mankind requires that they should declare the causes which impel them to the separation.

We hold these truths to be self-evident, that all men are created equal, that they are endowed by their Creator with certain unalienable Rights, that among these are Life, Liberty and the pursuit of Happiness.—That to secure these rights, Governments are instituted among Men, deriving their just powers from the consent of the governed, —That whenever any Form of Government becomes destructive of these ends, it is the Right of the People to alter or to abolish it, and to institute new Government, laying its foundation on such principles and organizing its powers in such form, as to them shall seem most likely to effect their Safety and Happiness. Prudence, indeed, will dictate that Governments long established should not be changed for light and transient causes; and accordingly all experience hath shewn, that mankind are more disposed to suffer, while evils are sufferable, than to right themselves by abolishing the forms to which they are accustomed. But when a long train of abuses and usurpations, pursuing invariably the same Object evinces a design to reduce them under absolute Despotism, it is their right, it is their duty, to throw off such Government, and to provide new Guards for their future security.—Such has been the patient sufferance of these Colonies; and such is now the necessity which constrains them to alter their former Systems of Government. The history of the present King of Great Britain is a history of repeated injuries and usurpations, all having in direct object the establishment of an absolute Tyranny over these States. To prove this, let Facts be submitted to a candid world.

He has refused his Assent to Laws, the most wholesome and necessary for the public good.

He has forbidden his Governors to pass Laws of immediate and pressing importance, unless suspended in their operation till his Assent should be obtained; and when so suspended, he has utterly neglected to attend to them.

He has refused to pass other Laws for the accommodation of large districts of people, unless those people would relinquish the right of Representation in the Legislature, a right inestimable to them and formidable to tyrants only.

He has called together legislative bodies at places unusual, uncomfortable, and distant from the depository of their public Records, for the sole purpose of fatiguing them into compliance with his measures.

THE DECLARATION OF INDEPENDENCE
IN CONGRESS, July 4, 1776.

He has dissolved Representative Houses repeatedly, for opposing with manly firmness his invasions on the rights of the people.

He has refused for a long time, after such dissolutions, to cause others to be elected; whereby the Legislative powers, incapable of Annihilation, have returned to the People at large for their exercise; the State remaining in the mean time exposed to all the dangers of invasion from without, and convulsions within.

He has endeavoured to prevent the population of these States; for that purpose obstructing the Laws for Naturalization of Foreigners; refusing to pass others to encourage their migrations hither, and raising the conditions of new Appropriations of Lands.

He has obstructed the Administration of Justice, by refusing his Assent to Laws for establishing Judiciary powers.

He has made Judges dependent on his Will alone, for the tenure of their offices, and the amount and payment of their salaries.

He has erected a multitude of New Offices, and sent hither swarms of Officers to harrass our people, and eat out their substance.

He has kept among us, in times of peace, Standing Armies without the Consent of our legislatures.

He has affected to render the Military independent of and superior to the Civil power.

He has combined with others to subject us to a jurisdiction foreign to our constitution, and unacknowledged by our laws; giving his Assent to their Acts of pretended Legislation:

For Quartering large bodies of armed troops among us:

For protecting them, by a mock Trial, from punishment for any Murders which they should commit on the Inhabitants of these States:

For cutting off our Trade with all parts of the world:

For imposing Taxes on us without our Consent:

For depriving us in many cases, of the benefits of Trial by Jury:

For transporting us beyond Seas to be tried for pretended offences:

For abolishing the free System of English Laws in a neighbouring Province, establishing therein an Arbitrary government, and enlarging its Boundaries so as to render it at once an example and fit instrument for introducing the same absolute rule into these Colonies:

For taking away our Charters, abolishing our most valuable Laws, and altering fundamentally the Forms of our Governments:

For suspending our own Legislatures, and declaring themselves invested with power to legislate for us in all cases whatsoever.

THE DECLARATION OF INDEPENDENCE
IN CONGRESS, July 4, 1776.

He has abdicated Government here, by declaring us out of his Protection and waging War against us.

He has plundered our seas, ravaged our Coasts, burnt our towns, and destroyed the lives of our people.

He is at this time transporting large Armies of foreign Mercenaries to compleat the works of death, desolation and tyranny, already begun with circumstances of Cruelty & perfidy scarcely paralleled in the most barbarous ages, and totally unworthy the Head of a civilized nation.

He has constrained our fellow Citizens taken Captive on the high Seas to bear Arms against their Country, to become the executioners of their friends and Brethren, or to fall themselves by their Hands.

He has excited domestic insurrections amongst us, and has endeavoured to bring on the inhabitants of our frontiers, the merciless Indian Savages, whose known rule of warfare, is an undistinguished destruction of all ages, sexes and conditions.

In every stage of these Oppressions We have Petitioned for Redress in the most humble terms: Our repeated Petitions have been answered only by repeated injury. A Prince whose character is thus marked by every act which may define a Tyrant, is unfit to be the ruler of a free people.

Nor have We been wanting in attentions to our British brethren. We have warned them from time to time of attempts by their legislature to extend an unwarrantable jurisdiction over us. We have reminded them of the circumstances of our emigration and settlement here. We have appealed to their native justice and magnanimity, and we have conjured them by the ties of our common kindred to disavow these usurpations, which, would inevitably interrupt our connections and correspondence. They too have been deaf to the voice of justice and of consanguinity. We must, therefore, acquiesce in the necessity, which denounces our Separation, and hold them, as we hold the rest of mankind, Enemies in War, in Peace Friends.

We, therefore, the Representatives of the United States of America, in General Congress, Assembled, appealing to the Supreme Judge of the world for the rectitude of our intentions, do, in the Name, and by Authority of the good People of these Colonies, solemnly publish and declare, That these United Colonies are, and of Right ought to be Free and Independent States; that they are Absolved from all Allegiance to the British Crown, and that all political connection between them and the State of Great Britain, is and ought to be totally dissolved; and that as Free and Independent States, they have full Power to levy War, conclude Peace, contract Alliances, establish Commerce, and to do all other Acts and Things which Independent States may of right do. And for the support of this Declaration, with a firm reliance on the protection of divine Providence, we mutually pledge to each other our Lives, our Fortunes and our sacred Honor.

THE DECLARATION OF INDEPENDENCE
IN CONGRESS, July 4, 1776.

Answer these questions.

1.70 Which full paragraph(s) are the preamble? _____

1.71 The center section lists the grievances against the crown and Parliament as well as the American attempts to gain a fair hearing. What are the phrases that begin and end this section?

a. Beginning phrase: _____

b. Ending phrase: _____

1.72 Which paragraph(s) are the statement of independence? _____

Do this activity.

1.73 In a class setting, read the preamble aloud and discuss what each phrase means. In an independent study setting, read the preamble (aloud, if possible) and write out what it means in your own words.

TEACHER CHECK _____ _____
                      initials   date

Look at the list of grievances in the Declaration. For each incident listed below give the phrase in the Declaration that refers to it (enough to identify it).

1.74 The dissolution of the colonial assemblies

_____

_____

1.75 The use of royal authority to veto colonial laws

_____

_____

1.76 The use of income from the Townshend Acts to pay salaries of officials

_____

_____

1.77 The Stamp Act

_____

_____

1.78 Use of Admiralty Courts

_____

_____

1.79 Changing the Massachusetts charter

_____

_____

1.80 Closing Boston Harbor

_____

_____

1.81 Encouraging Native American attacks

_____

_____

1.82 Hiring of Hessians

_____

_____

1.83 Quartering Act

_____

_____

1.84 Setting up a military government in Boston

_____

_____

1.85 Quebec Act

_____

_____

Review the material in this section in preparation for the Self Test. The Self Test will check your mastery of this particular section. The items missed on this Self Test will indicate specific areas where restudy is needed for mastery.

SELF TEST 1

Match the following people (each answer, 2 points).

1.01	_____ Boston radical; started Committees of Correspondence	a. George Grenville
1.02	_____ American commander at Ticonderoga and the invasion of Canada	b. Benjamin Franklin
1.03	_____ commander-in-chief of American army	c. Charles Townshend
1.04	_____ Prime Minister of Britain; Stamp Act	d. John Dickinson
1.05	_____ author of the Declaration of Independence	e. Lord North
1.06	_____ *Letters from a Farmer in Pennsylvania*; Olive Branch Petition	f. Samuel Adams
1.07	_____ Chancellor of the Exchequer; Britain	g. John Hancock
1.08	_____ Prime Minister who gave East India Company a monopoly on American tea sales	h. George Washington
1.09	_____ president of Second Continental Congress; large signer of Declaration of Independence	i. Benedict Arnold
1.010	_____ colonial representative in London before the war	j. Thomas Jefferson

Describe each of these giving the important points.

1.011 Stamp Act (5 points)

_____

_____

1.012 Townshend Acts (5 points)

_____

_____

1.013 Boston Massacre (5 points)

_____

_____

1.014 Boston Tea Party (4 points)

_____

_____

1.015 The Intolerable Acts (5 points)

_____

_____

_____

1.016 Quebec Act (5 points)

_____

_____

_____

1.017 Battle of Bunker Hill (5 points)

_____

_____

_____

_____

1.018 Colonial reaction to the Stamp Act (6 points)

a. _____ b. _____

c. _____

Complete these sentences (each answer, 3 points).

1.019 British policy toward the Thirteen Colonies was based on the economic theory of

_____ .

1.020 The laws that were passed in the late 1600s, but rarely enforced, that restricted America to

trade to the benefit of England were called the _____ Acts.

1.021 The _____ Act was passed when the Stamp Act was repealed

and stated that Parliament could tax the colonies.

1.022 The _____ were secret societies opposed to British power that

led mob action.

1.023 The _____ Act required colonists to house and feed British

troops.

1.024 The _____ Act kept high taxes on sugar and rum and allowed

violators to be tried in Admiralty Court.

1.025 The First Continental Congress met in response to the _____ Acts.

1.026 The Revolutionary War began at _____ .

1.027 The key fort, with its cannon, that was captured on Lake Champlain was Fort

_____ .

1.028 _____ was an influential pamphlet written by Thomas Paine

that urged America to become independent.

Answer true or false (each answer, 1 point).

1.029 _____ Britain was deeply in debt after the Seven Years War.

1.030 _____ The colonists carefully obeyed the trade laws before 1763.

1.031 _____ The American invasion of Canada encouraged the French colonists to rebel against the British.

1.032 _____ Congress voted for independence on July 4, 1776.

1.033 _____ The king's decision to use German mercenaries to fight in America turned many Americans against the British.

1.034 _____ The Olive Branch Petition was an offer of surrender by the American army after the defeat at Bunker Hill.

1.035 _____ The American army was organized from militia units.

1.036 _____ In 1773 Boston was the only city that refused to accept for sale the tea shipped in under the new monopoly to the East India Company.

1.037 _____ Britain wanted the Americans to bear some of the cost of their own defense.

1.038 _____ The colonies were always short of hard money because of British laws.

2. WAR

The Revolutionary War was fought from 1775 until 1783. Most of it was very discouraging for the Americans. They rarely won battles. They were always short of gunpowder, uniforms, boots, food, and cannons. Most of the soldiers in the army were militia. They only stayed for short periods of time. Some would return home each spring for planting or to deal with Native Americans in their state. The army was in a constant state of change, growing smaller and larger as men came and went. But, this very unlikely group held off the well-trained, well-supplied, well-disciplined British army for years.

Washington was forced by his circumstances to fight a defensive war. He wanted to attack and drive the British out of America, but he never had an army that could do that. Instead, he fought and retreated, forcing the British to keep their army ready to face him, but never giving them a decisive victory. The British captured cities but could not capture the hearts of the people. Eventually, the vengeful nations of Europe stepped in to reduce British power by helping the Americans. In the end, the war went to the Americans who won by simply surviving and not giving up.

SECTION OBJECTIVES

Review these objectives. When you have completed this section, you should be able to:

1. Identify the men who contributed to the Revolution.
3. Identify and describe the governing bodies that acted for the colonies/states.
4. Name the major battles of the war and to tell their significances.
5. Outline the terms of the peace agreements that the United States signed with Britain.

VOCABULARY

Study these words to enhance your learning success in this section.

asset (as′ et). An advantage.

enlistment (en list′ ment). The time for which a person joins some part of the armed forces.

guerrillas (gu ril′ u). Fighters who harass the enemy by sudden raids; ambushes; the plundering of supplies and the like.

mediocre (mē′ dē ō′ ker). Of average quality; ordinary.

morale (mu ral′). Mental condition in regard to courage, confidence, or enthusiasm.

America Alone

British situation. The British appeared to have huge advantages over their American opponents in this war. They had a professional army of thousands, trained and ready to go. They also had the means to hire Hessians to add to their strength (eventually 30,000 served under the British in America). The British navy controlled the Atlantic. This was a tremendous advantage. The army could be moved, supplied, and reinforced anywhere along the coast, where most of the American population and all of the American cities were located.

Also, the British could count on the support of Americans still loyal to the crown. About one-third of the colonists were Loyalists or Tories. These were formidable **assets**.

However, the British also had several weaknesses. They had to fight this war across an ocean 3,000 miles (4,839 km) away. New information and orders could take months to reach a commander in the field from London. Britain also had no great leaders in power to organize the fight and most of her generals were **mediocre**. The other countries of Europe were anxious to take down British power, and might be willing to support the Americans. Moreover, the British had to defeat and conquer a huge area of territory and an uncooperative population. An incomplete victory would be no victory.

American situation. The Americans had the advantage of fighting near their homes for a righteous cause. They had outstanding leadership in men like George Washington, Nathanael Greene, Benedict Arnold, and Daniel Morgan. They were a tough, capable people who had already proven their courage and strength by leaving the safety of Europe to tame a wilderness land. The Americans learned to shoot while hunting for food. They were usually better shots than the British soldiers. Moreover, the Americans had the wide spaces of the country in which to retreat and hide.

The Americans also had deep weaknesses. Only about one third of the people supported the Revolution. America did not have an effective central government. The Second Continental Congress became the first government because there was no other body that could do it. It had no official authority. A system of government for the colonies, the Articles of Confederation, was not set up until 1781. The Congress had no power to tax and the money it printed lost value until it was practically worthless. The different states fought with each other constantly and usually put the needs of their state above the needs of the "nation."

Boston. General Washington was camped with the American army around Boston in early 1776. He had been there since July and the army had been there since Lexington in April. Washington's main accomplishment through that time was that he managed to keep the army there at all. Most of the militia were there only for short periods of **enlistment**, some as short as eight months. Gradually, Washington convinced some of them to stay and others to join. But, he did not have the strength to threaten the British in Boston, at least, not until Henry Knox arrived from Ticonderoga in March of 1776 with the fort's cannons.

The cannons changed the entire situation. Washington had them installed on Dorchester Heights, a high hill directly across from Boston. From there Washington could fire at will on the British in the city. The new British commander, Sir William Howe, gathered his men to attack, but a storm prevented them from crossing the bay. Instead, the British abandoned Boston, withdrawing to Canada.

Charleston. The British hoped to gain the support of Loyalists in the South by a show of force there. A force was organized for an assault in the spring of 1776. A Loyalist force of about 1,500 that intended to join up with the British was destroyed by Patriot forces in February. The defeat disheartened the Loyalists who made no attempt to join with the British when they finally arrived. Orders from London calling off the assault because of the Loyalists' defeat reached the commander, Henry Clinton, too late.

The British assault force, including ten warships and thirty transports, reached Charleston in June, 1776. The city, however, was well prepared. Sturdy forts had been built on the approaches to the harbor, and they were well supplied. The defenders were organized and calm. The British assault failed, driven back by the steady fire from the forts. The South was left in peace for the time being.

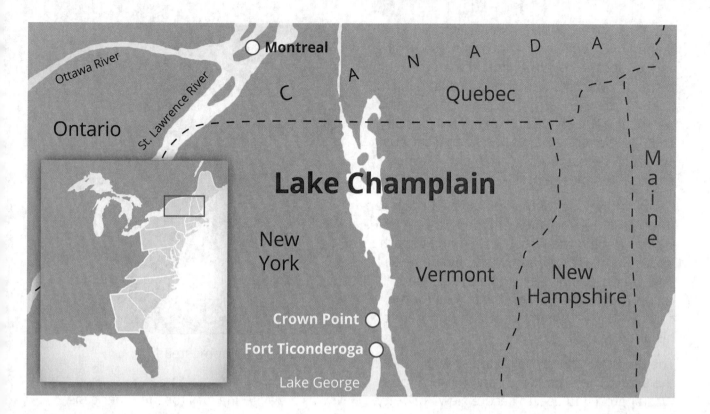

Lake Champlain. When Benedict Arnold retreated from Quebec in May of 1776, he headed back down Lake Champlain. The British governor in Canada, Sir Guy Carleton, followed. Carleton assembled a fleet to take troops down the lake. Arnold, now a brigadier general, constructed a ramshackle fleet to oppose them. The two sides met in October of 1776 on Lake Champlain. The American fleet was destroyed, but it succeeded in inflicting enough damage that Carleton withdrew for the season. Arnold's success at keeping the British from taking Fort Ticonderoga in 1776 was a key victory. It meant that the British invasion from Canada in 1777 had to start in Canada, not New York! Those would be precious miles and months for the Americans.

New York. The British withdrawal from Boston left Washington in a difficult position. The British had control of the seas and could attack anywhere they wanted along the coast. Washington would then have to march his men overland to meet them. Fortunately, Washington expected them to go to New York City, and they did. The army was shifted there to meet them.

The British arrived in July of 1776 with a huge force including more than 30,000 soldiers and 30 battleships. They took Staten Island to use as a base. The American position was impossible from the start. New York City is built on an island and the British controlled the waterways. They could land at will and prevent Washington from moving across the rivers. Washington had to defend everywhere at once. The British expected Washington to simply submit to British rule in the face of their control of the waterways and superior troop strength. They sent a few ships to fire on the city to prove their point. But, Washington refused to submit.

The British launched an assault on Long Island in August of 1776. The Americans had more than 10,000 men waiting for them. But, the British did not go straight up the hill into the fortifications as they did at Bunker Hill. Part of the British forces came around to attack from the rear. The inexperienced Americans panicked. By the end of the day, the survivors had retreated to Brooklyn Heights, near the ocean where the British navy prevented an escape.

But, Washington was not so easily trapped. He had his men leave their campfires burning and, under the cover of night, transferred the entire army across to Manhattan Island in small boats. The Americans retreated up the island leaving the British in control of New York City. The Battle of Long Island had been a serious American defeat, but the army had escaped and would fight again.

It was during this campaign that the British captured an American officer named Nathan Hale. He was behind the British lines trying to gather information. He was hung as a spy the next day without a trial. He said before he died, "I regret that I have but one life to lose for my country." He is remembered and honored for his bravery.

The British followed their success with more of the same. The Americans had built two forts, Washington and Lee, to secure New York City. Both held large supplies of American gunpowder, cannons, clothing, and war material. The British captured both forts and all of the 3,000 defenders.

| Nathan Hale's homestead

It was a staggering loss for the Americans. The British commander, William Howe, then settled down to enjoy the winter in the comfort of New York City since armies traditionally did not fight in the colder months.

These are the times that try men's souls. The summer soldier and the sunshine patriot will, in this crisis, shrink from the service of their country; but he that stands it now, deserves the love and thanks of man and woman. Tyranny, like hell, is not easily conquered; yet we have this consolation with us, that the harder the conflict, the more glorious the triumph. What we obtain too cheap, we esteem too lightly: it is dearness only that gives every thing its value.

Heaven knows how to put a proper price upon its goods; and it would be strange indeed if so celestial an article as FREEDOM should not be highly rated. Britain, with an army to enforce her tyranny, has declared that she has a right (not only to TAX) but "to BIND us in ALL CASES WHATSOEVER," and if being bound in that manner, is not slavery, then is there not such a thing as slavery upon earth. Even the expression is impious; for so unlimited a power can belong only to God.

THE AMERICAN CRISIS
Thomas Paine

Washington's men withdrew into New Jersey. They were in bad shape. They had been retreating for months. They lacked food and proper clothing. Thomas Paine, author of *Common Sense*, was with the army during this bleak hour.

On a drumhead he wrote an essay that even today stirs the hearts of those who must face unexpected hardship in fighting for what they believe.

In each case, check the side that had the advantage.

	British	Americans
2.1 size of army	☐	☐
2.2 professionalism	☐	☐
2.3 commanders	☐	☐
2.4 government	☐	☐
2.5 location of the war	☐	☐
2.6 hope of foreign alliances	☐	☐
2.7 money and supplies	☐	☐
2.8 control of the sea	☐	☐
2.9 shooting accuracy	☐	☐
2.10 national unity	☐	☐

Answer these questions.

2.11 What was Washington's main accomplishment from July 1775 until March 1776?

_____

2.12 What gave the Americans the advantage in Boston?

_____

2.13 Why was Arnold's defeat on Lake Champlain in 1776 so important to the Americans?

_____

2.14 What was the result of the 1776 assault on Charleston?

_____

2.15 What happened to the Americans at the Battle of Long Island?

_____

_____

2.16 Who was Nathan Hale and what happened to him?

_____

_____

2.17 What happened to Forts Washington and Lee?

_____

2.18 How did the Continental Army escape after the Battle of Long Island?

_____

2.19 What was the condition of Washington's army going into winter 1776?

_____

According to Thomas Paine.

2.20 Why is tyranny like hell? _____ .

2.21 Unlimited power belongs only to _____ .

2.22 Those that shrink from the service of their country are _____

_____ .

2.23 If we obtain something too easily we will _____ .

Trenton. By the end of 1776, Washington was in a fix. He had experienced nothing but defeat since the evacuation of Boston. **Morale** was low. Many people were calling for him to be replaced. The enlistments of most of his men would run out at the end of the year. By January, the Americans might not even have any army. The Americans, now in Pennsylvania, desperately needed a victory. So, Washington took a huge gamble and prepared to attack.

On Christmas night 1776, Washington and his army made a dangerous trip across the ice-choked Delaware River. Early the next morning, the Americans attacked the Hessian army at Trenton, New Jersey. Surprise was complete. Most of the Germans were still in bed, sleeping off the celebrations of the day before. It was all over in less than an hour. Washington's army captured over a thousand men and their supplies. The victory convinced many of the men to stay in the army for at least a little longer.

Princeton. British General Charles Cornwallis rushed to Trenton in an attempt to trap Washington's army in January of 1777. The larger, better supplied British force caught the Americans at Trenton with their backs to the river. But, again, the cagey Washington refused to be trapped. He left his fires burning and a few volunteers who made noise in the camp while the rest of the army snuck away after dark. The Americans swung around the British force and attacked their reinforcements at Princeton, winning yet another battle. From there Washington retreated to easily defended highlands near Morristown, Pennsylvania for the rest of the winter.

The twin victories at Trenton and Princeton saved the American cause. Volunteers came in from all over the colonies. Many of the experienced troops agreed to stay, some of them serving until the end of the war. Washington's command was secure and never was seriously questioned again. But, these were only small victories.

Washington, summer of 1777. Sir William Howe was in command of the British forces in New York. The British strategy for that year called for him to move his men up the Hudson River to meet General Burgoyne who was invading from Canada. Howe's orders, however, were not clear, and he had already committed his soldiers to a campaign against Washington in the central states.

Howe tried, at first, to draw Washington into a battle around New York. When that failed, he decided to take his army by sea up the Chesapeake to attack Philadelphia in July. He believed he had plenty of time to help Burgoyne should the need arise.

Howe fought two battles with Washington en route to Philadelphia. The Americans lost both at Brandywine Creek (September) and Germantown (October). But, again the American army was not captured.

The loss at Germantown, moreover, impressed foreign observers. The Americans had initiated the attack and had been driven off only after heavy fighting. Also, the men had fought well against the experienced British army. But, they could not keep Howe from capturing Philadelphia.

The capture of the capital should have been a major victory for the British. But, it accomplished very little. Congress simply moved elsewhere. There were very few government officials or offices to move. Howe again settled down to spend a comfortable winter in yet another American city. But, Washington's army was still in the field and America was not yet conquered.

| Washington and his men crossing the Delaware

Valley Forge. The Continental army faced many hardships in the long years of the Revolution. Perhaps the most famous was their stay at Valley Forge, outside of Philadelphia in the winter of 1777-78. The very name of the place has become synonymous with suffering.

Washington had to stay near Philadelphia in case Howe decided to attack, and Valley Forge was one of his few choices for winter quarters. The army came in having lost two major battles, and the nation's capital. Thanks to a lack of funds, hoarding, corruption, and poor transport the troops were constantly short of supplies. In December, Washington wrote to Congress that 2,873 of his men were unfit for duty because they were barefoot or otherwise in need of clothes. Men left bloody tracks in the snow from their unprotected feet. Food was scarce and disease common.

The army's main occupation that winter was survival. What was astonishing was that the army continued to exist. The dedicated men did not desert. In fact, the army managed to build its skills during this dark time. The Americans were good fighters as individuals, but they lacked training on how to work as a group. A German officer, Baron von Steuben, who spoke no English, drilled the men all through the long winter on how to maneuver and attack as a unit. In spite of the conditions, he managed to vastly improve the discipline and professionalism of the army. The hard work in Valley Forge would yield good fruit for the army in the future.

 Choose the correct match for each item.

2.24	_____ January 1777	a.	Trenton
2.25	_____ October 1777	b.	Princeton
2.26	_____ Winter 1777-78	c.	Germantown
2.27	_____ drilling by von Stueben	d.	Brandywine Creek
2.28	_____ capture of 1,000 Hessians	e.	Valley Forge
2.29	_____ Americans snuck behind Cornwallis to attack his reinforcements	f.	Philadelphia
2.30	_____ December 1776		
2.31	_____ captured by Howe		
2.32	_____ Washington's winter quarters		
2.33	_____ Howe's winter quarters		
2.34	_____ Americans crossed the icy Delaware		
2.35	_____ September 1777		
2.36	_____ time of great suffering		
2.37	_____ surprise attack, day after Christmas		
2.38	_____ should have been major victory for British, did not accomplish much		
2.39	_____ American army impressed foreign observers		

HISTORY & GEOGRAPHY 803

LIFEPAC TEST

NAME _____

DATE _____

SCORE _____

$$\frac{80}{100}$$

HISTORY & GEOGRAPHY 803: LIFEPAC TEST

Match these people (each answer, 2 points).

1. _____ Father of the Constitution
2. _____ Lost battles but won campaign in the South
3. _____ American general that turned traitor
4. _____ author of *Common Sense*
5. _____ president of the Constitutional Convention
6. _____ colonial representative in London right before the Revolution
7. _____ hanged as a spy during the New York campaign of 1776
8. _____ Boston radical, began Committees of Correspondence
9. _____ author of the Declaration of Independence
10. _____ American naval commander, *Bonhomme Richard*

a. George Washington
b. Benjamin Franklin
c. Nathanael Greene
d. Benedict Arnold
e. Samuel Adams
f. Thomas Jefferson
g. James Madison
h. John Paul Jones
i. Nathan Hale
j. Thomas Paine

Complete the following.

11. What was the Great Compromise of the Constitutional Convention? (5 points)

_____
_____
_____

12. Describe the set up and results of the Battle of Yorktown. (5 points)

_____
_____
_____

13. Why did British policy towards the colonies change after 1763? (5 points)

_____
_____
_____

14. Describe the most important provisions of each law (each answer, 2 points).

Stamp Act: _____

Quebec Act: _____

Quartering Act: _____

Townshend Acts: _____

Intolerable Acts: _____

15. What was Shays Rebellion and why was it important? (5 points)

_____

_____

Complete each sentence using a word from the list (each answer, 2 points).

Lexington	Ticonderoga	Saratoga
Rochambeau	Monmouth	Camden
Trenton	Cornwallis	Lafayette
Steuben		

16. The Revolutionary War began at _____ .

17. The Marquis de _____ was a wealthy French volunteer who became an American hero.

18. _____ was the commander of the French army in America during the Revolution.

19. _____ was the indecisive last major battle in the North during the Revolution.

20. Lord _____ was the British commander in the South after the capture of Charleston.

21. Baron von _____ drilled the American army at Valley Forge.

22. Henry Knox dragged the cannon from _____ to Boston.

23. Horatio Gates lost the humiliating battle of _____ when he brought a new American army south after the loss of Charleston.

24. _____ was the turning point of the Revolutionary War.

25. Washington led his army across the icy Delaware River to surprise the Hessians at _____ on the day after Christmas.

Name the legislature or constitution related to each item (each answer, 3 points).

26. _____ Declaration of Independence

27. _____ Stamp Act

28. _____ America's first constitution

29. _____ Northwest Ordinance

30. _____ enslaved people counted as three-fifths of a person

31. _____ America's first government

32. _____ reaction to the Intolerable Acts

33. _____ a firm league of friendship between the states

34. _____ checks and balances

35. _____ appointed Washington as commander-in-chief

The Turning Point

British plan. During the summer of 1777, the British had organized a master plan to cut New England off from the rest of the United States. The plan called for General Burgoyne to come down Lake Champlain and the Hudson River to Albany. Lieutenant Colonel St. Leger was to reach the same point by coming across from Lake Ontario and up the Mohawk River. In the meantime, General Howe was to come up the Hudson from New York and also reach Albany. This three-prong attack would conquer New York and isolate New England. The plan, however, required cooperation and the success of all three parts. As noted in the last section, General Howe received unclear orders from London and had already committed his troops to action in Pennsylvania. He never even made an attempt to join Burgoyne at Albany. The British master plan had all the makings of a grand disaster without the full support of all three commanders.

| The unsuccessful British attack plan in the summer of 1777

St. Leger and the Battle of Oriskany.

Lt. Colonel Barry St. Leger was to bring a British force up the Mohawk Valley for his part in the campaign. He had a mixed force of about one thousand British, German, and Loyalist soldiers. He also had about the same number of Iroquois allies. The Americans in the valley knew what would happen if the Iroquois and the Loyalists, who were supporters of several autocratic landlords from the region, were to reach the rich farms of the region. They were prepared and ready to fight, ferociously.

St. Leger reached the American Fort Stanwix at what is now Rome, New York in late summer of 1777. The fort refused to surrender and skillfully held off his siege. The militia of the nearby towns sent a force of 800 under the command of General Nicholas Herkimer to aid the fort.

St. Leger heard of the relief effort and sent 1,200 soldiers and Iroquois to meet them. The British force set up an ambush near Oriskany Creek. The Americans walked into the trap on August 6th. They were driven to retreat, but not before they inflicted heavy losses on the British. In the meantime, Fort Stanwix's defenders had taken advantage of the situation to raid the British camp and carry off many of their supplies.

By now the Continental Army had been alerted and a force of 1,000 men under General Benedict Arnold was on route to Stanwix. St. Leger's men heard rumors of the force, and received exaggerated reports of its size. The Iroquois and Loyalists began to panic. In late August, St. Leger began a retreat to his base on Lake Ontario. General Burgoyne was now the only one of the three commanders still pursuing the planned advance on Albany.

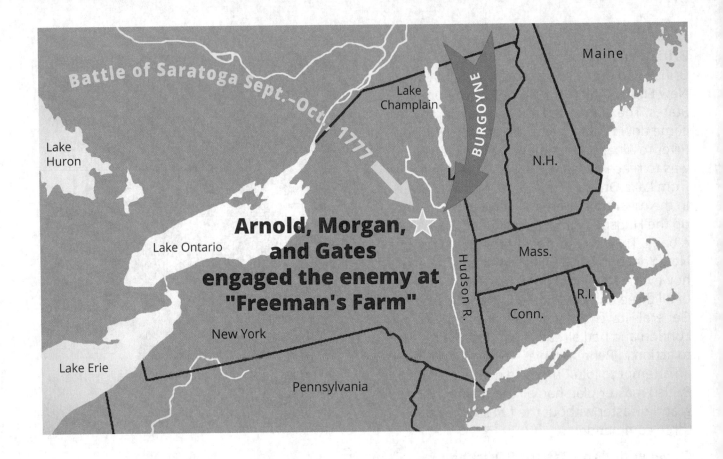

Battle of Saratoga Sept.–Oct., 1777

Lake Huron

Lake Ontario

Lake Erie

New York

Pennsylvania

Lake Champlain

Maine

N.H.

Mass.

R.I.

Conn.

Hudson R.

BURGOYNE

Arnold, Morgan, and Gates engaged the enemy at "Freeman's Farm"

Burgoyne. John "Gentleman Johnny" Burgoyne was a popular and arrogant British general. He believed he would have no trouble with the American militia. He started down the Richelieu River to Lake Champlain in June of 1777. He had about 7,000 British and German troops under his command. He was also accompanied by a large contingent of about 400 Iroquois People. Burgoyne was handicapped by a huge baggage train, hundreds of camp followers, including women and children, and over a hundred cannons he insisted be brought along, some of them to be dragged with the army through the wilderness.

The force floated down Lake Champlain and reached Fort Ticonderoga in early July. The fort was held by Major General Arthur St. Clair and 2,000 men. An alert British engineer noticed the high hill called Mount Defiance that towered above the fort. The steep sides made it difficult to climb and no one among the Americans dreamed the British could haul cannons up there. But, they did. St. Clair realized his danger and evacuated the fort before he and his men could be trapped.

Burgoyne then proceeded to show his ignorance of wilderness warfare. He set off to cross the 23 miles between Lake Champlain and the Hudson River Valley <u>building a road as he went</u>. He also dragged his own thirty carts of personal belongings as well as dozens of cannons. By now the alarm had gone out all over New England and Americans were swarming around Burgoyne like flies. They made him pay for every step he took through those miles of wilderness. Trees were felled across his path. Rivers were dammed and low areas flooded. It took Burgoyne an entire month to reach the Hudson. Then, he had to wait for his supplies to reach him.

The Americans feared not only the British but the Iroquois they had with him. They had good reason to believe that Burgoyne could not control them. In fact, on the trip south, some of the Iroquois captured and scalped a young woman named Jane McCrea, the fiancée of one of the Loyalist officers. Burgoyne did not punish the murderer because the other Indians would have left if he did. The Americans made good use of the story to convince New Englanders that Burgoyne did not even protect those who were loyal to the crown. What would happen to Patriots that happened to fall into his hands? More and more citizens took up their guns and went to join the growing horde opposing the British advance.

Burgoyne sent out a small force in mid-August to secure some horses that were rumored to be at Bennington. The entire German unit was destroyed by the Americans. The British unit sent to help was driven back. Burgoyne refused to take warning from the defeat or the news that neither Howe nor St. Leger were coming.

Saratoga. Burgoyne pressed on down the Hudson Valley toward Albany in September. He took only the minimum of supplies his army would need for the short trip to Albany, but kept his own baggage and the cannons. Snipers made it dangerous to leave the camp. The Americans again burned bridges, flooded lowlands, and felled trees to slow him down. Burgoyne often made only a mile a day or less and it was getting near winter.

General Horatio Gates was sent by Congress to command the American forces. Daniel Morgan, with his sharp-shooting riflemen, and Benedict Arnold were also sent. (Rifles, which were just coming into use, were more accurate than the muskets used by the British, but they took longer to reload.) Washington was too busy with Howe in Pennsylvania to come or send many men. Most of the soldiers in the army that faced Burgoyne were simply citizens who came to defend their homeland.

The two armies met twice on a piece of land called Freeman's Farm in September and October. The Americans fought from behind trees and let the British have the open field. Morgan and Arnold, not Gates, were responsible for the victories. Morgan's riflemen defied every rule of polite warfare by shooting from up in the trees deliberately aiming for the officers! General Benedict Arnold displayed his brilliance as a field commander by leading a furious attack in the second battle. He was severely wounded in the same leg that was injured in the attack on Quebec. Most of the time the British could not even get a good look, much less a clear shot, at their enemies. The British were routed in both battles.

His army in shambles, Burgoyne retreated, hoping to reach the safety of Ticonderoga. The men had no warm clothes and the weather was getting colder. British supplies of food were also low and the Americans continued to harass them. Burgoyne dug in on some high ground near the village of Saratoga for a rest. The American army surrounded him. With no other alternative, Burgoyne surrendered his entire army of about 5,000 men on October 17, 1777.

Complete these sentences.

2.40 The British plan for 1777 called for _____ to lead an attack down Lake Champlain, _____ to come up the Mohawk Valley, and _____ to come up the Hudson from New York City.

2.41 St. Leger was unable to capture _____ in New York and his forces were badly hurt in the battle at _____ .

2.42 Burgoyne took Fort _____ on Lake Champlain by putting cannon on Mount _____ .

2.43 Burgoyne carried _____ cart loads of his own belongings, dozens of _____ and hundreds of camp followers with him.

2.44 The Americans made good use of propaganda in the murder of _____ _____ by the Iroquois.

2.45 An entire German unit was wiped out by the Americans at _____ .

2.46 The Americans defeated Burgoyne's forces in two battles at _____ .

2.47 The leaders of the American victory were _____ and _____ .

2.48 The official American commander was _____ .

2.49 Burgoyne surrendered his entire army at _____ in October 1777.

Significance of Saratoga. The victory at Saratoga was the turning point of the war. The Americans had defeated and captured an entire British army. The British evacuated Ticonderoga and withdrew to Canada. The victory brought great cheer to the American side. The victory also brought the Patriot cause much needed allies.

Franklin in France. The Americans knew how badly the French wanted revenge for their losses in the Seven Years War. It was natural, therefore, to seek assistance from them for the American Rebellion. Benjamin Franklin was sent to France as an official envoy in September, 1776 to get a possible alliance. The French were willing to encourage the colonists, but were not willing to immediately risk war with Britain. However, they did provide valuable weapons and supplies through a trading company called *Hortalez et Cie*, thus staying officially neutral.

Franklin quickly became one of the most popular men in France, the darling of the frivolous French court. The aristocracy was very interested in the theories of the day that taught the superiority of "natural man." Franklin agreeably played the part of the noble rustic, much to the delight of the high-born ladies. He did not wear the rich clothes, sword, and wig normally expected of a court envoy. Instead, he dressed plainly and acted the part of the natural philosopher, even occasionally wearing a fur cap. The French courtiers were enchanted, but the French leaders wanted proof that America could fight and win a war before they committed.

The victory at Saratoga along with the surprising American showing at Germantown provided the proof the French wanted. They signed a treaty of Alliance with the Americans in February of 1778, while Washington's men hungered in Valley Forge. The French navy could now be used to protect American trade and threaten the British West Indies. The Spanish and Dutch also eventually joined the alliance. Britain now had a world war, not a colonial rebellion on its hands.

| The Marquis de Lafayette

Lafayette. The Marquis de Lafayette was one of the many assets America received from France throughout the Revolution. Lafayette was a very wealthy French aristocrat who joined the American cause in 1777 at the age of nineteen. He was assigned as an aide to General Washington, and the two became very close friends. He was gradually given opportunities to command which he handled skillfully to the advantage of the American cause. He donated a great deal of money to the patriot cause and used his influence with the king of France to arrange for a French army to come to America in 1779. He has long been hailed as a hero of the Revolution and is honored in America by numerous towns that bear his name.

Monmouth. By early 1778, Sir Henry Clinton had replaced Howe as commander of the British forces in America. News of the alliance with France reached him in Philadelphia, which the British still held. He was ordered to evacuate Philadelphia and return to New York. Clinton decided to march his army north and Washington went to meet him. A battle was fought at Monmouth Court House in New Jersey. It would be the last major battle in the North.

Washington sent an advance strike force under the command of General Charles Lee, who had been a British prisoner for a time and had a poor attitude. Lee attacked as ordered, but then withdrew without any reason. Washington came up with the rest of the army to find the strike force in a disorderly retreat. It was one of the few times Washington publicly lost his temper. He charged into the retreating lines, ordered Lee to surrender his command, rallied the men, and led the fight himself (Lee was later court-martialed). The battle ended indecisively, and the British succeeded in reaching New York safely. The two sides were now back where they had been in 1776, the British bottled up in New York, the Americans watching and waiting. Washington would remain there until 1781.

Western campaign. Most of the battles in the west were fought against the Native American Peoples who were encouraged by the British to make raids on the American settlements. Control of this region would enable the patriots to concentrate on the east and south. In 1778 George Rogers Clark and a band of frontiersmen overcame the British at Kaskasia, Cahokia, and Vincennes, the three major British forts in the west. These victories brought the west under American control. Colonel Henry Hamilton, a British officer, however, recaptured Vincennes. His victory was short-lived as George Rogers Clark led his men 180 miles through waist-deep swamps in the dead of winter to recapture the fort and bring the west under American control. This would prove vital in the years after the Revolution because the area south of the Great Lakes was in American hands, not British. The Americans received little trouble from the Native Americans and British in the west for the remainder of the war.

The war at sea. The tiny American navy, made up mostly of privateers, was no match for the British navy, which was the largest in the world. Yet, under the leadership of John Paul Jones and John Barry, using European ports, the navy managed to harass British ships near England.

One of the most famous American-British sea battles took place in 1779 between the *Bonhomme Richard*, under the command of John Paul Jones, and the British warship *Serapis*. The two engaged in savage combat for over three hours. The *Bonhomme Richard* was badly damaged and sinking. Yet, Jones refused to surrender saying, "I have not yet begun to fight!" He eventually captured the *Serapis*. This and other victories did little for the American cause except in the area of morale. The only real chance the Americans had at sea came with the alliance that brought the French navy in on their side.

Treachery. One of the most disheartening events of the Revolution occurred in 1780 when Benedict Arnold became a traitor. The hero of Ticonderoga and Saratoga was bitter over some setbacks in his military career. He also had married a Loyalist and become fond of rich living. In September of 1780, he offered to turn over his command, the American fort at West Point that protected the upper Hudson River, to the British. In exchange, he was to receive a large amount of money and a commission in the British army.

The man acting as the go-between, Major John André, was captured with the plans of the fort in Arnold's handwriting. Arnold fled to New York before he could be captured and André was hanged as a spy. West Point was strengthened and never fell into British hands. But, the loss of such a trusted and successful commander was a blow to the Americans.

Arnold fought the remainder of the Revolution as a British Brigadier General, a step below his American rank of Major General. He lived the rest of his life as a British subject reviled by his former countrymen. His name became synonymous with traitor in the American language. But, his brilliant work for the American cause was not forgotten. At Saratoga there is a very unusual memorial. It is a statue of a leg, the leg of Benedict Arnold. Injured at both Quebec and Saratoga, it was the only loyal part of the former American hero.

Complete these sentences.

2.50 _____ was the turning point of the Revolutionary War.

2.51 France formed an alliance with the Americans after the battles of _____

and _____ .

2.52 _____ was a wealthy French aristocrat who became an

American officer and hero.

2.53 America's representative in France was _____ who played

the part of the "natural man" for the court.

2.54 The last major battle in the North was _____ and it was indecisive.

2.55 _____ took control of the British forts in the west with a

small force of frontiersmen.

2.56 The Americans recaptured the fort at _____ from the

British after marching 180 miles through waist deep water in the winter.

2.57 _____ betrayed his country by offering to turn over the fort at

_____ to the British for money and an officer's commission.

2.58 _____ was court-martialed for retreating at Monmouth

Courthouse.

2.59 _____ was the American naval commander who said,

"I have not yet begun to fight," during the battle between the American ship

_____ and the British ship _____ .

2.60 _____ was the spy captured by the Americans with the

plans of West Point.

The End of the War

Georgia. The British plans had failed so miserably in the North that they decided to concentrate on the less populous South. Their plan was to capture each state, organize the Loyalists there to take control, and then move on to the next state. In 1779 a well-organized force captured Savannah and all of Georgia. An attempt to retake the city by a joint American-French force failed in October.

South Carolina. Sir Henry Clinton, in command in New York, now moved a force of about 10,000 south using the resources of the British navy. He successfully besieged Charleston avoiding the mistakes made in the earlier attempt. The city fell on May 12, 1780. The American commander, General Benjamin Lincoln, was captured along with 5,000 men, all of their supplies, and almost all of the Revolutionary leaders of South Carolina. It was the biggest single American disaster of the war.

Using Charleston as a base, Clinton sent out troops to secure the colony. In June, Clinton turned over command to Lord Cornwallis and returned to New York. Cornwallis set up a series of forts in the interior of South Carolina to protect the British gains. Soon all of South Carolina was under British control.

Camden. Congress sent a new army south to engage Cornwallis. They chose Horatio Gates, the official victor at Saratoga, to command the force. Gates lacked the skills needed for such a difficult job. The hastily assembled force was made up mainly of militia, which had never been in battle, and a few experienced units from the Continental Army. The two sides met at Camden, South Carolina in August 1780. It was a humiliating defeat for the Americans. Many of the inexperienced troops ran without firing a shot. The Continentals fought hard, but were overwhelmed when the rest of the army withdrew. Gates and the remains of his army fled north.

King's Mountain. The overconfident Cornwallis decided to attack North Carolina before South Carolina was fully secure. He sent an advance force of about a thousand Loyalists north under the command of Major Patrick Ferguson, a British officer. They ordered the North Carolina citizens to submit to the crown or face attack and occupation. The independent men of North Carolina not only refused, they gathered a force of backwoodsmen and went south to meet the British. They engaged the enemy at King's Mountain in South Carolina in October of 1780. It was one of the bloodiest battles of the war because the Patriots totally annihilated the Tory regiment.

Nathanael Greene. Congress now wisely asked Washington to recommend someone to take command of the shattered southern army. Washington chose Nathanael Greene. It was an ideal choice. Greene realized he did not have the strength to defeat Cornwallis in a pitched battle. So, he planned out and executed one of the most brilliant American campaigns of the war.

There were several bands of **guerrillas** active in the South. The most famous was under the command of Francis Marion, the "Swamp Fox." Greene made contact with these men and had his regular troops work with them. The guerrilla bands raided British outposts, harassed supply lines, and acted as scouts for the regular army. By coordinating with these bands, Greene managed to press the British and keep them off balance.

Greene used his regular army to draw Cornwallis into an extended chase all over Carolina. The British were drawn far from their supply bases and forced to take provisions from the local people. This made the British unpopular and strengthened the American cause in the South. Greene lost every major engagement he fought. But, he always inflicted severe losses on the British and escaped to fight again. "We fight, get beat, rise and fight again," was the way Greene described the campaign. By June of 1781, Greene and his guerrilla allies had made the Carolina countryside difficult for Cornwallis to handle. The British lost control of everything except the cities.

Cowpens. Greene had split his forces when he took command in 1780, in the hopes that Cornwallis would split his as well, giving the Americans a chance. Cornwallis cooperated sending a force of about a thousand after Daniel Morgan's eight hundred men. Morgan chose the place for the battle, a spot called the Cowpens. In January 1781, the British under Colonel Tarleton rode into the American trap. Faking a retreat, Morgan's men drew the British into a position to be attacked from all sides. Almost the entire force was killed or captured. It was the one major victory of the campaign.

A furious Cornwallis chased Morgan, who wisely withdrew. Then, Cornwallis took off in an exhausting chase to try and trap Greene. Greene's men managed to outrun him, and crossed the Dan River to safety in Virginia in February of 1781. Cornwallis was now far from his supply bases and constantly facing harassment from the Americans.

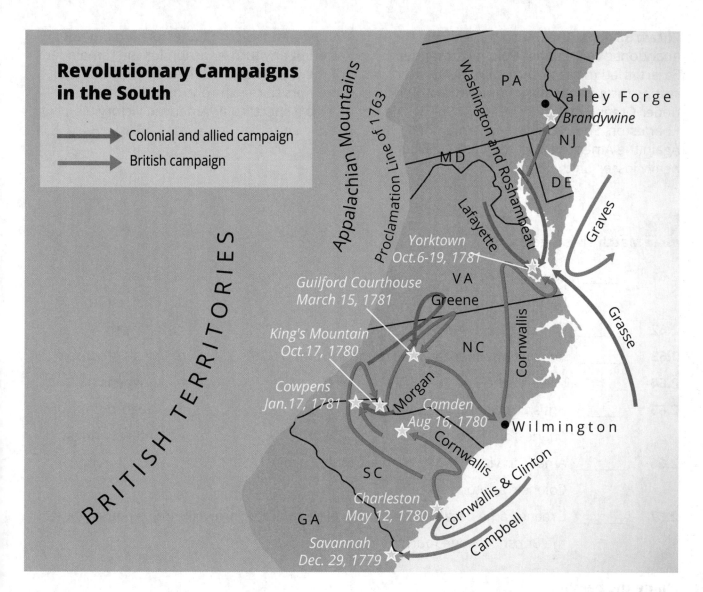

Revolutionary Campaigns in the South

→ Colonial and allied campaign
→ British campaign

Appalachian Mountains

Proclamation Line of 1763

Washington and Roshambeau

PA • Valley Forge
☆ *Brandywine*
NJ
MD
DE

Lafayette

Graves

Yorktown
Oct.6-19, 1781

VA
Greene

Grasse

Guilford Courthouse
March 15, 1781

Cornwallis

King's Mountain
Oct.17, 1780

NC

Cowpens
Jan.17, 1781

Morgan

Camden
Aug 16, 1780

• Wilmington

Cornwallis

Cornwallis & Clinton

BRITISH TERRITORIES

SC

Charleston
May 12, 1780

Cornwallis & Clinton

GA

Campbell

Savannah
Dec. 29, 1779

Guilford Courthouse. Greene came back into North Carolina after Cornwallis withdrew. He set his men up at a site he had selected in advance, Guilford Courthouse, North Carolina. Cornwallis chased him and arrived March 15th with a British force. The British technically won the battle because the Americans withdrew at the end of the day. But, Cornwallis lost one-fourth of his men, while the American casualties were light. Moreover, the American army was still intact. Cornwallis withdrew toward the sea to refit his force.

Falling forts. Greene then turned on the forts that held the Carolina interior. His forces were defeated at Hobkirk's Hill in April, but the British commander abandoned the nearby fort due to the heavy losses of men and supplies to the guerrilla forces. Other forts were captured by these forces while the army kept the British too busy to send aid. Greene's siege of another fort, Ninety-six, was broken by the British in May, but again the British decided the fort could not be held and withdrew. By June, almost the entire line of British forts were gone. Having lost most of the battles, Greene won the campaign. Most of the South was again in American hands.

Eutaw Springs. The British troops from the abandoned forts, under Colonel Alexander Stuart, tried to reach Cornwallis' army after resting through the hot summer. The Americans under Greene met them at Eutaw Springs near Charleston, South Carolina in September 1781. Again the Americans lost the battle, inflicting heavy losses on the British.

Stuart withdrew to Charleston and did not attempt any further action for the remainder of the war. The British made no other major attempts to regain control in the South. It was a spectacular American victory.

 Match these items.

2.61	_____ Loyalist force was destroyed by North Carolina backwoodsmen	a. Savannah
2.62	_____ loss of Lincoln and 5,000 men	b. Charleston
2.63	_____ humiliating American defeat under Horatio Gates	c. Camden
2.64	_____ taken by the British in 1779	d. King's Mountain
2.65	_____ British troops under Stuart defeat Greene near Charleston	e. Cowpens
		f. Guilford Courthouse
2.66	_____ American victory under Daniel Morgan against Colonel Tarleton's force	g. Eutaw Springs
2.67	_____ Greene came back from North Carolina to draw Cornwallis into a battle where the British lost one fourth of their men	

Name the person.

2.68 _____ the "Swamp Fox", Carolina guerrilla leader

2.69 _____ victorious commander at Cowpens

2.70 _____ American commander in the south who lost the battles and won the campaign

2.71 _____ victor at Saratoga, chosen by Congress to command American army in the South after the fall of Charleston

2.72 _____ British commander in the South after the withdrawal of Clinton

Yorktown. Lafayette had been sent south in 1781 with an American army to pursue Cornwallis, who was now busy in Virginia. Cornwallis was unable to pin down the cagey Frenchman. Meanwhile, Clinton decided he wanted some of Cornwallis' men to reinforce New York, for fear of an attack there. So, Cornwallis withdrew to Yorktown on Chesapeake Bay and set up a strong defensive position to wait for the British navy. But, it would be the French navy that came instead.

When Washington heard that Cornwallis was stationary on the sea coast, he grabbed a chance to capture a major British army. The Americans had the use of a French fleet under the command of Admiral de Grasse. Washington sent it to blockade the Chesapeake, cutting off Cornwallis' supply and escape route. The French navy successfully defeated the ships sent to relieve Cornwallis and blocked any hope of help from the sea.

While de Grasse moved into position, Washington and Rochambeau, the commander of the French army in America, moved south to trap Cornwallis. The American and French armies, numbering about 17,000, encircled the British camp which held about 10,000 men. Cornwallis was dug into a defensive position, but with the sea and the French navy behind him, he had no place to go.

The Allies set up siege lines under the direction of Rochambeau, who was an expert in this type of warfare. They began a steady pounding of the British lines with cannon fire. Slowly, the Americans and French moved closer and closer capturing the outer British defenses. With no hope of reinforcements or supplies, the result was inevitable. On October 17th, the British asked for surrender terms.

Cornwallis surrendered his entire command on October 19, 1781. The army marched out to the tune of "The World Turn'd Upside Down" and laid down their arms. Lord Cornwallis, claiming to be ill, sent General O'Hara to surrender for him.

O'Hara first moved to surrender to the French, but was directed to Washington. Washington declined to receive Cornwallis' sword (the customary mark of a surrender) since the general did not choose to deliver it in person. Instead, Washington directed that it be surrendered to Benjamin Lincoln, the general who had suffered the greatest American defeat of the war, at Charleston.

Yorktown was the last major battle of the war, although neither side knew that. Both armies remained in the field for another two years, awaiting events in Europe that would finally bring a conclusion. In Britain the war had become immensely unpopular as British losses mounted both in America and in other areas. A new government came to power that was determined to make peace.

Treaty of Paris. Peace talks were opened in France in 1782 with the American delegation. The Americans included Benjamin Franklin, John Adams, and John Jay. A treaty was negotiated and signed on September 3, 1783 in Paris. The terms were very generous to the Americans because the British wanted to break up America's alliance with the French in the event of future wars.

The Treaty of Paris gave the Americans almost everything they wanted. America's independence was recognized, and all of the land east of the Mississippi between Canada and Florida was recognized as hers. All British forces were to leave American land. The Mississippi was open to American commerce and American ships could fish in the Newfoundland waters. Spain received Florida back, and the French got back the islands of the West Indies captured in the war. Congress was to recommend that Loyalists be given back their land and all debts owed to Britain were recognized as valid. The military phase of the Revolution was now over, but it was still not clear what kind of government would rule in America. That part of the Revolution was unfinished.

Washington's finest hour. The American economy was in a shambles at the end of the war. The money issued by Congress was worthless and the army had never been properly paid. In May of 1782, several of Washington's officers sent him a memo asking him to use the army and set himself up as a new king. This was the pattern of history when a victorious general has led a successful rebellion against a king.

Washington coldly refused. When word of the peace treaty reached him in November of 1783, he defied the pattern of history and shocked most of the rulers of Europe by resigning his commission and retiring to private life. It was, in this author's opinion, the single greatest service Washington ever did for his country.

 Answer these question.

2.73 How was Cornwallis trapped at Yorktown?

_____

_____

2.74 What was the name of the French army commander at Yorktown?

_____

2.75 What was the name of the French naval commander at Yorktown?

_____

2.76 Who negotiated the Treaty of Paris for America?

_____

2.77 Who received Cornwallis' sword at the surrender at Yorktown?

_____

2.78 Why was Washington's decision to resign his commission so important? (Think about it.)

_____

_____

2.79 What were the nine important terms of the Treaty of Paris?

1. _____

2. _____

3. _____

4. _____

5. _____

6. _____

7. _____

8. _____

9. _____

↺ **Review the material in this section in preparation for the Self Test.** This Self Test will check your mastery of this particular section as well as your knowledge of the previous section.

SELF TEST 2

Match these people (each answer, 2 points).

2.01	_____	Lord Cornwallis
2.02	_____	Benedict Arnold
2.03	_____	Thomas Paine
2.04	_____	Burgoyne
2.05	_____	Benjamin Franklin
2.06	_____	Marquis de Lafayette
2.07	_____	Thomas Jefferson
2.08	_____	Samuel Adams
2.09	_____	George Rogers Clark
2.010	_____	John Paul Jones
2.011	_____	Benjamin Lincoln
2.012	_____	Nathanael Greene
2.013	_____	Daniel Morgan
2.014	_____	Rochambeau
2.015	_____	De Grasse

a. Boston radical; Committees of Correspondence

b. commanded greatest American defeat of the war; lost 5,000 men

c. British commander in the south, 1780-81

d. captured western British forts with small force of frontiersmen

e. French army commander

f. French admiral

g. author of *Common Sense* and *The American Crisis*

h. captain of the *Bonhomme Richard*

i. American commander in the South; lost all the battles but won the campaign

j. commanded riflemen at Freeman's Farm and the victorious Americans at Cowpens

k. French volunteer/hero in American army; close friend of Washington

l. British general; surrendered his entire army after campaign in Upstate New York

m. American hero turned traitor

n. American representative in France; played the "natural man" for the court

o. author of the Declaration of Independence

Choose the correct answer from the list (each answer, 3 points).

Saratoga	Long Island	Yorktown
Charleston	Camden	Oriskany
Monmouth Courthouse	Trenton	King's Mountain
Valley Forge		

2.016 The last major battle in the North was an inconclusive conflict fought at _____ _____ between Washington's army and the army of Sir Henry Clinton who was moving back to New York.

2.017 Washington made a risky crossing of the icy Delaware River to attack the Hessians at _____ the day after Christmas 1776.

2.018 The surrender of the British army at _____ was the turning point of the war.

2.019 British commander St. Leger won the Battle of _____ when he ambushed an American force coming to the aid of Fort Stanwix.

2.020 A Tory army marching to attack North Carolina was met by a force of backwoodsmen from that state who annihilated them in 1780 at _____ .

2.021 The American army spent a cold, difficult winter at _____ improving their drilling skills under the teaching of Baron von Steuben.

2.022 The surrender of the British army at _____ , after it was trapped by the French navy and the combined French/American army, was the final major battle of the war.

2.023 The British defeated Washington at the Battle of _____ in 1776 by coming around and attacking from the rear of his inexperienced army and driving them back to Brooklyn Heights, where they skillfully slipped away after dark.

2.024 _____ was successfully defended in 1776, but was taken in 1780 in the biggest American disaster of the war.

2.025 Horatio Gates was humiliatingly defeated at _____ when he tried to lead an army south in 1780 to engage the victorious British after the conquest of Georgia and South Carolina.

Answer these questions (each answer, 3 points).

2.026 What nation signed a treaty of alliance with the Americans in 1778?

_____

2.027 Where did the cannons come from that drove the British out of Boston in 1776?

_____

2.028 In the summer of 1777, Washington fought the Battles of Brandywine Creek and Germantown trying to stop the British from reaching what city?

_____

2.029 The British colonies were ruled using what economic theory?

_____

2.030 What was the law that guaranteed the French in Canada their traditional laws and extended their land?

_____

2.031 What was the law that united the colonies against taxation without representation and was repealed after just four months of being in effect?

_____

2.032 The Intolerable Acts were the British reaction to what event?

_____

2.033 What were three advantages the British had in the Revolution?

a. _____

b. _____

c. _____

Answer true or false (each answer, 1 point).

2.034 _____ The Americans had the advantage of location in the war.

2.035 _____ Forts Washington and Lee near New York City were never taken by the British.

2.036 _____ The American army that fought at Freeman's Farm was mainly citizen soldiers who came to defend their homes.

2.037 _____ Nathan Hale said, "I have not yet begun to fight."

2.038 _____ Guilford Courthouse and Eutaw Springs were both British victories that hurt the victors more than the losers.

2.039 _____ The Navigation Acts were rarely enforced until after the Seven Years War.

2.040 _____ The Treaty of Paris gave the Americans very little of what they wanted.

2.041 _____ The Treaty of Paris granted America independence and promised they could use the Mississippi River.

2.042 _____ George Washington was not a great strategist, but he was faithful and had the loyalty of his men.

2.043 _____ Colonists tried in Admiralty Courts did not have a jury and were presumed to be guilty.

80 / 100   SCORE _____   TEACHER _____ _____
initials   date

3. THE CONSTITUTION

A revolution is a tremendous change in events. The American Revolution changed the states of North America from separate colonies under a European monarchy, to a united nation under a Federal Republic. Thus, the Revolution is actually more than just the war. It also includes the process of establishing the new government in America.

It was not clear at the end of the Revolutionary War what sort of government the new nation would have. It was not even clear that it would be one nation. The people thought of themselves as citizens of their states, and might well have set up thirteen countries, with or without some sort of alliance between them.

The "government" that was set up during the war had very little authority and was not trusted by the people. The country was still unstable and could easily have slipped into a dictatorship of some kind.

The Revolution up until 1783 had been a revolt against the old system, now the Americans had to create a new one. This was not to be a war of guns, but a war of ideas. Victory was not to be won by conquest, but by compromise. The result of this part of the Revolution was the surprisingly successful Constitution of the United States of America.

SECTION OBJECTIVES

Review these objectives. When you have completed this section, you should be able to:

1. Identify the men who contributed to the Revolution.
3. Identify and describe the governing bodies that acted for the colonies/states.
6. Explain the Articles of Confederation and why they were replaced.
7. Describe the Constitutional Convention.
8. Describe the main features of the Constitution and the process by which it was approved.

VOCABULARY

Study these words to enhance your learning success in this section.

confederation (kun fed′ u rā shun). A group of countries or states joined together for a special purpose; a league.

executive (eg zek′ yu tiv). The person or branch of government that has the duty and power of putting laws into effect.

impeach (im pēch′). To accuse a public official of wrong conduct in office before a proper tribunal.

inflation (in flā′ shun). A rise in the price of goods.

ratify (rat′ u fī). To confirm or approve.

sovereign (sov′ ren). Independent of the control of another government or governments.

The Articles of Confederation

The first constitution of the United States was called the Articles of **Confederation**. It was adopted by the Second Continental Congress in 1777. However, it could not go into effect until all thirteen of the states **ratified** it. That did not happen until 1781, and by 1789, it was superseded by the new Constitution. These eight years were a stepping stone between America's first government under the Second Continental Congress, and her permanent government under the Constitution.

America's first constitution. The Articles of Confederation formed only a "firm league of friendship" between the thirteen **sovereign** states of America. It was less than a union, but more than an alliance. The states kept the power to tax, regulate commerce, and provide justice. The central government was very weak, for good reason. The states would not have accepted gaining their freedom from Britain just to lose it to a more local tyrant! The Articles provided an in-between step that allowed them time to accept the need for a strong central government.

The national government under the Articles was very weak. The states did not want a strong **executive**, like the king, to threaten their liberties. So, the Articles had no executive to enforce the laws. There was also no national system of courts or judges. The Confederation was ruled by a very weak Congress.

Congress was deliberately limited in its power. It could not raise taxes, it could only request money from the states. It also could not regulate commerce between the states. The voting in the Congress was one representative per state. All important matters had to be passed by two-thirds of the states and any changes to the Articles had to be unanimous. Congress was supposed to conduct the Confederation's foreign affairs (including those with the Native Americans), declare war, establish an army and navy, set up a postal service, and settle disputes between the states.

| The U.S. in 1783

But, without a steady source of income or authority to enforce its laws, Congress was severely shackled in its efforts to act for the nation.

The Northwest Territory. In spite of its weaknesses, the Congress under the Articles had one very notable success. That was the handling of the Northwest Territory. The Northwest Territory (or Old Northwest) was the land west of the established states and north of the Ohio River. This land came under the control of Congress shortly after the ratification of the Articles of Confederation.

Several of the original colonies had been granted in their charters rights to vast amounts of land west of the Appalachians. The states who did not have land claims there, notably Pennsylvania and Maryland, insisted that all of the western lands be given to the national government.

They argued the land-rich states could use land sales to pay off debts from the Revolution, while the states without excess land could not. Since all the states shared in the expense of the war, all should share in the bounty of the western land sales through the national government. Eventually, all the states agreed to this and the land outside the current boundaries was placed under the control of the national government.

The Land Ordinance. First of all, congress had to decide how to sell the land and what to do with the proceeds. These questions were answered with the Land Ordinance of 1785. The law required the land to be surveyed and divided for sale. It was divided into townships measuring six miles by six miles. The townships were further divided into thirty-six sections, each one square mile. The sixteenth section was sold to benefit public education. The money made from the sales was used to pay off the national debt.

Northwest Ordinance. The second decision Congress had to make, was how the land would be governed. Would the western lands be colonies for the east? Would they be subject to the control that Britain had once placed on America? These questions were answered for the Northwest and for all later U.S. territories by the Northwest Ordinance.

The Northwest Ordinance was a piece of legislation that was to have long-lasting effects in America. The Confederation Congress established the pattern that would be followed for over a hundred and fifty years of national expansion. The law required that new territories be under federal control until they had a population of 60,000. At that point, they could be admitted to the Confederation by Congress as a new state, having all the rights and privileges of the old ones. This farsighted piece of legislation ensured that America could grow with equal rights for citizens in newly added lands. America would be a free nation, not an empire.

Check the statements that were true of the Articles of Confederation.

3.1 _____ had a weak executive

3.2 _____ the states were sovereign

3.3 _____ Congress could not raise taxes

3.4 _____ it was only an alliance

3.5 _____ Congress could not declare war

3.6 _____ the national court system was weak

3.7 _____ the Congress could not pass any effective legislation

3.8 _____ Congress could handle Native Americans affairs

3.9 _____ commerce between the states was handled by Congress

3.10 _____ it was ratified in 1781

3.11 _____ it was the first government of the United States

3.12 _____ it was in effect for about twenty years

Complete these sentences.

3.13 The Confederation Congress passed the _____

to set up the government for the Northwest Territory.

3.14 All state land claims in the Northwest Territory were given to _____

_____ .

3.15 Money made from land sales in the Old Northwest were used to pay

_____ .

3.16 The Land Ordinance divided the Old Northwest into townships measuring _____

by _____ .

3.17 Townships, under the Land Ordinance, were divided into _____ sections of one square mile

each and section _____ was sold to benefit public education.

3.18 A territory could be admitted as a state when the population reached _____ .

Problems under the Articles. The biggest problem facing the Confederation Congress in the 1780s, was the national economy. The nation had immense debts and no way of paying them. Congress could only request money from the states and it never got all it requested. Foreign nations did not trust American credit. Several of the states were printing money, freely causing widespread **inflation**.

Congress also could not regulate trade between the states and that was causing more problems. Several of the states were putting tariffs on goods from other states. Trade with foreign nations was regulated as each state saw fit. Some of the states set very low tariffs to attract foreign trade, while others set high ones to protect their own manufacturers.

There also was unrest among the people. The bad economy had put many people into debt. Debtors and creditors clashed. Several of the states, like Rhode Island, deliberately allowed inflation to help the debtors. (Inflation means money loses value and debts are paid back later with the less valuable currency. Or put another way, you pay back less than you borrowed.) The Revolution had encouraged rebellion over taxes as well as a disrespect for law and property. These attitudes were coming back to haunt the new government.

Annapolis Convention. The problems over commerce were substantial enough to call a meeting in Annapolis, Maryland in 1786 to deal with them. Only five states sent delegates. With such a poor showing, nothing could be done. But, Alexander Hamilton of New York managed to have the convention accept his recommendation for a meeting in Philadelphia the following year to revise the Articles. That meeting might have met the same fate except for an event in Massachusetts that frightened the states into action.

Shays' Rebellion. Massachusetts had not inflated its currency. In fact, that state had raised taxes and refused to help debtors. Farmers, many of them veterans from the Revolution, faced the loss of their farms due to personal debts or unpaid taxes. In 1786 the western part of the state erupted in rebellion under the leadership of Daniel Shays, a former Revolutionary soldier. The rebels demanded lower taxes, debt relief, and more paper money (inflation, also called cheap money).

Shays' Rebellion forced the closure of several courts to prevent foreclosures and imprisonment for debtors. The alarmed wealthy merchants of the east, who controlled the government, raised an army under General Benjamin Lincoln to quell the rebellion. He did so in early 1787 after several small skirmishes in which a few of the rebels were killed. Shays fled the state and was later pardoned.

Shays' Rebellion frightened the property owners and wealthy businessmen of the Confederation. These were the men in power in the state governments due to the property requirements to vote and hold office. They understood the threat Shays and others were to the process of law and government. They saw the need for a stronger national government to restore order and prevent mob rule. The Confederation Congress reluctantly approved the meeting called by the Annapolis Convention now scheduled for the summer of 1787 in Philadelphia. Its stated purpose was to revise the Articles of Confederation. It would do much more than that.

 Answer true or false.

If the statement is false, change some of the nouns or adjectives to make it true.

3.19 _____ Inflation helps creditors.

3.20 _____ The Annapolis Convention was called to discuss problems over state boundaries.

3.21 _____ Seven states sent delegates to the Annapolis Convention.

3.22 _____ The largest problem facing the Confederation Congress was the economy.

3.23 _____ Shays' Rebellion occurred in Massachusetts.

3.24 _____ Shays' Rebellion was put down by an army under the command of General Benjamin Lincoln.

3.25 _____ The poor people of the Confederation were frightened by Shays' Rebellion.

3.26 _____ America had good credit abroad under the Confederation.

3.27 _____ Some of the states put tariffs on goods from other states.

3.28 _____ States under the Confederation had the same tariffs on foreign goods.

Constitutional Convention

The meeting called for by the Annapolis Convention finally began on May 25, 1787 in the State House in Philadelphia. (It was later renamed Independence Hall). The fifty-five delegates came from twelve of the thirteen states. (Independent Rhode Island refused to participate). They were all well-to-do men chosen by the wealthy members of the state assemblies. The most radical leaders of the Revolution, such as Samuel Adams and Patrick Henry, were not there.

The men who did come were basically conservative, men who wanted a strong central government to prevent further rebellions. Among them were George Washington, Benjamin Franklin, James Madison (whose careful work earned him the title "Father of the Constitution"),

Alexander Hamilton (a fierce advocate of a strong central government), and a host of lesser-known "Founding Fathers." Most of the delegates had served in the Revolution as either a soldier or administrator. They all understood the problems under the weak rule of Congress. Moreover, most had experience writing constitutions since all of the states had to write them after independence.

The delegates made several key decisions at the beginning. First of all, they elected George Washington as president of the convention. His immense prestige made him an obvious choice and gave the whole meeting a greater chance of success. The delegates also decided that their meetings would be completely secret. That enabled the men to debate and

| The delegates at the Constitutional Convention

compromise without being subject to outside pressure or having to explain their decisions before a final agreement was reached. (James Madison took detailed notes about the debates and decisions that were later published). Finally, the delegates decided not to revise the Articles, as they had been instructed. Instead, they decided to start over and write a whole new constitution. They had no authority to do this, but they felt that the Articles could not be amended to meet the country's needs.

Bundle of compromises. The Constitution of the United States was a bundle of compromises. The most important one involved the dispute over representation in Congress. The larger states supported the *Virginia Plan* which would have the states represented in Congress according to their population. This would give the more populous states more votes and the smaller states feared they would dominate the government. The smaller states, therefore, favored the *New Jersey Plan* in which each state had the same number of votes, no matter what its population. The larger states argued that they would pay more taxes without having any more representation.

This issue threatened to divide the convention and stop all progress on a constitution. Finally, an alternative, the *Connecticut Plan*, was proposed and approved. Under this plan, also called the *Great Compromise*, Congress was made up of two houses. Each state would have two representatives in the upper house, the Senate. But, the states would send representatives to the lower house, the House of Representatives, based on their population. Laws would have to pass both houses, so the Senate would protect the smaller states from being dominated by the larger. Also, laws involving money issues could only begin in the House of Representatives where the members more closely represented the percentage of taxes paid by each state. This compromise put the convention back on track.

Another issue the delegates had to face involved the counting of enslaved people. States in the South that had a larger number of slaves wanted them to be counted as part of the population to determine how many seats they got in the House of Representatives. Northern states wanted the enslaved people to count for taxation purposes. The compromise that was reached counted each slave as three-fifths of a person for both population and taxation purposes.

Most of the delegates wanted to end the slave trade (the importation of more Africans) because of the brutality it involved. But, several of the southern states would not accept giving Congress the authority to do that. By way of a compromise, Congress was denied that authority until the year 1807 (at which point it did end the trade). These were the key compromises of the Constitution.

Checks and balances. In their need to establish order and settle their own differences, the delegates did not forget they had just fought a war against a tyrannical government. They were determined not to create another one. Instead, they created a government in which power was divided among several branches, so that each would balance and check the others.

The power of government was divided between three branches of government: executive, legislative, and judicial. The executive, the president, could veto laws passed by Congress and appoint judges. The legislature, Congress, could override a veto, approve the appointment of judges and could **impeach** the president if he broke the law. The judiciary were judges appointed for life that could also be impeached by Congress and could declare a law unconstitutional (that is not expressly stated in the Constitution, but was assumed). Thus, each branch of the government had some control over the other. This division of power was a deliberate plan by the delegates to prevent any one person or part of the government from becoming too powerful.

The power of government was also divided between the states and the new federal government. The sovereignty of the states was kept. They simply lost certain powers to the national government. Any powers not specifically given to the national government were still kept by the states. For example, the states would run the police forces, set up schools, and handle many other local matters. But, the national government was given several key powers including the right to tax and to regulate commerce between the states.

The Results. The delegates at the Constitutional Convention debated in secrecy for almost four months. Finally, on September 17, 1787 they signed the final document. Of the original fifty-five delegates, only forty-two were still there. Three of those refused to sign it. The rest did and used their substantial means and prestige to have it ratified.

The delegates had acted without authorization when they wrote a new constitution. They did so again when they did not send the document to Congress, but to the states. Since Rhode Island had not even attended, they knew it was impossible to get all the states to ratify it. Therefore, the delegates agreed that it would go into effect as soon as nine of the thirteen states (two-thirds) had accepted it. This was also the basis for amending the Constitution.

The publication of the Constitution was a shock to the American public. They had been expecting some amendments to improve the Articles of Confederation. This was a completely new plan of government unlike any used before in history by a nation. It created a strong central government to replace the "union " of states. It raised fears of tyranny and taxation. The last major battle of the Revolution was to be fought over this document.

 Answer these questions.

3.29 How many states were represented at the convention? _____

3.30 What social class did the delegates come from? _____

3.31 What three important decisions did the delegates make at the beginning of the convention?

    a. _____

    b. _____

    c. _____

3.32 What were the two proposals that were not accepted on representation in Congress? (Give the name of the plan and describe it.)

    a. _____

    _____

    b. _____

    _____

3.33 What was the other name of the Great Compromise? _____

3.34 What was the Great Compromise?

_____

_____

_____

3.35 Why would the compromise on counting slaves be called the Three-Fifths Compromise?

_____

_____

3.36 What compromise was made on controlling the slave trade?

_____

3.37 What were the three branches of government power was divided between?

a. _____   b. _____

c. _____

3.38 What check did the

a. executive have on the legislature?

_____

b. legislature have on the executive?

_____

c. judiciary have on the legislature and executive?

_____

d. executive have on the judiciary?

_____

e. legislature have on the judiciary?

_____

3.39 What happened to the sovereignty of the states?

_____

_____

3.40 Did all of the delegates sign the Constitution? _____

3.41 How many states had to ratify the Constitution to put it into effect? _____

The Battle of Ratification

Battle Lines. The signing of the Constitution was followed by six months of heated public debate. The people that favored the document were called Federalists. Those that opposed it Anti-Federalists. Generally, the Federalists were from the wealthier classes. They were merchants who wanted a strong government to protect trade, property owners who feared lawlessness, and educated people who understood the problems of governing under the Articles. The Anti-Federalists were usually the poorer people, who feared that a strong central government might enforce payment of personal debts. These people distrusted governments of all sorts, especially strong ones. These were reinforced by the radicals of the Revolution. These people had fought for liberty from oppressive government and were not going to give it up now. Others believed in the independence of the states and did not want them to give up that much power to another government.

The Battle. The Federalists defended the Constitution in a whole storm of papers, speeches, articles, and essays. The most famous defense was the *The Federalist*, a series of essays originally published in New York and then in the other states. They were written by Alexander Hamilton, James Madison, and John Jay under the name *Publicus*. This brilliant analysis of the nature of republican government and the details of the Constitution was eventually put into book form and is still sold today.

The Anti-Federalists responded with attacks on the Constitution. They had one concern that drew the most attention. The Constitution did not protect the basic rights of the people. Many of the state constitutions included statements specifically protecting the right to trial by jury, freedom of speech, the right to petition the government and other important freedoms. Without these, the Anti-Federalists feared the people would have no protection from this

THE NEW NATION

Delaware
Pennsylvania
New Jersey
Georgia
Connecticut
Massachusetts
Maryland
South Carolina
New Hampshire
Virginia
New York
North Carolina
Rhode Island

The last two states to ratify were North Carolina and Rhode Island, both of which were notorious for being dedicated to individual rights and distrusting government.

NORTH CAROLINA
Ratified the Constitution:
November 1789

RHODE ISLAND
Ratified the Constitution:
May 1790

powerful new government. The Federalists agreed this was a valid consideration. They promised that the first order of business for the new Congress would be to pass amendments protecting the key freedoms of the people. (These were eventually passed and ratified as the Bill of Rights, the first ten amendments to the Constitution).

The Victory. The states called special conventions to vote on ratification beginning in the winter of 1787-88. The strong, well reasoned defense of the Federalists carried the day. The problems of the Articles of Confederation also drove many to accept the proposal. The promise of a Bill of Rights won over many others who opposed the new government.

Slowly the Federalists won over the necessary states. Delaware was the first state to ratify in December of 1787. Pennsylvania, New Jersey, Georgia, Connecticut, and Massachusetts followed that winter. In the spring, Maryland and South Carolina ratified it. The Constitution went into effect in June of 1788 when the ninth state, New Hampshire, approved it.

Two important states had not ratified the Constitution when it went into effect: Virginia, the first, largest, and most populous state, as well as the large, commercially important state of New York. Both of these states knew that the union was going to be formed with or without them. Realizing that they could not hope to prosper independent of the new order, both states ratified the Constitution in the summer of 1788. With these additions, the new government had enough support to make a solid start.

The two states that had still not ratified were North Carolina and Rhode Island, both of which were notorious for being dedicated to individual rights and distrusting government. Both finally realized they could not hope to go it alone in this case. But, North Carolina did not ratify the Constitution until November of 1789. Stubborn Rhode Island, which did not even send delegates to the convention, did not join the union until May of 1790, over a year after the first president took office.

In the end, all thirteen states approved the Constitution and created a powerful republic. The reasons why they did it were clearly spelled out in the document's preamble which states:

We the people of the United States, in order to form a more perfect union, establish justice, insure domestic tranquility, provide for the common defense, promote the general welfare, and secure the blessings of liberty to ourselves and our posterity, do ordain and establish this Constitution for the United States of America.

Preamble to The Constitution

✎ **Complete these sentences.**

3.42 People who supported the Constitution were called _____ while opponents were called _____ .

3.43 The most serious objection to the Constitution was corrected with the passage of the _____ , the first ten amendments.

3.44 _____ was the first state to ratify the Constitution.

3.45 The Constitution went into effect after the state of _____ ratified it.

3.46 The two important states that had not ratified the Constitution when it went into effect were _____ and _____ .

3.47 The two states that did not ratify the Constitution until over a year after the others were _____ and _____ .

List the six reasons why the Constitution was written, according to the preamble.

3.48 1. _____

2. _____

3. _____

4. _____

5. _____

6. _____

Memorize the Preamble to the Constitution and recite it for your teacher.

TEACHER CHECK _____ _____
                    initials   date

Before you take this last Self Test, you may want to do one or more of these self checks.

1. _____ Read the objectives. See if you can do them.
2. _____ Restudy the material related to any objectives that you cannot do.
3. _____ Use the **SQ3R** study procedure to review the material:
   a. **S**can the sections.
   b. **Q**uestion yourself.
   c. **R**ead to answer your questions.
   d. **R**ecite the answers to yourself.
   e. **R**eview areas you did not understand.
4. _____ Review all vocabulary, activities, and Self Tests, writing a correct answer for every wrong answer.

SELF TEST 3

Match the following (each answer, 2 points).

3.01	_____ Articles of Confederation	a. essays in favor of the Constitution
3.02	_____ Northwest Ordinance	b. representation in Congress would be based on population
3.03	_____ Land Ordinance of 1785	c. first ten amendments to Constitution
3.04	_____ Annapolis Convention	d. meeting of five states that called for the Constitutional Convention
3.05	_____ Shays' Rebellion	e. representation by state in the Senate and by population in the House
3.06	_____ Virginia Plan	f. Thomas Paine's essay that turned American opinion to independence
3.07	_____ Great Compromise	g. territory of 60,000 can be admitted as a state
3.08	_____ Bill of Rights	h. Northwest divided into towns of 36 square miles for sale to pay off debt
3.09	_____ *The Federalist*	i. America's first constitution
3.010	_____ *Common Sense*	j. frightened many property owners to support the Constitution

Name the person (each answer, 3 points).

3.011 _____ America's representative in France during the Revolution; played the "natural man," delegate to Constitutional Convention

3.012 _____ Commander-in-chief of American forces during the Revolution; president of the Constitutional Convention

3.013 _____ Author of the Declaration of Independence

3.014 _____ Father of the Constitution; took notes of the debate at the Constitutional Convention

3.015 _____ Hero at Ticonderoga and Saratoga; traitor at West Point

3.016 _____ American commander of southern army after Camden; lost all the battles; won the campaign

3.017 _____ French aristocrat; volunteer American soldier; American hero; gave his own money to the cause

3.018 _____ President of the Second Continental Congress; signed the Declaration of Independence in large letters

3.019 _____ Led a group of frontiersmen to capture British forts in the west, and 180 miles through waist-deep swamps to recapture Vincennes

3.020 _____ British commander in the south after the capture of Charleston; surrendered at Yorktown

Answer these questions (each answer, 4 points).

3.021 What battle was the turning point of the Revolutionary War?

_____

3.022 What were the three branches of government set up by the Constitution?

a. _____ b. _____

c. _____

3.023 How can the president check the power of Congress under the Constitution?

_____

3.024 How many states had to approve the Constitution before it went into effect?

_____

3.025 What was the economic theory used by the British to govern the colonies?

_____

3.026 What were the three American reactions to the Stamp Act?

a. _____ b. _____

c. _____

Answer true or false (each answer, 1 point).

3.027 _____ Rhode Island was the last of the thirteen states to ratify the Constitution.

3.028 _____ The Articles of Confederation did not allow Congress to raise taxes.

3.029 _____ The Confederation Congress could not declare war.

3.030 _____ The Constitution allowed slaves to count as one-third of a person for taxes and two-thirds for representation.

3.031 _____ The Constitution forbids Congress from ever regulating the slave trade.

3.032 _____ Under the Constitution, Congress can impeach the president for breaking the law.

3.033 _____ The Confederation Congress could regulate commerce between the states.

3.034 _____ Inflation helps debtors.

3.035 _____ Monmouth Courthouse was the last major battle in the North during the Revolutionary War.

3.036 _____ The Northwest Ordinance was passed by the Confederation Congress.

80 / 100   SCORE _____   TEACHER _____ _____
                                                    initials   date

Before taking the LIFEPAC Test, you may want to do one or more of these self checks.

1. _____ Read the objectives. See if you can do them.
2. _____ Restudy the material related to any objectives that you cannot do.
3. _____ Use the **SQ3R** study procedure to review the material.
4. _____ Review activities, Self Tests, and LIFEPAC vocabulary words.
5. _____ Restudy areas of weakness indicated by the last Self Test.

HISTORY & GEOGRAPHY 804
A Firm Foundation (1789–1820)

LIFEPAC Test is located in the center of the booklet. Please remove before starting the unit.

Author:
Theresa Buskey, B.A., J.D.

Editor:
Alan Christopherson, M.S.

Westover Studios Design Team:
Phillip Pettet, Creative Lead
Teresa Davis, DTP Lead
Nick Castro
Andi Graham
Jerry Wingo

Alpha Omega
PUBLICATIONS

804 N. 2nd Ave. E.
Rock Rapids, IA 51246-1759

A Firm Foundation (1789–1820)

Introduction

The first forty years after the ratification of the Constitution was a time of foundation building. The new Constitution had to be transformed from ideas on paper to a practical, working government. Even with a good plan, a weak original government would set precedents that would be hard to change. It was up to first president, George Washington, and his advisors to use the blueprint of the Constitution to build a good foundation for the structure of the United States.

The early years of our nation were complicated by events in Europe. The French Revolution began in 1789. The king of France was overthrown and executed. The Revolution degenerated into a bloodbath called the Reign of Terror (1793-94). A war began in Europe as other monarchs tried to interfere. Finally, General Napoleon Bonaparte seized power in France (1799) and conquered much of Europe. He was defeated by an alliance led by Britain (1813) and went into exile (1814). In 1815 he returned to be defeated again.

The war put America in a difficult position. France had been America's ally in the Revolution, but Britain was America's biggest trading partner. Both sides had interfered with American trade during the long years of conflict, but the actions of the British were especially infuriating. The hard-pressed American leaders did not want to get into a European war. By 1812, the long-suffering Americans could take no more; war was declared on Britain. The second war of independence, the War of 1812, finished laying the foundation of America. With the foundation laid, the country built toward its future.

Objectives

Read these objectives. The objectives tell you what you will be able to do when you have successfully completed this LIFEPAC. When you have finished this LIFEPAC, you should be able to:

1. Describe the important events of the first five presidential administrations.

2. Describe the Great Seal of the United States.

3. Describe the course and nature of America's problems with Britain that led to the War of 1812.

4. Describe the growth, policies, and decline of the Federalist Party.

5. Describe the growth and policies of the Democratic-Republican Party.

6. Describe the course and results of the War of 1812.

7. Describe how America changed after the War of 1812.

8. Describe the development of the power of the Supreme Court under John Marshall.

9. Explain the reasons behind U.S. policy decisions from 1789 to the early 1820s.

Survey the LIFEPAC. Ask yourself some questions about this study and write your questions here.

_____
_____
_____
_____
_____
_____
_____
_____
_____
_____
_____
_____
_____
_____
_____

1. FEDERALIST ERA

The Federalists led the victorious battle for the Constitution after the Constitutional Convention. When the first government was formed under the new plan in 1789, it was dominated by the same Federalists. They controlled the U.S. government through the Washington and Adams administrations, but they were driven from power in 1801 when Thomas Jefferson became president under the Democratic-Republican Party.

The republic faced many difficulties in the first twelve years under the Constitution. Washington had to establish exactly what all the descriptions of his duties meant and what the newly created post required of him. Alexander Hamilton, the first secretary of the treasury, had to repair the poor state of the nation's finances. A rebellion broke out against the new taxes which such repairs required. America had to deal with the French Revolution and a European war. Trade problems threatened war with both Britain and France. Controversy brewed over a treaty with Britain and a bribery scandal with France. Finally, the Federalists began their own decline by threatening freedom of speech in an attempt to control the passions of the era.

SECTION OBJECTIVES

Review these objectives. When you have completed this section, you should be able to:

1. Describe the important events of the first five presidential administrations.
2. Describe the Great Seal of the United States.
3. Describe the course and nature of America's problems with Britain that led to the War of 1812.
4. Describe the growth, policies, and decline of the Federalist Party.
5. Describe the growth and policies of the Democratic-Republican Party.
9. Explain the reasons behind U.S. policy decisions from 1789 to the early 1820s.

VOCABULARY

Study these words to enhance your learning success in this section.

agrarian (u grar' ē an). Concerning agriculture or rural matters.

bond (bond). A certificate issued by a government or company which promises to pay back, with interest; the money borrowed from the buyer of the certificate.

nominal (nom' i nal). In name only; not real or actual.

nullify (nul' i fī). To deprive of legal force; make void.

partisan (pär' ti zan). A very strong supporter of a party, cause, or faction.

repudiation (ri pyoo' dē ā' shun). The act of rejecting the validity of something.

Note: *All vocabulary words in this LIFEPAC appear in* **boldface** *print the first time they are used. If you are not sure of the meaning when you are reading, study the definitions given.*

Pronunciation Key: hat, āge, cãre, fär; let, ēqual, tėrm; it, īce; hot, ōpen, ôrder; oil; out; cup, pu̇t, rüle; child; long; thin; /ғʜ/ for then; /zh/ for measure; /u/ or /ə/ represents /a/ in about, /e/ in taken, /i/ in pencil, /o/ in lemon, and /u/ in circus.

AMERICA from **1789** to **1820**

George Washington
1789–1797

John Adams
1797–1801
Federalist

Thomas Jefferson
1801–1809
Democratic-Republican

James Madison
1809–1817
Democratic-Republican

James Monroe
1817–1825
Democratic-Republican

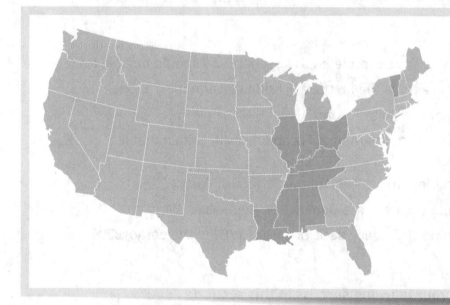

STATES ADMITTED TO THE UNION

Vermont	1791
Kentucky	1792
Tennessee	1796
Ohio	1803
Louisiana	1812
Indiana	1816
Mississippi	1817
Alabama	1819
Illinois	1819

POPULATION of the United States of America

1820   9,638,453

1790   3,929,000

Washington's First Term

There was never any doubt as to who would be elected as the first president of the United States. George Washington was the one person who had the public trust and the stature to take the job. He had the support of both the Federalists and Anti-Federalists. It can reasonably be argued that the position was created with him in mind. The Constitution required each state to choose electors who would then choose a president. When the vote was counted in April of 1789, the tally was unanimous for Washington. (He was the only president to receive a unanimous electoral vote). John Adams was chosen as vice president.

The same qualities that made Washington a great general also made him a superb first president. He did not like politics and accepted the presidency only because he felt the nation needed him. He commanded the respect of his subordinates and gave his tremendous prestige to the new post. He was careful, fair, and methodical. He chose wise counselors and listened to them before making his decisions. He provided the stability and thoughtful leadership the new nation so desperately needed in those early years.

Inauguration. Washington received word of his election at his home in Mount Vernon, Virginia. He immediately left on the long journey to New York City, which was America's temporary capital. He was greeted all along the route by cheering crowds. He took the oath of office on the balcony of Federal Hall, overlooking Wall Street, on April 30, 1789. He then gave an inaugural address in the chambers of the Senate.

Washington set a formal tone for the new office, mainly because of his own rather formal personality. He would bow, not shake hands, to greet visitors. He dressed richly and drove about in a handsome coach. Visitors could see him during his weekly open house or make an appointment. His wife Martha held a formal reception every Friday evening that the president attended. The office of president was less than a king, but more than a simple politician.

| George Washington's inauguration

Cabinet. The new Congress created three departments to help the president run the government: foreign affairs (state), war, and treasury. An attorney general, the attorney for the government, was added later. Washington choose men he knew and trusted to head these departments. They came to be his personal advisors and eventually met together to discuss decisions, forming the president's cabinet.

Washington stayed out of **partisan** politics as much as he could, but he recognized the conflicts of the day and represented both sides in his cabinet. Thomas Jefferson was the first secretary of state. He was a firm believer in a weak federal government, an **agrarian** country, and rule by the "common people." He eventually became the leader of the Democratic-Republican Party. Alexander Hamilton was the first secretary of the treasury. He was a Federalist leader who believed in a strong central government, a commercial nation, and rule by the "elite." The other cabinet members were Secretary of War Henry Knox and Attorney General Edmund Randolph.

Washington did not officially attach himself to either of the new political parties. However, mainly on the basis of Hamilton's arguments, he supported much of the Federalist agenda. As a result, Washington came under attack from the Anti-Federalists, who eventually developed into the Democratic-Republican Party.

Finances. The main problem facing the new government was the same one they had faced under the Articles of Confederation—money. The nation was deeply in debt and had no stable currency. Hamilton proposed the government pay the debt at full value and assume the Revolutionary War debts of the states as well. Hamilton intended to build the power of the federal government by establishing it financially and having the people look to it, not the state governments, for their money.

There was a tremendous amount of opposition to Hamilton's plan. Few people believed the **bonds** issued by the Revolutionary government would ever be paid. The war veterans and people who originally held the bonds had sold them for a fraction of what they were worth. Most were owned by wealthy men who could afford to hold them and wait. Many felt that it was unfair to give the profit to these men. Hamilton wanted the support of these wealthy citizens for the new government. He wanted to give the rich and well-born a stake in the new system.

Most of the southern states had already paid off their war debts. They objected to also paying off the northern debts through the federal government. Eventually, they agreed to the plan in exchange for placing the new national capital in the south, on the Potomac River between Maryland and Virginia. The rest of Hamilton's plan was accepted because Congress believed that a government should pay its lawful debts and knew it would be impossible to find the original owners of the bonds.

The third part of Hamilton's plan called for the establishment of a national bank. The bank would be partially owned by the government and would be used to deposit government funds. It also would issue a stable paper currency backed by the deposits in the bank.

The bank ran into violent opposition in Congress. Most of the supporters came from the north which favored a strong currency and bank to build trade and manufacturing. State's rights advocates did not want a large central bank which would compete with their state banks. The measure was passed after a heated debate and was sent to Washington for his signature.

Washington was deeply concerned about whether the bill was constitutional. He asked Jefferson (against) and Hamilton (for) to each give him a written opinion on the matter. Jefferson argued that the Constitution did not specifically authorize a bank. He favored a "strict construction" of the Constitution. The government could only do things specifically allowed by the Constitution, a position that would have severely limited federal power. Hamilton, on the other hand, persuasively argued for a "loose construction." The Constitution said that the Congress could pass any laws "necessary and proper" to carrying out the powers of the government. Since the government was authorized to collect taxes, a bank was both necessary and proper to fulfill that function. Washington agreed with Hamilton and signed the bill.

Money to pay the debts and finance the bank came from taxes. The primary tax of that day was the tariff, a tax on goods imported from other countries. A tariff also made foreign goods more expensive, thus protecting the few American manufacturers. This fit well with Hamilton's far-sighted plan for America to become a manufacturing nation. Congress also passed an excise tax on distilled liquor to supplement the tariff income.

The prosperity of the new government depended on trade which produced tariff income. Most of America's trade was with Britain. Thus, Hamilton and the Federalists came to favor England over France in foreign policy. This created yet another difference with Jefferson's supporters who favored France, a country that found itself in the middle of its own revolution.

Match these people.

1.1	_____ George Washington	a.	secretary of war
1.2	_____ John Adams	b.	attorney general
1.3	_____ Thomas Jefferson	c.	chosen unanimously by the electors
1.4	_____ Alexander Hamilton	d.	vice president
1.5	_____ Edmund Randolph	e.	secretary of state
1.6	_____ Henry Knox	f.	secretary of the treasury

Answer these questions.

1.7 What were Hamilton's three main proposals for the nation's finances?

a. _____

b. _____

c. _____

1.8 What did the southern states get in exchange for the federal government taking over the state's debts?

_____

1.9 What form of taxation was the main source of income for the new government?

_____

1.10 Why did some people not want the war bonds to be paid at full value?

_____

_____

_____

Put an *H* beside the policies supported by Hamilton and a *J* beside those supported by Jefferson.

1.11 _____ favored Britain

1.12 _____ strong central government

1.13 _____ agrarian society

1.14 _____ favored France

1.15 _____ weak federal government

1.16 _____ "strict construction" of Constitution

1.17 _____ "loose construction" of Constitution

1.18 _____ commercial society

THE GREAT SEAL

Nations are represented by symbols. The most famous symbol of the United States is our flag, the Stars and Stripes. Another important symbol is the Great Seal, which was adopted in 1782 by the nation's first government, the Second Continental Congress. Most people have probably seen the front or "obverse" of the Great Seal of the United States. It appears on federal buildings, vehicles, laws, and documents as well as coins and currency. The back or "reverse" is less well known, but it does appear on the back of the one-dollar bill. The Seal is rich with symbolism, much of which refers to the Christian foundation of our nation.

| The Great Seal of the United States

The Obverse of the Great Seal

On the obverse side of the seal are these symbols:

1. The Crest: At the top of the seal is a cluster of thirteen white stars on a blue field, which represents the original thirteen states. A ring of golden light is breaking through a white cloud which surrounds the stars. This light is a symbol of God's constant protection and guidance.

2. The National Coat of Arms: The remainder of the seal is our nation's coat of arms, which consists of these symbols;

   a. American Eagle: The eagle was selected to represent the United States because of its dignity, size, strength, and majestic appearance. The head and tail feathers are white, the claws and beak are yellow. Franklin wanted our symbol to be a turkey, but he was wisely outvoted by the committee.

   b. Shield: On the eagle's breast is a shield. The solid blue bar at the top represents the national government (originally just Congress). The seven white stripes and six red stripes stand for the first thirteen states.

   c. Scroll and Motto: Held by the eagle's beak is a golden scroll on which are written these words in Latin:
   E PLURIBUS UNUM
   The English translation of this motto is "One out of many." Many states make up the one nation, the United States of America.

   d. Thirteen Arrows: The eagle's left talon is clutching a bundle of thirteen arrows. This suggests that we will defend our nation.

   e. Olive Branch: The eagle's right talon is clutching a green olive branch with thirteen blue-tinted olives. The olive branch is a symbol of peace. Since the right side is considered to be more important, holding the olive branch in the right talon indicates that the United States prefers peace to war. The eagle is also facing the peace side rather than the war side.

The Reverse of the Great Seal

This part of the Great Seal is not as well known. The parts and their meanings are:

1. The Pyramid: In the center of the Seal is a pyramid built on the earth with a blue sky background. On the base of the pyramid are the Roman numerals MDCCLXXVI (1776), the year our nation was born. Thirteen layers of stone are in the pyramid, representing the original thirteen states. The pyramid is unfinished, indicating that our nation will continue to grow. The pyramid shape symbolizes the strength and stability of the United States.

2. The Eye: Above the pyramid is a large eye within a blue triangle surrounded by a golden light. The eye is a symbol that God is watching over our nation. The light represents God's glory and majesty.

3. Latin Mottoes:

   a. *ANNUIT COEPTIS* is written across the top of the Seal in golden letters. This means: *He (God) has favored our undertaking.*

   b. *NOVUS ORDO SECLORUM* is written in black letters on a golden scroll across the bottom. This means: *A new order of the ages.*

The Great Seal

On the Great Seal.

1.19 Name five ways that the original thirteen states are represented.

a. _____   b. _____

c. _____   d. _____

e. _____

1.20 Name two ways the presence of God is represented.

a. _____

b. _____

1.21 Why is the olive branch in the eagle's right talon? _____

_____

1.22 What does "E Pluribus Unum" mean? _____

Washington's Second Term

Washington wanted to retire after his first term. However, his friends urged him to stay on for another term for the sake of the country. He agreed and was unanimously re-elected in 1792. In March 1793, he was inaugurated in Philadelphia, which was the new temporary capital. Adams also returned as vice president.

European War. Washington received word of a general war in Europe a month into his second term. France was at war with Britain, Austria, Spain, and Prussia. France had been America's primary ally during the Revolution, and the treaty of alliance obligated the U.S. to aid them now. However, that treaty had been signed with the king of France who had been executed in the French Revolution. Supporters of the French Revolution wanted to honor the treaty. But even Jefferson was reluctant to get into another war. The Federalists feared the effect that war with Britain would have on trade and urged neutrality.

America was not strong militarily or politically. There was no army, and the new government had only been in place for four years. The pressures of a war could easily destroy all that had been built. Washington decided that the nation could not afford to be involved in a European war and issued a Proclamation of Neutrality on April 22nd. This continued to be the policy of the U.S. for most of the remaining years of this long war. American leaders desperately tried to keep out of the conflict as long as they could in order to buy time for their nation to grow strong.

Citizen Genêt. The republican government of France sent a new representative to America in April of 1793. He was Citizen (the title used by all in the Revolution) Edmond Genêt, an enthusiastic and tactless man. He had been commissioned to renew the treaty of friendship with America and obtain a new trade treaty. What he did was create a huge mess for Washington.

Genêt was received with joy by French supporters in America. He began at once to commission privateers to attack British shipping from American ports. He also tried to organize expeditions against the Spanish and British lands in America. Washington received him coolly, but Genêt did not take the hint. He ignored the Neutrality Proclamation and appealed to the American people to support France in the war. All this activity threatened to convince Britain that America was not truly neutral. Washington finally asked France to recall Genêt. He was stripped of his authority by a new government in France and stayed in the U.S. for fear of execution upon his return. American neutrality held.

Whiskey Rebellion. The excise tax passed by Congress during Washington's first administration had hit the northwestern farmers hard. It was difficult for these frontier farmers to make a profit shipping their grain to markets in the east because of the cost. Therefore, they routinely distilled their grain into liquor which was easier to transport and provided a good profit. The excise tax was immensely unpopular among these men and sparked a frontier revolt called the Whiskey Rebellion.

The Whiskey Rebellion began in 1794 in western Pennsylvania. The farmers there drew up resolutions against the tax, attacked the tax collectors, and terrorized court officials. The governor refused to act, so Washington called out the militia in the other states to enforce the law. The response was an army of over 13,000 men, more than Washington had for much of the Revolution. The rebellion scattered, and Washington pardoned the two culprits who were caught. The government's firmness made rebellious individuals use voting, rather than fighting, as the best means for pursuing their goals.

Problem with Britain. During his second term, Washington had to deal with the increasing problems with Great Britain. England still kept possession of several western forts in U.S. territory. It continued to support the Native American population there, hoping to use them as a buffer between the U.S. and Canada. As the war progressed with France, Britain began

| John Jay, negotiator with the British

seizing U.S. ships and cargoes trading with France or French colonies. The British also would search U.S. ships for British sailors who had become U.S. citizens. These men and many others who had never been British citizens were "impressed" or forced into serving in the British navy. Americans were outraged by this treatment of their vessels and citizens.

Jay's Treaty. Washington, hoping to avoid a war, and at the urging of the Federalists, sent John Jay to London to negotiate a settlement. He succeeded in obtaining a treaty in late 1794. The British agreed to evacuate the American forts, pay some compensation for the seized cargoes, and improve U.S. trading rights with Britain. However, the agreement mentioned nothing about ending their interference with American shipping or impressing of American sailors. The treaty restated the obligation of Americans to pay back debts owed to Britain from before the Revolution. Washington, believing it was the best he could get, submitted it to the Senate for approval.

The treaty was violently unpopular. Westerners were angry that it did not deal with the English support of the Native Americans. Southerners were angry that it did not require Britain to pay for slaves taken during the Revolution. Supporters of France saw it as a rejection of the nation's obligation to the French people. Patriotic Americans were angered by the extension of trade with a nation that freely mistreated American citizens. Even Hamilton, who needed the treaty to prevent a war and keep his financial system on track, did not like it. However, the pro-British, pro-trade Federalists dominated the Senate and after weeks of debate, it was approved. The nation was able to avoid a war for the time being.

Jay's Treaty did have one positive effect. Spain became nervous over the possibility of a British-American alliance in North America and settled some of her outstanding disputes with the U.S. A Spanish-American treaty was signed in 1795. It gave Americans the right to use the Mississippi and bring their goods through the Spanish-controlled port of New Orleans without paying any duty. It set the southern boundary of the U.S. and contained a Spanish promise to control Native Americans in their territory. This treaty helped restore the damaged national pride.

Farewell Address. Washington had come under savage attack for his policies and Jay's Treaty during his second administration. He was weary of public life and discouraged by the division of the government into factions. Washington believed political parties were a threat to the unity of the nation, but he had been unable to prevent them. Jefferson had even resigned from the cabinet because of Washington's support of Hamilton.

Washington announced that he would not accept re-election again. He set a "two-terms only" precedent which was followed by every president until Franklin Roosevelt in 1940. (After that, the president was limited to two terms by a constitutional amendment). He also published the *Farewell Address* that issued two warnings to the American people. The first was to avoid party politics. This was ignored. The second was that America should avoid all permanent alliances like the one made with France during the Revolution since they would draw us into foreign wars. This admonition became a key part of American foreign policy for generations. America did not sign a permanent military alliance again until after World War II (1938-1945).

 Complete the following.

1.23 Washington reacted to the War in Europe in 1793 by issuing the _____ _____ .

1.24 In 1793 France was at war with _____ _____ .

1.25 The French republican representative to the U.S. in 1793 was (including his title) _____ .

1.26 Name three things the French envoy did that threatened U.S. neutrality.

    a. _____

    b. _____

    c. _____

1.27 What were the problems America was having with Britain?

a. _____

b. _____

c. _____

d. _____

1.28 What did the British agree to do under Jay's Treaty?

a. _____

b. _____

c. _____

1.29 Why did so many Americans object to Jay's Treaty?

_____

_____

_____

1.30 What was the Whiskey Rebellion and how was it settled?

_____

_____

_____

1.31 What two things did Washington recommend that Americans avoid in the *Farewell Address*?

_____ and _____

1.32 Washington set the precedent that the president serves _____ terms.

Adams Administration

Election of 1796. The elections of George Washington had been uncontested. In the election of 1796, however, there were three candidates. Hamilton was too unpopular to run as a candidate, so the Federalist faction supported John Adams or Thomas Pinckney (backed by Hamilton). The Democratic-Republicans supported Thomas Jefferson. With Washington no longer acting as a unifying factor, the verbal mud flew back and forth, further separating the two developing political parties. Adams won by three electoral votes. The system at the time did not take political parties into account, and the runner-up in electoral votes, Thomas Jefferson, received the vice presidency. The messy situation of having a president from one political party and his vice president from another was eventually prevented by the 12th Amendment to the Constitution, adopted in 1804.

John Adams was a lawyer from Massachusetts and had been an active participant in the political end of the Revolution. He had worked to oppose the Stamp Act, followed his conscience in defending the British soldiers responsible for the Boston Massacre, served in the First and Second Continental Congress, and represented America in Europe during the Revolutionary War. He assisted in the negotiations with Britain at the end of the war and was America's first ambassador to the former mother country. He returned home in 1788 and was selected to serve under Washington as vice president.

Adams was a very capable statesman but tended to be cold and sharp in person. He and Thomas Jefferson had become friends during the Revolution. Their political differences would temporarily end their relationship until after both had retired from office. Adams and Hamilton did not get along at all. Adams represented the moderate part of the Federalist party while Hamilton's views were more extreme. This split would do tremendous damage to the Federalist Party.

Adams kept all of Washington's cabinet when he took office in 1797. Hamilton had resigned earlier, but most of the other cabinet members kept him informed of their activities and relied on his advice. This further aggravated the problems between the two men and their supporters. Adams also inherited from Washington the problems in Europe, and those would dominate his time in office.

XYZ Affair. The Jay Treaty had triggered a crisis with France. The French saw it as a **repudiation** of the French-American treaty signed during the Revolution. The latest French government, the Directory, began to seriously harass U.S. trade and insultingly refused to receive a new American ambassador. Adams sent a special three-man delegation to France to try to resolve the dispute.

The American delegation arrived in France in 1797 and was approached by three representatives of Talleyrand, the French foreign minister. These three coolly requested a huge bribe for both the Directory and Talleyrand before negotiations could even begin! The Americans firmly refused and left. They filed a full report with Adams, calling the three French representatives X, Y, and Z.

The XYZ Affair triggered a tremendous outcry when it became public in America. The insult to the national honor excited everyone. The extreme Federalists under Hamilton led the call for war. Taxes were raised to improve the navy and army. An aging George Washington was named as the **nominal** head of the army, with Alexander Hamilton in actual command. Americans put aside their own differences, and even Democratic-Republicans joined in the cry of "Millions for defense but not one cent for tribute."

Through it all, Adams kept his head. He realized the new nation could not afford a war. He proceeded with preparations, but with the support of the moderate Federalists, never called for declaration of war. An undeclared war went on between the ships of both sides for about two years. Finally, Talleyrand realized he could not afford to add America to the list of countries fighting France. He let Adams know that a new delegation would be received properly.

Convention of 1800. Adams authorized a new delegation to go to France in 1799 over the severe objections of much of his own party. The government in France had changed yet again by the time the Americans arrived. Napoleon Bonaparte was now the dictator of France, and he wanted to clear up foreign disputes to leave himself a free hand in Europe. The two sides negotiated (without bribes) the Convention of 1800. The Convention officially ended the old French-American treaty of alliance and temporarily settled the differences between the two nations. Adams had won the peace, but his refusal to give in to war hysteria cost him his popularity. He deserves a great deal of credit for stubbornly putting his country ahead of his political ambitions.

Alien and Sedition Acts. The Federalists had regained strength in Congress after the XYZ Affair. They took advantage of the anti-French hysteria to pass a series of laws in 1798 to suppress the Democratic-Republican opposition. The first part of the laws, the Alien Acts, had wide support in the country. These acts increased the time an immigrant must live in America to become a citizen from five to fourteen years. They also allowed the president to deport dangerous aliens or to imprison them during war time.

The Alien Acts were aimed at new immigrants who tended to support the more democratic party of Jefferson. They were also aimed at the hundreds of political refugees who had fled from the law in their own countries to cause trouble in America. The laws were never enforced, but their existence served to encourage many of the worst radicals to leave, and many others decided never to come.

The Sedition Act was aimed squarely at the rights of American citizens to free speech and freedom of the press. It required fines and imprisonment for such "crimes" as publishing any false, scandalous, or malicious statements against the government or organizing to oppose federal laws. This law was used very little, and then exclusively against Democratic-Republican publishers (only ten were convicted).

The Democratic-Republicans obviously led the opposition to the acts. Jefferson and Madison went overboard in opposing them. They succeeded in having the state legislatures in Kentucky and Virginia pass resolutions to **nullify** the laws. The Kentucky and Virginia Resolves were based on the theory that the federal government was a creation of the states, and the states could disallow its laws. Such a position would rob the federal government of all authority over the states. Fortunately, the other states did not join in this extreme position, but it was to be used again in the years leading up to the Civil War. The offensive laws were repealed or allowed to expire over the next two years.

Election of 1800. The election of 1800 was the first that can be described as a fight between

| John Adams was the only Federalist President.

two political parties. Adams faced an uphill battle for re-election. His Federalist Party was divided. The Hamilton wing openly fought against him. The Alien and Sedition Acts had given the Democratic-Republicans an issue to use against the Federalists. Moreover, after all the taxes and preparations, John Adams had not given the country the war they wanted. The well-organized Democratic-Republicans rallied behind Thomas Jefferson and Aaron Burr who ran as a president/vice president team.

The Democratic-Republicans won the election, but the rules for the election caused a serious problem. Each elector was to cast two votes, the one with the most votes became the president, the one in second place became the vice president. The Democratic-Republicans electors loyally cast their two votes, one each for Jefferson and Burr, who therefore tied! A tie was resolved by voting between the candidates in the House of Representatives, which was still under Federalist control. The Federalists supported Burr who was a professional politician, over the idealistic Jefferson. As a result, neither could get the necessary majority in thirty-five consecutive ballots. Finally, Jefferson won on the thirty-sixth when some of the Federalists abstained from voting. (They may have been convinced to do so by Hamilton, who had a strong dislike for Burr). This event brought about the 12th Amendment in 1804 which separated the voting for the two offices.

Federalist legacy. John Adams was the last Federalist president. The party slowly died after that. The divisions within the party hampered its ability to win elections. Its appeal to leadership by the elite did not fit with the growing democratic spirit of the nation. Moreover, once the Democratic-Republicans were in power, they began to support a strong federal government, gaining Federalist supporters as they moved toward Federalist ideas.

However, the Federalists left a rich legacy in America. They set up the basic structure of the national government, established a solid financial system, and protected the new nation from early wars that might have destroyed it. They also established the "loose construction" of the Constitution, giving the new government the flexibility to deal with the changes that were ahead.

Name the item or person.

1.33 _____ Allowed the president to deport dangerous aliens and increased the time of residency to become a citizen

1.34 _____ Party that won the 1800 elections

1.35 _____ Second president of the United States

1.36 _____ Treaty that triggered a crisis with France

1.37 _____ State resolutions to nullify Alien and Sedition Acts

1.38 _____ Agreement with France under Napoleon that ended the current disputes with America and the alliance

1.39 _____ An attempt by the French government to get bribes for negotiations

1.40 _____ Federalist law that attacked freedom of speech and the press

Answer these questions.

1.41 Who were the two leaders of the Federalist factions?

_____

1.42 What single decision cost John Adams his popularity?

_____

1.43 Publishers with what political party were prosecuted under the Sedition Act?

_____

1.44 What was the rallying cry of the nation preparing for war after the XYZ Affair?

_____

1.45 Who won the electoral vote in 1800?

_____

1.46 Who was Adams' vice president and why was that a problem?

_____

1.47 What was the legacy of the Federalists?

a. _____

b. _____

c. _____

d. _____

Review the material in this section in preparation for the Self Test. The Self Test will check your mastery of this particular section. The items missed on this Self Test will indicate specific areas where restudy is needed for mastery.

SELF TEST 1

Match these people (each answer, 2 points).

1.01 _____ Napoleon Bonaparte

1.02 _____ Alexander Hamilton

1.03 _____ Thomas Jefferson

1.04 _____ George Washington

1.05 _____ John Adams

1.06 _____ Edmond Genêt

1.07 _____ Edmund Randolph

1.08 _____ John Jay

1.09 _____ Aaron Burr

1.010 _____ Henry Knox

a. obtained an unpopular treaty with Britain under President Washington

b. first secretary of state

c. first secretary of the treasury

d. vice presidential candidate who tied with Jefferson in electoral votes in 1800

e. dictator of France

f. troublesome minister from France to America under Washington

g. unanimously chosen president by the electors

h. first and last Federalist president

i. first secretary of war

j. first attorney general

Name the item being described (each answer, 3 points).

1.011 _____ Political party that believed in rule by the elite, a strong central government, and was pro-British

1.012 _____ Political party that believed in rule by the common people, a weak federal government, and was pro-French

1.013 _____ Structure on the reverse of the Great Seal

1.014 _____ A revolt in Pennsylvania in 1794 against the excise tax

1.015 _____ The side that America fought with in the European war that began in 1793

1.016 _____ Scandal that erupted under John Adams when the French demanded a bribe before they would negotiate

1.017 _____ Laws passed by the Federalists to control immigrants and silence opposition to their government

1.018 _____ Agreement between America and France that ended their alliance and settled their current disputes

1.019 _____ The English translation of "E Pluribus Unum"

1.020 _____ Washington's statement that recommended the nation avoid political parties and foreign alliances

Answer these questions (each answer, 4 points).

1.021 What were the three parts of Hamilton's financial plan?

a. _____

b. _____

c. _____

1.022 What was Thomas Jefferson's argument against the National Bank?

_____

1.023 What are three legacies of the Federalist Era?

a. _____

b. _____

c. _____

1.024 What were some of the problems America was having with Britain under Washington?

a. _____

b. _____

c. _____

Answer true or false (each answer, 1 point).

1.025 _____ The national capital was to be built in the south in exchange for a lower tariff rate.

1.026 _____ Alexander Hamilton was vice president under John Adams.

1.027 _____ Citizen Genêt was a British ambassador who negotiated a treaty with the U.S.

1.028 _____ George Washington served two terms as president.

1.029 _____ "Millions for defense but not one cent for tribute" was the rally cry against the British during Washington's term.

1.030 _____ The French and British interfered with American trade.

1.031 _____ Washington did not attach himself to any political party.

1.032 _____ The obverse of the Great Seal has an eagle on it.

1.033 _____ Washington liked politics and eagerly sought the presidency.

1.034 _____ Hamilton favored an agrarian society with a weak federal government.

1.035 _____ John Adams' commitment to peace cost him his popularity.

80 / 100   SCORE _____   TEACHER _____ _____
                                              initials   date

2. JEFFERSONIAN DEMOCRACY

The election of Thomas Jefferson was a step in the continuing expansion of democracy in America. The old European idea of rule by the elite was slowly being replaced with the idea of rule by the people. Most of the states of the day still would only allow men who owned property to vote, but that was beginning to change. Jefferson was a warm advocate of the common people even though he was clearly a member of the upper class. He was acceptable to the old elites and yet reached out to the growing power of the people.

Jefferson found it impossible to maintain his ideal of a weak federal government when he was in charge. He would repeatedly act in ways not approved by "strict construction" of the Constitution. He justified such actions as being necessary for the "will of the people" and the protection of the country. They also firmly entrenched the idea of a strong, flexible federal government. Ironically, one of the reasons for the continuing decline of the Federalist Party was the fact that many of its supporters became very comfortable with Jefferson's government.

SECTION OBJECTIVES

Review these objectives. When you have completed this section, you should be able to:

1. Describe the important events of the first five presidential administrations.

3. Describe the course and nature of America's problems with Britain that led to the War of 1812.

4. Describe the growth, policies, and decline of the Federalist Party.

5. Describe the growth and policies of the Democratic-Republican Party.

9. Explain the reasons behind U.S. policy decisions from 1789 to the early 1820s.

VOCABULARY

Study these words to enhance your learning success in this section.

arbitrator (är' bi trā tor). One having the power to make authoritative decisions.

constituent (kon stich' oo ent). Someone represented by an elected official.

Enlightenment (en līt' n ment). A philosophical movement of the 18th century, concerned with making a rational re-examination of previously accepted ideas and institutions. It emphasized man's mind as the source of all knowledge and ridiculed faith.

lame duck (lām duk). An elected officeholder or assembly continuing in office during the period between the election of new people and their inauguration.

Democratic-Republicans in Power

Transitions. The election of 1800 was very important in the history of the United States. It was the first time that the ruling party had been defeated in an election. Often in a new republic, the losing party which still has control of the government and the army will use force to keep itself in power. The first change of party power is an important test for any new democracy. America passed that test. The Federalists unhappily but peacefully surrendered power to their political enemies.

Jefferson's election began twenty-five years of Democratic-Republican leadership in America. He immediately set a more informal tone for the presidency. He did not even arrive for his inauguration in a coach. He simply walked over from where he was staying. He shook hands with visitors and sat people at banquets without regard to their rank. He was even known to receive official callers wearing his bathrobe and slippers!

Thomas Jefferson was born into a wealthy Virginia family. He owned large tracts of land in the state and many slaves. He was a brilliant, well-educated man of many interests. He designed his own home, Monticello, near Charlottesville, Virginia, and filled it with many of his own inventions. He had been a member of the Virginia House of Burgesses, a representative at the Continental Congress (where he was the principle author of the Declaration of Independence), an American minister in France, secretary of state and vice president before he was elected to the presidency.

He was a follower of the **Enlightenment** and a "free thinker" where religion was concerned. He was not a Christian. He believed that man's nature was basically good, and by one's own strength evil could be overcome in the world.

Jefferson's policies. In spite of his anti-Federalist rhetoric, Jefferson took a more moderate course once in office. He did not overrule all of the Federalist financial policies. He promised to make full payment on the national debt. The

| The young Washington D.C.

National Bank was left in place as were the tariffs. The excise tax that fell so heavily on Jefferson's beloved farmers was repealed, however.

Jefferson slowly replaced the Federalist officeholders with people from his own party. Although it was done slowly, it was his administration that began the "spoils system" ("to the victor goes the spoils") which allowed government jobs to go to political supporters, rather than qualified workers. Jefferson overturned the Alien and Sedition Acts. The few men convicted under the Sedition Acts were pardoned and their fines returned. The residency requirement for citizenship was brought back down to five years, and the rest of the laws were not renewed when they expired.

Jefferson and his secretary of the treasury, Swiss-born Albert Gallatin, ran the government as cheaply as they could. They took advantage of a lull in the European fighting to vastly reduce the army and navy. They balanced the budget and put as much money as possible into paying off the national debt. In keeping with his philosophy of small government, Jefferson kept the taxes and government expenses low.

Midnight judges. Jefferson proved to be less moderate in dealing with Federalist judges. The **lame duck** Federalist Congress had passed the Judiciary Act of 1801 before the Democratic-Republicans came to power. It created about two hundred new jobs for judges and court officials. John Adams appointed Federalists to these jobs, the Senate quickly approved them, and Adams signed their commissions, (a few even on his last day in office). Rumor stated that some were signed after midnight that night. Jefferson and his party were understandably angered by these "midnight judges" that left the Federalists in power in the judicial branch.

The new Congress repealed the Judiciary Act of 1801, leaving many of the new appointees without jobs to take. Jefferson also ordered that many of the commissions signed by Adams simply not be delivered. One of the appointees, William Marbury, sued Secretary of State James Madison to get his commission. The case was brought in the Supreme Court under an earlier law, the Judiciary Act of 1789.

The chief justice of the Supreme Court was John Marshall, himself a last-minute Federalist appointee. Marshall used *Marbury v. Madison* (1803) to establish the Supreme Court as the final **arbitrator** of the Constitution. He ruled that the Judiciary Act of 1789 was unconstitutional in that it could not require the court to hear these kinds of cases. The Supreme Court was not the right place for Marbury to sue, so it could not make a decision for or against him. Thus Marshall avoided the issue of trying to force an unwilling president to deliver a questionable commission. He also established that the Supreme Court had the power to invalidate a law passed by Congress if it "conflicts" with the Constitution. That power is not given in the Constitution, and it gave the Federalist judiciary tremendous power that would be used more and more as American history progressed.

Jefferson was afraid of how the Federalist judges would use their power and decided to try to remove them. Federal judges were appointed for life under the Constitution and could only be removed by impeachment. Jefferson moved first to impeach John Pickering, a New England judge who was obviously insane.

After he was successfully removed, Jefferson set his sights higher.

In 1804 Jefferson brought impeachment proceedings in the Senate against Samuel Chase, a member of the Supreme Court. Chase was a Federalist judge who openly supported the Federalist agenda on the bench. He had been prominent in the conviction of the Democratic-Republican publishers under the Sedition Act. For impeachment, Jefferson had to prove that Chase was guilty of "high crimes and misdemeanors." The Senators decided that his conduct did not fit that description and acquitted him. Had they convicted him, Jefferson probably would have moved against John Marshall and other judges he did not like. Judges would have had to please the president in order to keep their jobs. The Senate's decision to abide by the plain meaning of the Constitution protected the independence of the federal judges.

Louisiana Purchase. America owned the eastern half of the Mississippi basin. The western half, the Louisiana Territory, was given to Spain after the French and Indian War. In late 1800 Napoleon convinced Spain to return the land to France. This was a dangerous turn of events for America. The west depended upon the Mississippi River and the port of New Orleans for the transport and sale of their products. Spain was an aging power who had agreed to let Americans use both the river and the port. France on the other hand, was an expanding power under Napoleon and might prove difficult to dislodge.

Jefferson acted quickly after he received news of the transfer. He sent James Monroe to France in 1803 to negotiate with the help of Robert Livingston, the American minister there. They were authorized to buy the port of New Orleans and as much land to the east as they could get for a maximum price of ten million dollars. When Monroe reached France he received a staggering surprise. Napoleon, having little success in his schemes in the New World, offered to sell all of Louisiana.

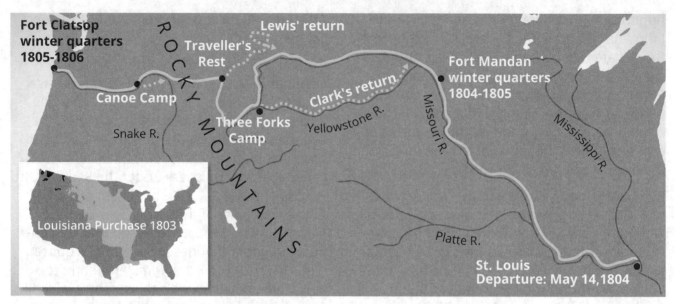

| The Lewis and Clark Expedition 1804-1806 and the Louisiana Purchase

The delegation had no authorization to buy so much land and had no way to contact Jefferson, who was across the Atlantic, for further instructions. The offer was just too good to refuse. Monroe and Livingston negotiated the sale of the land for fifteen million dollars, about three cents an acre.

The treaty put Jefferson in a very difficult position. He did not believe the Constitution authorized him to purchase such a large area of land. He wanted to get an amendment passed to permit it before going forward with the sale. Several of his advisors pointed out that Napoleon might not be willing to wait for that. In the end, the immense advantages of the sale overcame Jefferson's uncertainty. He submitted the treaty to the Senate who rapidly approved it.

The treaty was very popular, especially in the west. It removed the threat of a foreign power on the country's frontier. It guaranteed access to the Mississippi River and gave the country more land for expansion. All or part of fourteen states would eventually be created from the territory. The only losers in the deal were the Federalists, who saw their popularity sink in the light of Jefferson's success.

Lewis and Clark Expedition. The curious Jefferson commissioned a scientific/military expedition to explore and map the new territory. It was led by Jefferson's private secretary, Meriwether Lewis, and frontiersman William Clark, who was the younger brother of Revolutionary War hero George Rogers Clark. They were to try to reach the Pacific Ocean while taking notes on the animals, plants, geographical features, and Native Americans in the land.

The expedition left St. Louis, Missouri in May of 1804. They traveled up the Missouri, across the Rocky Mountains, and down the Columbia River to the Pacific Ocean. They were the first Americans to reach the Pacific overland. A Shoshone woman they met on the way named Sacajawea helped guide them over the mountains. On their return, Lewis and Clark took separate routes to increase the scope of their explorations. They eventually reunited to travel together down the Missouri toward home.

With almost all of their personnel, Lewis and Clark returned to St. Louis in September of 1806. Many people had given them up for dead because they had been gone so long. Their highly successful expedition expanded America's knowledge of the new land. It also gave America a solid claim to the rich Oregon Territory. Meriwether Lewis later became the governor of the very Louisiana Territory that he had explored.

Write true or false.

If the statement is false, change some nouns or adjectives to make it true.

2.1 _____ Jefferson's presidency was less formal than Washington's.

2.2 _____ The right of the Supreme Court to determine if laws are constitutional was set by *Marbury v. Marshall* in 1803.

2.3 _____ Thomas Jefferson brought impeachment proceedings against John Marshall in 1804.

2.4 _____ Thomas Jefferson reduced the army and navy when he was president.

2.5 _____ The treaty to purchase Louisiana was very unpopular.

2.6 _____ Lewis and Clark were the first Americans to reach the Pacific Ocean overland.

2.7 _____ Lewis and Clark traveled in the west for about a year.

2.8 _____ Pocahontas was a woman who helped Lewis and Clark.

2.9 _____ Jefferson's home in Virginia was Monticello.

Answer these questions.

2.10 Why was the election of 1800 important in the development of the American republic?

_____

_____

2.11 What (if anything) did Jefferson change in the Federalist finance system?

_____

2.12 Why were Americans concerned about France taking over Louisiana?

_____

_____

_____

2.13 What did Jefferson do about the Alien and Sedition Acts?

_____

_____

2.14 What was the financial and tax policy of Jefferson and Gallatin?

_____

_____

2.15 What did Jefferson believe he needed before he could accept the Louisiana Purchase?

_____

2.16 What route did Lewis and Clark follow to the Pacific?

_____

_____

Problems and Controversies

The Shores of Tripoli. The nations of the north coast of Africa (called the Barbary Coast) made a rich living attacking the ships that sailed in the Mediterranean. These pirates had routinely been paid off by the major trading nations to leave their ships alone. Jefferson objected to paying bribes and ransom (for captured sailors). He had long argued that the military should fight the pirates, not pay them.

The Pasha of Tripoli gave Jefferson his chance, when he declared war on the U.S. in 1801 because he was unhappy with his share of the tribute. Jefferson dispatched the reduced American navy to deal with the pirates more forcefully. The navy and the marines successfully fought a four-year war with the pirates, earning experience and international respect. (The marines immortalized the battles by including the "shores of Tripoli" in their hymn). Eventually, the Americans won a treaty with reduced payments. After a few years of fighting, the payments were stopped entirely.

Burr Conspiracy. Some New England Federalists were concerned that new states created in the Louisiana Territory would eliminate their influence in the federal government. They hatched a plot to take New England, New York and New Jersey out of the Union. They were joined in the plot by the Democratic-Republican vice president Aaron Burr who was out of favor with Jefferson. Burr ran for governor of New York in 1804, intending to use the office to support the plot. He was defeated with the help of Alexander Hamilton.

After the election, Burr challenged Hamilton to a duel and killed him. That incident ended Burr's political career and further depleted the Federalist Party. Burr fled to Pennsylvania after New York and New Jersey charged him with murder. In New York, he hatched a plot to invade Spanish territory, and possibly set up a separate government in the west. He organized a group of armed men and headed down the Ohio River. It is uncertain exactly what he intended to do, but one of his fellow conspirators, James Wilkinson, decided to back out and informed Jefferson of their actions.

Jefferson had Burr arrested and put on trial for treason in May of 1807. John Marshall was the judge at the trial which was held in Virginia. The Constitution requires two witnesses to convict someone of treason. Marshall interpreted it to mean that there had to be two witnesses to each separate act of treason. That was not possible and, in any case, the evidence was very confused. Much to Jefferson's disgust, Burr was acquitted. The stigma of the death of Hamilton and his trial led him to withdraw to Europe. He was never again politically active in America.

Growing problems with Britain. The country was so prosperous that Jefferson was overwhelmingly re-elected in 1804. However, there were dangerous clouds on the national horizon. Immediately after the sale of Louisiana, Napoleon declared war on Britain. In 1805 he defeated the Austrian and Russian armies in Austria at Austerlitz. Earlier that same year, Britain had destroyed the French fleet at Trafalgar, south of Spain. The combination of the two victories left France in control of Europe and Britain in control of the oceans.

The two sides were secure in their own areas and could not directly fight each other. So both began a campaign to starve each other into submission. Napoleon used his control of Europe to cut off its trade with Britain and Britain used its control of the seas to cut off all other trade with the entire continent. In 1806 and 1807 Britain issued Orders in Council (an order from the king on the advice of his council) that all neutral ships found on the sea sailing near French-controlled lands were to be seized. Such ships must stop first in Britain to have their cargo examined. France in turn ordered all ships that stopped in Britain to be seized if they came to France. American trade fell as both sides took ships and cargoes.

The British stepped up their impressment of sailors in a desperate attempt to keep their hard-pressed navy at full strength. Life in the British navy was incredibly harsh and inhumane. Many British sailors had deserted, obtained legal or fraudulent American citizenship, and had began serving on American ships for better pay and better conditions. It was these Englishmen that the British were "officially" after when they searched American merchant ships. They would claim that a man born English is always English. In fact, the British captains took many men who had never even been English, without any rebuke from London. The American navy had been so reduced under Jefferson that there was no way it could protect U.S. shipping and the British clearly knew this.

The contempt the British held for American rights was illustrated by the *Chesapeake-Leopard* affair in 1807. The American warship *Chesapeake* was approached by the British ship *Leopard* a few miles off the coast of Virginia. The British captain demanded the surrender of four deserters he claimed were aboard the American ship. Even though his guns were not ready, the

| The *Leopard* attacking the *Chesapeake*

American captain refused. The British opened fire, killing three men, injuring eighteen, and badly damaging the ship. The Americans surrendered, the British took the four men, and the Chesapeake limped back to port.

The British captain clearly exceeded his government's guidelines by attacking a neutral warship, but the British government was reluctant to admit error and refused the American demand to give up impressment. The American public cried out for war. Jefferson did not want one. America's small, poorly equipped army and navy proved the nation was not ready. Jefferson searched for an honorable alternative.

Embargo disaster. Jefferson decided to force the European powers to respect American rights by cutting off trade with them. He hoped that they needed American supplies badly enough that they would meet his demands. Congress passed Jefferson's Embargo Act in 1807. It forbade the export of <u>any</u> American goods on any ship. It was a long way from Jefferson's earlier position under Washington that the federal government did not even have the power to charter a bank!

The Embargo Act was an unqualified disaster. Legitimate trade came to a halt. The docks of the American port cities were deserted.

Thousands lost their jobs in the shipping, storage, exchange, and shipbuilding industries. Crops such as cotton, grain, and tobacco that supplied cash for western and southern farmers could not be sold abroad. The entire country suffered from the crisis. Napoleon added a humiliating note to the law when he began to "enforce" it in Europe by seizing any American vessels that happened to reach port there.

The embargo quickly raised a storm of opposition. Angry citizens called it the "O Grab Me" (embargo spelled backwards). A flourishing illegal trade grew along the U.S.-Canadian border. The New England states, which were the most dependent on trade, talked of leaving the Union. Jefferson's popularity plummeted, especially after he convinced Congress to pass tough laws to enforce the embargo.

The embargo also failed to cause any real harm to Britain. The British had good crops that year—enough to meet their food requirements. Some of the depleted trade was taken up by the new republics in South America. The English were not willing to consider any American demands to restore trade. Jefferson finally admitted defeat and signed the repeal of the law days before he left office. It had been in effect for fourteen months.

 Complete these sentences.

2.17 Aaron Burr killed _____ in a duel.

2.18 The French land victory at _____ and the British sea victory at _____ created a stalemate in the European war.

2.19 Aaron Burr was acquitted on the charge of _____ in 1807.

2.20 The British ship _____ attacked the American ship _____ in 1807 to recover four deserters; in the process the British killed three Americans and injured eighteen.

2.21 America fought a four year war with the pirates along the north coast of _____ under Thomas Jefferson.

2.22 Jefferson tried to deal with European interference with American ships by the _____ Act of 1807.

2.23 Aaron Burr's conspiracy was exposed by _____ , a co-conspirator who decided to back out.

2.24 British issued _____ in 1806 and 1807 that ordered their navy to seize all neutral ships headed for French-held Europe.

2.25 The British tried to keep their ships at full staff by the _____ of sailors on American ships.

2.26 Jefferson signed the _____ of the Embargo Act right before he left office.

HISTORY & GEOGRAPHY 804

LIFEPAC TEST

NAME _____

DATE _____

SCORE _____

HISTORY & GEOGRAPHY 804: LIFEPAC TEST

Put a *C* beside items that were a cause of the War of 1812, an *R* beside those that were results of the war, and a *P* beside those that were attempts to prevent war (each answer, 2 points).

1. _____ Embargo Act

2. _____ Impressment

3. _____ Nationalism

4. _____ Rise of American Manufacturing

5. _____ British support of Tecumseh

6. _____ Jay's Treaty

7. _____ *Chesapeake-Leopard* Affair

8. _____ Improvement in British-American relations

9. _____ Eliminated the Native American resistance on the frontier

10. _____ Orders in Council

Name the item described (each answer, 3 points).

11. _____ State ceded by Spain after Andrew Jackson defeated the Seminole Indians there

12. _____ Scandal under John Adams when the French would not negotiate without a bribe

13. _____ Political party that set up the basic government structure, a solid financial system and "loose construction"

14. _____ The obverse has an eagle holding an olive branch and thirteen arrows, the reverse has a pyramid

15. _____ western Mississippi land purchased by Jefferson in spite of his belief it was unconstitutional

16. _____ Laws passed by the Federalist Party to control immigrants and silence opposition to the government

17. _____ Revenue for transportation was to come from these under Henry Clay's American System

18. _____ Name for the time under the Monroe administration when the country was united and content

19. _____ Fort that was successfully defended in the Battle of Baltimore

20. _____ Federalist group that wanted to weaken the federal government near the end of the War of 1812

Match these people (each answer, 2 points).

21. _____ John Marshall
22. _____ Tecumseh
23. _____ Henry Clay
24. _____ Oliver Perry
25. _____ Alexander Hamilton
26. _____ Henry Knox
27. _____ Andrew Jackson
28. _____ Thomas Jefferson
29. _____ James Madison
30. _____ James Monroe

a. hero of the Battle of New Orleans
b. first secretary of war
c. first leader of Democratic-Republicans
d. Battle of Lake Erie
e. Anti-American Confederacy organizer
f. president; asked for war with Britain
g. Speaker of the House; War Hawk
h. Federalist chief justice; Supreme Court
i. first secretary of the treasury
j. president; warned Europe not to interfere in America

Choose the best answer (each answer, 3 points).

31. Thomas Jefferson opposed the National Bank because _____ .
    a. it would take capital from state banks
    b. it was not specifically permitted by the Constitution
    c. it would benefit mainly rich investors
    d. he was afraid of the power it would have

32. The most important issue facing Washington's administration was _____ .
    a. the Whiskey Rebellion
    b. British occupation of forts in the Old Northwest
    c. finances
    d. where to locate the capital

33. The Federalists declined as a political party because _____ .
    a. the Democratic-Republicans took over much of their agenda
    b. most of their support was in New England
    c. John Adams was unpopular
    d. Alexander Hamilton was killed in a duel

34. The significance of the election of 1800 was that _____ .
    a. Adams did not win a second term
    b. Jefferson introduced a more relaxed style of government
    c. the Federalists never won the presidency again
    d. there was a peaceful change in political power

35. The Treaty of Ghent did not cost America any territory because _____ .
    a. of the Battle of New Orleans
    b. Britain was exhausted from twenty years of war
    c. the British did not get the victories they expected
    d. Napoleon was threatening Europe again

36. America entered the War of 1812 at a disadvantage because _____ .
    a. New England opposed the war
    b. the army and navy were inadequate
    c. the National Bank was no longer in existence
    d. France was still seizing American ships

37. The goal of the U.S. in the War of 1812 was _____ .
    a. to capture Canada
    b. to end years of mistreatment by the British
    c. to force free trade
    d. prove the worth of her navy

38. New England opposed the War of 1812 because _____ .
    a. they opposed Madison
    b. It stopped trade
    c. they did not want Canadian land to add more states
    d. it stopped tariff revenue

39. Thomas Jefferson tried to impeach several judges because _____ .
    a. they were incompetent
    b. they were appointed by the lame duck Federalists
    c. he was afraid of the power of lifetime-appointed Federalist judges
    d. he wanted to expand the spoils system

40. Washington's greatest success as president was _____ .
    a. putting down the Whiskey Rebellion
    b. providing the nation with the early stability it needed
    c. choosing the best men for his cabinet
    d. establishing the First National Bank

Answer these questions.

2.27 Did the embargo accomplish its purpose? _____

Explain. _____

_____

2.28 What caused the war with the Barbary pirates?

_____

_____

2.29 How did Americans react to the embargo?

_____

_____

2.30 What plot was Aaron Burr involved with when he ran for governor of New York?

_____

_____

War Hawks

Elections of 1808 and 1810. Thomas Jefferson decided not to run for another term as president. He was afraid that the men who followed him might try to keep the office for life. So like Washington before him, he served only two terms. He retired to Monticello, helped found the University of Virginia, and renewed his broken friendship with John Adams who was living in retirement in Massachusetts. The two old friends and revolutionaries carried on a lively correspondence in their declining years. By a memorable act of Providence, John Adams and Thomas Jefferson both died on July 4, 1826, the fiftieth anniversary of the Declaration of Independence.

Thomas Jefferson was not active in the election of 1808, but he was pleased when his good friend and secretary of state, James Madison, was elected president. Madison defeated the Federalist candidate, C.C. Pinckney by more than a two-to-one margin in the electoral votes. With their pro-British agenda and New England power base, the Federalists were declining rapidly as more western states were added and anti-British sentiment grew.

The growing anger against Britain and the natural passage of time brought significant changes in Congress, most noticeably in the House of Representatives. In 1808 and particularly in 1810, a new crop of Representatives came to dominate the House. They were young men, often from the west. They had not fought or served in the Revolution. They had no first-hand experience of what the high cost of a war with Great Britain would be. They were eager to defend their nation's honor and expand her borders. History named them the "War Hawks."

War Hawks. The leader of the War Hawks was a young man who would be prominent in American politics for many decades. His name was Henry Clay. Clay was a brilliant speaker from Kentucky who was chosen as Speaker of the House in 1811. He used that position to appoint War Hawks to head important committees and dominate the House. Another member of the Hawks was John Calhoun of South Carolina. Calhoun also would be prominent on the American political stage for several decades to come.

The War Hawks were primarily from the west and the south. They were avidly in favor of war with Britain. They were men who had known no other country but the United States and were passionately nationalistic. They wanted to capture Canada and naively believed it would be a simple matter, since Britain was busy fighting in Europe. They also hoped to take Florida from Spain. The farmers from their states badly needed free trade in order to sell their goods abroad. The War Hawks' **constituents** also wanted to rid the frontier of attacks lead by Native Americans.

Tecumseh's Confederacy. One of the most remarkable leaders of the Native Americans resistance to the American pioneer flood was Tecumseh, a Shawnee leader from the Ohio country. He was a skilled orator who succeeded in organizing Native American people from all over the eastern Mississippi basin into an anti-American confederacy. He was assisted by his brother, "the Prophet," who claimed to have had a revelation and led a spiritual organization of the tribes.

In 1811 General William Henry Harrison led an American army to drive the confederation out of lands they had given away by treaty. Harrison was attacked by the Prophet not far from Tecumseh's headquarters at Tippecanoe.

| Henry Clay, Champion of the War Hawks

Harrison defeated the Native Americans and burned their settlement. He also found a large supply of British guns and powder in the settlement.

The defeat broke the power of the Prophet and dispersed the confederacy. Still, Tecumseh convinced many of the tribes to fight with the British during the upcoming War of 1812. He was killed in 1813 at the battle of the Thames in Canada.

The slide toward War. News of British supplies in the hands of the Native Americans further inflamed the War Hawks. They believed Britain was aiding and plotting with Tecumseh's Confederacy. They pushed ever harder for a war with Britain.

The situation was extremely difficult to resolve. Britain was fighting, possibly for its own survival, against one of the greatest dictators in history. Napoleon had conquered most of Europe, putting his family and friends on the thrones of its nations. Now he was looking for new lands to conquer. Britain was almost alone in trying to stop him. Meanwhile, America wanted to make wartime profits in trade without choosing sides. Britain was in no mood to compromise and neither were the War Hawks.

President Madison had searched desperately for a way to avoid a war. The Embargo Act was replaced in 1809 by the Non-Intercourse Act, which allowed trade with any nation except Britain or France. This was replaced in 1810 by Macon's Bill No. 2. This law allowed trade with all nations, but included what Congress hoped would be a enticing lure. If Britain or France would repeal their orders to capture U.S. ships, America would stop trading with their opponent.

Napoleon seized on this new law as a way to restore the American trade embargo against Britain. He publicly announced in November of 1810 that he would no longer seize American ships. Madison foolishly believed him and ordered all trade with Britain to be stopped. In fact, the French never had recalled their orders and continued to capture American ships. Britain demanded proof of the French decision and continued her own seizures. Relations between America and the former mother country continued to deteriorate.

War. America was totally unprepared for war. Jefferson had left the nation without a substantial navy or army. The War Hawks foolishly believed the war would be fought on land in Canada and refused to improve the navy in the time leading up to the war. Even when Congress did increase the size of the army, they were not able to overcome the lack of organization and trained officers. The army would have to rely on additions from the state militia, and many people felt the militia could not legally fight outside the United States. In fact, many of the militia refused to fight in Canada, which further undermined the military situation.

The nation's financial situation added to the military problems. The Democratic-Republicans had allowed the Charter for the hated National Bank to expire in 1811, leaving the nation without any central financial structure. Embargoes and trade problems had cut off the government's income from tariffs. The Democratic-Republicans, true to their Jeffersonian origins, opposed internal taxes needed to prepare for war. They finally agreed to them once war was already declared, which cut off any hope of having a nation ready in advance.

The hard realities of the situation did not disturb the well-organized War Hawks. They continued to press for war, confident that a simple invasion of Canada would force Britain to come to terms. Madison finally gave in to his own frustrations, pressure from the War Hawks, and the temptation of capturing Canada. He asked Congress to declare war in June of 1812. In support of the request, he sent a list of grievances, which included impressment, the seizure of American ships and British support of Native American attacks on Americans. Congress voted in favor of war on June 17th and 18th. The war Washington, Adams, and Jefferson avoided had finally arrived.

Complete the following.

2.31 Who won the presidential election of 1808? _____

2.32 Name two young War Hawks that would be important political leaders for decades.

_____

2.33 Who was the American commander at the Battle of Tippecanoe?

_____

2.34 Name four of the reasons why the War Hawks favored war.

   a. _____

   b. _____

   c. _____

   d. _____

2.35 What was significant about the day Adams and Jefferson died?

_____

2.36 What did Tecumseh do that threatened the U.S. frontier?

_____

_____

2.37 Give five reasons why the U.S. was not prepared for war.

   a. _____

   b. _____

   c. _____

   d. _____

   e. _____

2.38 What part of the country did the War Hawks come from?

_____

2.39 Why did the Battle of Tippecanoe increase American hostility toward Britain?

_____

2.40 Why was it significant that most of the War Hawks were young?

_____

_____

2.41 What territory did the War Hawks expect to capture easily? _____

2.42 What trick did Napoleon play on Madison in regard to Macon's Bill No. 2?

_____

_____

2.43 What month and year did America declare war on Britain?

_____

2.44 What were the reasons given by President Madison for declaring war?

a. _____

b. _____

c. _____

Review the material in this section in preparation for the Self Test. This Self Test will check your mastery of this particular section as well as your knowledge of the previous section.

SELF TEST 2

Name the item described (each answer, 3 points).

2.01 _____ Scandal under John Adams over an attempt by French official to demand bribes before negotiation

2.02 _____ Young representatives from the west and south, elected in 1808 and 1810, who favored war with Great Britain

2.03 _____ A revolt in Pennsylvania during George Washington's presidency against the excise tax

2.04 _____ Laws passed by the Federalists to control recent immigrants and restrict the free speech of Democratic-Republican publishers

2.05 _____ Land purchased from France in 1803 for 3 cents an acre that Jefferson was not sure he could constitutionally take

2.06 _____ Expedition to explore the land purchased from France; men were the first Americans to reach the Pacific Ocean by an overland route

2.07 _____ Political party of John Adams

2.08 _____ Political party of Thomas Jefferson

2.09 _____ Supreme Court decision that created the right of the court to invalidate a law passed by Congress as unconstitutional

2.010 _____ The disastrous law passed under Jefferson to cut off trade and force the European nations to honor U.S. neutrality

Answer these questions (each answer, 4 points).

2.011 What were three grievances America had against Britain under Washington that were named as reasons for the War of 1812?

a. _____

b. _____

c. _____

2.012 Did Jefferson follow "strict construction" after he became president? _____

Give an example. _____

_____

2.013 What was the *Chesapeake-Leopard* incident of 1807?

_____

_____

2.014 Name three legacies of the Federalist Era.

a. _____

b. _____

c. _____

2.015 What was the significance in American history of the election of 1800?

_____

2.016 What "war" was fought during Jefferson's administration?

_____

Match these people (each answer, 2 points).

2.017	_____ Thomas Jefferson	a. Alexander Hamilton set his financial policies
2.018	_____ George Washington	b. Shoshone woman who aided Lewis and Clark
2.019	_____ John Calhoun	c. chief justice of the Supreme Court
2.020	_____ John Marshall	d. representative from Kentucky; Speaker of the House
2.021	_____ Sacajawea	
2.022	_____ Aaron Burr	e. organized the Native Americans of the eastern Mississippi into an anti-American alliance
2.023	_____ Napoleon	f. representative from South Carolina
2.024	_____ James Madison	g. third president of the U.S.
2.025	_____ Tecumseh	h. dictator of France
2.026	_____ Henry Clay	i. president who finally asked for war with Britain
		j. led a conspiracy that possibly intended to create a new government in the west

Choose the letters of the correct answers (1 point for each letter, chosen or not).

2.027 Which of the following were part of the controversy between Jefferson and the Federalist judiciary? _____
a. Many were appointed after the election of 1800 under the Judiciary Act of 1801, which was also passed after the election.
b. The appointments, approval, and commissioning of the judges were hurried through procedures by the Federalists after the election of 1800.
c. Jefferson was able to successfully use impeachment to get rid of the Federalist judges he opposed.
d. The Democratic-Republican Congress used the Judiciary Act of 1801 to appoint their own judges to the bench.

2.028 Each of the following either moved America and Britain closer to war or were used to avoid it. Choose the ones that moved the nations toward war. _____
a. Orders in Council
b. Non-Intercourse Act
c. Jay's Treaty
d. Austerlitz and Trafalgar
e. Tecumseh's Confederacy
f. Washington's Farewell Address

80 / 100	SCORE _____	TEACHER _____ _____
		initials date

3. WAR OF 1812

The War of 1812 has been called the Second War for Independence, because it established America's reputation as a nation. Britain began acting like a bully by meddling in the Northwest Territory and disregarded America's rights on the open sea. The Americans stood up to the bully in the War of 1812. This time, the Americans fought alone, without any European allies. Britain could not blame American victories on the French. The war established a new respect for America and its armed forces, particularly the navy.

This was a war that began and ended with irony. The Orders in Council, a major cause of the war, were withdrawn days before war was declared because the drop in trade was hurting British merchants. The greatest American victory, the Battle of New Orleans, was fought after the peace treaty was signed that ended the war.

Those ironic twists almost perfectly describe this bumbling war. The Americans were unable to capture Canada, as they so arrogantly believed they could. The tiny American navy astounded the British by besting many of her warships in one-on-one battle. At one point, the British tried to dictate terms for peace, only to find that the Americans were doing much better than they had thought. It was a war of confusion that was fought in a series of small, scattered battles which ended in a draw. The war was ended by a treaty that was essentially a cease-fire agreement.

SECTION OBJECTIVES

Review these objectives. When you have completed this section, you should be able to:

1.   Describe the important events of the first five presidential administrations.
2.   Describe the growth, policies, and decline of the Federalist Party.
3.   Describe the growth and policies of the Democratic-Republican Party.
4.   Describe the course and results of the War of 1812.
5.   Describe how America changed after the War of 1812.
6.   Describe the development of the power of the Supreme Court under John Marshall.
7.   Explain the reasons behind U.S. policy decisions from 1789 to the early 1820s.

VOCABULARY

Study these words to enhance your learning success in this section.

annex (a neks'). To incorporate territory into an existing country.

arbitration (är' bi trā shun). The process by which the parties to a dispute submit their differences to the judgment of an impartial party appointed by mutual consent.

czar (zär). A king or emperor; especially one of the former emperors of Russia.

depression (di presh' en). A period of drastic decline in the national economy characterized by decreasing business activity, falling prices, and unemployment.

frigate (frig' it). A high speed, medium-sized sailing warship of the 17th-19th century.

nationalism (nash' un ul iz' em). Devotion to the interests of a particular nation.

speculate (spek′ yu lāt). To engage in the buying or selling of a commodity with an element of risk on the chance of great profit.

status quo (stā′ tus kwō). The existing condition or state of affairs.

Not the War They Planned

New England. New England bitterly opposed the War of 1812. It was often referred to there as "Mr. Madison's War." This region was the last stronghold of the pro-British Federalists. They believed that America should be helping Britain to defeat the despot Napoleon, not help him in defeating Britain! New England was also the center of American trade, which was mainly trade with Great Britain. The profits were so high in wartime that New England merchants continued to make money, even if only a few of their ships ran all the blockades. The war stopped the profits. Some of the New Englanders went so far as to support the British with loans and supplies during the war! The American war effort was handicapped by disunity in the nation.

Invasion of Canada. The mainspring of the American plan, the invasion of Canada, was a disaster. The American strategy called for a three-way invasion: from Detroit and Niagara, between the Great Lakes, and up Lake Champlain to Montreal. The Americans believed the Canadian people would not put up much of a fight for faraway Britain, especially since most of them were French. Instead, the Canadians fought bravely and fiercely—they were defending their homes against an alien invader. Many Canadians were former Americans who had been loyal to Britain during the Revolution. Forced to flee when threatened in America, they fought valiantly to prevent their new land from also falling to the Revolutionaries.

The attack from Detroit was under the command of General William Hull. Hull had been an officer in the Revolution but was now old and unsure of himself. He led an army into Canada but quickly retreated because of fears about his supply lines. The British commander, Isaac Brock, took advantage of Hull's hesitation and marched his army toward Detroit. Brock threatened that if he captured the city, he might not be able to control his Native American allies.

Fearful of such a result, Hull surrendered without firing a single shot. In August of 1812, Hull surrendered to a force that was much smaller than his own! He was later court-martialed and condemned to death but was pardoned by Madison for his services during the Revolution. His cowardice cost America control of the Detroit region.

General Stephen Van Rensselaer led the American attack from Niagara. His small army ran into stiff British resistance and was defeated when the militia reinforcements refused to cross the border. The militiamen stayed on the American side while the British killed their countrymen across the river. General Henry Dearborn, who commanded the attack toward Montreal, withdrew without seriously engaging the enemy when the militia under his command refused to leave the country. Meanwhile, the British and their Native American allies captured Fort Michilimackinac between Lake Huron and Lake Superior in July of 1812. The Canadian campaign of 1812 was a complete failure.

Naval War. The fiasco of the Canadian adventure was partially redeemed by the surprising American success at sea. The American **frigates** succeeded in defeating and capturing several of their British counterparts. This was a humiliating turn for the proud British navy and a boost for American morale.

The most famous American frigate, the *U.S.S. Constitution*, defeated and captured the *H.M.S. Guerriére* in August of 1812. The American

| Oliver Hazard Perry transferring his command over to the *Niagara*.

vessel, under the command of Isaac Hull, the nephew of disgraced William Hull, had more guns and a larger crew than its opponent. Moreover, British cannon fire bounced off the heavy oak sides of the *Constitution*, earning it the affectionate nickname "Old Ironsides."

The success of the *Constitution* was quickly followed by others. The *United States* under Stephen Decatur, a naval hero from the war against the Barbary pirates, captured the British frigate *Macedonian*. The *U.S.S. Wasp* defeated the *Frolic*, the *Essex* captured the *Alert,* and the *Hornet* took the *H.M.S. Peacock*. In October of 1812, the *Constitution* struck again under a new commander, William Bainbridge, and sunk the *Java*. The U.S. also suffered a loss in June of 1813 when the British frigate *Shannon* defeated the smaller *Chesapeake* (which had been so humiliated in the *Chesapeake-Leopard* Affair of 1807). Overall, the single ship combat tended to go to the Americans with thirteen wins to the British three.

The few losses did not seriously threaten the huge British navy, but it did humiliate them. Their navy commanders had mocked the Americans at the beginning of the war. Their overconfidence was badly misplaced. The American frigates were heavier, had larger crews, and carried more firepower than the British ships. American ships were all manned by patriots who were defending their nation's honor, not by poor, luckless men forced into service as with the British. The British finally ordered their frigates to sail in pairs to avoid any more single ship battles.

The naval campaign also included about five hundred American privateers. These were smaller, quicker ships that attacked and captured British merchant vessels for profit. They captured over a thousand ships during the war, some of them from the Irish Sea and the English Channel. These losses further angered the British government and a public already stung by the loss of the frigates. The English business class turned against the war as their losses mounted.

Canadian Campaign of 1813. Command of the troubled front at Detroit was given to William Henry Harrison, the hero of Tippecanoe. He quickly determined that he could not retake Detroit without having control of the Great Lakes. The lakes were the key for both transportation and communication along the U.S.-Canadian border. Captain Oliver Hazard Perry was given the task of gaining control of the waterways.

Perry's first job was to obtain a fleet. At Presque Isle on Lake Erie he spent the summer of 1813 building five ships. Five more were towed by oxen up the rapids of the Niagara River from Lake Ontario. In September Perry sailed his fleet to the western end of Lake Erie and met the British.

The Battle of Lake Erie was incredibly fierce. Perry's flagship, the *Lawrence,* was destroyed. He moved his command to the *Niagara* which broke through the British line, firing at them from both sides as it passed. The British were defeated, and the lake came under American control. "We have met the enemy and they are ours," Perry reported back to Washington. The victory was a sweet balm to America's shattered cause in the north.

The British withdrew from Detroit once they realized they could not hold it without support from the water. They retreated eastward and were met at the Thames River in Canada by Harrison and over three thousand American troops. The outnumbered British (with their Native American allies) were quickly defeated. The Americans thus regained control of the Detroit region. The great organizer, Tecumseh, was killed, which destroyed his confederacy and ended the Native American alliance with the British.

The campaign of 1813 had undone some of the damage of the previous year's fiasco, but Canada and the far northwest American frontier were still in British hands. A second attempt by the Americans under James Wilkinson and Wade Hampton to capture Montreal failed in 1813. The British succeeded in capturing Fort Niagara and burning the city of Buffalo, New York in that same year. The Canadian front was reduced to a stalemate for the remainder of the war.

Match these people.

3.1	_____	William Hull
3.2	_____	William Bainbridge
3. 3	_____	Oliver Perry
3.4	_____	Isaac Brock
3.5	_____	Stephen Decatur
3.6	_____	Henry Dearborn
3.7	_____	Stephen Van Rensselaer
3.8	_____	William Henry Harrison
3.9	_____	Isaac Hull

a. victor at the Battle of the Thames

b. British commander in Canada

c. victor at the Battle of Lake Erie

d. *Constitution* commander, captured the *Guerriere*

e. commander of the *United States*, hero of Barbary Coast war

f. *Constitution* commander, sunk the *Java*

g. cowardly officer who surrendered Detroit

h. failed in march on Montreal

i. lost battle in attack from *Niagara* because the militia would not leave the country

✎ Write the correct answer.

3.10 What bitter New Englanders named the war _____

3.11 Fort between Lakes Huron and Superior _____

3.12 Nickname of the *Constitution* _____

3.13 Message Perry sent after his victory _____

_____

3.14 Small, quick, American ships that captured over 1,000 British merchantmen for profit

_____

Answer these questions.

3.15 Why did New England oppose the War of 1812?

a. _____

b. _____

3.16 What did America primarily want to capture in the War of 1812? _____

3.17 Why did the American ships fare so well against the British in one-on-one ship battles?

_____

_____

3.18 Where did Captain Perry get his fleet?

_____

_____

To the Depths of Despair and Back

In 1814 events in Europe took an ominous turn against the Americans. In October 1813, Napoleon was seriously defeated in the Battle of the Nations at Leipzig. The loss forced him to abdicate in April of 1814 and exile himself to the Mediterranean island of Elba. That freed Britain to concentrate its massive military strength on America. By the spring of 1814, experienced, battle-hardened British officers and soldiers who had just won a great victory in Europe were now taking up positions in the New World.

Last attempt at Canada. In 1814 the Americans made one last attempt to invade Canada under the leadership of Generals Jacob Brown and Winfield Scott. These commanders led an army across the Niagara River and defeated the British at the Battle of Chippewa in July. The troops coming from Europe began adding their weight to the fray. Later that same month, the Americans were driven back at the Battle of Lundy's Lane. The Americans held the British at Fort Erie for several months and then withdrew, ending the last American attempt to bring Canada into the Union by force.

British strategy. The British ended the string of American naval victories by establishing a tight blockade all along the east coast. The blockade ruined the remainder of American trade and cut off all tariff revenue for the government. By the end of the war the nation's economy was in a shambles, and the government was almost bankrupt.

The British strategy was to inflict several large defeats on the Americans and force them to sign away large chunks of territory in exchange for peace. An army of over 10,000 was assembled in Canada for an invasion of New York along the traditional route down Lake Champlain. Another was assembled in the West Indies to move against New Orleans.

The British also used their control of the seas to land troops along the American coastline. Much of eastern Maine was captured. Several of the towns along the coast were plundered by the roving British navy, but with troops freed by the defeat of Napoleon, the British moved for bigger prizes.

The burning of Washington. The British fleet under Admiral George Cockburn had taken complete control of Chesapeake Bay in the summer of 1814. He and British general Robert Ross led an attack against the American capital in August. The Americans had not expected an attack there and had only slight defenses. The British disembarked without any resistance in Maryland and marched toward Washington. A hastily assembled militia force met them at the Battle of Bladensburg. The Americans quickly fled from the professional British army which marched into the capital unopposed.

Most of the population of the city fled before the British arrived. Government clerks had hidden or removed important papers. President Madison rode down to the front and fled with the retreating army. His wife Dolley Madison had been at the president's mansion all day packing up valuable goods and papers to take with her. She stayed until late in the afternoon, even when cannon fire could be heard in the distance. One of the last items she took out was the priceless painting of George Washington by Gilbert Stuart. She had the frame broken so the canvas could be moved easily. At last she also fled. Washington was almost deserted when the British arrived on the night of August 24, 1814.

The British burned most of the public buildings in Washington, including the capital and the president's house. They also burned the offices of the local newspaper. A huge thunderstorm put out most of the fires that night and contained the damage. The British withdrew to their ships, fearing that an American army was assembling to face them. The president's mansion was completely gutted by the fire. It was eventually repaired and the outside whitewashed to cover the black marks of the fire. It became known as the White House from then on.

Negotiations in Europe. Russia was a British ally in the war against Napoleon. The Russian czar sent a peace feeler in 1814, which resulted in British-American negotiations in Ghent, Belgium. The American delegation was led by future president John Quincy Adams, the son of John Adams. Henry Clay was also a delegate. The war was running very much in favor of the British when the two sides met for the first time.

The British negotiators made sweeping demands based on their confidence that the Americans

| The burning of the President's Mansion

were losing the war. The facts supported their view. Britain occupied parts of Maine and the upper Mississippi basin. A British army was moving down Lake Champlain, and another was organizing in the West Indies. The American capital had been sacked without any serious resistance. The British felt quite secure in dictating terms to their American counterparts.

The British demanded an independent Native American nation created out of the land west of the Mississippi, south of the Great Lakes. They also demanded permanent control of the Great Lakes, and a large part of land in Maine. The American delegation refused without even bothering to send the offer back to Madison for his decision. Both sides then waited for further developments in America. This was the low point of the war for the tattered United States. Things were about to improve.

Battle of Plattsburgh Bay. In the summer of 1814, the British advanced along the traditional Canadian-American invasion route, Lake Champlain. The British had to maintain control of the lake in order to move their supplies. The British fleet supporting the invasion was met by a weaker American force at Plattsburgh Bay in September. Once again, the balance of the war hung on a naval battle on an inland lake. The Americans under the command of Thomas Macdonough fought a desperate, bloody battle that ended in their favor. With supply and communication lines cut off by the American control of Lake Champlain, the British retreated.

Baltimore. Americans were infuriated by the attack on their capital. When Cockburn and Ross moved to attack the privateer center of Baltimore in September they met an angry, prepared enemy. The British attacked by both land and sea. The land attack was quickly blunted by a traditional American tactic. Early in the battle, some American sharp shooters succeeded in killing General Ross while he directed his men from the back of his horse. His successor was faced with stiff defenses and eventually withdrew.

Meanwhile, the navy tried to subdue Fort McHenry, which protected Baltimore harbor. The British bombarded the fort all during the night of September 13th to 14th. On board one of the British ships was a young American named Francis Scott Key. He had come aboard to negotiate for the release of a friend who had been captured a month before at the Battle of Bladensburg. He was detained during the attack on the fort. He watched most of the night in a state of high anxiety as the British pounded the fort with cannon fire. He was overjoyed when the first light of morning showed the Stars and Stripes still flying over the fort. He wrote out a poem in honor of the event which was set to the music of an English drinking song. It eventually became our national anthem, "The Star-Spangled Banner."

Key's poem celebrated the failure of the British assault on Baltimore. The army reboarded the ships after they had given up on the well-fortified Fort McHenry. The entire force withdrew from the region about a month later.

Treaty of Ghent. The British, who were expecting news of victories, were upset by reports of the failures in New York and Baltimore. The government offered the Duke of Wellington, the great British commander who had defeated Napoleon, a chance to take over the campaign in America. He informed the government that the only way to defeat the United States would be to control the Great Lakes. That would mean building a large fleet that could never be used on the ocean. As badly as the British wanted to teach the Americans a lesson, the cost was too high. Britain was exhausted and in deep financial trouble after twenty years of war in Europe. Napoleon was still alive and might return. (He did in 1815). The negotiators at Ghent were ordered to make a reasonable peace.

The two sides agreed to a return to the **status quo**. The fighting ended, and both sides retained the land they had when the war began. The Americans did not demand any statement or concession on the issues of impressment or ship seizures; the completion of the war in Europe had ended them anyway. In turn the British gave up their captured territory. They were never again to be an issue in British-American relations.

News of the Treaty of Ghent, signed in December of 1814, took several weeks to reach the United States. In those few weeks, the biggest land battle of the war was fought. The long-anticipated British invasion from the West Indies had finally taken place at New Orleans. The new peace started off quite unexpectedly.

Oh, say can you see by the dawn's early light
What so proudly we hailed at the twilight's last gleaming?
Whose broad stripes and bright stars thro' the perilous fight,
O'er the ramparts we watched were so gallantly streaming?
And the rocket's red glare, the bombs bursting in air,
Gave proof thro' the night that our flag was still there.
Oh, say does that star-spangled banner yet wave
O'er the land of the free and the home of the brave?

On the shore, dimly seen through the mists of the deep,
Where the foe's haughty host in dread silence reposes,
What is that which the breeze, o'er the towering steep,
As it fitfully blows, half conceals, half discloses?
Now it catches the gleam of the morning's first beam,
In full glory reflected now shines in the stream:
Tis the star-spangled banner! Oh long may it wave
O'er the land of the free and the home of the brave.

And where is that band who so vauntingly swore
That the havoc of war and the battle's confusion,
A home and a country should leave us no more!
Their blood has washed out their foul footsteps' pollution.
No refuge could save the hireling and slave,
From the terror of flight and the gloom of the grave:
And the star-spangled banner in triumph doth wave
O'er the land of the free and the home of the brave.

Oh! thus be it ever, when freemen shall stand
Between their loved home and the war's desolation!
Blest with victory and peace, may the Heav'n-rescued land
Praise the Pow'r that hath made and preserved us a nation.
Then conquer we must, when our cause it is just,
And this be our motto: "In God is our trust."
And the star-spangled banner in triumph shall wave
O'er the land of the free and the home of the brave.

THE STAR-SPANGLED BANNER
by Francis Scott Key

Answer these questions.

3.19 Why did the military situation change in 1814?

_____

3.20 What did the British negotiators demand when the two sides first met at Ghent in August of

1814? _____

_____

_____

3.21 Why did the demands of the British change by December of 1814?

_____

3.22 What was the British strategy in the War of 1812?

_____

3.23 Who faced the British at the Battle of Bladensburg?

_____

3.24 Who led the American negotiators at Ghent? _____

3.25 What eastern state did Britain occupy part of during the war? _____

3.26 How did the British end their embarrassing string of naval losses?

_____

3.27 What naval battle turned back the British advance into New York, and who was the American

commander?

_____

3.28 What did the British do in Washington in August of 1814?

_____

3.29 How did the British attack Baltimore?

_____

3.30 The "Star-Spangled Banner" was written about the defense of what?

_____

3.31 What two battles were fought during America's last invasion of Canada?

_____

3.32 What was the basic result of the Treaty of Ghent?

_____

Rewrite the first and last verse of the "Star-Spangled Banner" in prose, plainly writing what the author was saying.

3.33 _____

_____

_____

_____

_____

_____

_____

_____

_____

_____

_____

_____

_____

_____

_____

_____

_____

_____

_____

_____

_____

Write a two-page biography of any of these people, using at least three sources.

George Washington	John Adams	Thomas Jefferson
James Madison	Alexander Hamilton	Henry Knox
James Monroe	Aaron Burr	Abigail Adams
Dolley Madison	Martha Washington	John Jay
John Marshall	Meriwether Lewis	William Clark

TEACHER CHECK _____   _____

initials   date

Results

Andrew Jackson. The Creek People of the southeast Mississippi took advantage of the war in 1813 to attack and massacre the defenders of Fort Mims near Mobile, Alabama. The Creek People were certain to assist the British when they attacked in the south. Andrew Jackson, a senator from Tennessee and commander of the state militia, moved south to confront the Creek People. He led a well-organized, ruthless, and decisive campaign. After Jackson's victory at the Battle of Horseshoe Bend in March of 1814, he forced the Creek to concede a huge portion of territory that included much of the states of Georgia and Alabama. Impressed with Jackson's results, the secretary of war gave him command of the American army in the south in 1814.

The Americans knew the British were preparing a large army in the West Indies to gain control of the lower Mississippi. Jackson moved into Spanish Florida and took the city of Pensacola in November, cutting off an excellent invasion route for the British. Then he began to prepare for an invasion along the Gulf Coast. When the British landed near New Orleans, Jackson came in to defend the city.

Battle of New Orleans. Jackson set up a strong defensive position in front of the advancing British in the swampy land around the mouth of the Mississippi. His men built fortifications of logs and dirt on a platform of cotton bales and wood. The position was located with a swamp on one side and the Mississippi River on the other. The enemy could not easily go around them. The barricade was manned by about 7,000 men, including soldiers, free blacks, backwoodsmen, pirates, and Frenchmen.

The over-confident British with an army of 10,000, including many veterans of the Napoleonic Wars, decided on a frontal attack. On the morning of January 8, 1815 (two weeks after the Treaty of Ghent had been signed), the British marched straight at the Americans in formation. The Americans mowed them down like grass. Over 2,000 British soldiers were killed or wounded while the Americans lost less than fifty. It was the greatest American victory of the war, even if it did come after the war ended. It also made Andrew Jackson a national hero.

News of the victory reached the cities of the east coast just before news of the treaty in Europe. Americans went wild with joy. They had not lost any territory in the treaty, and they had a great victory to cap it off. The public rejoiced using the slogan, "Not One Inch of Territory Ceded or Lost." The American perception of the war was that they had won.

The Hartford Convention. New England, under Federalist leadership, continued to oppose the war right up to the end. Five of the New England states sent representatives, who were Federalists, to a meeting in Hartford, Connecticut in December of 1814 to discuss their grievances and options. Their continued opposition to the war led many people to question their loyalty. The secret meetings in December and January caused further concern.

The Hartford Convention issued a report requesting several changes in the basic structure of the government. The changes would have increased the power of the states at the

| The British, in formation, marching towards the Americans

expense of the federal government. The recommendations included restrictions on the federal government's ability to make war or restrict trade, both key New England issues. The Convention wanted the states to have more control over their own defense. They also wanted to increase New England's power in the national government by making the admission of new states more difficult.

The report of the Convention was taken to Washington by three special envoys from Massachusetts. They arrived in the capital about the same time as the news of the Battle of New Orleans and the Treaty of Ghent. Their proposals were ridiculed and they left in disgrace. The popular reaction against the Federalist proposals cost them what was left of their strength. They only nominated one more presidential candidate in 1816 before they disappeared into historical extinction.

Results of the War. The end of the war marked a turning point in British-American relations. Four boundary disputes between the two nations were referred to **arbitration** for solutions. All disputes in the future between America and the former mother country would be settled by negotiations, not war. Over the next years and decades, steps were taken to remove border forts and warships on the Great Lakes between the U.S. and Canada. Eventually, the two neighbors would come to share the longest unfortified boundary in the world. Feelings still ran high against the British for many years, but the journey down the long path to friendship had begun.

The major Native American threat of the frontier was extinguished during the War of 1812. Tecumseh's confederacy was destroyed at the Battle of the Thames, and the Native American Peoples of the south were subdued in the Battle of Horseshoe Bend. Both groups were forced to cede large areas of land to the U.S. government. The pioneers quickly began to migrate to the new areas, creating more states for the Union. Indiana, Mississippi, Alabama,

and Illinois were added to the nation within five years after the war.

The great manufacturing power of the United States was born as a result of the War of 1812. The war and trade embargoes had drastically cut imports from Europe and deprived wealthy Americans of their major investment, which was commerce. Many wealthy men, especially in New England, invested their idle money in building factories of their own to produce goods the nation could not get from Europe. Out of necessity, the engine of American manufacturing began.

The Second War for Independence gave the nations of Europe a new respect for the young nation. British naval officers no longer sneered at American ships and seamen. European powers no longer tried to get some of the new nation's land for themselves. The war had ended their hopes that the nation would fall apart, leaving them to pick up the richest pieces.

The War of 1812 marked the end of the nation's dangerous infancy. The first leaders had kept the peace long enough for the nation to gain the strength needed to fight alone. Americans had held their own against the greatest power of Europe and proved their mettle in battle. The war gave them a new sense of their own destiny which they believed was to expand their republic across the width of the continent.

Florida. After the war, Florida was the only land east of the Mississippi not in American hands. The proud Yankees wanted it and believed it was destined by Providence to be theirs. Andrew Jackson had already seized parts of West Florida during the War of 1812. Afterwards, the Americans **annexed** that land and opened negotiations with Spain for the rest of it.

Spain was reluctant to sell Florida. She had her own agenda and resented America's presence in West Florida. The Spanish government wanted to settle the boundaries of the whole Louisiana Territory and did not want America to support the rebelling Spanish colonies in Latin

America. Circumstances, in the form of Andrew Jackson, forced Spain to negotiate.

In the years after the war, Native Americans, runaway slaves, and thieves began using Florida as a base for raids into the United States. In 1818 the president sent Andrew Jackson "to deal with the Seminole People," who were using Florida as a base. Jackson interpreted his orders liberally and marched into Florida where he defeated the Seminoles. He also captured St. Marks and Pensacola, executing two British citizens who were aiding the Native American People.

The raids by Jackson convinced the Spanish government that they could not successfully defend Florida. Therefore, in 1819 they signed the Adams-Onis Treaty that ceded it to the United States. The treaty also settled the boundaries of the Louisiana Territory with Spain giving up all of its claim to the Oregon country. The United States agreed that Texas was Spanish territory and took responsibility for about 5 million dollars in claims that U.S. citizens had against Spain. The northern and southern bounds of the U.S. were now set. The only direction left to go was west.

 Complete these sentences.

3.34 The Battle of New Orleans made _____ a national hero.

3.35 The Federalists destroyed the last of their party with the proposals that were made at the _____ at the end of the War of 1812.

3.36 Andrew Jackson was given command of the army in 1814 after his success as a military commander against the _____ People.

3.37 The Battle of New Orleans took place _____ after the Treaty of Ghent was signed.

3.38 Jackson captured part of western _____ during the war and the American government later annexed it.

3.39 The Creek People were defeated at the Battle of _____ .

3.40 The Spanish government agreed to cede Florida after _____ made raids into the territory against the _____ People.

3.41 America obtained Florida and settled the boundaries of the Louisiana Territory by the _____ Treaty of 1819.

3.42 The lack of trade encouraged many wealthy New Englanders to invest in _____ during the War of 1812.

3.43 The Treaty of Ghent settled four boundary disputes by referring them to _____ .

3.44 The War of 1812 gave the nations of Europe a new _____ for the United States.

Answer these questions.

3.45 How did British-American relations change after the War of 1812?

_____

_____

_____

3.46 Why could pioneers flood onto the frontier after the war?

_____

_____

3.47 What mistake did the British make at New Orleans?

_____

_____

3.48 Who did the American public believe won the War of 1812?

_____

_____

3.49 What did America believe was its destiny?

_____

_____

Good Feelings

Nationalism. The War of 1812 produced a new feeling of nationalism in America. The nation believed that it had won a war against Great Britain. After that, the proud American navy thrashed the Barbary pirates so completely that all tribute payments were ended. The regional outlook of the New England Federalists had been discredited. Citizens of the United States began to think of themselves as just that—U.S. citizens. The older view that they were citizens of a state that was part of a Union declined for a time. This also led to a respect for the ideal of the "common man," the founder and defender of the great American republic.

The American System. Speaker of the House Henry Clay captured the pulse of the nation with his "American System." The American System was a group of proposals intended to benefit the entire nation. It included a protective tariff, a new national bank, money for roads and canals, and other improvements. Some of it became law.

The tariff was included in the American System in order to protect infant American factories that were born during the war. British manufacturers had not been able to sell their goods during the war, so they had collected their huge surpluses in warehouses, waiting to be sold. Once the Treaty of Ghent was signed, England began shipping boatloads of goods to America. Prices were driven so low that American factories were going out of business. In 1816 Congress passed the first protective tariff. It was different from earlier ones which were small and used to raise money. These new tariffs were high—20 to 25%—and were intended to make foreign goods more expensive so American goods could compete.

The absence of a national bank proved to be a disaster for the nation's finances. Any bank could print money, and many did, printing more than they could redeem in gold or silver. This made the currency decline rapidly in value,

causing inflation. Financial chaos had been a particular problem during the war. Under the leadership of Clay and Calhoun, a Second National Bank was chartered in 1816. The Democratic-Republicans had learned their lesson and supported it.

The Second National Bank was even larger than the first. Unfortunately, it got off to a bad start. The managers of the bank printed money freely, made loans improperly, and speculated in western land (a popular occupation at the time). The bank's new president, Nicholas Biddle, took over in 1819 and brought the institution under control. He reset policies, recalled risky loans, and reduced the money printed to match the gold reserves. The sudden change in policy was good for the bank, but it hurt the nation as a whole. It contributed to the Panic of 1819 (panic was a name for a depression). The bank foreclosed on many farms, especially in the west, which hurt its popular support.

The last part of Clay's American System was the proposal to use the extra revenue from the higher tariffs to build roads and canals. Clay believed that desperately needed improvements in transportation would allow western and southern farmers to increase their trade with the manufacturers of the north, benefiting everyone. One such road had already begun. The first national road, the Cumberland Road, was begun in 1811. It ran from Cumberland, Maryland to Vandalia, Illinois. It eventually connected to St. Louis on the Mississippi.

However, most of the improvements were needed inside the states, not between them. President Madison, and later Monroe, believed it was unconstitutional to use federal funds to benefit projects in one state, even if it would benefit the nation as a whole. So when Congress passed the Bonus Bill in 1817 (which would have given money from the new National Bank to the states for improvements), Madison vetoed it. The states were forced to finance the roads and canals themselves. Many did so by encouraging private citizens to build roads and charge for their use. These "turnpikes" spread all over the nation.

Era of Good Feelings. In 1816 James Monroe was elected president. He crushed his Federalist opponent 183 to 34 in the electoral vote. Monroe was the last president to have served in the Revolution and the last of the "Virginia Dynasty" (Washington, Jefferson, Madison, Monroe). He joined the army at eighteen and fought in several major battles of the Revolution, including Trenton where he was wounded in the shoulder. His political career included the Virginia legislature, the Confederation Congress, governor of Virginia, envoy to France and Britain, U.S. senator, as well as secretary of state and secretary of war under Madison. His appearance and manners resembled those of George Washington. He established a strict protocol for social events, following Washington's example. He was not a brilliant leader, but was a capable, experienced administrator who knew how to listen for "the will of the people."

James Monroe took over a nation still basking in the glow of the War of 1812. There was only one major political party, the Democratic-Republicans, and the nation was united as never before. Shortly after his election, Monroe took a tour of the country. He was greeted with widespread acclaim, even in New England. One newspaper spoke of an "Era of Good Feelings" that had come over America. This era lasted through much of the early part of the Monroe administration but gradually yielded to the rise of sectionalism which will be covered in the next LIFEPAC. However, the "good feelings" lasted until Monroe's re-election in 1820. He ran unopposed and won every electoral vote except one. That one was deliberately thrown away so that the honor of being unanimously elected would fall only on George Washington.

Western Land. The United States of America is a land whose national character and history were built on the frontier. From the time the first settlers arrived in 1603 until the early 1900s, the nation always was expanding into the frontier. The frontier changed from the east coast, to the foothills of the Appalachians, to the eastern Mississippi, to the west coast, and lastly, to the Great Plains. For much of our history the acquisition of new lands, the settling of that land, and the addition of new states have been major political issues in Washington.

| A log cabin on the frontier

The frontier of the Era of Good Feelings was the eastern Mississippi. This frontier saw huge gains in population after the war. The population of the territory/state of Illinois in 1820 was more than four times what it had been in 1810. In that same time period, the population of Kentucky and Mississippi more than doubled while that of Illinois multiplied four times and Alabama increased thirteen times over!

The move west was encouraged by increasingly easy terms to purchase government land. The Land Ordinance of 1795 had set the price at $1 per acre payable in two installments with a minimum purchase of 640 acres. In 1800 the law was changed to a minimum purchase of 320 acres and four payments. By 1804 the price was $2 an acre, but the minimum purchase was only 160 acres. After the Panic of 1819, further reductions were made in 1820. The price was reduced to $1.25 an acre with an 80-acre minimum, and the purchaser could keep whatever part of the land he managed to pay for, only losing the unpaid portion. These generous terms kept the American population moving west to claim land of their own.

The Marshall Court. John Marshall remained chief justice of the Supreme Court for thirty-four years (1801-1835). He used his position to pursue the Hamilton-Federalist goals of a strong central government and protection against the excesses of democracy. Using its self-created right to judicial review, the Marshall Court issued a series of important decisions.

Fletcher v. Peck (1810) was a suit brought after the Georgia legislature sold 35 million acres of land to speculators in a corrupt deal. In its next session, the legislature revoked the deal due to public outcry. Marshall ruled that it was a contract and could not be arbitrarily revoked. He placed property rights, even dubious ones, above the power of the legislature. He asserted the Supreme Court's right to declare *state* laws unconstitutional.

McCulloch v. Maryland (1819) was a suit over the right of the states to tax the National Bank. Following the Panic of 1819, popular opinion ran high against the bank. Maryland tried to destroy it by taxing it out of existence. Marshall ruled that the federal government had the right to create the bank under its implied powers in the Constitution (loose construction), and the states had no authority to tax the federally created National Bank.

Many other decisions followed the same lines of reasoning. States were not allowed to change the charter of a college after *Dartmouth College v. Woodard* (1819), because it was a contract and was protected by the Constitution. The decision in *Cohens v. Virginia* (1821) gave the Supreme Court the right to reverse the decisions of even the highest state courts. The court ruled in *Gibbons v. Ogden* (1824) that only the federal government could regulate interstate commerce. Elected officials who favored state's rights and the power of the legislature objected to these rulings but could not find any way to effectively challenge them.

Monroe Doctrine. The aftermath of the Napoleonic Wars restored the old monarchs of Europe to their thrones. From then on, these rulers were determined to stop any and all revolutions like the one in France. Rebellions in favor of democracy were crushed by an alliance of monarchs in both Italy and Spain in the early 1820s. The United States began to fear that the new republics in Latin America that had recently won their freedom from Spain might suffer a similar fate. Americans naturally favored the new republics as followers of their own example. The presence of large European armies in the Americas would have been a definite threat to the United States.

The U.S. had an unexpected ally in their support for the new republics. Britain was enjoying the new freedom she had in trading with Latin America. This had previously been restricted by

Spain. Britain proposed that she and the U.S. issue a joint statement against any European intervention. However, Secretary of State John Quincy Adams was suspicious of the motives behind Britain's offer. He saw no reason for the U.S. to ride behind British foreign policy.

At the urging of Adams, Monroe decided to follow a separate but parallel course with the British. He took advantage of his annual address to Congress in 1823 to announce the American policy which became known as the Monroe Doctrine. He stated, the American continents were closed to any further European colonization. An attempt by the powers of the Old World to intervene in America would be viewed as a hostile act against the United States. Furthermore, the U.S. would not interfere with any European colonies already in America, nor would she intervene in European conflicts.

The United States lacked the military strength to back up this sweeping statement. It was largely ignored outside the country, but American national pride supported the independent spirit in which it was made. In later years, when America had grown to be an international power, the Monroe Doctrine would become a major part of the nation's foreign policy.

Conclusion. The years from 1789 to the early 1820s were a time of foundation building in the United States. The institutions of the new republic were established along with the customs and protocols that accompany them. The nation faced and successfully completed a peaceful change of political authority in 1800. The power of government was reaching down towards the people and away from the elites. The nation's leaders remained calm in the light of severe provocation from Europe as the Napoleonic Wars raged. Finally, when they could stand no more, America had fought again for her independence, this time from the arrogance of the British. The nation came out of the war with her territory and pride intact. The east coast from Canada to Mexico was under her control, and the west called to her growing population. Finally, America boldly asserted her right to keep the Old World out of her neighborhood. The foundation was laid. Its strength would be tested by fire in the decades ahead.

 Complete the following.

3.50 What were the three parts of Henry Clay's American System?

a. _____   b. _____

c. _____

3.51 What was the minimum number of acres of western land that had to be purchased in each year?

a. 1795 _____   b. 1800 _____

c. 1804 _____   d. 1820 _____

3.52 What was the time after the election of James Monroe called?

_____

3.53 Name the Supreme Court decision that decided each issue.

    a. College charters are contracts protected by the Constitution

    _____

    b. States can not tax a federal bank

    _____

    c. Only the federal government can regulate interstate trade

    _____

    d. Legislatures can not revoke a contract they made earlier, even if it was dubious

    _____

    e. The Supreme Court can reverse the decision of the highest state courts

    _____

3.54 Name the four parts of the Monroe Doctrine.

    a. _____

    b. _____

    c. _____

    d. _____

3.55 What was the sentiment of the nation after the War of 1812? _____

3.56 What part of the American System was opposed by Presidents Madison and Monroe? Why?

    _____

    _____

3.57 Who brought the Second National Bank under better management?
    What was the name of the depression caused by his tightened monetary policies?

    a. _____   b. _____

3.58 What was the American frontier of the early 1800s? _____

3.59 What major European nation supported the new Latin American republics?

    _____

3.60 Who was the chief justice of the Supreme Court from 1801 to 1835?
    Whose ideas of government did he promote?

    a. _____   b. _____

3.61 Why was the National Bank unpopular after 1819, especially in the west?

    _____

    _____

3.62 Name the first national road, the year it was begun, and the cities it eventually ran between.

a. _____ b. _____

c. _____

3.63 What were privately built roads which charged people to use them? _____

↻ **Before you take this last Self Test, you may want to do one or more of these self checks.**

1. _____ Read the objectives. See if you can do them.
2. _____ Restudy the material related to any objectives that you cannot do.
3. _____ Use the **SQ3R** study procedure to review the material:
   a. **S**can the sections.
   b. **Q**uestion yourself.
   c. **R**ead to answer your questions.
   d. **R**ecite the answers to yourself.
   e. **R**eview areas you did not understand.
4. _____ Review all vocabulary, activities, and Self Tests, writing a correct answer for every wrong answer.

SELF TEST 3

Answer these questions (each answer, 4 points).

3.01 What was the main object of American strategy in the War of 1812?

_____

3.02 What are two of the things the British negotiators demanded when they first met with the Americans in Ghent in the summer of 1814?

a. _____ b. _____

3.03 What were the three parts of Henry Clay's proposed American System?

a. _____ b. _____

c. _____

3.04 What were two of the grievances that led to the War of 1812?

a. _____ b. _____

3.05 What were two of the parts of Alexander Hamilton's financial program?

a. _____ b. _____

Name the item described (each answer, 3 points).

3.06 _____ European interference in the Americas would be viewed as a hostile act by the U.S.

3.07 _____ Greatest American victory of the War of 1812, fought after the treaty was signed

3.08 _____ City burned by the British in the Chesapeake Bay campaign of 1814

3.09 _____ Political party that dominated the American government in the early 1800s

3.010 _____ Section of the country that opposed the War of 1812

3.011 _____ Group of Federalists who wanted to weaken the federal government near the end of the War of 1812

3.012 _____ Name given to the early part of the Monroe Administration because of the unity and good will of the nation

3.013 _____ A revolt against the excise tax in Pennsylvania under Washington

3.014 _____ "Old Ironsides," famous American frigate

3.015 _____ Song written about the siege of Fort McHenry in Baltimore

Match these people (each answer, 2 points).

3.016 _____ Andrew Jackson   a. American victor at the Battle of Lake Erie

3.017 _____ Henry Clay   b. American victor at the Battle of the Thames

3.018 _____ James Calhoun   c. Speaker of the House from Kentucky

3.019 _____ William H. Harrison   d. militia general, defeated the Creek People

3.020 _____ James Madison   e. chief justice of the Supreme Court

3.021 _____ Nicholas Biddle   f. British commander in Canada

3.022 _____ John Marshall   g. War Hawk from South Carolina

3.023 _____ William Hull   h. president of the Second National Bank

3.024 _____ Isaac Brock   i. president who asked for war with Britain

3.025 _____ Oliver Perry   j. American general, surrendered Detroit

Answer true or false (each answer, 1 point).

3.026 _____ The War of 1812 is also called the Second War for Independence.

3.027 _____ British navy was reduced in effectiveness by American naval victories in the War of 1812.

3.028 _____ American ships could not fight effectively against British ships.

3.029 _____ The British strategy in the War of 1812 was to capture key American cities and make the nation a colony again.

3.030 _____ The Battle of Plattsburgh Bay stopped the British invasion of New York coming down Lake Champlain.

3.031 _____ Americans were relieved and humiliated after the War of 1812.

3.032 _____ The War of 1812 encouraged the beginning of American manufacturing.

3.033 _____ America lost part of the Northwest Territory in the Treaty of Ghent.

3.034 _____ The military situation became worse for the Americans in 1814 when Napoleon went into exile.

3.035 _____ The steady improvement of British-American relations began after the War of 1812.

80 / 100   SCORE _____   TEACHER _____   _____
                                             initials   date

Before taking the LIFEPAC Test, you may want to do one or more of these self checks.

1. _____ Read the objectives. See if you can do them.

2. _____ Restudy the material related to any objectives that you cannot do.

3. _____ Use the **SQ3R** study procedure to review the material.

4. _____ Review activities, Self Tests, and LIFEPAC vocabulary words.

5. _____ Restudy areas of weakness indicated by the last Self Test.

HISTORY & GEOGRAPHY 804
A Firm Foundation (1789–1820)

LIFEPAC Test is located in the
center of the booklet. Please
remove before starting the unit.

Author:

Theresa Buskey, B.A., J.D.

Editor:

Alan Christopherson, M.S.

Westover Studios Design Team:

Phillip Pettet, Creative Lead

Teresa Davis, DTP Lead

Nick Castro

Andi Graham

Jerry Wingo

Alpha Omega
PUBLICATIONS

804 N. 2nd Ave. E.
Rock Rapids, IA 51246-1759

A Firm Foundation (1789–1820)

Introduction

The first forty years after the ratification of the Constitution was a time of foundation building. The new Constitution had to be transformed from ideas on paper to a practical, working government. Even with a good plan, a weak original government would set precedents that would be hard to change. It was up to first president, George Washington, and his advisors to use the blueprint of the Constitution to build a good foundation for the structure of the United States.

The early years of our nation were complicated by events in Europe. The French Revolution began in 1789. The king of France was overthrown and executed. The Revolution degenerated into a blood-bath called the Reign of Terror (1793-94). A war began in Europe as other monarchs tried to interfere. Finally, General Napoleon Bonaparte seized power in France (1799) and conquered much of Europe. He was defeated by an alliance led by Britain (1813) and went into exile (1814). In 1815 he returned to be defeated again.

The war put America in a difficult position. France had been America's ally in the Revolution, but Britain was America's biggest trading partner. Both sides had interfered with American trade during the long years of conflict, but the actions of the British were especially infuriating. The hard-pressed American leaders did not want to get into a European war. By 1812, the long-suffering Americans could take no more; war was declared on Britain. The second war of independence, the War of 1812, finished laying the foundation of America. With the foundation laid, the country built toward its future.

Objectives

Read these objectives. The objectives tell you what you will be able to do when you have successfully completed this LIFEPAC. When you have finished this LIFEPAC, you should be able to:

1. Describe the important events of the first five presidential administrations.

2. Describe the Great Seal of the United States.

3. Describe the course and nature of America's problems with Britain that led to the War of 1812.

4. Describe the growth, policies, and decline of the Federalist Party.

5. Describe the growth and policies of the Democratic-Republican Party.

6. Describe the course and results of the War of 1812.

7. Describe how America changed after the War of 1812.

8. Describe the development of the power of the Supreme Court under John Marshall.

9. Explain the reasons behind U.S. policy decisions from 1789 to the early 1820s.

Survey the LIFEPAC. Ask yourself some questions about this study and write your questions here.

1. FEDERALIST ERA

The Federalists led the victorious battle for the Constitution after the Constitutional Convention. When the first government was formed under the new plan in 1789, it was dominated by the same Federalists. They controlled the U.S. government through the Washington and Adams administrations, but they were driven from power in 1801 when Thomas Jefferson became president under the Democratic-Republican Party.

The republic faced many difficulties in the first twelve years under the Constitution. Washington had to establish exactly what all the descriptions of his duties meant and what the newly created post required of him. Alexander Hamilton, the first secretary of the treasury, had to repair the poor state of the nation's finances. A rebellion broke out against the new taxes which such repairs required. America had to deal with the French Revolution and a European war. Trade problems threatened war with both Britain and France. Controversy brewed over a treaty with Britain and a bribery scandal with France. Finally, the Federalists began their own decline by threatening freedom of speech in an attempt to control the passions of the era.

SECTION OBJECTIVES

Review these objectives. When you have completed this section, you should be able to:

1. Describe the important events of the first five presidential administrations.
2. Describe the Great Seal of the United States.
3. Describe the course and nature of America's problems with Britain that led to the War of 1812.
4. Describe the growth, policies, and decline of the Federalist Party.
5. Describe the growth and policies of the Democratic-Republican Party.
9. Explain the reasons behind U.S. policy decisions from 1789 to the early 1820s.

VOCABULARY

Study these words to enhance your learning success in this section.

agrarian (u grar' ē an). Concerning agriculture or rural matters.

bond (bond). A certificate issued by a government or company which promises to pay back, with interest; the money borrowed from the buyer of the certificate.

nominal (nom' i nal). In name only; not real or actual.

nullify (nul' i fī). To deprive of legal force; make void.

partisan (pär' ti zan). A very strong supporter of a party, cause, or faction.

repudiation (ri pyoo' dē ā' shun). The act of rejecting the validity of something.

Note: *All vocabulary words in this LIFEPAC appear in* **boldface** *print the first time they are used. If you are not sure of the meaning when you are reading, study the definitions given.*

Pronunciation Key: hat, āge, cãre, fär; let, ēqual, tėrm; it, īce; hot, ōpen, ôrder; oil; out; cup, pùt, rüle; child; long; thin; /ŦH/ for then; /zh/ for measure; /u/ or /ə/ represents /a/ in about, /e/ in taken, /i/ in pencil, /o/ in lemon, and /u/ in circus.

AMERICA from **1789** to **1820**

George Washington
1789–1797

John Adams
1797–1801
Federalist

Thomas Jefferson
1801–1809
Democratic-Republican

James Madison
1809–1817
Democratic-Republican

James Monroe
1817–1825
Democratic-Republican

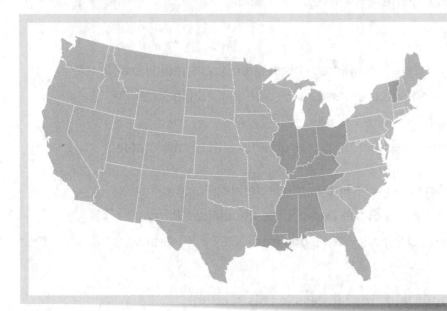

STATES ADMITTED TO THE UNION

Vermont	1791
Kentucky	1792
Tennessee	1796
Ohio	1803
Louisiana	1812
Indiana	1816
Mississippi	1817
Alabama	1819
Illinois	1819

POPULATION of the United States of America

1820 9,638,453

1790 3,929,000

Washington's First Term

There was never any doubt as to who would be elected as the first president of the United States. George Washington was the one person who had the public trust and the stature to take the job. He had the support of both the Federalists and Anti-Federalists. It can reasonably be argued that the position was created with him in mind. The Constitution required each state to choose electors who would then choose a president. When the vote was counted in April of 1789, the tally was unanimous for Washington. (He was the only president to receive a unanimous electoral vote). John Adams was chosen as vice president.

The same qualities that made Washington a great general also made him a superb first president. He did not like politics and accepted the presidency only because he felt the nation needed him. He commanded the respect of his subordinates and gave his tremendous prestige to the new post. He was careful, fair, and methodical. He chose wise counselors and listened to them before making his decisions. He provided the stability and thoughtful leadership the new nation so desperately needed in those early years.

Inauguration. Washington received word of his election at his home in Mount Vernon, Virginia. He immediately left on the long journey to New York City, which was America's temporary capital. He was greeted all along the route by cheering crowds. He took the oath of office on the balcony of Federal Hall, overlooking Wall Street, on April 30, 1789. He then gave an inaugural address in the chambers of the Senate.

Washington set a formal tone for the new office, mainly because of his own rather formal personality. He would bow, not shake hands, to greet visitors. He dressed richly and drove about in a handsome coach. Visitors could see him during his weekly open house or make an appointment. His wife Martha held a formal reception every Friday evening that the president attended. The office of president was less than a king, but more than a simple politician.

| George Washington's inauguration

Cabinet. The new Congress created three departments to help the president run the government: foreign affairs (state), war, and treasury. An attorney general, the attorney for the government, was added later. Washington choose men he knew and trusted to head these departments. They came to be his personal advisors and eventually met together to discuss decisions, forming the president's cabinet.

Washington stayed out of **partisan** politics as much as he could, but he recognized the conflicts of the day and represented both sides in his cabinet. Thomas Jefferson was the first secretary of state. He was a firm believer in a weak federal government, an **agrarian** country, and rule by the "common people." He eventually became the leader of the Democratic-Republican Party. Alexander Hamilton was the first secretary of the treasury. He was a Federalist leader who believed in a strong central government, a commercial nation, and rule by the "elite." The other cabinet members were Secretary of War Henry Knox and Attorney General Edmund Randolph.

Washington did not officially attach himself to either of the new political parties. However, mainly on the basis of Hamilton's arguments, he supported much of the Federalist agenda. As a result, Washington came under attack from the Anti-Federalists, who eventually developed into the Democratic-Republican Party.

Finances. The main problem facing the new government was the same one they had faced under the Articles of Confederation—money. The nation was deeply in debt and had no stable currency. Hamilton proposed the government pay the debt at full value and assume the Revolutionary War debts of the states as well. Hamilton intended to build the power of the federal government by establishing it financially and having the people look to it, not the state governments, for their money.

There was a tremendous amount of opposition to Hamilton's plan. Few people believed the **bonds** issued by the Revolutionary government would ever be paid. The war veterans and people who originally held the bonds had sold them for a fraction of what they were worth. Most were owned by wealthy men who could afford to hold them and wait. Many felt that it was unfair to give the profit to these men. Hamilton wanted the support of these wealthy citizens for the new government. He wanted to give the rich and well-born a stake in the new system.

Most of the southern states had already paid off their war debts. They objected to also paying off the northern debts through the federal government. Eventually, they agreed to the plan in exchange for placing the new national capital in the south, on the Potomac River between Maryland and Virginia. The rest of Hamilton's plan was accepted because Congress believed that a government should pay its lawful debts and knew it would be impossible to find the original owners of the bonds.

The third part of Hamilton's plan called for the establishment of a national bank. The bank would be partially owned by the government and would be used to deposit government funds. It also would issue a stable paper currency backed by the deposits in the bank.

The bank ran into violent opposition in Congress. Most of the supporters came from the north which favored a strong currency and bank to build trade and manufacturing. State's rights advocates did not want a large central bank which would compete with their state banks. The measure was passed after a heated debate and was sent to Washington for his signature.

Washington was deeply concerned about whether the bill was constitutional. He asked Jefferson (against) and Hamilton (for) to each give him a written opinion on the matter. Jefferson argued that the Constitution did not specifically authorize a bank. He favored a "strict construction" of the Constitution. The government could only do things specifically allowed by the Constitution, a position that would have severely limited federal power. Hamilton, on the other hand, persuasively argued for a "loose construction." The Constitution said that the Congress could pass any laws "necessary and proper" to carrying out the powers of the government. Since the government was authorized to collect taxes, a bank was both necessary and proper to fulfill that function. Washington agreed with Hamilton and signed the bill.

Money to pay the debts and finance the bank came from taxes. The primary tax of that day was the tariff, a tax on goods imported from other countries. A tariff also made foreign goods more expensive, thus protecting the few American manufacturers. This fit well with Hamilton's far-sighted plan for America to become a manufacturing nation. Congress also passed an excise tax on distilled liquor to supplement the tariff income.

The prosperity of the new government depended on trade which produced tariff income. Most of America's trade was with Britain. Thus, Hamilton and the Federalists came to favor England over France in foreign policy. This created yet another difference with Jefferson's supporters who favored France, a country that found itself in the middle of its own revolution.

Match these people.

1.1	_____ George Washington		a.	secretary of war
1.2	_____ John Adams		b.	attorney general
1.3	_____ Thomas Jefferson		c.	chosen unanimously by the electors
1.4	_____ Alexander Hamilton		d.	vice president
1.5	_____ Edmund Randolph		e.	secretary of state
1.6	_____ Henry Knox		f.	secretary of the treasury

Answer these questions.

1.7 What were Hamilton's three main proposals for the nation's finances?

a. _____

b. _____

c. _____

1.8 What did the southern states get in exchange for the federal government taking over the state's debts?

_____

1.9 What form of taxation was the main source of income for the new government?

_____

1.10 Why did some people not want the war bonds to be paid at full value?

_____

_____

_____

Put an *H* beside the policies supported by Hamilton and a *J* beside those supported by Jefferson.

1.11 _____ favored Britain

1.12 _____ strong central government

1.13 _____ agrarian society

1.14 _____ favored France

1.15 _____ weak federal government

1.16 _____ "strict construction" of Constitution

1.17 _____ "loose construction" of Constitution

1.18 _____ commercial society

THE GREAT SEAL

Nations are represented by symbols. The most famous symbol of the United States is our flag, the Stars and Stripes. Another important symbol is the Great Seal, which was adopted in 1782 by the nation's first government, the Second Continental Congress. Most people have probably seen the front or "obverse" of the Great Seal of the United States. It appears on federal buildings, vehicles, laws, and documents as well as coins and currency. The back or "reverse" is less well known, but it does appear on the back of the one-dollar bill. The Seal is rich with symbolism, much of which refers to the Christian foundation of our nation.

| The Great Seal of the United States

The Obverse of the Great Seal

On the obverse side of the seal are these symbols:

1. The Crest: At the top of the seal is a cluster of thirteen white stars on a blue field, which represents the original thirteen states. A ring of golden light is breaking through a white cloud which surrounds the stars. This light is a symbol of God's constant protection and guidance.

2. The National Coat of Arms: The remainder of the seal is our nation's coat of arms, which consists of these symbols;

    a. American Eagle: The eagle was selected to represent the United States because of its dignity, size, strength, and majestic appearance. The head and tail feathers are white, the claws and beak are yellow. Franklin wanted our symbol to be a turkey, but he was wisely outvoted by the committee.

    b. Shield: On the eagle's breast is a shield. The solid blue bar at the top represents the national government (originally just Congress). The seven white stripes and six red stripes stand for the first thirteen states.

    c. Scroll and Motto: Held by the eagle's beak is a golden scroll on which are written these words in Latin:
    E PLURIBUS UNUM
    The English translation of this motto is "One out of many." Many states make up the one nation, the United States of America.

    d. Thirteen Arrows: The eagle's left talon is clutching a bundle of thirteen arrows. This suggests that we will defend our nation.

    e. Olive Branch: The eagle's right talon is clutching a green olive branch with thirteen blue-tinted olives. The olive branch is a symbol of peace. Since the right side is considered to be more important, holding the olive branch in the right talon indicates that the United States prefers peace to war. The eagle is also facing the peace side rather than the war side.

The Reverse of the Great Seal

This part of the Great Seal is not as well known. The parts and their meanings are:

1. The Pyramid: In the center of the Seal is a pyramid built on the earth with a blue sky background. On the base of the pyramid are the Roman numerals MDCCLXXVI (1776), the year our nation was born. Thirteen layers of stone are in the pyramid, representing the original thirteen states. The pyramid is unfinished, indicating that our nation will continue to grow. The pyramid shape symbolizes the strength and stability of the United States.

2. The Eye: Above the pyramid is a large eye within a blue triangle surrounded by a golden light. The eye is a symbol that God is watching over our nation. The light represents God's glory and majesty.

3. Latin Mottoes:

    a. *ANNUIT COEPTIS* is written across the top of the Seal in golden letters. This means: *He (God) has favored our undertaking.*

    b. *NOVUS ORDO SECLORUM* is written in black letters on a golden scroll across the bottom. This means: *A new order of the ages.*

The Great Seal

On the Great Seal.

1.19 Name five ways that the original thirteen states are represented.

a. _____   b. _____

c. _____   d. _____

e. _____

1.20 Name two ways the presence of God is represented.

a. _____

b. _____

1.21 Why is the olive branch in the eagle's right talon? _____
_____

1.22 What does "E Pluribus Unum" mean? _____

Washington's Second Term

Washington wanted to retire after his first term. However, his friends urged him to stay on for another term for the sake of the country. He agreed and was unanimously re-elected in 1792. In March 1793, he was inaugurated in Philadelphia, which was the new temporary capital. Adams also returned as vice president.

European War. Washington received word of a general war in Europe a month into his second term. France was at war with Britain, Austria, Spain, and Prussia. France had been America's primary ally during the Revolution, and the treaty of alliance obligated the U.S. to aid them now. However, that treaty had been signed with the king of France who had been executed in the French Revolution. Supporters of the French Revolution wanted to honor the treaty. But even Jefferson was reluctant to get into another war. The Federalists feared the effect that war with Britain would have on trade and urged neutrality.

America was not strong militarily or politically. There was no army, and the new government had only been in place for four years. The pressures of a war could easily destroy all that had been built. Washington decided that the nation could not afford to be involved in a European war and issued a Proclamation of Neutrality on April 22nd. This continued to be the policy of the U.S. for most of the remaining years of this long war. American leaders desperately tried to keep out of the conflict as long as they could in order to buy time for their nation to grow strong.

Citizen Genêt. The republican government of France sent a new representative to America in April of 1793. He was Citizen (the title used by all in the Revolution) Edmond Genêt, an enthusiastic and tactless man. He had been commissioned to renew the treaty of friendship with America and obtain a new trade treaty. What he did was create a huge mess for Washington.

Genêt was received with joy by French supporters in America. He began at once to commission privateers to attack British shipping from American ports. He also tried to organize expeditions against the Spanish and British lands in America. Washington received him coolly, but Genêt did not take the hint. He ignored the Neutrality Proclamation and appealed to the American people to support France in the war. All this activity threatened to convince Britain that America was not truly neutral. Washington finally asked France to recall Genêt. He was stripped of his authority by a new government in France and stayed in the U.S. for fear of execution upon his return. American neutrality held.

Whiskey Rebellion. The excise tax passed by Congress during Washington's first administration had hit the northwestern farmers hard. It was difficult for these frontier farmers to make a profit shipping their grain to markets in the east because of the cost. Therefore, they routinely distilled their grain into liquor which was easier to transport and provided a good profit. The excise tax was immensely unpopular among these men and sparked a frontier revolt called the Whiskey Rebellion.

The Whiskey Rebellion began in 1794 in western Pennsylvania. The farmers there drew up resolutions against the tax, attacked the tax collectors, and terrorized court officials. The governor refused to act, so Washington called out the militia in the other states to enforce the law. The response was an army of over 13,000 men, more than Washington had for much of the Revolution. The rebellion scattered, and Washington pardoned the two culprits who were caught. The government's firmness made rebellious individuals use voting, rather than fighting, as the best means for pursuing their goals.

Problem with Britain. During his second term, Washington had to deal with the increasing problems with Great Britain. England still kept possession of several western forts in U.S. territory. It continued to support the Native American popluation there, hoping to use them as a buffer between the U.S. and Canada. As the war progressed with France, Britain began

| John Jay, negotiator with the British

seizing U.S. ships and cargoes trading with France or French colonies. The British also would search U.S. ships for British sailors who had become U.S. citizens. These men and many others who had never been British citizens were "impressed" or forced into serving in the British navy. Americans were outraged by this treatment of their vessels and citizens.

Jay's Treaty. Washington, hoping to avoid a war, and at the urging of the Federalists, sent John Jay to London to negotiate a settlement. He succeeded in obtaining a treaty in late 1794. The British agreed to evacuate the American forts, pay some compensation for the seized cargoes, and improve U.S. trading rights with Britain. However, the agreement mentioned nothing about ending their interference with American shipping or impressing of American sailors. The treaty restated the obligation of Americans to pay back debts owed to Britain from before the Revolution. Washington, believing it was the best he could get, submitted it to the Senate for approval.

The treaty was violently unpopular. Westerners were angry that it did not deal with the English support of the Native Americans. Southerners were angry that it did not require Britain to pay for slaves taken during the Revolution. Supporters of France saw it as a rejection of the nation's obligation to the French people. Patriotic Americans were angered by the extension of trade with a nation that freely mistreated American citizens. Even Hamilton, who needed the treaty to prevent a war and keep his financial system on track, did not like it. However, the pro-British, pro-trade Federalists dominated the Senate and after weeks of debate, it was approved. The nation was able to avoid a war for the time being.

Jay's Treaty did have one positive effect. Spain became nervous over the possibility of a British-American alliance in North America and settled some of her outstanding disputes with the U.S. A Spanish-American treaty was signed in 1795. It gave Americans the right to use the Mississippi and bring their goods through the Spanish-controlled port of New Orleans without paying any duty. It set the southern boundary of the U.S. and contained a Spanish promise to control Native Americans in their territory. This treaty helped restore the damaged national pride.

Farewell Address. Washington had come under savage attack for his policies and Jay's Treaty during his second administration. He was weary of public life and discouraged by the division of the government into factions. Washington believed political parties were a threat to the unity of the nation, but he had been unable to prevent them. Jefferson had even resigned from the cabinet because of Washington's support of Hamilton.

Washington announced that he would not accept re-election again. He set a "two-terms only" precedent which was followed by every president until Franklin Roosevelt in 1940. (After that, the president was limited to two terms by a constitutional amendment). He also published the *Farewell Address* that issued two warnings to the American people. The first was to avoid party politics. This was ignored. The second was that America should avoid all permanent alliances like the one made with France during the Revolution since they would draw us into foreign wars. This admonition became a key part of American foreign policy for generations. America did not sign a permanent military alliance again until after World War II (1938-1945).

Complete the following.

1.23 Washington reacted to the War in Europe in 1793 by issuing the _____

_____ .

1.24 In 1793 France was at war with _____

_____ .

1.25 The French republican representative to the U.S. in 1793 was (including his title)

_____ .

1.26 Name three things the French envoy did that threatened U.S. neutrality.

a. _____

b. _____

c. _____

1.27 What were the problems America was having with Britain?

a. _____

b. _____

c. _____

d. _____

1.28 What did the British agree to do under Jay's Treaty?

a. _____

b. _____

c. _____

1.29 Why did so many Americans object to Jay's Treaty?

_____

_____

_____

1.30 What was the Whiskey Rebellion and how was it settled?

_____

_____

_____

1.31 What two things did Washington recommend that Americans avoid in the *Farewell Address*?

_____ and _____

1.32 Washington set the precedent that the president serves _____ terms.

Adams Administration

Election of 1796. The elections of George Washington had been uncontested. In the election of 1796, however, there were three candidates. Hamilton was too unpopular to run as a candidate, so the Federalist faction supported John Adams or Thomas Pinckney (backed by Hamilton). The Democratic-Republicans supported Thomas Jefferson. With Washington no longer acting as a unifying factor, the verbal mud flew back and forth, further separating the two developing political parties. Adams won by three electoral votes. The system at the time did not take political parties into account, and the runner-up in electoral votes, Thomas Jefferson, received the vice presidency. The messy situation of having a president from one political party and his vice president from another was eventually prevented by the 12th Amendment to the Constitution, adopted in 1804.

John Adams was a lawyer from Massachusetts and had been an active participant in the political end of the Revolution. He had worked to oppose the Stamp Act, followed his conscience in defending the British soldiers responsible for the Boston Massacre, served in the First and Second Continental Congress, and represented America in Europe during the Revolutionary War. He assisted in the negotiations with Britain at the end of the war and was America's first ambassador to the former mother country. He returned home in 1788 and was selected to serve under Washington as vice president.

Adams was a very capable statesman but tended to be cold and sharp in person. He and Thomas Jefferson had become friends during the Revolution. Their political differences would temporarily end their relationship until after both had retired from office. Adams and Hamilton did not get along at all. Adams represented the moderate part of the Federalist party while Hamilton's views were more extreme. This split would do tremendous damage to the Federalist Party.

Adams kept all of Washington's cabinet when he took office in 1797. Hamilton had resigned earlier, but most of the other cabinet members kept him informed of their activities and relied on his advice. This further aggravated the problems between the two men and their supporters. Adams also inherited from Washington the problems in Europe, and those would dominate his time in office.

XYZ Affair. The Jay Treaty had triggered a crisis with France. The French saw it as a **repudiation** of the French-American treaty signed during the Revolution. The latest French government, the Directory, began to seriously harass U.S. trade and insultingly refused to receive a new American ambassador. Adams sent a special three-man delegation to France to try to resolve the dispute.

The American delegation arrived in France in 1797 and was approached by three representatives of Talleyrand, the French foreign minister. These three coolly requested a huge bribe for both the Directory and Talleyrand before negotiations could even begin! The Americans firmly refused and left. They filed a full report with

Adams, calling the three French representatives X, Y, and Z.

The XYZ Affair triggered a tremendous outcry when it became public in America. The insult to the national honor excited everyone. The extreme Federalists under Hamilton led the call for war. Taxes were raised to improve the navy and army. An aging George Washington was named as the **nominal** head of the army, with Alexander Hamilton in actual command. Americans put aside their own differences, and even Democratic-Republicans joined in the cry of "Millions for defense but not one cent for tribute."

Through it all, Adams kept his head. He realized the new nation could not afford a war. He proceeded with preparations, but with the support of the moderate Federalists, never called for declaration of war. An undeclared war went on between the ships of both sides for about two years. Finally, Talleyrand realized he could not afford to add America to the list of countries fighting France. He let Adams know that a new delegation would be received properly.

Convention of 1800. Adams authorized a new delegation to go to France in 1799 over the severe objections of much of his own party. The government in France had changed yet again by the time the Americans arrived. Napoleon Bonaparte was now the dictator of France, and he wanted to clear up foreign disputes to leave himself a free hand in Europe. The two sides negotiated (without bribes) the Convention of 1800. The Convention officially ended the old French-American treaty of alliance and temporarily settled the differences between the two nations. Adams had won the peace, but his refusal to give in to war hysteria cost him his popularity. He deserves a great deal of credit for stubbornly putting his country ahead of his political ambitions.

Alien and Sedition Acts. The Federalists had regained strength in Congress after the XYZ Affair. They took advantage of the anti-French hysteria to pass a series of laws in 1798 to suppress the Democratic-Republican opposition. The first part of the laws, the Alien Acts, had wide support in the country. These acts increased the time an immigrant must live in America to become a citizen from five to fourteen years. They also allowed the president to deport dangerous aliens or to imprison them during war time.

The Alien Acts were aimed at new immigrants who tended to support the more democratic party of Jefferson. They were also aimed at the hundreds of political refugees who had fled from the law in their own countries to cause trouble in America. The laws were never enforced, but their existence served to encourage many of the worst radicals to leave, and many others decided never to come.

The Sedition Act was aimed squarely at the rights of American citizens to free speech and freedom of the press. It required fines and imprisonment for such "crimes" as publishing any false, scandalous, or malicious statements against the government or organizing to oppose federal laws. This law was used very little, and then exclusively against Democratic-Republican publishers (only ten were convicted).

The Democratic-Republicans obviously led the opposition to the acts. Jefferson and Madison went overboard in opposing them. They succeeded in having the state legislatures in Kentucky and Virginia pass resolutions to **nullify** the laws. The Kentucky and Virginia Resolves were based on the theory that the federal government was a creation of the states, and the states could disallow its laws. Such a position would rob the federal government of all authority over the states. Fortunately, the other states did not join in this extreme position, but it was to be used again in the years leading up to the Civil War. The offensive laws were repealed or allowed to expire over the next two years.

Election of 1800. The election of 1800 was the first that can be described as a fight between

| John Adams was the only Federalist President.

two political parties. Adams faced an uphill battle for re-election. His Federalist Party was divided. The Hamilton wing openly fought against him. The Alien and Sedition Acts had given the Democratic-Republicans an issue to use against the Federalists. Moreover, after all the taxes and preparations, John Adams had not given the country the war they wanted. The well-organized Democratic-Republicans rallied behind Thomas Jefferson and Aaron Burr who ran as a president/vice president team.

The Democratic-Republicans won the election, but the rules for the election caused a serious problem. Each elector was to cast two votes, the one with the most votes became the president, the one in second place became the vice president. The Democratic-Republicans electors loyally cast their two votes, one each for Jefferson and Burr, who therefore tied! A tie was resolved by voting between the candidates in the House of Representatives, which was still under Federalist control. The Federalists supported Burr who was a professional politician, over the idealistic Jefferson. As a result, neither could get the necessary majority in thirty-five consecutive ballots. Finally, Jefferson won on the thirty-sixth when some of the Federalists abstained from voting. (They may have been convinced to do so by Hamilton, who had a strong dislike for Burr). This event brought about the 12th Amendment in 1804 which separated the voting for the two offices.

Federalist legacy. John Adams was the last Federalist president. The party slowly died after that. The divisions within the party hampered its ability to win elections. Its appeal to leadership by the elite did not fit with the growing democratic spirit of the nation. Moreover, once the Democratic-Republicans were in power, they began to support a strong federal government, gaining Federalist supporters as they moved toward Federalist ideas.

However, the Federalists left a rich legacy in America. They set up the basic structure of the national government, established a solid financial system, and protected the new nation from early wars that might have destroyed it. They also established the "loose construction" of the Constitution, giving the new government the flexibility to deal with the changes that were ahead.

Name the item or person.

1.33 _____ Allowed the president to deport dangerous aliens and increased the time of residency to become a citizen

1.34 _____ Party that won the 1800 elections

1.35 _____ Second president of the United States

1.36 _____ Treaty that triggered a crisis with France

1.37 _____ State resolutions to nullify Alien and Sedition Acts

1.38 _____ Agreement with France under Napoleon that ended the current disputes with America and the alliance

1.39 _____ An attempt by the French government to get bribes for negotiations

1.40 _____ Federalist law that attacked freedom of speech and the press

Answer these questions.

1.41 Who were the two leaders of the Federalist factions?

_____

1.42 What single decision cost John Adams his popularity?

_____

1.43 Publishers with what political party were prosecuted under the Sedition Act?

_____

1.44 What was the rallying cry of the nation preparing for war after the XYZ Affair?

_____

1.45 Who won the electoral vote in 1800?

_____

1.46 Who was Adams' vice president and why was that a problem?

_____

1.47 What was the legacy of the Federalists?

a. _____

b. _____

c. _____

d. _____

Review the material in this section in preparation for the Self Test. The Self Test will check your mastery of this particular section. The items missed on this Self Test will indicate specific areas where restudy is needed for mastery.

SELF TEST 1

Match these people (each answer, 2 points).

1.01	_____	Napoleon Bonaparte
1.02	_____	Alexander Hamilton
1.03	_____	Thomas Jefferson
1.04	_____	George Washington
1.05	_____	John Adams
1.06	_____	Edmond Genêt
1.07	_____	Edmund Randolph
1.08	_____	John Jay
1.09	_____	Aaron Burr
1.010	_____	Henry Knox

a. obtained an unpopular treaty with Britain under President Washington

b. first secretary of state

c. first secretary of the treasury

d. vice presidential candidate who tied with Jefferson in electoral votes in 1800

e. dictator of France

f. troublesome minister from France to America under Washington

g. unanimously chosen president by the electors

h. first and last Federalist president

i. first secretary of war

j. first attorney general

Name the item being described (each answer, 3 points).

1.011 _____ Political party that believed in rule by the elite, a strong central government, and was pro-British

1.012 _____ Political party that believed in rule by the common people, a weak federal government, and was pro-French

1.013 _____ Structure on the reverse of the Great Seal

1.014 _____ A revolt in Pennsylvania in 1794 against the excise tax

1.015 _____ The side that America fought with in the European war that began in 1793

1.016 _____ Scandal that erupted under John Adams when the French demanded a bribe before they would negotiate

1.017 _____ Laws passed by the Federalists to control immigrants and silence opposition to their government

1.018 _____ Agreement between America and France that ended their alliance and settled their current disputes

1.019 _____ The English translation of "E Pluribus Unum"

1.020 _____ Washington's statement that recommended the nation avoid political parties and foreign alliances

Answer these questions (each answer, 4 points).

1.021 What were the three parts of Hamilton's financial plan?

a. _____

b. _____

c. _____

1.022 What was Thomas Jefferson's argument against the National Bank?

_____

1.023 What are three legacies of the Federalist Era?

a. _____

b. _____

c. _____

1.024 What were some of the problems America was having with Britain under Washington?

a. _____

b. _____

c. _____

Answer true or false (each answer, 1 point).

1.025 _____ The national capital was to be built in the south in exchange for a lower tariff rate.

1.026 _____ Alexander Hamilton was vice president under John Adams.

1.027 _____ Citizen Genêt was a British ambassador who negotiated a treaty with the U.S.

1.028 _____ George Washington served two terms as president.

1.029 _____ "Millions for defense but not one cent for tribute" was the rally cry against the British during Washington's term.

1.030 _____ The French and British interfered with American trade.

1.031 _____ Washington did not attach himself to any political party.

1.032 _____ The obverse of the Great Seal has an eagle on it.

1.033 _____ Washington liked politics and eagerly sought the presidency.

1.034 _____ Hamilton favored an agrarian society with a weak federal government.

1.035 _____ John Adams' commitment to peace cost him his popularity.

80 / 100   SCORE _____   TEACHER _____ _____
                                                initials   date

2. JEFFERSONIAN DEMOCRACY

The election of Thomas Jefferson was a step in the continuing expansion of democracy in America. The old European idea of rule by the elite was slowly being replaced with the idea of rule by the people. Most of the states of the day still would only allow men who owned property to vote, but that was beginning to change. Jefferson was a warm advocate of the common people even though he was clearly a member of the upper class. He was acceptable to the old elites and yet reached out to the growing power of the people.

Jefferson found it impossible to maintain his ideal of a weak federal government when he was in charge. He would repeatedly act in ways not approved by "strict construction" of the Constitution. He justified such actions as being necessary for the "will of the people" and the protection of the country. They also firmly entrenched the idea of a strong, flexible federal government. Ironically, one of the reasons for the continuing decline of the Federalist Party was the fact that many of its supporters became very comfortable with Jefferson's government.

SECTION OBJECTIVES

Review these objectives. When you have completed this section, you should be able to:

1. Describe the important events of the first five presidential administrations.

3. Describe the course and nature of America's problems with Britain that led to the War of 1812.

4. Describe the growth, policies, and decline of the Federalist Party.

5. Describe the growth and policies of the Democratic-Republican Party.

9. Explain the reasons behind U.S. policy decisions from 1789 to the early 1820s.

VOCABULARY

Study these words to enhance your learning success in this section.

arbitrator (är' bi trā tor). One having the power to make authoritative decisions.

constituent (kon stich' oo ent). Someone represented by an elected official.

Enlightenment (en līt' n ment). A philosophical movement of the 18th century, concerned with making a rational re-examination of previously accepted ideas and institutions. It emphasized man's mind as the source of all knowledge and ridiculed faith.

lame duck (lām duk). An elected officeholder or assembly continuing in office during the period between the election of new people and their inauguration.

Democratic-Republicans in Power

Transitions. The election of 1800 was very important in the history of the United States. It was the first time that the ruling party had been defeated in an election. Often in a new republic, the losing party which still has control of the government and the army will use force to keep itself in power. The first change of party power is an important test for any new democracy. America passed that test. The Federalists unhappily but peacefully surrendered power to their political enemies.

Jefferson's election began twenty-five years of Democratic-Republican leadership in America. He immediately set a more informal tone for the presidency. He did not even arrive for his inauguration in a coach. He simply walked over from where he was staying. He shook hands with visitors and sat people at banquets without regard to their rank. He was even known to receive official callers wearing his bathrobe and slippers!

Thomas Jefferson was born into a wealthy Virginia family. He owned large tracts of land in the state and many slaves. He was a brilliant, well-educated man of many interests. He designed his own home, Monticello, near Charlottesville, Virginia, and filled it with many of his own inventions. He had been a member of the Virginia House of Burgesses, a representative at the Continental Congress (where he was the principle author of the Declaration of Independence), an American minister in France, secretary of state and vice president before he was elected to the presidency.

He was a follower of the **Enlightenment** and a "free thinker" where religion was concerned. He was not a Christian. He believed that man's nature was basically good, and by one's own strength evil could be overcome in the world.

Jefferson's policies. In spite of his anti-Federalist rhetoric, Jefferson took a more moderate course once in office. He did not overrule all of the Federalist financial policies. He promised to make full payment on the national debt. The

| The young Washington D.C.

National Bank was left in place as were the tariffs. The excise tax that fell so heavily on Jefferson's beloved farmers was repealed, however.

Jefferson slowly replaced the Federalist officeholders with people from his own party. Although it was done slowly, it was his administration that began the "spoils system" ("to the victor goes the spoils") which allowed government jobs to go to political supporters, rather than qualified workers. Jefferson overturned the Alien and Sedition Acts. The few men convicted under the Sedition Acts were pardoned and their fines returned. The residency requirement for citizenship was brought back down to five years, and the rest of the laws were not renewed when they expired.

Jefferson and his secretary of the treasury, Swiss-born Albert Gallatin, ran the government as cheaply as they could. They took advantage of a lull in the European fighting to vastly reduce the army and navy. They balanced the budget and put as much money as possible into paying off the national debt. In keeping with his philosophy of small government, Jefferson kept the taxes and government expenses low.

Midnight judges. Jefferson proved to be less moderate in dealing with Federalist judges. The **lame duck** Federalist Congress had passed the Judiciary Act of 1801 before the Democratic-Republicans came to power. It created about two hundred new jobs for judges and court officials. John Adams appointed Federalists to these jobs, the Senate quickly approved them, and Adams signed their commissions, (a few even on his last day in office). Rumor stated that some were signed after midnight that night. Jefferson and his party were understandably angered by these "midnight judges" that left the Federalists in power in the judicial branch.

The new Congress repealed the Judiciary Act of 1801, leaving many of the new appointees without jobs to take. Jefferson also ordered that many of the commissions signed by Adams simply not be delivered. One of the appointees, William Marbury, sued Secretary of State James Madison to get his commission. The case was brought in the Supreme Court under an earlier law, the Judiciary Act of 1789.

The chief justice of the Supreme Court was John Marshall, himself a last-minute Federalist appointee. Marshall used *Marbury v. Madison* (1803) to establish the Supreme Court as the final **arbitrator** of the Constitution. He ruled that the Judiciary Act of 1789 was unconstitutional in that it could not require the court to hear these kinds of cases. The Supreme Court was not the right place for Marbury to sue, so it could not make a decision for or against him. Thus Marshall avoided the issue of trying to force an unwilling president to deliver a questionable commission. He also established that the Supreme Court had the power to invalidate a law passed by Congress if it "conflicts" with the Constitution. That power is not given in the Constitution, and it gave the Federalist judiciary tremendous power that would be used more and more as American history progressed.

Jefferson was afraid of how the Federalist judges would use their power and decided to try to remove them. Federal judges were appointed for life under the Constitution and could only be removed by impeachment. Jefferson moved first to impeach John Pickering, a New England judge who was obviously insane.

After he was successfully removed, Jefferson set his sights higher.

In 1804 Jefferson brought impeachment proceedings in the Senate against Samuel Chase, a member of the Supreme Court. Chase was a Federalist judge who openly supported the Federalist agenda on the bench. He had been prominent in the conviction of the Democratic-Republican publishers under the Sedition Act. For impeachment, Jefferson had to prove that Chase was guilty of "high crimes and misdemeanors." The Senators decided that his conduct did not fit that description and acquitted him. Had they convicted him, Jefferson probably would have moved against John Marshall and other judges he did not like. Judges would have had to please the president in order to keep their jobs. The Senate's decision to abide by the plain meaning of the Constitution protected the independence of the federal judges.

Louisiana Purchase. America owned the eastern half of the Mississippi basin. The western half, the Louisiana Territory, was given to Spain after the French and Indian War. In late 1800 Napoleon convinced Spain to return the land to France. This was a dangerous turn of events for America. The west depended upon the Mississippi River and the port of New Orleans for the transport and sale of their products. Spain was an aging power who had agreed to let Americans use both the river and the port. France on the other hand, was an expanding power under Napoleon and might prove difficult to dislodge.

Jefferson acted quickly after he received news of the transfer. He sent James Monroe to France in 1803 to negotiate with the help of Robert Livingston, the American minister there. They were authorized to buy the port of New Orleans and as much land to the east as they could get for a maximum price of ten million dollars. When Monroe reached France he received a staggering surprise. Napoleon, having little success in his schemes in the New World, offered to sell all of Louisiana.

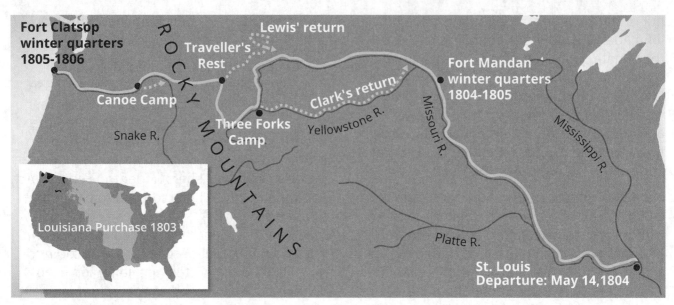

| The Lewis and Clark Expedition 1804-1806 and the Louisiana Purchase

The delegation had no authorization to buy so much land and had no way to contact Jefferson, who was across the Atlantic, for further instructions. The offer was just too good to refuse. Monroe and Livingston negotiated the sale of the land for fifteen million dollars, about three cents an acre.

The treaty put Jefferson in a very difficult position. He did not believe the Constitution authorized him to purchase such a large area of land. He wanted to get an amendment passed to permit it before going forward with the sale. Several of his advisors pointed out that Napoleon might not be willing to wait for that. In the end, the immense advantages of the sale overcame Jefferson's uncertainty. He submitted the treaty to the Senate who rapidly approved it.

The treaty was very popular, especially in the west. It removed the threat of a foreign power on the country's frontier. It guaranteed access to the Mississippi River and gave the country more land for expansion. All or part of fourteen states would eventually be created from the territory. The only losers in the deal were the Federalists, who saw their popularity sink in the light of Jefferson's success.

Lewis and Clark Expedition. The curious Jefferson commissioned a scientific/military expedition to explore and map the new territory. It was led by Jefferson's private secretary, Meriwether Lewis, and frontiersman William Clark, who was the younger brother of Revolutionary War hero George Rogers Clark. They were to try to reach the Pacific Ocean while taking notes on the animals, plants, geographical features, and Native Americans in the land.

The expedition left St. Louis, Missouri in May of 1804. They traveled up the Missouri, across the Rocky Mountains, and down the Columbia River to the Pacific Ocean. They were the first Americans to reach the Pacific overland. A Shoshone woman they met on the way named Sacajawea helped guide them over the mountains. On their return, Lewis and Clark took separate routes to increase the scope of their explorations. They eventually reunited to travel together down the Missouri toward home.

With almost all of their personnel, Lewis and Clark returned to St. Louis in September of 1806. Many people had given them up for dead because they had been gone so long. Their highly successful expedition expanded America's knowledge of the new land. It also gave America a solid claim to the rich Oregon Territory. Meriwether Lewis later became the governor of the very Louisiana Territory that he had explored.

Write true or false.

If the statement is false, change some nouns or adjectives to make it true.

2.1 _____ Jefferson's presidency was less formal than Washington's.

2.2 _____ The right of the Supreme Court to determine if laws are constitutional was set by *Marbury v. Marshall* in 1803.

2.3 _____ Thomas Jefferson brought impeachment proceedings against John Marshall in 1804.

2.4 _____ Thomas Jefferson reduced the army and navy when he was president.

2.5 _____ The treaty to purchase Louisiana was very unpopular.

2.6 _____ Lewis and Clark were the first Americans to reach the Pacific Ocean overland.

2.7 _____ Lewis and Clark traveled in the west for about a year.

2.8 _____ Pocahontas was a woman who helped Lewis and Clark.

2.9 _____ Jefferson's home in Virginia was Monticello.

Answer these questions.

2.10 Why was the election of 1800 important in the development of the American republic?

_____

_____

2.11 What (if anything) did Jefferson change in the Federalist finance system?

_____

2.12 Why were Americans concerned about France taking over Louisiana?

_____

_____

_____

2.13 What did Jefferson do about the Alien and Sedition Acts?

_____

_____

2.14 What was the financial and tax policy of Jefferson and Gallatin?

_____

_____

2.15 What did Jefferson believe he needed before he could accept the Louisiana Purchase?

_____

2.16 What route did Lewis and Clark follow to the Pacific?

_____

_____

Problems and Controversies

The Shores of Tripoli. The nations of the north coast of Africa (called the Barbary Coast) made a rich living attacking the ships that sailed in the Mediterranean. These pirates had routinely been paid off by the major trading nations to leave their ships alone. Jefferson objected to paying bribes and ransom (for captured sailors). He had long argued that the military should fight the pirates, not pay them.

The Pasha of Tripoli gave Jefferson his chance, when he declared war on the U.S. in 1801 because he was unhappy with his share of the tribute. Jefferson dispatched the reduced American navy to deal with the pirates more forcefully. The navy and the marines successfully fought a four-year war with the pirates, earning experience and international respect. (The marines immortalized the battles by including the "shores of Tripoli" in their hymn). Eventually, the Americans won a treaty with reduced payments. After a few years of fighting, the payments were stopped entirely.

Burr Conspiracy. Some New England Federalists were concerned that new states created in the Louisiana Territory would eliminate their influence in the federal government. They hatched a plot to take New England, New York and New Jersey out of the Union. They were joined in the plot by the Democratic-Republican vice president Aaron Burr who was out of favor with Jefferson. Burr ran for governor of New York in 1804, intending to use the office to support the plot. He was defeated with the help of Alexander Hamilton.

After the election, Burr challenged Hamilton to a duel and killed him. That incident ended Burr's political career and further depleted the Federalist Party. Burr fled to Pennsylvania after New York and New Jersey charged him with murder. In New York, he hatched a plot to invade Spanish territory, and possibly set up a separate government in the west. He organized a group of armed men and headed down the Ohio River. It is uncertain exactly what he intended to do, but one of his fellow conspirators, James Wilkinson, decided to back out and informed Jefferson of their actions.

Jefferson had Burr arrested and put on trial for treason in May of 1807. John Marshall was the judge at the trial which was held in Virginia. The Constitution requires two witnesses to convict someone of treason. Marshall interpreted it to mean that there had to be two witnesses to each separate act of treason. That was not possible and, in any case, the evidence was very confused. Much to Jefferson's disgust, Burr was acquitted. The stigma of the death of Hamilton and his trial led him to withdraw to Europe. He was never again politically active in America.

Growing problems with Britain. The country was so prosperous that Jefferson was overwhelmingly re-elected in 1804. However, there were dangerous clouds on the national horizon. Immediately after the sale of Louisiana, Napoleon declared war on Britain. In 1805 he defeated the Austrian and Russian armies in Austria at Austerlitz. Earlier that same year, Britain had destroyed the French fleet at Trafalgar, south of Spain. The combination of the two victories left France in control of Europe and Britain in control of the oceans.

The two sides were secure in their own areas and could not directly fight each other. So both began a campaign to starve each other into submission. Napoleon used his control of Europe to cut off its trade with Britain and Britain used its control of the seas to cut off all other trade with the entire continent. In 1806 and 1807 Britain issued Orders in Council (an order from the king on the advice of his council) that all neutral ships found on the sea sailing near French-controlled lands were to be seized. Such ships must stop first in Britain to have their cargo examined. France in turn ordered all ships that stopped in Britain to be seized if they came to France. American trade fell as both sides took ships and cargoes.

The British stepped up their impressment of sailors in a desperate attempt to keep their hard-pressed navy at full strength. Life in the British navy was incredibly harsh and inhumane. Many British sailors had deserted, obtained legal or fraudulent American citizenship, and had began serving on American ships for better pay and better conditions. It was these Englishmen that the British were "officially" after when they searched American merchant ships. They would claim that a man born English is always English. In fact, the British captains took many men who had never even been English, without any rebuke from London. The American navy had been so reduced under Jefferson that there was no way it could protect U.S. shipping and the British clearly knew this.

The contempt the British held for American rights was illustrated by the *Chesapeake-Leopard* affair in 1807. The American warship *Chesapeake* was approached by the British ship *Leopard* a few miles off the coast of Virginia. The British captain demanded the surrender of four deserters he claimed were aboard the American ship. Even though his guns were not ready, the

| The *Leopard* attacking the *Chesapeake*

American captain refused. The British opened fire, killing three men, injuring eighteen, and badly damaging the ship. The Americans surrendered, the British took the four men, and the Chesapeake limped back to port.

The British captain clearly exceeded his government's guidelines by attacking a neutral warship, but the British government was reluctant to admit error and refused the American demand to give up impressment. The American public cried out for war. Jefferson did not want one. America's small, poorly equipped army and navy proved the nation was not ready. Jefferson searched for an honorable alternative.

Embargo disaster. Jefferson decided to force the European powers to respect American rights by cutting off trade with them. He hoped that they needed American supplies badly enough that they would meet his demands. Congress passed Jefferson's Embargo Act in 1807. It forbade the export of <u>any</u> American goods on any ship. It was a long way from Jefferson's earlier position under Washington that the federal government did not even have the power to charter a bank!

The Embargo Act was an unqualified disaster. Legitimate trade came to a halt. The docks of the American port cities were deserted.

Thousands lost their jobs in the shipping, storage, exchange, and shipbuilding industries. Crops such as cotton, grain, and tobacco that supplied cash for western and southern farmers could not be sold abroad. The entire country suffered from the crisis. Napoleon added a humiliating note to the law when he began to "enforce" it in Europe by seizing any American vessels that happened to reach port there.

The embargo quickly raised a storm of opposition. Angry citizens called it the "O Grab Me" (embargo spelled backwards). A flourishing illegal trade grew along the U.S.-Canadian border. The New England states, which were the most dependent on trade, talked of leaving the Union. Jefferson's popularity plummeted, especially after he convinced Congress to pass tough laws to enforce the embargo.

The embargo also failed to cause any real harm to Britain. The British had good crops that year—enough to meet their food requirements. Some of the depleted trade was taken up by the new republics in South America. The English were not willing to consider any American demands to restore trade. Jefferson finally admitted defeat and signed the repeal of the law days before he left office. It had been in effect for fourteen months.

 Complete these sentences.

2.17 Aaron Burr killed _____ in a duel.

2.18 The French land victory at _____ and the British sea victory at _____ created a stalemate in the European war.

2.19 Aaron Burr was acquitted on the charge of _____ in 1807.

2.20 The British ship _____ attacked the American ship _____ in 1807 to recover four deserters; in the process the British killed three Americans and injured eighteen.

2.21 America fought a four year war with the pirates along the north coast of _____ under Thomas Jefferson.

2.22 Jefferson tried to deal with European interference with American ships by the _____ Act of 1807.

2.23 Aaron Burr's conspiracy was exposed by _____ , a co-conspirator who decided to back out.

2.24 British issued _____ in 1806 and 1807 that ordered their navy to seize all neutral ships headed for French-held Europe.

2.25 The British tried to keep their ships at full staff by the _____ of sailors on American ships.

2.26 Jefferson signed the _____ of the Embargo Act right before he left office.

HISTORY & GEOGRAPHY 804

LIFEPAC TEST

NAME   _____

DATE   _____

SCORE   _____

HISTORY & GEOGRAPHY 804: LIFEPAC TEST

Put a *C* beside items that were a cause of the War of 1812, an *R* beside those that were results of the war, and a *P* beside those that were attempts to prevent war (each answer, 2 points).

1. _____ Embargo Act

2. _____ Impressment

3. _____ Nationalism

4. _____ Rise of American Manufacturing

5. _____ British support of Tecumseh

6. _____ Jay's Treaty

7. _____ *Chesapeake-Leopard* Affair

8. _____ Improvement in British-American relations

9. _____ Eliminated the Native American resistance on the frontier

10. _____ Orders in Council

Name the item described (each answer, 3 points).

11. _____ State ceded by Spain after Andrew Jackson defeated the Seminole Indians there

12. _____ Scandal under John Adams when the French would not negotiate without a bribe

13. _____ Political party that set up the basic government structure, a solid financial system and "loose construction"

14. _____ The obverse has an eagle holding an olive branch and thirteen arrows, the reverse has a pyramid

15. _____ western Mississippi land purchased by Jefferson in spite of his belief it was unconstitutional

16. _____ Laws passed by the Federalist Party to control immigrants and silence opposition to the government

17. _____ Revenue for transportation was to come from these under Henry Clay's American System

18. _____ Name for the time under the Monroe administration when the country was united and content

19. _____ Fort that was successfully defended in the Battle of Baltimore

20. _____ Federalist group that wanted to weaken the federal government near the end of the War of 1812

Match these people (each answer, 2 points).

21. _____ John Marshall
22. _____ Tecumseh
23. _____ Henry Clay
24. _____ Oliver Perry
25. _____ Alexander Hamilton
26. _____ Henry Knox
27. _____ Andrew Jackson
28. _____ Thomas Jefferson
29. _____ James Madison
30. _____ James Monroe

a. hero of the Battle of New Orleans
b. first secretary of war
c. first leader of Democratic-Republicans
d. Battle of Lake Erie
e. Anti-American Confederacy organizer
f. president; asked for war with Britain
g. Speaker of the House; War Hawk
h. Federalist chief justice; Supreme Court
i. first secretary of the treasury
j. president; warned Europe not to interfere in America

Choose the best answer (each answer, 3 points).

31. Thomas Jefferson opposed the National Bank because _____ .
    a. it would take capital from state banks
    b. it was not specifically permitted by the Constitution
    c. it would benefit mainly rich investors
    d. he was afraid of the power it would have

32. The most important issue facing Washington's administration was _____ .
    a. the Whiskey Rebellion
    b. British occupation of forts in the Old Northwest
    c. finances
    d. where to locate the capital

33. The Federalists declined as a political party because _____ .
    a. the Democratic-Republicans took over much of their agenda
    b. most of their support was in New England
    c. John Adams was unpopular
    d. Alexander Hamilton was killed in a duel

34. The significance of the election of 1800 was that _____ .
    a. Adams did not win a second term
    b. Jefferson introduced a more relaxed style of government
    c. the Federalists never won the presidency again
    d. there was a peaceful change in political power

35. The Treaty of Ghent did not cost America any territory because _____ .
    a. of the Battle of New Orleans
    b. Britain was exhausted from twenty years of war
    c. the British did not get the victories they expected
    d. Napoleon was threatening Europe again

36. America entered the War of 1812 at a disadvantage because _____ .
    a. New England opposed the war
    b. the army and navy were inadequate
    c. the National Bank was no longer in existence
    d. France was still seizing American ships

37. The goal of the U.S. in the War of 1812 was _____ .
    a. to capture Canada
    b. to end years of mistreatment by the British
    c. to force free trade
    d. prove the worth of her navy

38. New England opposed the War of 1812 because _____ .
    a. they opposed Madison
    b. it stopped trade
    c. they did not want Canadian land to add more states
    d. it stopped tariff revenue

39. Thomas Jefferson tried to impeach several judges because _____ .
    a. they were incompetent
    b. they were appointed by the lame duck Federalists
    c. he was afraid of the power of lifetime-appointed Federalist judges
    d. he wanted to expand the spoils system

40. Washington's greatest success as president was _____ .
    a. putting down the Whiskey Rebellion
    b. providing the nation with the early stability it needed
    c. choosing the best men for his cabinet
    d. establishing the First National Bank

✎ **Answer these questions.**

2.27 Did the embargo accomplish its purpose? _____

Explain. _____

_____

2.28 What caused the war with the Barbary pirates?

_____

_____

2.29 How did Americans react to the embargo?

_____

_____

2.30 What plot was Aaron Burr involved with when he ran for governor of New York?

_____

_____

War Hawks

Elections of 1808 and 1810. Thomas Jefferson decided not to run for another term as president. He was afraid that the men who followed him might try to keep the office for life. So like Washington before him, he served only two terms. He retired to Monticello, helped found the University of Virginia, and renewed his broken friendship with John Adams who was living in retirement in Massachusetts. The two old friends and revolutionaries carried on a lively correspondence in their declining years. By a memorable act of Providence, John Adams and Thomas Jefferson both died on July 4, 1826, the fiftieth anniversary of the Declaration of Independence.

Thomas Jefferson was not active in the election of 1808, but he was pleased when his good friend and secretary of state, James Madison, was elected president. Madison defeated the Federalist candidate, C. C. Pinckney by more than a two-to-one margin in the electoral votes. With their pro-British agenda and New England power base, the Federalists were declining rapidly as more western states were added and anti-British sentiment grew.

The growing anger against Britain and the natural passage of time brought significant changes in Congress, most noticeably in the House of Representatives. In 1808 and particularly in 1810, a new crop of Representatives came to dominate the House. They were young men, often from the west. They had not fought or served in the Revolution. They had no first-hand experience of what the high cost of a war with Great Britain would be. They were eager to defend their nation's honor and expand her borders. History named them the "War Hawks."

War Hawks. The leader of the War Hawks was a young man who would be prominent in American politics for many decades. His name was Henry Clay. Clay was a brilliant speaker from Kentucky who was chosen as Speaker of the House in 1811. He used that position to appoint War Hawks to head important committees and dominate the House. Another member of the Hawks was John Calhoun of South Carolina. Calhoun also would be prominent on the American political stage for several decades to come.

The War Hawks were primarily from the west and the south. They were avidly in favor of war with Britain. They were men who had known no other country but the United States and were passionately nationalistic. They wanted to capture Canada and naively believed it would be a simple matter, since Britain was busy fighting in Europe. They also hoped to take Florida from Spain. The farmers from their states badly needed free trade in order to sell their goods abroad. The War Hawks' **constituents** also wanted to rid the frontier of attacks lead by Native Americans.

Tecumseh's Confederacy. One of the most remarkable leaders of the Native Americans resistance to the American pioneer flood was Tecumseh, a Shawnee leader from the Ohio country. He was a skilled orator who succeeded in organizing Native American people from all over the eastern Mississippi basin into an anti-American confederacy. He was assisted by his brother, "the Prophet," who claimed to have had a revelation and led a spiritual organization of the tribes.

In 1811 General William Henry Harrison led an American army to drive the confederation out of lands they had given away by treaty. Harrison was attacked by the Prophet not far from Tecumseh's headquarters at Tippecanoe.

| Henry Clay, Champion of the War Hawks

Harrison defeated the Native Americans and burned their settlement. He also found a large supply of British guns and powder in the settlement.

The defeat broke the power of the Prophet and dispersed the confederacy. Still, Tecumseh convinced many of the tribes to fight with the British during the upcoming War of 1812. He was killed in 1813 at the battle of the Thames in Canada.

The slide toward War. News of British supplies in the hands of the Native Americans further inflamed the War Hawks. They believed Britain was aiding and plotting with Tecumseh's Confederacy. They pushed ever harder for a war with Britain.

The situation was extremely difficult to resolve. Britain was fighting, possibly for its own survival, against one of the greatest dictators in history. Napoleon had conquered most of Europe, putting his family and friends on the thrones of its nations. Now he was looking for new lands to conquer. Britain was almost alone in trying to stop him. Meanwhile, America wanted to make wartime profits in trade without choosing sides. Britain was in no mood to compromise and neither were the War Hawks.

President Madison had searched desperately for a way to avoid a war. The Embargo Act was replaced in 1809 by the Non-Intercourse Act, which allowed trade with any nation except Britain or France. This was replaced in 1810 by Macon's Bill No. 2. This law allowed trade with all nations, but included what Congress hoped would be a enticing lure. If Britain or France would repeal their orders to capture U.S. ships, America would stop trading with their opponent.

Napoleon seized on this new law as a way to restore the American trade embargo against Britain. He publicly announced in November of 1810 that he would no longer seize American ships. Madison foolishly believed him and ordered all trade with Britain to be stopped. In fact, the French never had recalled their orders and continued to capture American ships. Britain demanded proof of the French decision and continued her own seizures. Relations between America and the former mother country continued to deteriorate.

War. America was totally unprepared for war. Jefferson had left the nation without a substantial navy or army. The War Hawks foolishly believed the war would be fought on land in Canada and refused to improve the navy in the time leading up to the war. Even when Congress did increase the size of the army, they were not able to overcome the lack of organization and trained officers. The army would have to rely on additions from the state militia, and many people felt the militia could not legally fight outside the United States. In fact, many of the militia refused to fight in Canada, which further undermined the military situation.

The nation's financial situation added to the military problems. The Democratic-Republicans had allowed the Charter for the hated National Bank to expire in 1811, leaving the nation without any central financial structure. Embargoes and trade problems had cut off the government's income from tariffs. The Democratic-Republicans, true to their Jeffersonian origins, opposed internal taxes needed to prepare for war. They finally agreed to them once war was already declared, which cut off any hope of having a nation ready in advance.

The hard realities of the situation did not disturb the well-organized War Hawks. They continued to press for war, confident that a simple invasion of Canada would force Britain to come to terms. Madison finally gave in to his own frustrations, pressure from the War Hawks, and the temptation of capturing Canada. He asked Congress to declare war in June of 1812. In support of the request, he sent a list of grievances, which included impressment, the seizure of American ships and British support of Native American attacks on Americans. Congress voted in favor of war on June 17th and 18th. The war Washington, Adams, and Jefferson avoided had finally arrived.

✎ **Complete the following.**

2.31 Who won the presidential election of 1808? _____

2.32 Name two young War Hawks that would be important political leaders for decades.

_____

2.33 Who was the American commander at the Battle of Tippecanoe?

_____

2.34 Name four of the reasons why the War Hawks favored war.

    a. _____

    b. _____

    c. _____

    d. _____

2.35 What was significant about the day Adams and Jefferson died?

_____

2.36 What did Tecumseh do that threatened the U.S. frontier?

_____

_____

2.37 Give five reasons why the U.S. was not prepared for war.

    a. _____

    b. _____

    c. _____

    d. _____

    e. _____

2.38 What part of the country did the War Hawks come from?

_____

2.39 Why did the Battle of Tippecanoe increase American hostility toward Britain?

_____

2.40 Why was it significant that most of the War Hawks were young?

_____

_____

2.41 What territory did the War Hawks expect to capture easily? _____

2.42 What trick did Napoleon play on Madison in regard to Macon's Bill No. 2?

_____

_____

2.43 What month and year did America declare war on Britain?

_____

2.44 What were the reasons given by President Madison for declaring war?

a. _____

b. _____

c. _____

Review the material in this section in preparation for the Self Test. This Self Test will check your mastery of this particular section as well as your knowledge of the previous section.

SELF TEST 2

Name the item described (each answer, 3 points).

2.01 _____ Scandal under John Adams over an attempt by French official to demand bribes before negotiation

2.02 _____ Young representatives from the west and south, elected in 1808 and 1810, who favored war with Great Britain

2.03 _____ A revolt in Pennsylvania during George Washington's presidency against the excise tax

2.04 _____ Laws passed by the Federalists to control recent immigrants and restrict the free speech of Democratic-Republican publishers

2.05 _____ Land purchased from France in 1803 for 3 cents an acre that Jefferson was not sure he could constitutionally take

2.06 _____ Expedition to explore the land purchased from France; men were the first Americans to reach the Pacific Ocean by an overland route

2.07 _____ Political party of John Adams

2.08 _____ Political party of Thomas Jefferson

2.09 _____ Supreme Court decision that created the right of the court to invalidate a law passed by Congress as unconstitutional

2.010 _____ The disastrous law passed under Jefferson to cut off trade and force the European nations to honor U.S. neutrality

Answer these questions (each answer, 4 points).

2.011 What were three grievances America had against Britain under Washington that were named as reasons for the War of 1812?

a. _____

b. _____

c. _____

2.012 Did Jefferson follow "strict construction" after he became president? _____

Give an example. _____

_____

2.013 What was the *Chesapeake-Leopard* incident of 1807?

_____

_____

2.014 Name three legacies of the Federalist Era.

a. _____

b. _____

c. _____

2.015 What was the significance in American history of the election of 1800?

_____

2.016 What "war" was fought during Jefferson's administration?

_____

Match these people (each answer, 2 points).

2.017	_____	Thomas Jefferson
2.018	_____	George Washington
2.019	_____	John Calhoun
2.020	_____	John Marshall
2.021	_____	Sacajawea
2.022	_____	Aaron Burr
2.023	_____	Napoleon
2.024	_____	James Madison
2.025	_____	Tecumseh
2.026	_____	Henry Clay

a. Alexander Hamilton set his financial policies

b. Shoshone woman who aided Lewis and Clark

c. chief justice of the Supreme Court

d. representative from Kentucky; Speaker of the House

e. organized the Native Americans of the eastern Mississippi into an anti-American alliance

f. representative from South Carolina

g. third president of the U.S.

h. dictator of France

i. president who finally asked for war with Britain

j. led a conspiracy that possibly intended to create a new government in the west

Choose the letters of the correct answers (1 point for each letter, chosen or not).

2.027 Which of the following were part of the controversy between Jefferson and the Federalist judiciary? _____
a. Many were appointed after the election of 1800 under the Judiciary Act of 1801, which was also passed after the election.
b. The appointments, approval, and commissioning of the judges were hurried through procedures by the Federalists after the election of 1800.
c. Jefferson was able to successfully use impeachment to get rid of the Federalist judges he opposed.
d. The Democratic-Republican Congress used the Judiciary Act of 1801 to appoint their own judges to the bench.

2.028 Each of the following either moved America and Britain closer to war or were used to avoid it.

Choose the ones that moved the nations toward war. _____
a. Orders in Council
b. Non-Intercourse Act
c. Jay's Treaty
d. Austerlitz and Trafalgar
e. Tecumseh's Confederacy
f. Washington's Farewell Address

80 / 100   SCORE _____   TEACHER _____ _____

initials   date

3. WAR OF 1812

The War of 1812 has been called the Second War for Independence, because it established America's reputation as a nation. Britain began acting like a bully by meddling in the Northwest Territory and disregarded America's rights on the open sea. The Americans stood up to the bully in the War of 1812. This time, the Americans fought alone, without any European allies. Britain could not blame American victories on the French. The war established a new respect for America and its armed forces, particularly the navy.

This was a war that began and ended with irony. The Orders in Council, a major cause of the war, were withdrawn days before war was declared because the drop in trade was hurting British merchants. The greatest American victory, the Battle of New Orleans, was fought after the peace treaty was signed that ended the war.

Those ironic twists almost perfectly describe this bumbling war. The Americans were unable to capture Canada, as they so arrogantly believed they could. The tiny American navy astounded the British by besting many of her warships in one-on-one battle. At one point, the British tried to dictate terms for peace, only to find that the Americans were doing much better than they had thought. It was a war of confusion that was fought in a series of small, scattered battles which ended in a draw. The war was ended by a treaty that was essentially a cease-fire agreement.

SECTION OBJECTIVES

Review these objectives. When you have completed this section, you should be able to:

1. Describe the important events of the first five presidential administrations.
2. Describe the growth, policies, and decline of the Federalist Party.
3. Describe the growth and policies of the Democratic-Republican Party.
4. Describe the course and results of the War of 1812.
5. Describe how America changed after the War of 1812.
6. Describe the development of the power of the Supreme Court under John Marshall.
7. Explain the reasons behind U.S. policy decisions from 1789 to the early 1820s.

VOCABULARY

Study these words to enhance your learning success in this section.

annex (a neks'). To incorporate territory into an existing country.

arbitration (är' bi trā shun). The process by which the parties to a dispute submit their differences to the judgment of an impartial party appointed by mutual consent.

czar (zär). A king or emperor; especially one of the former emperors of Russia.

depression (di presh' en). A period of drastic decline in the national economy characterized by decreasing business activity, falling prices, and unemployment.

frigate (frig' it). A high speed, medium-sized sailing warship of the 17th-19th century.

nationalism (nash' un ul iz' em). Devotion to the interests of a particular nation.

speculate (spek′ yu lāt). To engage in the buying or selling of a commodity with an element of risk on the chance of great profit.

status quo (stā′ tus kwō). The existing condition or state of affairs.

Not the War They Planned

New England. New England bitterly opposed the War of 1812. It was often referred to there as "Mr. Madison's War." This region was the last stronghold of the pro-British Federalists. They believed that America should be helping Britain to defeat the despot Napoleon, not help him in defeating Britain! New England was also the center of American trade, which was mainly trade with Great Britain. The profits were so high in wartime that New England merchants continued to make money, even if only a few of their ships ran all the blockades. The war stopped the profits. Some of the New Englanders went so far as to support the British with loans and supplies during the war! The American war effort was handicapped by disunity in the nation.

Invasion of Canada. The mainspring of the American plan, the invasion of Canada, was a disaster. The American strategy called for a three-way invasion: from Detroit and Niagara, between the Great Lakes, and up Lake Champlain to Montreal. The Americans believed the Canadian people would not put up much of a fight for faraway Britain, especially since most of them were French. Instead, the Canadians fought bravely and fiercely—they were defending their homes against an alien invader. Many Canadians were former Americans who had been loyal to Britain during the Revolution. Forced to flee when threatened in America, they fought valiantly to prevent their new land from also falling to the Revolutionaries.

The attack from Detroit was under the command of General William Hull. Hull had been an officer in the Revolution but was now old and unsure of himself. He led an army into Canada but quickly retreated because of fears about his supply lines. The British commander, Isaac Brock, took advantage of Hull's hesitation and marched his army toward Detroit. Brock threatened that if he captured the city, he might not be able to control his Native American allies.

Fearful of such a result, Hull surrendered without firing a single shot. In August of 1812, Hull surrendered to a force that was much smaller than his own! He was later court-martialed and condemned to death but was pardoned by Madison for his services during the Revolution. His cowardice cost America control of the Detroit region.

General Stephen Van Rensselaer led the American attack from Niagara. His small army ran into stiff British resistance and was defeated when the militia reinforcements refused to cross the border. The militiamen stayed on the American side while the British killed their countrymen across the river. General Henry Dearborn, who commanded the attack toward Montreal, withdrew without seriously engaging the enemy when the militia under his command refused to leave the country. Meanwhile, the British and their Native American allies captured Fort Michilimackinac between Lake Huron and Lake Superior in July of 1812. The Canadian campaign of 1812 was a complete failure.

Naval War. The fiasco of the Canadian adventure was partially redeemed by the surprising American success at sea. The American **frigates** succeeded in defeating and capturing several of their British counterparts. This was a humiliating turn for the proud British navy and a boost for American morale.

The most famous American frigate, the *U.S.S. Constitution*, defeated and captured the *H.M.S. Guerriére* in August of 1812. The American

| Oliver Hazard Perry transferring his command over to the *Niagara*.

vessel, under the command of Isaac Hull, the nephew of disgraced William Hull, had more guns and a larger crew than its opponent. Moreover, British cannon fire bounced off the heavy oak sides of the *Constitution*, earning it the affectionate nickname "Old Ironsides."

The success of the *Constitution* was quickly followed by others. The *United States* under Stephen Decatur, a naval hero from the war against the Barbary pirates, captured the British frigate *Macedonian*. The *U.S.S. Wasp* defeated the *Frolic*, the *Essex* captured the *Alert,* and the *Hornet* took the *H.M.S. Peacock*. In October of 1812, the *Constitution* struck again under a new commander, William Bainbridge, and sunk the *Java*. The U.S. also suffered a loss in June of 1813 when the British frigate *Shannon* defeated the smaller *Chesapeake* (which had been so humiliated in the *Chesapeake-Leopard* Affair of 1807). Overall, the single ship combat tended to go to the Americans with thirteen wins to the British three.

The few losses did not seriously threaten the huge British navy, but it did humiliate them. Their navy commanders had mocked the

Americans at the beginning of the war. Their overconfidence was badly misplaced. The American frigates were heavier, had larger crews, and carried more firepower than the British ships. American ships were all manned by patriots who were defending their nation's honor, not by poor, luckless men forced into service as with the British. The British finally ordered their frigates to sail in pairs to avoid any more single ship battles.

The naval campaign also included about five hundred American privateers. These were smaller, quicker ships that attacked and captured British merchant vessels for profit. They captured over a thousand ships during the war, some of them from the Irish Sea and the English Channel. These losses further angered the British government and a public already stung by the loss of the frigates. The English business class turned against the war as their losses mounted.

Canadian Campaign of 1813. Command of the troubled front at Detroit was given to William Henry Harrison, the hero of Tippecanoe. He quickly determined that he could not retake Detroit without having control of the Great Lakes. The lakes were the key for both transportation and communication along the U.S.-Canadian border. Captain Oliver Hazard Perry was given the task of gaining control of the waterways.

Perry's first job was to obtain a fleet. At Presque Isle on Lake Erie he spent the summer of 1813 building five ships. Five more were towed by oxen up the rapids of the Niagara River from Lake Ontario. In September Perry sailed his fleet to the western end of Lake Erie and met the British.

The Battle of Lake Erie was incredibly fierce. Perry's flagship, the *Lawrence,* was destroyed. He moved his command to the *Niagara* which broke through the British line, firing at them from both sides as it passed. The British were defeated, and the lake came under American control. "We have met the enemy and they are ours," Perry reported back to Washington. The victory was a sweet balm to America's shattered cause in the north.

The British withdrew from Detroit once they realized they could not hold it without support from the water. They retreated eastward and were met at the Thames River in Canada by Harrison and over three thousand American troops. The outnumbered British (with their Native American allies) were quickly defeated. The Americans thus regained control of the Detroit region. The great organizer, Tecumseh, was killed, which destroyed his confederacy and ended the Native American alliance with the British.

The campaign of 1813 had undone some of the damage of the previous year's fiasco, but Canada and the far northwest American frontier were still in British hands. A second attempt by the Americans under James Wilkinson and Wade Hampton to capture Montreal failed in 1813. The British succeeded in capturing Fort Niagara and burning the city of Buffalo, New York in that same year. The Canadian front was reduced to a stalemate for the remainder of the war.

Match these people.

3.1	_____ William Hull	a.	victor at the Battle of the Thames
3.2	_____ William Bainbridge	b.	British commander in Canada
3.3	_____ Oliver Perry	c.	victor at the Battle of Lake Erie
3.4	_____ Isaac Brock	d.	*Constitution* commander, captured the *Guerriere*
3.5	_____ Stephen Decatur	e.	commander of the *United States*, hero of Barbary Coast war
3.6	_____ Henry Dearborn	f.	*Constitution* commander, sunk the *Java*
3.7	_____ Stephen Van Rensselaer	g.	cowardly officer who surrendered Detroit
3.8	_____ William Henry Harrison	h.	failed in march on Montreal
3.9	_____ Isaac Hull	i.	lost battle in attack from *Niagara* because the militia would not leave the country

Write the correct answer.

3.10 What bitter New Englanders named the war _____

3.11 Fort between Lakes Huron and Superior _____

3.12 Nickname of the *Constitution* _____

3.13 Message Perry sent after his victory _____

_____

3.14 Small, quick, American ships that captured over 1,000 British merchantmen for profit

_____

Answer these questions.

3.15 Why did New England oppose the War of 1812?

a. _____

b. _____

3.16 What did America primarily want to capture in the War of 1812? _____

3.17 Why did the American ships fare so well against the British in one-on-one ship battles?

_____

_____

3.18 Where did Captain Perry get his fleet?

_____

_____

To the Depths of Despair and Back

In 1814 events in Europe took an ominous turn against the Americans. In October 1813, Napoleon was seriously defeated in the Battle of the Nations at Leipzig. The loss forced him to abdicate in April of 1814 and exile himself to the Mediterranean island of Elba. That freed Britain to concentrate its massive military strength on America. By the spring of 1814, experienced, battle-hardened British officers and soldiers who had just won a great victory in Europe were now taking up positions in the New World.

Last attempt at Canada. In 1814 the Americans made one last attempt to invade Canada under the leadership of Generals Jacob Brown and Winfield Scott. These commanders led an army across the Niagara River and defeated the British at the Battle of Chippewa in July. The troops coming from Europe began adding their weight to the fray. Later that same month, the Americans were driven back at the Battle of Lundy's Lane. The Americans held the British at Fort Erie for several months and then withdrew, ending the last American attempt to bring Canada into the Union by force.

British strategy. The British ended the string of American naval victories by establishing a tight blockade all along the east coast. The blockade ruined the remainder of American trade and cut off all tariff revenue for the government. By the end of the war the nation's economy was in a shambles, and the government was almost bankrupt.

The British strategy was to inflict several large defeats on the Americans and force them to sign away large chunks of territory in exchange for peace. An army of over 10,000 was assembled in Canada for an invasion of New York along the traditional route down Lake Champlain. Another was assembled in the West Indies to move against New Orleans.

The British also used their control of the seas to land troops along the American coastline. Much of eastern Maine was captured. Several of the towns along the coast were plundered by the roving British navy, but with troops freed by the defeat of Napoleon, the British moved for bigger prizes.

The burning of Washington. The British fleet under Admiral George Cockburn had taken complete control of Chesapeake Bay in the summer of 1814. He and British general Robert Ross led an attack against the American capital in August. The Americans had not expected an attack there and had only slight defenses. The British disembarked without any resistance in Maryland and marched toward Washington. A hastily assembled militia force met them at the Battle of Bladensburg. The Americans quickly fled from the professional British army which marched into the capital unopposed.

Most of the population of the city fled before the British arrived. Government clerks had hidden or removed important papers. President Madison rode down to the front and fled with the retreating army. His wife Dolley Madison had been at the president's mansion all day packing up valuable goods and papers to take with her. She stayed until late in the afternoon, even when cannon fire could be heard in the distance. One of the last items she took out was the priceless painting of George Washington by Gilbert Stuart. She had the frame broken so the canvas could be moved easily. At last she also fled. Washington was almost deserted when the British arrived on the night of August 24, 1814.

The British burned most of the public buildings in Washington, including the capital and the president's house. They also burned the offices of the local newspaper. A huge thunderstorm put out most of the fires that night and contained the damage. The British withdrew to their ships, fearing that an American army was assembling to face them. The president's mansion was completely gutted by the fire. It was eventually repaired and the outside whitewashed to cover the black marks of the fire. It became known as the White House from then on.

Negotiations in Europe. Russia was a British ally in the war against Napoleon. The Russian czar sent a peace feeler in 1814, which resulted in British-American negotiations in Ghent, Belgium. The American delegation was led by future president John Quincy Adams, the son of John Adams. Henry Clay was also a delegate. The war was running very much in favor of the British when the two sides met for the first time.

The British negotiators made sweeping demands based on their confidence that the Americans

| The burning of the President's Mansion

were losing the war. The facts supported their view. Britain occupied parts of Maine and the upper Mississippi basin. A British army was moving down Lake Champlain, and another was organizing in the West Indies. The American capital had been sacked without any serious resistance. The British felt quite secure in dictating terms to their American counterparts.

The British demanded an independent Native American nation created out of the land west of the Mississippi, south of the Great Lakes. They also demanded permanent control of the Great Lakes, and a large part of land in Maine. The American delegation refused without even bothering to send the offer back to Madison for his decision. Both sides then waited for further developments in America. This was the low point of the war for the tattered United States. Things were about to improve.

Battle of Plattsburgh Bay. In the summer of 1814, the British advanced along the traditional Canadian-American invasion route, Lake Champlain. The British had to maintain control of the lake in order to move their supplies. The British fleet supporting the invasion was met by a weaker American force at Plattsburgh Bay in September. Once again, the balance of the war hung on a naval battle on an inland lake. The Americans under the command of Thomas Macdonough fought a desperate, bloody battle that ended in their favor. With supply and communication lines cut off by the American control of Lake Champlain, the British retreated.

Baltimore. Americans were infuriated by the attack on their capital. When Cockburn and Ross moved to attack the privateer center of Baltimore in September they met an angry, prepared enemy. The British attacked by both land and sea. The land attack was quickly blunted by a traditional American tactic. Early in the battle, some American sharp shooters succeeded in killing General Ross while he directed his men from the back of his horse. His successor was faced with stiff defenses and eventually withdrew.

Meanwhile, the navy tried to subdue Fort McHenry, which protected Baltimore harbor. The British bombarded the fort all during the night of September 13th to 14th. On board one of the British ships was a young American named Francis Scott Key. He had come aboard to negotiate for the release of a friend who had been captured a month before at the Battle of Bladensburg. He was detained during the attack on the fort. He watched most of the night in a state of high anxiety as the British pounded the fort with cannon fire. He was overjoyed when the first light of morning showed the Stars and Stripes still flying over the fort. He wrote out a poem in honor of the event which was set to the music of an English drinking song. It eventually became our national anthem, "The Star-Spangled Banner."

Key's poem celebrated the failure of the British assault on Baltimore. The army reboarded the ships after they had given up on the well-fortified Fort McHenry. The entire force withdrew from the region about a month later.

Treaty of Ghent. The British, who were expecting news of victories, were upset by reports of the failures in New York and Baltimore. The government offered the Duke of Wellington, the great British commander who had defeated Napoleon, a chance to take over the campaign in America. He informed the government that the only way to defeat the United States would be to control the Great Lakes. That would mean building a large fleet that could never be used on the ocean. As badly as the British wanted to teach the Americans a lesson, the cost was too high. Britain was exhausted and in deep financial trouble after twenty years of war in Europe. Napoleon was still alive and might return. (He did in 1815). The negotiators at Ghent were ordered to make a reasonable peace.

The two sides agreed to a return to the **status quo**. The fighting ended, and both sides retained the land they had when the war began. The Americans did not demand any statement or concession on the issues of impressment or ship seizures; the completion of the war in Europe had ended them anyway. In turn the British gave up their captured territory. They were never again to be an issue in British-American relations.

News of the Treaty of Ghent, signed in December of 1814, took several weeks to reach the United States. In those few weeks, the biggest land battle of the war was fought. The long-anticipated British invasion from the West Indies had finally taken place at New Orleans. The new peace started off quite unexpectedly.

Oh, say can you see by the dawn's early light
What so proudly we hailed at the twilight's last gleaming?
Whose broad stripes and bright stars thro' the perilous fight,
O'er the ramparts we watched were so gallantly streaming?
And the rocket's red glare, the bombs bursting in air,
Gave proof thro' the night that our flag was still there.
Oh, say does that star-spangled banner yet wave
O'er the land of the free and the home of the brave?

On the shore, dimly seen through the mists of the deep,
Where the foe's haughty host in dread silence reposes,
What is that which the breeze, o'er the towering steep,
As it fitfully blows, half conceals, half discloses?
Now it catches the gleam of the morning's first beam,
In full glory reflected now shines in the stream:
Tis the star-spangled banner! Oh long may it wave
O'er the land of the free and the home of the brave.

And where is that band who so vauntingly swore
That the havoc of war and the battle's confusion,
A home and a country should leave us no more!
Their blood has washed out their foul footsteps' pollution.
No refuge could save the hireling and slave,
From the terror of flight and the gloom of the grave:
And the star-spangled banner in triumph doth wave
O'er the land of the free and the home of the brave.

Oh! thus be it ever, when freemen shall stand
Between their loved home and the war's desolation!
Blest with victory and peace, may the Heav'n-rescued land
Praise the Pow'r that hath made and preserved us a nation.
Then conquer we must, when our cause it is just,
And this be our motto: "In God is our trust."
And the star-spangled banner in triumph shall wave
O'er the land of the free and the home of the brave.

THE STAR-SPANGLED BANNER
by Francis Scott Key

Answer these questions.

3.19 Why did the military situation change in 1814?

_____

3.20 What did the British negotiators demand when the two sides first met at Ghent in August of

1814? _____

_____

_____

3.21 Why did the demands of the British change by December of 1814?

_____

3.22 What was the British strategy in the War of 1812?

_____

3.23 Who faced the British at the Battle of Bladensburg?

_____

3.24 Who led the American negotiators at Ghent? _____

3.25 What eastern state did Britain occupy part of during the war? _____

3.26 How did the British end their embarrassing string of naval losses?

_____

3.27 What naval battle turned back the British advance into New York, and who was the American

commander?

_____

3.28 What did the British do in Washington in August of 1814?

_____

3.29 How did the British attack Baltimore?

_____

3.30 The "Star-Spangled Banner" was written about the defense of what?

_____

3.31 What two battles were fought during America's last invasion of Canada?

_____

3.32 What was the basic result of the Treaty of Ghent?

_____

Rewrite the first and last verse of the "Star-Spangled Banner" in prose, plainly writing what the author was saying.

3.33 _____

_____

_____

_____

_____

_____

_____

_____

_____

_____

_____

_____

_____

_____

_____

_____

_____

_____

_____

_____

Write a two-page biography of any of these people, using at least three sources.

George Washington	John Adams	Thomas Jefferson
James Madison	Alexander Hamilton	Henry Knox
James Monroe	Aaron Burr	Abigail Adams
Dolley Madison	Martha Washington	John Jay
John Marshall	Meriwether Lewis	William Clark

TEACHER CHECK _____ _____

initials   date

Results

Andrew Jackson. The Creek People of the southeast Mississippi took advantage of the war in 1813 to attack and massacre the defenders of Fort Mims near Mobile, Alabama. The Creek People were certain to assist the British when they attacked in the south. Andrew Jackson, a senator from Tennessee and commander of the state militia, moved south to confront the Creek People. He led a well-organized, ruthless, and decisive campaign. After Jackson's victory at the Battle of Horseshoe Bend in March of 1814, he forced the Creek to concede a huge portion of territory that included much of the states of Georgia and Alabama. Impressed with Jackson's results, the secretary of war gave him command of the American army in the south in 1814.

The Americans knew the British were preparing a large army in the West Indies to gain control of the lower Mississippi. Jackson moved into Spanish Florida and took the city of Pensacola in November, cutting off an excellent invasion route for the British. Then he began to prepare for an invasion along the Gulf Coast. When the British landed near New Orleans, Jackson came in to defend the city.

Battle of New Orleans. Jackson set up a strong defensive position in front of the advancing British in the swampy land around the mouth of the Mississippi. His men built fortifications of logs and dirt on a platform of cotton bales and wood. The position was located with a swamp on one side and the Mississippi River on the other. The enemy could not easily go around them. The barricade was manned by about 7,000 men, including soldiers, free blacks, backwoodsmen, pirates, and Frenchmen.

The over-confident British with an army of 10,000, including many veterans of the Napoleonic Wars, decided on a frontal attack. On the morning of January 8, 1815 (two weeks after the Treaty of Ghent had been signed), the British marched straight at the Americans in formation. The Americans mowed them down like grass. Over 2,000 British soldiers were killed or wounded while the Americans lost less than fifty. It was the greatest American victory of the war, even if it did come after the war ended. It also made Andrew Jackson a national hero.

News of the victory reached the cities of the east coast just before news of the treaty in Europe. Americans went wild with joy. They had not lost any territory in the treaty, and they had a great victory to cap it off. The public rejoiced using the slogan, "Not One Inch of Territory Ceded or Lost." The American perception of the war was that they had won.

The Hartford Convention. New England, under Federalist leadership, continued to oppose the war right up to the end. Five of the New England states sent representatives, who were Federalists, to a meeting in Hartford, Connecticut in December of 1814 to discuss their grievances and options. Their continued opposition to the war led many people to question their loyalty. The secret meetings in December and January caused further concern.

The Hartford Convention issued a report requesting several changes in the basic structure of the government. The changes would have increased the power of the states at the

| The British, in formation, marching towards the Americans

expense of the federal government. The recommendations included restrictions on the federal government's ability to make war or restrict trade, both key New England issues. The Convention wanted the states to have more control over their own defense. They also wanted to increase New England's power in the national government by making the admission of new states more difficult.

The report of the Convention was taken to Washington by three special envoys from Massachusetts. They arrived in the capital about the same time as the news of the Battle of New Orleans and the Treaty of Ghent. Their proposals were ridiculed and they left in disgrace. The popular reaction against the Federalist proposals cost them what was left of their strength. They only nominated one more presidential candidate in 1816 before they disappeared into historical extinction.

Results of the War. The end of the war marked a turning point in British-American relations. Four boundary disputes between the two nations were referred to **arbitration** for solutions. All disputes in the future between America and the former mother country would be settled by negotiations, not war. Over the next years and decades, steps were taken to remove border forts and warships on the Great Lakes between the U.S. and Canada. Eventually, the two neighbors would come to share the longest unfortified boundary in the world. Feelings still ran high against the British for many years, but the journey down the long path to friendship had begun.

The major Native American threat of the frontier was extinguished during the War of 1812. Tecumseh's confederacy was destroyed at the Battle of the Thames, and the Native American Peoples of the south were subdued in the Battle of Horseshoe Bend. Both groups were forced to cede large areas of land to the U.S. government. The pioneers quickly began to migrate to the new areas, creating more states for the Union. Indiana, Mississippi, Alabama,

and Illinois were added to the nation within five years after the war.

The great manufacturing power of the United States was born as a result of the War of 1812. The war and trade embargoes had drastically cut imports from Europe and deprived wealthy Americans of their major investment, which was commerce. Many wealthy men, especially in New England, invested their idle money in building factories of their own to produce goods the nation could not get from Europe. Out of necessity, the engine of American manufacturing began.

The Second War for Independence gave the nations of Europe a new respect for the young nation. British naval officers no longer sneered at American ships and seamen. European powers no longer tried to get some of the new nation's land for themselves. The war had ended their hopes that the nation would fall apart, leaving them to pick up the richest pieces.

The War of 1812 marked the end of the nation's dangerous infancy. The first leaders had kept the peace long enough for the nation to gain the strength needed to fight alone. Americans had held their own against the greatest power of Europe and proved their mettle in battle. The war gave them a new sense of their own destiny which they believed was to expand their republic across the width of the continent.

Florida. After the war, Florida was the only land east of the Mississippi not in American hands. The proud Yankees wanted it and believed it was destined by Providence to be theirs. Andrew Jackson had already seized parts of West Florida during the War of 1812. Afterwards, the Americans **annexed** that land and opened negotiations with Spain for the rest of it.

Spain was reluctant to sell Florida. She had her own agenda and resented America's presence in West Florida. The Spanish government wanted to settle the boundaries of the whole Louisiana Territory and did not want America to support the rebelling Spanish colonies in Latin

America. Circumstances, in the form of Andrew Jackson, forced Spain to negotiate.

In the years after the war, Native Americans, runaway slaves, and thieves began using Florida as a base for raids into the United States. In 1818 the president sent Andrew Jackson "to deal with the Seminole People," who were using Florida as a base. Jackson interpreted his orders liberally and marched into Florida where he defeated the Seminoles. He also captured St. Marks and Pensacola, executing two British citizens who were aiding the Native American People.

The raids by Jackson convinced the Spanish government that they could not successfully defend Florida. Therefore, in 1819 they signed the Adams-Onis Treaty that ceded it to the United States. The treaty also settled the boundaries of the Louisiana Territory with Spain giving up all of its claim to the Oregon country. The United States agreed that Texas was Spanish territory and took responsibility for about 5 million dollars in claims that U.S. citizens had against Spain. The northern and southern bounds of the U.S. were now set. The only direction left to go was west.

Complete these sentences.

3.34 The Battle of New Orleans made _____ a national hero.

3.35 The Federalists destroyed the last of their party with the proposals that were made at the _____ at the end of the War of 1812.

3.36 Andrew Jackson was given command of the army in 1814 after his success as a military commander against the _____ People.

3.37 The Battle of New Orleans took place _____ after the Treaty of Ghent was signed.

3.38 Jackson captured part of western _____ during the war and the American government later annexed it.

3.39 The Creek People were defeated at the Battle of _____ .

3.40 The Spanish government agreed to cede Florida after _____ made raids into the territory against the _____ People.

3.41 America obtained Florida and settled the boundaries of the Louisiana Territory by the _____ Treaty of 1819.

3.42 The lack of trade encouraged many wealthy New Englanders to invest in _____ during the War of 1812.

3.43 The Treaty of Ghent settled four boundary disputes by referring them to _____ .

3.44 The War of 1812 gave the nations of Europe a new _____ for the United States.

Answer these questions.

3.45 How did British-American relations change after the War of 1812?

_____

_____

_____

3.46 Why could pioneers flood onto the frontier after the war?

_____

_____

3.47 What mistake did the British make at New Orleans?

_____

_____

3.48 Who did the American public believe won the War of 1812?

_____

_____

3.49 What did America believe was its destiny?

_____

_____

Good Feelings

Nationalism. The War of 1812 produced a new feeling of **nationalism** in America. The nation believed that it had won a war against Great Britain. After that, the proud American navy thrashed the Barbary pirates so completely that all tribute payments were ended. The regional outlook of the New England Federalists had been discredited. Citizens of the United States began to think of themselves as just that—U.S. citizens. The older view that they were citizens of a state that was part of a Union declined for a time. This also led to a respect for the ideal of the "common man," the founder and defender of the great American republic.

The American System. Speaker of the House Henry Clay captured the pulse of the nation with his "American System." The American System was a group of proposals intended to benefit the entire nation. It included a protective tariff, a new national bank, money for roads and canals, and other improvements. Some of it became law.

The tariff was included in the American System in order to protect infant American factories that were born during the war. British manufacturers had not been able to sell their goods during the war, so they had collected their huge surpluses in warehouses, waiting to be sold. Once the Treaty of Ghent was signed, England began shipping boatloads of goods to America. Prices were driven so low that American factories were going out of business. In 1816 Congress passed the first protective tariff. It was different from earlier ones which were small and used to raise money. These new tariffs were high—20 to 25%—and were intended to make foreign goods more expensive so American goods could compete.

The absence of a national bank proved to be a disaster for the nation's finances. Any bank could print money, and many did, printing more than they could redeem in gold or silver. This made the currency decline rapidly in value,

causing inflation. Financial chaos had been a particular problem during the war. Under the leadership of Clay and Calhoun, a Second National Bank was chartered in 1816. The Democratic-Republicans had learned their lesson and supported it.

The Second National Bank was even larger than the first. Unfortunately, it got off to a bad start. The managers of the bank printed money freely, made loans improperly, and **speculated** in western land (a popular occupation at the time). The bank's new president, Nicholas Biddle, took over in 1819 and brought the institution under control. He reset policies, recalled risky loans, and reduced the money printed to match the gold reserves. The sudden change in policy was good for the bank, but it hurt the nation as a whole. It contributed to the Panic of 1819 (panic was a name for a **depression**). The bank foreclosed on many farms, especially in the west, which hurt its popular support.

The last part of Clay's American System was the proposal to use the extra revenue from the higher tariffs to build roads and canals. Clay believed that desperately needed improvements in transportation would allow western and southern farmers to increase their trade with the manufacturers of the north, benefiting everyone. One such road had already begun. The first national road, the Cumberland Road, was begun in 1811. It ran from Cumberland, Maryland to Vandalia, Illinois. It eventually connected to St. Louis on the Mississippi.

However, most of the improvements were needed inside the states, not between them. President Madison, and later Monroe, believed it was unconstitutional to use federal funds to benefit projects in one state, even if it would benefit the nation as a whole. So when Congress passed the Bonus Bill in 1817 (which would have given money from the new National Bank to the states for improvements), Madison vetoed it. The states were forced to finance the roads and canals themselves. Many did so by encouraging private citizens to build roads and charge for their use. These "turnpikes" spread all over the nation.

Era of Good Feelings. In 1816 James Monroe was elected president. He crushed his Federalist opponent 183 to 34 in the electoral vote. Monroe was the last president to have served in the Revolution and the last of the "Virginia Dynasty" (Washington, Jefferson, Madison, Monroe). He joined the army at eighteen and fought in several major battles of the Revolution, including Trenton where he was wounded in the shoulder. His political career included the Virginia legislature, the Confederation Congress, governor of Virginia, envoy to France and Britain, U.S. senator, as well as secretary of state and secretary of war under Madison. His appearance and manners resembled those of George Washington. He established a strict protocol for social events, following Washington's example. He was not a brilliant leader, but was a capable, experienced administrator who knew how to listen for "the will of the people."

James Monroe took over a nation still basking in the glow of the War of 1812. There was only one major political party, the Democratic-Republicans, and the nation was united as never before. Shortly after his election, Monroe took a tour of the country. He was greeted with widespread acclaim, even in New England. One newspaper spoke of an "Era of Good Feelings" that had come over America. This era lasted through much of the early part of the Monroe administration but gradually yielded to the rise of sectionalism which will be covered in the next LIFEPAC. However, the "good feelings" lasted until Monroe's re-election in 1820. He ran unopposed and won every electoral vote except one. That one was deliberately thrown away so that the honor of being unanimously elected would fall only on George Washington.

Western Land. The United States of America is a land whose national character and history were built on the frontier. From the time the first settlers arrived in 1603 until the early 1900s, the nation always was expanding into the frontier. The frontier changed from the east coast, to the foothills of the Appalachians, to the eastern Mississippi, to the west coast, and lastly, to the Great Plains. For much of our history the acquisition of new lands, the settling of that land, and the addition of new states have been major political issues in Washington.

| A log cabin on the frontier

The frontier of the Era of Good Feelings was the eastern Mississippi. This frontier saw huge gains in population after the war. The population of the territory/state of Illinois in 1820 was more than four times what it had been in 1810. In that same time period, the population of Kentucky and Mississippi more than doubled while that of Illinois multiplied four times and Alabama increased thirteen times over!

The move west was encouraged by increasingly easy terms to purchase government land. The Land Ordinance of 1795 had set the price at $1 per acre payable in two installments with a minimum purchase of 640 acres. In 1800 the law was changed to a minimum purchase of 320 acres and four payments. By 1804 the price was $2 an acre, but the minimum purchase was only 160 acres. After the Panic of 1819, further reductions were made in 1820. The price was reduced to $1.25 an acre with an 80-acre minimum, and the purchaser could keep whatever part of the land he managed to pay for, only losing the unpaid portion. These generous terms kept the American population moving west to claim land of their own.

The Marshall Court. John Marshall remained chief justice of the Supreme Court for thirty-four years (1801-1835). He used his position to pursue the Hamilton-Federalist goals of a strong central government and protection against the excesses of democracy. Using its self-created right to judicial review, the Marshall Court issued a series of important decisions.

Fletcher v. Peck (1810) was a suit brought after the Georgia legislature sold 35 million acres of land to speculators in a corrupt deal. In its next session, the legislature revoked the deal due to public outcry. Marshall ruled that it was a contract and could not be arbitrarily revoked. He placed property rights, even dubious ones, above the power of the legislature. He asserted the Supreme Court's right to declare *state* laws unconstitutional.

McCulloch v. Maryland (1819) was a suit over the right of the states to tax the National Bank. Following the Panic of 1819, popular opinion ran high against the bank. Maryland tried to destroy it by taxing it out of existence. Marshall ruled that the federal government had the right to create the bank under its implied powers in the Constitution (loose construction), and the states had no authority to tax the federally created National Bank.

Many other decisions followed the same lines of reasoning. States were not allowed to change the charter of a college after *Dartmouth College v. Woodard* (1819), because it was a contract and was protected by the Constitution. The decision in *Cohens v. Virginia* (1821) gave the Supreme Court the right to reverse the decisions of even the highest state courts. The court ruled in *Gibbons v. Ogden* (1824) that only the federal government could regulate interstate commerce. Elected officials who favored state's rights and the power of the legislature objected to these rulings but could not find any way to effectively challenge them.

Monroe Doctrine. The aftermath of the Napoleonic Wars restored the old monarchs of Europe to their thrones. From then on, these rulers were determined to stop any and all revolutions like the one in France. Rebellions in favor of democracy were crushed by an alliance of monarchs in both Italy and Spain in the early 1820s. The United States began to fear that the new republics in Latin America that had recently won their freedom from Spain might suffer a similar fate. Americans naturally favored the new republics as followers of their own example. The presence of large European armies in the Americas would have been a definite threat to the United States.

The U.S. had an unexpected ally in their support for the new republics. Britain was enjoying the new freedom she had in trading with Latin America. This had previously been restricted by

Spain. Britain proposed that she and the U.S. issue a joint statement against any European intervention. However, Secretary of State John Quincy Adams was suspicious of the motives behind Britain's offer. He saw no reason for the U.S. to ride behind British foreign policy.

At the urging of Adams, Monroe decided to follow a separate but parallel course with the British. He took advantage of his annual address to Congress in 1823 to announce the American policy which became known as the Monroe Doctrine. He stated, the American continents were closed to any further European colonization. An attempt by the powers of the Old World to intervene in America would be viewed as a hostile act against the United States. Furthermore, the U.S. would not interfere with any European colonies already in America, nor would she intervene in European conflicts.

The United States lacked the military strength to back up this sweeping statement. It was largely ignored outside the country, but American national pride supported the independent spirit in which it was made. In later years, when

America had grown to be an international power, the Monroe Doctrine would become a major part of the nation's foreign policy.

Conclusion. The years from 1789 to the early 1820s were a time of foundation building in the United States. The institutions of the new republic were established along with the customs and protocols that accompany them. The nation faced and successfully completed a peaceful change of political authority in 1800. The power of government was reaching down towards the people and away from the elites. The nation's leaders remained calm in the light of severe provocation from Europe as the Napoleonic Wars raged. Finally, when they could stand no more, America had fought again for her independence, this time from the arrogance of the British. The nation came out of the war with her territory and pride intact. The east coast from Canada to Mexico was under her control, and the west called to her growing population. Finally, America boldly asserted her right to keep the Old World out of her neighborhood. The foundation was laid. Its strength would be tested by fire in the decades ahead.

 Complete the following.

3.50 What were the three parts of Henry Clay's American System?

a. _____   b. _____

c. _____

3.51 What was the minimum number of acres of western land that had to be purchased in each year?

a. 1795 _____   b. 1800 _____

c. 1804 _____   d. 1820 _____

3.52 What was the time after the election of James Monroe called?

_____

3.53 Name the Supreme Court decision that decided each issue.

   a. College charters are contracts protected by the Constitution

   _____

   b. States can not tax a federal bank

   _____

   c. Only the federal government can regulate interstate trade

   _____

   d. Legislatures can not revoke a contract they made earlier, even if it was dubious

   _____

   e. The Supreme Court can reverse the decision of the highest state courts

   _____

3.54 Name the four parts of the Monroe Doctrine.

   a. _____

   b. _____

   c. _____

   d. _____

3.55 What was the sentiment of the nation after the War of 1812? _____

3.56 What part of the American System was opposed by Presidents Madison and Monroe? Why?

   _____

   _____

3.57 Who brought the Second National Bank under better management?
   What was the name of the depression caused by his tightened monetary policies?

   a. _____   b. _____

3.58 What was the American frontier of the early 1800s? _____

3.59 What major European nation supported the new Latin American republics?

   _____

3.60 Who was the chief justice of the Supreme Court from 1801 to 1835?
   Whose ideas of government did he promote?

   a. _____   b. _____

3.61 Why was the National Bank unpopular after 1819, especially in the west?

   _____

   _____

3.62 Name the first national road, the year it was begun, and the cities it eventually ran between.

a. _____   b. _____

c. _____

3.63 What were privately built roads which charged people to use them? _____

↺ **Before you take this last Self Test, you may want to do one or more of these self checks.**

1. _____ Read the objectives. See if you can do them.

2. _____ Restudy the material related to any objectives that you cannot do.

3. _____ Use the **SQ3R** study procedure to review the material:

a. **S**can the sections.
b. **Q**uestion yourself.
c. **R**ead to answer your questions.
d. **R**ecite the answers to yourself.
e. **R**eview areas you did not understand.

4. _____ Review all vocabulary, activities, and Self Tests, writing a correct answer for every wrong answer.

SELF TEST 3

Answer these questions (each answer, 4 points).

3.01 What was the main object of American strategy in the War of 1812?

_____

3.02 What are two of the things the British negotiators demanded when they first met with the Americans in Ghent in the summer of 1814?

a. _____   b. _____

3.03 What were the three parts of Henry Clay's proposed American System?

a. _____   b. _____

c. _____

3.04 What were two of the grievances that led to the War of 1812?

a. _____   b. _____

3.05 What were two of the parts of Alexander Hamilton's financial program?

a. _____   b. _____

Name the item described (each answer, 3 points).

3.06 _____ European interference in the Americas would be viewed as a hostile act by the U.S.

3.07 _____ Greatest American victory of the War of 1812, fought after the treaty was signed

3.08 _____ City burned by the British in the Chesapeake Bay campaign of 1814

3.09 _____ Political party that dominated the American government in the early 1800s

3.010 _____ Section of the country that opposed the War of 1812

3.011 _____ Group of Federalists who wanted to weaken the federal government near the end of the War of 1812

3.012 _____ Name given to the early part of the Monroe Administration because of the unity and good will of the nation

3.013 _____ A revolt against the excise tax in Pennsylvania under Washington

3.014 _____ "Old Ironsides," famous American frigate

3.015 _____ Song written about the siege of Fort McHenry in Baltimore

Match these people (each answer, 2 points).

3.016 _____ Andrew Jackson

3.017 _____ Henry Clay

3.018 _____ James Calhoun

3.019 _____ William H. Harrison

3.020 _____ James Madison

3.021 _____ Nicholas Biddle

3.022 _____ John Marshall

3.023 _____ William Hull

3.024 _____ Isaac Brock

3.025 _____ Oliver Perry

a. American victor at the Battle of Lake Erie

b. American victor at the Battle of the Thames

c. Speaker of the House from Kentucky

d. militia general, defeated the Creek People

e. chief justice of the Supreme Court

f. British commander in Canada

g. War Hawk from South Carolina

h. president of the Second National Bank

i. president who asked for war with Britain

j. American general, surrendered Detroit

Answer true or false (each answer, 1 point).

3.026 _____ The War of 1812 is also called the Second War for Independence.

3.027 _____ British navy was reduced in effectiveness by American naval victories in the War of 1812.

3.028 _____ American ships could not fight effectively against British ships.

3.029 _____ The British strategy in the War of 1812 was to capture key American cities and make the nation a colony again.

3.030 _____ The Battle of Plattsburgh Bay stopped the British invasion of New York coming down Lake Champlain.

3.031 _____ Americans were relieved and humiliated after the War of 1812.

3.032 _____ The War of 1812 encouraged the beginning of American manufacturing.

3.033 _____ America lost part of the Northwest Territory in the Treaty of Ghent.

3.034 _____ The military situation became worse for the Americans in 1814 when Napoleon went into exile.

3.035 _____ The steady improvement of British-American relations began after the War of 1812.

80 / 100	SCORE _____	TEACHER _____ _____
		initials date

Before taking the LIFEPAC Test, you may want to do one or more of these self checks.

1. _____ Read the objectives. See if you can do them.
2. _____ Restudy the material related to any objectives that you cannot do.
3. _____ Use the **SQ3R** study procedure to review the material.
4. _____ Review activities, Self Tests, and LIFEPAC vocabulary words.
5. _____ Restudy areas of weakness indicated by the last Self Test.

HISTORY & GEOGRAPHY 803
The American Revolution (1763–1789)

LIFEPAC Test is located in the center of the booklet. Please remove before starting the unit.

Author:
Theresa Buskey, B.A., J.D.

Editor:
Alan Christopherson, M.S.

Westover Studios Design Team:
Phillip Pettet, Creative Lead
Teresa Davis, DTP Lead
Nick Castro
Andi Graham
Jerry Wingo

Alpha Omega
PUBLICATIONS

804 N. 2nd Ave. E.
Rock Rapids, IA 51246-1759

The American Revolution (1763–1789)

Introduction

The struggle for independence by the United States has often baffled historians. Raw courage and determination in many cases were the only resources the colonists had to depend upon. The American government during the war was ineffective and disorganized. The army lacked basic supplies and regular soldiers. Yet, these raw colonials defeated the greatest military power of their era, Great Britain.

Historians have also long debated the reasons for the war. At the end of the French and Indian War, the American colonies were joyfully, deeply British. No one dreamed in 1763 that there would be a war between the colonies and Britain just twelve years later. Those years were a litany of miscalculations on the part of Britain that drove the colonists further and further from the loyalty of 1763.

This LIFEPAC® will discuss the events that caused the Revolution. It will also present a history of the Revolution itself, the major battles, ideas, and events. Finally, this LIFEPAC will show how the colonists finally managed to create a stable government under the United States Constitution.

Objectives

Read these objectives. The objectives tell you what you will be able to do when you have successfully completed this LIFEPAC. When you have finished this LIFEPAC, you should be able to:

1. Identify the men who contributed to the Revolution.

2. Identify and describe the incidents and thinking which led to the Revolution.

3. Identify and describe the governing bodies that acted for the colonies/states.

4. Name the major battles of the war and tell their significances.

5. Outline the terms of the peace agreements that the United States signed with Great Britain.

6. Explain the Articles of Confederation and why they were replaced.

7. Describe the Constitutional Convention.

8. Describe the main features of the Constitution and the process by which it was approved.

Survey the LIFEPAC. Ask yourself some questions about this study and write your questions here.

1. GROWING CONFLICT

The American colonists were delighted with the outcome of the French and Indian War. The hated French had finally been driven out of their land. They were free to expand into the rich lands of the eastern Mississippi basin. They were proud to be British, part of the mighty British Empire.

But, even in the midst of the joy, the first signs of the difference between the colonists and the government in Britain appeared, the Proclamation of 1763. The king tried to block the colonists behind the Appalachian Mountains, but the colonists chose to ignore the order.
Worse was to come.

In the years that followed, the British tried to tax and control the colonies for the first time in colonial history. The Sugar Act, the Stamp Act, the Townshend Acts, and the Intolerable Acts beat a steady path to rebellion in the colonies. The colonists saw a conspiracy to deprive them of their liberty and reacted with resistance. The British saw no valid reason for the increasing resistance to their "lawful" decrees and reacted with more force. Finally, the colonists gave up hope of a peaceful settlement and chose to fight rather than submit.

SECTION OBJECTIVES

Review these objectives. When you have completed this section, you should be able to:

1.   Identify the men who contributed to the Revolution.

2.   Identify and describe the incidents and thinking which led to the Revolution.

3.   Identify and describe the governing bodies that acted for the colonies/states.

VOCABULARY

Study these words to enhance your learning success in this section.

arbitrary (är′ bi trer′ ē). Not going by any rule or law.

conservative (kon sėr′ va tiv). A person who is opposed to change.

militia (mu lish′ a). Army of citizens who are not regular soldiers.

moderate (mod′ er it). A person whose political views are not extreme in any way.

Prime Minister (prīm′ min′ i stir). The chief official in certain types of government.

propaganda (prop′ a gan′ da). Systematic efforts to spread opinions or beliefs.

protocol (prō′ tu kol). Rules (written or unwritten) for a procedure.

providential (prov′ u den′ shul). Good fortune happening by God's intervention (the Christian version of "good luck"-author).

radical (rad′ i kal). A person who favors extreme changes or reform.

Note: *All vocabulary words in this LIFEPAC appear in* **boldface** *print the first time they are used. If you are not sure of the meaning when you are reading, study the definitions given.*

Pronunciation Key: hat, āge, cãre, fär; let, ēqual, tėrm; it, īce; hot, ōpen, ôrder; oil; out; cup, pu̇t, rüle; child; long; thin; /ᵺH/ for then; /zh/ for measure; /u/ or /ə/ represents /a/ in about, /e/ in taken, /i/ in pencil, /o/ in lemon, and /u/ in circus.

Britain Flexes its Muscles

British attitudes. Britain was the greatest power on earth after the Seven Years (French and Indian) War. It had soundly defeated its great rival, France, and taken her North American empire. The British were proud and arrogant about their victory. They were confident of their own glory and were not in a mood to compromise with anyone, especially their backwoods colonies.

Moreover, the war had left Britain deeply in debt. The national debt had doubled and the new territory in America would be expensive to administer. Pontiac's War was launched by Native American tribes in the Great Lakes region, proving that the British needed to maintain troops in the colonies for their protection. That was expensive. The government felt it was high time the colonists bore some of the cost of their own defense.

Mercantilism. The popular economic theory of the 1700s was mercantilism. This theory held that only gold or silver was real wealth, and countries must work to obtain more of it. Colonies were used to doing this through trade. Colonies were to supply the mother country with raw materials such as wood, iron, and indigo. Then, the colonies would be a market for goods manufactured by the mother country, like cloth, hats, and tools. The colony was not to compete with the mother country by building its own manufacturing and industry. This theory held that the colony only existed to serve the mother country and should never be allowed to develop. It should be kept dependent on the mother country at all times.

British policy towards America was based on mercantilism. The Navigation Acts, which were passed mainly in the late 1600s, were intended to force the colonies to act in accord with this theory. One of the laws required that all trade with the colonies had to be on English or colonial ships.

| The American British Empire in 1763

Another required all colonial trade to go through England to be taxed. That meant that goods going from the colonies to the French West Indies, just south of Florida, had to go to England, be unloaded, stored, and taxed before they could go to their destination. The same was true in reverse for goods coming from the West Indies or Europe to the colonies. This gave English merchants a virtual monopoly on colonial trade, because the cost of going through England made foreign trade too expensive. Other laws stated that certain important goods like tobacco and naval supplies could only be sold to Britain, even if Britain could not possibly buy all that the colonies could produce. These laws would have crippled colonial trade, but until 1763 they were rarely enforced, and the colonists traded with many nations by smuggling.

There were other laws on the books by 1763 that were intended to keep the colonies economically backward and dependent on Britain. The colonies were forbidden to export wool cloth, hats or tools. They were also forbidden to build iron mills to make tools. The Molasses Act of 1733 put a high tax on molasses, sugar, and rum imported from non-British sources, primarily the French West Indies. The problem was that the British West Indies could not supply half of the molasses needed by the distilleries in New England. (The molasses was made into rum for sale at home and abroad). So, the law was routinely and easily avoided by smuggling.

One of the more damaging laws forbade the colonies to mint coins. British merchants could not pay for colonial products in hard money (coins). That meant the colonies were always short of coins they needed to pay for British goods. It also made it difficult for colonists to collect enough money to start any large businesses. The colonists had to barter for most of their goods and try to get coins by trade with French and Spanish lands. These restrictions were very unpopular in the colonies, but, obviously, very popular in London.

| George III, King of England

Changes in policy. After the Seven Years War, Britain began to change her policy toward the colonies. The British government had been content for over a hundred and fifty years to let the colonies govern themselves. Now, flush with pride in their victory, they felt it was time for Parliament to establish better control over the empire. There was also a strong feeling that since the British had spent both blood and treasure to protect the colonies, the colonies owed them something in return. What the British expected to get was loyalty and some income to help defray the huge costs of stationing troops in America.

George Grenville became **Prime Minister** of Great Britain in 1763. He moved quickly to meet the new mood of the king, George III, and Parliament. He began in 1763 by ordering that the Navigation Acts be strictly enforced. He obtained the Sugar Act of 1764 from the Parliament that decreased the high tax on French molasses but kept high taxes on sugar and rum. He arranged for this act to actually be enforced by customs offices and an Admiralty Court.

That court did not use a jury and the defendant was assumed to be guilty, not innocent as in regular courts. The colonists saw this as a threat to their English liberties. The next law was a Quartering Act in 1765 that required colonists to provide food and lodging for British troops. These acts angered the Americans, but it was the next one that set fire to the dynamite, the Stamp Act.

| An early U.S. Flag

 Answer these questions.

1.1 What was the popular economic theory of the 1700s?

_____

1.2 According to that theory what should a colony do for a mother country?

_____

_____

1.3 What were the goals of the British government toward the colonies in 1763?

a. _____

b. _____

1.4 What were the major parts of the Navigation Acts?

a. _____

b. _____

c. _____

1.5 What was the Molasses Act of 1733? Why would it have hurt the New England colonies and why didn't it? _____

_____

_____

1.6 Why were the colonies short of hard money? _____

_____

1.7 What did George Grenville do to anger the colonies in

1763? _____

1764? _____

1765? _____

The Stamp Act. Grenville proposed to raise a substantial amount of money in the colonies by the Stamp Act, passed in 1765. The law required all legal documents and public papers, such as wills, playing cards, newspapers, and bills of sale, to be marked with a stamp purchased from the government. Grenville thought this was a reasonable way to raise money. The amount charged for the stamps would be less than a similar stamp in Britain and the money would be used to pay British troops in the colonies. Even Benjamin Franklin, the colonial representative in London, who disapproved of the law expected the colonists to accept it after a few protests.

However, the Stamp Act was seen as a threat in America. It was the first time Britain had tried to directly tax the colonists. Taxes before had been on imports and were intended mostly to control trade. Any other taxes had only come from the colonial assemblies elected by the colonists. The tax fell on everyone from the card playing sailors to wealthy merchants or lawyers whose trade depended on documents. Moreover, the colonists were constantly short of the money needed to buy the stamps. Even worse, people who violated the act were to be tried in Admiralty Courts! The colonists thought Britain was trying to reduce them to virtual slavery with all these new laws.

It was the very visible Stamp Act that drew the wrath of the colonists, who were united in their opposition to it. The Americans said Parliament could not tax them, since there were no American representatives in Parliament. The battle cry that would open the Revolution was: "No taxation without representation." But, more than shouting slogans, the Americans began to organize, unite, and resist. This was the real legacy of the Stamp Act.

The controversy was a repeat of the conflict between Parliament and the king in England. The Glorious Revolution (1688) had established that political power in England would be in the hands of an elected body, Parliament, not an

| Patrick Henry

autocratic king. The colonists felt that if they indeed had the rights of Englishmen, then the political power in their land should be in the hands of their representatives. The British Parliament could not step in as a new monarch to rob the colonists of their traditional English liberties. Parliament thought of the colonists as subjects who should obey, not as citizens who should participate. This arrogant attitude was intolerable.

The House of Burgesses in Virginia debated and passed the Virginia Resolves, which declared the act illegal, stating that only Virginians could tax Virginians. The debate over the Resolves included a famous speech by **radical** member Patrick Henry. He said, "Caesar had his Brutus–Charles the First, his Cromwell–and George the Third–may profit by their example." When the **conservative** members of the Burgesses began to whisper, "Treason," Henry replied, "If this be treason, make the most of it."

The reaction to the Stamp Act came in three major ways: the Stamp Act Congress, boycotts, and mob action. The Massachusetts assembly invited all the colonies to send delegates to New York to discuss the Stamp Act.

Nine of the colonies sent delegates to what became known as the Stamp Act Congress. The delegates were wealthy, distinguished men from the elite of the colonies. They passed a Declaration of Rights and Grievances stating that only the colonies could tax their own citizens. Britain ignored it. It was, however, a significant step in uniting the colonies, most of which thought of themselves almost as separate nations.

A much more effective message was sent to Parliament when the colonies began to boycott British goods. They were very successful in organizing agreements not to import British products. Colonists found other sources to meet their needs, or self-sufficiently went without them. The boycott began to threaten the prosperity of the English merchants who complained to Parliament. Parliament listened.

The last way that the colonists resisted the Stamp Act was by mob action, this was also very effective. The "Sons of Liberty," secret societies opposed to the act, took the law into their own hands. They attacked stamp sellers, royal officials, and people who violated the boycott. On the date the law was to take effect, November 1, 1765, there were no officials to sell the hated stamps. All had resigned in fear of the mobs.

Faced with an outcry in Britain and the colonies, and knowing they were not collecting any revenue, Parliament repealed the Stamp Act four months after it went into effect. At the same time they passed the face-saving Declaratory Act, stating that Parliament had the right to tax the colonies. The colonists rejoiced at their victory and, with a few exceptions, ignored the dark implications of the Declaratory Act. They had acted together, sometimes with violence, and accomplished what they wanted. The lesson would be remembered.

 Name the requested item or person.

1.8 British Prime Minister who passed the Stamp Act

_____

1.9 Colonial representative in London who thought the Act would be obeyed

_____

1.10 Radical in House of Burgesses who said, "If this be treason, make the most of it."

_____

1.11 Burgesses statement against the Stamp Act

_____

1.12 Three ways the colonies reacted to the Stamp Act

    a. _____

    b. _____

    c. _____

1.13 Secret societies that led mob action against the Stamp Act

_____

1.14 The slogan against the tax

_____

1.15 Law stating that Parliament had a right to tax the colonies

_____

Answer these questions.

1.16 What did the Stamp Act require?

_____

_____

1.17 Why did the colonists object so much to it? (four reasons)

_____

_____

1.18 What did Patrick Henry mean in his speech about Brutus and Cromwell? (Look up the named people if you need to.)

_____

_____

Actions and Reactions

Townshend Acts. The failure of the Stamp Act did not help Britain's financial problems. The debt remained along with the huge expense of protecting North America. The king and the powerful people in Britain were furious. They wanted the rebellious colonies brought in line. Finally, Britain had another change in government (this happened frequently). The new Chancellor of the Exchequer (Treasury), Charles Townshend promised to pluck the colonial goose with a minimum of squawking.

Townshend succeeded in passing a series of laws through Parliament in 1767. Called the Townshend Acts, they were designed to increase revenue and control. The most important put a tax on a large number of goods such as paint, lead, glass, paper, and tea that the colonies imported from Britain. This was an indirect tax which Townshend thought the colonies would accept.

Another act greatly increased the power of customs officials to enforce the tax laws, including the use of writs of assistance which allowed **arbitrary** searches of homes and businesses. Another law threatened to shut down the New York assembly if it did not comply with the Quartering Act (it had refused up until that point). Moreover, the money raised was to be used to pay British officials, including governors, in the colonies. This meant the colonists could no longer hope to control royal officials by limiting their salary!

The colonists were alarmed. They had fought with royal governors often enough to know the loss of the power of the purse would leave them helpless against arbitrary rule. They also saw the strict enforcement procedures as a violation of the basic legal rights of all Englishmen. The threat to suspend the New York legislature threatened every assembly in the colonies.

The uneasy colonists began to believe there was a conspiracy afoot to take away their rights. The taxes themselves, however, did not create the unanimous outcry of the Stamp Act. They were subtle and indirect, but still not acceptable.

The colonists objected to the Townshend Acts, but the reactions were not as strong or as quick as under the Stamp Act. Radicals like Samuel Adams from Boston wrote pamphlets urging action. John Dickinson, a lawyer and legislator, wrote a series of widely read articles called *Letters from a Farmer in Pennsylvania,* which argued that the Parliament had no power over colonial affairs. Several colonial assemblies were dissolved for supporting that idea. A boycott was slowly pulled together. The colonists also engaged in widespread smuggling to bring in products and avoid paying the taxes.

Boston Massacre. Massachusetts, founded by independent-minded Puritans, had always been a restive colony. Boston quickly became a center for the opposition to Britain. The Sons of Liberty were especially active there, interfering with the British officials and creating public disturbances. Finally, the government sent in British soldiers to keep order. The presence of soldiers in the midst of an angry population was asking for trouble, and it came.

On the evening of March 5, 1770, a crowd decided to entertain themselves by throwing snowballs at a soldier guarding the Customs House. Troops were sent to his aid. The crowd threw snowballs and debris at them. Despite the efforts of Captain Preston, the commander, to prevent it, someone opened fire on the mob. Five people were killed. The colonial **propaganda** called the incident the Boston Massacre.

Radicals spread the news all through the colonies. The public story made martyrs out of the dead. The soldiers involved were tried for murder. John Adams, patriot and future president, took the unpopular job of defending them. He did so well that only two were convicted and those received light sentences. The results added to colonial distrust and anger.

| The Boston Massacre

Repeal. In Britain, the boycotts slowly began to have some effect on commerce. Thanks in part to colonial interference, the taxes were bringing in very little money. Moreover, the British government realized it was foolish to tax their own goods they were trying to sell in America. Lord North, who was now in control of the government, repealed the taxes in 1770, except for the tax on tea. The king and others insisted it must remain as a symbol of the government's right to tax.

The repeal calmed the **moderates** and relieved the conservatives, but radicals still looked for a confrontation with the British. Samuel Adams of Boston took the lead in organizing groups to communicate between the towns in Massachusetts. These *Committees of Correspondence* were set up to exchange information and the latest news. They also kept the rebellious spirit active. Eventually, they were set up by all the colonies to communicate with each other, laying the foundation for future cooperation.

Answer true or false.

If the statement is false, change some of the nouns or adjectives to make it true.

1.19 _____ The Townshend duties taxed goods imported from France.

1.20 _____ Charles Townshend was the Prime Minister.

1.21 _____ Money from the Townshend taxes was to be used to pay British officials in the colonies.

1.22 _____ The Townshend Acts threatened to dissolve the Massachusetts assembly if it did not comply with the Stamp Act.

1.23 _____ The colonists did not react as fiercely to the Townshend Acts as they had to the Stamp Act.

1.24 _____ *Letters from a Farmer in Pennsylvania* argued that colonial assemblies had no power over affairs in the colonies.

1.25 _____ The Townshend Acts were also met with a boycott.

1.26 _____ Lord West repealed all of the Townshend duties except the tax on paint.

1.27 _____ Committees of Correspondence encouraged communication and cooperation between the colonies.

1.28 _____ Britain was deeply in debt and was paying to protect America.

Describe the following.

1.29 The Townshend Acts

_____

_____

_____

_____

1.30 The Boston Massacre

_____

_____

_____

_____

Boston Tea Party. In 1773, the British East India Company was in serious financial trouble. Lord North decided to help it by giving it a monopoly on the sale of tea to the American colonies. The prices were set so that, even with the tax, it was cheaper than tea smuggled in from other sources. The colonists distrusted the monopoly and saw the lower price as a way to sneak the tax by them. They made sure that none of the tea was ever sold in America.

The colonies reacted differently to the tea when it arrived. Pennsylvania stuck it in a warehouse to rot. Charleston also stored it, and later sold it to support the Revolution. But, it was the reaction of the Sons of Liberty in Boston that gained the most fame. Three tea ships were floating in Boston harbor on the night of December 16, 1773. None had been able to unload their cargo. That evening a group of colonists, thinly disguised as Native American people, boarded the ships, took the tea, and dumped it into the harbor. The entire protest, known as the Boston Tea Party, was orderly and completely without violence. They simply refused to accept the tea. The tea party was repeated in New York harbor by a group of patriots there.

The Intolerable Acts. The reaction in London to the Tea Party was one of uncontrolled fury. The public destruction of valuable property in defiance of the king was the last straw. Public opinion was united behind Lord North and the king as they decided that Boston must be brought to heel. A series of laws called the Coercive Acts in Britain, and the Intolerable Acts in America were rapidly passed by Parliament.

The most important of the Intolerable Acts was the Boston Port Bill. It ordered the port of Boston blockaded and closed until the tea was paid for, with the tax. The implication of this was staggering. The closing of the harbor would mean the destruction of the city which depended on commerce for its supplies, jobs, and revenue. An entire city was being destroyed for the non-violent actions of a few individuals, clearly an excessive and dangerous use of force.

The other parts of the Intolerable Acts were equally as odious. The Massachusetts charter was changed so that all important officials were appointed and controlled by the Crown. Town meetings were forbidden without the express approval of the governor. A military governor was appointed for Boston and more troops were sent in, putting it under military rule.

The British government expected the other colonies to see this as a matter only involving Boston and stay out of it. They expected other port cities to jump at the chance to take over some of Boston's trade. In fact, the other colonies did not see it that way. They realized that if Britain could successfully use that kind of force against Boston, it would likely be used later against other colonies. They acted, therefore, in support of Boston, sending supplies to the city by land from as far away as South Carolina.

Quebec Act. Passed with the Intolerable Acts in Britain was a piece of legislation called the Quebec Act. It was not a part of the laws aimed at the colonies, but the touchy Americans assumed it was. The law confirmed the rights of the French in Quebec to follow their own customs (which did not include the usual traditions of English liberty) and protected the Catholic religion. Moreover, it extended the boundaries of Quebec down into the Ohio Valley south of the Great Lakes. That cut the Americans off from any possibility of controlling that coveted land, and put the land under a foreign system of government. The Quebec Act was a wise attempt by Parliament to win the support of the citizens in the former French lands. The Americans saw it as a spread of hated Catholicism, and a further attempt to contain their liberties.

The First Continental Congress. The primary response to the Intolerable Acts was the First Continental Congress. The colonies realized they needed to act together. Using the Committees of Correspondence, they set up a meeting for September 1774 in Philadelphia. Every colony except Georgia sent delegates. The fifty-four delegates included Samuel and John Adams from Massachusetts, John Jay from New York, as well as George Washington and Patrick Henry from Virginia.

The Congress accomplished several things during the seven weeks it met. They passed a Declaration of Rights that included life, liberty, property, the right to assemble and to tax themselves. Several acts of Parliament were declared to be illegal and an Association was formed to enforce a *full stoppage* of trade until the acts were repealed. A petition was sent to the king to address the colonial complaints.

| The First Continental Congress

The Congress further agreed to meet again in May of 1775 if their demands had not been met by then.

Choose the correct word(s) to complete these sentences.

1.31 Lord North gave the _____ a monopoly on the sale of tea to America to in 1773.

1.32 The tea that was shipped to the city of _____ was stored and later sold to support the Revolution.

1.33 A second tea party occurred in the city of _____ after the one at Boston.

1.34 The _____ Bill closed Boston harbor until the tea and tax were paid for.

1.35 The _____ Act protected the traditional customs of the French in Quebec and expanded their territory.

1.36 The primary colonial response to the Intolerable Acts was to organize the _____

_____ .

1.37 The Intolerable Acts were the British reaction to the _____ .

✎ **Describe the following.**

1.38 The Intolerable Acts

_____

_____

_____

1.39 The Boston Tea Party

_____

_____

_____

1.40 The actions of the First Continental Congress

_____

_____

_____

1.41 The American view of the Quebec Act

_____

_____

_____

Rebellion

Lexington and Concord. All of the American colonies had **militias** in the 1700s. They had been been organized to protect the colonists from the Native Americans and the French. In the wake of the occupation of Boston, the militias began to drill and collect supplies to defend themselves against British troops. The Massachusetts assembly, which had been meeting illegally, chose the city of Concord as a major supply depot for the militia. The assembly also began meeting there to be out of the reach of General Gage, the military commander of Boston.

Gage found out about the supplies and decided to destroy them. He also hoped to arrest some of the colonial leaders such as Samuel Adams and John Hancock, who were staying in Lexington. In April of 1775, Gage sent over 700 men to Lexington during the night. Paul Revere, a Boston silversmith who had worked for many years as a courier for the Sons of Liberty, rode to warn the patriots. In accordance with plans laid in advance, two lights were put in the steeple of the Old North Church to let the patriots know that the soldiers were coming across the Charles River. Revere only made it as far as Lexington before he was captured by a British patrol. But, other riders brought word to Concord.

When the British arrived at Lexington on the morning of April 19th, they were met by two companies of militia drawn up in battle order.

Battle order in the 1700s was two lines of men, one behind the other, close together. This was the standard because of the type of weapon they used, muskets. Muskets were very inaccurate and could not be counted on to hit a target more than 100 yards away. The only way to be sure of hitting anything was to have a large mass of men, firing together at the target at close range. Military **protocol** required that this be done on an open field until one side withdrew leaving the victors in command of the field.

The American commander realized that he was heavily outnumbered. When he was ordered to disperse, he began to do so. As the Americans began to leave, someone fired a shot. That bullet has been called "The Shot Heard Around the World" because it started the Revolutionary War. When the British officers finally got their men back under control, eight Americans were dead.

The British went on to Concord where they destroyed some supplies. There, they confronted a larger militia force who forced them to retreat. The retreat quickly became dangerous. The Americans, contrary to all the rules of gentlemanly warfare, began firing at the soldiers from behind trees, rocks, and buildings as they withdrew. The arrival of reinforcements at Lexington kept the British from being destroyed. Even then, it was a long march back to Boston as the militia opened fire from any vantage point they could find all along the route back. In the end, about seventy British soldiers were killed. America was at war with Britain.

Capture of Lake Champlain. Roads in the colonies were terrible. The best and most reliable transportation was by water. In central New York, there was a key water route that almost bridged the gap between Canada and the Atlantic coast. The Riechelieu River connected the St. Lawrence with Lake Champlain. The southern end of the lake was only 23 miles from the Hudson River, which flowed through Albany to New York City. This key route was protected by two old forts, Ticonderoga and Crown Point. Both forts were taken by a New England force under Ethan Allen and Benedict Arnold in May of 1775, to protect New England from a Canadian-based invasion. The forts were in bad shape, but Ticonderoga had a large supply of good cannon, something the colonists needed. Henry Knox, who would eventually become the first Secretary of War, went to Ticonderoga to get them. In the dead of winter in 1775-76, he moved 59 cannons across miles of wilderness to give the British a nasty surprise.

Bunker Hill. Militia from all over New England began to gather around Boston after Lexington and Concord. The slowly assembling citizen's army was put under the command of Artemas Ward of Massachusetts. Ward decided to fortify Bunker Hill on the Charlestown Peninsula facing Boston. By mistake, his men put up their fortifications on nearby Breeds Hill, but the battle that followed was named for the place where it should have happened.

The British foolishly decided to make a frontal attack on the entrenched, protected Americans at the top of the hill. They probably believed that the amateurs would run at the first sight of a regular army. The Americans did not bring enough gunpowder with them for a long battle, but they were determined to stay.

On June 17, 1775, about 2,000 British soldiers in neat lines marched up the hill toward the Americans. The militia calmly waited and held their fire until they "could see the whites of their eyes." Then, the Americans opened fire, mowing down the unprotected "Redcoats." The British retreated and came again, with the same result. The Americans held until they ran out of gunpowder and then managed to retreat. The British had lost almost half of their men, dead or wounded. Even though the British took the hill, the heavy losses made it more of an American victory. One colonial leader commented that he would gladly sell the British another hill at the same price.

A Colonial army. The Second Continental Congress assembled in May of 1775 as they had arranged. This time all thirteen colonies were represented, and Benjamin Franklin, newly returned from London, was a Pennsylvania delegate. The Congress at that time still did not want independence, nor did most of the country. They saw the fighting more as a civil war in defense of their rights. Congress, however, agreed to take on the assembling forces around Boston as an *American* army and to appoint a commander-in-chief. They chose George Washington for the post. It was a **providential** choice.

Washington was the son of a wealthy Virginia planter and had increased his fortune by marrying a rich widow, Martha Custis. He had been a colonial officer in the French and Indian War. He was not a brilliant strategist, but he was very determined and faithful. He was able to win and hold the loyalty of the men who served under him. His religious beliefs were private, but appeared to follow traditional Christianity, not Deism. He believed deeply in the patriot cause and took a fearful chance when he agreed to lead the army. He would have been hanged as a traitor if the Americans had lost.

Washington did accept the commission from the Congress to lead the new "army." He refused to accept any pay, however, and asked only to be reimbursed for his expenses. He left at once for Boston and took command two weeks after Bunker Hill on July 2, 1775.

![pencil icon] **Choose the correct match for each item.**

1.42 _____ Ethan Allen

1.43 _____ Shot Heard Around the World

1.44 _____ Artemas Ward

1.45 _____ valuable cannons captured

1.46 _____ fortified Breeds Hill

1.47 _____ militia fires along the road at British in retreat

1.48 _____ British destroy supplies, but are forced to retreat

1.49 _____ protects water route from Canada to New York

1.50 _____ Americans forced to quit when they run out of gunpowder

a. Lexington and Concord

b. Ticonderoga

c. Bunker Hill

1.51 _____ About half of the British forces are killed or wounded

1.52 _____ April 1775

1.53 _____ May 1775

1.54 _____ June 1775

Complete these sentences.

1.55 The assembled militia around Boston were taken as an American army by the _____

_____ .

1.56 After the occupation of Boston, the American _____ began to drill and gather supplies.

1.57 Congress appointed _____ as commander-in-chief of the colonial army.

Olive Branch Petition. Congress was still hoping that the British government would come to terms and they could end this revolt. The Americans blamed most of what had happened on Parliament. They still declared their loyalty to the king. In July of 1775, the Congress made one last attempt to stop the war. At the insistence of John Dickinson of Delaware, the colonists prepared a petition directed to the king in July of 1775. The "Olive Branch Petition" affirmed their loyalty to the crown and asked the king to intervene with Parliament on behalf of the colonists. The petition was sent to Britain in the hands of one of William Penn's descendants. The king refused to even receive him. Instead he declared the colonies to be in rebellion.

The king further alienated the colonists by hiring German soldiers to fight the Americans. This was a common practice among European powers. Germany was divided into many small states, each with their own army. The kings would hire out these well-disciplined men to raise money. The Americans were shocked by the involvement of the foreign "Hessians" (many of the mercenaries came from the German state of Hesse) and many who had favored the king now joined the patriots.

Invasion of Canada. The war continued even while Congress and the country debated what to do. Several of the colonial leaders thought that the French Canadians might be persuaded to join the rebellion. In any case, New England needed to be secure from invasion from the North. So, American Generals Richard Montgomery and Benedict Arnold led an assault on Canada in late 1775.

Montgomery led his forces up from Lake Champlain and successfully captured Montreal. He then met up with Arnold at Quebec. Arnold's men had been struck by disease and reduced to eating shoe leather on their long march through the wilds of Maine. Still, the commanders attempted an attack in December. It failed miserably. Montgomery was killed. Arnold was wounded in the leg and retreated after a siege failed. The French, who had been treated generously by the Quebec Act, did not join the Americans; they remained firmly on the British side.

Common sense. The double life most Americans were leading, fighting British soldiers while declaring loyalty to the British crown, was shattered in early 1776 by the publication of a pamphlet called *Common Sense*. *Common Sense* was written by Thomas Paine, a recently arrived English immigrant. It was one of the most influential pamphlets ever written. Paine argued that British control over America was a violation of common sense. Why should an island rule over a continent? The colonists had no reason to be loyal to a king who had treated them so harshly. The Americans had a clear choice between independence or tyranny.

Common Sense was a phenomenal best seller. The pamphlet sold hundreds of thousands of copies in a few months. Public opinion turned in favor of independence. The American people decided to cross the line from loyal subjects defending their rights to a free and independent nation. Delegates at the Second Continental Congress were instructed by their state governments to vote for independence.

Declaration of Independence. On June 7, 1776 Richard Henry Lee of Virginia proposed to the Second Continental Congress that "These United Colonies are, and of right ought to be, free and independent states..." Debate began on the proposal and, since it was expected to pass, a committee was appointed to write a document explaining their reasons. The committee included Thomas Jefferson, John Adams, and Benjamin Franklin. As the best writer in the group, Jefferson was elected to do the writing. The other members only made suggestions after they had seen his draft of the paper.

| The signing of the Declaration of Independence

Jefferson's document became one of the most famous in American history. It included a brilliant preamble which was accepted by Congress without any changes. The remainder, a list of the acts of tyranny committed by the king and the actual statement that the colonies were now independent, were accepted with some changes. The document was accepted by Congress on July 4, 1776. A perfect copy was written and signed later by fifty-six of the delegates, including the president of the congress, John Hancock, who deliberately signed in very large letters. That bold act was the origin of the American saying that a person's signature is their "John Hancock."

The Fourth of July is celebrated as Independence Day in the United States. Congress voted for independence, in favor of Lee's proposal, on July 2, 1776. The day the Declaration of Independence was accepted, July 4th, has become the holiday. That document is simply too vibrant and stirring to take a second place to anything. You will study why as you examine the document in the next few pages.

Match these items.

1.58 _____ American general killed; invasion of Canada		a. Richard Henry Lee
1.59 _____ Congressman who insisted on one more petition to the king in July of 1775		b. Thomas Paine
		c. Thomas Jefferson
1.60 _____ author of *Common Sense*		d. Richard Montgomery
1.61 _____ American general wounded in the invasion of Canada		e. John Dickinson
		f. Benedict Arnold
1.62 _____ Congressman who proposed independence		g. John Hancock
1.63 _____ author of the Declaration of Independence		
1.64 _____ president of the Second Continental Congress		

Complete these sentences.

1.65 The Second Continental Congress sent a petition called the _____ Petition to request the king's help in July of 1775.

1.66 Montgomery succeeded in capturing the Canadian city of _____ .

1.67 American public opinion was turned in favor of independence by the popular pamphlet called _____ .

1.68 Congress voted for independence on _____ .

1.69 The American Revolution was fought for _____ months before independence was declared.

The unanimous Declaration of the thirteen united States of America,

When in the Course of human events, it becomes necessary for one people to dissolve the political bands which have connected them with another, and to assume among the powers of the earth, the separate and equal station to which the Laws of Nature and of Nature's God entitle them, a decent respect to the opinions of mankind requires that they should declare the causes which impel them to the separation.

We hold these truths to be self-evident, that all men are created equal, that they are endowed by their Creator with certain unalienable Rights, that among these are Life, Liberty and the pursuit of Happiness.—That to secure these rights, Governments are instituted among Men, deriving their just powers from the consent of the governed, —That whenever any Form of Government becomes destructive of these ends, it is the Right of the People to alter or to abolish it, and to institute new Government, laying its foundation on such principles and organizing its powers in such form, as to them shall seem most likely to effect their Safety and Happiness. Prudence, indeed, will dictate that Governments long established should not be changed for light and transient causes; and accordingly all experience hath shewn, that mankind are more disposed to suffer, while evils are sufferable, than to right themselves by abolishing the forms to which they are accustomed. But when a long train of abuses and usurpations, pursuing invariably the same Object evinces a design to reduce them under absolute Despotism, it is their right, it is their duty, to throw off such Government, and to provide new Guards for their future security.—Such has been the patient sufferance of these Colonies; and such is now the necessity which constrains them to alter their former Systems of Government. The history of the present King of Great Britain is a history of repeated injuries and usurpations, all having in direct object the establishment of an absolute Tyranny over these States. To prove this, let Facts be submitted to a candid world.

He has refused his Assent to Laws, the most wholesome and necessary for the public good.

He has forbidden his Governors to pass Laws of immediate and pressing importance, unless suspended in their operation till his Assent should be obtained; and when so suspended, he has utterly neglected to attend to them.

He has refused to pass other Laws for the accommodation of large districts of people, unless those people would relinquish the right of Representation in the Legislature, a right inestimable to them and formidable to tyrants only.

He has called together legislative bodies at places unusual, uncomfortable, and distant from the depository of their public Records, for the sole purpose of fatiguing them into compliance with his measures.

THE DECLARATION OF INDEPENDENCE
IN CONGRESS, July 4, 1776.

He has dissolved Representative Houses repeatedly, for opposing with manly firmness his invasions on the rights of the people.

He has refused for a long time, after such dissolutions, to cause others to be elected; whereby the Legislative powers, incapable of Annihilation, have returned to the People at large for their exercise; the State remaining in the mean time exposed to all the dangers of invasion from without, and convulsions within.

He has endeavoured to prevent the population of these States; for that purpose obstructing the Laws for Naturalization of Foreigners; refusing to pass others to encourage their migrations hither, and raising the conditions of new Appropriations of Lands.

He has obstructed the Administration of Justice, by refusing his Assent to Laws for establishing Judiciary powers.

He has made Judges dependent on his Will alone, for the tenure of their offices, and the amount and payment of their salaries.

He has erected a multitude of New Offices, and sent hither swarms of Officers to harrass our people, and eat out their substance.

He has kept among us, in times of peace, Standing Armies without the Consent of our legislatures.

He has affected to render the Military independent of and superior to the Civil power.

He has combined with others to subject us to a jurisdiction foreign to our constitution, and unacknowledged by our laws; giving his Assent to their Acts of pretended Legislation:

For Quartering large bodies of armed troops among us:

For protecting them, by a mock Trial, from punishment for any Murders which they should commit on the Inhabitants of these States:

For cutting off our Trade with all parts of the world:

For imposing Taxes on us without our Consent:

For depriving us in many cases, of the benefits of Trial by Jury:

For transporting us beyond Seas to be tried for pretended offences:

For abolishing the free System of English Laws in a neighbouring Province, establishing therein an Arbitrary government, and enlarging its Boundaries so as to render it at once an example and fit instrument for introducing the same absolute rule into these Colonies:

For taking away our Charters, abolishing our most valuable Laws, and altering fundamentally the Forms of our Governments:

For suspending our own Legislatures, and declaring themselves invested with power to legislate for us in all cases whatsoever.

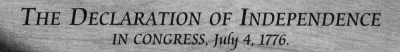

THE DECLARATION OF INDEPENDENCE
IN CONGRESS, July 4, 1776.

He has abdicated Government here, by declaring us out of his Protection and waging War against us.

He has plundered our seas, ravaged our Coasts, burnt our towns, and destroyed the lives of our people.

He is at this time transporting large Armies of foreign Mercenaries to compleat the works of death, desolation and tyranny, already begun with circumstances of Cruelty & perfidy scarcely paralleled in the most barbarous ages, and totally unworthy the Head of a civilized nation.

He has constrained our fellow Citizens taken Captive on the high Seas to bear Arms against their Country, to become the executioners of their friends and Brethren, or to fall themselves by their Hands.

He has excited domestic insurrections amongst us, and has endeavoured to bring on the inhabitants of our frontiers, the merciless Indian Savages, whose known rule of warfare, is an undistinguished destruction of all ages, sexes and conditions.

In every stage of these Oppressions We have Petitioned for Redress in the most humble terms: Our repeated Petitions have been answered only by repeated injury. A Prince whose character is thus marked by every act which may define a Tyrant, is unfit to be the ruler of a free people.

Nor have We been wanting in attentions to our British brethren. We have warned them from time to time of attempts by their legislature to extend an unwarrantable jurisdiction over us. We have reminded them of the circumstances of our emigration and settlement here. We have appealed to their native justice and magnanimity, and we have conjured them by the ties of our common kindred to disavow these usurpations, which, would inevitably interrupt our connections and correspondence. They too have been deaf to the voice of justice and of consanguinity. We must, therefore, acquiesce in the necessity, which denounces our Separation, and hold them, as we hold the rest of mankind, Enemies in War, in Peace Friends.

We, therefore, the Representatives of the United States of America, in General Congress, Assembled, appealing to the Supreme Judge of the world for the rectitude of our intentions, do, in the Name, and by Authority of the good People of these Colonies, solemnly publish and declare, That these United Colonies are, and of Right ought to be Free and Independent States; that they are Absolved from all Allegiance to the British Crown, and that all political connection between them and the State of Great Britain, is and ought to be totally dissolved; and that as Free and Independent States, they have full Power to levy War, conclude Peace, contract Alliances, establish Commerce, and to do all other Acts and Things which Independent States may of right do. And for the support of this Declaration, with a firm reliance on the protection of divine Providence, we mutually pledge to each other our Lives, our Fortunes and our sacred Honor.

The Declaration of Independence
IN CONGRESS, July 4, 1776.

✎ **Answer these questions.**

1.70 Which full paragraph(s) are the preamble? _____

1.71 The center section lists the grievances against the crown and Parliament as well as the American attempts to gain a fair hearing. What are the phrases that begin and end this section?

    a. Beginning phrase: _____

    b. Ending phrase: _____

1.72 Which paragraph(s) are the statement of independence? _____

Do this activity.

1.73 In a class setting, read the preamble aloud and discuss what each phrase means. In an independent study setting, read the preamble (aloud, if possible) and write out what it means in your own words.

TEACHER CHECK _____ _____
                                       initials   date

Look at the list of grievances in the Declaration. For each incident listed below give the phrase in the Declaration that refers to it (enough to identify it).

1.74 The dissolution of the colonial assemblies

_____

_____

1.75 The use of royal authority to veto colonial laws

_____

_____

1.76 The use of income from the Townshend Acts to pay salaries of officials

_____

_____

1.77 The Stamp Act

_____

_____

1.78 Use of Admiralty Courts

_____

_____

1.79 Changing the Massachusetts charter

_____

_____

1.80 Closing Boston Harbor

_____

_____

1.81 Encouraging Native American attacks

_____

_____

1.82 Hiring of Hessians

_____

_____

1.83 Quartering Act

_____

_____

1.84 Setting up a military government in Boston

_____

_____

1.85 Quebec Act

_____

_____

Review the material in this section in preparation for the Self Test. The Self Test will check your mastery of this particular section. The items missed on this Self Test will indicate specific areas where restudy is needed for mastery.

SELF TEST 1

Match the following people (each answer, 2 points).

1.01 _____ Boston radical; started
Committees of Correspondence

1.02 _____ American commander at Ticonderoga
and the invasion of Canada

1.03 _____ commander-in-chief of American army

1.04 _____ Prime Minister of Britain; Stamp Act

1.05 _____ author of the Declaration of Independence

1.06 _____ *Letters from a Farmer in Pennsylvania*;
Olive Branch Petition

1.07 _____ Chancellor of the Exchequer; Britain

1.08 _____ Prime Minister who gave East India Company
a monopoly on American tea sales

1.09 _____ president of Second Continental Congress;
large signer of Declaration of Independence

1.010 _____ colonial representative in London before the war

a. George Grenville

b. Benjamin Franklin

c. Charles Townshend

d. John Dickinson

e. Lord North

f. Samuel Adams

g. John Hancock

h. George Washington

i. Benedict Arnold

j. Thomas Jefferson

Describe each of these giving the important points.

1.011 Stamp Act (5 points)

_____

_____

1.012 Townshend Acts (5 points)

_____

_____

_____

1.013 Boston Massacre (5 points)

_____

_____

1.014 Boston Tea Party (4 points)

_____

_____

1.015 The Intolerable Acts (5 points)

_____

_____

_____

1.016 Quebec Act (5 points)

_____

_____

_____

1.017 Battle of Bunker Hill (5 points)

_____

_____

_____

_____

1.018 Colonial reaction to the Stamp Act (6 points)

a. _____   b. _____

c. _____

Complete these sentences (each answer, 3 points).

1.019 British policy toward the Thirteen Colonies was based on the economic theory of

_____ .

1.020 The laws that were passed in the late 1600s, but rarely enforced, that restricted America to trade to the benefit of England were called the _____ Acts.

1.021 The _____ Act was passed when the Stamp Act was repealed and stated that Parliament could tax the colonies.

1.022 The _____ were secret societies opposed to British power that led mob action.

1.023 The _____ Act required colonists to house and feed British troops.

1.024 The _____ Act kept high taxes on sugar and rum and allowed violators to be tried in Admiralty Court.

1.025 The First Continental Congress met in response to the _____ Acts.

1.026 The Revolutionary War began at _____ .

1.027 The key fort, with its cannon, that was captured on Lake Champlain was Fort

_____ .

1.028 _____ was an influential pamphlet written by Thomas Paine that urged America to become independent.

Answer true or false (each answer, 1 point).

1.029 _____ Britain was deeply in debt after the Seven Years War.

1.030 _____ The colonists carefully obeyed the trade laws before 1763.

1.031 _____ The American invasion of Canada encouraged the French colonists to rebel against the British.

1.032 _____ Congress voted for independence on July 4, 1776.

1.033 _____ The king's decision to use German mercenaries to fight in America turned many Americans against the British.

1.034 _____ The Olive Branch Petition was an offer of surrender by the American army after the defeat at Bunker Hill.

1.035 _____ The American army was organized from militia units.

1.036 _____ In 1773 Boston was the only city that refused to accept for sale the tea shipped in under the new monopoly to the East India Company.

1.037 _____ Britain wanted the Americans to bear some of the cost of their own defense.

1.038 _____ The colonies were always short of hard money because of British laws.

80 / 100   SCORE _____   TEACHER _____ _____
                                                    initials   date

2. WAR

The Revolutionary War was fought from 1775 until 1783. Most of it was very discouraging for the Americans. They rarely won battles. They were always short of gunpowder, uniforms, boots, food, and cannons. Most of the soldiers in the army were militia. They only stayed for short periods of time. Some would return home each spring for planting or to deal with Native Americans in their state. The army was in a constant state of change, growing smaller and larger as men came and went. But, this very unlikely group held off the well-trained, well-supplied, well-disciplined British army for years.

Washington was forced by his circumstances to fight a defensive war. He wanted to attack and drive the British out of America, but he never had an army that could do that. Instead, he fought and retreated, forcing the British to keep their army ready to face him, but never giving them a decisive victory. The British captured cities but could not capture the hearts of the people. Eventually, the vengeful nations of Europe stepped in to reduce British power by helping the Americans. In the end, the war went to the Americans who won by simply surviving and not giving up.

SECTION OBJECTIVES

Review these objectives. When you have completed this section, you should be able to:

1. Identify the men who contributed to the Revolution.
3. Identify and describe the governing bodies that acted for the colonies/states.
4. Name the major battles of the war and to tell their significances.
5. Outline the terms of the peace agreements that the United States signed with Britain.

VOCABULARY

Study these words to enhance your learning success in this section.

asset (as′ et). An advantage.

enlistment (en list′ ment). The time for which a person joins some part of the armed forces.

guerrillas (gu ril′ u). Fighters who harass the enemy by sudden raids; ambushes; the plundering of supplies and the like.

mediocre (mē′ dē ō′ ker). Of average quality; ordinary.

morale (mu ral′). Mental condition in regard to courage, confidence, or enthusiasm.

America Alone

British situation. The British appeared to have huge advantages over their American opponents in this war. They had a professional army of thousands, trained and ready to go. They also had the means to hire Hessians to add to their strength (eventually 30,000 served under the British in America). The British navy controlled the Atlantic. This was a tremendous advantage. The army could be moved, supplied, and reinforced anywhere along the coast, where most of the American population and all of the American cities were located.

Also, the British could count on the support of Americans still loyal to the crown. About one-third of the colonists were Loyalists or Tories. These were formidable **assets**.

However, the British also had several weaknesses. They had to fight this war across an ocean 3,000 miles (4,839 km) away. New information and orders could take months to reach a commander in the field from London. Britain also had no great leaders in power to organize the fight and most of her generals were **mediocre**. The other countries of Europe were anxious to take down British power, and might be willing to support the Americans. Moreover, the British had to defeat and conquer a huge area of territory and an uncooperative population. An incomplete victory would be no victory.

American situation. The Americans had the advantage of fighting near their homes for a righteous cause. They had outstanding leadership in men like George Washington, Nathanael Greene, Benedict Arnold, and Daniel Morgan. They were a tough, capable people who had already proven their courage and strength by leaving the safety of Europe to tame a wilderness land. The Americans learned to shoot while hunting for food. They were usually better shots than the British soldiers. Moreover, the Americans had the wide spaces of the country in which to retreat and hide.

The Americans also had deep weaknesses. Only about one third of the people supported the Revolution. America did not have an effective central government. The Second Continental Congress became the first government because there was no other body that could do it. It had no official authority. A system of government for the colonies, the Articles of Confederation, was not set up until 1781. The Congress had no power to tax and the money it printed lost value until it was practically worthless. The different states fought with each other constantly and usually put the needs of their state above the needs of the "nation."

Boston. General Washington was camped with the American army around Boston in early 1776. He had been there since July and the army had been there since Lexington in April. Washington's main accomplishment through that time was that he managed to keep the army there at all. Most of the militia were there only for short periods of **enlistment**, some as short as eight months. Gradually, Washington convinced some of them to stay and others to join. But, he did not have the strength to threaten the British in Boston, at least, not until Henry Knox arrived from Ticonderoga in March of 1776 with the fort's cannons.

The cannons changed the entire situation. Washington had them installed on Dorchester Heights, a high hill directly across from Boston. From there Washington could fire at will on the British in the city. The new British commander, Sir William Howe, gathered his men to attack, but a storm prevented them from crossing the bay. Instead, the British abandoned Boston, withdrawing to Canada.

Charleston. The British hoped to gain the support of Loyalists in the South by a show of force there. A force was organized for an assault in the spring of 1776. A Loyalist force of about 1,500 that intended to join up with the British was destroyed by Patriot forces in February. The defeat disheartened the Loyalists who made no attempt to join with the British when they finally arrived. Orders from London calling off the assault because of the Loyalists' defeat reached the commander, Henry Clinton, too late.

The British assault force, including ten warships and thirty transports, reached Charleston in June, 1776. The city, however, was well prepared. Sturdy forts had been built on the approaches to the harbor, and they were well supplied. The defenders were organized and calm. The British assault failed, driven back by the steady fire from the forts. The South was left in peace for the time being.

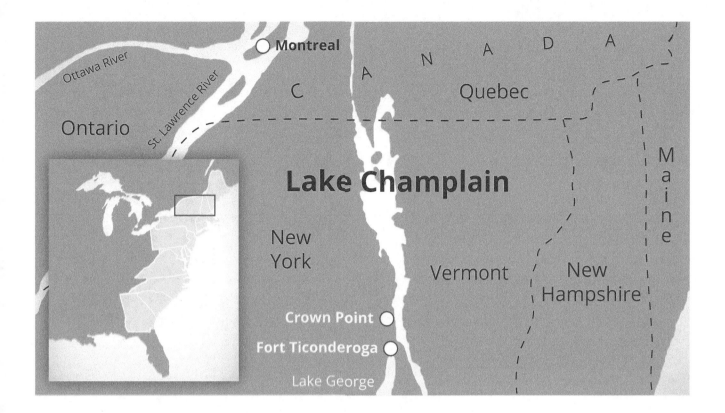

Lake Champlain. When Benedict Arnold retreated from Quebec in May of 1776, he headed back down Lake Champlain. The British governor in Canada, Sir Guy Carleton, followed. Carleton assembled a fleet to take troops down the lake. Arnold, now a brigadier general, constructed a ramshackle fleet to oppose them. The two sides met in October of 1776 on Lake Champlain. The American fleet was destroyed, but it succeeded in inflicting enough damage that Carleton withdrew for the season. Arnold's success at keeping the British from taking Fort Ticonderoga in 1776 was a key victory. It meant that the British invasion from Canada in 1777 had to start in Canada, not New York! Those would be precious miles and months for the Americans.

New York. The British withdrawal from Boston left Washington in a difficult position. The British had control of the seas and could attack anywhere they wanted along the coast. Washington would then have to march his men overland to meet them. Fortunately, Washington expected them to go to New York City, and they did. The army was shifted there to meet them.

The British arrived in July of 1776 with a huge force including more than 30,000 soldiers and 30 battleships. They took Staten Island to use as a base. The American position was impossible from the start. New York City is built on an island and the British controlled the waterways. They could land at will and prevent Washington from moving across the rivers. Washington had to defend everywhere at once. The British expected Washington to simply submit to British rule in the face of their control of the waterways and superior troop strength. They sent a few ships to fire on the city to prove their point. But, Washington refused to submit.

The British launched an assault on Long Island in August of 1776. The Americans had more than 10,000 men waiting for them. But, the British did not go straight up the hill into the fortifications as they did at Bunker Hill. Part of the British forces came around to attack from the rear. The inexperienced Americans panicked. By the end of the day, the survivors had retreated to Brooklyn Heights, near the ocean where the British navy prevented an escape.

But, Washington was not so easily trapped. He had his men leave their campfires burning and, under the cover of night, transferred the entire army across to Manhattan Island in small boats. The Americans retreated up the island leaving the British in control of New York City. The Battle of Long Island had been a serious American defeat, but the army had escaped and would fight again.

It was during this campaign that the British captured an American officer named Nathan Hale. He was behind the British lines trying to gather information. He was hung as a spy the next day without a trial. He said before he died, "I regret that I have but one life to lose for my country." He is remembered and honored for his bravery.

The British followed their success with more of the same. The Americans had built two forts, Washington and Lee, to secure New York City. Both held large supplies of American gunpowder, cannons, clothing, and war material. The British captured both forts and all of the 3,000 defenders.

| Nathan Hale's homestead

It was a staggering loss for the Americans. The British commander, William Howe, then settled down to enjoy the winter in the comfort of New York City since armies traditionally did not fight in the colder months.

These are the times that try men's souls. The summer soldier and the sunshine patriot will, in this crisis, shrink from the service of their country; but he that stands it now, deserves the love and thanks of man and woman. Tyranny, like hell, is not easily conquered; yet we have this consolation with us, that the harder the conflict, the more glorious the triumph. What we obtain too cheap, we esteem too lightly: it is dearness only that gives every thing its value.

Heaven knows how to put a proper price upon its goods; and it would be strange indeed if so celestial an article as FREEDOM should not be highly rated. Britain, with an army to enforce her tyranny, has declared that she has a right (not only to TAX) but "to BIND us in ALL CASES WHATSOEVER," and if being bound in that manner, is not slavery, then is there not such a thing as slavery upon earth. Even the expression is impious; for so unlimited a power can belong only to God.

THE AMERICAN CRISIS
Thomas Paine

Washington's men withdrew into New Jersey. They were in bad shape. They had been retreating for months. They lacked food and proper clothing. Thomas Paine, author of *Common Sense*, was with the army during this bleak hour. On a drumhead he wrote an essay that even today stirs the hearts of those who must face unexpected hardship in fighting for what they believe.

In each case, check the side that had the advantage.

		British	Americans
2.1	size of army	☐	☐
2.2	professionalism	☐	☐
2.3	commanders	☐	☐
2.4	government	☐	☐
2.5	location of the war	☐	☐
2.6	hope of foreign alliances	☐	☐
2.7	money and supplies	☐	☐
2.8	control of the sea	☐	☐
2.9	shooting accuracy	☐	☐
2.10	national unity	☐	☐

Answer these questions.

2.11 What was Washington's main accomplishment from July 1775 until March 1776?

_____

2.12 What gave the Americans the advantage in Boston?

_____

2.13 Why was Arnold's defeat on Lake Champlain in 1776 so important to the Americans?

_____

2.14 What was the result of the 1776 assault on Charleston?

_____

2.15 What happened to the Americans at the Battle of Long Island?

_____

_____

2.16 Who was Nathan Hale and what happened to him?

_____

_____

2.17 What happened to Forts Washington and Lee?

_____

2.18 How did the Continental Army escape after the Battle of Long Island?

_____

2.19 What was the condition of Washington's army going into winter 1776?

_____

According to Thomas Paine.

2.20 Why is tyranny like hell? _____ .

2.21 Unlimited power belongs only to _____ .

2.22 Those that shrink from the service of their country are _____

_____ .

2.23 If we obtain something too easily we will _____ .

Trenton. By the end of 1776, Washington was in a fix. He had experienced nothing but defeat since the evacuation of Boston. Morale was low. Many people were calling for him to be replaced. The enlistments of most of his men would run out at the end of the year. By January, the Americans might not even have any army. The Americans, now in Pennsylvania, desperately needed a victory. So, Washington took a huge gamble and prepared to attack.

On Christmas night 1776, Washington and his army made a dangerous trip across the ice-choked Delaware River. Early the next morning, the Americans attacked the Hessian army at Trenton, New Jersey. Surprise was complete. Most of the Germans were still in bed, sleeping off the celebrations of the day before. It was all over in less than an hour. Washington's army captured over a thousand men and their supplies. The victory convinced many of the men to stay in the army for at least a little longer.

Princeton. British General Charles Cornwallis rushed to Trenton in an attempt to trap Washington's army in January of 1777. The larger, better supplied British force caught the Americans at Trenton with their backs to the river. But, again, the cagey Washington refused to be trapped. He left his fires burning and a few volunteers who made noise in the camp while the rest of the army snuck away after dark. The Americans swung around the British force and attacked their reinforcements at Princeton, winning yet another battle. From there Washington retreated to easily defended highlands near Morristown, Pennsylvania for the rest of the winter.

The twin victories at Trenton and Princeton saved the American cause. Volunteers came in from all over the colonies. Many of the experienced troops agreed to stay, some of them serving until the end of the war. Washington's command was secure and never was seriously questioned again. But, these were only small victories.

Washington, summer of 1777. Sir William Howe was in command of the British forces in New York. The British strategy for that year called for him to move his men up the Hudson River to meet General Burgoyne who was invading from Canada. Howe's orders, however, were not clear, and he had already committed his soldiers to a campaign against Washington in the central states.

Howe tried, at first, to draw Washington into a battle around New York. When that failed, he decided to take his army by sea up the Chesapeake to attack Philadelphia in July. He believed he had plenty of time to help Burgoyne should the need arise.

Howe fought two battles with Washington en route to Philadelphia. The Americans lost both at Brandywine Creek (September) and Germantown (October). But, again the American army was not captured.

The loss at Germantown, moreover, impressed foreign observers. The Americans had initiated the attack and had been driven off only after heavy fighting. Also, the men had fought well against the experienced British army. But, they could not keep Howe from capturing Philadelphia.

The capture of the capital should have been a major victory for the British. But, it accomplished very little. Congress simply moved elsewhere. There were very few government officials or offices to move. Howe again settled down to spend a comfortable winter in yet another American city. But, Washington's army was still in the field and America was not yet conquered.

| Washington and his men crossing the Delaware

Valley Forge. The Continental army faced many hardships in the long years of the Revolution. Perhaps the most famous was their stay at Valley Forge, outside of Philadelphia in the winter of 1777-78. The very name of the place has become synonymous with suffering.

Washington had to stay near Philadelphia in case Howe decided to attack, and Valley Forge was one of his few choices for winter quarters. The army came in having lost two major battles, and the nation's capital. Thanks to a lack of funds, hoarding, corruption, and poor transport the troops were constantly short of supplies. In December, Washington wrote to Congress that 2,873 of his men were unfit for duty because they were barefoot or otherwise in need of clothes. Men left bloody tracks in the snow from their unprotected feet. Food was scarce and disease common.

The army's main occupation that winter was survival. What was astonishing was that the army continued to exist. The dedicated men did not desert. In fact, the army managed to build its skills during this dark time. The Americans were good fighters as individuals, but they lacked training on how to work as a group. A German officer, Baron von Steuben, who spoke no English, drilled the men all through the long winter on how to maneuver and attack as a unit. In spite of the conditions, he managed to vastly improve the discipline and professionalism of the army. The hard work in Valley Forge would yield good fruit for the army in the future.

 Choose the correct match for each item.

2.24 _____ January 1777		a. Trenton
2.25 _____ October 1777		b. Princeton
2.26 _____ Winter 1777-78		c. Germantown
2.27 _____ drilling by von Stueben		d. Brandywine Creek
2.28 _____ capture of 1,000 Hessians		e. Valley Forge
2.29 _____ Americans snuck behind Cornwallis to attack his reinforcements		f. Philadelphia
2.30 _____ December 1776		
2.31 _____ captured by Howe		
2.32 _____ Washington's winter quarters		
2.33 _____ Howe's winter quarters		
2.34 _____ Americans crossed the icy Delaware		
2.35 _____ September 1777		
2.36 _____ time of great suffering		
2.37 _____ surprise attack, day after Christmas		
2.38 _____ should have been major victory for British, did not accomplish much		
2.39 _____ American army impressed foreign observers		

HISTORY & GEOGRAPHY 803

LIFEPAC TEST

NAME _____

DATE _____

SCORE _____

HISTORY & GEOGRAPHY 803: LIFEPAC TEST

Match these people (each answer, 2 points).

1. _____ Father of the Constitution
2. _____ Lost battles but won campaign in the South
3. _____ American general that turned traitor
4. _____ author of *Common Sense*
5. _____ president of the Constitutional Convention
6. _____ colonial representative in London right before the Revolution
7. _____ hanged as a spy during the New York campaign of 1776
8. _____ Boston radical, began Committees of Correspondence
9. _____ author of the Declaration of Independence
10. _____ American naval commander, *Bonhomme Richard*

a. George Washington
b. Benjamin Franklin
c. Nathanael Greene
d. Benedict Arnold
e. Samuel Adams
f. Thomas Jefferson
g. James Madison
h. John Paul Jones
i. Nathan Hale
j. Thomas Paine

Complete the following.

11. What was the Great Compromise of the Constitutional Convention? (5 points)

_____

_____

_____

12. Describe the set up and results of the Battle of Yorktown. (5 points)

_____

_____

_____

13. Why did British policy towards the colonies change after 1763? (5 points)

_____

_____

_____

14. Describe the most important provisions of each law (each answer, 2 points).

    Stamp Act: _____

    Quebec Act: _____

    Quartering Act: _____

    Townshend Acts: _____

    Intolerable Acts: _____

15. What was Shays Rebellion and why was it important? (5 points)

    _____

    _____

Complete each sentence using a word from the list (each answer, 2 points).

Lexington	Ticonderoga	Saratoga
Rochambeau	Monmouth	Camden
Trenton	Cornwallis	Lafayette
Steuben		

16. The Revolutionary War began at _____ .

17. The Marquis de _____ was a wealthy French volunteer who became an American hero.

18. _____ was the commander of the French army in America during the Revolution.

19. _____ was the indecisive last major battle in the North during the Revolution.

20. Lord _____ was the British commander in the South after the capture of Charleston.

21. Baron von _____ drilled the American army at Valley Forge.

22. Henry Knox dragged the cannon from _____ to Boston.

23. Horatio Gates lost the humiliating battle of _____ when he brought a new American army south after the loss of Charleston.

24. _____ was the turning point of the Revolutionary War.

25. Washington led his army across the icy Delaware River to surprise the Hessians at _____ on the day after Christmas.

Name the legislature or constitution related to each item (each answer, 3 points).

26. _____   Declaration of Independence

27. _____   Stamp Act

28. _____   America's first constitution

29. _____   Northwest Ordinance

30. _____   enslaved people counted as three-fifths of a person

31. _____   America's first government

32. _____   reaction to the Intolerable Acts

33. _____   a firm league of friendship between the states

34. _____   checks and balances

35. _____   appointed Washington as commander-in-chief

The Turning Point

British plan. During the summer of 1777, the British had organized a master plan to cut New England off from the rest of the United States. The plan called for General Burgoyne to come down Lake Champlain and the Hudson River to Albany. Lieutenant Colonel St. Leger was to reach the same point by coming across from Lake Ontario and up the Mohawk River. In the meantime, General Howe was to come up the Hudson from New York and also reach Albany. This three-prong attack would conquer New York and isolate New England. The plan, however, required cooperation and the success of all three parts. As noted in the last section, General Howe received unclear orders from London and had already committed his troops to action in Pennsylvania. He never even made an attempt to join Burgoyne at Albany. The British master plan had all the makings of a grand disaster without the full support of all three commanders.

| The unsuccessful British attack plan in the summer of 1777

St. Leger and the Battle of Oriskany.

Lt. Colonel Barry St. Leger was to bring a British force up the Mohawk Valley for his part in the campaign. He had a mixed force of about one thousand British, German, and Loyalist soldiers. He also had about the same number of Iroquois allies. The Americans in the valley knew what would happen if the Iroquois and the Loyalists, who were supporters of several autocratic landlords from the region, were to reach the rich farms of the region. They were prepared and ready to fight, ferociously.

St. Leger reached the American Fort Stanwix at what is now Rome, New York in late summer of 1777. The fort refused to surrender and skillfully held off his siege. The militia of the nearby towns sent a force of 800 under the command of General Nicholas Herkimer to aid the fort.

St. Leger heard of the relief effort and sent 1,200 soldiers and Iroquois to meet them. The British force set up an ambush near Oriskany Creek. The Americans walked into the trap on August 6th. They were driven to retreat, but not before they inflicted heavy losses on the British. In the meantime, Fort Stanwix's defenders had taken advantage of the situation to raid the British camp and carry off many of their supplies.

By now the Continental Army had been alerted and a force of 1,000 men under General Benedict Arnold was on route to Stanwix. St. Leger's men heard rumors of the force, and received exaggerated reports of its size. The Iroquois and Loyalists began to panic. In late August, St. Leger began a retreat to his base on Lake Ontario. General Burgoyne was now the only one of the three commanders still pursuing the planned advance on Albany.

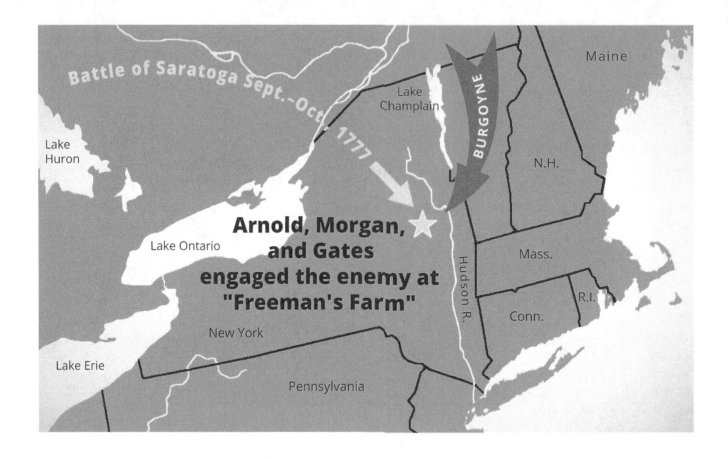

Battle of Saratoga Sept.–Oct. 1777

Lake Huron

Lake Ontario

Lake Erie

Lake Champlain

BURGOYNE

Maine

N.H.

Mass.

Hudson R.

R.I.

Conn.

New York

Pennsylvania

Arnold, Morgan, and Gates engaged the enemy at "Freeman's Farm"

Burgoyne. John "Gentleman Johnny" Burgoyne was a popular and arrogant British general. He believed he would have no trouble with the American militia. He started down the Richelieu River to Lake Champlain in June of 1777. He had about 7,000 British and German troops under his command. He was also accompanied by a large contingent of about 400 Iroquois People. Burgoyne was handicapped by a huge baggage train, hundreds of camp followers, including women and children, and over a hundred cannons he insisted be brought along, some of them to be dragged with the army through the wilderness.

The force floated down Lake Champlain and reached Fort Ticonderoga in early July. The fort was held by Major General Arthur St. Clair and 2,000 men. An alert British engineer noticed the high hill called Mount Defiance that towered above the fort. The steep sides made it difficult to climb and no one among the Americans dreamed the British could haul cannons up there. But, they did. St. Clair realized his danger and evacuated the fort before he and his men could be trapped.

Burgoyne then proceeded to show his ignorance of wilderness warfare. He set off to cross the 23 miles between Lake Champlain and the Hudson River Valley building a road as he went. He also dragged his own thirty carts of personal belongings as well as dozens of cannons. By now the alarm had gone out all over New England and Americans were swarming around Burgoyne like flies. They made him pay for every step he took through those miles of wilderness. Trees were felled across his path. Rivers were dammed and low areas flooded. It took Burgoyne an entire month to reach the Hudson. Then, he had to wait for his supplies to reach him.

The Americans feared not only the British but the Iroquois they had with him. They had good reason to believe that Burgoyne could not control them. In fact, on the trip south, some of the Iroquois captured and scalped a young woman named Jane McCrea, the fiancée of one of the Loyalist officers. Burgoyne did not punish the murderer because the other Indians would have left if he did. The Americans made good use of the story to convince New Englanders that Burgoyne did not even protect those who were loyal to the crown. What would happen to Patriots that happened to fall into his hands? More and more citizens took up their guns and went to join the growing horde opposing the British advance.

Burgoyne sent out a small force in mid-August to secure some horses that were rumored to be at Bennington. The entire German unit was destroyed by the Americans. The British unit sent to help was driven back. Burgoyne refused to take warning from the defeat or the news that neither Howe nor St. Leger were coming.

Saratoga. Burgoyne pressed on down the Hudson Valley toward Albany in September. He took only the minimum of supplies his army would need for the short trip to Albany, but kept his own baggage and the cannons. Snipers made it dangerous to leave the camp. The Americans again burned bridges, flooded lowlands, and felled trees to slow him down. Burgoyne often made only a mile a day or less and it was getting near winter.

General Horatio Gates was sent by Congress to command the American forces. Daniel Morgan, with his sharp-shooting riflemen, and Benedict Arnold were also sent. (Rifles, which were just coming into use, were more accurate than the muskets used by the British, but they took longer to reload.) Washington was too busy with Howe in Pennsylvania to come or send many men. Most of the soldiers in the army that faced Burgoyne were simply citizens who came to defend their homeland.

The two armies met twice on a piece of land called Freeman's Farm in September and October. The Americans fought from behind trees and let the British have the open field. Morgan and Arnold, not Gates, were responsible for the victories. Morgan's riflemen defied every rule of polite warfare by shooting from up in the trees deliberately aiming for the officers! General Benedict Arnold displayed his brilliance as a field commander by leading a furious attack in the second battle. He was severely wounded in the same leg that was injured in the attack on Quebec. Most of the time the British could not even get a good look, much less a clear shot, at their enemies. The British were routed in both battles.

His army in shambles, Burgoyne retreated, hoping to reach the safety of Ticonderoga. The men had no warm clothes and the weather was getting colder. British supplies of food were also low and the Americans continued to harass them. Burgoyne dug in on some high ground near the village of Saratoga for a rest. The American army surrounded him. With no other alternative, Burgoyne surrendered his entire army of about 5,000 men on October 17, 1777.

✎ **Complete these sentences.**

2.40 The British plan for 1777 called for _____ to lead an attack

down Lake Champlain, _____ to come up the Mohawk Valley,

and _____ to come up the Hudson from New York City.

2.41 St. Leger was unable to capture _____ in New York and his

forces were badly hurt in the battle at _____ .

2.42 Burgoyne took Fort _____ on Lake Champlain by putting

cannon on Mount _____ .

2.43 Burgoyne carried _____ cart loads of his own belongings, dozens of

_____ and hundreds of camp followers with him.

2.44 The Americans made good use of propaganda in the murder of _____

_____ by the Iroquois.

2.45 An entire German unit was wiped out by the Americans at

_____ .

2.46 The Americans defeated Burgoyne's forces in two battles at

_____ .

2.47 The leaders of the American victory were _____

and _____ .

2.48 The official American commander was _____ .

2.49 Burgoyne surrendered his entire army at _____ in October 1777.

Significance of Saratoga. The victory at Saratoga was the turning point of the war. The Americans had defeated and captured an entire British army. The British evacuated Ticonderoga and withdrew to Canada. The victory brought great cheer to the American side. The victory also brought the Patriot cause much needed allies.

Franklin in France. The Americans knew how badly the French wanted revenge for their losses in the Seven Years War. It was natural, therefore, to seek assistance from them for the American Rebellion. Benjamin Franklin was sent to France as an official envoy in September, 1776 to get a possible alliance. The French were willing to encourage the colonists, but were not willing to immediately risk war with Britain. However, they did provide valuable weapons and supplies through a trading company called *Hortalez et Cie*, thus staying officially neutral.

Franklin quickly became one of the most popular men in France, the darling of the frivolous French court. The aristocracy was very interested in the theories of the day that taught the superiority of "natural man." Franklin agreeably played the part of the noble rustic, much to the delight of the high-born ladies. He did not wear the rich clothes, sword, and wig normally expected of a court envoy. Instead, he dressed plainly and acted the part of the natural philosopher, even occasionally wearing a fur cap. The French courtiers were enchanted, but the French leaders wanted proof that America could fight and win a war before they committed.

The victory at Saratoga along with the surprising American showing at Germantown provided the proof the French wanted. They signed a treaty of Alliance with the Americans in February of 1778, while Washington's men hungered in Valley Forge. The French navy could now be used to protect American trade and threaten the British West Indies. The Spanish and Dutch also eventually joined the alliance. Britain now had a world war, not a colonial rebellion on its hands.

| The Marquis de Lafayette

Lafayette. The Marquis de Lafayette was one of the many assets America received from France throughout the Revolution. Lafayette was a very wealthy French aristocrat who joined the American cause in 1777 at the age of nineteen. He was assigned as an aide to General Washington, and the two became very close friends. He was gradually given opportunities to command which he handled skillfully to the advantage of the American cause. He donated a great deal of money to the patriot cause and used his influence with the king of France to arrange for a French army to come to America in 1779. He has long been hailed as a hero of the Revolution and is honored in America by numerous towns that bear his name.

Monmouth. By early 1778, Sir Henry Clinton had replaced Howe as commander of the British forces in America. News of the alliance with France reached him in Philadelphia, which the British still held. He was ordered to evacuate Philadelphia and return to New York. Clinton decided to march his army north and Washington went to meet him. A battle was fought at Monmouth Court House in New Jersey. It would be the last major battle in the North.

Washington sent an advance strike force under the command of General Charles Lee, who had been a British prisoner for a time and had a poor attitude. Lee attacked as ordered, but then withdrew without any reason. Washington came up with the rest of the army to find the strike force in a disorderly retreat. It was one of the few times Washington publicly lost his temper. He charged into the retreating lines, ordered Lee to surrender his command, rallied the men, and led the fight himself (Lee was later court-martialed). The battle ended indecisively, and the British succeeded in reaching New York safely. The two sides were now back where they had been in 1776, the British bottled up in New York, the Americans watching and waiting. Washington would remain there until 1781.

Western campaign. Most of the battles in the west were fought against the Native American Peoples who were encouraged by the British to make raids on the American settlements. Control of this region would enable the patriots to concentrate on the east and south. In 1778 George Rogers Clark and a band of frontiersmen overcame the British at Kaskasia, Cahokia, and Vincennes, the three major British forts in the west. These victories brought the west under American control. Colonel Henry Hamilton, a British officer, however, recaptured Vincennes. His victory was short-lived as George Rogers Clark led his men 180 miles through waist-deep swamps in the dead of winter to recapture the fort and bring the west under American control. This would prove vital in the years after the Revolution because the area south of the Great Lakes was in American hands, not British. The Americans received little trouble from the Native Americans and British in the west for the remainder of the war.

The war at sea. The tiny American navy, made up mostly of privateers, was no match for the British navy, which was the largest in the world. Yet, under the leadership of John Paul Jones and John Barry, using European ports, the navy managed to harass British ships near England.

One of the most famous American-British sea battles took place in 1779 between the *Bonhomme Richard*, under the command of John Paul Jones, and the British warship *Serapis*. The two engaged in savage combat for over three hours. The *Bonhomme Richard* was badly damaged and sinking. Yet, Jones refused to surrender saying, "I have not yet begun to fight!" He eventually captured the *Serapis*. This and other victories did little for the American cause except in the area of morale. The only real chance the Americans had at sea came with the alliance that brought the French navy in on their side.

Treachery. One of the most disheartening events of the Revolution occurred in 1780 when Benedict Arnold became a traitor. The hero of Ticonderoga and Saratoga was bitter over some setbacks in his military career. He also had married a Loyalist and become fond of rich living. In September of 1780, he offered to turn over his command, the American fort at West Point that protected the upper Hudson River, to the British. In exchange, he was to receive a large amount of money and a commission in the British army.

The man acting as the go-between, Major John André, was captured with the plans of the fort in Arnold's handwriting. Arnold fled to New York before he could be captured and André was hanged as a spy. West Point was strengthened and never fell into British hands. But, the loss of such a trusted and successful commander was a blow to the Americans.

Arnold fought the remainder of the Revolution as a British Brigadier General, a step below his American rank of Major General. He lived the rest of his life as a British subject reviled by his former countrymen. His name became synonymous with traitor in the American language. But, his brilliant work for the American cause was not forgotten. At Saratoga there is a very unusual memorial. It is a statue of a leg, the leg of Benedict Arnold. Injured at both Quebec and Saratoga, it was the only loyal part of the former American hero.

Complete these sentences.

2.50 _____ was the turning point of the Revolutionary War.

2.51 France formed an alliance with the Americans after the battles of _____

and _____ .

2.52 _____ was a wealthy French aristocrat who became an

American officer and hero.

2.53 America's representative in France was _____ who played

the part of the "natural man" for the court.

2.54 The last major battle in the North was _____ and it was indecisive.

2.55 _____ took control of the British forts in the west with a

small force of frontiersmen.

2.56 The Americans recaptured the fort at _____ from the

British after marching 180 miles through waist deep water in the winter.

2.57 _____ betrayed his country by offering to turn over the fort at

_____ to the British for money and an officer's commission.

2.58 _____ was court-martialed for retreating at Monmouth

Courthouse.

2.59 _____ was the American naval commander who said,

"I have not yet begun to fight," during the battle between the American ship

_____ and the British ship _____ .

2.60 _____ was the spy captured by the Americans with the

plans of West Point.

The End of the War

Georgia. The British plans had failed so miserably in the North that they decided to concentrate on the less populous South. Their plan was to capture each state, organize the Loyalists there to take control, and then move on to the next state. In 1779 a well-organized force captured Savannah and all of Georgia. An attempt to retake the city by a joint American-French force failed in October.

South Carolina. Sir Henry Clinton, in command in New York, now moved a force of about 10,000 south using the resources of the British navy. He successfully besieged Charleston avoiding the mistakes made in the earlier attempt. The city fell on May 12, 1780. The American commander, General Benjamin Lincoln, was captured along with 5,000 men, all of their supplies, and almost all of the Revolutionary leaders of South Carolina. It was the biggest single American disaster of the war.

Using Charleston as a base, Clinton sent out troops to secure the colony. In June, Clinton turned over command to Lord Cornwallis and returned to New York. Cornwallis set up a series of forts in the interior of South Carolina to protect the British gains. Soon all of South Carolina was under British control.

Camden. Congress sent a new army south to engage Cornwallis. They chose Horatio Gates, the official victor at Saratoga, to command the force. Gates lacked the skills needed for such a difficult job. The hastily assembled force was made up mainly of militia, which had never been in battle, and a few experienced units from the Continental Army. The two sides met at Camden, South Carolina in August 1780. It was a humiliating defeat for the Americans. Many of the inexperienced troops ran without firing a shot. The Continentals fought hard, but were overwhelmed when the rest of the army withdrew. Gates and the remains of his army fled north.

King's Mountain. The overconfident Cornwallis decided to attack North Carolina before South Carolina was fully secure. He sent an advance force of about a thousand Loyalists north under the command of Major Patrick Ferguson, a British officer. They ordered the North Carolina citizens to submit to the crown or face attack and occupation. The independent men of North Carolina not only refused, they gathered a force of backwoodsmen and went south to meet the British. They engaged the enemy at King's Mountain in South Carolina in October of 1780. It was one of the bloodiest battles of the war because the Patriots totally annihilated the Tory regiment.

Nathanael Greene. Congress now wisely asked Washington to recommend someone to take command of the shattered southern army. Washington chose Nathanael Greene. It was an ideal choice. Greene realized he did not have the strength to defeat Cornwallis in a pitched battle. So, he planned out and executed one of the most brilliant American campaigns of the war.

There were several bands of **guerrillas** active in the South. The most famous was under the command of Francis Marion, the "Swamp Fox." Greene made contact with these men and had his regular troops work with them. The guerrilla bands raided British outposts, harassed supply lines, and acted as scouts for the regular army. By coordinating with these bands, Greene managed to press the British and keep them off balance.

Greene used his regular army to draw Cornwallis into an extended chase all over Carolina. The British were drawn far from their supply bases and forced to take provisions from the local people. This made the British unpopular and strengthened the American cause in the South. Greene lost every major engagement he fought. But, he always inflicted severe losses on the British and escaped to fight again. "We fight, get beat, rise and fight again," was the way Greene described the campaign. By June of 1781, Greene and his guerrilla allies had made the Carolina countryside difficult for Cornwallis to handle. The British lost control of everything except the cities.

Cowpens. Greene had split his forces when he took command in 1780, in the hopes that Cornwallis would split his as well, giving the Americans a chance. Cornwallis cooperated sending a force of about a thousand after Daniel Morgan's eight hundred men. Morgan chose the place for the battle, a spot called the Cowpens. In January 1781, the British under Colonel Tarleton rode into the American trap. Faking a retreat, Morgan's men drew the British into a position to be attacked from all sides. Almost the entire force was killed or captured. It was the one major victory of the campaign.

A furious Cornwallis chased Morgan, who wisely withdrew. Then, Cornwallis took off in an exhausting chase to try and trap Greene. Greene's men managed to outrun him, and crossed the Dan River to safety in Virginia in February of 1781. Cornwallis was now far from his supply bases and constantly facing harassment from the Americans.

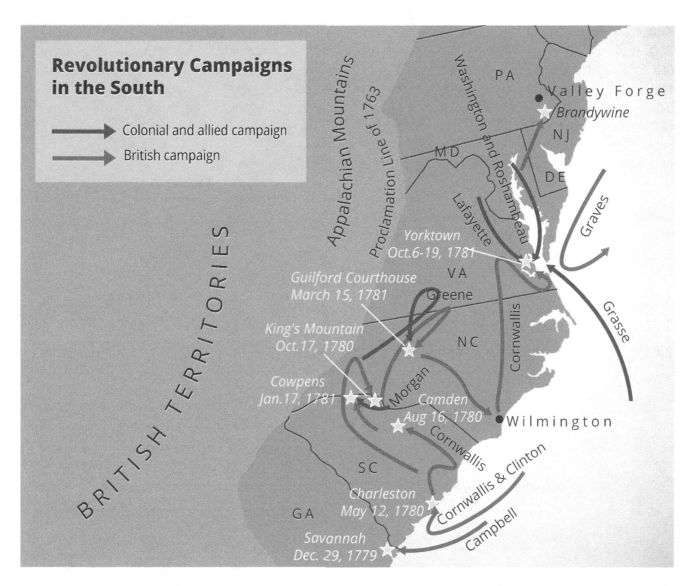

Revolutionary Campaigns in the South

→ Colonial and allied campaign
→ British campaign

BRITISH TERRITORIES

Appalachian Mountains

Proclamation Line of 1763

Washington and Roshambeau

PA

Valley Forge

Brandywine

NJ

MD

DE

Lafayette

Graves

Yorktown Oct. 6-19, 1781

VA

Greene

Grasse

Guilford Courthouse March 15, 1781

Cornwallis

King's Mountain Oct. 17, 1780

NC

Cowpens Jan. 17, 1781

Morgan

Camden Aug 16, 1780

•Wilmington

Cornwallis

SC

Cornwallis & Clinton

Charleston May 12, 1780

GA

Campbell

Savannah Dec. 29, 1779

Guilford Courthouse. Greene came back into North Carolina after Cornwallis withdrew. He set his men up at a site he had selected in advance, Guilford Courthouse, North Carolina. Cornwallis chased him and arrived March 15th with a British force. The British technically won the battle because the Americans withdrew at the end of the day. But, Cornwallis lost one-fourth of his men, while the American casualties were light. Moreover, the American army was still intact. Cornwallis withdrew toward the sea to refit his force.

Falling forts. Greene then turned on the forts that held the Carolina interior. His forces were defeated at Hobkirk's Hill in April, but the British commander abandoned the nearby fort due to the heavy losses of men and supplies to the guerrilla forces. Other forts were captured by these forces while the army kept the British too busy to send aid. Greene's siege of another fort, Ninety-six, was broken by the British in May, but again the British decided the fort could not be held and withdrew. By June, almost the entire line of British forts were gone. Having lost most of the battles, Greene won the campaign. Most of the South was again in American hands.

Eutaw Springs. The British troops from the abandoned forts, under Colonel Alexander Stuart, tried to reach Cornwallis' army after resting through the hot summer. The Americans under Greene met them at Eutaw Springs near Charleston, South Carolina in September 1781. Again the Americans lost the battle, inflicting heavy losses on the British.

Stuart withdrew to Charleston and did not attempt any further action for the remainder of the war. The British made no other major attempts to regain control in the South. It was a spectacular American victory.

 Match these items.

2.61	_____	Loyalist force was destroyed by North Carolina backwoodsmen	a. Savannah
			b. Charleston
2.62	_____	loss of Lincoln and 5,000 men	c. Camden
2.63	_____	humiliating American defeat under Horatio Gates	d. King's Mountain
2.64	_____	taken by the British in 1779	e. Cowpens
2.65	_____	British troops under Stuart defeat Greene near Charleston	f. Guilford Courthouse
			g. Eutaw Springs
2.66	_____	American victory under Daniel Morgan against Colonel Tarleton's force	
2.67	_____	Greene came back from North Carolina to draw Cornwallis into a battle where the British lost one fourth of their men	

Name the person.

2.68	_____	the "Swamp Fox", Carolina guerrilla leader
2.69	_____	victorious commander at Cowpens
2.70	_____	American commander in the south who lost the battles and won the campaign
2.71	_____	victor at Saratoga, chosen by Congress to command American army in the South after the fall of Charleston
2.72	_____	British commander in the South after the withdrawal of Clinton

Yorktown. Lafayette had been sent south in 1781 with an American army to pursue Cornwallis, who was now busy in Virginia. Cornwallis was unable to pin down the cagey Frenchman. Meanwhile, Clinton decided he wanted some of Cornwallis' men to reinforce New York, for fear of an attack there. So, Cornwallis withdrew to Yorktown on Chesapeake Bay and set up a strong defensive position to wait for the British navy. But, it would be the French navy that came instead.

When Washington heard that Cornwallis was stationary on the sea coast, he grabbed a chance to capture a major British army. The Americans had the use of a French fleet under the command of Admiral de Grasse. Washington sent it to blockade the Chesapeake, cutting off Cornwallis' supply and escape route. The French navy successfully defeated the ships sent to relieve Cornwallis and blocked any hope of help from the sea.

While de Grasse moved into position, Washington and Rochambeau, the commander of the French army in America, moved south to trap Cornwallis. The American and French armies, numbering about 17,000, encircled the British camp which held about 10,000 men. Cornwallis was dug into a defensive position, but with the sea and the French navy behind him, he had no place to go.

The Allies set up siege lines under the direction of Rochambeau, who was an expert in this type of warfare. They began a steady pounding of the British lines with cannon fire. Slowly, the Americans and French moved closer and closer capturing the outer British defenses. With no hope of reinforcements or supplies, the result was inevitable. On October 17th, the British asked for surrender terms.

Cornwallis surrendered his entire command on October 19, 1781. The army marched out to the tune of "The World Turn'd Upside Down" and laid down their arms. Lord Cornwallis, claiming to be ill, sent General O'Hara to surrender for him.

O'Hara first moved to surrender to the French, but was directed to Washington. Washington declined to receive Cornwallis' sword (the customary mark of a surrender) since the general did not choose to deliver it in person. Instead, Washington directed that it be surrendered to Benjamin Lincoln, the general who had suffered the greatest American defeat of the war, at Charleston.

Yorktown was the last major battle of the war, although neither side knew that. Both armies remained in the field for another two years, awaiting events in Europe that would finally bring a conclusion. In Britain the war had become immensely unpopular as British losses mounted both in America and in other areas. A new government came to power that was determined to make peace.

Treaty of Paris. Peace talks were opened in France in 1782 with the American delegation. The Americans included Benjamin Franklin, John Adams, and John Jay. A treaty was negotiated and signed on September 3, 1783 in Paris. The terms were very generous to the Americans because the British wanted to break up America's alliance with the French in the event of future wars.

The Treaty of Paris gave the Americans almost everything they wanted. America's independence was recognized, and all of the land east of the Mississippi between Canada and Florida was recognized as hers. All British forces were to leave American land. The Mississippi was open to American commerce and American ships could fish in the Newfoundland waters. Spain received Florida back, and the French got back the islands of the West Indies captured in the war. Congress was to recommend that Loyalists be given back their land and all debts owed to Britain were recognized as valid. The military phase of the Revolution was now over, but it was still not clear what kind of government would rule in America. That part of the Revolution was unfinished.

Washington's finest hour. The American economy was in a shambles at the end of the war. The money issued by Congress was worthless and the army had never been properly paid. In May of 1782, several of Washington's officers sent him a memo asking him to use the army and set himself up as a new king. This was the pattern of history when a victorious general has led a successful rebellion against a king.

Washington coldly refused. When word of the peace treaty reached him in November of 1783, he defied the pattern of history and shocked most of the rulers of Europe by resigning his commission and retiring to private life. It was, in this author's opinion, the single greatest service Washington ever did for his country.

 Answer these question.

2.73 How was Cornwallis trapped at Yorktown?

_____

_____

2.74 What was the name of the French army commander at Yorktown?

_____

2.75 What was the name of the French naval commander at Yorktown?

_____

2.76 Who negotiated the Treaty of Paris for America?

_____

2.77 Who received Cornwallis' sword at the surrender at Yorktown?

_____

2.78 Why was Washington's decision to resign his commission so important? (Think about it.)

_____

_____

2.79 What were the nine important terms of the Treaty of Paris?

1. _____

2. _____

3. _____

4. _____

5. _____

6. _____

7. _____

8. _____

9. _____

Review the material in this section in preparation for the Self Test. This Self Test will check your mastery of this particular section as well as your knowledge of the previous section.

SELF TEST 2

Match these people (each answer, 2 points).

2.01	_____	Lord Cornwallis
2.02	_____	Benedict Arnold
2.03	_____	Thomas Paine
2.04	_____	Burgoyne
2.05	_____	Benjamin Franklin
2.06	_____	Marquis de Lafayette
2.07	_____	Thomas Jefferson
2.08	_____	Samuel Adams
2.09	_____	George Rogers Clark
2.010	_____	John Paul Jones
2.011	_____	Benjamin Lincoln
2.012	_____	Nathanael Greene
2.013	_____	Daniel Morgan
2.014	_____	Rochambeau
2.015	_____	De Grasse

a. Boston radical; Committees of Correspondence

b. commanded greatest American defeat of the war; lost 5,000 men

c. British commander in the south, 1780-81

d. captured western British forts with small force of frontiersmen

e. French army commander

f. French admiral

g. author of *Common Sense* and *The American Crisis*

h. captain of the *Bonhomme Richard*

i. American commander in the South; lost all the battles but won the campaign

j. commanded riflemen at Freeman's Farm and the victorious Americans at Cowpens

k. French volunteer/hero in American army; close friend of Washington

l. British general; surrendered his entire army after campaign in Upstate New York

m. American hero turned traitor

n. American representative in France; played the "natural man" for the court

o. author of the Declaration of Independence

Choose the correct answer from the list (each answer, 3 points).

Saratoga   Long Island   Yorktown

Charleston   Camden   Oriskany

Monmouth Courthouse   Trenton   King's Mountain

Valley Forge

2.016 The last major battle in the North was an inconclusive conflict fought at _____

_____ between Washington's army and the army of Sir Henry

Clinton who was moving back to New York.

2.017 Washington made a risky crossing of the icy Delaware River to attack the Hessians at

_____ the day after Christmas 1776.

2.018 The surrender of the British army at _____ was the turning

point of the war.

2.019 British commander St. Leger won the Battle of _____ when he

ambushed an American force coming to the aid of Fort Stanwix.

2.020 A Tory army marching to attack North Carolina was met by a force of backwoodsmen from

that state who annihilated them in 1780 at _____ .

2.021 The American army spent a cold, difficult winter at _____

improving their drilling skills under the teaching of Baron von Steuben.

2.022 The surrender of the British army at _____ , after it

was trapped by the French navy and the combined French/American army, was the final

major battle of the war.

2.023 The British defeated Washington at the Battle of _____ in 1776

by coming around and attacking from the rear of his inexperienced army and driving them

back to Brooklyn Heights, where they skillfully slipped away after dark.

2.024 _____ was successfully defended in 1776, but was taken in

1780 in the biggest American disaster of the war.

2.025 Horatio Gates was humiliatingly defeated at _____ when he tried

to lead an army south in 1780 to engage the victorious British after the conquest of Georgia

and South Carolina.

Answer these questions (each answer, 3 points).

2.026 What nation signed a treaty of alliance with the Americans in 1778?

_____

2.027 Where did the cannons come from that drove the British out of Boston in 1776?

_____

2.028 In the summer of 1777, Washington fought the Battles of Brandywine Creek and Germantown trying to stop the British from reaching what city?

_____

2.029 The British colonies were ruled using what economic theory?

_____

2.030 What was the law that guaranteed the French in Canada their traditional laws and extended their land?

_____

2.031 What was the law that united the colonies against taxation without representation and was repealed after just four months of being in effect?

_____

2.032 The Intolerable Acts were the British reaction to what event?

_____

2.033 What were three advantages the British had in the Revolution?

a. _____

b. _____

c. _____

Answer true or false (each answer, 1 point).

2.034 _____ The Americans had the advantage of location in the war.

2.035 _____ Forts Washington and Lee near New York City were never taken by the British.

2.036 _____ The American army that fought at Freeman's Farm was mainly citizen soldiers who came to defend their homes.

2.037 _____ Nathan Hale said, "I have not yet begun to fight."

2.038 _____ Guilford Courthouse and Eutaw Springs were both British victories that hurt the victors more than the losers.

2.039 _____ The Navigation Acts were rarely enforced until after the Seven Years War.

2.040 _____ The Treaty of Paris gave the Americans very little of what they wanted.

2.041 _____ The Treaty of Paris granted America independence and promised they could use the Mississippi River.

2.042 _____ George Washington was not a great strategist, but he was faithful and had the loyalty of his men.

2.043 _____ Colonists tried in Admiralty Courts did not have a jury and were presumed to be guilty.

80/100

SCORE _____   TEACHER _____ _____
                                     initials   date

3. THE CONSTITUTION

A revolution is a tremendous change in events. The American Revolution changed the states of North America from separate colonies under a European monarchy, to a united nation under a Federal Republic. Thus, the Revolution is actually more than just the war. It also includes the process of establishing the new government in America.

It was not clear at the end of the Revolutionary War what sort of government the new nation would have. It was not even clear that it would be one nation. The people thought of themselves as citizens of their states, and might well have set up thirteen countries, with or without some sort of alliance between them.

The "government" that was set up during the war had very little authority and was not trusted by the people. The country was still unstable and could easily have slipped into a dictatorship of some kind.

The Revolution up until 1783 had been a revolt against the old system, now the Americans had to create a new one. This was not to be a war of guns, but a war of ideas. Victory was not to be won by conquest, but by compromise. The result of this part of the Revolution was the surprisingly successful Constitution of the United States of America.

SECTION OBJECTIVES

Review these objectives. When you have completed this section, you should be able to:

1. Identify the men who contributed to the Revolution.
3. Identify and describe the governing bodies that acted for the colonies/states.
6. Explain the Articles of Confederation and why they were replaced.
7. Describe the Constitutional Convention.
8. Describe the main features of the Constitution and the process by which it was approved.

VOCABULARY

Study these words to enhance your learning success in this section.

confederation (kun fed' u rā shun). A group of countries or states joined together for a special purpose; a league.

executive (eg zek' yu tiv). The person or branch of government that has the duty and power of putting laws into effect.

impeach (im pēch'). To accuse a public official of wrong conduct in office before a proper tribunal.

inflation (in flā' shun). A rise in the price of goods.

ratify (rat' u fī). To confirm or approve.

sovereign (sov' ren). Independent of the control of another government or governments.

The Articles of Confederation

The first constitution of the United States was called the Articles of **Confederation**. It was adopted by the Second Continental Congress in 1777. However, it could not go into effect until all thirteen of the states **ratified** it. That did not happen until 1781, and by 1789, it was superseded by the new Constitution. These eight years were a stepping stone between America's first government under the Second Continental Congress, and her permanent government under the Constitution.

America's first constitution. The Articles of Confederation formed only a "firm league of friendship" between the thirteen **sovereign** states of America. It was less than a union, but more than an alliance. The states kept the power to tax, regulate commerce, and provide justice. The central government was very weak, for good reason. The states would not have accepted gaining their freedom from Britain just to lose it to a more local tyrant! The Articles provided an in-between step that allowed them time to accept the need for a strong central government.

The national government under the Articles was very weak. The states did not want a strong **executive**, like the king, to threaten their liberties. So, the Articles had no executive to enforce the laws. There was also no national system of courts or judges. The Confederation was ruled by a very weak Congress.

Congress was deliberately limited in its power. It could not raise taxes, it could only request money from the states. It also could not regulate commerce between the states. The voting in the Congress was one representative per state. All important matters had to be passed by two-thirds of the states and any changes to the Articles had to be unanimous. Congress was supposed to conduct the Confederation's foreign affairs (including those with the Native Americans), declare war, establish an army and navy, set up a postal service, and settle disputes between the states.

| The U.S. in 1783

But, without a steady source of income or authority to enforce its laws, Congress was severely shackled in its efforts to act for the nation.

The Northwest Territory. In spite of its weaknesses, the Congress under the Articles had one very notable success. That was the handling of the Northwest Territory. The Northwest Territory (or Old Northwest) was the land west of the established states and north of the Ohio River. This land came under the control of Congress shortly after the ratification of the Articles of Confederation.

Several of the original colonies had been granted in their charters rights to vast amounts of land west of the Appalachians. The states who did not have land claims there, notably Pennsylvania and Maryland, insisted that all of the western lands be given to the national government.

They argued the land-rich states could use land sales to pay off debts from the Revolution, while the states without excess land could not. Since all the states shared in the expense of the war, all should share in the bounty of the western land sales through the national government. Eventually, all the states agreed to this and the land outside the current boundaries was placed under the control of the national government.

The Land Ordinance. First of all, congress had to decide how to sell the land and what to do with the proceeds. These questions were answered with the Land Ordinance of 1785. The law required the land to be surveyed and divided for sale. It was divided into townships measuring six miles by six miles. The townships were further divided into thirty-six sections, each one square mile. The sixteenth section was sold to benefit public education. The money made from the sales was used to pay off the national debt.

Northwest Ordinance. The second decision Congress had to make, was how the land would be governed. Would the western lands be colonies for the east? Would they be subject to the control that Britain had once placed on America? These questions were answered for the Northwest and for all later U.S. territories by the Northwest Ordinance.

The Northwest Ordinance was a piece of legislation that was to have long-lasting effects in America. The Confederation Congress established the pattern that would be followed for over a hundred and fifty years of national expansion. The law required that new territories be under federal control until they had a population of 60,000. At that point, they could be admitted to the Confederation by Congress as a new state, having all the rights and privileges of the old ones. This farsighted piece of legislation ensured that America could grow with equal rights for citizens in newly added lands. America would be a free nation, not an empire.

 Check the statements that were true of the Articles of Confederation.

3.1 _____ had a weak executive

3.2 _____ the states were sovereign

3.3 _____ Congress could not raise taxes

3.4 _____ it was only an alliance

3.5 _____ Congress could not declare war

3.6 _____ the national court system was weak

3.7 _____ the Congress could not pass any effective legislation

3.8 _____ Congress could handle Native Americans affairs

3.9 _____ commerce between the states was handled by Congress

3.10 _____ it was ratified in 1781

3.11 _____ it was the first government of the United States

3.12 _____ it was in effect for about twenty years

Complete these sentences.

3.13 The Confederation Congress passed the _____

to set up the government for the Northwest Territory.

3.14 All state land claims in the Northwest Territory were given to _____

_____ .

3.15 Money made from land sales in the Old Northwest were used to pay

_____ .

3.16 The Land Ordinance divided the Old Northwest into townships measuring _____

by _____ .

3.17 Townships, under the Land Ordinance, were divided into _____ sections of one square mile

each and section _____ was sold to benefit public education.

3.18 A territory could be admitted as a state when the population reached _____ .

Problems under the Articles. The biggest problem facing the Confederation Congress in the 1780s, was the national economy. The nation had immense debts and no way of paying them. Congress could only request money from the states and it never got all it requested. Foreign nations did not trust American credit. Several of the states were printing money, freely causing widespread **inflation**.

Congress also could not regulate trade between the states and that was causing more problems. Several of the states were putting tariffs on goods from other states. Trade with foreign nations was regulated as each state saw fit. Some of the states set very low tariffs to attract foreign trade, while others set high ones to protect their own manufacturers.

There also was unrest among the people. The bad economy had put many people into debt. Debtors and creditors clashed. Several of the states, like Rhode Island, deliberately allowed inflation to help the debtors. (Inflation means money loses value and debts are paid back later with the less valuable currency. Or put another way, you pay back less than you borrowed.) The Revolution had encouraged rebellion over taxes as well as a disrespect for law and property. These attitudes were coming back to haunt the new government.

Annapolis Convention. The problems over commerce were substantial enough to call a meeting in Annapolis, Maryland in 1786 to deal with them. Only five states sent delegates. With such a poor showing, nothing could be done. But, Alexander Hamilton of New York managed to have the convention accept his recommendation for a meeting in Philadelphia the following year to revise the Articles. That meeting might have met the same fate except for an event in Massachusetts that frightened the states into action.

Shays' Rebellion. Massachusetts had not inflated its currency. In fact, that state had raised taxes and refused to help debtors. Farmers, many of them veterans from the Revolution, faced the loss of their farms due to personal debts or unpaid taxes. In 1786 the western part of the state erupted in rebellion under the leadership of Daniel Shays, a former Revolutionary soldier. The rebels demanded lower taxes, debt relief, and more paper money (inflation, also called cheap money).

Shays' Rebellion forced the closure of several courts to prevent foreclosures and imprisonment for debtors. The alarmed wealthy merchants of the east, who controlled the government, raised an army under General Benjamin Lincoln to quell the rebellion. He did so in early 1787 after several small skirmishes in which a few of the rebels were killed. Shays fled the state and was later pardoned.

Shays' Rebellion frightened the property owners and wealthy businessmen of the Confederation. These were the men in power in the state governments due to the property requirements to vote and hold office. They understood the threat Shays and others were to the process of law and government. They saw the need for a stronger national government to restore order and prevent mob rule. The Confederation Congress reluctantly approved the meeting called by the Annapolis Convention now scheduled for the summer of 1787 in Philadelphia. Its stated purpose was to revise the Articles of Confederation. It would do much more than that.

 Answer true or false.

If the statement is false, change some of the nouns or adjectives to make it true.

3.19 _____ Inflation helps creditors.

3.20 _____ The Annapolis Convention was called to discuss problems over state boundaries.

3.21 _____ Seven states sent delegates to the Annapolis Convention.

3.22 _____ The largest problem facing the Confederation Congress was the economy.

3.23 _____ Shays' Rebellion occurred in Massachusetts.

3.24 _____ Shays' Rebellion was put down by an army under the command of General Benjamin Lincoln.

3.25 _____ The poor people of the Confederation were frightened by Shays' Rebellion.

3.26 _____ America had good credit abroad under the Confederation.

3.27 _____ Some of the states put tariffs on goods from other states.

3.28 _____ States under the Confederation had the same tariffs on foreign goods.

Constitutional Convention

The meeting called for by the Annapolis Convention finally began on May 25, 1787 in the State House in Philadelphia. (It was later renamed Independence Hall). The fifty-five delegates came from twelve of the thirteen states. (Independent Rhode Island refused to participate). They were all well-to-do men chosen by the wealthy members of the state assemblies. The most radical leaders of the Revolution, such as Samuel Adams and Patrick Henry, were not there.

The men who did come were basically conservative, men who wanted a strong central government to prevent further rebellions. Among them were George Washington, Benjamin Franklin, James Madison (whose careful work earned him the title "Father of the Constitution"),

Alexander Hamilton (a fierce advocate of a strong central government), and a host of lesser-known "Founding Fathers." Most of the delegates had served in the Revolution as either a soldier or administrator. They all understood the problems under the weak rule of Congress. Moreover, most had experience writing constitutions since all of the states had to write them after independence.

The delegates made several key decisions at the beginning. First of all, they elected George Washington as president of the convention. His immense prestige made him an obvious choice and gave the whole meeting a greater chance of success. The delegates also decided that their meetings would be completely secret. That enabled the men to debate and

| The delegates at the Constitutional Convention

compromise without being subject to outside pressure or having to explain their decisions before a final agreement was reached. (James Madison took detailed notes about the debates and decisions that were later published). Finally, the delegates decided not to revise the Articles, as they had been instructed. Instead, they decided to start over and write a whole new constitution. They had no authority to do this, but they felt that the Articles could not be amended to meet the country's needs.

Bundle of compromises. The Constitution of the United States was a bundle of compromises. The most important one involved the dispute over representation in Congress. The larger states supported the *Virginia Plan* which would have the states represented in Congress according to their population. This would give the more populous states more votes and the smaller states feared they would dominate the government. The smaller states, therefore, favored the *New Jersey Plan* in which each state had the same number of votes, no matter what its population. The larger states argued that they would pay more taxes without having any more representation.

This issue threatened to divide the convention and stop all progress on a constitution. Finally, an alternative, the *Connecticut Plan*, was proposed and approved. Under this plan, also called the *Great Compromise*, Congress was made up of two houses. Each state would have two representatives in the upper house, the Senate. But, the states would send representatives to the lower house, the House of Representatives, based on their population. Laws would have to pass both houses, so the Senate would protect the smaller states from being dominated by the larger. Also, laws involving money issues could only begin in the House of Representatives where the members more closely represented the percentage of taxes paid by each state. This compromise put the convention back on track.

Another issue the delegates had to face involved the counting of enslaved people. States in the South that had a larger number of slaves wanted them to be counted as part of the population to determine how many seats they got in the House of Representatives. Northern states wanted the enslaved people to count for taxation purposes. The compromise that was reached counted each slave as three-fifths of a person for both population and taxation purposes.

Most of the delegates wanted to end the slave trade (the importation of more Africans) because of the brutality it involved. But, several of the southern states would not accept giving Congress the authority to do that. By way of a compromise, Congress was denied that authority until the year 1807 (at which point it did end the trade). These were the key compromises of the Constitution.

Checks and balances. In their need to establish order and settle their own differences, the delegates did not forget they had just fought a war against a tyrannical government. They were determined not to create another one. Instead, they created a government in which power was divided among several branches, so that each would balance and check the others.

The power of government was divided between three branches of government: executive, legislative, and judicial. The executive, the president, could veto laws passed by Congress and appoint judges. The legislature, Congress, could override a veto, approve the appointment of judges and could **impeach** the president if he broke the law. The judiciary were judges appointed for life that could also be impeached by Congress and could declare a law unconstitutional (that is not expressly stated in the Constitution, but was assumed). Thus, each branch of the government had some control over the other. This division of power was a deliberate plan by the delegates to prevent any one person or part of the government from becoming too powerful.

The power of government was also divided between the states and the new federal government. The sovereignty of the states was kept. They simply lost certain powers to the national government. Any powers not specifically given to the national government were still kept by the states. For example, the states would run the police forces, set up schools, and handle many other local matters. But, the national government was given several key powers including the right to tax and to regulate commerce between the states.

The Results. The delegates at the Constitutional Convention debated in secrecy for almost four months. Finally, on September 17, 1787 they signed the final document. Of the original fifty-five delegates, only forty-two were still there. Three of those refused to sign it. The rest did and used their substantial means and prestige to have it ratified.

The delegates had acted without authorization when they wrote a new constitution. They did so again when they did not send the document to Congress, but to the states. Since Rhode Island had not even attended, they knew it was impossible to get all the states to ratify it. Therefore, the delegates agreed that it would go into effect as soon as nine of the thirteen states (two-thirds) had accepted it. This was also the basis for amending the Constitution.

The publication of the Constitution was a shock to the American public. They had been expecting some amendments to improve the Articles of Confederation. This was a completely new plan of government unlike any used before in history by a nation. It created a strong central government to replace the "union " of states. It raised fears of tyranny and taxation. The last major battle of the Revolution was to be fought over this document.

 Answer these questions.

3.29 How many states were represented at the convention? _____

3.30 What social class did the delegates come from? _____

3.31 What three important decisions did the delegates make at the beginning of the convention?

   a. _____

   b. _____

   c. _____

3.32 What were the two proposals that were not accepted on representation in Congress? (Give the name of the plan and describe it.)

   a. _____

   _____

   b. _____

   _____

3.33 What was the other name of the Great Compromise? _____

3.34 What was the Great Compromise?

_____

_____

_____

3.35 Why would the compromise on counting slaves be called the Three-Fifths Compromise?

_____

_____

3.36 What compromise was made on controlling the slave trade?

_____

3.37 What were the three branches of government power was divided between?

a. _____   b. _____

c. _____

3.38 What check did the

a. executive have on the legislature?

_____

b. legislature have on the executive?

_____

c. judiciary have on the legislature and executive?

_____

d. executive have on the judiciary?

_____

e. legislature have on the judiciary?

_____

3.39 What happened to the sovereignty of the states?

_____

_____

3.40 Did all of the delegates sign the Constitution? _____

3.41 How many states had to ratify the Constitution to put it into effect? _____

The Battle of Ratification

Battle Lines. The signing of the Constitution was followed by six months of heated public debate. The people that favored the document were called Federalists. Those that opposed it Anti-Federalists. Generally, the Federalists were from the wealthier classes. They were merchants who wanted a strong government to protect trade, property owners who feared lawlessness, and educated people who understood the problems of governing under the Articles. The Anti-Federalists were usually the poorer people, who feared that a strong central government might enforce payment of personal debts. These people distrusted governments of all sorts, especially strong ones. These were reinforced by the radicals of the Revolution. These people had fought for liberty from oppressive government and were not going to give it up now. Others believed in the independence of the states and did not want them to give up that much power to another government.

The Battle. The Federalists defended the Constitution in a whole storm of papers, speeches, articles, and essays. The most famous defense was the *The Federalist*, a series of essays originally published in New York and then in the other states. They were written by Alexander Hamilton, James Madison, and John Jay under the name *Publicus*. This brilliant analysis of the nature of republican government and the details of the Constitution was eventually put into book form and is still sold today.

The Anti-Federalists responded with attacks on the Constitution. They had one concern that drew the most attention. The Constitution did not protect the basic rights of the people. Many of the state constitutions included statements specifically protecting the right to trial by jury, freedom of speech, the right to petition the government and other important freedoms. Without these, the Anti-Federalists feared the people would have no protection from this

THE NEW NATION

Delaware
Pennsylvania
New Jersey
Georgia
Connecticut
Massachusetts
Maryland
South Carolina
New Hampshire
Virginia
New York
North Carolina
Rhode Island

The last two states to ratify were North Carolina and Rhode Island, both of which were notorious for being dedicated to individual rights and distrusting government.

NORTH CAROLINA
Ratified the Constitution:
November 1789

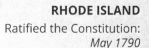

RHODE ISLAND
Ratified the Constitution:
May 1790

powerful new government. The Federalists agreed this was a valid consideration. They promised that the first order of business for the new Congress would be to pass amendments protecting the key freedoms of the people. (These were eventually passed and ratified as the Bill of Rights, the first ten amendments to the Constitution).

The Victory. The states called special conventions to vote on ratification beginning in the winter of 1787-88. The strong, well reasoned defense of the Federalists carried the day. The problems of the Articles of Confederation also drove many to accept the proposal. The promise of a Bill of Rights won over many others who opposed the new government.

Slowly the Federalists won over the necessary states. Delaware was the first state to ratify in December of 1787. Pennsylvania, New Jersey, Georgia, Connecticut, and Massachusetts followed that winter. In the spring, Maryland and South Carolina ratified it. The Constitution went into effect in June of 1788 when the ninth state, New Hampshire, approved it.

Two important states had not ratified the Constitution when it went into effect: Virginia, the first, largest, and most populous state, as well as the large, commercially important state of New York. Both of these states knew that the union was going to be formed with or without them. Realizing that they could not hope to prosper independent of the new order, both states ratified the Constitution in the summer of 1788. With these additions, the new government had enough support to make a solid start.

The two states that had still not ratified were North Carolina and Rhode Island, both of which were notorious for being dedicated to individual rights and distrusting government. Both finally realized they could not hope to go it alone in this case. But, North Carolina did not ratify the Constitution until November of 1789. Stubborn Rhode Island, which did not even send delegates to the convention, did not join the union until May of 1790, over a year after the first president took office.

In the end, all thirteen states approved the Constitution and created a powerful republic. The reasons why they did it were clearly spelled out in the document's preamble which states:

We the people of the United States, in order to form a more perfect union, establish justice, insure domestic tranquility, provide for the common defense, promote the general welfare, and secure the blessings of liberty to ourselves and our posterity, do ordain and establish this Constitution for the United States of America.

Preamble to The Constitution

Complete these sentences.

3.42 People who supported the Constitution were called _____ while opponents were called _____ .

3.43 The most serious objection to the Constitution was corrected with the passage of the _____ , the first ten amendments.

3.44 _____ was the first state to ratify the Constitution.

3.45 The Constitution went into effect after the state of _____ ratified it.

3.46 The two important states that had not ratified the Constitution when it went into effect were _____ and _____ .

3.47 The two states that did not ratify the Constitution until over a year after the others were _____ and _____ .

List the six reasons why the Constitution was written, according to the preamble.

3.48 1. _____

2. _____

3. _____

4. _____

5. _____

6. _____

Memorize the Preamble to the Constitution and recite it for your teacher.

TEACHER CHECK _____ _____

initials   date

Before you take this last Self Test, you may want to do one or more of these self checks.

1. _____ Read the objectives. See if you can do them.
2. _____ Restudy the material related to any objectives that you cannot do.
3. _____ Use the **SQ3R** study procedure to review the material:
   a. **S**can the sections.
   b. **Q**uestion yourself.
   c. **R**ead to answer your questions.
   d. **R**ecite the answers to yourself.
   e. **R**eview areas you did not understand.
4. _____ Review all vocabulary, activities, and Self Tests, writing a correct answer for every wrong answer.

SELF TEST 3

Match the following (each answer, 2 points).

3.01	_____	Articles of Confederation
3.02	_____	Northwest Ordinance
3.03	_____	Land Ordinance of 1785
3.04	_____	Annapolis Convention
3.05	_____	Shays' Rebellion
3.06	_____	Virginia Plan
3.07	_____	Great Compromise
3.08	_____	Bill of Rights
3.09	_____	*The Federalist*
3.010	_____	*Common Sense*

a. essays in favor of the Constitution

b. representation in Congress would be based on population

c. first ten amendments to Constitution

d. meeting of five states that called for the Constitutional Convention

e. representation by state in the Senate and by population in the House

f. Thomas Paine's essay that turned American opinion to independence

g. territory of 60,000 can be admitted as a state

h. Northwest divided into towns of 36 square miles for sale to pay off debt

i. America's first constitution

j. frightened many property owners to support the Constitution

Name the person (each answer, 3 points).

3.011 _____ America's representative in France during the Revolution; played the "natural man," delegate to Constitutional Convention

3.012 _____ Commander-in-chief of American forces during the Revolution; president of the Constitutional Convention

3.013 _____ Author of the Declaration of Independence

3.014 _____ Father of the Constitution; took notes of the debate at the Constitutional Convention

3.015 _____ Hero at Ticonderoga and Saratoga; traitor at West Point

3.016 _____ American commander of southern army after Camden; lost all the battles; won the campaign

3.017 _____ French aristocrat; volunteer American soldier; American hero; gave his own money to the cause

3.018 _____ President of the Second Continental Congress; signed the Declaration of Independence in large letters

3.019 _____ Led a group of frontiersmen to capture British forts in the west, and 180 miles through waist-deep swamps to recapture Vincennes

3.020 _____ British commander in the south after the capture of Charleston; surrendered at Yorktown

Answer these questions (each answer, 4 points).

3.021 What battle was the turning point of the Revolutionary War?

_____

3.022 What were the three branches of government set up by the Constitution?

a. _____ b. _____

c. _____

3.023 How can the president check the power of Congress under the Constitution?

_____

3.024 How many states had to approve the Constitution before it went into effect?

_____

3.025 What was the economic theory used by the British to govern the colonies?

_____

3.026 What were the three American reactions to the Stamp Act?

a. _____ b. _____

c. _____

Answer true or false (each answer, 1 point).

3.027 _____ Rhode Island was the last of the thirteen states to ratify the Constitution.

3.028 _____ The Articles of Confederation did not allow Congress to raise taxes.

3.029 _____ The Confederation Congress could not declare war.

3.030 _____ The Constitution allowed slaves to count as one-third of a person for taxes and two-thirds for representation.

3.031 _____ The Constitution forbids Congress from ever regulating the slave trade.

3.032 _____ Under the Constitution, Congress can impeach the president for breaking the law.

3.033 _____ The Confederation Congress could regulate commerce between the states.

3.034 _____ Inflation helps debtors.

3.035 _____ Monmouth Courthouse was the last major battle in the North during the Revolutionary War.

3.036 _____ The Northwest Ordinance was passed by the Confederation Congress.

80 / 100

SCORE _____ TEACHER _____ _____

initials   date

Before taking the LIFEPAC Test, you may want to do one or more of these self checks.

1. _____ Read the objectives. See if you can do them.
2. _____ Restudy the material related to any objectives that you cannot do.
3. _____ Use the **SQ3R** study procedure to review the material.
4. _____ Review activities, Self Tests, and LIFEPAC vocabulary words.
5. _____ Restudy areas of weakness indicated by the last Self Test.

HISTORY & GEOGRAPHY 806
The Civil War (1855–1880)

LIFEPAC Test is located in the center of the booklet. Please remove before starting the unit.

Author:
Theresa Buskey, B.A., J.D.

Editor:
Alan Christopherson, M.S.

Westover Studios Design Team:
Phillip Pettet, Creative Lead
Teresa Davis, DTP Lead
Nick Castro
Andi Graham
Jerry Wingo

Alpha Omega
PUBLICATIONS

804 N. 2nd Ave. E.
Rock Rapids, IA 51246-1759

The Civil War (1855–1880)

Introduction

"A house divided against itself cannot stand. I believe this government cannot endure permanently half slave and half free. I do not expect the Union to be dissolved—I do not expect the house to fall—but I do expect it will cease to be divided. It will become all one thing, or all the other." Abraham Lincoln spoke these words in 1858, just two years before the beginning of his presidency and the Civil War. They reflected the storm gathering across the nation that would soon empty its heavy clouds on the heads of the Union in one of America's costliest wars.

The years from 1855 to 1880 were some of the darkest in the history of our nation. In fact, the nation almost ceased to exist during those years. In some cases, the Civil War literally pitted brother against brother. It finally settled the issue of slavery and the permanence of the Union. The years that followed the war were blackened by revenge, greed, and failure to protect the newly freed slaves. The restoration of the Union was as much in question as its survival once was, but again the nation survived. A South without slavery was reintegrated into a stronger United States of America.

This LIFEPAC® will cover the critical years from 1855 to 1880. We will present the increasing hostility and distrust between the North and the South, the events within and those that led to the Civil War, and finally the difficult post-war Reconstruction.

Objectives

Read these objectives. The objectives tell you what you will be able to do when you have successfully completed this LIFEPAC. When you have finished this LIFEPAC, you should be able to:

1. Discuss why and how the North and South split.

2. Name the major events that led up to the Civil War.

3. Describe how secession occurred.

4. List the advantages of both sides in the Civil War.

5. Describe the major battles and the course of the Civil War.

6. Describe Reconstruction.

7. Describe the background and policies of Civil War-era presidents.

8. Describe the post-Civil War corruption.

9. Explain the status of black Americans during and after Reconstruction.

Survey the LIFEPAC. Ask yourself some questions about this study and write your questions here.

_____

_____

_____

_____

_____

_____

_____

_____

_____

_____

_____

_____

_____

_____

_____

_____

_____

_____

_____

1. INCREASING DISUNION

The era of compromise had ended with the Kansas-Nebraska Act in 1854. The Whig Party had fallen apart over disagreements about slavery, and the Democratic Party was soon split over it also. Several denominations, including Baptists, Methodists, and Presbyterians also split between North and South over the controversy. The two sides were becoming more hardened and less willing to discuss their positions. The Union was in grave danger.

The rhetoric of the two sides left less and less room for compromise during the last few years of the 1850s. The publicity of the Lincoln-Douglas debates gave a national following to Abraham Lincoln who steadfastly opposed slavery as immoral. The pro-slavery Dred Scott decision by the Supreme Court was denounced in the North as invalid. A financial crash that did not disturb the South as much as the North was seen in their own eyes as proof of the South's superior position.

A whole series of violent incidents marked the last five years before the Civil War. A small civil war broke out in "Bleeding Kansas" over the issue of whether or not it would be a slave state. On the Senate floor, a Southern congressman beat a Northern senator with a cane. John Brown led a raid into Virginia, intending to start up a slave revolt and instead became an abolitionist martyr. The verbal hostility of previous years became increasingly physical.

The South felt threatened by the growing abolitionist movement and political power of the North. The last straw was the election of a Republican president in 1860. The Republican Party was a Northern, anti-slavery party, and the South would not tolerate such a party to rule over them. Eleven states seceded from the Union. The war began in April of 1861 when the Southern army at Charleston fired on a federal outpost named Fort Sumter in their harbor.

SECTION OBJECTIVES

Review these objectives. When you have completed this section, you should be able to:

1. Discuss why and how the North and South split.
2. Name the major events that led up to the Civil War.
3. Describe how secession occurred.
4. List the advantages of both sides in the Civil War.
7. Describe the background and policies of Civil War-era presidents.

VOCABULARY

Study these words to enhance your learning success in this section.

arsenal (är′ se nal). A building for the manufacture or storage of arms, ammunition, and military equipment.

disavow (dis a vou′). To deny responsibility.

egalitarian (ē gal i ter′ ē an). Marked by a belief in human equality, especially in respect to social, economic, and political rights and privileges.

exacerbate (ig zas′ er bāt). To make more violent, bitter, or severe.

AMERICA from 1855 to 1880

Franklin Pierce
1853-1857
Democratic

James Buchanan
1857-1861
Democratic

Abraham Lincoln*
1861-1865
Republican

Andrew Johnson
1865-1869
Republican

Ulysses S. Grant
1869-1877
Republican

Rutherford B. Hayes
1877-1881
Republican

STATES ADMITTED TO THE UNION

Minnesota	1858
Oregon	1859
Kansas	1861
West Virginia	1863
Nevada	1864
Nebraska	1867
Colorado	1876

POPULATION of the United States of America

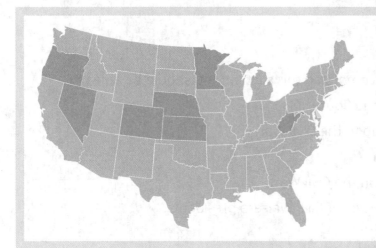

Year	Population
1880	50,189,209
1850	23,191,876
1820	9,638,453
1790	3,929,000

*assassinated while in office

repercussion (rē per kush' un). A widespread, indirect, or unforeseen effect of an act, action, or event.

segregate (seg' re gāt). To separate people of different races by having separate facilities like schools, restaurants, and theatres for each race.

Note: *All vocabulary words in this LIFEPAC appear in* **boldface** *print the first time they are used. If you are not sure of the meaning when you are reading, study the definitions given.*

Pronunciation Key: h**a**t, **ā**ge, c**ã**re, f**ä**r; l**e**t, **ē**qual, t**ė**rm; **i**t, **ī**ce; h**o**t, **ō**pen, **ô**rder; **oi**l; **ou**t; c**u**p, p**u̇**t, r**ü**le; **ch**ild; lo**ng**; **th**in; /ŦH/ for **th**en; /zh/ for mea**s**ure; /u/ or /ə/ represents /a/ in **a**bout, /e/ in tak**e**n, /i/ in penc**i**l, /o/ in lem**o**n, and /u/ in circ**u**s.

Division and Violence

The South. The slave states of the South in 1855 had a unique culture; they thought of themselves as virtually a separate nation. They believed they had a better way of life than the North. The South clung to older notions of an "aristocratic" class long after it had been abandoned by the rest of the nation. Its population was stagnant, and few immigrants came to the South because there were few opportunities there. The population was more uniformly people of British background whose families had lived in America for generations. A strict class system existed with wealthy planters at the top and slaves at the bottom. Southerners believed this was an ideal society and looked down on the **egalitarian** North.

The South was agricultural. It had little manufacturing. The factories that did exist were smaller and employed fewer people than those in either the North or northwest. The main cash crop was cotton with tobacco, rice, and sugar cane as alternatives in some areas. These crops were very labor intensive and were raised primarily on large plantations by enslaved people. Only about one-quarter of Southern families owned slaves. Those that did not often practiced subsistence agriculture. Even those without slaves supported the plantation system. Even the poorest white man had status above the enslaved black people.

By 1855 the South was very concerned about the threat from the North to their way of life. The North's growing population had given them complete control of the House of Representatives. The Compromise of 1850 had left the North in control of the Senate. The North had its own political party, the Republicans, which was rapidly gaining popularity and offices. The South equated the Republican Party with the radical abolitionists who spoke of fighting and slave revolts in order to end slavery in the South. The Republican Party pledged not to attack slavery where it existed, but only to prevent its spread. Most Southerners did not trust those statements. The Democratic Party still had supporters in both the North and South. Southerners looked to it as one of the last united institutions in the nation.

Abolitionists. Anti-slavery sentiment had existed in America for many years, but the serious, organized movement that so frightened the South began in the 1830s. In 1831 William Lloyd Garrison began publishing the anti-slavery newspaper, the *Liberator*. In 1833 Parliament voted to end slavery in the British West Indies. That same year, the American Anti-Slavery Society was formed with about sixty members. Within five years, it had grown to about 250,000 people. Hundreds of other societies devoted to the end of human bondage

UNITED STATES 1854–1861

States in 1854

States admitted 1855-61
(dates of admittance)

Territories in 1861
(boundaries are future states)

were formed all over the North in the late 1830s. Many of these people were Christians putting feet on their faith. These organizations worked by lobbying, organizing rallies, printing literature, publishing stories, and petitioning the government.

However, abolitionists were unpopular radicals for many years. The South and Southern sympathizers reacted to their work with repression and violence. Abolitionist works were banned in the South. People were imprisoned for even possessing them. Mobs attacked prominent abolitionists. Printing presses were destroyed, and anti-slavery speakers were pelted with filth when they spoke. Even Northern politicians tried to distance themselves from the abolitionist views. It had been an unspoken policy of both the Democrats and the Whigs to avoid the issue of slavery entirely, which they did for many years.

Gradually, these determined advocates won their point in the North. The issue of slavery was finally taken out of hiding. The continued discussions forced people to look and see what was happening in their nation. Millions of people were being held in bondage. The Fugitive Slave Act brought the issue home to many in the North. Eventually, when the Whigs and Democrats still avoided the issue, the Republicans took it up to squarely and rapidly become a powerful force in the North.

Bleeding Kansas. After the Kansas-Nebraska Act of 1854, Kansas was to choose for itself on the issue of slavery. It was west of the slave state of Missouri, and many Southerners expected to make it a slave state as well. Most of the settlers came from the North with its larger population. Some of the Northerners were sponsored by abolitionist societies who wanted to make sure that Kansas had a good supply of anti-slave settlers. Missouri responded by sending its own pro-slave settlers supported by well-armed bands of Missouri citizens. Both sides were hostile and violent in what became known as "Bleeding Kansas."

Conflict in both the political and physical areas ruled in Kansas. When the territory voted for its first legislature in 1855, Missouri pro-slavers crossed the border and voted illegally, giving the pro-slavery people control of the new government. The free-soil supporters formed their own illegal government at Topeka to counter it. A pro-slavery "posse" invaded the anti-slavery town of Lawrence in 1856 to arrest members of the illegal government, looting and burning the town. A violent (and possibly insane) abolitionist named John Brown butchered five pro-slavery men in Pottawatomie Creek in response.

By 1857 Kansas had enough people to apply for statehood. The majority of the population was anti-slavery, but the legislature was under the control of the pro-slavery group. The state had to vote on the issue of slavery to comply with "popular sovereignty," so the legislature created a shifty document known as the Lecompton Constitution. The people were allowed to vote only on the constitution, with or without slavery. But the constitution itself protected slavery. Even if the people voted for it to be free, Kansas would still be a slave state. The free-soil people boycotted the election, and the constitution passed with slavery. It was sent to Washington as the basis for admitting Kansas to the Union.

The Caning of Sumner. Charles Sumner was a radical abolitionist member of the Senate. In May of 1856, he delivered a scathing two-day speech on "The Crime against Kansas." His colorful rhetoric was very insulting to the South. He also made some vulgar insults against South Carolina's Senator Andrew Butler. The speech was not well received by his Northern colleagues. Even William Seward, abolitionist leader of Congress, did not approve of his language.

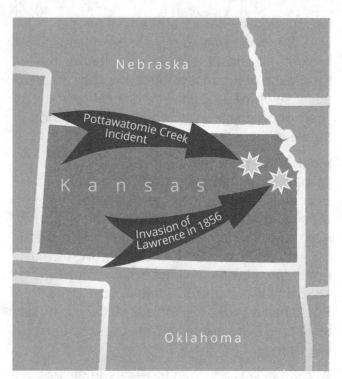

| Bleeding Kansas

Sumner's speech was considered a personal insult by Congressman Preston Brooks, a relative of Butler's. He decided to deal with the senator personally. Brooks decided against challenging him to a duel, since he believed Sumner to be his social inferior, and it was likely the Northerner would refuse. Instead, he decided to beat him to redress the insult.

On May 22nd, Brooks walked into the Senate chamber and approached Sumner, who was sitting at his desk. He raised his cane and proceeded to beat the helpless man about the head and shoulders until the cane broke. Finally, someone stopped Brooks, and Sumner was carried away unconscious.

What was remarkable about the incident was the difference between the reactions in the North and the South. People in the North saw it as a use of force to stop anti-slavery speech, and it drew a great deal of abolitionist publicity. Sumner was voted back into his seat in the Senate, even though it was three years before he was well enough to serve. In the South, Brooks was hailed as a hero. Hundreds of people sent him new canes to replace the one he had broken. His constituents voted him back into the House of Representatives after he resigned because of the incident. The difference in the reactions highlighted a dangerous separation between the two sides.

Election of 1856. In 1856, the Democrats managed to unite behind one candidate, James Buchanan. Most of the potential candidates for president were tainted by the Kansas-Nebraska Act and could not gain the support of Northern Democrats. Buchanan had been acting as the American minister in Great Britain from 1852-1856 and was therefore "safe" on the issue. Buchanan avoided the topic of slavery as much as possible and argued for the preservation of the Union.

Buchanan was opposed by the Republican candidate John Frémont, called "the Pathfinder" for his work mapping routes and sites for forts in the west. The Republicans campaigned on the issue of no slavery in the territories. "Free soil, free men, and Frémont" was their slogan. Millard Fillmore was a candidate for the Know-Nothing Party and also had the support of the dying Whig Party. The two-year-old Republican Party made a remarkable showing, winning eleven states, all in the North. However, the still barely unified Democrats won the election, putting James Buchanan in the White House.

James Buchanan. James Buchanan (1791-1868) was the only U.S. president never to marry. He entered the White House with impressive credentials. He had been born to immigrant parents in Pennsylvania and became a prosperous lawyer in that state. He began his political career as a Federalist, but eventually became a strong Democrat supporter of Andrew Jackson. He had served in the Pennsylvania legislature and as a soldier in the War of 1812. He had

| James Buchanan, the only U.S. president never to marry

served in both the House and Senate in Washington. He was secretary of state under James Polk and represented America in both Russia and Britain.

Buchanan lacked strong convictions on the issue of slavery and tended to be pro-Southern in his policies. He did not have the fortitude or the foresight to deal with the rising divisions in the nation. When the Lecompton Constitution was presented to Congress, Buchanan backed it without quibbling about its origins. Stephen Douglas showed that he was made of sterner stuff. He had proposed popular sovereignty for the territories, and he meant it to be just that! He successfully opposed the admission of Kansas under the dubious document. Instead, it was sent back for a vote on the whole constitution. The anti-slavery voters in Kansas rejected it. But with the ongoing conflict, it was not until 1861 that the state was finally able to organize a genuine constitution and be admitted to the Union.

Complete these sentences.

1.1 Congressman _____ beat Senator _____

with a cane over a speech the senator made.

1.2 The three candidates in the 1856 election were _____ ,

_____ , and _____ .

1.3 One of the last united political institutions in 1855 was the _____ Party.

1.4 The Lecompton Constitution was supported in Washington by _____ ,

but was successfully opposed by _____ .

1.5 The anti-slavery movement seriously took off in the decade of the _____ .

1.6 The main source of livelihood in the South was _____ .

1.7 Buchanan's policies tended to favor the _____ .

1.8 Pro-slavery partisans looted and burned the town of _____ , Kansas in 1856.

1.9 By 1857 most of the people in Kansas were _____- slavery.

1.10 The speech that got Charles Sumner into trouble was entitled

"_____ ."

1.11 _____ murdered five pro-slavery men in Pottawatomie Creek in

response to the invasion of Lawrence.

1.12 The Republican slogan in 1856 was _____ .

Answer these questions.

1.13 What made the South think the North was a threat to their way of life?

_____

_____

_____

1.14 How had the Democrats and Whigs dealt with the slavery issue before 1855?

_____

1.15 What was wrong with the Lecompton Constitution?

_____

_____

_____

1.16 Why did Kansas become known as "Bleeding Kansas?"

_____

_____

1.17 Why was Buchanan chosen as the Democratic candidate in 1856?

_____

_____

Dred Scott Decision. The tense situation in 1857 was **exacerbated** by the decision of the Supreme Court in *Dred Scott v. Sandford*. Dred Scott was an enslaved man who had lived for five years in the North with his master. He sued for his freedom on the basis of his long residence on free soil. It was a test case financed by abolitionists. It eventually reached the Supreme Court.

The Supreme Court of 1857 had nine justices, five from the South. Seven of the justices were Democrats, and two were Republicans. The Chief Justice, Roger Taney, was a Southerner and wrote the opinion of the court. The court ruled that Scott was not a citizen and could not sue in federal court. That is all the court needed to rule to end the case; unfortunately, it went further. Taney ruled that Scott was not free. He was considered property protected under the Fifth Amendment. It was therefore unconstitutional for the federal government to bar slavery *anywhere* in the United States!

The **repercussions** of the decision were vast. At one stroke, the Supreme Court claimed all of the country to be slave territory. Popular sovereignty no longer applied because people could not vote to keep constitutionally-protected slaves out of their states. All of the compromises to limit the spread of slavery were in one swoop declared unconstitutional. The court made a political decision based on its own prejudices.

The South rejoiced at the decision. The North swore to defy it, justifiably believing that it was a political decision by a Southern-dominated court that went beyond the issues of the case. Northern Democrats who supported popular sovereignty were now forced farther away from their Southern counterparts who supported the Dred Scott decision. Southerners were alarmed by the voices in the North that threatened to defy the courts and deny slave owners protection for their "property." The decision widened the North-South rift still further.

Panic of 1857. The nation was struck with one of its periodic depressions in 1857. Businesses had over-extended themselves during a boom time by speculating in land and railroads. The collapse closed thousands of businesses and caused widespread unemployment. It hit the manufacturing and grain-growing sections of the nation the hardest. The South rode out the panic comfortably because of the high international demand for cotton. Southerners saw the entire depression as proof of their superior way of life.

The Panic of 1857 created a clamor for higher tariffs in the North. Tariffs had been lowered in order to please the South. Northerners resented what they saw as a Southern blockade on Northern prosperity. Thus, the depression contributed to the division in the nation.

Lincoln-Douglas Debates. Democratic Senator Stephen Douglas was up for re-election in 1858. His Republican opponent was a tall, thin, back-country lawyer named Abraham Lincoln. Lincoln challenged Douglas to a series of debates which were held all over Illinois. Because of the prominence of Douglas and the growing reputation of Lincoln, the debates drew nationwide attention.

Douglas had a substantial advantage in the election. He was a well-known figure with several years of experience in Washington and an excellent orator. In Illinois he had redeemed himself for the Kansas-Nebraska Act by his opposition to the Lecompton Constitution. Illinois still generally favored popular sovereignty which was Douglas' primary position. In contrast, Lincoln had only served one term in the House of Representatives at the national level and had a high, thin voice. His Republican party was considered a threat to the Union in the South. Northern voters took that into consideration.

However, Lincoln was passionate about his subject and addressed the issues in clear, honest terms. He openly stated that he believed slavery was morally wrong. He did not believe it could be constitutionally ended where it already existed, but the spread of it should be prevented at all costs. He challenged Douglas on the issue of popular sovereignty, saying that slavery was an issue for the entire nation, not just the people who happened to move to a territory before a specific date. Moreover, Douglas and popular sovereignty denied the moral issues entirely, treating slavery and slaves as just another choice for voters. Lincoln also asked how Douglas could support popular sovereignty in the light of the Dred Scott decision, which stripped it of all constitutional support.

Douglas responded with a mix of politics and reasoning. He pointedly poked fun at Lincoln's lack of political experience and his background as a working man. He accused Lincoln of

| The capture of John Brown, depicted by an early sketch artist

favoring equality between black and white people (a charge which Lincoln refuted). Douglas also argued that even with the Dred Scott decision, popular sovereignty still had force. He said that slavery could not exist without state laws to protect slaves as property. Therefore, when states refused to pass such laws, slavery could not safely exist there, even if constitutional.

Douglas won the senate race, but the debates cost him his chance at the presidency. Newspapers had printed the texts of the debates all over the nation. Southern voters read about Douglas' proposal for states to annul Dred Scott by not passing the state laws needed to protect slavery. That proposal cost Douglas his support in the South. Lincoln was upset by the loss but he accepted it as "a slip, not a fall." The debates had made him a national Republican figure.

Harper's Ferry Raid. After the murders in Kansas at Pottawatomie Creek, John Brown and much of his family had fled to Canada. From there, he planned a grand attack on slavery. His scheme was to invade the South, seize weapons, lead the slaves in a revolt, and set up stronghold sanctuaries for black people in

| Abolitionist John Brown

| Stephen Douglas

the South. From these strongholds, he would organize an army to overrun the South. He chose to begin by attacking the federal **arsenal** at Harper's Ferry, Virginia.

In October of 1859, Brown and about twenty men captured the arsenal, taking several hostages. They held the building for over a day and killed several people. The black people that Brown had expected to rally to his aid never came. Instead, a detachment of federal troops arrived under the command of Colonel Robert E. Lee. Brown was quickly captured and most of his men with him.

John Brown's trial for treason drew phenomenal national attention. Brown behaved in a brave and dignified manner during the trial. His courageous devotion to freedom made many abolitionists overlook his violent nature and methods. Brown showed many signs of insanity, and it would have been wise to confine him to an asylum. Instead he was quickly tried, found guilty, and hanged. His death made him a martyr for the anti-slavery cause.

Brown gained a reputation in death that he never had in life. Abolitionists ignored his past and hailed him as a saint. There were

demonstrations throughout the North on the day he was executed. A popular song was written about him that became a marching song in the Civil War. It ran, in part:

> *John Brown's body lies a-moul'ring*
> *in the grave,*
> *His soul is marching on.*

The raid made the South even more suspicious of the North. Many knowledgeable moderates condemned Brown and his methods, but the South saw the public support for this murderous man and believed that was the direction the North was headed itself. The division grew.

The Election of 1860. The Democratic Party finally split over the issue of slavery in 1860. The party was unable to name a candidate at their first convention. A second convention was held and the Southern states walked out, as they had at the first. The Northern Democrats then nominated Stephen Douglas. Douglas ran on a platform of popular sovereignty and strict enforcement of the Fugitive Slave Act. The Southern Democrats met at their own convention and nominated John C. Breckinridge of Kentucky. Breckinridge campaigned on the basis of enforcing the Dred Scott Decision.

To add to the confusion, a group of Know-Nothings and Whigs formed a middle-of-the-road Constitutional Union Party and nominated John Bell of Tennessee.

The Republicans had a clear chance at victory with their opposition divided three ways. They nominated Abraham Lincoln over the better-known William Seward because Lincoln was less controversial. The Republicans also created a platform to keep themselves from being a one-issue party. The platform included: protective tariffs for the North, federal money for internal improvements for the west, free homesteads for farmers, a Northern railroad across the nation for the northwest, protection of the rights of immigrants, and its primary stand, no extension of slavery into the territories. Lincoln won the election, taking almost all the electoral votes in the North along with Oregon and California. However, in the popular vote he won just under 40%, making him a minority president.

 Answer these questions.

1.18 Why did Dred Scott argue he should be free?

_____

1.19 What did John Brown attack in 1859?

_____

1.20 Who commanded the troops that captured Brown?

_____

1.21 What caused the Panic of 1857?

_____

1.22 What made Lincoln a national figure?

_____

1.23 What was the only necessary part of the ruling in the Dred Scott case?

_____

1.24 What was the unnecessary and controversial part of the Dred Scott decision?

_____

_____

1.25 How did Douglas defend the idea of popular sovereignty after Dred Scott?

_____

_____

1.26 What happened to John Brown after his raid into Virginia?

_____

1.27 Name the candidates and their parties in the 1860 election.

a. _____

b. _____

c. _____

d. _____

1.28 What was the constitutional effect of the Dred Scott decision?

_____

1.29 What was Lincoln's opinion of slavery and what to do about it?

_____

_____

1.30 What happened to John Brown's reputation after his death?

_____

1.31 What were the proposals of the Republican platform in 1860?

a. _____

b. _____

c. _____

d. _____

e. _____

f. _____

1.32 Why did each of the following increase the South's desire to separate from the North?

Dred Scott

a. _____

_____

Panic of 1857

b. _____

_____

John Brown's raid

c. _____

_____

Secession

The South Secedes. There were four long months between the time Lincoln was elected in November of 1860 and the day he became president in March of 1861. The South took full advantage of the lull. Convinced that its unique and superior culture could not survive under a hated Republican president, South Carolina called a special constitutional convention in December of 1860. The Convention voted to secede from the Union. Six other states from the deep South quickly followed suit.

The seven states met together in February of 1861 and formed their own government. They called themselves the Confederate States of America or the Confederacy. They elected Jefferson Davis of Mississippi as president of the new "nation." The capital was established at Montgomery, Alabama. (It was later moved to Richmond, Virginia when that state seceded.)

President James Buchanan, with his pro-South advisors, was no match for the crisis. He made several speeches that accomplished nothing. He essentially said that a state could not secede, but that the federal government had no power to stop it if it did! He refused to strengthen the garrisons at federal forts in the South, as was recommended by the elderly General Winfield Scott. He did try to send reinforcements to Fort Sumter in South Carolina, but the effort was inadequate and the troops were forced to return.

Crittenden Compromise. As the crises matured, several attempts were made to work out a compromise. The most promising was a series of constitutional amendments proposed by Senator John Crittenden of Kentucky. The Crittenden Compromise would have guaranteed the protection of slavery where it already existed. It would have barred slavery in the territories north of the Missouri Compromise line of 36° 30' and protected it in all territories, present or future, south of it. Any states formed

| A modern photo of Fort Sumter

in the Southern territories would have popular sovereignty on the subject. The compromise failed because Lincoln was loyal to his beliefs and his party's platform. He refused to consider allowing slavery in the territories. It might have failed anyway, given the control the radicals had in the Confederate States.

In the end, the South seceded without any opposition from Buchanan. Most Southerners believed the North would never fight. The Northern factories needed Southern cotton too badly. Southern pride would not allow them to consider the possibility that the factory workers, shopkeepers, and fishermen of the North could put up any serious opposition. Pride went before the fall.

Abraham Lincoln. Abraham Lincoln (1809-1865) was one of the greatest men ever to occupy the presidency. He was born to a poor family in Kentucky. His family later moved to Indiana and then Illinois. Abe, as he was known, was a strong man who spent most of his youth working with his hands. His political propaganda called him the "Rail Splitter" for all the logs he had split over the years to make fences.

He had very little formal education (maybe a year) yet he loved to read, often walking miles to borrow a book. He failed in business and eventually got into law and politics in Illinois.

Abraham Lincoln entered the presidency with deceptively poor qualifications. He had served four terms in the Illinois House of Representatives and one in the U.S. House. Those were his only political qualifications. Yet, Lincoln had also been a popular Whig and Republican speaker in Illinois. He knew how to organize and administer political power. He had learned how to express himself in speech-making and in the courtroom in a way that persuaded his listeners. He had a reputation for integrity that earned him the nickname "Honest Abe." He had a strong will and the strength of convictions. Moreover, he was no Buchanan. He was willing to put force behind his beliefs and would accept the consequences.

Lincoln was sworn in on March 3, 1861. He tried to steer a moderate path in his inaugural address. He denied any intention of interfering with slavery where it already existed. There would be no conflict unless the South started one. He was still hoping to avoid a war, but he made it clear he would defend the Union. The South could not simply pull out because it did not like the outcome of a fairly contested election, for that made a mockery of democracy.

Fort Sumter. Fort Sumter was one of the few Southern federal forts still in Union hands when Lincoln became president. It was located at the mouth of the harbor for the city of Charleston, South Carolina. The fort's commander, Robert Anderson, steadfastly refused Southern demands to surrender his command, but his supplies were running low. Lincoln knew that sending reinforcements to the fort would touch off a strong reaction in that state. In the end, he compromised. He sent a boatload of provisions, but no new troops.

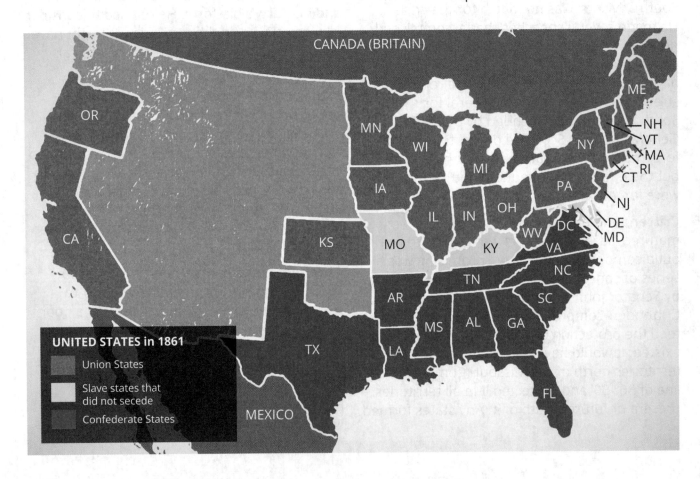

CANADA (BRITAIN)

UNITED STATES in 1861
- Union States
- Slave states that did not secede
- Confederate States

MEXICO

South Carolina was notified of the delivery of the provisions. Its leaders chose to interpret it as an aggressive act. Before the relief ship could arrive, the Carolinians decided to act. On April 12, 1861, under the command of General Pierre Beauregard, the cannons in the city opened fire on the fort. The garrison surrendered the next day.

The attack on Fort Sumter was the official beginning of the Civil War. It united the North in favor of war. Lincoln immediately called for volunteers to put down the rebellion. More men responded than the army could supply. Lincoln also suspended civil rights in areas that had Southern sympathizers. He ordered a blockade of Southern ports, and he ordered federal funds spent to support the war without Congressional approval (Congress was not in session). These actions were arguably unconstitutional, but they were in line with the extraordinary powers used by presidents in wartime. Without a strong, immediate action, there might not have been any country to uphold the Constitution.

The greatest area of concern was the border states. Four of these, Arkansas, Tennessee, North Carolina, and Virginia, seceded once they realized the North would fight to force them to stay in the Union. The northwest counties of Virginia did not vote for secession. The people in these counties seceded from Virginia and formed a new state that was loyal to the Union. West Virginia was admitted to the United States in 1863. The other border/slave states, Missouri, Kentucky, Maryland, and Delaware, stayed in the Union. However, Maryland was kept in by a declaration of martial law by Lincoln. He could not risk having Washington D.C. cut off from the rest of the nation. Thus, the sides were drawn—eleven to twenty-three.

Complete these sentences.

1.33 The Southern attack on _____ began the Civil War.

1.34 Seven states seceded after the election of Republican candidate

_____ .

1.35 After the war began, _____ more states seceded.

1.36 The most serious attempt to prevent the secession of the South was the

_____ Compromise.

1.37 _____ was president of the United States when the

Confederacy was organized.

1.38 The slave states that stayed in the Union were _____ ,

_____ , _____ ,

and _____ .

1.39 Because of his integrity, Abraham Lincoln was nicknamed _____

_____ .

1.40 _____ was the first state to secede.

1.41 The actions taken by Lincoln as commander-in-chief when the war began included

a. _____ , b. _____ ,

c. _____ , and d. _____ .

1.42 Lincoln's national political experience was limited to one term in the _____

_____ .

1.43 Lincoln sent _____ to Fort Sumter in 1861.

1.44 The Confederate states elected _____ as president.

1.45 The two Confederate capitals were _____ and

_____ .

1.46 The western counties of Virginia formed a new state called _____

and joined the Union in _____ .

Facing Off

Northern Advantages. The North had significant advantages in the Civil War. Money was needed to pursue a war, and the North had four-fifths of the available capital in the nation. The North also had a larger population, 22 million to the South's 9 million (including the 3.5 million slaves). The North had more of the raw materials needed for war, such as coal and iron. Moreover, the North had more factories, farms, and railroads.

Railroads were vital, being used to move troops and supplies. The South was hampered because it never had the resources to build tracks during the war. In order to repair damaged tracks or lay new ones, they had to tear up old ones.

The North controlled the navy and had more ships for moving supplies, so the Union was able to blockade the South. This cut off imports of badly needed manufactured goods. It prevented the South from selling its cotton, which robbed them of their primary income. The blockade eventually led to severe shortages of basic supplies to the South, which hampered their war effort. While the South was cut off from trade with Europe, the Union was not. Throughout the war, the North was able to sell grain and purchase military equipment by trading with Europe.

| A Northern railroad train, one of the Union's advantages

The Northern armies were eventually augmented by black soldiers. Black men formed one-tenth of the total Union troops by the end of the war. They served in **segregated** companies, led by white officers. They were paid less than white soldiers for part of the war. The South refused to recognize them as prisoners of war, treating them as escaped slaves. In spite of this, black volunteers fought courageously and were a dependable asset to the Union. On the other hand, the South would not even consider employing black soldiers until the very last, desperate days of the war.

The North had the advantage of an established government led by a strong president. Lincoln was an excellent leader whose authority was sustained by a government backed with eighty years of success. By contrast, the South had no united history to sustain them. Their entire government was built on the idea of states' rights and secession from another government. Jefferson Davis had difficulty maintaining his authority over the independent-minded Southern states.

Problems with central authority and the blockade made it difficult for the South to raise money for war. The states' rights Confederacy did not favor taxes, and the banks had little to offer in loans. The Confederate government printed money to pay its bills, which pushed up prices to many, many times what they were at the beginning of the war. The inflation added to Southern difficulties in prosecuting a war.

Southern Advantages. The South had some of the advantages the original thirteen colonies did during the War for Independence. In terms of ideals, the Rebels were fighting for independence and protecting their way of life. The North initially did not fight to end slavery, but only to preserve the Union by forcing the South to stay. Strategically, the South only had to survive to win. Southerners could fight a defensive war, protecting their homes and land. The North had to conquer the entire South and force it back into the Union. A simple draw would be a Confederate victory.

| Union soldiers

The South also had better quality officers than were available in the North. The gentlemen of the South had a long tradition of military training and service. Robert E. Lee, for example, had been an officer in the U.S. Army when the war began. He resigned when his home state of Virginia seceded and rose quickly to become the leader of the Confederate army. Other talented Southern officers included Thomas (Stonewall) Jackson, James Longstreet, and Jeb Stuart.

By contrast, the North did not have as many high-quality military leaders. The Northern generals seemed to be either overly cautious or foolhardy. Lincoln changed his commanders several times before he found a successful general in Ulysses S. Grant.

The Confederacy began the war with high hopes. They sincerely believed in the superiority of their way of life and their people. They did not believe the North would fight. Even if they did, no Northern shopkeeper could stand in a fight with a Southern gentleman. They expected that the North and Europe needed Southern cotton. If the North proved to be stubborn, Europe would be likely to intervene on behalf of the South to protect its own textile industries.

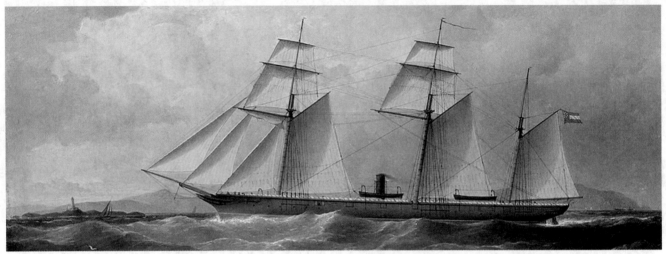

| On July 29, 1862, Hull "No. 290" steamed out of the Mersey from the Laird's Birkenhead Yard and into Civil War history. Soon taking her given name, ALABAMA, the Commerce Raider set out on a tour with devastating results for the American North's commercial shipping interests the world over. The screw sloop-of-war proved to be a fast, capable ship under the command of Captain Raphael Semmes, capturing or destroying 69 ships in less than two years.

Reactions Abroad. The best chance for the Confederacy lay in gaining support from the nations of Europe. The monarchs of Europe had good reason to want to see the United States divided. The failure of the American democratic experiment would strengthen the hand of the European aristocrats. These same aristocrats had a natural preference for the class-conscious culture of the South. Moreover, an independent Confederacy would be a supplier for European factories and a purchaser of European goods without the protective tariffs of the North.

English manufacturers were particularly dependent upon Southern cotton to supply their spindles and looms. The blockade threw thousands of textile workers out of their jobs. However, at the same time, the North was supplying much of Britain's wheat and corn. Britain would have had to risk its food supply if it supported the Confederacy for the sake of its cotton supply. Also, cotton suppliers in India and Egypt stepped up production to fill the need. Union demands for war goods also helped relieve employment problems. Thus, Britain was never pushed to intervene by the problems in its economy.

Britain did come very close to war over an incident in the fall of 1861, however. An American warship stopped a British steamer, the *Trent*, leaving the West Indies. Two passengers were arrested and taken back to the U.S. The men were Confederate diplomats en route to Europe. The British government was furious over this seizure of civilian passengers and threatened war. The incident was settled by releasing the men along with a U.S. statement **disavowing** their capture.

There was nevertheless a strong pro-Confederacy attitude in the British government at the beginning of the war. The government considered recognizing the Confederate nation especially when the South garnered a string of victories early in the war. Many ships for the Confederate navy were built in Britain during the war. Careful Union diplomacy limited this activity. What destroyed all hope of both British and French aid to the Confederacy was the Emancipation Proclamation in 1862. Once the war was reframed as a fight against slavery, neither of the great powers of Europe would raise their hands to aid the South. Thus, the aid the U.S. had during the Revolution was denied to the Confederacy in the Civil War.

Put an *N* beside the factors that were an advantage for the North and an *S* beside those that were an advantage for the South.

1.47 _____ ideals at the beginning of the war

1.48 _____ population

1.49 _____ manufacturing

1.50 _____ military personnel

1.51 _____ strategic position

1.52 _____ government

1.53 _____ navy

1.54 _____ hope for foreign allies

1.55 _____ black soldiers

1.56 _____ capital

1.57 _____ military tradition

1.58 _____ railroads

1.59 _____ farms

Answer these questions.

1.60 What effect did the blockade have on the South? _____

_____

_____

1.61 Why did the nations of Europe tend to favor the South? _____

_____

_____

1.62 What did the North provide for Britain that offset the loss of Southern cotton?

_____

_____

1.63 What happened in the *Trent* incident? _____

_____

_____

_____

1.64 What ended all hope of European aid to the Confederacy?

_____

Review the material in this section in preparation for the Self Test. The Self Test will check your mastery of this particular section. The items missed on this Self Test will indicate specific areas where restudy is needed for mastery.

SELF TEST 1

Match these people (each answer, 2 points).

1.01	_____ John Brown	a.	Confederate general
1.02	_____ James Buchanan	b.	violent abolitionist martyr
1.03	_____ Abraham Lincoln	c.	beaten by a Congressman in the U.S. Senate
1.04	_____ Stephen Douglas	d.	offered a compromise after secession
1.05	_____ Charles Sumner	e.	first Republican presidential candidate
1.06	_____ Dred Scott	f.	slave who lived in the North and sued for his freedom
1.07	_____ Robert E. Lee	g.	U.S. president when the Confederacy began
1.08	_____ Jefferson Davis	h.	president of the Confederacy
1.09	_____ John Frémont	i.	his election prompted Southern secession
1.010	_____ John Crittenden	j.	won the 1858 senate race in Illinois

Choose the correct word(s) to complete each sentence (each answer, 3 points).

1.011 Twisted, illegal version of popular sovereignty produced the pro-slavery _____ Constitution in Kansas.

1.012 The _____ Party opposed the spread of slavery but agreed it could not be abolished where it already existed.

1.013 The Civil War began when Confederate forces fired on _____ .

1.014 John Brown was executed for his attack on the arsenal at _____ , Virginia.

1.015 The _____ - _____ Debates centered on the issue of slavery and made Abraham Lincoln a national figure.

1.016 The Supreme Court declared that slavery was legal in all of the U.S. in the

_____ Decision.

1.017 The South had little difficulty with the Panic of 1857 because of the high price of

_____ on the international market.

1.018 The era of compromise was ended by the _____ - _____ Act.

1.019 _____ was the first state to secede.

1.020 Any hope of European aid to the Confederacy was ended by the

_____ .

Complete these items (each answer, 3 points).

1.021 Name four advantages the North had in the Civil War.

a. _____   b. _____

c. _____   d. _____

1.022 Name two advantages the South had at the beginning of the war.

a. _____   b. _____

1.023 Give two reasons why the nations of Europe might have supported the South.

a. _____   b. _____

1.024 Name two border/slave states that did not secede.

a. _____   b. _____

Answer true or false (each answer, 2 points).

1.025 _____ Abraham Lincoln believed that the U.S. could not continue to be part slave and part free.

1.026 _____ Britain almost went to war with the Union after two Confederate officials were arrested on the British steamer the _Trent_.

1.027 _____ The South received a tremendous number of immigrants in the years leading up to the Civil War.

1.028 _____ The Democratic Party split in two in 1860.

1.029 _____ James Buchanan did little to solve the divisions in the nation.

1.030 _____ Black soldiers in the Union army served in segregated units, usually with white officers.

1.031 _____ The blockade of the South hurt textile manufacturers in Britain.

1.032 _____ Abraham Lincoln was a well-educated man with many years of national experience when he became president.

1.033 _____ Lincoln believed slavery was morally wrong.

1.034 _____ The American abolitionist movement began its serious growth in the 1830s.

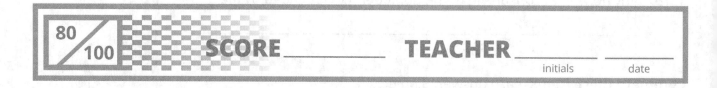

80 / 100   SCORE _____   TEACHER _____ _____

initials   date

| Painting by Civil War artist Dale Gallon

2. CIVIL WAR

The horrors of the Civil War were its nature and its cost. It was a *civil war*, fought between countrymen, friends, and family. Many of the opposing army officers had served together in the Mexican War. It was not uncommon for relatives to be on opposing sides. Senator John Crittenden, whose name is attached to the compromise, had sons who fought on opposite sides. One Union navy officer boarded a captured ship only to find his dead Confederate son aboard. Abraham Lincoln's sister-in-law was married to a Confederate general. She came to live in the White House for a time after her husband was killed in the war. It was a very personal war.

It was also a very bloody war. More Americans died in the Civil War than in World War I, Korea, or Vietnam. Only World War II cost America more lives. In fact, all the battle deaths in all the other wars before World War II added together does not equal the total from this "family conflict."

An estimated 620,000 died in battle and from disease and accidents (figures from the Civil War Trust). Thousands lost legs, arms, and/or their health.

The reason for the bloodshed was an advancement in technology without an appropriate change in military thinking. Since its invention, the soldier's firearm had been an inaccurate, slow-firing musket. By the 1860s, faster firing, very accurate rifles were in general use and artillery was improving. Standard military tactics, based on the older weapons, would send large numbers of men to attack enemy positions even if they had built barricades to protect themselves. The weapons were so poor that an attacking army had a good chance of overrunning an enemy position if it had enough men. The newer weapons made such attacks suicidal. However, all of the Civil War commanders only knew the old mass-attack tactics and used them to the bitter end.

SECTION OBJECTIVES

Review these objectives. When you have completed this section, you should be able to:

4.   List the advantages of both sides in the Civil War.

5.   Describe the major battles and the course of the Civil War.

7.   Describe the background and policies of Civil War-era presidents.

VOCABULARY

Study these words to enhance your learning success in this section.

amputate (am' pyu tāt). To cut off, especially a limb of a person.

anesthetic (an' es thet' ik). A substance that cause a loss of feeling in all or part of the body.

chaplain (chap len). A member of the clergy serving in a special group or place, like a prison or the military.

conscription (kon skrip' shun). Forced enrollment of people, mostly for military service.

division (di vizh' in). A large military unit that has all the necessary services to work as a self-contained unit and act independently.

morale (mo ral'). Moral or mental condition in regard to courage, confidence, or enthusiasm.

repulse (ri puls'). To drive back; repel.

Bull Run to Fredericksburg (1861-62)

First Bull Run. After Fort Sumter in April of 1861, Lincoln called for the state militia to come into service for three months. By May he realized the ill-trained, short-term militia would not be enough. A new call was put out for volunteers for a three-year enlistment. By summer, thousands of men were being organized into an army near Washington. A similar call had been made in the Confederacy, and its army was forming in Virginia near Richmond. The two capitals and their respective armies were only 120 miles apart.

Winfield Scott, the old commander of the U.S. army, wanted a slow, steady strategy to defeat the South. His plan called for a naval blockade to strangle Southern ports and the Mississippi River. In the meantime, the army would cut the South into pieces. This basic plan was the one followed by the Union throughout the war, even after Scott retired because of poor health. Scott wanted to take the time to drill and prepare the very untried Union troops before mounting any attacks, but the president and the American public were too impatient to wait.

Lincoln pressed the new Union field commander, Irvin McDowell, to attack at once. McDowell argued that his troops were untrained and not ready, but Lincoln prevailed. In July, the Union army moved south to attack the Confederacy. On July 21st, under the command of General Joe Johnston, the Union army met the Confederates near a creek called Bull Run and a town called Manassas Junction. The Northern public was convinced that it would be an easy victory. Many of the people of Washington brought picnic lunches and drove out to watch what they thought would be the only battle of the war.

The battle was a disaster for the Union. The green troops fought well at first, but as the equally green Confederate lines began to break, General Thomas Jackson stood his ground. A Confederate colleague yelled for the men to fight behind Jackson who was standing "like a stone wall." Jackson thus earned a

| The aftermath of First Bull Run

nickname (Stonewall) and the beginning of a famous reputation as a general. Confederate reinforcements arrived, and it was the Union lines that began to break. The North retreated and then ran in disarray. However the disorganized, untrained Confederates failed to follow up on the Union defeat. Both armies were left intact.

The defeat cleared up Union hopes of keeping the war short. The Union began the difficult preparations for a long war, but no one had any idea how long and difficult it would actually be. In the meantime, the South was delighted with the victory, which they saw as a vindication of their superiority. They did not expect a long war and became overconfident.

McClellan in Charge. McDowell was replaced by George McClellan. McClellan proved to be an excellent organizer. He trained and drilled the Union army for months. He also built up defenses around Washington to protect the capital from any enemy attack. He built a professional, well-organized, well-supplied army which was named the Army of the Potomac.

However, McClellan was cautious to the point of near cowardice. He refused to attack until he had everything where he wanted it and believed he had a large numerical advantage. As Lincoln so aptly put it, McClellan had a "case of the slows."

Forts Henry and Donelson. The Union strategy in the west was to gain control of the Mississippi River and its major tributaries. That would give the Union firm control of the border states of Missouri and Kentucky as well as a dominant position in Tennessee. It would cut off Louisiana, Arkansas, and Texas from the rest of the Confederacy. Attacks from the North were under the command of General Ulysses S. Grant. Grant had been out of the army for several years before the war and had a reputation for drinking that haunted his whole career,

but he was a fighter. He promptly went after two key river forts near the Tennessee-Kentucky border.

Fort Henry on the Tennessee River fell quickly to Grant and his supporting navy gunboats on February 6th of 1862. Nearby Fort Donelson on the Cumberland River was more difficult. The fort's better guns badly damaged the Union navy ships, but Grant managed to get his troops around the forts and set up a siege. The garrison tried, but was unable to break out and on February the 16th, the Confederate commander asked for terms of surrender. U.S. Grant insisted that nothing "except unconditional and immediate surrender can be accepted." The Confederates complied, and the Union general won the nickname "Unconditional Surrender" Grant.

| Battles for control of the Mississippi

The fall of the forts led the Confederate army to evacuate Nashville which then fell into Union hands. It was the first captured state capital. This was welcome news to victory-hungry President Lincoln and the Union. It made Grant a hero. More good news came in April with the capture of Island Number Ten, a heavily fortified Confederate position near where the Ohio and Mississippi Rivers met.

Shiloh. Grant promptly moved south after the victory at Donelson to Pittsburg Landing on the Tennessee River. He was headed for Corinth, an important railroad junction 22 miles away. Grant failed to prepare any defenses, believing the Confederates would not attack. However, they did attack on April 6th near a hill called Shiloh and caught the Union army by surprise.

The Battle of Shiloh lasted for two days. It was a confused and vicious fight. Many soldiers mistakenly fired on their own troops. Confederate commander Albert Johnston was killed. Union men took cover in a sunken road and slaughtered their Confederate attackers. The Southern army responded by raining artillery on the immobilized Union troops. The field caught fire, burning many of the wounded to death. The Union lines held, however, and reinforcements arriving the next day forced the Confederates to retreat.

About 4,000 Americans died in the two days of the Battle of Shiloh, and more would die later due to their wounds. The total of the casualties (dead or wounded) was around 13,000 from the Union and 10,000 from the Confederacy. Grant's exhausted, victorious army could not even follow the retreating rebels, who were allowed to escape. The bloodshed shocked both the North and South. Lincoln was pressured to fire Grant, but he said, "I can't spare this man—he fights."

| Admiral David Farragut

New Orleans. Admiral David Farragut led a federal naval attack on New Orleans in April. The city was the largest in the South and a key port for the entire Mississippi River. It was protected by two huge forts in the harbor. At first, Farragut tried to batter the forts into submission. Once that failed, he decided to slip by them at night. He lost only one boat in the attempt, and with the city at his mercy, New Orleans surrendered.

In May Farragut headed up the Mississippi to capture the capital of Louisiana, Baton Rouge. Meanwhile, General Henry Halleck took over active command of Grant's forces while the latter was in temporary disgrace. Halleck marched south, forcing the Confederate army to evacuate Corinth. In June the Union navy forced the surrender of Memphis. Only the fortress city of Vicksburg, Mississippi (in between Farragut and Halleck) kept the Union from complete control of the nation's largest river system.

Complete the following.

2.1   Explain why there were so many battle casualties in the Civil War.

_____

_____

2.2   What were the positive results of McClellan's command?

_____

_____

_____

2.3   Why was McClellan not a good field commander?

_____

_____

2.4   Name the only American war to date that caused more deaths than the Civil War.

_____

2.5   According to the *World Almanac*, how many Americans died in battle and from disease and

accidents in the Civil War? _____

Name the battle or place.

2.6   _____   "Stonewall" Jackson got his nickname

2.7   _____   "Unconditional Surrender" Grant got his nickname

2.8   _____   Admiral Farragut sailed his ships past the harbor forts at night

2.9   _____   Irvin McDowell was the Union commander

2.10   _____   green Confederate troops routed green Union troops

2.11   _____   fort on the Tennessee River fell easily to Grant

2.12   _____   Bloody battle cost 23,000 Union and Confederate casualties

2.13   _____   Washington citizens took picnic lunches out to watch

2.14   _____   the fall of these two forts set up the Union occupation of Nashville

2.15   _____   Grant was surprised by the Confederates at Pittsburg Landing

2.16 _____ important railroad junction, the goal of Grant after Donelson

2.17 _____ defeat that made the Union realize it would not be an easy war

2.18 _____ Lincoln and public opinion forced a Union attack with untrained troops against the wishes of the commander

Battle of the Ironclads. The Union's blockade of the South developed slowly. The North captured several key islands along the Southern coast early in the war to use as bases for the blockade fleet. But the thousands of miles of Southern coast could not all be watched. Eventually, the navy began to concentrate on the few Southern ports that had dock facilities to handle cotton bales, the South's currency in trade. This and the eventual capture of these ports made the blockade increasingly effective.

The South countered by using fast, dark-colored ships to run the blockade. The ships would take cotton from the South to British ports in the West Indies to trade for manufactured goods. The demand for luxury items in the South made the risky voyages very profitable. A ship owner could make a profit if his vessel made just two successful trips before it was captured. Eventually, Jefferson Davis' government insisted that half of all cargo space on the ships be used for war material, not silks and perfume.

The South tried to break the blockade. They almost succeeded, using the captured Union steamship *Merrimac*. When the Union withdrew from Norfolk Navy Yard shortly after the outset of the Civil War, the Union Navy sank the *Merrimac* to keep it from falling into enemy hands. The Confederates recovered and salvaged the steam-powered ship, and modified it by covering it with iron plates. They rearmed and renamed the ship the *Virginia* and used it with devastating effect to attack the wooden ships that blockaded Chesapeake Bay. The Union ships' cannon fire bounced harmlessly off of the steel-covered ship.

Fortunately, the Union had also developed an ironclad vessel. The *Monitor* arrived in time to confront the *Virginia* when it made its second appearance in the bay. The two ships fought an inconclusive four-hour battle because neither side had developed armor-piercing artillery shells. Out of both ammunition and resolve, the ships returned to their home ports. Eventually, the Union Navy claimed the battle's victory because the blockade was not broken. Later, both ships were lost. The Confederacy destroyed the *Virginia* (*Merrimac*), and the North lost the *Monitor* and its crew in a storm off the coast of Cape Hatteras. The battle of the *Monitor* and the *Merrimac* was the first battle in history to be fought between armor-plated ships.

| The *Monitor* and the *Merrimac*

Peninsular Campaign. McClellan had finally agreed to attack in the spring of 1862. He decided against a direct attack to the South. Instead, he had his entire army transported by sea to the peninsula between the York and the James River on Chesapeake Bay in Virginia. He hoped to outflank the Confederates and capture Richmond, which would be about 70 miles from his landing point. Lincoln reluctantly approved the plan, but insisted that a large number of troops be left behind to defend Washington.

McClellan landed safely with more than 100,000 men and in April of 1862 began to march toward Richmond. They confronted the Confederate army under the command of Joe Johnston in the inconclusive two-day battle of Fair Oaks (Seven Pines). Johnston was wounded and Robert E. Lee was given command of the Confederate forces which he called the Army of Northern Virginia.

| Lincoln and McClellan meeting at Antietam

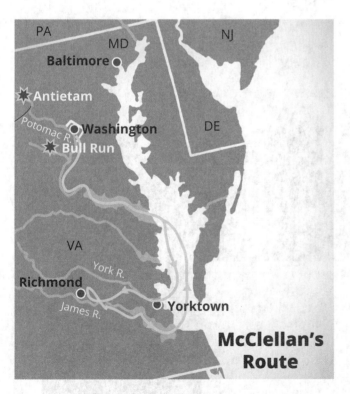

Stonewall Jackson used a smaller Confederate force to tie up McClellan's reinforcements around Washington in the Shenandoah Valley. Moving quickly and winning several small battles, Jackson convinced the Union high command that an attack on Washington was taking place. After fighting enough to insure the Union troops would remain there looking for him, Jackson slipped away and joined up with Lee.

Using information gained by Jeb Stuart's cavalry, which made a spectacular ride all the way around McClellan's army, Lee attacked on June 26th. The Seven Days' Battles raged from June 26th to July 1st with a series of savage battles in what are now the suburbs of Richmond. Lee succeeded in forcing McClellan to retreat to the James River. McClellan believed he was hopelessly outnumbered and refused to take the offensive again. He was finally ordered to return his army to Washington in the hopes it could be used from there.

Second Bull Run. While McClellan was in Virginia, the army around Washington was under the command of John Pope. Pope advanced toward Richmond in July, believing that McClellan's army on the peninsula would keep Lee too busy to stop him. But Lee realized the caliber of his opponents. Lee was certain that McClellan would be too busy moving his army to interfere with the Confederate army for a time, so Lee left a small force on the peninsula and led the rest of the army north to deal with Pope before McClellan's troops could join him. Lee sent Jackson to circle around Pope and cut his lines of supply and communication. As Lee expected, Pope turned his army and tried to find Jackson to do battle. Then Lee brought the Army of Northern Virginia to Jackson's aid.

The Battle of Second Bull Run went badly for the Union. Pope was very confused. He had finally cornered Jackson on August 29th after an exhausting search and had attacked him hard. Jackson managed to hold on for that day, and the next day Lee arrived. Pope never knew he was there until the Confederate army attacked from the side (flank). The Union army was routed.

That summer was the beginning of Lee's spectacular reputation as a general. Robert E. Lee was a devout Christian man from an aristocratic, but not very wealthy, Southern family. He gained several properties by his marriage into the family of George Washington's wife. He did not really believe slavery was just, but like so many in his day, he owned slaves and accepted "the institution." He fought for the Confederacy because he would not fight against his home state of Virginia. Most experts agree that he was the best general on either side during the Civil War. As at Second Bull Run, he routinely took chances, and he out-maneuvered and out-fought his Union opponents. By the end of the war, the soldiers of the Confederacy loved him and trusted him completely, even when he was wrong.

Confederate Soldier

Union Soldier

Antietam. Lee decided it was time for the Confederacy to go on the offensive. A rebel victory in Union territory might convince Britain to recognize the Confederacy and convince the North to give up the war. So Lee and his army moved into Maryland, heading for the capital of Pennsylvania. McClellan, whose command had been reduced after the peninsula campaign, was given command again under public pressure. He took his reorganized army out to meet Lee.

Lee divided his army to capture Harper's Ferry and press an attack to the north. McClellan learned of the plans when a lost copy of Lee's orders accidentally got into Union hands, but McClellan did not move fast enough to trap Lee with his army spread out. The two sides met near Antietam Creek on September 17th. It was the single bloodiest day of the long, bloody war. In one day, there were over 20,000 casualties between the two armies. Militarily, the battle was a draw. Lee's lines held but he retreated the next day. History records a Union victory because they took the field.

Emancipation Proclamation. Lincoln's goal had always been to restore the Union, but he began to see that the North needed a more specific, moral war aim—the end of slavery. He was reluctant to act because he did not want to drive the Northern border states into the arms of the Confederacy, but he had decided by the summer of 1862 to make the move. However, he wanted to wait until after a Union victory to make the announcement. Antietam gave him that chance.

On September 22nd, Lincoln issued the Emancipation Proclamation. It declared that all of the slaves in any state still in rebellion on January 1, 1863 would be forever free. It did not affect the slaves in the Northern border states and did not free any slaves until the South was effectively under Northern control. However, the document meant the end of slavery in the U.S. The North now had a moral cause. Britain, which had waged a world-wide campaign against slavery, would not aid the Confederacy to protect it.

Fredericksburg. McClellan was so slow following Lee that Lincoln lost all patience and finally removed him from command in November. He was replaced by Ambrose E. Burnside. The general was a handsome man with thick side whiskers that were thereafter called "side burns" in his honor. He immediately began an offensive, but he would prove as foolhardy as McClellan was hesitant.

Burnside decided to move his army to the east around Lee's right flank and march from there to Richmond. Burnside successfully moved the army and prepared to cross the Rappahannock River opposite the city of Fredericksburg. However, he insisted on waiting for pontoon bridges to cross. They took more than a week to arrive. By that time, Lee's scouts had warned him of the Union's location and he had set up strong defenses on the high ground near the city.

Faced with a strongly entrenched Confederate army, Burnside should have withdrawn to fight somewhere else. Instead, he attacked on December 13th. Wave after wave of Union soldiers were sent up the hill towards the Confederate guns. By the day's end, Union casualties were 13,000. General Lee said after that carnage, "It is well war is so terrible, or we should grow too fond of it."

Burnside's failures prompted Lincoln to again change generals. This time he choose General Joseph Hooker. Hooker had a reputation as a fighter, and he began to rebuild the army during the winter months in preparation for another summer of fighting. By that point, the war was more than a year and a half old. The Union had captured the upper and lower reaches of the Mississippi, but they had been completely unable to use their superior numbers and supplies to penetrate the eastern Confederate defenses. Richmond was still 120 miles away.

Name the person, event, battle, or item.

2.19 _____ freed all enslaved people in any state still in rebellion on January 1, 1863

2.20 _____ McClellan faced Johnston in the Peninsular Campaign

2.21 _____ Union ironclad that fought the *Merrimac* to a draw

2.22 _____ Lee fought using information from Stuart's ride around the Union army

2.23 _____ Lee advanced into Maryland and was almost trapped when his plans were discovered

2.24 _____ Lee trapped Pope before McClellan could come to his aid

2.25 _____ the best general in the Civil War

2.26 _____ it gave the war its single bloodiest day

2.27 _____ Burnside attacked entrenched Confederate positions on the Rappahannock River

2.28 _____ general who circled behind Pope and drew him away from Richmond

2.29 _____ gave the North a moral cause and kept Britain from supporting the Confederacy

2.30 _____ Confederate vessel that almost broke the blockade on Chesapeake Bay

2.31 _____ cotton from the South would be taken here by blockade runners

2.32 _____ Lee became the Confederate commander after Johnston was injured in this battle

2.33 _____ Lee forced McClellan back to the James River and effectively ended the Peninsular Campaign

2.34 _____ this battle gave Lincoln the "victory" he needed to release the Emancipation Proclamation

2.35 _____ Burnside waited too long for pontoon boats

2.36 _____ removed from Union command for not pursuing Lee

Murfreesboro to Chattanooga (1863)

Murfreesboro. The Union army in the west had been spread out to occupy captured territory. As a result, it had been largely ineffective through the end of 1862. A Confederate invasion of Tennessee floundered in October of 1862. A new Union commander, William Rosecrans, pursued the Confederates into southern Tennessee. They met at the Battle of Murfreesboro beginning on December 31, 1862. The battle raged for three days with a one-day break in the middle. The total casualties for both sides were over 20,000 men. The results were inconclusive. The Confederates retreated, and it was six months before that specific Union army took the offensive again.

Vicksburg. Grant was now in charge of an army in Tennessee. At the end of 1862, he headed south for Vicksburg. Vicksburg was a fortified city on a high bluff overlooking a bend in the Mississippi River. If the Union was to control the river, the city had to be taken. After a delay due to the Confederate cavalry destroying his supply depot and one failed first attempt to get around the city's defenses, Grant decided on more direct measures.

Grant fought his way south along the west bank of the Mississippi River. Eventually, he crossed the river below Vicksburg and came at the city from the east, which was the only level entrance. Grant assaulted the city on May 22nd and was **repulsed**. He set up trenches that blocked all entry into the city and then began a siege. His guns bombarded the city non-stop. Federal gunboats trained their fire on the city and kept Grant supplied with everything his army needed. The people of the city moved into caves to protect themselves and were reduced to living on mule, rat, and dog meat.

The result was inevitable. The Confederacy had no army to send to relieve Vicksburg. Believing he would get better terms on Independence Day than any other time all summer, the Confederate commander surrendered on July 4, 1863. The Confederacy had been divided, and now the Union had complete control of the Mississippi River. Grant had proven himself as the kind of determined, aggressive general that Lincoln wanted.

Chancellorsville. Union General Joseph Hooker moved to attack Lee in the spring of 1863. Lee still held his position at Fredericksburg. Hooker tried to move around Lee's army to the west, past their left flank. For some reason, Hooker lost his nerve just as the move was showing signs of success. He retreated to defensive positions at Chancellorsville, west of Fredericksburg.

Lee quickly moved to attack Hooker in what would be one of his greatest victories. Lee's army was about half the size of Hooker's. Nevertheless, Lee divided the Army of Northern Virginia into two parts. Lee's portion attacked from the front while the other part, under Stonewall Jackson, attacked the Union's right flank. The Union army was taken by surprise and the right flank collapsed.

The Battle of Chancellorsville lasted for four days beginning on May 2nd. The Confederates were never able to completely break the Union lines, but they did maul them fiercely. Attacked on two sides, the Union army literally fought for its life. As at Shiloh, the underbrush caught fire, burning many of the wounded to death. Hooker retreated, but the South did not get off unscathed. In the evening while scouting the area for possible night attack, Stonewall Jackson was accidentally shot by friendly fire. He died on May 10th. Lee would never find an adequate replacement for his brilliant subordinate.

| The Ghosts of Gettysburg

Gettysburg. In the early summer Lee headed north again to try for a major victory on Union soil. The cavalry from the two armies clashed near Brandy Station on June 9th. The Confederates took the field, but for the first time the Union cavalry equated itself well against the famous rebel horsemen. Another part of the Southern army captured some badly-needed supplies by defeating the Union garrison at Winchester. In the meantime, Hooker refused to pursue Lee and insisted he must attack Richmond. Lincoln relieved him of command and replaced him with George Meade. Meade was from Pennsylvania, and Lincoln hoped he would prove persistent in chasing Lee, who was now in his home state.

| George Meade

Lee marched north toward Harrisburg with the Union army in pursuit. On July 1, some of Lee's troops came into the town of Gettysburg, Pennsylvania searching for shoes. They were met by an advance force of Meade's army. Both sides called for reinforcements and the crucial three-day-long Battle of Gettysburg had begun.

The Confederates forced the Union troops out of the city on the first day of the battle. The Union troops took up defensive positions on a series of hills outside the city. Their line was shaped like a fish hook. Robert E. Lee now made one of his few mistakes. He tried to drive the Union army, which was larger than his, out of strong defenses on the top of a hill. The Confederates both suffered and inflicted huge losses as they repeatedly attacked the Union lines on the second day.

On the third day, Lee decided to make a frontal attack on the Union army. He ordered General George Pickett to march 13,000 men straight up on the Union position. Pickett's charge was a slaughter. Half the men who marched up that day did not come back. Lee blamed only himself for having asked his men to do the impossible. The next day, the Army of Northern Virginia retreated.

Gettysburg was the turning point of the war. The Confederate army would never again have the strength to mount a major offensive. It would never again threaten the North with invasion. However, Meade failed to follow up his victory. Lee and his army were allowed to escape and continue to protect the Confederacy. The war would continue for almost two more years.

The Union and the Confederacy had over 20,000 casualties each at Gettysburg. The Union built a cemetery on the site. It was dedicated on November 19, 1863. The main speaker addressed the crowd for two hours. Abraham Lincoln spoke for only two minutes, but it was Lincoln's words which were remembered. The Gettysburg Address still rings through the years as one of Lincoln's finest speeches.

Four score and seven years ago, our fathers brought forth upon this continent a new nation: conceived in liberty, and dedicated to the proposition that all men are created equal.

Now we are engaged in a great civil war...testing whether that nation, or any nation so conceived and so dedicated...can long endure. We are met on a great battlefield of that war.

We have come to dedicate a portion of that field as a final resting place for those who here gave their lives that this nation might live. It is altogether fitting and proper that we should do this.

But, in a larger sense, we cannot dedicate...we cannot consecrate... we cannot hallow this ground. The brave men, living and dead, who struggled here have consecrated it, far above our poor power to add or detract. The world will little note, nor long remember, what we say here, but it can never forget what they did here.

It is for us the living, rather, to be dedicated here to the unfinished work which they who fought here have thus far so nobly advanced. It is rather for us to be here dedicated to the great task remaining before us...that from these honored dead we take increased devotion to that cause for which they gave the last full measure of devotion...that we here highly resolve that these dead shall not have died in vain...that this nation, under God, shall have a new birth of freedom...and that government of the people...by the people...for the people...shall not perish from this earth.

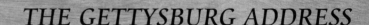

THE GETTYSBURG ADDRESS

Abraham Lincoln, November 19, 1863

Name the battle.

2.37 _____ turning point of the war

2.38 _____ Hooker was defeated by Lee

2.39 _____ Union victory gave them control of the Mississippi

2.40 _____ inconclusive battle in Tennessee under Union leader Rosecrans

2.41 _____ Confederate forces surrendered on the Fourth of July

2.42 _____ four-day battle beginning May 2, 1863

2.43 _____ the opposing armies met when the Confederates came into town looking for shoes

2.44 _____ fought in Pennsylvania

2.45 _____ Grant was unable to win by a direct attack, but won instead by siege

2.46 _____ Pickett's Charge was Lee's last attempt to break the Union lines

2.47 _____ Meade fought Lee

2.48 _____ Lee attacked the Union army from two directions with a smaller army and won

2.49 _____ Stonewall Jackson was shot and later died

2.50 _____ Lincoln's immortal words dedicated a cemetery there

Answer these questions.

2.51 What does "four score and seven years ago" mean? (Look it up.) _____

2.52 Why did Lincoln feel they could not dedicate the cemetery?

_____

_____

2.53 What did Lincoln say he and his listeners must dedicated themselves to do?

_____

2.54 To what was Lincoln highly resolved?

_____

2.55 What did Meade fail to do at Gettysburg that prolonged the war?

_____

_____

The armies. The two opposing armies were at once both similar and different. One important similarity was that both suffered under the limited medical knowledge in the 1860s. The simple idea that a wound should be cleaned to prevent infection was unknown in the mid-19th century. Diseases such as typhoid, dysentery, and pneumonia killed far more soldiers than bullets. The medical treatment for any serious injury to an arm or leg was **amputation**. Treatment was often done without **anaesthetic**. Surgery was usually done with an anaesthetic which had been discovered in the 1840s. However, it was also done with dirty instruments that spread infections.

The North had one advantage in the medical area, determined female volunteers. Northern women established the United States Sanitary Commission in 1861, modeled after the work of the British visionary Florence Nightingale in the Crimean War. The doctors had noticed that a clean camp or hospital resulted in fewer deaths. The Commission worked to provide clean housing for the troops as well as insuring they had ways to bathe and wash their clothes. The Commission also tried to track down missing soldiers and notify families of deaths. The women began to volunteer as nurses in the army hospitals, a revolutionary idea for the time.

The South suffered from a lack of resources to keep its own army clean. As the war progressed, the Confederate army could barely keep its men clothed. It was not surprising that Lee's army was looking for shoes at Gettysburg; they were constantly in need of them. They also lacked uniforms, blankets, soap, and food. The main reason was the poor system of roads and railroads in the South. Even when the supplies were available, it was often impossible to get them to the army in the field.

The Northern army, by contrast, was well-fed and supplied throughout the war. This difference was mainly due to the superior resources of the North. The North had more supplies for its men, and it had better means of transportation to deliver them. The better supplies and cleanliness meant the typical Union soldier was healthier than his Confederate opponent, but poor leadership squandered that and other advantages for most of the war.

Both armies had trouble getting enough soldiers to replace those that deserted, died, or were injured. The Confederacy passed the first **conscription** in American history in April of 1862. The Confederate conscription law made all white men between the ages of eighteen and thirty-five liable to be drafted for three years service in the army. There were ways around it, however. A man could legally hire a substitute, and many did. One key exception was that one white man on every plantation with at least twenty enslaved people was exempt. The complaints were so loud, that the law made this war to defend slavery "a rich man's war, but a poor man's fight." Even with the law, the South was desperately short of soldiers by the end of the war. They simply did not have a large enough population to compete with the North in manpower.

The North also passed a conscription law in 1863, when the number of volunteers fell due to defeats and reports of the horrible battles. The Northern law also allowed a person to hire a substitute or escape service by the payment of a $300 fee. That was a huge amount for a

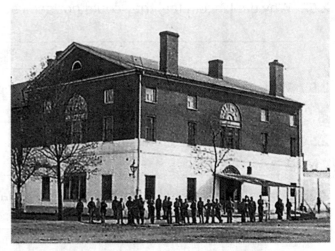

| Old Capital Prison, Washington D.C.

working man, and only the well-to-do could afford that escape. However, the Union army was mainly filled by volunteers who collected bonuses for signing, which they would not get if they were drafted. However, the draft was unpopular and sparked a riot in New York City in July of 1863. The disorder raged for almost a week and was finally suppressed by Union troops called in from the Army of the Potomac.

Another problem experienced by both armies was what to do with prisoners. It had been the long-standing military tradition to parole prisoners on the condition that they would not fight any more, or to exchange them between the armies. However, the South's refusal to recognize black soldiers as prisoners of war and the realization that the South could not afford to replace its soldiers led the North to stop paroles and exchanges. Both sides then had to house and care for thousands of enemy prisoners. More than 50,000 died in the poorly run prison camps. The worst ones were in the South, where there were few resources to spare for Union prisoners.

The worst of the worst among the prison camps was Andersonville prison in Georgia. It was a log stockade with no housing and the only water supply was a sluggish stream that ran through its center. Food was limited to a little cornmeal each day. There was no medical care of any kind. Thirteen thousand Northern soldiers died at that prison. The survivors were little better than living skeletons. The commander of the camp, Captain Henry Wirz, was executed after the war.

As the long, bloody war dragged on, revivals broke out in the army camps. Men who were facing death chose to face God first. The interest in the things of God grew stronger as the war continued. **Chaplains** became common in the army, for they had been rare in previous wars. *Christian History* estimates that a total of between 200,000 and 300,000 soldiers from the two sides accepted Christ as their Savior during the war. (Vol. XI, No. 1, page 30). Leading the list

of committed Christians who served on both sides were Generals Robert E. Lee and Stonewall Jackson.

Chickamauga and Chattanooga. Chattanooga in southeast Tennessee was a key Confederate city after Vicksburg was besieged and captured. The city was an important rail junction that made it the western door to the Confederacy. Confederate General Braxton Bragg, who had met William Rosencrans at the Battle of Murfreesboro, had withdrawn to Chattanooga to set up defenses. All the while, Rosencrans refused to move for months after the battle. In August of 1863, the Union army finally began to move on Chattanooga.

Bragg was not in the same class with Lee and Jackson. He was unsure of himself and acted with excessive caution. The Union army swung around the city, and Bragg became concerned for his supply lines to Atlanta. In early September, Bragg evacuated Chattanooga without firing a single shot in its defense. Rosencrans followed without pausing to rest his army, and the two armies met near Chickamauga Creek on September 19th and 20th.

| Robert E. Lee and "Stonewall" Jackson

| Ulysses S. Grant and William Tecumseh Sherman

Bragg received reinforcements just before the battle. General James Longstreet from Lee's Army of Northern Virginia arrived with two **divisions**. The Confederates broke the Union right flank on the second day of the battle. That part of the army fled the field in wild disarray. A complete collapse was prevented by General George Thomas who held his Union army on the left flank despite everything. His spirited defense allowed the Union army to escape to Chattanooga and earned him the nickname "the Rock of Chickamauga."

Chickamauga was to be the last major Confederate victory. Bragg failed to follow it up. He and his army took up positions in the mountains around the Union army in Chattanooga and began a siege. But unlike the South at Vicksburg, the North had troops it could send to the rescue.

In October of 1863, Ulysses S. Grant was made supreme commander of all Union troops in the west. Rosencrans was also replaced by George Thomas. Grant acted promptly to establish a river supply route to the Union army in Chattanooga. He then brought into the city two more armies under Generals William T. Sherman and Joseph Hooker. When they were in place, Grant attacked the surrounding Confederates on November 24th.

Hooker's men assaulted the tall, heavily-fortified Lookout Mountain; but the enemy troops there were in bad shape and quickly fell to the Union under the cover of low-lying clouds. When the clouds lifted late in the day, the Stars and Stripes were flying at the top. The newspapers dubbed it the "battle above the clouds."

Sherman attacked the Confederate right flank with little success on the first day. On the second day, Thomas' men were sent to attack some rifle pits in the center of the Confederate line. The men, with pride still wounded from their embarrassing defeat at Chickamauga, took not only the pits but (without orders) drove straight up into the Confederate lines. Thomas' army broke through the rebel defenses at their strongest point and forced them to retreat. Combined with September's capture of Knoxville by General Burnside, the Battle of Chattanooga gave the Union control of Tennessee and an upper hand in the west.

Complete these sentences.

2.56 The Union commander at Chickamauga was _____ and
the Confederate commander was _____ .

2.57 The first conscription law in U.S. history was passed by the _____
government in 1862.

2.58 An estimated _____ to _____ soldiers
became Christians during the war.

2.59 The center of the Confederate line at Chattanooga was overrun by men under the command
of _____ .

2.60 The worst of the Civil War prison camps was _____ in Georgia.

2.61 Northern women established the United States _____
which helped the Union army stay cleaner and healthier.

2.62 A Northern man could avoid the draft by _____ or
_____ .

2.63 The _____ army was better supplied throughout the war.

2.64 _____ was the last major Confederate victory.

2.65 George Thomas earned the nickname "the _____ Chickamauga"
by his stand when the rest of the Union army was fleeing.

2.66 The fighting on Lookout Mountain on November 24th was called the _____
_____ .

2.67 _____ became the supreme Union commander in the
west in October of 1863.

2.68 The standard treatment for any severe injury to a leg or arm was _____ .

2.69 A riot in New York City in July of 1863 was sparked by _____ .

2.70 _____ was a key railroad junction that Bragg evacuated
without firing a shot.

Wilderness to Ford's Theater (1864-65)

Wilderness. Lincoln believed that he had finally found the man he needed to defeat Lee. In March of 1864, Ulysses S. Grant was promoted to the rank of lieutenant general (the first man since George Washington to hold that rank) and given command of all Union forces. He was faced with the task of destroying two major Confederate armies, one in Tennessee now under Joseph Johnston, and the Army of Northern Virginia under Lee. Grant assigned Sherman to command the Union army in Tennessee and advance on Atlanta, Georgia. Grant himself went to the front with the Army of the Potomac that would have to face Robert E. Lee.

The Army of the Potomac marched into Virginia yet again in May of 1864. They came through a heavily wooded area called the Wilderness. Lee attacked there, in an area where the superior Union numbers could not be used effectively because of dense brush, poor visibility, and rough ground. The battle was a mass of confusion. The Union lost about 17,000 men in two days of fighting, and neither side could claim victory. The major difference between Grant and previous commanders was what happened after the battle. Instead of retreating, as every other commander had before him, Grant kept going.

Grant-Lee Duel. Grant shifted his army left and tried to go around Lee. Lee shifted skillfully and met him at Spotsylvania Court House. Again there were huge losses on both sides and victory for neither. Grant could replace his losses, but Lee could not, and Grant knew it. He continued to shift left, forcing Lee to move to meet him, and fighting battles almost daily. Grant was quite content with this strategy and was determined to "fight it out on this line if it takes all summer." It would and then some.

Cold Harbor. As Lee continued to move and block his advance on Richmond, Grant began to lose patience. When the Confederates set up new defensive lines at a town called Cold Harbor, Grant decided to make a strong frontal attack instead of maneuvering again. He sent about a dozen assaults at the Confederate lines, all of which were failures. The Union army suffered over 7,000 casualties in a half an hour. The Confederate lines held.

The slow progress and massive casualties attracted horror in the North. "Butcher Grant" was condemned for his lack of concern for human life, but Grant paid no attention. He had a job to do, and he would keep at it until it was done.

Siege of Petersburg. Grant decided to move yet again in mid-June. This time, he shifted his army south across the James River and marched on the town of Petersburg. Petersburg was a rail junction near Richmond. Most of the trains coming into the Confederate capital came by this route. If Grant captured it, the capital would be at his mercy; however, Lee had time to set up defenses and repulse the Union attack. Grant settled in for a siege.

Atlanta. While Grant was busy in Virginia, William Tecumseh Sherman moved south toward Atlanta, Georgia from Chattanooga. He was opposed by Joseph Johnston's Confederate army. The two sides practiced classic military maneuvering as Sherman worked his way closer and closer to Atlanta from May to July. Johnston's strategy was delay. He fought small battles and withdrew, never allowing Sherman the chance he wanted to destroy the Confederate army. By July Johnston had withdrawn to the strong defenses around Atlanta.

Johnston's strategy was not popular with the Confederate government who wanted Sherman stopped. The Confederate command wanted a more aggressive general, so Johnston was replaced in July by John Bell Hood. Hood attacked Sherman immediately and repeatedly. All the attacks failed and cost the Confederate army irreplaceable soldiers.

In August, Sherman began to shell the city. Morale among the soldiers and citizens fell as the capture of Atlanta seemed imminent. At the end of August, Sherman worked his way around the city and cut off the last railroad link to the Confederacy. Without his supply lines, Hood evacuated the city. Sherman occupied it on August 2nd.

Shenandoah Valley. When Grant settled in to besiege Petersburg, another Union army under David Hunter was working its way down the key Shenandoah Valley. The valley ran northeast in Virginia toward Washington D.C. It was a rich, fertile area that supplied the Confederate army with food. The Union had been unable to gain control of it thus far in the war.

Lee sent Jubal Early to the valley. He was able to stop Hunter and even threatened Washington for a short time. Grant was determined to end this threat that distracted him from concentrating on Lee. He sent Philip Sheridan in with express orders to clear the valley so clean of everything that "a crow could not cross it without carrying its own food." Early succeeded in surprising Sheridan's men at Cedar Creek on October 19th. The Confederates were forced back and were not able to challenge the Union after that. Sheridan proceeded to obey his orders, burning crops and buildings, driving off livestock, and depriving the Confederacy of anything of value in the valley. Using these methods, the Union finally took control of the valley.

This was total war. Prior to the Civil War, American armies avoided harming farms, industries, or any non-military target. But Grant, Sherman, and Sheridan realized that the farms and industries kept the army going. The destruction brought the war home to the ordinary people whose support was vital if the war was to continue. The Union began a new policy to destroy anything that might aid the Confederate army in the hope it would force the civilian population to sue for peace.

| David Farragut and his crew

Mobile. The port of Mobile, Alabama was a major port for blockade runners during the war. By mid-1864, it was also one of the few Confederate ports still open. The city's defenses included three forts, four gunboats (including one ironclad), underwater obstacles, and mines (called torpedoes). Admiral David Farragut, the commander who captured New Orleans, had organized a fleet to take the city. They attacked on August 5, 1864.

One of the Union ironclads was blown up by a torpedo early in the attack. When the other ships hesitated, Farragut gave the famous order, "Damn the torpedoes! Full speed ahead!" The fleet got past the outer defenses and into the harbor. The engines on the Confederate ironclad failed, and the forts were pounded into submission. The port was captured on August 23rd, but the city itself would not surrender for months.

| Civil War-era Navy

Election of 1864. The elections came around in 1864 with Lincoln running for a second term as president. The American democracy was still the only major one in the world and very much a unique experiment. It was astonishing that in the midst of Civil War carnage a regular election could even be held; but it proceeded in an orderly fashion, displaying the incredible strength and flexibility of the American republic.

The war was unpopular, having dragged on far longer than anyone dreamed it should have. A group of Northern Democrats called the Copperheads violently opposed the war, some to the point of treason. Other "War Democrats" supported the war and the Republican president. These joined with the Republicans in 1864 to form the temporary National Union Party and nominate Lincoln for president. One of the War Democrats named Andrew Johnson was nominated as his vice-president.

The remaining Democrats nominated George McClellan, the army general dismissed for his hesitancy in battle. Their platform was defeatist, calling the war a failure. McClellan, as a soldier who had fought in the war, disavowed the plank, but he would have been under immense pressure to negotiate an end to the war had he won. The Democrats had a chance as long as the war was going badly, but the victories at Atlanta, Mobile, and the Shenandoah Valley revived the Republican cause. Many Americans agreed with Lincoln's slogan "Don't swap horses in the middle of the river." Lincoln won easily and that ended the Confederacy's last realistic hope. The war would continue.

Name the person, event, battle, or item.

2.71 _____ rail junction near Richmond, besieged by Grant beginning June 1864

2.72 _____ man Lee sent to Shenandoah Valley to confront Hunter

2.73 _____ Grant lost 7,000 men in a half an hour in a vain attack on Confederate lines

2.74 _____ the dense trees kept Grant from using his superior numbers against Lee

2.75 _____ man who said "Damn the torpedoes! Full speed ahead!"

2.76 _____ Democratic nominee for president 1864

2.77 _____ Lincoln's running mate in 1864

2.78 _____ Union commander that captured Atlanta

2.79 _____ the name of the anti-war Northern Democrats

2.80 _____ Union man who laid waste to the Shenandoah Valley

2.81 _____ Confederate port captured August 23, 1864

2.82 _____ group of Democrats that joined with the Republicans in 1864

2.83 _____ commander who replaced Johnston in the west and immediately attacked Sherman

2.84 _____ rank given to Grant when he took command of all Union troops

Answer these questions.

2.85 How was Grant different from all previous Union commanders?

_____

_____

2.86 What event ended the Confederacy's last hope?

_____

2.87 What was Grant's strategy to defeat Lee?

_____

_____

2.88 What is total war?

_____

_____

Nashville. General Hood still had a Confederate army around Atlanta after Sherman captured the city. He unsuccessfully tried to cut Sherman's supply lines and force him to retreat. After several attempts through the fall, Hood decided on a desperate strategy. He would march north toward the Union-held city of Nashville. He hoped to force Sherman to abandon Atlanta and pursue him.

However, Sherman had other plans. He kept his army in Georgia and sent George Thomas, the "Rock of Chickamauga," north to take over the defense of Nashville. Thomas built up an army in the city as Hood worked his way north, pressing a small Union force that was fighting a delaying retreat in front of him. Hood reached Nashville in early December. By that time, Thomas had built up an army that was larger than his Confederate attackers.

Hood lacked the men to overrun the heavy defenses at Nashville. He also did not have enough men to effectively besiege it. He could not go around it without risking an attack by Thomas' forces. Out of all options except retreat, he stayed until Thomas was ready to attack.

On December 15th and 16th, the Union army attacked and destroyed Hood's army. The scattered remains fled south. What was left was no longer a threat to the Union.

Sherman's March to the Sea. William Tecumseh Sherman realized that with Hood's army to the north there was no one in the Confederacy that could stop him. He therefore proposed to take the war into the heart of the rebel states and make Georgia howl. Grant and Lincoln gave him permission to march from Atlanta to the sea, living off the land and destroying everything of value in his path. He destroyed much of Atlanta and marched out on November 15, 1864. During the march he had no communication with the North. He literally disappeared for a month.

Sherman's march to the sea was devastating to Georgia and the South. It aroused bitter hatred and fear. It showed that the Confederate armies could no longer protect their people. Buildings, railroads, farms, crops, and homes were systematically destroyed all along Sherman's route. Sherman's army ate well on captured food and had enough left over to supply the horde of escaping slaves that joined them along the route. Sherman reached the coast and contacted the blockade fleet on December 10th. Resupplied by the fleet, he captured Savannah on December 21st.

After Savannah, Sherman and his men headed north into South Carolina. That state had been the leader in the secession. The Union army was particularly vicious there. The capital of Columbia was burned on February 17th. Sherman cut the railroad lines into Charleston, forcing that city to surrender to the Union forces that were besieging it. Shortly after that, a combined force from the army and navy captured Wilmington, N.C. which was the last open Confederate port. Meanwhile, Sherman marched into North Carolina. The remaining Confederate army under the command of Joseph Johnston did not have the strength to even slow him down.

Petersburg. While Sheridan and Sherman had been moving, Grant had been in place at Petersburg. All through the end of 1864 and the first part of 1865, he had kept up the pressure on the Confederate defenses. Grant had tried several unsuccessful assaults with devastating losses; however, the fighting, disease, and desertions had steadily reduced the Confederate army. They were now desperately short of basic supplies and were hungry. Grant had slowly spread his lines west, forcing Lee to spread his own limited army out further and further. Grant hoped to eventually outflank Lee (move around the side of his army) and fight a decisive battle.

Lee decided to attempt an attack before the Union succeeded in encircling his army. The Confederate attack on March 25th successfully captured Fort Stedman, a focal point on the Union lines. Lee hoped to use it to threaten Grant's supply lines, but the Union counter-attacked and recaptured the fort the same day.

Meanwhile, Philip Sheridan had finished the Shenandoah Valley and rejoined the Union

| Appomattox Court House, where the Confederate Army surrendered

army at Petersburg. Grant now sent him around Lee's lines to the west to attack Five Forks which controlled Lee's last remaining supply line. The attack on April 1st was successful. Grant ordered a general attack all along the Union lines. The Confederate defenders were spread too thin, and their lines broke. Lee ordered a retreat and informed Jefferson Davis that he could no longer protect Richmond.

Appomattox Court House. After the fall of Petersburg, the Confederate government abandoned Richmond and fled south. Lee also headed south, hoping to join up with Johnston's forces in South Carolina. Grant followed in close pursuit. In the meantime, Sheridan got between Lee and Johnston, forcing the former to turn west. Things went from bad to worse for the Confederate army when food rations failed to arrive. At Sayler's Creek, the Union army attacked the retreating Confederates, capturing their supply wagons and thousands of prisoners. Finally, Lee realized he had no choice "but to go and see General Grant." He then added, "I would rather die a thousand deaths."

Lee and Grant met on April 9th in a small settlement called Appomattox Court House. Lee chose to surrender rather than disband his army and continue fighting a guerrilla war that would drive the nation into further barbarism and bloodshed. Grant returned the favor by granting the Army of Northern Virginia full parole if they laid down their arms. This meant that Lee and the other Confederate leaders would not be hanged as traitors. Grant even allowed the soldiers to keep their horses and sent rations over to the hungry Confederate army. The Army of Northern Virginia formally surrendered on April 12, 1865, four years to the day after Fort Sumter.

For all practical purposes, the war was over. Joseph Johnston realized he had no hope of continuing alone. On April 26th, he surrendered to Sherman on the same terms given to General Lee. Jefferson Davis was captured by Union cavalry on May 10th in Georgia. The last battle of the war was fought three days later near Brownsville, Texas.

Conclusions. The Civil War cost the United States over 600,000 men. Slavery was ended, and the notion that a state could leave the Union was abandoned. The United States was again one nation, and its government was stronger than ever before. Union industry had grown stronger under the demands of a war economy. The South, on the other hand, was devastated. Four million black Americans were no longer slaves, but they had no jobs and no education. Victory brought both great gain and great pain.

Ford's Theatre. The last wound that convulsed the nation was the assassination of Abraham Lincoln. Lincoln had held the Union together and pressed forward with the war. He had managed the infighting in his cabinet, opponents in Congress, poor generals, bad luck, and disappointment with skill and courage for four years. After Appomattox, the president decided to relax. He and his wife went to Ford's Theatre on April 14, 1865 to see a comedy. There, he was shot in the back of the head by a deranged actor named John Wilkes Booth, who thought he was avenging the South. Lincoln was carried across the street and died early on April 15th.

Booth fled from the scene. He was tracked by federal troops and shot after being cornered in a barn. Several people who had conspired with him to kill other members of the U.S. government were hanged. Lincoln's body was taken back to Springfield, Illinois in a slow-moving train for burial. His death coming so close on the heels of victory plunged the nation into grief and inspired a cry for revenge that echoed ominously through the South.

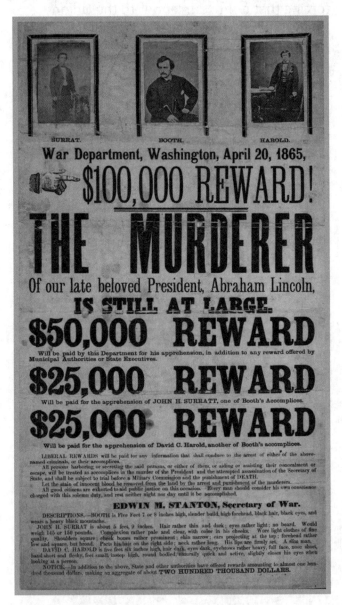

| John Wilkes Booth's Wanted Poster

Answer true or false.

If the answer is false, change it to make it true. Merely adding the word "not" is not sufficient.

2.89 _____ Sherman marched from Nashville to the sea, destroying anything of military value in his path.

2.90 _____ The Confederate army in Tennessee was virtually destroyed outside of Nashville in December 1864.

2.91 _____ Lee retreated from Petersburg in January of 1865.

2.92 _____ Over six hundred thousand men died in the Civil War.

2.93 _____ Lincoln was assassinated by John Wilkes Booth.

2.94 _____ Lee surrendered at Richmond in April, 1865.

2.95 _____ Grant led the troops that captured Five Forks.

2.96 _____ George Thomas was the Union victor at Nashville.

2.97 _____ Sherman captured Savannah in December 1864.

2.98 _____ The Confederate government was captured when Richmond fell.

2.99 _____ The surrender of Lee ended the war for all practical purposes.

2.100 _____ Lincoln's assassination occurred at Ford's Theater on April 14, 1865.

2.101 _____ Grant allowed the Confederate soldiers to keep their rifles after they surrendered.

2.102 _____ Booth was hanged after a trial.

2.103 _____ By the end, the Confederate army at Petersburg was hungry and short of basic supplies.

2.104 _____ Meade forced Lee to spread his defensive lines further and further at Petersburg.

Write a one-page paper.

2.105 Write a paper on the Emancipation Proclamation, a Civil War battle, a general, weapons used in the war, or the living conditions of the soldiers.

TEACHER CHECK _____ _____
                                    initials   date

↺ **Review the material in this section in preparation for the Self Test.** This Self Test will check your mastery of this particular section as well as your knowledge of the previous section.

SELF TEST 2

Match the correct person. Some answers will be used more than once (each answer, 2 points).

2.01	_____ devastated the Shenandoah Valley	a. Robert E. Lee
2.02	_____ led the Union army at Gettysburg	b. Ulysses S. Grant
2.03	_____ president of the Confederacy	c. George McClellan
2.04	_____ led the Confederate army at Gettysburg	d. Stonewall Jackson
2.05	_____ the "Rock of Chickamauga"	e. William T. Sherman
2.06	_____ dismissed from Union command for being repeatedly hesitant	f. David Farragut
2.07	_____ Gettysburg Address	g. John Brown
2.08	_____ first U.S. lieutenant general since Washington	h. George Meade
2.09	_____ Union commander who defeated Hood at Nashville	i. Jefferson Davis
2.010	_____ captured Vicksburg	j. Abraham Lincoln
2.011	_____ Lee's brilliant subordinate, shot by friendly fire at Chancellorsville	k. George Thomas
2.012	_____ captured New Orleans and Mobile	l. Joseph Johnston
2.013	_____ delayed Sherman on his way to Atlanta, relieved of command for not being aggressive	m. Philip Sheridan
2.014	_____ abolitionist martyr, attacked Harpers Ferry to start slave uprising	
2.015	_____ devastated Georgia in a march to the sea	

Put a *U* beside the Union victories and a *C* beside the Confederate victories (each answer, 1 point).

In cases where a victor was not clear, choose the side that benefited most from the results of the battle.

2.016 _____ Chancellorsville

2.017 _____ Gettysburg

2.018 _____ Antietam

2.019 _____ First Bull Run

2.020 _____ Peninsular Campaign

2.021 _____ *Monitor* and *Merrimac*

2.022 _____ Shiloh

2.023 _____ Chickamauga

2.024 _____ Petersburg

2.025 _____ Fredericksburg

Name the person, event, or term (each answer, 2 points).

2.026 _____ Act that ended the era of compromise

2.027 _____ Supreme Court decision that protected slavery in all the states

2.028 _____ document that freed the slaves in all states still in rebellion on January 1, 1863

2.029 _____ battle that was the turning point of the Civil War

2.030 _____ man who was the outgoing U.S. president when the Confederate states were first organized

2.031 _____ the worst prison camp in the Civil War

2.032 _____ killed more soldiers than bullets did during the Civil War

2.033 _____ place where Robert E. Lee surrendered

2.034 _____ man who killed Abraham Lincoln

2.035 _____ first state to secede from the Union

Answer these questions (each answer, 3 points).

2.036 What were two advantages the South had in the Civil War?

a. _____

b. _____

2.037 How was Grant different from all previous Union commanders?

_____

_____

2.038 What were two reasons why Britain did not support the Confederacy?

a. _____

b. _____

2.039 What was the political stand of the Republican Party and Abraham Lincoln on slavery in the election of 1860?

_____

_____

2.040 Why was the Kansas Territory called "Bleeding Kansas?"

_____

_____

2.041 Which army had the advantage in the area of supplies and why?

_____

_____

2.042 What was remarkable about the election of 1864?

_____

_____

2.043 Why were there so many battle casualties in the Civil War?

_____

_____

Answer true or false (each answer, 1 point).

2.044 _____ Soldiers in both armies became more interested in God as the war continued.

2.045 _____ More Americans died in the Civil War than in any other war fought by the U.S.

2.046 _____ The fall of Vicksburg gave the Union control of the Ohio River.

2.047 _____ Missouri was a slave state that stayed in the Union.

2.048 _____ Ulysses S. Grant is considered by most experts to have been the best general in the Civil War.

2.049 _____ The first Southern states seceded directly after the election of Abraham Lincoln.

2.050 _____ The Union government passed America's first conscription law.

2.051 _____ Black soldiers were quickly incorporated with white soldiers on equal terms in the Union army.

2.052 _____ Both sides expected a long, hard war from the beginning.

2.053 _____ Lincoln came to national attention through his work as secretary of state.

80 / 100 SCORE _____ TEACHER _____ _____
initials   date

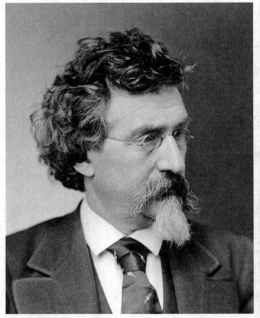

| Mathew Brady, the most famous photographer of the Civil War

3. RECONSTRUCTION

The nation faced many problems at the end of the Civil War. The victorious Union had to decide how much to punish the South for secession. The South had to form new state governments acceptable to the North. The rights of the newly freed black Americans needed to be defined, and those rights had to be protected. Moreover, the South itself was in ruins and lacked the funds needed to rebuild.

Many of the people in the North called for harsh treatment of the former Confederate States. However, Abraham Lincoln was not among them. In his second Inaugural Address about a month before his death, Lincoln spoke of his own goals in the victory which was quickly approaching.

> *With malice toward none, with charity for all, with firmness in the right as God gives us to see the right, let us strive on to finish the work we are in, to bind up the nation's wounds, to care for him who shall have borne the battle and for his widow and orphan, to do all which may achieve and cherish a just and lasting peace among ourselves and with all nations.*

Unfortunately for the South, Lincoln did not survive to pursue his peace. The new president, Andrew Johnson, did not have Lincoln's flexibility or political skill. After he butted heads with Congress, the Radical Republicans in that body set up their own harsh "Reconstruction" of the South over the president's vetoes. They even **impeached** Johnson for opposing them.

The Southern states all had acceptable state governments by 1870. By 1877 all of those states had white Democrats in complete control. That same year, newly elected President Rutherford B. Hayes moved out the last federal troops in the South that were supporting occupation governments. That was the final end of the long ordeal known as Reconstruction.

SECTION OBJECTIVES

Review these objectives. When you have completed this section, you should be able to:

6.   Describe Reconstruction.

7.   Describe the background and policies of Civil War-era presidents.

8.   Describe the post-Civil War corruption.

9.   Explain the status of black Americans during and after Reconstruction.

VOCABULARY

Study these words to enhance your learning success in this section.

alderman (äl' der man). Member of a city legislature.

filibuster (fil' a bus ter). In the U.S. Senate, a senator or group of senators refuse to stop debating a bill and thus prevent it from passing.

impeach (im pēch'). To charge a public official with misconduct in office in front of the proper authority for a trial.

posthumous (päs chu mus). Born after the death of the father.

Presidential Reconstruction

Andrew Johnson (1808-1875). Andrew Johnson was the first U.S. president to be impeached by Congress. Johnson was born to poor working parents in North Carolina. His father died when he was three. He had no formal education. At the age of thirteen, he was apprenticed to a tailor, which is probably when he learned to read.

As a youth, Johnson worked his way to Tennessee where he set up a successful tailoring business. He married the daughter of a shoemaker. She taught him to write, do simple arithmetic, and encouraged him to read. Johnson's business prospered, and he purchased property (including slaves) in Tennessee.

As Johnson's social position improved, he went into politics as a Jacksonian Democrat. He developed a powerful voice and used it to influence crowds. He won his first election in 1829 as an **alderman**, and he rarely lost after that. He served as a mayor, state representative, state senator, and governor in Tennessee. He served as a member of both the U.S. House and Senate.

Andrew Johnson believed in the right of Southerners to own enslaved people, but was an even stronger supporter of the Union. He was a member of the U.S. Senate in 1860 and was the only Southern senator who refused to secede with his state. Lincoln appointed him as military governor of his home state of Tennessee as it was conquered by the Union. As a prominent member of the War Democrats who supported Lincoln throughout the Civil War, he was an obvious choice for vice president in 1864. He filled out the ticket of the National Union Party which combined the Republicans and War Democrats to nominate Lincoln in 1864. He became president when Lincoln died.

Johnson's Reconstruction Plan. In 1863 Lincoln had established a plan to readmit the Confederate States to the Union. It was called the 10 percent plan. It required that only 10 percent of the voters in a state take an oath of loyalty to the Union. These would elect a state government that accepted the abolition of slavery. Then the state would be readmitted to the Union with all rights and privileges. Several conquered Confederate states had complied with these terms and sent representatives to Congress by 1864.

Congress refused to allow the new Congressmen to take their seats. (Congress has this right under the Constitution). Many in Congress felt that Lincoln's plan was too lenient. They hoped that Johnson, who hated rich planters because of his own humble background, would take a harder line with the South.

However, Johnson was a Southern Democrat and a follower of Andrew Jackson (a believer in restricted government). He set up a Reconstruction program in 1865 based on Lincoln's plans. Once 10% of voters had taken a loyalty oath, they were to vote for members of a special state convention. The convention had to approve the Thirteenth Amendment (which ended slavery), repudiate Confederate debts, and repeal the state's secession from Union. Certain high-level Confederates and those owning more than $20,000 in property were required to get a presidential pardon to vote, but Johnson granted those freely.

The Southern states quickly complied with these easy terms. The new state governments moved with equal swiftness in passing "Black Codes" that insured the black population would continue to be a subjugated people. The codes varied from state to state, but they basically worked to keep blacks as a cheap labor supply for the South. Black workers had to sign labor contracts with their employers. They lost all of their pay or could be dragged back by force if they tried to leave before the contract was finished. They could not vote, serve on juries, and in many states they could not own or lease land. Some states even declared that black people without jobs could be arrested for "idleness." They would be forced to work to pay their fines or serve on chain gangs rented out by the government. Everything possible was done to insure that the only change in the South was that black people were no longer *technically* slaves.

Abolitionists in the North were furious at the blatant defiance to the goals of the Union. To make matters worse, many of newly elected Southern Congressmen had been high-ranking Confederates, including Alexander Stephens, the Confederate vice president! The Republicans had enjoyed complete control of Congress during the war years. Several pro-Northern laws had passed during those four years, including a Homestead Act (giving free land to settlers), a high tariff, and subsidies for a Northern railroad across the nation. Northern Republicans were not anxious to surrender power, especially on such easy terms.

Johnson vs. Congress. An angry Congress now challenged Johnson's easy terms for the South. They were led by Thaddeus Stevens, a representative with a long history of championing the cause of black Americans. He led a group called the "Radical Republicans," Congressmen who pushed for a harsh policy toward the South. They were especially concerned with securing the rights of the newly freed black people, hoping to secure them as Republican voters.

Under the leadership of Stevens, Congress again refused to give the former Confederate states their seats in the national legislature. Then Congress formed the Joint (House-Senate) Committee on Reconstruction. Stevens, as chairman of the House members, quickly became the strongest influence on the committee. Stevens used his position to pursue plans that offered more protection to the newly freed slaves and less power to their defeated masters.

At first, Congress simply tried to modify the Johnson-Lincoln Plan to include more protection for the freedmen. In February of 1866,

| Andrew Johnson and a group of freedmen

Congress passed a law extending the life of the Freedmen's Bureau. The Freedmen's Bureau was a organization created to aid black people in their change from slaves to citizens. It operated as an early welfare agency, distributing clothes and food, providing education, settling disputes with employers, and hopefully settling the newly freed men on their own small farms. Southerners resented the Bureau, especially in its attempts to educate black people. Johnson vetoed the law to continue the Bureau because it interfered with the rights of the Southern states.

The now very angry Congress passed the Civil Rights Act which gave black people the rights of citizenship and tried to offset some of the Black Codes. Johnson vetoed that law as well, but in April Congress overrode the veto, making the bill a law. It was the first time Congress had ever successfully overridden a presidential veto on a piece of major legislation. It would be the first of many for President Johnson.

Congress wanted to insure that a future Democratic Congress could not undo the Civil Rights Act, so they passed the Fourteenth Amendment to the Constitution and sent it to the states. The Amendment made all freedmen citizens. It also ended the representation in Congress of any state that did not allow them to vote. However, it did not *require* that states allow black people to vote. Even many Northern states did not allow that. The Amendment barred certain Confederates from office and voided Confederate debts.

Johnson opposed the Fourteenth Amendment, but he had no power to prevent it. The loss of Lincoln was keenly felt as the relationship between the president and Congress deteriorated. Lincoln, the flexible political genius, would have understood the need to compromise with and then lead Congress, but Johnson was simply defiant. He went on a speaking tour in the summer of 1866, trying to influence the congressional elections. He hoped to get a Congress that favored his Reconstruction plan. Instead, his "swing around the circle" gained votes for the radicals. Johnson's fiery speeches were mercilessly heckled and rapidly became shouting matches between the president and the crowd. In the end, the 1866 elections expanded the number of Radical Republicans in Washington.

Johnson compounded his problems by failing to recognize dangerous reality. He encouraged the Southern states to reject the Fourteenth Amendment. Tennessee was the only one of the former Confederate states to vote in favor of the amendment. Congress now had solid, veto-proof majorities in both houses, and decided to set up its own Reconstruction plan when it met in 1867.

 Answer these questions.

3.1 Under Johnson and Lincoln's plan, what percent of Southern voters had to take a loyalty oath

to begin rebuilding the state government? _____

3.2 What did the state conventions have to do before they could reform as a government under Johnson's plan?

a. _____

b. _____

c. _____

3.3   What were the Republican Congressmen who favored harsh treatment of the South called?

_____

3.4   What Amendment to the Constitution ended slavery? _____

3.5   What was Andrew Johnson's trade? _____

3.6   What law did Congress pass to offset the Black Codes?

_____

3.7   What organization tried to aid the black people in the transition to freedom?

_____

3.8   How did Congress react to Johnson's veto of the Civil Rights Bill?

_____

3.9   What were the terms of the Fourteenth Amendment?

a.   _____

b.   _____

c.   _____

d.   _____

3.10 Why did Johnson make his "swing around the circle?"

_____

_____

3.11 Why did Johnson veto the extension of the Freedman's Bureau?

_____

3.12 What laws had the Republican Congress passed when the Democratic South was in rebellion?

a.   _____

b.   _____

c.   _____

3.13 What was the purpose of the "Black Codes?"

_____

_____

3.14 Which former Confederate state did accept the Fourteenth Amendment before 1867?

_____

3.15 What party nominated Johnson for vice president in 1864?

_____

3.16 What was unusual about Andrew Johnson as a senator in 1860?

_____

3.17 What Congressional committee tried to change Johnson's Reconstruction plan?

_____

3.18 Who was the leader of the Radical Republicans? _____

Radical Reconstruction

Occupation. Beginning in March of 1867, Congress began to model Reconstruction according to its own ideas, overriding every presidential veto. With the exception of Tennessee, the South was divided into five military districts run by a general and controlled by federal troops. The state governments were placed under military control, and former Confederate leaders were denied the right to vote. The states were required to ratify the Fourteenth Amendment and guarantee the right of black people to vote before they were allowed to form a new government. Moreover, another law was passed that required all of Johnson's orders to the army be issued through Ulysses S. Grant, whom the Republicans felt could be trusted to interpret them as Congress wished.

Southern reaction to the new laws was bitterly hostile. Not only were their own white leaders denied the right to even vote, black people would be voting! They were especially bitter at the hypocrisy that some Northern states still denied black people the right to vote. The rapid registration of black voters and the fact these new citizens voted Republican enforced Southern fears of a political conspiracy to take over the South. But by 1870, all of the states had new governments and constitutions that met Congressional criteria.

As a result of the new laws, Republican governments came to power in most of the states. Most of them also had a minority of black representatives, which inflamed the bigoted South. (Only in South Carolina did black representatives constitute a majority in the state assembly.) A few black Americans were also elected to the U.S. House and Senate. The Radical Republicans tried to protect these gains by passing the Fifteenth Amendment which guaranteed freedmen the right to vote. It was ratified in 1870.

Impeachment. Congress was so successful in pushing its own agenda that it began to reach for more power by getting rid of their main annoyance, the president. They tried to do this by passing the Tenure of Office Act (over Johnson's veto). This law supposedly forbade the president to fire any official approved by the Senate without the approval of that same body. This meant Johnson could not legally dismiss members of his own cabinet, his own personal advisors!

As expected, Johnson violated the law in 1868 when he dismissed Secretary of War Edwin Stanton who was a Radical supporter. Congress immediately voted to impeach Johnson for "high crimes and misdemeanors" as required by the Constitution. Most of the charges stemmed from firing Stanton, although he was also accused of verbal assaults on Congress.

The impeachment trial in the Senate was a huge show. The House prosecuted the case badly. Johnson's skillful attorneys showed that Johnson's only crime was opposing Congress. Still the Radical control of the Senate meant the vote would be close, and in the end Johnson was acquitted by a single vote. Seven Republican senators had voted in his favor, defying their own party for the sake of justice. Johnson had been stubborn and impolitic, but the Senate jury decided he had not committed a crime. The vote saved the presidency from a dangerous precedent. Impeachment could not be used as a political tool to remove an unpopular president.

Carpetbaggers and Scalawags. In the meantime, Reconstruction governments came to be dominated by Northerners who had traveled south and Southerners who decided to cooperate with Reconstruction. The former were called "carpetbaggers," because they supposedly traveled south with their possessions in a carpetbag to get rich yielding political power in the South. The latter group were called "scalawags" and were considered traitors to the Southern cause.

Some of the carpetbaggers did get rich by using their elected offices for personal gain. Others came south because they saw the Southern country while serving in the war and wanted to settle there. Still others came to bring Northern justice and ideas to the "backward" South. They were extremely unpopular, and stealing done by a prominent few of them reflected badly on the entire group.

The scalawags also had mixed reasons for cooperating. Many felt that they had lost the war and that cooperation was the proper course of action. Others saw the Republican Party as the only chance to put white people back in power. Still others were just switching sides to make a quick buck.

The corruption in the Reconstruction governments mirrored corruption in the entire nation. It varied, depending on the honesty of the men in power, but it also attracted a great deal of attention. As the years passed, Northerners saw the corruption as a reason to end Reconstruction. They eventually became tired of trying to control the South and believed that *white* Southerners should control their democratic governments.

| Sharecropper

Reconstruction governments did do some good. They instituted badly needed reforms in Southern governments. Public schools were established, tax systems were modernized, and internal improvements had begun. But the leaders of the old South would not tolerate being dominated by Northeners who promoted equality. The deep racial hatred of the Southern white people controlled their views of government and justice. They eventually found ways to regain power: violence, intimidation, and fraud.

"Redeemers." Some bitter Southern whites resorted to secret associations and terror to regain control of their governments. The Ku Klux Klan, formed in Tennessee in 1866, was the most infamous of these organizations. Dressed in white masks, these men would attack Northern Republicans, male teachers at freedmen schools, and Southerners who cooperated with the Reconstruction governments. But most of their fury was unleashed on black people who dared to exercise their newfound rights.

Black Americans were threatened, beaten, or killed for voting, getting an education, not acting in a subservient manner, or daring to challenge a white man in court.

Using these methods, the Klan and other organizations drove the Republicans out of the South. Only Democratic votes were acceptable, and by 1877, all the Southern states were "redeemed" as white Democrats came back into power. They remained in power for a long time. The deep bitterness of the Reconstruction period kept the Republican Party from having any large following in the South for many years.

Situation in the South. The South settled down to a new form of society. The old aristocratic planter society was gone. The lack of cash after the war meant that landowners had no way to pay laborers to work their fields. This led to the "share crop" system. In exchange for use of the land and tools, a worker (usually black) would raise a crop and split it with the landowner (usually white).

The white storekeepers and landowners charged high prices for tools and supplies. They also paid low prices for crops such as cotton. This led to a type of debt-slavery that kept thousands of black Americans in poverty for generations. High costs drove many of the landowners into debt and forced them to rely on heavily on cotton for needed cash. The concentration on one crop exhausted the soil and made poverty worse.

The Fourteenth Amendment gave black people the rights of citizenship, but equality was carefully evaded. Separate facilities were set up all over the South for eating, traveling, and learning. Tax dollars from the white-controlled legislatures invariably favored white facilities. Black schools received much less money than white schools; that is, until the system was overthrown in the 1960s.

The Fifteenth Amendment, which gave black people the right to vote, was virtually ignored. Black people who dared to vote faced the threat of violence from the Klan and other white supremacist organizations. Southern governments resorted to fraud and restrictive laws to prevent black Americans from voting. For example, some states required voters to pass literacy tests. White people routinely passed and black people routinely failed. Other states passed "grandfather clauses" that only allowed men to vote if their ancestors had in 1860. Poverty, poor education, and denial of the right to vote kept black Americans from truly being free, even after a devastating war had been fought for just that purpose.

Seward's Folly. By 1867 Andrew Johnson was little more than a figurehead, but his administration did manage one true victory, the purchase of Alaska. That territory was the property of the nation of Russia in the early 1860s. The czar saw the cold land in North America as a liability in the event of war with Britain. So he offered to sell it to the United States, which was another nation often at odds with the English.

Johnson's secretary of state was William Seward, a man who favored expansion, and he willingly negotiated a treaty offering Russia $7.2 million for the land (about two cents an acre). Most of the people in the United States saw no use for a piece of land so far north. It could not be used for farms, which is what most Americans wanted. The popular press called it "Seward's Folly" or "Seward's Icebox." Nevertheless, Congress approved the treaty, and the land has since repaid its purchase price many times over in oil, gold, fish, and minerals.

Complete these sentences.

3.19 Northern men who became part of the Reconstruction governments in the South were called _____ .

3.20 The South was divided into _____ military districts under Radical Reconstruction.

3.21 The purchase of Alaska was mocked by calling it _____ .

3.22 Many black farmers were put into debt-slavery by the _____ system.

3.23 Southern white people regained control of their governments using terror and secret societies like the _____ .

3.24 Freedmen were given the right to vote by the _____ Amendment.

3.25 _____ Republicans voted to acquit Johnson at his impeachment.

3.26 The Radical Congress required Johnson to issue all his orders to the army through _____ .

3.27 The United States paid _____ dollars for Alaska.

3.28 Johnson was impeached for violating the _____ Act.

3.29 Due to bitter feelings over Reconstruction, the South was dominated by the _____ Party for many years.

3.30 _____ were Southern men who cooperated with Reconstruction.

3.31 A Southern state was "_____" when white Democrats were again in power.

3.32 Johnson was impeached when he fired _____ .

Answer these questions.

3.33 How did the South avoid the Fifteenth Amendment?

a. _____

b. _____

c. _____

3.34 Why did Northern people begin to oppose Reconstruction as time went by?

a. _____

b. _____

c. _____

3.35 How did the Southern Democrats regain control of their governments?

_____

_____

3.36 What good did Reconstruction governments do?

a. _____

b. _____

c. _____

3.37 Why did the South continue to rely on cotton and what did it do to the soil?

a. _____

b. _____

3.38 How did the education system in the South hurt black Americans?

_____

_____

3.39 Why was the outcome of Johnson's impeachment so important?

_____

_____

Era of Good Stealings

Election of 1868. General Ulysses S. Grant slowly turned against Andrew Johnson. By the time Johnson was impeached, Grant was openly siding with the Republicans in Congress. His immense popularity made him an obvious choice for president in 1868. He was nominated by the Republicans along with a platform that called for harsh Reconstruction and repayment of Union Civil War debts. The Democrats nominated New York's Governor Horatio Seymour to oppose him. Their platform denounced Radical Reconstruction and called for debts to be repaid in inflationary paper money, not specie.

The Republican campaign involved a great deal of "waving the bloody shirt" (reminding the public about the war). The Democrats were accused of supporting the rebellion. "Vote as you shot" was a popular Republican slogan. Grant won the election by a comfortable majority. However, many white people in the South could not vote, and the black voters gave Grant the margin of victory. The unpopular Andrew Johnson was not even considered for the Democratic nomination, but he remained active in Tennessee politics. He was again elected to the U.S. Senate in 1875, just prior to his death.

Ulysses S. Grant (1822-1885). Ulysses S. Grant was an honest man who had one of the most corrupt administrations in American history. He was an excellent general, but one of the nation's worst presidents. He was born in Ohio to a tanner. His father had a prosperous business, and the shy Ulysses was given a good education. He became an excellent horseman, but had a distinct lack of business sense and no interest in his father's profession.

His father succeeded in getting him an appointment to West Point in 1839. Grant was an average student who did well in mathematics and horsemanship. He served in the Mexican War and received a promotion for his conduct. After the war, he married a classmate's sister and continued his career in the army.

| Ulysses S. Grant as President

In 1853, he was posted in an isolated fort in California, far from his beloved and growing family. He lost money in several schemes, began drinking, and eventually resigned from the army.

Until the Civil War, he worked at a variety of unsuccessful jobs. When the war began, he helped organize volunteers and was eventually given a colonel's command because the army badly needed experienced officers. He quickly gained fame for his victories in the west and was promoted to command of the entire Union army in 1864. He was the man who finally cornered Robert E. Lee. He was praised, even in the South, for the generous terms he gave to his defeated foe.

Grant was not well suited for the presidency. He was shy, naive, and a poor judge of character. His own honesty is supported by historians, but he constantly chose men for important offices who were extremely dishonest. He was easily swayed by these men to do what they wanted, and he continued to be loyal to them after their misdeeds were exposed. The result was an out-of-control administration that can be called the "Era of Good Stealings."

The new president was in a mess from the beginning. His cabinet was generally made up of friends without any consideration of their abilities. (Hamilton Fish, his very competent secretary of state, was an exception). The nation was in need of civil service reform to end the system of giving government jobs to pay off political supporters. Grant initially favored reform, but his "friends" talked him out of it. Grant's in-laws especially benefitted from the old plan, many of them landing government jobs. Grant also abandoned his initial plans to ease up on Reconstruction after pressure from the party.

Boss Tweed. The necessities of war had created an atmosphere of waste and fraud. Many businessmen had become rich supplying the needs of the army. Graft, corruption, and dishonesty became the dominant features of the get-rich-quick mindset. Cheating the government, investors, buyers, and anyone else became commonplace. Judges, police, and legislators were routinely bribed to look the other way. Millions were made by entrepreneurs who overcharged their own railroads for construction costs, sold stocks at inflated prices, paid bribes to get government contracts, and then set prices unreasonably high on the railroad routes they controlled.

One of the worst examples of governmental corruption was Boss Tweed in New York City. He gained control of the Democratic Party and absolute control of the city government. He and his ring stole as much as $200 million dollars by overcharging the treasury for goods and services (for example: $138,000 for two days work by a plasterer). He was brought down by

| Boss Tweed, with a Thomas Nast caricature of him

evidence published by the New York *Times* and by the anti-Tweed cartoons of Thomas Nast. (Both refused huge bribes not to publish). New York attorney Samuel Tilden led the prosecution team that finally put Tweed in jail in 1873.

Black Friday. James Fisk and Jay Gould were in the unsavory category of wealthy financial pirates. In 1869 they hatched a scheme to "corner the gold market," which would involve buying up gold and holding it until the price went sky high during a panic. Then they could sell the gold they had at an incredible profit. However, they had to make sure that the U.S. government would not sell its own supply of gold to stabilize the market once the panic began. They paid a large bribe to Grant's brother-in-law to convince the president to hold the government gold.

The pair tried their scheme on "Black Friday," September 24. The price of gold shot up, driving many businessmen to near ruin. However, Grant did not block the sale of government gold and the whole scheme collapsed. A congressional investigation did not implicate Grant, but the scandal did touch his family.

Crédit Mobilier. Another scandal hit the administration in 1872. Crédit Mobilier was a railroad construction company created by officers of the Union Pacific Railway. They used the company to build the transcontinental railroad, charging double the actual construction costs. The owners made sure Washington would not interfere by giving Crédit Mobilier stock to key congressmen and Grant's vice-president. When it was exposed by a newspaper, it reflected badly on the lack of control and honesty in the government. Pressure for reform began to mount.

Alabama Claims. During the Civil War, Britain had allowed ships to be built for the Confederacy in British shipyards. They were fitted with guns in other countries and were used to raid Union shipping throughout the war. The most notorious was the *Alabama*. The ship was built in Britain, armed in Portugal, and sailed by a British crew! It never entered a Confederate port, even though it flew a Confederate flag and captured over sixty Union merchant vessels. U.S. officials in Britain had been pressing the British government to pay for damages caused by that and other British/Confederate privateers.

The British government felt the pressure to settle the dispute, for their officials felt the claim was legitimate. Others feared a bad precedent if a revolt broke out in Ireland, and America supplied them with the same type of raiders. So in 1871, Britain and the U.S. signed the Treaty of Washington which submitted the entire dispute to an arbitration panel in Geneva, Switzerland. The arbitrators awarded the U.S. $15.5 million. The award restored good relations between the two nations.

Election of 1872. By 1872 the scandals of "Grantism" had created a large reform movement. Reformers in the Republican party refused to support Grant when it was clear he would run again. Instead, they formed the Liberal Republican Party and nominated Horace Greeley, the famous editor of the New York *Tribune*. Greeley was a bad choice due to his ragged appearance, lack of flexibility, and emotionalism. The Democrats, desperate for office, also supported the rabidly anti-Confederate Greeley.

After a vicious campaign, Grant won the election with a larger margin than in 1868. As with most third-party movements in U.S. history, the Liberal Republicans were absorbed into one of the larger parties once it took over their ideals. In this case, the Republicans sponsored tariff reform, amnesty for Confederate leaders, and a wave toward civil service reform, all of which stole the reformer's thunder.

| Horace Greeley, editor of the New York Tribune and Liberal Republican Presidential Candidate

Panic of 1873. Grant's second term had a hard shock when the nation went into a financial panic in 1873. The country had again overextended on credit. When purchases no longer kept up with what businesses needed to pay their debts, the economy crashed. It began with the bankruptcy of a large New York banking firm and quickly spread as thousands of other companies folded. It was the nation's longest depression to date, lasting six years.

The government of that day did not even consider using tax dollars to fix the economy. That was well understood to be the job of private businesses only. However, there was a vigorous debate over a correct monetary policy that would aid the economy. "Hard money" people wanted all money to be gold, silver, or paper notes backed by a certain amount of gold. "Soft" or "cheap money" advocates wanted paper money that circulated without a set value. The latter causes inflation and makes it easier for debtors to pay off their debts. It is known today that a hard money policy decreases the money supply and when begun during a depression it tends to make the depression worse.

Grant was a hard money man. He supported the Resumption Act of 1875 that promised to redeem all Civil War-issued paper money for its face value in gold. That decision worsened the depression and gave the Democrats control of the House of Representatives after the 1874 elections. It led to the creation of another third party called the Greenbacks who elected several members of Congress in 1878.

Further Scandals. Yet another scandal, the Whiskey Ring, surfaced in 1875. It was a system of payoffs designed to cheat the government out of money from the whiskey excise tax. Treasury agents took bribes to ignore untaxed whiskey. It was uncovered by a new secretary of the treasury and implicated several of President Grant's friends, including his personal secretary. Grant allowed the investigation at first, but began to interfere with it as it touched his friends. Eventually, the secretary was tried and Grant obtained his acquittal by sending the court a letter saying the president believed he was innocent.

William Belknap, Grant's secretary of war, was impeached in 1876 for taking bribes from men who received contracts to supply goods to the Native Americans. The supplier made a handsome profit by giving the Native Americans inferior goods while charging for quality ones. Belknap resigned, managing to avoid a conviction. The string of scandals severely damaged Grant's reputation.

Name these items, events, or people.

3.40 _____ policy that called for all money to be gold, silver, or paper notes backed by a certain amount of gold

3.41 _____ Democratic candidate in 1868

3.42 _____ Democrat who ran New York City, stealing millions

3.43 _____ company that constructed track for the Union Pacific, charging way over the costs and giving stock to congressmen

3.44 _____ law that promised to redeem all Civil War paper money for gold

3.45 _____ scheme to cheat the government out of excise tax income

3.46 _____ third party created by Grant's hard money policy

3.47 _____ treaty that submitted the *Alabama* dispute to arbitration

3.48 _____ plan to end rewarding political supporters with government jobs

3.49 _____ name given the day Fisk and Gould tried to corner the gold market

3.50 _____ third party that sought reform in 1872

3.51 _____ secretary of war, resigned over bribery scandal

3.52 _____ amount of money awarded to the U.S. for *Alabama* claims

3.53 _____ cartoonist who helped bring down Boss Tweed

Answer true or false.

3.54 _____ Ulysses S. Grant was a great president.

3.55 _____ "Waving the bloody shirt" was reminding the electorate of the war.

3.56 _____ Grant was dishonest.

3.57 _____ The Democratic Party absorbed the Liberal Republicans by taking their ideas.

3.58 _____ During his administration, Grant's brother-in-law, personal secretary, and secretary of war were implicated in bribery scandals.

3.59 _____ "Vote as you shot" was a Democratic slogan.

3.60 _____ Corruption was a major problem in government and business after the Civil War.

End of Reconstruction

Election of 1876. Grant, encouraged by his political leeches, seriously considered running for a third term. By large majority, the House of Representatives published a resolution opposing third terms as protection against dictators. Grant took the point, and the Republicans looked for another man.

The former president proved as inept in business after the war as he had been before it. He invested his savings in a banking company called Grant & Ward. Ward was dishonest, and Grant lost everything in 1884 when the company failed. He started writing articles about the Civil War in order to support his family, but shortly after that he developed throat cancer (he was a heavy cigar smoker). He wrote his memoirs as the disease slowly took his life. He died soon after it was completed, and the success of the book gave his family a very comfortable income. The Civil War was the one pure success of Ulysses S. Grant.

The Republicans almost nominated Maine congressman James Blaine, but evidence of a bribery scandal ended his chances. America was tired of corruption and wanted an honest candidate. The Republicans finally chose Rutherford B. Hayes, governor of Ohio and a Union war veteran. He had been an honest, competent governor and supported civil service reform. The Democrats chose Samuel Tilden, governor of New York and one of key men in smashing the Tweed Ring, to oppose Hayes. The Republicans again waved the bloody shirt while the Democrats condemned the years of scandal-ridden Republican rule.

Tilden won the popular vote by a small margin and clearly had 184 out of the 185 electoral votes needed to win the election. Hayes had 165 electoral votes. The remaining electoral votes were in dispute. The Republican and Democratic parties submitted different totals for four states: Oregon, Louisiana, Florida, and South Carolina. Hayes needed twenty of these to win, and the Republicans claimed that he had them. (There were grounds for the dispute. For example, in South Carolina there were more votes than registered voters, and the Ku Klux Klan was busy all over the South stopping Republican votes.)

The Republican Senate and the Democratic House fought over which had authority to settle the dispute. In the end, they set up a joint committee with seven Senate Republicans, seven House Democrats, and one independent, a member of the Supreme Court, to decide the issue. At the last minute, the only independent on the Court resigned, leaving only Republicans, which gave that party an 8 to 7 majority on the election committee. Not surprisingly, the committee gave all of the disputed votes to Hayes by an 8 to 7 vote. Democrats threatened to **filibuster** the acceptance of the results, and some were talking about taking up arms. By now it was February, and the new president was supposed to take office on March 4th.

Compromise of 1877. Eventually, the two sides worked out a compromise. The Democrats agreed to accept the election of Hayes in exchange for the end of Reconstruction. Hayes also promised, but did not deliver, subsidies for a transcontinental railroad in the South. As a result of the Compromise of 1877, Hayes was named the president-elect just three days before inauguration. The deal kept the peace, but gave Southern white people complete control of their states without further fear of federal intervention.

Rutherford B. Hayes (1822-1893). Rutherford B. Hayes entered the White House with much of the nation doubting he had won the election. Hayes had been born **posthumously** to a prosperous store owner in Ohio. His uncle became his guardian and saw that he had a good private school education. He graduated from Harvard in 1842 and took up the practice of law in Ohio. He served as an officer in the

Civil War, reaching the temporary rank of major general. He was elected to the U.S. House while still in combat. (He refused to leave his post to campaign, but won anyway.) He also served three terms as governor of Ohio before he was chosen as president. His was the most questionable election in U.S. history.

Hayes removed the last Union troops from occupation duty shorty after taking office in 1877. This was the official end of Reconstruction. Hayes pushed for civil service reform, but the spoils-minded Congress refused to pass it. Hayes himself appointed men based on ability, not party loyalty, which earned the wrath of the Republicans. Hayes supported hard money policies that did not help the depression, but did build confidence in the security of the American monetary system.

Hayes' wife, Lucy Webb Hayes, had a college degree. She was the first among the nation's First Ladies to have one. She was active in many social causes, including abolition and temperance. She earned the nickname "Lemonade Lucy" because she banned alcoholic beverages from the White House. She and her husband introduced the custom of an annual Easter egg roll for children on the White House lawn.

Conclusion. The Civil War settled two issues: slavery and secession. Other positive results were more elusive. Black people were free, guaranteed citizenship and the right to vote by constitutional amendments, but those rights were flagrantly violated. However, those amendments were on the books and would be effectively resurrected years later. The South remained a hostile place for black people, Republicans, and Northerners for many years. After winning the war, the North lacked the will or political skill to reintegrate the nation on friendly terms. Given the nature of a civil war, perhaps that was impossible.

| Rutherford B. Hayes

The Union was actually lenient to the Confederacy. No Confederate leaders were ever tried for treason. Jefferson Davis was kept in custody for two years and then released. Robert E. Lee was allowed to return home unmolested and became the president of Washington College, later named Washington and Lee. The South was fully represented in Congress by 1870, and the original privileged class was back in power by 1877. Considering that they led an armed rebellion against the government, this was an amazing show of tolerance. Awful as it was, the Civil War barely interrupted the American tradition of growth, expansion, and democracy.

Answer these questions.

3.61 What was the heart of the controversy in the 1876 election?

_____

_____

3.62 How did Hayes fight the spoils system?

_____

_____

3.63 What two issues did the Civil War settle?

_____

3.64 What were the terms of the Compromise of 1877?

_____

_____

_____

3.65 What was the official end of Reconstruction?

_____

3.66 Why was Hayes awarded all the disputed votes in the election of 1876?

_____

_____

3.67 What were some of the unusual things about First Lady Lucy Hayes?

_____

_____

3.68 Who was the Democratic candidate in 1876, and what were his qualifications?

_____

_____

3.69 How many Confederate leaders were tried for treason?

_____

3.70 What were Hayes' qualifications for president?

_____

_____

Before you take this last Self Test, you may want to do one or more of these self checks.

1. _____ Read the objectives. See if you can do them.
2. _____ Restudy the material related to any objectives that you cannot do.
3. _____ Use the **SQ3R** study procedure to review the material:
   a. **S**can the sections.
   b. **Q**uestion yourself.
   c. **R**ead to answer your questions.
   d. **R**ecite the answers to yourself.
   e. **R**eview areas you did not understand.
4. _____ Review all vocabulary, activities, and Self Tests, writing a correct answer for every wrong answer.

SELF TEST 3

Name the event, item, person, or battle (each answer, 4 points).

3.01 _____ first U.S. president in history to be impeached

3.02 _____ "Seward's Folly"

3.03 _____ Amendment that ended slavery

3.04 _____ Democratic hoodlum who ran New York City after the Civil War

3.05 _____ Grant-era scandal; railroad construction scam that gave stock to several government representatives

3.06 _____ Amendment that gave black Americans the right to vote

3.07 _____ Reconstruction under Congressional control

3.08 _____ post-Civil War laws to subjugate black people in the South

3.09 _____ Presidential document that ended slavery in the South

3.010 _____ Amendment that made black Americans citizens

3.011 _____ Hayes was awarded the election in exchange for removing the last troops from the South

3.012 _____ first state to secede from the Union

3.013 _____ Union victory that placed the whole Mississippi under their control

3.014 _____ Northern men who came to power in the South during Reconstruction

3.015 _____ began the Civil War

Choose the person who best fits the description (each answer, 2 points).

Abraham Lincoln	Ulysses S. Grant	Robert E. Lee
Rutherford B. Hayes	Thaddeus Stevens	Stonewall Jackson
Stephen Douglas	Dred Scott	Jefferson Davis
John Brown		

3.016 _____ little education; Illinois attorney; flexible; good organizer

3.017 _____ an enslaved man who asked the Supreme Court to set him free after living in the North

3.018 _____ had trouble maintaining authority over the independent-minded Confederacy; imprisoned for two years after the war

3.019 _____ brilliant general; followed his state not his nation; college president

3.020 _____ Radical Republican leader

3.021 _____ opposed Lecompton Constitution; Northern Democratic candidate for president (1860); supported popular sovereignty

3.022 _____ violent; possibly insane; became a popular abolitionist martyr

3.023 _____ good general; honest; corrupt administration; Whiskey Ring

3.024 _____ Southern; Christian general; killed by his own men

3.025 _____ Union officer; governor of Ohio; opposed the spoils system; most controversial presidential election in history

Answer true or false (each answer, 1 point).

3.026 _____ Lincoln supported harsh measures against the South after the war.

3.027 _____ Andrew Johnson was the only Southern senator who did not secede with his state.

3.028 _____ Alaska was purchased from Russia for $7.2 million by Secretary of State William Seward.

3.029 _____ The Ku Klux Klan was very ineffective after the Civil War.

3.030 _____ Scalawags were army deserters during the Civil War.

3.031 _____ Republicans after the war often campaigned by "waving the bloody shirt."

3.032 _____ George McClellan was an excellent organizer, but so over-cautious that he proved to be a poor general.

3.033 _____ Grant was not thrown out of the army after Shiloh because Lincoln would not fire a general who was willing to fight.

3.034 _____ Abolitionist Senator Charles Sumner was beaten in the Senate for an anti-Southern speech.

3.035 _____ The Kansas-Nebraska Act brought the nation closer to war.

3.036 _____ The battle of the *Merrimac* and the *Monitor* was the first in history between ironclad vessels.

3.037 _____ Fredericksburg, Chickamauga, and New Orleans were all taken by the Union after a long siege.

3.038 _____ Copperheads were Northern Democrats who opposed the war.

3.039 _____ The re-election of Lincoln in 1864 ended the last Confederate hope of a negotiated peace that would leave them independent.

3.040 _____ The Civil War effectively ended at Appomattox Court House when Lee's army surrendered.

3.041 _____ The Confederate government was formed before Lincoln was inaugurated.

3.042 _____ The *Alabama* was a British-built ship with a British crew that sailed under a Confederate flag and captured Union ships.

3.043 _____ Fisk and Gould tried to corner the oil market on black Thursday.

3.044 _____ Corruption was a major problem in government and industry after the Civil War.

3.045 _____ The assassination of Lincoln made matters worse for the South.

80 / 100   SCORE _____   TEACHER _____ _____
initials   date

Before taking the LIFEPAC Test, you may want to do one or more of these self checks.

1. _____ Read the objectives. See if you can do them.
2. _____ Restudy the material related to any objectives that you cannot do.
3. _____ Use the **SQ3R** study procedure to review the material.
4. _____ Review activities, Self Tests, and LIFEPAC vocabulary words.
5. _____ Restudy areas of weakness indicated by the last Self Test.

NOTES

HISTORY & GEOGRAPHY 805
A Growing Nation (1820–1855)

LIFEPAC Test is located in the center of the booklet. Please remove before starting the unit.

Author:
Theresa Buskey, B.A., J.D.

Editor:
Alan Christopherson, M.S.

Westover Studios Design Team:
Phillip Pettet, Creative Lead
Teresa Davis, DTP Lead
Nick Castro
Andi Graham
Jerry Wingo

Alpha Omega
PUBLICATIONS

804 N. 2nd Ave. E.
Rock Rapids, IA 51246-1759

A Growing Nation (1820–1855)

Introduction

1820 to 1855 were turbulent years in American history. Ten different presidents served during those thirty-five years. Only five had served in the first thirty years of the nation. All of the first five presidents except one, John Adams, had served two terms in office. Of the next ten, only one, Andrew Jackson, succeeded in obtaining a second term. The upheaval in the presidency was simply a reflection of the upheaval in the nation.

This was an era of new political parties, expansion, and the rise of sectionalism. The long-ruling Democratic-Republicans fell victim to their own success as they split into factions. Two of these emerged as opposing political parties, the Democrats and the Whigs. The two alternated in control of the government throughout this time period. By 1855, the issue that would not go away, slavery, produced yet another party, the Republicans.

The nation continued to grow at an alarming rate during these years. American immigrants in Spanish/Mexican Texas took over that land and eventually brought it into the Union. A war with Mexico added all of the Southwest and California. Settlements were reached with Britain over Maine and Oregon. A small piece of Mexican land was purchased in 1853 as a railroad route across Arizona and New Mexico. By 1855, all of the land that would create the contiguous 48 states was under U.S. control. Nine new states were added to the nation between 1820 and 1855 as their population grew to reach the required minimum. The natural problems caused by such rapid growth were part of the upheaval of the era.

Slavery and North-South differences were major issues from 1820 to 1855. The country was, at first, divided into three sections: North, South, and West. As the West matured, it joined either the North or South on the slavery issue. Prior to that two-way division, each section had its own agenda and its own representative giant in Washington. Henry Clay from the West, John Calhoun from the South, and Daniel Webster from the North were renowned in their own time for their oratory and their leadership. These men would provide much of the statesmanship that would keep the nation together until after they had died.

Objectives

Read these objectives. The objectives tell you what you will be able to do when you have successfully completed this LIFEPAC. When you have finished this LIFEPAC, you should be able to:

1. Name the leaders of the era and explain their accomplishments.

2. Describe the presidency of Andrew Jackson and its effect on America.

3. Trace the development of the slavery and tariff issues from 1820 to 1855.

4. Define Manifest Destiny and describe its course in America.

5. Describe the course of the Texas Revolution and Mexican War.

6. Define the Industrial Revolution and name the people, innovations, and inventions that contributed to it.

7. Describe the effects of the Industrial Revolution in America.

8. Describe the Second Great Awakening and the reform movements that followed it.

9. Describe the compromises that kept the nation together and what ended them.

10. Describe the changes in America and American life in this era.

Survey the LIFEPAC. Ask yourself some questions about this study and write your questions here.

_____

_____

_____

_____

_____

_____

_____

_____

_____

_____

_____

_____

_____

_____

_____

_____

_____

1. JACKSONIAN ERA

Andrew Jackson's election as president was, like Jefferson's before him, a step in the expansion of democracy in America. The right to vote had been expanding as more and more states dropped property requirements for voters. Jackson, therefore, was elected by the votes of ordinary working people, not the land-owning aristocrats who dominated the voting population a few years before that. His election was a turning point in our history. He was the people's president.

Andrew Jackson was also a man who would shape the government in his own fashion. He had strong opinions and the will, popular support, and party machinery to force them through. He believed he had the support of the people and saw no reason to compromise with Congress or the Supreme Court. His enemies called him "King Andrew I" with good reason. He did exactly what he wanted and changed the face of American government and politics forever.

SECTION OBJECTIVES

Review these objectives. When you have completed this section, you should be able to:

1. Name the leaders of the era and explain their accomplishments.
2. Describe the presidency of Andrew Jackson and its effect on America.
3. Trace the development of the slavery and tariff issues from 1820 to 1855.
9. Describe the compromises that kept the nation together and what ended them.
10. Describe the changes in America and American life in this era.

VOCABULARY

Study these words to enhance your learning success in this section.

abolitionist (ab ō lish' un ist). Person seeking to abolish (end) something, especially slavery.

caucus (kaw' kus). A closed meeting of a group of persons from the same political party to choose a candidate or decide on policy.

censure (sen' chur). An official reprimand.

duel (doo' ul). A formal combat with weapons fought between two persons in the presence of witnesses.

mandate (man' dāt). An authorization to act given to a representative.

nullification (nul i fi kā' shun). The action of a state attempting to prevent the enforcement within its territory of a law of the United States.

Note: *All vocabulary words in this LIFEPAC appear in* **boldface** *print the first time they are used. If you are not sure of the meaning when you are reading, study the definitions given.*

Pronunciation Key: hat, āge, cãre, fär; let, ēqual, tėrm; it, īce; hot, ōpen, ôrder; oil; out; cup, pu̇t, rüle; child; long; thin; /₮H/ for then; /zh/ for measure; /u/ or /ə/ represents /a/ in about, /e/ in taken, /i/ in pencil, /o/ in lemon, and /u/ in circus.

AMERICA from 1820 to 1855

James Monroe
1817–1825
Democratic-Republican

John Quincy Adams
1825-1829
Democratic-Republican

Andrew Jackson
1829-1837
Democratic

Martin Van Buren
1837-1841
Democratic

William H. Harrison*
1841
Whig

John Tyler
1841-1845
Whig

James K. Polk
1845-1849
Democratic

Zachary Taylor*
1849-1850
Whig

Millard Fillmore
1850-1853
Whig

Franklin Pierce
1853-1857
Democratic

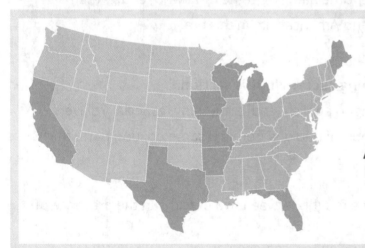

STATES ADMITTED TO THE UNION

Maine	1820		
Missouri	1821	**Texas**	1845
Arkansas	1836	**Iowa**	1846
Michigan	1837	**Wisconsin**	1848
Florida	1845	**California**	1850

POPULATION of the United States of America

1850	23,191,876
1820	9,638,453
1790	3,929,000

*died while in office

Setting the Times

Giants in Washington. By the beginning of the War of 1812, three men who would be among the most prominent of their era had begun careers in Washington. Henry Clay of Kentucky became a member of the House of Representatives in 1811. He was joined that same year by John Calhoun of South Carolina. They were leaders of the War Hawks who pushed for the war with Britain. Two years later, Daniel Webster of Massachusetts joined the House. These men would serve in Washington in the House, Senate, President's Cabinet, and even the vice presidency until the early 1850s. None of them ever became president, although they all tried. However, no discussion of this era would be complete without an understanding of these men and their influence.

Henry Clay was born in Virginia but moved to Kentucky as a young man to practice law. Clay was a notable speaker and an ambitious, natural leader. He was elected to the House of Representatives, where he often served as the Speaker, and the Senate. He also served one term as secretary of state and ran unsuccessfully for president several times, usually as a Whig. Clay was called the Great Compromiser for his ability to wrangle agreements and resolve crises in the difficult years leading up to the Civil War. He exercised tremendous influence in Congress. He used it to promote programs and compromises to benefit the whole nation. Clay was an ardent nationalist who earned the title of statesman for his work on behalf of the American people.

John Calhoun was born in South Carolina and practiced law there until a wealthy marriage enabled him to concentrate on politics. His federal employment included the House of Representatives, Senate, secretary of war, secretary of state, and vice president. In many ways he reflects the splitting up of the nation that occurred between the Era of Good Feelings and the Civil War. He began his career as a strong Jeffersonian Democratic nationalist.

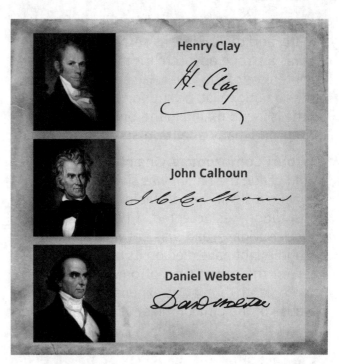

| Henry Clay, John Calhoun, and Daniel Webster, with their Respective Autographs

He favored a strong federal government and supported Clay's American System to benefit the entire nation. However, as time went on he began to focus more and more on the narrow needs of his own state and region. He opposed the tariffs that protected the northern manufacturers, and became very defensive of the South's "peculiar institution," slavery. In the end, Calhoun became the leading proponent of the doctrine of **nullification** and states' rights. Ironically, he believed this was a way to save the Union by protecting the South. His philosophies became the basis for the Confederacy.

Daniel Webster was born in New Hampshire but moved to Massachusetts as a young man to practice law. He gained tremendous fame as an orator and was one of the best paid attorneys in the nation. He argued and won several key cases before the Supreme Court, including *McCulloch v. Maryland* (states cannot tax the national bank) and *Gibbons v. Ogden* (federal government controls interstate commerce).

He served in the House of Representatives, the Senate, and the cabinet as secretary of state. He was a strong advocate for the manufacturing interests of the North. He opposed slavery, but as a nationalist, he supported compromises on the issue to maintain the Union, something that turned many **abolitionists** against him.

Missouri Compromise. One of the issues that would divide the nation was slavery. It had not been a significant problem when the new Constitution was accepted in 1789. Slavery, although widespread, was not very profitable and might have died on its own had it not been for the cotton gin. Cotton was a popular fiber for cloth, but it was expensive to produce because of the difficulty in separating the fiber

from the seeds. In 1793 Eli Whitney invented the cotton gin to help his southern friends. It provided a simple and easy way to separate cotton fiber from the seeds. With the machine, one person could now separate the same amount of cotton that 50 people used to do by hand. Suddenly, cotton production became very profitable.

In the years after 1793, the South concentrated on growing cotton. It purchased its manufactured goods from the North or Europe and its food from the West. Thus, it became completely dependent on cotton for its prosperity. Labor-intensive cotton production, it was believed, depended upon slavery. The institution of slavery, which had been in decline,

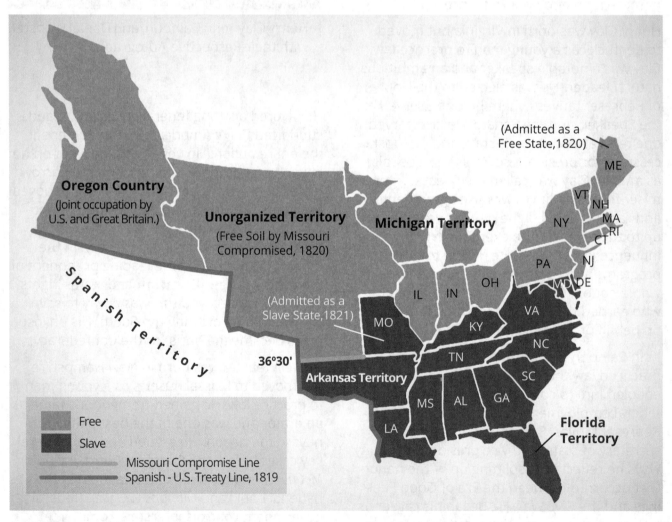

| The Missouri Compromise

rebounded. The South quickly became protective of slavery as the key to their region's wealth and cast a cautious eye to the North and those who opposed it.

The population of the northern states continued to grow in the early 1800s as manufacturing cities provided jobs for more and more people. The South, on the other hand, was stagnant in population. Thus, the North began to significantly outnumber the South in the House of Representatives. However, the slave-holding states were able to protect their interests by controlling half of the Senate. In 1819 the count was 11 slave and 11 free states. That year Missouri asked to be admitted as a slave-holding state.

The North-dominated House of Representatives voted to gradually end slavery in Missouri before admitting it. The South clearly saw the threat. If slavery could not expand with the nation, the slave-holding states would be gradually overwhelmed by the admission of more and more free states. A deadlock occurred that was finally broken by Henry Clay, who led the compromise effort. The result was the Missouri Compromise of 1820. Under its terms, Missouri was admitted as a slave state and Maine, now finally separated from Massachusetts, was admitted as a free state, thereby maintaining the Senate balance. Moreover, slavery was prohibited in all states created in the Louisiana Purchase north of 36° 30' latitude, the southern boundary of Missouri.

The compromise did not solve the slavery issue; it simply kept the political balance between the pro-slave and anti-slave forces. Both sides knew how touchy this issue was and that it might divide the nation. The Missouri Compromise swept the issue of slavery aside for another thirty-five years for the sake of the Union. The North and West continued to grow in size and strength during that time while the moral opposition to slavery also grew. In the end, the issue would have to be faced squarely, but not until the North was stronger.

Tariff Issue. The secondary issue of the South was the tariff. Tariffs raised the price of manufactured goods brought in from abroad. This protected American manufacturers by cutting off cheaper foreign goods. The South, however, had very little manufacturing. All tariffs did was raise the prices they had to pay for things like shoes, farm equipment, and luxury goods. Thus, the tariff became the hot- button issue of the 1820s to 1850s while both sides were avoiding the slavery problem.

Match these people (answers will be used more than once).

1.1	_____ lawyer from Massachusetts	a.	Henry Clay
1.2	_____ served as secretary of state	b.	John Calhoun
1.3	_____ served as vice president	c.	Eli Whitney
1.4	_____ invented the cotton gin	d.	Daniel Webster
1.5	_____ senator from Kentucky		
1.6	_____ Speaker of the House		
1.7	_____ argued _McCulloch v. Maryland_		
1.8	_____ supported states' rights		
1.9	_____ nationalist to the end		
1.10	_____ ran for president as a Whig		
1.11	_____ one of America's highest-paid lawyers		
1.12	_____ made cotton production profitable		
1.13	_____ strong advocate of manufacturing interests		
1.14	_____ Great Compromiser		
1.15	_____ senator from South Carolina		

Answer these questions.

1.16 What were the two issues related to the South?

a. _____

b. _____

1.17 What were the terms of the Missouri Compromise?

a. _____

b. _____

c. _____

1.18 What made cotton and slavery suddenly so profitable in the South?

_____

Election of 1824. The Democratic-Republican party was still the only viable party in 1824, but the unity shown in the unopposed election of James Monroe in 1820 was gone. The tides of change were moving against the stable political powers of Jefferson's party. The first sign was the growing opposition to the nominating procedure. Democratic-Republicans chose their candidate for the presidency in a secret congressional **caucus**. Since there was only one party, the nomination gave the man the office. This process of establishing "King Caucus" was widely denounced in 1824. In fact, the opposition hurt William Crawford who was the official nominee of the caucus that year.

Instead of the united support given to Monroe, the Democratic-Republicans were split four ways in 1824. John Quincy Adams, son of President John Adams, was the candidate of the North. Andrew Jackson and Henry Clay were both candidates from the West. William Crawford was the Southern candidate. Clay and Adams were men of experience with a wide range of government background. Andrew Jackson, the hero of the Battle of New Orleans, had immense popularity all over the country, even if he had fewer qualifications for the job.

Jackson received the largest part of the popular vote (42%), followed by Adams (32%), Crawford (13%), and Clay (13%), whose support in the West had been taken by the popular general. The electoral vote, however, did not give Jackson the majority he needed to become the next president. Under the Constitution, the election had to be decided by the House of Representatives.

Only the top three candidates in the electoral vote could be considered by the House. That left out Clay who had received the lowest count in that crucial vote. Clay, however, was the popular Speaker of the House of Representatives and was in position to influence the outcome of the election. Crawford had suffered a stroke and was unfit to take office, so he was never a factor in the House election. Clay and Jackson had a personal feud that dated back to Jackson's invasion of Florida in the Seminole conflict after the War of 1812. Clay had denounced Jackson in the House for his actions and made himself a bitter enemy. Clay, therefore, chose to support Adams.

John Quincy Adams was elected president by the House on the very first vote because of the influence of Henry Clay. Adams immediately offered Clay the position of secretary of state. This was a prize political plum because it was the office that had launched many of the presidents. Clay unwisely accepted and sealed his own political coffin.

Jackson and his supporters screamed that a deal had been cut trading the presidency to Adams in exchange for the Secretary's position for Clay. It is unlikely that Clay and Adams made an "official" deal for the office. However, the prompt repayment of Adams' political debt to Clay looked corrupt. Jackson and his allies had a ready-made issue for the 1828 election in the "corrupt bargain" between Adams and Clay. Moreover, Jackson was furious that the "will of the people" had been thwarted in such a fashion, and an angry Andrew Jackson was a dangerous opponent.

After the election, the Democratic-Republican Party split. The supporters of Jackson became known as the Democrats, the same party that still exists under that name. The supporters of Adams called themselves the National Republicans and later took the name Whigs, a patriotic name from the Revolutionary War. Andrew Jackson and his Democrats spent the entire four years between the presidential elections building the support they needed to crush Adams and Clay.

John Quincy Adams. John Quincy Adams (1767-1848) was arguably one of the most qualified men ever to assume the presidency. He was extremely honest and hard working. He had seen much of the world traveling with his father as a boy. He was well educated and had written political papers during the early years of the nation. He served his country as a diplomat in Prussia, the Netherlands, Great Britain and Russia. He led the American delegation at Ghent at the end of the War of 1812. He served as a senator from Massachusetts. He also proved to be a highly successful secretary of state under James Monroe. In that position, he created the Monroe Doctrine and negotiated the purchase of Florida from Spain. He also obtained an agreement with Britain for the joint occupation of Oregon and brushed off a Russian attempt to lay claim to the same area.

Adams, however, was not a popular or even very likable man. He had a cold personality, like his father. He had gained his position by ability, not by winning friends and influencing people. He was too honest to make use of public offices to gain support, refusing to throw out hard-working government employees to reward his own people. The "corrupt bargain" also hurt his popular support. His plans for the country were hampered on every turn by his lack of popularity and the violent opposition of the Democrats. His term as president was, therefore, the least notable part of a long and distinguished government career.

In his first address to Congress, Adams proposed an ambitious slate of national improvements including roads, canals, a national university, and an observatory. Americans fighting for survival on the frontier found these intellectual proposals ridiculous! The proposals flew in the face of the rising mood of sectionalism and states' rights. The West and the South in particular had no interest in paying high tariffs for such things. Adam's domestic agenda went nowhere, beat back at every turn by the Democrats. He further alienated the West by trying to control the wild speculation on land and by aiding the Cherokee, who were being evicted from their land by the state of Georgia.

Adams also failed to accomplish anything in foreign affairs, which should have been his best field. Britain's foreign minister, still upset

BORN TO COMMAND.

OF VETO MEMORY.

HAD I BEEN CONSULTED.

KING ANDREW THE FIRST.

| "King" Andrew Jackson

over the independent American action with the Monroe Doctrine, refused to discuss removing restrictions on American trade with the British West Indies. Adams and Clay also wanted America to participate in the Panama Congress of 1826, a meeting of the American republics to discuss mutual problems and goals. The Senate took so long to confirm the delegates that the one who survived the trip arrived after the meeting had ended. The incident was an acute embarrassment to Adams.

Tariff of Abominations. Jackson's supporters came up with an unusual way to embarrass Adams during the election year of 1828. They proposed an incredibly high tariff, as high as 45% on some items. Included with it was a tariff on raw materials like wool. The Democrats assumed that New England would be unwilling to accept the tariff on the raw materials they needed for their factories. The tariff bill would therefore fail and cause further problems for Adams in the tariff-hungry North.

The Jacksonians had not counted on just how tariff hungry the North was, however. The tariff passed by a narrow margin and was signed by Adams. The states of the South, particularly the older ones, were furious and called it the "Tariff of Abominations." The old South was the section most affected by the bill because it was the least productive area of the nation. Cotton farming exhausted the soil, and the older farms of the southeastern seaboard were in decline. The rest of the nation did not feel the effects as badly because they were growing and expanding. Thus, the higher prices on goods fell heaviest in the Southern states that had a long tradition of political activism.

The Election of 1828. The election of 1828 brought in a new low in mud-slinging. The need to appeal to the less educated voters brought out a type of campaigning that avoided, rather than stressed, the issues. Adams was accused of purchasing gambling equipment for the White House. (He had bought a billiard table with his own money). He was also accused of drawing excessive salaries during his many government jobs and helping a Russian nobleman get his hands on a pretty servant girl while serving as minister in that nation.

Adams did not engage in any of the wild personal attacks, but his supporters did. Jackson's many **duels** and quarrels were paraded out with embellishments. His mother was accused of being a prostitute. The most serious and painful allegations were charges of adultery and bigamy against Jackson and his wife. According to the official story, Andrew Jackson had unknowingly married his wife, Rachel, before her divorce from her first husband was final. The couple remarried when they found out the divorce had actually been granted almost two years after their first marriage ceremony. The entire episode was very humiliating

for Mrs. Jackson, and her husband was furious when it was dragged into the campaign.

The heart of Jackson's campaign was an attack on the "corruption" in Washington, the clearest example being the "corrupt bargain" between Clay and Adams that had given the latter the presidency in 1824. "Jackson and Reform" was the main slogan of the Democrats. Honest, hard-working John Quincy Adams was successfully portrayed in the public mind as the dishonest leader of a gang of corrupt politicians.

Andrew Jackson won both the popular and the electoral vote. He had 178 electoral votes to Adam's 83. Thus, America elected its first president who was not from the old American aristocracy. Jackson was wealthy, but he was a self-made man, a man of the people. The election is sometimes called a revolution because it was the end of the elite that had so effectively run the nation since the Revolutionary War. The power of the vote had reached the masses of the American people, and they chose a man like themselves to run their country.

Adams' Glorious Sunset. John Quincy Adams was not a man to retire into obscurity. He was elected to the House of Representatives and served there with distinction for seventeen years. He earned the affectionate nickname "Old Man Eloquent" for his determination in debates. His greatest achievement was his opposition to the *Gag Rule*. It was a series of resolutions pushed through by the South in 1836 that prevented any petition on slavery from being heard by the House. Adams believed it was an unconstitutional attack on the right to petition. He fought it consistently, trying repeatedly to introduce such petitions until the rule was abolished in 1844. John Quincy Adams collapsed at his desk in the House in February 1848 and, too weak to be removed, died in the Speaker's room two days later.

Check the items that were true of John Quincy Adams.

1.19 ☐ won the election of 1828

1.20 ☐ served as vice president

1.21 ☐ was second in the popular vote in 1824 and 1828

1.22 ☐ was accused of a "corrupt bargain" with William Crawford

1.23 ☐ was capable but not popular

1.24 ☐ won the support of the caucus in 1824

1.25 ☐ served in the House of Representatives after being president

1.26 ☐ wanted to spend government money on national improvements

1.27 ☐ was elected president as a Democratic-Republican

1.28 ☐ was successful in foreign but not domestic affairs as president

1.29 ☐ won the presidency because of Henry Clay

1.30 ☐ was one of three major candidates in 1824

1.31 ☐ led the Panama Congress of 1826

1.32 ☐ was very successful as secretary of state

Answer these questions.

1.33 What was the slogan for Jackson's campaign in 1828?

_____

1.34 What was the tariff of 1828 called?

_____

1.35 Who won the popular vote in 1824?

_____

1.36 What was John Quincy Adams' nickname in the House of Representatives?

_____

1.37 What was the Gag Rule?

_____

_____

1.38 Which of the major candidates was barred from the House election in 1824?

_____

1.39 What were the most serious personal attacks on Jackson in the 1828 campaign?

_____

Jackson's First Administration

Andrew Jackson. Andrew Jackson (1767-1845) was one of the most colorful and probably the most violent tempered president our country has ever had. He was born to poor Scotch-Irish immigrants in Carolina in a log cabin. His father died days before he was born. He grew up very wild and mischievous with a limited education. He joined the militia during the Revolution at the age of thirteen. His two brothers and his mother died during that time. Jackson himself was captured and slashed with a sword across the hand and face for refusing to clean a British officer's boots.

Jackson wasted an inheritance from his grand-father in Ireland and eventually took up the practice of law in Tennessee. His fierce atti-tude and determination in law brought him a measure of success. He made more money by speculating in land and eventually acquired a large plantation named "The Hermitage" near Nashville. He also earned a reputation as a dan-gerous enemy, fighting constantly over slights to his "honor." Two of his duels left him with bullets in his body for years afterward.

Jackson was a popular man who became well-connected with one of two political cliques that dominated Tennessee. He served without distinction in the House of Representatives and the Senate from 1796 to 1798. He returned to Tennessee and served as a justice of the state's supreme court. His greatest fame was won as the elected general of the state militia in the war with the Creek People and as commander of the U.S. army in the Battle of New Orleans. It was as a militia leader that he won his nick-name "Old Hickory" for his toughness.

Old Hickory was wildly popular with the com-mon people of America, especially in the West. He was no eastern aristocrat but a man who, like many on the frontier, had made it on his own in spite of fierce obstacles. He took with him into the White House many of the prej-udices of the West, including a hatred of the Native Americans, a distrust of banks, and a determination to expand the nation. He had little respect for the compromise and debate of the democratic process. In fact, he was more comfortable with the command of a general than the leadership of a president. He took the presidency to new heights as he insisted on using the power of the office as he saw fit. He changed the office and the nation.

Inauguration. The extent of the change in Washington could be seen by Jackson's inaugu-ration. It was a wild affair. The president-elect walked to the Capitol to take the oath of office and then to the White House for a reception. All along the route he shook hands and greeted the throngs of people in attendance. The White House reception was thrown open to everyone who wanted to attend. Hundreds of people mobbed the place. They stood on the furniture to get a look at the president. China and glass were broken. Curtains and upholstery ripped. The crush got so heavy that Jackson had to leave to avoid injury! The situation was finally relieved when the staff wisely began serving spiked punch on the lawn. The crowd quickly abandoned the house. One well-heeled Wash-ington resident said it was the rule of "King Mob."

| Crowds at Jackson's Inauguration

Spoils System. Andrew Jackson brought the spoils system to the national government on a large scale. The spoils system was based on the concept, "To the victors go the spoils of the enemy." In this case, it was jobs in the government. Jackson firmly believed in rotation in office, and that in a democracy government jobs should not be held for life. He also believed that he needed to change out the "corrupt" officeholders from the Adams' administration. What he wound up doing was initiating the replacement of government employees with people whose primary qualification was their loyalty to the Democratic cause. In all, he replaced less than 10% of the people on the government payroll, but the damage was done. For many years after that, government jobs were given to party loyalists. The quality and honesty of government service suffered accordingly.

Eaton Scandal. Andrew Jackson's mediocre Cabinet was quickly bogged down in a scandal over the wife of Secretary of War John Eaton. Eaton had married the pretty daughter of a tavern keeper who had a very poor moral reputation. The wives of the other members of the administration refused to socialize with her. "Old Hickory" was very taken with Peggy Eaton and believed she was the victim of baseless gossip. He also remembered the gossip about his own beloved wife who had died shortly after he was elected, and he unwisely became a public champion for Mrs. Eaton. Jackson tried unsuccessfully to force Washington society to accept Peggy Eaton. Led by the well-born wife of Vice President John Calhoun, the ladies refused. Even Jackson's niece, who was his official hostess, left rather than entertain Mrs. Eaton in the White House.

The cabinet's limited ability suffered in the discord. Jackson eventually began seeking advice on policy from an informal group of advisors and friends, called the "kitchen cabinet" by his opponents. Secretary of State Martin Van Buren took advantage of the situation to ingratiate

| Andrew Jackson

himself with the president. As a widower, Van Buren socialized freely with Mrs. Eaton and won the president's favor by doing so. As the discord in the cabinet grew worse, Van Buren resigned, knowing that would pressure the other secretaries to do the same. They did so, relieving Jackson of a difficult situation by removing the Eatons from the Washington elite. Van Buren was rewarded with the vice presidency during Jackson's second term.

Webster-Hayne Debate. The long-standing debate over the power of the states versus the power of the federal government was a key part of the conflict of the early 1800s. Early in 1830 the question was raised in the Senate and resulted in a spectacular debate between Robert Hayne of South Carolina and Daniel Webster of Massachusetts. The Webster-Hayne Debate was a memorable part of the long North-South conflict that preceded the Civil War.

The debate began over the unlikely topic of a resolution by the New England states to restrict the sale of land in the West. Hayne used the occasion to attack the northeast and the Tariff of Abominations. He publicly argued in favor of the doctrine of nullification. This doctrine taught that any state could nullify a law of the United States that was contrary to the Constitution as they understood it. Nullification had been espoused by no lesser person than Vice President Calhoun in a 1828 document called the "South Carolina Exposition." Hayne saw it as a way to protect his region from domination by the rest of the Union.

The gallery of the Senate was full as people came to listen to Webster's reply. He used all of his great skill to speak in favor of the Union and federal power to force obedience from the states. He argued that if the states were free to go their own way at will, then the country was united only by a "rope of sand." He attacked nullification as a danger to the nation. Webster's arguments were summarized in his stirring statement, "Liberty and Union, now and forever, one and inseparable." Webster's speech was printed and widely read, making him a hero among those who favored a strong Union.

Split with Calhoun. No one was certain where Jackson stood on the issue of states' rights. He consistently opposed internal improvements within any one state and sought to keep federal taxes and expenses low—basic pro-state positions. He was also a slave-owning plantation farmer, but he had not made any clear statements one way or the other. The states' rights supporters, led by Calhoun, hoped to gain his public support for their favorite cause. They chose a party celebrating Thomas Jefferson's birthday as the ideal occasion. A whole series of toasts were offered celebrating the Jeffersonian ideals of the sovereignty of the states. Jackson, however, had been warned of what would happen and had carefully prepared his own toast. When his turn came he spoke the words, "Our Union: It must be preserved!" A shaken Calhoun tried to salvage the evening with the answer, "The Union, next to our liberty, most dear!" However, the damage was done. Jackson had declared himself as a Union man.

Vice President John Calhoun was hoping to be Andrew Jackson's successor. As a potential future president, Calhoun hid his personal views and publicly supported the Union. He had deliberately not attached his name to the "South Carolina Exposition" on nullification. However, his presidential hopes were dashed when he and Jackson split over the Peggy Eaton scandal as well as personal and policy differences. Calhoun retired from the vice presidency near the end of his term and returned to the Senate as the leader of those who espoused nullification and the power of the states.

The National Bank. Andrew Jackson had a passionate distrust of the National Bank, which he called the "moneyed monster." The director, Nicholas Biddle, did little to help the situation by his "loans" and payments to prominent congressmen, including Daniel Webster. Jackson believed the bank was a danger to the nation. He shared the Western distrust of powerful financial institutions that foreclosed on farm mortgages. He did not understand national finances or the way the bank helped the West by its sound money policy.

Henry Clay, who was likely to be the National Republican presidential candidate, saw the bank as a way to undermine Old Hickory's popularity. The bank was due to be rechartered in 1836. Clay forced a bill through Congress rechartering the National Bank in 1832, a presidential election year. He assumed Jackson would have to sign it and alienate his Western followers or veto it and alienate the businessmen of the nation.

Jackson did veto the bill, sending a scathing message back to Congress. Jackson attacked the bank in violent, colorful terms that set the issue as a war between the rich and the poor. His arguments had little substance but a great deal of popular appeal among the financially ignorant public who loved him. Clay foolishly believed the message would harm Jackson because of its angry tone and lack of intelligent argument.

Election of 1832. The election of 1832 was the first in which the candidates were chosen by national political conventions. Jackson on the Democratic ticket squared off against Henry Clay who had received the National Republican nomination. The National Bank was the central issue of the campaign. Clay had copies of Jackson's veto printed up to use against him. The veto message, however, was accepted as truth by the general public and cemented Jackson's image as a defender of the common man. Wealthier people who had reason to be concerned by the attack did not vote for him anyway. Jackson won the election easily.

 Match these items (answers may be used more than once).

1.40 _____ party loyalists get government jobs		a. Spoils system
1.41 _____ King Mob		b. Jackson inauguration
1.42 _____ "Liberty and Union, now and forever, one and inseparable."		c. Webster-Hayne Debate
		d. National Bank
1.43 _____ Nicholas Biddle		e. Eaton Scandal
1.44 _____ Van Buren used it to gain Jackson's favor		f. Jefferson birthday dinner
1.45 _____ issue in 1832 election		
1.46 _____ rotation in office		
1.47 _____ Calhoun tried to get a states' rights position by Jackson		
1.48 _____ "Our Union: It must be preserved!"		
1.49 _____ senator publicly supported nullification		
1.50 _____ hurt the honesty and quality of government service		
1.51 _____ Jackson's "moneyed monster"		
1.52 _____ Jackson insisted on publicly supporting a woman against moral rumors		
1.53 _____ caused the resignation of the entire cabinet		
1.54 _____ Jackson had to flee the building to avoid injury		
1.55 _____ Jackson vetoed it in 1832		
1.56 _____ nullification would mean Union joined by a "rope of sand"		
1.57 _____ Congress passed bill to recharter it in 1832		

Answer these questions.

1.58 What injury gave Jackson a personal hatred for the British?

_____

_____

1.59 How did Jackson get the bullets that stayed in his body?

_____

1.60 What were three Western prejudices Jackson took to the White House?

a. _____

b. _____

c. _____

1.61 What is the doctrine of nullification?

_____

_____

1.62 What was the name of Jackson's group of informal advisors?

_____

1.63 Who was Jackson's first vice president?

_____

1.64 Who was vice president during Jackson's second term?

_____

1.65 Why did Henry Clay force a rechartering of the National Bank?

_____

_____

_____

_____

The End of the Jacksonian Era

Nullification Crisis. The Tariff of Abominations was a major issue in South Carolina. Congress voted in 1832 to reduce the tariff to more moderate levels, but it did not satisfy the Carolina "nullies." That same year they gained control of the state legislature and declared the tariff null and void in South Carolina. They also threatened to leave the Union if the federal government tried to enforce it.

Andrew Jackson was not about to take such a threat calmly. He sent reinforcements and supplies to federal forts in South Carolina. He also quietly prepared a larger army for use, if needed. He then denounced nullification and privately threatened to hang its supporters. The Southern leaders, especially Calhoun, knew Jackson well enough to take his threats seriously.

Jackson requested the passage of the Force Bill in early 1833 to grant authorization for troops to collect the tariffs in South Carolina. Calhoun led the assault on the bill. He had a great deal of support because of the rise of sectionalism in the nation. The nationalism of the post-War of 1812 era had given way to local loyalties to states and regions. Calhoun and Webster traded brilliant oratory in the Senate trying to force their views. Henry Clay finally brokered a compromise. A new tariff was passed that would gradually reduce the tax over the next ten years. Calhoun, realizing that he was on the verge of civil war, accepted the compromise and convinced his state to drop the nullification. South Carolina agreed but added the empty gesture of nullifying the Force Bill which had been signed into law.

Trail of Tears. The issue of what to do with the Native Americans who still owned large stretches of land east of the Mississippi had been left unanswered for years. Jackson was not a man to avoid an issue. In 1830 he proposed moving the tribes to new land west of the Mississippi where they would be "forever" free of encroachment by white settlers. Jackson deluded himself into believing this was a benevolent policy that was in the best interest of the Native Americans.

Many members of Congress opposed the Removal Act, particularly those who were strong Christians or who came from districts

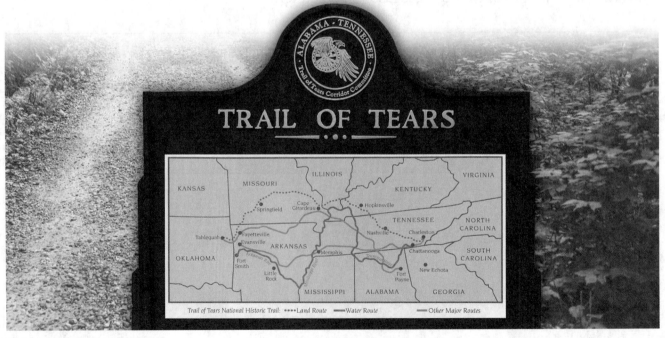

| National Historic Trail

with strong Christian constituents. However, Jackson put the full force of his persuasive and political powers behind the act. It was passed in 1830, granting the Native Americans land in the West and the money to move them.

Jackson moved enthusiastically to carry out his program. Many of the tribes accepted the inevitable and signed treaties giving up their land. They moved west suffering from hunger, disease, and exposure on the way. Georgia, Mississippi, and Alabama made it clear they would seize the Native American land whether treaties were signed or not. Jackson did nothing to discourage them.

The Cherokee People of Georgia, who had largely taken up American life, fought back. They refused to sign a new treaty and challenged Georgia in court when the state annexed their land. The Cherokee won. The Supreme Court said the state of Georgia had no authority over the federal treaties that gave the Native Americans their land, but it was no use. Andrew Jackson would not give the Supreme Court the backing it needed to protect the Native Americans. Jackson is reported to have said, "John Marshall has made his decision; now let him enforce it."

The Cherokee were finally removed by the army in 1838. They were crowded into prison camps and then forced to make the long journey west. About four thousand Cherokee died on the way. They called it "the Trail of Tears."

Some of the Native American People chose to go to war rather than leave. The Sauk People in the Northwest Territory fought under the leadership of their chief, Black Hawk. The Black Hawk War quickly ended in a victory by the American army. The Sauks were removed to Iowa. The Seminoles took advantage of the wild terrain of Florida to hold out until 1842. The Seminole War was the longest and most expensive war with a Native American people in American history. They were finally defeated and moved west also.

The Native American removal was one of the blackest marks on an already poor American record. Thousands of Native Americans died after being forced to surrender their land to the greed of white settlers. Even then, the promise that their new land would not be taken was never kept. Within a generation, they were facing the same pressure to give up their land to new settlers who had crossed the Mississippi. The whole thing was all the more tragic because of how many people believed it was good for the Native Americans. Sinful human beings have an incredible ability to justify their own wrongdoing.

National Bank. Jackson saw the election of 1832 as a **mandate** from the people in his battle with the National Bank. Therefore, he decided to kill the bank instead of just letting it run until its charter ended in 1836. He first had to fire his secretary of the treasury and appoint a new one that would go along with his plan. That accomplished, he began to remove federal money from the National Bank and put it into "pet banks" in various states. The banks were chosen in large part for their loyalty to Jackson, and some funds were wasted in the process. Henry Clay succeeded in convincing Congress to **censure** Jackson for this "unconstitutional" action. The rebuff had no effect on Jackson's actions.

Nicholas Biddle reacted in a way that confirmed Jackson's worst fears about the National Bank. He deliberately reduced credit to the point that businesses began to fail and the country fell on hard times. It was just this kind of power that Jackson did not want a private corporation to have! Jackson refused to budge even when hit with a long stream of petitions from struggling businessmen. He told them to take their petitions to Biddle. In the end, public pressure forced Biddle to surrender, relax credit, and close the bank.

The return to good times brought about a spiral of inflation and land speculation. Many of the western banks began issuing money with no reliable value. Jackson inadvertently encouraged the national self-confidence that fueled the speculation. In 1835, he became the only U.S. president ever to pay off the entire national debt! Fearful of the effects of wild speculation, Jackson issued the *Specie Circular*, a decree that all land purchased from the federal government had to be paid for in *specie*: gold or silver coins. That set the scene for the Panic of 1837.

Analysis. Andrew Jackson was a highly successful president. He did just about everything he wanted to do in office even if it was not good for the nation. He considered the president to be the representative of the people and acted independently of the other branches of government. He vetoed more laws than any president before him. He used his popularity to push through laws he wanted and to destroy the National Bank. His forceful foreign policy reopened American trade with the British West Indies and gained payments from Europe for American ships seized during the Napoleonic Wars. His actions as president increased the power and prestige of the office. His strong response to the Nullification Crisis undoubtedly saved the Union. He was so popular when he left office that he was even able to handpick his own successor whose term is considered a part of the Jacksonian Era.

Election of 1836. Jackson decided not to run again and made sure that Martin Van Buren received the Democratic nomination for president in 1836. The National Republicans had adopted the name of Whig by then and ran several candidates. Van Buren defeated the Whigs, led by William Henry Harrison, using Jackson's popularity. However, Van Buren inherited all the problems and enemies Jackson had created during his eight years in office. He took them on without having either the general's popularity or his fiery will. It was a disastrous combination.

Martin Van Buren. Martin Van Buren (1782-1862) was the first American president born after the Declaration of Independence. He was born in New York where he practiced law as a young man. He served in the New York legislature and the Senate. He won the governorship of New York in 1828 but gave it up to serve as Jackson's secretary of state. Van Buren was a professional politician known as the "Little Magician" for his skill at manipulating events to his advantage. He won the election solely on the support of Andrew Jackson. He had deliberately built his friendship with Old Hickory for just such a purpose.

The Panic of 1837. Land speculation in the West had become a major American pastime. Thousands of people bought land hoping to hold it and sell it for a profit later. The purchases were often made with loans from unstable banks. People were making huge profits only as long as credit was available. The prosperity of the nation was on shifting ground, and it gave way in 1837 just after Van Buren took office.

Jackson's destruction of the National Bank had removed one of the major safeguards in the American banking system. His *Specie Circular* had caused a sudden demand for gold and silver that drained Eastern bank reserves. Crop failures and a financial panic in England hit at the same time. British banks called in (demanded payment for) their foreign loans. Banks in America closed, people lost their savings, businesses closed, land sales fell, tariff income fell as trade was reduced, and unemployment hit the masses of common people.

Van Buren's popularity, never very high, quickly plummeted. He could do little to help in the situation. He did get federal money moved to an independent treasury to protect it from being lost when pet banks collapsed. His popularity was also hurt by anti-slave forces who opposed the Seminole War (they did not want another slave state in Florida) and pro-slave forces who wanted him to annex Texas. His single term was largely unfruitful.

Complete these sentences.

1.66 _____ was the only president ever to pay off the entire national debt.

1.67 The Cherokee called their removal west the _____ .

1.68 Jackson removed federal money from the National Bank and put it into so-called _____ banks.

1.69 In 1832 South Carolina voted to nullify the _____ .

1.70 Jackson's financial policies led to the _____ that hurt Van Buren.

1.71 Henry Clay succeeded in convincing the Senate to _____ Jackson because of the removal of federal funds from the National Bank.

1.72 The Panic of 1837 was largely caused by _____ in land.

1.73 The _____ War was the longest and most expensive Indian war in American history.

1.74 The Supreme Court sided with the _____ Native Americans in their legal fight with the state of Georgia.

1.75 The _____ Bill authorized troops to enforce the tariff in South Carolina.

1.76 Jackson privately threatened to _____ the nullifiers.

1.77 The Sauk People fought the _____ War to avoid removal from their land.

1.78 Andrew Jackson's hand-picked successor was _____ .

1.79 The Southern states annexed Native American land in defiance of the Supreme Court because _____ would not support the Native Americans.

1.80 "Little Magician" was the nickname of _____ .

Answer these questions.

1.81 What was the compromise that ended the Nullification Crisis?

_____

_____

_____

1.82 What did Jackson think he would accomplish with the Removal Act?

_____

_____

1.83 How did Jackson kill the National Bank?

_____

_____

Review the material in this section in preparation for the Self Test. The Self Test will check your mastery of this particular section. The items missed on this Self Test will indicate specific areas where restudy is needed for mastery.

SELF TEST 1

Match these people (each answer, 2 points).

1.01	_____ inventor of the cotton gin	a. Henry Clay
1.02	_____ leader of nullification and states' rights	b. Andrew Jackson
1.03	_____ "Old Hickory"	c. Daniel Webster
1.04	_____ his wife's social problems caused Jackson's entire cabinet to resign	d. John Calhoun
		e. Martin Van Buren
1.05	_____ won the presidency in 1824 in the House of Representatives with a "corrupt bargain"	f. John Quincy Adams
		g. John Eaton
1.06	_____ president of the Bank of the U.S.	h. Robert Hayne
1.07	_____ the Little Magician	i. Nicholas Biddle
1.08	_____ Massachusetts representative, defender of the Union	j. Eli Whitney
1.09	_____ the Great Compromiser	
1.010	_____ pro-nullification senator who had a famous debate with Webster	

Name the item or person described (each answer, 4 points).

1.011 _____ tax passed in 1828 to embarrass Adams by how high it was; it passed anyway, to the anger of the old South

1.012 _____ no slavery in the Louisiana Territory north of 36° 30', Maine admitted as a free state, Missouri as a slave state

1.013 _____ machine that led to the South becoming dependent on cotton and slavery

1.014 _____ political party created by Andrew Jackson

1.015 _____ political party led by Henry Clay after the split of the Democratic-Republicans

1.016 _____ "Old Man Eloquent," successfully opposed the Gag Rule in Congress, collapsed and died in the House of Representatives

1.017 _____ depression caused by land speculation and Jackson's financial policies that hurt Van Buren's presidency

1.018 _____ government jobs were given to loyal supporters of the newly-elected leaders

1.019 _____ the name the Cherokee used to described their forced trip west of the Mississippi, away from their land

1.020 _____ presidential decree by Andrew Jackson that all payments for land must be made in gold or silver

Complete the following (each answer, 5 points).

1.021 What was the Doctrine of Nullification?

_____

_____

_____

1.022 Why was the presidency of John Quincy Adams so unsuccessful?

_____

_____

_____

1.023 Briefly describe Andrew Jackson's personal history before he was president.

_____

_____

_____

_____

1.024 What did Jackson do to face the Nullification Crisis and how was it resolved?

_____

_____

_____

1.025 Why did Henry Clay try to recharter the National Bank early and what was the effect?

_____

_____

_____

1.026 Describe Andrew Jackson's first inaugural reception at the White House.

_____

_____

_____

_____

Answer true or false (each answer, 1 point).

1.027 _____ Jackson's group of informal advisors were called the "parlor cabinet."

1.028 _____ Henry Clay was never elected president.

1.029 _____ Jackson's campaign slogan in 1828, when he first won the presidency, was "Jackson and Reform."

1.030 _____ John Calhoun began his political career as a strong nationalist.

1.031 _____ The slavery issue was avoided in the early 1800s, but the North and South opposed each other over the tariff instead.

1.032 _____ John Calhoun was the spokesman for the western part of the nation.

1.033 _____ The South was very independent, producing its own food, cash crops, and manufactured goods.

1.034 _____ Before the time of Andrew Jackson presidential candidates were chosen by national convention of political parties.

1.035 _____ Andrew Jackson hand-picked Daniel Webster as his successor.

1.036 _____ The Seminole War was one of the shortest Indian wars in American history.

80 / 100   SCORE _____   TEACHER _____ _____

initials   date

2. MANIFEST DESTINY

In 1845 a newspaper article in the *Democratic Review* spoke of America's "manifest destiny" to move across the continent to claim the land given by God for her fast-growing population. The term quickly became popular. It became the historical title for the great American drive to gain land from sea to sea.

America had always been a land with a frontier. The frontier moved as older sections filled up with people and became more "civilized." The American urge to move west was almost an addiction. Thousands did it, hoping for a better life. They faced intense hardships and death, but these hardy people built the wild lands of the West into the cities, farms, and industries we know today.

This section will cover the last major phase of manifest destiny from 1840 to 1853, the expansion to the Pacific Ocean. Differences with Great Britain were settled on the borders of Maine and the Oregon Territory. Texas became independent from Mexico and joined the Union. A war with Mexico brought in the American southwest and California. Finally, in 1853 a piece of land, called the Gadsden Purchase, was bought from Mexico to allow a coast-to-coast railroad. Thus, manifest destiny was fulfilled, and America had all of the land that would become the forty-eight contiguous states.

SECTION OBJECTIVES

Review these objectives. When you have completed this section, you should be able to:

1. Name the leaders of the era and explain their accomplishments.
2. Describe the presidency of Andrew Jackson and its effect on America.
3. Trace the development of the slavery and tariff issues from 1820 to 1855.
4. Define Manifest Destiny and describe its course in America.
5. Describe the course of the Texas Revolution and Mexican War.
9. Describe the compromises that kept the nation together and what ended them.
10. Describe the changes in America and American life in this era.

VOCABULARY

Study these words to enhance your learning success in this section.

artillery (är til' u rē). A branch of the army armed with large-caliber, crew-served mounted firearms.

asylum (a sī' lum). Protection from arrest and extradition given to political or other refugees by a nation.

continental divide (kon' ti nen' tl de vīd). A ridge of land separating streams that flow to opposite sides of a continent.

protégé (prōt' e zhā). A person under the care and protection of an influential person, usually for the furthering of his career.

siesta (sē es' ta). An afternoon nap or rest.

The Northern Border

Log Cabin Campaign. The election of 1840 gave the Whigs a chance at the presidency. Martin Van Buren ran for re-election on the Democratic ticket in spite of his fall in popularity. The Whigs chose William Henry Harrison with running mate John Tyler. Henry Clay wanted the nomination, but Clay's political opinions were too well-known. The Whigs wanted a noncontroversial candidate. They chose Harrison because he was a popular general who won victories against the Native Americans at Tippecanoe and the British at the Thames. Moreover, his views on the issues of the day were unknown. In fact, he deliberately avoided taking any positions on such things as tariffs, the National Bank and internal improvements.

The real focus of the campaign was created when a Democratic newspaper gave the Whigs a slogan. The paper derided Harrison as a man who would be content with "a pension, a log cabin, and a barrel of hard cider." The Whigs jumped at the accusation calling Harrison the "Log Cabin and Hard Cider" candidate, a poor, hard-working common man. (Harrison was actually a wealthy land owner.) All over the country rallies were held with log cabins mounted on wagons and barrels of hard cider. The catchy phrase "Tippecanoe and Tyler, too" added to the circus atmosphere of the campaign. Harrison won by a large electoral but small popular margin.

William Henry Harrison. William Henry Harrison (1773-1841) was sixty-eight years old at the time of his election. He had been born in Virginia on his family's plantation. His father had signed the Declaration of Independence and served in the Continental Congress. Harrison joined the army as a young man and served until 1798. He later served as an official in the Northwest Territory and was one of that region's first representatives to Congress. He served for twelve years as the governor of the Indiana Territory. It was as the head of that

| Log Cabin and Hard Cider

territory's militia that he won the battle of Tippecanoe in 1811. He was a general in the War of 1812 and won the Battle of the Thames in Ontario. After that, he served in the House and the Senate. He ran for President as a Whig in 1836 and lost before winning in 1840.

Harrison had the shortest administration of any president in American history. He gave a very long inaugural address in cold, rainy weather and caught a cold. Less than a month later, the cold developed into pneumonia. On April 4, 1841, 31 days after his inauguration, Harrison died. (Presidential inaugurations took place in March until the 20th Amendment to the Constitution in 1933 changed it to January.)

Tyler, Too. John Tyler (1790-1862) was the first man to move from the vice presidency to the presidency because the latter died in office. He had, like Harrison, been born into an established Virginia family. He took up the practice of law with his father as a young man. He served in the House, the Senate, and as governor of Virginia before becoming vice president.

Tyler was a Democrat in Whig clothing. He had been put on the ticket as a supporter of states' rights to draw the Southern vote. His succession to the presidency doomed the Whig agenda. He proceeded to veto a new National Bank, higher tariffs, and internal improvements passed by the nationalistic Whig Congress. He quickly lost all of his Whig support in the government. His entire cabinet, except Secretary of State Daniel Webster, resigned. His enemies took to calling Tyler "His Accidency."

Maine's Boundary. Daniel Webster did not resign because he was in the middle of negotiations with Great Britain. Relations with the former mother country had reached one of their periodic boiling points. In 1837 a small, short-lived rebellion in Canada had been aided by many northern Americans before it was put down. An American vessel supplying the rebels with arms was attacked and destroyed by British troops on the American side of the Niagara River. In 1840 a Canadian citizen who claimed to have been a part of the raid was arrested for murder. The British government threatened war if the man was executed. (He was later acquitted.) The tension grew in 1841 when the British officials in the Bahamas gave **asylum** to a group of Virginia slaves who had rebelled and captured an American ship.

The two sides finally came to the negotiating table over the boundary of Maine. Both claimed parts of the land along the border. The treaty of 1783, which ended the Revolution, was not very clear on the matter. In the early 1840s, lumberjacks from Canada and the U.S. were fighting over the right to harvest trees in the disputed area. The fighting expanded and the militia was called in. The so-called "Aroostook War" threatened to become a real one. The two sides met and finally set an agreeable border. The Webster-Ashburton Treaty of 1842 gave the Americans more of the land but gave the British access to a route they needed for a military road. It also settled all of the other outstanding differences between the countries, except for the question of Oregon.

Congress was furious at the treaty. They were in no mood to give up land that they thought

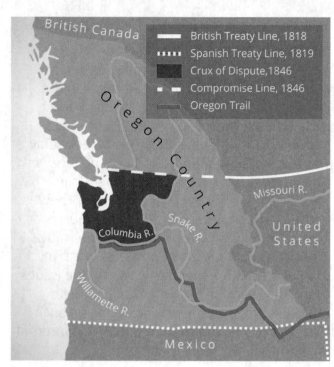

| Oregon Territory

was rightfully American. Webster, however, showed them an ancient map that implied that the British had rightful claim to the entire area in dispute! The treaty easily passed the Senate after that. Ironically, the British accepted the treaty because they had an ancient map that showed the Americans had rightful claim to the whole area!

Oregon Territory. Both Britain and America had claims to the beautiful and fertile Oregon Territory. At that time, Oregon included all of the land between California and the southern tip of Alaska west of the **continental divide**. Spain had given up her claim to the area in the Adams-Onis Treaty which had given Florida to the United States and set the borders of the Louisiana Territory. A Russian claim south of latitude 54° 40' was extinguished by treaty in the 1820s. Unable to settle their own differences there, Britain and the U.S. had agreed to occupy the land jointly in 1818. That agreement was renewed in 1827, since neither side would compromise.

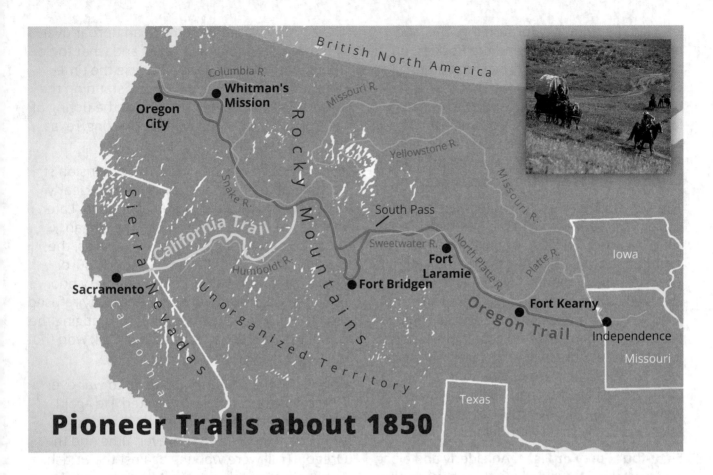

Pioneer Trails about 1850

The crux of the debate was a section of land north of the Columbia River up to the 49th parallel, the border between Canada and the U.S. on the east side of the Rocky Mountains. America wanted this land because it included Puget Sound, the only good harbor along the entire section of seacoast. The British were willing to concede the land south of the Columbia, but steadfastly refused to extend the previously established 49th parallel border requested by the Americans. The Americans on the other hand, did not want a section of land on the Pacific coast without access to a harbor. Matters stood this way for years.

Oregon Trail. The Rocky Mountains had been explored by mountain men who lived in the wild, trapping fur animals. Their knowledge provided the information Americans needed to reach their most western lands. One of these men named Jedidiah Smith discovered South Pass, a route over the Rockies that could be

traversed by a wagon. That pass was surveyed in 1842 by John Frémont, an American army officer. Slowly, the information needed to bring people and their wagons safely into Oregon was accumulated.

The British had established the first permanent settlements in Oregon. These were fur-trading posts organized by the Hudson Bay Company around 1825 under the leadership of John McLoughlin, known as "the Father of Oregon." The first permanent American settlement was a group of missionaries who settled in the Willamette Valley in 1834. In 1836 Presbyterian missionary Marcus Whitman brought his wife over the long, dangerous route to live in Oregon. She was the first of a flood of women and children who came with their men to make Oregon their home.

Americans became enraptured with reports coming out of Oregon. The missionaries, trappers, and explorers sent glowing reports of the land and its suitability for farming. The land between the Mississippi and the Rockies, on the other hand, was labeled "The Great American Desert" by an army explorer. That vast grassland was believed to be unsuitable for settled farming. It was primarily an obstacle to Oregon and California-bound settlers. Beginning in 1843, thousands of pioneers risked the dangers of the desert to reach the riches of Oregon.

The Oregon Trail was the route these brave souls traveled. It began in Independence, Missouri and covered 2,000 of the hardest miles ever regularly traveled by families and animals. The trip took six months. Native Americans attacked and rivers flooded. People ran out of food. Wagons broke and draft animals died. Hundreds of people also died and were buried along the route in lonely graves with bare wood markers. There had been only a handful of Americans in Oregon in 1840. By 1850, there were over 12,000. The Americans were going to take Oregon by sheer numbers.

Fifty-four Forty or Fight. An elderly and ailing Andrew Jackson decided to take a hand in the election of 1844. He hand picked the Democratic candidate James K. Polk, a strong expansionist, and campaigned for him by letters from his sickbed. He also persuaded Tyler not to run because he would take votes from Polk. The Whigs nominated the venerable Henry Clay.

The country was at the time in an uproar over whether or not to annex Texas and what to do about Oregon. Clay decided to use the time-honored method of avoiding any stand on the issues. Polk, on the other hand, at the urging of Jackson, spoke out in favor of annexing Texas and acquiring all of Oregon.

The Democrats cashed in on the expansionist attitude of the nation. Their campaign clearly called for America to have all of Oregon. Later, that desire was summarized by the slogan, "Fifty-four Forty or Fight!" In other words, the U.S. would get all of Oregon up to 54° 40' or would go to war with Britain. It was very poor diplomacy but great politics. Henry Clay refused to commit one way or the other, misjudging the popularity of the issues yet again. Polk won the election on a very close vote.

Polk was not as determined to go to war over Oregon as his campaign indicated. He again offered to set the boundary at 49° and was refused by the British. However, time and the Oregon Trail were working against the British. The rapid expansion of the American population in the territory endangered the British claims. The Americans could just take all of the land that they wanted, and the tiny British population could not oppose them. In 1846 the British themselves offered to extend the 49th parallel border, and the Americans quickly agreed.

Match these people.

2.1	_____ Father of Oregon	a. William H. Harrison
2.2	_____ discovered South Pass	b. John Tyler
2.3	_____ Whig candidate in 1844	c. James K. Polk
2.4	_____ Democratic candidate in 1844	d. Henry Clay
2.5	_____ president with the shortest administration	e. Daniel Webster
2.6	_____ first vice president to become president because of a death	f. Jedidiah Smith
		g. John McLoughlin

Complete these sentences.

2.7 William Henry Harrison's 1840 campaign called him the _____ and

_____ candidate.

2.8 _____ did not get the Whig nomination in 1840 because he had

publicly expressed his opinions on the issues.

2.9 Tyler was a Whig president, but he held _____ ideas on the issues.

2.10 The boundary of Maine was settled by the _____ Treaty.

2.11 Thousands of Americans reached Oregon by traveling the _____

from Independence, Missouri.

2.12 Britain and America disputed the Oregon land north of the _____

and south of the _____ .

2.13 America wanted the disputed Oregon land because it wanted a _____

on the Pacific coast.

2.14 The slogan for those who wanted all of the Oregon Territory was _____

_____ .

2.15 The catchy, rhyming phase used by Harrison's campaign in 1840 was _____

_____ .

2.16 President John Tyler's enemies called him "_____ ."

2.17 The battle that broke out between lumberjacks in Maine over disputed land was called the

_____ War.

2.18 The Great Plains were called the Great _____ in the 1840s.

2.19 The border of Oregon was set at the _____ parallel.

2.20 Tyler vetoed _____ , _____ , and

_____ .

2.21 Polk won the 1844 election because he publicly favored annexing _____

and acquiring all of _____ .

2.22 _____ was a missionary who brought his wife to Oregon in 1836.

2.23 Congress accepted the Webster-Ashburton Treaty because Webster found a map that showed

that _____ had claim to the entire area in dispute.

2.24 The Oregon Trail was about _____ miles long.

Texas and Polk

Americans in Texas. America's claims to Texas were surrendered in 1819 by the Adams-Onis Treaty with Spain; however, land-hungry Americans wanted to farm the rich lands of east Texas that faced them across the border. Spain agreed to allow some to enter under special conditions. Moses Austin negotiated one such agreement with Spain in 1820. Austin was given a large tract of land along the Brazos River and given permission to settle three hundred families there. The settlers had to become Catholics, be of good character, and swear allegiance to the king of Spain. The Spanish government hoped to gain a tax-paying population for their vast domain and defenses against the Native American Peoples of the region.

Moses Austin died before he could execute his agreement. His son, Stephen Austin, settled the "First Three Hundred" in Texas beginning in 1821. In that same year, Mexico won its independence from Spain. Austin made the difficult journey to Mexico City to have his agreement confirmed by the new government. It was, and many others were granted in the years that followed. One important late settler was Sam Houston, a former Tennessee governor and friend of Andrew Jackson.

By 1835 about 30,000 Americans were living in Texas. Most were law-abiding settlers but some were men avoiding the law in America. "G.T.T." (Gone to Texas) was a note that was often left behind when a man found it necessary to get out from under the jurisdiction of the United States.

In spite of the requirement that they swear allegiance to the Mexican government, most of the settlers continued to think of themselves as Americans. They often defied the requirement of becoming Catholic and brought enslaved people into Texas in violation of the law. The independent settlers clashed with corrupt local officials and soldiers who were often little more than uniformed bandits. The Americans also were disturbed by the continuous instability of the Mexican government.

A revolt broke out in Texas in 1832 over a decree that forbade any more Americans to settle in the land. A revolt was also going on in Mexico City. The new president, General Antonio Lopez de Santa Anna, accepted the changes in Texas. Stephen Austin went to Mexico City in 1833 to petition that Texas become a separate state in the Mexican federation and allow American immigration. He was arrested and spent almost a year in jail before he was released.

The Texas Revolution. The last straw came in 1835. Santa Anna suspended the constitution and declared himself dictator. Several of the Mexican states, including Texas, rose in revolt. Fighting began in Texas in October when Santa Anna's soldiers tried to force the settlers to turn in their weapons. It began as a fight for their rights under the suspended Mexican Constitution.

Santa Anna sent his brother-in-law and an army to occupy San Antonio to control the situation. The Texians (as they called themselves) set up a temporary government and put Sam Houston in command of the army. A request was sent to the United States for volunteers. They poured in from all over the South. The Americans attacked San Antonio, capturing it in December of 1835. This alarmed Santa Anna. He assembled an army of about 8,000 and invaded Texas, arriving at San Antonio on February 23, 1836.

The troops that had been left to hold San Antonio had taken shelter in a mission/ fortress called the Alamo. Houston sent Colonel Jim Bowie with orders to blow up the Alamo and retreat. Bowie and the resident commander, William Travis, decided to ignore their orders and defend the fort. They had 183 men including a group of Tennessee volunteers led by the famous backwoodsman, Davy Crockett.

The Battle of the Alamo has become a vibrant part of American folklore, even though the defense of the mission was in violation of the orders of Sam Houston. The men who held the fort acted with the highest courage and forced Santa Anna to pay a horrendous price for his victory. They also delayed the advance of his army for two critical weeks which bought Houston time to organize.

The defenders of the Alamo refused to surrender, even when surrounded by an army perhaps 30 times their numbers. Santa Anna besieged the mission unsuccessfully from February 23 to March 6. The expert American marksmen held the walls against all attacks. Finally, on the 6th, the Mexicans stormed the walls, overwhelming them by sheer numbers. The Americans fought hand-to-hand as they ran out of ammunition. On the dictator's orders, all of the defenders were killed. Santa Anna lost over a thousand of his own men in the siege to the defenders' 183.

Remember the Alamo. The Texan leaders had been meeting to discuss their plans when the Alamo was under attack. They confirmed Houston as commander of the army and decided to declare Texas independent on March 2. News of the Alamo angered and aroused the Texans. Further fuel was added later in the month when Santa Anna ordered the cold-blooded murder of 400 men who had surrendered at Goliad. To cries of "Remember the Alamo! Remember Goliad!", the Texans rallied to defend themselves.

The wily Sam Houston led the Mexicans on a long, winding chase through the rough Texas countryside. The retreat was unpopular, but Houston managed to hold it together. Every day his army grew larger while Santa Anna's grew wearier and smaller. Finally, on April 21, the Texans attacked at San Jacinto during the Mexican siesta. Over a thousand Mexican soldiers were killed or wounded while the Americans lost less than forty. Santa Anna was captured and signed a treaty giving Texas its independence.

Annexation Question. Andrew Jackson, who was president at the time, was in a quandary. Santa Anna repudiated the treaty he signed after San Jacinto as soon as he was safely back in Mexico. Extending official recognition to the Lone Star Republic (the flag of Texas had one star) might spark an unpopular war with Mexico. Jackson delayed until after the election of Van Buren and then recognized the Texas Republic just before he left office.

Texas wanted to be part of the United States and promptly applied for admission in 1837. A two-thirds majority was needed to approve the treaty of annexation and it failed. The reason was slavery. The northern states refused to admit such a large, slave-holding land. An attempt was made again in 1844, but it also failed for the same reason. However, popular opinion was building in favor of annexation.

In 1844 James K. Polk made Texas a major issue in his campaign. When Polk won the election, President John Tyler believed it was a mandate to add Texas to the Union. He arranged for Congress to annex the territory by a joint resolution requiring only a simple majority.

| Davy Crockett at the Alamo, preparing to die

Annexation passed in December of 1844 and Texas became a state one year later.

James K. Polk. James K. Polk (1795-1849) added more territory to the United States than any other president. Polk was born in North Carolina to Irish immigrants. His father speculated in land and became wealthy in America. The younger Polk graduated from the University of North Carolina and took up the practice of law in Tennessee. He became a close friend and **protégé** of Andrew Jackson earning the name "Young Hickory" because of the General's support. He served seven terms in the House of Representatives and was Speaker of the House under Jackson's presidency. He also was elected to one term as governor of Tennessee. The Democratic Party could not agree on Van Buren or his chief rival, Lewis Cass, for their candidate in 1844. With Jackson's backing, Polk was offered as a compromise candidate. He was the first "dark horse" candidate, a virtual unknown chosen when better-known candidates were not acceptable for some reason.

Polk was a highly successful president. He set four goals to accomplish while in office. He achieved all of them. The first two were to lower the tariff and establish an independent treasury. The latter was needed because the Whigs had repealed Van Buren's treasury plans and were unable to re-establish a national bank. The Walker Tariff (named after Secretary of the Treasury Robert Walker) passed in 1846. It lowered most of the tariffs and eliminated some altogether. The independent treasury was set up that same year and handled America's government funds until the Federal Reserve was set up in 1913.

Polk's third goal was to settle the Oregon boundary dispute, which was accomplished in 1846. Polk's last goal was to add California to the United States. This proved to be the most difficult and costly of his goals.

In 1844 California was owned by Mexico. It was sparsely populated with a few thousand

| Disputed Texas

Mexicans and even fewer foreigners, mostly Americans. Manifest Destiny Americans wanted the fertile lands of its coastal valleys and the fine harbor at San Francisco. Mexico, still smarting from the annexation of Texas, had broken off diplomatic relations and refused all offers to buy California. Tensions were also high because Mexico had defaulted on payments of claims it owed U.S. citizens. In 1845 Mexico refused to even receive the new American minister. Polk decided to get what he wanted by war.

Events in Texas. The treaty signed by Santa Anna had set the southern border of Texas at the Rio Grande River. Mexico claimed that the real border was the Nueces River further to the north. While he had been trying to negotiate for California, Polk had kept U.S. troops out of the disputed area. In January 1846 he ordered General Zachary Taylor to take up a position on the Rio Grande River. As he hoped, the Mexicans attacked Taylor on April 25, 1846, killing or wounding sixteen men. Polk sent a message to Congress asking for a declaration of war because of the shedding of "American blood on American soil" by the Mexicans. Congress passed the war resolution by a wide margin.

Answer true or false.

If the statement is false, change some nouns or adjectives to make it true.

2.25 _____ Moses Austin settled the "First Three Hundred" families on the Brazos River in Texas.

2.26 _____ Most of the defenders of the Alamo were killed.

2.27 _____ The annexation of Texas stalled over the issue of slavery.

2.28 _____ Texans won their independence at the Battle of Goliad.

2.29 _____ Andrew Jackson recognized the Lone Star Republic just before he left office.

2.30 _____ James K. Polk was called "Young Hickory."

2.31 _____ America had surrendered its claims to Texas in the Webster-Ashburton Treaty.

2.32 _____ Henry Clay was the first "dark horse" candidate for president.

2.33 _____ Polk was a successful president.

2.34 _____ Americans brought enslaved people into Texas in violation of Mexican law.

Answer these questions.

2.35 What are the names of three of the men who died at the Alamo?

　　a. _____　　b. _____

　　c. _____

2.36 What were James K. Polk's four goals for his presidency?

　　a. _____　　b. _____

　　c. _____　　d. _____

2.37 What did G.T.T. mean?

　　_____

2.38 How did Polk provoke a war with Mexico?

　　_____

　　_____

2.39 What event in Mexico triggered the Texas Revolution?

　　_____

　　_____

2.40 What were the two rally cries of the Texas Revolution?

_____

_____

2.41 What was Sam Houston's strategy after the Alamo?

_____

_____

The Mexican War

Politics of War. Mexican-American relations had been bad for some time. Revolution after revolution had rocked the Mexican Republic since its creation in 1821. During these upheavals, Americans were killed, their property taken, treaties were ignored, and damages were promised but not paid. The proud Mexicans had also said that the annexation of Texas would be a declaration of war. However, the main reason that the war began in 1846 was Polk's desire for California. There was a serious concern that Mexico could not hold California, and it might wind up in hostile British hands. Polk wanted it safely in American hands along with the New Mexico territory to complete America's sea-to-sea Manifest Destiny.

The war was controversial in its own time. Many people questioned whether or not America had really been the innocent victim of a Mexican attack, as Polk declared. Illinois representative Abraham Lincoln tried to force the president to admit that Mexicans attacked Americans on Mexican soil. Abolitionists feared the war was a conspiracy to add slave territory to the nation. John Calhoun opposed the declaration of war, fearing the new land would divide the nation. Webster and Clay opposed it as a creation of the Democratic president. (Both of them lost sons in the battles that followed.)

The controversy did not keep the war from being generally popular, however, especially as American victories mounted. Thousands of volunteers poured into the army from all over the nation to supplement the professional army. The professional army was small, especially compared to the large army Mexico had amassed (needed because of the continuous upheaval there). However, the American army had a superior collection of junior officers who had been trained at the military academy at West Point. Many of the men who would lead the North and South in the coming years received their battle training in the Mexican War. Robert E. Lee, Ulysses S. Grant, Thomas J. (Stonewall) Jackson, George Meade, George McClellan, and George Pickett were a few of the many future Civil War leaders who served in Mexico. Thus, the war was one of the last united acts of the nation before the division over slavery became unavoidable.

New Mexico and California. The territory coveted by the United States quickly and easily came under American control. Neither New Mexico nor California had any substantial forces to oppose an American invasion. Under the command of Colonel Stephen Kearny, troops marched from Fort Leavenworth, Kansas to New Mexico in June of 1846. The more than

1,500 troops traveled down the Santa Fe Trail, a road set up by American merchants to trade with that isolated Mexican outpost. Kearny captured the city and the territory easily.

California was captured in a very colorful manner. John C. Frémont, an army topographer, had already explored much of the West, creating accurate maps and suggesting sites for forts. He appeared in California in 1845, supposedly on a scientific expedition, but probably under secret orders from President Polk to be ready to take it in the event of war. In any case, Frémont led a rebellion in June of 1846 that declared California an independent republic called the "Bear Flag Republic." By the time word reached Frémont of the war with Mexico, most of northern California was already in his hands. The rest followed shortly.

The situation was complicated when Commodore Robert Stockton sailed in with official orders to seize California. He took Santa Barbara and Los Angeles. He was joined by Kearny who had arrived overland from New Mexico with the same orders. The two commanders retook Los Angeles when it rebelled in September of 1846 and quarreled over who was in command. Frémont arrived and added his dubious authority to the fray. Kearny had Frémont arrested and sent back to Washington for a court martial. He was found guilty but was released by President Polk's orders. Thus, California was captured.

Northern Mexico Campaign. Zachary Taylor, whose troops had been attacked along the Rio Grande, did not wait for the official declaration from Washington. He knew he had a war with Mexico even though the politicians had not officially declared it. "Old Rough and Ready," as Taylor was known, was a popular commander. He was an easy-going man who dressed without regard for military protocol, often wearing a straw hat. He was a capable but not brilliant commander who was determined to press on with the job.

| Battle in Northern Mexico

In May, Taylor met the Mexican army at Palo Alto and Resaca de la Palma, both north of the Rio Grande. In both cases, the Americans won with far lighter casualties than the Mexicans. The skillful American **artillery** proved decisive in both victories. Taylor then went to the aid of Fort Texas which he had established near the mouth of the Rio Grande. He renamed it Fort Brown after the commander who had died defending it during the siege by the Mexican army. Acting without orders, Taylor then crossed the Rio Grande and captured the city of Matamoros without firing a shot.

The quick series of victories made Taylor a hero. The Whigs immediately began to talk of having him run for president in 1848, and Taylor did nothing to discourage the talk. Polk, a hard-core Jacksonian Democrat, was alarmed by the general's popularity. The president tried unsuccessfully to appoint a Democratic general to gain the laurels of victory, but Congress refused to cooperate.

In June Taylor was ordered south. He attacked the city of Monterrey in September of 1846. It was heavily fortified and American losses were heavy. The Americans eventually captured the town, using a technique borrowed from the Texans who took San Antonio during their revolution. The soldiers burrowed through the adobe walls of the city buildings, moving closer and closer to the city center, house by house. The Mexicans finally surrendered and received generous peace terms from the general. The terms were so generous that they were later repudiated by the U.S. government. Taylor was now ordered to hold what he had taken and send a large part of his army south to assist General Winfield Scott in a planned attack on the Mexican capital.

Taylor, however, believed his orders were intended to quiet him and cut off his political popularity. He ignored them and marched his reduced army south, reaching Buena Vista near the city of Saltillo in February of 1847. There he

| California's Bear Flag

was met by a huge army under the command of the revived Mexican dictator, Santa Anna.

Santa Anna had been in exile in Cuba when the war began. In exchange for a large bribe and passage into Mexico, he had offered to give America the land they wanted. Naively, James Polk believed him. Santa Anna returned to Mexico, took over the government and announced a great war to defend the nation against the barbarian invaders. He assembled an army of over 20,000 to meet Taylor who had about 6,500. He offered Taylor a chance to surrender in the face of the superior numbers. Taylor refused, even though he was outnumbered three to one.

The Battle of Buena Vista lasted two days. It was marked by the daring and skill of the junior officers who held out against the incredible odds. Taylor refused to retreat, even when some of his men recommended it. Again, the American artillery proved decisive, and it was the Mexicans who retreated. This remarkable victory confirmed Taylor's growing reputation as a national hero. He remained in northern Mexico for the rest of the war.

Doniphan. Kearny had divided his command at Santa Fe. A group of Missouri Mounted Volunteers were sent south under the command of Colonel Alexander Doniphan. They were supposed to pacify the Navajos, and then go through El Paso and Chihuahua City to meet up with General Taylor. Doniphan proceeded to do just that with his group of ragtag volunteer backwoodsmen. This undisciplined gang defeated a much larger Mexican army at El Brazito on Christmas Day 1846. They also won the Battle of the Sacramento near Chihuahua in February of 1847 and then occupied the city.

The "lost" regiment finally met up with Taylor at Saltillo in May of 1847, having marched several thousand miles and won two major victories against larger armies. Most of them took their pay, which they received for the first time in the campaign, and headed home.

Match these people (answers may be used more than once).

2.42 _____	Old Rough and Ready	a. John Frémont
2.43 _____	army topographer	b. Zachary Taylor
2.44 _____	victor at Palo Alto and Buena Vista	c. Alexander Doniphan
2.45 _____	commander, Missouri Mounted Volunteers	d. Stephen Kearny
2.46 _____	founder of the Bear Flag Republic	e. Robert Stockton
2.47 _____	captured Santa Fe	f. Santa Anna
2.48 _____	naval officer, took Los Angeles	g. James Polk
2.49 _____	Mexican dictator, again	
2.50 _____	captured Matamoros	
2.51 _____	captured Monterrey	
2.52 _____	captured Chihuahua	
2.53 _____	a Jacksonian Democrat	
2.54 _____	victories made Whigs talk of making him president	
2.55 _____	took advantage of Polk's naiveté	

Answer these questions.

2.56 Where were America's superior junior officers of the Mexican War educated?

_____

2.57 The Mexican War provided battle training for the officers of what future war?

_____

2.58 What were two reasons why the Mexican War was controversial?

_____

_____

2.59 Why did Taylor ignore his orders to stay in Monterrey?

_____

_____

2.60 What part of the army contributed decisively to the victories at Palo Alto, Resaca de la Palma, and Buena Vista? _____

Campaign Against Mexico City. General Winfield Scott was the highest-ranking general in the American army during the Mexican War. He was a man who loved pomp, good food, and fancy uniforms. His men called him "Old Fuss and Feathers." He was quick-tempered, touchy, and blunt. He stayed out of the early part of the war because of differences with President Polk. However, he was a brilliant military man, and he proved it in the campaign to capture Mexico City.

In October of 1846, Scott proposed to lead a campaign against the Mexican capital. It was a bold idea. He would have to march from Veracruz on the Gulf of Mexico across miles of poorly mapped, heavily defended territory. He would have to penetrate deep into enemy territory with only a thin supply line. It was a difficult military venture.

| Mexican Cession

Scott sailed to Mexico with over 10,000 men in 1847. In March he landed his men away from Veracruz and attacked it from the landward side where the defenses were weakest. The siege lasted only a few days. Scott left a small force to occupy the city and moved quickly toward Mexico City.

Santa Anna received word that Scott was coming and went to meet him. The Mexican army set up defenses in a narrow mountain pass near Cerro Gordo. Scott's rapid advance reached the site before the defenses were fully in place. Captain Robert E. Lee, working with the engineers, found and cut a way around the enemy to allow an attack from two sides. The outnumbered Americans won the two-day battle, clearing the road to Mexico City.

At this point, Polk tried again to negotiate the peace he wanted. Nicholas P. Trist, a State Department clerk, was sent to attempt negotiations. The Mexican government refused, but Santa Anna sent a secret offer to Scott. In exchange for $10,000 up front, and $90,000 more after a treaty was signed, Santa Anna would arrange for a treaty that gave the Americans what they wanted. Scott decided to try it and sent the $10,000. The Americans did not get their treaty. Santa Anna pocketed the money and used the time to prepare his defenses.

Scott advanced on the capital in August of 1847. During this part of the campaign, he was cut off from his communications and supplies. He either had to win or surrender. Santa Anna had strong defenses in place to protect the city. Scott took the first of these at Contreras and Churubusco on the 19th and 20th.

The Mexicans then asked for an armistice. Scott granted one for two weeks, believing the enemy wanted to negotiate. Again, Santa Anna used the time to improve his defenses. When the armistice ended, the Americans attacked again, winning a battle at Molino del Rey. They then captured the fortress of Chapultepec which cleared the way right up to the city gates. Santa Anna fled and the city authorities sued for peace. On September 14, 1847, Scott rode into the central plaza of the city and the Stars and Stripes were raised.

Treaty of Guadalupe Hidalgo. Nicholas Trist had been recalled by the president in October. He ignored the order and opened negotiations with the new Mexican government. The two sides met at Guadalupe Hidalgo, a city north of the capital. Faced with an army in their capital, the Mexicans gave the Americans everything they wanted.

The treaty ceded to America all of California and the land between it and Texas north of the Gila River. America agreed to pay 15 million dollars for the land and assume all of Mexico's debts to American citizens for damage claims. Mexico also recognized the Rio Grande as the border of Texas. The treaty was signed on February 2, 1848.

Polk was facing growing pressure to annex all of Mexico. However, when the treaty arrived, the president decided to submit it to the Senate because it gave him what he had originally wanted. He chose to ignore the fact that Trist was not authorized to negotiate for the United States. He may have been motivated by a fear that the government in Mexico would change again and repudiate it. The Senate approved it on March 10.

Results of the War. The Mexican Cession added more than 525,000 square miles (1,360,000 square kilometers) to the nation. It was the largest single piece of land ever to become part of the United States. However, Congress had tremendous difficulty trying to organize the new land into official territories. The sticking point was slavery.

David Wilmot of Pennsylvania had introduced a proposal in 1846, while the war was still in progress. It specified that no slavery would ever be allowed to exist in any land acquired from Mexico as a result of the war. The South fought the Wilmot Proviso with a passion. It passed in the House but failed in the Senate; however, it would not go away. It was introduced repeatedly to acrimonious debate.

After the war, other proposals were offered, some allowing slavery, some forbidding it, and some leaving it up to the citizens of each territory to decide for themselves (popular sovereignty). No agreements could be reached. The issue of organizing the new land hung on the deepening chasm of slavery. It was finally brought to a crisis by the sudden changes that had occurred in California.

California Gold Rush. It was expected that it would be years before any part of the Mexican Cession would have the 60,000 people needed to apply for statehood. However, in 1848, just days before the Treaty of Guadalupe Hidalgo was signed, gold was discovered in the Sierra Nevada Mountains of California. What followed was one of the largest mass migrations in history. Approximately 80,000 people came to California in 1849 hoping to strike it rich. Just about the same number came the next few years. Some left after failing to get rich, but many stayed to make their homes in the West.

The "forty-niners," as they were called, came mainly from the United States by three routes. The largest group came overland via the trading and wagon trails. Another group sailed south to Panama, crossed the Isthmus, and came north by sea to California. Still another group took the difficult ocean route around the southern tip of South America. Hundreds of ships reached the West Coast and were promptly abandoned as all the men aboard went searching for gold. Rotting ships filled San Francisco harbor, which had became a major city overnight.

California's population rapidly exceeded the 60,000 needed for statehood. The official population count in 1850 was over 90,000! In 1849 California organized a government and applied for admission as a state, skipping the intermediate step of territory. The real problem arose because the new state constitution barred slavery. The stage was set for a major sectional battle.

Election of 1848. The Whigs jumped at the chance to run the popular general, Zachary Taylor, for president in 1848. They again bypassed Henry Clay and Daniel Webster, both of whom wanted the nomination. The Democrats nominated General Lewis Cass, a veteran of the War of 1812. President Polk had promised not to run again if he was elected; his health would not permit it in any case. Martin Van Buren ran as a third-party candidate for the anti-slavery Free-Soil Party.

The Whigs and the Democrats avoided the slavery issue. In fact, they avoided most of the issues. The Free-Soil Party, on the other hand, came out openly against slavery in the territories. They also advocated internal improvements and free land for settlers. Their slogan was "free soil, free speech, free labor, and free men." However, it was a contest of personalities, not issues, and the popular Taylor won.

| Gold Prospector by the River

Zachary Taylor. Zachary Taylor (1784-1850) was the son of a wealthy Virginia planter. His father fought in the Revolution, and it was no surprise when Zachary joined the army as a young man. Taylor fought in the Black Hawk and Seminole Indian Wars before becoming a national hero in the Mexican War. He had no political experience and knew very little about national or international affairs. In fact, he had never even voted in a presidential election!

The intense controversy in Congress over the organization of the Mexican Cession was beyond Taylor. He bungled back and forth, unable to resolve the issues. Before any resolution could be worked out, Taylor died in 1850 and Millard Fillmore, his vice president, came to power.

The Last Piece. The growing American population in California and Oregon was causing communication problems. The populated West Coast lands were thousands of miles and months of travel away from the center of government in the East. Several people proposed to build a railroad across the country to connect the two coasts more conveniently.

The most attractive route was across what is now New Mexico and Arizona south of the Gila River. The Rocky Mountains were lower through that part of the West. Unfortunately, that land belonged to Mexico.

In 1853 James Gadsden was sent as the American minister to Mexico. He was authorized to negotiate for the land needed for a railroad route. Gadsden's efforts prospered because Santa Anna was once again (for the sixth time) in power, and the old dictator needed money. He agreed to sell the United States a section of land south of the Gila River for $10 million. The Gadsden Purchase was the last piece of land acquired for what would become the forty-eight contiguous states. Manifest Destiny had been fulfilled.

| Gadsden Purchase

✎ **Complete these sentences.**

2.61 The Mexican War was ended by the Treaty of _____ .

2.62 The sticking point over organizing the land acquired from Mexico was the issue of

_____ .

2.63 Winfield Scott's nickname was _____ .

2.64 California's population grew rapidly after the discovery of _____ in 1848.

2.65 _____ was elected president in 1848.

2.66 Martin Van Buren ran for president in 1848 as a candidate of the _____

Party.

2.67 The last part of the contiguous states added to the Union was the _____

Purchase.

2.68 The men who arrived in California in 1849 were called _____ .

2.69 Winfield Scott led a brilliant campaign that conquered _____ in

September of 1847.

2.70 The man who negotiated the treaty that ended the war with Mexico was

_____ .

2.71 The three routes to California in the rush after 1848 were:

a. _____

b. _____

c. _____

2.72 America paid _____ dollars to Mexico for the land ceded by them after

the war.

2.73 The defense of Mexico City was under the command of the dictator,

_____ .

2.74 California organized a government in the year _____ and wanted to become

a state without ever being a _____ .

2.75 The slogan of the Free-Soil Party in 1848 was _____

_____ .

2.76 The Gadsden Purchase was made because the U.S. needed the land for a _____

line to the West Coast.

2.77 The two-day battle at the mountain pass near _____ cleared the road to Mexico City for the Americans.

2.78 The land taken from Mexico by the war was called the _____ _____ .

2.79 After the Mexican War, Mexico recognized the _____ as the border of Texas.

2.80 The _____ Proviso that proposed to forbid slavery in land acquired from Mexico did not become law.

2.81 The constitution of California did not allow _____ .

2.82 _____ became president after Taylor died in 1850.

2.83 During the Mexican War, _____ was the highest ranking general in the U.S. army.

Review the material in this section in preparation for the Self Test. This Self Test will check your mastery of this particular section as well as your knowledge of the previous section.

SELF TEST 2

Match these items (each answer, 2 points).

2.01 _____ Wilmot Proviso

2.02 _____ Missouri Compromise

2.03 _____ Tariff of Abominations

2.04 _____ Gag Rule

2.05 _____ *Specie Circular*

2.06 _____ Pet Banks

2.07 _____ Manifest Destiny

2.08 _____ Trail of Tears

2.09 _____ Log Cabin and Hard Cider

2.010 _____ Gadsden Purchase

a. America should move across the continent, claiming the land

b. Harrison's presidential campaign

c. no petitions on slavery

d. Native American removal to west of Mississippi

e. needed for railroad to the Pacific

f. no slavery north of 36° 30′

g. passed in 1828 to embarrass President Adams, infuriated the South

h. government funds placed there under Jackson

i. no slavery in territory from Mexico

j. federal land must be purchased with gold or silver

Name the item or person (each answer, 3 points).

2.011 The three national leaders from the South, West, and North who never became president:

a. _____ b. _____

c. _____

2.012 _____ Name for land acquired after the Mexican War

2.013 _____ Slogan for those who wanted all of Oregon

2.014 _____ One rally cry of the Texas Revolution

2.015 _____ State that was an independent republic for 10 years before joining the Union

2.016 _____ Polk went to war with Mexico to get this state

2.017 _____ The crisis that almost divided the nation under Andrew Jackson

2.018 _____ The "moneyed monster" hated by Jackson and eventually destroyed by him

Answer these questions (each answer, 3 points).

2.019 The United States peacefully resolved border disputes with Great Britain over which two territories in the 1840s?

_____

2.020 How did the Mexican War start?

_____

_____

2.021 What campaign won the Mexican War for America and who led it?

_____

_____

2.022 What happened at the Alamo in 1836?

_____

_____

_____

2.023 What were Zachary Taylor's qualifications for president?

_____

_____

2.024 What were the terms of the Treaty of Guadalupe Hidalgo?

_____

_____

_____

_____

2.025 What was the "corrupt bargain" that Jackson claimed John Quincy Adams used to win the presidency?

_____

_____

2.026 Why could Congress not agree on organizing the new territories after the Mexican War?

_____

_____

2.027 Why was James Polk chosen as the Democratic candidate for president?

_____

_____

2.028 What happened to the Democratic-Republican Party after the election of John Quincy Adams?

_____

_____

Match these people (each answer, 2 points).

2.029 _____ became president at Harrison's death, a Whig with Democrat ideas	a.	Andrew Jackson
2.030 _____ brilliant American general, highest-ranking officer during Mexican War	b.	Sam Houston
2.031 _____ served in House of Representatives for years after presidency	c.	William H. Harrison
2.032 _____ the Great Compromiser	d.	Henry Clay
2.033 _____ hero of New Orleans, the people's president	e.	James K. Polk
2.034 _____ Jackson's hand-picked successor, the Little Magician	f.	Zachary Taylor
2.035 _____ victor at Buena Vista, Old Rough and Ready	g.	Winfield Scott
2.036 _____ Texan, victor at San Jacinto against Santa Anna	h.	Martin Van Buren
2.037 _____ added more territory to the Union than any other president	i.	John Quincy Adams
2.038 _____ president for only 31 days	j.	John Tyler

80 / 100   SCORE _____   TEACHER _____ _____

initials   date

3. GROWTH AND DIVISION

America grew in the early 1800s in more than just size. The Industrial Revolution brought manufacturing growth which would eventually make America a world power. Innovations in transportation, agriculture, manufacturing, and communications caused unprecedented changes in American life. Trade grew and the various parts of the frontier were brought into the national economy as transport became easier. Life became easier as machines took over backbreaking manual labor. The new industries created large pools of wealth that further fed the growth of industry and commerce.

American life also saw changes as immigration brought in large numbers of new citizens.

A revival broke out in the early 1800s that led thousands to the Lord. A reform movement followed the revival and touched many areas of American life.

The great tragedy of the era was the continuation of slavery and the South's stubborn defense of it. The Kansas-Nebraska Act destroyed the Missouri Compromise and much of the remaining trust between the anti-slavery North and the pro-slavery South. The anti-slavery Republican Party was formed and leaped onto the national scene. The breakup of the Union was drawing near.

SECTION OBJECTIVES

Review these objectives. When you have completed this section, you should be able to:

1. Name the leaders of the era and explain their accomplishments.
3. Trace the development of the slavery and tariff issues from 1820 to 1855.
4. Define Manifest Destiny and describe its course in America.
6. Define the Industrial Revolution and name the people, innovations, and inventions that contributed to it.
7. Describe the effects of the Industrial Revolution in America.
8. Describe the Second Great Awakening and the reform movements that followed it.
9. Describe the compromises that kept the nation together and what ended them.
10. Describe the changes in America and American life in this era.

VOCABULARY

Study these words to enhance your learning success in this section.

comptroller (komp trō′ ler). A public official who audits government accounts.

denomination (di nom i nā′ shun). A religious organization uniting in a single administrative body a number of local congregations.

heresy (her′ e sē). A belief different from the standard beliefs of the church.

patent (pat′ nt). A document that gives an inventor the sole right to make, use or sell his invention for so many years.

platform (plat′ form). Statement of policies and ideas adopted by a political party.

polygamy (po lig' a mē). Marriage to more than one person at one time, usually the taking of several wives by one man.

propaganda (prop a gan' da). The spreading of ideas or information for the purpose of helping or injuring a cause, institution, or person.

temperance (tem' pe rens). Moderation in or abstinence from the use of intoxicating drinks.

The Industrial Revolution

Not all revolutions are violent. Second only to the War for Independence, the greatest revolution in American history was the Industrial Revolution. This revolution was the change from a farming and handcrafting society to one of industry and machine manufacturing. It began in England in the 1700s and eventually spread to reach much of the world. It began in America, in a small way, late in that same century, but it did not become an important part of American culture until the War of 1812. It was the embargoes and blockades of that war that pushed American manufacturing to begin its spectacular rise.

Textiles. The revolution had its most successful beginning in the textile industry. Britain had developed many of the machines used in the mass production of cloth in the late 1700s. These machines spun several spools of yarn or thread instead of the one at a time that could be done by hand. British inventors had also invented the power loom that allowed cloth to be woven more quickly. These inventions were protected by laws that prohibited plans of the machines or people who knew them from leaving the country.

However, the laws did not stop Samuel Slater, the "Father of the Factory System (in America). Slater was a skilled mechanic familiar with the British textile machines. He memorized the plans for the machines and succeeded in reaching the United States in disguise. In 1791 with the financial backing of Moses Brown, a New England capitalist, Slater opened America's first factory for spinning thread in Rhode Island.

The new factory was opened in time to cash in on the flood of cotton from the South. Eli Whitney invented the cotton gin in 1793, allowing for the cheap production of this textile fiber. The factories of the North were soon busy turning Southern cotton into cotton thread. These same factories began to weave it into cloth when the power loom was added to the American system in 1814. The textile industry received another boost in 1846 when Elias Howe **patented** the sewing machine. It was further perfected by Isaac Singer who made it popular. It was the first in a long line of labor-saving devices that began to appear

| Cotton Gin

in American homes, not just factories. It also allowed the factories to begin mass-producing clothes from their inexpensive thread and cloth.

Most of the factories were located in the northeast for several reasons. The machines were powered at first by water wheels that required fast-moving streams. The steep hills and swift streams of New England were ideal for these kinds of factories. The poor soil of New England encouraged people to try the alternative of manufacturing. Northern seaports provided a ready way to bring in raw material and export finished goods. New England also had a ready supply of capital from its many wealthy shipping entrepreneurs. Moreover, the northeast was the most densely populated part of the nation, providing the factories with needed workers. The West, by contrast, was sparsely populated by poor farmers, and the South was populated by rich plantation owners whose money was in cotton and slaves.

Mass Production. Eli Whitney made very little money on his cotton gin. He obtained a patent for the device, but others still produced the simple machine. By the time Whitney had gone through the courts and put the illegal manufacturers out of business, his patent had almost expired, so he had to earn his fortune another way. The way he chose once again revolutionized American manufacturing.

Whitney came up with the idea of mass production of interchangeable parts for guns. Prior to that time, each part of a gun was made by hand and it fit only that particular gun. If a part broke, a new one had to be handmade to replace it. Whitney had the parts made in large groups, each exactly alike. That way, a broken part could be easily and quickly replaced. The guns could be manufactured and maintained at a lesser cost. Whitney reportedly proved his point by taking ten guns to Washington for government officials to see. He took them apart, scrambled the pieces, and reassembled them into ten working guns!

Mass production of interchangeable parts spread to all areas of manufacturing. The cheap production of many goods brought those goods within reach for more and more people. It also gave the North a vast manufacturing engine that would be vital in the coming war with the South.

Factory Workers. The factory system was very beneficial to the nation by providing new jobs, cheaper goods, and economic prosperity; but it also had a downside. Many factory workers were shamefully exploited. Wages were low and hours were long. Thirteen- or fourteen-hour days, six days a week were common. Unions were considered conspiracies, and strikes for better pay often were broken up by the law. Working conditions were bad and often unsafe. An injured or ill worker had no protection from losing their job.

The worst abuse was the employment of children in the factories. Children, often under the age of ten, were put to work tending the machines for pitiful wages. They worked the same hours as the adults, deprived of their childhood and frequently their health by years of labor. Working also meant they could not get an education, and that often meant they would be unskilled laborers for all their lives. This child abuse was one of the blackest marks on the growth of industry in America and would continue for many years.

Gradually, improvements were made. Martin Van Buren set a precedent in 1840 when he limited workers on federal projects to ten hours a day. Slowly, the states began to pass laws limiting working hours. In 1842 the Supreme Court ruled that labor unions were not automatically illegal conspiracies. However, it would be many years before unions could build up the strength to effectively challenge the power of the employers.

Farming. Farming also profited from the Industrial Revolution. The thickly matted soil of the West had been hard on the heavy wooden plows that existed in the 1700s. In 1837 John Deere invented a light, sharp steel plow for western farmers. A few years earlier, Cyrus McCormick had patented a mechanical reaper. This remarkable invention allowed a man to harvest his grain by himself faster than he could with several helpers.

The new plow and reaper allowed a farmer to produce substantially more food than he needed for his family. Suddenly, farming was not just a way to survive, it was a way to make a profit!! Fertile western farms began to supply food for cotton-growing southern plantations and cotton-spinning northern factories. The different parts of the country specialized and depended upon the others for what they did not produce themselves.

Communication. The single greatest revolution in the history of communication was the invention of the telegraph by Samuel Morse. Morse invented a way to send messages instantly over a wire using a series of dots and dashes called Morse Code. In 1844 he sent a message from Washington to Baltimore, "What hath God wrought?" opening the era of instant communications! Soon, telegraph wires were all over the nation, allowing news and information to speed across the American expanse. In 1866 after five failures, Cyrus Field succeeded in laying a telegraph cable between Canada and Great Britain. The Old and New World were suddenly just a few seconds apart.

| McCormick's Reaper advertisement, the caption read, "The People's Favorite! The World-Renowned McCormick Twine Binder! Victorious in over 100 Field Trials! New and Valuable Improvements for 1884!"

Match these people (some answers will be used more than once).

3.1 _____ Father of the Factory System

3.2 _____ cotton gin

3.3 _____ interchangeable parts for guns

3.4 _____ invented the telegraph

3.5 _____ opened America's first thread-spinning factory

3.6 _____ invented the sewing machine

3.7 _____ steel plow

3.8 _____ improved and popularized the sewing machine

3.9 _____ "What hath God wrought?"

3.10 _____ mechanical reaper

3.11 _____ memorized British machine plans and came to America

3.12 _____ laid a telegraph cable from Europe to North America

a. Cyrus McCormick

b. Cyrus Field

c. John Deere

d. Elias Howe

e. Eli Whitney

f. Isaac Singer

g. Samuel Morse

h. Samuel Slater

Complete the following.

3.13 Where did the worldwide Industrial Revolution begin? _____

3.14 How did the new farm machines change Western farming?

_____

3.15 Name three reasons why factories developed in the Northeast.

a. _____

b. _____

c. _____

3.16 Name four ways the factory system exploited workers.

a. _____

b. _____

c. _____

d. _____

3.17 What was the Industrial Revolution?

_____

_____

Transportation Needs. Improvements in transportation were a vital part of the Industrial Revolution. At the time of the American Revolution, transportation was very poor. Roads were unpaved, muddy, rutted, and often impassable for wagons. The most reliable transportation was by water, but the rivers did not go to every farm. Since most farms produced only for the needs of the family, it was not a vital concern until the Industrial Revolution. However, before farms could provide food for cities devoted to manufacturing, they needed reliable ways to ship their produce.

Roads. The first improvements in overland transportation came through privately owned turnpikes at the end of the 1700s. The Lancaster Turnpike was a pioneer in this field. It was a wide road with a hard surface and was built by a private company. The company made a substantial profit charging tolls for commerce between Philadelphia and Lancaster, Pennsylvania. Its success encouraged many other companies to invest in these arteries. Commerce flourished along these routes, encouraging more of the same.

The Cumberland Road, also called the National Road, was built with public funds. It ran from Cumberland, Maryland to Vandalia, Illinois (completed in 1852). Connecting roads made it a fairly direct route between Baltimore on Chesapeake Bay, and St. Louis on the Mississippi River. It was a huge stimulant to trade, western migration, and the development of the cities of the frontier.

However, public roads were difficult to build. It was very expensive to build roads in the middle of the wilderness, miles from major sources of supplies, manpower, and food. States' rights advocates, like the Democrats, objected violently to using federal funds for any project inside one state. Moreover, the Northeast did not want to aid roads that would encourage their population to move west. So, additions to the national road that would connect it with major cities in Kentucky, for example, were

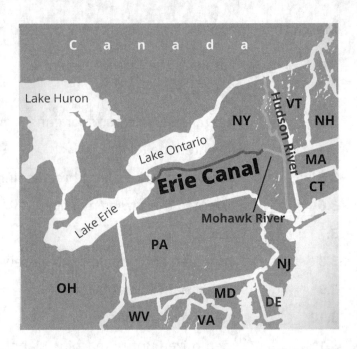

routinely voted down or vetoed, especially by Andrew Jackson. Nevertheless, with dedicated state spending, the hard-surface roads were gradually expanded.

The Steamboat. The mighty rivers of America, especially the Mississippi, were major trade routes. However, prior to 1807 they were basically one-way streets. Shipping goods downstream from a farm in Illinois to New Orleans, for example, was slow but simple. A farmer only had to build a raft and float it carefully down the river. However, going upstream carrying cargo of any bulk was incredibly difficult and too expensive to be very profitable.

That all changed in 1807 when Robert Fulton built a workable steamboat. It used a steam engine (which had been invented by other people) to drive a paddle wheel on the side of the ship. Fulton's ship, the *Clermont*, was called "Fulton's Folly" by his detractors. No one was laughing, however, when the ship steamed up the Hudson River from New York City to Albany in 32 hours—an unheard-of feat!

The steamboats rapidly spread to all the navigable rivers of the nation. They especially came to dominate trade on the Mississippi where a thousand or more people were working by 1860. Cities along the upper reaches of the river flourished as trade expanded. The Supreme Court decision of *Gibbons v. Ogden* in 1824 prohibited the states from controlling interstate trade on these rivers. That opened up these vital routes to healthy competition and rapid expansion.

Canal Craze. Even with better roads, water transportation was still better for large quantities of bulky cargo, but the rivers did not connect many of the vital inland water routes. This problem was corrected by a surge of canal building in the early 1800s.

The most famous and most successful of the internal canals was the Erie Canal in New York State. The Erie Canal connected Lake Erie with the Atlantic Ocean through the Mohawk and Hudson Rivers. It was promoted by New York Governor DeWitt Clinton. The federal government would not contribute any funds, so the difficult project was built entirely with New York money. Clinton's opponents called it "Clinton's Ditch." The determined governor persevered from 1817 until 1825, when the canal finally opened.

The canal was an unprecedented success. The time required to ship a ton of grain from Buffalo to New York City fell from twenty days to six days, and the cost dropped from $100 to $5! The Erie Canal connected New York City to the entire Midwest by the Great Lakes. The city quickly became the premier port on the eastern seaboard because of the influx of produce from the West. Land values along the canal shot up. Industry flourished with a ready source of raw materials and a cheap method for shipping out finished goods. "Clinton's Ditch" was New York's gold mine!

Other states observed the success and tried to copy it. A flurry of canal construction occurred in the 1820s and '30s. Several canals were built to connect the Mississippi and the Great Lakes. This also benefitted the trade going into New York City via the Erie Canal. One of the most

unusual canals connected the Susquehanna River above Chesapeake Bay to the Ohio River; it used a special railroad to lift the barges over the Allegheny Mountains. Many of these canals were a commercial success for a short time, but none rivaled the economic impact of the Erie Canal.

Ocean Trade. The steamboats and canals brought American products to seaports for trade with the world. America led the world in the mid-1800s in the development of a new ocean vessel, the clipper ship. Clipper ships were streamlined vessels built with a huge collection of sails. They were built for speed, not bulk, to carry valuable cargoes quickly. They quickly took over the tea trade to the Far East and were the vessel of choice for the impatient thousands heading to the California gold fields.

However, the majestic clippers were put out of business by the development of ocean-going steamships. These unlovely, slower ships were reliable and could carry much more cargo. By the time of the Civil War, the beautiful clippers were losing their cargoes to the cheaper transport of the smoke-belching steamers.

Railroad. The success of the canals was quickly ended by the incredible story of the railroads. These speedy monsters could go anywhere tracks could be laid. They were not dependent upon waterways or limited by hills and mountains. Railroads could carry bulky cargo even to cities that had no nearby river or lake.

Rail lines were used in the early 1800s to connect major cities using horse-drawn coaches. It was in Britain that the newly developed steam engine was first adapted to pull these coaches. It was also in Britain that the standard gauge (rail separation) of 4 feet 8 1/2 inches was set. (This was the standard width for wagon axles in Britain because the deep ruts in the old Roman roads were that distance apart. It had been the width of Roman chariot axles and became the railroad width in Britain, Canada, and the United States!)

The first American company to try the new technology was the Baltimore and Ohio Company which began service in 1830 with thirteen miles of track. That same year the B&O publicized its new venture by staging a race between a horse-drawn rail coach and one drawn by the *Tom Thumb*, an American-built locomotive. The *Tom Thumb* was winning until it broke down and the horse crossed the finish line first. It did not matter—the railroad had arrived.

The railroad expanded rapidly and quickly took up a vital role in the nation. From the thirteen miles set up by the B&O in 1830, the rail lines grew to about 30,000 miles by 1860! Most of these tracks were in the industrial North and the rapidly expanding West around the Great Lakes. The railroad gave the farmers of Ohio, Illinois, and Indiana direct access to the markets of the northeast. This vital river of iron replaced the Mississippi as the main trade route of the West. That stopped the South from choking off the West by their control of the Mississippi seaports during the Civil War.

| Early Steam Locomotive

 Answer these questions.

3.18 Why was better transportation needed for the Industrial Revolution?

_____

_____

3.19 Why didn't the federal government build more roads?

_____

_____

3.20 Why was the railroad important to the West in the Civil War?

_____

_____

3.21 Why were so many canals built in the years after 1825?

_____

_____

3.22 What put the clipper ships out of business?

_____

Match these items (some answers will be used more than once).

3.23 _____ *Gibbons v. Ogden* gave these unfettered competition

3.24 _____ built by private companies that made a profit on tolls

3.25 _____ *Clermont*

3.26 _____ *Tom Thumb's* owners

3.27 _____ had 30,000 miles by 1860

3.28 _____ made New York City the most important Eastern port

3.29 _____ the National Road

3.30 _____ major land artery between Chesapeake Bay and the Mississippi

3.31 _____ took over the tea trade with the Far East because of their speed

3.32 _____ dropped the cost of shipping a ton of grain from Buffalo to New York City from $100 to $5

3.33 _____ ocean vessels built for speed

3.34 _____ made the rivers into two-way streets

3.35 _____ first railroad in the U.S.

3.36 _____ pioneer connected Lancaster and Philadelphia

3.37 _____ Clinton's Ditch

3.38 _____ connected Mississippi River and Great Lakes

3.39 _____ one used to connect the Susquehanna and Ohio Rivers and used a railroad to get over the Allegheny Mountains

3.40 _____ its success ended the success of canals

3.41 _____ transport for large quantities of bulk cargo, did not require waterways

a. steamboats

b. clipper ships

c. turnpikes

d. railroads

e. canals

f. Erie Canal

g. Cumberland Road

h. Baltimore and Ohio

Changing American Life

Immigration. The population of the United States continued to grow at a remarkable rate in the early 1800s. Since colonial times, the population had continued to double every 23 years! By 1860 America had the fourth-largest national population in the world. Much of this was due to the country's remarkable birthrate; but by the early 1800s, the native-born citizens were being supplemented by immigrants from Europe. The rate of immigration skyrocketed in the 1840s, primarily from Ireland and Germany.

Ireland was a land held in near slavery by Great Britain. In order to feed their families, the Irish peasants were forced to rent land from British landlords. British law restricted the rights of Catholics who made up most of the Irish population. The last straw was the Potato Famine from 1845-1847. The Irish people lived on potatoes and in those years the crops were destroyed by a blight. An estimated 2 million people died of starvation and disease. Boatloads of Irishmen left their homeland out of desperation. Hundreds of thousands came to America during those bleak years.

Irish immigrants were too poor to buy land and supplies. They could not move west; therefore, they tended to congregate in the cities of the East Coast. They had little education and quickly filled the ranks of the unskilled laborers. Many found work building the canals and railroads. They often lived in filthy city tenements and faced death from the diseases bred by poor sanitation. Moreover, the Catholic Irish were distrusted by the more established Protestant Americans. They were often denied jobs because of their ancestry. "No Irish Need Apply" was a common note added to a job offer.

The concentration of Irish immigrants in the cities slowly built their political power. Politicians found it necessary to cater to the "Irish vote." Some Irish, notably Tammany Hall in New York City, built extensive political control organizations called "machines" that literally controlled the city. Irishmen came to dominate the police and fire departments of many Northeastern cities. In time, the Irish found a piece of the American pie.

The other large group of immigrants came from Germany. Most of these people were farmers displaced by hard times or political upheaval. A few of the immigrants were intellectuals who fled in 1848 after revolutions for greater freedom failed in Europe. As with the Irish, hundreds of thousands of German immigrants came in the 1800s. Unlike the Irish, the German newcomers usually had some money. As a result, they did not stay in the eastern cities. They moved west, often to the northern states of the upper Mississippi River, such as Wisconsin and Michigan. They built prosperous farms and integrated into American life. They brought their love of *bier* (beer) and their brewing skills to their new homeland, as well as their tradition of hard work.

Know-Nothing Party. The 1840s and '50s saw a rise of anti-immigrant feelings in America. The sudden influx of Irish and German people alarmed native-born Americans. The poverty of many of the immigrants left them dependent on charity and public support. Many of the newcomers were also Catholic, and anti-Catholicism was still strong in the United States. Several incidents of anti-Catholic violence occurred in the mid-1800s. The strongest evidence of the anti-immigrant sentiment was the creation of the Know-Nothing Party.

The Know-Nothing Party developed from the Order of the Star Spangled Banner, created in 1849. It was a political organization that called for strict control on immigration, deportation of poor immigrants, and long waiting periods for citizenship and the right to vote. It was called the Know-Nothing Party because of its secrecy. Its rally cry was "America for the Americans."

The party won several elections on the local and state level in the 1850s, but they were never able to successfully push their agenda. The controversy over slavery split the movement and ended its day of glory. It disappeared after a dismal showing in the 1856 elections.

The Second Great Awakening. In the 1730s and '40s, The Great Awakening had turned the hearts of many of the American colonists to God. Revival struck the nation again in the late 1790s. This visitation of God's Spirit was called the Second Great Awakening, and it lasted into the 1830s. This revival did not have the prominent leaders the first one had with George Whitefield and Jonathan Edwards. It also was less intense, but it lasted longer and covered a larger area.

The fervor of American Christianity had gone cold in the years since the Great Awakening. The spread of the frontier had taken people further and further from organized churches. The needs of survival had drawn hearts away from God, and the roughness of frontier life had pushed aside the Savior's gentle touch. However, the preachers of the early 1800s found a way to reach the scattered masses of the frontier: the camp meeting.

Camp meetings were large gatherings of people to hear several days of preaching and teaching from the Word of God. The place was advertised in advance, and people would come from all over the region and camp at the site. Hundreds and sometimes thousands of people would attend. People were attracted to the meetings by a chance to socialize and to enjoy some stimulation in their monotonous wilderness lives. They often came away changed by the message of Christ's love and salvation.

The camp meeting revivals were often extremely emotional. People would sing, dance, shout, and shake. Salvation was often accompanied by hysterical weeping and repenting. The emotionalism was criticized by many, and some preachers tried to control it.

| A Circuit-Riding Preacher

The revival eventually spread to the cities due to the work of traveling evangelists who came out of the Awakening. The most famous was Charles Finney who preached to large crowds in the cities in the 1820s to the 1850s. Finney saw a great mass of people turn to God in New York City where he primarily worked. Another great city evangelist was D. L. Moody who worked out of Chicago beginning in the 1850s. Moody went on to found the Moody Bible Institute in that city. Both men concentrated on preaching individual salvation and the Bible as the Word of God.

The Methodists and Baptists which welcomed greater emotionalism were the **denominations** that grew the most during this revival. The new congregations were served by "circuit riders," pastors who traveled hundreds of miles visiting each church on his circuit in turn. The most renowned of these traveling pastors was Francis Asbury (1745-1816), who was the leader of the American Methodist Church. He traveled thousands of miles a year on horseback, via frontier roads or trails to serve the people under his care.

Other Sects. Other sects developed in the 1800s which most evangelical Christians would call **heresies**. The deist tradition of the founding fathers led to the development of Unitarianism in the early 1800s. This belief stripped the gospel of the doctrines of sin, grace, and salvation. Unitarians believed there was no trinity, only one God, hence the name *Unitarian*. They also said that Jesus was not God, man was essentially good, and good works were the way to "salvation." Thus, man needed only himself, not God.

Another prominent sect was the Church of Jesus Christ of Latter-Day Saints (Mormons). The Mormon religion was founded in the 1830s by Joseph Smith. Smith claimed to have had a vision in which an angel told him to dig up some golden plates written in an ancient language. Given a way to translate the tablets, Smith claimed to have written the Book of Mormon from them. This book is the basis of Mormon beliefs.

The Mormon religion began in Missouri, and later Smith and his followers moved to Illinois. They were distrusted and persecuted there. Eventually, Smith was murdered and most of his followers left under the leadership of Brigham Young. Young led the group to the dry, empty wilderness of Utah to allow them to live in peace and follow their own ways, which included **polygamy**.

In the mid-1800s, the well-organized Mormons irrigated and built the state into a prosperous community. The number of believers grew due to high birthrates and aggressive missionary work. The powerful hierarchy of the church clashed with the federal government when the population grew large enough to allow a territory to be organized. Much of the conflict centered on the practice of polygamy, which traditional Christians found repulsive. Eventually, the Mormons gave up that practice, and Utah was allowed to become a state in 1896.

| Carrie Nation, a colorful Temperance Leader

Reform Movements. The revival of Christianity caused a renewed interest in reforms. The reform movement dealt with prisons, treatment of the insane, debt law, drinking, working conditions, and women's rights. In the early 1800s, many laws were passed reforming problems in these areas. Imprisonment for debt was gradually ended. Brutal forms of punishment like whipping and branding were eliminated. The concept of trying to reform, not just punish, criminals was introduced. This was especially applied to young children drawn into a life of crime. Improvements were made in the brutal treatment of the insane. Dorthea Dix led the way in this area, traveling all over the nation publicizing the way insane people were caged and tied like animals.

The **temperance** movement also gained force in this time period. Heavy drinking was an American tradition, especially on the frontier. It came under increasing attacks by reformers as Christianity reasserted itself. Men were encouraged to "take the pledge," which was an oath never to drink again. Thousands did so in well-organized temperance rallies. The movement also made good use of public advertisements on the evils of drinking.

The campaign for women's rights also began in the early 1800s. At that time, women could not vote, all of their property belonged to their husbands, and the husbands were even free to beat them, to a certain extent. The movement for women's rights grew out of women participating in the abolitionist movement. The political activism of that cause led many women to question why they were denied full protection of the law and the right to vote.

The official beginning of the modern movement for women's rights was at the Seneca Falls Convention. A few of the pioneers of the women's movement met at the Convention in 1848 and drew up a statement of rights for women. It was based on the Declaration of Independence, declaring that "all men *and* women are created equal." It drew a tremendous amount of ridicule in the press. Many of the original supporters backed away from it, but the women would not be silenced. Gradually, colleges began to admit women, and laws were passed giving them rights to their own property. However, it would be many years before legal equality was achieved.

Another important movement was the growing support for public education. Massachusetts had led the way in colonial times, but education was primarily a privilege of the rich through the 1700s. The situation began to change with the expansion of the right to vote. Poor working men who voted began to demand education for their children. Gradually the wealthy members of society began to realize the advantages of having education available to all, preventing illiterate voters from controlling the elections. The idea that good citizens need to be educated pushed the state governments to pay for elementary education for everyone. Reformers also created better textbooks and set up training schools for teachers.

The most noticeable reform movement of the early to mid-1800s was the abolitionist movement. The case for eliminating slavery had been gaining momentum for years. Slavery was abolished in Great Britain in 1833, thanks to the impressive labor of William Wilberforce, a wealthy evangelical Christian. This freed the slaves in the nearby British West Indies and encouraged the movement in America.

Moderate abolitionists wanted to end slavery slowly, possibly with compensation for slave owners. They hoped to use moral persuasion and increasingly anti-slavery laws to end the institution. This had been the successful pattern in Britain, but Britain did not have a place like the southern United States.

It was the extreme abolitionists who attracted the most attention, however. They were led by William Garrison who founded the anti-slavery newspaper, *The Liberator,* in 1831. Garrison condemned slavery in violent terms that disturbed more moderate abolitionists. He received many death threats and was attacked by mobs several times while giving speeches that presented his views. He continued to publish the newspaper until 1865 which was when the 13th amendment to the Constitution was ratified by the states and slavery officially ended.

Another man who for a short time also published a newspaper that supported the anti-slavery movement was Elijah P. Lovejoy. His presses were repeatedly destroyed, and he was eventually killed by a mob in 1837. The death of Lovejoy gave the anti-slavery movement their first martyr.

Men like Garrison and Lovejoy caused reactions of fear and hatred in the South. Southerners defended their peculiar institution all the more. They argued that their slaves were part of their families and better off than poor factory workers in the North. The two sides found it increasingly difficult even to discuss the issue, much less reach agreement on it.

Complete these sentences.

3.42 The _____ was a Christian revival from the 1790s to the 1830s.

3.43 The _____ Party was a political party that was anti-immigrant.

3.44 The two largest groups of immigrants in the early 1800s came from _____ and _____ .

3.45 Mormons got into trouble with the government largely over the practice of _____ .

3.46 Many Irishmen came to America because of the _____ in 1845-1847.

3.47 The frontier revivals of the early 1800s were spread by means of large, emotional _____ .

3.48 The modern women's rights movement began at the _____ _____ in 1848.

3.49 _____ believe in only one God, not a Trinity, and that man is good.

3.50 Extreme abolitionist William Garrison started the newspaper, _____ , in 1831.

3.51 The _____ movement used ads and pledges to reduce drinking in America.

3.52 The creator of Mormonism was _____ .

3.53 _____ was largely responsible for ending slavery in Great Britain.

3.54 The two denominations that grew most from the revivals of the early 1800s were the _____ and the _____ .

3.55 _____ led the Mormons out of Illinois to form their own community in what would become the state of _____ .

3.56 Six of the areas that reformers tried to change in the early 1800s were.

_____ , _____ ,

_____ , _____ ,

_____ , and _____ .

Answer true or false.

3.57 _____ Circuit riders were pastors of several churches spread over a large area.

3.58 _____ Irish immigrants were usually very poor.

3.59 _____ German immigrants tended to stay in the cities of the Northeast.

3.60 _____ The reform movements were partly a result of the Second Great Awakening.

3.61 _____ D. L. Moody was the early leader of the American Methodist Church.

3.62 _____ Moderate abolitionists wanted to end slavery immediately.

3.63 _____ America in the early 1800s was generally anti-Catholic.

3.64 _____ "America for the Americans," was the rally cry of Dorthea Dix.

3.65 _____ *The Book of Mormon* was supposedly taken from the words spoken by an angel to Brigham Young.

3.66 _____ D. L. Moody was an evangelist who worked out of Chicago.

The Great Divide

Last Compromise. California opened a hornet's nest when it requested admission into the Union in 1849. The Union had exactly fifteen slave and fifteen free states at the time. That meant the South could block any anti-slavery laws by its control of half of the votes in the Senate. Loss of that veto power was a serious threat to the South, or so they believed. The South was not about to lose it without a fight, and the Union was again threatened. Into the gap stepped the old giants: Clay, Webster, and Calhoun, for their last major appearance on the public stage. All of them would be dead by 1852. Clay, "the Great Compromiser," proposed a series of laws that would save the Union. Calhoun opposed them, but died before the debate concluded. Webster spoke strongly in support of compromise for the sake of the country, a stand that brought him heavy condemnation from abolitionists. Eventually, a compromise was worked out and accepted by the nation, with a sigh of relief.

The Compromise of 1850 was a series of agreements that tried to balance each other. The first allowed California to join the Union as a free state. That permanently cost the South its veto in the Senate. In exchange, slavery would not be barred in the remaining states in the Mexican Cession. They would have popular sovereignty on the issue of slavery (chosen for themselves).

The state of Texas claimed a large piece of territory that is now part of the states of New Mexico, Colorado, Wyoming, Kansas and Oklahoma. That land was taken from Texas. In exchange, Texas received $10 million in compensation.

The moderate abolitionists had been trying for years to restrict or eliminate slavery in Washington D.C. as a step on their agenda of gradual abolition. The Compromise gave them an end to the slave trade, but not slavery, in the American capital. The South was also given a much stronger fugitive slave act because of the many concessions they made.

The Fugitive Slave Act of 1850 was something the South had wanted for a long time. For many years abolitionists had been running the "Underground Railroad" to help enslaved people escape to Canada. The Railroad was actually a series of houses on the road north, called "stations," where slaves could hide and receive help to reach the next stop. People who helped on the route were called "conductors" and the escaping slaves "passengers." One remarkable conductor, Harriet Tubman, herself an escaped slave, returned to the South repeatedly and led over 300 people to freedom on the Railroad.

The Underground Railroad infuriated the South. Only a small percentage of enslaved people escaped that way, but it was the principle that grated on slave owners. In their eyes, their property was being stolen by a well-organized conspiracy and the officials in the North were not doing anything to stop it. Southerners had been arguing for a stronger federal law to stop the "thefts." They got it as part of the Compromise of 1850.

The law regarding fugitive slaves was harsh. A black person who was accused of being a runaway slave could not testify in their own behalf or post bail, nor would the case be heard by a jury. The commissioner who decided the case was paid five dollars if the prisoner was released and ten dollars if they were not, a practice that sounded very much like a bribe. Federal officials were required to act as slave catchers. Any private person who aided an escaping slave or refused to aid in their capture was subject to fines or imprisonment.

The law was a serious mistake. It caused many people who had not opposed slavery to become abolitionists and many moderates to become extremists. The injustices of the law inflamed the North. Free black people who were captured by "slave catchers" had no possible way to prove they were not slaves. Escaped slaves who had lived in the North for years were sent back to angry masters. Honest men who opposed slavery and helped their fellow

| Underground Railroad

man reach freedom went to jail or lost their worldly wealth for helping them. The people of the North now saw the effects of slavery in their own towns and cities. Southerners became increasingly frustrated as the law was ignored, avoided, and condemned.

The reaction in the North was strong. Mobs freed slaves who were taken under the Fugitive Slave Act. At times, troops had to be used to guard black captives and escort them south. Northern states tried to hamper the law by refusing to aid federal officials and denying the use of state jails. "The Bloodhound Bill" or the "Man-Stealing Law," as it was called, was opposed in print all over the North. The law did a great deal to unify the North and lay the ground work for the Civil War.

Millard Fillmore. Millard Fillmore (1800-1874) became president in 1850 when Zachary Taylor died. Fillmore was born in New York. He had been apprenticed to a cloth maker as a boy but eventually went into the practice of law in his home state. He served in the House of Representatives in New York and Washington. He was serving as **comptroller** of New York when he was chosen to run with Zachary Taylor. Since Taylor was from the South, a New Yorker was added to balance the Whig ticket to represent the whole nation.

Fillmore was a good friend and follower of Henry Clay. He had presided over the Senate as vice president during the debates on the Compromise of 1850. He favored the Compromise even though Taylor opposed it and had threatened to veto it, so Fillmore put his new administration firmly behind the bills, which were stalled in Congress. The Compromise passed and Fillmore signed it. It was the one significant accomplishment of his presidency, and it preserved the Union for ten more years.

Election of 1852. By 1852, Northern opposition to the Fugitive Slave Law had divided the Whig party. Fillmore, who supported the law, did not get the nomination. Instead, the Whigs relied on one of their favorite tricks, nominating a war hero. In this case, they nominated Winfield Scott, "Old Fuss and Feathers," the brilliant commander of the campaign against Mexico City. Their **platform** supported the Compromise of 1850 even though Scott opposed slavery. The Whigs were badly split because the Northerners hated the party platform.

The Democrats were also divided and wound up nominating a "dark horse" candidate, Franklin Pierce. Pierce was a pro-slavery northerner who warmly supported all of the Compromise of 1850. Other than that, Pierce and Scott were both distinguished by their lack of controversial stands on any issues. However, Scott's personal stand against slavery and his pompous nature cost him the election. The slavery issue had successfully split the Whigs. Their party was nearing extinction.

Franklin Pierce. Franklin Pierce (1804-1869) won the Democratic nomination only after the four primary candidates had fought to a draw at the convention. Pierce was born to a wealthy family in New Hampshire. His father served in the Revolution and was governor of the state

| Perry's visit to Japan

for a time. Franklin became a lawyer and a member of the state House of Representatives. He later served in both the House and the Senate in Washington. He also served without distinction as a general in the Mexican War. He was virtually unknown outside of New Hampshire when he was nominated for president in 1852.

Pierce was an easygoing man who tended to listen to the pro-Southern voices in his Cabinet. He was an expansionist, and his Southern friends specifically wanted lands suitable for the expansion of slavery. Pierce's foreign policy was a mixed bag, however, with a success that was not his doing and a failure that was.

The success came from Millard Fillmore. As president, Fillmore had dispatched Commodore Matthew Perry to the Far East to expand American trade in the Pacific. Perry carried a letter addressed to the ruler of Japan. Japan was at that time a completely closed society. It had refused to trade with the West, even imprisoning sailors shipwrecked on its shores. Perry, by a show of force with his modern gunboats, persuaded the Japanese to take his letter. Using tact and threats, Perry convinced the Japanese to open up their nation to trade with the United States. The treaty was approved by the Senate in 1854. It marked a turning point for Japan which changed from a medieval feudal kingdom to a world power in less than a hundred years.

Pierce's failure was an embarrassing attempt to add Cuba to the United States. Cuba, with its large slave-run sugar plantations, was a prize plum for the South as a way to add slave states to the Union. Pierce tried to purchase the island, but Spain absolutely refused. In 1854, Spanish officials seized an American steamer, the *Black Warrior*, in Cuba which triggered a crisis. The American ministers in Spain, Britain, and France were instructed to meet and draw up a plan for acquiring Cuba. The plan they

drew up, the Ostend Manifesto, called for taking the island by force if Spain refused an offer of $120 million for it and if Spanish ownership endangered American interests.

The Ostend Manifesto became public and the reaction was wild. Northern abolitionists condemned the scheme as a blueprint for piracy. The publication of the secret plan was an acute embarrassment to the administration. Pierce dropped all attempts to take Cuba. The infighting over slavery had finally done what France, Britain, Mexico, and Spain could not do: halt the advance of Manifest Destiny.

 Answer these questions.

3.67 What were the six major terms of the Compromise of 1850?

a. _____

b. _____

c. _____

d. _____

e. _____

f. _____

3.68 Where did the three old "giants" in the Congress stand on the Compromise?

Clay _____

Calhoun _____

Webster _____

3.69 How did the death of Zachary Taylor help the Compromise of 1850?

_____

_____

3.70 Why did the Southern states want Cuba?

_____

_____

3.71 What did Commodore Perry do that resulted in Japan becoming a world power?

_____

_____

3.72 What was the Ostend Manifesto and what happened when it became public?

_____

_____

_____

3.73 What was the Underground Railroad?

_____

_____

Check the items that are true of the Fugitive Slave Act.

3.74 ☐ It hurt the abolitionist cause in the North.

3.75 ☐ An accused fugitive could post bail until his trial.

3.76 ☐ People helping enslaved people escape could be fined or imprisoned.

3.77 ☐ The commissioner got more money for returning a slave than he did for releasing a free man.

3.78 ☐ Northern mobs would sometimes free captured fugitives.

3.79 ☐ Franklin Pierce did not support it.

3.80 ☐ A captured black person could not testify in their own behalf.

3.81 ☐ Federal officials were required to act as slave catchers.

3.82 ☐ Harriet Tubman supported it.

Uncle Tom's Cabin. The anti-slavery sentiment in the North received an incredible and unexpected boost in 1852. In that year, Harriet Beecher Stowe published the anti-slavery novel *Uncle Tom's Cabin*. Melding true stories taken from the files of the abolitionists, she wrote a compelling tale of a faithful slave named Tom. Tom was a committed Christian who obeyed his masters out of respect for God. He was sold twice in the novel, once to pay off a debt his master owed and another time when his master died. During his journeys he met other enslaved people and heard their heart-rending stories. The book also followed another slave named Eliza, who succeeded in fleeing to Canada when she was threatened with separation from her small son. Tom, in the meantime, was well- treated by his first two masters, but was beaten to death by the third, Simon Legree.

Uncle Tom's Cabin was one of the most successful pieces of **propaganda** in history. The phenomenal impact of the novel cannot be overstated. It sold hundreds of thousands of copies in the first year and millions thereafter. It was translated into several languages and became a popular stage play. It turned the nation against the evils of slavery. Lincoln reportedly said to Mrs. Stowe when they met in 1862, "So you're the little woman who wrote the book that made this great war."

The novel had a wide impact. It gave strength to the abolitionist cause and later to the Union in the Civil War. Its popularity in Britain made it difficult for that government to support the Confederacy. It spelled out in cold blood exactly what the North opposed. Southerners condemned it as an unfair and dishonest portrayal of slavery. However, they could not erase the image of faithful Tom dying of his wounds or desperate Eliza clutching her young child, racing across the ice floes of the Ohio River just a few yards ahead of the slave catchers.

Today, there are mixed reviews of the novel, some saying that the portrayal of the characters supports stereotyping and discrimination.

| A scene from *Uncle Tom's Cabin*

This doesn't change the fact that the story had the desired effect at that time period and impacted the views of many white people.

Kansas-Nebraska Act. The deaths of Clay, Calhoun, and Webster left the Senate in the control of lesser men. Dominant among these was the "Little Giant," Stephen Douglas, senator from Illinois. Douglas was a Democrat with no strong opinions on slavery. However, Illinois favored popular sovereignty. Douglas also had an eye on the presidency and needed Southern support to get it. Moreover, he had investments in Chicago and railroads. He wanted to organize the territories of the Midwest to allow a railroad to cross the center of the nation. Southern states opposed organizing those territories because they were north of the no-slavery line established by the Missouri Compromise and would become free states. Ignoring the problems he was about to create, Douglas found a way to get Southern support to organize the territories. In 1854 he dropped the bomb that undid the key compromises holding the nation together.

As the chairman of the Committee on Territories, Douglas proposed the Kansas-Nebraska Act to organize those territories. To gain the support of the South, the law would allow the people of the state to make decisions about slavery themselves. The carefully negotiated, long-standing Missouri Compromise was swept aside. Douglas used his influence and oratory skills to ram the law through Congress regardless of the consequences. Pliable Franklin Pierce signed it.

Northerners screamed in dismay. They felt betrayed. The carefully negotiated terms the North had accepted in 1820 had been dumped without compensation or agreement. Any territory might now become slave-holding, in spite of agreements to the contrary. The law turned even more Northerners against slavery because slaveholders could not be trusted to keep their bargains.

Douglas underestimated the reaction and results of his actions. He ended the era of compromise. The North steadfastly refused to enforce the Fugitive Slave Law now that the South was no longer honoring its agreements. That caused more bitterness in the South and more division in the nation. So, the Kansas-Nebraska Act doomed both the Missouri Compromise and the Compromise of 1850. The two sides no longer trusted each other enough to work out or keep delicate compromises.

Republican Party. The slavery issue had shattered the Whig party. It now created a new party. In 1854 the Republican Party was organized specifically opposing the spread of slavery. Spurred by the betrayal of the Kansas-Nebraska Act, the party gained strength quickly. The Republicans gathered up the remains of the northern Whig party, Know-Nothings, and supporters of free soil. They quickly became a national party, electing a Speaker of the House in 1856 and making a serious showing in the presidential election of that year.

The problem with the Republican Party was that it was clearly a Northern party. Until that time, the Whigs and the Democrats had support in both the North and the South. Thus, both parties had to compromise to please both parts of their membership. Unfortunately, the Kansas-Nebraska Act had broken the thin threads that held the parties together. The Democrats were also dividing on the slavery issue. They would present a united candidate in 1856, but in 1860 the Democratic Party would divide into Northern and Southern parts. Cooperation would yield to partisanship, which would yield to war.

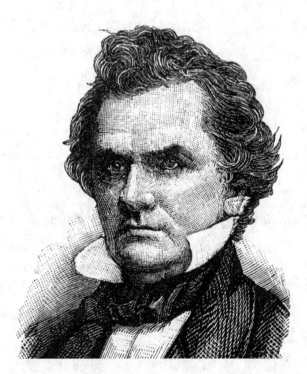

| Stephen Douglas

✏️ **Complete these sentences.**

3.83 The anti-slavery novel _____ was one of the most successful pieces of propaganda in history.

3.84 The chief architect of the Kansas-Nebraska Act was _____ .

3.85 The _____ Party was organized to oppose the spread of slavery.

3.86 _____ was the author of _Uncle Tom's Cabin_.

3.87 The Republican Party was a party from the _____ section of the nation.

Put a _K_ beside the items that were in whole or part a result of the Kansas-Nebraska Act.

3.88 _____ The rapid growth of the Republican Party

3.89 _____ The success of _Uncle Tom's Cabin_

3.90 _____ Popular sovereignty in Kansas and Nebraska

3.91 _____ The Missouri Compromise was overturned

3.92 _____ A new compromise was created

3.93 _____ Douglas acted heedlessly

3.94 _____ North-South distrust

3.95 _____ The Compromise of 1850 became stronger

3.96 _____ The Ostend Manifesto

↻ **Before you take this last Self Test, you may want to do one or more of these self checks.**

1. _____ Read the objectives. See if you can do them.

2. _____ Restudy the material related to any objectives that you cannot do.

3. _____ Use the **SQ3R** study procedure to review the material:
   a. **S**can the sections.
   b. **Q**uestion yourself.
   c. **R**ead to answer your questions.
   d. **R**ecite the answers to yourself.
   e. **R**eview areas you did not understand.

4. _____ Review all vocabulary, activities, and Self Tests, writing a correct answer for every wrong answer.

SELF TEST 3

Choose the person who matches each item. Some answers will be used more than once (each answer, 2 points).

3.01	_____ Kansas-Nebraska Act	a. William Henry Harrison
3.02	_____ destroyed the National Bank	b. Eli Whitney
3.03	_____ cotton gin	c. Cyrus McCormick
3.04	_____ first textile factory in U.S.	d. Andrew Jackson
3.05	_____ telegraph	e. Joseph Smith
3.06	_____ steamboat	f. Henry Clay
3.07	_____ Erie Canal	g. Zachary Taylor
3.08	_____ Missouri Compromise	h. Stephen Douglas
3.09	_____ Buena Vista victory	i. Samuel Slater
3.010	_____ Mexico City victory	j. Commodore Matthew Perry
3.011	_____ interchangeable parts	k. Winfield Scott
3.012	_____ Mormon religion	l. Harriet Tubman
3.013	_____ over 300 slaves escaped to freedom	m. DeWitt Clinton
3.014	_____ treaty with Japan	n. Harriet Beecher Stowe
3.015	_____ Compromise of 1850	o. Samuel Morse
3.016	_____ *Uncle Tom's Cabin*	p. Robert Fulton
3.017	_____ the mechanical reaper	
3.018	_____ Father of the Factory System	
3.019	_____ "Log Cabin and Hard Cider"	
3.020	_____ Eaton scandal	
3.021	_____ became secretary of state due to a "corrupt bargain"	
3.022	_____ his death left Millard Fillmore as president	
3.023	_____ his followers founded the state of Utah	
3.024	_____ "Old Fuss and Feathers"	
3.025	_____ picked Martin Van Buren as his successor	

Name the item described (each answer, 3 points).

3.026 _____ change from farming and handcrafting to industry and machine manufacturing

3.027 _____ secretive, anti-immigrant political party of the late 1840s

3.028 _____ Christian revival in 1790s to 1830s

3.029 _____ mission/fortress in Texas that was defended to the death by patriots, including Davy Crockett and Jim Bowie

3.030 _____ organization that helped slaves escape to Canada

3.031 _____ act that ended the Missouri Compromise and the era of compromises

3.032 _____ privately-owned toll roads that were the first improvements in American transportation

3.033 _____ the reason so many Irish came to America in 1845-1847

3.034 _____ the "Man-Stealing Law" that imprisoned people who helped slaves escape and denied recaptured slaves the right to a fair trial

3.035 _____ anti-slavery, Northern political party founded in 1854 that grew rapidly

Answer true or false (each answer, 1 point).

3.036 _____ Most factories were located in the Northeast because it had water power and a supply of capital.

3.037 _____ Factory workers were often shamefully exploited.

3.038 _____ Steamboats had little effect on the trade on the Mississippi River.

3.039 _____ Canals put the railroads out of business.

3.040 _____ Most of the immigrants in the 1840s and '50s came from Ireland, Britain, and France.

3.041 _____ Children were not employed in early factories.

3.042 _____ Mormons were persecuted because they practiced polygamy.

3.043 _____ Temperance was one of the reform movements of the mid-1800s.

3.044 _____ California became a state as part of the Missouri Compromise.

3.045 _____ The Ostend Manifesto was an anti-slavery document.

3.046 _____ Franklin Pierce wanted to add Cuba to the United States.

3.047 _____ Slavery was ended in Washington D.C. as part of the Compromise of 1850.

3.048 _____ Daniel Webster was a firm abolitionist, opposing the Compromise of 1850 because of his beliefs.

3.049 _____ The Wilmot Proviso would have forbidden slavery in the Mexican Cession.

3.050 _____ Manifest Destiny was the belief America would spread over the continent.

3.051 _____ John Tyler was a strong Whig, an admirer of Henry Clay.

3.052 _____ James Polk tried very hard to keep America out of a war with Mexico.

3.053 _____ John Quincy Adams supported the Gag Rule.

3.054 _____ Andrew Jackson successfully fought nullification.

3.055 _____ John Calhoun was a Southern leader.

3.056 _____ The Gadsden Treaty ended the Mexican War.

Before taking the LIFEPAC Test, you may want to do one or more of these self checks.

1. _____ Read the objectives. See if you can do them.
2. _____ Restudy the material related to any objectives that you cannot do.
3. _____ Use the **SQ3R** study procedure to review the material.
4. _____ Review activities, Self Tests, and LIFEPAC vocabulary words.
5. _____ Restudy areas of weakness indicated by the last Self Test.

HISTORY & GEOGRAPHY 805
A Growing Nation (1820–1855)

LIFEPAC Test is located in the center of the booklet. Please remove before starting the unit.

Author:

Theresa Buskey, B.A., J.D.

Editor:

Alan Christopherson, M.S.

Westover Studios Design Team:

Phillip Pettet, Creative Lead

Teresa Davis, DTP Lead

Nick Castro

Andi Graham

Jerry Wingo

Alpha Omega
PUBLICATIONS

804 N. 2nd Ave. E.
Rock Rapids, IA 51246-1759

A Growing Nation (1820–1855)

Introduction

1820 to 1855 were turbulent years in American history. Ten different presidents served during those thirty-five years. Only five had served in the first thirty years of the nation. All of the first five presidents except one, John Adams, had served two terms in office. Of the next ten, only one, Andrew Jackson, succeeded in obtaining a second term. The upheaval in the presidency was simply a reflection of the upheaval in the nation.

This was an era of new political parties, expansion, and the rise of sectionalism. The long-ruling Democratic-Republicans fell victim to their own success as they split into factions. Two of these emerged as opposing political parties, the Democrats and the Whigs. The two alternated in control of the government throughout this time period. By 1855, the issue that would not go away, slavery, produced yet another party, the Republicans.

The nation continued to grow at an alarming rate during these years. American immigrants in Spanish/Mexican Texas took over that land and eventually brought it into the Union. A war with Mexico added all of the Southwest and California. Settlements were reached with Britain over Maine and Oregon. A small piece of Mexican land was purchased in 1853 as a railroad route across Arizona and New Mexico. By 1855, all of the land that would create the contiguous 48 states was under U.S. control. Nine new states were added to the nation between 1820 and 1855 as their population grew to reach the required minimum. The natural problems caused by such rapid growth were part of the upheaval of the era.

Slavery and North-South differences were major issues from 1820 to 1855. The country was, at first, divided into three sections: North, South, and West. As the West matured, it joined either the North or South on the slavery issue. Prior to that two-way division, each section had its own agenda and its own representative giant in Washington. Henry Clay from the West, John Calhoun from the South, and Daniel Webster from the North were renowned in their own time for their oratory and their leadership. These men would provide much of the statesmanship that would keep the nation together until after they had died.

Objectives

Read these objectives. The objectives tell you what you will be able to do when you have successfully completed this LIFEPAC. When you have finished this LIFEPAC, you should be able to:

1. Name the leaders of the era and explain their accomplishments.

2. Describe the presidency of Andrew Jackson and its effect on America.

3. Trace the development of the slavery and tariff issues from 1820 to 1855.

4. Define Manifest Destiny and describe its course in America.

5. Describe the course of the Texas Revolution and Mexican War.

6. Define the Industrial Revolution and name the people, innovations, and inventions that contributed to it.

7. Describe the effects of the Industrial Revolution in America.

8. Describe the Second Great Awakening and the reform movements that followed it.

9. Describe the compromises that kept the nation together and what ended them.

10. Describe the changes in America and American life in this era.

Survey the LIFEPAC. Ask yourself some questions about this study and write your questions here.

1. JACKSONIAN ERA

Andrew Jackson's election as president was, like Jefferson's before him, a step in the expansion of democracy in America. The right to vote had been expanding as more and more states dropped property requirements for voters. Jackson, therefore, was elected by the votes of ordinary working people, not the land-owning aristocrats who dominated the voting population a few years before that. His election was a turning point in our history. He was the people's president.

Andrew Jackson was also a man who would shape the government in his own fashion. He had strong opinions and the will, popular support, and party machinery to force them through. He believed he had the support of the people and saw no reason to compromise with Congress or the Supreme Court. His enemies called him "King Andrew I" with good reason. He did exactly what he wanted and changed the face of American government and politics forever.

SECTION OBJECTIVES

Review these objectives. When you have completed this section, you should be able to:

1. Name the leaders of the era and explain their accomplishments.
2. Describe the presidency of Andrew Jackson and its effect on America.
3. Trace the development of the slavery and tariff issues from 1820 to 1855.
9. Describe the compromises that kept the nation together and what ended them.
10. Describe the changes in America and American life in this era.

VOCABULARY

Study these words to enhance your learning success in this section.

abolitionist (ab ō lish' un ist). Person seeking to abolish (end) something, especially slavery.

caucus (kaw' kus). A closed meeting of a group of persons from the same political party to choose a candidate or decide on policy.

censure (sen' chur). An official reprimand.

duel (doo' ul). A formal combat with weapons fought between two persons in the presence of witnesses.

mandate (man' dāt). An authorization to act given to a representative.

nullification (nul i fi kā' shun). The action of a state attempting to prevent the enforcement within its territory of a law of the United States.

Note: *All vocabulary words in this LIFEPAC appear in* **boldface** *print the first time they are used. If you are not sure of the meaning when you are reading, study the definitions given.*

Pronunciation Key: hat, āge, cãre, fär; let, ēqual, tėrm; it, īce; hot, ōpen, ôrder; oil; out; cup, put, rüle; child; long; thin; /ŦH/ for then; /zh/ for measure; /u/ or /ə/ represents /a/ in about, /e/ in taken, /i/ in pencil, /o/ in lemon, and /u/ in circus.

AMERICA from 1820 to 1855

James Monroe
1817–1825
Democratic-Republican

John Quincy Adams
1825-1829
Democratic-Republican

Andrew Jackson
1829-1837
Democratic

Martin Van Buren
1837-1841
Democratic

William H. Harrison*
1841
Whig

John Tyler
1841-1845
Whig

James K. Polk
1845-1849
Democratic

Zachary Taylor*
1849-1850
Whig

Millard Fillmore
1850-1853
Whig

Franklin Pierce
1853-1857
Democratic

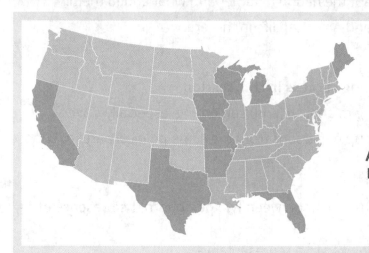

STATES ADMITTED TO THE UNION

Maine	1820		
Missouri	1821	**Texas**	1845
Arkansas	1836	**Iowa**	1846
Michigan	1837	**Wisconsin**	1848
Florida	1845	**California**	1850

POPULATION of the United States of America

1850 — 23,191,876

1820 — 9,638,453

1790 — 3,929,000

*died while in office

Setting the Times

Giants in Washington. By the beginning of the War of 1812, three men who would be among the most prominent of their era had begun careers in Washington. Henry Clay of Kentucky became a member of the House of Representatives in 1811. He was joined that same year by John Calhoun of South Carolina. They were leaders of the War Hawks who pushed for the war with Britain. Two years later, Daniel Webster of Massachusetts joined the House. These men would serve in Washington in the House, Senate, President's Cabinet, and even the vice presidency until the early 1850s. None of them ever became president, although they all tried. However, no discussion of this era would be complete without an understanding of these men and their influence.

Henry Clay was born in Virginia but moved to Kentucky as a young man to practice law. Clay was a notable speaker and an ambitious, natural leader. He was elected to the House of Representatives, where he often served as the Speaker, and the Senate. He also served one term as secretary of state and ran unsuccessfully for president several times, usually as a Whig. Clay was called the Great Compromiser for his ability to wrangle agreements and resolve crises in the difficult years leading up to the Civil War. He exercised tremendous influence in Congress. He used it to promote programs and compromises to benefit the whole nation. Clay was an ardent nationalist who earned the title of statesman for his work on behalf of the American people.

John Calhoun was born in South Carolina and practiced law there until a wealthy marriage enabled him to concentrate on politics. His federal employment included the House of Representatives, Senate, secretary of war, secretary of state, and vice president. In many ways he reflects the splitting up of the nation that occurred between the Era of Good Feelings and the Civil War. He began his career as a strong Jeffersonian Democratic nationalist.

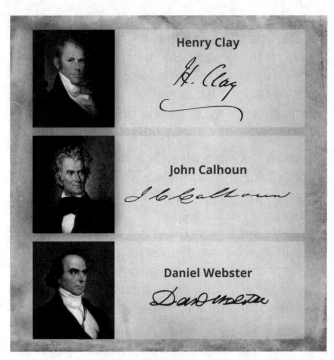

Henry Clay

John Calhoun

Daniel Webster

| Henry Clay, John Calhoun, and Daniel Webster, with their Respective Autographs

He favored a strong federal government and supported Clay's American System to benefit the entire nation. However, as time went on he began to focus more and more on the narrow needs of his own state and region. He opposed the tariffs that protected the northern manufacturers, and became very defensive of the South's "peculiar institution," slavery. In the end, Calhoun became the leading proponent of the doctrine of **nullification** and states' rights. Ironically, he believed this was a way to save the Union by protecting the South. His philosophies became the basis for the Confederacy.

Daniel Webster was born in New Hampshire but moved to Massachusetts as a young man to practice law. He gained tremendous fame as an orator and was one of the best paid attorneys in the nation. He argued and won several key cases before the Supreme Court, including *McCulloch v. Maryland* (states cannot tax the national bank) and *Gibbons v. Ogden* (federal government controls interstate commerce).

He served in the House of Representatives, the Senate, and the cabinet as secretary of state. He was a strong advocate for the manufacturing interests of the North. He opposed slavery, but as a nationalist, he supported compromises on the issue to maintain the Union, something that turned many **abolitionists** against him.

Missouri Compromise. One of the issues that would divide the nation was slavery. It had not been a significant problem when the new Constitution was accepted in 1789. Slavery, although widespread, was not very profitable and might have died on its own had it not been for the cotton gin. Cotton was a popular fiber for cloth, but it was expensive to produce because of the difficulty in separating the fiber

from the seeds. In 1793 Eli Whitney invented the cotton gin to help his southern friends. It provided a simple and easy way to separate cotton fiber from the seeds. With the machine, one person could now separate the same amount of cotton that 50 people used to do by hand. Suddenly, cotton production became very profitable.

In the years after 1793, the South concentrated on growing cotton. It purchased its manufactured goods from the North or Europe and its food from the West. Thus, it became completely dependent on cotton for its prosperity. Labor-intensive cotton production, it was believed, depended upon slavery. The institution of slavery, which had been in decline,

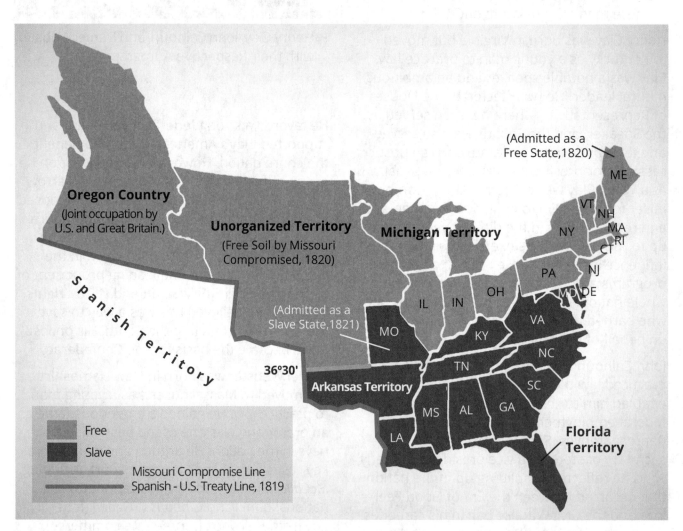

| The Missouri Compromise

rebounded. The South quickly became protective of slavery as the key to their region's wealth and cast a cautious eye to the North and those who opposed it.

The population of the northern states continued to grow in the early 1800s as manufacturing cities provided jobs for more and more people. The South, on the other hand, was stagnant in population. Thus, the North began to significantly outnumber the South in the House of Representatives. However, the slave-holding states were able to protect their interests by controlling half of the Senate. In 1819 the count was 11 slave and 11 free states. That year Missouri asked to be admitted as a slave-holding state.

The North-dominated House of Representatives voted to gradually end slavery in Missouri before admitting it. The South clearly saw the threat. If slavery could not expand with the nation, the slave-holding states would be gradually overwhelmed by the admission of more and more free states. A deadlock occurred that was finally broken by Henry Clay, who led the compromise effort. The result was the Missouri Compromise of 1820. Under its terms, Missouri was admitted as a slave state and Maine, now finally separated from Massachusetts, was admitted as a free state, thereby maintaining the Senate balance. Moreover, slavery was prohibited in all states created in the Louisiana Purchase north of 36° 30′ latitude, the southern boundary of Missouri.

The compromise did not solve the slavery issue; it simply kept the political balance between the pro-slave and anti-slave forces. Both sides knew how touchy this issue was and that it might divide the nation. The Missouri Compromise swept the issue of slavery aside for another thirty-five years for the sake of the Union. The North and West continued to grow in size and strength during that time while the moral opposition to slavery also grew. In the end, the issue would have to be faced squarely, but not until the North was stronger.

Tariff Issue. The secondary issue of the South was the tariff. Tariffs raised the price of manufactured goods brought in from abroad. This protected American manufacturers by cutting off cheaper foreign goods. The South, however, had very little manufacturing. All tariffs did was raise the prices they had to pay for things like shoes, farm equipment, and luxury goods. Thus, the tariff became the hot- button issue of the 1820s to 1850s while both sides were avoiding the slavery problem.

Match these people (answers will be used more than once).

1.1	_____ lawyer from Massachusetts	a.	Henry Clay
1.2	_____ served as secretary of state	b.	John Calhoun
1.3	_____ served as vice president	c.	Eli Whitney
1.4	_____ invented the cotton gin	d.	Daniel Webster
1.5	_____ senator from Kentucky		
1.6	_____ Speaker of the House		
1.7	_____ argued _McCulloch v. Maryland_		
1.8	_____ supported states' rights		
1.9	_____ nationalist to the end		
1.10	_____ ran for president as a Whig		
1.11	_____ one of America's highest-paid lawyers		
1.12	_____ made cotton production profitable		
1.13	_____ strong advocate of manufacturing interests		
1.14	_____ Great Compromiser		
1.15	_____ senator from South Carolina		

Answer these questions.

1.16 What were the two issues related to the South?

a. _____

b. _____

1.17 What were the terms of the Missouri Compromise?

a. _____

b. _____

c. _____

1.18 What made cotton and slavery suddenly so profitable in the South?

_____

Election of 1824. The Democratic-Republican party was still the only viable party in 1824, but the unity shown in the unopposed election of James Monroe in 1820 was gone. The tides of change were moving against the stable political powers of Jefferson's party. The first sign was the growing opposition to the nominating procedure. Democratic-Republicans chose their candidate for the presidency in a secret congressional **caucus**. Since there was only one party, the nomination gave the man the office. This process of establishing "King Caucus" was widely denounced in 1824. In fact, the opposition hurt William Crawford who was the official nominee of the caucus that year.

Instead of the united support given to Monroe, the Democratic-Republicans were split four ways in 1824. John Quincy Adams, son of President John Adams, was the candidate of the North. Andrew Jackson and Henry Clay were both candidates from the West. William Crawford was the Southern candidate. Clay and Adams were men of experience with a wide range of government background. Andrew Jackson, the hero of the Battle of New Orleans, had immense popularity all over the country, even if he had fewer qualifications for the job.

Jackson received the largest part of the popular vote (42%), followed by Adams (32%), Crawford (13%), and Clay (13%), whose support in the West had been taken by the popular general. The electoral vote, however, did not give Jackson the majority he needed to become the next president. Under the Constitution, the election had to be decided by the House of Representatives.

Only the top three candidates in the electoral vote could be considered by the House. That left out Clay who had received the lowest count in that crucial vote. Clay, however, was the popular Speaker of the House of Representatives and was in position to influence the outcome of the election. Crawford had suffered a stroke and was unfit to take office, so he was never a factor in the House election. Clay and Jackson had a personal feud that dated back to Jackson's invasion of Florida in the Seminole conflict after the War of 1812. Clay had denounced Jackson in the House for his actions and made himself a bitter enemy. Clay, therefore, chose to support Adams.

John Quincy Adams was elected president by the House on the very first vote because of the influence of Henry Clay. Adams immediately offered Clay the position of secretary of state. This was a prize political plum because it was the office that had launched many of the presidents. Clay unwisely accepted and sealed his own political coffin.

Jackson and his supporters screamed that a deal had been cut trading the presidency to Adams in exchange for the Secretary's position for Clay. It is unlikely that Clay and Adams made an "official" deal for the office. However, the prompt repayment of Adams' political debt to Clay looked corrupt. Jackson and his allies had a ready-made issue for the 1828 election in the "corrupt bargain" between Adams and Clay. Moreover, Jackson was furious that the "will of the people" had been thwarted in such a fashion, and an angry Andrew Jackson was a dangerous opponent.

After the election, the Democratic-Republican Party split. The supporters of Jackson became known as the Democrats, the same party that still exists under that name. The supporters of Adams called themselves the National Republicans and later took the name Whigs, a patriotic name from the Revolutionary War. Andrew Jackson and his Democrats spent the entire four years between the presidential elections building the support they needed to crush Adams and Clay.

John Quincy Adams. John Quincy Adams (1767-1848) was arguably one of the most qualified men ever to assume the presidency. He was extremely honest and hard working. He had seen much of the world traveling with his father as a boy. He was well educated and had written political papers during the early years of the nation. He served his country as a diplomat in Prussia, the Netherlands, Great Britain and Russia. He led the American delegation at Ghent at the end of the War of 1812. He served as a senator from Massachusetts. He also proved to be a highly successful secretary of state under James Monroe. In that position, he created the Monroe Doctrine and negotiated the purchase of Florida from Spain. He also obtained an agreement with Britain for the joint occupation of Oregon and brushed off a Russian attempt to lay claim to the same area.

Adams, however, was not a popular or even very likable man. He had a cold personality, like his father. He had gained his position by ability, not by winning friends and influencing people. He was too honest to make use of public offices to gain support, refusing to throw out hard-working government employees to reward his own people. The "corrupt bargain" also hurt his popular support. His plans for the country were hampered on every turn by his lack of popularity and the violent opposition of the Democrats. His term as president was, therefore, the least notable part of a long and distinguished government career.

In his first address to Congress, Adams proposed an ambitious slate of national improvements including roads, canals, a national university, and an observatory. Americans fighting for survival on the frontier found these intellectual proposals ridiculous! The proposals flew in the face of the rising mood of sectionalism and states' rights. The West and the South in particular had no interest in paying high tariffs for such things. Adam's domestic agenda went nowhere, beat back at every turn by the Democrats. He further alienated the West by trying to control the wild speculation on land and by aiding the Cherokee, who were being evicted from their land by the state of Georgia.

Adams also failed to accomplish anything in foreign affairs, which should have been his best field. Britain's foreign minister, still upset

| "King" Andrew Jackson

over the independent American action with the Monroe Doctrine, refused to discuss removing restrictions on American trade with the British West Indies. Adams and Clay also wanted America to participate in the Panama Congress of 1826, a meeting of the American republics to discuss mutual problems and goals. The Senate took so long to confirm the delegates that the one who survived the trip arrived after the meeting had ended. The incident was an acute embarrassment to Adams.

Tariff of Abominations. Jackson's supporters came up with an unusual way to embarrass Adams during the election year of 1828. They proposed an incredibly high tariff, as high as 45% on some items. Included with it was a tariff on raw materials like wool. The Democrats assumed that New England would be unwilling to accept the tariff on the raw materials they needed for their factories. The tariff bill would therefore fail and cause further problems for Adams in the tariff-hungry North.

The Jacksonians had not counted on just how tariff hungry the North was, however. The tariff passed by a narrow margin and was signed by Adams. The states of the South, particularly the older ones, were furious and called it the "Tariff of Abominations." The old South was the section most affected by the bill because it was the least productive area of the nation. Cotton farming exhausted the soil, and the older farms of the southeastern seaboard were in decline. The rest of the nation did not feel the effects as badly because they were growing and expanding. Thus, the higher prices on goods fell heaviest in the Southern states that had a long tradition of political activism.

The Election of 1828. The election of 1828 brought in a new low in mud-slinging. The need to appeal to the less educated voters brought out a type of campaigning that avoided, rather than stressed, the issues. Adams was accused of purchasing gambling equipment for the White House. (He had bought a billiard table with his own money). He was also accused of drawing excessive salaries during his many government jobs and helping a Russian nobleman get his hands on a pretty servant girl while serving as minister in that nation.

Adams did not engage in any of the wild personal attacks, but his supporters did. Jackson's many **duels** and quarrels were paraded out with embellishments. His mother was accused of being a prostitute. The most serious and painful allegations were charges of adultery and bigamy against Jackson and his wife. According to the official story, Andrew Jackson had unknowingly married his wife, Rachel, before her divorce from her first husband was final. The couple remarried when they found out the divorce had actually been granted almost two years <u>after</u> their first marriage ceremony. The entire episode was very humiliating for Mrs. Jackson, and her husband was furious when it was dragged into the campaign.

The heart of Jackson's campaign was an attack on the "corruption" in Washington, the clearest example being the "corrupt bargain" between Clay and Adams that had given the latter the presidency in 1824. "Jackson and Reform" was the main slogan of the Democrats. Honest, hard-working John Quincy Adams was successfully portrayed in the public mind as the dishonest leader of a gang of corrupt politicians.

Andrew Jackson won both the popular and the electoral vote. He had 178 electoral votes to Adam's 83. Thus, America elected its first president who was not from the old American aristocracy. Jackson was wealthy, but he was a self-made man, a man of the people. The election is sometimes called a revolution because it was the end of the elite that had so effectively run the nation since the Revolutionary War. The power of the vote had reached the masses of the American people, and they chose a man like themselves to run their country.

Adams' Glorious Sunset. John Quincy Adams was not a man to retire into obscurity. He was elected to the House of Representatives and served there with distinction for seventeen years. He earned the affectionate nickname "Old Man Eloquent" for his determination in debates. His greatest achievement was his opposition to the *Gag Rule*. It was a series of resolutions pushed through by the South in 1836 that prevented any petition on slavery from being heard by the House. Adams believed it was an unconstitutional attack on the right to petition. He fought it consistently, trying repeatedly to introduce such petitions until the rule was abolished in 1844. John Quincy Adams collapsed at his desk in the House in February 1848 and, too weak to be removed, died in the Speaker's room two days later.

Check the items that were true of John Quincy Adams.

1.19 ☐ won the election of 1828

1.20 ☐ served as vice president

1.21 ☐ was second in the popular vote in 1824 and 1828

1.22 ☐ was accused of a "corrupt bargain" with William Crawford

1.23 ☐ was capable but not popular

1.24 ☐ won the support of the caucus in 1824

1.25 ☐ served in the House of Representatives after being president

1.26 ☐ wanted to spend government money on national improvements

1.27 ☐ was elected president as a Democratic-Republican

1.28 ☐ was successful in foreign but not domestic affairs as president

1.29 ☐ won the presidency because of Henry Clay

1.30 ☐ was one of three major candidates in 1824

1.31 ☐ led the Panama Congress of 1826

1.32 ☐ was very successful as secretary of state

Answer these questions.

1.33 What was the slogan for Jackson's campaign in 1828?

_____

1.34 What was the tariff of 1828 called?

_____

1.35 Who won the popular vote in 1824?

_____

1.36 What was John Quincy Adams' nickname in the House of Representatives?

_____

1.37 What was the Gag Rule?

_____

_____

1.38 Which of the major candidates was barred from the House election in 1824?

_____

1.39 What were the most serious personal attacks on Jackson in the 1828 campaign?

_____

Jackson's First Administration

Andrew Jackson. Andrew Jackson (1767-1845) was one of the most colorful and probably the most violent tempered president our country has ever had. He was born to poor Scotch-Irish immigrants in Carolina in a log cabin. His father died days before he was born. He grew up very wild and mischievous with a limited education. He joined the militia during the Revolution at the age of thirteen. His two brothers and his mother died during that time. Jackson himself was captured and slashed with a sword across the hand and face for refusing to clean a British officer's boots.

Jackson wasted an inheritance from his grandfather in Ireland and eventually took up the practice of law in Tennessee. His fierce attitude and determination in law brought him a measure of success. He made more money by speculating in land and eventually acquired a large plantation named "The Hermitage" near Nashville. He also earned a reputation as a dangerous enemy, fighting constantly over slights to his "honor." Two of his duels left him with bullets in his body for years afterward.

Jackson was a popular man who became well-connected with one of two political cliques that dominated Tennessee. He served without distinction in the House of Representatives and the Senate from 1796 to 1798. He returned to Tennessee and served as a justice of the state's supreme court. His greatest fame was won as the elected general of the state militia in the war with the Creek People and as commander of the U.S. army in the Battle of New Orleans. It was as a militia leader that he won his nickname "Old Hickory" for his toughness.

Old Hickory was wildly popular with the common people of America, especially in the West. He was no eastern aristocrat but a man who, like many on the frontier, had made it on his own in spite of fierce obstacles. He took with him into the White House many of the prejudices of the West, including a hatred of the Native Americans, a distrust of banks, and a determination to expand the nation. He had little respect for the compromise and debate of the democratic process. In fact, he was more comfortable with the command of a general than the leadership of a president. He took the presidency to new heights as he insisted on using the power of the office as he saw fit. He changed the office and the nation.

Inauguration. The extent of the change in Washington could be seen by Jackson's inauguration. It was a wild affair. The president-elect walked to the Capitol to take the oath of office and then to the White House for a reception. All along the route he shook hands and greeted the throngs of people in attendance. The White House reception was thrown open to everyone who wanted to attend. Hundreds of people mobbed the place. They stood on the furniture to get a look at the president. China and glass were broken. Curtains and upholstery ripped. The crush got so heavy that Jackson had to leave to avoid injury! The situation was finally relieved when the staff wisely began serving spiked punch on the lawn. The crowd quickly abandoned the house. One well-heeled Washington resident said it was the rule of "King Mob."

| Crowds at Jackson's Inauguration

Spoils System. Andrew Jackson brought the spoils system to the national government on a large scale. The spoils system was based on the concept, "To the victors go the spoils of the enemy." In this case, it was jobs in the government. Jackson firmly believed in rotation in office, and that in a democracy government jobs should not be held for life. He also believed that he needed to change out the "corrupt" officeholders from the Adams' administration. What he wound up doing was initiating the replacement of government employees with people whose primary qualification was their loyalty to the Democratic cause. In all, he replaced less than 10% of the people on the government payroll, but the damage was done. For many years after that, government jobs were given to party loyalists. The quality and honesty of government service suffered accordingly.

Eaton Scandal. Andrew Jackson's mediocre Cabinet was quickly bogged down in a scandal over the wife of Secretary of War John Eaton. Eaton had married the pretty daughter of a tavern keeper who had a very poor moral reputation. The wives of the other members of the administration refused to socialize with her. "Old Hickory" was very taken with Peggy Eaton and believed she was the victim of baseless gossip. He also remembered the gossip about his own beloved wife who had died shortly after he was elected, and he unwisely became a public champion for Mrs. Eaton. Jackson tried unsuccessfully to force Washington society to accept Peggy Eaton. Led by the well-born wife of Vice President John Calhoun, the ladies refused. Even Jackson's niece, who was his official hostess, left rather than entertain Mrs. Eaton in the White House.

The cabinet's limited ability suffered in the discord. Jackson eventually began seeking advice on policy from an informal group of advisors and friends, called the "kitchen cabinet" by his opponents. Secretary of State Martin Van Buren took advantage of the situation to ingratiate

| Andrew Jackson

himself with the president. As a widower, Van Buren socialized freely with Mrs. Eaton and won the president's favor by doing so. As the discord in the cabinet grew worse, Van Buren resigned, knowing that would pressure the other secretaries to do the same. They did so, relieving Jackson of a difficult situation by removing the Eatons from the Washington elite. Van Buren was rewarded with the vice presidency during Jackson's second term.

Webster-Hayne Debate. The long-standing debate over the power of the states versus the power of the federal government was a key part of the conflict of the early 1800s. Early in 1830 the question was raised in the Senate and resulted in a spectacular debate between Robert Hayne of South Carolina and Daniel Webster of Massachusetts. The Webster-Hayne Debate was a memorable part of the long North-South conflict that preceded the Civil War.

The debate began over the unlikely topic of a resolution by the New England states to restrict the sale of land in the West. Hayne used the occasion to attack the northeast and the Tariff of Abominations. He publicly argued in favor of the doctrine of nullification. This doctrine taught that any state could nullify a law of the United States that was contrary to the Constitution as they understood it. Nullification had been espoused by no lesser person than Vice President Calhoun in a 1828 document called the "South Carolina Exposition." Hayne saw it as a way to protect his region from domination by the rest of the Union.

The gallery of the Senate was full as people came to listen to Webster's reply. He used all of his great skill to speak in favor of the Union and federal power to force obedience from the states. He argued that if the states were free to go their own way at will, then the country was united only by a "rope of sand." He attacked nullification as a danger to the nation. Webster's arguments were summarized in his stirring statement, "Liberty and Union, now and forever, one and inseparable." Webster's speech was printed and widely read, making him a hero among those who favored a strong Union.

Split with Calhoun. No one was certain where Jackson stood on the issue of states' rights. He consistently opposed internal improvements within any one state and sought to keep federal taxes and expenses low—basic pro-state positions. He was also a slave-owning plantation farmer, but he had not made any clear statements one way or the other. The states' rights supporters, led by Calhoun, hoped to gain his public support for their favorite cause. They chose a party celebrating Thomas Jefferson's birthday as the ideal occasion. A whole series of toasts were offered celebrating the Jeffersonian ideals of the sovereignty of the states. Jackson, however, had been warned of what would happen and had carefully prepared his own toast. When his turn came he spoke the words, "Our Union: It must be preserved!" A shaken Calhoun tried to salvage the evening with the answer, "The Union, next to our liberty, most dear!" However, the damage was done. Jackson had declared himself as a Union man.

Vice President John Calhoun was hoping to be Andrew Jackson's successor. As a potential future president, Calhoun hid his personal views and publicly supported the Union. He had deliberately not attached his name to the "South Carolina Exposition" on nullification. However, his presidential hopes were dashed when he and Jackson split over the Peggy Eaton scandal as well as personal and policy differences. Calhoun retired from the vice presidency near the end of his term and returned to the Senate as the leader of those who espoused nullification and the power of the states.

The National Bank. Andrew Jackson had a passionate distrust of the National Bank, which he called the "moneyed monster." The director, Nicholas Biddle, did little to help the situation by his "loans" and payments to prominent congressmen, including Daniel Webster. Jackson believed the bank was a danger to the nation. He shared the Western distrust of powerful financial institutions that foreclosed on farm mortgages. He did not understand national finances or the way the bank helped the West by its sound money policy.

Henry Clay, who was likely to be the National Republican presidential candidate, saw the bank as a way to undermine Old Hickory's popularity. The bank was due to be rechartered in 1836. Clay forced a bill through Congress rechartering the National Bank in 1832, a presidential election year. He assumed Jackson would have to sign it and alienate his Western followers or veto it and alienate the businessmen of the nation.

Jackson did veto the bill, sending a scathing message back to Congress. Jackson attacked the bank in violent, colorful terms that set the issue as a war between the rich and the poor. His arguments had little substance but a great deal of popular appeal among the financially ignorant public who loved him. Clay foolishly believed the message would harm Jackson because of its angry tone and lack of intelligent argument.

Election of 1832. The election of 1832 was the first in which the candidates were chosen by national political conventions. Jackson on the Democratic ticket squared off against Henry Clay who had received the National Republican nomination. The National Bank was the central issue of the campaign. Clay had copies of Jackson's veto printed up to use against him. The veto message, however, was accepted as truth by the general public and cemented Jackson's image as a defender of the common man. Wealthier people who had reason to be concerned by the attack did not vote for him anyway. Jackson won the election easily.

Match these items (answers may be used more than once).

1.40 _____ party loyalists get government jobs		a. Spoils system
1.41 _____ King Mob		b. Jackson inauguration
1.42 _____ "Liberty and Union, now and forever, one and inseparable."		c. Webster-Hayne Debate
1.43 _____ Nicholas Biddle		d. National Bank
1.44 _____ Van Buren used it to gain Jackson's favor		e. Eaton Scandal
1.45 _____ issue in 1832 election		f. Jefferson birthday dinner

1.46 _____ rotation in office

1.47 _____ Calhoun tried to get a states' rights position by Jackson

1.48 _____ "Our Union: It must be preserved!"

1.49 _____ senator publicly supported nullification

1.50 _____ hurt the honesty and quality of government service

1.51 _____ Jackson's "moneyed monster"

1.52 _____ Jackson insisted on publicly supporting a woman against moral rumors

1.53 _____ caused the resignation of the entire cabinet

1.54 _____ Jackson had to flee the building to avoid injury

1.55 _____ Jackson vetoed it in 1832

1.56 _____ nullification would mean Union joined by a "rope of sand"

1.57 _____ Congress passed bill to recharter it in 1832

Answer these questions.

1.58 What injury gave Jackson a personal hatred for the British?

_____

_____

1.59 How did Jackson get the bullets that stayed in his body?

_____

1.60 What were three Western prejudices Jackson took to the White House?

a. _____

b. _____

c. _____

1.61 What is the doctrine of nullification?

_____

_____

1.62 What was the name of Jackson's group of informal advisors?

_____

1.63 Who was Jackson's first vice president?

_____

1.64 Who was vice president during Jackson's second term?

_____

1.65 Why did Henry Clay force a rechartering of the National Bank?

_____

_____

_____

_____

The End of the Jacksonian Era

Nullification Crisis. The Tariff of Abominations was a major issue in South Carolina. Congress voted in 1832 to reduce the tariff to more moderate levels, but it did not satisfy the Carolina "nullies." That same year they gained control of the state legislature and declared the tariff null and void in South Carolina. They also threatened to leave the Union if the federal government tried to enforce it.

Andrew Jackson was not about to take such a threat calmly. He sent reinforcements and supplies to federal forts in South Carolina. He also quietly prepared a larger army for use, if needed. He then denounced nullification and privately threatened to hang its supporters. The Southern leaders, especially Calhoun, knew Jackson well enough to take his threats seriously.

Jackson requested the passage of the Force Bill in early 1833 to grant authorization for troops to collect the tariffs in South Carolina. Calhoun led the assault on the bill. He had a great deal of support because of the rise of sectionalism in the nation. The nationalism of the post-War of 1812 era had given way to local loyalties to states and regions. Calhoun and Webster traded brilliant oratory in the Senate trying to force their views. Henry Clay finally brokered a compromise. A new tariff was passed that would gradually reduce the tax over the next ten years. Calhoun, realizing that he was on the verge of civil war, accepted the compromise and convinced his state to drop the nullification. South Carolina agreed but added the empty gesture of nullifying the Force Bill which had been signed into law.

Trail of Tears. The issue of what to do with the Native Americans who still owned large stretches of land east of the Mississippi had been left unanswered for years. Jackson was not a man to avoid an issue. In 1830 he proposed moving the tribes to new land west of the Mississippi where they would be "forever" free of encroachment by white settlers. Jackson deluded himself into believing this was a benevolent policy that was in the best interest of the Native Americans.

Many members of Congress opposed the Removal Act, particularly those who were strong Christians or who came from districts

| National Historic Trail

with strong Christian constituents. However, Jackson put the full force of his persuasive and political powers behind the act. It was passed in 1830, granting the Native Americans land in the West and the money to move them.

Jackson moved enthusiastically to carry out his program. Many of the tribes accepted the inevitable and signed treaties giving up their land. They moved west suffering from hunger, disease, and exposure on the way. Georgia, Mississippi, and Alabama made it clear they would seize the Native American land whether treaties were signed or not. Jackson did nothing to discourage them.

The Cherokee People of Georgia, who had largely taken up American life, fought back. They refused to sign a new treaty and challenged Georgia in court when the state annexed their land. The Cherokee won. The Supreme Court said the state of Georgia had no authority over the federal treaties that gave the Native Americans their land, but it was no use. Andrew Jackson would not give the Supreme Court the backing it needed to protect the Native Americans. Jackson is reported to have said, "John Marshall has made his decision; now let him enforce it."

The Cherokee were finally removed by the army in 1838. They were crowded into prison camps and then forced to make the long journey west. About four thousand Cherokee died on the way. They called it "the Trail of Tears."

Some of the Native American People chose to go to war rather than leave. The Sauk People in the Northwest Territory fought under the leadership of their chief, Black Hawk. The Black Hawk War quickly ended in a victory by the American army. The Sauks were removed to Iowa. The Seminoles took advantage of the wild terrain of Florida to hold out until 1842. The Seminole War was the longest and most expensive war with a Native American people in American history. They were finally defeated and moved west also.

The Native American removal was one of the blackest marks on an already poor American record. Thousands of Native Americans died after being forced to surrender their land to the greed of white settlers. Even then, the promise that their new land would not be taken was never kept. Within a generation, they were facing the same pressure to give up their land to new settlers who had crossed the Mississippi. The whole thing was all the more tragic because of how many people believed it was good for the Native Americans. Sinful human beings have an incredible ability to justify their own wrongdoing.

National Bank. Jackson saw the election of 1832 as a **mandate** from the people in his battle with the National Bank. Therefore, he decided to kill the bank instead of just letting it run until its charter ended in 1836. He first had to fire his secretary of the treasury and appoint a new one that would go along with his plan. That accomplished, he began to remove federal money from the National Bank and put it into "pet banks" in various states. The banks were chosen in large part for their loyalty to Jackson, and some funds were wasted in the process. Henry Clay succeeded in convincing Congress to **censure** Jackson for this "unconstitutional" action. The rebuff had no effect on Jackson's actions.

Nicholas Biddle reacted in a way that confirmed Jackson's worst fears about the National Bank. He deliberately reduced credit to the point that businesses began to fail and the country fell on hard times. It was just this kind of power that Jackson did not want a private corporation to have! Jackson refused to budge even when hit with a long stream of petitions from struggling businessmen. He told them to take their petitions to Biddle. In the end, public pressure forced Biddle to surrender, relax credit, and close the bank.

The return to good times brought about a spiral of inflation and land speculation. Many of the western banks began issuing money with no reliable value. Jackson inadvertently encouraged the national self-confidence that fueled the speculation. In 1835, he became the only U.S. president ever to pay off the entire national debt! Fearful of the effects of wild speculation, Jackson issued the *Specie Circular*, a decree that all land purchased from the federal government had to be paid for in *specie*: gold or silver coins. That set the scene for the Panic of 1837.

Analysis. Andrew Jackson was a highly successful president. He did just about everything he wanted to do in office even if it was not good for the nation. He considered the president to be the representative of the people and acted independently of the other branches of government. He vetoed more laws than any president before him. He used his popularity to push through laws he wanted and to destroy the National Bank. His forceful foreign policy reopened American trade with the British West Indies and gained payments from Europe for American ships seized during the Napoleonic Wars. His actions as president increased the power and prestige of the office. His strong response to the Nullification Crisis undoubtedly saved the Union. He was so popular when he left office that he was even able to handpick his own successor whose term is considered a part of the Jacksonian Era.

Election of 1836. Jackson decided not to run again and made sure that Martin Van Buren received the Democratic nomination for president in 1836. The National Republicans had adopted the name of Whig by then and ran several candidates. Van Buren defeated the Whigs, led by William Henry Harrison, using Jackson's popularity. However, Van Buren inherited all the problems and enemies Jackson had created during his eight years in office. He took them on without having either the general's popularity or his fiery will. It was a disastrous combination.

Martin Van Buren. Martin Van Buren (1782-1862) was the first American president born after the Declaration of Independence. He was born in New York where he practiced law as a young man. He served in the New York legislature and the Senate. He won the governorship of New York in 1828 but gave it up to serve as Jackson's secretary of state. Van Buren was a professional politician known as the "Little Magician" for his skill at manipulating events to his advantage. He won the election solely on the support of Andrew Jackson. He had deliberately built his friendship with Old Hickory for just such a purpose.

The Panic of 1837. Land speculation in the West had become a major American pastime. Thousands of people bought land hoping to hold it and sell it for a profit later. The purchases were often made with loans from unstable banks. People were making huge profits only as long as credit was available. The prosperity of the nation was on shifting ground, and it gave way in 1837 just after Van Buren took office.

Jackson's destruction of the National Bank had removed one of the major safeguards in the American banking system. His *Specie Circular* had caused a sudden demand for gold and silver that drained Eastern bank reserves. Crop failures and a financial panic in England hit at the same time. British banks called in (demanded payment for) their foreign loans. Banks in America closed, people lost their savings, businesses closed, land sales fell, tariff income fell as trade was reduced, and unemployment hit the masses of common people.

Van Buren's popularity, never very high, quickly plummeted. He could do little to help in the situation. He did get federal money moved to an independent treasury to protect it from being lost when pet banks collapsed. His popularity was also hurt by anti-slave forces who opposed the Seminole War (they did not want another slave state in Florida) and pro-slave forces who wanted him to annex Texas. His single term was largely unfruitful.

Complete these sentences.

1.66 _____ was the only president ever to pay off the entire national debt.

1.67 The Cherokee called their removal west the _____ .

1.68 Jackson removed federal money from the National Bank and put it into so-called _____ banks.

1.69 In 1832 South Carolina voted to nullify the _____ .

1.70 Jackson's financial policies led to the _____ that hurt Van Buren.

1.71 Henry Clay succeeded in convincing the Senate to _____ Jackson because of the removal of federal funds from the National Bank.

1.72 The Panic of 1837 was largely caused by _____ in land.

1.73 The _____ War was the longest and most expensive Indian war in American history.

1.74 The Supreme Court sided with the _____ Native Americans in their legal fight with the state of Georgia.

1.75 The _____ Bill authorized troops to enforce the tariff in South Carolina.

1.76 Jackson privately threatened to _____ the nullifiers.

1.77 The Sauk People fought the _____ War to avoid removal from their land.

1.78 Andrew Jackson's hand-picked successor was _____ .

1.79 The Southern states annexed Native American land in defiance of the Supreme Court because _____ would not support the Native Americans.

1.80 "Little Magician" was the nickname of _____ .

Answer these questions.

1.81 What was the compromise that ended the Nullification Crisis?

_____

_____

_____

1.82 What did Jackson think he would accomplish with the Removal Act?

_____

_____

1.83 How did Jackson kill the National Bank?

_____

_____

Review the material in this section in preparation for the Self Test. The Self Test will check your mastery of this particular section. The items missed on this Self Test will indicate specific areas where restudy is needed for mastery.

SELF TEST 1

Match these people (each answer, 2 points).

1.01	_____ inventor of the cotton gin	a. Henry Clay
1.02	_____ leader of nullification and states' rights	b. Andrew Jackson
1.03	_____ "Old Hickory"	c. Daniel Webster
1.04	_____ his wife's social problems caused Jackson's entire cabinet to resign	d. John Calhoun
		e. Martin Van Buren
1.05	_____ won the presidency in 1824 in the House of Representatives with a "corrupt bargain"	f. John Quincy Adams
		g. John Eaton
1.06	_____ president of the Bank of the U.S.	h. Robert Hayne
1.07	_____ the Little Magician	i. Nicholas Biddle
1.08	_____ Massachusetts representative, defender of the Union	j. Eli Whitney
1.09	_____ the Great Compromiser	
1.010	_____ pro-nullification senator who had a famous debate with Webster	

Name the item or person described (each answer, 4 points).

1.011 _____ tax passed in 1828 to embarrass Adams by how high it was; it passed anyway, to the anger of the old South

1.012 _____ no slavery in the Louisiana Territory north of 36° 30', Maine admitted as a free state, Missouri as a slave state

1.013 _____ machine that led to the South becoming dependent on cotton and slavery

1.014 _____ political party created by Andrew Jackson

1.015 _____ political party led by Henry Clay after the split of the Democratic-Republicans

1.016 _____ "Old Man Eloquent," successfully opposed the Gag Rule in Congress, collapsed and died in the House of Representatives

1.017 _____ depression caused by land speculation and Jackson's financial policies that hurt Van Buren's presidency

1.018 _____ government jobs were given to loyal supporters of the newly-elected leaders

1.019 _____ the name the Cherokee used to described their forced trip west of the Mississippi, away from their land

1.020 _____ presidential decree by Andrew Jackson that all payments for land must be made in gold or silver

Complete the following (each answer, 5 points).

1.021 What was the Doctrine of Nullification?

_____

_____

_____

1.022 Why was the presidency of John Quincy Adams so unsuccessful?

_____

_____

_____

_____

1.023 Briefly describe Andrew Jackson's personal history before he was president.

_____

_____

_____

_____

1.024 What did Jackson do to face the Nullification Crisis and how was it resolved?

_____

_____

_____

1.025 Why did Henry Clay try to recharter the National Bank early and what was the effect?

_____

_____

_____

1.026 Describe Andrew Jackson's first inaugural reception at the White House.

_____

_____

_____

_____

Answer true or false (each answer, 1 point).

1.027 _____ Jackson's group of informal advisors were called the "parlor cabinet."

1.028 _____ Henry Clay was never elected president.

1.029 _____ Jackson's campaign slogan in 1828, when he first won the presidency, was "Jackson and Reform."

1.030 _____ John Calhoun began his political career as a strong nationalist.

1.031 _____ The slavery issue was avoided in the early 1800s, but the North and South opposed each other over the tariff instead.

1.032 _____ John Calhoun was the spokesman for the western part of the nation.

1.033 _____ The South was very independent, producing its own food, cash crops, and manufactured goods.

1.034 _____ Before the time of Andrew Jackson presidential candidates were chosen by national convention of political parties.

1.035 _____ Andrew Jackson hand-picked Daniel Webster as his successor.

1.036 _____ The Seminole War was one of the shortest Indian wars in American history.

80/100 SCORE _____ TEACHER _____ _____
initials date

2. MANIFEST DESTINY

In 1845 a newspaper article in the *Democratic Review* spoke of America's "manifest destiny" to move across the continent to claim the land given by God for her fast-growing population. The term quickly became popular. It became the historical title for the great American drive to gain land from sea to sea.

America had always been a land with a frontier. The frontier moved as older sections filled up with people and became more "civilized." The American urge to move west was almost an addiction. Thousands did it, hoping for a better life. They faced intense hardships and death, but these hardy people built the wild lands of the West into the cities, farms, and industries we know today.

This section will cover the last major phase of manifest destiny from 1840 to 1853, the expansion to the Pacific Ocean. Differences with Great Britain were settled on the borders of Maine and the Oregon Territory. Texas became independent from Mexico and joined the Union. A war with Mexico brought in the American southwest and California. Finally, in 1853 a piece of land, called the Gadsden Purchase, was bought from Mexico to allow a coast-to-coast railroad. Thus, manifest destiny was fulfilled, and America had all of the land that would become the forty-eight contiguous states.

SECTION OBJECTIVES

Review these objectives. When you have completed this section, you should be able to:

1. Name the leaders of the era and explain their accomplishments.
2. Describe the presidency of Andrew Jackson and its effect on America.
3. Trace the development of the slavery and tariff issues from 1820 to 1855.
4. Define Manifest Destiny and describe its course in America.
5. Describe the course of the Texas Revolution and Mexican War.
9. Describe the compromises that kept the nation together and what ended them.
10. Describe the changes in America and American life in this era.

VOCABULARY

Study these words to enhance your learning success in this section.

artillery (är til' u rē). A branch of the army armed with large-caliber, crew-served mounted firearms.

asylum (a sī' lum). Protection from arrest and extradition given to political or other refugees by a nation.

continental divide (kon' ti nen' tl de vīd). A ridge of land separating streams that flow to opposite sides of a continent.

protégé (prōt' e zhā). A person under the care and protection of an influential person, usually for the furthering of his career.

siesta (sē es' ta). An afternoon nap or rest.

The Northern Border

Log Cabin Campaign. The election of 1840 gave the Whigs a chance at the presidency. Martin Van Buren ran for re-election on the Democratic ticket in spite of his fall in popularity. The Whigs chose William Henry Harrison with running mate John Tyler. Henry Clay wanted the nomination, but Clay's political opinions were too well-known. The Whigs wanted a noncontroversial candidate. They chose Harrison because he was a popular general who won victories against the Native Americans at Tippecanoe and the British at the Thames. Moreover, his views on the issues of the day were unknown. In fact, he deliberately avoided taking any positions on such things as tariffs, the National Bank and internal improvements.

The real focus of the campaign was created when a Democratic newspaper gave the Whigs a slogan. The paper derided Harrison as a man who would be content with "a pension, a log cabin, and a barrel of hard cider." The Whigs jumped at the accusation calling Harrison the "Log Cabin and Hard Cider" candidate, a poor, hard-working common man. (Harrison was actually a wealthy land owner.) All over the country rallies were held with log cabins mounted on wagons and barrels of hard cider. The catchy phrase "Tippecanoe and Tyler, too" added to the circus atmosphere of the campaign. Harrison won by a large electoral but small popular margin.

William Henry Harrison. William Henry Harrison (1773-1841) was sixty-eight years old at the time of his election. He had been born in Virginia on his family's plantation. His father had signed the Declaration of Independence and served in the Continental Congress. Harrison joined the army as a young man and served until 1798. He later served as an official in the Northwest Territory and was one of that region's first representatives to Congress. He served for twelve years as the governor of the Indiana Territory. It was as the head of that

| Log Cabin and Hard Cider

territory's militia that he won the battle of Tippecanoe in 1811. He was a general in the War of 1812 and won the Battle of the Thames in Ontario. After that, he served in the House and the Senate. He ran for President as a Whig in 1836 and lost before winning in 1840.

Harrison had the shortest administration of any president in American history. He gave a very long inaugural address in cold, rainy weather and caught a cold. Less than a month later, the cold developed into pneumonia. On April 4, 1841, 31 days after his inauguration, Harrison died. (Presidential inaugurations took place in March until the 20th Amendment to the Constitution in 1933 changed it to January.)

Tyler, Too. John Tyler (1790-1862) was the first man to move from the vice presidency to the presidency because the latter died in office. He had, like Harrison, been born into an established Virginia family. He took up the practice of law with his father as a young man. He served in the House, the Senate, and as governor of Virginia before becoming vice president.

Tyler was a Democrat in Whig clothing. He had been put on the ticket as a supporter of states' rights to draw the Southern vote. His succession to the presidency doomed the Whig agenda. He proceeded to veto a new National Bank, higher tariffs, and internal improvements passed by the nationalistic Whig Congress. He quickly lost all of his Whig support in the government. His entire cabinet, except Secretary of State Daniel Webster, resigned. His enemies took to calling Tyler "His Accidency."

Maine's Boundary. Daniel Webster did not resign because he was in the middle of negotiations with Great Britain. Relations with the former mother country had reached one of their periodic boiling points. In 1837 a small, short-lived rebellion in Canada had been aided by many northern Americans before it was put down. An American vessel supplying the rebels with arms was attacked and destroyed by British troops on the American side of the Niagara River. In 1840 a Canadian citizen who claimed to have been a part of the raid was arrested for murder. The British government threatened war if the man was executed. (He was later acquitted.) The tension grew in 1841 when the British officials in the Bahamas gave **asylum** to a group of Virginia slaves who had rebelled and captured an American ship.

The two sides finally came to the negotiating table over the boundary of Maine. Both claimed parts of the land along the border. The treaty of 1783, which ended the Revolution, was not very clear on the matter. In the early 1840s, lumberjacks from Canada and the U.S. were fighting over the right to harvest trees in the disputed area. The fighting expanded and the militia was called in. The so-called "Aroostook War" threatened to become a real one. The two sides met and finally set an agreeable border. The Webster-Ashburton Treaty of 1842 gave the Americans more of the land but gave the British access to a route they needed for a military road. It also settled all of the other outstanding differences between the countries, except for the question of Oregon.

Congress was furious at the treaty. They were in no mood to give up land that they thought

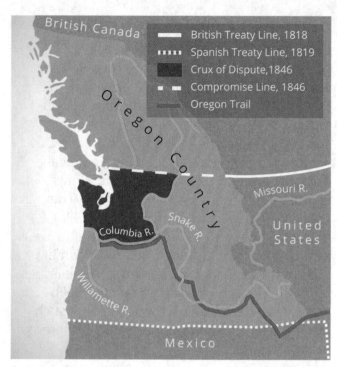

| Oregon Territory

was rightfully American. Webster, however, showed them an ancient map that implied that the British had rightful claim to the entire area in dispute! The treaty easily passed the Senate after that. Ironically, the British accepted the treaty because they had an ancient map that showed the Americans had rightful claim to the whole area!

Oregon Territory. Both Britain and America had claims to the beautiful and fertile Oregon Territory. At that time, Oregon included all of the land between California and the southern tip of Alaska west of the **continental divide**. Spain had given up her claim to the area in the Adams-Onis Treaty which had given Florida to the United States and set the borders of the Louisiana Territory. A Russian claim south of latitude 54° 40' was extinguished by treaty in the 1820s. Unable to settle their own differences there, Britain and the U.S. had agreed to occupy the land jointly in 1818. That agreement was renewed in 1827, since neither side would compromise.

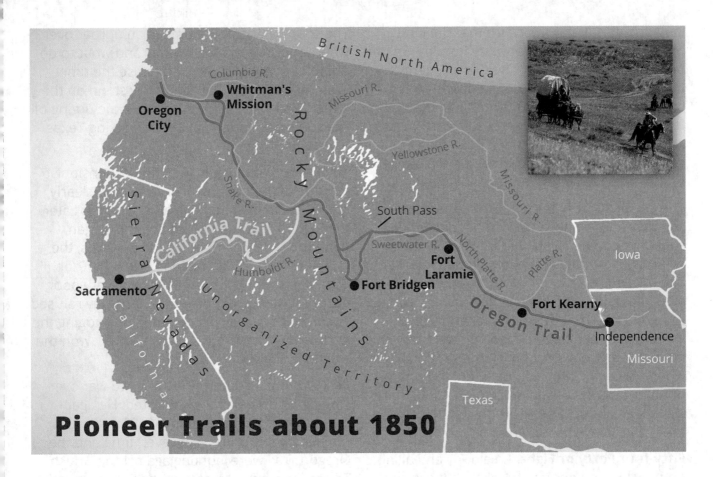

Pioneer Trails about 1850

The crux of the debate was a section of land north of the Columbia River up to the 49th parallel, the border between Canada and the U.S. on the east side of the Rocky Mountains. America wanted this land because it included Puget Sound, the only good harbor along the entire section of seacoast. The British were willing to concede the land south of the Columbia, but steadfastly refused to extend the previously established 49th parallel border requested by the Americans. The Americans on the other hand, did not want a section of land on the Pacific coast without access to a harbor. Matters stood this way for years.

Oregon Trail. The Rocky Mountains had been explored by mountain men who lived in the wild, trapping fur animals. Their knowledge provided the information Americans needed to reach their most western lands. One of these men named Jedidiah Smith discovered South Pass, a route over the Rockies that could be

traversed by a wagon. That pass was surveyed in 1842 by John Frémont, an American army officer. Slowly, the information needed to bring people and their wagons safely into Oregon was accumulated.

The British had established the first permanent settlements in Oregon. These were fur-trading posts organized by the Hudson Bay Company around 1825 under the leadership of John McLoughlin, known as "the Father of Oregon." The first permanent American settlement was a group of missionaries who settled in the Willamette Valley in 1834. In 1836 Presbyterian missionary Marcus Whitman brought his wife over the long, dangerous route to live in Oregon. She was the first of a flood of women and children who came with their men to make Oregon their home.

Americans became enraptured with reports coming out of Oregon. The missionaries, trappers, and explorers sent glowing reports of the land and its suitability for farming. The land between the Mississippi and the Rockies, on the other hand, was labeled "The Great American Desert" by an army explorer. That vast grass-land was believed to be unsuitable for settled farming. It was primarily an obstacle to Oregon and California-bound settlers. Beginning in 1843, thousands of pioneers risked the dangers of the desert to reach the riches of Oregon.

The Oregon Trail was the route these brave souls traveled. It began in Independence, Missouri and covered 2,000 of the hardest miles ever regularly traveled by families and animals. The trip took six months. Native Americans attacked and rivers flooded. People ran out of food. Wagons broke and draft animals died. Hundreds of people also died and were buried along the route in lonely graves with bare wood markers. There had been only a handful of Americans in Oregon in 1840. By 1850, there were over 12,000. The Americans were going to take Oregon by sheer numbers.

Fifty-four Forty or Fight. An elderly and ailing Andrew Jackson decided to take a hand in the election of 1844. He hand picked the Democratic candidate James K. Polk, a strong expansionist, and campaigned for him by letters from his sickbed. He also persuaded Tyler not to run because he would take votes from Polk. The Whigs nominated the venerable Henry Clay.

The country was at the time in an uproar over whether or not to annex Texas and what to do about Oregon. Clay decided to use the time-honored method of avoiding any stand on the issues. Polk, on the other hand, at the urging of Jackson, spoke out in favor of annexing Texas and acquiring all of Oregon.

The Democrats cashed in on the expansionist attitude of the nation. Their campaign clearly called for America to have all of Oregon. Later, that desire was summarized by the slogan, "Fifty-four Forty or Fight!" In other words, the U.S. would get all of Oregon up to 54° 40' or would go to war with Britain. It was very poor diplomacy but great politics. Henry Clay refused to commit one way or the other, misjudging the popularity of the issues yet again. Polk won the election on a very close vote.

Polk was not as determined to go to war over Oregon as his campaign indicated. He again offered to set the boundary at 49° and was refused by the British. However, time and the Oregon Trail were working against the British. The rapid expansion of the American population in the territory endangered the British claims. The Americans could just take all of the land that they wanted, and the tiny British population could not oppose them. In 1846 the British themselves offered to extend the 49th parallel border, and the Americans quickly agreed.

Match these people.

2.1	_____ Father of Oregon	a. William H. Harrison
2.2	_____ discovered South Pass	b. John Tyler
2.3	_____ Whig candidate in 1844	c. James K. Polk
2.4	_____ Democratic candidate in 1844	d. Henry Clay
2.5	_____ president with the shortest administration	e. Daniel Webster
2.6	_____ first vice president to become president because of a death	f. Jedidiah Smith
		g. John McLoughlin

✎ **Complete these sentences.**

2.7 William Henry Harrison's 1840 campaign called him the _____ and _____ candidate.

2.8 _____ did not get the Whig nomination in 1840 because he had publicly expressed his opinions on the issues.

2.9 Tyler was a Whig president, but he held _____ ideas on the issues.

2.10 The boundary of Maine was settled by the _____ Treaty.

2.11 Thousands of Americans reached Oregon by traveling the _____ from Independence, Missouri.

2.12 Britain and America disputed the Oregon land north of the _____ and south of the _____ .

2.13 America wanted the disputed Oregon land because it wanted a _____ on the Pacific coast.

2.14 The slogan for those who wanted all of the Oregon Territory was _____ .

2.15 The catchy, rhyming phase used by Harrison's campaign in 1840 was _____ .

2.16 President John Tyler's enemies called him "_____ ."

2.17 The battle that broke out between lumberjacks in Maine over disputed land was called the _____ War.

2.18 The Great Plains were called the Great _____ in the 1840s.

2.19 The border of Oregon was set at the _____ parallel.

2.20 Tyler vetoed _____ , _____ , and _____ .

2.21 Polk won the 1844 election because he publicly favored annexing _____ and acquiring all of _____ .

2.22 _____ was a missionary who brought his wife to Oregon in 1836.

2.23 Congress accepted the Webster-Ashburton Treaty because Webster found a map that showed that _____ had claim to the entire area in dispute.

2.24 The Oregon Trail was about _____ miles long.

Texas and Polk

Americans in Texas. America's claims to Texas were surrendered in 1819 by the Adams-Onis Treaty with Spain; however, land-hungry Americans wanted to farm the rich lands of east Texas that faced them across the border. Spain agreed to allow some to enter under special conditions. Moses Austin negotiated one such agreement with Spain in 1820. Austin was given a large tract of land along the Brazos River and given permission to settle three hundred families there. The settlers had to become Catholics, be of good character, and swear allegiance to the king of Spain. The Spanish government hoped to gain a tax-paying population for their vast domain and defenses against the Native American Peoples of the region.

Moses Austin died before he could execute his agreement. His son, Stephen Austin, settled the "First Three Hundred" in Texas beginning in 1821. In that same year, Mexico won its independence from Spain. Austin made the difficult journey to Mexico City to have his agreement confirmed by the new government. It was, and many others were granted in the years that followed. One important late settler was Sam Houston, a former Tennessee governor and friend of Andrew Jackson.

By 1835 about 30,000 Americans were living in Texas. Most were law-abiding settlers but some were men avoiding the law in America. "G.T.T." (Gone to Texas) was a note that was often left behind when a man found it necessary to get out from under the jurisdiction of the United States.

In spite of the requirement that they swear allegiance to the Mexican government, most of the settlers continued to think of themselves as Americans. They often defied the requirement of becoming Catholic and brought enslaved people into Texas in violation of the law. The independent settlers clashed with corrupt local officials and soldiers who were often little more than uniformed bandits. The Americans also were disturbed by the continuous instability of the Mexican government.

A revolt broke out in Texas in 1832 over a decree that forbade any more Americans to settle in the land. A revolt was also going on in Mexico City. The new president, General Antonio Lopez de Santa Anna, accepted the changes in Texas. Stephen Austin went to Mexico City in 1833 to petition that Texas become a separate state in the Mexican federation and allow American immigration. He was arrested and spent almost a year in jail before he was released.

The Texas Revolution. The last straw came in 1835. Santa Anna suspended the constitution and declared himself dictator. Several of the Mexican states, including Texas, rose in revolt. Fighting began in Texas in October when Santa Anna's soldiers tried to force the settlers to turn in their weapons. It began as a fight for their rights under the suspended Mexican Constitution.

Santa Anna sent his brother-in-law and an army to occupy San Antonio to control the situation. The Texians (as they called themselves) set up a temporary government and put Sam Houston in command of the army. A request was sent to the United States for volunteers. They poured in from all over the South. The Americans attacked San Antonio, capturing it in December of 1835. This alarmed Santa Anna. He assembled an army of about 8,000 and invaded Texas, arriving at San Antonio on February 23, 1836.

The troops that had been left to hold San Antonio had taken shelter in a mission/ fortress called the Alamo. Houston sent Colonel Jim Bowie with orders to blow up the Alamo and retreat. Bowie and the resident commander, William Travis, decided to ignore their orders and defend the fort. They had 183 men including a group of Tennessee volunteers led by the famous backwoodsman, Davy Crockett.

The Battle of the Alamo has become a vibrant part of American folklore, even though the defense of the mission was in violation of the orders of Sam Houston. The men who held the fort acted with the highest courage and forced Santa Anna to pay a horrendous price for his victory. They also delayed the advance of his army for two critical weeks which bought Houston time to organize.

The defenders of the Alamo refused to surrender, even when surrounded by an army perhaps 30 times their numbers. Santa Anna besieged the mission unsuccessfully from February 23 to March 6. The expert American marksmen held the walls against all attacks. Finally, on the 6th, the Mexicans stormed the walls, overwhelming them by sheer numbers. The Americans fought hand-to-hand as they ran out of ammunition. On the dictator's orders, all of the defenders were killed. Santa Anna lost over a thousand of his own men in the siege to the defenders' 183.

Remember the Alamo. The Texan leaders had been meeting to discuss their plans when the Alamo was under attack. They confirmed Houston as commander of the army and decided to declare Texas independent on March 2. News of the Alamo angered and aroused the Texans. Further fuel was added later in the month when Santa Anna ordered the cold-blooded murder of 400 men who had surrendered at Goliad. To cries of "Remember the Alamo! Remember Goliad!", the Texans rallied to defend themselves.

The wily Sam Houston led the Mexicans on a long, winding chase through the rough Texas countryside. The retreat was unpopular, but Houston managed to hold it together. Every day his army grew larger while Santa Anna's grew wearier and smaller. Finally, on April 21, the Texans attacked at San Jacinto during the Mexican siesta. Over a thousand Mexican soldiers were killed or wounded while the Americans lost less than forty. Santa Anna was captured and signed a treaty giving Texas its independence.

Annexation Question. Andrew Jackson, who was president at the time, was in a quandary. Santa Anna repudiated the treaty he signed after San Jacinto as soon as he was safely back in Mexico. Extending official recognition to the Lone Star Republic (the flag of Texas had one star) might spark an unpopular war with Mexico. Jackson delayed until after the election of Van Buren and then recognized the Texas Republic just before he left office.

Texas wanted to be part of the United States and promptly applied for admission in 1837. A two-thirds majority was needed to approve the treaty of annexation and it failed. The reason was slavery. The northern states refused to admit such a large, slave-holding land. An attempt was made again in 1844, but it also failed for the same reason. However, popular opinion was building in favor of annexation.

In 1844 James K. Polk made Texas a major issue in his campaign. When Polk won the election, President John Tyler believed it was a mandate to add Texas to the Union. He arranged for Congress to annex the territory by a joint resolution requiring only a simple majority.

| Davy Crockett at the Alamo, preparing to die

Annexation passed in December of 1844 and Texas became a state one year later.

James K. Polk. James K. Polk (1795-1849) added more territory to the United States than any other president. Polk was born in North Carolina to Irish immigrants. His father speculated in land and became wealthy in America. The younger Polk graduated from the University of North Carolina and took up the practice of law in Tennessee. He became a close friend and **protégé** of Andrew Jackson earning the name "Young Hickory" because of the General's support. He served seven terms in the House of Representatives and was Speaker of the House under Jackson's presidency. He also was elected to one term as governor of Tennessee. The Democratic Party could not agree on Van Buren or his chief rival, Lewis Cass, for their candidate in 1844. With Jackson's backing, Polk was offered as a compromise candidate. He was the first "dark horse" candidate, a virtual unknown chosen when better-known candidates were not acceptable for some reason.

Polk was a highly successful president. He set four goals to accomplish while in office. He achieved all of them. The first two were to lower the tariff and establish an independent treasury. The latter was needed because the Whigs had repealed Van Buren's treasury plans and were unable to re-establish a national bank. The Walker Tariff (named after Secretary of the Treasury Robert Walker) passed in 1846. It lowered most of the tariffs and eliminated some altogether. The independent treasury was set up that same year and handled America's government funds until the Federal Reserve was set up in 1913.

Polk's third goal was to settle the Oregon boundary dispute, which was accomplished in 1846. Polk's last goal was to add California to the United States. This proved to be the most difficult and costly of his goals.

In 1844 California was owned by Mexico. It was sparsely populated with a few thousand

| Disputed Texas

Mexicans and even fewer foreigners, mostly Americans. Manifest Destiny Americans wanted the fertile lands of its coastal valleys and the fine harbor at San Francisco. Mexico, still smarting from the annexation of Texas, had broken off diplomatic relations and refused all offers to buy California. Tensions were also high because Mexico had defaulted on payments of claims it owed U.S. citizens. In 1845 Mexico refused to even receive the new American minister. Polk decided to get what he wanted by war.

Events in Texas. The treaty signed by Santa Anna had set the southern border of Texas at the Rio Grande River. Mexico claimed that the real border was the Nueces River further to the north. While he had been trying to negotiate for California, Polk had kept U.S. troops out of the disputed area. In January 1846 he ordered General Zachary Taylor to take up a position on the Rio Grande River. As he hoped, the Mexicans attacked Taylor on April 25, 1846, killing or wounding sixteen men. Polk sent a message to Congress asking for a declaration of war because of the shedding of "American blood on American soil" by the Mexicans. Congress passed the war resolution by a wide margin.

Answer true or false.

If the statement is false, change some nouns or adjectives to make it true.

2.25 _____ Moses Austin settled the "First Three Hundred" families on the Brazos River in Texas.

2.26 _____ Most of the defenders of the Alamo were killed.

2.27 _____ The annexation of Texas stalled over the issue of slavery.

2.28 _____ Texans won their independence at the Battle of Goliad.

2.29 _____ Andrew Jackson recognized the Lone Star Republic just before he left office.

2.30 _____ James K. Polk was called "Young Hickory."

2.31 _____ America had surrendered its claims to Texas in the Webster-Ashburton Treaty.

2.32 _____ Henry Clay was the first "dark horse" candidate for president.

2.33 _____ Polk was a successful president.

2.34 _____ Americans brought enslaved people into Texas in violation of Mexican law.

Answer these questions.

2.35 What are the names of three of the men who died at the Alamo?

a. _____   b. _____

c. _____

2.36 What were James K. Polk's four goals for his presidency?

a. _____   b. _____

c. _____   d. _____

2.37 What did G.T.T. mean?

_____

2.38 How did Polk provoke a war with Mexico?

_____

_____

2.39 What event in Mexico triggered the Texas Revolution?

_____

_____

2.40 What were the two rally cries of the Texas Revolution?

_____

_____

2.41 What was Sam Houston's strategy after the Alamo?

_____

_____

The Mexican War

Politics of War. Mexican-American relations had been bad for some time. Revolution after revolution had rocked the Mexican Republic since its creation in 1821. During these upheavals, Americans were killed, their property taken, treaties were ignored, and damages were promised but not paid. The proud Mexicans had also said that the annexation of Texas would be a declaration of war. However, the main reason that the war began in 1846 was Polk's desire for California. There was a serious concern that Mexico could not hold California, and it might wind up in hostile British hands. Polk wanted it safely in American hands along with the New Mexico territory to complete America's sea-to-sea Manifest Destiny.

The war was controversial in its own time. Many people questioned whether or not America had really been the innocent victim of a Mexican attack, as Polk declared. Illinois representative Abraham Lincoln tried to force the president to admit that Mexicans attacked Americans on Mexican soil. Abolitionists feared the war was a conspiracy to add slave territory to the nation. John Calhoun opposed the declaration of war, fearing the new land would divide the nation. Webster and Clay opposed it as a creation of the Democratic president. (Both of them lost sons in the battles that followed.)

The controversy did not keep the war from being generally popular, however, especially as American victories mounted. Thousands of volunteers poured into the army from all over the nation to supplement the professional army. The professional army was small, especially compared to the large army Mexico had amassed (needed because of the continuous upheaval there). However, the American army had a superior collection of junior officers who had been trained at the military academy at West Point. Many of the men who would lead the North and South in the coming years received their battle training in the Mexican War. Robert E. Lee, Ulysses S. Grant, Thomas J. (Stonewall) Jackson, George Meade, George McClellan, and George Pickett were a few of the many future Civil War leaders who served in Mexico. Thus, the war was one of the last united acts of the nation before the division over slavery became unavoidable.

New Mexico and California. The territory coveted by the United States quickly and easily came under American control. Neither New Mexico nor California had any substantial forces to oppose an American invasion. Under the command of Colonel Stephen Kearny, troops marched from Fort Leavenworth, Kansas to New Mexico in June of 1846. The more than

HISTORY & GEOGRAPHY 805

LIFEPAC TEST

NAME _____

DATE _____

SCORE _____

HISTORY & GEOGRAPHY 805: LIFEPAC TEST

Match the president with the events of his administration. Some answers will be used more than once (each answer, 2 points).

1.	_____ shortest administration in history	a. John Quincy Adams
2.	_____ Mexican War	b. Andrew Jackson
3.	_____ Panic of 1837	c. Martin Van Buren
4.	_____ Tariff of Abominations	d. William H. Harrison
5.	_____ "corrupt bargain"	e. John Tyler
6.	_____ Nullification Crisis	f. James K. Polk
7.	_____ *Specie Circular*	g. Zachary Taylor
8.	_____ Compromise of 1850	h. Millard Fillmore
9.	_____ Kansas-Nebraska Act	i. Franklin Pierce
10.	_____ boundary of Maine settled	
11.	_____ boundary of Oregon settled	
12.	_____ died in office unable to resolve organization of the Mexican Cession	
13.	_____ National Bank closed	
14.	_____ Texas Revolution	
15.	_____ California's Bear Flag Republic	

Name the item described (each answer, 3 points).

16. _____ No slavery north of 36° 30' in the Louisiana Purchase, Maine admitted as a free state

17. _____ Fugitive Slave Act, California admitted as a free state

18. _____ Native Americans of the Southeast were forced to move to land beyond the Mississippi River

19. _____ America was destined to move across and occupy the entire continent

20. _____ Rally cry for Americans who wanted to claim all of the Oregon Territory

21. _____ Majestic, streamlined sailing ships that took over the high-speed ocean trade of the early to mid-1800s

22. _____ Most successful internal canal in American history

23. _____ Secondary issue fought over by the North and South after the slavery issue was avoided by the Missouri Compromise

24. _____ government jobs are given to the loyal followers of whoever won the election

25. _____ route taken by people from eastern America to reach Oregon over land

Match these people (each answer, 2 points).

26. _____ author of *Uncle Tom's Cabin*   a. Winfield Scott

27. _____ Mexican dictator, fought Americans   b. Henry Clay
        in Texas and in the Mexican War
                                                        c. John Calhoun

28. _____ conductor on Underground Railroad   d. Daniel Webster

29. _____ cotton gin, interchangeable parts   e. Harriet Beecher Stowe

30. _____ steel plow   f. Eli Whitney

31. _____ Great Compromiser   g. Sam Houston

32. _____ victor of Mexico City campaign   h. Stephen Douglas

33. _____ brought British textile machine   i. Samuel Morse
        information to America
                                                         j. Harriet Tubman

34. _____ sewing machine   k. Nicholas Biddle

35. _____ defender of the South, Doctrine of Nullification   l. Samuel Slater

36. _____ president of National Bank   m. John Deere

37. _____ victor in Texas Revolution   n. Elias Howe

38. _____ telegraph   o. Santa Anna

39. _____ great orator from the North, debated Hayne
        on the subject of states' rights and nullification

40. _____ pushed the Kansas-Nebraska Act through Congress

Answer true or false (each answer, 1 point).

41. _____ *Uncle Tom's Cabin* was very effective anti-slavery propaganda.

42. _____ Andrew Jackson made the American government more elitist and less responsible to the desires of the common man.

43. _____ The cotton gin made slavery very profitable and protected in the South.

44. _____ The Whig party favored states' rights, low taxes and slavery.

45. _____ Americans settled in Texas when it was still part of Mexico.

46. _____ The Mexican War was a training ground for the Civil War.

47. _____ Irish immigrants were usually poor and settled on farms in the Far West.

48. _____ John Tyler was the only president of this era to serve two terms.

49. _____ John Quincy Adams was more successful as a member of the House of Representatives than as president.

50. _____ Nullification was a doctrine that said any state could leave the Union if it did not like the way it was being run.

1,500 troops traveled down the Santa Fe Trail, a road set up by American merchants to trade with that isolated Mexican outpost. Kearny captured the city and the territory easily.

California was captured in a very colorful manner. John C. Frémont, an army topographer, had already explored much of the West, creating accurate maps and suggesting sites for forts. He appeared in California in 1845, supposedly on a scientific expedition, but probably under secret orders from President Polk to be ready to take it in the event of war. In any case, Frémont led a rebellion in June of 1846 that declared California an independent republic called the "Bear Flag Republic." By the time word reached Frémont of the war with Mexico, most of northern California was already in his hands. The rest followed shortly.

The situation was complicated when Commodore Robert Stockton sailed in with official orders to seize California. He took Santa Barbara and Los Angeles. He was joined by Kearny who had arrived overland from New Mexico with the same orders. The two commanders retook Los Angeles when it rebelled in September of 1846 and quarreled over who was in command. Frémont arrived and added his dubious authority to the fray. Kearny had Frémont arrested and sent back to Washington for a court martial. He was found guilty but was released by President Polk's orders. Thus, California was captured.

Northern Mexico Campaign. Zachary Taylor, whose troops had been attacked along the Rio Grande, did not wait for the official declaration from Washington. He knew he had a war with Mexico even though the politicians had not officially declared it. "Old Rough and Ready," as Taylor was known, was a popular commander. He was an easy-going man who dressed without regard for military protocol, often wearing a straw hat. He was a capable but not brilliant commander who was determined to press on with the job.

| Battle in Northern Mexico

In May, Taylor met the Mexican army at Palo Alto and Resaca de la Palma, both north of the Rio Grande. In both cases, the Americans won with far lighter casualties than the Mexicans. The skillful American **artillery** proved decisive in both victories. Taylor then went to the aid of Fort Texas which he had established near the mouth of the Rio Grande. He renamed it Fort Brown after the commander who had died defending it during the siege by the Mexican army. Acting without orders, Taylor then crossed the Rio Grande and captured the city of Matamoros without firing a shot.

The quick series of victories made Taylor a hero. The Whigs immediately began to talk of having him run for president in 1848, and Taylor did nothing to discourage the talk. Polk, a hard-core Jacksonian Democrat, was alarmed by the general's popularity. The president tried unsuccessfully to appoint a Democratic general to gain the laurels of victory, but Congress refused to cooperate.

In June Taylor was ordered south. He attacked the city of Monterrey in September of 1846. It was heavily fortified and American losses were heavy. The Americans eventually captured the town, using a technique borrowed from the Texans who took San Antonio during their revolution. The soldiers burrowed through the adobe walls of the city buildings, moving closer and closer to the city center, house by house. The Mexicans finally surrendered and received generous peace terms from the general. The terms were so generous that they were later repudiated by the U.S. government. Taylor was now ordered to hold what he had taken and send a large part of his army south to assist General Winfield Scott in a planned attack on the Mexican capital.

Taylor, however, believed his orders were intended to quiet him and cut off his political popularity. He ignored them and marched his reduced army south, reaching Buena Vista near the city of Saltillo in February of 1847. There he

| California's Bear Flag

was met by a huge army under the command of the revived Mexican dictator, Santa Anna.

Santa Anna had been in exile in Cuba when the war began. In exchange for a large bribe and passage into Mexico, he had offered to give America the land they wanted. Naively, James Polk believed him. Santa Anna returned to Mexico, took over the government and announced a great war to defend the nation against the barbarian invaders. He assembled an army of over 20,000 to meet Taylor who had about 6,500. He offered Taylor a chance to surrender in the face of the superior numbers. Taylor refused, even though he was outnumbered three to one.

The Battle of Buena Vista lasted two days. It was marked by the daring and skill of the junior officers who held out against the incredible odds. Taylor refused to retreat, even when some of his men recommended it. Again, the American artillery proved decisive, and it was the Mexicans who retreated. This remarkable victory confirmed Taylor's growing reputation as a national hero. He remained in northern Mexico for the rest of the war.

Doniphan. Kearny had divided his command at Santa Fe. A group of Missouri Mounted Volunteers were sent south under the command of Colonel Alexander Doniphan. They were supposed to pacify the Navajos, and then go through El Paso and Chihuahua City to meet up with General Taylor. Doniphan proceeded to do just that with his group of ragtag volunteer backwoodsmen. This undisciplined gang defeated a much larger Mexican army at El Brazito on Christmas Day 1846. They also won the Battle of the Sacramento near Chihuahua in February of 1847 and then occupied the city.

The "lost" regiment finally met up with Taylor at Saltillo in May of 1847, having marched several thousand miles and won two major victories against larger armies. Most of them took their pay, which they received for the first time in the campaign, and headed home.

Match these people (answers may be used more than once).

2.42	_____ Old Rough and Ready	a. John Frémont
2.43	_____ army topographer	b. Zachary Taylor
2.44	_____ victor at Palo Alto and Buena Vista	c. Alexander Doniphan
2.45	_____ commander, Missouri Mounted Volunteers	d. Stephen Kearny
2.46	_____ founder of the Bear Flag Republic	e. Robert Stockton
2.47	_____ captured Santa Fe	f. Santa Anna
2.48	_____ naval officer, took Los Angeles	g. James Polk
2.49	_____ Mexican dictator, again	
2.50	_____ captured Matamoros	
2.51	_____ captured Monterrey	
2.52	_____ captured Chihuahua	
2.53	_____ a Jacksonian Democrat	
2.54	_____ victories made Whigs talk of making him president	
2.55	_____ took advantage of Polk's naiveté	

Answer these questions.

2.56 Where were America's superior junior officers of the Mexican War educated?

_____

2.57 The Mexican War provided battle training for the officers of what future war?

_____

2.58 What were two reasons why the Mexican War was controversial?

_____

_____

2.59 Why did Taylor ignore his orders to stay in Monterrey?

_____

_____

2.60 What part of the army contributed decisively to the victories at Palo Alto, Resaca de la Palma, and Buena Vista? _____

Campaign Against Mexico City. General Winfield Scott was the highest-ranking general in the American army during the Mexican War. He was a man who loved pomp, good food, and fancy uniforms. His men called him "Old Fuss and Feathers." He was quick-tempered, touchy, and blunt. He stayed out of the early part of the war because of differences with President Polk. However, he was a brilliant military man, and he proved it in the campaign to capture Mexico City.

In October of 1846, Scott proposed to lead a campaign against the Mexican capital. It was a bold idea. He would have to march from Veracruz on the Gulf of Mexico across miles of poorly mapped, heavily defended territory. He would have to penetrate deep into enemy territory with only a thin supply line. It was a difficult military venture.

| Mexican Cession

Scott sailed to Mexico with over 10,000 men in 1847. In March he landed his men away from Veracruz and attacked it from the landward side where the defenses were weakest. The siege lasted only a few days. Scott left a small force to occupy the city and moved quickly toward Mexico City.

Santa Anna received word that Scott was coming and went to meet him. The Mexican army set up defenses in a narrow mountain pass near Cerro Gordo. Scott's rapid advance reached the site before the defenses were fully in place. Captain Robert E. Lee, working with the engineers, found and cut a way around the enemy to allow an attack from two sides. The outnumbered Americans won the two-day battle, clearing the road to Mexico City.

At this point, Polk tried again to negotiate the peace he wanted. Nicholas P. Trist, a State Department clerk, was sent to attempt negotiations. The Mexican government refused, but Santa Anna sent a secret offer to Scott. In exchange for $10,000 up front, and $90,000 more after a treaty was signed, Santa Anna would arrange for a treaty that gave the Americans what they wanted. Scott decided to try it and sent the $10,000. The Americans did not get their treaty. Santa Anna pocketed the money and used the time to prepare his defenses.

Scott advanced on the capital in August of 1847. During this part of the campaign, he was cut off from his communications and supplies. He either had to win or surrender. Santa Anna had strong defenses in place to protect the city. Scott took the first of these at Contreras and Churubusco on the 19th and 20th.

The Mexicans then asked for an armistice. Scott granted one for two weeks, believing the enemy wanted to negotiate. Again, Santa Anna used the time to improve his defenses. When the armistice ended, the Americans attacked again, winning a battle at Molino del Rey. They then captured the fortress of Chapultepec which cleared the way right up to the city gates. Santa Anna fled and the city authorities sued for peace. On September 14, 1847, Scott rode into the central plaza of the city and the Stars and Stripes were raised.

Treaty of Guadalupe Hidalgo. Nicholas Trist had been recalled by the president in October. He ignored the order and opened negotiations with the new Mexican government. The two sides met at Guadalupe Hidalgo, a city north of the capital. Faced with an army in their capital, the Mexicans gave the Americans everything they wanted.

The treaty ceded to America all of California and the land between it and Texas north of the Gila River. America agreed to pay 15 million dollars for the land and assume all of Mexico's debts to American citizens for damage claims. Mexico also recognized the Rio Grande as the border of Texas. The treaty was signed on February 2, 1848.

Polk was facing growing pressure to annex all of Mexico. However, when the treaty arrived, the president decided to submit it to the Senate because it gave him what he had originally wanted. He chose to ignore the fact that Trist was not authorized to negotiate for the United States. He may have been motivated by a fear that the government in Mexico would change again and repudiate it. The Senate approved it on March 10.

Results of the War. The Mexican Cession added more than 525,000 square miles (1,360,000 square kilometers) to the nation. It was the largest single piece of land ever to become part of the United States. However, Congress had tremendous difficulty trying to organize the new land into official territories. The sticking point was slavery.

David Wilmot of Pennsylvania had introduced a proposal in 1846, while the war was still in progress. It specified that no slavery would ever be allowed to exist in any land acquired from Mexico as a result of the war. The South fought the Wilmot Proviso with a passion. It passed in the House but failed in the Senate; however, it would not go away. It was introduced repeatedly to acrimonious debate.

After the war, other proposals were offered, some allowing slavery, some forbidding it, and some leaving it up to the citizens of each territory to decide for themselves (popular sovereignty). No agreements could be reached. The issue of organizing the new land hung on the deepening chasm of slavery. It was finally brought to a crisis by the sudden changes that had occurred in California.

California Gold Rush. It was expected that it would be years before any part of the Mexican Cession would have the 60,000 people needed to apply for statehood. However, in 1848, just days before the Treaty of Guadalupe Hidalgo was signed, gold was discovered in the Sierra Nevada Mountains of California. What followed was one of the largest mass migrations in history. Approximately 80,000 people came to California in 1849 hoping to strike it rich. Just about the same number came the next few years. Some left after failing to get rich, but many stayed to make their homes in the West.

The "forty-niners," as they were called, came mainly from the United States by three routes. The largest group came overland via the trading and wagon trails. Another group sailed south to Panama, crossed the Isthmus, and came north by sea to California. Still another group took the difficult ocean route around the southern tip of South America. Hundreds of ships reached the West Coast and were promptly abandoned as all the men aboard went searching for gold. Rotting ships filled San Francisco harbor, which had became a major city overnight.

California's population rapidly exceeded the 60,000 needed for statehood. The official population count in 1850 was over 90,000! In 1849 California organized a government and applied for admission as a state, skipping the intermediate step of territory. The real problem arose because the new state constitution barred slavery. The stage was set for a major sectional battle.

Election of 1848. The Whigs jumped at the chance to run the popular general, Zachary Taylor, for president in 1848. They again bypassed Henry Clay and Daniel Webster, both of whom wanted the nomination. The Democrats nominated General Lewis Cass, a veteran of the War of 1812. President Polk had promised not to run again if he was elected; his health would not permit it in any case. Martin Van Buren ran as a third-party candidate for the anti-slavery Free-Soil Party.

The Whigs and the Democrats avoided the slavery issue. In fact, they avoided most of the issues. The Free-Soil Party, on the other hand, came out openly against slavery in the territories. They also advocated internal improvements and free land for settlers. Their slogan was "free soil, free speech, free labor, and free men." However, it was a contest of personalities, not issues, and the popular Taylor won.

| Gold Prospector by the River

Zachary Taylor. Zachary Taylor (1784-1850) was the son of a wealthy Virginia planter. His father fought in the Revolution, and it was no surprise when Zachary joined the army as a young man. Taylor fought in the Black Hawk and Seminole Indian Wars before becoming a national hero in the Mexican War. He had no political experience and knew very little about national or international affairs. In fact, he had never even voted in a presidential election!

The intense controversy in Congress over the organization of the Mexican Cession was beyond Taylor. He bungled back and forth, unable to resolve the issues. Before any resolution could be worked out, Taylor died in 1850 and Millard Fillmore, his vice president, came to power.

The Last Piece. The growing American population in California and Oregon was causing communication problems. The populated West Coast lands were thousands of miles and months of travel away from the center of government in the East. Several people proposed to build a railroad across the country to connect the two coasts more conveniently.

The most attractive route was across what is now New Mexico and Arizona south of the Gila River. The Rocky Mountains were lower through that part of the West. Unfortunately, that land belonged to Mexico.

In 1853 James Gadsden was sent as the American minister to Mexico. He was authorized to negotiate for the land needed for a railroad route. Gadsden's efforts prospered because Santa Anna was once again (for the sixth time) in power, and the old dictator needed money. He agreed to sell the United States a section of land south of the Gila River for $10 million. The Gadsden Purchase was the last piece of land acquired for what would become the forty-eight contiguous states. Manifest Destiny had been fulfilled.

| Gadsden Purchase

✏️ **Complete these sentences.**

2.61 The Mexican War was ended by the Treaty of _____.

2.62 The sticking point over organizing the land acquired from Mexico was the issue of

_____.

2.63 Winfield Scott's nickname was _____.

2.64 California's population grew rapidly after the discovery of _____ in 1848.

2.65 _____ was elected president in 1848.

2.66 Martin Van Buren ran for president in 1848 as a candidate of the _____

Party.

2.67 The last part of the contiguous states added to the Union was the _____

Purchase.

2.68 The men who arrived in California in 1849 were called _____.

2.69 Winfield Scott led a brilliant campaign that conquered _____ in

September of 1847.

2.70 The man who negotiated the treaty that ended the war with Mexico was

_____.

2.71 The three routes to California in the rush after 1848 were:

a. _____

b. _____

c. _____

2.72 America paid _____ dollars to Mexico for the land ceded by them after

the war.

2.73 The defense of Mexico City was under the command of the dictator,

_____.

2.74 California organized a government in the year _____ and wanted to become

a state without ever being a _____.

2.75 The slogan of the Free-Soil Party in 1848 was _____

_____.

2.76 The Gadsden Purchase was made because the U.S. needed the land for a _____

line to the West Coast.

2.77 The two-day battle at the mountain pass near _____ cleared the road to Mexico City for the Americans.

2.78 The land taken from Mexico by the war was called the _____ _____ .

2.79 After the Mexican War, Mexico recognized the _____ as the border of Texas.

2.80 The _____ Proviso that proposed to forbid slavery in land acquired from Mexico did not become law.

2.81 The constitution of California did not allow _____ .

2.82 _____ became president after Taylor died in 1850.

2.83 During the Mexican War, _____ was the highest ranking general in the U.S. army.

Review the material in this section in preparation for the Self Test. This Self Test will check your mastery of this particular section as well as your knowledge of the previous section.

SELF TEST 2

Match these items (each answer, 2 points).

2.01 _____ Wilmot Proviso

2.02 _____ Missouri Compromise

2.03 _____ Tariff of Abominations

2.04 _____ Gag Rule

2.05 _____ *Specie Circular*

2.06 _____ Pet Banks

2.07 _____ Manifest Destiny

2.08 _____ Trail of Tears

2.09 _____ Log Cabin and Hard Cider

2.010 _____ Gadsden Purchase

a. America should move across the continent, claiming the land

b. Harrison's presidential campaign

c. no petitions on slavery

d. Native American removal to west of Mississippi

e. needed for railroad to the Pacific

f. no slavery north of 36° 30'

g. passed in 1828 to embarrass President Adams, infuriated the South

h. government funds placed there under Jackson

i. no slavery in territory from Mexico

j. federal land must be purchased with gold or silver

Name the item or person (each answer, 3 points).

2.011 The three national leaders from the South, West, and North who never became president:

a. _____ b. _____

c. _____

2.012 _____ Name for land acquired after the Mexican War

2.013 _____ Slogan for those who wanted all of Oregon

2.014 _____ One rally cry of the Texas Revolution

2.015 _____ State that was an independent republic for 10 years before joining the Union

2.016 _____ Polk went to war with Mexico to get this state

2.017 _____ The crisis that almost divided the nation under Andrew Jackson

2.018 _____ The "moneyed monster" hated by Jackson and eventually destroyed by him

Answer these questions (each answer, 3 points).

2.019   The United States peacefully resolved border disputes with Great Britain over which two territories in the 1840s?

_____

2.020   How did the Mexican War start?

_____

_____

2.021   What campaign won the Mexican War for America and who led it?

_____

_____

2.022   What happened at the Alamo in 1836?

_____

_____

_____

2.023   What were Zachary Taylor's qualifications for president?

_____

_____

2.024   What were the terms of the Treaty of Guadalupe Hidalgo?

_____

_____

_____

_____

2.025   What was the "corrupt bargain" that Jackson claimed John Quincy Adams used to win the presidency?

_____

_____

2.026   Why could Congress not agree on organizing the new territories after the Mexican War?

_____

_____

2.027 Why was James Polk chosen as the Democratic candidate for president?

_____

_____

2.028 What happened to the Democratic-Republican Party after the election of John Quincy Adams?

_____

_____

Match these people (each answer, 2 points).

2.029 _____ became president at Harrison's death, a Whig with Democrat ideas

2.030 _____ brilliant American general, highest-ranking officer during Mexican War

2.031 _____ served in House of Representatives for years after presidency

2.032 _____ the Great Compromiser

2.033 _____ hero of New Orleans, the people's president

2.034 _____ Jackson's hand-picked successor, the Little Magician

2.035 _____ victor at Buena Vista, Old Rough and Ready

2.036 _____ Texan, victor at San Jacinto against Santa Anna

2.037 _____ added more territory to the Union than any other president

2.038 _____ president for only 31 days

a.   Andrew Jackson

b.   Sam Houston

c.   William H. Harrison

d.   Henry Clay

e.   James K. Polk

f.   Zachary Taylor

g.   Winfield Scott

h.   Martin Van Buren

i.   John Quincy Adams

j.   John Tyler

80 / 100   SCORE _____   TEACHER _____ _____

initials   date

3. GROWTH AND DIVISION

America grew in the early 1800s in more than just size. The Industrial Revolution brought manufacturing growth which would eventually make America a world power. Innovations in transportation, agriculture, manufacturing, and communications caused unprecedented changes in American life. Trade grew and the various parts of the frontier were brought into the national economy as transport became easier. Life became easier as machines took over backbreaking manual labor. The new industries created large pools of wealth that further fed the growth of industry and commerce.

American life also saw changes as immigration brought in large numbers of new citizens.

A revival broke out in the early 1800s that led thousands to the Lord. A reform movement followed the revival and touched many areas of American life.

The great tragedy of the era was the continuation of slavery and the South's stubborn defense of it. The Kansas-Nebraska Act destroyed the Missouri Compromise and much of the remaining trust between the anti-slavery North and the pro-slavery South. The anti-slavery Republican Party was formed and leaped onto the national scene. The breakup of the Union was drawing near.

SECTION OBJECTIVES

Review these objectives. When you have completed this section, you should be able to:

1. Name the leaders of the era and explain their accomplishments.
3. Trace the development of the slavery and tariff issues from 1820 to 1855.
4. Define Manifest Destiny and describe its course in America.
6. Define the Industrial Revolution and name the people, innovations, and inventions that contributed to it.
7. Describe the effects of the Industrial Revolution in America.
8. Describe the Second Great Awakening and the reform movements that followed it.
9. Describe the compromises that kept the nation together and what ended them.
10. Describe the changes in America and American life in this era.

VOCABULARY

Study these words to enhance your learning success in this section.

comptroller (komp trō' ler). A public official who audits government accounts.

denomination (di nom i nā' shun). A religious organization uniting in a single administrative body a number of local congregations.

heresy (her' e sē). A belief different from the standard beliefs of the church.

patent (pat' nt). A document that gives an inventor the sole right to make, use or sell his invention for so many years.

platform (plat' form). Statement of policies and ideas adopted by a political party.

polygamy (po lig' a mē). Marriage to more than one person at one time, usually the taking of several wives by one man.

propaganda (prop a gan' da). The spreading of ideas or information for the purpose of helping or injuring a cause, institution, or person.

temperance (tem' pe rens). Moderation in or abstinence from the use of intoxicating drinks.

The Industrial Revolution

Not all revolutions are violent. Second only to the War for Independence, the greatest revolution in American history was the Industrial Revolution. This revolution was the change from a farming and handcrafting society to one of industry and machine manufacturing. It began in England in the 1700s and eventually spread to reach much of the world. It began in America, in a small way, late in that same century, but it did not become an important part of American culture until the War of 1812. It was the embargoes and blockades of that war that pushed American manufacturing to begin its spectacular rise.

Textiles. The revolution had its most successful beginning in the textile industry. Britain had developed many of the machines used in the mass production of cloth in the late 1700s. These machines spun several spools of yarn or thread instead of the one at a time that could be done by hand. British inventors had also invented the power loom that allowed cloth to be woven more quickly. These inventions were protected by laws that prohibited plans of the machines or people who knew them from leaving the country.

However, the laws did not stop Samuel Slater, the "Father of the Factory System (in America). Slater was a skilled mechanic familiar with the British textile machines. He memorized the plans for the machines and succeeded in reaching the United States in disguise. In 1791 with the financial backing of Moses Brown, a New England capitalist, Slater opened America's first factory for spinning thread in Rhode Island.

The new factory was opened in time to cash in on the flood of cotton from the South. Eli Whitney invented the cotton gin in 1793, allowing for the cheap production of this textile fiber. The factories of the North were soon busy turning Southern cotton into cotton thread. These same factories began to weave it into cloth when the power loom was added to the American system in 1814. The textile industry received another boost in 1846 when Elias Howe **patented** the sewing machine. It was further perfected by Isaac Singer who made it popular. It was the first in a long line of labor-saving devices that began to appear

| Cotton Gin

in American homes, not just factories. It also allowed the factories to begin mass-producing clothes from their inexpensive thread and cloth.

Most of the factories were located in the northeast for several reasons. The machines were powered at first by water wheels that required fast-moving streams. The steep hills and swift streams of New England were ideal for these kinds of factories. The poor soil of New England encouraged people to try the alternative of manufacturing. Northern seaports provided a ready way to bring in raw material and export finished goods. New England also had a ready supply of capital from its many wealthy shipping entrepreneurs. Moreover, the northeast was the most densely populated part of the nation, providing the factories with needed workers. The West, by contrast, was sparsely populated by poor farmers, and the South was populated by rich plantation owners whose money was in cotton and slaves.

Mass Production. Eli Whitney made very little money on his cotton gin. He obtained a patent for the device, but others still produced the simple machine. By the time Whitney had gone through the courts and put the illegal manufacturers out of business, his patent had almost expired, so he had to earn his fortune another way. The way he chose once again revolutionized American manufacturing.

Whitney came up with the idea of mass production of interchangeable parts for guns. Prior to that time, each part of a gun was made by hand and it fit only that particular gun. If a part broke, a new one had to be handmade to replace it. Whitney had the parts made in large groups, each exactly alike. That way, a broken part could be easily and quickly replaced. The guns could be manufactured and maintained at a lesser cost. Whitney reportedly proved his point by taking ten guns to Washington for government officials to see. He took them apart, scrambled the pieces, and reassembled them into ten working guns!

Mass production of interchangeable parts spread to all areas of manufacturing. The cheap production of many goods brought those goods within reach for more and more people. It also gave the North a vast manufacturing engine that would be vital in the coming war with the South.

Factory Workers. The factory system was very beneficial to the nation by providing new jobs, cheaper goods, and economic prosperity; but it also had a downside. Many factory workers were shamefully exploited. Wages were low and hours were long. Thirteen- or fourteen-hour days, six days a week were common. Unions were considered conspiracies, and strikes for better pay often were broken up by the law. Working conditions were bad and often unsafe. An injured or ill worker had no protection from losing their job.

The worst abuse was the employment of children in the factories. Children, often under the age of ten, were put to work tending the machines for pitiful wages. They worked the same hours as the adults, deprived of their childhood and frequently their health by years of labor. Working also meant they could not get an education, and that often meant they would be unskilled laborers for all their lives. This child abuse was one of the blackest marks on the growth of industry in America and would continue for many years.

Gradually, improvements were made. Martin Van Buren set a precedent in 1840 when he limited workers on federal projects to ten hours a day. Slowly, the states began to pass laws limiting working hours. In 1842 the Supreme Court ruled that labor unions were not automatically illegal conspiracies. However, it would be many years before unions could build up the strength to effectively challenge the power of the employers.

Farming. Farming also profited from the Industrial Revolution. The thickly matted soil of the West had been hard on the heavy wooden plows that existed in the 1700s. In 1837 John Deere invented a light, sharp steel plow for western farmers. A few years earlier, Cyrus McCormick had patented a mechanical reaper. This remarkable invention allowed a man to harvest his grain by himself faster than he could with several helpers.

The new plow and reaper allowed a farmer to produce substantially more food than he needed for his family. Suddenly, farming was not just a way to survive, it was a way to make a profit!! Fertile western farms began to supply food for cotton-growing southern plantations and cotton-spinning northern factories. The different parts of the country specialized and depended upon the others for what they did not produce themselves.

Communication. The single greatest revolution in the history of communication was the invention of the telegraph by Samuel Morse. Morse invented a way to send messages instantly over a wire using a series of dots and dashes called Morse Code. In 1844 he sent a message from Washington to Baltimore, "What hath God wrought?" opening the era of instant communications! Soon, telegraph wires were all over the nation, allowing news and information to speed across the American expanse. In 1866 after five failures, Cyrus Field succeeded in laying a telegraph cable between Canada and Great Britain. The Old and New World were suddenly just a few seconds apart.

| McCormick's Reaper advertisement, the caption read, "The People's Favorite! The World-Renowned McCormick Twine Binder! Victorious in over 100 Field Trials! New and Valuable Improvements for 1884!"

Match these people (some answers will be used more than once).

3.1	_____	Father of the Factory System	a. Cyrus McCormick
3.2	_____	cotton gin	b. Cyrus Field
3.3	_____	interchangeable parts for guns	c. John Deere
3.4	_____	invented the telegraph	d. Elias Howe
3.5	_____	opened America's first thread-spinning factory	e. Eli Whitney
3.6	_____	invented the sewing machine	f. Isaac Singer
3.7	_____	steel plow	g. Samuel Morse
3.8	_____	improved and popularized the sewing machine	h. Samuel Slater
3.9	_____	"What hath God wrought?"	
3.10	_____	mechanical reaper	
3.11	_____	memorized British machine plans and came to America	
3.12	_____	laid a telegraph cable from Europe to North America	

Complete the following.

3.13 Where did the worldwide Industrial Revolution begin? _____

3.14 How did the new farm machines change Western farming?

_____

3.15 Name three reasons why factories developed in the Northeast.

a. _____

b. _____

c. _____

3.16 Name four ways the factory system exploited workers.

a. _____

b. _____

c. _____

d. _____

3.17 What was the Industrial Revolution?

_____

_____

Transportation Needs. Improvements in transportation were a vital part of the Industrial Revolution. At the time of the American Revolution, transportation was very poor. Roads were unpaved, muddy, rutted, and often impassable for wagons. The most reliable transportation was by water, but the rivers did not go to every farm. Since most farms produced only for the needs of the family, it was not a vital concern until the Industrial Revolution. However, before farms could provide food for cities devoted to manufacturing, they needed reliable ways to ship their produce.

Roads. The first improvements in overland transportation came through privately owned turnpikes at the end of the 1700s. The Lancaster Turnpike was a pioneer in this field. It was a wide road with a hard surface and was built by a private company. The company made a substantial profit charging tolls for commerce between Philadelphia and Lancaster, Pennsylvania. Its success encouraged many other companies to invest in these arteries. Commerce flourished along these routes, encouraging more of the same.

The Cumberland Road, also called the National Road, was built with public funds. It ran from Cumberland, Maryland to Vandalia, Illinois (completed in 1852). Connecting roads made it a fairly direct route between Baltimore on Chesapeake Bay, and St. Louis on the Mississippi River. It was a huge stimulant to trade, western migration, and the development of the cities of the frontier.

However, public roads were difficult to build. It was very expensive to build roads in the middle of the wilderness, miles from major sources of supplies, manpower, and food. States' rights advocates, like the Democrats, objected violently to using federal funds for any project inside one state. Moreover, the Northeast did not want to aid roads that would encourage their population to move west. So, additions to the national road that would connect it with major cities in Kentucky, for example, were

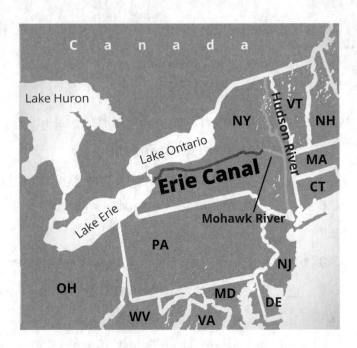

routinely voted down or vetoed, especially by Andrew Jackson. Nevertheless, with dedicated state spending, the hard-surface roads were gradually expanded.

The Steamboat. The mighty rivers of America, especially the Mississippi, were major trade routes. However, prior to 1807 they were basically one-way streets. Shipping goods downstream from a farm in Illinois to New Orleans, for example, was slow but simple. A farmer only had to build a raft and float it carefully down the river. However, going upstream carrying cargo of any bulk was incredibly difficult and too expensive to be very profitable.

That all changed in 1807 when Robert Fulton built a workable steamboat. It used a steam engine (which had been invented by other people) to drive a paddle wheel on the side of the ship. Fulton's ship, the *Clermont*, was called "Fulton's Folly" by his detractors. No one was laughing, however, when the ship steamed up the Hudson River from New York City to Albany in 32 hours—an unheard-of feat!

The steamboats rapidly spread to all the navigable rivers of the nation. They especially came to dominate trade on the Mississippi where a thousand or more people were working by 1860. Cities along the upper reaches of the river flourished as trade expanded. The Supreme Court decision of *Gibbons v. Ogden* in 1824 prohibited the states from controlling interstate trade on these rivers. That opened up these vital routes to healthy competition and rapid expansion.

Canal Craze. Even with better roads, water transportation was still better for large quantities of bulky cargo, but the rivers did not connect many of the vital inland water routes. This problem was corrected by a surge of canal building in the early 1800s.

The most famous and most successful of the internal canals was the Erie Canal in New York State. The Erie Canal connected Lake Erie with the Atlantic Ocean through the Mohawk and Hudson Rivers. It was promoted by New York Governor DeWitt Clinton. The federal government would not contribute any funds, so the difficult project was built entirely with New York money. Clinton's opponents called it "Clinton's Ditch." The determined governor persevered from 1817 until 1825, when the canal finally opened.

The canal was an unprecedented success. The time required to ship a ton of grain from Buffalo to New York City fell from twenty days to six days, and the cost dropped from $100 to $5! The Erie Canal connected New York City to the entire Midwest by the Great Lakes. The city quickly became the premier port on the eastern seaboard because of the influx of produce from the West. Land values along the canal shot up. Industry flourished with a ready source of raw materials and a cheap method for shipping out finished goods. "Clinton's Ditch" was New York's gold mine!

Other states observed the success and tried to copy it. A flurry of canal construction occurred in the 1820s and '30s. Several canals were built to connect the Mississippi and the Great Lakes. This also benefitted the trade going into New York City via the Erie Canal. One of the most

unusual canals connected the Susquehanna River above Chesapeake Bay to the Ohio River; it used a special railroad to lift the barges over the Allegheny Mountains. Many of these canals were a commercial success for a short time, but none rivaled the economic impact of the Erie Canal.

Ocean Trade. The steamboats and canals brought American products to seaports for trade with the world. America led the world in the mid-1800s in the development of a new ocean vessel, the clipper ship. Clipper ships were streamlined vessels built with a huge collection of sails. They were built for speed, not bulk, to carry valuable cargoes quickly. They quickly took over the tea trade to the Far East and were the vessel of choice for the impatient thousands heading to the California gold fields.

However, the majestic clippers were put out of business by the development of ocean-going steamships. These unlovely, slower ships were reliable and could carry much more cargo. By the time of the Civil War, the beautiful clippers were losing their cargoes to the cheaper transport of the smoke-belching steamers.

Railroad. The success of the canals was quickly ended by the incredible story of the railroads. These speedy monsters could go anywhere tracks could be laid. They were not dependent upon waterways or limited by hills and mountains. Railroads could carry bulky cargo even to cities that had no nearby river or lake.

Rail lines were used in the early 1800s to connect major cities using horse-drawn coaches. It was in Britain that the newly developed steam engine was first adapted to pull these coaches. It was also in Britain that the standard gauge (rail separation) of 4 feet 8 1/2 inches was set. (This was the standard width for wagon axles in Britain because the deep ruts in the old Roman roads were that distance apart. It had been the width of Roman chariot axles and became the railroad width in Britain, Canada, and the United States!)

The first American company to try the new technology was the Baltimore and Ohio Company which began service in 1830 with thirteen miles of track. That same year the B&O publicized its new venture by staging a race between a horse-drawn rail coach and one drawn by the *Tom Thumb*, an American-built locomotive. The *Tom Thumb* was winning until it broke down and the horse crossed the finish line first. It did not matter—the railroad had arrived.

The railroad expanded rapidly and quickly took up a vital role in the nation. From the thirteen miles set up by the B&O in 1830, the rail lines grew to about 30,000 miles by 1860! Most of these tracks were in the industrial North and the rapidly expanding West around the Great Lakes. The railroad gave the farmers of Ohio, Illinois, and Indiana direct access to the markets of the northeast. This vital river of iron replaced the Mississippi as the main trade route of the West. That stopped the South from choking off the West by their control of the Mississippi seaports during the Civil War.

| Early Steam Locomotive

 Answer these questions.

3.18 Why was better transportation needed for the Industrial Revolution?

_____

_____

3.19 Why didn't the federal government build more roads?

_____

_____

3.20 Why was the railroad important to the West in the Civil War?

_____

_____

3.21 Why were so many canals built in the years after 1825?

_____

_____

3.22 What put the clipper ships out of business?

_____

Match these items (some answers will be used more than once).

3.23 _____ _Gibbons v. Ogden_ gave these unfettered competition

3.24 _____ built by private companies that made a profit on tolls

3.25 _____ _Clermont_

3.26 _____ _Tom Thumb's_ owners

3.27 _____ had 30,000 miles by 1860

3.28 _____ made New York City the most important Eastern port

3.29 _____ the National Road

3.30 _____ major land artery between Chesapeake Bay and
the Mississippi

3.31 _____ took over the tea trade with the Far East because of their speed

3.32 _____ dropped the cost of shipping a ton of grain from Buffalo to New York City from
$100 to $5

3.33 _____ ocean vessels built for speed

3.34 _____ made the rivers into two-way streets

3.35 _____ first railroad in the U.S.

3.36 _____ pioneer connected Lancaster and Philadelphia

3.37 _____ Clinton's Ditch

3.38 _____ connected Mississippi River and Great Lakes

3.39 _____ one used to connect the Susquehanna and Ohio Rivers and used a railroad to get
over the Allegheny Mountains

3.40 _____ its success ended the success of canals

3.41 _____ transport for large quantities of bulk cargo, did not require waterways

a. steamboats

b. clipper ships

c. turnpikes

d. railroads

e. canals

f. Erie Canal

g. Cumberland Road

h. Baltimore and Ohio

Changing American Life

Immigration. The population of the United States continued to grow at a remarkable rate in the early 1800s. Since colonial times, the population had continued to double every 23 years! By 1860 America had the fourth-largest national population in the world. Much of this was due to the country's remarkable birthrate; but by the early 1800s, the native-born citizens were being supplemented by immigrants from Europe. The rate of immigration skyrocketed in the 1840s, primarily from Ireland and Germany.

Ireland was a land held in near slavery by Great Britain. In order to feed their families, the Irish peasants were forced to rent land from British landlords. British law restricted the rights of Catholics who made up most of the Irish population. The last straw was the Potato Famine from 1845-1847. The Irish people lived on potatoes and in those years the crops were destroyed by a blight. An estimated 2 million people died of starvation and disease. Boatloads of Irishmen left their homeland out of desperation. Hundreds of thousands came to America during those bleak years.

Irish immigrants were too poor to buy land and supplies. They could not move west; therefore, they tended to congregate in the cities of the East Coast. They had little education and quickly filled the ranks of the unskilled laborers. Many found work building the canals and railroads. They often lived in filthy city tenements and faced death from the diseases bred by poor sanitation. Moreover, the Catholic Irish were distrusted by the more established Protestant Americans. They were often denied jobs because of their ancestry. "No Irish Need Apply" was a common note added to a job offer.

The concentration of Irish immigrants in the cities slowly built their political power. Politicians found it necessary to cater to the "Irish vote." Some Irish, notably Tammany Hall in New York City, built extensive political control

organizations called "machines" that literally controlled the city. Irishmen came to dominate the police and fire departments of many Northeastern cities. In time, the Irish found a piece of the American pie.

The other large group of immigrants came from Germany. Most of these people were farmers displaced by hard times or political upheaval. A few of the immigrants were intellectuals who fled in 1848 after revolutions for greater freedom failed in Europe. As with the Irish, hundreds of thousands of German immigrants came in the 1800s. Unlike the Irish, the German newcomers usually had some money. As a result, they did not stay in the eastern cities. They moved west, often to the northern states of the upper Mississippi River, such as Wisconsin and Michigan. They built prosperous farms and integrated into American life. They brought their love of *bier* (beer) and their brewing skills to their new homeland, as well as their tradition of hard work.

Know-Nothing Party. The 1840s and '50s saw a rise of anti-immigrant feelings in America. The sudden influx of Irish and German people alarmed native-born Americans. The poverty of many of the immigrants left them dependent on charity and public support. Many of the newcomers were also Catholic, and anti-Catholicism was still strong in the United States. Several incidents of anti-Catholic violence occurred in the mid-1800s. The strongest evidence of the anti-immigrant sentiment was the creation of the Know-Nothing Party.

The Know-Nothing Party developed from the Order of the Star Spangled Banner, created in 1849. It was a political organization that called for strict control on immigration, deportation of poor immigrants, and long waiting periods for citizenship and the right to vote. It was called the Know-Nothing Party because of its secrecy. Its rally cry was "America for the Americans."

The party won several elections on the local and state level in the 1850s, but they were never able to successfully push their agenda. The controversy over slavery split the movement and ended its day of glory. It disappeared after a dismal showing in the 1856 elections.

The Second Great Awakening. In the 1730s and '40s, The Great Awakening had turned the hearts of many of the American colonists to God. Revival struck the nation again in the late 1790s. This visitation of God's Spirit was called the Second Great Awakening, and it lasted into the 1830s. This revival did not have the prominent leaders the first one had with George Whitefield and Jonathan Edwards. It also was less intense, but it lasted longer and covered a larger area.

The fervor of American Christianity had gone cold in the years since the Great Awakening. The spread of the frontier had taken people further and further from organized churches. The needs of survival had drawn hearts away from God, and the roughness of frontier life had pushed aside the Savior's gentle touch. However, the preachers of the early 1800s found a way to reach the scattered masses of the frontier: the camp meeting.

Camp meetings were large gatherings of people to hear several days of preaching and teaching from the Word of God. The place was advertised in advance, and people would come from all over the region and camp at the site. Hundreds and sometimes thousands of people would attend. People were attracted to the meetings by a chance to socialize and to enjoy some stimulation in their monotonous wilderness lives. They often came away changed by the message of Christ's love and salvation.

The camp meeting revivals were often extremely emotional. People would sing, dance, shout, and shake. Salvation was often accompanied by hysterical weeping and repenting. The emotionalism was criticized by many, and some preachers tried to control it.

| A Circuit-Riding Preacher

The revival eventually spread to the cities due to the work of traveling evangelists who came out of the Awakening. The most famous was Charles Finney who preached to large crowds in the cities in the 1820s to the 1850s. Finney saw a great mass of people turn to God in New York City where he primarily worked. Another great city evangelist was D. L. Moody who worked out of Chicago beginning in the 1850s. Moody went on to found the Moody Bible Institute in that city. Both men concentrated on preaching individual salvation and the Bible as the Word of God.

The Methodists and Baptists which welcomed greater emotionalism were the **denominations** that grew the most during this revival. The new congregations were served by "circuit riders," pastors who traveled hundreds of miles visiting each church on his circuit in turn. The most renowned of these traveling pastors was Francis Asbury (1745-1816), who was the leader of the American Methodist Church. He traveled thousands of miles a year on horseback, via frontier roads or trails to serve the people under his care.

Other Sects. Other sects developed in the 1800s which most evangelical Christians would call **heresies**. The deist tradition of the founding fathers led to the development of Unitarianism in the early 1800s. This belief stripped the gospel of the doctrines of sin, grace, and salvation. Unitarians believed there was no trinity, only one God, hence the name *Unitarian*. They also said that Jesus was not God, man was essentially good, and good works were the way to "salvation." Thus, man needed only himself, not God.

Another prominent sect was the Church of Jesus Christ of Latter-Day Saints (Mormons). The Mormon religion was founded in the 1830s by Joseph Smith. Smith claimed to have had a vision in which an angel told him to dig up some golden plates written in an ancient language. Given a way to translate the tablets, Smith claimed to have written the Book of Mormon from them. This book is the basis of Mormon beliefs.

The Mormon religion began in Missouri, and later Smith and his followers moved to Illinois. They were distrusted and persecuted there. Eventually, Smith was murdered and most of his followers left under the leadership of Brigham Young. Young led the group to the dry, empty wilderness of Utah to allow them to live in peace and follow their own ways, which included **polygamy**.

In the mid-1800s, the well-organized Mormons irrigated and built the state into a prosperous community. The number of believers grew due to high birthrates and aggressive missionary work. The powerful hierarchy of the church clashed with the federal government when the population grew large enough to allow a territory to be organized. Much of the conflict centered on the practice of polygamy, which traditional Christians found repulsive. Eventually, the Mormons gave up that practice, and Utah was allowed to become a state in 1896.

| Carrie Nation, a colorful Temperance Leader

Reform Movements. The revival of Christianity caused a renewed interest in reforms. The reform movement dealt with prisons, treatment of the insane, debt law, drinking, working conditions, and women's rights. In the early 1800s, many laws were passed reforming problems in these areas. Imprisonment for debt was gradually ended. Brutal forms of punishment like whipping and branding were eliminated. The concept of trying to reform, not just punish, criminals was introduced. This was especially applied to young children drawn into a life of crime. Improvements were made in the brutal treatment of the insane. Dorthea Dix led the way in this area, traveling all over the nation publicizing the way insane people were caged and tied like animals.

The **temperance** movement also gained force in this time period. Heavy drinking was an American tradition, especially on the frontier. It came under increasing attacks by reformers as Christianity reasserted itself. Men were encouraged to "take the pledge," which was an oath never to drink again. Thousands did so in well-organized temperance rallies. The movement also made good use of public advertisements on the evils of drinking.

The campaign for women's rights also began in the early 1800s. At that time, women could not vote, all of their property belonged to their husbands, and the husbands were even free to beat them, to a certain extent. The movement for women's rights grew out of women participating in the abolitionist movement. The political activism of that cause led many women to question why they were denied full protection of the law and the right to vote.

The official beginning of the modern movement for women's rights was at the Seneca Falls Convention. A few of the pioneers of the women's movement met at the Convention in 1848 and drew up a statement of rights for women. It was based on the Declaration of Independence, declaring that "all men *and* women are created equal." It drew a tremendous amount of ridicule in the press. Many of the original supporters backed away from it, but the women would not be silenced. Gradually, colleges began to admit women, and laws were passed giving them rights to their own property. However, it would be many years before legal equality was achieved.

Another important movement was the growing support for public education. Massachusetts had led the way in colonial times, but education was primarily a privilege of the rich through the 1700s. The situation began to change with the expansion of the right to vote. Poor working men who voted began to demand education for their children. Gradually the wealthy members of society began to realize the advantages of having education available to all, preventing illiterate voters from controlling the elections. The idea that good citizens need to be educated pushed the state governments to pay for elementary education for everyone. Reformers also created better textbooks and set up training schools for teachers.

The most noticeable reform movement of the early to mid-1800s was the abolitionist movement. The case for eliminating slavery had been gaining momentum for years. Slavery was abolished in Great Britain in 1833, thanks to the impressive labor of William Wilberforce, a wealthy evangelical Christian. This freed the slaves in the nearby British West Indies and encouraged the movement in America.

Moderate abolitionists wanted to end slavery slowly, possibly with compensation for slave owners. They hoped to use moral persuasion and increasingly anti-slavery laws to end the institution. This had been the successful pattern in Britain, but Britain did not have a place like the southern United States.

It was the extreme abolitionists who attracted the most attention, however. They were led by William Garrison who founded the anti-slavery newspaper, *The Liberator,* in 1831. Garrison condemned slavery in violent terms that disturbed more moderate abolitionists. He received many death threats and was attacked by mobs several times while giving speeches that presented his views. He continued to publish the newspaper until 1865 which was when the 13th amendment to the Constitution was ratified by the states and slavery officially ended.

Another man who for a short time also published a newspaper that supported the anti-slavery movement was Elijah P. Lovejoy. His presses were repeatedly destroyed, and he was eventually killed by a mob in 1837. The death of Lovejoy gave the anti-slavery movement their first martyr.

Men like Garrison and Lovejoy caused reactions of fear and hatred in the South. Southerners defended their peculiar institution all the more. They argued that their slaves were part of their families and better off than poor factory workers in the North. The two sides found it increasingly difficult even to discuss the issue, much less reach agreement on it.

Complete these sentences.

3.42 The _____ was a Christian revival from the 1790s to the 1830s.

3.43 The _____ Party was a political party that was anti-immigrant.

3.44 The two largest groups of immigrants in the early 1800s came from _____ and _____ .

3.45 Mormons got into trouble with the government largely over the practice of _____ .

3.46 Many Irishmen came to America because of the _____ in 1845-1847.

3.47 The frontier revivals of the early 1800s were spread by means of large, emotional _____ .

3.48 The modern women's rights movement began at the _____ _____ in 1848.

3.49 _____ believe in only one God, not a Trinity, and that man is good.

3.50 Extreme abolitionist William Garrison started the newspaper, _____ , in 1831.

3.51 The _____ movement used ads and pledges to reduce drinking in America.

3.52 The creator of Mormonism was _____ .

3.53 _____ was largely responsible for ending slavery in Great Britain.

3.54 The two denominations that grew most from the revivals of the early 1800s were the _____ and the _____ .

3.55 _____ led the Mormons out of Illinois to form their own community in what would become the state of _____ .

3.56 Six of the areas that reformers tried to change in the early 1800s were.

_____ , _____ ,

_____ , _____ ,

_____ , and _____ .

Answer true or false.

3.57 _____ Circuit riders were pastors of several churches spread over a large area.

3.58 _____ Irish immigrants were usually very poor.

3.59 _____ German immigrants tended to stay in the cities of the Northeast.

3.60 _____ The reform movements were partly a result of the Second Great Awakening.

3.61 _____ D. L. Moody was the early leader of the American Methodist Church.

3.62 _____ Moderate abolitionists wanted to end slavery immediately.

3.63 _____ America in the early 1800s was generally anti-Catholic.

3.64 _____ "America for the Americans," was the rally cry of Dorthea Dix.

3.65 _____ *The Book of Mormon* was supposedly taken from the words spoken by an angel to Brigham Young.

3.66 _____ D. L. Moody was an evangelist who worked out of Chicago.

The Great Divide

Last Compromise. California opened a hornet's nest when it requested admission into the Union in 1849. The Union had exactly fifteen slave and fifteen free states at the time. That meant the South could block any anti-slavery laws by its control of half of the votes in the Senate. Loss of that veto power was a serious threat to the South, or so they believed. The South was not about to lose it without a fight, and the Union was again threatened. Into the gap stepped the old giants: Clay, Webster, and Calhoun, for their last major appearance on the public stage. All of them would be dead by 1852. Clay, "the Great Compromiser," proposed a series of laws that would save the Union. Calhoun opposed them, but died before the debate concluded. Webster spoke strongly in support of compromise for the sake of the country, a stand that brought him heavy condemnation from abolitionists. Eventually, a compromise was worked out and accepted by the nation, with a sigh of relief.

The Compromise of 1850 was a series of agreements that tried to balance each other. The first allowed California to join the Union as a free state. That permanently cost the South its veto in the Senate. In exchange, slavery would not be barred in the remaining states in the Mexican Cession. They would have popular sovereignty on the issue of slavery (chosen for themselves).

The state of Texas claimed a large piece of territory that is now part of the states of New Mexico, Colorado, Wyoming, Kansas and Oklahoma. That land was taken from Texas. In exchange, Texas received $10 million in compensation.

The moderate abolitionists had been trying for years to restrict or eliminate slavery in Washington D.C. as a step on their agenda of gradual abolition. The Compromise gave them an end to the slave trade, but not slavery, in the American capital. The South was also given a much stronger fugitive slave act because of the many concessions they made.

The Fugitive Slave Act of 1850 was something the South had wanted for a long time. For many years abolitionists had been running the "Underground Railroad" to help enslaved people escape to Canada. The Railroad was actually a series of houses on the road north, called "stations," where slaves could hide and receive help to reach the next stop. People who helped on the route were called "conductors" and the escaping slaves "passengers." One remarkable conductor, Harriet Tubman, herself an escaped slave, returned to the South repeatedly and led over 300 people to freedom on the Railroad.

The Underground Railroad infuriated the South. Only a small percentage of enslaved people escaped that way, but it was the principle that grated on slave owners. In their eyes, their property was being stolen by a well-organized conspiracy and the officials in the North were not doing anything to stop it. Southerners had been arguing for a stronger federal law to stop the "thefts." They got it as part of the Compromise of 1850.

The law regarding fugitive slaves was harsh. A black person who was accused of being a runaway slave could not testify in their own behalf or post bail, nor would the case be heard by a jury. The commissioner who decided the case was paid five dollars if the prisoner was released and ten dollars if they were not, a practice that sounded very much like a bribe. Federal officials were required to act as slave catchers. Any private person who aided an escaping slave or refused to aid in their capture was subject to fines or imprisonment.

The law was a serious mistake. It caused many people who had not opposed slavery to become abolitionists and many moderates to become extremists. The injustices of the law inflamed the North. Free black people who were captured by "slave catchers" had no possible way to prove they were not slaves. Escaped slaves who had lived in the North for years were sent back to angry masters. Honest men who opposed slavery and helped their fellow

| Underground Railroad

man reach freedom went to jail or lost their worldly wealth for helping them. The people of the North now saw the effects of slavery in their own towns and cities. Southerners became increasingly frustrated as the law was ignored, avoided, and condemned.

The reaction in the North was strong. Mobs freed slaves who were taken under the Fugitive Slave Act. At times, troops had to be used to guard black captives and escort them south. Northern states tried to hamper the law by refusing to aid federal officials and denying the use of state jails. "The Bloodhound Bill" or the "Man-Stealing Law," as it was called, was opposed in print all over the North. The law did a great deal to unify the North and lay the ground work for the Civil War.

Millard Fillmore. Millard Fillmore (1800-1874) became president in 1850 when Zachary Taylor died. Fillmore was born in New York. He had been apprenticed to a cloth maker as a boy but eventually went into the practice of law in his home state. He served in the House of Representatives in New York and Washington. He was serving as **comptroller** of New York when he was chosen to run with Zachary Taylor. Since Taylor was from the South, a New Yorker was added to balance the Whig ticket to represent the whole nation.

Fillmore was a good friend and follower of Henry Clay. He had presided over the Senate as vice president during the debates on the Compromise of 1850. He favored the Compromise even though Taylor opposed it and had threatened to veto it, so Fillmore put his new administration firmly behind the bills, which were stalled in Congress. The Compromise passed and Fillmore signed it. It was the one significant accomplishment of his presidency, and it preserved the Union for ten more years.

Election of 1852. By 1852, Northern opposition to the Fugitive Slave Law had divided the Whig party. Fillmore, who supported the law, did not get the nomination. Instead, the Whigs relied on one of their favorite tricks, nominating a war hero. In this case, they nominated Winfield Scott, "Old Fuss and Feathers," the brilliant commander of the campaign against Mexico City. Their **platform** supported the Compromise of 1850 even though Scott opposed slavery. The Whigs were badly split because the Northerners hated the party platform.

The Democrats were also divided and wound up nominating a "dark horse" candidate, Franklin Pierce. Pierce was a pro-slavery northerner who warmly supported all of the Compromise of 1850. Other than that, Pierce and Scott were both distinguished by their lack of controversial stands on any issues. However, Scott's personal stand against slavery and his pompous nature cost him the election. The slavery issue had successfully split the Whigs. Their party was nearing extinction.

Franklin Pierce. Franklin Pierce (1804-1869) won the Democratic nomination only after the four primary candidates had fought to a draw at the convention. Pierce was born to a wealthy family in New Hampshire. His father served in the Revolution and was governor of the state

| Perry's visit to Japan

for a time. Franklin became a lawyer and a member of the state House of Representatives. He later served in both the House and the Senate in Washington. He also served without distinction as a general in the Mexican War. He was virtually unknown outside of New Hampshire when he was nominated for president in 1852.

Pierce was an easygoing man who tended to listen to the pro-Southern voices in his Cabinet. He was an expansionist, and his Southern friends specifically wanted lands suitable for the expansion of slavery. Pierce's foreign policy was a mixed bag, however, with a success that was not his doing and a failure that was.

The success came from Millard Fillmore. As president, Fillmore had dispatched Commodore Matthew Perry to the Far East to expand American trade in the Pacific. Perry carried a letter addressed to the ruler of Japan. Japan was at that time a completely closed society. It had refused to trade with the West, even imprisoning sailors shipwrecked on its shores. Perry, by a show of force with his modern gunboats, persuaded the Japanese to take his letter. Using tact and threats, Perry convinced the Japanese to open up their nation to trade with the United States. The treaty was approved by the Senate in 1854. It marked a turning point for Japan which changed from a medieval feudal kingdom to a world power in less than a hundred years.

Pierce's failure was an embarrassing attempt to add Cuba to the United States. Cuba, with its large slave-run sugar plantations, was a prize plum for the South as a way to add slave states to the Union. Pierce tried to purchase the island, but Spain absolutely refused. In 1854, Spanish officials seized an American steamer, the *Black Warrior*, in Cuba which triggered a crisis. The American ministers in Spain, Britain, and France were instructed to meet and draw up a plan for acquiring Cuba. The plan they

drew up, the Ostend Manifesto, called for taking the island by force if Spain refused an offer of $120 million for it and if Spanish ownership endangered American interests.

The Ostend Manifesto became public and the reaction was wild. Northern abolitionists condemned the scheme as a blueprint for piracy. The publication of the secret plan was an acute embarrassment to the administration. Pierce dropped all attempts to take Cuba. The infighting over slavery had finally done what France, Britain, Mexico, and Spain could not do: halt the advance of Manifest Destiny.

 Answer these questions.

3.67 What were the six major terms of the Compromise of 1850?

a. _____

b. _____

c. _____

d. _____

e. _____

f. _____

3.68 Where did the three old "giants" in the Congress stand on the Compromise?

Clay _____

Calhoun _____

Webster _____

3.69 How did the death of Zachary Taylor help the Compromise of 1850?

_____

_____

3.70 Why did the Southern states want Cuba?

_____

_____

3.71 What did Commodore Perry do that resulted in Japan becoming a world power?

_____

_____

3.72 What was the Ostend Manifesto and what happened when it became public?

_____

_____

_____

3.73 What was the Underground Railroad?

_____

_____

Check the items that are true of the Fugitive Slave Act.

3.74 ☐ It hurt the abolitionist cause in the North.

3.75 ☐ An accused fugitive could post bail until his trial.

3.76 ☐ People helping enslaved people escape could be fined or imprisoned.

3.77 ☐ The commissioner got more money for returning a slave than he did for releasing a free man.

3.78 ☐ Northern mobs would sometimes free captured fugitives.

3.79 ☐ Franklin Pierce did not support it.

3.80 ☐ A captured black person could not testify in their own behalf.

3.81 ☐ Federal officials were required to act as slave catchers.

3.82 ☐ Harriet Tubman supported it.

Uncle Tom's Cabin. The anti-slavery sentiment in the North received an incredible and unexpected boost in 1852. In that year, Harriet Beecher Stowe published the anti-slavery novel *Uncle Tom's Cabin*. Melding true stories taken from the files of the abolitionists, she wrote a compelling tale of a faithful slave named Tom. Tom was a committed Christian who obeyed his masters out of respect for God. He was sold twice in the novel, once to pay off a debt his master owed and another time when his master died. During his journeys he met other enslaved people and heard their heart-rending stories. The book also followed another slave named Eliza, who succeeded in fleeing to Canada when she was threatened with separation from her small son. Tom, in the meantime, was well- treated by his first two masters, but was beaten to death by the third, Simon Legree.

Uncle Tom's Cabin was one of the most successful pieces of **propaganda** in history. The phenomenal impact of the novel cannot be overstated. It sold hundreds of thousands of copies in the first year and millions thereafter. It was translated into several languages and became a popular stage play. It turned the nation against the evils of slavery. Lincoln reportedly said to Mrs. Stowe when they met in 1862, "So you're the little woman who wrote the book that made this great war."

The novel had a wide impact. It gave strength to the abolitionist cause and later to the Union in the Civil War. Its popularity in Britain made it difficult for that government to support the Confederacy. It spelled out in cold blood exactly what the North opposed. Southerners condemned it as an unfair and dishonest portrayal of slavery. However, they could not erase the image of faithful Tom dying of his wounds or desperate Eliza clutching her young child, racing across the ice floes of the Ohio River just a few yards ahead of the slave catchers.

Today, there are mixed reviews of the novel, some saying that the portrayal of the characters supports stereotyping and discrimination.

| A scene from *Uncle Tom's Cabin*

This doesn't change the fact that the story had the desired effect at that time period and impacted the views of many white people.

Kansas-Nebraska Act. The deaths of Clay, Calhoun, and Webster left the Senate in the control of lesser men. Dominant among these was the "Little Giant," Stephen Douglas, senator from Illinois. Douglas was a Democrat with no strong opinions on slavery. However, Illinois favored popular sovereignty. Douglas also had an eye on the presidency and needed Southern support to get it. Moreover, he had investments in Chicago and railroads. He wanted to organize the territories of the Midwest to allow a railroad to cross the center of the nation. Southern states opposed organizing those territories because they were north of the no-slavery line established by the Missouri Compromise and would become free states. Ignoring the problems he was about to create, Douglas found a way to get Southern support to organize the territories. In 1854 he dropped the bomb that undid the key compromises holding the nation together.

As the chairman of the Committee on Territories, Douglas proposed the Kansas-Nebraska Act to organize those territories. To gain the support of the South, the law would allow the people of the state to make decisions about slavery themselves. The carefully negotiated, long-standing Missouri Compromise was swept aside. Douglas used his influence and oratory skills to ram the law through Congress regardless of the consequences. Pliable Franklin Pierce signed it.

Northerners screamed in dismay. They felt betrayed. The carefully negotiated terms the North had accepted in 1820 had been dumped without compensation or agreement. Any territory might now become slave-holding, in spite of agreements to the contrary. The law turned even more Northerners against slavery because slaveholders could not be trusted to keep their bargains.

Douglas underestimated the reaction and results of his actions. He ended the era of compromise. The North steadfastly refused to enforce the Fugitive Slave Law now that the South was no longer honoring its agreements. That caused more bitterness in the South and more division in the nation. So, the Kansas-Nebraska Act doomed both the Missouri Compromise and the Compromise of 1850. The two sides no longer trusted each other enough to work out or keep delicate compromises.

Republican Party. The slavery issue had shattered the Whig party. It now created a new party. In 1854 the Republican Party was organized specifically opposing the spread of slavery. Spurred by the betrayal of the Kansas-Nebraska Act, the party gained strength quickly. The Republicans gathered up the remains of the northern Whig party, Know-Nothings, and supporters of free soil. They quickly became a national party, electing a Speaker of the House in 1856 and making a serious showing in the presidential election of that year.

The problem with the Republican Party was that it was clearly a Northern party. Until that time, the Whigs and the Democrats had support in both the North and the South. Thus, both parties had to compromise to please both parts of their membership. Unfortunately, the Kansas-Nebraska Act had broken the thin threads that held the parties together. The Democrats were also dividing on the slavery issue. They would present a united candidate in 1856, but in 1860 the Democratic Party would divide into Northern and Southern parts. Cooperation would yield to partisanship, which would yield to war.

| Stephen Douglas

Complete these sentences.

3.83 The anti-slavery novel _____ was one of the most successful pieces of propaganda in history.

3.84 The chief architect of the Kansas-Nebraska Act was _____ .

3.85 The _____ Party was organized to oppose the spread of slavery.

3.86 _____ was the author of *Uncle Tom's Cabin*.

3.87 The Republican Party was a party from the _____ section of the nation.

Put a *K* beside the items that were in whole or part a result of the Kansas-Nebraska Act.

3.88 _____ The rapid growth of the Republican Party

3.89 _____ The success of *Uncle Tom's Cabin*

3.90 _____ Popular sovereignty in Kansas and Nebraska

3.91 _____ The Missouri Compromise was overturned

3.92 _____ A new compromise was created

3.93 _____ Douglas acted heedlessly

3.94 _____ North-South distrust

3.95 _____ The Compromise of 1850 became stronger

3.96 _____ The Ostend Manifesto

Before you take this last Self Test, you may want to do one or more of these self checks.

1. _____ Read the objectives. See if you can do them.

2. _____ Restudy the material related to any objectives that you cannot do.

3. _____ Use the **SQ3R** study procedure to review the material:
   a. **S**can the sections.
   b. **Q**uestion yourself.
   c. **R**ead to answer your questions.
   d. **R**ecite the answers to yourself.
   e. **R**eview areas you did not understand.

4. _____ Review all vocabulary, activities, and Self Tests, writing a correct answer for every
wrong answer.

SELF TEST 3

Choose the person who matches each item. Some answers will be used more than once (each answer, 2 points).

3.01	_____	Kansas-Nebraska Act	a.	William Henry Harrison
3.02	_____	destroyed the National Bank	b.	Eli Whitney
3.03	_____	cotton gin	c.	Cyrus McCormick
3.04	_____	first textile factory in U.S.	d.	Andrew Jackson
3.05	_____	telegraph	e.	Joseph Smith
3.06	_____	steamboat	f.	Henry Clay
3.07	_____	Erie Canal	g.	Zachary Taylor
3.08	_____	Missouri Compromise	h.	Stephen Douglas
3.09	_____	Buena Vista victory	i.	Samuel Slater
3.010	_____	Mexico City victory	j.	Commodore Matthew Perry
3.011	_____	interchangeable parts	k.	Winfield Scott
3.012	_____	Mormon religion	l.	Harriet Tubman
3.013	_____	over 300 slaves escaped to freedom	m.	DeWitt Clinton
3.014	_____	treaty with Japan	n.	Harriet Beecher Stowe
3.015	_____	Compromise of 1850	o.	Samuel Morse
3.016	_____	*Uncle Tom's Cabin*	p.	Robert Fulton
3.017	_____	the mechanical reaper		
3.018	_____	Father of the Factory System		
3.019	_____	"Log Cabin and Hard Cider"		
3.020	_____	Eaton scandal		
3.021	_____	became secretary of state due to a "corrupt bargain"		
3.022	_____	his death left Millard Fillmore as president		
3.023	_____	his followers founded the state of Utah		
3.024	_____	"Old Fuss and Feathers"		
3.025	_____	picked Martin Van Buren as his successor		

Name the item described (each answer, 3 points).

3.026 _____ change from farming and handcrafting to industry and machine manufacturing

3.027 _____ secretive, anti-immigrant political party of the late 1840s

3.028 _____ Christian revival in 1790s to 1830s

3.029 _____ mission/fortress in Texas that was defended to the death by patriots, including Davy Crockett and Jim Bowie

3.030 _____ organization that helped slaves escape to Canada

3.031 _____ act that ended the Missouri Compromise and the era of compromises

3.032 _____ privately-owned toll roads that were the first improvements in American transportation

3.033 _____ the reason so many Irish came to America in 1845-1847

3.034 _____ the "Man-Stealing Law" that imprisoned people who helped slaves escape and denied recaptured slaves the right to a fair trial

3.035 _____ anti-slavery, Northern political party founded in 1854 that grew rapidly

Answer true or false (each answer, 1 point).

3.036 _____ Most factories were located in the Northeast because it had water power and a supply of capital.

3.037 _____ Factory workers were often shamefully exploited.

3.038 _____ Steamboats had little effect on the trade on the Mississippi River.

3.039 _____ Canals put the railroads out of business.

3.040 _____ Most of the immigrants in the 1840s and '50s came from Ireland, Britain, and France.

3.041 _____ Children were not employed in early factories.

3.042 _____ Mormons were persecuted because they practiced polygamy.

3.043 _____ Temperance was one of the reform movements of the mid-1800s.

3.044 _____ California became a state as part of the Missouri Compromise.

3.045 _____ The Ostend Manifesto was an anti-slavery document.

3.046 _____ Franklin Pierce wanted to add Cuba to the United States.

3.047 _____ Slavery was ended in Washington D.C. as part of the Compromise of 1850.

3.048 _____ Daniel Webster was a firm abolitionist, opposing the Compromise of 1850 because of his beliefs.

3.049 _____ The Wilmot Proviso would have forbidden slavery in the Mexican Cession.

3.050 _____ Manifest Destiny was the belief America would spread over the continent.

3.051 _____ John Tyler was a strong Whig, an admirer of Henry Clay.

3.052 _____ James Polk tried very hard to keep America out of a war with Mexico.

3.053 _____ John Quincy Adams supported the Gag Rule.

3.054 _____ Andrew Jackson successfully fought nullification.

3.055 _____ John Calhoun was a Southern leader.

3.056 _____ The Gadsden Treaty ended the Mexican War.

80 / 100

SCORE _____ TEACHER _____ _____

initials   date

Before taking the LIFEPAC Test, you may want to do one or more of these self checks.

1. _____ Read the objectives. See if you can do them.
2. _____ Restudy the material related to any objectives that you cannot do.
3. _____ Use the **SQ3R** study procedure to review the material.
4. _____ Review activities, Self Tests, and LIFEPAC vocabulary words.
5. _____ Restudy areas of weakness indicated by the last Self Test.

HISTORY & GEOGRAPHY 807
Gilded Age to Progressive Era (1880–1915)

LIFEPAC Test is located in the center of the booklet. Please remove before starting the unit.

Author:
Theresa Buskey, B.A., J.D.

Editor:
Alan Christopherson, M.S.

Westover Studios Design Team:
Phillip Pettet, Creative Lead
Teresa Davis, DTP Lead
Nick Castro
Andi Graham
Jerry Wingo

Alpha Omega
PUBLICATIONS

804 N. 2nd Ave. E.
Rock Rapids, IA 51246-1759

Gilded Age to Progressive Era (1880–1915)

Introduction

The era from 1880 to 1915 was one of great changes. The Civil War had settled the burning political questions that had dominated the government before 1860. The last of the frontier was being opened by the railroad and settled by hardy pioneers, but the major change in this era was the tremendous growth of big business and industry. At the beginning of the 19th century, America had been an internationally unimportant nation of small farmers. America at the end of the 19th century was a wealthy, industrial world power, status it has never lost.

The change did not come without conflict. The new, huge industrial powers abused their strength. The American public at first welcomed the stronger, more efficient industries. The incredible wealth collected by the men who owned them was seen as their rightful reward. However, as these rich men exploited their workers, paid off politicians, and ruthlessly eliminated their competitors, the American attitude began to change.

Since the Revolution, Americans had always favored small government that interfered as little as possible in the lives of its citizens. Slowly, there arose a cry to control these great corporations before they robbed the nation of its most precious possession, government by the people. That cry brought down the Gilded Age, the age of wild growth, wealth, and poverty. The demand for reforms ushered in the Progressive Era, a rewriting of the basic laws of the American system. This LIFEPAC® will cover this change and what it meant to American history.

Objectives

Read these objectives. The objectives tell you what you will be able to do when you have successfully completed this LIFEPAC. When you have finished this LIFEPAC, you should be able to:

1. Describe the social, political, technological, and industrial developments of the Gilded Age.

2. Describe the last years of the Western frontier.

3. Describe the presidents of the Gilded Age and their policies.

4. Describe the development of unions and reform movements from 1865 to 1915.

5. Describe the causes, course, and consequences of the Spanish-American War.

6. Describe the course of the Progressive Movement.

7. Describe the personality of Theodore Roosevelt and his effect on the presidency.

8. Name the Progressive presidents and describe their policies.

Survey the LIFEPAC. Ask yourself some questions about this study and write your questions here.

1. THE GILDED AGE

One of the most famous American authors of the late 1800s, Mark Twain, published a novel in 1873 called the *Gilded Age*. It was written in collaboration with another author and gave a snapshot of its era. The greedy business-men and corrupt politicians in the novel were mirror images of the people in power at the end of the 19th century. Thus, the name of the novel has become the name of the entire era, from about 1865 to 1900.

Gilding is a process that puts a thin layer of gold over the top of something less valuable. The result is beautiful and valuable on the sur-face, but underneath it can be worthless, dirty, and scarred. That was the late 1800s.

The gold surface of the 1880s and 1890s was the wealth and power of the United States. New American millionaires spent lavishly on homes, art, carriages, clothes, and travel accommodations. Museums, libraries, theaters, and schools were built all over the nation. New inventions like telephones, street cars, electric lights, and phonographs became popular and common. By 1900 America was the wealthiest nation in the world in total assets and income per person.

However, there was a less valuable center under the gold surface. Wealthy "captains of industry" virtually controlled the government which gave them subsidies, incredibly high tar-iffs, and protective legislation. A few powerful individuals routinely would control an entire industry, setting prices and making huge prof-its. Many of the workers in the new industries labored under horrible conditions and lived in worse ones. Cities and whole states were run by corrupt political machines that traded favors for votes and money. Thus, "gilded" is an accurate description of this complex era.

SECTION OBJECTIVES

Review these objectives. When you have completed this section, you should be able to:

1. Describe the social, political, technological, and industrial developments of the Gilded Age.
2. Describe the last years of the Western frontier.
3. Describe the presidents of the Gilded Age and their policies.
4. Describe the development of unions and reform movements from 1865 to 1915.

VOCABULARY

Study these words to enhance your learning success in this section.

anarchist (an' ə r kist). Person seeking to establish complete freedom by eliminating all government.

assimilate (ə sim' ə lāt). To absorb into the cultural tradition of a population or group.

bankrupt (ban' krəpt). To declare a person unable to meet their debts by law, their available assets are taken by the court to be given to their creditors.

capitalist (kap' ət l əst). A system in which capital goods (money, factories, land) are privately owned and controlled. Decisions about prices, production, and distribution are based on private decisions in response to free market competition.

AMERICA from **1880** to **1915**

Rutherford B. Hayes
1877-1881
Republican

James A. Garfield*
1881
Republican

Chester A. Arthur
1881-1885
Republican

Grover Cleveland
1885-1889
Democratic

Benjamin Harrison
1889-1893
Republican

Grover Cleveland
1893-1897
Democratic

William McKinley*
1897-1901
Republican

Theodore Roosevelt
1901-1909
Republican

William H. Taft
1909-1913
Republican

Woodrow Wilson
1913-1921
Democratic

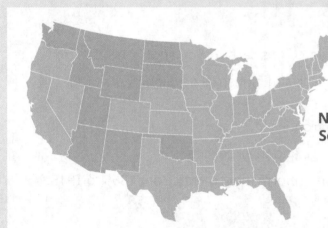

STATES ADMITTED TO THE UNION

State	Year	State	Year
North Dakota	1889	Wyoming	1890
South Dakota	1889	Utah	1896
Washington	1889	Oklahoma	1907
Montana	1889	New Mexico	1912
Idaho	1890	Arizona	1912

POPULATION of the United States of America

Year	Population
1910	92,228,496
1880	50,189,209
1850	23,191,876
1820	9,638,453
1790	3,929,000

*assassinated while in office

communist (käm' yə nəst). (In the 1890s and early 1900s) A person who advocated following the teachings of Marx, who believed that private property should be eliminated by a rebellion of the working class. Then, all goods should be owned in common and be available to all as needed. (This was before the totalitarian communist Soviet Union had been created. Thus, communism was not at this time a type of treason that favored the expansion of Soviet power. It was an unrealistic hope for a perfect society created by a class war in which everyone had the same things and was absolutely equal.)

creditor (kred' ət ər). One to whom a debt is owed.

injunction (in jənk' shən). A writ issued by a court which orders a person to do or refrain from doing a specific act.

largess (lär jes'). Liberal giving to others.

monopoly (mə näp' ə lē). Complete control of a product or service.

philanthropy (fə lan' thər pē). Goodwill to fellow man, often accomplished by giving large gifts for the benefit of others.

socialist (sōsh' ə ləst). Person or system that advocates collective or government ownership of the means of production and distribution. It is usually less extreme than communism in that it allows some private property.

Note: *All vocabulary words in this LIFEPAC appear in* **boldface** *print the first time they are used. If you are not sure of the meaning when you are reading, study the definitions given.*

Pronunciation Key: hat, āge, cãre, fär; let, ēqual, tėrm; it, īce; hot, ōpen, ôrder; oil; out; cup, pu̇t, rüle; child; long; thin; /ŦH/ for then; /zh/ for measure; /u/ or /ə/ represents /a/ in about, /e/ in taken, /i/ in pencil, /o/ in lemon, and /u/ in circus.

Rise of Industry

America had always been a nation of farmers, but in the 1890s, the value of the nation's manufacturing was for the first time greater than the value of its agriculture. This change was brought about by the railroads, investment capital, new inventions, and old-fashioned ingenuity. Moreover, it was a permanent change. America would never be the same again.

Railroads and the newer industries required more capital (money), than a single or a few investors could assemble. Railroads, for example, needed researchers to improve the trains, locomotives, miles of track, cars, repairmen, builders, conductors, stations, station workers, rails, ties, equipment, and supervisors, just to name a few. The amount of capital needed for such an industry was staggering, so in the late 1800s a new form of business became popular to meet this need, the corporation.

A corporation is formed when a group of people organize a company under the laws of a state and sell *stock* in it. The people who purchase the stock become the *stockholders*, who are the legal owners of the company. They are entitled to receive part of the company's profits by way of *dividends* paid on the stock. Thousands of people can contribute to forming a company this way, raising millions in capital. The stockholders vote for a board of directors who run the company for them. (Usually, the board is controlled by the people who own the most stock.)

American law treats corporations as persons. That allows them to pay taxes, enter into contracts, and sue or be sued. That also means that if a corporation goes **bankrupt**, the stockholders lose only their stock. **Creditors** cannot try to get the money they are owed from the "owners." The stockholders are not liable for the debts of another "person," the corporation. Thus, a corporation is a way to raise a large amount of capital without exposing the investors to the dangers of a major business failure.

Railroads. The railroads were the first of the new breed of giant corporations. At the beginning of the Civil War (1860), the United States had 30,000 miles of railroad track. By 1900 it had 193,000 miles, more than all of Europe. These rivers of steel opened up all of the United States for trade. Midwestern farmers could ship their wheat to the cities of the East or to ports to go abroad. Manufactured goods could be produced in whatever part of the country had the needed raw materials and factories. From there, the goods could be sent by rail to any market in the nation. It was this huge domestic market that the new industries supplied quickly and cheaply.

A transcontinental railroad had been a major American goal for years, but there was little profit in building a railroad through miles of empty land. Such an endeavor needed government encouragement. However, competition between the North and the South for this priceless avenue had deadlocked government support before the Civil War.

The North took advantage of the absence of Southern congressmen during the war to authorize subsidies to build a railroad from Omaha, Nebraska, to Sacramento, California. The Union Pacific built west from Omaha, while the Central Pacific built east from Sacramento. Both railroads received 20 square miles of land (in 640-acre sections, on alternate sides of the track) for every mile of track they laid. On this rail line across the nation, they also received generous loans for every mile laid. The rich government benefits made it a race between the two companies to build as much as they could.

The Union Pacific Railroad built across the flat prairie and made spectacular progress. Using mainly Irish laborers, the company built 1,086

miles of track between 1862 and 1869, in one case building 10 miles in a day (using shovels and carts)! The rich government support and press for speed enabled the Crédit Mobilier scandal. Union Pacific officials had hired their own construction company (Crédit Mobilier) that overcharged for the building of the tracks, pocketing huge profits that were shared with cooperative legislators.

Building east, the Central Pacific had to deal with more treacherous terrain through the Sierra Nevada Mountains. Central Pacific used mainly unskilled Chinese workers and was able to build only 689 miles of track. Nevertheless, the Central's main investors, called the Big Four, also made huge profits hiring their own construction companies to do the work.

The two sides met in May of 1869 at Promontory Point near Ogden, Utah. At a wild, joyous ceremony a golden spike was driven into the last rail that united the nation. It was a remarkable feat of engineering and determination, in spite of the graft involved. It firmly joined the far-off Western states to the older portion of the nation and enabled the spread of commerce across the continent. By the end of the century, there would be five such lifelines crossing the nation.

Railroads meant life and prosperity for cities, towns, and states. Consequently, the state and federal governments continued for years to give land grants to railroad companies for building tracks. Cities also were expected to give land and money for the privilege of having the railroad reach their town. In the end, the railroads wound up owning millions of acres of land and controlling millions of dollars of capital.

The railroad improved in more ways than just miles during the late 1800s. Air brakes that stopped the trains more safely were put into general use in the 1870s. Rails were made of more durable steel as opposed to the older, less stable iron rails. Pullman sleeping cars and

| Transcontinental Railroad Completion

dining cars made travel comfortable, even luxurious. The railroads became safe, comfortable modes of long-distance travel.

The railroads which triggered the industrial era by opening new markets across the nation also led in the establishment of huge corporate powerhouses. Smaller railroads were increasingly bought out by larger ones which grew into huge networks. Cornelius Vanderbilt, Leland Stanford, Collis Huntington, Henry Villard, and James Hill were among the men who built fortunes by consolidating rail lines into huge corporations.

These companies increased their profits by using a whole range of various schemes. Competition was decreased by "pools" in which the railroads agreed to divide the business in a certain area. Each would be free to charge as much as they could on their share because no other company would try to take it away. The

railroads would normally charge less for carrying freight long distances, for which there was competition, than for short ones which were frequently controlled by one company. This lack of uniform rates hit small, local producers, especially farmers, the hardest. Large industries also would routinely receive rebates for putting all of their business with one company, a benefit unavailable to small operators. High railroad rates could ruin a farmer's profit on his crop or drive a small manufacturing firm out of business, and often did.

Steel. The second major industry of this era was steel manufacturing. Steel is made by purifying iron to make a stronger, more versatile metal. It was rare and expensive until just prior to the Civil War. In the 1850s, the Bessemer process was developed to make steel cheaply from iron. Having all the abundant natural resources needed to produce steel, America was in a unique position to capitalize on the new discovery. By 1900 the U.S. was exceeding both Britain and Germany in steel production.

Andrew Carnegie was a poor Scottish immigrant who made his way up the ladder of success by hard work and shrewd investments. He realized the value of the Bessemer process and invested heavily in it. Moreover, he brought all of the steps needed to produce the steel under his personal control. He owned the mines that produced the iron ore, the barges and railroads that carried it, and the factories that produced it. By 1900 Carnegie was producing one-fourth of the nation's Bessemer steel. He sold his empire in 1901 to banker J.P. Morgan for $480 million. Morgan used it to form a new corporation, U.S. Steel, which was the first billion-dollar corporation in American history.

Standard Oil. Perhaps the most controversial of the new corporations was John D. Rockefeller's Standard Oil. Petroleum (oil), was increasingly being used for lubrication of machines, heating, fuel, and especially kerosene for lighting. This new industry came to be dominated by Rockefeller who organized his Standard Oil Company in 1870.

John D. Rockefeller practiced the kind of ruthless business suitable for a pirate. He concentrated on controlling the **refining** business as a choke point to control the entire industry. He ran his business with careful attention to costs, bringing down prices and forcing competitors out of business. He used his power to get rebates from the railroads. He even got rebates on his competitors' shipments! His ruthless practices gave him control of oil production in the U.S., but they also produced a cheaper, higher quality product for the American public.

Rockefeller formed a new type of business, the trust, to control the entire oil industry. The trust took stock from several companies and ran them together to eliminate competition.

The companies that joined the trust became rich under Rockefeller's leadership. Those that refused were driven to bankruptcy. The Standard Oil Trust eventually controlled more than 90% of the oil production in America.

| Andrew Carnegie

| John D. Rockefeller

Rockefeller's success led to the creation of new industry-wide trusts. The sugar, tobacco, leather, farm implement, and meat-packing industries (among many others) came to be dominated by trusts. This type of business, however, was successfully challenged in state courts. Eventually, the trusts became "holding companies," corporations created just to control other corporations. Also, banking giants like J.P. Morgan gained control of whole industries by putting themselves on the board of several different companies at the same time. The public, however, continued to refer to these huge, industry-dominating, **monopoly**-seeking corporations as "trusts."

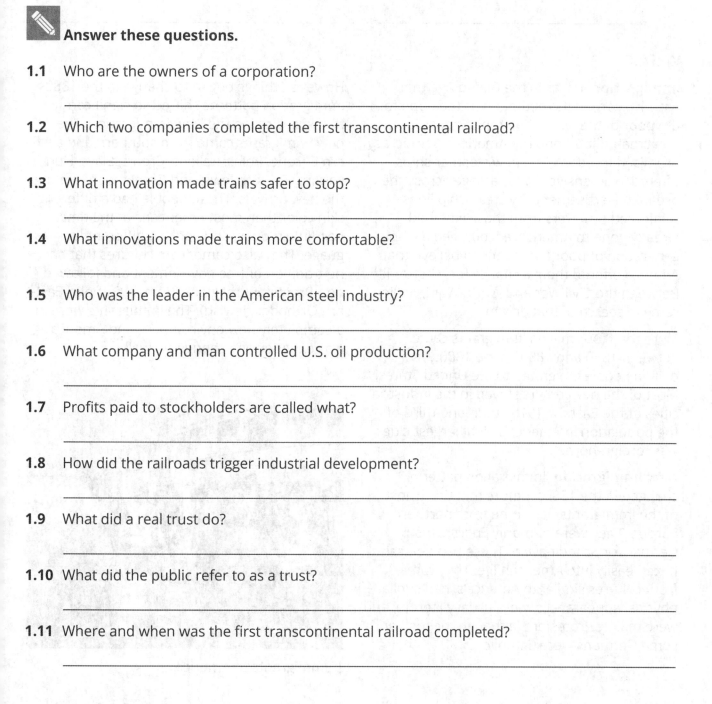

Answer these questions.

1.1   Who are the owners of a corporation?

_____

1.2   Which two companies completed the first transcontinental railroad?

_____

1.3   What innovation made trains safer to stop?

_____

1.4   What innovations made trains more comfortable?

_____

1.5   Who was the leader in the American steel industry?

_____

1.6   What company and man controlled U.S. oil production?

_____

1.7   Profits paid to stockholders are called what?

_____

1.8   How did the railroads trigger industrial development?

_____

1.9   What did a real trust do?

_____

1.10 What did the public refer to as a trust?

_____

1.11 Where and when was the first transcontinental railroad completed?

_____

1.12 What was unfair about the way railroads charged for hauling goods?

_____

_____

_____

1.13 What process made steel cheap enough for general use?

_____

1.14 What type of corporation replaced the trust?

_____

Workers

Immigration. It was in the Gilded Age that America earned its reputation as the hope for the poor of the world. The rapid industrialization created jobs, and the American democracy promised freedom. The new steamer ships offered inexpensive, swift passage across the ocean. Advertisements by steamship lines, reinforced by letters from those who had already gone to America, encouraged a whole generation of poor Europeans to believe that America offered them a chance for a better life. Between the Civil War and World War I, millions came in search of that dream.

More than four million immigrants came between 1860 and 1880. In the 1880s, five million people emigrated to the United States. Most of the newcomers stayed in the industrial cities of the East. By 1910 about one-third of the population in America's eight largest cities was foreign-born.

New Immigration. Immigration patterns changed in the 1880s. Before that time most of the immigrants had come from northern Europe. They were primarily English, Irish, German, or Scandinavian. These people **assimilated** easily into American life. They came from cultures similar to America's, had similar physical appearances, were usually literate, and were mainly Protestant (although the Irish and some Germans were Catholic).

However, things began to change in the 1880s. Immigration patterns shifted so significantly that it was called the New Immigration. The new immigrants came from southern and eastern Europe. Poles, Italians, Croats, Slavs, Hungarians, Russian Jews, and Greeks were among the new arrivals. These people had a different skin color than most Americans at the time, had little money, and spoke a different language. They also came from cultures that had no tradition of free government and followed non-Protestant religions (Roman Catholic, Eastern Orthodox, Jewish). The immigrants were in a completely new environment and America was experiencing change, as well.

| Immigrants to America

The new immigrants huddled together in the cities once they arrived in this strange new land. They formed small islands of home for themselves. Districts called "Little Italy" or "Little Poland" became common in the larger cities. There, the bewildered newcomers could speak their own language, wear their native costumes, buy their own kind of food, and worship in their own churches. It was their children who eventually entered the American mainstream. The adults usually did not, because the change was simply too great.

Working and living conditions. The immigrants were the backbone of the new industrial giants. Working for low wages and rarely making any demands, they were perfect workers for corporations greedy for profits. The wages they received were higher than they would get in Europe, and they knew they could be easily replaced if they made any demands. Women and children were also employed at even lower wages, but the immigrants did not object. Their families needed the money.

These unskilled industrial workers had no rights or protection on the job. Safety precautions were few, and injured workers were simply fired. Illness might also cost a man his job. Any time business was bad, the entire work force might be laid off with no promise of being rehired. Job security was non-existent.

The laborers often lived in squalid tenements, which were all they could afford. These were dark, filthy, rat-infested, fire-trap apartments grouped together in some of the worst city slums in the world. There was little or no sanitation. Diseases spread quickly. Life was harsh and often short.

The new immigrants were a boon to the political machines that ran America's big cities. Used to autocratic government, they were ideal clients for the machine system. The political bosses would help them find jobs, give them food in hard times, help smooth over legal problems, and provide services. In exchange, the new citizens would vote as the bosses told them. They did not understand enough about the ideals of American government to realize this was not the way it was supposed to work.

Policy changes. The New Immigration created a wave of anti-immigrant feeling in America. Older Americans had strong prejudices against the olive-skinned newcomers and their strange, separate ways of life. Anti-Catholicism had always been strong in Protestant America, and it added fuel to the flames. Organized labor objected to the foreigners who were often used as strike-breakers, were hard to organize because they did not speak English, and were willing to work for low wages (which seemed high to them). Pressure built to restrict immigration, which had never been done before in U.S. history.

Beginning in 1880, the open door to immigration was slowly narrowed. The first to feel the pinch were Chinese immigrants on the West Coast. European Americans felt a strong hatred for these racially different, hard-working people who emigrated to California in large numbers after the Civil War. They worked for low wages and kept their own customs. In response to public pressure in 1882, Congress barred all Chinese immigration for ten years and later extended it.

Other restrictions were not so blatant. Also in 1882, paupers and criminals were barred from emigrating. Three years later, contract-worker emigration, which brought in workers by paying their passage in exchange for low-wage employment, was banned. Later anarchists, insane persons, polygamists, and people with contagious diseases were barred. Many of the most vocal "nativists" also wanted a literacy test. It was passed by Congress, only to be vetoed three times. The presidents saw it as a test of opportunity, not ability. It was finally passed over the president's veto in 1917, during the anti-foreign feeling of World War I.

| The Haymarket Riot

Labor movement. The huge new industries profited their owners greatly and their workers hardly at all. Workers faced long hours, poor safety precautions, low wages, and no job security while they were making millions for their employers. The workers realized they needed to band together to force owners to improve conditions and wages. In the years after the Civil War, they began to form unions to press their demands.

Industrial leaders were strongly opposed to unions. They routinely fired workers who joined a union or tried to organize one. The owners were especially vicious in breaking up strikes (work stoppages) to force an owner to consider the workers' demands. Strikebreakers (gangs of thugs) were often hired to attack strikers picketing a business. The owners also took full advantage of their political power.

The police, and sometimes the army, were called in to break up strikes. The courts were very cooperative about issuing **injunctions** against striking unions. Labor disputes, therefore, often became violent as working men despaired of a fair chance to improve their conditions.

The violence and the way strikes interfered with commerce made most Americans suspicious of unions. This was especially true of strikes in key industries like the railroads, which delivered the nation's goods, and the coal mines, which heated its homes. Few middle-class people had ever seen the inside of a factory or a mine, nor had they ever tried to live on a laborer's wages. Also, a few anarchists, **socialists**, and **communists** were involved with the unions, and they gave the movement a bad name among the very pro-**capitalist** American public.

Thus, the unions had to overcome ruthless owners, skeptical public opinion, and hostile government action while trying to organize an effective force to push their demands.

The first unions to organize after the Civil War were severely damaged by the 1873 depression. No man would risk his job by joining a union when jobs were scarce. One of the unions that did manage to survive the depression was the Knights of Labor, the first national union, which was organized in 1869. It was initially a secret society organized to protect its members from the hostility of their employers. It was intended to be a union for all workers in all trades. Moreover, it had wide social and political goals that made it more of a lobbying organization rather than a labor organization.

The Knights came to the height of their power under Terence Powderly in the early 1880s. Powderly relaxed the secrecy, discouraged strikes, and pushed a wide social agenda that included government ownership of public utilities and the end of child labor. Membership vaulted after two successful strikes against Jay Gould's railroad in 1885. (Powderly had opposed the strikes.) Membership reached a height of about 700,000.

However, 1886 proved to be a destructive year for the Knights. A third strike against the Gould railroad failed, causing a fall in membership. Powderly was criticized for failing to support the strike. Another strike against the McCormick Reaper factory in Chicago proved to be an even greater disaster. The strike became violent when non-striking workers were attacked as they left the factory on May third. The police intervened and several strikers were killed. A protest was held the next day at Haymarket Square. As the speeches were ending, the police moved in to break up the meeting. Someone threw a dynamite bomb into the crowd. A policeman was killed and several people were injured.

The Haymarket Riot caused a nationwide panic and a wave of anti-union feeling. Several anarchists were arrested, and eight were convicted in the witch-hunt that followed. The Knights of Labor never recovered from their association with the riot. After 1886, the leadership of the national labor movement was passed to the American Federation of Labor, organized in 1886 after the riot. That meant it could not be associated with the Haymarket Riot.

The AFL became a far more effective force than the Knights of Labor for several reasons. The AFL did not try to organize everyone into one large union. Instead, each trade organized its own union for the simple goal of getting the best wages and conditions for its people. These individual unions pooled their resources to form strike funds and a central support structure which allowed striking workers to hold out until businesses met their demands.

The new federation was led from 1886 until 1924 (except for one year) by Samuel Gompers, a cigar maker and an effective labor leader. Gompers concentrated on specific labor issues, such as the eight-hour work day, and avoided more utopian political ideas. He also stressed that the union supported capitalism; it just wanted more of the benefits for the workers. The AFL did engage in some political lobbying, but it was specifically for labor goals. The strongest demand was simply for the right to organize and strike peacefully without being arrested for violating anti-union laws and injunctions. These narrow, specific goals gained the support of working men. The AFL rapidly grew in strength, comfortably surviving the 1893 depression.

✏️ **Name the item, event, or person.**

1.15 _____ Immigration after 1880 that came from southern and eastern Europe

1.16 _____ leader of the AFL, 1886-1924

1.17 _____ damaged the development of unions in 1873

1.18 _____ number of immigrants in the 1880s

1.19 _____ leader of the Knights of Labor at its height

1.20 _____ immigrant group hated in California

1.21 _____ 1885 events that increased Knights of Labor membership

1.22 _____ political group that benefited from the ignorance of the immigrants in American cities

1.23 _____ 1886 event that irreparably damaged the reputation of the Knights of Labor

1.24 _____ immigration test finally made into law in 1917

Answer these questions.

1.25 Why were the New Immigrants so disliked in America?

_____

_____

1.26 Why was the AFL more successful than the Knights of Labor?

_____

_____

1.27 Why did most middle-class Americans oppose unions?

_____

_____

_____

1.28 What were the restrictions put on immigration after 1882?

_____

_____

_____

Gilded Society

Social Darwinism. Social and political reformers in the Gilded Age faced formidable obstacles. One of the greatest was the attitude of the American people. America had always been a nation of freedom, a land where people could make money without restrictions or interference. *Laissez-faire* capitalism was the dominant view of the day. This philosophy stated that a nation would prosper when government interfered as little as possible in business. Encouraged by hefty donations and bribes, the U.S. government was a warm supporter of laissez-faire.

Popular opinion supported not only laissez-faire but also the anti-reform idea of Social Darwinism. The latter was an offshoot of Darwin's *Origin of the Species*, the book that described the theory of evolution. Darwin taught, among other things, that in nature each species prospers by competition in which the strongest survive and dominate. Led by a British philosopher named Herbert Spencer, this idea was applied to people. The rich were the strong who climbed to the top by their own ability. The poor, on the other hand, were poor because they were failures and they deserved to be poor. Thus, any reforms to benefit the poor would violate natural law to the harm of the human species! This contradicted the concept of Christian charity, and was never fully accepted in America, although ruthless industrialists did use it to justify their actions and impede reform.

The rich and powerful "captains of industry" were also widely admired in the Gilded Age. They were seen as the finest examples of the success of the American system. They had earned their wealth by their own cleverness and hard work. It was believed that anyone could become a millionaire in America. Andrew Carnegie, who had been a poor immigrant, was the prime example of what hard work and skill could bring to a man in this great land. Thousands of "rags to riches" stories about poor boys who became rich filled the bookshelves and gave dreams to hard-working men and boys. It was difficult for reformers to attack these heroes and their often underhanded methods.

New rich. The greatest glitter of the Gilded Age came from the incredibly wealthy new industrialists. High society took the air of a European royal court as the new rich competed in ways of showing off their wealth. Fortunes were spent on antiques and art from Europe. Lavish clothes, large yachts, and expensive parties were all part of the social scene. The Vanderbilts built a 70-room mansion called The Breakers at Newport, Rhode Island as a summer home. It included two rooms that were built in France, shipped over, and reassembled. They referred to it without joking as a "cottage." Another Vanderbilt, Consuelo, married an English Duke in exchange for a large cash settlement.

The new rich did not keep all of their money for themselves. The tradition of **philanthropy** was strong in America, despite Social Darwinism. John D. Rockefeller helped start the University of Chicago. Cornell in New York, and Stanford in California were both universities built with money from wealthy industrialists. The premier philanthropist, however, was Andrew Carnegie. He believed it was a sin to die rich; and a rich man's duty was to give away his excess money. Carnegie, therefore, dedicated the latter part of his life to philanthropy. He is best known for the many public libraries established all over America with his grants.

American life. Ordinary people had more money in the Gilded Age, as well. Cities were growing in population, and they began to add civic attractions for their population. With donations from wealthy individuals and other funds, large cities established libraries, museums, operas, and symphony orchestras. The first large department stores were built in the late

1800s by John Wanamaker in Philadelphia and Marshall Field in Chicago. Professional police and fire departments were established to protect city property. Sanitation laws, boards of health, safe water supplies, sewage systems, and trash removal added to the comfort and safety of city life.

Middle-class America had time and money for new amusements in the late 1800s. Vaudeville, a form of comedic theater, became popular with its acrobats, singers, and comics. The circus emerged as a favorite family amusement, led by P. T. Barnum, the master showman who founded the Barnum & Bailey Circus in 1881. "Buffalo Bill" Cody's Wild West Show with live buffalo, staged fights with Native Americans and stunt shooting toured the country beginning in the 1880s.

Sports also began their climb to the height of popularity in the Gilded Age. Baseball had been a popular game even before the Civil War. The National League of professional teams was started in 1876. Football, boxing, and horse racing were popular. The low-framed "safety" bicycle created a national craze as cycling clubs spread all over the nation. Tennis, imported from England, gained a following. For the less active, croquet and archery offered a pass at friendly competition. Thus, many of the activities that are part of modern American life had their foundations in the Gilded Age.

Inventions. Life in America was transformed in the late 1800s by a cornucopia of new and improved inventions. The typewriter (1867), cash register (1879), adding machine (1891), and telephone (1875) transformed the business office. Electric streetcars allowed cities to spread out in all directions and still bring people in for business or pleasure. Refrigeration and better canning techniques improved the supply of healthy food. The Kodak camera (1888) made photography available to everyone and gave us a record of American life.

| "The Breakers"

The most famous inventor of the turn of the century was Thomas Alva Edison (1847-1931). Edison was a creative genius who approached inventing like a business. He set up a laboratory, and had a group of paid assistants who worked on creating useful inventions. He decided what he wanted to create, and experimented until he found a way to do it. He was not dismayed by failures. He thought of them as discoveries of what did not work. He invented the phonograph, the electric light bulb, the storage battery, and a duplicating machine. He also made improvements on the typewriter, the stock ticker machine, motion pictures, the electric generator, and the electric train. He patented 1,093 inventions in his lifetime and left a brighter, more automated America as his legacy.

| A Collage of Invention: A Kodak Camera, Edison and his Light Bulb, the First Typewriter, the First Subway

Match these items.

1.29 _____ Social Darwinism

1.30 _____ Carnegie

1.31 _____ Kodak

1.32 _____ laissez-faire

1.33 _____ University of Chicago

1.34 _____ The Breakers

1.35 _____ National League

a. Vanderbilt summer cottage

b. established libraries all over America

c. business with a minimum of government interference

d. professional baseball organization

e. made photography available to everyone

f. theory based on evolution that the rich were superior and the poor were inferior; interfered with reform

g. founded with money from John D. Rockefeller

Match these people.

1.36 _____ John Wanamaker	a.	creator of the theory of evolution
1.37 _____ P. T. Barnum	b.	Wild West Show
1.38 _____ Thomas Edison	c.	department store, Philadelphia
1.39 _____ Herbert Spencer	d.	great philanthropist
1.40 _____ Andrew Carnegie	e.	philosopher, Social Darwinism
1.41 _____ Buffalo Bill Cody	f.	inventor, 1,093 patents
1.42 _____ Charles Darwin	g.	master showman, circus founder

Complete these items.

1.43 Name five of the important inventions of the late 1800s.

_____

_____

1.44 Name three things invented by Thomas Edison.

_____

_____

1.45 Name three things improved by Thomas Edison.

_____

_____

1.46 Name three reasons why the attitude of the American people did not support reform in the Gilded Age.

a. _____

b. _____

c. _____

Wild West

The Gilded Age was the era of the Wild West that is usually shown on TV and in the movies. This was the opening of the last frontier of the contiguous states, the Great Plains. It was the time of the Indian Wars, America's final drive to take the land from its original owners. It was the time of the great cattle drives, wild mining towns, and rough frontier justice. It was the arrival of the Gilded Age homesteaders that transformed this wild prairie into America's breadbasket.

Plains Indians. Much of the land between the Mississippi and the Rocky Mountains had been set aside as a home for the Native Americans by Andrew Jackson. The land known as the "Great American Desert" was believed to be worthless for farming. However, after the Civil War, Americans decided they wanted the land after all. In 1867 Congress decided to put all of the Native Americans there onto two reservations (Oklahoma and the Black Hills of North Dakota).

The Plains Indians were nomadic and war-like. They fought harder and more effectively against forced confinement to reservations than their farming cousins east of the Mississippi River had. Between 1865 and 1890, the U.S. army fought hundreds of battles with the Native Americans of the plains. In the end, repeating rifles (which did not have to be reloaded after every shot), the mobility of the railroad, the extermination of the buffalo (the Plains Indian's main source of food), and European diseases finally subdued the last of the Native American tribes. Several of the battles and their leaders have become legend.

In 1875 the land given to the Sioux people was invaded by hordes of greedy miners after gold was discovered there. Led by Sitting Bull and Crazy Horse, the Sioux fought back. In 1876 Lieutenant-Colonel George A. Custer rashly attacked a group of well-armed warriors near the Little Big Horn River in Montana. He and his entire command of 264 men were killed, but reinforcements drove the Sioux into Canada where hunger forced them to surrender.

Chief Joseph was the leader of the Nez Percé people. In 1877 he and his people refused to surrender their land and began to fight with the troops sent to force the move. Chief Joseph realized he could not win and began a skillful retreat toward Canada. He was finally cornered less than 50 miles from the border. With his people cold and hungry, he agreed to move to a reservation.

| Members of the Nez Percé

The most notorious Native American leader was Geronimo of the Apache people. He was placed on reservations several times in his life. He repeatedly escaped and led raids against white settlements in the U.S. and Mexico, using the mountains to hide. He proved very difficult to find. He finally surrendered for the last time in 1886 and was sent to Fort Sill, Oklahoma, where he lived the rest of his life.

The unofficial policy of the army and the government during these years was extermination of the Native American people. That was not the announced policy, but it was the effect. Incidents of soldiers murdering peaceful tribes, including women and children, were all too common. In 1881 Helen Hunt Jackson wrote *A Century of Dishonor*, which detailed the fraud, murder, and deceit practiced on the Native Americans in the previous hundred years. This book touched the conscience of the nation, and reform pressures eventually brought about the Dawes Act of 1887.

The Dawes Act ended tribal ownership of land, gave every Native American family its own land, and promised them full title to the land and citizenship after twenty-five years. It was an improvement over the policy of consolidation and destruction. However, the law ignored the Indian culture and their way of land management. (It was eventually reversed in 1934.) A lack of respect for non-European cultures was a common trait of all Western peoples before the middle of the 20th century. Even Christians made this error, not recognizing that the love of Christ does not require Western ways of worship and life.

Pioneer Miners. The leaders in the white settlement of the Wild West were the miners. The discovery of gold and silver brought waves of miners to Colorado, Montana, Nevada, and Idaho. These men established wild boomtowns near the strikes. After the surface metal was exhausted, the individual prospectors wandered away or found new occupations. They were followed, however, by corporations who set up major industries to get at the deeper metals. Industrial mining brought in jobs for miners, engineers, machine specialists and shopkeepers. Gold, silver and copper were the leading reasons for the growth of cities and towns in the mountain states of the West. Railroads followed to take out the ore and bring in supplies. Mining took the lead in the Western mountains, while it was cattle that did so on the plains.

Cattle drives. After the Civil War, the plains were covered with herds of wild cattle (escaped remnants of those brought over by Spain). The herds were worthless in the sparsely populated Western states, but very valuable to beef-hungry Eastern cities. The problem was how to get them back East. After the Civil War, the railroads provided the solution.

| Cattle Drive Trails

Under the leadership of clever businessmen, stations were set up on the transcontinental railroad to collect cattle for shipment to meat-processing centers in Kansas City and Chicago. The herds were brought to "cowtowns" like Abilene, Kansas by long "drives." Cattlemen would raise the cows on the unfenced, government-owned prairie land at virtually no cost. Then, the herds would be slowly driven to the rail junctions along established routes like the Chisholm and Goodnight-Loving Trails. Huge profits were reaped by the cattle owners who completed the long drives in the 1870s and early 1880s.

Opportunity on the prairie was very appealing to the American cowboy. These hard-working men entered American folklore on the long drives to market. It was their job to guard, move, brand, and control the huge herds. To do this, they lived out on the prairie with their charges, only rarely coming to town to spend their pay with wild abandon. Novels and short stories written in the East popularized the life of a cowboy on the open range. Later, movies and TV did the same.

It was all over in a short time, however. Open-range cattle raising was so profitable that hundreds of people and corporations jumped into the business. The result was an oversupply of beef, a drop in beef prices, and the over-grazing of good grasslands. The railroads were also bringing in settlers who bought up and fenced the range lands. The death blow came during the winter of 1886-87. Freezing temperatures and harsh blizzards killed thousands of cattle. The stockmen who survived did so by getting legal title to grasslands, growing feed for the winter, and investing in higher quality breeds of cattle. The spread of the railroad brought transport to all areas of the West, eliminating the need for the long drive. Cowboys lost their major function and became ranch hands, but they never lost their mystique for generations of Americans.

Homesteaders. The millions of acres of land in the last part of the West were settled with inordinate speed. Americans settled more acres between 1870 and 1900 than they had in the previous two hundred and fifty years! The Homestead Act and the railroads were the reasons for this incredible achievement.

The Homestead Act was passed by the Republican Congress during the Civil War. It gave 160 acres of free land to any citizen who lived on it for five years and improved it. (The South had previously opposed homestead laws as a way to increase the number of free states.) By 1900 about 80 million acres of land had been given away. However, even more land had been sold outright or given to railroads and states under various grants. This land was sold to settlers, speculators, or developers. In all, 500 million acres of land was disposed of by the U.S. government by 1900.

The railroads allowed the people to reach this **largess** quickly and easily. The dangerous months of travel by covered wagon were replaced by days of travel in relative comfort. Services and supplies were within easy reach of the new settlers. They no longer had to survive unaided on the "frontier." In fact, by the time of the 1890 census (American law requires a census every ten years), there no longer was a discernible frontier. For the first time in American history, there was no longer a line of settlement with open land to the West. There was still a tremendous amount of land available, but it was spread out in between established cities and towns. The frontier was gone.

The farmers of the plains faced major problems in establishing agriculture. The region was much drier than the East and needed special equipment to work the heavy soil. This equipment was expensive. More than 160 acres was needed in the drier regions to have a profitable farm. Nevertheless, the Great Plains quickly became a wheat- and corn-growing region, supplying American and foreign cities with grain.

These business farms depended upon a single cash crop and bought their own food from local stores.

Western farmers were hurt in the late 1800s by a variety of problems. The vast productive power of the plains produced huge crops that forced prices down. Railroads took a hefty cut of farmer's profits, sometimes eliminating them entirely. While manufactured goods were protected and overpriced due to high tariffs, farm products had no protection from competition. Farmers who went into debt to pay for expensive machinery often lacked the means to repay. They either sold out or carried debt and interest payments for years.

The problems of debt and railroad extortion forced the incredibly independent American farmers to organize. In 1867 they formed the Grange which became an important social/political organization for farmers. The Grange worked at first for self-improvement for farmers and later tackled some of the thorny issues of late 19th century agriculture. Its work for railroad regulation and debt relief was largely ineffective. However, its torch was taken up by the Farmer's Alliance, the Populists, and later, by the Progressive Movement.

 Complete these sentences.

1.47 _____ was the leader of the Nez Percé people who tried to retreat to Canada.

1.48 The pioneer settlers in the Western mountain states were _____ .

1.49 Helen Hunt Jackson's book, _____ , pricked the American conscience about the treatment of the Native American people.

1.50 The Homestead Act gave any citizen _____ acres of free land if they lived on it for _____ years.

1.51 The American _____ became a folk hero during the cattle drives of the 1870s and 1880s.

1.52 The _____ people fought back when their land was invaded by gold-hungry miners in 1875.

1.53 Cattle were taken to railroad "cowtowns" along trails like the _____ and the _____-_____ .

1.54 Overproduction of open-range cattle caused a _____ in prices and _____-_____ of grassland.

1.55 The _____ was a social/political organization for farmers.

1.56 The things that contributed to the conquest of the Plains Indians were:

a. _____

b. _____

c. _____

d. _____

1.57 The Apache leader who proved difficult to confine was _____ .

1.58 The death blow to the open-range cattle business was _____ .

1.59 The American frontier had disappeared by the census of _____ .

1.60 _____ and all of his men were killed at Little Big Horn in 1876.

1.61 The _____ Act ended tribal ownership of land and tried to make the Indians into independent farmers.

1.62 The farms of the Great Plains specialized in growing _____ and _____ .

1.63 The major political issues of the Grange were _____ relief and control of the _____ .

1.64 The two reasons for the speed of settlement on the Great Plains were the _____ and the _____ .

↺ **Review the material in this section in preparation for the Self Test.** The Self Test will check your mastery of this particular section. The items missed on this Self Test will indicate specific areas where restudy is needed for mastery.

SELF TEST 1

Match these people (each answer, 2 points).

1.01	_____	Andrew Carnegie	a.	master circus showman
1.02	_____	Samuel Gompers	b.	author of the _Gilded Age_
1.03	_____	P. T. Barnum	c.	leader of Nez Percé people
1.04	_____	John D. Rockefeller	d.	founder of Standard Oil
1.05	_____	Geronimo	e.	leader of AFL
1.06	_____	Thomas Edison	f.	wealthy railroad man, built The Breakers
1.07	_____	Terence Powderly	g.	philanthropist, steel-making industrialist
1.08	_____	Chief Joseph	h.	leader of the Knights of Labor
1.09	_____	Mark Twain	i.	Apache leader
1.010	_____	Cornelius Vanderbilt	j.	inventor

Complete these sentences (each answer, 3 points).

1.011 Large corporations that controlled a certain industry with a near monopoly were called

_____ .

1.012 The first of the large, post Civil War corporate industries was the _____ .

1.013 The _____ gave the Native Americans land as individuals, not as a tribe, and tried to make them into independent farmers.

1.014 The _____ was a shift of people coming to America from South and East Europe instead of the North.

1.015 The Knights of Labor never recovered from their association with the

_____ in 1886.

1.016 _____-_____ was a philosophy that a nation would prosper when government interfered as little as possible with business.

1.017 The _____ gave 160 acres to any citizen who improved it and lived on it for five years.

1.018 _____ was a philosophy which taught that the poor were failures that deserved to be poor because they could not compete successfully.

1.019 The era from 1865 to 1900 was called the _____ .

1.020 The census of 1890 showed that America no longer had a _____ .

Answer these questions (each number, 3 points).

1.021 What made open-range cattle raising profitable?

_____

_____

1.022 Who are the owners of a corporation and who runs it?

_____

_____

1.023 What two railroads completed the first transcontinental railroad?

_____

_____

1.024 Why did organized labor oppose immigration?

_____

_____

1.025 Why was the AFL more effective than the Knights of Labor?

_____

_____

1.026 What two things contributed to the rapid settlement of the plains?

_____

_____

1.027 Why were the railroads a problem for Midwestern farmers?

_____

_____

1.028 Why were immigrants considered ideal employees for the industrial giants?

_____

_____

1.029 How would the industries fight strikes?

_____

_____

1.030 Why were the captains of industry admired in America?

_____

_____

Match these items (each answer, 2 points).

1.031 _____ middle-class

1.032 _____ dividend

1.033 _____ Grange

1.034 _____ Promontory Point

1.035 _____ U.S. Steel

1.036 _____ Standard Oil

1.037 _____ capitalism

1.038 _____ Bessemer

1.039 _____ *A Century of Dishonor*

1.040 _____ Chisholm

a. controlled more than 90% of American petroleum production

b. process to make steel cheaply

c. company profits paid on stock

d. book that detailed abuse of the Indians

e. system of private ownership as a means of production

f. long drive cattle trail

g. people spend money on professional amusements

h. first billion-dollar corporation

i. sought debt relief and railroad regulation

j. place where the two sides of the first transcontinental railroad met

80/100   SCORE _____   TEACHER _____ _____
initials   date

2. GILDED POLITICS

After 1877, the Civil War ceased to be the major issue in American politics. The tariff, civil service reform, currency issues, and regulation of trusts were the largest issues leading up to the turn of the century. Local and state politics, however, were dominated by political machines, not issues. The machines and the trusts had the money and power to get what they wanted from the government, most of the time. However, increasing calls for reform battled the power of the industrialists and the party bosses. A few reform laws did make it onto the books, but most were not seriously enforced until the Progressive Era (after 1900). Thus, 1880-1900 was a time when the rich and powerful had the government mainly where they wanted it, very docile and obedient.

The presidents of this era were a lackluster bunch. The near-impeachment of Johnson had badly hurt the power of the presidency. The corruption of the Grant administration further discredited the office. Moreover, the next president, Hayes, obtained the office by very questionable means. Thus, by 1880 the presidency was not a powerful, well-respected office. Congress was recognized as the leader of the nation. Men of vision and ambition were turning to business, not politics. It was mainly men of mediocrity that occupied the White House in the years leading up to 1900.

SECTION OBJECTIVES

Review these objectives. When you have completed this section, you should be able to:

1. Describe the social, political, technological, and industrial developments of the Gilded Age.
3. Describe the presidents of the Gilded Age and their policies.
4. Describe the development of unions and reform movements from 1865 to 1915.
5. Describe the causes, course, and consequences of the Spanish-American War.

VOCABULARY

Study these words to enhance your learning success in this section.

armistice (är′ mə stəs). A halt to a war or fight by agreement between the opponents.

co-sign (kō′ sīn). Person who agrees to be responsible for a debt if the original debtor defaults.

decimate (des′ ə māt). To destroy a large part of. Literally, to destroy one tenth.

deficit (def′ ə sət). More expenses than income.

imperialism (im pir′ ē ə liz əm). The policy of expanding the power and dominion of a nation, especially by acquiring new territories and by gaining indirect economic or political control over other lands.

patronage (pā′ trə nij). The power to make appointments to government jobs on a basis other than merit alone.

Garfield to First Cleveland

Neither political party was able to dominate between 1880 and 1900. The Democrats always had control of the South, but Republican strength in the West and North offset that. The Republicans held the presidency for all but two terms, but the elections were usually close. In only four of the 20 years between 1877 and 1897 did the same party control Congress and the presidency. Thus, policy was often based on compromise between the two parties and even within factions of the same party.

Election of 1880. Rutherford B. Hayes decided not to run again in 1880. He probably could not have won the Republican nomination anyway. The bosses were angry with him for his opposition to using federal jobs to reward party loyalty, the source of the bosses' power. Hayes had an especially strong enemy in Senator Roscoe Conkling of New York. Conkling controlled New York politics by his control of political **patronage** there. He was in no mood to yield his power to a reformist president. Hayes had fired Conkling's man, Chester A. Arthur, who was in charge of the New York Custom House, the nation's largest collection spot for tariff revenue.

The Republican convention was badly split over a candidate. Conkling's faction supported a return of Ulysses S. Grant who had provided the "era of good stealing" for them. Conkling's "Stalwarts" were opposed in the convention by James Blaine of Maine who had the support of the "Half-Breed" Republican faction. The two sides could not defeat each other and finally compromised on James A. Garfield of Ohio. The Stalwarts were compensated by the nomination of Chester A. Arthur for vice president. The Democrats nominated General Winfield Hancock, a Union war veteran with a spotless record. Garfield won by less than 7,000 votes.

James A. Garfield (1831-1881). James A. Garfield was the last president to be born in a log cabin. He was born in Ohio to pioneer

| The Assassination of Garfield

farmers. His father died when he was two, but his mother succeeded in raising the family on their farm. Garfield worked for a short time as a driver on the Ohio barge canal but later obtained an education and went into teaching. He worked as a college professor and became president of Hiram College in Ohio. He fought in the Civil War, reaching the rank of major general. He was elected to the U.S. House of Representatives while still in the army. He was re-elected eight times and served on several influential committees. He was a Republican leader in the House under Hayes, gaining the confidence of both the Stalwarts and the Half-Breeds. He was elected to the Senate but was nominated for the presidency before he could take office.

Garfield named James Blaine, the Half-Breed leader, to the plum post of Secretary of State and favored his faction in other political appointments. Conkling opposed many of Garfield's nominations, especially when he made an appointment to the New York Custom House without consulting the New York senator. When it looked like this man would be appointed in spite of Conkling's opposition, the old party boss resigned, expecting to be triumphantly returned to office by the New York legislature. He was disappointed. The legislature chose someone else, and he never returned to office.

In the meantime, President Garfield was shot on July 2, 1881 by a man who had been denied a political office. Garfield lingered for eleven weeks, but finally died on September 19th. The assassin, Charles J. Guiteau, was tried and hanged. The president's murder raised a nationwide cry in favor of civil service reform and was largely responsible for Congress finally passing a reform bill in 1883.

Chester A. Arthur (1829-1886). Chester A. Arthur was a machine politician. He reached the presidency without ever having been elected to any political office other than the vice presidency. He was born in Vermont, the son of a pastor/teacher. He went to college in upstate New York and eventually practiced law in New York City. He served in various office positions in the New York militia during the Civil War. After the war, he became an associate of Roscoe Conkling's and was appointed as collector of customs at the huge New York Custom House. Arthur used his control of the over 1,000 jobs at the Custom House to support the Republican Party. Party loyalists got the jobs in exchange for votes, support, and a portion of their salary to the party's treasury. Arthur lost the job under Hayes when he refused to obey the president's order to stop collecting political "donations" from federal employees. Arthur was given the vice-presidential nomination in 1880 to gain Stalwart support for Garfield.

The reformers, called Mugwumps, had few hopes for Arthur. They expected him to blindly follow the policies of the bosses who had made him. However, he rose to the occasion of his advancement and surprised everyone with his independence. He strongly supported civil service reform and had the pleasure of finally seeing it made into law.

The pressure for reform was intense after Garfield's assassination. However, the Republican Congress stalled on the issue until the congressional elections of 1882. The Republicans lost control of the House that year and feared they would lose the presidency in 1884.

Consequently, to keep their own men in office when the Democrats took over, they passed the Pendleton Act of 1883 before the new Congress took office. Arthur signed it into law.

The Pendleton Act forbade the practice of taking a portion of the officeholders' salaries to support the party that gave them the job. It also set up a merit system for appointment to federal offices under the supervision of the Civil Service Commission. The president was given the authority to classify which jobs would be filled by competitive exams. The others would still be available for patronage.

Arthur appointed the author of the law as the first commissioner. He also moved with vigor to classify federal jobs under the commission. By the end of his term, about ten percent of all federal jobs were classified, awarded on merit. Succeeding presidents expanded the number of classified jobs, usually when it looked like their party would lose them after an election. The system expanded until, by the 1940s, 90% of all federal jobs were awarded on merit, not political activism. The reform took time, but the spoilsmanship begun by Andrew Jackson was finally being eliminated.

Arthur further surprised reformers by supporting fraud prosecutions against some former political allies. He appointed a commission to examine the high tariffs and vetoed extravagant legislation. He also signed a law that authorized the purchase of a modest number of modern naval ships (the Navy had been allowed to deteriorate since the Civil War). His independence made him unpopular with the bosses, and he developed a terminal illness that led him to not press for renomination in 1884. He died less than two years after leaving office.

Election of 1884. The Republicans easily nominated James Blaine for president in 1884. He was, however, a controversial nominee. The Republican star had a history of questionable dealings in his public career. The Republican

Mugwumps either gave him little support or supported the Democrats who had the sense to nominate an honest reform candidate named Grover Cleveland.

The only major issue dividing the parties was the tariff. (The Republicans wanted it high and the Democrats wanted to lower it.) Neither candidate had served in the Civil War, so the bloody shirt was not waved very much. The lack of issues and Blaine's reputation led the election to dissolve into heavy mudslinging. The Republicans thought they had a winning mud-ball when it was discovered that the bachelor Cleveland had an illegitimate son. The smear campaign backfired, however, when Cleveland admitted it and was admired for his honesty. The campaign was waged between Blaine's public reputation and Cleveland's private one. Cleveland won by a small popular majority.

Grover Cleveland (1837-1908). Grover Cleveland was the only president to serve two non-consecutive terms. (He was elected again in 1892 after four years out of office). He was born in New Jersey, the son of a pastor. He attended various schools in New York but never went to college. His father died when he was 16. He and his brothers worked to support his mother and sisters. He studied law with a firm in Buffalo, New York and was admitted to the bar in 1859. He paid for a substitute to serve for him in the Civil War so that he could continue to support his family. He served in a couple of minor offices before being elected as mayor of Buffalo in 1881. He proved to be a strong reformer in office, blocking many corrupt city contracts. His reputation and lack of political enemies gained him the governor's office in 1882. He earned the hatred of Tammany Hall, the New York City machine, with his support for reforms. He quickly gained a national reputation, and the Democrats nominated him in 1884 to run against the tainted James Blaine.

| Grover Cleveland's Wedding

Grover Cleveland, the first Democratic president since the Civil War, was an exception to the lackluster presidents of the Gilded Age. He was a strong reformer, but he was limited by Congress and the demands of his own party. Still, he began to polish the tarnished image of the presidency by his leadership and integrity. He also added a bit of social spice by being the first president to marry while in office. The forty-nine-year-old Cleveland married twenty-one-year-old Frances Folsom, his ward, in 1886.

Reformer Cleveland. Cleveland was besieged with Democratic office-seekers. After nearly a quarter century out of power, the Democrats wanted the spoils of victory. Cleveland found it impossible to ignore the pressure. By the end of his term, he had replaced two-thirds of the federal employees with Democratic workers. He tried to check the qualifications of the applicants and often refused those who were unfit. He also doubled the number of jobs classified under the Civil Service Commission. The overall result was that he angered both the Democratic bosses who thought he should have given them more jobs, and the reformers who thought he should have given less jobs.

Currency was a major issue of the era. The Grange Movement was one of several supporters of inflationary currency that would increase prices and ease agricultural debt. It was believed that this could be done by increasing the money supply by using paper currency and silver money. The economically stagnant South and the agricultural West generally supported paper currency and silver coinage. However, the industrial powers of the North favored hard currency with gold as the basis for all U.S. money.

The United States currency in the 1880s was, by law, always redeemable in gold. The government had to keep on hand enough gold to satisfy any demands by people holding paper money. Supporters of a larger money supply and silver interests had passed the Bland-Allison Act in 1878. It required the treasury to buy silver and mint silver dollar coins with 16 ounces of silver for the value of every 1 ounce of gold. These silver dollars could also be redeemed for gold.

During Cleveland's first administration, the opening of new silver mines in the West drove down the price of silver. This made the silver dollars less valuable than their gold counterparts. Observant citizens began to obtain silver dollars and then redeem them one-for-one for the more valuable gold. The result was a drain on the gold reserves in the U.S. treasury. Cleveland tried to get the Bland-Allison Act repealed, but Congress refused. The treasury sold bonds for gold which brought in needed reserves, but the drain continued.

The Grange also favored control of the railroads. The life or death control railroads had over many farmers required regulation to insure fair treatment. Under Grange pressure, several Midwestern states had passed laws to regulate the railroads. However, their efforts were shattered in 1886 when the Supreme Court ruled that states could not regulate railroads engaged in interstate commerce. Since most of the railroads ran between states, this effectively ended any hope of state regulation. Only the federal government could act.

Responding to heavy public pressure, Congress passed the Interstate Commerce Act in 1887. The Act banned rate discrimination, rebates, and pooling. It forbade charging more for short hauls than long hauls. It also required that rates be "reasonable and just." The most important part of the law set up the Interstate Commerce Commission (I.C.C.) to enforce the new law.

The Commission was not terribly effective in its early years. The railroad bosses still had tremendous power in the government, but it was an important first step. The federal government finally acknowledged that unbridled capitalism could have unreasonable and unfair results for the nation. It was the first tentative step into regulation of the economy. Cleveland was, for all his reform ideas, a laissez-faire man and signed the law reluctantly. Over the years, however, it turned out to be one of the most significant accomplishments of his administration.

Cleveland also earned the enmity of the G.A.R. (Grand Army of the Republic), the Union veteran's organization, by his tight control over granting pensions. Cleveland carefully examined private requests for pensions to make sure the applicant was truly disabled in the war. Previous Republican presidents had routinely approved such requests without examining them to appease the politically powerful G.A.R. Cleveland also vetoed the Dependent Pension Bill in 1887. This law would have given a government pension to any man who served at least 90 days in the war and who was currently disabled. He further infuriated the G.A.R. by trying to return captured Southern battle flags, but he was forced to back down by the outcry against him.

The reason the G.A.R. and Congress thought veterans should freely be rewarded was because the treasury had a huge surplus. The high tariffs were bringing in more money than the government needed. Cleveland courageously attacked the high tariffs in his annual message to Congress in 1887. He requested that the tariffs be reduced, believing it was unfair to take money the government did not need. The Republicans accused him of favoring free trade, which was an unpopular idea in those protectionist times. The conflict created the issue for the 1888 campaign.

Choose the correct person for each item.

2.1 _____ first Democratic president since the Civil War   a. James Garfield

2.2 _____ senator, political boss of New York   b. James Blaine

2.3 _____ doubled the number of classified federal jobs   c. Chester Arthur

2.4 _____ assassinated by disgruntled office seeker   d. Roscoe Conkling

2.5 _____ tried to get Bland-Allison repealed   e. Grover Cleveland

2.6 _____ Democratic candidate, 1880   f. Ulysses Grant

2.7 _____ mayor, governor, president in four years   g. Winfield Hancock

2.8 _____ Garfield's Secretary of State

2.9 _____ president, previously never held elected office

2.10 _____ vetoed Dependent Pension Bill

2.11 _____ fired at N.Y. Custom House for disobeying Hayes

2.12 _____ signed Interstate Commerce Act

2.13 _____ Stalwart leader

2.14 _____ Half-Breed faction leader

2.15 _____ signed civil service reform law

2.16 _____ Republican candidate, 1884

2.17 _____ candidate wanted by Stalwarts in 1880

2.18 _____ House leader, had Stalwart and Half-Breed faction confidence

2.19 _____ resigned over president's appointments; expected to be re-elected; was not

2.20 _____ president made by Conkling

2.21 _____ accused of having illegitimate son

2.22 _____ paid a substitute in the Civil War

2.23 _____ son of Ohio pioneers

2.24 _____ angered veterans by granting only legitimate pension requests

2.25 _____ opposed high tariffs that produced treasury surpluses

Answer these questions.

2.26 What were the reformers called?

_____

2.27 Which political party dominated the government between 1880 and 1900?

_____

2.28 Why were people trading in silver dollars for gold ones under Cleveland?

_____

_____

_____

2.29 Which sections of the country favored paper currency and silver coinage?

_____

2.30 What did the Bland-Allison Act require?

_____

_____

2.31 What was the name of the civil service reform law?

_____

2.32 What percentage of federal jobs were classified under Arthur?

_____

2.33 What made the public clamor for civil service reform?

_____

2.34 What did the Interstate Commerce Act forbid?

_____

_____

Harrison to McKinley

Election of 1888. Cleveland was re-nominated by the Democrats in 1888. His stand on the tariff issue had made him vulnerable, but he was still the party's best chance. The Republicans considered James Blaine, but he refused when it became clear he did not have the full support of the party. Instead, a compromise candidate, Benjamin Harrison, was chosen.

The tariff was the main issue of the campaign. It was the focus of the literature, speeches, and rhetoric. Because there was a definite issue, the mud slinging was lower than the previous election. The Republicans argued that the tariff protected American jobs and a budget surplus was good. They accused the Democrats of favoring Britain, who wanted decreased tariffs to help their trade. That was a serious accusation in anti-British America, especially among the Irish voters. The Republicans also raised a huge amount of money from industrialists frightened by the prospect of losing their high tariffs. The money went to buy Republican votes, sometimes literally. Cleveland won the popular vote, but lost the election because Harrison received the most electoral votes.

Benjamin Harrison (1833-1901). Benjamin Harrison was the grandson of former president and war hero, William Henry Harrison. Benjamin was born in Ohio and raised on the family farm there. He received a college education and began the practice of law in 1854. He moved to Indiana and held several appointed and elected positions in that state. During the Civil War, he organized and led a volunteer regiment. He rose to the rank of brigadier general on the basis of his ability as a commander. After the war, he served on a government commission and was elected to the U.S. Senate. He had almost 100,000 less votes than Cleveland, but won the election 233 to 168 in the official electoral votes. (This is possible because Harrison won in the large states that had more electoral votes. The state winner gets all of that state's electoral votes.)

Billion-dollar Congress. The 1888 election gave the Republicans control of Congress as well as the presidency. They quickly moved to spend the nation's surplus so they could justify the high tariffs. This Fifty-first Congress became known as the "Billion-dollar Congress." It was the first to appropriate almost a billion dollars, an enormous amount for its day, in peacetime. The huge surplus was successfully spent, and it did not seriously trouble our nation again for many years.

The main beneficiary of the Republican largess was the G.A.R. The Pension Act of 1890 gave a full pension to any Union veteran who served at least ninety days and could not, for any reason, now do manual labor. The number of people drawing pensions went up by half again under Harrison. So did the cost.

The pressure for control of the trusts had been mounting for years. The cold, efficient work of John D. Rockefeller and his fellow trust builders in eliminating their competition had aroused tremendous anger. The Fifty-first Congress acknowledged the importance of the issue by passing the Sherman Anti-Trust Act in 1890. This law declared that any combination of companies that was in restraint of trade was illegal. Mere size was not enough; the trust had to be interfering with competition and interstate trade.

The government did not successfully use the law against any monopoly for years. It was, however, successfully used in 1894 to break up a railroad strike. The union was accused of interfering with interstate trade. However, the law was now on the books, a testament to the growing public outcry for reform. It would see action early in the coming century under the command of the Progressives.

Eastern congressmen were anxious to raise the tariff to new heights, but they needed Western support to do it. In the end, a deal was made and the Easterners received support for a new

| Carnegie Steel Plant

tariff. In exchange, they agreed to support increased coinage of silver. Western farmers believed this would help depressed farm prices and rising farm debt. Western silver mining states wanted it for more obvious reasons.

The Sherman Silver Purchase Act of 1890 was the Western end of the deal. It required that the treasury buy about twice as much silver as it had been under the old Bland-Allison Law. The metal was to be made into coins at the old ratio of 16 ounces of silver for every 1 ounce of gold. It did nothing to relieve farm problems.

The industrial Northeast received the McKinley Tariff as its part in the bargain. It pushed the rates to the highest in peacetime history. A bounty of two cents a pound was given to U.S. sugar producers to help eliminate the surplus. A few agricultural products were also protected by tariffs to quiet farm protest, but American farmers had little foreign competition for the U.S. food market. The "protection" did them no good.

The tariff was a disaster. The farmers saw an immediate increase in the prices of their dry-goods, equipment, clothes, and other supplies. The prices on their products continued to be low. The voters reacted with anger at the high tariff and free-spending of the Billion-dollar Congress. A challenge to the old order was in the air.

Populist revolt. Rising industrialist power over the government, unregulated railroad abuses, falling prices for farm products, and rising farm debt had created an angry U.S. farm community. By 1890 farmers had organized the Farmer's Alliance to press their demands. There were two main Alliances, one in the Northwest which worked independently and one in the South which worked within the Democratic Party. (Southern farmers would not risk losing white control of the government by splitting with the Democratic Party.) The Alliances were able to elect many of their people in the West and the South. They also contributed to the election of a Democratic House of Representatives in 1890.

The Alliances decided they needed to step out of the two main parties to press their demands. In 1892, they held a convention in Omaha, Nebraska, and formed the People's (Populist) Party. The Farmer's Alliance was joined by the Grangers, Mugwumps, Greenbacks, labor unions, and a wide variety of reform-minded individuals. They nominated General James Weaver, a former Greenback, for president. The Populists, however, still lacked Southern support. The Southern Democrats would not split from their party and risk a return of black power.

The Populists had an astonishing reform platform. The platform called, first of all, for free coinage of silver. It also endorsed (among other things) a new banking system; income tax (to replace land taxes and tariffs that did not touch industrial income); government ownership of railroads, the telegraph system, and the telephone companies; an eight-hour workday; restrictions on immigration; and direct election of U.S. senators (they were still appointed by the state legislatures).

Election of 1892. The Republicans renominated Harrison and the Democrats again chose Cleveland. The stage was set for a repeat fight with the added interest of the Populist vote.

| Pullman Car of the Late 1890s

The campaign again focused on the tariff. Republicans argued that the tariff gave Americans high wages. A wave of strikes, mainly over wages, flew in the face of this argument. The worst was at Carnegie's Homestead Steel plant near Pittsburgh, after the company cut wages. Three hundred armed Pinkerton detectives battled with the strikers, and several people died. Soldiers were called in to break up the strike, which collapsed. The publicity hurt the Republican cause and helped elect Cleveland by a reasonable popular and substantial electoral margin. Weaver received over a million votes in his party's first appearance at the poles.

Second Cleveland. The second Cleveland administration was doomed by a major depression that hit the nation early in 1893. It was caused by over-speculation, strikes, and the depression in farm prices. Cleveland had no tools to effectively deal with the crisis. He did, however, insist that the Sherman Silver Act had to be repealed because of the drain on the nation's gold reserves. He called a special session of Congress in 1893 to do just that.

The fight over repealing the Sherman Silver Act was substantial. Silver coinage had become an issue far beyond the question of what it actually accomplished. It was supported by the poorer classes and opposed by the wealthier ones. It was an issue of class conflict, not one of actual policy. The issue was particularly sensitive as the working class was losing what little it had in the depression. A young congressman from Nebraska, William Jennings Bryan, made a spellbinding speech against repealing the act, but Cleveland was able to force a repeal. It damaged his own party substantially and did not completely halt the decline in the gold reserves.

The continued drain on the treasury forced the government to sell bonds for gold. When even this was not enough, Cleveland negotiated a new bond sale through J. P. Morgan, the banking giant. The sale restored confidence in the U.S. monetary system, but it created a political cramp for the president. Morgan and his people received a substantial commission for their part in the bond sale. This left Cleveland open to charges of currying favor with the powerful

men of the banking industry. This was an especially onerous charge leveled by the rising Populists.

The second major debacle of Cleveland's administration was his handling of the Pullman strike in 1894. The Pullman Palace Car Company built and leased sleeping cars for the railroads. Due to the depression, Pullman cut wages in 1894 without reducing the high rent it charged for homes in the company town. The workers went on strike. They were supported by the American Railway Union under Eugene Debs. The workers refused to work on any train that had Pullman cars. The railroad obtained an injunction against the strikers for interfering with the delivery of the mail and interstate commerce. Since obeying the injunction would mean ending the strike, Debs refused. Some of the strikers in Chicago reacted with violence. Urged by his attorney general, who was a corporate lawyer, Cleveland sent in the army to break up the strike.

The nation was alarmed by how quickly the courts and the government jumped to do the bidding of the railroads. More alarms were raised when the courts refused to use the Sherman Anti-Trust Act against the huge sugar trust that controlled virtually all sugar production in America. Protest books, such as *Progress and Poverty*, *Wealth Against Commonwealth*, and *Coin's Financial School*, condemning the hypocrisy of the Gilded Age were widely read and discussed. The alliance between powerful businesses and the government was being threatened by a rising tide of voter rebellion.

Cleveland tried to obtain a reduction in the tariff, as he had promised in the 1892 campaign, but the depression and the spending of the Fifty-first Congress had left the government short of money. The Democratic Party was still reeling from the silver coinage fight. The Wilson-Gorman Bill that finally came out of Congress only slightly reduced the tariffs and was burdened with hundreds of amendments, including an income tax and a payoff to the sugar trust. Cleveland allowed the law to pass. The popular income tax provision was quickly struck down by the courts, further alienating the Populists.

 Answer these questions.

2.35 What was the Fifty-first Congress (elected in 1888) called?

_____

2.36 Who were the presidential candidates and their parties in 1888?

_____

_____

2.37 Who were the presidential candidates and their parties in 1892?

_____

_____

_____

2.38 Which two laws passed in 1890 were the result of a Northern-Western deal?

_____

2.39 What was the group that spoke for the farmers and reform in 1890?

_____

2.40 What event doomed Cleveland's second administration?

_____

2.41 What was the main issue of the 1888 and 1892 campaigns?

_____

2.42 What law was passed in response to public pressure to control the trusts?

_____

2.43 What political party was formed in 1892 in Omaha, Nebraska?

_____

2.44 Cleveland damaged his own party forcing the repeal of what law?

_____

2.45 Cleveland sent in the Army to halt which strike? _____

2.46 What was the name of the Nebraska congressman who supported silver coinage?

_____

2.47 Who won the popular presidential vote in 1888?

_____

2.48 Who was the main beneficiary of Republican spending in the Fifty-first Congress?

_____

2.49 What issue became an emotional class conflict more than a debate of merits?

_____

2.50 What tariff law did Cleveland allow even though it did not make serious reductions?

_____

2.51 What action to increase the gold reserves got Cleveland in political trouble?

_____

2.52 What were the major problems affecting the farmers?

_____

2.53 Who was the head of the American Railway Union?

_____

2.54 What events challenged Republican claims in the 1892 campaign that the tariff protected high American wages? _____

2.55 What alarmed the nation about the response to the Pullman Strike of 1894?

_____

2.56 What did Congress do with the 1888 budget surplus? _____

2.57 What were seven of the planks in the Populist Platform in 1892?

a. _____   b. _____

c. _____   d. _____

e. _____   f. _____

g. _____

Election of 1896. The 1896 campaign vaulted into the limelight a man who would be the most important figure in the Democratic Party for many years, William Jennings Bryan. Bryan had been a Congressman and had lost a bid for the Senate in 1894. He worked as an editor and lecturer until the 1896 Democratic convention when he appeared as a delegate from Nebraska.

The convention was dominated by pro-silver men. They repudiated Cleveland and would not even consider him as a candidate. The convention had no clear candidate until Bryan took the platform to speak in support of free coinage of silver. It was probably the most famous convention speech in American history.

Bryan spoke in favor of the laboring class, against the rich industrialists and the government they controlled. He spoke in the ideas of the day, in favor of silver, which was the issue of the downtrodden. He scathingly attacked those who favored the gold standard. "We will answer their demands for a gold standard by saying to them: 'You shall not press down upon the brow of labor this crown of thorns, you shall not crucify mankind upon a cross of gold.'"

The "Cross of Gold" speech ignited the Democratic convention and made Bryan their candidate even though he was only 36 years old.

The Populist Party was in a quandary because the Democrats had taken their main issue, silver coinage. Therefore, they nominated Bryan. The alarmed Republicans nominated William McKinley, a man who strongly favored the business interests. McKinley was promoted and managed by Marcus Hanna, a wealthy Ohio businessman. Hanna spent the time and money to secure McKinley's nomination on the first ballot and then went on to manage his campaign.

Bryan was the first presidential candidate to go to the people. Before that time, candidates did not usually actively campaign. It was considered undignified. Subordinates did all of the campaigning. Bryan, on the other hand, toured the nation, speaking in favor of silver and the working people. He made hundreds of emotional speeches, even in the industrial North.

The money powers were terrified of Bryan. Silver was so cheap that a silver dollar would actually be worth about 50 cents in gold.

The bankers could see all of their loans being repaid at half the value using silver dollars. The industrialists could see their profits destroyed in the resulting financial chaos. Hanna took full advantage of the panic over the silver issue. He raised millions of dollars from wealthy businessmen to create the largest campaign fund to date.

Hanna used his money to flood the nation with literature and rallies. The Republican campaign emphasized prosperity issues. The depression was blamed on the Democrats. McKinley was the candidate of stability and business. "McKinley and a full dinner pail," was his slogan. A careful smear campaign created fear that Bryan's election would doom the nation to economic disorder and depression.

McKinley stayed at home and conducted a "Front Porch Campaign." Loyal Republicans were brought to his home in Ohio to hear their candidate give a carefully prepared speech. The issues he addressed were chosen in advance based on what was important to that particular group. McKinley won by a convincing popular and electoral majority. Bryan won the South and part of the West, but McKinley won in the population centers in the North and East.

William McKinley (1843-1901). William McKinley was the last president of the Gilded Age. He favored business, did not enforce the antitrust laws, raised the tariff, and ignored cries for reform. He was personally a very charming man, religious, and devoted to his invalid wife. He was born in Ohio to prosperous Scotch-Irish parents. His father owned an iron manufacturing business. William received a good education, but he withdrew from college because of illness. He was eighteen when the Civil War began and immediately volunteered. In spite of his youth, he reached the temporary rank of major. He was the last Civil War veteran to be president. After the war, he studied law and began practicing in Canton, Ohio.

| William Jennings Bryan

McKinley entered local politics in the late 1860s. He was elected to the U.S. House of Representatives in 1876. He served in the House, with one break, until 1890. In that election, public anger over his tariff and the Billion-dollar Congress cost him and many other Republicans their seats. McKinley was thereafter twice elected governor and became friends with Marcus Hanna. Hanna bailed him out of a serious jam in the Panic of 1893. McKinley became responsible for some debts he had **co-signed** for a friend. Hanna raised the $100,000 needed to pay the debts. Hanna began working to win the presidency for McKinley in 1892 and did so in 1896.

First administration. McKinley allowed the trusts to grow as they wanted, thus repaying his debts to the industrialists who financed his campaign. Moreover, the treasury was operating at a **deficit**. A new tariff bill, the Dingley Tariff, was passed in 1897. Again burdened with hundreds of amendments, it raised the tariffs back to near the levels of the McKinley Tariff of 1890 (some categories were even higher).

The triumphant "gold-bugs" wanted to put the nation's currency officially on the gold standard. That would value all of the nation's currency on gold only. There were too many Silverites left in Congress to do it right away, but by 1900 enough had been voted out for the Gold Standard Act to pass. The problem of the gold reserves was solved by the discovery of new gold fields and the development of new techniques to extract gold from other ores. Moreover, the nation came out of the depression in 1897 and entered an era of prosperity. Thus, McKinley would have ridden comfortably through his presidency with little to note had it not been for foreign affairs, specifically a war with Spain.

Complete these sentences.

2.58 The _____ officially tied all U.S. money to a value of gold in 1900.

2.59 The most famous convention speech in U.S. history was Bryan's _____ speech in 1896.

2.60 The farmers, reformers, and anti-industrialists (poorer working people) took up

_____ as their key issue in the early to mid-1890s.

2.61 The Populist Party nominated _____ in 1896.

2.62 McKinley owed his nomination and election to _____ .

2.63 McKinley's campaign slogan was _____ .

2.64 The most important man in the Democratic Party for years after 1896 was

_____ .

2.65 The _____ Tariff again raised the tariff rates.

2.66 _____ was the first presidential candidate to take his

campaign to the people.

2.67 McKinley's campaign convinced Americans that the election of _____

_____ would bring depression and disorder.

2.68 _____ raised the largest campaign fund to date for McKinley.

2.69 McKinley conducted a _____ campaign from his home.

2.70 A silver "dollar" would have been worth _____ at the 16 to 1 ratio in 1896.

2.71 America came out of the Panic of 1893 in _____ .

America Becomes a World Power

International interest. American foreign policy had been very stable since the Republic was founded. America avoided all involvement with European wars and problems. In return, Americans expected European powers to honor the Monroe Doctrine and stay out of the Americas. This was the policy of a militarily weak, agrarian nation, busy with the job of filling up its empty spaces.

Things were changing by the end of the 1800s. The industrial boom after the Civil War had made the United States one of the richest nations on earth. In the first decades after the war, the nation had maintained its traditional isolation. There were railroads to build, Indians to defeat, cattle to drive, and industries to build. By the 1890s, the frontier was gone, and America was looking to expand in other parts of the world. The nation had slowly been building a steel navy to protect its growing commerce.

This was the age of European **imperialism**. European powers like Britain, France, and Germany were taking colonies in Africa and Asia. America, now among the world's wealthiest nations, began to hunger for her share. Moreover, Social Darwinism dictated that the strong and powerful dominate the weak and less capable. Surely that meant more expansion for the great American Republic! Further impetus was added by the work of Captain Alfred Mahan. His popular book, *The Influence of Sea Power upon History, 1660-1783*, taught that sea power gave victory and world power to its possessors.

A whole string of international incidents focused American attention on the outside world in the late 1880s and 1890s. The U.S. had come close to war with Germany over the Samoan Islands (1889), with Italy over the lynching of some Italian citizens (1891), with Chile over an attack on U.S. sailors (1892), and with Britain over a boundary dispute in South America (1895-96). In 1893 American white planters on the island of Hawaii overthrew the native ruler, Queen Liluokalani. Honest President Cleveland refused to annex the island when it became clear that the people of Hawaii did not want it, only the white-controlled government did. Many Americans clamored to take the islands (they were annexed in 1898). America was growing in power and anxious to prove it. It was also becoming increasingly imperialistic.

Revolt in Cuba. Cuba was one of the last Spanish possessions in the New World. Having lost all of Latin America, Spain was determined to keep her Caribbean Islands. The oppressed Cuban people broke out in one of their regular revolts in 1895. The rebels burned villages, destroyed crops and attacked officials. The Spanish government reacted harshly with arrests, torture, and executions. Civilians were rounded up into detention camps where they could not aid the rebels. There, they died from diseases spread by the lack of decent sanitation.

The American public was always willing to support people fighting for their freedom. Cuba also had attracted a great deal of American investments that were in jeopardy, but the leading cause of U.S. interest in the Cuban revolt was "yellow journalism." Two powerful New York City newspapers, the *Journal* and the *World*, were fighting a battle for sales. The nearby revolt gave the newspapers a creative source for sensational stories. William R. Hearst and Joseph Pulitzer (the newspapers' owners) were far more interested in good stories than true ones. The vivid, creative, and often false tales of abuse and murder raised a war cry from the American public.

Congress followed the American public in pressing for war. McKinley and his business backers, however, did not want that. McKinley, who had seen enough war as a young man, refused to give into the war cries until events forced his hand. The first event was a letter written by the Spanish ambassador in Washington calling McKinley a politician without good faith who was interested mainly in following the direction of his party. The private letter was stolen and published. The reaction forced the unfortunate Spanish diplomat to resign. The second event was the destruction of the *Maine* a few days after the letter was published.

The U.S. battleship *Maine* was sent to Havana, Cuba to protect and evacuate Americans if the situation grew worse. On February 15, 1898 the ship blew up in the harbor with the loss of over 250 American seamen. A U.S. investigation blamed a Spanish mine. The American public screamed for revenge. (Another U.S. investigation in the 1970s concluded the explosion was probably caused by combustion in the ship's coal supply, but no one will ever be sure of what happened.)

Angry Americans blamed Spain for destroying the *Maine* and killing U.S. sailors. A strong president might have been able to resist the popularity of war and work for a diplomatic solution. Spain was willing to negotiate, but she was not willing to grant Cuba independence. Fearful of losing the election in 1900 if he did not give in, McKinley finally requested armed intervention in Cuba on April 11th. Congress agreed, Spain declared war, and Congress followed suit on April 25th.

Spanish-American War. The war between the new rising world power, America, and the aging world power, Spain, began a long way from Cuba. A U.S. Pacific squadron, under Commodore George Dewey, had been ordered to attack the Spanish fleet in the Philippines (southwest of Japan) in the event of war. Dewey attacked the Spanish fleet in Manila Bay on May 1, 1898. He destroyed it with a minimum of U.S. casualties. He then blockaded the harbor until U.S. troops could arrive to take the city. They finally arrived and took the city on August 13th, the day after the war ended.

Back in Cuba, the U.S. fleet was blockading the island and searching for their Spanish counterparts. The Spanish fleet, under Admiral Pascual Cervera, was finally located, safely in Santiago Harbor at the east end of the island. The U.S. fleet blockaded the harbor and sent for the army to help take the city from the land side.

The U.S. army had been fighting only Indians since the Civil War and was too small to handle a major war. As in the past, the government called for volunteers and thousands responded. The volunteers were taken to Florida for training. There they drilled in woolen uniforms, which was all the army had available at the time.

Among the volunteers, two were particularly worth noting. One was Democratic General Joseph Wheeler, formerly of the Confederate Army. At the age of 61, "Fighting Joe" volunteered to wear a Union uniform. He led the attack on Santiago. His willingness and that of other Southern volunteers helped with the ongoing national reconciliation.

The second famous volunteer was Theodore Roosevelt. T.R. had been assistant secretary of the navy when the war began. He had been one of the Republicans pushing hard for the war. When it came, he quickly resigned and helped form the First United States Volunteer Cavalry,

| Battle of Santiago

better known as the "Rough Riders." The Rough Riders were a mixed bag of adventurers that included cowboys, Eastern college graduates, and policemen. Lieutenant-Colonel Roosevelt was the group's second in command but their prime organizer and leader.

When the navy finally located and trapped the Spanish fleet, 17,000 of the new volunteer troops were sent to assist. Among the troops sent to Cuba were about half of the Rough Riders, including T.R. The U.S. force made a very confused, and fortunately unopposed, landing near Santiago on June 22nd. They fought their way inland to take the city's defenses, which

were set up in the hills around it. The Rough Riders had their moment of glory on July 1st when Roosevelt led them on a charge up Kettle Hill to capture its defenses. (They went up on foot because they were not able to bring their horses.) The American army then captured San Juan Hill which set up a siege of the city. Roosevelt and the Rough Riders became associated in the public mind with the capture of San Juan Hill and the eventual victory in Cuba.

With the city under siege, Admiral Cervera tried to escape from the trap. On July 3rd, the Spanish fleet sailed out of the harbor with the Americans in full pursuit. The faster American ships

| Theodore Roosevelt and His "Rough Riders"

overtook and destroyed the Spanish fleet. The Americans suffered no serious damage, and Santiago surrendered on July 17th. An invasion of nearby Puerto Rico on July 25th was unopposed. Spain signed a preliminary armistice on August 12th. The "splendid little war," as soon-to-be Secretary of State John Hay called it, lasted less than four months.

There were very few battle-related deaths in the Spanish-American War, despite the fact it was conducted in an atmosphere of sheer chaos. However, there were a significant number of deaths from tropical diseases, specifically yellow fever which hit the army stationed in Santiago. In total, less than 400 men died of bullets, while many times that number died of diseases. Roosevelt, who had both political clout and no army career to protect, was one of several men who insisted the army get out of Cuba before it was decimated. Most of the army was removed by the end of July and back in the states by August.

Imperialism or not. At the end of the war, America was in possession of the Philippines, Cuba, Puerto Rico and several other small islands. A strong division rent the nation over what to do with these territories. The Philippines, which had not been part of the war aims, were especially troubling. The Congress had passed the Teller Amendment in 1898 which declared the U.S. had no ambitions to annex Cuba, but the nation was heavily divided about the rest. An Anti-Imperialist League sprang up to fight against keeping these foreign lands, but much of the nation was ready to be a world power and take on the "responsibility" of caring for less developed lands.

Eventually, McKinley decided to keep them all. Spain gave Cuba its freedom under U.S. protection. The U.S. took Puerto Rico as the spoils of war (it is still a U.S. territory, not a state) and purchased the Philippines for $20 million. The treaty was very controversial, however. It only passed in the Senate by one vote and that only because William Jennings Bryan decided to support it.

Cuba. Cuba remained under U.S. occupation until 1902. During that time, the Americans invested in many helpful improvements for the island. The most significant was to bring yellow fever under control by cleaning up the breeding areas of the disease-carrying mosquitoes. Eventually, Cuba was given its independence, but only after it accepted the Platt Amendment as a part of its constitution. The Platt Amendment restricted Cuba from forming alliances with other nations and gave America the right to intervene on the island to maintain order. In effect, Cuba was free, but only as free as America permitted.

Philippines. A revolt against Spanish rule in the Philippines had been going on before 1898. Its leader, Emilo Aguinaldo, expected his nation to receive its independence after America won the war. When it became clear that was not what McKinley had in mind, Aguinaldo continued his rebellion against the Americans. A bloody, nasty guerrilla war was fought between the two sides until 1901. The Anti-Imperialists were furious at this turnabout of Americans killing men who were fighting for their independence. Eventually, Aguinaldo was captured and the rebellion was broken. The U.S gradually gave the Philippines more home rule in the early 1900s, but the Filipinos would have to wait until 1946 for their independence.

Open Door policy. America soundly defeated one of the old European powers in the Spanish-American War. This war is the point historians use to mark America's transition to a world power. The first test of this new status came in China.

China, unlike Japan, had never embraced Western technology. It was, therefore, a very weak nation at the end of the 1800s. Several European powers were in the process of carving it up into private trading zones. Americans wanted this huge land to be open to all traders.

In 1899, Secretary of State John Hay announced a new "Open Door" policy for China. He asked that all European nations honor China's boundaries and allow everyone to trade freely there. Many of the powers were only marginally interested, but Hays declared the policy established. The Open Door policy was aided by the fact that no one nation had a clear advantage in China and no chance of taking the whole country for themselves. Moreover, the most powerful nation of the day, Britain, also favored free trade in China.

In 1900, the Chinese people tried to drive out the foreigners during the Boxer Rebellion. The U.S. was one of the nations that sent in troops to rescue trapped foreigners in the capital of Beijing. Afterwards, Hay announced America supported an Open Door protecting China's territorial and commercial independence. This policy was largely successful, since China was never divided up into colonies. Many nations traded with her up until World War II. America was now acting on a larger stage than just the Western Hemisphere.

Match these people.

2.72	_____ Theodore Roosevelt	a. led Filipino revolt against Spain and U.S.
2.73	_____ Alfred Mahan	b. Secretary of State
2.74	_____ Pascual Cervera	c. wrote *The Influence of Sea Power on History*
2.75	_____ William R. Hearst	d. Confederate general, fought in Spanish-American War for the U.S.
2.76	_____ Joseph Wheeler	
2.77	_____ William J. Bryan	e. Rough Riders' leader
2.78	_____ Emilo Aguinaldo	f. newspaper owner
2.79	_____ John Hay	g. defeated Spanish fleet, Manila Bay
2.80	_____ George Dewey	h. Spanish admiral, Santiago fleet
		i. supported Spanish treaty to use as a campaign issue in 1900

Name the item described.

2.81 _____ sensational writing, not very factual, used by the *World* and the *Journal* to encourage war

2.82 _____ battleship that blew up in Havana harbor

2.83 _____ U.S. policy toward China, 1900

2.84 _____ U.S. declared it would not annex Cuba

2.85 _____ bought by U.S. for $20 million

2.86 _____ event that recognized U.S. as a world power

2.87 _____ First United States Volunteer Cavalry

2.88 _____ opposed U.S. keeping land taken in Spanish war

2.89 _____ islands, American planters overthrew Queen Liluokalani

2.90 _____ Chinese tried to drive out foreigners

2.91 _____ disease brought under control by U.S. during Cuban occupation

2.92 _____ part of Cuban constitution that limited its freedom

2.93 _____ hill taken by the Rough Riders

2.94 _____ island taken by U.S. forces on July 25, 1898

2.95 _____ approximate length of the Spanish-American War

2.96 _____ city captured by U.S. in Cuba

Review the material in this section in preparation for the Self Test. This Self Test will check your mastery of this particular section as well as your knowledge of the previous section.

SELF TEST 2

Match these people. Some answers will be used more than once (each answer, 2 points).

2.01	_____ Assistant Secretary of the Navy	a. James Garfield
2.02	_____ led the Rough Riders	b. William McKinley
2.03	_____ signed first civil service reform	c. William J. Bryan
2.04	_____ Billion-dollar Congress, Sherman Anti-Trust Act	d. Chester A. Arthur
2.05	_____ first Democratic president after Civil War	e. Theodore Roosevelt
2.06	_____ Populist candidate	f. James Blaine
2.07	_____ served two non-consecutive terms	g. Benjamin Harrison
2.08	_____ shot by angry office seeker	h. Grover Cleveland
2.09	_____ "Cross of Gold" speech	
2.010	_____ protegé of Senator Roscoe Conkling, ran N.Y. Custom House until fired	
2.011	_____ Republican Half-Breed faction leader	
2.012	_____ made vice presidential candidate to win Stalwart support	
2.013	_____ strong reformer, improved the tarnished image of the presidency	
2.014	_____ Republican candidate, never became president	
2.015	_____ Democratic party leader for years after 1896	

Answer these questions (each answer, 3 points).

2.016 What was the emotional issue of the working people in the late 1800s?

a. _____

What did they think it would accomplish?

b. _____

2.017 Between the Civil War and the Spanish-American War, what did the army do?

_____

2.018 What is the philosophy that government should leave business alone?

_____

2.019 What nation's revolt led America into war with Spain?

_____

2.020 What event marked the establishment of the U.S. as a world power?

_____

2.021 What was the movement that grew out of the Farmer's Alliances combining the demands of several reform movements? _____

2.022 What was the main source of American revenue in the late 1800s that businessmen strongly supported? _____

2.023 What did the Billion-dollar Congress do with the surplus?

_____

2.024 What was the nation's first major union movement? _____

Choose the best match. Each answer is used only once (each answer, 2 points).

2.025 _____ limited Cuban freedom

2.026 _____ gave away free land to settlers

2.027 _____ Rockefeller's trust

2.028 _____ allowed the plains to be settled quickly

2.029 _____ basis of U.S. approach to Chinese trade

2.030 _____ civil service reform

2.031 _____ written to control the railroads

2.032 _____ idea that the poor are poor because they are inferior people

2.033 _____ Carnegie used Bessemer process

2.034 _____ used against unions in restraint of trade

a. Sherman Anti-Trust Act

b. Interstate Commerce Act

c. Standard Oil

d. Social Darwinism

e. Railroads

f. Steel production

g. Pendleton Act

h. Platt Amendment

i. Homestead Act

j. Open Door policy

Answer true or false (each answer, 2 points).

2.035	_____	The Gilded Age was a time of progress and reform.
2.036	_____	Most of the presidents of the Gilded Age were outstanding leaders.
2.037	_____	The AFL emphasized labor issues such as wages and hours.
2.038	_____	McKinley was a very pro-business president.
2.039	_____	The Spanish-American War lasted almost a year.
2.040	_____	Farmers wanted controls on the railroads.
2.041	_____	New Immigrants came from south and eastern Europe.
2.042	_____	Republicans after the Civil War gave away a tremendous amount of money in pensions to gain the political support of veterans.
2.043	_____	The U.S. peacefully took control of the Philippines.
2.044	_____	Striking unions were opposed by the law, the government and the corporations during the Gilded Age.
2.045	_____	Living and working conditions for immigrant industrial workers were usually excellent.
2.046	_____	The destruction of the U.S. fleet in Manila made America go to war with Spain.

80 / 100   SCORE _____   TEACHER _____ _____
initials   date

3. THE PROGRESSIVE ERA

The pressure for reforms had been building since the end of the Civil War. It finally blew the lid off the kettle of traditionalism in the early 20th century. Between about 1900 and 1917, America faced a storm of reforms that touched political, social, and economic life. It was called the Progressive Era, and it had no precedent in American history.

Americans had always been champions of small government. For all of its one hundred and twenty-year existence, the Revolutionary spirit that had driven out the British had opposed large, powerful governments. The basic opinion of most Americans was that the job of government was to stay out of people's way. The restricted government that easily managed a nation of farmers and small business could not control the power of corporate trusts, the exploitation of friendless workers, and the corruption of political machines. Either the government had to expand to control these things, or it had to accept being controlled by them.

The Progressive Movement was the end result of a series of reform movements that had gained increasing respect in the late 1800s. It began with the Grange which passed its demands onto the Farmer's Alliances and then on to the Populists. The difference was that the Progressives succeeded! They started with reforms in the place that needed them most, the cities. The movement expanded into states and, under the leadership of dynamic Theodore Roosevelt, jumped into the national arena. This section will study this remarkable period.

SECTION OBJECTIVES

Review these objectives. When you have completed this section, you should be able to:

1. Describe the development of unions and reform movements from 1865 to 1915.
2. Describe the course of the Progressive Movement.
3. Describe the personality of Theodore Roosevelt and his effect on the presidency.
4. Name the Progressive presidents and describe their policies.

VOCABULARY

Study these words to enhance your learning success in this section.

adulteration (ə dəl tə rā′ shən). Making something impure by adding foreign or inferior substances, especially by replacing valuable ingredients with less costly inferior ones.

libel (lī′ bəl). The publication of false written statements that harm a person's reputation to a degree that he can sue for damages.

recall (ri kol′). The right by which an official may be removed by the vote of the people.

referendum (ref ə ren′ dəm). Submitting a proposal to a popular vote.

suffrage (səf′ rij). The right of voting.

Roosevelt

Progressive birth. The Progressive Movement was a widespread and unusual reform movement. It did not have any one single leader. The work was accomplished by many people in many different places and walks of life. The early 1900s were very prosperous times for America and it was remarkable that such a large reform movement would happen then. Prosperous people do not usually demand major changes from their government and society, but in the early 1900s they did.

The reforms began in the cities in the 1890s. The depression in 1893 had caused tremendous suffering in the cities and starkly emphasized the need for changes. City governments were run by party bosses who traded city jobs and contracts for profit and votes. Honest men normally stayed away. That began to change as angry voters in city after city voted for reformers beginning in the late-1890s. Machines in cities like Detroit, Toledo, New York, St. Louis and San Francisco fell to reformers.

| La Follette

The new city governments had wide support among the middle class, which was the mainstay of the Progressive Movement. They used that support to change the way Gilded Age cities had been run. One of the first changes was in the area of public utilities. Electricity, gas, water, and garbage pickup were all handled by private companies. The Gilded Age city machines sold the right to supply these services, took bribes on the sales and allowed the company to charge whatever it could, regardless of the quality of service! The reformers ended the sale of public services for bribes and placed those services under more effective control. Other city reforms included using experts, not politicians, to run the city by appointing city managers. Action was also taken against unsafe housing, prostitution, and political and police corruption.

An excellent example of the city reformer was Samuel Jones, mayor of Toledo. "Golden Rule"

Jones was a wealthy businessman who treated his employees as he would want to be treated. He took that idea with him into city management in 1897. He required open bidding for city contracts, initiated civil service reform, and led drives for more parks, schools, and city facilities. He so infuriated his party's bosses that he had to run as an independent, but he continued to be re-elected until his death.

State reforms. Many of the states were also hit with the effects of Progressivism. The model for the new movement was Wisconsin, under the leadership of Governor Robert La Follette. The Wisconsin state government had, like most, been dominated by a few powerful state industries (railroads in Wisconsin). La Follette was elected governor in 1900 and proceeded to work steadily for reforms. He established a system of primary elections for candidates, which meant that the party bosses and the railroads could no longer choose the candidates.

He established an effective railroad commission to control rates within the state. He forced the railroads to pay taxes on the full value of their holdings. He also initiated state civil service reform.

The "Wisconsin Idea" spread to other states. In California, Hiram Johnson broke the Southern Pacific Railroad's control over state politics. Charles Evans Hughes pushed similar reforms in New York. Reform movements succeeded in Oregon, Iowa, Kansas, Minnesota, North Dakota, and Missouri. Even in states where they did not take the governor's office, the Progressives often were able to get enough votes in the legislature to force some reforms. Secret ballots, primary elections, voter **referendums, recall** elections, tax reform, and regulatory commissions became common as the people demanded their government be returned to them.

Muckraking. Writers added fuel to the flames with their popular stories of corruption and scandal. Roosevelt named them "Muckrakers" for a character in the book *Pilgrim's Progress* who was so busy digging in the muck that he never saw the crown above his head. T.R. meant it as a criticism, but the Muckrakers proudly took on the name and kept themselves busy in the nation's mud holes.

The main Muckrakers were popular magazines who discovered that these articles sold well. *McClure's*, *Munsey's*, *Cosmopolitan*, and *Collier's* were among the magazines that competed for the most sensational stories. Careful of the powerful men they were attacking and the **libel** laws, the articles were well- researched and carefully documented. The writers exposed corruption in government, bribery by businesses, the abuses of child labor, the **adulteration** of medicines, and the conditions of the poor. One of the most famous, the *History of the Standard Oil Company*, by Ida Tarbell, used public documents and interviews to prove that the company had succeeded using bribery, extortion, and ruthlessness.

The public ate up these articles. The constant supply of information about the abuses around them pushed the reform movement. The Muckrakers and the Progressives fed each other. The writers provided the proof and motivation the reformers needed. The reformers provided the reading audience the writers needed.

Anti-liquor movement. Part of the Progressive Movement was an active temperance campaign. Reformers saw alcohol as the basis of many of the vices of the city (similar to drug addiction today). The leading groups in this battle were the Woman's Christian Temperance Union and the Anti-Saloon League. The latter was well organized and financed. It attacked liquor sales at their most obvious and despised source, the local saloon. Under pressure from these reformers, many "dry" laws outlawing, regulating, and restricting the sale of alcohol were passed. Eventually, the movement was rewarded with the 18th Amendment in 1919 which outlawed liquor sales in all of the United States until its repeal in 1933.

Election of 1900. McKinley, as the popular leader of a victorious nation, easily won the Republican nomination in 1900. The dynamic Theodore Roosevelt, who had returned from the war to become governor of New York, was chosen as his running mate. The Democrats nominated William Jennings Bryan again. Even though it was a dead issue, Bryan insisted on a free silver plank in the party platform. McKinley again stayed on his front porch while the popular T.R. toured the nation. The Republicans campaigned for "Four more years of a full dinner pail." Bryan tried to campaign against imperialism but lost the election by a larger margin than in 1896.

Roosevelt was deliberately put into the vice presidency to make use of his popular appeal and keep him powerless. He was an independent, energetic man who quickly became a Progressive leader. The party bosses in New York supported his move to the ceremonial job of vice president to get him out of their state. However, as Marcus Hanna realized, the "cowboy" was now only one heartbeat from the presidency. The boss' fears were realized when McKinley was assassinated in September of 1901 by an anarchist. The Progressive Movement had its first president.

Theodore Roosevelt (1858-1919). Theodore Roosevelt revitalized the office of the presidency. He was a man of boundless energy, self-confidence, and bravado. He loved a good fight and was immensely popular. He had a personal following that rivaled Andrew Jackson's. He remade the presidency in his own image and left it as one of the most powerful offices in the world. He is considered to be among our nation's greatest presidents.

Roosevelt was born to a wealthy New York City family. He was a sickly child who overcame his own ill health by forceful exercise. He developed a tremendous love for the "strenuous life." He was an athlete and an avid outdoorsman the rest of his life. He was tutored at home until he went to Harvard in 1876. After college, he went into politics as a Republican. He served in the state legislature and worked for reforms with then Governor Grover Cleveland.

Tragedy struck T.R.'s life in 1884. His young wife died in childbirth, and on the same day his mother died. Roosevelt resigned from politics and moved West to live on some ranches he owned. He worked as a cowboy with his men. The long hours and hard work helped him recover from his grief. At first, his men thought he was a silly dude, but his willingness to work hard and his ability to fight with his fists soon won their respect.

He returned to New York in 1886 to run for mayor of New York City and lost. He served on the Civil Service Commission and as police commissioner in New York City. He proved to be an honest reformer in both jobs. Roosevelt campaigned for McKinley in 1896 and was rewarded with a position as assistant secretary of the navy. He resigned at the beginning of the Spanish-American War to organize the

| Theodore Roosevelt

Rough Riders. His exploits in the war added to his growing reputation and enabled him to win election as the governor of New York. From there, he was moved up to the vice presidency. McKinley's death made him president at the young age of 42, and he quickly became a favorite with the newspapers. He lived up to his image as a reformer, leader, and devoted family man.

T.R. had remarried in 1886 after he returned from the West. He and his new wife, Edith Carow, had five children. Edith also raised T.R.'s daughter from his first marriage, Alice (named after her dead mother). The Roosevelts' lively household was part of their father's popularity. He loved his children and played wild games with them on the White House lawn. Stories of the boys sliding down the White House banister and bringing a pony upstairs only added to his colorful presidency. T.R. was a man who enjoyed living and the public ate it up. The "Teddy Bear" was a measure of his popularity. It quickly became a best-selling toy after Roosevelt sportingly refused to shoot a captured bear cub on one of his hunting trips.

Reform. Roosevelt was astute enough to realize he had to work with the leaders of the Republican Party. Therefore, he reassured them that he would follow McKinley's policies and then set off to carefully form his own. His approach to government was what he called the "Square Deal." Everyone did not get the best cards in the game, but the dealing must be done fairly. He began by going against the trusts which had grown fat and prosperous under McKinley's presidency.

T.R. created a sensation in 1902 when he ordered the rarely used Sherman Anti-Trust Act into action. Suit was brought against Northern Securities Company, a J.P. Morgan holding company that controlled most of the railroads in the Northwest. The case went all the way to the Supreme Court. In 1904 the Court ruled against the company and forced it to dissolve. It was the first significant victory for the "trust busters." Roosevelt initiated more than forty such actions during his presidency, and he won a respectable percentage of them; but he did not move against many of the trusts. He used the threat of anti-trust action to force the corporations to accept more regulation, which they did.

Roosevelt was the first president since the Civil War who actually led the government. He proposed legislation and followed it through the process. Today, we expect that of a president. It was T.R. who established the custom.

One of his first laws was the Elkins Act of 1903 which prohibited rebates (still a problem) by railroads. The law imposed heavy fines on <u>both</u> the railroad and the shipper who participated in a rebate scheme. Standard Oil was one of the companies fined under the law.

An even more effective law was the Hepburn Act of 1906. This gave some teeth to the powerless Interstate Commerce Commission. The I.C.C. was expanded and given the power to set rates, if shippers complained. The railroads could still challenge in court (they had tied up previous decisions for years that way), but under the Hepburn Act, the I.C.C. rates held until the court made its decision, and the railroad, not the government, had to prove its case.

Name the item, term, or person.

3.1 _____ wrote stories about corruption and social evils

3.2 _____ government level where Progressive Movement began

3.3 _____ state that lead in Progressive reform

3.4 _____ law prohibiting rebates

3.5 _____ first major success of Sherman Anti-Trust Act

3.6 _____ toy named after Theodore Roosevelt

3.7 _____ author of the *History of Standard Oil Company*

3.8 _____ McKinley's campaign promised four more years of it

3.9 _____ T.R.'s approach to government

3.10 _____ law that gave the I.C.C. some power

3.11 _____ reform governor of Wisconsin

3.12 _____ reform mayor of Toledo

3.13 _____ event that emphasized the need for city reforms

3.14 _____ two groups that led the temperance movement

Complete these items.

3.15 Why did the party bosses support Roosevelt's nomination as vice president?

_____

_____

3.16 Name eight of the reforms of the Progressive Movement.

a. _____   b. _____

c. _____   d. _____

e. _____   f. _____

g. _____   h. _____

3.17 How did Theodore Roosevelt change the presidency?

_____

_____

1902 Coal Strike. Roosevelt also exemplified the growing Progressive concern for the working man. In 1902 the hard coal miners of Pennsylvania went on strike. These were men who had been shamelessly exploited for years by low wages, high rent, dangerous conditions, and long hours. The United Mine Workers Union was careful to keep the strike peaceful and thereby gained public sympathy for the strikers. The mine owners, however, refused to negotiate. Coal was the nation's major source of heat, and the situation grew desperate as winter approached and coal supplies ran low.

Roosevelt, unlike the presidents before him, did not automatically side with the owner. As a crisis loomed, he brought both sides to the White House and offered to arbitrate. The United Mine Workers agreed; the owners refused. T.R. furiously threatened to send in the army to mine the coal. That threat turned the tide. The owners agreed and the miners went to work, pending the decision of the arbitrators. The arbitrators gave the miners some but not all of what they wanted. It was not a total victory, but for the first time the government had given the workers a fair hearing. It was a significant turning point for labor, although their battle was far from completed.

Roosevelt also recognized that the problems with corporations and labor unions required more supervision. In 1903 he convinced Congress to establish the Department of Commerce and Labor. Among other things, this new organization investigated corporations and laid the groundwork for later trust busting.

Conservation. For generations, Americans had used their resources as if they were limitless. In the early 1900s, with the end of the frontier, many far sighted individuals realized the nation needed to conserve its resources. T.R., the hunter and avid outdoorsman, was an early leader in the conservation movement. Roosevelt set aside millions of acres of forest land, water sources, and mineral lands for public, not private, use. The Newlands Act of 1902 set up a fund from land sales for Western irrigation projects. Roosevelt wanted the land used carefully and scientifically in a manner that would make it productive for many years. The nation no longer had an endless supply of new land. T.R. realized that we had to take care of what we had.

Big Stick in Panama. America had been hoping for years to build a canal across Central America. Such a canal would save thousands of miles and weeks of travel for ships going from the east to the West Coast. After the Spanish-American War, the new territories in the Pacific seemed particularly vulnerable without a quick way to get the navy from one ocean to another to protect them.

An old British-American treaty required the two nations to share ownership of any such canal. Obviously, times had changed and the now powerful U.S. was not willing to share such an American canal with anyone. The British recognized this and signed the Hay-Pauncefote Treaty in 1901. It gave the U.S. full rights to any canal as well as the right to fortify it. In exchange, the Americans promised that the canal would be open to all nations.

Roosevelt was not a man to wait on any important issue. A French company had tried to build a canal across Panama and failed. It offered its holdings to the U.S. government for the very low price of $40 million. After deciding against an alternate route through Nicaragua, a treaty was negotiated with Colombia which owned Panama. The treaty would have given the U.S. a permanent lease on a six-mile wide strip of land needed for the canal. America offered to pay $10 million up front and $250,000 a year for the lease.

The Colombian congress rejected the treaty. Roosevelt was furious. His philosophy in foreign affairs was based on a proverb, "Speak softly and carry a big stick, you will go far." Colombia was about to feel the weight of his "Big Stick."

| Construction of the Locks on the Panama Canal, 1910

| Modern-Day picture of the Canal

Panama had revolted against Colombia a number of times in the past. With the encouragement of a representative of the French canal company, they did so again in November of 1903. This time the American navy stopped the Colombians from coming in to put down the revolt. Roosevelt recognized the revolutionary government at once and sent them the same treaty he had offered Colombia (the only change was the canal zone was now ten miles wide). It was immediately accepted.

The Americans did succeed in building the massive canal under the leadership of George W. Goethals, a West Point engineer. He was aided by Colonel William Gorgas who had eliminated yellow fever in Cuba. This intrepid medical pioneer made the disease-ridden canal zone safe for the thousands of men needed to complete the project. The canal cost $400 million to build and opened in 1914, just in time for World War I. The rough handling of Colombia, however, soured American relations with Latin America, leaving a dark blot on an otherwise momentous accomplishment.

Roosevelt Corollary. T.R. added his own "corollary" to the Monroe Doctrine, which warned Europeans to stay out of the American nations.

Roosevelt's addition was that if any American nation were doing something wrong, the U.S. would intervene as a type of policeman so that Europe would not have to do so. This corollary came out of debt problems in Latin America.

Venezuela had defaulted on its debts to Europe in the early 1900s. Germany and Britain, therefore, blockaded its ports and bombarded a city in 1902 to force the nation to honor its just debts. The American public was aroused over this "violation" of the Monroe Doctrine. Roosevelt stepped in and was able to arrange arbitration to settle that issue.

In 1904, however, Santa Domingo (Dominican Republic) also found itself unable to pay its debts. Fearful of another European attack in America's backyard, Roosevelt decided to act. He published his "corollary" and used it to justify moving American officials to the island to take charge of its finances. The U.S. took over the custom houses in Santa Domingo, the main source of revenue. The Americans then used the money to make payments on the debts for almost forty years. This heavy-handed use of the Monroe Doctrine would be American policy in the Caribbean through the 1920s.

Election of 1904. Roosevelt longed to be elected president on his own to prove he was more than a political accident. The bosses really did not want to nominate him in 1904, but the death of Marcus Hanna left them without another candidate. T.R. received the nomination. The Democrats bypassed two-time loser Bryan and nominated Alton Parker, a New York judge. Roosevelt campaigned for his "square deal" and won by the largest popular majority to date.

Second administration. Roosevelt's major reform laws in his second administration were the Hepburn Act (discussed earlier) as well as food and drug acts. The latter had been inspired by the Upton Sinclair novel, *The Jungle*. One of the most famous Muckraker works, *The Jungle* exposed the incredibly gross and unsanitary conditions in the meat-packing industry. An investigation ordered by Roosevelt confirmed the worst of it. Roosevelt responded with the Meat Inspection Act that required meat packers to submit to federal health inspections. A follow-up bill, the Pure Food and Drug Act, set standards for processed foods and medicines.

Roosevelt's popularity faced a serious test when speculation caused a panic in 1907. The corporations immediately blamed Roosevelt and his reform policy; but it was a short depression that affected mainly the banking industry, and Roosevelt emerged from it as popular as ever. It did pave the way for currency reform, however. It became clear during the panic that the nation needed a way to expand the supply of money in a crisis. (On the gold standard, a nation cannot easily increase its money supply without getting more gold.) Congress passed a law that allowed national banks to issue currency in an emergency, using different backing.

Russo-Japanese War. Russia had been expanding in the Far East for years. Japan watched in alarm as the great bear reached into Manchuria (northern China) and Korea. Fearful of the czar's intentions, Japan attacked the Russian fleet at Port Arthur (west of Korea) in 1904,

| Big Stick in the Caribbean cartoon

destroying it. The resulting war gave Japan a series of rapid victories that humiliated Imperial Russia. Japan was too weak to continue the war and quietly asked Roosevelt to mediate in 1905.

Roosevelt knew it would be a thankless job, but he agreed to bring the combatants to the U.S. for talks. He put on the pressure until an agreement was reached that both accepted and neither liked. Japan thought she did not get enough for her victories and Russia felt the U.S. interfered before she had a chance to win. Thus, Roosevelt won the anger of the two nations, but he was also awarded the 1906 Nobel Peace Prize for his efforts.

Moroccan Crisis. Tensions that would eventually lead to World War I were mounting in Europe. In 1905 Germany refused to recognize French control of Morocco (on the North coast of Africa). Roosevelt stepped in when he realized a general European war was possible. He convinced both sides to meet at a conference in Spain in 1906. There America supported the French claims and Germany backed down, this time.

Gentlemen's Agreement. Roosevelt had other problems with Japan. Japanese immigrants had been coming to the American West Coast in record numbers. In 1906 San Francisco decided to send Japanese children to segregated schools. The Japanese saw this as a racial insult, and it triggered an international crisis. Roosevelt had no official power over the decisions of a city school board and yet it had the potential to start a war. The president eventually worked out a plan. Under a "Gentlemen's Agreement," the school board rescinded its order and the diplomats settled California's fear of large scale Asian immigration. The secret agreement was that Japan would limit the number of people it allowed to leave for America. This set relations with Japan on a more even keel for the time being.

Great White Fleet. Roosevelt was concerned that the Japanese might interpret his willingness to negotiate as an inability to fight. Therefore, he sent part of the U.S. navy (now the second largest on earth) on a tour around the world in 1907. The tour of the "Great White Fleet" was a resounding success. The ships were greeted by cheering crowds all over the world, including Japan. It returned in triumph in 1909 just as Roosevelt retired from the presidency.

Complete these sentences.

3.18 The _____ Act used money from sale of Western lands to finance irrigation projects.

3.19 The 1904 Democratic candidate for president was _____ .

3.20 The novel that brought food and drug reform was _____ by _____ .

3.21 In 1902 Panama was a part of _____ .

3.22 Theodore Roosevelt's foreign policy was based on the proverb, "Speak softly and carry a _____ ."

3.23 Roosevelt won the Noble Peace Prize for negotiating an end to the _____ .

3.24 The _____ Crisis of 1905 almost started a war in Europe.

3.25 The nation faced a panic under Roosevelt in _____ .

3.26 Roosevelt recognized the need for more control over corporations and workers when he created the Department of _____ .

3.27 The _____ to the Monroe Doctrine said the U.S. would correct wrongs in American nations to prevent European intervention.

3.28 Japan began a war in 1904 by attacking the Russian fleet at

_____ .

3.29 The _____ toured the world between 1907 and 1909.

3.30 _____ was the engineer in charge of construction of the

Panama Canal.

3.31 The Panama Canal cost _____ and opened in _____ .

3.32 Japan and America had a crisis in 1906 when San Francisco decided to

_____ .

3.33 The U.S. took over the custom houses on _____ to pay that

nation's debts.

3.34 Germany and Britain blockaded _____ in 1902 after it failed to

pay its debts.

3.35 _____ eliminated yellow fever in Cuba and in the canal zone.

3.36 The _____ Act required federal health inspections of

meat-packing plants.

3.37 The _____ Act set standards for processed food and medicine.

Answer these questions.

3.38 How did Roosevelt handle the 1902 hard coal strike?

_____

_____

_____

3.39 How did America get the Panama canal lease after Colombia refused it?

_____

_____

_____

3.40 What was the Gentlemen's Agreement that ended the crisis between the U.S. and Japan in

1906? _____

_____

_____

Taft

Election of 1908. Roosevelt had promised not to run in 1908, and he felt bound by that promise even though he was only 50 years old. However, he was so incredibly popular that, like Andrew Jackson, he was able to name his successor. He named his friend, Secretary of War William H. Taft, as the man he wanted to continue his policies. Roosevelt used his big stick to force Taft's nomination through on the first ballot at the party convention. The Democrats nominated William J. Bryan again. Taft won easily, largely on Roosevelt's popularity. Roosevelt took off on an extended hunting trip in Africa. His big business enemies toasted the good health of the lions.

William Howard Taft (1857-1930). William Howard Taft never wanted to be president. What he did want to be was a Supreme Court justice. He had a good legal mind and enjoyed being a judge. However, he had an ambitious wife, and his family was active in Republican politics. Therefore, he got into several political jobs that eventually led him to the White House.

Taft was born in Ohio, the son of a lawyer who was a prominent Republican. Taft attended Cincinnati Law School and was admitted to the Ohio bar in 1880. He became a successful lawyer, but his family pushed him toward a political career. He was appointed to and then elected to the Cincinnati Superior Court. He later served as a federal attorney and a federal court of appeals judge.

In 1900 he was appointed by McKinley as part of a commission to govern the Philippines and later he became the territory's first American governor. Taft did some of his best work in the Philippines. He built schools, roads, and harbor facilities. He arranged new courts, set up government offices for record keeping, pushed for land reform, and encouraged the development of limited self-government. The public took note of his work, and in 1904 Roosevelt had him take over as secretary of war in his cabinet.

| Taft Campaigning

Taft proved equally capable as a cabinet member. He worked well with Roosevelt and proved to be a capable administrator. Roosevelt felt comfortable leaving him in control when he retired. Taft, however, was a large, amiable man (he weighed over 300 pounds) who was ill suited to follow the energetic Roosevelt in office. Taft was a good man and a good administrator, but he lacked Roosevelt's drive, his zeal for reform, and his public flair. The result was disappointing, to the nation and to the president.

Republican Problems. Roosevelt had been the leader of the Progressive Republicans, and he gave their support to Taft when he retired. Taft promptly alienated them. The Republican platform had called for tariff reform, and Taft called a special session of Congress in 1909 to do that. Tariff reduction passed the House but was torpedoed by amendments in the Senate. The resulting Payne-Aldrich Tariff lowered only a few rates slightly. The Progressives were furious. Taft made matters worse by signing the bill and then defending it as the "best bill that the Republican Party ever passed."

Taft lost even more Progressive support over the fight between Secretary of the Interior Richard Ballinger, and the chief of the Division of Forestry, Gifford Pinchot, a Roosevelt pal and conservationist. Roosevelt had used his authority to prevent the sale of water sources and mineral lands on dubious legal grounds. Ballinger reversed some of these decisions and put the land up for sale. Pinchot accused Ballinger and the administration of turning against T.R.'s policies, favoring the corporations (who wanted the land), and making the sales illegally. A congressional investigation cleared Ballinger of the charges and Taft dismissed Pinchot. Progressives saw it as another failure by Taft to support their agenda.

The Progressives also wanted the president's support to break the power of Joseph Cannon, the dictatorial Speaker of the House of Representatives. The Progressives of the two parties were finally able to do so by joining forces. They stripped Cannon of his power to control legislation in the House that he had used to block reform laws. Taft did not support the effort, and the Progressives no longer counted him as one of their own.

Roosevelt returned from abroad and helped to split the Republicans further in 1910. He made fiery speeches in favor of "New Nationalism" in which the government would control political and social problems. The division in the party gave the Democrats control of the House in 1910 and weakened Republican control of the Senate.

Taft did have several successes in the continuing Progressive reform. His administration started almost twice as many anti-trust suits as Roosevelt had. Standard Oil and the American Tobacco Company were ordered to dissolve by the Supreme Court in 1911. Moreover, the new Democratic House began an investigation into the control Wall Street bankers had over corporations (the so-called "Money Trust"). It revealed a great deal about the way Morgan had spread

| The Wright Brothers and Their First Flight

his power by gaining control of companies that used his bank for loans. Moreover, under Taft, Congress passed the Sixteenth (allowed income tax) and Seventeenth (direct election of senators) Amendments to the Constitution.

Dollar Diplomacy. Taft's foreign policy was called "Dollar Diplomacy." The idea was to use American money as a way to expand U.S. influence abroad. Taft encouraged investment in Manchuria, the Caribbean, Panama, and Central America. It did not have any significant results. For example, Taft tried to get a U.S.-built railroad in China but failed when Japan and Russia would not cooperate. Taft also failed in an attempt to get mutual tariff reductions with Canada in 1911. Relations with the rest of the Americas remained tense as Taft used U.S. troops to quell disorder in the Caribbean and Nicaragua. Thus, Taft was left with a divided party, an unsuccessful foreign policy, and growing opposition from T.R. by the end of his term.

Technology advances. Two key advances in travel hit the U.S. during the Progressive Era, the airplane and the automobile. Orville and Wilbur Wright succeeded in the first powered airplane flight on December 17, 1903. It would be many years, however, before this new technology could be used on a large scale.

Automobiles, however, were poised to begin their takeover of the American road. The automobile had been invented in Europe, but it came to the people in America. The same year the Wright brothers first flew, Henry Ford organized the Ford Motor Company. Ford succeeded in using the moving assembly line to make cars faster and cheaper than ever before. His Model T became the first popular American car by bringing the price down within the reach of most Americans. (A Model T cost $390 in 1915 and $260 in 1925). Other companies took notice, and the industry soon expanded to a leading position in American manufacturing, eventually replacing the railroads.

Bull Moose Party. Robert La Follette, who had led the reforms in Wisconsin and was now a U.S. senator, formed the National Progressive Republican League in 1911. The League was pushing to get the Republican nomination for La Follette instead of Taft. In early 1912 Theodore Roosevelt, furious with Taft for abandoning his policies, decided he would run again. La Follette could not compete with the Rough Rider's popularity and quickly lost his support.

T.R. easily won most of the new primary elections, but Taft was now angry and put up an unusually strong fight. As president, Taft had the votes of the delegates outside the primary system, and he controlled the party machinery at the convention. Moreover, T.R. had frightened the milder Progressives with some of his demands, which included a scheme to control judicial decisions (a very radical idea). Thus, Taft won the nomination on the first vote. Roosevelt and his followers yelled fraud and left to form their own party.

The Progressive Party convention in August of 1912 nominated Theodore Roosevelt for president. T.R. claimed he felt "as strong as a Bull Moose" and gave the party its popular name, the Bull Moose Party. The party platform favored all the traditional Progressive reforms plus women's **suffrage**, minimum wage laws, government pensions, unemployment compensation, and control of the stock market. It was a radical platform and more than most Americans wanted.

The Election of 1912. The Republicans and the Progressives were obviously going to split the Republican vote. The Democrats realized they had an excellent chance to win the White House if they could select a decent candidate. They chose Woodrow Wilson, the reform governor of New Jersey. Wilson campaigned for a reform package he called the "New Freedom." Wilson emphasized the need to enforce anti-trust legislation and allow businesses to compete freely without monopolies. He did not favor adding extensively to the power of the federal government as the Bull Moose platform did.

The result was inevitable. Wilson won with 41% of the popular vote and a huge electoral majority (435 votes). Roosevelt took 27% of the popular vote and 88 electoral votes. Taft had the worst defeat in history for a president running for re-election. He won 23% of the popular vote and only 8 electoral votes. Taft happily retired and eventually did sit on the Supreme Court.

Name the person(s) related to each item.

3.41 _____ Dollar Diplomacy

3.42 _____ Bull Moose Party

3.43 _____ New Freedom

3.44 _____ 1908 Democratic candidate

3.45 _____ New Nationalism

3.46 _____ first powered airplane flight

3.47 _____ worst loss for president seeking re-election

3.48 _____ organized Republican Progressive League

3.49 _____ dictatorial Speaker of the House

3.50 _____ Model T

3.51 _____ Roosevelt's hand-picked successor

3.52 _____ governor of the Philippines

3.53 _____ Supreme Court justice

3.54 _____ used moving assembly line to make cheap cars

3.55 _____ secretary of the interior, reversed some of T.R.'s bans on sale of land

3.56 _____ Sixteenth and Seventeenth Amendments

3.57 _____ Progressive Party presidential candidate

3.58 _____ fired for accusations against the secretary of the interior

Answer these questions.

3.59 What three events cost Taft his support from Progressive Republicans?

a. _____ b. _____

c. _____

3.60 What was the purpose of Dollar Diplomacy? _____

_____

3.61 What were four of the planks in the Progressive Party platform?

a. _____ b. _____

c. _____ d. _____

3.62 What sort of an anti-trust record did Taft have? _____

_____

_____

Wilson

Woodrow Wilson (1856-1924). Woodrow Wilson was one of America's most successful and respected presidents. He was born in Virginia, the son of a Presbyterian minister. He grew up in Georgia and North Carolina during the Civil War Era and had Southern sympathies all his life. He graduated from Princeton in 1879. He tried a career in law before becoming a college professor, an expert in the theory of politics. He became the president of Princeton University in 1902 and quickly became well-known for his reform efforts there.

His reputation attracted the attention of the New Jersey Democratic bosses who needed an honest candidate for governor. They offered Wilson the nomination in 1910, and he accepted with the understanding the bosses would not influence his decisions. Wilson won the election and quickly transformed New Jersey into a Progressive state. Primaries, anti-corruption laws, corporate regulation, and other reforms were signed by the governor. His growing national reputation, and the fact he gained the support

| Woodrow Wilson and His Wife

of William J. Bryan, won Wilson the Democratic nomination and the presidency in 1912.

Wilson's reforms. Wilson was, like T.R. before him, an active leader and unusually successful in getting what he wanted from Congress. Three goals reached by Wilson were tariff reform, banking reform, and stronger anti-trust legislation. He started with the tariff. The Democrats had never been tied as tightly to the tariff as the Republicans so the new Democratic Congress was open to reductions.

Wilson took the lead by going to Congress in person to speak for the bill (no president since Jefferson had done that). The Underwood Tariff Bill was passed in 1913. It was the first major reduction of the tariff since the Civil War. Wilson got it past the Senate by a direct appeal to the American people. The new law reduced the overall tariff rates, eliminated duties on many items (raw wool, steel rails, sugar, and others), and set up an income tax to replace the lost revenue.

Wilson also made a personal appeal to Congress for banking reform. The nation needed a banking system that could expand the money supply to meet the demand. Bankers wanted a private system of banks tied closely to the money trust that controlled the nation's financial center at Wall Street in New York City. Reformers and agricultural representatives like Bryan (now secretary of state) wanted a government-owned system.

The Federal Reserve System, created in 1913, was a compromise. The twelve Federal Reserve Banks that served the system were privately owned, but the controlling Federal Reserve Board was government appointed. The new system allowed for more control and stability in the banking system. It also allowed the Federal Reserve Board to expand the money supply as needed. It has served the nation well and continues to operate today.

The last major item on Wilson's card was anti-trust legislation. The Clayton Anti-Trust Act of 1914 tried to fill holes in the Sherman Act. It also exempted unions from anti-trust laws, a much-needed reform. The Federal Trade Commission was also established to prevent trusts. The commission used its powers to order corporations to "cease and desist" from actions that were leading toward monopolies.

Wilson's administration also saw many other reforms. Laws were passed creating loans for farmers, requiring better treatment of sailors, providing income for disabled federal workers, restricting child labor, and setting an eight-hour day for railroad workers. Thus, Wilson was probably America's most successful Progressive president.

Foreign problems. Wilson was an idealist who did not favor using money or military to expand American power. He did not like Dollar Diplomacy and immediately stopped pressing Wall Street for foreign loans and investments. However, in spite of his ideals, he did use the army to deal with disorders in Nicaragua, Haiti, and Santo Domingo. The U.S. increasingly thought of the Caribbean as its own lake. Wilson was successful in expanding self-government in the Philippines in preparation for eventually giving that nation its independence. Wilson and Bryan also settled a dispute with Japan over another anti-Japanese law in California and a dispute with Britain over tolls for the Panama Canal. Thus, Wilson's results in foreign policy were mixed, but his biggest test, before World War I, was Mexico.

Mexico. Mexico had been ruled by a dictator, Díaz, for years before 1910. That year a reform leader of the people, Francisco Madero, became president. He was murdered in 1913 by General Victoriano Huerta just a few weeks before Wilson became president. The resulting disorder threatened American investments and U.S. citizens who lived in Mexico. Wilson refused to intervene. However, he could not stomach a murderer like Huerta, so Wilson refused to recognize Huerta's government and pressed him to resign.

Wilson allowed arms to be sold to Huerta's opponents in the hope of getting rid of him. The situation became severe in 1914 when some American navy sailors were arrested in the Mexican port of Tampico. The men were released, but Huerta refused to salute the U.S. flag as the American admiral demanded. Wilson then asked for and received permission to use force. American troops captured the city of Vera Cruz. This cut off Huerta's supplies and nearly began another Mexican war. At this point, Argentina, Brazil, and Chile offered to mediate. Wilson promptly accepted, and the matter was settled peacefully.

Huerta was finally driven from power in 1914 and was succeeded by Carranza. Carranza found himself fighting his own war with a former ally, "Pancho" Villa. Villa earned American wrath by killing several U.S. citizens in Mexico and then raiding a town in New Mexico in 1916. With Carranza's reluctant permission, General John Pershing pursued Villa deep into Mexico. The expedition failed to capture him and eventually had to withdraw in the face of mounting Mexican hostility. Wilson had tried not to intervene but wound up doing so anyway. He accomplished very little except to further darken relations with Latin America.

Conclusion. The Progressive Movement expanded federal powers into new areas. The old pre-Civil War government that was never involved in private business was gone. The new, huge corporations had proven that they needed government control or they would exploit their wealth and power. The curbs on their power were main focus of the reform movement. It also addressed the social problems (poverty, vice, sanitation) of the growing cities. The Progressive Movement could claim only three presidents, but two of those three, Roosevelt and Wilson, were among the best men ever to hold the office. Even Taft, who did not have their charisma or leadership skills, kept the reforms moving. As a result, the Progressive Movement was a remarkable success.

| Pancho Villa

Anti-trust laws, corporation commissions, labor laws, primary elections, anti-corruption laws, and direct election of senators were among its many results. The ideals of Progressivism became a part of the American system and still exist today. However, the oncoming conflict of World War I, which began in 1914, changed the nation's focus and ended this era.

Complete these sentences.

3.63 Woodrow Wilson refused to recognize the government of General

_____ in Mexico.

3.64 General _____ followed Mexican bandit, _____

_____ , deep into Mexico after he attacked a town in New Mexico.

3.65 _____ ended the Progressive Era.

3.66 Wilson strengthened the anti-trust laws with the _____ Anti-Trust Act.

3.67 Wilson was the first president to appear before Congress to speak for a bill since

_____ .

3.68 The _____ Commission was established to prevent trusts.

3.69 Wilson's three main goals in office were _____ ,

_____ , and _____ .

3.70 The _____ Bill was the first major tariff reduction since the Civil War.

3.71 The Federal Reserve System set up twelve privately owned Federal Reserve Banks that were

controlled by the government appointed _____ .

3.72 Wilson used the army to quell disorders in _____ ,

_____ , and _____ .

3.73 Wilson's Secretary of State was _____ .

3.74 Wilson had been governor of _____ and president of

_____ University.

3.75 The three Progressive presidents were _____ ,

_____ , and _____ .

3.76 Mexico and the U.S. almost went to war in 1914 when some American sailors were arrested

in the city of _____ . The dispute was successfully mediated by

_____ , _____ , and _____ .

Before you take this last Self Test, you may want to do one or more of these self checks.

1. _____ Read the objectives. See if you can do them.
2. _____ Restudy the material related to any objectives that you cannot do.
3. _____ Use the **SQ3R** study procedure to review the material:
   a. **S**can the sections.
   b. **Q**uestion yourself.
   c. **R**ead to answer your questions.
   d. **R**ecite the answers to yourself.
   e. **R**eview areas you did not understand.
4. _____ Review all vocabulary, activities, and Self Tests, writing a correct answer for every wrong answer.

SELF TEST 3

Name the Progressive president (each answer, 2 points).

3.01 _____   vice president, took office when president was assassinated

3.02 _____   Dollar Diplomacy

3.03 _____   mediated the 1902 coal strike without favoring the owners

3.04 _____   Federal Reserve System

3.05 _____   lost Progressive support during his term

3.06 _____   advocate of the "strenuous life"

3.07 _____   former college professor and president

3.08 _____   sent troops into Mexico after Pancho Villa

3.09 _____   messed up tariff reform

3.010 _____   used the "Big Stick" to get canal treaty with Panama

3.011 _____   created the "right" of the U.S. to intervene in other American nations to prevent European intervention

3.012 _____   major tariff reduction

3.013 _____   Nobel Peace Prize for mediating Russo-Japanese War

3.014 _____   supported Richard Ballinger on the sale of government land, fired Gifford Pinchot who objected

3.015 _____   first to really use the Sherman Anti-Trust Act

Complete these sentences (each answer, 3 points).

3.016 Progressive reforms began at the _____ level of government.

3.017 Writers who exposed corruption and social problems were called

_____ .

3.018 William J. Bryan was vaulted to the leadership of the Democratic Party by his

_____ speech at the 1896 convention.

3.019 The _____ marked America's emergence as a world

power.

3.020 Roosevelt's philosophy of government, that everyone should be treated fairly, was called the

_____ .

3.021 _____ was the philosophy, based on evolution, that the poor

were inferior and deserved their poverty.

3.022 The _____ were the first corporate giants in the U.S.

3.023 The _____ were the first national union movement in the U.S.

3.024 The reform movement in between the Farmer's Alliance and the Progressive Movement was

called the _____ .

3.025 After the Civil War, the army fought hundreds of battles with the

_____ .

Choose the correct match for each item (each answer, 2 points).

3.026	_____ Progressive split off Republicans	a.	laissez-faire
3.027	_____ Pure Food and Drug Act	b.	Standard Oil
3.028	_____ California allows Japanese in schools,	c.	*Maine*
	Japan restricts emigration to U.S.	d.	Grange
3.029	_____ no government interference in business	e.	Open Door Policy
3.030	_____ all nations trade freely with China	f.	Hepburn Act
3.031	_____ revenue from land sales goes to irrigation projects	g.	Newlands Act
3.032	_____ most famous trust	h.	*The Jungle*
3.033	_____ explosion began war with Spain	i.	Bull Moose Party
3.034	_____ gave Interstate Commerce Commission some real	j.	Gentlemen's
	power		Agreement
3.035	_____ reform movement, sought debt relief and railroad regulation		

Match these people (each item, 2 points).

3.036	_____	Democratic president; two non-consecutive terms
3.037	_____	led pursuit of Pancho Villa in Mexico
3.038	_____	made fortune in steel; gave much of it away
3.039	_____	Republican leader of Half-Breeds; presidential candidate stained by corruption charges
3.040	_____	made Model T cheaply; using moving assembly line
3.041	_____	eliminated yellow fever; Cuba, Panama
3.042	_____	pro-business president; front porch campaign
3.043	_____	pro-silver coinage; Democratic leader; Wilson's secretary of state
3.044	_____	Wisconsin governor; Progressive leader
3.045	_____	AFL organizer; favored capitalism

a. William J. Bryan

b. William McKinley

c. Andrew Carnegie

d. Samuel Gompers

e. Henry Ford

f. Robert La Follette

g. William Gorgas

h. John Pershing

i. Grover Cleveland

j. James Blaine

80 / 100

SCORE _____ TEACHER _____ _____

initials   date

Before taking the LIFEPAC Test, you may want to do one or more of these self checks.

1. _____ Read the objectives. See if you can do them.
2. _____ Restudy the material related to any objectives that you cannot do.
3. _____ Use the **SQ3R** study procedure to review the material.
4. _____ Review activities, Self Tests, and LIFEPAC vocabulary words.
5. _____ Restudy areas of weakness indicated by the last Self Test.

HISTORY & GEOGRAPHY 807
Gilded Age to Progressive Era (1880–1915)

LIFEPAC Test is located in the center of the booklet. Please remove before starting the unit.

Author:
Theresa Buskey, B.A., J.D.

Editor:
Alan Christopherson, M.S.

Westover Studios Design Team:
Phillip Pettet, Creative Lead
Teresa Davis, DTP Lead
Nick Castro
Andi Graham
Jerry Wingo

804 N. 2nd Ave. E.
Rock Rapids, IA 51246-1759

Gilded Age to Progressive Era (1880–1915)

Introduction

The era from 1880 to 1915 was one of great changes. The Civil War had settled the burning political questions that had dominated the government before 1860. The last of the frontier was being opened by the railroad and settled by hardy pioneers, but the major change in this era was the tremendous growth of big business and industry. At the beginning of the 19th century, America had been an internationally unimportant nation of small farmers. America at the end of the 19th century was a wealthy, industrial world power, status it has never lost.

The change did not come without conflict. The new, huge industrial powers abused their strength. The American public at first welcomed the stronger, more efficient industries. The incredible wealth collected by the men who owned them was seen as their rightful reward. However, as these rich men exploited their workers, paid off politicians, and ruthlessly eliminated their competitors, the American attitude began to change.

Since the Revolution, Americans had always favored small government that interfered as little as possible in the lives of its citizens. Slowly, there arose a cry to control these great corporations before they robbed the nation of its most precious possession, government by the people. That cry brought down the Gilded Age, the age of wild growth, wealth, and poverty. The demand for reforms ushered in the Progressive Era, a rewriting of the basic laws of the American system. This LIFEPAC® will cover this change and what it meant to American history.

Objectives

Read these objectives. The objectives tell you what you will be able to do when you have successfully completed this LIFEPAC. When you have finished this LIFEPAC, you should be able to:

1. Describe the social, political, technological, and industrial developments of the Gilded Age.

2. Describe the last years of the Western frontier.

3. Describe the presidents of the Gilded Age and their policies.

4. Describe the development of unions and reform movements from 1865 to 1915.

5. Describe the causes, course, and consequences of the Spanish-American War.

6. Describe the course of the Progressive Movement.

7. Describe the personality of Theodore Roosevelt and his effect on the presidency.

8. Name the Progressive presidents and describe their policies.

Survey the LIFEPAC. Ask yourself some questions about this study and write your questions here.

_____

_____

_____

_____

_____

_____

_____

_____

_____

_____

_____

_____

_____

_____

_____

_____

_____

_____

1. THE GILDED AGE

One of the most famous American authors of the late 1800s, Mark Twain, published a novel in 1873 called the *Gilded Age*. It was written in collaboration with another author and gave a snapshot of its era. The greedy business-men and corrupt politicians in the novel were mirror images of the people in power at the end of the 19th century. Thus, the name of the novel has become the name of the entire era, from about 1865 to 1900.

Gilding is a process that puts a thin layer of gold over the top of something less valuable. The result is beautiful and valuable on the sur-face, but underneath it can be worthless, dirty, and scarred. That was the late 1800s.

The gold surface of the 1880s and 1890s was the wealth and power of the United States. New American millionaires spent lavishly on homes, art, carriages, clothes, and travel accommodations. Museums, libraries, theaters, and schools were built all over the nation. New inventions like telephones, street cars, electric lights, and phonographs became popular and common. By 1900 America was the wealthiest nation in the world in total assets and income per person.

However, there was a less valuable center under the gold surface. Wealthy "captains of industry" virtually controlled the government which gave them subsidies, incredibly high tar-iffs, and protective legislation. A few powerful individuals routinely would control an entire industry, setting prices and making huge prof-its. Many of the workers in the new industries labored under horrible conditions and lived in worse ones. Cities and whole states were run by corrupt political machines that traded favors for votes and money. Thus, "gilded" is an accurate description of this complex era.

SECTION OBJECTIVES

Review these objectives. When you have completed this section, you should be able to:

1.   Describe the social, political, technological, and industrial developments of the Gilded Age.

2.   Describe the last years of the Western frontier.

3.   Describe the presidents of the Gilded Age and their policies.

4.   Describe the development of unions and reform movements from 1865 to 1915.

VOCABULARY

Study these words to enhance your learning success in this section.

anarchist (an' ə r kist). Person seeking to establish complete freedom by eliminating all government.

assimilate (ə sim' ə lāt). To absorb into the cultural tradition of a population or group.

bankrupt (ban' krəpt). To declare a person unable to meet their debts by law, their available assets are taken by the court to be given to their creditors.

capitalist (kap' ət l əst). A system in which capital goods (money, factories, land) are privately owned and controlled. Decisions about prices, production, and distribution are based on private decisions in response to free market competition.

AMERICA from 1880 to 1915

Rutherford B. Hayes
1877-1881
Republican

James A. Garfield*
1881
Republican

Chester A. Arthur
1881-1885
Republican

Grover Cleveland
1885-1889
Democratic

Benjamin Harrison
1889-1893
Republican

Grover Cleveland
1893-1897
Democratic

William McKinley*
1897-1901
Republican

Theodore Roosevelt
1901-1909
Republican

William H. Taft
1909-1913
Republican

Woodrow Wilson
1913-1921
Democratic

STATES ADMITTED TO THE UNION

North Dakota	1889	**Wyoming**	1890
South Dakota	1889	**Utah**	1896
Washington	1889	**Oklahoma**	1907
Montana	1889	**New Mexico**	1912
Idaho	1890	**Arizona**	1912

POPULATION of the United States of America

Year	Population
1910	92,228,496
1880	50,189,209
1850	23,191,876
1820	9,638,453
1790	3,929,000

*assassinated while in office

communist (käm′ yə nəst). (In the 1890s and early 1900s) A person who advocated following the teachings of Marx, who believed that private property should be eliminated by a rebellion of the working class. Then, all goods should be owned in common and be available to all as needed. (This was before the totalitarian communist Soviet Union had been created. Thus, communism was not at this time a type of treason that favored the expansion of Soviet power. It was an unrealistic hope for a perfect society created by a class war in which everyone had the same things and was absolutely equal.)

creditor (kred′ ət ər). One to whom a debt is owed.

injunction (in jənk′ shən). A writ issued by a court which orders a person to do or refrain from doing a specific act.

largess (lär jes′). Liberal giving to others.

monopoly (mə näp′ ə lē). Complete control of a product or service.

philanthropy (fə lan′ thər pē). Goodwill to fellow man, often accomplished by giving large gifts for the benefit of others.

socialist (sōsh′ ə ləst). Person or system that advocates collective or government ownership of the means of production and distribution. It is usually less extreme than communism in that it allows some private property.

Note: *All vocabulary words in this LIFEPAC appear in* **boldface** *print the first time they are used. If you are not sure of the meaning when you are reading, study the definitions given.*

Pronunciation Key: hat, āge, cãre, fär; let, ēqual, tėrm; it, īce; hot, ōpen, ôrder; oil; out; cup, pu̇t, rüle; child; long; thin; /ŦH/ for then; /zh/ for measure; /u/ or /ə/ represents /a/ in about, /e/ in taken, /i/ in pencil, /o/ in lemon, and /u/ in circus.

Rise of Industry

America had always been a nation of farmers, but in the 1890s, the value of the nation's manufacturing was for the first time greater than the value of its agriculture. This change was brought about by the railroads, investment capital, new inventions, and old-fashioned ingenuity. Moreover, it was a permanent change. America would never be the same again.

Railroads and the newer industries required more capital (money), than a single or a few investors could assemble. Railroads, for example, needed researchers to improve the trains, locomotives, miles of track, cars, repairmen, builders, conductors, stations, station workers, rails, ties, equipment, and supervisors, just to name a few. The amount of capital needed for such an industry was staggering, so in the late 1800s a new form of business became popular to meet this need, the corporation.

A corporation is formed when a group of people organize a company under the laws of a state and sell *stock* in it. The people who purchase the stock become the *stockholders*, who are the legal owners of the company. They are entitled to receive part of the company's profits by way of *dividends* paid on the stock. Thousands of people can contribute to forming a company this way, raising millions in capital. The stockholders vote for a board of directors who run the company for them. (Usually, the board is controlled by the people who own the most stock.)

American law treats corporations as persons. That allows them to pay taxes, enter into contracts, and sue or be sued. That also means that if a corporation goes **bankrupt**, the stockholders lose only their stock. **Creditors** cannot try to get the money they are owed from the "owners." The stockholders are not liable for the debts of another "person," the corporation. Thus, a corporation is a way to raise a large amount of capital without exposing the investors to the dangers of a major business failure.

Railroads. The railroads were the first of the new breed of giant corporations. At the beginning of the Civil War (1860), the United States had 30,000 miles of railroad track. By 1900 it had 193,000 miles, more than all of Europe. These rivers of steel opened up all of the United States for trade. Midwestern farmers could ship their wheat to the cities of the East or to ports to go abroad. Manufactured goods could be produced in whatever part of the country had the needed raw materials and factories. From there, the goods could be sent by rail to any market in the nation. It was this huge domestic market that the new industries supplied quickly and cheaply.

A transcontinental railroad had been a major American goal for years, but there was little profit in building a railroad through miles of empty land. Such an endeavor needed government encouragement. However, competition between the North and the South for this priceless avenue had deadlocked government support before the Civil War.

The North took advantage of the absence of Southern congressmen during the war to authorize subsidies to build a railroad from Omaha, Nebraska, to Sacramento, California. The Union Pacific built west from Omaha, while the Central Pacific built east from Sacramento. Both railroads received 20 square miles of land (in 640-acre sections, on alternate sides of the track) for every mile of track they laid. On this rail line across the nation, they also received generous loans for every mile laid. The rich government benefits made it a race between the two companies to build as much as they could.

The Union Pacific Railroad built across the flat prairie and made spectacular progress. Using mainly Irish laborers, the company built 1,086

miles of track between 1862 and 1869, in one case building 10 miles in a day (using shovels and carts)! The rich government support and press for speed enabled the Crédit Mobilier scandal. Union Pacific officials had hired their own construction company (Crédit Mobilier) that overcharged for the building of the tracks, pocketing huge profits that were shared with cooperative legislators.

Building east, the Central Pacific had to deal with more treacherous terrain through the Sierra Nevada Mountains. Central Pacific used mainly unskilled Chinese workers and was able to build only 689 miles of track. Nevertheless, the Central's main investors, called the Big Four, also made huge profits hiring their own construction companies to do the work.

The two sides met in May of 1869 at Promontory Point near Ogden, Utah. At a wild, joyous ceremony a golden spike was driven into the last rail that united the nation. It was a remarkable feat of engineering and determination, in spite of the graft involved. It firmly joined the far-off Western states to the older portion of the nation and enabled the spread of commerce across the continent. By the end of the century, there would be five such lifelines crossing the nation.

Railroads meant life and prosperity for cities, towns, and states. Consequently, the state and federal governments continued for years to give land grants to railroad companies for building tracks. Cities also were expected to give land and money for the privilege of having the railroad reach their town. In the end, the railroads wound up owning millions of acres of land and controlling millions of dollars of capital.

The railroad improved in more ways than just miles during the late 1800s. Air brakes that stopped the trains more safely were put into general use in the 1870s. Rails were made of more durable steel as opposed to the older, less stable iron rails. Pullman sleeping cars and

| Transcontinental Railroad Completion

dining cars made travel comfortable, even luxurious. The railroads became safe, comfortable modes of long-distance travel.

The railroads which triggered the industrial era by opening new markets across the nation also led in the establishment of huge corporate powerhouses. Smaller railroads were increasingly bought out by larger ones which grew into huge networks. Cornelius Vanderbilt, Leland Stanford, Collis Huntington, Henry Villard, and James Hill were among the men who built fortunes by consolidating rail lines into huge corporations.

These companies increased their profits by using a whole range of various schemes. Competition was decreased by "pools" in which the railroads agreed to divide the business in a certain area. Each would be free to charge as much as they could on their share because no other company would try to take it away. The railroads would normally charge less for carrying freight long distances, for which there was competition, than for short ones which were frequently controlled by one company. This lack of uniform rates hit small, local producers, especially farmers, the hardest. Large industries also would routinely receive rebates for putting all of their business with one company, a benefit unavailable to small operators. High railroad rates could ruin a farmer's profit on his crop or drive a small manufacturing firm out of business, and often did.

Steel. The second major industry of this era was steel manufacturing. Steel is made by purifying iron to make a stronger, more versatile metal. It was rare and expensive until just prior to the Civil War. In the 1850s, the Bessemer process was developed to make steel cheaply from iron. Having all the abundant natural resources needed to produce steel, America was in a unique position to capitalize on the new discovery. By 1900 the U.S. was exceeding both Britain and Germany in steel production.

Andrew Carnegie was a poor Scottish immigrant who made his way up the ladder of success by hard work and shrewd investments. He realized the value of the Bessemer process and invested heavily in it. Moreover, he brought all of the steps needed to produce the steel under his personal control. He owned the mines that produced the iron ore, the barges and railroads that carried it, and the factories that produced it. By 1900 Carnegie was producing one-fourth of the nation's Bessemer steel. He sold his empire in 1901 to banker J.P. Morgan for $480 million. Morgan used it to form a new corporation, U.S. Steel, which was the first billion-dollar corporation in American history.

Standard Oil. Perhaps the most controversial of the new corporations was John D. Rockefeller's Standard Oil. Petroleum (oil), was increasingly being used for lubrication of machines, heating, fuel, and especially kerosene for lighting. This new industry came to be dominated by Rockefeller who organized his Standard Oil Company in 1870.

John D. Rockefeller practiced the kind of ruthless business suitable for a pirate. He concentrated on controlling the **refining** business as a choke point to control the entire industry. He ran his business with careful attention to costs, bringing down prices and forcing competitors out of business. He used his power to get rebates from the railroads. He even got rebates on his competitors' shipments! His ruthless practices gave him control of oil production in the U.S., but they also produced a cheaper, higher quality product for the American public.

Rockefeller formed a new type of business, the trust, to control the entire oil industry. The trust took stock from several companies and ran them together to eliminate competition.

The companies that joined the trust became rich under Rockefeller's leadership. Those that refused were driven to bankruptcy. The Standard Oil Trust eventually controlled more than 90% of the oil production in America.

| Andrew Carnegie

| John D. Rockefeller

Rockefeller's success led to the creation of new industry-wide trusts. The sugar, tobacco, leather, farm implement, and meat-packing industries (among many others) came to be dominated by trusts. This type of business, however, was successfully challenged in state courts. Eventually, the trusts became "holding companies," corporations created just to control other corporations. Also, banking giants like J.P. Morgan gained control of whole industries by putting themselves on the board of several different companies at the same time. The public, however, continued to refer to these huge, industry-dominating, **monopoly**-seeking corporations as "trusts."

 Answer these questions.

1.1 Who are the owners of a corporation?

_____

1.2 Which two companies completed the first transcontinental railroad?

_____

1.3 What innovation made trains safer to stop?

_____

1.4 What innovations made trains more comfortable?

_____

1.5 Who was the leader in the American steel industry?

_____

1.6 What company and man controlled U.S. oil production?

_____

1.7 Profits paid to stockholders are called what?

_____

1.8 How did the railroads trigger industrial development?

_____

1.9 What did a real trust do?

_____

1.10 What did the public refer to as a trust?

_____

1.11 Where and when was the first transcontinental railroad completed?

_____

1.12 What was unfair about the way railroads charged for hauling goods?

_____

_____

_____

1.13 What process made steel cheap enough for general use?

_____

1.14 What type of corporation replaced the trust?

_____

Workers

Immigration. It was in the Gilded Age that America earned its reputation as the hope for the poor of the world. The rapid industrialization created jobs, and the American democracy promised freedom. The new steamer ships offered inexpensive, swift passage across the ocean. Advertisements by steamship lines, reinforced by letters from those who had already gone to America, encouraged a whole generation of poor Europeans to believe that America offered them a chance for a better life. Between the Civil War and World War I, millions came in search of that dream.

More than four million immigrants came between 1860 and 1880. In the 1880s, five million people emigrated to the United States. Most of the newcomers stayed in the industrial cities of the East. By 1910 about one-third of the population in America's eight largest cities was foreign-born.

New Immigration. Immigration patterns changed in the 1880s. Before that time most of the immigrants had come from northern Europe. They were primarily English, Irish, German, or Scandinavian. These people **assimilated** easily into American life. They came from cultures similar to America's, had similar physical appearances, were usually literate, and were mainly Protestant (although the Irish and some Germans were Catholic).

However, things began to change in the 1880s. Immigration patterns shifted so significantly that it was called the New Immigration. The new immigrants came from southern and eastern Europe. Poles, Italians, Croats, Slavs, Hungarians, Russian Jews, and Greeks were among the new arrivals. These people had a different skin color than most Americans at the time, had little money, and spoke a different language. They also came from cultures that had no tradition of free government and followed non-Protestant religions (Roman Catholic, Eastern Orthodox, Jewish). The immigrants were in a completely new environment and America was experiencing change, as well.

| Immigrants to America

The new immigrants huddled together in the cities once they arrived in this strange new land. They formed small islands of home for themselves. Districts called "Little Italy" or "Little Poland" became common in the larger cities. There, the bewildered newcomers could speak their own language, wear their native costumes, buy their own kind of food, and worship in their own churches. It was their children who eventually entered the American mainstream. The adults usually did not, because the change was simply too great.

Working and living conditions. The immigrants were the backbone of the new industrial giants. Working for low wages and rarely making any demands, they were perfect workers for corporations greedy for profits. The wages they received were higher than they would get in Europe, and they knew they could be easily replaced if they made any demands. Women and children were also employed at even lower wages, but the immigrants did not object. Their families needed the money.

These unskilled industrial workers had no rights or protection on the job. Safety precautions were few, and injured workers were simply fired. Illness might also cost a man his job. Any time business was bad, the entire work force might be laid off with no promise of being rehired. Job security was non-existent.

The laborers often lived in squalid tenements, which were all they could afford. These were dark, filthy, rat-infested, fire-trap apartments grouped together in some of the worst city slums in the world. There was little or no sanitation. Diseases spread quickly. Life was harsh and often short.

The new immigrants were a boon to the political machines that ran America's big cities. Used to autocratic government, they were ideal clients for the machine system. The political bosses would help them find jobs, give them food in hard times, help smooth over legal problems, and provide services. In exchange, the new citizens would vote as the bosses told them. They did not understand enough about the ideals of American government to realize this was not the way it was supposed to work.

Policy changes. The New Immigration created a wave of anti-immigrant feeling in America. Older Americans had strong prejudices against the olive-skinned newcomers and their strange, separate ways of life. Anti-Catholicism had always been strong in Protestant America, and it added fuel to the flames. Organized labor objected to the foreigners who were often used as strike-breakers, were hard to organize because they did not speak English, and were willing to work for low wages (which seemed high to them). Pressure built to restrict immigration, which had never been done before in U.S. history.

Beginning in 1880, the open door to immigration was slowly narrowed. The first to feel the pinch were Chinese immigrants on the West Coast. European Americans felt a strong hatred for these racially different, hard-working people who emigrated to California in large numbers after the Civil War. They worked for low wages and kept their own customs. In response to public pressure in 1882, Congress barred all Chinese immigration for ten years and later extended it.

Other restrictions were not so blatant. Also in 1882, paupers and criminals were barred from emigrating. Three years later, contract-worker emigration, which brought in workers by paying their passage in exchange for low-wage employment, was banned. Later **anarchists**, insane persons, polygamists, and people with contagious diseases were barred. Many of the most vocal "nativists" also wanted a literacy test. It was passed by Congress, only to be vetoed three times. The presidents saw it as a test of opportunity, not ability. It was finally passed over the president's veto in 1917, during the anti-foreign feeling of World War I.

| The Haymarket Riot

Labor movement. The huge new industries profited their owners greatly and their workers hardly at all. Workers faced long hours, poor safety precautions, low wages, and no job security while they were making millions for their employers. The workers realized they needed to band together to force owners to improve conditions and wages. In the years after the Civil War, they began to form unions to press their demands.

Industrial leaders were strongly opposed to unions. They routinely fired workers who joined a union or tried to organize one. The owners were especially vicious in breaking up strikes (work stoppages) to force an owner to consider the workers' demands. Strikebreakers (gangs of thugs) were often hired to attack strikers picketing a business. The owners also took full advantage of their political power.

The police, and sometimes the army, were called in to break up strikes. The courts were very cooperative about issuing **injunctions** against striking unions. Labor disputes, therefore, often became violent as working men despaired of a fair chance to improve their conditions.

The violence and the way strikes interfered with commerce made most Americans suspicious of unions. This was especially true of strikes in key industries like the railroads, which delivered the nation's goods, and the coal mines, which heated its homes. Few middle-class people had ever seen the inside of a factory or a mine, nor had they ever tried to live on a laborer's wages. Also, a few anarchists, **socialists**, and **communists** were involved with the unions, and they gave the movement a bad name among the very pro-**capitalist** American public.

Thus, the unions had to overcome ruthless owners, skeptical public opinion, and hostile government action while trying to organize an effective force to push their demands.

The first unions to organize after the Civil War were severely damaged by the 1873 depression. No man would risk his job by joining a union when jobs were scarce. One of the unions that did manage to survive the depression was the Knights of Labor, the first national union, which was organized in 1869. It was initially a secret society organized to protect its members from the hostility of their employers. It was intended to be a union for all workers in all trades. Moreover, it had wide social and political goals that made it more of a lobbying organization rather than a labor organization.

The Knights came to the height of their power under Terence Powderly in the early 1880s. Powderly relaxed the secrecy, discouraged strikes, and pushed a wide social agenda that included government ownership of public utilities and the end of child labor. Membership vaulted after two successful strikes against Jay Gould's railroad in 1885. (Powderly had opposed the strikes.) Membership reached a height of about 700,000.

However, 1886 proved to be a destructive year for the Knights. A third strike against the Gould railroad failed, causing a fall in membership. Powderly was criticized for failing to support the strike. Another strike against the McCormick Reaper factory in Chicago proved to be an even greater disaster. The strike became violent when non-striking workers were attacked as they left the factory on May third. The police intervened and several strikers were killed. A protest was held the next day at Haymarket Square. As the speeches were ending, the police moved in to break up the meeting. Someone threw a dynamite bomb into the crowd. A policeman was killed and several people were injured.

The Haymarket Riot caused a nationwide panic and a wave of anti-union feeling. Several anarchists were arrested, and eight were convicted in the witch-hunt that followed. The Knights of Labor never recovered from their association with the riot. After 1886, the leadership of the national labor movement was passed to the American Federation of Labor, organized in 1886 after the riot. That meant it could not be associated with the Haymarket Riot.

The AFL became a far more effective force than the Knights of Labor for several reasons. The AFL did not try to organize everyone into one large union. Instead, each trade organized its own union for the simple goal of getting the best wages and conditions for its people. These individual unions pooled their resources to form strike funds and a central support structure which allowed striking workers to hold out until businesses met their demands.

The new federation was led from 1886 until 1924 (except for one year) by Samuel Gompers, a cigar maker and an effective labor leader. Gompers concentrated on specific labor issues, such as the eight-hour work day, and avoided more utopian political ideas. He also stressed that the union supported capitalism; it just wanted more of the benefits for the workers. The AFL did engage in some political lobbying, but it was specifically for labor goals. The strongest demand was simply for the right to organize and strike peacefully without being arrested for violating anti-union laws and injunctions. These narrow, specific goals gained the support of working men. The AFL rapidly grew in strength, comfortably surviving the 1893 depression.

Name the item, event, or person.

1.15 _____ Immigration after 1880 that came from southern and eastern Europe

1.16 _____ leader of the AFL, 1886-1924

1.17 _____ damaged the development of unions in 1873

1.18 _____ number of immigrants in the 1880s

1.19 _____ leader of the Knights of Labor at its height

1.20 _____ immigrant group hated in California

1.21 _____ 1885 events that increased Knights of Labor membership

1.22 _____ political group that benefited from the ignorance of the immigrants in American cities

1.23 _____ 1886 event that irreparably damaged the reputation of the Knights of Labor

1.24 _____ immigration test finally made into law in 1917

Answer these questions.

1.25 Why were the New Immigrants so disliked in America?

_____

_____

1.26 Why was the AFL more successful than the Knights of Labor?

_____

_____

1.27 Why did most middle-class Americans oppose unions?

_____

_____

_____

1.28 What were the restrictions put on immigration after 1882?

_____

_____

_____

Gilded Society

Social Darwinism. Social and political reformers in the Gilded Age faced formidable obstacles. One of the greatest was the attitude of the American people. America had always been a nation of freedom, a land where people could make money without restrictions or interference. *Laissez-faire* capitalism was the dominant view of the day. This philosophy stated that a nation would prosper when government interfered as little as possible in business. Encouraged by hefty donations and bribes, the U.S. government was a warm supporter of laissez-faire.

Popular opinion supported not only laissez-faire but also the anti-reform idea of Social Darwinism. The latter was an offshoot of Darwin's *Origin of the Species*, the book that described the theory of evolution. Darwin taught, among other things, that in nature each species prospers by competition in which the strongest survive and dominate. Led by a British philosopher named Herbert Spencer, this idea was applied to people. The rich were the strong who climbed to the top by their own ability. The poor, on the other hand, were poor because they were failures and they deserved to be poor. Thus, any reforms to benefit the poor would violate natural law to the harm of the human species! This contradicted the concept of Christian charity, and was never fully accepted in America, although ruthless industrialists did use it to justify their actions and impede reform.

The rich and powerful "captains of industry" were also widely admired in the Gilded Age. They were seen as the finest examples of the success of the American system. They had earned their wealth by their own cleverness and hard work. It was believed that anyone could become a millionaire in America. Andrew Carnegie, who had been a poor immigrant, was the prime example of what hard work and skill could bring to a man in this great land. Thousands of "rags to riches" stories about poor boys who became rich filled the bookshelves and gave dreams to hard-working men and boys. It was difficult for reformers to attack these heroes and their often underhanded methods.

New rich. The greatest glitter of the Gilded Age came from the incredibly wealthy new industrialists. High society took the air of a European royal court as the new rich competed in ways of showing off their wealth. Fortunes were spent on antiques and art from Europe. Lavish clothes, large yachts, and expensive parties were all part of the social scene. The Vanderbilts built a 70-room mansion called The Breakers at Newport, Rhode Island as a summer home. It included two rooms that were built in France, shipped over, and reassembled. They referred to it without joking as a "cottage." Another Vanderbilt, Consuelo, married an English Duke in exchange for a large cash settlement.

The new rich did not keep all of their money for themselves. The tradition of **philanthropy** was strong in America, despite Social Darwinism. John D. Rockefeller helped start the University of Chicago. Cornell in New York, and Stanford in California were both universities built with money from wealthy industrialists. The premier philanthropist, however, was Andrew Carnegie. He believed it was a sin to die rich; and a rich man's duty was to give away his excess money. Carnegie, therefore, dedicated the latter part of his life to philanthropy. He is best known for the many public libraries established all over America with his grants.

American life. Ordinary people had more money in the Gilded Age, as well. Cities were growing in population, and they began to add civic attractions for their population. With donations from wealthy individuals and other funds, large cities established libraries, museums, operas, and symphony orchestras. The first large department stores were built in the late

1800s by John Wanamaker in Philadelphia and Marshall Field in Chicago. Professional police and fire departments were established to protect city property. Sanitation laws, boards of health, safe water supplies, sewage systems, and trash removal added to the comfort and safety of city life.

Middle-class America had time and money for new amusements in the late 1800s. Vaudeville, a form of comedic theater, became popular with its acrobats, singers, and comics. The circus emerged as a favorite family amusement, led by P. T. Barnum, the master showman who founded the Barnum & Bailey Circus in 1881. "Buffalo Bill" Cody's Wild West Show with live buffalo, staged fights with Native Americans and stunt shooting toured the country beginning in the 1880s.

Sports also began their climb to the height of popularity in the Gilded Age. Baseball had been a popular game even before the Civil War. The National League of professional teams was started in 1876. Football, boxing, and horse racing were popular. The low-framed "safety" bicycle created a national craze as cycling clubs spread all over the nation. Tennis, imported from England, gained a following. For the less active, croquet and archery offered a pass at friendly competition. Thus, many of the activities that are part of modern American life had their foundations in the Gilded Age.

Inventions. Life in America was transformed in the late 1800s by a cornucopia of new and improved inventions. The typewriter (1867), cash register (1879), adding machine (1891), and telephone (1875) transformed the business office. Electric streetcars allowed cities to spread out in all directions and still bring people in for business or pleasure. Refrigeration and better canning techniques improved the supply of healthy food. The Kodak camera (1888) made photography available to everyone and gave us a record of American life.

| "The Breakers"

The most famous inventor of the turn of the century was Thomas Alva Edison (1847-1931). Edison was a creative genius who approached inventing like a business. He set up a laboratory, and had a group of paid assistants who worked on creating useful inventions. He decided what he wanted to create, and experimented until he found a way to do it. He was not dismayed by failures. He thought of them as discoveries of what did not work. He invented the phonograph, the electric light bulb, the storage battery, and a duplicating machine. He also made improvements on the typewriter, the stock ticker machine, motion pictures, the electric generator, and the electric train. He patented 1,093 inventions in his lifetime and left a brighter, more automated America as his legacy.

| A Collage of Invention: A Kodak Camera, Edison and his Light Bulb, the First Typewriter, the First Subway

 Match these items.

1.29 _____ Social Darwinism

1.30 _____ Carnegie

1.31 _____ Kodak

1.32 _____ laissez-faire

1.33 _____ University of Chicago

1.34 _____ The Breakers

1.35 _____ National League

a. Vanderbilt summer cottage

b. established libraries all over America

c. business with a minimum of government interference

d. professional baseball organization

e. made photography available to everyone

f. theory based on evolution that the rich were superior and the poor were inferior; interfered with reform

g. founded with money from John D. Rockefeller

Match these people.

1.36	_____ John Wanamaker	a.	creator of the theory of evolution
1.37	_____ P. T. Barnum	b.	Wild West Show
1.38	_____ Thomas Edison	c.	department store, Philadelphia
1.39	_____ Herbert Spencer	d.	great philanthropist
1.40	_____ Andrew Carnegie	e.	philosopher, Social Darwinism
1.41	_____ Buffalo Bill Cody	f.	inventor, 1,093 patents
1.42	_____ Charles Darwin	g.	master showman, circus founder

Complete these items.

1.43 Name five of the important inventions of the late 1800s.

_____

_____

1.44 Name three things invented by Thomas Edison.

_____

_____

1.45 Name three things improved by Thomas Edison.

_____

_____

1.46 Name three reasons why the attitude of the American people did not support reform in the Gilded Age.

a. _____

b. _____

c. _____

Wild West

The Gilded Age was the era of the Wild West that is usually shown on TV and in the movies. This was the opening of the last frontier of the contiguous states, the Great Plains. It was the time of the Indian Wars, America's final drive to take the land from its original owners. It was the time of the great cattle drives, wild mining towns, and rough frontier justice. It was the arrival of the Gilded Age homesteaders that transformed this wild prairie into America's breadbasket.

Plains Indians. Much of the land between the Mississippi and the Rocky Mountains had been set aside as a home for the Native Americans by Andrew Jackson. The land known as the "Great American Desert" was believed to be worthless for farming. However, after the Civil War, Americans decided they wanted the land after all. In 1867 Congress decided to put all of the Native Americans there onto two reservations (Oklahoma and the Black Hills of North Dakota).

The Plains Indians were nomadic and war-like. They fought harder and more effectively against forced confinement to reservations than their farming cousins east of the Mississippi River had. Between 1865 and 1890, the U.S. army fought hundreds of battles with the Native Americans of the plains. In the end, repeating rifles (which did not have to be reloaded after every shot), the mobility of the railroad, the extermination of the buffalo (the Plains Indian's main source of food), and European diseases finally subdued the last of the Native American tribes. Several of the battles and their leaders have become legend.

In 1875 the land given to the Sioux people was invaded by hordes of greedy miners after gold was discovered there. Led by Sitting Bull and Crazy Horse, the Sioux fought back. In 1876 Lieutenant-Colonel George A. Custer rashly attacked a group of well-armed warriors near the Little Big Horn River in Montana. He and his entire command of 264 men were killed, but reinforcements drove the Sioux into Canada where hunger forced them to surrender.

Chief Joseph was the leader of the Nez Percé people. In 1877 he and his people refused to surrender their land and began to fight with the troops sent to force the move. Chief Joseph realized he could not win and began a skillful retreat toward Canada. He was finally cornered less than 50 miles from the border. With his people cold and hungry, he agreed to move to a reservation.

| Members of the Nez Percé

The most notorious Native American leader was Geronimo of the Apache people. He was placed on reservations several times in his life. He repeatedly escaped and led raids against white settlements in the U.S. and Mexico, using the mountains to hide. He proved very difficult to find. He finally surrendered for the last time in 1886 and was sent to Fort Sill, Oklahoma, where he lived the rest of his life.

The unofficial policy of the army and the government during these years was extermination of the Native American people. That was not the announced policy, but it was the effect. Incidents of soldiers murdering peaceful tribes, including women and children, were all too common. In 1881 Helen Hunt Jackson wrote *A Century of Dishonor*, which detailed the fraud, murder, and deceit practiced on the Native Americans in the previous hundred years. This book touched the conscience of the nation, and reform pressures eventually brought about the Dawes Act of 1887.

The Dawes Act ended tribal ownership of land, gave every Native American family its own land, and promised them full title to the land and citizenship after twenty-five years. It was an improvement over the policy of consolidation and destruction. However, the law ignored the Indian culture and their way of land management. (It was eventually reversed in 1934.) A lack of respect for non-European cultures was a common trait of all Western peoples before the middle of the 20th century. Even Christians made this error, not recognizing that the love of Christ does not require Western ways of worship and life.

Pioneer Miners. The leaders in the white settlement of the Wild West were the miners. The discovery of gold and silver brought waves of miners to Colorado, Montana, Nevada, and Idaho. These men established wild boom-towns near the strikes. After the surface metal was exhausted, the individual prospectors wandered away or found new occupations. They were followed, however, by corporations who set up major industries to get at the deeper metals. Industrial mining brought in jobs for miners, engineers, machine specialists and shopkeepers. Gold, silver and copper were the leading reasons for the growth of cities and towns in the mountain states of the West. Railroads followed to take out the ore and bring in supplies. Mining took the lead in the Western mountains, while it was cattle that did so on the plains.

Cattle drives. After the Civil War, the plains were covered with herds of wild cattle (escaped remnants of those brought over by Spain). The herds were worthless in the sparsely populated Western states, but very valuable to beef-hungry Eastern cities. The problem was how to get them back East. After the Civil War, the railroads provided the solution.

| Cattle Drive Trails

Under the leadership of clever businessmen, stations were set up on the transcontinental railroad to collect cattle for shipment to meat-processing centers in Kansas City and Chicago. The herds were brought to "cowtowns" like Abilene, Kansas by long "drives." Cattlemen would raise the cows on the unfenced, government-owned prairie land at virtually no cost. Then, the herds would be slowly driven to the rail junctions along established routes like the Chisholm and Goodnight-Loving Trails. Huge profits were reaped by the cattle owners who completed the long drives in the 1870s and early 1880s.

Opportunity on the prairie was very appealing to the American cowboy. These hard-working men entered American folklore on the long drives to market. It was their job to guard, move, brand, and control the huge herds. To do this, they lived out on the prairie with their charges, only rarely coming to town to spend their pay with wild abandon. Novels and short stories written in the East popularized the life of a cowboy on the open range. Later, movies and TV did the same.

It was all over in a short time, however. Open-range cattle raising was so profitable that hundreds of people and corporations jumped into the business. The result was an oversupply of beef, a drop in beef prices, and the over-grazing of good grasslands. The railroads were also bringing in settlers who bought up and fenced the range lands. The death blow came during the winter of 1886-87. Freezing temperatures and harsh blizzards killed thousands of cattle. The stockmen who survived did so by getting legal title to grasslands, growing feed for the winter, and investing in higher quality breeds of cattle. The spread of the railroad brought transport to all areas of the West, eliminating the need for the long drive. Cowboys lost their major function and became ranch hands, but they never lost their mystique for generations of Americans.

Homesteaders. The millions of acres of land in the last part of the West were settled with inordinate speed. Americans settled more acres between 1870 and 1900 than they had in the previous two hundred and fifty years! The Homestead Act and the railroads were the reasons for this incredible achievement.

The Homestead Act was passed by the Republican Congress during the Civil War. It gave 160 acres of free land to any citizen who lived on it for five years and improved it. (The South had previously opposed homestead laws as a way to increase the number of free states.) By 1900 about 80 million acres of land had been given away. However, even more land had been sold outright or given to railroads and states under various grants. This land was sold to settlers, speculators, or developers. In all, 500 million acres of land was disposed of by the U.S. government by 1900.

The railroads allowed the people to reach this **largess** quickly and easily. The dangerous months of travel by covered wagon were replaced by days of travel in relative comfort. Services and supplies were within easy reach of the new settlers. They no longer had to survive unaided on the "frontier." In fact, by the time of the 1890 census (American law requires a census every ten years), there no longer was a discernible frontier. For the first time in American history, there was no longer a line of settlement with open land to the West. There was still a tremendous amount of land available, but it was spread out in between established cities and towns. The frontier was gone.

The farmers of the plains faced major problems in establishing agriculture. The region was much drier than the East and needed special equipment to work the heavy soil. This equipment was expensive. More than 160 acres was needed in the drier regions to have a profitable farm. Nevertheless, the Great Plains quickly became a wheat- and corn-growing region, supplying American and foreign cities with grain.

These business farms depended upon a single cash crop and bought their own food from local stores.

Western farmers were hurt in the late 1800s by a variety of problems. The vast productive power of the plains produced huge crops that forced prices down. Railroads took a hefty cut of farmer's profits, sometimes eliminating them entirely. While manufactured goods were protected and overpriced due to high tariffs, farm products had no protection from competition. Farmers who went into debt to pay for expensive machinery often lacked the means to repay. They either sold out or carried debt and interest payments for years.

The problems of debt and railroad extortion forced the incredibly independent American farmers to organize. In 1867 they formed the Grange which became an important social/political organization for farmers. The Grange worked at first for self-improvement for farmers and later tackled some of the thorny issues of late 19th century agriculture. Its work for railroad regulation and debt relief was largely ineffective. However, its torch was taken up by the Farmer's Alliance, the Populists, and later, by the Progressive Movement.

 Complete these sentences.

1.47 _____ was the leader of the Nez Percé people who tried to retreat to Canada.

1.48 The pioneer settlers in the Western mountain states were _____ .

1.49 Helen Hunt Jackson's book, _____ , pricked the American conscience about the treatment of the Native American people.

1.50 The Homestead Act gave any citizen _____ acres of free land if they lived on it for _____ years.

1.51 The American _____ became a folk hero during the cattle drives of the 1870s and 1880s.

1.52 The _____ people fought back when their land was invaded by gold-hungry miners in 1875.

1.53 Cattle were taken to railroad "cowtowns" along trails like the _____ and the _____-_____ .

1.54 Overproduction of open-range cattle caused a _____ in prices and _____-_____ of grassland.

1.55 The _____ was a social/political organization for farmers.

1.56 The things that contributed to the conquest of the Plains Indians were:

a. _____

b. _____

c. _____

d. _____

1.57 The Apache leader who proved difficult to confine was _____ .

1.58 The death blow to the open-range cattle business was _____ .

1.59 The American frontier had disappeared by the census of _____ .

1.60 _____ and all of his men were killed at Little Big Horn in 1876.

1.61 The _____ Act ended tribal ownership of land and tried to make the Indians into independent farmers.

1.62 The farms of the Great Plains specialized in growing _____ and _____ .

1.63 The major political issues of the Grange were _____ relief and control of the _____ .

1.64 The two reasons for the speed of settlement on the Great Plains were the _____ and the _____ .

Review the material in this section in preparation for the Self Test. The Self Test will check your mastery of this particular section. The items missed on this Self Test will indicate specific areas where restudy is needed for mastery.

SELF TEST 1

Match these people (each answer, 2 points).

1.01	_____ Andrew Carnegie	a.	master circus showman
1.02	_____ Samuel Gompers	b.	author of the *Gilded Age*
1.03	_____ P. T. Barnum	c.	leader of Nez Percé people
1.04	_____ John D. Rockefeller	d.	founder of Standard Oil
1.05	_____ Geronimo	e.	leader of AFL
1.06	_____ Thomas Edison	f.	wealthy railroad man, built The Breakers
1.07	_____ Terence Powderly	g.	philanthropist, steel-making industrialist
1.08	_____ Chief Joseph	h.	leader of the Knights of Labor
1.09	_____ Mark Twain	i.	Apache leader
1.010	_____ Cornelius Vanderbilt	j.	inventor

Complete these sentences (each answer, 3 points).

1.011 Large corporations that controlled a certain industry with a near monopoly were called

_____ .

1.012 The first of the large, post Civil War corporate industries was the _____ .

1.013 The _____ gave the Native Americans land as individuals, not as a tribe, and tried to make them into independent farmers.

1.014 The _____ was a shift of people coming to America from South and East Europe instead of the North.

1.015 The Knights of Labor never recovered from their association with the _____ in 1886.

1.016 _____-_____ was a philosophy that a nation would prosper when government interfered as little as possible with business.

1.017 The _____ gave 160 acres to any citizen who improved it and lived on it for five years.

1.018 _____ was a philosophy which taught that the poor were failures that deserved to be poor because they could not compete successfully.

1.019 The era from 1865 to 1900 was called the _____ .

1.020 The census of 1890 showed that America no longer had a _____ .

Answer these questions (each number, 3 points).

1.021 What made open-range cattle raising profitable?

_____

_____

1.022 Who are the owners of a corporation and who runs it?

_____

_____

1.023 What two railroads completed the first transcontinental railroad?

_____

_____

1.024 Why did organized labor oppose immigration?

_____

_____

1.025 Why was the AFL more effective than the Knights of Labor?

_____

_____

1.026 What two things contributed to the rapid settlement of the plains?

_____

_____

1.027 Why were the railroads a problem for Midwestern farmers?

_____

_____

1.028 Why were immigrants considered ideal employees for the industrial giants?

_____

_____

1.029 How would the industries fight strikes?

_____

_____

1.030 Why were the captains of industry admired in America?

_____

_____

Match these items (each answer, 2 points).

1.031	_____ middle-class	a. controlled more than 90% of American petroleum production
1.032	_____ dividend	b. process to make steel cheaply
1.033	_____ Grange	c. company profits paid on stock
1.034	_____ Promontory Point	d. book that detailed abuse of the Indians
1.035	_____ U.S. Steel	e. system of private ownership as a means of production
1.036	_____ Standard Oil	
1.037	_____ capitalism	f. long drive cattle trail
1.038	_____ Bessemer	g. people spend money on professional amusements
1.039	_____ _A Century of Dishonor_	h. first billion-dollar corporation
1.040	_____ Chisholm	i. sought debt relief and railroad regulation
		j. place where the two sides of the first transcontinental railroad met

80/100   SCORE _____   TEACHER _____ _____
                                            initials   date

2. GILDED POLITICS

After 1877, the Civil War ceased to be the major issue in American politics. The tariff, civil service reform, currency issues, and regulation of trusts were the largest issues leading up to the turn of the century. Local and state politics, however, were dominated by political machines, not issues. The machines and the trusts had the money and power to get what they wanted from the government, most of the time. However, increasing calls for reform battled the power of the industrialists and the party bosses. A few reform laws did make it onto the books, but most were not seriously enforced until the Progressive Era (after 1900). Thus, 1880-1900 was a time when the rich and powerful had the government mainly where they wanted it, very docile and obedient.

The presidents of this era were a lackluster bunch. The near-impeachment of Johnson had badly hurt the power of the presidency. The corruption of the Grant administration further discredited the office. Moreover, the next president, Hayes, obtained the office by very questionable means. Thus, by 1880 the presidency was not a powerful, well-respected office. Congress was recognized as the leader of the nation. Men of vision and ambition were turning to business, not politics. It was mainly men of mediocrity that occupied the White House in the years leading up to 1900.

SECTION OBJECTIVES

Review these objectives. When you have completed this section, you should be able to:

1. Describe the social, political, technological, and industrial developments of the Gilded Age.

3. Describe the presidents of the Gilded Age and their policies.

4. Describe the development of unions and reform movements from 1865 to 1915.

5. Describe the causes, course, and consequences of the Spanish-American War.

VOCABULARY

Study these words to enhance your learning success in this section.

armistice (är′ mə stəs). A halt to a war or fight by agreement between the opponents.

co-sign (kō′ sīn). Person who agrees to be responsible for a debt if the original debtor defaults.

decimate (des′ ə māt). To destroy a large part of. Literally, to destroy one tenth.

deficit (def′ ə sət). More expenses than income.

imperialism (im pir′ ē ə liz əm). The policy of expanding the power and dominion of a nation, especially by acquiring new territories and by gaining indirect economic or political control over other lands.

patronage (pā′ trə nij). The power to make appointments to government jobs on a basis other than merit alone.

Garfield to First Cleveland

Neither political party was able to dominate between 1880 and 1900. The Democrats always had control of the South, but Republican strength in the West and North offset that. The Republicans held the presidency for all but two terms, but the elections were usually close. In only four of the 20 years between 1877 and 1897 did the same party control Congress and the presidency. Thus, policy was often based on compromise between the two parties and even within factions of the same party.

Election of 1880. Rutherford B. Hayes decided not to run again in 1880. He probably could not have won the Republican nomination anyway. The bosses were angry with him for his opposition to using federal jobs to reward party loyalty, the source of the bosses' power. Hayes had an especially strong enemy in Senator Roscoe Conkling of New York. Conkling controlled New York politics by his control of political **patronage** there. He was in no mood to yield his power to a reformist president. Hayes had fired Conkling's man, Chester A. Arthur, who was in charge of the New York Custom House, the nation's largest collection spot for tariff revenue.

The Republican convention was badly split over a candidate. Conkling's faction supported a return of Ulysses S. Grant who had provided the "era of good stealing" for them. Conkling's "Stalwarts" were opposed in the convention by James Blaine of Maine who had the support of the "Half-Breed" Republican faction. The two sides could not defeat each other and finally compromised on James A. Garfield of Ohio. The Stalwarts were compensated by the nomination of Chester A. Arthur for vice president. The Democrats nominated General Winfield Hancock, a Union war veteran with a spotless record. Garfield won by less than 7,000 votes.

James A. Garfield (1831-1881). James A. Garfield was the last president to be born in a log cabin. He was born in Ohio to pioneer

| The Assassination of Garfield

farmers. His father died when he was two, but his mother succeeded in raising the family on their farm. Garfield worked for a short time as a driver on the Ohio barge canal but later obtained an education and went into teaching. He worked as a college professor and became president of Hiram College in Ohio. He fought in the Civil War, reaching the rank of major general. He was elected to the U.S. House of Representatives while still in the army. He was re-elected eight times and served on several influential committees. He was a Republican leader in the House under Hayes, gaining the confidence of both the Stalwarts and the Half-Breeds. He was elected to the Senate but was nominated for the presidency before he could take office.

Garfield named James Blaine, the Half-Breed leader, to the plum post of Secretary of State and favored his faction in other political appointments. Conkling opposed many of Garfield's nominations, especially when he made an appointment to the New York Custom House without consulting the New York senator. When it looked like this man would be appointed in spite of Conkling's opposition, the old party boss resigned, expecting to be triumphantly returned to office by the New York legislature. He was disappointed. The legislature chose someone else, and he never returned to office.

In the meantime, President Garfield was shot on July 2, 1881 by a man who had been denied a political office. Garfield lingered for eleven weeks, but finally died on September 19th. The assassin, Charles J. Guiteau, was tried and hanged. The president's murder raised a nationwide cry in favor of civil service reform and was largely responsible for Congress finally passing a reform bill in 1883.

Chester A. Arthur (1829-1886). Chester A. Arthur was a machine politician. He reached the presidency without ever having been elected to any political office other than the vice presidency. He was born in Vermont, the son of a pastor/teacher. He went to college in upstate New York and eventually practiced law in New York City. He served in various office positions in the New York militia during the Civil War. After the war, he became an associate of Roscoe Conkling's and was appointed as collector of customs at the huge New York Custom House. Arthur used his control of the over 1,000 jobs at the Custom House to support the Republican Party. Party loyalists got the jobs in exchange for votes, support, and a portion of their salary to the party's treasury. Arthur lost the job under Hayes when he refused to obey the president's order to stop collecting political "donations" from federal employees. Arthur was given the vice-presidential nomination in 1880 to gain Stalwart support for Garfield.

The reformers, called Mugwumps, had few hopes for Arthur. They expected him to blindly follow the policies of the bosses who had made him. However, he rose to the occasion of his advancement and surprised everyone with his independence. He strongly supported civil service reform and had the pleasure of finally seeing it made into law.

The pressure for reform was intense after Garfield's assassination. However, the Republican Congress stalled on the issue until the congressional elections of 1882. The Republicans lost control of the House that year and feared they would lose the presidency in 1884.

Consequently, to keep their own men in office when the Democrats took over, they passed the Pendleton Act of 1883 before the new Congress took office. Arthur signed it into law.

The Pendleton Act forbade the practice of taking a portion of the officeholders' salaries to support the party that gave them the job. It also set up a merit system for appointment to federal offices under the supervision of the Civil Service Commission. The president was given the authority to classify which jobs would be filled by competitive exams. The others would still be available for patronage.

Arthur appointed the author of the law as the first commissioner. He also moved with vigor to classify federal jobs under the commission. By the end of his term, about ten percent of all federal jobs were classified, awarded on merit. Succeeding presidents expanded the number of classified jobs, usually when it looked like their party would lose them after an election. The system expanded until, by the 1940s, 90% of all federal jobs were awarded on merit, not political activism. The reform took time, but the spoilsmanship begun by Andrew Jackson was finally being eliminated.

Arthur further surprised reformers by supporting fraud prosecutions against some former political allies. He appointed a commission to examine the high tariffs and vetoed extravagant legislation. He also signed a law that authorized the purchase of a modest number of modern naval ships (the Navy had been allowed to deteriorate since the Civil War). His independence made him unpopular with the bosses, and he developed a terminal illness that led him to not press for renomination in 1884. He died less than two years after leaving office.

Election of 1884. The Republicans easily nominated James Blaine for president in 1884. He was, however, a controversial nominee. The Republican star had a history of questionable dealings in his public career. The Republican

Mugwumps either gave him little support or supported the Democrats who had the sense to nominate an honest reform candidate named Grover Cleveland.

The only major issue dividing the parties was the tariff. (The Republicans wanted it high and the Democrats wanted to lower it.) Neither candidate had served in the Civil War, so the bloody shirt was not waved very much. The lack of issues and Blaine's reputation led the election to dissolve into heavy mudslinging. The Republicans thought they had a winning mud-ball when it was discovered that the bachelor Cleveland had an illegitimate son. The smear campaign backfired, however, when Cleveland admitted it and was admired for his honesty. The campaign was waged between Blaine's public reputation and Cleveland's private one. Cleveland won by a small popular majority.

Grover Cleveland (1837-1908). Grover Cleveland was the only president to serve two non-consecutive terms. (He was elected again in 1892 after four years out of office). He was born in New Jersey, the son of a pastor. He attended various schools in New York but never went to college. His father died when he was 16. He and his brothers worked to support his mother and sisters. He studied law with a firm in Buffalo, New York and was admitted to the bar in 1859. He paid for a substitute to serve for him in the Civil War so that he could continue to support his family. He served in a couple of minor offices before being elected as mayor of Buffalo in 1881. He proved to be a strong reformer in office, blocking many corrupt city contracts. His reputation and lack of political enemies gained him the governor's office in 1882. He earned the hatred of Tammany Hall, the New York City machine, with his support for reforms. He quickly gained a national reputation, and the Democrats nominated him in 1884 to run against the tainted James Blaine.

| Grover Cleveland's Wedding

Grover Cleveland, the first Democratic president since the Civil War, was an exception to the lackluster presidents of the Gilded Age. He was a strong reformer, but he was limited by Congress and the demands of his own party. Still, he began to polish the tarnished image of the presidency by his leadership and integrity. He also added a bit of social spice by being the first president to marry while in office. The forty-nine-year-old Cleveland married twenty-one-year-old Frances Folsom, his ward, in 1886.

Reformer Cleveland. Cleveland was besieged with Democratic office-seekers. After nearly a quarter century out of power, the Democrats wanted the spoils of victory. Cleveland found it impossible to ignore the pressure. By the end of his term, he had replaced two-thirds of the federal employees with Democratic workers. He tried to check the qualifications of the applicants and often refused those who were unfit. He also doubled the number of jobs classified under the Civil Service Commission. The overall result was that he angered both the Democratic bosses who thought he should have given them more jobs, and the reformers who thought he should have given less jobs.

Currency was a major issue of the era. The Grange Movement was one of several supporters of inflationary currency that would increase prices and ease agricultural debt. It was believed that this could be done by increasing the money supply by using paper currency and silver money. The economically stagnant South and the agricultural West generally supported paper currency and silver coinage. However, the industrial powers of the North favored hard currency with gold as the basis for all U.S. money.

The United States currency in the 1880s was, by law, always redeemable in gold. The government had to keep on hand enough gold to satisfy any demands by people holding paper money. Supporters of a larger money supply and silver interests had passed the Bland-Allison Act in 1878. It required the treasury to buy silver and mint silver dollar coins with 16 ounces of silver for the value of every 1 ounce of gold. These silver dollars could also be redeemed for gold.

During Cleveland's first administration, the opening of new silver mines in the West drove down the price of silver. This made the silver dollars less valuable than their gold counterparts. Observant citizens began to obtain silver dollars and then redeem them one-for-one for the more valuable gold. The result was a drain on the gold reserves in the U.S. treasury. Cleveland tried to get the Bland-Allison Act repealed, but Congress refused. The treasury sold bonds for gold which brought in needed reserves, but the drain continued.

The Grange also favored control of the railroads. The life or death control railroads had over many farmers required regulation to insure fair treatment. Under Grange pressure, several Midwestern states had passed laws to regulate the railroads. However, their efforts were shattered in 1886 when the Supreme Court ruled that states could not regulate railroads engaged in interstate commerce. Since most of the railroads ran between states, this effectively ended any hope of state regulation. Only the federal government could act.

Responding to heavy public pressure, Congress passed the Interstate Commerce Act in 1887. The Act banned rate discrimination, rebates, and pooling. It forbade charging more for short hauls than long hauls. It also required that rates be "reasonable and just." The most important part of the law set up the Interstate Commerce Commission (I.C.C.) to enforce the new law.

The Commission was not terribly effective in its early years. The railroad bosses still had tremendous power in the government, but it was an important first step. The federal government finally acknowledged that unbridled capitalism could have unreasonable and unfair results for the nation. It was the first tentative step into regulation of the economy. Cleveland was, for all his reform ideas, a laissez-faire man and signed the law reluctantly. Over the years, however, it turned out to be one of the most significant accomplishments of his administration.

Cleveland also earned the enmity of the G.A.R. (Grand Army of the Republic), the Union veteran's organization, by his tight control over granting pensions. Cleveland carefully examined private requests for pensions to make sure the applicant was truly disabled in the war. Previous Republican presidents had routinely approved such requests without examining them to appease the politically powerful G.A.R. Cleveland also vetoed the Dependent Pension Bill in 1887. This law would have given a government pension to any man who served at least 90 days in the war and who was currently disabled. He further infuriated the G.A.R. by trying to return captured Southern battle flags, but he was forced to back down by the outcry against him.

The reason the G.A.R. and Congress thought veterans should freely be rewarded was because the treasury had a huge surplus. The high tariffs were bringing in more money than the government needed. Cleveland courageously attacked the high tariffs in his annual message to Congress in 1887. He requested that the tariffs be reduced, believing it was unfair to take money the government did not need. The Republicans accused him of favoring free trade, which was an unpopular idea in those protectionist times. The conflict created the issue for the 1888 campaign.

Choose the correct person for each item.

2.1 _____ first Democratic president since the Civil War

2.2 _____ senator, political boss of New York

2.3 _____ doubled the number of classified federal jobs

2.4 _____ assassinated by disgruntled office seeker

2.5 _____ tried to get Bland-Allison repealed

2.6 _____ Democratic candidate, 1880

2.7 _____ mayor, governor, president in four years

2.8 _____ Garfield's Secretary of State

2.9 _____ president, previously never held elected office

2.10 _____ vetoed Dependent Pension Bill

2.11 _____ fired at N.Y. Custom House for disobeying Hayes

2.12 _____ signed Interstate Commerce Act

2.13 _____ Stalwart leader

2.14 _____ Half-Breed faction leader

2.15 _____ signed civil service reform law

2.16 _____ Republican candidate, 1884

2.17 _____ candidate wanted by Stalwarts in 1880

2.18 _____ House leader, had Stalwart and Half-Breed faction confidence

2.19 _____ resigned over president's appointments; expected to be re-elected; was not

2.20 _____ president made by Conkling

2.21 _____ accused of having illegitimate son

2.22 _____ paid a substitute in the Civil War

2.23 _____ son of Ohio pioneers

2.24 _____ angered veterans by granting only legitimate pension requests

2.25 _____ opposed high tariffs that produced treasury surpluses

a. James Garfield

b. James Blaine

c. Chester Arthur

d. Roscoe Conkling

e. Grover Cleveland

f. Ulysses Grant

g. Winfield Hancock

Answer these questions.

2.26 What were the reformers called?

_____

2.27 Which political party dominated the government between 1880 and 1900?

_____

2.28 Why were people trading in silver dollars for gold ones under Cleveland?

_____

_____

_____

2.29 Which sections of the country favored paper currency and silver coinage?

_____

2.30 What did the Bland-Allison Act require?

_____

_____

2.31 What was the name of the civil service reform law?

_____

2.32 What percentage of federal jobs were classified under Arthur?

_____

2.33 What made the public clamor for civil service reform?

_____

2.34 What did the Interstate Commerce Act forbid?

_____

_____

Harrison to McKinley

Election of 1888. Cleveland was re-nominated by the Democrats in 1888. His stand on the tariff issue had made him vulnerable, but he was still the party's best chance. The Republicans considered James Blaine, but he refused when it became clear he did not have the full support of the party. Instead, a compromise candidate, Benjamin Harrison, was chosen.

The tariff was the main issue of the campaign. It was the focus of the literature, speeches, and rhetoric. Because there was a definite issue, the mud slinging was lower than the previous election. The Republicans argued that the tariff protected American jobs and a budget surplus was good. They accused the Democrats of favoring Britain, who wanted decreased tariffs to help their trade. That was a serious accusation in anti-British America, especially among the Irish voters. The Republicans also raised a huge amount of money from industrialists frightened by the prospect of losing their high tariffs. The money went to buy Republican votes, sometimes literally. Cleveland won the popular vote, but lost the election because Harrison received the most electoral votes.

Benjamin Harrison (1833-1901). Benjamin Harrison was the grandson of former president and war hero, William Henry Harrison. Benjamin was born in Ohio and raised on the family farm there. He received a college education and began the practice of law in 1854. He moved to Indiana and held several appointed and elected positions in that state. During the Civil War, he organized and led a volunteer regiment. He rose to the rank of brigadier general on the basis of his ability as a commander. After the war, he served on a government commission and was elected to the U.S. Senate. He had almost 100,000 less votes than Cleveland, but won the election 233 to 168 in the official electoral votes. (This is possible because Harrison won in the large states that had more electoral votes. The state winner gets all of that state's electoral votes.)

Billion-dollar Congress. The 1888 election gave the Republicans control of Congress as well as the presidency. They quickly moved to spend the nation's surplus so they could justify the high tariffs. This Fifty-first Congress became known as the "Billion-dollar Congress." It was the first to appropriate almost a billion dollars, an enormous amount for its day, in peacetime. The huge surplus was successfully spent, and it did not seriously trouble our nation again for many years.

The main beneficiary of the Republican largess was the G.A.R. The Pension Act of 1890 gave a full pension to <u>any</u> Union veteran who served at least ninety days and could not, for <u>any</u> reason, now do manual labor. The number of people drawing pensions went up by half again under Harrison. So did the cost.

The pressure for control of the trusts had been mounting for years. The cold, efficient work of John D. Rockefeller and his fellow trust builders in eliminating their competition had aroused tremendous anger. The Fifty-first Congress acknowledged the importance of the issue by passing the Sherman Anti-Trust Act in 1890. This law declared that any combination of companies that was in restraint of trade was illegal. Mere size was not enough; the trust had to be interfering with competition and interstate trade.

The government did not successfully use the law against any monopoly for years. It was, however, successfully used in 1894 to break up a railroad strike. The union was accused of interfering with interstate trade. However, the law was now on the books, a testament to the growing public outcry for reform. It would see action early in the coming century under the command of the Progressives.

Eastern congressmen were anxious to raise the tariff to new heights, but they needed Western support to do it. In the end, a deal was made and the Easterners received support for a new

| Carnegie Steel Plant

tariff. In exchange, they agreed to support increased coinage of silver. Western farmers believed this would help depressed farm prices and rising farm debt. Western silver mining states wanted it for more obvious reasons.

The Sherman Silver Purchase Act of 1890 was the Western end of the deal. It required that the treasury buy about twice as much silver as it had been under the old Bland-Allison Law. The metal was to be made into coins at the old ratio of 16 ounces of silver for every 1 ounce of gold. It did nothing to relieve farm problems.

The industrial Northeast received the McKinley Tariff as its part in the bargain. It pushed the rates to the highest in peacetime history. A bounty of two cents a pound was given to U.S. sugar producers to help eliminate the surplus. A few agricultural products were also protected by tariffs to quiet farm protest, but American farmers had little foreign competition for the U.S. food market. The "protection" did them no good.

The tariff was a disaster. The farmers saw an immediate increase in the prices of their dry-goods, equipment, clothes, and other supplies. The prices on their products continued to be low. The voters reacted with anger at the high tariff and free-spending of the Billion-dollar Congress. A challenge to the old order was in the air.

Populist revolt. Rising industrialist power over the government, unregulated railroad abuses, falling prices for farm products, and rising farm debt had created an angry U.S. farm community. By 1890 farmers had organized the Farmer's Alliance to press their demands. There were two main Alliances, one in the Northwest

which worked independently and one in the South which worked within the Democratic Party. (Southern farmers would not risk losing white control of the government by splitting with the Democratic Party.) The Alliances were able to elect many of their people in the West and the South. They also contributed to the election of a Democratic House of Representatives in 1890.

The Alliances decided they needed to step out of the two main parties to press their demands. In 1892, they held a convention in Omaha, Nebraska, and formed the People's (Populist) Party. The Farmer's Alliance was joined by the Grangers, Mugwumps, Greenbacks, labor unions, and a wide variety of reform-minded individuals. They nominated General James Weaver, a former Greenback, for president. The Populists, however, still lacked Southern support. The Southern Democrats would not split from their party and risk a return of black power.

The Populists had an astonishing reform platform. The platform called, first of all, for free coinage of silver. It also endorsed (among other things) a new banking system; income tax (to replace land taxes and tariffs that did not touch industrial income); government ownership of railroads, the telegraph system, and the telephone companies; an eight-hour workday; restrictions on immigration; and direct election of U.S. senators (they were still appointed by the state legislatures).

Election of 1892. The Republicans renominated Harrison and the Democrats again chose Cleveland. The stage was set for a repeat fight with the added interest of the Populist vote.

| Pullman Car of the Late 1890s

The campaign again focused on the tariff. Republicans argued that the tariff gave Americans high wages. A wave of strikes, mainly over wages, flew in the face of this argument. The worst was at Carnegie's Homestead Steel plant near Pittsburgh, after the company cut wages. Three hundred armed Pinkerton detectives battled with the strikers, and several people died. Soldiers were called in to break up the strike, which collapsed. The publicity hurt the Republican cause and helped elect Cleveland by a reasonable popular and substantial electoral margin. Weaver received over a million votes in his party's first appearance at the poles.

Second Cleveland. The second Cleveland administration was doomed by a major depression that hit the nation early in 1893. It was caused by over-speculation, strikes, and the depression in farm prices. Cleveland had no tools to effectively deal with the crisis. He did, however, insist that the Sherman Silver Act had to be repealed because of the drain on the nation's gold reserves. He called a special session of Congress in 1893 to do just that.

The fight over repealing the Sherman Silver Act was substantial. Silver coinage had become an issue far beyond the question of what it actually accomplished. It was supported by the poorer classes and opposed by the wealthier ones. It was an issue of class conflict, not one of actual policy. The issue was particularly sensitive as the working class was losing what little it had in the depression. A young congressman from Nebraska, William Jennings Bryan, made a spellbinding speech against repealing the act, but Cleveland was able to force a repeal. It damaged his own party substantially and did not completely halt the decline in the gold reserves.

The continued drain on the treasury forced the government to sell bonds for gold. When even this was not enough, Cleveland negotiated a new bond sale through J. P. Morgan, the banking giant. The sale restored confidence in the U.S. monetary system, but it created a political cramp for the president. Morgan and his people received a substantial commission for their part in the bond sale. This left Cleveland open to charges of currying favor with the powerful

HISTORY & GEOGRAPHY 807

LIFEPAC TEST

NAME _____

DATE _____

SCORE _____

HISTORY & GEOGRAPHY 807: LIFEPAC TEST

Answer these questions (each answer, 3 points).

1. What was the era from 1865 to 1900 called?

   _____

2. What form of currency became an emotional issue of poorer working people in the late 1800s?

   _____

3. What event marked America's emergence as a world power?

   _____

4. What two things caused the Great Plains to be settled so quickly?

   a. _____

   b. _____

5. What banking reform finally gave the nation a flexible money supply?

   _____

6. What was the first major corporate industry in America?

   _____

7. How did Theodore Roosevelt get permission for a canal after Colombia refused?

   _____

   _____

8. How was open range cattle raising profitable in the 1870s and 80s?

   _____

   _____

   _____

9. What did the Pendleton Act do?

   _____

   _____

   _____

Put the first letter of the correct president'(s) name in the blank (each blank, 2 points).

Garfield	Arthur	Cleveland	Harrison
McKinley	Roosevelt	Taft	Wilson

10. _____ , _____ , _____ Progressive presidents

11. _____ , _____ assassinated in office

12. _____ , _____ Democrats

13. _____ served two non-consecutive terms

14. _____ started the Civil Service Commission off well

15. _____ Spanish-American War, front porch campaign, very pro-business

16. _____ Rough Rider, first to seriously use anti-trust laws

17. _____ , _____ split the Republican vote in 1912

18. _____ governor of Philippines, Dollar Diplomacy, failed to reduce tariff

19. _____ had problems with Mexico, reduced the tariff, used army in the Caribbean

Choose the correct item, thing, or person (each answer, 3 points).

20. _____ Roosevelt's foreign policy for action, based on a proverb

21. _____ immigrants that came from the south and east in the 1880s, not northern Europe

22. _____ Democratic leader, "Cross of Gold" speech

23. _____ Congress under Harrison that spent a huge surplus

24. _____ first major law written to control monopolies

25. _____ America's first popular automobile

26. _____ group that received generous pensions from Republican governments

27. _____ census year in which there was no longer a frontier

28. _____ explosion of this ship started war with Spain

29. _____ American trade policy with China

Answer true or false (each answer, 1 point).

30. _____ America changed its policy of no interference in business because corporations abused their power.

31. _____ Wilson's primary agenda was tariff reform, civil service reform, and farm loans.

32. _____ Wealthy industrialists often both exploited workers and engaged in philanthropy.

33. _____ Most Americans had more money and more ways to spend it at the end of the 1800s.

34. _____ The Republican Party opposed high tariffs and opposed the gold standard.

35. _____ Roosevelt was an unpopular, but successful, president.

36. _____ Progressive reform began at the national level.

37. _____ Most of the presidents from the Civil War until 1900 were mediocre and were not national leaders.

38. _____ The Progressive Movement had wide popular support, but was not very successful.

39. _____ Muckrakers were politicians who dug up negative stories about their opponents.

BONUS (4 points for a completely correct answer).

40. Name the three post-Civil War reform movements that began among farmers and led into Progressivism.

_____

_____

_____

men of the banking industry. This was an especially onerous charge leveled by the rising Populists.

The second major debacle of Cleveland's administration was his handling of the Pullman strike in 1894. The Pullman Palace Car Company built and leased sleeping cars for the railroads. Due to the depression, Pullman cut wages in 1894 without reducing the high rent it charged for homes in the company town. The workers went on strike. They were supported by the American Railway Union under Eugene Debs. The workers refused to work on any train that had Pullman cars. The railroad obtained an injunction against the strikers for interfering with the delivery of the mail and interstate commerce. Since obeying the injunction would mean ending the strike, Debs refused. Some of the strikers in Chicago reacted with violence. Urged by his attorney general, who was a corporate lawyer, Cleveland sent in the army to break up the strike.

The nation was alarmed by how quickly the courts and the government jumped to do the bidding of the railroads. More alarms were raised when the courts refused to use the Sherman Anti-Trust Act against the huge sugar trust that controlled virtually all sugar production in America. Protest books, such as *Progress and Poverty*, *Wealth Against Commonwealth*, and *Coin's Financial School*, condemning the hypocrisy of the Gilded Age were widely read and discussed. The alliance between powerful businesses and the government was being threatened by a rising tide of voter rebellion.

Cleveland tried to obtain a reduction in the tariff, as he had promised in the 1892 campaign, but the depression and the spending of the Fifty-first Congress had left the government short of money. The Democratic Party was still reeling from the silver coinage fight. The Wilson-Gorman Bill that finally came out of Congress only slightly reduced the tariffs and was burdened with hundreds of amendments, including an income tax and a payoff to the sugar trust. Cleveland allowed the law to pass. The popular income tax provision was quickly struck down by the courts, further alienating the Populists.

 Answer these questions.

2.35 What was the Fifty-first Congress (elected in 1888) called?

_____

2.36 Who were the presidential candidates and their parties in 1888?

_____

_____

2.37 Who were the presidential candidates and their parties in 1892?

_____

_____

_____

2.38 Which two laws passed in 1890 were the result of a Northern-Western deal?

_____

2.39 What was the group that spoke for the farmers and reform in 1890?

_____

2.40 What event doomed Cleveland's second administration?

_____

2.41 What was the main issue of the 1888 and 1892 campaigns?

_____

2.42 What law was passed in response to public pressure to control the trusts?

_____

2.43 What political party was formed in 1892 in Omaha, Nebraska?

_____

2.44 Cleveland damaged his own party forcing the repeal of what law?

_____

2.45 Cleveland sent in the Army to halt which strike? _____

2.46 What was the name of the Nebraska congressman who supported silver coinage?

_____

2.47 Who won the popular presidential vote in 1888?

_____

2.48 Who was the main beneficiary of Republican spending in the Fifty-first Congress?

_____

2.49 What issue became an emotional class conflict more than a debate of merits?

_____

2.50 What tariff law did Cleveland allow even though it did not make serious reductions?

_____

2.51 What action to increase the gold reserves got Cleveland in political trouble?

_____

2.52 What were the major problems affecting the farmers?

_____

2.53 Who was the head of the American Railway Union?

_____

2.54 What events challenged Republican claims in the 1892 campaign that the tariff protected

high American wages? _____

2.55 What alarmed the nation about the response to the Pullman Strike of 1894?

_____

2.56 What did Congress do with the 1888 budget surplus? _____

2.57 What were seven of the planks in the Populist Platform in 1892?

a. _____   b. _____

c. _____   d. _____

e. _____   f. _____

g. _____

Election of 1896. The 1896 campaign vaulted into the limelight a man who would be the most important figure in the Democratic Party for many years, William Jennings Bryan. Bryan had been a Congressman and had lost a bid for the Senate in 1894. He worked as an editor and lecturer until the 1896 Democratic convention when he appeared as a delegate from Nebraska.

The convention was dominated by pro-silver men. They repudiated Cleveland and would not even consider him as a candidate. The convention had no clear candidate until Bryan took the platform to speak in support of free coinage of silver. It was probably the most famous convention speech in American history.

Bryan spoke in favor of the laboring class, against the rich industrialists and the government they controlled. He spoke in the ideas of the day, in favor of silver, which was the issue of the downtrodden. He scathingly attacked those who favored the gold standard. "We will answer their demands for a gold standard by saying to them: 'You shall not press down upon the brow of labor this crown of thorns, you shall not crucify mankind upon a cross of gold.'"

The "Cross of Gold" speech ignited the Democratic convention and made Bryan their candidate even though he was only 36 years old.

The Populist Party was in a quandary because the Democrats had taken their main issue, silver coinage. Therefore, they nominated Bryan. The alarmed Republicans nominated William McKinley, a man who strongly favored the business interests. McKinley was promoted and managed by Marcus Hanna, a wealthy Ohio businessman. Hanna spent the time and money to secure McKinley's nomination on the first ballot and then went on to manage his campaign.

Bryan was the first presidential candidate to go to the people. Before that time, candidates did not usually actively campaign. It was considered undignified. Subordinates did all of the campaigning. Bryan, on the other hand, toured the nation, speaking in favor of silver and the working people. He made hundreds of emotional speeches, even in the industrial North.

The money powers were terrified of Bryan. Silver was so cheap that a silver dollar would actually be worth about 50 cents in gold.

The bankers could see all of their loans being repaid at half the value using silver dollars. The industrialists could see their profits destroyed in the resulting financial chaos. Hanna took full advantage of the panic over the silver issue. He raised millions of dollars from wealthy businessmen to create the largest campaign fund to date.

Hanna used his money to flood the nation with literature and rallies. The Republican campaign emphasized prosperity issues. The depression was blamed on the Democrats. McKinley was the candidate of stability and business. "McKinley and a full dinner pail," was his slogan. A careful smear campaign created fear that Bryan's election would doom the nation to economic disorder and depression.

McKinley stayed at home and conducted a "Front Porch Campaign." Loyal Republicans were brought to his home in Ohio to hear their candidate give a carefully prepared speech. The issues he addressed were chosen in advance based on what was important to that particular group. McKinley won by a convincing popular and electoral majority. Bryan won the South and part of the West, but McKinley won in the population centers in the North and East.

William McKinley (1843-1901). William McKinley was the last president of the Gilded Age. He favored business, did not enforce the antitrust laws, raised the tariff, and ignored cries for reform. He was personally a very charming man, religious, and devoted to his invalid wife. He was born in Ohio to prosperous Scotch-Irish parents. His father owned an iron manufacturing business. William received a good education, but he withdrew from college because of illness. He was eighteen when the Civil War began and immediately volunteered. In spite of his youth, he reached the temporary rank of major. He was the last Civil War veteran to be president. After the war, he studied law and began practicing in Canton, Ohio.

| William Jennings Bryan

McKinley entered local politics in the late 1860s. He was elected to the U.S. House of Representatives in 1876. He served in the House, with one break, until 1890. In that election, public anger over his tariff and the Billion-dollar Congress cost him and many other Republicans their seats. McKinley was thereafter twice elected governor and became friends with Marcus Hanna. Hanna bailed him out of a serious jam in the Panic of 1893. McKinley became responsible for some debts he had **co-signed** for a friend. Hanna raised the $100,000 needed to pay the debts. Hanna began working to win the presidency for McKinley in 1892 and did so in 1896.

First administration. McKinley allowed the trusts to grow as they wanted, thus repaying his debts to the industrialists who financed his campaign. Moreover, the treasury was operating at a **deficit**. A new tariff bill, the Dingley Tariff, was passed in 1897. Again burdened with hundreds of amendments, it raised the tariffs back to near the levels of the McKinley Tariff of 1890 (some categories were even higher).

The triumphant "gold-bugs" wanted to put the nation's currency officially on the gold standard. That would value all of the nation's currency on gold only. There were too many Silverites left in Congress to do it right away, but by 1900 enough had been voted out for the Gold Standard Act to pass. The problem of the gold reserves was solved by the discovery of new gold fields and the development of new techniques to extract gold from other ores. Moreover, the nation came out of the depression in 1897 and entered an era of prosperity. Thus, McKinley would have ridden comfortably through his presidency with little to note had it not been for foreign affairs, specifically a war with Spain.

Complete these sentences.

2.58 The _____ officially tied all U.S. money to a value of gold in 1900.

2.59 The most famous convention speech in U.S. history was Bryan's _____ speech in 1896.

2.60 The farmers, reformers, and anti-industrialists (poorer working people) took up

_____ as their key issue in the early to mid-1890s.

2.61 The Populist Party nominated _____ in 1896.

2.62 McKinley owed his nomination and election to _____ .

2.63 McKinley's campaign slogan was _____ .

2.64 The most important man in the Democratic Party for years after 1896 was

_____ .

2.65 The _____ Tariff again raised the tariff rates.

2.66 _____ was the first presidential candidate to take his

campaign to the people.

2.67 McKinley's campaign convinced Americans that the election of _____

_____ would bring depression and disorder.

2.68 _____ raised the largest campaign fund to date for McKinley.

2.69 McKinley conducted a _____ campaign from his home.

2.70 A silver "dollar" would have been worth _____ at the 16 to 1 ratio in 1896.

2.71 America came out of the Panic of 1893 in _____ .

America Becomes a World Power

International interest. American foreign policy had been very stable since the Republic was founded. America avoided all involvement with European wars and problems. In return, Americans expected European powers to honor the Monroe Doctrine and stay out of the Americas. This was the policy of a militarily weak, agrarian nation, busy with the job of filling up its empty spaces.

Things were changing by the end of the 1800s. The industrial boom after the Civil War had made the United States one of the richest nations on earth. In the first decades after the war, the nation had maintained its traditional isolation. There were railroads to build, Indians to defeat, cattle to drive, and industries to build. By the 1890s, the frontier was gone, and America was looking to expand in other parts of the world. The nation had slowly been building a steel navy to protect its growing commerce.

This was the age of European **imperialism**. European powers like Britain, France, and Germany were taking colonies in Africa and Asia. America, now among the world's wealthiest nations, began to hunger for her share. Moreover, Social Darwinism dictated that the strong and powerful dominate the weak and less capable. Surely that meant more expansion for the great American Republic! Further impetus was added by the work of Captain Alfred Mahan. His popular book, *The Influence of Sea Power upon History, 1660-1783*, taught that sea power gave victory and world power to its possessors.

A whole string of international incidents focused American attention on the outside world in the late 1880s and 1890s. The U.S. had come close to war with Germany over the Samoan Islands (1889), with Italy over the lynching of some Italian citizens (1891), with Chile over an attack on U.S. sailors (1892), and with Britain over a boundary dispute in South America (1895-96). In 1893 American white planters on the island of Hawaii overthrew the native ruler, Queen Liluokalani. Honest President Cleveland refused to annex the island when it became clear that the people of Hawaii did not want it, only the white-controlled government did. Many Americans clamored to take the islands (they were annexed in 1898). America was growing in power and anxious to prove it. It was also becoming increasingly imperialistic.

Revolt in Cuba. Cuba was one of the last Spanish possessions in the New World. Having lost all of Latin America, Spain was determined to keep her Caribbean Islands. The oppressed Cuban people broke out in one of their regular revolts in 1895. The rebels burned villages, destroyed crops and attacked officials. The Spanish government reacted harshly with arrests, torture, and executions. Civilians were rounded up into detention camps where they could not aid the rebels. There, they died from diseases spread by the lack of decent sanitation.

The American public was always willing to support people fighting for their freedom. Cuba also had attracted a great deal of American investments that were in jeopardy, but the leading cause of U.S. interest in the Cuban revolt was "yellow journalism." Two powerful New York City newspapers, the *Journal* and the *World*, were fighting a battle for sales. The nearby revolt gave the newspapers a creative source for sensational stories. William R. Hearst and Joseph Pulitzer (the newspapers' owners) were far more interested in good stories than true ones. The vivid, creative, and often false tales of abuse and murder raised a war cry from the American public.

Congress followed the American public in pressing for war. McKinley and his business backers, however, did not want that. McKinley, who had seen enough war as a young man, refused to give into the war cries until events forced his hand. The first event was a letter written by the Spanish ambassador in Washington calling McKinley a politician without good faith who was interested mainly in following the direction of his party. The private letter was stolen and published. The reaction forced the unfortunate Spanish diplomat to resign. The second event was the destruction of the *Maine* a few days after the letter was published.

The U.S. battleship *Maine* was sent to Havana, Cuba to protect and evacuate Americans if the situation grew worse. On February 15, 1898 the ship blew up in the harbor with the loss of over 250 American seamen. A U.S. investigation blamed a Spanish mine. The American public screamed for revenge. (Another U.S. investigation in the 1970s concluded the explosion was probably caused by combustion in the ship's coal supply, but no one will ever be sure of what happened.)

Angry Americans blamed Spain for destroying the *Maine* and killing U.S. sailors. A strong president might have been able to resist the popularity of war and work for a diplomatic solution. Spain was willing to negotiate, but she was not willing to grant Cuba independence. Fearful of losing the election in 1900 if he did not give in, McKinley finally requested armed intervention in Cuba on April 11th. Congress agreed, Spain declared war, and Congress followed suit on April 25th.

Spanish-American War. The war between the new rising world power, America, and the aging world power, Spain, began a long way from Cuba. A U.S. Pacific squadron, under Commodore George Dewey, had been ordered to attack the Spanish fleet in the Philippines (southwest of Japan) in the event of war. Dewey attacked the Spanish fleet in Manila Bay on May 1, 1898. He destroyed it with a minimum of U.S. casualties. He then blockaded the harbor until U.S. troops could arrive to take the city. They finally arrived and took the city on August 13th, the day after the war ended.

Back in Cuba, the U.S. fleet was blockading the island and searching for their Spanish counterparts. The Spanish fleet, under Admiral Pascual Cervera, was finally located, safely in Santiago Harbor at the east end of the island. The U.S. fleet blockaded the harbor and sent for the army to help take the city from the land side.

The U.S. army had been fighting only Indians since the Civil War and was too small to handle a major war. As in the past, the government called for volunteers and thousands responded. The volunteers were taken to Florida for training. There they drilled in woolen uniforms, which was all the army had available at the time.

Among the volunteers, two were particularly worth noting. One was Democratic General Joseph Wheeler, formerly of the Confederate Army. At the age of 61, "Fighting Joe" volunteered to wear a Union uniform. He led the attack on Santiago. His willingness and that of other Southern volunteers helped with the ongoing national reconciliation.

The second famous volunteer was Theodore Roosevelt. T.R. had been assistant secretary of the navy when the war began. He had been one of the Republicans pushing hard for the war. When it came, he quickly resigned and helped form the First United States Volunteer Cavalry,

| Battle of Santiago

better known as the "Rough Riders." The Rough Riders were a mixed bag of adventurers that included cowboys, Eastern college graduates, and policemen. Lieutenant-Colonel Roosevelt was the group's second in command but their prime organizer and leader.

When the navy finally located and trapped the Spanish fleet, 17,000 of the new volunteer troops were sent to assist. Among the troops sent to Cuba were about half of the Rough Riders, including T.R. The U.S. force made a very confused, and fortunately unopposed, landing near Santiago on June 22nd. They fought their way inland to take the city's defenses, which

were set up in the hills around it. The Rough Riders had their moment of glory on July 1st when Roosevelt led them on a charge up Kettle Hill to capture its defenses. (They went up on foot because they were not able to bring their horses.) The American army then captured San Juan Hill which set up a siege of the city. Roosevelt and the Rough Riders became associated in the public mind with the capture of San Juan Hill and the eventual victory in Cuba.

With the city under siege, Admiral Cervera tried to escape from the trap. On July 3rd, the Spanish fleet sailed out of the harbor with the Americans in full pursuit. The faster American ships

| Theodore Roosevelt and His "Rough Riders"

overtook and destroyed the Spanish fleet. The Americans suffered no serious damage, and Santiago surrendered on July 17th. An invasion of nearby Puerto Rico on July 25th was unopposed. Spain signed a preliminary **armistice** on August 12th. The "splendid little war," as soon-to-be Secretary of State John Hay called it, lasted less than four months.

There were very few battle-related deaths in the Spanish-American War, despite the fact it was conducted in an atmosphere of sheer chaos. However, there were a significant number of deaths from tropical diseases, specifically yellow fever which hit the army stationed in Santiago. In total, less than 400 men died of bullets, while many times that number died of diseases. Roosevelt, who had both political clout and no army career to protect, was one of several men who insisted the army get out of Cuba before it was **decimated**. Most of the army was removed by the end of July and back in the states by August.

Imperialism or not. At the end of the war, America was in possession of the Philippines, Cuba, Puerto Rico and several other small islands. A strong division rent the nation over what to do with these territories. The Philippines, which had not been part of the war aims, were especially troubling. The Congress had passed the Teller Amendment in 1898 which declared the U.S. had no ambitions to annex Cuba, but the nation was heavily divided about the rest. An Anti-Imperialist League sprang up to fight against keeping these foreign lands, but much of the nation was ready to be a world power and take on the "responsibility" of caring for less developed lands.

Eventually, McKinley decided to keep them all. Spain gave Cuba its freedom under U.S. protection. The U.S. took Puerto Rico as the spoils of war (it is still a U.S. territory, not a state) and purchased the Philippines for $20 million. The treaty was very controversial, however. It only passed in the Senate by one vote and that only

because William Jennings Bryan decided to support it.

Cuba. Cuba remained under U.S. occupation until 1902. During that time, the Americans invested in many helpful improvements for the island. The most significant was to bring yellow fever under control by cleaning up the breeding areas of the disease-carrying mosquitoes. Eventually, Cuba was given its independence, but only after it accepted the Platt Amendment as a part of its constitution. The Platt Amendment restricted Cuba from forming alliances with other nations and gave America the right to intervene on the island to maintain order. In effect, Cuba was free, but only as free as America permitted.

Philippines. A revolt against Spanish rule in the Philippines had been going on before 1898. Its leader, Emilo Aguinaldo, expected his nation to receive its independence after America won the war. When it became clear that was not what McKinley had in mind, Aguinaldo continued his rebellion against the Americans. A bloody, nasty guerrilla war was fought between the two sides until 1901. The Anti-Imperialists were furious at this turnabout of Americans killing men who were fighting for their independence. Eventually, Aguinaldo was captured and the rebellion was broken. The U.S gradually gave the Philippines more home rule in the early 1900s, but the Filipinos would have to wait until 1946 for their independence.

Open Door policy. America soundly defeated one of the old European powers in the Spanish-American War. This war is the point historians use to mark America's transition to a world power. The first test of this new status came in China.

China, unlike Japan, had never embraced Western technology. It was, therefore, a very weak nation at the end of the 1800s. Several European powers were in the process of carving it up into private trading zones. Americans wanted this huge land to be open to all traders.

In 1899, Secretary of State John Hay announced a new "Open Door" policy for China. He asked that all European nations honor China's boundaries and allow everyone to trade freely there. Many of the powers were only marginally interested, but Hays declared the policy established. The Open Door policy was aided by the fact that no one nation had a clear advantage in China and no chance of taking the whole country for themselves. Moreover, the most powerful nation of the day, Britain, also favored free trade in China.

In 1900, the Chinese people tried to drive out the foreigners during the Boxer Rebellion. The U.S. was one of the nations that sent in troops to rescue trapped foreigners in the capital of Beijing. Afterwards, Hay announced America supported an Open Door protecting China's territorial and commercial independence. This policy was largely successful, since China was never divided up into colonies. Many nations traded with her up until World War II. America was now acting on a larger stage than just the Western Hemisphere.

Match these people.

2.72	_____	Theodore Roosevelt		a.	led Filipino revolt against Spain and U.S.
2.73	_____	Alfred Mahan		b.	Secretary of State
2.74	_____	Pascual Cervera		c.	wrote *The Influence of Sea Power on History*
2.75	_____	William R. Hearst		d.	Confederate general, fought in Spanish-American War for the U.S.
2.76	_____	Joseph Wheeler			
2.77	_____	William J. Bryan		e.	Rough Riders' leader
2.78	_____	Emilo Aguinaldo		f.	newspaper owner
2.79	_____	John Hay		g.	defeated Spanish fleet, Manila Bay
2.80	_____	George Dewey		h.	Spanish admiral, Santiago fleet
				i.	supported Spanish treaty to use as a campaign issue in 1900

Name the item described.

2.81 _____ sensational writing, not very factual, used by the *World* and the *Journal* to encourage war

2.82 _____ battleship that blew up in Havana harbor

2.83 _____ U.S. policy toward China, 1900

2.84 _____ U.S. declared it would not annex Cuba

2.85 _____ bought by U.S. for $20 million

2.86 _____ event that recognized U.S. as a world power

2.87 _____ First United States Volunteer Cavalry

2.88 _____ opposed U.S. keeping land taken in Spanish war

2.89 _____ islands, American planters overthrew Queen Liluokalani

2.90 _____ Chinese tried to drive out foreigners

2.91 _____ disease brought under control by U.S. during Cuban occupation

2.92 _____ part of Cuban constitution that limited its freedom

2.93 _____ hill taken by the Rough Riders

2.94 _____ island taken by U.S. forces on July 25, 1898

2.95 _____ approximate length of the Spanish-American War

2.96 _____ city captured by U.S. in Cuba

Review the material in this section in preparation for the Self Test. This Self Test will check your mastery of this particular section as well as your knowledge of the previous section.

SELF TEST 2

Match these people. Some answers will be used more than once (each answer, 2 points).

2.01 _____ Assistant Secretary of the Navy

2.02 _____ led the Rough Riders

2.03 _____ signed first civil service reform

2.04 _____ Billion-dollar Congress, Sherman Anti-Trust Act

2.05 _____ first Democratic president after Civil War

2.06 _____ Populist candidate

2.07 _____ served two non-consecutive terms

2.08 _____ shot by angry office seeker

2.09 _____ "Cross of Gold" speech

2.010 _____ protegé of Senator Roscoe Conkling, ran N.Y. Custom House until fired

2.011 _____ Republican Half-Breed faction leader

2.012 _____ made vice presidential candidate to win Stalwart support

2.013 _____ strong reformer, improved the tarnished image of the presidency

2.014 _____ Republican candidate, never became president

2.015 _____ Democratic party leader for years after 1896

a. James Garfield

b. William McKinley

c. William J. Bryan

d. Chester A. Arthur

e. Theodore Roosevelt

f. James Blaine

g. Benjamin Harrison

h. Grover Cleveland

Answer these questions (each answer, 3 points).

2.016 What was the emotional issue of the working people in the late 1800s?

a. _____

What did they think it would accomplish?

b. _____

2.017 Between the Civil War and the Spanish-American War, what did the army do?

_____

2.018 What is the philosophy that government should leave business alone?

_____

2.019 What nation's revolt led America into war with Spain?

_____

2.020 What event marked the establishment of the U.S. as a world power?

_____

2.021 What was the movement that grew out of the Farmer's Alliances combining the demands of several reform movements? _____

2.022 What was the main source of American revenue in the late 1800s that businessmen strongly supported? _____

2.023 What did the Billion-dollar Congress do with the surplus?

_____

2.024 What was the nation's first major union movement? _____

Choose the best match. Each answer is used only once (each answer, 2 points).

2.025 _____ limited Cuban freedom	a.	Sherman Anti-Trust Act
2.026 _____ gave away free land to settlers	b.	Interstate Commerce Act
2.027 _____ Rockefeller's trust	c.	Standard Oil
2.028 _____ allowed the plains to be settled quickly	d.	Social Darwinism
2.029 _____ basis of U.S. approach to Chinese trade	e.	Railroads
2.030 _____ civil service reform	f.	Steel production
2.031 _____ written to control the railroads	g.	Pendleton Act
2.032 _____ idea that the poor are poor because they are inferior people	h.	Platt Amendment
2.033 _____ Carnegie used Bessemer process	i.	Homestead Act
2.034 _____ used against unions in restraint of trade	j.	Open Door policy

Answer true or false (each answer, 2 points).

2.035	_____	The Gilded Age was a time of progress and reform.
2.036	_____	Most of the presidents of the Gilded Age were outstanding leaders.
2.037	_____	The AFL emphasized labor issues such as wages and hours.
2.038	_____	McKinley was a very pro-business president.
2.039	_____	The Spanish-American War lasted almost a year.
2.040	_____	Farmers wanted controls on the railroads.
2.041	_____	New Immigrants came from south and eastern Europe.
2.042	_____	Republicans after the Civil War gave away a tremendous amount of money in pensions to gain the political support of veterans.
2.043	_____	The U.S. peacefully took control of the Philippines.
2.044	_____	Striking unions were opposed by the law, the government and the corporations during the Gilded Age.
2.045	_____	Living and working conditions for immigrant industrial workers were usually excellent.
2.046	_____	The destruction of the U.S. fleet in Manila made America go to war with Spain.

80 / 100   SCORE _____   TEACHER _____ _____
initials   date

3. THE PROGRESSIVE ERA

The pressure for reforms had been building since the end of the Civil War. It finally blew the lid off the kettle of traditionalism in the early 20th century. Between about 1900 and 1917, America faced a storm of reforms that touched political, social, and economic life. It was called the Progressive Era, and it had no precedent in American history.

Americans had always been champions of small government. For all of its one hundred and twenty-year existence, the Revolutionary spirit that had driven out the British had opposed large, powerful governments. The basic opinion of most Americans was that the job of government was to stay out of people's way. The restricted government that easily managed a nation of farmers and small business could not control the power of corporate trusts, the exploitation of friendless workers, and the corruption of political machines. Either the government had to expand to control these things, or it had to accept being controlled by them.

The Progressive Movement was the end result of a series of reform movements that had gained increasing respect in the late 1800s. It began with the Grange which passed its demands onto the Farmer's Alliances and then on to the Populists. The difference was that the Progressives succeeded! They started with reforms in the place that needed them most, the cities. The movement expanded into states and, under the leadership of dynamic Theodore Roosevelt, jumped into the national arena. This section will study this remarkable period.

SECTION OBJECTIVES

Review these objectives. When you have completed this section, you should be able to:

1. Describe the development of unions and reform movements from 1865 to 1915.
2. Describe the course of the Progressive Movement.
3. Describe the personality of Theodore Roosevelt and his effect on the presidency.
4. Name the Progressive presidents and describe their policies.

VOCABULARY

Study these words to enhance your learning success in this section.

adulteration (ə dəl tə rā' shən). Making something impure by adding foreign or inferior substances, especially by replacing valuable ingredients with less costly inferior ones.

libel (lī' bəl). The publication of false written statements that harm a person's reputation to a degree that he can sue for damages.

recall (ri kol'). The right by which an official may be removed by the vote of the people.

referendum (ref ə ren' dəm). Submitting a proposal to a popular vote.

suffrage (səf' rij). The right of voting.

Roosevelt

Progressive birth. The Progressive Movement was a widespread and unusual reform movement. It did not have any one single leader. The work was accomplished by many people in many different places and walks of life. The early 1900s were very prosperous times for America and it was remarkable that such a large reform movement would happen then. Prosperous people do not usually demand major changes from their government and society, but in the early 1900s they did.

The reforms began in the cities in the 1890s. The depression in 1893 had caused tremendous suffering in the cities and starkly emphasized the need for changes. City governments were run by party bosses who traded city jobs and contracts for profit and votes. Honest men normally stayed away. That began to change as angry voters in city after city voted for reformers beginning in the late-1890s. Machines in cities like Detroit, Toledo, New York, St. Louis and San Francisco fell to reformers.

The new city governments had wide support among the middle class, which was the mainstay of the Progressive Movement. They used that support to change the way Gilded Age cities had been run. One of the first changes was in the area of public utilities. Electricity, gas, water, and garbage pickup were all handled by private companies. The Gilded Age city machines sold the right to supply these services, took bribes on the sales and allowed the company to charge whatever it could, regardless of the quality of service! The reformers ended the sale of public services for bribes and placed those services under more effective control. Other city reforms included using experts, not politicians, to run the city by appointing city managers. Action was also taken against unsafe housing, prostitution, and political and police corruption.

An excellent example of the city reformer was Samuel Jones, mayor of Toledo. "Golden Rule"

| La Follette

Jones was a wealthy businessman who treated his employees as he would want to be treated. He took that idea with him into city management in 1897. He required open bidding for city contracts, initiated civil service reform, and led drives for more parks, schools, and city facilities. He so infuriated his party's bosses that he had to run as an independent, but he continued to be re-elected until his death.

State reforms. Many of the states were also hit with the effects of Progressivism. The model for the new movement was Wisconsin, under the leadership of Governor Robert La Follette. The Wisconsin state government had, like most, been dominated by a few powerful state industries (railroads in Wisconsin). La Follette was elected governor in 1900 and proceeded to work steadily for reforms. He established a system of primary elections for candidates, which meant that the party bosses and the railroads could no longer choose the candidates.

He established an effective railroad commission to control rates within the state. He forced the railroads to pay taxes on the full value of their holdings. He also initiated state civil service reform.

The "Wisconsin Idea" spread to other states. In California, Hiram Johnson broke the Southern Pacific Railroad's control over state politics. Charles Evans Hughes pushed similar reforms in New York. Reform movements succeeded in Oregon, Iowa, Kansas, Minnesota, North Dakota, and Missouri. Even in states where they did not take the governor's office, the Progressives often were able to get enough votes in the legislature to force some reforms. Secret ballots, primary elections, voter **referendums, recall** elections, tax reform, and regulatory commissions became common as the people demanded their government be returned to them.

Muckraking. Writers added fuel to the flames with their popular stories of corruption and scandal. Roosevelt named them "Muckrakers" for a character in the book *Pilgrim's Progress* who was so busy digging in the muck that he never saw the crown above his head. T.R. meant it as a criticism, but the Muckrakers proudly took on the name and kept themselves busy in the nation's mud holes.

The main Muckrakers were popular magazines who discovered that these articles sold well. *McClure's*, *Munsey's*, *Cosmopolitan*, and *Collier's* were among the magazines that competed for the most sensational stories. Careful of the powerful men they were attacking and the **libel** laws, the articles were well- researched and carefully documented. The writers exposed corruption in government, bribery by businesses, the abuses of child labor, the **adulteration** of medicines, and the conditions of the poor. One of the most famous, the *History of the Standard Oil Company*, by Ida Tarbell, used public documents and interviews to prove that the company had succeeded using bribery, extortion, and ruthlessness.

The public ate up these articles. The constant supply of information about the abuses around them pushed the reform movement. The Muckrakers and the Progressives fed each other. The writers provided the proof and motivation the reformers needed. The reformers provided the reading audience the writers needed.

Anti-liquor movement. Part of the Progressive Movement was an active temperance campaign. Reformers saw alcohol as the basis of many of the vices of the city (similar to drug addiction today). The leading groups in this battle were the Woman's Christian Temperance Union and the Anti-Saloon League. The latter was well organized and financed. It attacked liquor sales at their most obvious and despised source, the local saloon. Under pressure from these reformers, many "dry" laws outlawing, regulating, and restricting the sale of alcohol were passed. Eventually, the movement was rewarded with the 18th Amendment in 1919 which outlawed liquor sales in all of the United States until its repeal in 1933.

Election of 1900. McKinley, as the popular leader of a victorious nation, easily won the Republican nomination in 1900. The dynamic Theodore Roosevelt, who had returned from the war to become governor of New York, was chosen as his running mate. The Democrats nominated William Jennings Bryan again. Even though it was a dead issue, Bryan insisted on a free silver plank in the party platform. McKinley again stayed on his front porch while the popular T.R. toured the nation. The Republicans campaigned for "Four more years of a full dinner pail." Bryan tried to campaign against imperialism but lost the election by a larger margin than in 1896.

Roosevelt was deliberately put into the vice presidency to make use of his popular appeal and keep him powerless. He was an independent, energetic man who quickly became a Progressive leader. The party bosses in New York supported his move to the ceremonial job of vice president to get him out of their state. However, as Marcus Hanna realized, the "cowboy" was now only one heartbeat from the presidency. The boss' fears were realized when McKinley was assassinated in September of 1901 by an anarchist. The Progressive Movement had its first president.

Theodore Roosevelt (1858-1919). Theodore Roosevelt revitalized the office of the presidency. He was a man of boundless energy, self-confidence, and bravado. He loved a good fight and was immensely popular. He had a personal following that rivaled Andrew Jackson's. He remade the presidency in his own image and left it as one of the most powerful offices in the world. He is considered to be among our nation's greatest presidents.

Roosevelt was born to a wealthy New York City family. He was a sickly child who overcame his own ill health by forceful exercise. He developed a tremendous love for the "strenuous life." He was an athlete and an avid outdoorsman the rest of his life. He was tutored at home until he went to Harvard in 1876. After college, he went into politics as a Republican. He served in the state legislature and worked for reforms with then Governor Grover Cleveland.

Tragedy struck T.R.'s life in 1884. His young wife died in childbirth, and on the same day his mother died. Roosevelt resigned from politics and moved West to live on some ranches he owned. He worked as a cowboy with his men. The long hours and hard work helped him recover from his grief. At first, his men thought he was a silly dude, but his willingness to work hard and his ability to fight with his fists soon won their respect.

He returned to New York in 1886 to run for mayor of New York City and lost. He served on the Civil Service Commission and as police commissioner in New York City. He proved to be an honest reformer in both jobs. Roosevelt campaigned for McKinley in 1896 and was rewarded with a position as assistant secretary of the navy. He resigned at the beginning of the Spanish-American War to organize the

| Theodore Roosevelt

Rough Riders. His exploits in the war added to his growing reputation and enabled him to win election as the governor of New York. From there, he was moved up to the vice presidency. McKinley's death made him president at the young age of 42, and he quickly became a favorite with the newspapers. He lived up to his image as a reformer, leader, and devoted family man.

T.R. had remarried in 1886 after he returned from the West. He and his new wife, Edith Carow, had five children. Edith also raised T.R.'s daughter from his first marriage, Alice (named after her dead mother). The Roosevelts' lively household was part of their father's popularity. He loved his children and played wild games with them on the White House lawn. Stories of the boys sliding down the White House banister and bringing a pony upstairs only added to his colorful presidency. T.R. was a man who enjoyed living and the public ate it up. The "Teddy Bear" was a measure of his popularity. It quickly became a best-selling toy after Roosevelt sportingly refused to shoot a captured bear cub on one of his hunting trips.

Reform. Roosevelt was astute enough to realize he had to work with the leaders of the Republican Party. Therefore, he reassured them that he would follow McKinley's policies and then set off to carefully form his own. His approach to government was what he called the "Square Deal." Everyone did not get the best cards in the game, but the dealing must be done fairly. He began by going against the trusts which had grown fat and prosperous under McKinley's presidency.

T.R. created a sensation in 1902 when he ordered the rarely used Sherman Anti-Trust Act into action. Suit was brought against Northern Securities Company, a J.P. Morgan holding company that controlled most of the railroads in the Northwest. The case went all the way to the Supreme Court. In 1904 the Court ruled against the company and forced it to dissolve. It was the first significant victory for the "trust busters." Roosevelt initiated more than forty such actions during his presidency, and he won a respectable percentage of them; but he did not move against many of the trusts. He used the threat of anti-trust action to force the corporations to accept more regulation, which they did.

Roosevelt was the first president since the Civil War who actually led the government. He proposed legislation and followed it through the process. Today, we expect that of a president. It was T.R. who established the custom.

One of his first laws was the Elkins Act of 1903 which prohibited rebates (still a problem) by railroads. The law imposed heavy fines on <u>both</u> the railroad and the shipper who participated in a rebate scheme. Standard Oil was one of the companies fined under the law.

An even more effective law was the Hepburn Act of 1906. This gave some teeth to the powerless Interstate Commerce Commission. The I.C.C. was expanded and given the power to set rates, if shippers complained. The railroads could still challenge in court (they had tied up previous decisions for years that way), but under the Hepburn Act, the I.C.C. rates held until the court made its decision, and the railroad, not the government, had to prove its case.

Name the item, term, or person.

3.1 _____ wrote stories about corruption and social evils

3.2 _____ government level where Progressive Movement began

3.3 _____ state that lead in Progressive reform

3.4 _____ law prohibiting rebates

3.5 _____ first major success of Sherman Anti-Trust Act

3.6 _____ toy named after Theodore Roosevelt

3.7 _____ author of the *History of Standard Oil Company*

3.8 _____ McKinley's campaign promised four more years of it

3.9 _____ T.R.'s approach to government

3.10 _____ law that gave the I.C.C. some power

3.11 _____ reform governor of Wisconsin

3.12 _____ reform mayor of Toledo

3.13 _____ event that emphasized the need for city reforms

3.14 _____ two groups that led the temperance movement

Complete these items.

3.15 Why did the party bosses support Roosevelt's nomination as vice president?

_____

_____

3.16 Name eight of the reforms of the Progressive Movement.

a. _____ b. _____

c. _____ d. _____

e. _____ f. _____

g. _____ h. _____

3.17 How did Theodore Roosevelt change the presidency?

_____

_____

1902 Coal Strike. Roosevelt also exemplified the growing Progressive concern for the working man. In 1902 the hard coal miners of Pennsylvania went on strike. These were men who had been shamelessly exploited for years by low wages, high rent, dangerous conditions, and long hours. The United Mine Workers Union was careful to keep the strike peaceful and thereby gained public sympathy for the strikers. The mine owners, however, refused to negotiate. Coal was the nation's major source of heat, and the situation grew desperate as winter approached and coal supplies ran low.

Roosevelt, unlike the presidents before him, did not automatically side with the owner. As a crisis loomed, he brought both sides to the White House and offered to arbitrate. The United Mine Workers agreed; the owners refused. T.R. furiously threatened to send in the army to mine the coal. That threat turned the tide. The owners agreed and the miners went to work, pending the decision of the arbitrators. The arbitrators gave the miners some but not all of what they wanted. It was not a total victory, but for the first time the government had given the workers a fair hearing. It was a significant turning point for labor, although their battle was far from completed.

Roosevelt also recognized that the problems with corporations and labor unions required more supervision. In 1903 he convinced Congress to establish the Department of Commerce and Labor. Among other things, this new organization investigated corporations and laid the groundwork for later trust busting.

Conservation. For generations, Americans had used their resources as if they were limitless. In the early 1900s, with the end of the frontier, many far sighted individuals realized the nation needed to conserve its resources. T.R., the hunter and avid outdoorsman, was an early leader in the conservation movement. Roosevelt set aside millions of acres of forest land, water sources, and mineral lands for public, not private, use. The Newlands Act of 1902 set up a fund from land sales for Western irrigation projects. Roosevelt wanted the land used carefully and scientifically in a manner that would make it productive for many years. The nation no longer had an endless supply of new land. T.R. realized that we had to take care of what we had.

Big Stick in Panama. America had been hoping for years to build a canal across Central America. Such a canal would save thousands of miles and weeks of travel for ships going from the east to the West Coast. After the Spanish-American War, the new territories in the Pacific seemed particularly vulnerable without a quick way to get the navy from one ocean to another to protect them.

An old British-American treaty required the two nations to share ownership of any such canal. Obviously, times had changed and the now powerful U.S. was not willing to share such an American canal with anyone. The British recognized this and signed the Hay-Pauncefote Treaty in 1901. It gave the U.S. full rights to any canal as well as the right to fortify it. In exchange, the Americans promised that the canal would be open to all nations.

Roosevelt was not a man to wait on any important issue. A French company had tried to build a canal across Panama and failed. It offered its holdings to the U.S. government for the very low price of $40 million. After deciding against an alternate route through Nicaragua, a treaty was negotiated with Colombia which owned Panama. The treaty would have given the U.S. a permanent lease on a six-mile wide strip of land needed for the canal. America offered to pay $10 million up front and $250,000 a year for the lease.

The Colombian congress rejected the treaty. Roosevelt was furious. His philosophy in foreign affairs was based on a proverb, "Speak softly and carry a big stick, you will go far." Colombia was about to feel the weight of his "Big Stick."

| Construction of the Locks on the Panama Canal, 1910

| Modern-Day picture of the Canal

Panama had revolted against Colombia a number of times in the past. With the encouragement of a representative of the French canal company, they did so again in November of 1903. This time the American navy stopped the Colombians from coming in to put down the revolt. Roosevelt recognized the revolutionary government at once and sent them the same treaty he had offered Colombia (the only change was the canal zone was now ten miles wide). It was immediately accepted.

The Americans did succeed in building the massive canal under the leadership of George W. Goethals, a West Point engineer. He was aided by Colonel William Gorgas who had eliminated yellow fever in Cuba. This intrepid medical pioneer made the disease-ridden canal zone safe for the thousands of men needed to complete the project. The canal cost $400 million to build and opened in 1914, just in time for World War I. The rough handling of Colombia, however, soured American relations with Latin America, leaving a dark blot on an otherwise momentous accomplishment.

Roosevelt Corollary. T.R. added his own "corollary" to the Monroe Doctrine, which warned Europeans to stay out of the American nations.

Roosevelt's addition was that if any American nation were doing something wrong, the U.S. would intervene as a type of policeman so that Europe would not have to do so. This corollary came out of debt problems in Latin America.

Venezuela had defaulted on its debts to Europe in the early 1900s. Germany and Britain, therefore, blockaded its ports and bombarded a city in 1902 to force the nation to honor its just debts. The American public was aroused over this "violation" of the Monroe Doctrine. Roosevelt stepped in and was able to arrange arbitration to settle that issue.

In 1904, however, Santa Domingo (Dominican Republic) also found itself unable to pay its debts. Fearful of another European attack in America's backyard, Roosevelt decided to act. He published his "corollary" and used it to justify moving American officials to the island to take charge of its finances. The U.S. took over the custom houses in Santa Domingo, the main source of revenue. The Americans then used the money to make payments on the debts for almost forty years. This heavy-handed use of the Monroe Doctrine would be American policy in the Caribbean through the 1920s.

Election of 1904. Roosevelt longed to be elected president on his own to prove he was more than a political accident. The bosses really did not want to nominate him in 1904, but the death of Marcus Hanna left them without another candidate. T.R. received the nomination. The Democrats bypassed two-time loser Bryan and nominated Alton Parker, a New York judge. Roosevelt campaigned for his "square deal" and won by the largest popular majority to date.

Second administration. Roosevelt's major reform laws in his second administration were the Hepburn Act (discussed earlier) as well as food and drug acts. The latter had been inspired by the Upton Sinclair novel, *The Jungle*. One of the most famous Muckraker works, *The Jungle* exposed the incredibly gross and unsanitary conditions in the meat-packing industry. An investigation ordered by Roosevelt confirmed the worst of it. Roosevelt responded with the Meat Inspection Act that required meat packers to submit to federal health inspections. A follow-up bill, the Pure Food and Drug Act, set standards for processed foods and medicines.

Roosevelt's popularity faced a serious test when speculation caused a panic in 1907. The corporations immediately blamed Roosevelt and his reform policy; but it was a short depression that affected mainly the banking industry, and Roosevelt emerged from it as popular as ever. It did pave the way for currency reform, however. It became clear during the panic that the nation needed a way to expand the supply of money in a crisis. (On the gold standard, a nation cannot easily increase its money supply without getting more gold.) Congress passed a law that allowed national banks to issue currency in an emergency, using different backing.

Russo-Japanese War. Russia had been expanding in the Far East for years. Japan watched in alarm as the great bear reached into Manchuria (northern China) and Korea. Fearful of the czar's intentions, Japan attacked the Russian fleet at Port Arthur (west of Korea) in 1904,

| Big Stick in the Caribbean cartoon

destroying it. The resulting war gave Japan a series of rapid victories that humiliated Imperial Russia. Japan was too weak to continue the war and quietly asked Roosevelt to mediate in 1905.

Roosevelt knew it would be a thankless job, but he agreed to bring the combatants to the U.S. for talks. He put on the pressure until an agreement was reached that both accepted and neither liked. Japan thought she did not get enough for her victories and Russia felt the U.S. interfered before she had a chance to win. Thus, Roosevelt won the anger of the two nations, but he was also awarded the 1906 Nobel Peace Prize for his efforts.

Moroccan Crisis. Tensions that would eventually lead to World War I were mounting in Europe. In 1905 Germany refused to recognize French control of Morocco (on the North coast of Africa). Roosevelt stepped in when he realized a general European war was possible. He convinced both sides to meet at a conference in Spain in 1906. There America supported the French claims and Germany backed down, this time.

Gentlemen's Agreement. Roosevelt had other problems with Japan. Japanese immigrants had been coming to the American West Coast in record numbers. In 1906 San Francisco decided to send Japanese children to segregated schools. The Japanese saw this as a racial insult, and it triggered an international crisis. Roosevelt had no official power over the decisions of a city school board and yet it had the potential to start a war. The president eventually worked out a plan. Under a "Gentlemen's Agreement," the school board rescinded its order and the diplomats settled California's fear of large scale Asian immigration. The secret agreement was that Japan would limit the number of people it allowed to leave for America. This set relations with Japan on a more even keel for the time being.

Great White Fleet. Roosevelt was concerned that the Japanese might interpret his willingness to negotiate as an inability to fight. Therefore, he sent part of the U.S. navy (now the second largest on earth) on a tour around the world in 1907. The tour of the "Great White Fleet" was a resounding success. The ships were greeted by cheering crowds all over the world, including Japan. It returned in triumph in 1909 just as Roosevelt retired from the presidency.

 Complete these sentences.

3.18 The _____ Act used money from sale of Western lands to finance irrigation projects.

3.19 The 1904 Democratic candidate for president was _____ .

3.20 The novel that brought food and drug reform was _____

by _____ .

3.21 In 1902 Panama was a part of _____ .

3.22 Theodore Roosevelt's foreign policy was based on the proverb, "Speak softly and carry a

_____ ."

3.23 Roosevelt won the Noble Peace Prize for negotiating an end to the

_____ .

3.24 The _____ Crisis of 1905 almost started a war in Europe.

3.25 The nation faced a panic under Roosevelt in _____ .

3.26 Roosevelt recognized the need for more control over corporations and workers when he

created the Department of _____ .

3.27 The _____ to the Monroe Doctrine said the U.S. would correct

wrongs in American nations to prevent European intervention.

3.28 Japan began a war in 1904 by attacking the Russian fleet at

_____ .

3.29 The _____ toured the world between 1907 and 1909.

3.30 _____ was the engineer in charge of construction of the

Panama Canal.

3.31 The Panama Canal cost _____ and opened in _____ .

3.32 Japan and America had a crisis in 1906 when San Francisco decided to

_____ .

3.33 The U.S. took over the custom houses on _____ to pay that

nation's debts.

3.34 Germany and Britain blockaded _____ in 1902 after it failed to

pay its debts.

3.35 _____ eliminated yellow fever in Cuba and in the canal zone.

3.36 The _____ Act required federal health inspections of

meat-packing plants.

3.37 The _____ Act set standards for processed food and medicine.

Answer these questions.

3.38 How did Roosevelt handle the 1902 hard coal strike?

_____

_____

_____

3.39 How did America get the Panama canal lease after Colombia refused it?

_____

_____

_____

3.40 What was the Gentlemen's Agreement that ended the crisis between the U.S. and Japan in

1906? _____

_____

_____

Taft

Election of 1908. Roosevelt had promised not to run in 1908, and he felt bound by that promise even though he was only 50 years old. However, he was so incredibly popular that, like Andrew Jackson, he was able to name his successor. He named his friend, Secretary of War William H. Taft, as the man he wanted to continue his policies. Roosevelt used his big stick to force Taft's nomination through on the first ballot at the party convention. The Democrats nominated William J. Bryan again. Taft won easily, largely on Roosevelt's popularity. Roosevelt took off on an extended hunting trip in Africa. His big business enemies toasted the good health of the lions.

William Howard Taft (1857-1930). William Howard Taft never wanted to be president. What he did want to be was a Supreme Court justice. He had a good legal mind and enjoyed being a judge. However, he had an ambitious wife, and his family was active in Republican politics. Therefore, he got into several political jobs that eventually led him to the White House.

Taft was born in Ohio, the son of a lawyer who was a prominent Republican. Taft attended Cincinnati Law School and was admitted to the Ohio bar in 1880. He became a successful lawyer, but his family pushed him toward a political career. He was appointed to and then elected to the Cincinnati Superior Court. He later served as a federal attorney and a federal court of appeals judge.

In 1900 he was appointed by McKinley as part of a commission to govern the Philippines and later he became the territory's first American governor. Taft did some of his best work in the Philippines. He built schools, roads, and harbor facilities. He arranged new courts, set up government offices for record keeping, pushed for land reform, and encouraged the development of limited self-government. The public took note of his work, and in 1904 Roosevelt had him take over as secretary of war in his cabinet.

| Taft Campaigning

Taft proved equally capable as a cabinet member. He worked well with Roosevelt and proved to be a capable administrator. Roosevelt felt comfortable leaving him in control when he retired. Taft, however, was a large, amiable man (he weighed over 300 pounds) who was ill suited to follow the energetic Roosevelt in office. Taft was a good man and a good administrator, but he lacked Roosevelt's drive, his zeal for reform, and his public flair. The result was disappointing, to the nation and to the president.

Republican Problems. Roosevelt had been the leader of the Progressive Republicans, and he gave their support to Taft when he retired. Taft promptly alienated them. The Republican platform had called for tariff reform, and Taft called a special session of Congress in 1909 to do that. Tariff reduction passed the House but was torpedoed by amendments in the Senate. The resulting Payne-Aldrich Tariff lowered only a few rates slightly. The Progressives were furious. Taft made matters worse by signing the bill and then defending it as the "best bill that the Republican Party ever passed."

Taft lost even more Progressive support over the fight between Secretary of the Interior Richard Ballinger, and the chief of the Division of Forestry, Gifford Pinchot, a Roosevelt pal and conservationist. Roosevelt had used his authority to prevent the sale of water sources and mineral lands on dubious legal grounds. Ballinger reversed some of these decisions and put the land up for sale. Pinchot accused Ballinger and the administration of turning against T.R.'s policies, favoring the corporations (who wanted the land), and making the sales illegally. A congressional investigation cleared Ballinger of the charges and Taft dismissed Pinchot. Progressives saw it as another failure by Taft to support their agenda.

The Progressives also wanted the president's support to break the power of Joseph Cannon, the dictatorial Speaker of the House of Representatives. The Progressives of the two parties were finally able to do so by joining forces. They stripped Cannon of his power to control legislation in the House that he had used to block reform laws. Taft did not support the effort, and the Progressives no longer counted him as one of their own.

Roosevelt returned from abroad and helped to split the Republicans further in 1910. He made fiery speeches in favor of "New Nationalism" in which the government would control political and social problems. The division in the party gave the Democrats control of the House in 1910 and weakened Republican control of the Senate.

Taft did have several successes in the continuing Progressive reform. His administration started almost twice as many anti-trust suits as Roosevelt had. Standard Oil and the American Tobacco Company were ordered to dissolve by the Supreme Court in 1911. Moreover, the new Democratic House began an investigation into the control Wall Street bankers had over corporations (the so-called "Money Trust"). It revealed a great deal about the way Morgan had spread

| The Wright Brothers and Their First Flight

his power by gaining control of companies that used his bank for loans. Moreover, under Taft, Congress passed the Sixteenth (allowed income tax) and Seventeenth (direct election of senators) Amendments to the Constitution.

Dollar Diplomacy. Taft's foreign policy was called "Dollar Diplomacy." The idea was to use American money as a way to expand U.S. influence abroad. Taft encouraged investment in Manchuria, the Caribbean, Panama, and Central America. It did not have any significant results. For example, Taft tried to get a U.S.-built railroad in China but failed when Japan and Russia would not cooperate. Taft also failed in an attempt to get mutual tariff reductions with Canada in 1911. Relations with the rest of the Americas remained tense as Taft used U.S. troops to quell disorder in the Caribbean and Nicaragua. Thus, Taft was left with a divided party, an unsuccessful foreign policy, and growing opposition from T.R. by the end of his term.

Technology advances. Two key advances in travel hit the U.S. during the Progressive Era, the airplane and the automobile. Orville and Wilbur Wright succeeded in the first powered airplane flight on December 17, 1903. It would be many years, however, before this new technology could be used on a large scale.

Automobiles, however, were poised to begin their takeover of the American road. The automobile had been invented in Europe, but it came to the people in America. The same year the Wright brothers first flew, Henry Ford organized the Ford Motor Company. Ford succeeded in using the moving assembly line to make cars faster and cheaper than ever before. His Model T became the first popular American car by bringing the price down within the reach of most Americans. (A Model T cost $390 in 1915 and $260 in 1925). Other companies took notice, and the industry soon expanded to a leading position in American manufacturing, eventually replacing the railroads.

Bull Moose Party. Robert La Follette, who had led the reforms in Wisconsin and was now a U.S. senator, formed the National Progressive Republican League in 1911. The League was pushing to get the Republican nomination for La Follette instead of Taft. In early 1912 Theodore Roosevelt, furious with Taft for abandoning his policies, decided he would run again. La Follette could not compete with the Rough Rider's popularity and quickly lost his support.

T.R. easily won most of the new primary elections, but Taft was now angry and put up an unusually strong fight. As president, Taft had the votes of the delegates outside the primary system, and he controlled the party machinery at the convention. Moreover, T.R. had frightened the milder Progressives with some of his demands, which included a scheme to control judicial decisions (a very radical idea). Thus, Taft won the nomination on the first vote. Roosevelt and his followers yelled fraud and left to form their own party.

The Progressive Party convention in August of 1912 nominated Theodore Roosevelt for president. T.R. claimed he felt "as strong as a Bull Moose" and gave the party its popular name, the Bull Moose Party. The party platform favored all the traditional Progressive reforms plus women's **suffrage**, minimum wage laws, government pensions, unemployment compensation, and control of the stock market. It was a radical platform and more than most Americans wanted.

The Election of 1912. The Republicans and the Progressives were obviously going to split the Republican vote. The Democrats realized they had an excellent chance to win the White House if they could select a decent candidate. They chose Woodrow Wilson, the reform governor of New Jersey. Wilson campaigned for a reform package he called the "New Freedom." Wilson emphasized the need to enforce anti-trust legislation and allow businesses to compete freely without monopolies. He did not favor adding extensively to the power of the federal government as the Bull Moose platform did.

The result was inevitable. Wilson won with 41% of the popular vote and a huge electoral majority (435 votes). Roosevelt took 27% of the popular vote and 88 electoral votes. Taft had the worst defeat in history for a president running for re-election. He won 23% of the popular vote and only 8 electoral votes. Taft happily retired and eventually did sit on the Supreme Court.

Name the person(s) related to each item.

3.41 _____ Dollar Diplomacy

3.42 _____ Bull Moose Party

3.43 _____ New Freedom

3.44 _____ 1908 Democratic candidate

3.45 _____ New Nationalism

3.46 _____ first powered airplane flight

3.47 _____ worst loss for president seeking re-election

3.48 _____ organized Republican Progressive League

3.49 _____ dictatorial Speaker of the House

3.50 _____ Model T

3.51 _____ Roosevelt's hand-picked successor

3.52 _____ governor of the Philippines

3.53 _____ Supreme Court justice

3.54 _____ used moving assembly line to make cheap cars

3.55 _____ secretary of the interior, reversed some of T.R.'s bans on sale of land

3.56 _____ Sixteenth and Seventeenth Amendments

3.57 _____ Progressive Party presidential candidate

3.58 _____ fired for accusations against the secretary of the interior

Answer these questions.

3.59 What three events cost Taft his support from Progressive Republicans?

a. _____   b. _____

c. _____

3.60 What was the purpose of Dollar Diplomacy? _____
_____

3.61 What were four of the planks in the Progressive Party platform?

a. _____   b. _____

c. _____   d. _____

3.62 What sort of an anti-trust record did Taft have? _____
_____
_____

Wilson

Woodrow Wilson (1856-1924). Woodrow Wilson was one of America's most successful and respected presidents. He was born in Virginia, the son of a Presbyterian minister. He grew up in Georgia and North Carolina during the Civil War Era and had Southern sympathies all his life. He graduated from Princeton in 1879. He tried a career in law before becoming a college professor, an expert in the theory of politics. He became the president of Princeton University in 1902 and quickly became well-known for his reform efforts there.

His reputation attracted the attention of the New Jersey Democratic bosses who needed an honest candidate for governor. They offered Wilson the nomination in 1910, and he accepted with the understanding the bosses would not influence his decisions. Wilson won the election and quickly transformed New Jersey into a Progressive state. Primaries, anti-corruption laws, corporate regulation, and other reforms were signed by the governor. His growing national reputation, and the fact he gained the support

| Woodrow Wilson and His Wife

of William J. Bryan, won Wilson the Democratic nomination and the presidency in 1912.

Wilson's reforms. Wilson was, like T.R. before him, an active leader and unusually successful in getting what he wanted from Congress. Three goals reached by Wilson were tariff reform, banking reform, and stronger anti-trust legislation. He started with the tariff. The Democrats had never been tied as tightly to the tariff as the Republicans so the new Democratic Congress was open to reductions.

Wilson took the lead by going to Congress in person to speak for the bill (no president since Jefferson had done that). The Underwood Tariff Bill was passed in 1913. It was the first major reduction of the tariff since the Civil War. Wilson got it past the Senate by a direct appeal to the American people. The new law reduced the overall tariff rates, eliminated duties on many items (raw wool, steel rails, sugar, and others), and set up an income tax to replace the lost revenue.

Wilson also made a personal appeal to Congress for banking reform. The nation needed a banking system that could expand the money supply to meet the demand. Bankers wanted a private system of banks tied closely to the money trust that controlled the nation's financial center at Wall Street in New York City. Reformers and agricultural representatives like Bryan (now secretary of state) wanted a government-owned system.

The Federal Reserve System, created in 1913, was a compromise. The twelve Federal Reserve Banks that served the system were privately owned, but the controlling Federal Reserve Board was government appointed. The new system allowed for more control and stability in the banking system. It also allowed the Federal Reserve Board to expand the money supply as needed. It has served the nation well and continues to operate today.

The last major item on Wilson's card was anti-trust legislation. The Clayton Anti-Trust Act of 1914 tried to fill holes in the Sherman Act. It also exempted unions from anti-trust laws, a much-needed reform. The Federal Trade Commission was also established to prevent trusts. The commission used its powers to order corporations to "cease and desist" from actions that were leading toward monopolies.

Wilson's administration also saw many other reforms. Laws were passed creating loans for farmers, requiring better treatment of sailors, providing income for disabled federal workers, restricting child labor, and setting an eight-hour day for railroad workers. Thus, Wilson was probably America's most successful Progressive president.

Foreign problems. Wilson was an idealist who did not favor using money or military to expand American power. He did not like Dollar Diplomacy and immediately stopped pressing Wall Street for foreign loans and investments. However, in spite of his ideals, he did use the army to deal with disorders in Nicaragua, Haiti, and Santo Domingo. The U.S. increasingly thought of the Caribbean as its own lake. Wilson was successful in expanding self-government in the Philippines in preparation for eventually giving that nation its independence. Wilson and Bryan also settled a dispute with Japan over another anti-Japanese law in California and a dispute with Britain over tolls for the Panama Canal. Thus, Wilson's results in foreign policy were mixed, but his biggest test, before World War I, was Mexico.

Mexico. Mexico had been ruled by a dictator, Díaz, for years before 1910. That year a reform leader of the people, Francisco Madero, became president. He was murdered in 1913 by General Victoriano Huerta just a few weeks before Wilson became president. The resulting disorder threatened American investments and U.S. citizens who lived in Mexico. Wilson refused to intervene. However, he could not stomach a murderer like Huerta, so Wilson refused to recognize Huerta's government and pressed him to resign.

Wilson allowed arms to be sold to Huerta's opponents in the hope of getting rid of him. The situation became severe in 1914 when some American navy sailors were arrested in the Mexican port of Tampico. The men were released, but Huerta refused to salute the U.S. flag as the American admiral demanded. Wilson then asked for and received permission to use force. American troops captured the city of Vera Cruz. This cut off Huerta's supplies and nearly began another Mexican war. At this point, Argentina, Brazil, and Chile offered to mediate. Wilson promptly accepted, and the matter was settled peacefully.

Huerta was finally driven from power in 1914 and was succeeded by Carranza. Carranza found himself fighting his own war with a former ally, "Pancho" Villa. Villa earned American wrath by killing several U.S. citizens in Mexico and then raiding a town in New Mexico in 1916. With Carranza's reluctant permission, General John Pershing pursued Villa deep into Mexico. The expedition failed to capture him and eventually had to withdraw in the face of mounting Mexican hostility. Wilson had tried not to intervene but wound up doing so anyway. He accomplished very little except to further darken relations with Latin America.

Conclusion. The Progressive Movement expanded federal powers into new areas. The old pre-Civil War government that was never involved in private business was gone. The new, huge corporations had proven that they needed government control or they would exploit their wealth and power. The curbs on their power were main focus of the reform movement. It also addressed the social problems (poverty, vice, sanitation) of the growing cities. The Progressive Movement could claim only three presidents, but two of those three, Roosevelt and Wilson, were among the best men ever to hold the office. Even Taft, who did not have their charisma or leadership skills, kept the reforms moving. As a result, the Progressive Movement was a remarkable success.

| Pancho Villa

Anti-trust laws, corporation commissions, labor laws, primary elections, anti-corruption laws, and direct election of senators were among its many results. The ideals of Progressivism became a part of the American system and still exist today. However, the oncoming conflict of World War I, which began in 1914, changed the nation's focus and ended this era.

Complete these sentences.

3.63 Woodrow Wilson refused to recognize the government of General

_____ in Mexico.

3.64 General _____ followed Mexican bandit, _____

_____ , deep into Mexico after he attacked a town in New Mexico.

3.65 _____ ended the Progressive Era.

3.66 Wilson strengthened the anti-trust laws with the _____ Anti-Trust Act.

3.67 Wilson was the first president to appear before Congress to speak for a bill since

_____ .

3.68 The _____ Commission was established to prevent trusts.

3.69 Wilson's three main goals in office were _____ ,

_____ , and _____ .

3.70 The _____ Bill was the first major tariff reduction since the Civil War.

3.71 The Federal Reserve System set up twelve privately owned Federal Reserve Banks that were

controlled by the government appointed _____ .

3.72 Wilson used the army to quell disorders in _____ ,

_____ , and _____ .

3.73 Wilson's Secretary of State was _____ .

3.74 Wilson had been governor of _____ and president of

_____ University.

3.75 The three Progressive presidents were _____ ,

_____ , and _____ .

3.76 Mexico and the U.S. almost went to war in 1914 when some American sailors were arrested

in the city of _____ . The dispute was successfully mediated by

_____ , _____ , and _____ .

Before you take this last Self Test, you may want to do one or more of these self checks.

1. _____ Read the objectives. See if you can do them.
2. _____ Restudy the material related to any objectives that you cannot do.
3. _____ Use the **SQ3R** study procedure to review the material:
   a. **S**can the sections.
   b. **Q**uestion yourself.
   c. **R**ead to answer your questions.
   d. **R**ecite the answers to yourself.
   e. **R**eview areas you did not understand.
4. _____ Review all vocabulary, activities, and Self Tests, writing a correct answer for every wrong answer.

SELF TEST 3

Name the Progressive president (each answer, 2 points).

3.01 _____ vice president, took office when president was assassinated

3.02 _____ Dollar Diplomacy

3.03 _____ mediated the 1902 coal strike without favoring the owners

3.04 _____ Federal Reserve System

3.05 _____ lost Progressive support during his term

3.06 _____ advocate of the "strenuous life"

3.07 _____ former college professor and president

3.08 _____ sent troops into Mexico after Pancho Villa

3.09 _____ messed up tariff reform

3.010 _____ used the "Big Stick" to get canal treaty with Panama

3.011 _____ created the "right" of the U.S. to intervene in other American nations to prevent European intervention

3.012 _____ major tariff reduction

3.013 _____ Nobel Peace Prize for mediating Russo-Japanese War

3.014 _____ supported Richard Ballinger on the sale of government land, fired Gifford Pinchot who objected

3.015 _____ first to really use the Sherman Anti-Trust Act

Complete these sentences (each answer, 3 points).

3.016 Progressive reforms began at the _____ level of government.

3.017 Writers who exposed corruption and social problems were called

_____ .

3.018 William J. Bryan was vaulted to the leadership of the Democratic Party by his

_____ speech at the 1896 convention.

3.019 The _____ marked America's emergence as a world

power.

3.020 Roosevelt's philosophy of government, that everyone should be treated fairly, was called the

_____ .

3.021 _____ was the philosophy, based on evolution, that the poor

were inferior and deserved their poverty.

3.022 The _____ were the first corporate giants in the U.S.

3.023 The _____ were the first national union movement in the U.S.

3.024 The reform movement in between the Farmer's Alliance and the Progressive Movement was

called the _____ .

3.025 After the Civil War, the army fought hundreds of battles with the

_____ .

Choose the correct match for each item (each answer, 2 points).

3.026 _____ Progressive split off Republicans		a. laissez-faire
3.027 _____ Pure Food and Drug Act		b. Standard Oil
3.028 _____ California allows Japanese in schools,		c. *Maine*
Japan restricts emigration to U.S.		d. Grange
3.029 _____ no government interference in business		e. Open Door Policy
3.030 _____ all nations trade freely with China		f. Hepburn Act
3.031 _____ revenue from land sales goes to irrigation projects		g. Newlands Act
3.032 _____ most famous trust		h. *The Jungle*
3.033 _____ explosion began war with Spain		i. Bull Moose Party
3.034 _____ gave Interstate Commerce Commission some real		j. Gentlemen's
power		Agreement
3.035 _____ reform movement, sought debt relief and railroad regulation		

Match these people (each item, 2 points).

3.036	_____ Democratic president; two non-consecutive terms	a. William J. Bryan
3.037	_____ led pursuit of Pancho Villa in Mexico	b. William McKinley
3.038	_____ made fortune in steel; gave much of it away	c. Andrew Carnegie
3.039	_____ Republican leader of Half-Breeds; presidential candidate stained by corruption charges	d. Samuel Gompers
		e. Henry Ford
3.040	_____ made Model T cheaply; using moving assembly line	f. Robert La Follette
3.041	_____ eliminated yellow fever; Cuba, Panama	g. William Gorgas
3.042	_____ pro-business president; front porch campaign	h. John Pershing
3.043	_____ pro-silver coinage; Democratic leader; Wilson's secretary of state	i. Grover Cleveland
		j. James Blaine
3.044	_____ Wisconsin governor; Progressive leader	
3.045	_____ AFL organizer; favored capitalism	

80/100   SCORE _____   TEACHER _____ _____
initials   date

Before taking the LIFEPAC Test, you may want to do one or more of these self checks.

1. _____ Read the objectives. See if you can do them.
2. _____ Restudy the material related to any objectives that you cannot do.
3. _____ Use the **SQ3R** study procedure to review the material.
4. _____ Review activities, Self Tests, and LIFEPAC vocabulary words.
5. _____ Restudy areas of weakness indicated by the last Self Test.

HISTORY & GEOGRAPHY 806
The Civil War (1855–1880)

LIFEPAC Test is located in the center of the booklet. Please remove before starting the unit.

Author:
Theresa Buskey, B.A., J.D.

Editor:
Alan Christopherson, M.S.

Westover Studios Design Team:
Phillip Pettet, Creative Lead
Teresa Davis, DTP Lead
Nick Castro
Andi Graham
Jerry Wingo

Alpha Omega
PUBLICATIONS

**804 N. 2nd Ave. E.
Rock Rapids, IA 51246-1759**

The Civil War (1855–1880)

Introduction

"A house divided against itself cannot stand. I believe this government cannot endure permanently half slave and half free. I do not expect the Union to be dissolved—I do not expect the house to fall—but I do expect it will cease to be divided. It will become all one thing, or all the other." Abraham Lincoln spoke these words in 1858, just two years before the beginning of his presidency and the Civil War. They reflected the storm gathering across the nation that would soon empty its heavy clouds on the heads of the Union in one of America's costliest wars.

The years from 1855 to 1880 were some of the darkest in the history of our nation. In fact, the nation almost ceased to exist during those years. In some cases, the Civil War literally pitted brother against brother. It finally settled the issue of slavery and the permanence of the Union. The years that followed the war were blackened by revenge, greed, and failure to protect the newly freed slaves. The restoration of the Union was as much in question as its survival once was, but again the nation survived. A South without slavery was reintegrated into a stronger United States of America.

This LIFEPAC® will cover the critical years from 1855 to 1880. We will present the increasing hostility and distrust between the North and the South, the events within and those that led to the Civil War, and finally the difficult post-war Reconstruction.

Objectives

Read these objectives. The objectives tell you what you will be able to do when you have successfully completed this LIFEPAC. When you have finished this LIFEPAC, you should be able to:

1. Discuss why and how the North and South split.

2. Name the major events that led up to the Civil War.

3. Describe how secession occurred.

4. List the advantages of both sides in the Civil War.

5. Describe the major battles and the course of the Civil War.

6. Describe Reconstruction.

7. Describe the background and policies of Civil War-era presidents.

8. Describe the post-Civil War corruption.

9. Explain the status of black Americans during and after Reconstruction.

Survey the LIFEPAC. Ask yourself some questions about this study and write your questions here.

1. INCREASING DISUNION

The era of compromise had ended with the Kansas-Nebraska Act in 1854. The Whig Party had fallen apart over disagreements about slavery, and the Democratic Party was soon split over it also. Several denominations, including Baptists, Methodists, and Presbyterians also split between North and South over the controversy. The two sides were becoming more hardened and less willing to discuss their positions. The Union was in grave danger.

The rhetoric of the two sides left less and less room for compromise during the last few years of the 1850s. The publicity of the Lincoln-Douglas debates gave a national following to Abraham Lincoln who steadfastly opposed slavery as immoral. The pro-slavery Dred Scott decision by the Supreme Court was denounced in the North as invalid. A financial crash that did not disturb the South as much as the North was seen in their own eyes as proof of the South's superior position.

A whole series of violent incidents marked the last five years before the Civil War. A small civil war broke out in "Bleeding Kansas" over the issue of whether or not it would be a slave state. On the Senate floor, a Southern congressman beat a Northern senator with a cane. John Brown led a raid into Virginia, intending to start up a slave revolt and instead became an abolitionist martyr. The verbal hostility of previous years became increasingly physical.

The South felt threatened by the growing abolitionist movement and political power of the North. The last straw was the election of a Republican president in 1860. The Republican Party was a Northern, anti-slavery party, and the South would not tolerate such a party to rule over them. Eleven states seceded from the Union. The war began in April of 1861 when the Southern army at Charleston fired on a federal outpost named Fort Sumter in their harbor.

SECTION OBJECTIVES

Review these objectives. When you have completed this section, you should be able to:

1. Discuss why and how the North and South split.
2. Name the major events that led up to the Civil War.
3. Describe how secession occurred.
4. List the advantages of both sides in the Civil War.
7. Describe the background and policies of Civil War-era presidents.

VOCABULARY

Study these words to enhance your learning success in this section.

arsenal (är′ se nal). A building for the manufacture or storage of arms, ammunition, and military equipment.

disavow (dis a vou′). To deny responsibility.

egalitarian (ē gal i ter′ ē an). Marked by a belief in human equality, especially in respect to social, economic, and political rights and privileges.

exacerbate (ig zas′ er bāt). To make more violent, bitter, or severe.

AMERICA from **1855** to **1880**

Franklin Pierce
1853-1857
Democratic

James Buchanan
1857-1861
Democratic

Abraham Lincoln*
1861-1865
Republican

Andrew Johnson
1865-1869
Republican

Ulysses S. Grant
1869-1877
Republican

Rutherford B. Hayes
1877-1881
Republican

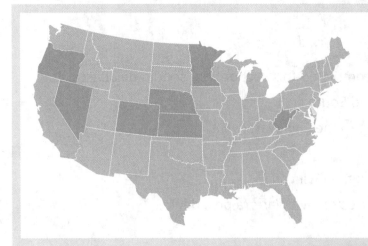

STATES ADMITTED TO THE UNION

Minnesota	1858
Oregon	1859
Kansas	1861
West Virginia	1863
Nevada	1864
Nebraska	1867
Colorado	1876

POPULATION of the United States of America

Year	Population
1880	50,189,209
1850	23,191,876
1820	9,638,453
1790	3,929,000

*assassinated while in office

repercussion (rē per kush' un). A widespread, indirect, or unforeseen effect of an act, action, or event.

segregate (seg' re gāt). To separate people of different races by having separate facilities like schools, restaurants, and theatres for each race.

Note: *All vocabulary words in this LIFEPAC appear in* **boldface** *print the first time they are used. If you are not sure of the meaning when you are reading, study the definitions given.*

Pronunciation Key: h**a**t, **ā**ge, c**ã**re, f**ä**r; l**e**t, **ē**qual, t**ė**rm; **i**t, **ī**ce; h**o**t, **ō**pen, **ô**rder; **oi**l; **ou**t; c**u**p, p**u̇**t, r**ü**le; **ch**ild; lo**ng**; **th**in; /**ŦH**/ for **th**en; /zh/ for mea**s**ure; /u/ or /ə/ represents /a/ in **a**bout, /e/ in tak**e**n, /i/ in penc**i**l, /o/ in lem**o**n, and /u/ in circ**u**s.

Division and Violence

The South. The slave states of the South in 1855 had a unique culture; they thought of themselves as virtually a separate nation. They believed they had a better way of life than the North. The South clung to older notions of an "aristocratic" class long after it had been abandoned by the rest of the nation. Its population was stagnant, and few immigrants came to the South because there were few opportunities there. The population was more uniformly people of British background whose families had lived in America for generations. A strict class system existed with wealthy planters at the top and slaves at the bottom. Southerners believed this was an ideal society and looked down on the **egalitarian** North.

The South was agricultural. It had little manufacturing. The factories that did exist were smaller and employed fewer people than those in either the North or northwest. The main cash crop was cotton with tobacco, rice, and sugar cane as alternatives in some areas. These crops were very labor intensive and were raised primarily on large plantations by enslaved people. Only about one-quarter of Southern families owned slaves. Those that did not often practiced subsistence agriculture. Even those without slaves supported the plantation system. Even the poorest white man had status above the enslaved black people.

By 1855 the South was very concerned about the threat from the North to their way of life. The North's growing population had given them complete control of the House of Representatives. The Compromise of 1850 had left the North in control of the Senate. The North had its own political party, the Republicans, which was rapidly gaining popularity and offices. The South equated the Republican Party with the radical abolitionists who spoke of fighting and slave revolts in order to end slavery in the South. The Republican Party pledged not to attack slavery where it existed, but only to prevent its spread. Most Southerners did not trust those statements. The Democratic Party still had supporters in both the North and South. Southerners looked to it as one of the last united institutions in the nation.

Abolitionists. Anti-slavery sentiment had existed in America for many years, but the serious, organized movement that so frightened the South began in the 1830s. In 1831 William Lloyd Garrison began publishing the anti-slavery newspaper, the *Liberator*. In 1833 Parliament voted to end slavery in the British West Indies. That same year, the American Anti-Slavery Society was formed with about sixty members. Within five years, it had grown to about 250,000 people. Hundreds of other societies devoted to the end of human bondage

CANADA (BRITAIN)

Washington Territory

OR
(1859)

Dakota Territory

MN
(1858)

WI

ME

NH
VT
MA
RI
CT

NY

MI

Nevada
Territory   Utah
Territory   Colorado
Territory

Nebraska Territory

IA

PA

NJ
DE
MD

CA

IL   IN   OH

WV
VA

KS
(1861)

MO

KY

New Mexico Territory

Indian
Territory

AR

TN

NC

SC

MS   AL   GA

TX

LA

FL

UNITED STATES 1854–1861

States in 1854

States admitted 1855-61
(dates of admittance)

Territories in 1861
(boundaries are future states)

MEXICO

were formed all over the North in the late 1830s. Many of these people were Christians putting feet on their faith. These organizations worked by lobbying, organizing rallies, printing literature, publishing stories, and petitioning the government.

However, abolitionists were unpopular radicals for many years. The South and Southern sympathizers reacted to their work with repression and violence. Abolitionist works were banned in the South. People were imprisoned for even possessing them. Mobs attacked prominent abolitionists. Printing presses were destroyed, and anti-slavery speakers were pelted with filth when they spoke. Even Northern politicians tried to distance themselves from the abolitionist views. It had been an unspoken policy of both the Democrats and the Whigs to avoid the issue of slavery entirely, which they did for many years.

Gradually, these determined advocates won their point in the North. The issue of slavery was finally taken out of hiding. The continued discussions forced people to look and see what was happening in their nation. Millions of people were being held in bondage. The Fugitive Slave Act brought the issue home to many in the North. Eventually, when the Whigs and Democrats still avoided the issue, the Republicans took it up to squarely and rapidly become a powerful force in the North.

Bleeding Kansas. After the Kansas-Nebraska Act of 1854, Kansas was to choose for itself on the issue of slavery. It was west of the slave state of Missouri, and many Southerners expected to make it a slave state as well. Most of the settlers came from the North with its larger population. Some of the Northerners were sponsored by abolitionist societies who wanted to make sure that Kansas had

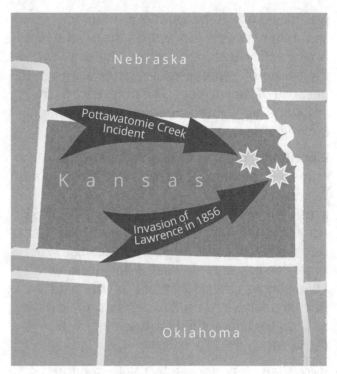

a good supply of anti-slave settlers. Missouri responded by sending its own pro-slave settlers supported by well-armed bands of Missouri citizens. Both sides were hostile and violent in what became known as "Bleeding Kansas."

Conflict in both the political and physical areas ruled in Kansas. When the territory voted for its first legislature in 1855, Missouri pro-slavers crossed the border and voted illegally, giving the pro-slavery people control of the new government. The free-soil supporters formed their own illegal government at Topeka to counter it. A pro-slavery "posse" invaded the anti-slavery town of Lawrence in 1856 to arrest members of the illegal government, looting and burning the town. A violent (and possibly insane) abolitionist named John Brown butchered five pro-slavery men in Pottawatomie Creek in response.

By 1857 Kansas had enough people to apply for statehood. The majority of the population was anti-slavery, but the legislature was under the control of the pro-slavery group. The state had to vote on the issue of slavery to comply with "popular sovereignty," so the legislature created a shifty document known as the Lecompton Constitution. The people were allowed to vote only on the constitution, with or without slavery. But the constitution itself protected slavery. Even if the people voted for it to be free, Kansas would still be a slave state. The free-soil people boycotted the election, and the constitution passed with slavery. It was sent to Washington as the basis for admitting Kansas to the Union.

The Caning of Sumner. Charles Sumner was a radical abolitionist member of the Senate. In May of 1856, he delivered a scathing two-day speech on "The Crime against Kansas." His colorful rhetoric was very insulting to the South. He also made some vulgar insults against South Carolina's Senator Andrew Butler. The speech was not well received by his Northern colleagues. Even William Seward, abolitionist leader of Congress, did not approve of his language.

| Bleeding Kansas

Sumner's speech was considered a personal insult by Congressman Preston Brooks, a relative of Butler's. He decided to deal with the senator personally. Brooks decided against challenging him to a duel, since he believed Sumner to be his social inferior, and it was likely the Northerner would refuse. Instead, he decided to beat him to redress the insult.

On May 22nd, Brooks walked into the Senate chamber and approached Sumner, who was sitting at his desk. He raised his cane and proceeded to beat the helpless man about the head and shoulders until the cane broke. Finally, someone stopped Brooks, and Sumner was carried away unconscious.

What was remarkable about the incident was the difference between the reactions in the North and the South. People in the North saw it as a use of force to stop anti-slavery speech, and it drew a great deal of abolitionist publicity. Sumner was voted back into his seat in the Senate, even though it was three years before he was well enough to serve. In the South, Brooks was hailed as a hero. Hundreds of people sent him new canes to replace the one he had broken. His constituents voted him back into the House of Representatives after he resigned because of the incident. The difference in the reactions highlighted a dangerous separation between the two sides.

Election of 1856. In 1856, the Democrats managed to unite behind one candidate, James Buchanan. Most of the potential candidates for president were tainted by the Kansas-Nebraska Act and could not gain the support of Northern Democrats. Buchanan had been acting as the American minister in Great Britain from 1852-1856 and was therefore "safe" on the issue. Buchanan avoided the topic of slavery as much as possible and argued for the preservation of the Union.

| James Buchanan, the only U.S. president never to marry

Buchanan was opposed by the Republican candidate John Frémont, called "the Pathfinder" for his work mapping routes and sites for forts in the west. The Republicans campaigned on the issue of no slavery in the territories. "Free soil, free men, and Frémont" was their slogan. Millard Fillmore was a candidate for the Know-Nothing Party and also had the support of the dying Whig Party. The two-year-old Republican Party made a remarkable showing, winning eleven states, all in the North. However, the still barely unified Democrats won the election, putting James Buchanan in the White House.

James Buchanan. James Buchanan (1791-1868) was the only U.S. president never to marry. He entered the White House with impressive credentials. He had been born to immigrant parents in Pennsylvania and became a prosperous lawyer in that state. He began his political career as a Federalist, but eventually became a strong Democrat supporter of Andrew Jackson. He had served in the Pennsylvania legislature and as a soldier in the War of 1812. He had

served in both the House and Senate in Washington. He was secretary of state under James Polk and represented America in both Russia and Britain.

Buchanan lacked strong convictions on the issue of slavery and tended to be pro-Southern in his policies. He did not have the fortitude or the foresight to deal with the rising divisions in the nation. When the Lecompton Constitution was presented to Congress, Buchanan backed it without quibbling about its origins. Stephen Douglas showed that he was made of sterner stuff. He had proposed popular sovereignty for the territories, and he meant it to be just that! He successfully opposed the admission of Kansas under the dubious document. Instead, it was sent back for a vote on the whole constitution. The anti-slavery voters in Kansas rejected it. But with the ongoing conflict, it was not until 1861 that the state was finally able to organize a genuine constitution and be admitted to the Union.

Complete these sentences.

1.1 Congressman _____ beat Senator _____

with a cane over a speech the senator made.

1.2 The three candidates in the 1856 election were _____ ,

_____ , and _____ .

1.3 One of the last united political institutions in 1855 was the _____ Party.

1.4 The Lecompton Constitution was supported in Washington by _____ ,

but was successfully opposed by _____ .

1.5 The anti-slavery movement seriously took off in the decade of the _____ .

1.6 The main source of livelihood in the South was _____ .

1.7 Buchanan's policies tended to favor the _____ .

1.8 Pro-slavery partisans looted and burned the town of _____ , Kansas in 1856.

1.9 By 1857 most of the people in Kansas were _____ - slavery.

1.10 The speech that got Charles Sumner into trouble was entitled

"_____ ."

1.11 _____ murdered five pro-slavery men in Pottawatomie Creek in

response to the invasion of Lawrence.

1.12 The Republican slogan in 1856 was _____ .

Answer these questions.

1.13 What made the South think the North was a threat to their way of life?

_____

_____

_____

1.14 How had the Democrats and Whigs dealt with the slavery issue before 1855?

_____

1.15 What was wrong with the Lecompton Constitution?

_____

_____

_____

1.16 Why did Kansas become known as "Bleeding Kansas?"

_____

_____

1.17 Why was Buchanan chosen as the Democratic candidate in 1856?

_____

_____

Dred Scott Decision. The tense situation in 1857 was **exacerbated** by the decision of the Supreme Court in *Dred Scott v. Sandford*. Dred Scott was an enslaved man who had lived for five years in the North with his master. He sued for his freedom on the basis of his long residence on free soil. It was a test case financed by abolitionists. It eventually reached the Supreme Court.

The Supreme Court of 1857 had nine justices, five from the South. Seven of the justices were Democrats, and two were Republicans. The Chief Justice, Roger Taney, was a Southerner and wrote the opinion of the court. The court ruled that Scott was not a citizen and could not sue in federal court. That is all the court needed to rule to end the case; unfortunately, it went further. Taney ruled that Scott was not free. He was considered property protected under the Fifth Amendment. It was therefore unconstitutional for the federal government to bar slavery *anywhere* in the United States!

The **repercussions** of the decision were vast. At one stroke, the Supreme Court claimed all of the country to be slave territory. Popular sovereignty no longer applied because people could not vote to keep constitutionally-protected slaves out of their states. All of the compromises to limit the spread of slavery were in one swoop declared unconstitutional. The court made a political decision based on its own prejudices.

The South rejoiced at the decision. The North swore to defy it, justifiably believing that it was a political decision by a Southern-dominated court that went beyond the issues of the case. Northern Democrats who supported popular sovereignty were now forced farther away from their Southern counterparts who supported the Dred Scott decision. Southerners were alarmed by the voices in the North that threatened to defy the courts and deny slave owners protection for their "property." The decision widened the North-South rift still further.

Panic of 1857. The nation was struck with one of its periodic depressions in 1857. Businesses had over-extended themselves during a boom time by speculating in land and railroads. The collapse closed thousands of businesses and caused widespread unemployment. It hit the manufacturing and grain-growing sections of the nation the hardest. The South rode out the panic comfortably because of the high international demand for cotton. Southerners saw the entire depression as proof of their superior way of life.

The Panic of 1857 created a clamor for higher tariffs in the North. Tariffs had been lowered in order to please the South. Northerners resented what they saw as a Southern blockade on Northern prosperity. Thus, the depression contributed to the division in the nation.

Lincoln-Douglas Debates. Democratic Senator Stephen Douglas was up for re-election in 1858. His Republican opponent was a tall, thin, back-country lawyer named Abraham Lincoln. Lincoln challenged Douglas to a series of debates which were held all over Illinois. Because of the prominence of Douglas and the growing reputation of Lincoln, the debates drew nationwide attention.

Douglas had a substantial advantage in the election. He was a well-known figure with several years of experience in Washington and an excellent orator. In Illinois he had redeemed himself for the Kansas-Nebraska Act by his opposition to the Lecompton Constitution. Illinois still generally favored popular sovereignty which was Douglas' primary position. In contrast, Lincoln had only served one term in the House of Representatives at the national level and had a high, thin voice. His Republican party was considered a threat to the Union in the South. Northern voters took that into consideration.

However, Lincoln was passionate about his subject and addressed the issues in clear, honest terms. He openly stated that he believed slavery was morally wrong. He did not believe it could be constitutionally ended where it already existed, but the spread of it should be prevented at all costs. He challenged Douglas on the issue of popular sovereignty, saying that slavery was an issue for the entire nation, not just the people who happened to move to a territory before a specific date. Moreover, Douglas and popular sovereignty denied the moral issues entirely, treating slavery and slaves as just another choice for voters. Lincoln also asked how Douglas could support popular sovereignty in the light of the Dred Scott decision, which stripped it of all constitutional support.

Douglas responded with a mix of politics and reasoning. He pointedly poked fun at Lincoln's lack of political experience and his background as a working man. He accused Lincoln of

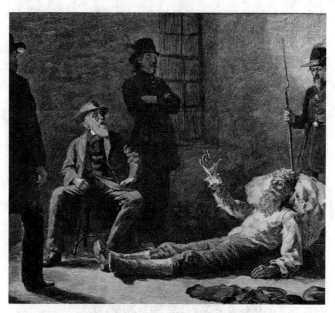

| The capture of John Brown, depicted by an early sketch artist

favoring equality between black and white people (a charge which Lincoln refuted). Douglas also argued that even with the Dred Scott decision, popular sovereignty still had force. He said that slavery could not exist without state laws to protect slaves as property. Therefore, when states refused to pass such laws, slavery could not safely exist there, even if constitutional.

Douglas won the senate race, but the debates cost him his chance at the presidency. Newspapers had printed the texts of the debates all over the nation. Southern voters read about Douglas' proposal for states to annul Dred Scott by not passing the state laws needed to protect slavery. That proposal cost Douglas his support in the South. Lincoln was upset by the loss but he accepted it as "a slip, not a fall." The debates had made him a national Republican figure.

Harper's Ferry Raid. After the murders in Kansas at Pottawatomie Creek, John Brown and much of his family had fled to Canada. From there, he planned a grand attack on slavery. His scheme was to invade the South, seize weapons, lead the slaves in a revolt, and set up stronghold sanctuaries for black people in

| Abolitionist John Brown

| Stephen Douglas

the South. From these strongholds, he would organize an army to overrun the South. He chose to begin by attacking the federal **arsenal** at Harper's Ferry, Virginia.

In October of 1859, Brown and about twenty men captured the arsenal, taking several hostages. They held the building for over a day and killed several people. The black people that Brown had expected to rally to his aid never came. Instead, a detachment of federal troops arrived under the command of Colonel Robert E. Lee. Brown was quickly captured and most of his men with him.

John Brown's trial for treason drew phenomenal national attention. Brown behaved in a brave and dignified manner during the trial. His courageous devotion to freedom made many abolitionists overlook his violent nature and methods. Brown showed many signs of insanity, and it would have been wise to confine him to an asylum. Instead he was quickly tried, found guilty, and hanged. His death made him a martyr for the anti-slavery cause.

Brown gained a reputation in death that he never had in life. Abolitionists ignored his past and hailed him as a saint. There were

demonstrations throughout the North on the day he was executed. A popular song was written about him that became a marching song in the Civil War. It ran, in part:

> *John Brown's body lies a-moul'ring in the grave,*
> *His soul is marching on.*

The raid made the South even more suspicious of the North. Many knowledgeable moderates condemned Brown and his methods, but the South saw the public support for this murderous man and believed that was the direction the North was headed itself. The division grew.

The Election of 1860. The Democratic Party finally split over the issue of slavery in 1860. The party was unable to name a candidate at their first convention. A second convention was held and the Southern states walked out, as they had at the first. The Northern Democrats then nominated Stephen Douglas. Douglas ran on a platform of popular sovereignty and strict enforcement of the Fugitive Slave Act. The Southern Democrats met at their own convention and nominated John C. Breckinridge of Kentucky. Breckinridge campaigned on the basis of enforcing the Dred Scott Decision.

To add to the confusion, a group of Know-Nothings and Whigs formed a middle-of-the-road Constitutional Union Party and nominated John Bell of Tennessee.

The Republicans had a clear chance at victory with their opposition divided three ways. They nominated Abraham Lincoln over the better-known William Seward because Lincoln was less controversial. The Republicans also created a platform to keep themselves from being a one-issue party. The platform included: protective tariffs for the North, federal money for internal improvements for the west, free homesteads for farmers, a Northern railroad across the nation for the northwest, protection of the rights of immigrants, and its primary stand, no extension of slavery into the territories. Lincoln won the election, taking almost all the electoral votes in the North along with Oregon and California. However, in the popular vote he won just under 40%, making him a minority president.

 Answer these questions.

1.18 Why did Dred Scott argue he should be free?

_____

1.19 What did John Brown attack in 1859?

_____

1.20 Who commanded the troops that captured Brown?

_____

1.21 What caused the Panic of 1857?

_____

1.22 What made Lincoln a national figure?

_____

1.23 What was the only necessary part of the ruling in the Dred Scott case?

_____

1.24 What was the unnecessary and controversial part of the Dred Scott decision?

_____

_____

1.25 How did Douglas defend the idea of popular sovereignty after Dred Scott?

_____

_____

1.26 What happened to John Brown after his raid into Virginia?

_____

1.27 Name the candidates and their parties in the 1860 election.

a. _____

b. _____

c. _____

d. _____

1.28 What was the constitutional effect of the Dred Scott decision?

_____

1.29 What was Lincoln's opinion of slavery and what to do about it?

_____

_____

1.30 What happened to John Brown's reputation after his death?

_____

1.31 What were the proposals of the Republican platform in 1860?

a. _____

b. _____

c. _____

d. _____

e. _____

f. _____

1.32 Why did each of the following increase the South's desire to separate from the North?

Dred Scott

a. _____

_____

Panic of 1857

b. _____

_____

John Brown's raid

c. _____

_____

Secession

The South Secedes. There were four long months between the time Lincoln was elected in November of 1860 and the day he became president in March of 1861. The South took full advantage of the lull. Convinced that its unique and superior culture could not survive under a hated Republican president, South Carolina called a special constitutional convention in December of 1860. The Convention voted to secede from the Union. Six other states from the deep South quickly followed suit.

The seven states met together in February of 1861 and formed their own government. They called themselves the Confederate States of America or the Confederacy. They elected Jefferson Davis of Mississippi as president of the new "nation." The capital was established at Montgomery, Alabama. (It was later moved to Richmond, Virginia when that state seceded.)

President James Buchanan, with his pro-South advisors, was no match for the crisis. He made several speeches that accomplished nothing. He essentially said that a state could not secede, but that the federal government had no power to stop it if it did! He refused to strengthen the garrisons at federal forts in the South, as was recommended by the elderly General Winfield Scott. He did try to send reinforcements to Fort Sumter in South Carolina, but the effort was inadequate and the troops were forced to return.

Crittenden Compromise. As the crises matured, several attempts were made to work out a compromise. The most promising was a series of constitutional amendments proposed by Senator John Crittenden of Kentucky. The Crittenden Compromise would have guaranteed the protection of slavery where it already existed. It would have barred slavery in the territories north of the Missouri Compromise line of 36° 30' and protected it in all territories, present or future, south of it. Any states formed

| A modern photo of Fort Sumter

in the Southern territories would have popular sovereignty on the subject. The compromise failed because Lincoln was loyal to his beliefs and his party's platform. He refused to consider allowing slavery in the territories. It might have failed anyway, given the control the radicals had in the Confederate States.

In the end, the South seceded without any opposition from Buchanan. Most Southerners believed the North would never fight. The Northern factories needed Southern cotton too badly. Southern pride would not allow them to consider the possibility that the factory workers, shopkeepers, and fishermen of the North could put up any serious opposition. Pride went before the fall.

Abraham Lincoln. Abraham Lincoln (1809-1865) was one of the greatest men ever to occupy the presidency. He was born to a poor family in Kentucky. His family later moved to Indiana and then Illinois. Abe, as he was known, was a strong man who spent most of his youth working with his hands. His political propaganda called him the "Rail Splitter" for all the logs he had split over the years to make fences.

He had very little formal education (maybe a year) yet he loved to read, often walking miles to borrow a book. He failed in business and eventually got into law and politics in Illinois.

Abraham Lincoln entered the presidency with deceptively poor qualifications. He had served four terms in the Illinois House of Representatives and one in the U.S. House. Those were his only political qualifications. Yet, Lincoln had also been a popular Whig and Republican speaker in Illinois. He knew how to organize and administer political power. He had learned how to express himself in speech-making and in the courtroom in a way that persuaded his listeners. He had a reputation for integrity that earned him the nickname "Honest Abe." He had a strong will and the strength of convictions. Moreover, he was no Buchanan. He was willing to put force behind his beliefs and would accept the consequences.

Lincoln was sworn in on March 3, 1861. He tried to steer a moderate path in his inaugural address. He denied any intention of interfering with slavery where it already existed. There would be no conflict unless the South started one. He was still hoping to avoid a war, but he made it clear he would defend the Union. The South could not simply pull out because it did not like the outcome of a fairly contested election, for that made a mockery of democracy.

Fort Sumter. Fort Sumter was one of the few Southern federal forts still in Union hands when Lincoln became president. It was located at the mouth of the harbor for the city of Charleston, South Carolina. The fort's commander, Robert Anderson, steadfastly refused Southern demands to surrender his command, but his supplies were running low. Lincoln knew that sending reinforcements to the fort would touch off a strong reaction in that state. In the end, he compromised. He sent a boatload of provisions, but no new troops.

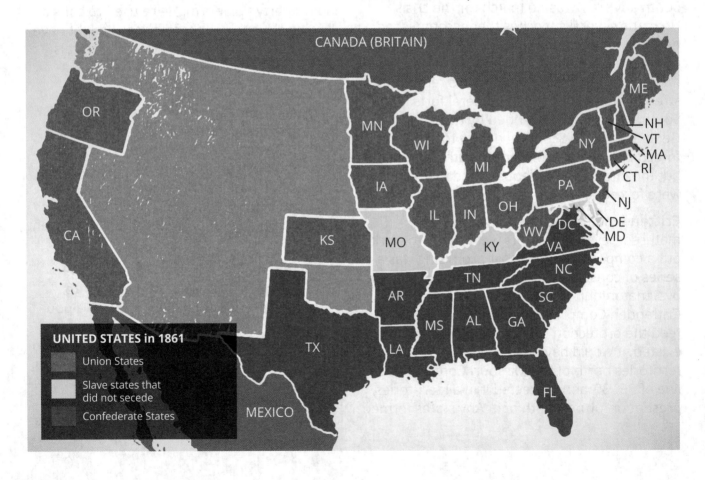

CANADA (BRITAIN)

ME
OR
MN
NH
WI
NY
VT
MI
MA
RI
IA
PA
CT
IL
IN
OH
NJ
CA
KS
MO
WV
DC
DE
KY
VA
MD
TN
NC
AR
SC
MS
AL
GA
TX
LA
FL
MEXICO

UNITED STATES in 1861
- Union States
- Slave states that did not secede
- Confederate States

South Carolina was notified of the delivery of the provisions. Its leaders chose to interpret it as an aggressive act. Before the relief ship could arrive, the Carolinians decided to act. On April 12, 1861, under the command of General Pierre Beauregard, the cannons in the city opened fire on the fort. The garrison surrendered the next day.

The attack on Fort Sumter was the official beginning of the Civil War. It united the North in favor of war. Lincoln immediately called for volunteers to put down the rebellion. More men responded than the army could supply. Lincoln also suspended civil rights in areas that had Southern sympathizers. He ordered a blockade of Southern ports, and he ordered federal funds spent to support the war without Congressional approval (Congress was not in session). These actions were arguably unconstitutional, but they were in line with the extraordinary powers used by presidents in wartime. Without a strong, immediate action, there might not have been any country to uphold the Constitution.

The greatest area of concern was the border states. Four of these, Arkansas, Tennessee, North Carolina, and Virginia, seceded once they realized the North would fight to force them to stay in the Union. The northwest counties of Virginia did not vote for secession. The people in these counties seceded from Virginia and formed a new state that was loyal to the Union. West Virginia was admitted to the United States in 1863. The other border/slave states, Missouri, Kentucky, Maryland, and Delaware, stayed in the Union. However, Maryland was kept in by a declaration of martial law by Lincoln. He could not risk having Washington D.C. cut off from the rest of the nation. Thus, the sides were drawn—eleven to twenty-three.

 Complete these sentences.

1.33 The Southern attack on _____ began the Civil War.

1.34 Seven states seceded after the election of Republican candidate

_____ .

1.35 After the war began, _____ more states seceded.

1.36 The most serious attempt to prevent the secession of the South was the

_____ Compromise.

1.37 _____ was president of the United States when the

Confederacy was organized.

1.38 The slave states that stayed in the Union were _____ ,

_____ , _____ ,

and _____ .

1.39 Because of his integrity, Abraham Lincoln was nicknamed _____

_____ .

1.40 _____ was the first state to secede.

1.41 The actions taken by Lincoln as commander-in-chief when the war began included

a. _____ , b. _____ ,

c. _____ , and d. _____ .

1.42 Lincoln's national political experience was limited to one term in the _____

_____ .

1.43 Lincoln sent _____ to Fort Sumter in 1861.

1.44 The Confederate states elected _____ as president.

1.45 The two Confederate capitals were _____ and

_____ .

1.46 The western counties of Virginia formed a new state called _____

and joined the Union in _____ .

Facing Off

Northern Advantages. The North had significant advantages in the Civil War. Money was needed to pursue a war, and the North had four-fifths of the available capital in the nation. The North also had a larger population, 22 million to the South's 9 million (including the 3.5 million slaves). The North had more of the raw materials needed for war, such as coal and iron. Moreover, the North had more factories, farms, and railroads.

Railroads were vital, being used to move troops and supplies. The South was hampered because it never had the resources to build tracks during the war. In order to repair damaged tracks or lay new ones, they had to tear up old ones.

The North controlled the navy and had more ships for moving supplies, so the Union was able to blockade the South. This cut off imports of badly needed manufactured goods. It prevented the South from selling its cotton, which robbed them of their primary income. The blockade eventually led to severe shortages of basic supplies to the South, which hampered their war effort. While the South was cut off from trade with Europe, the Union was not. Throughout the war, the North was able to sell grain and purchase military equipment by trading with Europe.

| A Northern railroad train, one of the Union's advantages

The Northern armies were eventually augmented by black soldiers. Black men formed one-tenth of the total Union troops by the end of the war. They served in **segregated** companies, led by white officers. They were paid less than white soldiers for part of the war. The South refused to recognize them as prisoners of war, treating them as escaped slaves. In spite of this, black volunteers fought courageously and were a dependable asset to the Union. On the other hand, the South would not even consider employing black soldiers until the very last, desperate days of the war.

The North had the advantage of an established government led by a strong president. Lincoln was an excellent leader whose authority was sustained by a government backed with eighty years of success. By contrast, the South had no united history to sustain them. Their entire government was built on the idea of states' rights and secession from another government. Jefferson Davis had difficulty maintaining his authority over the independent-minded Southern states.

Problems with central authority and the blockade made it difficult for the South to raise money for war. The states' rights Confederacy did not favor taxes, and the banks had little to offer in loans. The Confederate government printed money to pay its bills, which pushed up prices to many, many times what they were at the beginning of the war. The inflation added to Southern difficulties in prosecuting a war.

Southern Advantages. The South had some of the advantages the original thirteen colonies did during the War for Independence. In terms of ideals, the Rebels were fighting for independence and protecting their way of life. The North initially did not fight to end slavery, but only to preserve the Union by forcing the South to stay. Strategically, the South only had to survive to win. Southerners could fight a defensive war, protecting their homes and land. The North had to conquer the entire South and force it back into the Union. A simple draw would be a Confederate victory.

| Union soldiers

The South also had better quality officers than were available in the North. The gentlemen of the South had a long tradition of military training and service. Robert E. Lee, for example, had been an officer in the U.S. Army when the war began. He resigned when his home state of Virginia seceded and rose quickly to become the leader of the Confederate army. Other talented Southern officers included Thomas (Stonewall) Jackson, James Longstreet, and Jeb Stuart.

By contrast, the North did not have as many high-quality military leaders. The Northern generals seemed to be either overly cautious or foolhardy. Lincoln changed his commanders several times before he found a successful general in Ulysses S. Grant.

The Confederacy began the war with high hopes. They sincerely believed in the superiority of their way of life and their people. They did not believe the North would fight. Even if they did, no Northern shopkeeper could stand in a fight with a Southern gentleman. They expected that the North and Europe needed Southern cotton. If the North proved to be stubborn, Europe would be likely to intervene on behalf of the South to protect its own textile industries.

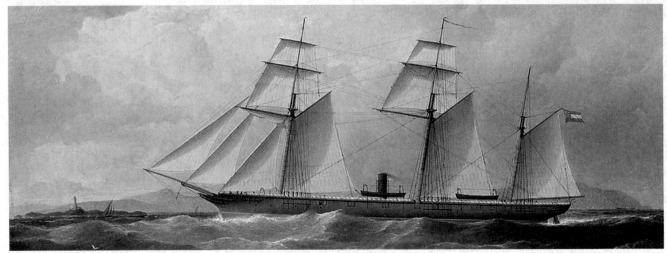

| On July 29, 1862, Hull "No. 290" steamed out of the Mersey from the Laird's Birkenhead Yard and into Civil War history. Soon taking her given name, ALABAMA, the Commerce Raider set out on a tour with devastating results for the American North's commercial shipping interests the world over. The screw sloop-of-war proved to be a fast, capable ship under the command of Captain Raphael Semmes, capturing or destroying 69 ships in less than two years.

Reactions Abroad. The best chance for the Confederacy lay in gaining support from the nations of Europe. The monarchs of Europe had good reason to want to see the United States divided. The failure of the American democratic experiment would strengthen the hand of the European aristocrats. These same aristocrats had a natural preference for the class-conscious culture of the South. Moreover, an independent Confederacy would be a supplier for European factories and a purchaser of European goods without the protective tariffs of the North.

English manufacturers were particularly dependent upon Southern cotton to supply their spindles and looms. The blockade threw thousands of textile workers out of their jobs. However, at the same time, the North was supplying much of Britain's wheat and corn. Britain would have had to risk its food supply if it supported the Confederacy for the sake of its cotton supply. Also, cotton suppliers in India and Egypt stepped up production to fill the need. Union demands for war goods also helped relieve employment problems. Thus, Britain was never pushed to intervene by the problems in its economy.

Britain did come very close to war over an incident in the fall of 1861, however. An American warship stopped a British steamer, the *Trent*, leaving the West Indies. Two passengers were arrested and taken back to the U.S. The men were Confederate diplomats en route to Europe. The British government was furious over this seizure of civilian passengers and threatened war. The incident was settled by releasing the men along with a U.S. statement **disavowing** their capture.

There was nevertheless a strong pro-Confederacy attitude in the British government at the beginning of the war. The government considered recognizing the Confederate nation especially when the South garnered a string of victories early in the war. Many ships for the Confederate navy were built in Britain during the war. Careful Union diplomacy limited this activity. What destroyed all hope of both British and French aid to the Confederacy was the Emancipation Proclamation in 1862. Once the war was reframed as a fight against slavery, neither of the great powers of Europe would raise their hands to aid the South. Thus, the aid the U.S. had during the Revolution was denied to the Confederacy in the Civil War.

Put an N beside the factors that were an advantage for the North and an S beside those that were an advantage for the South.

1.47 _____ ideals at the beginning of the war

1.48 _____ population

1.49 _____ manufacturing

1.50 _____ military personnel

1.51 _____ strategic position

1.52 _____ government

1.53 _____ navy

1.54 _____ hope for foreign allies

1.55 _____ black soldiers

1.56 _____ capital

1.57 _____ military tradition

1.58 _____ railroads

1.59 _____ farms

Answer these questions.

1.60 What effect did the blockade have on the South? _____

_____

_____

1.61 Why did the nations of Europe tend to favor the South? _____

_____

_____

1.62 What did the North provide for Britain that offset the loss of Southern cotton?

_____

_____

1.63 What happened in the *Trent* incident? _____

_____

_____

1.64 What ended all hope of European aid to the Confederacy?

_____

Review the material in this section in preparation for the Self Test. The Self Test will check your mastery of this particular section. The items missed on this Self Test will indicate specific areas where restudy is needed for mastery.

SELF TEST 1

Match these people (each answer, 2 points).

1.01 _____ John Brown

1.02 _____ James Buchanan

1.03 _____ Abraham Lincoln

1.04 _____ Stephen Douglas

1.05 _____ Charles Sumner

1.06 _____ Dred Scott

1.07 _____ Robert E. Lee

1.08 _____ Jefferson Davis

1.09 _____ John Frémont

1.010 _____ John Crittenden

a. Confederate general

b. violent abolitionist martyr

c. beaten by a Congressman in the U.S. Senate

d. offered a compromise after secession

e. first Republican presidential candidate

f. slave who lived in the North and sued for his freedom

g. U.S. president when the Confederacy began

h. president of the Confederacy

i. his election prompted Southern secession

j. won the 1858 senate race in Illinois

Choose the correct word(s) to complete each sentence (each answer, 3 points).

1.011 Twisted, illegal version of popular sovereignty produced the pro-slavery _____ Constitution in Kansas.

1.012 The _____ Party opposed the spread of slavery but agreed it could not be abolished where it already existed.

1.013 The Civil War began when Confederate forces fired on _____ .

1.014 John Brown was executed for his attack on the arsenal at _____ , Virginia.

1.015 The _____ - _____ Debates centered on the issue of slavery and made Abraham Lincoln a national figure.

1.016 The Supreme Court declared that slavery was legal in all of the U.S. in the

_____ Decision.

1.017 The South had little difficulty with the Panic of 1857 because of the high price of

_____ on the international market.

1.018 The era of compromise was ended by the _____ - _____ Act.

1.019 _____ was the first state to secede.

1.020 Any hope of European aid to the Confederacy was ended by the

_____ .

Complete these items (each answer, 3 points).

1.021 Name four advantages the North had in the Civil War.

a. _____   b. _____

c. _____   d. _____

1.022 Name two advantages the South had at the beginning of the war.

a. _____   b. _____

1.023 Give two reasons why the nations of Europe might have supported the South.

a. _____   b. _____

1.024 Name two border/slave states that did not secede.

a. _____   b. _____

Answer true or false (each answer, 2 points).

1.025 _____ Abraham Lincoln believed that the U.S. could not continue to be part slave and part free.

1.026 _____ Britain almost went to war with the Union after two Confederate officials were arrested on the British steamer the _Trent_.

1.027 _____ The South received a tremendous number of immigrants in the years leading up to the Civil War.

1.028 _____ The Democratic Party split in two in 1860.

1.029 _____ James Buchanan did little to solve the divisions in the nation.

1.030 _____ Black soldiers in the Union army served in segregated units, usually with white officers.

1.031 _____ The blockade of the South hurt textile manufacturers in Britain.

1.032 _____ Abraham Lincoln was a well-educated man with many years of national experience when he became president.

1.033 _____ Lincoln believed slavery was morally wrong.

1.034 _____ The American abolitionist movement began its serious growth in the 1830s.

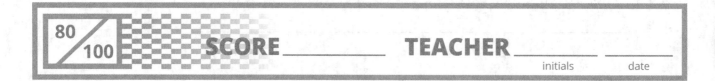

80 / 100   SCORE _____   TEACHER _____ _____
initials   date

| Painting by Civil War artist Dale Gallon

2. CIVIL WAR

The horrors of the Civil War were its nature and its cost. It was a *civil war*, fought between countrymen, friends, and family. Many of the opposing army officers had served together in the Mexican War. It was not uncommon for relatives to be on opposing sides. Senator John Crittenden, whose name is attached to the compromise, had sons who fought on opposite sides. One Union navy officer boarded a captured ship only to find his dead Confederate son aboard. Abraham Lincoln's sister-in-law was married to a Confederate general. She came to live in the White House for a time after her husband was killed in the war. It was a very personal war.

It was also a very bloody war. More Americans died in the Civil War than in World War I, Korea, or Vietnam. Only World War II cost America more lives. In fact, all the battle deaths in all the other wars before World War II added together does not equal the total from this "family conflict."

An estimated 620,000 died in battle and from disease and accidents (figures from the Civil War Trust). Thousands lost legs, arms, and/or their health.

The reason for the bloodshed was an advancement in technology without an appropriate change in military thinking. Since its invention, the soldier's firearm had been an inaccurate, slow-firing musket. By the 1860s, faster firing, very accurate rifles were in general use and artillery was improving. Standard military tactics, based on the older weapons, would send large numbers of men to attack enemy positions even if they had built barricades to protect themselves. The weapons were so poor that an attacking army had a good chance of overrunning an enemy position if it had enough men. The newer weapons made such attacks suicidal. However, all of the Civil War commanders only knew the old mass-attack tactics and used them to the bitter end.

SECTION OBJECTIVES

Review these objectives. When you have completed this section, you should be able to:

4.   List the advantages of both sides in the Civil War.

5.   Describe the major battles and the course of the Civil War.

7.   Describe the background and policies of Civil War-era presidents.

VOCABULARY

Study these words to enhance your learning success in this section.

amputate (am' pyu tāt). To cut off, especially a limb of a person.

anesthetic (an' es thet' ik). A substance that cause a loss of feeling in all or part of the body.

chaplain (chap len). A member of the clergy serving in a special group or place, like a prison or the military.

conscription (kon skrip' shun). Forced enrollment of people, mostly for military service.

division (di vizh' in). A large military unit that has all the necessary services to work as a self-contained unit and act independently.

morale (mo ral'). Moral or mental condition in regard to courage, confidence, or enthusiasm.

repulse (ri puls'). To drive back; repel.

Bull Run to Fredericksburg (1861-62)

First Bull Run. After Fort Sumter in April of 1861, Lincoln called for the state militia to come into service for three months. By May he realized the ill-trained, short-term militia would not be enough. A new call was put out for volunteers for a three-year enlistment. By summer, thousands of men were being organized into an army near Washington. A similar call had been made in the Confederacy, and its army was forming in Virginia near Richmond. The two capitals and their respective armies were only 120 miles apart.

Winfield Scott, the old commander of the U.S. army, wanted a slow, steady strategy to defeat the South. His plan called for a naval blockade to strangle Southern ports and the Mississippi River. In the meantime, the army would cut the South into pieces. This basic plan was the one followed by the Union throughout the war, even after Scott retired because of poor health. Scott wanted to take the time to drill and prepare the very untried Union troops before mounting any attacks, but the president and the American public were too impatient to wait.

Lincoln pressed the new Union field commander, Irvin McDowell, to attack at once. McDowell argued that his troops were untrained and not ready, but Lincoln prevailed. In July, the Union army moved south to attack the Confederacy. On July 21st, under the command of General Joe Johnston, the Union army met the Confederates near a creek called Bull Run and a town called Manassas Junction. The Northern public was convinced that it would be an easy victory. Many of the people of Washington brought picnic lunches and drove out to watch what they thought would be the only battle of the war.

The battle was a disaster for the Union. The green troops fought well at first, but as the equally green Confederate lines began to break, General Thomas Jackson stood his ground. A Confederate colleague yelled for the men to fight behind Jackson who was standing "like a stone wall." Jackson thus earned a

| The aftermath of First Bull Run

nickname (Stonewall) and the beginning of a famous reputation as a general. Confederate reinforcements arrived, and it was the Union lines that began to break. The North retreated and then ran in disarray. However the disorganized, untrained Confederates failed to follow up on the Union defeat. Both armies were left intact.

The defeat cleared up Union hopes of keeping the war short. The Union began the difficult preparations for a long war, but no one had any idea how long and difficult it would actually be. In the meantime, the South was delighted with the victory, which they saw as a vindication of their superiority. They did not expect a long war and became overconfident.

McClellan in Charge. McDowell was replaced by George McClellan. McClellan proved to be an excellent organizer. He trained and drilled the Union army for months. He also built up defenses around Washington to protect the capital from any enemy attack. He built a professional, well-organized, well-supplied army which was named the Army of the Potomac.

However, McClellan was cautious to the point of near cowardice. He refused to attack until he had everything where he wanted it and believed he had a large numerical advantage. As Lincoln so aptly put it, McClellan had a "case of the slows."

Forts Henry and Donelson. The Union strategy in the west was to gain control of the Mississippi River and its major tributaries. That would give the Union firm control of the border states of Missouri and Kentucky as well as a dominant position in Tennessee. It would cut off Louisiana, Arkansas, and Texas from the rest of the Confederacy. Attacks from the North were under the command of General Ulysses S. Grant. Grant had been out of the army for several years before the war and had a reputation for drinking that haunted his whole career,

but he was a fighter. He promptly went after two key river forts near the Tennessee-Kentucky border.

Fort Henry on the Tennessee River fell quickly to Grant and his supporting navy gunboats on February 6th of 1862. Nearby Fort Donelson on the Cumberland River was more difficult. The fort's better guns badly damaged the Union navy ships, but Grant managed to get his troops around the forts and set up a siege. The garrison tried, but was unable to break out and on February the 16th, the Confederate commander asked for terms of surrender. U.S. Grant insisted that nothing "except unconditional and immediate surrender can be accepted." The Confederates complied, and the Union general won the nickname "Unconditional Surrender" Grant.

| Battles for control of the Mississippi

The fall of the forts led the Confederate army to evacuate Nashville which then fell into Union hands. It was the first captured state capital. This was welcome news to victory-hungry President Lincoln and the Union. It made Grant a hero. More good news came in April with the capture of Island Number Ten, a heavily fortified Confederate position near where the Ohio and Mississippi Rivers met.

Shiloh. Grant promptly moved south after the victory at Donelson to Pittsburg Landing on the Tennessee River. He was headed for Corinth, an important railroad junction 22 miles away. Grant failed to prepare any defenses, believing the Confederates would not attack. However, they did attack on April 6th near a hill called Shiloh and caught the Union army by surprise.

The Battle of Shiloh lasted for two days. It was a confused and vicious fight. Many soldiers mistakenly fired on their own troops. Confederate commander Albert Johnston was killed. Union men took cover in a sunken road and slaughtered their Confederate attackers. The Southern army responded by raining artillery on the immobilized Union troops. The field caught fire, burning many of the wounded to death. The Union lines held, however, and reinforcements arriving the next day forced the Confederates to retreat.

About 4,000 Americans died in the two days of the Battle of Shiloh, and more would die later due to their wounds. The total of the casualties (dead or wounded) was around 13,000 from the Union and 10,000 from the Confederacy. Grant's exhausted, victorious army could not even follow the retreating rebels, who were allowed to escape. The bloodshed shocked both the North and South. Lincoln was pressured to fire Grant, but he said, "I can't spare this man—he fights."

| Admiral David Farragut

New Orleans. Admiral David Farragut led a federal naval attack on New Orleans in April. The city was the largest in the South and a key port for the entire Mississippi River. It was protected by two huge forts in the harbor. At first, Farragut tried to batter the forts into submission. Once that failed, he decided to slip by them at night. He lost only one boat in the attempt, and with the city at his mercy, New Orleans surrendered.

In May Farragut headed up the Mississippi to capture the capital of Louisiana, Baton Rouge. Meanwhile, General Henry Halleck took over active command of Grant's forces while the latter was in temporary disgrace. Halleck marched south, forcing the Confederate army to evacuate Corinth. In June the Union navy forced the surrender of Memphis. Only the fortress city of Vicksburg, Mississippi (in between Farragut and Halleck) kept the Union from complete control of the nation's largest river system.

Complete the following.

2.1 Explain why there were so many battle casualties in the Civil War.

_____

_____

2.2 What were the positive results of McClellan's command?

_____

_____

_____

2.3 Why was McClellan not a good field commander?

_____

_____

2.4 Name the only American war to date that caused more deaths than the Civil War.

_____

2.5 According to the *World Almanac*, how many Americans died in battle and from disease and

accidents in the Civil War? _____

Name the battle or place.

2.6 _____ "Stonewall" Jackson got his nickname

2.7 _____ "Unconditional Surrender" Grant got his nickname

2.8 _____ Admiral Farragut sailed his ships past the harbor forts
at night

2.9 _____ Irvin McDowell was the Union commander

2.10 _____ green Confederate troops routed green Union troops

2.11 _____ fort on the Tennessee River fell easily to Grant

2.12 _____ Bloody battle cost 23,000 Union and Confederate
casualties

2.13 _____ Washington citizens took picnic lunches out to watch

2.14 _____ the fall of these two forts set up the Union occupation
of Nashville

2.15 _____ Grant was surprised by the Confederates at Pittsburg
Landing

2.16 _____ important railroad junction, the goal of Grant after Donelson

2.17 _____ defeat that made the Union realize it would not be an easy war

2.18 _____ Lincoln and public opinion forced a Union attack with untrained troops against the wishes of the commander

Battle of the Ironclads. The Union's blockade of the South developed slowly. The North captured several key islands along the Southern coast early in the war to use as bases for the blockade fleet. But the thousands of miles of Southern coast could not all be watched. Eventually, the navy began to concentrate on the few Southern ports that had dock facilities to handle cotton bales, the South's currency in trade. This and the eventual capture of these ports made the blockade increasingly effective.

The South countered by using fast, dark-colored ships to run the blockade. The ships would take cotton from the South to British ports in the West Indies to trade for manufactured goods. The demand for luxury items in the South made the risky voyages very profitable. A ship owner could make a profit if his vessel made just two successful trips before it was captured. Eventually, Jefferson Davis' government insisted that half of all cargo space on the ships be used for war material, not silks and perfume.

The South tried to break the blockade. They almost succeeded, using the captured Union steamship *Merrimac*. When the Union withdrew from Norfolk Navy Yard shortly after the outset of the Civil War, the Union Navy sank the *Merrimac* to keep it from falling into enemy hands. The Confederates recovered and salvaged the steam-powered ship, and modified it by covering it with iron plates. They rearmed and renamed the ship the *Virginia* and used it with devastating effect to attack the wooden ships that blockaded Chesapeake Bay. The Union ships' cannon fire bounced harmlessly off of the steel-covered ship.

Fortunately, the Union had also developed an ironclad vessel. The *Monitor* arrived in time to confront the *Virginia* when it made its second appearance in the bay. The two ships fought an inconclusive four-hour battle because neither side had developed armor-piercing artillery shells. Out of both ammunition and resolve, the ships returned to their home ports. Eventually, the Union Navy claimed the battle's victory because the blockade was not broken. Later, both ships were lost. The Confederacy destroyed the *Virginia* (*Merrimac*), and the North lost the *Monitor* and its crew in a storm off the coast of Cape Hatteras. The battle of the *Monitor* and the *Merrimac* was the first battle in history to be fought between armor-plated ships.

| The *Monitor* and the *Merrimac*

Peninsular Campaign. McClellan had finally agreed to attack in the spring of 1862. He decided against a direct attack to the South. Instead, he had his entire army transported by sea to the peninsula between the York and the James River on Chesapeake Bay in Virginia. He hoped to outflank the Confederates and capture Richmond, which would be about 70 miles from his landing point. Lincoln reluctantly approved the plan, but insisted that a large number of troops be left behind to defend Washington.

McClellan landed safely with more than 100,000 men and in April of 1862 began to march toward Richmond. They confronted the Confederate army under the command of Joe Johnston in the inconclusive two-day battle of Fair Oaks (Seven Pines). Johnston was wounded and Robert E. Lee was given command of the Confederate forces which he called the Army of Northern Virginia.

| Lincoln and McClellan meeting at Antietam

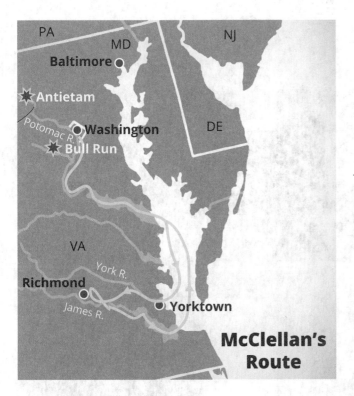

McClellan's Route

Stonewall Jackson used a smaller Confederate force to tie up McClellan's reinforcements around Washington in the Shenandoah Valley. Moving quickly and winning several small battles, Jackson convinced the Union high command that an attack on Washington was taking place. After fighting enough to insure the Union troops would remain there looking for him, Jackson slipped away and joined up with Lee.

Using information gained by Jeb Stuart's cavalry, which made a spectacular ride all the way around McClellan's army, Lee attacked on June 26th. The Seven Days' Battles raged from June 26th to July 1st with a series of savage battles in what are now the suburbs of Richmond. Lee succeeded in forcing McClellan to retreat to the James River. McClellan believed he was hopelessly outnumbered and refused to take the offensive again. He was finally ordered to return his army to Washington in the hopes it could be used from there.

Second Bull Run. While McClellan was in Virginia, the army around Washington was under the command of John Pope. Pope advanced toward Richmond in July, believing that McClellan's army on the peninsula would keep Lee too busy to stop him. But Lee realized the caliber of his opponents. Lee was certain that McClellan would be too busy moving his army to interfere with the Confederate army for a time, so Lee left a small force on the peninsula and led the rest of the army north to deal with Pope before McClellan's troops could join him. Lee sent Jackson to circle around Pope and cut his lines of supply and communication. As Lee expected, Pope turned his army and tried to find Jackson to do battle. Then Lee brought the Army of Northern Virginia to Jackson's aid.

The Battle of Second Bull Run went badly for the Union. Pope was very confused. He had finally cornered Jackson on August 29th after an exhausting search and had attacked him hard. Jackson managed to hold on for that day, and the next day Lee arrived. Pope never knew he was there until the Confederate army attacked from the side (flank). The Union army was routed.

That summer was the beginning of Lee's spectacular reputation as a general. Robert E. Lee was a devout Christian man from an aristocratic, but not very wealthy, Southern family. He gained several properties by his marriage into the family of George Washington's wife. He did not really believe slavery was just, but like so many in his day, he owned slaves and accepted "the institution." He fought for the Confederacy because he would not fight against his home state of Virginia. Most experts agree that he was the best general on either side during the Civil War. As at Second Bull Run, he routinely took chances, and he out-maneuvered and out-fought his Union opponents. By the end of the war, the soldiers of the Confederacy loved him and trusted him completely, even when he was wrong.

Confederate Soldier

Union Soldier

Antietam. Lee decided it was time for the Confederacy to go on the offensive. A rebel victory in Union territory might convince Britain to recognize the Confederacy and convince the North to give up the war. So Lee and his army moved into Maryland, heading for the capital of Pennsylvania. McClellan, whose command had been reduced after the peninsula campaign, was given command again under public pressure. He took his reorganized army out to meet Lee.

Lee divided his army to capture Harper's Ferry and press an attack to the north. McClellan learned of the plans when a lost copy of Lee's orders accidentally got into Union hands, but McClellan did not move fast enough to trap Lee with his army spread out. The two sides met near Antietam Creek on September 17th. It was the single bloodiest day of the long, bloody war. In one day, there were over 20,000 casualties between the two armies. Militarily, the battle was a draw. Lee's lines held but he retreated the next day. History records a Union victory because they took the field.

Emancipation Proclamation. Lincoln's goal had always been to restore the Union, but he began to see that the North needed a more specific, moral war aim—the end of slavery. He was reluctant to act because he did not want to drive the Northern border states into the arms of the Confederacy, but he had decided by the summer of 1862 to make the move. However, he wanted to wait until after a Union victory to make the announcement. Antietam gave him that chance.

On September 22nd, Lincoln issued the Emancipation Proclamation. It declared that all of the slaves in any state still in rebellion on January 1, 1863 would be forever free. It did not affect the slaves in the Northern border states and did not free any slaves until the South was effectively under Northern control. However, the document meant the end of slavery in the U.S. The North now had a moral cause. Britain, which had waged a world-wide campaign against slavery, would not aid the Confederacy to protect it.

Fredericksburg. McClellan was so slow following Lee that Lincoln lost all patience and finally removed him from command in November. He was replaced by Ambrose E. Burnside. The general was a handsome man with thick side whiskers that were thereafter called "side burns" in his honor. He immediately began an offensive, but he would prove as foolhardy as McClellan was hesitant.

Burnside decided to move his army to the east around Lee's right flank and march from there to Richmond. Burnside successfully moved the army and prepared to cross the Rappahannock River opposite the city of Fredericksburg. However, he insisted on waiting for pontoon bridges to cross. They took more than a week to arrive. By that time, Lee's scouts had warned him of the Union's location and he had set up strong defenses on the high ground near the city.

Faced with a strongly entrenched Confederate army, Burnside should have withdrawn to fight somewhere else. Instead, he attacked on December 13th. Wave after wave of Union soldiers were sent up the hill towards the Confederate guns. By the day's end, Union casualties were 13,000. General Lee said after that carnage, "It is well war is so terrible, or we should grow too fond of it."

Burnside's failures prompted Lincoln to again change generals. This time he choose General Joseph Hooker. Hooker had a reputation as a fighter, and he began to rebuild the army during the winter months in preparation for another summer of fighting. By that point, the war was more than a year and a half old. The Union had captured the upper and lower reaches of the Mississippi, but they had been completely unable to use their superior numbers and supplies to penetrate the eastern Confederate defenses. Richmond was still 120 miles away.

Name the person, event, battle, or item.

2.19 _____ freed all enslaved people in any state still in rebellion on January 1, 1863

2.20 _____ McClellan faced Johnston in the Peninsular Campaign

2.21 _____ Union ironclad that fought the *Merrimac* to a draw

2.22 _____ Lee fought using information from Stuart's ride around the Union army

2.23 _____ Lee advanced into Maryland and was almost trapped when his plans were discovered

2.24 _____ Lee trapped Pope before McClellan could come to his aid

2.25 _____ the best general in the Civil War

2.26 _____ it gave the war its single bloodiest day

2.27 _____ Burnside attacked entrenched Confederate positions on the Rappahannock River

2.28 _____ general who circled behind Pope and drew him away from Richmond

2.29 _____ gave the North a moral cause and kept Britain from supporting the Confederacy

2.30 _____ Confederate vessel that almost broke the blockade on Chesapeake Bay

2.31 _____ cotton from the South would be taken here by blockade runners

2.32 _____ Lee became the Confederate commander after Johnston was injured in this battle

2.33 _____ Lee forced McClellan back to the James River and effectively ended the Peninsular Campaign

2.34 _____ this battle gave Lincoln the "victory" he needed to release the Emancipation Proclamation

2.35 _____ Burnside waited too long for pontoon boats

2.36 _____ removed from Union command for not pursuing Lee

Murfreesboro to Chattanooga (1863)

Murfreesboro. The Union army in the west had been spread out to occupy captured territory. As a result, it had been largely ineffective through the end of 1862. A Confederate invasion of Tennessee floundered in October of 1862. A new Union commander, William Rosecrans, pursued the Confederates into southern Tennessee. They met at the Battle of Murfreesboro beginning on December 31, 1862. The battle raged for three days with a one-day break in the middle. The total casualties for both sides were over 20,000 men. The results were inconclusive. The Confederates retreated, and it was six months before that specific Union army took the offensive again.

Vicksburg. Grant was now in charge of an army in Tennessee. At the end of 1862, he headed south for Vicksburg. Vicksburg was a fortified city on a high bluff overlooking a bend in the Mississippi River. If the Union was to control the river, the city had to be taken. After a delay due to the Confederate cavalry destroying his supply depot and one failed first attempt to get around the city's defenses, Grant decided on more direct measures.

Grant fought his way south along the west bank of the Mississippi River. Eventually, he crossed the river below Vicksburg and came at the city from the east, which was the only level entrance. Grant assaulted the city on May 22nd and was **repulsed**. He set up trenches that blocked all entry into the city and then began a siege. His guns bombarded the city non-stop. Federal gunboats trained their fire on the city and kept Grant supplied with everything his army needed. The people of the city moved into caves to protect themselves and were reduced to living on mule, rat, and dog meat.

The result was inevitable. The Confederacy had no army to send to relieve Vicksburg. Believing he would get better terms on Independence Day than any other time all summer, the Confederate commander surrendered on July 4, 1863. The Confederacy had been divided, and now the Union had complete control of the Mississippi River. Grant had proven himself as the kind of determined, aggressive general that Lincoln wanted.

Chancellorsville. Union General Joseph Hooker moved to attack Lee in the spring of 1863. Lee still held his position at Fredericksburg. Hooker tried to move around Lee's army to the west, past their left flank. For some reason, Hooker lost his nerve just as the move was showing signs of success. He retreated to defensive positions at Chancellorsville, west of Fredericksburg.

Lee quickly moved to attack Hooker in what would be one of his greatest victories. Lee's army was about half the size of Hooker's. Nevertheless, Lee divided the Army of Northern Virginia into two parts. Lee's portion attacked from the front while the other part, under Stonewall Jackson, attacked the Union's right flank. The Union army was taken by surprise and the right flank collapsed.

The Battle of Chancellorsville lasted for four days beginning on May 2nd. The Confederates were never able to completely break the Union lines, but they did maul them fiercely. Attacked on two sides, the Union army literally fought for its life. As at Shiloh, the underbrush caught fire, burning many of the wounded to death. Hooker retreated, but the South did not get off unscathed. In the evening while scouting the area for possible night attack, Stonewall Jackson was accidentally shot by friendly fire. He died on May 10th. Lee would never find an adequate replacement for his brilliant subordinate.

| The Ghosts of Gettysburg

Gettysburg. In the early summer Lee headed north again to try for a major victory on Union soil. The cavalry from the two armies clashed near Brandy Station on June 9th. The Confederates took the field, but for the first time the Union cavalry equated itself well against the famous rebel horsemen. Another part of the Southern army captured some badly-needed supplies by defeating the Union garrison at Winchester. In the meantime, Hooker refused to pursue Lee and insisted he must attack Richmond. Lincoln relieved him of command and replaced him with George Meade. Meade was from Pennsylvania, and Lincoln hoped he would prove persistent in chasing Lee, who was now in his home state.

| George Meade

Lee marched north toward Harrisburg with the Union army in pursuit. On July 1, some of Lee's troops came into the town of Gettysburg, Pennsylvania searching for shoes. They were met by an advance force of Meade's army. Both sides called for reinforcements and the crucial three-day-long Battle of Gettysburg had begun.

The Confederates forced the Union troops out of the city on the first day of the battle. The Union troops took up defensive positions on a series of hills outside the city. Their line was shaped like a fish hook. Robert E. Lee now made one of his few mistakes. He tried to drive the Union army, which was larger than his, out of strong defenses on the top of a hill. The Confederates both suffered and inflicted huge losses as they repeatedly attacked the Union lines on the second day.

On the third day, Lee decided to make a frontal attack on the Union army. He ordered General George Pickett to march 13,000 men straight up on the Union position. Pickett's charge was a slaughter. Half the men who marched up that day did not come back. Lee blamed only himself for having asked his men to do the impossible. The next day, the Army of Northern Virginia retreated.

Gettysburg was the turning point of the war. The Confederate army would never again have the strength to mount a major offensive. It would never again threaten the North with invasion. However, Meade failed to follow up his victory. Lee and his army were allowed to escape and continue to protect the Confederacy. The war would continue for almost two more years.

The Union and the Confederacy had over 20,000 casualties each at Gettysburg. The Union built a cemetery on the site. It was dedicated on November 19, 1863. The main speaker addressed the crowd for two hours. Abraham Lincoln spoke for only two minutes, but it was Lincoln's words which were remembered. The Gettysburg Address still rings through the years as one of Lincoln's finest speeches.

Four score and seven years ago, our fathers brought forth upon this continent a new nation: conceived in liberty, and dedicated to the proposition that all men are created equal.

Now we are engaged in a great civil war…testing whether that nation, or any nation so conceived and so dedicated…can long endure. We are met on a great battlefield of that war.

We have come to dedicate a portion of that field as a final resting place for those who here gave their lives that this nation might live. It is altogether fitting and proper that we should do this.

But, in a larger sense, we cannot dedicate…we cannot consecrate… we cannot hallow this ground. The brave men, living and dead, who struggled here have consecrated it, far above our poor power to add or detract. The world will little note, nor long remember, what we say here, but it can never forget what they did here.

It is for us the living, rather, to be dedicated here to the unfinished work which they who fought here have thus far so nobly advanced. It is rather for us to be here dedicated to the great task remaining before us…that from these honored dead we take increased devotion to that cause for which they gave the last full measure of devotion…that we here highly resolve that these dead shall not have died in vain…that this nation, under God, shall have a new birth of freedom…and that government of the people…by the people…for the people…shall not perish from this earth.

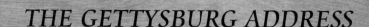

THE GETTYSBURG ADDRESS

Abraham Lincoln, November 19, 1863

Name the battle.

2.37 _____ turning point of the war

2.38 _____ Hooker was defeated by Lee

2.39 _____ Union victory gave them control of the Mississippi

2.40 _____ inconclusive battle in Tennessee under Union leader Rosecrans

2.41 _____ Confederate forces surrendered on the Fourth of July

2.42 _____ four-day battle beginning May 2, 1863

2.43 _____ the opposing armies met when the Confederates came into town looking for shoes

2.44 _____ fought in Pennsylvania

2.45 _____ Grant was unable to win by a direct attack, but won instead by siege

2.46 _____ Pickett's Charge was Lee's last attempt to break the Union lines

2.47 _____ Meade fought Lee

2.48 _____ Lee attacked the Union army from two directions with a smaller army and won

2.49 _____ Stonewall Jackson was shot and later died

2.50 _____ Lincoln's immortal words dedicated a cemetery there

Answer these questions.

2.51 What does "four score and seven years ago" mean? (Look it up.) _____

2.52 Why did Lincoln feel they could not dedicate the cemetery?

_____

_____

2.53 What did Lincoln say he and his listeners must dedicated themselves to do?

_____

2.54 To what was Lincoln highly resolved?

_____

2.55 What did Meade fail to do at Gettysburg that prolonged the war?

_____

_____

The armies. The two opposing armies were at once both similar and different. One important similarity was that both suffered under the limited medical knowledge in the 1860s. The simple idea that a wound should be cleaned to prevent infection was unknown in the mid-19th century. Diseases such as typhoid, dysentery, and pneumonia killed far more soldiers than bullets. The medical treatment for any serious injury to an arm or leg was **amputation**. Treatment was often done without **anaesthetic**. Surgery was usually done with an anaesthetic which had been discovered in the 1840s. However, it was also done with dirty instruments that spread infections.

The North had one advantage in the medical area, determined female volunteers. Northern women established the United States Sanitary Commission in 1861, modeled after the work of the British visionary Florence Nightingale in the Crimean War. The doctors had noticed that a clean camp or hospital resulted in fewer deaths. The Commission worked to provide clean housing for the troops as well as insuring they had ways to bathe and wash their clothes. The Commission also tried to track down missing soldiers and notify families of deaths. The women began to volunteer as nurses in the army hospitals, a revolutionary idea for the time.

The South suffered from a lack of resources to keep its own army clean. As the war progressed, the Confederate army could barely keep its men clothed. It was not surprising that Lee's army was looking for shoes at Gettysburg; they were constantly in need of them. They also lacked uniforms, blankets, soap, and food. The main reason was the poor system of roads and railroads in the South. Even when the supplies were available, it was often impossible to get them to the army in the field.

The Northern army, by contrast, was well-fed and supplied throughout the war. This difference was mainly due to the superior resources of the North. The North had more supplies for its men, and it had better means of transportation to deliver them. The better supplies and cleanliness meant the typical Union soldier was healthier than his Confederate opponent, but poor leadership squandered that and other advantages for most of the war.

Both armies had trouble getting enough soldiers to replace those that deserted, died, or were injured. The Confederacy passed the first **conscription** in American history in April of 1862. The Confederate conscription law made all white men between the ages of eighteen and thirty-five liable to be drafted for three years service in the army. There were ways around it, however. A man could legally hire a substitute, and many did. One key exception was that one white man on every plantation with at least twenty enslaved people was exempt. The complaints were so loud, that the law made this war to defend slavery "a rich man's war, but a poor man's fight." Even with the law, the South was desperately short of soldiers by the end of the war. They simply did not have a large enough population to compete with the North in manpower.

The North also passed a conscription law in 1863, when the number of volunteers fell due to defeats and reports of the horrible battles. The Northern law also allowed a person to hire a substitute or escape service by the payment of a $300 fee. That was a huge amount for a

| Old Capital Prison, Washington D.C.

HISTORY & GEOGRAPHY 806

LIFEPAC TEST

NAME _____

DATE _____

SCORE _____

HISTORY & GEOGRAPHY 806: LIFEPAC TEST

Choose the best answer (each answer, 4 points).

1. The North won the Civil War because _____ .
   a. it had better generals
   b. it had more resources
   c. the South could not break the blockade

2. The most important failure of Reconstruction was _____ .
   a. share cropping
   b. not adequately protecting the rights of freedmen
   c. Southern corruption

3. The greatest cause of the high numbers of dead in the Civil War was _____ .
   a. out of date military tactics
   b. accurate artillery fire
   c. lack of medical knowledge

4. The primary reason for the Civil War was conflict over _____ .
   a. slavery
   b. states' rights
   c. Lincoln's election

5. The Republican Party _____ in 1860.
   a. was abolitionist
   b. opposed states' rights
   c. opposed the extension of slavery

Name the person, event, battle, or item (each answer, 3 points).

6. _____   where the Civil War effectively ended

7. _____   turning point of the Civil War

8. _____   document issued by Lincoln that declared slavery ended in the Confederacy

9. _____   the most brilliant general of the Civil War

10. _____   man who assassinated Lincoln

11. _____   Amendment that ended slavery

12. _____   land called "Seward's Folly"

13. _____ "Four score and seven years ago, our fathers brought forth upon this continent ... " (name the speech)

14. _____ one of our worst presidents, had a scandal ridden administration, Union general

15. _____ Union general, devastated Georgia on march to the sea

16. _____ laws passed by Southern states after the Civil War that ensured black people would still be subjugated

17. _____ nickname for Kansas as popular sovereignty was practiced there

18. _____ Supreme Court decision, protected slavery in all states

19. _____ Amendment that made freedmen citizens

20. _____ last attempt at compromise before the Civil War

Answer these questions (each answer, 3 points).

21. What was different about Grant as the Union commander in Virginia?

    _____

22. What was the outcome of Andrew Johnson's impeachment trial?

    _____

    _____

23. Why was the Northern army better supplied that the Southern one?

    _____

    _____

24. Why was the battle of Antietam specifically important to Lincoln?

    _____

    _____

25. What did the South do that caused Congress and the North to challenge Johnson's Reconstruction plans?

    _____

    _____

Match these items (each answer, 2 points).

26. _____ anti-war Northern Democrats

27. _____ scam to cheat the government out of excise tax income

28. _____ prison camp

29. _____ pro-slavery legal document that mocked popular sovereignty in Kansas

30. _____ gave the North control of the Mississippi

31. _____ rude awakening for the Union which had hoped for an easy war

32. _____ used violence to regain white control of the South

33. _____ attempt by John Brown to start a slave uprising

34. _____ made Lincoln a name in national politics

35. _____ early welfare agency, set up schools for former slaves

a. Lecompton Constitution

b. Lincoln-Douglas Debates

c. Harpers Ferry Raid

d. Vicksburg

e. Copperheads

f. Freedmen's Bureau

g. Ku Klux Klan

h. Whiskey Ring

i. First Bull Run

j. Andersonville

working man, and only the well-to-do could afford that escape. However, the Union army was mainly filled by volunteers who collected bonuses for signing, which they would not get if they were drafted. However, the draft was unpopular and sparked a riot in New York City in July of 1863. The disorder raged for almost a week and was finally suppressed by Union troops called in from the Army of the Potomac.

Another problem experienced by both armies was what to do with prisoners. It had been the long-standing military tradition to parole prisoners on the condition that they would not fight any more, or to exchange them between the armies. However, the South's refusal to recognize black soldiers as prisoners of war and the realization that the South could not afford to replace its soldiers led the North to stop paroles and exchanges. Both sides then had to house and care for thousands of enemy prisoners. More than 50,000 died in the poorly run prison camps. The worst ones were in the South, where there were few resources to spare for Union prisoners.

The worst of the worst among the prison camps was Andersonville prison in Georgia. It was a log stockade with no housing and the only water supply was a sluggish stream that ran through its center. Food was limited to a little cornmeal each day. There was no medical care of any kind. Thirteen thousand Northern soldiers died at that prison. The survivors were little better than living skeletons. The commander of the camp, Captain Henry Wirz, was executed after the war.

As the long, bloody war dragged on, revivals broke out in the army camps. Men who were facing death chose to face God first. The interest in the things of God grew stronger as the war continued. **Chaplains** became common in the army, for they had been rare in previous wars. *Christian History* estimates that a total of between 200,000 and 300,000 soldiers from the two sides accepted Christ as their Savior during the war. (Vol. XI, No. 1, page 30). Leading the list

of committed Christians who served on both sides were Generals Robert E. Lee and Stonewall Jackson.

Chickamauga and Chattanooga. Chattanooga in southeast Tennessee was a key Confederate city after Vicksburg was besieged and captured. The city was an important rail junction that made it the western door to the Confederacy. Confederate General Braxton Bragg, who had met William Rosencrans at the Battle of Murfreesboro, had withdrawn to Chattanooga to set up defenses. All the while, Rosencrans refused to move for months after the battle. In August of 1863, the Union army finally began to move on Chattanooga.

Bragg was not in the same class with Lee and Jackson. He was unsure of himself and acted with excessive caution. The Union army swung around the city, and Bragg became concerned for his supply lines to Atlanta. In early September, Bragg evacuated Chattanooga without firing a single shot in its defense. Rosencrans followed without pausing to rest his army, and the two armies met near Chickamauga Creek on September 19th and 20th.

| Robert E. Lee and "Stonewall" Jackson

| Ulysses S. Grant and William Tecumseh Sherman

Bragg received reinforcements just before the battle. General James Longstreet from Lee's Army of Northern Virginia arrived with two **divisions**. The Confederates broke the Union right flank on the second day of the battle. That part of the army fled the field in wild disarray. A complete collapse was prevented by General George Thomas who held his Union army on the left flank despite everything. His spirited defense allowed the Union army to escape to Chattanooga and earned him the nickname "the Rock of Chickamauga."

Chickamauga was to be the last major Confederate victory. Bragg failed to follow it up. He and his army took up positions in the mountains around the Union army in Chattanooga and began a siege. But unlike the South at Vicksburg, the North had troops it could send to the rescue.

In October of 1863, Ulysses S. Grant was made supreme commander of all Union troops in the west. Rosencrans was also replaced by George Thomas. Grant acted promptly to establish a river supply route to the Union army in Chattanooga. He then brought into the city two more

armies under Generals William T. Sherman and Joseph Hooker. When they were in place, Grant attacked the surrounding Confederates on November 24th.

Hooker's men assaulted the tall, heavily-fortified Lookout Mountain; but the enemy troops there were in bad shape and quickly fell to the Union under the cover of low-lying clouds. When the clouds lifted late in the day, the Stars and Stripes were flying at the top. The newspapers dubbed it the "battle above the clouds."

Sherman attacked the Confederate right flank with little success on the first day. On the second day, Thomas' men were sent to attack some rifle pits in the center of the Confederate line. The men, with pride still wounded from their embarrassing defeat at Chickamauga, took not only the pits but (without orders) drove straight up into the Confederate lines. Thomas' army broke through the rebel defenses at their strongest point and forced them to retreat. Combined with September's capture of Knoxville by General Burnside, the Battle of Chattanooga gave the Union control of Tennessee and an upper hand in the west.

Complete these sentences.

2.56 The Union commander at Chickamauga was _____ and the Confederate commander was _____ .

2.57 The first conscription law in U.S. history was passed by the _____ government in 1862.

2.58 An estimated _____ to _____ soldiers became Christians during the war.

2.59 The center of the Confederate line at Chattanooga was overrun by men under the command of _____ .

2.60 The worst of the Civil War prison camps was _____ in Georgia.

2.61 Northern women established the United States _____ which helped the Union army stay cleaner and healthier.

2.62 A Northern man could avoid the draft by _____ or _____ .

2.63 The _____ army was better supplied throughout the war.

2.64 _____ was the last major Confederate victory.

2.65 George Thomas earned the nickname "the _____ Chickamauga" by his stand when the rest of the Union army was fleeing.

2.66 The fighting on Lookout Mountain on November 24th was called the _____ _____ .

2.67 _____ became the supreme Union commander in the west in October of 1863.

2.68 The standard treatment for any severe injury to a leg or arm was _____ .

2.69 A riot in New York City in July of 1863 was sparked by _____ .

2.70 _____ was a key railroad junction that Bragg evacuated without firing a shot.

Wilderness to Ford's Theater (1864-65)

Wilderness. Lincoln believed that he had finally found the man he needed to defeat Lee. In March of 1864, Ulysses S. Grant was promoted to the rank of lieutenant general (the first man since George Washington to hold that rank) and given command of all Union forces. He was faced with the task of destroying two major Confederate armies, one in Tennessee now under Joseph Johnston, and the Army of Northern Virginia under Lee. Grant assigned Sherman to command the Union army in Tennessee and advance on Atlanta, Georgia. Grant himself went to the front with the Army of the Potomac that would have to face Robert E. Lee.

The Army of the Potomac marched into Virginia yet again in May of 1864. They came through a heavily wooded area called the Wilderness. Lee attacked there, in an area where the superior Union numbers could not be used effectively because of dense brush, poor visibility, and rough ground. The battle was a mass of confusion. The Union lost about 17,000 men in two days of fighting, and neither side could claim victory. The major difference between Grant and previous commanders was what happened after the battle. Instead of retreating, as every other commander had before him, Grant kept going.

Grant-Lee Duel. Grant shifted his army left and tried to go around Lee. Lee shifted skillfully and met him at Spotsylvania Court House. Again there were huge losses on both sides and victory for neither. Grant could replace his losses, but Lee could not, and Grant knew it. He continued to shift left, forcing Lee to move to meet him, and fighting battles almost daily. Grant was quite content with this strategy and was determined to "fight it out on this line if it takes all summer." It would and then some.

Cold Harbor. As Lee continued to move and block his advance on Richmond, Grant began to lose patience. When the Confederates set up new defensive lines at a town called Cold

Harbor, Grant decided to make a strong frontal attack instead of maneuvering again. He sent about a dozen assaults at the Confederate lines, all of which were failures. The Union army suffered over 7,000 casualties in a half an hour. The Confederate lines held.

The slow progress and massive casualties attracted horror in the North. "Butcher Grant" was condemned for his lack of concern for human life, but Grant paid no attention. He had a job to do, and he would keep at it until it was done.

Siege of Petersburg. Grant decided to move yet again in mid-June. This time, he shifted his army south across the James River and marched on the town of Petersburg. Petersburg was a rail junction near Richmond. Most of the trains coming into the Confederate capital came by this route. If Grant captured it, the capital would be at his mercy; however, Lee had time to set up defenses and repulse the Union attack. Grant settled in for a siege.

Atlanta. While Grant was busy in Virginia, William Tecumseh Sherman moved south toward Atlanta, Georgia from Chattanooga. He was opposed by Joseph Johnston's Confederate army. The two sides practiced classic military maneuvering as Sherman worked his way closer and closer to Atlanta from May to July. Johnston's strategy was delay. He fought small battles and withdrew, never allowing Sherman the chance he wanted to destroy the Confederate army. By July Johnston had withdrawn to the strong defenses around Atlanta.

Johnston's strategy was not popular with the Confederate government who wanted Sherman stopped. The Confederate command wanted a more aggressive general, so Johnston was replaced in July by John Bell Hood. Hood attacked Sherman immediately and repeatedly. All the attacks failed and cost the Confederate army irreplaceable soldiers.

In August, Sherman began to shell the city. Morale among the soldiers and citizens fell as the capture of Atlanta seemed imminent. At the end of August, Sherman worked his way around the city and cut off the last railroad link to the Confederacy. Without his supply lines, Hood evacuated the city. Sherman occupied it on August 2nd.

Shenandoah Valley. When Grant settled in to besiege Petersburg, another Union army under David Hunter was working its way down the key Shenandoah Valley. The valley ran northeast in Virginia toward Washington D.C. It was a rich, fertile area that supplied the Confederate army with food. The Union had been unable to gain control of it thus far in the war.

Lee sent Jubal Early to the valley. He was able to stop Hunter and even threatened Washington for a short time. Grant was determined to end this threat that distracted him from concentrating on Lee. He sent Philip Sheridan in with express orders to clear the valley so clean of everything that "a crow could not cross it without carrying its own food." Early succeeded in surprising Sheridan's men at Cedar Creek on October 19th. The Confederates were forced back and were not able to challenge the Union after that. Sheridan proceeded to obey his orders, burning crops and buildings, driving off livestock, and depriving the Confederacy of anything of value in the valley. Using these methods, the Union finally took control of the valley.

This was total war. Prior to the Civil War, American armies avoided harming farms, industries, or any non-military target. But Grant, Sherman, and Sheridan realized that the farms and industries kept the army going. The destruction brought the war home to the ordinary people whose support was vital if the war was to continue. The Union began a new policy to destroy anything that might aid the Confederate army in the hope it would force the civilian population to sue for peace.

| David Farragut and his crew

Mobile. The port of Mobile, Alabama was a major port for blockade runners during the war. By mid-1864, it was also one of the few Confederate ports still open. The city's defenses included three forts, four gunboats (including one ironclad), underwater obstacles, and mines (called torpedoes). Admiral David Farragut, the commander who captured New Orleans, had organized a fleet to take the city. They attacked on August 5, 1864.

One of the Union ironclads was blown up by a torpedo early in the attack. When the other ships hesitated, Farragut gave the famous order, "Damn the torpedoes! Full speed ahead!" The fleet got past the outer defenses and into the harbor. The engines on the Confederate ironclad failed, and the forts were pounded into submission. The port was captured on August 23rd, but the city itself would not surrender for months.

| Civil War-era Navy

Election of 1864. The elections came around in 1864 with Lincoln running for a second term as president. The American democracy was still the only major one in the world and very much a unique experiment. It was astonishing that in the midst of Civil War carnage a regular election could even be held; but it proceeded in an orderly fashion, displaying the incredible strength and flexibility of the American republic.

The war was unpopular, having dragged on far longer than anyone dreamed it should have. A group of Northern Democrats called the Copperheads violently opposed the war, some to the point of treason. Other "War Democrats" supported the war and the Republican president. These joined with the Republicans in 1864 to form the temporary National Union Party and nominate Lincoln for president. One of the War Democrats named Andrew Johnson was nominated as his vice-president.

The remaining Democrats nominated George McClellan, the army general dismissed for his hesitancy in battle. Their platform was defeatist, calling the war a failure. McClellan, as a soldier who had fought in the war, disavowed the plank, but he would have been under immense pressure to negotiate an end to the war had he won. The Democrats had a chance as long as the war was going badly, but the victories at Atlanta, Mobile, and the Shenandoah Valley revived the Republican cause. Many Americans agreed with Lincoln's slogan "Don't swap horses in the middle of the river." Lincoln won easily and that ended the Confederacy's last realistic hope. The war would continue.

Name the person, event, battle, or item.

2.71 _____ rail junction near Richmond, besieged by Grant beginning June 1864

2.72 _____ man Lee sent to Shenandoah Valley to confront Hunter

2.73 _____ Grant lost 7,000 men in a half an hour in a vain attack on Confederate lines

2.74 _____ the dense trees kept Grant from using his superior numbers against Lee

2.75 _____ man who said "Damn the torpedoes! Full speed ahead!"

2.76 _____ Democratic nominee for president 1864

2.77 _____ Lincoln's running mate in 1864

2.78 _____ Union commander that captured Atlanta

2.79 _____ the name of the anti-war Northern Democrats

2.80 _____ Union man who laid waste to the Shenandoah Valley

2.81 _____ Confederate port captured August 23, 1864

2.82 _____ group of Democrats that joined with the Republicans in 1864

2.83 _____ commander who replaced Johnston in the west and immediately attacked Sherman

2.84 _____ rank given to Grant when he took command of all Union troops

Answer these questions.

2.85 How was Grant different from all previous Union commanders?

_____

_____

2.86 What event ended the Confederacy's last hope?

_____

2.87 What was Grant's strategy to defeat Lee?

_____

_____

2.88 What is total war?

_____

_____

Nashville. General Hood still had a Confederate army around Atlanta after Sherman captured the city. He unsuccessfully tried to cut Sherman's supply lines and force him to retreat. After several attempts through the fall, Hood decided on a desperate strategy. He would march north toward the Union-held city of Nashville. He hoped to force Sherman to abandon Atlanta and pursue him.

However, Sherman had other plans. He kept his army in Georgia and sent George Thomas, the "Rock of Chickamauga," north to take over the defense of Nashville. Thomas built up an army in the city as Hood worked his way north, pressing a small Union force that was fighting a delaying retreat in front of him. Hood reached Nashville in early December. By that time, Thomas had built up an army that was larger than his Confederate attackers.

Hood lacked the men to overrun the heavy defenses at Nashville. He also did not have enough men to effectively besiege it. He could not go around it without risking an attack by Thomas' forces. Out of all options except retreat, he stayed until Thomas was ready to attack.

On December 15th and 16th, the Union army attacked and destroyed Hood's army. The scattered remains fled south. What was left was no longer a threat to the Union.

Sherman's March to the Sea. William Tecumseh Sherman realized that with Hood's army to the north there was no one in the Confederacy that could stop him. He therefore proposed to take the war into the heart of the rebel states and make Georgia howl. Grant and Lincoln gave him permission to march from Atlanta to the sea, living off the land and destroying everything of value in his path. He destroyed much of Atlanta and marched out on November 15, 1864. During the march he had no communication with the North. He literally disappeared for a month.

Sherman's march to the sea was devastating to Georgia and the South. It aroused bitter hatred and fear. It showed that the Confederate armies could no longer protect their people. Buildings, railroads, farms, crops, and homes were systematically destroyed all along Sherman's route. Sherman's army ate well on captured food and had enough left over to supply the horde of escaping slaves that joined them along the route. Sherman reached the coast and contacted the blockade fleet on December 10th. Resupplied by the fleet, he captured Savannah on December 21st.

After Savannah, Sherman and his men headed north into South Carolina. That state had been the leader in the secession. The Union army was particularly vicious there. The capital of Columbia was burned on February 17th. Sherman cut the railroad lines into Charleston, forcing that city to surrender to the Union forces that were besieging it. Shortly after that, a combined force from the army and navy captured Wilmington, N.C. which was the last open Confederate port. Meanwhile, Sherman marched into North Carolina. The remaining Confederate army under the command of Joseph Johnston did not have the strength to even slow him down.

Petersburg. While Sheridan and Sherman had been moving, Grant had been in place at Petersburg. All through the end of 1864 and the first part of 1865, he had kept up the pressure on the Confederate defenses. Grant had tried several unsuccessful assaults with devastating losses; however, the fighting, disease, and desertions had steadily reduced the Confederate army. They were now desperately short of basic supplies and were hungry. Grant had slowly spread his lines west, forcing Lee to spread his own limited army out further and further. Grant hoped to eventually outflank Lee (move around the side of his army) and fight a decisive battle.

Lee decided to attempt an attack before the Union succeeded in encircling his army. The Confederate attack on March 25th successfully captured Fort Stedman, a focal point on the Union lines. Lee hoped to use it to threaten Grant's supply lines, but the Union counter-attacked and recaptured the fort the same day.

Meanwhile, Philip Sheridan had finished the Shenandoah Valley and rejoined the Union

| Appomattox Court House, where the Confederate Army surrendered

army at Petersburg. Grant now sent him around Lee's lines to the west to attack Five Forks which controlled Lee's last remaining supply line. The attack on April 1st was successful. Grant ordered a general attack all along the Union lines. The Confederate defenders were spread too thin, and their lines broke. Lee ordered a retreat and informed Jefferson Davis that he could no longer protect Richmond.

Appomattox Court House. After the fall of Petersburg, the Confederate government abandoned Richmond and fled south. Lee also headed south, hoping to join up with Johnston's forces in South Carolina. Grant followed in close pursuit. In the meantime, Sheridan got between Lee and Johnston, forcing the former to turn west. Things went from bad to worse for the Confederate army when food rations failed to arrive. At Sayler's Creek, the Union army attacked the retreating Confederates, capturing their supply wagons and thousands of prisoners. Finally, Lee realized he had no choice "but to go and see General Grant." He then added, "I would rather die a thousand deaths."

Lee and Grant met on April 9th in a small settlement called Appomattox Court House. Lee chose to surrender rather than disband his army and continue fighting a guerrilla war that would drive the nation into further barbarism and bloodshed. Grant returned the favor by granting the Army of Northern Virginia full parole if they laid down their arms. This meant that Lee and the other Confederate leaders would not be hanged as traitors. Grant even allowed the soldiers to keep their horses and sent rations over to the hungry Confederate army. The Army of Northern Virginia formally surrendered on April 12, 1865, four years to the day after Fort Sumter.

For all practical purposes, the war was over. Joseph Johnston realized he had no hope of continuing alone. On April 26th, he surrendered to Sherman on the same terms given to General Lee. Jefferson Davis was captured by Union cavalry on May 10th in Georgia. The last battle of the war was fought three days later near Brownsville, Texas.

Conclusions. The Civil War cost the United States over 600,000 men. Slavery was ended, and the notion that a state could leave the Union was abandoned. The United States was again one nation, and its government was stronger than ever before. Union industry had grown stronger under the demands of a war economy. The South, on the other hand, was devastated. Four million black Americans were no longer slaves, but they had no jobs and no education. Victory brought both great gain and great pain.

Ford's Theatre. The last wound that convulsed the nation was the assassination of Abraham Lincoln. Lincoln had held the Union together and pressed forward with the war. He had managed the infighting in his cabinet, opponents in Congress, poor generals, bad luck, and disappointment with skill and courage for four years. After Appomattox, the president decided to relax. He and his wife went to Ford's Theatre on April 14, 1865 to see a comedy. There, he was shot in the back of the head by a deranged actor named John Wilkes Booth, who thought he was avenging the South. Lincoln was carried across the street and died early on April 15th.

Booth fled from the scene. He was tracked by federal troops and shot after being cornered in a barn. Several people who had conspired with him to kill other members of the U.S. government were hanged. Lincoln's body was taken back to Springfield, Illinois in a slow-moving train for burial. His death coming so close on the heels of victory plunged the nation into grief and inspired a cry for revenge that echoed ominously through the South.

| John Wilkes Booth's Wanted Poster

Answer true or false.

If the answer is false, change it to make it true. Merely adding the word "not" is not sufficient.

2.89 _____ Sherman marched from Nashville to the sea, destroying anything of military value in his path.

2.90 _____ The Confederate army in Tennessee was virtually destroyed outside of Nashville in December 1864.

2.91 _____ Lee retreated from Petersburg in January of 1865.

2.92 _____ Over six hundred thousand men died in the Civil War.

2.93 _____ Lincoln was assassinated by John Wilkes Booth.

2.94 _____ Lee surrendered at Richmond in April, 1865.

2.95 _____ Grant led the troops that captured Five Forks.

2.96 _____ George Thomas was the Union victor at Nashville.

2.97 _____ Sherman captured Savannah in December 1864.

2.98 _____ The Confederate government was captured when Richmond fell.

2.99 _____ The surrender of Lee ended the war for all practical purposes.

2.100 _____ Lincoln's assassination occurred at Ford's Theater on April 14, 1865.

2.101 _____ Grant allowed the Confederate soldiers to keep their rifles after they surrendered.

2.102 _____ Booth was hanged after a trial.

2.103 _____ By the end, the Confederate army at Petersburg was hungry and short of basic supplies.

2.104 _____ Meade forced Lee to spread his defensive lines further and further at Petersburg.

Write a one-page paper.

2.105 Write a paper on the Emancipation Proclamation, a Civil War battle, a general, weapons used in the war, or the living conditions of the soldiers.

TEACHER CHECK _____ _____
                                    initials   date

↺ **Review the material in this section in preparation for the Self Test.** This Self Test will check your mastery of this particular section as well as your knowledge of the previous section.

SELF TEST 2

Match the correct person. Some answers will be used more than once (each answer, 2 points).

2.01 _____ devastated the Shenandoah Valley

2.02 _____ led the Union army at Gettysburg

2.03 _____ president of the Confederacy

2.04 _____ led the Confederate army at Gettysburg

2.05 _____ the "Rock of Chickamauga"

2.06 _____ dismissed from Union command for being repeatedly hesitant

2.07 _____ Gettysburg Address

2.08 _____ first U.S. lieutenant general since Washington

2.09 _____ Union commander who defeated Hood at Nashville

2.010 _____ captured Vicksburg

2.011 _____ Lee's brilliant subordinate, shot by friendly fire at Chancellorsville

2.012 _____ captured New Orleans and Mobile

2.013 _____ delayed Sherman on his way to Atlanta, relieved of command for not being aggressive

2.014 _____ abolitionist martyr, attacked Harpers Ferry to start slave uprising

2.015 _____ devastated Georgia in a march to the sea

a. Robert E. Lee

b. Ulysses S. Grant

c. George McClellan

d. Stonewall Jackson

e. William T. Sherman

f. David Farragut

g. John Brown

h. George Meade

i. Jefferson Davis

j. Abraham Lincoln

k. George Thomas

l. Joseph Johnston

m. Philip Sheridan

Put a *U* beside the Union victories and a *C* beside the Confederate victories (each answer, 1 point).

In cases where a victor was not clear, choose the side that benefited most from the results of the battle.

2.016 _____ Chancellorsville

2.017 _____ Gettysburg

2.018 _____ Antietam

2.019 _____ First Bull Run

2.020 _____ Peninsular Campaign

2.021 _____ *Monitor* and *Merrimac*

2.022 _____ Shiloh

2.023 _____ Chickamauga

2.024 _____ Petersburg

2.025 _____ Fredericksburg

Name the person, event, or term (each answer, 2 points).

2.026 _____ Act that ended the era of compromise

2.027 _____ Supreme Court decision that protected slavery in all the states

2.028 _____ document that freed the slaves in all states still in rebellion on January 1, 1863

2.029 _____ battle that was the turning point of the Civil War

2.030 _____ man who was the outgoing U.S. president when the Confederate states were first organized

2.031 _____ the worst prison camp in the Civil War

2.032 _____ killed more soldiers than bullets did during the Civil War

2.033 _____ place where Robert E. Lee surrendered

2.034 _____ man who killed Abraham Lincoln

2.035 _____ first state to secede from the Union

Answer these questions (each answer, 3 points).

2.036 What were two advantages the South had in the Civil War?

a. _____

b. _____

2.037 How was Grant different from all previous Union commanders?

_____

_____

2.038 What were two reasons why Britain did not support the Confederacy?

a. _____

b. _____

2.039 What was the political stand of the Republican Party and Abraham Lincoln on slavery in the election of 1860?

_____

_____

2.040 Why was the Kansas Territory called "Bleeding Kansas?"

_____

_____

2.041 Which army had the advantage in the area of supplies and why?

_____

_____

2.042 What was remarkable about the election of 1864?

_____

_____

2.043 Why were there so many battle casualties in the Civil War?

_____

_____

Answer true or false (each answer, 1 point).

2.044 _____ Soldiers in both armies became more interested in God as the war continued.

2.045 _____ More Americans died in the Civil War than in any other war fought by the U.S.

2.046 _____ The fall of Vicksburg gave the Union control of the Ohio River.

2.047 _____ Missouri was a slave state that stayed in the Union.

2.048 _____ Ulysses S. Grant is considered by most experts to have been the best general in the Civil War.

2.049 _____ The first Southern states seceded directly after the election of Abraham Lincoln.

2.050 _____ The Union government passed America's first conscription law.

2.051 _____ Black soldiers were quickly incorporated with white soldiers on equal terms in the Union army.

2.052 _____ Both sides expected a long, hard war from the beginning.

2.053 _____ Lincoln came to national attention through his work as secretary of state.

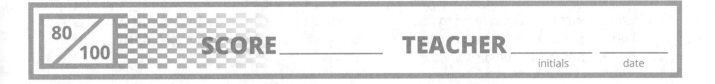

80 / 100   SCORE _____   TEACHER _____ _____
                                                    initials   date

| Mathew Brady, the most famous photographer of the Civil War

3. RECONSTRUCTION

The nation faced many problems at the end of the Civil War. The victorious Union had to decide how much to punish the South for secession. The South had to form new state governments acceptable to the North. The rights of the newly freed black Americans needed to be defined, and those rights had to be protected. Moreover, the South itself was in ruins and lacked the funds needed to rebuild.

Many of the people in the North called for harsh treatment of the former Confederate States. However, Abraham Lincoln was not among them. In his second Inaugural Address about a month before his death, Lincoln spoke of his own goals in the victory which was quickly approaching.

> *With malice toward none, with charity for all, with firmness in the right as God gives us to see the right, let us strive on to finish the work we are in, to bind up the nation's wounds, to care for him who shall have borne the battle and for his widow and orphan, to do all which may achieve and cherish a just and lasting peace among ourselves and with all nations.*

Unfortunately for the South, Lincoln did not survive to pursue his peace. The new president, Andrew Johnson, did not have Lincoln's flexibility or political skill. After he butted heads with Congress, the Radical Republicans in that body set up their own harsh "Reconstruction" of the South over the president's vetoes. They even **impeached** Johnson for opposing them.

The Southern states all had acceptable state governments by 1870. By 1877 all of those states had white Democrats in complete control. That same year, newly elected President Rutherford B. Hayes moved out the last federal troops in the South that were supporting occupation governments. That was the final end of the long ordeal known as Reconstruction.

SECTION OBJECTIVES

Review these objectives. When you have completed this section, you should be able to:

6. Describe Reconstruction.
7. Describe the background and policies of Civil War-era presidents.
8. Describe the post-Civil War corruption.
9. Explain the status of black Americans during and after Reconstruction.

VOCABULARY

Study these words to enhance your learning success in this section.

alderman (äl′ der man). Member of a city legislature.

filibuster (fil′ a bus ter). In the U.S. Senate, a senator or group of senators refuse to stop debating a bill and thus prevent it from passing.

impeach (im pēch′). To charge a public official with misconduct in office in front of the proper authority for a trial.

posthumous (päs chu mus). Born after the death of the father.

Presidential Reconstruction

Andrew Johnson (1808-1875). Andrew Johnson was the first U.S. president to be impeached by Congress. Johnson was born to poor working parents in North Carolina. His father died when he was three. He had no formal education. At the age of thirteen, he was apprenticed to a tailor, which is probably when he learned to read.

As a youth, Johnson worked his way to Tennessee where he set up a successful tailoring business. He married the daughter of a shoemaker. She taught him to write, do simple arithmetic, and encouraged him to read. Johnson's business prospered, and he purchased property (including slaves) in Tennessee.

As Johnson's social position improved, he went into politics as a Jacksonian Democrat. He developed a powerful voice and used it to influence crowds. He won his first election in 1829 as an **alderman**, and he rarely lost after that. He served as a mayor, state representative, state senator, and governor in Tennessee. He served as a member of both the U.S. House and Senate.

Andrew Johnson believed in the right of Southerners to own enslaved people, but was an even stronger supporter of the Union. He was a member of the U.S. Senate in 1860 and was the only Southern senator who refused to secede with his state. Lincoln appointed him as military governor of his home state of Tennessee as it was conquered by the Union. As a prominent member of the War Democrats who supported Lincoln throughout the Civil War, he was an obvious choice for vice president in 1864. He filled out the ticket of the National Union Party which combined the Republicans and War Democrats to nominate Lincoln in 1864. He became president when Lincoln died.

Johnson's Reconstruction Plan. In 1863 Lincoln had established a plan to readmit the Confederate States to the Union. It was called the 10 percent plan. It required that only 10 percent of the voters in a state take an oath of loyalty to the Union. These would elect a state government that accepted the abolition of slavery. Then the state would be readmitted to the Union with all rights and privileges. Several conquered Confederate states had complied with these terms and sent representatives to Congress by 1864.

Congress refused to allow the new Congressmen to take their seats. (Congress has this right under the Constitution). Many in Congress felt that Lincoln's plan was too lenient. They hoped that Johnson, who hated rich planters because of his own humble background, would take a harder line with the South.

However, Johnson was a Southern Democrat and a follower of Andrew Jackson (a believer in restricted government). He set up a Reconstruction program in 1865 based on Lincoln's plans. Once 10% of voters had taken a loyalty oath, they were to vote for members of a special state convention. The convention had to approve the Thirteenth Amendment (which ended slavery), repudiate Confederate debts, and repeal the state's secession from Union. Certain high-level Confederates and those owning more than $20,000 in property were required to get a presidential pardon to vote, but Johnson granted those freely.

The Southern states quickly complied with these easy terms. The new state governments moved with equal swiftness in passing "Black Codes" that insured the black population would continue to be a subjugated people. The codes varied from state to state, but they basically worked to keep blacks as a cheap labor supply for the South. Black workers had to sign labor contracts with their employers. They lost all of their pay or could be dragged back by force if they tried to leave before the contract was finished. They could not vote, serve on juries, and in many states they could not own or lease land. Some states even declared that black people without jobs could be arrested for "idleness." They would be forced to work to pay their fines or serve on chain gangs rented out by the government. Everything possible was done to insure that the only change in the South was that black people were no longer *technically* slaves.

Abolitionists in the North were furious at the blatant defiance to the goals of the Union. To make matters worse, many of newly elected Southern Congressmen had been high-ranking Confederates, including Alexander Stephens, the Confederate vice president! The Republicans had enjoyed complete control of Congress during the war years. Several pro-Northern laws had passed during those four years, including a Homestead Act (giving free land to settlers), a high tariff, and subsidies for a Northern railroad across the nation. Northern Republicans were not anxious to surrender power, especially on such easy terms.

Johnson vs. Congress. An angry Congress now challenged Johnson's easy terms for the South. They were led by Thaddeus Stevens, a representative with a long history of championing the cause of black Americans. He led a group called the "Radical Republicans," Congressmen who pushed for a harsh policy toward the South. They were especially concerned with securing the rights of the newly freed black people, hoping to secure them as Republican voters.

Under the leadership of Stevens, Congress again refused to give the former Confederate states their seats in the national legislature. Then Congress formed the Joint (House-Senate) Committee on Reconstruction. Stevens, as chairman of the House members, quickly became the strongest influence on the committee. Stevens used his position to pursue plans that offered more protection to the newly freed slaves and less power to their defeated masters.

At first, Congress simply tried to modify the Johnson-Lincoln Plan to include more protection for the freedmen. In February of 1866,

| Andrew Johnson and a group of freedmen

Congress passed a law extending the life of the Freedmen's Bureau. The Freedmen's Bureau was a organization created to aid black people in their change from slaves to citizens. It operated as an early welfare agency, distributing clothes and food, providing education, settling disputes with employers, and hopefully settling the newly freed men on their own small farms. Southerners resented the Bureau, especially in its attempts to educate black people. Johnson vetoed the law to continue the Bureau because it interfered with the rights of the Southern states.

The now very angry Congress passed the Civil Rights Act which gave black people the rights of citizenship and tried to offset some of the Black Codes. Johnson vetoed that law as well, but in April Congress overrode the veto, making the bill a law. It was the first time Congress had ever successfully overridden a presidential veto on a piece of major legislation. It would be the first of many for President Johnson.

Congress wanted to insure that a future Democratic Congress could not undo the Civil Rights Act, so they passed the Fourteenth Amendment to the Constitution and sent it to the states. The Amendment made all freedmen citizens. It also ended the representation in Congress of any state that did not allow them to vote. However, it did not *require* that states allow black people

to vote. Even many Northern states did not allow that. The Amendment barred certain Confederates from office and voided Confederate debts.

Johnson opposed the Fourteenth Amendment, but he had no power to prevent it. The loss of Lincoln was keenly felt as the relationship between the president and Congress deteriorated. Lincoln, the flexible political genius, would have understood the need to compromise with and then lead Congress, but Johnson was simply defiant. He went on a speaking tour in the summer of 1866, trying to influence the congressional elections. He hoped to get a Congress that favored his Reconstruction plan. Instead, his "swing around the circle" gained votes for the radicals. Johnson's fiery speeches were mercilessly heckled and rapidly became shouting matches between the president and the crowd. In the end, the 1866 elections expanded the number of Radical Republicans in Washington.

Johnson compounded his problems by failing to recognize dangerous reality. He encouraged the Southern states to reject the Fourteenth Amendment. Tennessee was the only one of the former Confederate states to vote in favor of the amendment. Congress now had solid, veto-proof majorities in both houses, and decided to set up its own Reconstruction plan when it met in 1867.

 Answer these questions.

3.1 Under Johnson and Lincoln's plan, what percent of Southern voters had to take a loyalty oath to begin rebuilding the state government? _____

3.2 What did the state conventions have to do before they could reform as a government under Johnson's plan?

    a. _____

    b. _____

    c. _____

3.3 What were the Republican Congressmen who favored harsh treatment of the South called?

_____

3.4 What Amendment to the Constitution ended slavery? _____

3.5 What was Andrew Johnson's trade? _____

3.6 What law did Congress pass to offset the Black Codes?

_____

3.7 What organization tried to aid the black people in the transition to freedom?

_____

3.8 How did Congress react to Johnson's veto of the Civil Rights Bill?

_____

3.9 What were the terms of the Fourteenth Amendment?

a. _____

b. _____

c. _____

d. _____

3.10 Why did Johnson make his "swing around the circle?"

_____

_____

3.11 Why did Johnson veto the extension of the Freedman's Bureau?

_____

3.12 What laws had the Republican Congress passed when the Democratic South was in rebellion?

a. _____

b. _____

c. _____

3.13 What was the purpose of the "Black Codes?"

_____

_____

3.14 Which former Confederate state did accept the Fourteenth Amendment before 1867?

_____

3.15 What party nominated Johnson for vice president in 1864?

_____

3.16 What was unusual about Andrew Johnson as a senator in 1860?

_____

3.17 What Congressional committee tried to change Johnson's Reconstruction plan?

_____

3.18 Who was the leader of the Radical Republicans? _____

Radical Reconstruction

Occupation. Beginning in March of 1867, Congress began to model Reconstruction according to its own ideas, overriding every presidential veto. With the exception of Tennessee, the South was divided into five military districts run by a general and controlled by federal troops. The state governments were placed under military control, and former Confederate leaders were denied the right to vote. The states were required to ratify the Fourteenth Amendment and guarantee the right of black people to vote before they were allowed to form a new government. Moreover, another law was passed that required all of Johnson's orders to the army be issued through Ulysses S. Grant, whom the Republicans felt could be trusted to interpret them as Congress wished.

Southern reaction to the new laws was bitterly hostile. Not only were their own white leaders denied the right to even vote, black people would be voting! They were especially bitter at the hypocrisy that some Northern states still denied black people the right to vote. The rapid registration of black voters and the fact these new citizens voted Republican enforced Southern fears of a political conspiracy to take over the South. But by 1870, all of the states had new governments and constitutions that met Congressional criteria.

As a result of the new laws, Republican governments came to power in most of the states. Most of them also had a minority of black representatives, which inflamed the bigoted South. (Only in South Carolina did black representatives

constitute a majority in the state assembly.) A few black Americans were also elected to the U.S. House and Senate. The Radical Republicans tried to protect these gains by passing the Fifteenth Amendment which guaranteed freedmen the right to vote. It was ratified in 1870.

Impeachment. Congress was so successful in pushing its own agenda that it began to reach for more power by getting rid of their main annoyance, the president. They tried to do this by passing the Tenure of Office Act (over Johnson's veto). This law supposedly forbade the president to fire any official approved by the Senate without the approval of that same body. This meant Johnson could not legally dismiss members of his own cabinet, his own personal advisors!

As expected, Johnson violated the law in 1868 when he dismissed Secretary of War Edwin Stanton who was a Radical supporter. Congress immediately voted to impeach Johnson for "high crimes and misdemeanors" as required by the Constitution. Most of the charges stemmed from firing Stanton, although he was also accused of verbal assaults on Congress.

The impeachment trial in the Senate was a huge show. The House prosecuted the case badly. Johnson's skillful attorneys showed that Johnson's only crime was opposing Congress. Still the Radical control of the Senate meant the vote would be close, and in the end Johnson was acquitted by a single vote. Seven Republican senators had voted in his favor, defying their own party for the sake of justice. Johnson had been stubborn and impolitic, but the Senate jury decided he had not committed a crime. The vote saved the presidency from a dangerous precedent. Impeachment could not be used as a political tool to remove an unpopular president.

Carpetbaggers and Scalawags. In the meantime, Reconstruction governments came to be dominated by Northerners who had traveled south and Southerners who decided to cooperate with Reconstruction. The former were called "carpetbaggers," because they supposedly traveled south with their possessions in a carpetbag to get rich yielding political power in the South. The latter group were called "scalawags" and were considered traitors to the Southern cause.

Some of the carpetbaggers did get rich by using their elected offices for personal gain. Others came south because they saw the Southern country while serving in the war and wanted to settle there. Still others came to bring Northern justice and ideas to the "backward" South. They were extremely unpopular, and stealing done by a prominent few of them reflected badly on the entire group.

The scalawags also had mixed reasons for cooperating. Many felt that they had lost the war and that cooperation was the proper course of action. Others saw the Republican Party as the only chance to put white people back in power. Still others were just switching sides to make a quick buck.

The corruption in the Reconstruction governments mirrored corruption in the entire nation. It varied, depending on the honesty of the men in power, but it also attracted a great deal of attention. As the years passed, Northerners saw the corruption as a reason to end Reconstruction. They eventually became tired of trying to control the South and believed that *white* Southerners should control their democratic governments.

| Sharecropper

Reconstruction governments did do some good. They instituted badly needed reforms in Southern governments. Public schools were established, tax systems were modernized, and internal improvements had begun. But the leaders of the old South would not tolerate being dominated by Northerners who promoted equality. The deep racial hatred of the Southern white people controlled their views of government and justice. They eventually found ways to regain power: violence, intimidation, and fraud.

"Redeemers." Some bitter Southern whites resorted to secret associations and terror to regain control of their governments. The Ku Klux Klan, formed in Tennessee in 1866, was the most infamous of these organizations. Dressed in white masks, these men would attack Northern Republicans, male teachers at freedmen schools, and Southerners who cooperated with the Reconstruction governments. But most of their fury was unleashed on black people who dared to exercise their newfound rights.

Black Americans were threatened, beaten, or killed for voting, getting an education, not acting in a subservient manner, or daring to challenge a white man in court.

Using these methods, the Klan and other organizations drove the Republicans out of the South. Only Democratic votes were acceptable, and by 1877, all the Southern states were "redeemed" as white Democrats came back into power. They remained in power for a long time. The deep bitterness of the Reconstruction period kept the Republican Party from having any large following in the South for many years.

Situation in the South. The South settled down to a new form of society. The old aristocratic planter society was gone. The lack of cash after the war meant that landowners had no way to pay laborers to work their fields. This led to the "share crop" system. In exchange for use of the land and tools, a worker (usually black) would raise a crop and split it with the landowner (usually white).

The white storekeepers and landowners charged high prices for tools and supplies. They also paid low prices for crops such as cotton. This led to a type of debt-slavery that kept thousands of black Americans in poverty for generations. High costs drove many of the landowners into debt and forced them to rely on heavily on cotton for needed cash. The concentration on one crop exhausted the soil and made poverty worse.

The Fourteenth Amendment gave black people the rights of citizenship, but equality was carefully evaded. Separate facilities were set up all over the South for eating, traveling, and learning. Tax dollars from the white-controlled legislatures invariably favored white facilities. Black schools received much less money than white schools; that is, until the system was overthrown in the 1960s.

The Fifteenth Amendment, which gave black people the right to vote, was virtually ignored. Black people who dared to vote faced the

threat of violence from the Klan and other white supremacist organizations. Southern governments resorted to fraud and restrictive laws to prevent black Americans from voting. For example, some states required voters to pass literacy tests. White people routinely passed and black people routinely failed. Other states passed "grandfather clauses" that only allowed men to vote if their ancestors had in 1860. Poverty, poor education, and denial of the right to vote kept black Americans from truly being free, even after a devastating war had been fought for just that purpose.

Seward's Folly. By 1867 Andrew Johnson was little more than a figurehead, but his administration did manage one true victory, the purchase of Alaska. That territory was the property of the nation of Russia in the early 1860s. The czar saw the cold land in North America as a liability in the event of war with Britain. So he offered to sell it to the United States, which was another nation often at odds with the English.

Johnson's secretary of state was William Seward, a man who favored expansion, and he willingly negotiated a treaty offering Russia $7.2 million for the land (about two cents an acre). Most of the people in the United States saw no use for a piece of land so far north. It could not be used for farms, which is what most Americans wanted. The popular press called it "Seward's Folly" or "Seward's Icebox." Nevertheless, Congress approved the treaty, and the land has since repaid its purchase price many times over in oil, gold, fish, and minerals.

Complete these sentences.

3.19 Northern men who became part of the Reconstruction governments in the South were

called _____ .

3.20 The South was divided into _____ military districts under Radical Reconstruction.

3.21 The purchase of Alaska was mocked by calling it _____ .

3.22 Many black farmers were put into debt-slavery by the _____ system.

3.23 Southern white people regained control of their governments using terror and secret societies

like the _____ .

3.24 Freedmen were given the right to vote by the _____ Amendment.

3.25 _____ Republicans voted to acquit Johnson at his impeachment.

3.26 The Radical Congress required Johnson to issue all his orders to the army through

_____ .

3.27 The United States paid _____ dollars for Alaska.

3.28 Johnson was impeached for violating the _____ Act.

3.29 Due to bitter feelings over Reconstruction, the South was dominated by the

_____ Party for many years.

3.30 _____ were Southern men who cooperated with Reconstruction.

3.31 A Southern state was "_____" when white Democrats were again in power.

3.32 Johnson was impeached when he fired _____ .

Answer these questions.

3.33 How did the South avoid the Fifteenth Amendment?

a. _____

b. _____

c. _____

3.34 Why did Northern people begin to oppose Reconstruction as time went by?

a. _____

b. _____

c. _____

3.35 How did the Southern Democrats regain control of their governments?

_____

_____

3.36 What good did Reconstruction governments do?

a. _____

b. _____

c. _____

3.37 Why did the South continue to rely on cotton and what did it do to the soil?

a. _____

b. _____

3.38 How did the education system in the South hurt black Americans?

_____

_____

3.39 Why was the outcome of Johnson's impeachment so important?

_____

_____

Era of Good Stealings

Election of 1868. General Ulysses S. Grant slowly turned against Andrew Johnson. By the time Johnson was impeached, Grant was openly siding with the Republicans in Congress. His immense popularity made him an obvious choice for president in 1868. He was nominated by the Republicans along with a platform that called for harsh Reconstruction and repayment of Union Civil War debts. The Democrats nominated New York's Governor Horatio Seymour to oppose him. Their platform denounced Radical Reconstruction and called for debts to be repaid in inflationary paper money, not specie.

The Republican campaign involved a great deal of "waving the bloody shirt" (reminding the public about the war). The Democrats were accused of supporting the rebellion. "Vote as you shot" was a popular Republican slogan. Grant won the election by a comfortable majority. However, many white people in the South could not vote, and the black voters gave Grant the margin of victory. The unpopular Andrew Johnson was not even considered for the Democratic nomination, but he remained active in Tennessee politics. He was again elected to the U.S. Senate in 1875, just prior to his death.

Ulysses S. Grant (1822-1885). Ulysses S. Grant was an honest man who had one of the most corrupt administrations in American history. He was an excellent general, but one of the nation's worst presidents. He was born in Ohio to a tanner. His father had a prosperous business, and the shy Ulysses was given a good education. He became an excellent horseman, but had a distinct lack of business sense and no interest in his father's profession.

His father succeeded in getting him an appointment to West Point in 1839. Grant was an average student who did well in mathematics and horsemanship. He served in the Mexican War and received a promotion for his conduct. After the war, he married a classmate's sister and continued his career in the army.

| Ulysses S. Grant as President

In 1853, he was posted in an isolated fort in California, far from his beloved and growing family. He lost money in several schemes, began drinking, and eventually resigned from the army.

Until the Civil War, he worked at a variety of unsuccessful jobs. When the war began, he helped organize volunteers and was eventually given a colonel's command because the army badly needed experienced officers. He quickly gained fame for his victories in the west and was promoted to command of the entire Union army in 1864. He was the man who finally cornered Robert E. Lee. He was praised, even in the South, for the generous terms he gave to his defeated foe.

Grant was not well suited for the presidency. He was shy, naive, and a poor judge of character. His own honesty is supported by historians, but he constantly chose men for important offices who were extremely dishonest. He was easily swayed by these men to do what they wanted, and he continued to be loyal to them after their misdeeds were exposed. The result was an out-of-control administration that can be called the "Era of Good Stealings."

The new president was in a mess from the beginning. His cabinet was generally made up of friends without any consideration of their abilities. (Hamilton Fish, his very competent secretary of state, was an exception). The nation was in need of civil service reform to end the system of giving government jobs to pay off political supporters. Grant initially favored reform, but his "friends" talked him out of it. Grant's in-laws especially benefitted from the old plan, many of them landing government jobs. Grant also abandoned his initial plans to ease up on Reconstruction after pressure from the party.

Boss Tweed. The necessities of war had created an atmosphere of waste and fraud. Many businessmen had become rich supplying the needs of the army. Graft, corruption, and dishonesty became the dominant features of the get-rich-quick mindset. Cheating the government, investors, buyers, and anyone else became commonplace. Judges, police, and legislators were routinely bribed to look the other way. Millions were made by entrepreneurs who overcharged their own railroads for construction costs, sold stocks at inflated prices, paid bribes to get government contracts, and then set prices unreasonably high on the railroad routes they controlled.

One of the worst examples of governmental corruption was Boss Tweed in New York City. He gained control of the Democratic Party and absolute control of the city government. He and his ring stole as much as $200 million dollars by overcharging the treasury for goods and services (for example: $138,000 for two days work by a plasterer). He was brought down by

| Boss Tweed, with a Thomas Nast caricature of him

evidence published by the New York *Times* and by the anti-Tweed cartoons of Thomas Nast. (Both refused huge bribes not to publish). New York attorney Samuel Tilden led the prosecution team that finally put Tweed in jail in 1873.

Black Friday. James Fisk and Jay Gould were in the unsavory category of wealthy financial pirates. In 1869 they hatched a scheme to "corner the gold market," which would involve buying up gold and holding it until the price went sky high during a panic. Then they could sell the gold they had at an incredible profit. However, they had to make sure that the U.S. government would not sell its own supply of gold to stabilize the market once the panic began. They paid a large bribe to Grant's brother-in-law to convince the president to hold the government gold.

The pair tried their scheme on "Black Friday," September 24. The price of gold shot up, driving many businessmen to near ruin. However, Grant did not block the sale of government gold and the whole scheme collapsed. A congressional investigation did not implicate Grant, but the scandal did touch his family.

Crédit Mobilier. Another scandal hit the administration in 1872. Crédit Mobilier was a railroad construction company created by officers of the Union Pacific Railway. They used the company to build the transcontinental railroad, charging double the actual construction costs. The owners made sure Washington would not interfere by giving Crédit Mobilier stock to key congressmen and Grant's vice-president. When it was exposed by a newspaper, it reflected badly on the lack of control and honesty in the government. Pressure for reform began to mount.

Alabama Claims. During the Civil War, Britain had allowed ships to be built for the Confederacy in British shipyards. They were fitted with guns in other countries and were used to raid Union shipping throughout the war. The most notorious was the *Alabama*. The ship was built in Britain, armed in Portugal, and sailed by a British crew! It never entered a Confederate port, even though it flew a Confederate flag and captured over sixty Union merchant vessels. U.S. officials in Britain had been pressing the British government to pay for damages caused by that and other British/Confederate privateers.

The British government felt the pressure to settle the dispute, for their officials felt the claim was legitimate. Others feared a bad precedent if a revolt broke out in Ireland, and America supplied them with the same type of raiders. So in 1871, Britain and the U.S. signed the Treaty of Washington which submitted the entire dispute to an arbitration panel in Geneva, Switzerland. The arbitrators awarded the U.S. $15.5 million. The award restored good relations between the two nations.

Election of 1872. By 1872 the scandals of "Grantism" had created a large reform movement. Reformers in the Republican party refused to support Grant when it was clear he would run again. Instead, they formed the Liberal Republican Party and nominated Horace Greeley, the famous editor of the New York *Tribune*. Greeley was a bad choice due to his ragged appearance, lack of flexibility, and emotionalism. The Democrats, desperate for office, also supported the rabidly anti-Confederate Greeley.

After a vicious campaign, Grant won the election with a larger margin than in 1868. As with most third-party movements in U.S. history, the Liberal Republicans were absorbed into one of the larger parties once it took over their ideals. In this case, the Republicans sponsored tariff reform, amnesty for Confederate leaders, and a wave toward civil service reform, all of which stole the reformer's thunder.

| Horace Greeley, editor of the New York Tribune and Liberal Republican Presidential Candidate

Panic of 1873. Grant's second term had a hard shock when the nation went into a financial panic in 1873. The country had again overextended on credit. When purchases no longer kept up with what businesses needed to pay their debts, the economy crashed. It began with the bankruptcy of a large New York banking firm and quickly spread as thousands of other companies folded. It was the nation's longest depression to date, lasting six years.

The government of that day did not even consider using tax dollars to fix the economy. That was well understood to be the job of private businesses <u>only</u>. However, there was a vigorous debate over a correct monetary policy that would aid the economy. "Hard money" people wanted all money to be gold, silver, or paper notes backed by a certain amount of gold. "Soft" or "cheap money" advocates wanted paper money that circulated without a set value. The latter causes inflation and makes it easier for debtors to pay off their debts. It is known today that a hard money policy decreases the money supply and when begun during a depression it tends to make the depression worse.

Grant was a hard money man. He supported the Resumption Act of 1875 that promised to redeem all Civil War-issued paper money for its face value in gold. That decision worsened the depression and gave the Democrats control of the House of Representatives after the 1874 elections. It led to the creation of another third party called the Greenbacks who elected several members of Congress in 1878.

Further Scandals. Yet another scandal, the Whiskey Ring, surfaced in 1875. It was a system of payoffs designed to cheat the government out of money from the whiskey excise tax. Treasury agents took bribes to ignore untaxed whiskey. It was uncovered by a new secretary of the treasury and implicated several of President Grant's friends, including his personal secretary. Grant allowed the investigation at first, but began to interfere with it as it touched his friends. Eventually, the secretary was tried and Grant obtained his acquittal by sending the court a letter saying the president believed he was innocent.

William Belknap, Grant's secretary of war, was impeached in 1876 for taking bribes from men who received contracts to supply goods to the Native Americans. The supplier made a handsome profit by giving the Native Americans inferior goods while charging for quality ones. Belknap resigned, managing to avoid a conviction. The string of scandals severely damaged Grant's reputation.

✎ **Name these items, events, or people.**

3.40 _____ policy that called for all money to be gold, silver, or paper notes backed by a certain amount of gold

3.41 _____ Democratic candidate in 1868

3.42 _____ Democrat who ran New York City, stealing millions

3.43 _____ company that constructed track for the Union Pacific, charging way over the costs and giving stock to congressmen

3.44 _____ law that promised to redeem all Civil War paper money for gold

3.45 _____ scheme to cheat the government out of excise tax income

3.46 _____ third party created by Grant's hard money policy

3.47 _____ treaty that submitted the *Alabama* dispute to arbitration

3.48 _____ plan to end rewarding political supporters with government jobs

3.49 _____ name given the day Fisk and Gould tried to corner the gold market

3.50 _____ third party that sought reform in 1872

3.51 _____ secretary of war, resigned over bribery scandal

3.52 _____ amount of money awarded to the U.S. for *Alabama* claims

3.53 _____ cartoonist who helped bring down Boss Tweed

Answer true or false.

3.54 _____ Ulysses S. Grant was a great president.

3.55 _____ "Waving the bloody shirt" was reminding the electorate of the war.

3.56 _____ Grant was dishonest.

3.57 _____ The Democratic Party absorbed the Liberal Republicans by taking their ideas.

3.58 _____ During his administration, Grant's brother-in-law, personal secretary, and secretary of war were implicated in bribery scandals.

3.59 _____ "Vote as you shot" was a Democratic slogan.

3.60 _____ Corruption was a major problem in government and business after the Civil War.

End of Reconstruction

Election of 1876. Grant, encouraged by his political leeches, seriously considered running for a third term. By large majority, the House of Representatives published a resolution opposing third terms as protection against dictators. Grant took the point, and the Republicans looked for another man.

The former president proved as inept in business after the war as he had been before it. He invested his savings in a banking company called Grant & Ward. Ward was dishonest, and Grant lost everything in 1884 when the company failed. He started writing articles about the Civil War in order to support his family, but shortly after that he developed throat cancer (he was a heavy cigar smoker). He wrote his memoirs as the disease slowly took his life. He died soon after it was completed, and the success of the book gave his family a very comfortable income. The Civil War was the one pure success of Ulysses S. Grant.

The Republicans almost nominated Maine congressman James Blaine, but evidence of a bribery scandal ended his chances. America was tired of corruption and wanted an honest candidate. The Republicans finally chose Rutherford B. Hayes, governor of Ohio and a Union war veteran. He had been an honest, competent governor and supported civil service reform. The Democrats chose Samuel Tilden, governor of New York and one of key men in smashing the Tweed Ring, to oppose Hayes. The Republicans again waved the bloody shirt while the Democrats condemned the years of scandal-ridden Republican rule.

Tilden won the popular vote by a small margin and clearly had 184 out of the 185 electoral votes needed to win the election. Hayes had 165 electoral votes. The remaining electoral votes were in dispute. The Republican and Democratic parties submitted different totals for four states: Oregon, Louisiana, Florida, and South Carolina. Hayes needed twenty of these to win, and the Republicans claimed that he had them. (There were grounds for the dispute. For example, in South Carolina there were more votes than registered voters, and the Ku Klux Klan was busy all over the South stopping Republican votes.)

The Republican Senate and the Democratic House fought over which had authority to settle the dispute. In the end, they set up a joint committee with seven Senate Republicans, seven House Democrats, and one independent, a member of the Supreme Court, to decide the issue. At the last minute, the only independent on the Court resigned, leaving only Republicans, which gave that party an 8 to 7 majority on the election committee. Not surprisingly, the committee gave all of the disputed votes to Hayes by an 8 to 7 vote. Democrats threatened to **filibuster** the acceptance of the results, and some were talking about taking up arms. By now it was February, and the new president was supposed to take office on March 4th.

Compromise of 1877. Eventually, the two sides worked out a compromise. The Democrats agreed to accept the election of Hayes in exchange for the end of Reconstruction. Hayes also promised, but did not deliver, subsidies for a transcontinental railroad in the South. As a result of the Compromise of 1877, Hayes was named the president-elect just three days before inauguration. The deal kept the peace, but gave Southern white people complete control of their states without further fear of federal intervention.

Rutherford B. Hayes (1822-1893). Rutherford B. Hayes entered the White House with much of the nation doubting he had won the election. Hayes had been born **posthumously** to a prosperous store owner in Ohio. His uncle became his guardian and saw that he had a good private school education. He graduated from Harvard in 1842 and took up the practice of law in Ohio. He served as an officer in the

Civil War, reaching the temporary rank of major general. He was elected to the U.S. House while still in combat. (He refused to leave his post to campaign, but won anyway.) He also served three terms as governor of Ohio before he was chosen as president. His was the most questionable election in U.S. history.

Hayes removed the last Union troops from occupation duty shorty after taking office in 1877. This was the official end of Reconstruction. Hayes pushed for civil service reform, but the spoils-minded Congress refused to pass it. Hayes himself appointed men based on ability, not party loyalty, which earned the wrath of the Republicans. Hayes supported hard money policies that did not help the depression, but did build confidence in the security of the American monetary system.

Hayes' wife, Lucy Webb Hayes, had a college degree. She was the first among the nation's First Ladies to have one. She was active in many social causes, including abolition and temperance. She earned the nickname "Lemonade Lucy" because she banned alcoholic beverages from the White House. She and her husband introduced the custom of an annual Easter egg roll for children on the White House lawn.

Conclusion. The Civil War settled two issues: slavery and secession. Other positive results were more elusive. Black people were free, guaranteed citizenship and the right to vote by constitutional amendments, but those rights were flagrantly violated. However, those amendments were on the books and would be effectively resurrected years later. The South remained a hostile place for black people, Republicans, and Northerners for many years. After winning the war, the North lacked the will or political skill to reintegrate the nation on friendly terms. Given the nature of a civil war, perhaps that was impossible.

| Rutherford B. Hayes

The Union was actually lenient to the Confederacy. No Confederate leaders were ever tried for treason. Jefferson Davis was kept in custody for two years and then released. Robert E. Lee was allowed to return home unmolested and became the president of Washington College, later named Washington and Lee. The South was fully represented in Congress by 1870, and the original privileged class was back in power by 1877. Considering that they led an armed rebellion against the government, this was an amazing show of tolerance. Awful as it was, the Civil War barely interrupted the American tradition of growth, expansion, and democracy.

Answer these questions.

3.61 What was the heart of the controversy in the 1876 election?

_____

_____

3.62 How did Hayes fight the spoils system?

_____

_____

3.63 What two issues did the Civil War settle?

_____

3.64 What were the terms of the Compromise of 1877?

_____

_____

_____

3.65 What was the official end of Reconstruction?

_____

3.66 Why was Hayes awarded all the disputed votes in the election of 1876?

_____

_____

3.67 What were some of the unusual things about First Lady Lucy Hayes?

_____

_____

3.68 Who was the Democratic candidate in 1876, and what were his qualifications?

_____

_____

3.69 How many Confederate leaders were tried for treason?

_____

3.70 What were Hayes' qualifications for president?

_____

_____

Before you take this last Self Test, you may want to do one or more of these self checks.

1. _____ Read the objectives. See if you can do them.
2. _____ Restudy the material related to any objectives that you cannot do.
3. _____ Use the **SQ3R** study procedure to review the material:
    a. **S**can the sections.
    b. **Q**uestion yourself.
    c. **R**ead to answer your questions.
    d. **R**ecite the answers to yourself.
    e. **R**eview areas you did not understand.
4. _____ Review all vocabulary, activities, and Self Tests, writing a correct answer for every wrong answer.

SELF TEST 3

Name the event, item, person, or battle (each answer, 4 points).

3.01 _____ first U.S. president in history to be impeached

3.02 _____ "Seward's Folly"

3.03 _____ Amendment that ended slavery

3.04 _____ Democratic hoodlum who ran New York City after the Civil War

3.05 _____ Grant-era scandal; railroad construction scam that gave stock to several government representatives

3.06 _____ Amendment that gave black Americans the right to vote

3.07 _____ Reconstruction under Congressional control

3.08 _____ post-Civil War laws to subjugate black people in the South

3.09 _____ Presidential document that ended slavery in the South

3.010 _____ Amendment that made black Americans citizens

3.011 _____ Hayes was awarded the election in exchange for removing the last troops from the South

3.012 _____ first state to secede from the Union

3.013 _____ Union victory that placed the whole Mississippi under their control

3.014 _____ Northern men who came to power in the South during Reconstruction

3.015 _____ began the Civil War

Choose the person who best fits the description (each answer, 2 points).

Abraham Lincoln	Ulysses S. Grant	Robert E. Lee
Rutherford B. Hayes	Thaddeus Stevens	Stonewall Jackson
Stephen Douglas	Dred Scott	Jefferson Davis
John Brown		

3.016 _____ little education; Illinois attorney; flexible; good organizer

3.017 _____ an enslaved man who asked the Supreme Court to set him free after living in the North

3.018 _____ had trouble maintaining authority over the independent-minded Confederacy; imprisoned for two years after the war

3.019 _____ brilliant general; followed his state not his nation; college president

3.020 _____ Radical Republican leader

3.021 _____ opposed Lecompton Constitution; Northern Democratic candidate for president (1860); supported popular sovereignty

3.022 _____ violent; possibly insane; became a popular abolitionist martyr

3.023 _____ good general; honest; corrupt administration; Whiskey Ring

3.024 _____ Southern; Christian general; killed by his own men

3.025 _____ Union officer; governor of Ohio; opposed the spoils system; most controversial presidential election in history

Answer true or false (each answer, 1 point).

3.026 _____ Lincoln supported harsh measures against the South after the war.

3.027 _____ Andrew Johnson was the only Southern senator who did not secede with his state.

3.028 _____ Alaska was purchased from Russia for $7.2 million by Secretary of State William Seward.

3.029 _____ The Ku Klux Klan was very ineffective after the Civil War.

3.030 _____ Scalawags were army deserters during the Civil War.

3.031 _____ Republicans after the war often campaigned by "waving the bloody shirt."

3.032 _____ George McClellan was an excellent organizer, but so over-cautious that he proved to be a poor general.

3.033 _____ Grant was not thrown out of the army after Shiloh because Lincoln would not fire a general who was willing to fight.

3.034 _____ Abolitionist Senator Charles Sumner was beaten in the Senate for an anti-Southern speech.

3.035 _____ The Kansas-Nebraska Act brought the nation closer to war.

3.036 _____ The battle of the *Merrimac* and the *Monitor* was the first in history between ironclad vessels.

3.037 _____ Fredericksburg, Chickamauga, and New Orleans were all taken by the Union after a long siege.

3.038 _____ Copperheads were Northern Democrats who opposed the war.

3.039 _____ The re-election of Lincoln in 1864 ended the last Confederate hope of a negotiated peace that would leave them independent.

3.040 _____ The Civil War effectively ended at Appomattox Court House when Lee's army surrendered.

3.041 _____ The Confederate government was formed before Lincoln was inaugurated.

3.042 _____ The *Alabama* was a British-built ship with a British crew that sailed under a Confederate flag and captured Union ships.

3.043 _____ Fisk and Gould tried to corner the oil market on black Thursday.

3.044 _____ Corruption was a major problem in government and industry after the Civil War.

3.045 _____ The assassination of Lincoln made matters worse for the South.

80/100 SCORE _____ TEACHER _____ _____
initials   date

Before taking the LIFEPAC Test, you may want to do one or more of these self checks.

1. _____ Read the objectives. See if you can do them.

2. _____ Restudy the material related to any objectives that you cannot do.

3. _____ Use the **SQ3R** study procedure to review the material.

4. _____ Review activities, Self Tests, and LIFEPAC vocabulary words.

5. _____ Restudy areas of weakness indicated by the last Self Test.

HISTORY & GEOGRAPHY 810
Recent America and Review (1990–Present)

LIFEPAC Test is located in the center of the booklet. Please remove before starting the unit.

Author:
Theresa Buskey, B.A., J.D.

Editor:
Alan Christopherson, M.S.

Westover Studios Design Team:
Phillip Pettet, Creative Lead
Teresa Davis, DTP Lead
Nick Castro
Andi Graham
Jerry Wingo

Alpha Omega
PUBLICATIONS

804 N. 2nd Ave. E.
Rock Rapids, IA 51246-1759

Recent America and Review (1990–Present)

Introduction

The first part of this LIFEPAC® will deal with recent developments in American history since 1990. It is very difficult to analyze this part of history because it happened too recently. History can only fully be understood in perspective, or in the context of what happened before and after it. The most recent events in America do not yet have that perspective, but they can be reported pending the passage of time.

The last two sections of this LIFEPAC are a review of the year's material done in an outline form. This form deals only with major concepts and is the essence of what you should have learned this year.

Carefully study the major events of each presidency, war, and the development of any conflicts. These should be reviews for you. If any concept is not clear, look it up in the appropriate LIFEPAC or elsewhere. Do not leave yourself uncertain of any concept or event.

Objectives

Read these objectives. The objectives tell you what you will be able to do when you have successfully completed this LIFEPAC. When you have finished this LIFEPAC, you should be able to:

1. List the major recent domestic and foreign political events.

2. Describe the technical advances around the turn of the century.

3. Describe the moral decline in America and list Christian organizations that are trying to fight it.

4. Describe how America was settled and became an independent nation.

5. Match the presidents with the events of their administration.

6. Describe the wars and major events of U.S. history.

7. Describe important trends in ideas and conflicts in U.S. history.

8. Describe how and when America acquired new territories.

9. Place major American historical events in chronological order.

Survey the LIFEPAC. Ask yourself some questions about this study and write your questions here.

1. RECENT AMERICA

This section is the most recent history of the United States, covering the politics at the turn of the **millennium**. This part of history is your history. Your parents lived and voted during these events. If you wish, you can ask them their opinions and ideas about what living during these times were like. Do not be surprised if some of their opinions are very strong. This is living history which is still being made. It has strong effects on the people who live through it.

This section is a snapshot of the turn from the second to third millennium after the birth of Christ. Changes in American society include changes in technology, ideas, and morals. Some of these changes are good and some are not. Whether or not these changes are good is based solely on one thing, whether or not they agree with the Word of God. As Christians, we affirm that it is our only standard.

SECTION OBJECTIVES

Review these objectives. When you have completed this section, you should be able to:

1. List the recent major domestic and foreign political events.
2. Describe the technical advances around the turn of the century.
3. Describe the moral decline in America and list Christian organizations that are trying to fight it.

VOCABULARY

Study these words to enhance your learning success in this section.

allegation (al′ i gā′ shən). Declare without proof.

atrocity (ə-tros′ ītē). A horrible event.

line-item veto (līn ĭt′ əm vēt′ ō). A government executive's power to refuse to enact a single line of or portion of a law.

millennium (mə len′ ē əm). A period of a thousand years.

modem (mō′ dem). An electronic device that enables a computer to send or receive information by telephone or other communication lines.

paranoid (par′ ə noid). Characterized by excessive or irrational suspiciousness and distrustfulness of others.

perjury (pər′ jə rē). The violation of an oath or vow by swearing to what is untrue.

software (sôft′ wâr). Written or printed data, such as programs, routines, and symbolic languages, essential to the operation of computers.

trajectory (trəjek′ tə rē). The path of a moving particle or body, especially in three dimensions.

Note: *All vocabulary words in this LIFEPAC appear in* **boldface** *print the first time they are used. If you are not sure of the meaning when you are reading, study the definitions given.*

Pronunciation Key: hat, āge, cãre, fär; let, ēqual, tėrm; it, īce; hot, ōpen, ôrder; oil; out; cup, pu̇t, rüle; child; long; thin; /ᵮH/ for then; /zh/ for measure; /u/ or /ə/ represents /a/ in about, /e/ in taken, /i/ in pencil, /o/ in lemon, and /u/ in circus.

AMERICA from **1990** to **Present**

George H. W. Bush
1989-1993
Republican

William J. Clinton
1993-2001
Democratic

George W. Bush
2001-2009
Republican

Barack H. Obama
2009-2017
Democratic

Donald J. Trump
2017-
Republican

STATES ADMITTED TO THE UNION

None

POPULATION of the United States of America

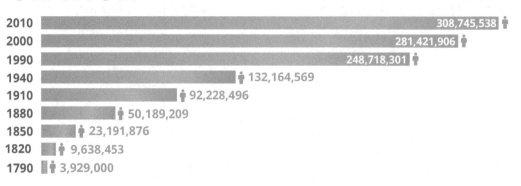

Year	Population
2010	308,745,538
2000	281,421,906
1990	248,718,301
1940	132,164,569
1910	92,228,496
1880	50,189,209
1850	23,191,876
1820	9,638,453
1790	3,929,000

Politics in the 1990s

George H. W. Bush Administration. In 1989 the U.S. signed the North American Free Trade Agreement (NAFTA) with Canada. It allowed nations to sell their goods in the other NAFTA countries without any tariffs or restrictions. Late in 1992, the pact was expanded to include Mexico. It was ratified by the Senate in 1993, and took effect in January of 1994. Many of the provisions were introduced gradually, and its effects are still uncertain.

The African nation of Somalia collapsed into clan warfare in 1992. A drought devastated crops, and fighting made it impossible for relief agencies to distribute food. With the threat of millions starving to death, George H. W. Bush ordered the U.S. military to lead a U.N. effort to protect relief workers. The troops came in unopposed, but several soldiers died in street fighting while they were there. U.S. forces remained until 1994.

The collapse of communism caused a chain reaction all over the world. Dictators lost support since their communist backers were gone, or the U.S. no longer had reason to keep them as allies. Free elections were held in many new places in the 1990s, such as South Africa, Nicaragua, Taiwan, and Uganda. Some of those elections led to greater freedoms, but some were only brief breaks between dictators. Regardless, the early 1990s were a time of hope for the expansion of democracy all over the world. Only time would tell if the expansion would continue.

Communism did not collapse completely. In 1999 three prominent nations were still communist: North Korea, Cuba, and China. The economies of North Korea and Cuba suffered deeply from the loss of their powerful protector, the U.S.S.R., but the entrenched communist leadership refused to allow reforms.

China had begun economic reforms before 1990. It no longer had a communist economic system, but was rapidly becoming more like the West with private ownership and control of business, but in 1989, demonstrations for political freedom were crushed by the government. Students occupying Tiananmen Square (in the Chinese capital of Beijing) who demanded free elections were attacked by the army. The student leaders were executed. In a lie by communist leaders, the government announced that students had attacked and killed soldiers in the square. Chinese leaders denied the event, although millions of people saw the demonstration and the army's attack on international television.

Election of 1992. President George H. W. Bush's popularity soared during the Persian Gulf War and he was easily renominated by the Republicans. The Democratic nomination went to the governor of Arkansas, William Jefferson Clinton. Billionaire Ross Perot ran an independent campaign that focused mainly on the growing national debt.

In 1990 the nation slipped into a recession that lasted until the 1992 election, which deeply hurt Bush's popularity. Clinton ran an intense, well-organized campaign. He won with 43% of the popular vote. George H. W. Bush drew 38% and Perot took 19% of the popular vote, illustrating how concerned many people were about the country's huge debt.

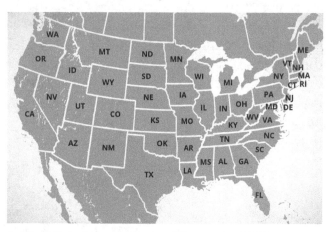

| The Continental United States in 2010

William Jefferson Clinton. Clinton was born William Jefferson Blythe IV in Arkansas in 1946. His father died when he was a baby. His mother remarried when he was four and he took his stepfather's name of Clinton. Bill attended public and private schools, showing an early interest in politics. He graduated from Georgetown University in 1968 and then studied at Oxford University in England for two years as a Rhodes Scholar. He received his law degree from Yale in 1973.

Clinton quickly turned to politics after graduation, losing in a race for the U.S. House in 1974. He served as attorney general from 1976 until he was elected governor of Arkansas in 1978. Clinton lost the governorship in 1980, but regained it two years later. He held that office until he became president in 1993.

Deficits and Debts. The end of the Cold War drew national attention back to domestic problems. The budget deficit and the national debt were two primary ones. In 1992 the deficit was $290,000,000,000. That means the government spent 290 billion more dollars in a year than it made! The national debt that year reached $4,064,000,000,000, which was $15,846 per American citizen. One reason George H. W. Bush had been so helpless in the recession of 1990, was that the deficit made it difficult for the government to increase spending to help the economy.

Increased emphasis on spending controls, and a soaring taxable income, slowly reduced the deficit in the 1990s. By the end of 1996 the deficit had been reduced to $107 billion. In 1998 the thriving U.S. economy almost eliminated the deficit. If the money taken for Social Security taxes was included, there was no deficit in 1998. However, the huge national debt still reached $5.6 trillion by the end of 1998.

Contract with America. Under the leadership of Newt Gingrich, a Republican Congressman, the Republican Party made a major push for control of Congress in 1994. They published a list of conservative proposals called the "Contract with America." They proposed a list of laws, including a line-item veto, an amendment to balance the budget, tax reforms, and term limits, to Congress within 100 days if the Republicans were given control. Many Republican candidates signed the contract, and it worked. The Congress elected in 1994 was Republican for the first time in forty years. Gingrich became Speaker of the House. The contract terms were brought before Congress, but several did not pass in the Senate.

The Republican Congress and the Democratic president did not work well together. Conflicts over just how the budget should be cut led to brief shutdowns of the government in 1995 and 1996.

The worst act of domestic terrorism in U.S. history took place in April of 1995. A bomb exploded in front of the Federal Building in Oklahoma City. The blast destroyed the front of the building and killed 168 people. Included among the dead were many small children from a daycare center inside. Timothy McVeigh, an ex-soldier with a paranoid fear of the federal government, was convicted of the bombing and condemned to death.

Foreign Affairs. In 1994 Clinton ended the American Cold War policy of allowing any Cuban who escaped the island to come to the U.S. Castro, in response to the rapid disintegration of the Cuban economy, had given his people permission to leave. Thousands took advantage of the chance, leaving the island in anything that would float. Rather than try to settle so many refugees in the U.S., Clinton began a policy of returning them to Cuba.

Haiti, the poorest nation in the Western Hemisphere, had chosen its first freely elected president in 1990, Jean-Bertrand Aristide. He was overthrown by a military coup in 1991 and exiled. After U.N. sanctions failed to restore him to power, the U.S. prepared for an invasion in 1994. Last-minute negotiations by former president Jimmy Carter led the military government to step down, and Aristide returned with the support of U.S. troops to aid in the transition.

Communism's collapse triggered a number of wars in the 1990s. Some of the worst were in Yugoslavia, the region where World War I began. Muslims, Croats, Albanians, and Serbs who hated each other had been together in that one nation under communism. After 1990, the nation split into four parts and brutal fighting quickly followed. The wars were marked by repeated atrocities, primarily by the Serbs. The U.S. and U.N. mediated repeatedly and used air strikes to force cooperation and end the massacres. An agreement in Daytona in 1995 brought a cease fire in Bosnia, one of the new nations. However, the fighting never completely stopped and new battles broke out in Kosovo, part of Serbia, in 1998.

Elections of 1996 and 1998. After the 1990 recession, the American economy boomed as inflation stayed low. Bill Clinton rode the economic prosperity to victory over his Republican opponent Bob Dole in the 1996 election. However, the Republicans kept control of Congress both in 1996 and 1998.

After the 1998 election, the House voted to impeach Clinton on two charges of **perjury**. A trial was held in the Senate. It lasted slightly over a month. There were only three witnesses, and they all testified by video tape. Public opinion ran strongly against impeachment and the president was acquitted. The vote for impeachment did not even receive a majority of votes, let alone the two-thirds majority needed for conviction.

| The aftermath in 1995 from the bombing of the Federal Building in Oklahoma City

Give the requested information.

1.1   The three remaining communist nations in 1999

_____

1.2   Site of the Chinese army attack on student demonstrators in 1989

_____

1.3   Man who bombed the Federal Building in Oklahoma City, 1995

_____

1.4   Party that won control of Congress in 1994 for the first time in forty years

_____

1.5   Nation the U.S. sent soldiers to protect relief workers, 1992

_____

1.6   Free trade agreement between the U.S., Canada, and Mexico

_____

1.7   Former communist nation, site of brutal wars in Serbia and Bosnia

_____

1.8   Haiti's first freely elected president

_____

1.9   Reason why George H. W. Bush was so popular in 1990

_____

1.10   Reason H. W. Bush lost his popularity between 1990 and 1992

_____

1.11   Document that stated the conservative goals of the Republican candidates, 1994

_____

1.12   Speaker of the House, 1993-1998

_____

1.13   The charges made against President Clinton in 1998

_____

1.14   The number of witnesses that testified during the Senate trial following the House vote to impeach President Clinton

_____

1.15 How the elected president was restored in Haiti, 1994

_____

_____

1.16 Amount of the deficit in 1992 _____

1.17 Independent candidate in 1992 that emphasized the national debt

_____

1.18 The change in U.S. policy toward Cuban refugees in 1994

_____

1.19 The result of Clinton's Senate impeachment trial in 1999

_____

_____

1.20 Amount of the national debt at the end of 1998 _____

Millennium's Last Decade

Technology. At the end of the second millennium, the most remarkable changes in American society were improvements in technology, led by incredible advances in computers. These advances led to improvements in communications, satellite usage, and medicine.

The computer has a long history. A tabulating machine was developed as early as 1888 for use in the 1890 census. The company that was created to sell that machine eventually became IBM (International Business Machines), which was the largest computer company in the world. Computer development really took off because of World War II. Both sides needed computing power to calculate weapons **trajectories** and break enemy codes. Electronic machines used for complex calculations were invaluable. However, the hard work to produce computing machines bore most of its fruit after the war.

The first general use computer was developed at the University of Pennsylvania in 1946. It was called ENIAC (Electronic Numerical Integrator And Computer). It weighed 30 tons and covered 1,500 square feet (the size of a small house). It could do thousands of calculations per second. Any current personal computer that costs less than $500 is faster and more powerful.

The first commercial computer was the UNIVAC 1 of the 1950s. Less than 50 of these expensive machines were sold to the U.S. government and businesses. These "first generation" computers used vacuum tubes to handle data. The second generation (beginning in the 1960s) used transistors that were smaller and faster than ungainly vacuum tubes. Smaller and faster still were integrated circuits, tiny silicon chips, developed for the third generation in the late 60s and early 70s. Fourth generation computers use microprocessors which are single chips that contain all of the basic functions of a computer. The first of these were developed in the mid-1970s.

These smaller, faster computers have expanded their influence all over the nation. They are embedded in cars to control gas flow, in wristwatches to keep time, in greeting cards to record messages and play simple tunes, and DVR's to record television shows. They control payroll in almost all businesses, record sales, prepare documents, calculate taxes, and modify pictures. Almost every major business function in the U.S. is either prepared or controlled by computers.

The first home computer was the Altair, which was sold in 1975 to people whose hobby was home electronics. In 1977, the Apple Computer Company was founded to sell the first popular home computer, the Apple II. In 1981 IBM entered the field of home (or personal) computers and quickly dominated the market. By 2008, more than 78% of American homes had a computer, an unbelievable idea in the 1950s-70s when they were huge, heavy, and expensive.

One of the uses of a home computer is finding information on the internet (interconnected network of networks). The internet connects millions of computers by using modems to communicate over telephone and other communication lines. Businesses, governments, charities, and ordinary people set up "websites" on the internet (also called the World Wide Web) that can be "visited" by computer. These sites give information about products, places, history, and ideas that is available to anyone with a computer and the right software. The internet is also used to send emails (electronic mail), letters via computer.

The internet began as an interconnection of government and military computers in the 1960s. Eventually, universities and other large institutions set up their own Nets. By the 1990s, the system had expanded to include anyone who wanted to buy the software. Businesses (providers) were established to connect people for a fee. Since the beginning of the new millennium the internet has grown vastly in speed and resources.

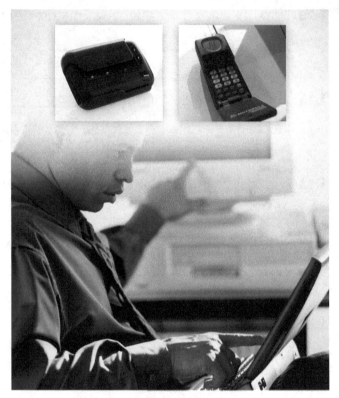

| Common technology of the 1990s

The net includes reliable sources and useful tools, unreliable sources, and bad or dangerous sources. No young person should utilize the internet without adult permission and supervision. There are many sites on the internet which no child or Christian should visit. There are programs and services that try to block out the worst of the garbage, including racist propaganda, altered history, and "adult" content. Internet use should be discussed with responsible parents before it is done.

The smaller and faster computers have also been used to improve communication. Besides email, telephone lines can also be used to send a "fax" or facsimile, a copy of any document from one fax machine to another. This technology came into general use in the 1980s after the size and cost of the machinery came down.

Prior to the 1980s, most people could make phone calls and receive messages only when they were in a building near a telephone. In the last part of the millennium, pagers (beepers), and cellular phones (which are smaller than a deck of cards) changed that. They use a combination of radio waves and telephone lines to send messages to people wherever they happen to be. This allows people to have instant communication almost anywhere!

Satellites, which are used for communication and gathering information, also use the new computer technology. There are thousands of satellites in orbit around earth. They are used to monitor weather, stars, enemy airplanes, rainforest fires, solar flares, and other things. They are also used to relay radio signals, allowing instant communications across the globe. Recently they have also been used for navigation, telling ships, cars, and people on the ground exactly where they are on the earth.

New technology has also led to improvements in medicine. Improvements in engineering has led to the creation of artificial heart valves, joints, limbs, and even hearts. In 1982 Barney Clark survived for over a hundred days with a man-made heart called *The Jarvik-7*. Artificial legs have become so advanced that people can wear them to run marathons! Joint replacement has become routine.

Medical advances have also caused problems. Machines can keep a person's body alive long after the brain has stopped functioning. Doctors and families must often decide whether or not someone is truly dead and should be taken off life-supporting machines. So much can be done to keep someone alive that patients and families must often choose when they want to stop the medicine and allow the body to die naturally.

Moral Decline. One of the most marked changes in American society was the decline of morals and ethics at the turn of the new millennium. Some of the most serious problems have been with the family. By God's design, families are the basic unit of any society. They uphold values for all their members as well as provide the earthly security and love needed in life.

The biggest single pressure on the family in America, is divorce. About half of all marriages ended in divorce in the year 2000. Divorce destroys the couple and tears apart the closest relationships of any children involved. Children of divorced parents are more likely to have problems with depression, drug abuse, and in establishing their own families. Many children of divorce are raised in single parent homes; which means the child only has one parent to provide for their physical, financial, and emotional needs.

Experts debate why divorce is so common in America. Americans are taught by the entertainment media (TV, movies, music, and magazines) to pursue what makes them personally happy. A good marriage takes work, commitment, and sacrifice, especially during the unhappy times which inevitably come. The nation's moral decline has made divorce acceptable. In America in the mid-1900s, a divorce was scandalous and society pressured couples to remain married. Divorce in some places is common; and even encouraged, if one partner is simply not "happy."

The family is bombarded by the poor moral climate of the United States. Moral purity before and during marriage is considered old-fashioned. Many people believe marriage should be for anyone who wants it (including two men or two women), so they attempt to change the laws to make that possible. God's laws regarding marriage are mocked and ignored. The simple belief that God's Word is truth is considered narrow-minded and prejudiced.

The dismissal of God leads Americans to treat human beings (made in His image) with less respect. Abortion, or the murder of children before birth, is commonplace and vigorously protected by law. States are passing laws allowing people to choose to die if they are seriously ill (euthanasia). Killing someone who is very sick is often considered an act of mercy, not murder.

Christian Reaction. God's people began to fight the collapse of decency using socio-political means. Many large para-church (not connected to, but coming alongside the church) organizations were founded to fight part of the battle. Chuck Colson, one of the men convicted during Watergate, became a Christian in prison. He founded Prison Fellowship in 1976 as an outreach to the huge prison population. He has become a well known speaker on morals and ethics. Focus on the Family was started in 1977 by Dr. James Dobson, a doctor of child development. It works to encourage and build up families. The National Right to Life Committee fights abortion and euthanasia. These organizations are some of the ways Christians try to be "salt" and "light" in the dark climate threatening America.

Match these items.

1.21 _____	a copy of a document sent by phone lines	a. Internet
1.22 _____	letters sent from one computer to another	b. ENIAC
1.23 _____	uses radio waves and phone lines to reach a person almost anywhere	c. UNIVAC 1
		d. Altair
1.24 _____	interconnected network of networks	e. technology
1.25 _____	first home computer	f. IBM
1.26 _____	first popular home computer	g. fax
1.27 _____	company that made tabulating machines in the late 1800s; was the world's largest computer firm	h. cell phone
		i. email
		j. Apple II
1.28 _____	first computer sold for commercial use	
1.29 _____	first general use computer; developed in 1946	
1.30 _____	improvements in this area contributed to remarkable changes in American society	

Matching.

1.31 _____	organization that opposes abortion and euthanasia	a. Focus on the Family
1.32 _____	organization with an outreach to convicts	b. abortion
1.33 _____	ending the life of someone seriously ill	c. Right to Life
1.34 _____	organization that supports and encourage families	d. Prison Fellowship
1.35 _____	ending the life of a baby before it is born	e. euthanasia

Complete these items.

1.36 What is the largest problem that families faced around the new millennium?

_____

1.37 Give two reasons why the answer in 1.36 is so common.

_____

1.38 Complete.

a. Name the organization founded by Chuck Colson. _____

b. Man who survived 100 days with a man-made heart. _____

c. Name the organization founded by Dr. James Dobson. _____

d. Programs and services for the internet block: _____

_____

1.39 Name two ways that humans are treated with less respect in modern America.

_____

1.40 What problem is caused by medical machines that can keep bodies alive?

_____

1.41 What are two major functions of satellites?

_____

_____

1.42 What was the major component to handle calculations in each generation of computers?

a. First _____   b. Second _____

c. Third _____   d. Fourth _____

1.43 Where did the internet first develop?

_____

1.44 Assignment: Choose a major news story in America today. Do some research on the background of it using newspapers, magazines or the internet. Follow the story for two weeks in the newspapers, online, or the TV news. Write a 500-word paper about it that includes your personal views. (Continue on with this LIFEPAC in the meantime.)

TEACHER CHECK _____ _____
                                                   initials   date

The New Millennium's First Decade

George W. Bush Administration. George W. Bush was the Republican elected president in 2000. He was only the second president whose father had also been president. He was also only the second president who had lost the popular vote but won the electoral election.

Among other policies, George W. Bush focused on education. He worked with congress to pass the "No Child Left Behind" legislation. Schools would be given grades just like the students. Schools were required to show progress in key areas of education such as reading and math or they would be penalized. Some of these penalties included a loss of federal money. Teacher requirements also became stricter.

War on Terrorism. George W. Bush was only president a few months when terrorists attacked the United States. On September 11, 2001 terrorists hijacked four airplanes intending to use them as weapons against Americans. Two planes flew into the twin towers of the World Trade Center, one flew into the Pentagon, and the passengers of the fourth kept it from reaching its target. At days end, over 3000 people were dead and Americans felt unsafe in their own country.

As terrorist attacks caused changes in American policy at home and abroad, George W. Bush and his leadership team established the Department of Home Security. This department was tasked with keeping U.S. citizens safe from terrorist attacks on U.S. soil. The department was also responsible for securing America's borders.

After the attacks, it soon became apparent they were masterminded by Osama bin Laden and his Al Qaeda terrorist organization. The terrorists were centered in Afghanistan. Afghanistan was ruled by the Taliban. The Taliban placed strict rules on the people of the country and gave harsh punishments to those who disobeyed. The Taliban refused to cooperate with the U.S. and its allies and stop supporting terrorists. As a result, the U.S. and its allies invaded Afghanistan and removed the Taliban from power. However, the

U.S. was unable to locate bin Laden who was hiding in the mountainous regions of the country.

The Taliban were removed from power and replaced with a democratic form of government. Al Qaeda has not been completely removed from the country, but their influence has lessened. The U.S. and its allies remain in Afghanistan helping establish the newly elected government.

Iraq War. Saddam Hussein was Iraq's dictator from 1979-2003. He attacked other nations and his own people in an effort to remain in power. In 2003 the U.S. led a coalition of nations to forcefully remove Saddam Hussein from power. There were **allegations** that Hussein was stockpiling weapons of mass destruction which could be used against other nations. These allegations proved to be false, but the documentation of Hussein's **atrocities** against his own people was not.

Hussein was quickly removed from power and went into hiding. Once found, he was tried, convicted, and killed for his crimes. Unfortunately, Iraq's change to a democracy did not go smoothly. Fighting continues to take place in Iraq. The U.S. military and others are working hard to train Iraq police to maintain stability in the nation.

The Obama Administration. As the Democratic party's candidate, Barack Obama was elected President of the U.S. in 2008. He took office in January of 2009. Millions of people in the U.S. and around the world watched his inauguration. Obama was the first African American to be elected president of the U.S. His administration inherited a terrible economic crisis. The unemployment rate was rising and many businesses were closing their doors. Along with the U.S. economy, Obama would need to deal with the struggles of the nation being at war in Iraq and Afghanistan.

Donald J. Trump Administration. The Republican nominee for president in 2016 was businessman Donald J. Trump. Although his opponent, the Democrat Hillary Clinton had more popular votes, he won the election by winning the most electoral votes. Hillary Clinton's run for the presidency was notable since she was the first woman ever to be nominated by a major political party. This was the fifth presidential election in history where the losing candidate had the most popular votes.

 Match these items.

1.45	_____ former dictator of Iraq	a.	Taliban
1.46	_____ president on September 11, 2001	b.	Al Qaeda
1.47	_____ first African American president	c.	George W. Bush
1.48	_____ leader who planned the September 11 attacks on the U.S.	d.	Barack Obama
		e.	Saddam Hussein
1.49	_____ former rulers in Afghanistan	f.	Osama bin Laden
1.50	_____ terrorist organization		

Answer true or false.

1.51 _____ The "No Child Left Behind" legislation was designed to help the children of soldiers.

1.52 _____ In 2000, George W. Bush was elected by the majority of Americans.

1.53 _____ The Taliban were easy-going leaders who let the people of Afghanistan do what they please.

1.54 _____ Saddam Hussein was killed for his crimes against his people.

1.55 _____ The U.S. led a group of nations to war against Saddam Hussein.

1.56 _____ Osama bin Laden hid in the mountains of Iraq.

Review the material in this section in preparation for the Self Test. The Self Test will check your mastery of this particular section. The items missed on this Self Test will indicate specific areas where restudy is needed for mastery.

SELF TEST 1

Match these people (each answer, 2 points).

1.01 _____ founder of Focus on the Family

1.02 _____ president during the economic boom of the 1990s; faced impeachment in 1998

1.03 _____ blew up the Oklahoma Federal Building in 1995

1.04 _____ founder of Prison Fellowship

1.05 _____ led the Republican takeover of Congress in 1994; Speaker of the House (1994-1998)

1.06 _____ ran as a third party candidate for president in 1992; emphasized the national debt

1.07 _____ the second president whose father had been a president

1.08 _____ president; sent troops to Somalia to protect relief workers; lost in 1992 due to a recession

1.09 _____ inherited an economic crisis when he took office in 2009

1.010 _____ leader of Al Qaeda

a. George H. W. Bush

b. Bill Clinton

c. Osama bin Laden

d. Newt Gingrich

e. Ross Perot

f. Timothy McVeigh

g. Chuck Colson

h. James Dobson

i. Barack Obama

j. George W. Bush

Explain or describe each item (each answer, 5 points).

1.011 Improvements in technology

_____

_____

_____

1.012 Problem caused by medical machines when people are dying

_____

_____

_____

1.013 The event in Tiananmen Square, China in 1989

_____

_____

_____

1.014 Considerations when using the internet

_____

_____

_____

1.015 Why divorce is so common

_____

_____

_____

Name the item, event, nation, or idea (each answer, 3 points).

1.016 _____ letter from one computer to another

1.017 _____ free trade agreement between the U.S., Canada, and Mexico

1.018 _____ list of promises made by Republicans in the 1994 election, to be fulfilled if they were elected

1.019 _____ uses radio waves and telephone lines to reach people away from buildings

1.020 _____ the first popular home computer

1.021 _____ there was no deficit in 1998 if this was included

1.022 _____ Jimmy Carter convinced the military government to leave before a U.S. invasion

1.023 _____ a document copy sent by telephone lines

1.024 _____ put in orbit to gather information and relay communications

1.025 _____ the first general use computer; developed in1946

1.026 _____ the three remaining communist nations in 1999

_____

_____

1.027 _____ handled data in first generation computers

1.028 _____ the murder of children before they are born

Answer true or false (each answer, 2 points).

1.029 _____ America, as a nation, was less focused on Christian values in the 1990s than it was in the 1950s.

1.030 _____ Euthanasia is the greatest problem for families in the 1990s.

1.031 _____ Altair was the first computer sold for commercial use (1950s).

1.032 _____ Budget deficits were reduced in the 1990s.

1.033 _____ The end of communism brought prosperity and peace to the nation of Yugoslavia.

1.034 _____ After September 11, 2001, the Office of Homeland Security was established by President George W. Bush.

1.035 _____ Many nations that had never had free elections had them in the early 1990s.

1.036 _____ Saddam Hussein led the Al Qaeda terrorist organization.

1.037 _____ By 1998, the U.S. national debt was more than $5,000 billion.

1.038 _____ Modern television and magazines tell Americans to do what makes them happy.

1.039 _____ The September 11 terrorists flew airplanes in buildings.

1.040 _____ The Taliban were in power in Iraq before the U.S. and its allies invaded.

1.041 _____ Barack Obama was elected the first African American U.S. President.

77 / 97   SCORE _____   TEACHER _____ _____
initials   date

2. BEFORE THE CIVIL WAR

This section is an outline review of what you studied about the United States before the Civil War. The outline will note the most important events, people, ideas, and developments in our nation. It will restate what you should have learned in the past year. The ideas it will review include colonization, expansion of the frontier, development of political freedoms, separation from England, early political problems, and the disagreement on slavery that finally split the nation.

SECTION OBJECTIVES

Review these objectives. When you have completed this section, you should be able to:

4. Describe how America was settled and became an independent nation.

5. Match the presidents with the events of their administration.

6. Describe the wars and major events of U.S. history.

7. Describe important trends in ideas and conflicts in U.S. history.

8. Describe how and when America acquired new territories.

9. Place major American historical events in chronological order.

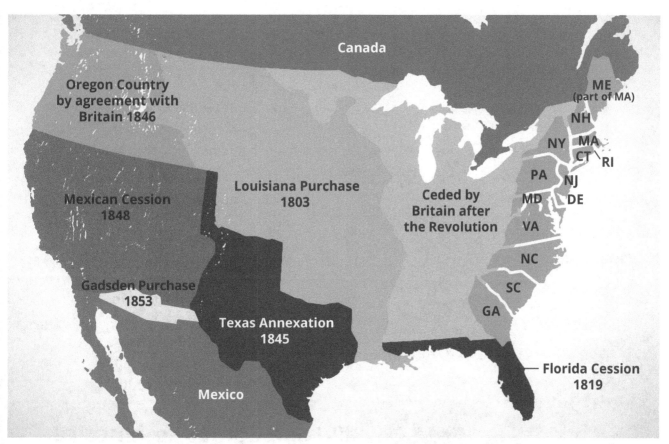

| Major land acquisitions prior to the Civil War

Quest and Conquest

I. Europe Awakens

   A. Crusades, about AD 1100-1300

      1. Wars to free the Holy Land from Muslim control

      2. Results

         a. Created a demand for Eastern goods in Europe

         b. Trade developed between Europe and Far East (Indies)

   B. Marco Polo, late 1200s

      1. Traveled overland to China and lived there 20 years

      2. Wrote a popular book that increased interest in the Far East

   C. Henry the Navigator (1394-1460)

      1. Portuguese prince

      2. Saw the need for a water route to Asia

         a. Land route was dangerous and subject to tolls (expensive)

         b. Water route could carry larger cargoes, cheaper

      3. Set up a navigational school, the best in Europe

      4. Ordered voyages along African coast

         a. Bartholomeu Diaz reached Cape of Good Hope, 1488

         b. Vasco da Gama reached India around Africa, 1498

II. Voyages of Columbus

   A. Experienced, ambitious Italian sailor

   B. His plan

      1. To reach Far East by sailing west from Europe

      2. Underestimated the distance

      3. Did not know about America

      4. Plan accepted by Spain, 1492

   C. First Voyage

      1. Ships—*Niña*, *Pinta*, *Santa Maria*

      2. Landed San Salvador-Oct. 12, 1492

      3. Explored for three months

   D. Three later Voyages

      1. Explored the Caribbean and the coast of Central America

      2. Established Isabela, 1st European colony in America

      3. Always believed he found the Indies (called the natives Indians)

   E. Results

      1. Not the first European to America— Leif Ericson was first in about AD 1000 (Vikings)

      2. Established permanent contact between Europe and America

      3. Europe became the main cultural source for America

      4. Continents named after Amerigo Vespucci, another explorer

III. Spanish Claims and Conquests

   A. Gradually realized it was not Asia

      1. Treaty of Tordesillas (1494) divided all of the new land between Spain and Portugal

      2. Generated tremendous interest in Spain—*conquistadors* came to get rich and claim land for Spain

   B. Balboa–crossed the Isthmus of Panama, found the Pacific Ocean

   C. Ponce de León–explored Florida looking for the fountain of youth

Europe Comes to America

D. Magellan–led the first successful circum-navigation of the world

  1. Sailed south of South America through Straits of Magellan

  2. Named the Pacific Ocean

  3. Died in the Philippines

  4. One ship, Victoria, reached Spain safely with eighteen men

E. Wealthy Empires were conquered, Aztec (Cortes) and Inca (Pizzaro),

  1. Spain concentrated on the rich southern lands; Northern lands left open or sparsely controlled

  2. Gold and silver attracted other European nations

F. De Soto–discovered Mississippi, explored AL, MS, AR, and GA

G. Coronado–searched for seven cities of gold; explored U.S. Southwest; discovered the Grand Canyon

H. Results

  1. Spain had a claim to most of America up into the Southern U.S.

The Chase

I. Other Europeans came to the New World looking for a route to Asia and gold or silver

II. English Efforts

  A. John Cabot, the *Matthew* (1497)

    1. Explored the coast of Canada

    2. Found the Grand Banks, one of the finest fishing spots in the ocean

  B. English problems prevented exploration for almost 100 years

    C. Sea Dogs, raided Spanish shipping in New World, explored

| Jolliet and Marquette

  D. Francis Drake–greatest Sea Dog

    1. Raided Spanish American towns

    2. Sailed around the world on the *Golden Hind*, attacking Spanish towns and ships (1577-1580)

      a. Explored the U.S. West coast

      b. Traded for spices in Far East

III. Henry Hudson

  A. Sailed for England and Netherlands

  B. Searched Arctic regions for a Northern route around either America (Northwest Passage) or Europe (Northeast Passage)

  C. Claimed Hudson River and New York for the Dutch (1609)

  D. Claimed Baffin Strait and Hudson Bay for England (1610)

IV. French Exploration

  A. French fishing boats came annually to Grand Banks in the early 1500s

  B. Jacques Cartier–explored the St. Lawrence River (1530s-40s)

Europe Comes to America

C. Samuel de Champlain–Father of New France

1. Founded Quebec, first successful French settlement (1608)

2. Made friends with the Huron and Algonquin but became enemies of the Iroquois

3. Explored upper New York State, named Lake Champlain there

4. Explored the Great Lakes as far west as Lake Huron

D. Fur Trade

1. Furs were popular in Europe, a source of wealth for New France

2. *Coureurs de bois*, runners of the woods, explored, set up trading posts to get furs

3. France's claim in N. America was expanded and secured

4. Few Frenchmen lived in the large area of New France

E. Jolliet and Marquette

1. Explored the Mississippi down to the Arkansas River (1673)

2. Realized the river went south to the Gulf of Mexico

F. La Salle

1. Followed the Mississippi all the way to its mouth (1682)

2. Claimed <u>all</u> of the land drained by the river for France

The First Colonies

I. Spanish

A. Founded Augustine, Florida, the first successful European settlement in the U.S. (1565)

B. Santa Fe, New Mexico (1610)

C. San Diego, California (1769)

D. Missions in California, Spain had over twenty by 1823

E. Colonial Life

1. King's representative had absolute power

2. Native Americans enslaved, Africans brought to work as slaves on the land for the wealthy Spanish owners

3. Strict hierarchy with the Spanish at the top, Native Americans or enslaved people at the bottom

II. French

A. Most settlements were trading forts

B. Colonial Life

1. Had the best relations with Native Americans among the Europeans

a. French were few in number, not a threat to Native American lands

b. Wanted to trade with the Native Americans for furs, did not displace them

2. Not attractive to settlers

a. Colony was under the absolute control of the king

b. No religious freedom (must be Catholic)

c. Land owned by the rich, farmers could only be serfs

d. King controlled and took most of the profit on the fur trade

III. Dutch, New Netherlands

A. Hudson River region

B. Owned by Dutch West India Company

C. Developed profitable fur trade

D. Company sent 30 families in 1624 to establish the first settlements

Europe Comes to America

E. Purchased Manhattan Island for $24 worth of trade goods

F. Colonial Life

   1. Despotic rule by Company directors, poor administrators

   2. *Patroon* (landowner) system

     a. Company members given huge tracts of land if they settled fifty people on it

     b. Created a wealthy aristocracy who controlled the land

IV. English

  A. Roanoke (Virginia)

   1. The Lost Colony, settled 1587

   2. Established by Sir Walter Raleigh

   3. Ships returned 1590, colony was abandoned, no trace was ever found of the people

  B. Jamestown (Virginia)

   1. First successful English colony

   2. Financed by London Company

   3. Built on swampy peninsula on the James River, unhealthy

   4. First settlers arrived 1607

     a. Searched for gold

     b. Sixty of the first 100 died

   5. 1608 new group arrived under Captain John Smith

     a. Set up discipline, saved the colony

     b. Men worked or were expelled

     c. Native Americans helped feed the colonists

   6. Winter 1609-1610, "starving time," only 60 people survived

   7. John Rolfe discovered a cash crop in 1612, tobacco, gave the colony a profitable trade item

   8. "Headright" established in 1618

     a. Every settler was given 50 acres of his own land

     b. Encouraged land-hungry English farmers to come

   9. Events of 1619

     a. House of Burgesses, colonial assembly, organized

     b. A shipload of women brought over as wives for the mostly male colonists

     c. First enslaved Africans imported

   10. Became a crown colony under the king's rule in 1624

  C. Why the Native Americans consistently lost the battle for America

   1. Europeans had better weapons

   2. European diseases killed the Native Americans at an alarming rate

   3. Different groups did not unite

   4. Overwhelmed by the continuous inflow of colonists

Europe Comes to America

Complete these activities.

2.1 What two events aroused European interest in the Far East?

a. _____

b. _____

2.2 Name the English explorer or company who:

a. explored the Canadian coast and found the Grand Banks

_____

b. explored the west coast of the U.S. on a voyage around the world

_____

c. financed the first successful English colony _____

d. founded Roanoke _____

e. claimed Hudson Bay for England _____

2.3 Where was New Netherlands located and who controlled the colony?

_____

2.4 What major lakes and two rivers were the basis of New France?

_____

_____

2.5 Who organized the effort to find the first water route to Asia, and what was the route?

_____

2.6 Who established permanent contact between Europe and the New World?

_____

2.7 Name the French explorer for each region or result.

a. Mississippi River as far south as the Arkansas River _____

b. St. Lawrence River _____

c. Upper New York State, founded Quebec _____

d. Mississippi River to its mouth _____

2.8 What were the three important events for the Virginia Colony in 1619?

a. _____

b. _____

c. _____

2.9 Name the Spanish *conquistador* for each area or event.

a. Discovered the Mississippi _____

b. The Pacific Ocean across Isthmus of Panama _____

c. Florida _____

d. Led the first circumnavigation of the world _____

e. Southwest U.S. _____

2.10 What two mistakes did Columbus make on his plan to reach Asia?

a. _____

_____

b. _____

_____

2.11 Name of the Dutch land system _____

2.12 Europeans who had the best relations with the Native Americans _____

2.13 The first successful British colony was _____

2.14 Each Virginia colonist got 50 acres of land under _____

2.15 Profitable Virginian crop _____

2.16 What event caused Spain to concentrate on the South and attracted other Europeans to

America? _____

2.17 Give two reasons why the Native Americans lost their battle with the Europeans

a. _____

_____

b. _____

_____

2.18 What was the main commodity of New France? _____

English Colonies

I. New England

A. Plymouth Plantation (1620)

1. Separatists were persecuted in England, so they left

2. The *Mayflower* landed at Plymouth Bay, MA in 1620

3. Charter for Virginia, so they were illegally in Massachusetts

4. Made a government

a. Mayflower Compact

b. Precursor of written constitutions in America

5. Aided by Squanto, an English speaking member of the Patuxet tribe

6. First harvest in 1621 was good, held a day of Thanksgiving

7. Were absorbed by the larger Massachusetts Bay Colony, 1691

B. Massachusetts Bay (1628)

1. Founded by Puritans (wanted to purify the English church) who were also persecuted

2. Massachusetts Bay Company

a. Organized by wealthy Puritans

b. Given a royal charter for lands north of Cape Cod

c. Took their charter to America

3. Well planned and financed

4. Strict, religious colony

a. Only Puritan churches

b. Only church members voted

c. Puritan aristocrats controlled the government

| Jamestown settlement in Virginia

d. Tended to drive out dissidents to start new colonies

C. Rhode Island (1636)

1. Roger Williams, fled Mass. Bay

a. Believed the government and the church should be separate

b. Believed the land belonged to Native Americans, not the king

2. Took refuge with Native Americans, then bought land from them to found Providence in 1636

a. Complete freedom of religion (first colony to do so)

b. All free men could vote

D. Connecticut (1636)

1. Organized by Thomas Hooker

a. Puritan pastor

b. Believed non-church members should vote

c. Led group of like-minded people to settle the Connecticut River valley

2. After several towns settled, they organized a government

British America

a. Fundamental Orders of Connecticut; first true constitution in America

b. All free men could vote

E. New Hampshire (1623)

1. Settled by people from Massachusetts Bay

2. Taken over by that colony in 1643

3. Became its own colony, 1680

F. Maine

1. Settled from Massachusetts Bay

2. Bay Colony purchased it in 1677

3. Part of Massachusetts until 1820

II. Middle Colonies

A. New York

1. Settled by Dutch West India Co.

2. King Charles II (England) gave the land to his brother, the Duke of York (1664)

a. Duke sent warships to capture the colony

b. Surrendered without a fight

c. Renamed New York

3. Autocratic government, grew slowly

4. Became a royal colony when the Duke became King James II, 1685

B. New Jersey

1. Land given to two wealthy friends of the Duke of York

2. Attracted settlers with promises of an assembly, religious freedom, and delayed quit-rents

3. Colony sold to the Quakers, a pacifist, persecuted religion

4. Became royal colony in 1702 in combination with New York

5. Given separate governor in 1738

C. Pennsylvania and Delaware

1. William Penn

a. Wealthy Quaker, friend of the monarchy

b. Granted large tract of land to pay off a debt by Charles II

2. Penn set up a "holy experiment"

a. Complete religious freedom

b. An assembly

c. No state church

d. Liberal land sales

e. Paid the Native Americans for the land

3. Quickly attracted many settlers

4. Separated in 1701, but both were owned by the Penn family until the Revolution

III. Southern Colonies

A. Maryland

1. Lord Baltimore (George Calvert)

a. Catholic friend of James II

b. Given land in America

2. Established as a refuge for Catholics

3. Protestants soon outnumbered Catholics

a. Toleration Act passed by assembly to protect Catholics

b. Full religious freedom for Christians who believed in the Trinity

4. Catholic Calverts lost control of the colony from 1691 to 1715

British America

5. Anglican Calverts owned the colony from 1715 to 1776

B. Carolinas

1. Land granted to group of wealthy, powerful men who supported Charles II

2. Leader, Earl of Shaftesbury

3. South Carolina

a. Had an excellent harbor at Charleston

b. Settled by aristocrats, many from West Indies who brought enslaved people

c. Developed a cash crop, plantation economy

d. Slave-supported, aristocratic culture

4. North Carolina

a. No major ports

b. Settled by small, independent-minded farmers from Virginia

5. Separated into two royal colonies in 1729

C. Georgia

1. Organized as a refuge for debtors

2. Leader, James Oglethorpe

3. Ruled by a paternalistic board of trustees

4. Strict laws retarded growth

5. Buffer colony between British and Spanish America, subject to wars

6. Became a royal colony with a plantation economy

IV. Colonial Growth

A. Government types

1. The original charters were granted to three groups

a. Company—to a corporation

b. Proprietor—to a person or group of people

c. Self-governing—to the people living on the land

2. Company and most proprietary colonies fail

a. Owners expected to profit by renting land like in Europe

b. Colonists insisted on owning their land and refused to pay rents = no profits

c. By the Revolution, only three proprietary (PA, DE, and MD) colonies remained, no corporate colonies at all

3. At the Revolution, there were two self-governing colonies (Connecticut & Rhode Island)

4. Most (8 out of 13) colonies were royal colonies by 1776

B. Government structure

1. Executive

a. Governor, appointed by king or proprietor, elected in self-governing colonies

b. Held a tremendous amount of power

2. Council

a. Had to approve all laws

b. Appointed by governor, usually wealthy men

3. Assembly

a. Elected by the voters

b. Voters had to own land or wealth, easy in America

c. Used control over finances to control the governor

British America

Name the person, colony, or item.

2.19 _____ settled by the Dutch West India Company

2.20 _____ organized by wealthy Puritans who took their royal charter with them to America

2.21 _____ refuge for Catholics

2.22 _____ founder of Rhode Island

2.23 _____ by the time of the Revolution, the most common type of colony

2.24 _____ founder of Delaware

2.25 _____ three parts of a typical colonial government

_____

_____

2.26 _____ document used to create a government for Separatists who landed illegally in Massachusetts

2.27 _____ three types of charters originally granted for colonies

_____

_____

2.28 _____ power used by colonial assemblies to control the royal governor

2.29 _____ settled by small independent farmers from Virginia

2.30 _____ given to the Duke of York by Charles II

2.31 _____ man from Patuxet tribe, aided the Plymouth Colony

2.32 _____ settled by aristocrats from West Indies; excellent harbor; plantation economy

2.33 _____ first colony to have complete freedom of religion

2.34 _____ first true constitution in America

2.35 _____ founder of Connecticut

2.36 _____ many Northeastern colonies were founded by dissidents driven out of this strict religious colony

2.37 _____ Quaker holy experiment

2.38 _____ three remaining proprietary colonies at the Revolution

_____

_____

2.39 _____ organized as refuge for debtors and a buffer between British and Spanish America

2.40 _____ eventually a U.S. state; part of Massachusetts until 1820

2.41 _____ primary reason proprietary and corporate colonies were not profitable

2.42 _____ people who could vote in Massachusetts Bay Colony

C. Lifestyles

   1. New England

      a. Settled mainly by Puritans

      b. Small farms and towns

      c. Lifestyle of hard work and thrift

      d. Town meetings

         (1) Men debate local issues

         (2) Pure democracy

      e. First region to support public education so that all people could read the Bible

      f. Poor farmland forced people to turn to the sea for more income

         (1) Fishing

         (2) Whaling

         (3) Shipbuilding

      g. Birthplace of traditional American moral values and work ethic

   2. Middle Colonies

      a. Richer soil and larger farms than New England

      b. Called the "Bread Colonies"

      c. Religious toleration

      d. Mix of many peoples and styles of worship

      e. Commerce important, Philadelphia was the largest port in the Colonies by 1750s

      f. Wealth leads to demand for luxury goods and artisans

      g. Birthplace of American tolerance and ideas of equality

   3. Southern Colonies

      a. Large, plantation farms based on cash crops (indigo, rice, tobacco)

      b. Tremendous need for workers

         (1) Indentured servants not willing to work beyond their term

         (2) Need filled with enslaved Africans

      c. Strict social divisions

         (1) Resembled Europe with aristocracy above and workers (slaves) below

         (2) Little of the tolerance of the other colonies

         (3) No large manufacturing or middle class

      d. Tradition of independence and political leadership

D. Religion

   1. Denominations

      a. Largest–Congregationalist

         (1) Puritan churches

British America

(2) Often tax supported

b. 2nd largest–Anglican

    (1) State church of Britain

    (2) Fashionable church of the wealthy

    (3) Tax supported in the South

c. Presbyterians–3rd largest group

d. Other groups

    (1) Quakers

    (2) Roman Catholic

    (3) Baptist

    (4) Methodist (began shortly before the Revolution)

e. Deism–religion of the Enlightenment

    (1) God was the creator but was not active in the world

    (2) Belief of many early American leaders (Franklin, Jefferson)

2. Great Awakening

a. Tremendous revival in 1730s and 1740s

b. Jonathan Edwards

    (1) Pastor, Massachusetts

    (2) Became one of America's first theologians

c. George Whitefield

    (1) Popular British evangelist

    (2) Preached all over the Colonies to large crowds

V. Colonial History, 1600s

A. New England Confederation

1. Formed by four of the "proper" religious colonies

2. Central board to deal with defense and common problems

B. King Philip's War

| American theologian Jonathan Edwards

1. Philip, ruler of the Wampanoag people, friends of Plymouth

2. Initiated a war to drive out all of the settlers in 1675

3. The Native Americans could not sustain the war

C. Bacon's Rebellion

1. Rebellion in Virginia, led by Nathaniel Bacon

2. Crushed, but Bacon's Laws passed to address complaints

D. Dominion of New England

1. James II tried to control New England by combining it with New York and New Jersey under strict royal governor Andros

2. Restricted town meetings, forced rent payments; very unpopular

E. Glorious Revolution

1. James II overthrown, making Parliament supreme

British America

2. Andros overthrown in America

3. Colonies given back charters with improvements in equality

Wars with France

I. Repeated Conflicts

A. France and Britain fought series of wars that included North America

   1. British advantages in America

      a. Larger population with people concentrated together

      c. Self-sufficient in food

      d. Had some manufacturing

      e. British navy could supply and protect

      f. Allies, powerful Iroquois

   2. French advantages in America

      a. Single, central government

      b. Capable generals on the spot

B. King William's War (1689-1697)

   1. "War of the League of Augsburg" in Europe

   2. No loss of territory

C. Queen Anne's War (1701-1713)

   1. "War of the Spanish Succession"

   2. Due to victories in Europe, Britain given Nova Scotia and Newfoundland

D. King George's War (1740-1748)

   1. "War of the Austrian Succession"

   2. No loss of territory

II. French and Indian War (1754-1763)

A. Started in America by militia Colonel George Washington's attack on the French near Pittsburgh

B. Albany Congress

   1. Congress of all the colonies called to secure the loyalty of the Iroquois in the coming war

   2. Addressed the problem of the lack of unity among the colonies

   3. Benjamin Franklin's Albany Plan to set up a limited central government was rejected

C. Braddock's Defeat

   1. British General Edward Braddock sent to America

      a. Trained in European warfare, formal confrontations between armies lined up in ranks against each other

      b. Ignored warnings about surprise attacks

   2. Marched in formation to attack Fort Dusquesne (Pittsburgh)

   3. French with Native American allies attacked from behind trees

      a. Braddock killed

      b. British routed

D. French victorious, 1756 and 1757

E. Organizer of Victory–William Pitt

   1. Became British leader in 1757

   2. Selected more energetic generals

   3. Organized supplies and strategy

   4. Concentrated on French forts, especially on the St. Lawrence Seaway

F. Quebec (1759)

   1. Set on a bluff above the St. Lawrence, it controlled the river

   2. British climbed the bluff and forced the French to fight

British America

3. British victory, both commanders killed

G. Treaty of Paris (1763)

1. France gave Britain all of her land east of the Mississippi and along the St. Lawrence

2. Spain given the French land west of the Mississippi (later returned)

3. France kept only two small islands in North America

H. Results

1. Britain was the dominant world power, unwilling to compromise

2. Britain deeply in debt

3. Colonists began process of thinking and acting together

4. Americans gained military training

    5. Lack of unity and support by colonists disturbed Britain

III. After the Victory

A. Pontiac's War (1763)

1. Pontiac, an Ottawa chief, organized the tribes south of the Great Lakes against the colonists

2. Many forts taken, but not Detroit and Pittsburgh

3. Native Americans did not receive expected French aid for the war

B. Proclamation of 1763

1. British wanted to separate the Native Americans and the colonists to avoid another war

2. Forbade colonists from settling west of the Appalachian Mountains.

3. Colonial reaction

  a. Believed expansion was their right

  b. Ignored it, moved west

4. British frustrated by the disobedience

British America

Complete these sentences.

2.43 Colonial Colonel _____ was instrumental in starting the French and Indian War.

2.44 The _____ were the largest denomination in the colonies in the mid-1700s.

2.45 The _____ was a major revival in the American colonies in the 1730s and 40s.

2.46 _____ was an attempt by the leader of the Wampanoag people to drive out the colonists in 1675.

2.47 _____ was the section of the colonies settled mainly by Puritans with small farms.

2.48 The _____ was the fashionable church of the colonies, usually supported by taxes in the South.

2.49 _____ , _____ and _____ were ways that New Englanders supplemented their income from the sea.

2.50 Formed in the 1600s, the _____ was a loose alliance formed by four of the "proper" religious colonies of the North.

2.51 France lost all but two islands of its American colonial empire due to the _____ War.

2.52 _____ was the religion of the Enlightenment.

2.53 _____ was the section of the colonies which had large plantations farmed first by indentured servants and then enslaved people.

2.54 _____ was the British leader in the mid-1700 war with France who was the "Organizer of Victory."

2.55 _____ was the British commander who ignored the advice of the Americans and was killed while marching openly to Fort Dusquesne.

2.56 _____ of Britain and _____ of Massachusetts were the leading preachers of the Great Awakening.

✎ **Name the item(s).**

2.57 The American and European names for the three wars between France and Britain (1689-
1748) _____

_____

_____

2.58 The Bread Colonies _____

2.59 Colonial section that was the birthplace of American moral values and work ethic

_____

2.60 Attempt to combine most of the Northern colonies during the reign of James II

_____

2.61 Colonial congress called to insure the loyalty of the Iroquois; tried to set up a central colonial
government _____

2.62 Section of the colonies that was the birthplace of American tolerance

_____

2.63 First section of the colonies to establish public education

_____

2.64 Decree that tried to forbid Americans from settling west of the Appalachian Mountains

_____

2.65 Four significant results of the French and Indian War

a. _____

b. _____

c. _____

d. _____

Growing Conflict

I. Britain Flexes its Muscles

  A. Britain wanted colonies to pay some costs of the war and protection

  B. Mercantilism (an economic theory)

    1. Colonies existed to benefit the mother country

    2. Navigation Acts (1600s)

      a. Restrictions on American trade and manufacturing

      b. Never enforced before 1763

  C. Prime Minister Grenville

    1. Order Navigation Acts strictly enforced by Admiralty Courts, 1763

      a. No jury

      b. Defendant presumed guilty

    2. Quartering Act, 1765, colonists must provide lodging for soldiers

    3. Stamp Act, 1765

      a. Must pay for stamp on all legal papers

      b. First direct tax on colonists

      c. Aroused strong reaction, so Americans began to organize

  D. Stamp Act reaction in America

    1. Stamp Act Congress

    2. Boycott of British goods

    3. Mob action

      a. Attacked stamp sellers, royal officials, and boycott violators

      b. All the stamp sellers resigned

    4. Act repealed after four months

      E. Declaratory Act, states Parliament had the right to tax the colonies

II. Actions and Reaction

  A. Townshend Acts, 1767

    1. Tax on goods imported from Britain: tea, paint, lead, and glass

    2. Gave customs officials power to search without a warrant

    3. Threatened to close the New York assembly if it did not comply with the Quartering Act

    4. Money raised was to be used to pay British officials so they no longer were under the financial control of the colonists

    5. Colonial response: gradual boycott, smuggling, and agitation

  B. Boston Massacre, March 5, 1770

    1. Crowd threw debris at British soldiers

    2. Soldiers fired, five people died

    3. Fueled anti-British propaganda

  C. Due to unrest and boycott, Townsend taxes repealed except the tax on tea, 1770

    1. Calmed the moderates

    2. Samuel Adams set up Committees of Correspondence to allow colonies to have constant communication

  D. Boston Tea Party, December 16, 1773

    1. British East India Co. given a monopoly on sale of tea

    2. Americans distrusted monopoly and saw it as hiding the tax

    3. Boston crowd disguised as Native Americans boarded the ships, threw the tea into the harbor, no violence

  E. Intolerable Acts, British overreaction to the Boston Tea Party

The American Revolution

1. Port of Boston closed until tea paid for, with the tax (meant hardship for the whole city)

2. King appointed all important officials in Massachusetts

3. Town meetings forbidden

4. Boston under military rule

5. Quebec Act, colonists <u>believed</u> it was part of the Intolerable Acts

    a. French customs and religion protected in Quebec

    b. Quebec given the land of the Ohio Valley which the American colonies wanted

F. First Continental Congress, response to Intolerable Acts

    1. Met Sept. 1774, Philadelphia

    2. Sent petitions and resolutions

    3. Agreed to meet in May 1775 if situation not resolved

III. Rebellion

A. Lexington and Concord

    1. By 1775, colonial militias were training and collecting weapons

    2. General Gage, British military governor of Boston, sent soldiers to capture the supplies and leaders

    3. Lexington

        a. Met colonial militia in battle formation

        b. "Shot heard round the world" was fired, beginning of the Revolution

        4. British forced to retreat by militia force at Concord

5. British attacked by snipers all the way back to Boston

B. Ethan Allen and Benedict Arnold captured Lake Champlain forts (Ticonderoga, Crown Point), May 1775, moved fort cannons to Boston

C. Bunker Hill

    1. Militia gathered outside Boston, fortified Breeds Hill

    2. British attack, June 17, 1775

    3. British take the hill only after heavy losses, Americans retreat

D. Second Continental Congress, met as arranged, May, 1775

    1. Put Washington in command of the army at Boston

    2. Olive Branch Petition sent to the king, rejected

    3. *Common Sense*

        a. Influential pamphlet written by Thomas Paine, early 1776

        b. Turned public opinion in favor of independence

    4. Declaration of Independence

        a. Written by Thomas Jefferson to explain the decision to be independent

        b. Independence declared July 2

        c. Declaration signed on July 4, 1776

War

I. America Alone

A. British advantages in the war

    1. Professional army

    2. Large navy to control the coast

    3. One-third of Americans loyal to the British (Tories)

The American Revolution

4. British government stable, could raise taxes and give orders

5. American government had little authority, could not raise taxes

B. American advantages

1. Excellent leadership, whereas British generals were mediocre

3. Fighting at home

4. America able to get foreign aid

5. American's had a "cause"

C. Early course of the War

1. Boston: British occupation army forced to withdraw when cannon from Fort Ticonderoga set up above the city, March, 1776

2. New York

a. Battle of Long Island, August, 1776

(1) Americans defeated and trapped by Gen. Howe

(2) Washington left his campfires burning so they could escape

b. British captured New York City and nearby forts

c. Americans retreated to poor winter quarters in New Jersey

3. Trenton

a. Washington needed victory to keep his army together

b. Surprise attack across the Delaware R. on Christmas night, victory

4. Princeton

a. British under Cornwallis tried to trap Washington at Trenton

b. Americans escaped, attacked, defeated reinforcements

c. Twin victories revived American morale

D. Washington, 1777-78

1. Howe moved to take American capital, Philadelphia

2. Americans lost two battles as British move toward the city

a. Brandywine Creek, September

b. Germantown, October (Americans impressed foreign observers with their fighting)

3. Howe took Philadelphia, little result, Congress moved to new location

4. Valley Forge

a. American winter quarters near Philadelphia, 1777-78

b. Food scare, cold, Americans suffered from lack of supplies

c. Baron von Steuben, drilled the soldiers to work together

The American Revolution

Choose the correct item, person, or battle for each description.

2.66 _____ congress; met in response to Intolerable Acts

2.67 _____ protected the customs and religion of French in Canada

2.68 _____ American defeat began the Revolutionary War

2.69 _____ five people in Boston killed after throwing things at soldiers in March 1770

2.70 _____ laws that restricted American trade and manufacturing was not enforced until 1763

2.71 _____ laws that taxed tea, increased search power of customs officials, and used the money to pay royal officials

2.72 _____ colonists threw monopoly tea into Boston harbor in 1773

2.73 _____ Washington led his men on a successful surprise attack across the Delaware River, Christmas night, 1776

2.74 _____ first direct tax; colonists react with a Congress, boycott, and mob action; repealed after four months

2.75 _____ city; captured by British after the Battle of Long Island

2.76 _____ closed Boston harbor; put the city under military rule

2.77 _____ American militia driven off fortified hill above Boston, in June, 1775

2.78 _____ pamphlet by Thomas Paine, turned public opinion in favor of independence

2.79 _____ American winter quarters, 1777-78; scene of great suffering and time of training for the army

2.80 _____ economic theory that colonies exist to benefit the mother country

2.81 _____ congress appointed Washington; declared independence; Olive Branch Petition

2.82 _____ side in the Revolution that had the advantage in leadership and location

2.83 _____ side in the Revolution that had the advantage in government, army, and navy

2.84 _____ important city captured by British under Howe in 1777

2.85 _____ author—Declaration of Independence

2.86 _____ created Committees of Correspondence

2.87 _____ source of the cannons that drove British out of Boston in March, 1776

2.88 _____ American officers who captured Ticonderoga

_____

2.89 _____ three British generals

_____

_____

II. Turning Point

  A. British plan, divide New York into three parts, 1777

  B. General Howe to come from South, but he never tried to do it

  C. Lt. Colonel St. Leger to come from west

    1. Moved up Mohawk Valley

    2. Unable to capture the American Fort Stanwix at Rome, New York

    3. Eventually retreated

  D. Gen. Burgoyne to come from the North down Lake Champlain

    1. Brought along a huge train of baggage and built a road as he went, progress <u>very</u> slow

    2. Captured Ticonderoga, July, 1777

    3. American defenders did everything possible to slow him

    4. Saratoga, turning point of the war, September and October

      a. Horatio Gates sent to command the American army

      b. American victory, Burgoyne and his entire army surrender

      c. Convinced France to join as an American ally, February, 1778

  E. Campaigns of 1778

    1. Monmouth, indecisive

      a. British under Gen. Clinton evacuated Philadelphia and retreated to New York City

      b. Washington intercepted them

    2. George Rogers Clark captured key forts in the West in 1778, putting the region under American control

  F. Benedict Arnold offered to give the American fort at West Point to the British, September, 1780

    1. Go-between caught

    2. Arnold fled to the British

    3. Lived as British subject the rest of his life, hated by Americans

III. The End of the War

  A. British successes in the South

    1. Captured Savannah, Georgia in 1779

The American Revolution

2. Clinton captured Charleston, South Carolina in May, 1780

   a. Gen. Benjamin Lincoln and 5,000 men captured

   b. Biggest disaster for America during the war

   c. Cornwallis set up string of forts in the state and soon controlled South Carolina

3. Camden, August, 1780

   a. Gates sent with American army to confront Cornwallis

   b. Hastily assembled force

   c. Americans defeated, fled

B. King's Mountain, October, 1780

   1. Overconfident Cornwallis sends a Tory force into North Carolina

   2. Defeated and destroyed

C. Nathanael Greene's campaign

   1. Greene chosen by Washington to take command in the South

   2. Conducted a brilliant campaign

     a. Worked with guerrilla bands harassing the British

     b. Drew Cornwallis into a long, fruitless chase in Carolina

     c. Never won a battle, but always inflicted heavy losses and kept his army intact

   3. Heavy losses force British to withdraw to Charleston, Carolinas free by September, 1781

D. Yorktown, October, 1781

   1. Combined America-French army under Washington and Rochambeau set up siege of Cornwallis

2. French navy blocked escape

3. Entire British army in the South trapped, surrendered

4. Final battle of the war

E. Treaty of Paris, September 3, 1783

   1. Britain accepted American independence

   2. Gave America all land east of Mississippi

   3. Terms generous because British want to break up American-French alliance

F. Washington could have tried to become king, but returned to private life instead

The Constitution

I. Articles of Confederation, America's first constitution from 1781-89

A. Terms

   1. "Firm league of friendship" between the sovereign states

   2. Federal government had no power to tax, control commerce or provide justice

   3. No executive to enforce laws

   4. Each state had one vote in the Congress, two-thirds had to approve important matters

   5. Without tax power, it had no steady income to fulfill powers it did have: war, foreign affairs, and a postal service

B. Northwest Territory, the one notable success of the Confederation

   1. Land west of Appalachians, north of Ohio River put under the control of Congress

The American Revolution

    2. Land Ordinance, sold the land to pay war debts

    3. Northwest Ordinance

        a. Land organized into territories under national control

        b. Once a territory's population reached 60,000 it could be admitted as a state

        c. New lands have equal rights with the old ones, made America a free nation, not an empire

  C. Shay's Rebellion

    1. Debtors in Massachusetts revolt

    2. Army raised to suppress them

    3. Frightened well-to-do people into seeking a reform of the Articles

    4. Meeting set to reform the Articles in Philadelphia in 1787

II. Constitutional Convention

  A. Early key decisions

    1. Washington elected as chairman, gave prestige to the convention

    2. Meetings held in secret, kept delegates free from outside pressure, allowed compromise

    3. Articles were too awkward to revise, started over

  B. Compromises on new constitution

    1. Representation in Congress

        a. Virginia Plan, by population

        b. Connecticut Plan, by state

        c. Great Compromise: Senate by state; House by population

    2. Slaves counted as three-fifths of a person for taxation and representation purposes

| The Constitutional Convention

    3. Congress not allowed to outlaw the slave trade until 1807

  C. Checks and Balances, to keep government from becoming too powerful

    1. Power divided into three parts: executive (president), legislative (Congress), and judicial (courts)

    2. Checks

        a. President can veto laws passed by Congress

        b. Congress can override a veto

        c. Congress can impeach a president or judges

    3. States gave up certain powers to the Federal government but kept he rest for themselves

    4. Federal government could tax and control interstate commerce

  D. Forty-two delegates signed it on September 17, 1787

    1. Sent it to the states, not Congress

    2. Announced it would be effective when two-thirds (9) states accepted it

The American Revolution

III. The Battle for Ratification

A. Federalists favored the constitution

1. Generally wealthy people who wanted more order

2. *The Federalist*, a series of essays by Madison, Hamilton, and John Jay defended the constitution

B. Anti-federalists opposed it

1. Feared tyranny from a strong government

2. Did not want the states to lose so much power

3. Strongest argument: no protection of individual rights

C. Federalists promised a Bill of Rights under the new government (it was passed as the first 10 amendments)

D. Federalists slowly won over the needed states

1. Became official in June, 1788

2. Large states of New York and Virginia ratified it

3. Eventually all thirteen ratified it

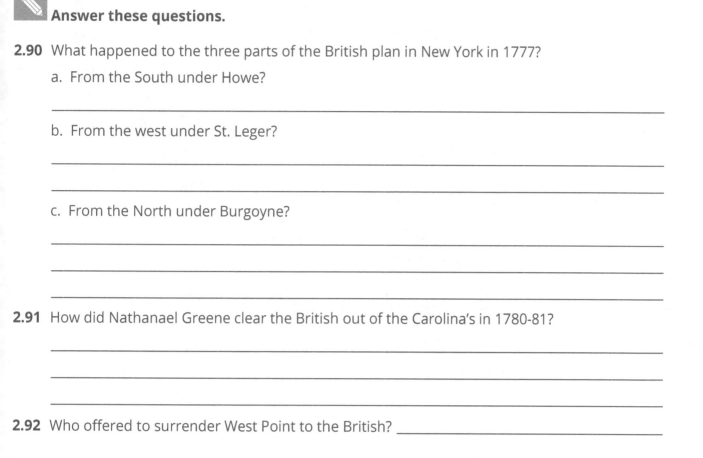

The American Revolution

Answer these questions.

2.90 What happened to the three parts of the British plan in New York in 1777?

a. From the South under Howe?

_____

b. From the west under St. Leger?

_____

_____

c. From the North under Burgoyne?

_____

_____

_____

2.91 How did Nathanael Greene clear the British out of the Carolina's in 1780-81?

_____

_____

_____

2.92 Who offered to surrender West Point to the British? _____

2.93 What were the weaknesses of the Articles of Confederation?

_____

_____

_____

2.94 How did the Confederation Congress handle the land in the Northwest?

_____

_____

_____

_____

2.95 What pushed people to reform the Articles of Confederation in 1786-87?

_____

2.96 What was the turning point of the Revolutionary War?

_____

2.97 What happened at the Battle of Yorktown?

_____

_____

2.98 What were the terms of the Treaty of Paris (1783)?

_____

_____

2.99 At the constitutional convention:

a. What was the Great Compromise over representation?

_____

b. What was the compromise over counting slaves?

_____

c. Who was chosen to lead the convention?

_____

d. Why were the meetings held in secret?

_____

e. What was the compromise over the slave trade?

_____

2.100 How is the power of the federal government divided in the constitution?

_____

2.101 What was the strongest argument against ratifying the constitution?

_____

2.102 What was the name of the group that favored ratifying the constitution?

_____

2.103 What is the U.S. Bill of Rights? _____

2.104 What was _The Federalist_? _____

Federalist Era

I. Washington's First Term

  A. Chosen as first president under the new constitution, April, 1789

    1. Only unanimous choice of electors in U.S. history

    2. His prestige and fairness established the power of the new office

  B. Cabinet

    1. Thomas Jefferson; Secretary of State

    2. Alexander Hamilton; Secretary of the Treasury

    3. Henry Knox; Secretary of War

    4. Edmund Randolph; Attorney General

  C. Parties developed quickly

    1. Federalists

      a. Led by Hamilton

      b. Wanted a strong central government

      c. Loose construction of the Constitution

      d. Favored Britain

    2. Democratic-Republicans (D-R)

      a. Led by Jefferson

      b. Wanted weak central government

      c. Strict construction of the constitution

      d. Favored France

  D. Main problem, finances

    1. U.S. deeply in debt and had no stable currency

    2. Hamilton's plan

      a. National government assume all state war debts (bonds)

      b. Bonds paid at full value

      c. A national bank would hold government deposits and issue currency

      d. Money raised by tariffs and excise tax on whiskey

    3. Washington concerned that a bank might not be constitutional

      a. Jefferson argued for strict construction: government can only do exactly what the Constitution allows

      b. Hamilton argued for loose construction: government can do any reasonable thing needed to fulfill its purposes

      c. President accepted Hamilton's argument and signed the bill

    4. Hamilton's plan stabilized America's finances

II. Washington's Second Term

  A. War in Europe

    1. France at war, America obligated to help

    2. Even pro-French Jefferson did not want U.S. in a European war

    3. Declaration of Neutrality by U.S.

  B. Whiskey Rebellion, 1794

    1. Farmers in Pennsylvania rebel against the tax on whiskey

    2. Washington sent an army

    3. Firmness caused opposition to turn to votes, not guns

  C. Problems with Britain

    1. Kept possession of several Western forts in U.S. lands

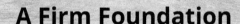

A Firm Foundation

2. Began seizing U.S. ships, cargo, and "impressing" sailors, forcing them to serve in the British navy

D. Jay's Treaty

   1. John Jay sent to Britain to resolve outstanding issues

   2. A weak, unpopular treaty, did not resolve impressment issue

   3. Treaty encouraged Spain to settle its differences with America

E. Washington refused third term and urged the nation to avoid alliances

III. Adams Administration

A. Election of 1796

   1. First contested election

   2. John Adams, Federalist, previously vice president, won

   3. Thomas Jefferson, D-R, in 2nd place became vice president

   4. Only time those offices held by men of different parties (rules changed in 1804)

B. XYZ Affair

   1. Jay Treaty triggered a crisis with France who began harassing U.S. ships

   2. Three delegates sent to France to negotiate in 1797

   3. French officials, called X, Y and Z, demanded a bribe

   4. Americans refused and left

   5. Adams avoided a war because he knew the nation was too weak to fight

C. Convention of 1800

   1. Revolutionary France was at war with most of Europe, could not also afford war with U.S.

   2. New delegation sent in 1799 and was received properly

   3. U.S. signed Convention with Napoleon, new French dictator

      a. End U.S.-French alliance

      b. Settled differences

   4. Adams' unwillingness to go to war cost him popularity

D. Alien and Sedition Acts, 1798

   1. Passed by Federalist Congress during war hysteria

   2. Alien Act made it harder to become a citizen and allowed the "dangerous" aliens to be deported

   3. Sedition Act made malicious, false or scandalous speech a crime

      a. Used against D-R newspapers

      b. Jefferson and Madison tried unsuccessfully to have the states nullify the laws (South would use that tactic again)

   4. Repealed or allowed to expire

E. Election of 1800

   1. Federalists divided

   2. Jefferson and Aaron Burr ran as a team, neither got electoral majority

   3. Jefferson won after 35 ballots

   4. Constitution changed (1804) so president and vice president were voted for separately

   5. Federalist party began to decline

A Firm Foundation

F. Federalist legacy

1. Set up basic institutions of our government

2. Kept the nation out of dangerous European war

3. Set up a strong government under loose construction

Jeffersonian Democracy

I. D-R in Power

A. Election in 1800 the first in which the ruling party was voted out of office and left peacefully

1. A key test of a new democracy

2. Began 25 years of D-R rule

B. Jefferson's policies

1. Kept Federalist financial policies

2. Ended the excise tax

3. Ran the government cheaply

4. Reduced the navy

5. Replaced government employees with his own supporters (began the spoils system)

C. Midnight Judges

1. Appointed at the last minute by Federalists who had been voted out of office

2. Jefferson refused to deliver some of the commissions

3. One named Marbury sued

a. *Marbury v. Madison*

b. Set the precedent that the Supreme Court can declare laws unconstitutional

D. Louisiana Purchase

1. Napoleon sold the west part of the Mississippi River basin to the U.S.

2. Jefferson approved but hesitated because it was not authorized by the Constitution

3. U.S. paid $3 million, 3¢ an acre

E. Lewis and Clark Expedition, 1804-1806

1. Meriwether Lewis and William Clark sent to explore the new lands

2. Traveled up Missouri River, across the Rocky Mountains, down the Columbia R. to the Pacific

3. Gone over 2 years, greatly increased the knowledge of the new land

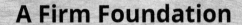

A Firm Foundation

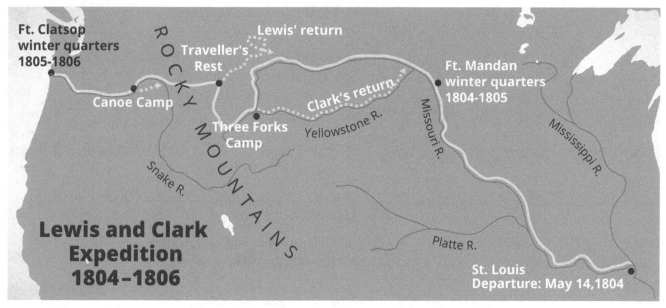

| Lewis and Clark Expedition route and the Louisiana Purchase

Name the item, person, or event.

2.105 _____ first Secretary of State

2.106 _____ French refused to negotiate without a bribe; caused a call for war

2.107 _____ election year of the first successful, peaceful change of political power

2.108 _____ rebellion against the excise tax; Washington met it with force

2.109 _____ political party that favored France; weak government; strict construction

2.110 _____ Jefferson approved paying three million for western part of Mississippi River land

2.111 _____ expedition; explored the Louisiana Purchase in 1804-1806

2.112 _____ Secretary of the Treasury who set up a national bank; had the federal government pay war debts at full value and established tariffs and excise taxes

2.113 _____ Washington's declaration in response to the war in Europe, despite a treaty with France

2.114 _____   political party of Alexander Hamilton and John Adams

2.115 _____   agreement with Napoleon that ended the U.S.–French alliance

2.116 _____   laws that restricted the rights of immigrants and free speech (1798), hurt the Federalist Party

2.117 _____   lawsuit that established that the Supreme Court can declare laws unconstitutional

2.118 _____   president who ended the excise tax and ran the government cheaply

2.119 _____   president who lost his popularity by keeping the nation out of a war with France

2.120 _____   political party that favored loose construction, a strong government in Britain

2.121 _____   unpopular treaty with Britain that failed to resolve the issue of impressment

2.122 _____   only president ever elected by a unanimous electoral vote

2.123 _____   three parts of the Federalist legacy

       _____

       _____

II. Problems and Controversies

   A. Jefferson sent the American navy to wage a successful war against the Barbary pirates (North Africa) to protect trade in the Mediterranean

   B. Some New England states wanted to take their states out of the union

      1. Aaron Burr, a leader of the plot

      2. Arrested, tried for treason, and acquitted, but career ruined

   C. Growing Problems with Britain

      1. War between France and Britain, both seized U.S. ships

      2. U.S. Navy too weak to protect trade

         a. British increased impressment of American sailors

         b. Orders in Council, seized neutral ships going to France

      3. *Chesapeake-Leopard* Affair, 1807

         a. British demanded "deserters" on U.S. warship near Virginia

         b. British opened fire, killed 3, injured 18, removed 4 men

   D. Embargo Disaster

      1. Jefferson signed the Embargo Act of 1807 to deal with British

      2. Forbade the export of any goods

      3. Did not hurt the British, but did tremendous damage to the U.S.

         a. Legitimate trade stopped

         b. Massive job loss

         c. Jefferson's popularity fell

      4. Jefferson repealed it just before leaving office

III. War Hawks

   A. Elections of 1808 and 1810

      1. James Madison, D-R, won the presidency in 1808

      2. Younger men who wanted war were elected (War Hawks)

      3. War Hawks take lead in Congress

         a. Henry Clay, Kentucky, leader

         b. John Calhoun, South Carolina

         c. Mainly from the South and West, very nationalistic

   B. Tecumseh's Confederacy

      1. Shawnee leader, Tecumseh organized the Native Americans all along the eastern Mississippi River

      2. General William Henry Harrison defeated part of the group at Tippecanoe in 1811

         a. Broke up the confederation

         b. Found British guns amongst the Native Americans

   C. Slide toward War

      1. War Hawks press for war even though the nation is very unprepared

      2. War Hawks think they can seize Canada while Britain is busy in Europe

      3. Under pressure, Madison asked for war, declared June, 1812

War of 1812

I. Not the War They Planned

   A. New England did not support war

   B. Invasion of Canada, failure

      1. The Canadians fought hard to protect their homes

A Firm Foundation

| The Battle of Lake Erie, 1812

2. Many militiamen refused to cross the border

3. British capture Detroit and Michilimackinac in 1812

C. Naval War

1. American frigates successful against British counterparts

   a. Americans win most of the single ship battles

   b. Humiliating to the British

   c. American ships heavier, better armed and crews were free men fighting for their country

2. *U.S.S. Constitution*

   a. Most famous warship

b. "Old Ironsides," cannon balls bounced off heavy oak sides

3. American privateers capturing British merchant ships made the war unpopular

D. Canadian Campaign, 1813

1. William H. Harrison put in charge

2. Ordered Oliver Perry to get the British off the Great Lakes

   a. Towed ships in and built some on Lake Erie

   b. Battle of Lake Erie, British defeated

3. British retreated from Detroit

4. Defeated by Harrison at Thames River, Tecumseh killed

5. Americans did not take Montreal

A Firm Foundation

6. British took Fort Niagara and burned Buffalo

II. To the Depths of Despair and Back

A. Napoleon was defeated and sent into exile in 1814, leaving the British free to focus on the U.S.

B. British move troops from Europe

1. Occupied much of eastern Maine

2. Set up blockade that ruined the U.S. economy

3. Invaded New York

4. Burned Washington, August 1814

C. Peace talks in Ghent, Belgium

1. British demanded a Native American Nation west of Mississippi, control of the Great Lakes and part of Maine

2. U.S. delegates refused

D. Tide turns

1. Battle of Plattsburgh Bay

a. Battle on Lake Champlain

b. British defeated and invasion of New York was stopped

2. British attack on Baltimore failed

E. Treaty of Ghent, December 1814

1. British reverses; forced them to offer a better treaty

2. Agreed to a return to the borders set before the war

3. News of the treaty reached America too late to stop a British invasion of New Orleans

a. Andrew Jackson defended the city

b. British defeated with heavy losses two weeks after the peace treaty was signed

F. Results

1. Americans see it as a victory; they did not lose any territory

2. Danger from Native Americans reduced, settlers move West

3. Trade problems helped to create American manufacturing

4. U.S. proved it could survive

5. After the war, Andrew Jackson was sent into Florida to deal with Native Americans raiders, convinced Spain to cede the territory to the U.S.

6. U.S. controlled all land between Canada and Mexico east of the Mississippi River

III. Good Feelings

A. National pride high after the war

B. American System

1. Proposed by Henry Clay

a. Tariff to protect new industries in the North

b. A new national bank to stabilize the money supply

c. Federal money for roads and canals to benefit Western and Southern farmers

2. Madison refused to use federal money for use within a state

C. James Monroe, D-R, easily won the presidency in 1816

1. Nation united and proud

2. D-R was the only strong party

3. Monroe was re-elected without opposition in 1820

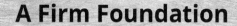

A Firm Foundation

4. Called the Era of Good Feelings—the time between the War of 1812 and the rise of sectionalism

D. Western land

1. Land prices were low and the amount of land a man had to buy was steadily reduced from 1795-1820

2. Massive increase in population on the east side of the Mississippi River in the years after War of 1812

E. Under Chief Justice John Marshall, the Supreme Court increased the power of the federal government and protected property rights

F. Monroe Doctrine

1. Monarchs of Europe back in power after the Napoleonic wars

2. U.S. feared for the new republics in South America

3. Monroe told Europe not to meddle in the Americas

4. U.S. did not have the power to enforce it at the time

A Firm Foundation

Complete these sentences.

2.124 _____ was an Shawnee leader who organized a confederation of the tribes along the eastern Mississippi.

2.125 The *U.S.S.* _____ was the most famous American warship of the War of 1812.

2.126 The new congressmen who favored war in 1808 and 1810 were called the

_____ .

2.127 Jefferson sent the American navy to fight the _____ on the north coast of Africa.

2.128 The War Hawks hoped to invade _____ while Britain was busy in Europe.

2.129 The British fired on an American warship to recapture four "deserters" in the

_____ Affair in 1807.

2.130 The _____ Act was a disaster ruining U.S. trade without hurting Britain in 1807.

2.131 The British lost control of the Great Lakes at the Battle of _____ in 1813.

2.132 Jefferson, Madison, and Monroe were all part of the _____ political party.

2.133 The British invasion on New York was stopped at the Battle of _____ on Lake Champlain.

2.134 The major issue between the U.S. and Britain during the Napoleonic wars was the _____ of American sailors.

2.135 The British burned the city of _____ in 1814, but were unable to capture _____ later in the year.

2.136 The Treaty of _____ ended the War of 1812.

2.137 _____ was involved in a plot to take some of the Northeastern states out of the union, but was acquitted of treason.

2.138 The amount of land that had to be purchased at one time in the West steadily _____ from 1795-1820.

2.139 _____ was the Chief Justice of the Supreme Court whose decisions made the federal government stronger and protected rights.

2.140 Henry Clay's idea to benefit all parts of the nation by tariffs and spending on internal improvements was called the _____ .

2.141 The _____ warned Europe not the meddle in the Americas.

2.142 _____ won a victory against the British near _____ weeks after the Treaty of Ghent was signed.

2.143 The time of unity between the War of 1812 and the rise of sectionalism was called the _____ .

2.144 The British were able to concentrate on fighting in America in 1814 because _____ _____ .

Check the items that were results of the War of 1812.

2.145 ☐ Nationalism

2.146 ☐ Loss of U.S. territory in Maine

2.147 ☐ Danger from Native Americans decreased

2.148 ☐ Americans moved West

2.149 ☐ American manufacturing was established

2.150 ☐ The War Hawks were first elected

2.151 ☐ The Embargo Act was passed

Jacksonian Era

I. Setting the Times

A. Giants in Washington, leaders whose statesmanship held the nation together, 1820-1855

1. Henry Clay, Kentucky

a. Great Compromiser

b. Very influential in Congress

2. John Calhoun, South Carolina

a. Began his career as a nationalist

b. Became a leading proponent of nullification (states can void federal laws)

3. Daniel Webster, Massachusetts

a. Famous orator

b. Anti-slavery, but willing to compromise for the Union

B. Missouri Compromise

1. Cotton gin made cotton growing very profitable in the 1800s

a. Slavery, which had been in decline, grew rapidly

b. Cotton became the main crop of the South and Southerners became very protective of slavery

2. North was growing in population, but the South was not

a. North controlled the House of Representatives

b. North and South were equal in the Senate

c. South saw the balance in the Senate as their protection

3. 1819, Missouri requested admission to the Union

a. Northern states wanted slavery ended there first

b. Southern states demanded that slavery be allowed to expand with the nation

4. Clay initiates a compromise

a. Missouri admitted as a slave state

b. Maine admitted as a free state

c. No slavery in any new states north of 36° 30', the southern border of Missouri

5. Kept the balance of power

C. Tariff issue

1. Agricultural South did not support tariffs that raised the price of manufactured goods

2. Since all sides avoided debating slavery, the tariff was the sectional issue of the era

D. Election of 1824

1. D-R still the only party, but had four sectional candidates

a. West, Henry Clay and Andrew Jackson

b. North, John Quincy Adams

c. South, William Crawford

2. Jackson had the largest popular vote, but did not get an electoral majority, went to the House

a. Clay supported Adams, who won

b. Adams named Clay Secretary of State

c. Jackson believed Clay's appointment proved corruption, and the D-R split

(1) National Republicans (Whigs) supported Adams

(2) Democrats supported Jackson

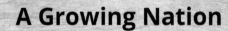

A Growing Nation

E. Adam's presidency unproductive

　1. Tariff of Abominations

　　a. Incredibly high tariff proposed by Democrats to embarrass Adams

　　b. Became law and made the South very angry

　2. Adams' foreign and domestic policy went nowhere

F. Election of 1828

　1. Jackson won

　2. Called the Jacksonian Revolution, end of the rule by the elite in America

　3. Adams, "Old Man Eloquent," served in the House with distinction

II. Jackson's First Administration

A. Spoils System

　1. Jackson was the president most associated with the spoils system, "To the victor go the spoils of the enemy." (jobs)

　2. He believed in rotation in office to reduce corruption

　3. In fact, he established a poor system that lasted for years

　　a. Jobs went to faithful party people, regardless of their ability

　　b. Result was corruption and poor quality in government

B. Eaton Scandal

　1. Secretary of War, John Eaton, had a wife, Peggy, with a poor moral reputation

　2. Washington society refused to associate with her

| President Andrew Jackson

　3. Jackson unwisely became her champion and tried to force her into society, with no success

　4. Discord split the cabinet until Martin Van Buren led them all to resign, ending the crisis (Van Buren was rewarded with the vice presidency)

C. Webster-Haynes Debate

　1. The nation had long debated over which had more power, the federal government or the states that created it

　2. Haynes and Webster debated the issue in relation to the tariff

　3. Haynes, a Southerner, argued that states could nullify federal laws

　4. Webster eloquently argued for the Union and was widely acclaimed for his speech

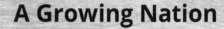

A Growing Nation

D. Jackson declared himself as a supporter of the union; Calhoun, his V. P., split with him to return to the Senate

E. The National Bank

1. Jackson had a distrust of banks

2. National Bank under Nicholas Biddle was very powerful and corrupt, but it did stabilize the national finances

3. Clay proposed rechartering the bank to make an election issue

   a. Jackson vetoed it

   b. Clay made it an issue in 1832 and the people supported Jackson

4. Jackson easily won re-election in 1832

III. The End of the Jacksonian Era

A. Nullification Crisis (1832)

1. South Carolina declared the tariff null and void in their state

2. Jackson prepared troops and denounced nullification

3. Clay brokered a compromise

   a. Tariff rates reduced gradually over the next ten years

   b. Nullification dropped (temporary)

B. Trail of Tears

1. Native Americans east of the Mississippi were forced to move West

2. Cherokee of Georgia fought removal in court and won, but Jackson refused to protect them

   a. Army moved them by force

   b. Trail of Tears, about four thousand died along the way

      3. American army defeated the tribes who refused to move

| The Oregon Boundary Dispute

4. The land they were given in the West was supposed to be theirs forever, but American settlers would soon want that too

C. National Bank

1. Jackson began moving money out of the National Bank into state "pet banks," owned by loyal supporters

2. Biddle reduced credit and created a depression (panic)

3. Jackson refused to budge and forced the bank to close

4. Rebound caused wild land speculation and banks printed money without any controls

5. *Specie Circular*, Jackson required land to be purchased with gold or silver, 1836

A Growing Nation

D. Election of 1836

  1. Jackson was so popular that he could choose his successor, Van Buren

  2. Van Buren won, inheriting all of Jackson's problems and enemies

     a. Land speculation widespread

     b. *Specie Circular* forced people to pay in coin, not on credit

     c. Sales and prices fell, part of the cause of the Panic of 1837

  3. Van Buren became unpopular and was ineffective as president

Manifest Destiny

I. Northern Border

   A. Whig candidate William Henry Harrison won in 1840

      1. Died after one month in office

      2. Vice president John Tyler became president

         a. Favored Democratic agenda

         b. Vetoed a new national bank, higher tariffs, and internal improvements

         c. Lost all support in Congress, whole cabinet resigned, except Secretary of State Webster

   B. Maine border dispute with Britain resolved by Webster-Ashburn Treaty, 1842

   C. Oregon claimed by both the U.S. and Britain

   D. "Fifty-four Forty or Fight"

      1. Oregon and Texas were issues in the election of 1844

      2. Democrat James K. Polk wanted all of Oregon and to annex Texas

      3. The Democrats wanted all of Oregon, up to 54° 40'

      4. Polk won the election, but accepted a British offer to divide Oregon at 49° in 1846

II. Texas and Polk

   A. Background

      1. Spain allowed some Americans to settle in Spanish Texas

      2. Mexico became independent in 1821, and settlement continued

      3. Tensions grew between American settlers and the unstable Mexican government

   B. Texas Revolution

      1. Santa Anna took over in Mexico as a dictator in 1835

      2. Texas rebelled, set up a government and called for U.S. volunteers, who quickly came

      3. Alamo, San Antonio

         a. Santa Anna brought in an army of 8,000 in 1836

         b. Texans held a mission/fort called the Alamo (183 men)

         c. Alamo held out for two weeks, inflicting heavy casualties on the Mexicans

         d. Defenders refused to surrender, all were killed

      4. Texans rallied and defeated Santa Anna at the Battle of San Jacinto, April, 1836

   C. Texas applied for admission to the Union in 1837

      1. Mexico threatened war if it was annexed

      2. Disagreements about slavery

A Growing Nation

3. Jackson stalled, Van Buren and Tyler did not act, Texas was a republic during those years

4. Polk made annexation a campaign issue in 1844 and Texas became a state in 1845

D. Mexico broke off relations with the U.S., tensions grew

1. Polk tried to negotiate the purchase of California with no success

2. Texans claimed border was at the Rio Grande River, Mexicans claim it was further north at Nueces River

3. Polk sent soldiers south of the Nueces in 1846 to provoke a war so he could get California

4. Mexicans attacked, Congress declared war, April, 1846

A Growing Nation

Complete these items.

2.152 Describe the spoils system and its effects.

_____

_____

2.153 Why did Jackson believe Adam's election in 1824 was corrupt?

_____

_____

2.154 Name the three parts of the Missouri Compromise.

_____

_____

2.155 What made slavery so profitable in the South in the 1800s?

_____

2.156 What was the Nullification Crisis of 1832 about and how was it resolved?

_____

_____

2.157 Describe the Trail of Tears.

_____

_____

HISTORY & GEOGRAPHY 810

LIFEPAC TEST

NAME _____

DATE _____

SCORE _____

$$\frac{80}{100}$$

HISTORY & GEOGRAPHY 810: LIFEPAC TEST

Put these events in chronological order (20 points, take off only one point for every event out of correct order).

1. _____ World War I
2. _____ French and Indian War
3. _____ Great Depression
4. _____ Progressive Era
5. _____ Persian Gulf War
6. _____ Roaring Twenties
7. _____ Civil War
8. _____ Henry Clay Era Begins
9. _____ Gilded Age
10. _____ Vietnam War

11. _____ Federalist Era
12. _____ Fall of Communism in Europe
13. _____ Battle of Saratoga
14. _____ Attack on Pearl Harbor
15. _____ Louisiana Purchase
16. _____ British burned Washington
17. _____ Korean War
18. _____ Founding of Plymouth colony
19. _____ Travels of Marco Polo
20. _____ Founding of St. Augustine, FL

Match these items (each answer, 1 point).

21. _____ America's first constitution
22. _____ U.S. gained California and the Southwest
23. _____ conflict between the U.S. and U.S.S.R. (1945-91)
24. _____ territories with enough people became states
25. _____ turning point of the Pacific War, WWII
26. _____ British response to the Boston Tea Party
27. _____ corrected by the Pendleton Act, civil service reform
28. _____ marked the U.S. becoming a world power
29. _____ turning point of the Civil War
30. _____ 3 branches of government: executive, legislative, judicial
31. _____ political party formed to stop the spread of slavery
32. _____ law that gave free land to settlers who lived on it
33. _____ Europe was not to meddle in America
34. _____ tax on documents, united the colonies in opposition
35. _____ put Medieval Europe in contact with Asian products
36. _____ French demanded a bribe to negotiate with the U.S.

a. Intolerable Acts
b. Republican
c. Stamp Act
d. Watergate
e. Mexican War
f. Articles of Confederation
g. Constitution
h. Nullification
i. Cold War
j. Spoils system
k. XYZ Affair
l. Crusades
m. Reconstruction
n. Spanish-American War

37. _____ scandal that forced President Nixon to resign
38. _____ states declared national laws invalid
39. _____ occupation of the South after the Civil War
40. _____ American spy plane was shot down over the U.S.S.R.

o. Homestead Act
p. Northwest Ordinance
q. Gettysburg
r. Midway
s. U-2 incident
t. Monroe Doctrine

Describe briefly the <u>historical importance</u> of the following (each answer, 2 points).

41. Kansas-Nebraska Act _____
42. Treaty of Versailles _____
43. *Common Sense* _____
44. Battle of Yorktown _____
45. New Deal _____
46. *Uncle Tom's Cabin* _____
47. Voyages of Columbus _____
48. Civil Rights Movement _____
49. Stock Market Crash of 1929 _____
50. Gulf of Tonkin Resolution _____

Name the president associated with the following (each answer, 2 points).

51. Revolutionary War leader, Whiskey Rebellion, Jay's Treaty, 1789-1797 _____
52. Rough Riders, Panama Canal, Square Deal, 1901-1909 _____
53. Great Society, Vietnam build up, experienced legislator, 1963-1969 _____
54. Fight with the National Bank, Battle of New Orleans, Peggy Eaton, 1829-1837 _____
55. Containment created, Korean War, Fair Deal, 1945-1953 _____
56 Emancipation Proclamation, assassinated, Gettysburg Address, 1861-1865 _____
57. Iran Hostage Crisis, end of Détente, Camp David Accords, 1977-1981 _____
58. 1st Sec. of State, Declaration of Independence, Embargo Act, 1801-1809 _____
59. Fourteen Points, World War I, Federal Reserve System, 1913-1921 _____
60. 1st Vice president, Alien and Sedition Acts, only Federalist president, 1797-1801

_____

61. Easy Reconstruction, 1st ever impeached, Lincoln's vice president, 1865-1869

_____

62 "Return to Normalcy," Teapot Dome Scandal, corrupt administration, 1921-1923

_____

63. Persian Gulf War, Savings and Loan Crisis, Soviet Union dissolved, 1989-1993

_____

64. Peace Corps, assassinated in Dallas, New Frontier, 1961-1963 _____

65. World War II, New Deal, elected to four terms, Good Neighbor Policy, 1933-1945

_____

Match these people (each answer, 1 point).

66. _____ founder of Rhode Island; religious freedom

67. _____ Civil Rights Movement leader

68. _____ general in WWII and Korea

69. _____ Soviet reformer

70. _____ WWI American general

71. _____ set up the new nation's finances; loose construction of the Constitution

72. _____ Democratic Congressman; favored free coinage of silver; Scopes Monkey Trial

73. _____ Quaker; founded Delaware and Pennsylvania

74. _____ Prince of Portugal; led the effort to reach Asia around Africa

75. _____ Union Civil War general; poor president

a. Douglas MacArthur

b. William J. Bryan

c. Henry the Navigator

d. William Penn

e. Ulysses S. Grant

f. Alexander Hamilton

g. Mikhail Gorbachev

h. Martin L. King

i. Roger Williams

j. John Pershing

Bonus!
On a separate sheet of paper, list the most recent presidents beginning with Grover Cleveland in chronological order (10 points maximum).

2.158 What happened to the national bank under Andrew Jackson?

_____

_____

2.159 What was the Tariff of Abominations?

_____

_____

2.160 What portion of Oregon did Polk say he wanted and what did he accept?

_____

_____

2.161 What happened at the Alamo in 1836?

_____

_____

2.162 What did Webster and Haynes debate?

_____

_____

2.163 How did Polk start a war with Mexico?

_____

_____

Match these items.

2.164 _____ battle that won Texas' independence

2.165 _____ Jackson's chosen successor, had to deal with the results of the anti-bank policies and the _Specie Circular_

2.166 _____ South Carolina representative, separated from Jackson over states' rights

2.167 _____ Kentucky representative; the Great Compromiser

2.168 _____ favored annexation of Texas and all of Oregon in the election of 1844

2.169 _____ his wife caused a scandal when Jackson tried to force society to accept her

2.170 _____ Massachusetts representative; favored the union; great orator

a. Henry Clay

b. Daniel Webster

c. John Calhoun

d. San Jacinto

e. John Eaton

f. James K. Polk

g. Martin Van Buren

III. The Mexican War

A. American army

1. Small professional army augmented with volunteers from all over the nation

2. The army officers trained at West Point were a superior group

3. Training ground for the Civil War

B. California and New Mexico were quickly captured by the Americans

C. Northern Mexico Campaign

1. Made Zachary Taylor a hero

2. Series of victories in Texas and Mexico

D. Mexico City Campaign

1. Winfield Scott commanded

2. In 1847, led a bold campaign that captured the Mexican capital

E. Treaty of Guadalupe Hidalgo

1. Ended the war

2. U.S. given California and all the land north of the Gila River, Arizona between California and Texas

3. America paid $15 million and assumed Mexican debts to American citizens

F. California Gold Rush

1. Gold discovered in 1848

2. Thousands swarm to the territory

3. Population grew so fast it applied for statehood in 1849

G. Election of 1848

1. Whigs and Democrats avoided the topic of slavery

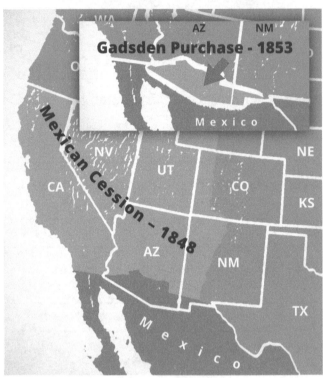

| The Mexican Cession and Gadsden Purchase

2. New Free Soil Party came out against slavery in the territories

3. Popular general Zachary Taylor won the election

H. Gadsden Purchase, southern AZ and NM

1. Land purchased from Mexico in 1853 for a railroad route to California

2. Completed the land of the 48 continental United States Growth and Division

Growth and Division

I. The Industrial Revolution

A. A change from agriculture and handcrafts to industry and machine manufacturing

1. Began in Britain in the 1700s

2. Began in America, War of 1812

A Growing Nation

B. Textiles, first major industry

1. Machines to spin thread and weave cloth invented in Britain

2. Samuel Slater learned how to build the machines and came to the U.S.

    a. Father of the Factory System

    b. Built the first American factory to spin thread in 1791

3. New factories cashed in on the production of cheap cotton due to the cotton gin

4. The sewing machine was invented in 1846

5. Most factories in the Northeast

    a. Large population with poor soil for agriculture

    b. Shipping industry to bring in materials and export finished goods

    c. Shipping industry owners had money to invest (West-poor pioneers; Southern money in land and slaves)

    d. Swift rivers for power

C. Mass production of interchangeable parts developed by Eli Whitney for making guns

1. Allowed uniform goods to be built quickly and cheaply

2. Repairs were simplified

3. Brought down prices

D. Factory workers were often shamefully exploited

E. Farming Improvements

1. Steel plow invented by John Deere, 1837

2. Mechanical reaper by Cyrus McCormick in 1830s

3. Farmers produced more food than they needed and sold it for a profit, feeding city workers

F. Communication

1. Telegraph invented by Samuel Morse, 1844

2. Telegraph cable laid across the Atlantic in 1866

G. Roads, poor in 1700s, dirt trails

1. Turnpikes, better roads with hard surfaces, privately owned, 1800s

2. Cumberland Road, the National Road, built with public money from Maryland to Illinois (finished 1852)

3. States gradually financed hard surface roads

H. Steamboat

1. Invented by Robert Fulton in 1807

2. Made rivers into two-way highways

3. Trade flourished on the Mississippi

4. Supreme Court ruled that states could not control interstate river trade, allowed free competition

I. Canals

1. Erie Canal opened, 1825

    a. Connected Lake Erie with the Hudson River

    b. Provided a safe, cheap shipping route from the Great Lakes to the Atlantic

    c. Made New York City into a major port

2. Many successful canals built in the following years

A Growing Nation

J. Railroads replaced canals

1. Carried bulk cargo anywhere tracks could be laid

2. First American steam railroad service began in 1830

3. 30,000 miles of track laid by 1860

4. Linked the Midwest farmers with the Eastern cities

II. Changing American Life

A. Immigration

1. Helped to build population

2. U.S. fourth most populous nation on Earth by 1860

3. Irish, major group in the 1800s

a. Came in 1845-47 to escape the potato famine in Ireland

b. Too poor to move West, stayed in Eastern cities

4. Germans–prosperous group came in high numbers to avoid upheavals in Europe

B. Second Great Awakening

1. Revival from about 1790-1830

2. Baptist and Methodist churches grew substantially

3. Emphasis on personal salvation and the Bible

C. Mormons

1. A distortion of Christianity created by Joseph Smith in the 1830s

2. Practiced polygamy, distrusted and driven out of the East

3. Brigham Young led them to Utah

| The Underground Railroad

4. Eventually gave up polygamy to gain statehood for Utah in 1896

D. Many reform movements came after the revival

1. Education, prison, temperance

2. Largest group, the anti-slavery (abolitionist) movement

a. Slavery ended in Britain, 1833

b. Encouraged U.S. movement

c. Grew rapidly in the North after the 1830s

d. South reacted with fear

III. The Great Divide

A. Last Compromise

1. California requested admission in 1849 as a free state

2. Slave and Free states equal in the Senate

3. South fought losing that balance

A Growing Nation

4. Clay brokered a last compromise

    a. Calhoun opposed it but died in the middle of the debate

    b. Webster supported it for the sake of the Union

5. Compromise of 1850

    a. California admitted as a free state

    b. Slavery could not be barred in the rest of the Mexican Cession, those states would choose for themselves

    c. Fugitive Slave Act

B. Fugitive Slave Act

1. Underground Railroad helped slaves escape to Canada

2. Few slaves escaped this way but it angered Southern slave owners

3. Harsh law

    a. Captured black person could not testify or post bail

    b. No jury

    c. Fines and prison for those who helped slaves escape

    d. Federal officials forced to act as slave catchers

4. Inflamed, the North as black people were dragged back to slavery and people who helped them were put in prison

5. Mobs freed captured slaves and states refused to follow the law

C. Election of 1852

1. Whigs divided on slavery and the Compromise

2. Pro-South Northern Democrat, Franklin Pierce elected

D. *Uncle Tom's Cabin,* Harriet B. Stowe

1. One of the most influential books in history, published in 1852

2. Novel that portrayed slavery from stories in abolitionist files

3. Sold millions of copies, made into a popular stage play

4. Inflamed the North against slavery

E. Kansas-Nebraska Act, 1854

1. Ended the era of compromise

2. Stephen Douglas proposed to organize Kansas and Nebraska with popular sovereignty (choose for themselves) on slavery

    a. Those lands were north of the Missouri Compromise line

    b. For personal reasons, Douglas forced the law through and Pierce signed it

3. Huge outcry in the North, violation of long-standing agreement to limit slavery

    a. Fugitive Slave Law a dead law in much of the North

    b. Further compromises would not be trusted

F. Republican Party, 1854

1. Whig party broken over slavery

2. Remains of Northern Whigs formed the Republican Party that opposed the spread of slavery

3. Quickly became a major party in the North

4. Political unity of former Whigs and Democrats who avoided discussing slavery was gone, slavery now was the topic

A Growing Nation

Name the person or item.

2.171 _____ law that ended the era of compromise by giving popular sovereignty to land north of the Missouri Compromise line

2.172 _____ admitted California as a free state and gave the South a Fugitive Slave law

2.173 _____ political party that opposed the spread of slavery, quickly became a major party in the North in 1854

2.174 _____ Robert Fulton's invention that made two-way trade possible on rivers

2.175 _____ American war hero in north Mexico; elected president in 1848

2.176 _____ invention that replaced canals; linked the Midwest with the East

2.177 _____ treaty gave California and the Southwest to the U.S.

2.178 _____ reason California's population grew so fast after 1848

2.179 _____ the revolution from agriculture and handcrafts to industry and machine manufacturing

2.180 _____ revival in 1790-1830; Baptists and Methodists grew

2.181 _____ inventor of the telegraph

2.182 _____ business in the Northeast that provided money and transport for the Industrial Revolution there

2.183 _____ religion created by Joseph Smith; practiced polygamy; people moved to Utah

2.184 _____ invention of Cyrus McCormick

2.185 _____ major reform movement grew rapidly in the North from the 1830s; encouraged by success in Britain

2.186 _____ law that inflamed the North because it dragged free black people back to slavery and imprisoned those who aided them

2.187 _____ best-selling novel that portrayed the evils of slavery

2.188 _____ U.S. general; brilliant campaign against Mexico City

2.189 _____ invented interchangeable parts and mass production

2.190 _____ most successful canal; allowed shipping from the Great Lakes to the Atlantic Ocean

2.191 _____ immigrant group; escaped a potato famine in 1845-47

2.192 _____ inventor of the steel plow

2.193 _____ land purchased from Mexico to make southern Arizona and New Mexico completed the 48 contiguous states

2.194 _____ brought British thread spinning technology to the U.S. and started the first factory using it

2.195 _____ Cumberland Road was built with federal money, but most roads built in the 1800s were privately or state financed

2.196 _____ first industry developed in the Industrial Revolution

Review the material in this section in preparation for the Self Test. The Self Test will check your mastery of this particular section as well as your knowledge of the previous section.

SELF TEST 2

Match these items (each answer, 2 points).

2.01 _____ sparked European interest in the Far East

2.02 _____ slavery was forbidden north of Missouri; Missouri and Maine admitted to the union

2.03 _____ port of Boston closed; city under military rule; a reaction to the Boston Tea Party

2.04 _____ revival in colonial America; Whitefield

2.05 _____ Napoleonic wars in Europe; Washington burned; British impressing U.S. sailors

2.06 _____ lacking in the Constitution; added by the first 10 amendments

2.07 _____ began the Revolutionary War

2.08 _____ made New York City a major port; joined the Great Lakes to the Atlantic

2.09 _____ Santa Anna defeated; the Alamo

2.010 _____ pamphlet by Paine that convinced Americans to seek independence

2.011 _____ French officials demanded a bribe to negotiate; set off anti-French war hysteria

2.012 _____ first constitution; government could not collect taxes; Northwest Ordinance

2.013 _____ novel by Harriet B. Stowe inflamed the North against slavery

2.014 _____ last compromise; California admitted free state; Fugitive Slave Law

2.015 _____ France lost Canada; Britain world power

2.016 _____ Polk started war to get California; Zachary Taylor a hero; training for the Civil War

2.017 _____ turning point of the Revolutionary War; Burgoyne surrendered an army

2.018 _____ political party that set up the institutions of our government; loose construction

2.019 _____ navigation Acts; policy that colonies were to benefit Britain

2.020 _____ ended the Revolution; Cornwallis defeated

2.021 _____ land sold to U.S. by Napoleon for 3¢ an acre; explored by Lewis and Clark

2.022 _____ five who threw debris at British troops killed in 1770

2.023 _____ forbade colonists from settling west of the Appalachians

2.024 _____ party formed 1854; opposed the spread of slavery

2.025 _____ first direct tax on colonies; reaction: mobs, boycott, congress

a.   Crusades; Marco Polo's book

b.   Erie Canal

c.   *Uncle Tom's Cabin*

d.   Compromise of 1850

e.   XYZ Affair

f.   Louisiana Purchase

g.   Republican

h.   Texas Revolution

i.   Stamp Act

j.   War of 1812

k.   Proclamation of 1763

l.   Mercantilism

m.   Great Awakening

n.   French and Indian War

o.   Mexican War

p.   Missouri Compromise

q.   Boston Massacre

r.   Intolerable Acts

s.   Lexington

t.   Saratoga

u.   *Common Sense*

v.   Articles of Confederation

w.   Federalists

x.   Yorktown

y.   Bill of Rights

Match these people (each answer, 1 point).

2.026 _____ revolutionary hero (Saratoga); traitor

2.027 _____ New Orleans; president; closed the National
Bank; spoils system; followers formed the
Democratic Party

2.028 _____ wanted all of Oregon; split it with Britain;
got California by a war

2.029 _____ explored Northern Canada for the English and
New York for the Netherlands

2.030 _____ author—Declaration of Independence;
Embargo Act, Democratic-Republican Party

2.031 _____ Tippecanoe, president—died after one month

2.032 _____ Great Compromiser; began as a War Hawk

2.033 _____ victorious general—Revolution; led Constitution
Convention; got all electoral votes-presidency

2.034 _____ invented the steamboat

2.035 _____ led campaign to clear South Carolina; Revolution

2.036 _____ won presidency with Clay's support; followers
Whigs; served in the House after presidency

2.037 _____ creator of Mormon religion

2.038 _____ stabilized finances for new U.S.; bonds paid in full;
national bank; Federalist leader

2.039 _____ Alien and Sedition Acts; lost popularity—refused
to go to war with France; last Federalist president

2.040 _____ Supreme Court Chief; built government power

2.041 _____ found the Americas by sailing west to reach Asia;
explored the Caribbean and Central American coast

2.042 _____ found the Grand Banks exploring the Canadian coast
for England

2.043 _____ organized the search for an all-water route to Asia

a. George Washington

b. Thomas Jefferson

c. Benedict Arnold

d. Nathanael Greene

e. Alexander Hamilton

f. John Adams

g. William H. Harrison

h. Andrew Jackson

i. John Marshall

j. Henry Clay

k. Robert Fulton

l. Joseph Smith

m. John Quincy Adams

n. James K. Polk

o. Columbus

p. Prince Henry

q. Henry Hudson

r. John Cabot

Name the colony, country, or section (each answer, 2 points).

2.044 _____ colony founded by wealthy Puritans; only church members could vote; exiled dissidents started many new colonies

2.045 _____ founded as a place for debtors; a buffer between Spanish and British America; last of the original 13 colonies

2.046 _____ nation that first explored the St. Lawrence; Great Lakes and Mississippi River

2.047 _____ nation of Coronado; Balboa; Ponce de Leon, and De Soto

2.048 _____ American ally during the Revolution; signed Convention of 1800; had the best relations with the Native Americans of all the European powers

2.049 _____ nation that settled Roanoke; signed Jay's Treaty; lost the battles of New Orleans, Plattsburgh, and Baltimore in the War of 1812

2.050 _____ House of Burgesses; headright gave settlers land; first successful English colony thanks to tobacco

2.051 _____ colony first settled by the Dutch on the Hudson River; given to the brother of Charles II of England in the 1660s

2.052 _____ colony founded by Roger Williams; first to grant full religious freedom, did not attend the Constitutional Convention

2.053 _____ Quaker holy experiment colony; religious freedom; paid the Native Americans for their land; owned by the same family until the Revolution

2.054 _____ section of the U.S. that protected slavery to grow cotton; opposed tariffs; home of John C. Calhoun

2.055 _____ colony founded by the Calvert family as a refuge for Catholics; Toleration Act-religious freedom for all who believe in the Trinity

2.056 _____ colony founded by Separatists fleeing persecution; created a government under the Mayflower Compact

Answer these questions (each answer, 2 points).

2.057 What was so important about the Kansas-Nebraska Act?

_____

_____

_____

2.058 What were two advantages the Americans had in the Revolutionary War?

_____

_____

_____

2.059 What was the Industrial Revolution?

_____

_____

_____

80 / 100   SCORE _____   TEACHER _____ _____
                                              initials   date

3. CIVIL WAR TO END OF COLD WAR

This section of the LIFEPAC will review American history after about 1855. Those years saw the division of the nation, a civil war, the growth of industrial power, reforms, world wars, a large depression, a cold war, and social upheaval. This outline will review the key concepts and events of this time period for you.

SECTION OBJECTIVES

Review these objectives. When you have completed this section, you should be able to:

5. Match the presidents with the events of their administration.

6. Describe the wars and major events of U.S. history.

7. Describe important trends in ideas and conflicts in U.S. history.

8. Describe how and when America acquired new territories.

9. Place major American historical events in chronological order.

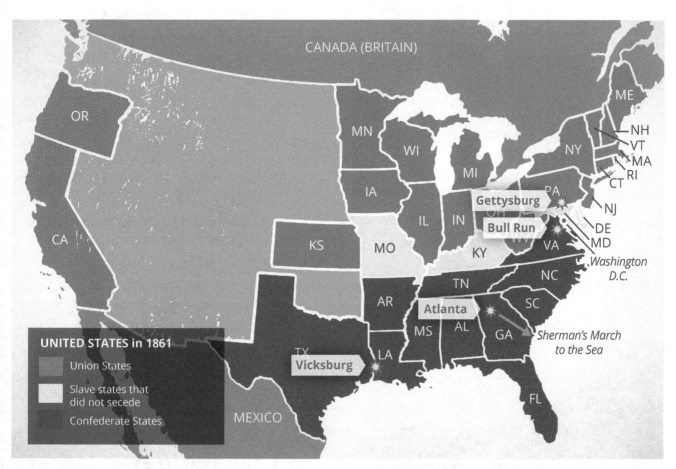

| America during the Civil War

Increasing Disunion

I. Division and Violence

    A. South, different from the North

        1. Aristocratic, class system supported by slavery

        2. Little manufacturing

        3. Felt threatened by abolitionist movement which developed in the 1830s

    B. Bleeding Kansas

        1. Northern and Southern settlers moved in and fought for control

        2. Admitted as a free state after the war began in 1861

    C. Charles Sumner, an abolitionist, was beaten on the Senate floor by a Southern Congressman, 1856

    D. Democrat James Buchanan was elected president in 1856

        1. Lacked convictions on the issues

        2. Pro-Southern

    E. *Dred Scott* Decision

        1. Test case by abolitionists

        2. Tried to free a slave who had lived with his master in the North

        3. Ruling: slave is property protected by the constitution

        4. Effect

            a. Slavery could not be barred anywhere in U.S.

            b. All compromises that limited slavery were unconstitutional

            c. North vows to defy it, South alarmed

    F. Lincoln-Douglas Debates, 1858

        1. Debates between candidates for Senator from Illinois

        2. Douglas supported popular sovereignty

        3. Lincoln said slavery was wrong and should not spread

        4. Debates printed in newspapers all over the nation

        5. Douglas won; but Lincoln became a national figure

    G. Harper's Ferry Raid, 1859

        1. John Brown tried to start a slave rebellion in the South with violence

        2. Attacked the Harper's Ferry arsenal

        3. Captured, tried, and hung

        4. Became an abolitionist martyr

    H. Election of 1860

        1. Democrats finally split over slavery: two candidates

        2. Republicans win with Lincoln

II. Secession

    A. South seceded

        1. Believed a Republican president would destroy their culture

        2. Seven states seceded before Lincoln's inauguration

        3. Formed the Confederate States, Jefferson Davis, president

    B. Fort Sumter, April 12, 1861

        1. Lincoln tried to send provisions to federal Fort Sumter in Charleston harbor, South Carolina

        2. Rebels fired on the fort, beginning the Civil War

        3. Lincoln called for volunteers and ordered a blockade

The Civil War

4. Four more states seceded

III. Facing Off

A. Northern Advantages

1. Money, resources, and industry

2. Larger population

3. Navy for blockade and trade

4. Black soldiers

5. Strong, established government with a solid taxation system

B. Southern Advantages

1. Had only to survive to win

2. Fighting for their homes

3. Higher quality army officers

Civil War

I. Bull Run to Fredericksburg (1861-62)

A. First Bull Run, July, 1861

1. Lincoln pressed for battle before the troops were ready

2. Union defeated

3. Hope of a quick war gone

B. McClellan in charge, Union army

1. Excellent organizer and trainer

2. Built an effective, professional army

3. Cowardly, cautious

C. Forts Henry and Donelson on the Tennessee and Cumberland Rivers taken by Ulysses S. Grant, February, 1862

1. Made Grant a hero

2. Union then took Nashville

D. Shiloh, April, 1862

1. Grant caught by surprise

2. Bloody, two-day battle

3. Union held with heavy losses

4. Bloodshed shocked the nation, Lincoln refused to fire Grant

E. New Orleans and Baton Rouge were taken in a sea battle by Admiral David Farragut, April, 1862

1. Union secured the northern part of the Mississippi by summer

2. Only Vicksburg left in Confederate hands on the river

F. Battle of the Ironclads

1. Confederacy built an iron-plated ship, the *Merrimac*, to break the Union blockade

2. Union ships could not sink it

3. Met by a Union ironclad, the *Monitor*, March, 1862

4. Neither able to damage the other, Union blockade held

G. Peninsular Campaign, 1862

1. McClellan had the army brought to Virginia by sea

2. Confederate commander, Robert

3. Union army retreated to the sea

4. McClellan refused to fight any more

5. Lincoln ordered the army brought back to Washington

H. Second Bull Run, August, 1862

1. Second Union army advanced overland toward Richmond (Confederate capital)

2. Lee and Jackson routed them

3. Summer of 1862 established Lee's reputation as the best general of the war

I. Antietam, September, 1862

The Civil War

1. Offensive by Lee into Maryland

2. Battle a draw, but Lee retreated

J. Emancipation Proclamation

1. Issued by Lincoln after the Union "victory" at Antietam

2. Freed all slaves in rebel states (but many people did not comply)

3. Gave the war a moral goal

4. Blocked British intervention

K. Fredericksburg, December, 1862

1. New Union general, Burnside, attacked entrenched Confederate positions

2. Union troops slaughtered, retreat

L. Murfreesburo-bloody, inconclusive battle in Tennessee, kept Union army off the field for six months

M. Vicksburg–besieged by Grant and surrendered July 4, 1863

N. Chancellorsville–Lee's great victory

1. Defeated much larger Union army under Hooker

2. Lee's brilliant subordinate Gen. Stonewall Jackson was killed

O. Gettysburg–July 1-3, 1863

1. Lee advanced into Pennsylvania

2. Union in defensive positions,

3. Confederates take heavy losses

4. Picketts's charge, last attempt by Lee to overrun the Union

5. Lee retreated

6. Gettysburg Address, by Lincoln

| Union soldiers operating a cannon

a. His most famous speech

b. Two minute speech, stated the essential purposes of the war

P. The armies

1. Poor medical care

2. South always short of supplies, North was well-supplied

3. Both sides conscript soldiers, but men could hire substitutes–made it a "rich man's war, but a poor man's fight."

4. Prison camps poorly run, high death rates, particularly in the South (Andersonville, the worst)

5. Religious revivals on both sides

Q. Chickamauga (Tennessee)–last major Confederate victory, September, 1863

R. Victorious Confederates besieged Union-held Chattanooga

The Civil War

1. Grant put in command of the Union army in the West

2. Relieved the siege of Chattanooga, gave the Union control in the West

II. Wilderness to Ford's Theater (1864-65)

A. Wilderness, May, 1964, inconclusive

   1. Grant put in supreme command of Union Army, marched into Virginia

   2. Lee attacked in heavy woods where Union size no advantage

   3. Heavy losses, but Grant picked up and kept attacking

B. Grant kept moving left, fighting battles and forcing Lee's army to its knees

C. Besieged Petersburg, rail center for Richmond, June, 1864

D. Sherman captured Atlanta, Georgia in August, 1864

E. Union General Sheridan razed the Shenandoah Valley in Virginia

F. Admiral Farragut captured the port of Mobile, Alabama in August, 1864

G. Lincoln re-elected in 1864, with Andrew Johnson, a pro-Union Southern Democrat as vice president

H. Last of the Confederate army in the West defeated at Nashville in December

I. Sherman burned Atlanta and marched to the sea, destroying all valuable things in his way

   1. Resupplied by the U.S. fleet, he captured Savannah, Georgia

   2. Captured Charleston, South Carolina, the last major Confederate port

      J. Petersburg captured, April 1865, Lee

retreated, Confederates abandoned Richmond

K. Appomattox Courthouse

   1. Grant pursued and cornered Lee

   2. Lee surrendered and received gracious terms on April 12, 1865

L. Lincoln assassinated at Ford's Theatre on April 15th

M. On June 19th, 1865, the remaining enslaved black people were freed in Texas (since not all states complied to Emancipation); Juneteenth

Reconstruction

I. Presidential Reconstruction

A. Johnson used Lincoln's plan to readmit Confederate States

   1. 10% must take loyalty oath

   2. Then vote for convention to set up new government

   3. Must accept 13th Amendment (ended slavery), repudiate debts, and repeal secession

   4. South quickly complied

B. Congress opposed the easy terms

   1. Southern Black Codes made black people live like slaves again

   2. Several high-ranking Confederates elected to Congress

   3. Led by Thaddeus Stevens, the "Radical Republicans" refused to allow the Southern congressmen to take their seats

   4. Passed a Civil Rights Bill over Johnson's veto and the 14th Amendment (protected citizenship)

   5. Relations between the president and Congress deteriorate

The Civil War

6. Republicans got veto-proof majority in 1866 elections

II. Radical Reconstruction under Congress
   A. Occupation
      1. South divided into five military districts
      2. States had to ratify the 14th Amendment and give black people the right to vote; Republicans came to power in the South
      3. 15th Amendment protecting the right to vote, ratified in 1870
   B. Impeachment
      1. Tenure in Office Act–forbade the president to dismiss officials approved by the Senate
      2. Johnson violated it and the House voted to impeach him (bring to trial)
      3. Acquitted in the Senate by one vote
   C. Carpetbaggers (Northerners in the South) and Scalawags (Southerners who cooperated with the new government) ran the South
      1. Many were corrupt, as was government all over the U.S.
      2. Did reform Southern tax, school and transportation
      3. Hated in the South, especially because black people voted and took office
   D. Redeemers, used violence to regain white Democratic control
      1. Attacked black people who exercised their rights, Northerners and teachers for the Freedmen
      2. Drove the Republicans out of the South by 1877

3. South stayed Democratic for years
E. Situation in the South
   1. Due to lack of cash, most land-owners use "share crop" system, black people worked the land and paid with part of the crop
   2. Black people were separated and denied the right to vote, kept as lower class citizens until the 1960s
F. Johnson's Secretary of State, Seward, purchased Alaska in 1867
   1. Ridiculed as "Seward's Folly"
   2. Rich in resources

III. Era of Good Stealing
   A. Ulysses S. Grant, who favored Radical Reconstruction, was elected president in 1868
      1. Among the nation's worst presidents with a very corrupt administration
      2. He was honest, but easily misled
   B. Black Friday–two financiers tried to corner the gold market
      1. Bribe paid to Grant's brother-in-law to keep U.S. gold from being sold to stabilize the market
      2. Grant did not cooperate and the scheme collapsed
      3. Investigation did not implicate the president
   C. Crédit Mobilier
      1. Charged huge amounts to build transcontinental railroad
      2. Stock given to Congressmen and the vice president
      3. Brought calls for reform

The Civil War

D. Grant re-elected in 1872, but Republicans forced to make some reforms

E. Panic of 1873 lasted six years and was worsened by Grant's hard money policies (money given a set value in gold or silver)

F. Whiskey Ring, scandal

　1. Some of Grant's friends in office were taking bribes to cut the whiskey tax for some producers

　2. Grant interfered with investigation; helped the acquittal of one friend

G. Secretary of War impeached in 1876 for taking bribes on awarding contracts

IV. End of Reconstruction

　A. Election of 1876

　　1. Republican Rutherford B. Hayes, Democrat Samuel Tilden

　　2. Tilden won the popular vote; electoral votes were disputed

　　4. Commission with a majority of Republicans awarded all the disputed votes to Hayes

　　5. Democrats threatened a filibuster or a revolt

　B. Compromise of 1877

　　1. Hayes became president

　　2. Ended reconstruction

　　3. Hayes named the winner just three days before his inauguration

　C. Hayes administration

　　1. Favored civil service reform to control the spoils system, Congress refused

　　2. Appointed honest, capable men

　　3. Hard money policy built confidence in the economy

　D. Conclusion–Civil War settled the issues of slavery and secession, but civil rights for black people would not come for almost a hundred years

The Civil War

 Name the battle, person, or event.

3.1	_____	event that prompted the first seven states to secede
3.2	_____	event that prompted four more states to secede
3.3	_____	under Johnson's reconstruction plan the percent of the population that had to take a loyalty oath before a new government could be set up
3.4	_____	Amendment that protected the citizenship of Freedmen
3.5	_____	group that used violence to restore white Democratic control of the South
3.6	_____	document that freed the slaves in the rebel states
3.7	_____	Abolitionist martyr; Harper's Ferry Raid

3.8 _____ one of the worst presidents in U.S. history due to scandals like Crédit Mobilier

3.9 _____ court decision that protected slavery in all the U.S.

3.10 _____ law that was used to impeach President Johnson

3.11 _____ Amendment the Southern states had to ratify under Radical Reconstruction

3.12 _____ made Lincoln a national figure

3.13 _____ Seward's Folly

3.14 _____ state in which Northern and Southern settlers fought for control

3.15 _____ the Northerners and Southerners who ran the South during Reconstruction

3.16 _____ attempt to corner the gold market under Grant

3.17 _____ Amendment that ended slavery

3.18 _____ terms of the compromise of 1877

3.19 _____ policy that paper money is given a value in gold or silver

3.20 _____ laws in the South that made Freedmen practically slaves again

3.21 _____ Amendment that supposedly protected Freedmen's voting rights

3.22 _____ scandal involving bribes to avoid paying the whiskey tax

3.23 _____ Abolitionist beaten by a Southern Congressman in the Senate

3.24 _____ an option for a rich man who was conscripted and didn't want a fight

3.25 _____ hero of Forts Henry and Donelson who almost lost his command over Shiloh

3.26 _____ method of working the land in the South after the Civil War

3.27 _____ movement that frightened the South, grew beginning in the 1830s

✏️ Put an *S* by the Southern victories, people, advantages, or events and an *N* by the ones for the North.

3.28 _____ Gettysburg

3.29 _____ First Bull Run

3.30 _____ David Farragut

3.31 _____ Robert E. Lee

3.32 _____ Fredericksburg

3.33 _____ results of Pickett's charge

3.34 _____ Petersburg

3.35 _____ had more money

3.36 _____ Peninsular Campaign

3.37 _____ Merrimac

3.38 _____ Hooker

3.39 _____ had only to survive to win

3.40 _____ Chickamauga

3.41 _____ Jefferson Davis

3.42 _____ Vicksburg

3.43 _____ McClellan

3.44 _____ Stonewall Jackson

3.45 _____ Chancellorsville

3.46 _____ had better officers

3.47 _____ had larger population

3.48 _____ Chattanooga

3.49 _____ Baton Rouge

3.50 _____ Burnside

3.51 _____ Appomattox Courthouse

3.52 _____ Ulysses S. Grant

3.53 _____ Sherman's march to the sea

The Gilded Age

I. Rise of Industry

   A. Railroads were the first of the new, huge corporations

      1. Allowed trade all over the U.S.

      2. Transcontinental railroad

         a. Completed in 1869 at Promontory Point, Utah

         b. Five routes finished by 1900

      3. Corporations were given large grants of land and money to lay rails, results: wealth, corruption

      4. Gave rebates to large shippers and did not have uniform rates

      5. Farmers were hurt by lack of control over transporting crops

   B. Steel–Bessemer process made inexpensive steel available in 1850s

      1. U.S. was a major producer by 1900

      2. Andrew Carnegie's corporation

         a. Produced 1/4 the nation's steel by 1900

         b. Sold it to banker J.P. Morgan who created the first billion dollar company, U.S. Steel

   C. Standard Oil

      1. Owned by John D. Rockefeller

      2. Practiced ruthless competition

      3. Trust that controlled more than 90% of oil production and sales in the U.S.

      4. Other monopolies copied it

Gilded Age to Progressive Era

II. Workers

   A. Immigration

      1. America offered the chance for work and freedom attracting people from all over the world

      2. 5 million people came to U.S. in 1880s

      3. Prior to 1880s, most immigrants came from Northern Europe

   B. New Immigration, after 1880

      1. Came from Southern Europe

      2. Arrived poor with different languages and physical appearances, less education, non-Protestant

   C. Conditions

      1. Low wages, no job protection, seldom complained

      2. City slums were squalid, unhealthy

      3. Cities controlled by corrupt bosses, provided services for votes

   D. Restrictions grew due to prejudice against the new immigrants

   E. Labor Movement

      1. Owners opposed unions by firing those who joined, using force and political power to stop them

      2. Public did not trust unions

      3. Knights of Labor, first national union, organized in 1869

         a. Terence Powderly led it to its high point 1880s

         b. Wanted many social reforms

         c. Lost support after the Haymarket Riot of 1886

      4. American Federation of Labor

| A luxurious mansion built during the Gilded Age

         a. Concentrated on only labor issues like wages and hours

         b. Led by Samuel Gompers (1886-1924)

         c. Biggest demand–the right to organize and strike

III. Gilded Society

   A. Gilded Age named for the glitter on the surface, corruption underneath

   B. Social Darwinism–the rich were rich because they were better workers

      1. Based on Darwin's theories

      2. Impeded reforms because the poor "deserved to be poor"

   C. New Rich

      1. New industries created great wealth for the owners

      2. Wealthy spent on expensive clothes, homes, and philanthropy

Gilded Age to Progressive Era

D. American Life

1. Most ordinary people had more money to spend as well

2. City services improved and entertainment expanded

3. Spectator and participation sports grew more popular

E. Inventions improved life

1. Business machines

2. Electric street cars

3. Refrigeration and canning

4. Kodak camera

5. Thomas Edison, greatest inventor of the era (light bulb)

IV. Wild West, settling of the Great Plains

A. Plains Indians, nomadic, warlike

1. Forced onto reservations by a series of wars, 1865-1890

2. Lost due to repeating rifles, destruction of the buffalo, army mobility, and European diseases

3. Little Big Horn–Colonel George Custer and his men massacred

4. Chief Joseph and the Nez Perce people refused to go to a reservation, skillful retreat toward Canada, finally cornered, surrendered

5. Geronimo (Apache)–raided U.S. settlements for years

6. *Century of Dishonor*–book that detailed the genocide and fraud against Native Americans

7. Dawes Act gave Native Americans land and citizenship, but ignored their culture

| The U.S. Army in Cuba during the Spanish-American War

B. Miners led settlement in the barren West, they were followed by corporations and settlers

C. Cattle Drives

1. Cattle raised on open range

2. Driven to railroad junctions for shipment east to the cities

3. Made cowboys part of the American folklore

4. Ended by 1890

D. Homestead Act of 1862

1. Gave 160 acres of land to anyone who lived on it for five years

2. Railroad brought in settlers

3. Frontier gone by 1890

4. High costs for new equipment and shipping crops hurt farmers who organized the Granges to improve farming conditions

Gilded Age to Progressive Era

Gilded Politics

I. Garfield to First Cleveland

   A. No party dominated 1880-1900

   B. Corrupt party bosses faced off with reformers

   C. Republican James Garfield won in 1880, but was assassinated in 1881 by a disgruntled office seeker

   D. New president Chester A. Arthur was a protegé of a party boss

      1. Assassination caused a public outcry for civil service reform

      2. Pendleton Act–merit system for federal jobs–passed

      3. Arthur used it to move federal jobs out of the spoils system

      4. By 1940s, 90% of federal jobs were on the merit system

   E. Grover Cleveland elected in 1884

      1. Honest reformer

      2. Did not give Democrats the spoils jobs they wanted but gave enough to anger reformers

      3. Currency issue, Grange wanted inflationary paper money and silver coins to help farm prices

      4. Pushed for regulation of railroads

      5. Interstate Commerce Act, 1887, passed to regulate the railroads, not very effective at first

      6. High tariffs brought in more money than needed, Cleveland tried to reduce the tariff

II. Harrison to McKinley

   A. Benjamin Harrison, Republican, elected in 1888 over tariff issue

      1. Business made huge donations to Republican party to protect the tariff

      2. Billion Dollar Congress, spent the huge surplus

      3. Sherman Anti-Trust Act passed to appease public opinion about monopolies, but was not enforced

      4. McKinley Tariff raised the rates

   B. Populist Revolt

      1. Populist Party formed in 1892

      2. Wanted: free coinage of silver (inflation), income tax, government ownership of railroads, eight hour day

   C. People, angry over the Republican spending and tariff, re-elected Cleveland in 1892

      1. Depression hit the nation

      2. Repealed silver coinage, the issue of the poorer classes

      3. Sent the army to break up Pullman Strike in 1894

   D. Reformers angry over government support of business interests

   E. William Jennings Bryan won Democratic nomination with the "Cross of Gold" speech favoring silver coinage in 1896

   F. Republicans nominated William McKinley and raised millions for his election, with the threat of financial chaos under Bryan, McKinley won

      1. Favored business, did not regulate trusts or railroads

      2. Raised the tariff

Gilded Age to Progressive Era

3. Tied U.S. currency to gold

III. America Becomes a World Power

A. America had become an industrial power and was looking to expand her power in the world by the 1890s

B. Cuba revolted against Spain in 1895

1. American opinion favored Cuba

2. Press sensationalized the war

3. U.S. battleship *Maine* sent to Havana to protect Americans

    a. Explodes on February 15, 1898

    b. Americans blamed Spain

    c. U.S. declared war April 25th

C. Spanish-American War

1. Commodore George Dewey destroyed the Spanish fleet in Manila, Philippines; islands occupied at the end of the war

2. Volunteers filled out the army

    a. Theodore Roosevelt led the volunteer "Rough Riders"

    b. Army sent to take Santiago

    c. City surrendered in July

    d. Roosevelt became a hero

3. Spanish fleet at Santiago destroyed in July

4. Armistice signed August 12th

5. Less than 400 battle deaths, many more died of diseases

D. Imperialism or Not

1. Nation debated over the captured Philippines and Puerto Rico

2. McKinley decided to keep both, treaty passed by only one vote

3. Philippines fought for its independence until 1901

E. Cuba

1. Occupied until 1902

2. U.S. invested in the island, cleaned up yellow fever

3. Given independence with the Platt Amendment in their constitution (gave the U.S. the right to intervene there)

F. Open Door Policy toward China

1. All nations to trade freely there

2. Sec. of State John Hay created it in 1899, largely successful

3. Due to the fact no one nation had a clear advantage, China never became a colony

The Progressive Era

I. Roosevelt

A. Progressive birth, early 1900s

1. Pressure for reform had been building since the Civil War

2. Heir to the Grange and Populists

3. Began in the cities as reform-minded men were voted in

    a. Public utilities controlled, not supplied based on bribes

    b. Open bidding for contracts

    c. City waste and vice attacked

    d. More parks and services

4. Movement had wide support in the prosperous middle class

B. State Reforms

1. Model, Wisconsin under Robert La Follette

Gilded Age to Progressive Era

a. Primary elections: the people choose the candidates

b. Effective railroad control

c. Fair taxes on corporations

2. Spread to other states

C. Muckraking, reporting on corruption and scandal

1. Mainly popular magazines

2. Fed the Progressive Movement, exposing the need for reform

D. Temperance Movement, anti-liquor

1. Part of Progressive Movement

2. Led to the 18th Amendment that forbade the sale of liquor

E. Roosevelt became president

1. McKinley re-elected in 1900 in a race against Bryan

a. Theodore Roosevelt (TR) chosen as vice president

b. McKinley assassinated in 1901

2. Popular, progressive president that revitalized the presidency

F. Reform under TR

1. Called the Square Deal

2. Used the Sherman Anti-Trust Act against a J.P. Morgan company, and won in 1904

3. Won anti-trust suits

4. Elkins Act forbade railroad rebates

5. Hepburn Act gave power to the Interstate Commerce Commission

G. 1902 Coal Strike, TR did not side with the owners, forced negotiations

H. Reserved millions of acres for national parks

| Big Stick in the Caribbean cartoon

I. Big Stick in Panama

1. U.S. needed a canal to connect the Atlantic and Pacific

2. TR supported a revolt in Panama when Colombia refused to lease land there for a canal

3. New Panamanian government signed the lease

4. Canal built by George Goethals, opened in 1914

J. Roosevelt Corollary to Monroe Doctrine: U.S. would police problems in the Americas so Europe would not

K. Second Administration, elected on his own in 1904

1. Food and Drug purity acts due to Muckrakers like Upton Sinclair, *The Jungle*, exposed unsanitary meat packing

2. Panic in 1907 brought banking reform that allowed banks to expand the money supply

3. Negotiated an end to the Russo-Japanese War in 1905 and was awarded the Nobel Peace Prize

Gilded Age to Progressive Era

    4. Sent the new U.S. fleet on a successful world tour

II. Taft

  A. TR was able to name William H. Taft as his successor in 1908

  B. Lost Progressive support due to several controversies

  C. Expanded anti-trust suits

  D. Congress passed the 16th Amendment (income tax) and 17th Amendment (direct election of senators)

  E. Dollar Diplomacy, tried to use U.S. investments as a way to expand American influence abroad

  F. Bull Moose Party

    1. TR furious with Taft, ran again in 1912 under the Progressive Party, the Bull Moose Party

    2. Split the Republican vote

    3. Democrat Woodrow Wilson won

III. Wilson

  A. Also a Progressive reformer

    1. Underwood Tariff Bill, first major reduction since the Civil War

    2. Created Federal Reserve System, banks privately owned but main board government appointed

    3. Clayton Anti-Trust Act

      a. Exempted unions

      b. Federal Trade Commission established to prevent trusts

    4. Signed many other reforms

    B. Used the army to settle Caribbean problems

| Woodrow Wilson

  C. Mexico

    1. Wilson refused to recognize a new leader, Huerta, that killed the last president

    2. Sold weapons to his opponents

    3. Huerta removed in 1914, but civil war broke out

    4. U.S. troops pursued Pancho Villa who raided across the border

      a. Never caught him

      b. U.S. Army in Mexico angered the people there, withdrew

    5. Policy accomplished only bad relations with our neighbor

  D. Conclusion: Progressive Era expanded government power over corporations and all American life

Gilded Age to Progressive Era

Match these people.

3.54	_____	Democratic leader of the 1890s; favored silver coinage	a. J.P. Morgan
			b. Andrew Carnegie
3.55	_____	TR's chosen successor; angered Progressives	c. John D. Rockefeller
3.56	_____	assassinated by disgruntled office seeker	d. Terence Powderly
3.57	_____	banker; created U.S. Steel Corporation	e. Samuel Gompers
3.58	_____	Admiral that defeated Spanish fleet at Manila in the Philippines	f. Chester A. Arthur
			g. James Garfield
3.59	_____	Progressive; led reform in Wisconsin	h. Benjamin Harrison
3.60	_____	Progressive president; Federal Reserve System; won after Republican Party split	i. William Jennings Bryan
			j. George Dewey
3.61	_____	president who was a protegé of a party boss, but signed Civil Service reform	k. William McKinley
			l. Theodore Roosevelt
3.62	_____	built a steel empire using Bessemer process	m. William H. Taft
3.63	_____	leader of the Knights of Labor	n. Woodrow Wilson
3.64	_____	president during Spanish American War; pro-business; assassinated	o. Robert La Follette
3.65	_____	Standard Oil Trust	
3.66	_____	leader of the American Federation of Labor	
3.67	_____	elected president in 1888 over the tariff issue	
3.68	_____	Spanish-American War hero; Progressive president; led the Bull Moose Party in 1912	

Match these items.

3.69 _____ Anti-liquor campaign; 18th Amendment

3.70 _____ worked to improve farming conditions

3.71 _____ Muckraking exposé on meat packing

3.72 _____ gave power to the Interstate Commerce Commission

3.73 _____ the rich were rich because they were better workers

3.74 _____ book that exposed mistreatment of Native Americans

3.75 _____ places where Progressive reform began

3.76 _____ gave land to anyone who lived on it 5 years

3.77 _____ law forbidding railroad rebates

3.78 _____ first of the new huge corporations (late 1800s)

3.79 _____ new party formed in 1892; wanted free coinage silver, 8 hour day, income tax

3.80 _____ U.S. battleship blown up in Havana harbor

3.81 _____ Taft's foreign policy

3.82 _____ allowed the U.S. to intervene in Cuba

3.83 _____ gave Native Americans land and citizenship

3.84 _____ Union that focused only on labor issues

3.85 _____ Union that had a social agenda; Haymarket Riot

3.86 _____ first major tariff reduction after the Civil War

3.87 _____ open range cattle taken to railroad junctions to be shipped East, created the cowboy image

3.88 _____ established a merit system for government positions

3.89 _____ W. J. Bryan favored this kind of coinage

3.90 _____ TR used the big stick to get the necessary treaty in spite of Colombia

3.91 _____ shift in people coming to the U.S., now came from Southern, not Northern Europe in the 1880s

3.92 _____ set up the Federal Trade Commission and exempted unions

3.93 _____ allowed monopolies to be broken up, but was not used much before TR

3.94 _____ TR's Progressive/reform policy

a. Homestead Act

b. railroads

c. New Immigration

d. Knights of Labor

e. American Federation of Labor

f. _Century of Dishonor_

g. Dawes Act

h. cattle drives

i. Pendleton Act

j. Grange

k. Populist Party

l. Silver coinage

m. Sherman Anti-Trust

n. _Maine_

o. Platt Amendment

p. cities

q. Temperance

r. Square Deal

s. Hepburn Act

t. Elkins Act

u. Panama Canal

v. _The Jungle_

w. Dollar Diplomacy

x. Underwood Tariff

y. Clayton Anti-Trust

z. Social Darwinism

Answer these questions.

3.95 What were the conditions for immigrant workers in the 1880s?

_____

_____

3.96 Why were the late 1900s called the Gilded Age?

_____

3.97 What factors led to the defeat of the Plains Indians?

_____

_____

3.98 What did the U.S. do with the territory captured during the Spanish-American War?

_____

World War I

I. Neutral America

   A. Causes of World War I

      1. Alliances

         a. Triple Alliance–Germany, Austria-Hungary, and Italy (Central Powers)

         b. Triple Entente–France, Russia, and Britain (allies)

      2. National pride

      3. Arms race

   B. War began in 1914

      1. Heir to the Austrian throne was assassinated in Sarajevo, Bosnia

      2. Austria demanded redress from Serbia for encouraging terrorism

      3. Austria declared war; alliances dragged the other nations into it

      C. Stalemate

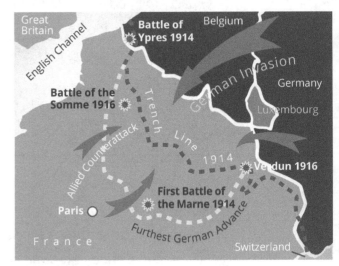

| The Western Front during World War I

      1. Germany quickly invaded France through neutral Belgium

      2. French stopped them, both sides dug defenses across France

      3. Trench warfare–brutal

         a. Parallel trenches on either side of "no man's land"

A World in Conflict

      b. Attacked into strong defenses, heavy casualties, little gain

      c. Front hardly moved for years

D. First war that used aircraft

E. American reaction

   1. Wanted to stay neutral

   2. Most favored the allies

F. American Trade

   1. Mainly with the allies

      a. Britain controlled the seas

      b. Allies could get credit, Central Powers could not

   2. Germany decided to use U-boats (subs) to blockade the allies

      a. Destroyed ships and men

      b. Seen in America as a violation of international law

G. Building crisis

   1. 1915, British liner *Lusitania* sunk, killing more than 100 Americans

   2. U.S. protests ended the blockade temporarily

   3. Wilson was re-elected in 1916 on the promise of staying out of war

   4. Zimmerman Note

      a. Offered Mexico the land taken in 1848 for fighting the U.S.

      b. Published in 1917

   5. Germany began unrestricted submarine warfare in early 1917

      a. Believed it could win before the U.S. got fully into the war

      b. After several ships sunk, U.S. declared war in April 1917

      6. Russia withdrew from the war after the Communist Revolution

| Images of the Great Depression

II. The Great War

   A. Wilson saw the war as a crusade "to make the world safe for democracy"

      1. Nation liked the idealistic goal

      2. American economy was gradually organized to support the war

   B. Took the U.S. almost a year to train, equip, and ship a substantial army

   C. American Expeditionary Force

      1. Commander–John Pershing

      2. As the numbers grew, Pershing insisted the U.S. take over one part of the front

A World in Conflict

3. Allies wanted the U.S. men as replacements, but the U.S. did get a front eventually

D. End of the war, 1918

1. Germans moved troops from Russia hoping to crush the allies before the Americans arrived

2. American action

a. Château-Thierry

b. Cleared Belleau woods

c. Cleared the St. Mihiel salient

d. Meuse-Argonne Offensive, greatest U.S. battle of the war

3. Germans were losing ground, asked for an armistice, the war ended November, 1918

4. More Americans died in an influenza pandemic in 1918-19 than in the war

5. U.S. deaths in war–over 100,000

III. The Peace that Failed

A. Fourteen Points–Wilson's proposal for a just peace,

1. Open negotiations

2. Self-government for many of the oppressed people of Europe

3. An association of nations

4. Hailed by liberals world-wide

5. Germans ask for peace, believing the Points would govern the final treaty

B. Treaty of Versailles

1. Wilson planned badly

a. Took no senators and only one minor Republican

b. Personally led the team, away from the U.S. for six months

2. Treaty was negotiated in secret, Germans not allowed to attend

3. France and Britain were determined to crush Germany

4. A harsh treaty resulted

a. Germany forced to accept responsibility for the war

b. Paid a huge indemnity, lost territory to France

c. Productive areas put under French control for years

d. Italy given land it was promised for joining the allies

e. Poland, Estonia, Latvia, Lithuania, Czechoslovakia & Yugoslavia created

f. League of Nations created (Wilson believed it would repair the damage done by the treaty)

g. Austria-Hungary separated

5. Treaty pleased no one, especially liberals and the Germans

C. Senate under Republican control, dragged its feet on ratifying it

1. Wilson collapsed on a national speaking tour to push the treaty

2. Ill and out of touch, Wilson refused to compromise

3. Treaty failed, U.S. made a separate peace with Germany

D. Bitterness and economic pressure on Germany set up World War II

The Great Depression

I. Roaring Twenties

A. Warren Harding (Rep.) elected, 1920

1. Called for a "return to normalcy"

A World in Conflict

2. People tired of wars and crusades

3. Reverted to traditional isolation

B. Wave of anti-foreign hatred hit the U.S. after the "Great War"

C. Five Power Naval Treaty, 1922, restricted the number of large ships, partially diffused the arms race

D. Harding died in 1923 as scandals began to break (bad president)

   1. Kickbacks in the Veteran's Bureau

   2. Illegal schemes at the Attorney General's office

   3. Teapot Dome Scandal–oil leases sold to company after a bribe

E. Calvin Coolidge became president

   1. Famous for how little he spoke

   2. Pro-business like Harding

   3. Nation was prospering, he was popular as were his policies

   4. Won ill will in Europe by insisting that war debts to the U.S. be paid in full

   5. Elected on his own in 1924

F. 1920s were a time of prosperity

   1. Named the Roaring Twenties for the free spending, illegal drinking, fads

   2. New affordable products such as automobiles, refrigerators, radios

   3. People spent unwisely, using credit

   4. 18th Amendment made liquor illegal

      a. Widely violated through "speakeasies," illegal saloons

      c. Money went to organized crime

   5. "Flappers," women danced, drank, smoked, and wore shorter skirts

6. Charles Lindbergh a hero by flying solo across the Atlantic in 1927

G. Fundamentalism

   1. Modernists produced liberal Christianity: evolution, no miracles, no need for atonement, just a code of ethics

   2. Fundamentalists defended Biblical truth

   3. Scopes Monkey Trial, 1925

      a. Trial of John Scopes who taught evolution to challenge a law forbidding it

      b. Charles Darrow defended, William Bryan aided the state

      c. Media circus, ridiculed Christianity and faith

      d. Scopes was convicted, but it was overturned on appeal

H. Herbert Hoover (Republican) elected, 1928

II. Crash

A. Economic Warnings, before 1929

   1. Farm economy very bad

   2. Wealthy taking most of the money made in the decade

   3. Overuse of credit

   4. Wild speculation on the Stock Market

B. Stock Market crashed in October, 1929

   1. Prices fell by half in 10 weeks

   2. Everyone lost confidence in the economy and stopped spending

   3. Business cut back, people lost jobs, banks closed

C. Results

   1. 25% unemployment in 1933

A World in Conflict

2. New factory construction stopped

3. Men roamed the country, looking for jobs

4. Drought in the Plains destroyed crops, blowing dust everywhere

5. Thousands of farmers left

6. People were desperate

D. Hoover's response

1. Tried to rebuild confidence

2. Hawley-Smoot Tariff raised the rates and prices making the depression worse

3. Set up some public works projects, called for private aid

4. Did not believe in federal money for relief

5. Bonus Army

a. Veterans came to Washington to get bonuses due in 1945

b. Congress refused and the army drove the men away

c. Hoover's falling popularity hurt even more

E. Hoover and the Republican Party lost in 1932 (blamed for the depression); Franklin D. Roosevelt (FDR) won

III. New Deal, FDR's national policy

A. Hundred Days, time of rapid passage of laws to meet the crisis

1. Bank holiday restored confidence in the banking system

2. Set up dozens of agencies to deal with problems

3. Social Security-pensions

4. All the activity gave hope and confidence even though things only improved slightly

B. FDR was re-elected easily in 1936

1. Tried and failed to pack the Supreme Court with his own people, lost support in Congress

2. Protected and encouraged unions

3. Good Neighbor Policy improved relations in the Western Hemisphere

C. Depression continued until World War II ended it in 1942

World War II

I. War Comes Again

A. Dictators took advantage of the world wide depression to gain power in Germany, Italy, and Japan

1. Hitler's rise to power brought the start of the Holocaust around 1933 (genocide against Jews)

2. The Nazi party gained power

B. American attitude, strict isolation, refused to be a world leader

C. Appeasement-democracies did not stop aggression by dictators

1. Japan took Manchuria, 1931

2. Italy took Ethiopia, 1935

3. Hitler rearmed Germany and put soldiers along the French border

4. Hitler took Austria, 1938

5. Hitler demanded the Sudetenland, part of Czechoslovakia

a. British Prime Minister Neville Chamberlain came to Munich

b. Gave Hitler the land in exchange for a promise not to take any more

A World in Conflict

c. Chamberlain claimed to have gotten "peace in our time"

6. Hitler took all of Czechoslovakia, 1939

7. Stalin (U.S.S.R.) & Hitler agreed to divide Poland and not attack each other, 1939

D. War

1. France and Britain promised war if Poland was invaded

2. Poland invaded September, 1939

   a. Began World War II

   b. *Blitzkrieg*, lightning war, used by the Nazis (Germans)

      (1) Speed, surprise, fire power

      (2) Conquered in three weeks

3. Phony War, no actual fighting until 1940

4. Hitler took Denmark, Norway, Belgium, and the Netherlands in quick succession

5. France fell June, 1940

6. Most of the British army escaped by boats across the English Channel from Dunkirk

7. Germany took most of France, leaving part as a satellite nation called Vichy France

E. Britain Alone

1. Hitler expected Britain to sue for peace, but under Winston Churchill's leadership they flatly refused

2. Battle of Britain

   a. Battle for control of the skies

   b. Hitler could not invade until the Royal Air Force was destroyed

c. RAF survived, so Hitler next tried to bomb Britain into submission, that also failed

3. The Blitz, 1940-41, bombs dropped every day but Britain refused to give up

4. June, 1941, Hitler gave up on Britain and attacked the U.S.S.R.

F. Arsenal of Democracy

1. America gradually became less neutral, supporting Britain

2. Lend-lease, 1941, FDR lent or leased weapons to Britain until after the war

3. Atlantic Charter, 1941, FDR and Churchill set common goals for the war

G. Pearl Harbor

1. Japanese attacked the U.S. fleet in Hawaii, December 7, 1941

2. United the nation in favor of war

3. War declared on Japan; Germany and Italy declared war on the U.S.

4. U.S., Britain, and U.S.S.R. joined forces, called the allies

5. Germany, Italy, and Japan–Axis

H. Homefront

1. America went to full employment

2. Consumer goods unavailable

3. People united for a long fight

4. Production was incredible

   a. Created a synthetic rubber industry from scratch

   b. Cargo ships were built in days

   c. Made half the weapons in the world by the war's end

A World in Conflict

I. Japanese citizens on the West coast were held in internment camps during the war

J. Roosevelt broke tradition, was re-elected in 1940 and 1944

    1. Died in office, April, 1945

    2. Harry S. Truman, new president

II. War in Europe

  A. Commanders

    1. Gen. George Marshall–organized the war effort from the U.S.

    2. Gen. Dwight D. Eisenhower–led U.S. invasion of N. Africa and the Allied invasion of France

    3. Gen. George Patton–controversial, war-loving tank commander

    4. Gen. Omar Bradley–calm leader, led U.S. in the invasion of France

  B. Battle of the Atlantic

    1. Germans used "wolf packs," groups of submarines, to attack the ships bringing vital supplies to the Allied war effort

    2. Allies used convoys, airplanes, radar, and sonar to protect ships

    3. Gradually Germans lost control of the Atlantic and Allied supplies got through

  C. North Africa invasion, Allied victory

    1. First European experience for the Americans during WWII

    2. British defeated the Germans at El Alamein in October, 1942, their first victory of the war

    3. Germans trapped in between the British

from Egypt and allies with free French from Morocco

D. Stalingrad, turning point in Europe

    1. Soviets had retreated carefully in front of the German invasion letting the huge land and cold winters bog them down

    2. City attacked in summer, 1942, but was not taken

    3. Soviets counterattacked in the winter, trapping and capturing a German army

E. Italy, Allied advance

    1. Sicily attacked in July, 1943, and Italy surrendered

    3. Germany occupied the country and kept fighting fiercely, retreating slowly

    4. Not taken until 1945

F. D-day, invasion of France (June 6, 1944)

    1. Huge force built up in Britain

    3. Successful, but with heavy losses

    4. Paris liberated in October, 1944

G. Battle of the Bulge (December 1944)

    1. Hitler threw his remaining strength at the allies, Hitler's last offensive

    2. Forced a bulge in the lines, but the allies held

H. V-E Day, Victory in Europe

    1. Yalta Conference, Allied leaders

      a. Decided to divide and occupy Germany and Austria

      b. Stalin promised free elections in East Europe and was given a free hand there

      c. Soviet army already occupied those lands

A World in Conflict

2. Soviets took Berlin and trashed it

3. Hitler committed suicide

4. Surrender–May 7, 1945

I. Holocaust

1. Murder of about six million Jews in Nazi concentration camps (1933-1945)

2. Many Nazi leaders were prosecuted afterwards for it

III. War in Asia

A. Commanders

1. Gen. Douglas MacArthur-U.S. Army in the Pacific

2. Admiral Chester Nimitz-Pacific navy

B. Japanese conquered most of the South Pacific in 1941-42

C. Coral Sea, May, 1942

1. 1st navy battle in which the ships never saw each other, planes did the fighting

2. Japanese won, but stopped their invasion of Port Moresby, New Guinea

D. Midway, Pacific turning point, June, 1942

1. U.S. set a trap for the Japanese

2. Japanese lost, took heavy losses, and had no victories after that

E. Island hopping–U.S. strategy

1. Americans attacked only key islands, not all of them, used each island as a base to attack the next one

3. Ships and planes would bombard the island then the soldiers would go ashore

4. Once U.S. invaded, victory was only a matter of time

5. Japanese made suicidal defenses of the islands

F. Closing in

1. After capturing the Marianas Island in June 1944, Japan was in bomber range

2. Iwo Jima between the Marianas and Japan taken in February 1945, the many volcanic caves had to be taken one at a time

3. Okinawa, 350 miles from Japan, taken in the spring of 1945

4. Estimates were an invasion of Japan would cost 1 million men

5. Instead, U.S. dropped two atomic bombs developed by the "Manhattan Project"

6. Japan surrendered, September 2, 1945

A World in Conflict

✎ **Complete these sentences.**

3.99 _____ saw World War I (WWI) as a crusade for democracy and he wanted to use the Fourteen Points to bring it to a just conclusion.

3.100 _____ was the American strategy in the Pacific during World War II (WWII).

3.101 America got into WWI primarily due to German _____ attacks and into WWII due to a Japanese attack on _____ .

3.102 _____ and _____ were characteristics of the Roaring Twenties.

3.103 The _____ of 1929 started the Great Depression.

3.104 The early part of FDR's administration when laws were passed quickly to restore confidence was called the _____ .

3.105 Hitler conquered the nations of _____ _____ in 1940.

3.106 WWII began when _____ in 1939.

3.107 FDR's national policy was called the _____ .

3.108 _____ was the commander of the U.S. forces in WWI.

3.109 WWI began when _____ .

3.110 The _____ Trial of the 1920s ridiculed Christianity.

3.111 Unemployment reached 25% during the _____ .

3.112 _____ commanded the Allied invasion of France in WWII.

3.113 Giving Hitler the Sudetenland was an act of _____ .

3.114 The _____ forced Germany to pay a huge indemnity and blamed it for WWI.

3.115 The _____ made Russia withdraw from WWI.

3.116 The _____ Amendment forbade the sale of liquor in the U.S.

3.117 During WWII the turning point in Europe was _____ while the turning point in the Pacific was _____ .

3.118 The U.S. Army commander in the Pacific during WWII was _____ .

3.119 WWII was ended when _____ .

3.120 _____ administration was famous for a "return to normalcy" and scandals like the Teapot Dome.

3.121 _____ became president when FDR died in office.

3.122 The three causes of WWI were _____

_____ .

3.123 _____ was president when the Great Depression began.

3.124 _____ ended the Great Depression.

3.125 The allies, after the U.S. joined them in WWII, invaded first _____ ,

then _____ and, finally, _____ in Europe.

3.126 The U.S. _____ Project developed the atomic bomb.

3.127 During WWI the fighting stalemated into _____ warfare for years

while in WWII the Nazi's used _____ , lightning war, to avoid

repeating it.

3.128 _____ was a pro-business president famous for not speaking much.

3.129 _____ was Hitler's last offensive of WWII.

3.130 The _____ was the murder of about 6 million people by the Nazis

during WWII.

Hot or Cold

I. Origins of the Cold War

  A. Definition: A conflict of ideas, economics, propaganda, and intimidation between the U.S. and the U.S.S.R. from 1945 to 1991.

  B. Features

    1. Nuclear arms race, fear of nuclear war was a main reason the "superpowers" never fought each other

    2. Competition for allies

    3. Limited "hot" wars

    4. America opposed the evils and lies of practical communism

  C. United Nations, set up to replace the League of Nations in 1945

    1. Quickly approved by the Senate

    2. U.S. and U.S.S.R. have vetoes on the powerful Security Council

  D. Post-war problems

    1. U.S. hoped to enjoy Soviet cooperation for a time after the war, but it did not happen

    2. Stalin set up communist governments in Eastern Europe and cut them off from the West

    3. East Germany cut off and made communist

    4. Western sections united to make free West Germany

    5. Soviets refused to leave Iran in 1946, until the U.S. threatened force

  E. Containment

    1. U.S.S.R. was threatening Turkey and Greece in 1947

    2. Truman announced a policy to contain communism where it already existed

      a. Aid was given to Turkey and Greece which remained free

      b. Was the basic American policy for the whole Cold War

  F. Marshall Plan

    1. Aid to Europe to recover from the war and block communism

    2. Phenomenal success

  G. Berlin Airlift, 1948-49

    1. Soviets cut off all land routes to West Berlin

    2. City supplied by air

    3. Soviets quit when it was clear the U.S. would support the city

  H. NATO, America's first permanent alliance since the Revolution

    1. North Atlantic Treaty Organization

    2. Bound nations to protect each other against any attack

  I. Iron Curtain, name give to the division between free and communist Europe

II. Heating Up, Cooling Down

  A. 1949, a bad year for the West

    1. U.S.S.R. set off an atomic bomb

    2. China fell to the communists under Mao Zedong

  B. Korean War, 1950-53

    1. Korea was divided

    2. Communist North attacked the South in 1950

    3. U.N. authorized a defense

    4. Under Douglas MacArthur the U.S. led in the fighting

Cold War America

5. U.N. forces were trapped in the South at the Pusan Perimeter

   a. Made an amphibious landing at Inchon behind enemy lines

   b. Pushed into the North near the Chinese border

   c. Chinese "volunteers" drove them back

   d. Eventually, stalemated near the old border, 38th Parallel

6. Truman wanted to limit the war and refused to attack China

   a. Publicly opposed by MacArthur

   b. Truman fired MacArthur in 1951, a very unpopular move

7. Peace talks stalled over the return of prisoners, it finally was resolved when Stalin died

C. Thaw, a time of negotiations and better relations under a new Soviet leader, Nikita Khrushchev, 1950s

1. Wanted peaceful coexistence

2. Met with Pres. Eisenhower

3. Still crushed a democratic revolt in Hungary, 1956

D. Middle East

1. U.S. supported Israel (recreated in 1948); Soviets supported the Arabs

2. Eisenhower Doctrine, U.S. would use force to aid any Middle Eastern nation threatened by communism

E. *Sputnik*, 1957

1. World's first artificial satellite

2. Launched by the U.S.S.R.

   3. Shocked the U.S. into pushing its own space program

   a. NASA (National Aeronautics and Space Administration) was created to lead it

   b. America became the world leader in space technology

F. U-2 Affair, 1960

1. U.S. spy plane was shot down over the Soviet Union

2. Broke up a summit

G. Cuba, island 70 miles from Florida

1. Taken over by a communist dictator, Fidel Castro in 1959

2. Bay of Pigs Invasion, 1961

   a. American-trained Cubans tried to overthrow Castro

   b. It was a disastrous failure, an embarrassment to the U.S.

3. Cuban Missile Crisis, 1962

   a. One of the most dangerous events of the Cold War

   b. Soviets were building missile sites in Cuba

   c. Kennedy blockaded the island to stop the missile delivery

   d. Seizing Soviet ships would have been an act of war

   e. Soviet ships turned back

   f. U.S. promised not to invade Cuba and the missile sites were dismantled

H. Berlin Wall, begun, 1961

1. East Germans were escaping by the thousands to West Germany through Berlin

2. East Germans built a wall around the city to block the escape route

3. Called the *Schandmaurer*, wall of shame

Cold War America

III. Vietnam

  A. French tried to retake their colony after the war but were stopped by communist rebels

  B. International agreement gave the North to the communists and the South to another group in 1954

  C. The South, fearing a communist takeover, refused to reunite

  D. Communists organized a revolt in the South in 1957, the U.S. supported the Southern government

    1. Southern government was corrupt and unpopular

    2. Communists kept the rebels well supplied

    3. South could not defeat the rebels

    4. When the U.S. allowed a coup against a cruel Southern leader in 1963, it made the new government look like an American puppet

  E. Gulf of Tonkin, 1964

    1. N. Vietnamese supposedly fired on a U.S. ship in the gulf

    2. Pres. Johnson used the incident to get a Congressional resolution that gave him permission to do whatever was necessary to protect U.S. forces there

    3. Gulf of Tonkin Resolution was a blank check to conduct a war

    4. Johnson began sending U.S. soldiers to do the fighting, not just train and advise

    5. By 1969, over a half a million Americans were fighting; they could not drive the communists out of the South

  F. Effects at home: large scale, violent protests against involvement

  G. Tet Offensive, 1968

    1. Massive communist attack that proved the strength of the enemy

    2. Increased American distrust of the government and the war

  H. U.S. withdrawal

    1. Nixon tried to hand the war over to S. Vietnam, "Vietnamization"

    2. Nixon pressed the war and pursued negotiations

    3. A "cease fire" in 1973 allowed the U.S. soldiers to leave

    4. The communists over ran the South in 1975, thousands fled

    5. One of the longest wars in U.S. history

Between War and Watergate

I. Truman/Eisenhower

  A. The post-war economy boomed

    1. Inflation was a serious problem as people spent their war savings

    2. Republican Congress refused to continue wartime price controls and rejected Truman's liberal programs

  B. Election of 1948

    1. Democrats split over civil rights

    2. Republican, Thomas Dewey, saw an easy victory and did little

    3. Truman led a strong campaign against the "do nothing" Congress and was elected

    4. New Democratic Congress did not pass most of his "Fair Deal"

  C. Cold War produced anti-communist fever in the U.S.

Cold War America

1. The notorious Chambers and Rosenberg spy cases fueled fears
2. Truman had the loyalty of federal employees investigated

D. Election of 1952

1. Truman did not run, supported Democrat Adlai Stevenson
2. WWII hero Dwight D. Eisenhower ran (Republican) and won
3. Republican slogan "I Like Ike"

E. Joseph McCarthy, U.S. Senator

1. Made accusations about communist activity in the U.S. to create fear
2. Ruined many people's careers
3. Lost popularity in televised hearings in 1953 and was censured by Senate

F. Black Americans were kept separate from white Americans, prevented from voting, given inferior schools and services, and denied protection under the law in the 100 years after the Civil War (there are still lasting effects of inequality)

G. Civil Rights–Beginnings

1. Montgomery Bus Boycott, 1955

   a. Beginning of the modern Civil Rights Movement
   b. Rosa Parks refused to sit in the back of the bus as segregation laws required
   c. Rev. Martin Luther King led a successful, peaceful boycott that led to the integration of bus system
   d. Gave Dr. King a national reputation

2. *Brown v. Board of Education,* forbade segregation in schools and ordered the beginning of integration in 1954

| Civil rights leader, Martin Luther King Jr.

3. Eisenhower ordered the army to escort black students at Central High School in Little Rock, Arkansas in 1957 when mobs tried to stop integration there

H. Eisenhower was re-elected in 1956

1. Time of prosperity and growth
2. Set up interstate highway plan

II. Kennedy/Johnson

A. John Kennedy (Democrat) elected president in 1960 with a Democrat Congress

B. New Frontier, Kennedy's program

1. Plan for national education, medical insurance, transportation, etc.
2. Most of it failed due to conservative opposition
3. Peace Corps was one success

   a. Sent volunteers to aid Third World countries
   b. Reaped goodwill for America

Cold War America

C. Foreign Affairs
1. Alliance for Progress, promoted reform with aid to Latin America
2. Signed treaty banning nuclear tests except underground
3. Set up a "hotline" to allow communication with the Soviet Union in a crisis

D. Civil Rights Movemen (1960s)
1. Dr. Martin Luther King
   a. Began nationwide movement after success in Montgomery
   b. Used non-violent, peaceful protest to press for change
   c. Won national fame
2. Black protesters peacefully sat, walked or ate, violating segregation laws
3. Birmingham, Alabama, 1963
   a. King led marches to protest segregation there
   b. Police attacked the marchers
   c. National TV showed the travesty
   d. Led Kennedy to propose a stronger civil rights law
4. March on Washington, 1963
   a. To support the civil rights bill and press for racial equality
   b. Met at Lincoln Memorial
   c. King gave his most famous speech, "I Have a Dream"

E. Kennedy assassinated, November, 1963
1. Lee Harvey Oswald was captured and killed before a trial
2. Many believe his death was due to an unproven conspiracy
   F. Lyndon Johnson became president

1. Very experienced legislator
2. Pushed through the Civil Rights Act and part of the New Frontier

G. Election of 1964
1. Republican candidate was the very conservative Barry Goldwater
2. Both Johnson and the Democrats in Congress won

H. Great Society, Johnson's program
1. The deficit soared as Congress gave Johnson what he wanted: Medicare, Medicaid, War on Poverty
2. Began deep American involvement in Vietnam
   a. Cost hurt the Great Society
   b. War hurt his popularity and people's trust of him
   c. Did not run again in 1968

I. Civil Rights Movement, continued
1. After 1963, emphasis shifted to black voter registration
2. Voting Rights Act of 1965 was passed after more violence against the marchers
3. Riots began in 1965 over how slowly things were changing
   a. Some black people began to call for violence and "Black Power"
   b. Movement lost much of its moral standing and support
4. King continued to support non-violent protest
   a. Assassinated, April, 1968
   b. James Earl Ray convicted
5. Results, ended 100 years of legal inequality for black Americans and paved the way for future efforts for equality

Cold War America

Answer these questions.

3.131 What was the Cold War?

_____

_____

_____

3.132 What was the successful method used by Dr. Martin Luther King?

_____

3.133 What court decision ended school segregation?

_____

3.134 What were the successes of the Kennedy Administration?

_____

3.135 What resolution gave the president a free hand in Vietnam and began the use of U.S. soldiers there?

_____

3.136 Why was Senator Joseph McCarthy censured?

_____

_____

3.137 What was the military course of the Korean War?

_____

_____

_____

3.138 Why was 1949 a bad year for the free world?

_____

_____

3.139 What were the results of the Civil Rights Movement?

_____

_____

3.140 What happened in the Cuban Missile Crisis?

_____

_____

Name the item, crisis, or person.

3.141 Assassinated Martin Luther King _____

3.142 Johnson's legislative program _____

3.143 Two laws passed due to violence against Civil Rights protesters

_____

_____

3.144 *Schandmaurer*, blocked the escape of East Germans _____

3.145 Truman's legislative program _____

3.146 U.S. spy plane shot down over U.S.S.R. _____

3.147 U.S. Cold War policy toward the U.S.S.R. _____

3.148 Successful post-WWII aid to Europe _____

3.149 1st U.S. permanent alliance since 1770s _____

3.150 Popular commander in Korean War, fired for insubordination

_____

3.151 Boycott that began the Civil Rights Movement _____

3.152 WWII hero whose presidency was a time of prosperity _____

3.153 Dr. M. L. King's most famous speech _____

3.154 World's first artificial satellite _____

3.155 One of America's longest and most controversial wars _____

3.156 Assassinated John Kennedy _____

3.157 Group targeted by fears in the 1950s _____

3.158 Post-WWII League of Nations _____

3.159 North Vietnamese offensive that proved they were still a strong enemy

_____

3.160 Organization that led the U.S. space program _____

III. Nixon

  A. Election of 1968

    1. Robert Kennedy, Democrat, leading anti-war candidate assassinated

    2. Hubert Humphery, Johnson's vice president, nominated at Democratic convention torn by violence

    3. Richard M. Nixon, Republican, won

  B. Social Changes

    1. Mass youth rebellion, 1960s-70s

      a. Rejected traditional values

      b. Increased drug use

      c. Wanted life without responsibility

    2. Results in the 1980s and 90s

      a. Higher divorce rates

      b. More illegitimate children

      c. Abortion

      d. Doctor assisted suicide

  C. Domestic Issues

    1. Main one: Inflation

      a. With stagnant economy, called stagflation

      b. Nixon tried price controls, ineffective, 1971

    2. Supreme Court

      a. Very active under Earl Warren

      b. Expanded individual rights into new, controversial areas

      c. Nixon named Warren Burger (conservative) to replace him

      d. New court did not throw out the Warren Court decisions

      e. Busing

        (1) Ordered to racially balance school districts, 1970s

        (2) Expensive and unpopular

        (3) Continued into the 80s

    3. Anti-war protests

      a. Continued as Nixon withdrew from Vietnam

      b. Often violent

  D. Nixon won re-election in 1972 over liberal Democrat George McGovern

  E. Détente, 1970s Cold War thaw

    1. Nixon made diplomatic contact with communist China, treating it as a rival to the U.S.S.R.

    2. Went to China in 1972 and allowed it to replace Taiwan in the United Nations

    3. Soviet Union improved its ties with the U.S. under Leonid Brezhnev, but never ended its quest for world power

  F. Watergate

    1. Republicans tried to "bug" the Democratic party headquarters at the Watergate Hotel in June of 1972

    2. The burglars were caught

    3. An investigation showed that Nixon's staff was involved

    4. Nixon had been taping the conversations in his office

      a. Prosecutors wanted the tapes

      b. Nixon fought releasing them

      c. Eventually the prosecutors won in court

    5. Nixon resigned from office, August, 1974, after the tapes showed he approved a cover-up of the truth right after burglary

    6. Gerald Ford, who was the 1st appointed vice president, became president

Cold War America

Unexpected Victory

I. Aftershocks of Vietnam

  A. Gerald Ford lost popularity when he pardoned Nixon

  B. Home Problems

    1. Inflation, still a major problem

      a. Continued unemployment and inflation

      b. Ford's "Whip Inflation Now" campaign failed

    2. Nelson Rockefeller appointed vice president

    3. Congress refused to aid South Vietnam when the North invaded in 1975

  C. *Mayaguez*, Ford ordered the navy to rescue an American merchant ship seized by Cambodia, May, 1975

  D. Election of 1976

    1. Gerald Ford narrowly won the Republican nomination

    2. Democrat Jimmy Carter campaigned as an honest outsider and won

      a. Did not know how to work with Congress

      b. Could not lead effectively

  E. Economic Problems

    1. Energy

      a. Oil costs rose in the 1970s

      b. Carter tried to set up an energy program, but prices rose more

      c. Prices finally dropped in the 1980s due to increased production

    2. Inflation

      a. The Federal Reserve Board began to increase interest rates in 1979

      b. Higher rates caused a recession, slowed inflation

  F. Foreign Policy Successes

    1. Camp David Accords,

      a. Carter invited the leaders of Israel and Egypt to negotiate

      b. Became the basis of a treaty between the two nations

    2. Treaty to give the Panama Canal to Panama was approved, 1978

  G. Death of Détente

    1. A push for human rights was the center of Carter's foreign policy

      a. Soviet Union resented the pressure for personal freedom

      b. Nuclear arms negotiations begun under Détente stalled

    2. In Dec. 1979 the U.S.S.R. invaded Afghanistan ending Détente

  H. Iran Hostage Crisis, 1979-81

    1. Central event of Carter's years

    2. 52 Americans from the Iran embassy were held hostage for 444 days with the support of the Islamic government

      a. Rescue attempt failed

      b. Iran's war with Iraq (1980-88) finally forced Iran to release the people to recover assets in the U.S.

      c. Hurt U.S. prestige abroad

  I. Election of 1980

    1. Carter won Democratic nomination

    2. Ronald Reagan (Republican) won the election

II. Healing and Change

  A. Terrorism, especially by Middle East groups, was a problem in the 1980s

Cold War America

B. Reaganomics

1. Reagan's efforts to reduce the size and influence of government

2. Tax cuts and increases in military spending for the Cold War increased the deficit

3. A recession due to increased interest rates ended by 1984 and high inflation did not return

C. Foreign Affairs

1. Reagan's confidence in America and anti-communist beliefs undid some of the U.S. self-doubt from Vietnam

2. Supported the *Contras*, guerrillas fighting the communist regime in Nicaragua

   a. Massacres and cruelty led to questions about U.S. support

   b. Congress barred more aid

3. Invaded the island of Grenada to stop a communist revolt, 1983

4. "Star Wars"

   a. Strategic Defense Initiative

   b. Space based missile defense system proposed by Reagan

   c. Limited work done on it

D. Election of 1984

1. Reagan won by a huge majority

2. Democratic opponent was Walter Mondale, his running mate was the first woman to run on a major party ticket

E. Changes in the U.S.S.R.

1. A new leader, Mikhail Gorbachev, realized the Soviet Union was behind the West in technology and its economy was in trouble

2. He began reforms

   a. *Perestroika* (restructuring) to increase productivity

   b. *Glasnost* (openness) to allow more freedom of ideas

3. Sought reductions in the arms race and peace to reduce the costs of the Soviet military

4. Reagan was ridiculed for being slow to trust the changes

   a. Met Gorbachev several times

   b. Signed the first treaty to reduce the number of nuclear weapons

F. Iran Contra Affair

1. Complicated scandal

2. Reagan sold weapons to Iran hoping to influence them to help free U.S. hostages in Lebanon

3. The profits from the sales were used to aid the *Contras*, which was illegal

4. Several of Reagan's aides were convicted, but he was not

G. Reagan's vice president, George H. W. Bush, won the 1988 election

III. Miraculous Victory

A. Savings and Loan Crisis

1. Lax rules and fraud led many to close for lack of funds

2. George H. W. Bush signed law to cover the losses in 1989

3. Cost hundreds of billions

B. Miracle Year, 1989

1. Soviet Union had withdrawn from Afghanistan, cut back its military in Europe and refused to protect Iron Curtain governments

Cold War America

2. With the withdrawal of Soviet force, communism collapsed in Eastern Europe

3. In 1989 there were democratic reforms or revolts in every Iron Curtain nation

4. East Germany opened its borders with the West in November, 1989

   a. People began to tear down the Berlin Wall

   b. Germany reunited in 1990

C. U.S. invaded Panama in 1989 to overthrow a drug-running dictator

D. Persian Gulf War, 1990-91

   1. Iraq brutally conquered its neighbor, Kuwait

   2. George H. W. Bush organized a U.S. led coalition under the U.N.

      a. Built an army in Saudi Arabia

      b. Massive bombing raids from January 16-February 24 on Iraq

      c. Land invasion began February 24 and was victorious in only 100 hours of fighting

   3. Gave America and George H. W. Bush tremendous worldwide prestige

E. Cold War Finale, 1991

   1. Soviet communists tried a coup to retake control and failed

   2. U.S.S.R. dissolved, creating fifteen new nations

   3. The U.S. had won the Cold War

NOTE: Review Section 1 on post-1990 history for Self Test 3 and the LIFEPAC Test

Cold War America

Choose the correct person.

3.161	_____ Whip Inflation Now	a. Richard Nixon
3.162	_____ Iran Hostage Crisis	b. Gerald Ford
3.163	_____ Iran-Contra Affair	c. Jimmy Carter
3.164	_____ *Perestroika*	d. Ronald Reagan
3.165	_____ Watergate	e. Mikhail Gorbachev
3.166	_____ Persian Gulf War	f. George H. W. Bush
3.167	_____ Camp David Accords	
3.168	_____ Pardoned Nixon	
3.169	_____ put Warren Burger on the Supreme Court	
3.170	_____ Savings and Loan Crisis	
3.171	_____ *Mayaguez*	
3.172	_____ the end of Détente	
3.173	_____ "Star Wars"	
3.174	_____ Made the first official contact with communist China	
3.175	_____ *Glasnost*	
3.176	_____ invasion of Grenada	
3.177	_____ invasion of Panama	
3.178	_____ Panama Canal Treaty	
3.179	_____ ended support for communist governments in East Europe	

Answer these questions.

3.180 What was the major economic problem of the 1970s?

_____

_____

3.181 What happened in the Watergate scandal?

_____

_____

_____

3.182 Why was 1989 such an incredible year in Europe?

_____

_____

_____

3.183 What was accomplished in the Persian Gulf War?

_____

_____

3.184 During the Iran Hostage Crisis who was held and for how long?

_____

_____

3.185 When did the Soviet Union dissolve? _____

3.186 What ended Détente? _____

3.187 What did busing try to accomplish?

_____

_____

3.188 What led to many of the social problems of the 1980s, like divorce and abortion?

_____

_____

Do this activity.

3.189 Memorize the names of the presidents of the United States in chronological order and recite the list for your teacher.

TEACHER CHECK _____ _____
                              initials   date

Before you take this last Self Test, you may want to do one or more of these self checks.

1. _____ Read the objectives. See if you can do them.
2. _____ Restudy the material related to any objectives that you cannot do.
3. _____ Use the SQ3R study procedure to review the material:

   a. Scan the sections.
   b. Question yourself.
   c. Read to answer your questions.
   d. Recite the answers to yourself.
   e. Review areas you did not understand.
4. _____ Review all vocabulary, activities, and Self Tests, writing a correct answer for every wrong answer.

SELF TEST 3

Match these people (each answer, 1 point).

Abbreviations: President–P; Vice president–VP; World War–WW

3.01	_____ Black American Civil Rights leader	a. Abraham Lincoln
3.02	_____ Soviet leader; his reforms ended communism	b. Ulysses S. Grant
3.03	_____ became president when Franklin Roosevelt died;	c. William Clinton
	Fair Deal; began containment	d. Robert E. Lee
3.04	_____ P 1980-88; Iran-Contra Affair; "Star Wars"	e. John D. Rockefeller
3.05	_____ Lincoln's VP; 1st P impeached; easy Reconstruction	f. Ronald Reagan
3.06	_____ Great Compromiser before the Civil War	g. Harry Truman
3.07	_____ Confederate general	h. Theodore Roosevelt
3.08	_____ P 1929-1933; blamed for the Great Depression	i. Lyndon B. Johnson
3.09	_____ P resigned over Watergate; visited communist China	j. Winston Churchill
3.010	_____ P assassinated in 1963; Peace Corps; New Frontier	k. Franklin Roosevelt
3.011	_____ Standard Oil owner; monopolies copied his ways	l. George Washington
3.012	_____ P 1921-23; "Return to Normalcy" many scandals	m. Martin L. King
3.013	_____ Progressive P; built Panama Canal; Square Deal	n. Jimmy Carter
3.014	_____ Union general; P 1869-1877; corrupt administration	o. Henry Clay
3.015	_____ WWII & Korean general; fired for insubordination	p. Andrew Johnson
3.016	_____ incredibly popular P 1829-37; hero of New Orleans;	q. Douglas MacArthur
	closed the National Bank; used the spoils system	r. Grover Cleveland
3.017	_____ British Prime Minister during WWII	s. John Kennedy
3.018	_____ P during the Civil War; Emancipation Proclamation	t. Richard Nixon
3.019	_____ appointed VP; became P 1974, "Whip Inflation Now"	u. William J. Bryan
3.020	_____ supported silver coinage but not evolution	v. Gerald Ford
3.021	_____ 2nd P impeached; elected 1992	w. Woodrow Wilson
3.022	_____ P during Persian Gulf War; Savings & Loan crisis	x. Warren Harding
3.023	_____ 1st P; Revolutionary War general	y. Dwight Eisenhower
3.024	_____ P two non-consecutive terms, 1885 &1893; reformer	z. George H. W. Bush

3.025 _____ P during WWII, gave hope in the Great Depression   aa. Mikhail Gorbachev

3.026 _____ P 1977-81; Iran Hostage Crisis; Camp David Accords   bb. Thomas Jefferson

3.027 _____ Progressive P; led during WWI; Fourteen Points   cc. Andrew Jackson

3.028 _____ author–Declaration of Independence; strict   dd. Herbert Hoover
construction of Constitution; Louisiana Purchase

3.029 _____ WWII hero; P 1953-61; time of prosperity

3.030 _____ VP who became P when Kennedy died; Great Society; began the deep U.S.
involvement in Vietnam

Match these items (each answer, 1 point).

3.031	_____ pamphlet by Thomas Paine that turned the colonies in favor of independence	a. Missouri Compromise
3.032	_____ Wall of Shame, symbol of the Cold War	b. *Common Sense*
3.033	_____ time of wealth and corruption after Reconstruction	c. Reconstruction
3.034	_____ greatest economic problem of the 1970s	d. Progressive Era
3.035	_____ era of free spending and fast living after WWI	e. *Dred Scott* Decision
3.036	_____ Alaska	f. Cuban Missile Crisis
3.037	_____ plan to end the Great Depression, F. Roosevelt	g. Seward's Folly
3.038	_____ occupation of the South after the Civil War	h. 13th Amendment
3.039	_____ law to control monopolies	i. Sherman Anti-Trust
3.040	_____ ended slavery in America	j. Treaty of Versailles
3.041	_____ no slavery north of 36° 30' except in Missouri	k. New Deal
3.042	_____ non-violent protests to end racial discrimination that began with the Montgomery Bus Boycott	l. Appeasement
		m. Technology
		n. NATO
3.043	_____ Supreme Court ruled that slavery could not be forbidden anywhere in the U.S.	o. Containment
		p. Berlin Wall
3.044	_____ land bought from France in the western Mississippi basin for 3¢ an acre	q. Louisiana Purchase
		r. Federalist
3.045	_____ document whose unfairness led to WWII	s. United Nations
3.046	_____ U.S. blockaded a Soviet ally to stop delivery of weapons that could have reached the American mainland, Soviets backed down	t. Civil Rights Movement
		u. Détente
		v. Inflation
3.047	_____ giving in to dictators before WWII, especially Hitler at Munich about Czechoslovakia	w. Gilded Age
		x. Roaring Twenties
3.048	_____ political party of John Adams, set up our basic institutions of government	
3.049	_____ improvements helped change American society	
3.050	_____ basic U.S. strategy during the Cold War	
3.051	_____ organization of nations to keep the peace that was created toward the end of WWII	

3.052 _____ America's first permanent alliance after the Revolutionary War

3.053 _____ Cold War thaw in the 1970s

3.054 _____ time of reform from the late 1800s to WWI

Name the war or major crisis (each answer, 3 points).

3.055 Impressment of American sailors by the British, Washington was burned, War Hawks,

_____

3.056 Shiloh, Gettysburg, Bull Run, Appomattox Courthouse, Sherman's march to the sea

_____

3.057 U-boats, Austrian heir killed in Sarajevo, Meuse-Argonne, trench warfare

_____

3.058 Lexington, Saratoga, Yorktown, alliance with France against Britain

_____

3.059 British-French war, Braddock was ambushed, training ground for the Revolution, William Pitt

organized victory _____

3.060 Training ground for the Civil War, heroes–Zachary Taylor & Winfield Scott, U.S. got California,

1847-48 _____

3.061 U.N. coalition drove Iraq out of Kuwait in 100-hour ground war, 1990-91

_____

3.062 U.N. forces fought to a stalemate on the 38th parallel in a divided nation with a communist

North (1950-53) _____

3.063 25% unemployment, Stock crash of 1929 _____

3.064 Destruction of the _Maine_ in Havana Harbor, San Juan Hill, Rough Riders, America became a

world power, 1898 _____

3.065 Island hopping in the Pacific to reach Japan, Atomic bombs, Holocaust, Pearl Harbor, D-day

_____

3.066 One of America's longest and most controversial wars, Gulf of Tonkin Resolution

_____

3.067 In the space provided or on a separate piece of paper, list the most recent presidents of the United States (beginning with Grover Cleveland) in chronological order (10 points).

Before taking the LIFEPAC Test, you may want to do one or more of these self checks.

1. _____ Read the objectives. See if you can do them.

2. _____ Restudy the material related to any objectives that you cannot do.

3. _____ Use the **SQ3R** study procedure to review the material.

4. _____ Review activities, Self Tests, and LIFEPAC vocabulary words.

5. _____ Restudy areas of weakness indicated by the last Self Test.

HISTORY & GEOGRAPHY 809
Cold War America (1945–1990)

LIFEPAC Test is located in the center of the booklet. Please remove before starting the unit.

Author:
Theresa Buskey, B.A., J.D.

Editor:
Alan Christopherson, M.S.

Westover Studios Design Team:
Phillip Pettet, Creative Lead
Teresa Davis, DTP Lead
Nick Castro
Andi Graham
Jerry Wingo

Alpha Omega
PUBLICATIONS

804 N. 2nd Ave. E.
Rock Rapids, IA 51246-1759

Cold War America (1945–1990)

Introduction

From 1945 to 1991, the U.S. and the Union of Soviet Socialist Republics (U.S.S.R.) met in a conflict called the "Cold War." It was a conflict of ideas, economics, propaganda, and intimidation. During all of those years, the two sides never directly fought each other in a "hot" war. However, during those years, international politics revolved around the confrontation between the two super powers.

One of the most important features of the Cold War was a massive arms race, particularly in the area of atomic weapons. By the end of the era, both sides had enough nuclear bombs to destroy all life on earth. This "mutually assured destruction," the ability of both sides to destroy the other if the bombs were ever used, was one of the main reasons the two sides never quite went to war. Both sides were aware that a U.S.-Soviet war could be the end for everyone on the planet.

The Cold War was a world war. Each super-power could count on the support of allies or satellites all over the world. Both fought tenaciously for the hearts of the non-aligned (neutral) nations. Civil wars became part of the Cold War as the Soviets and the Americans supported different sides. However, even in "hot" wars like Korea and Vietnam, the two great powers were careful to avoid expanding the wars beyond that place. These were "limited" wars, carefully restricted to prevent the dreaded World War III.

At the heart of the conflict was the difference between the ideas of the two sides. America was a republic that favored freedom of ideas and a free market economic system. The Soviet Union was a communist nation. Communism is a system that allows no freedom of thought and has an economy completely owned and run by the government. Moreover, communism is a system of flagrant lies. Its governments claim they are utopias where the workers have everything they need, when in reality, people barely have enough of anything. The truth about corruption, poverty, inefficiency, and failure is never reported. Eventually, communism collapsed in the Soviet Union under the weight of its own stupidity. That collapse finally ended the Cold War

Objectives

Read these objectives. The objectives tell you what you will be able to do when you have successfully completed this LIFEPAC. When you have finished this LIFEPAC, you should be able to:

1. Describe the course of the Cold War and the incidents within it.

2. Name the presidents of the Cold War and the events that happened during their administration.

3. Describe the course of the Civil Rights Movement.

4. Describe events in America and changes in American thinking during the Cold War era.

5. Name the important people on both sides of the Cold War.

Survey the LIFEPAC. Ask yourself some questions about this study and write your questions here.

1. HOT OR COLD?

The Cold War developed very quickly after World War II. Americans thought the Soviets would be willing to work with their allies after the defeat of Germany. Events quickly proved that assumption wrong.

Stalin was obsessed with protecting his nation by creating a buffer of loyal nations in Eastern Europe. Because these countries were occupied by Soviet troops, the Western nations could not stop it, except by starting another war. Stalin ignored his wartime promises and set up communist governments all over East Europe without allowing free elections.

These actions of Soviet aggression in the Middle East convinced America to abandon her traditional isolation. There was a very real fear that without the support of the United States,

much of the world might be forced under the control of a communist dictatorship. Therefore, America took the leadership of the free world to contain communism at all costs.

The threat communism posed to the free world dominated American policy and thinking for forty-five years. It was especially strong in the first half of the era, up until the 1970s. During this time, the line between cold and hot war was often dangerously thin. Two "limited" wars were fought between communist and non-communist forces in Korea and Vietnam. Incidents like the Berlin blockade, the Berlin Wall, and the Cuban Missile Crisis threatened to escalate to war. The danger of an earth-destroying war was all too real.

SECTION OBJECTIVES

Review these objectives. When you have completed this section, you should be able to:

1. Describe the course of the Cold War and the incidents within it.
2. Name the presidents of the Cold War and the events that happened during their administration.
4. Describe events in America and changes in American thinking during the Cold War era.
5. Name the important people on both sides of the Cold War.

VOCABULARY

Study these words to enhance your learning success in this section.

espionage (es' pē ə näzh). The use of spies to obtain information about the plans of a foreign government.

fait accompli (fāt' ak om plē'). A thing accomplished and presumably irreversible.

ideology (īd ē äl' ə jē). A systematic body of concepts about human life or culture.

summit (səm' ət). A conference of the highest-level officials (such as heads of government).

Note: *All vocabulary words in this LIFEPAC appear in* **boldface** *print the first time they are used. If you are not sure of the meaning when you are reading, study the definitions given.*

Pronunciation Key: hat, āge, cãre, fär; let, ēqual, tėrm; it, īce; hot, ōpen, ôrder; oil; out; cup, půt, rüle; child; long; thin; /ŦH/ for then; /zh/ for measure; /u/ or /ə/ represents /a/ in about, /e/ in taken, /i/ in pencil, /o/ in lemon, and /u/ in circus.

AMERICA from 1945 to 1990

Harry S. Truman
1945-1953
Democratic

Dwight D. Eisenhower
1953-1961
Republican

John F. Kennedy*
1961-1963
Democratic

Lyndon B. Johnson
1963-1969
Democratic

Richard M. Nixon
1969-1974
Republican

Gerald R. Ford
1974-1977
Republican

James E. Carter
1977-1981
Democratic

Ronald Reagan
1981-1989
Republican

George H. W. Bush
1989-1993
Republican

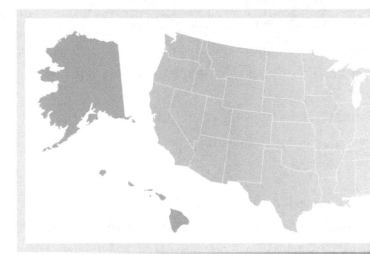

STATES ADMITTED TO THE UNION

Alaska 1959
Hawaii 1959

POPULATION of the United States of America

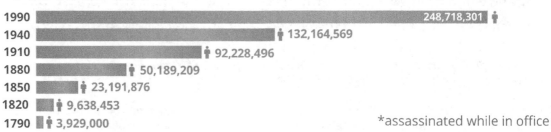

Year	Population
1990	248,718,301
1940	132,164,569
1910	92,228,496
1880	50,189,209
1850	23,191,876
1820	9,638,453
1790	3,929,000

*assassinated while in office

Origins of the Cold War

Harry S. Truman (1884-1972). Harry S. Truman was unprepared when he suddenly became president in 1945 upon the death of Franklin Roosevelt. He knew nothing of foreign policy and had not been kept up-to-date on anything the president was doing. He did not even know about the project to develop the atomic bomb before Roosevelt's death. Yet, he managed to face his own ignorance and rose to be considered, by some, among America's best presidents.

Harry Truman was born and lived most of his life in Missouri. He was widely read but never obtained a college degree. After high school, he worked at various jobs until 1917. He was an artillery officer in France during World War I. After the war, he tried his hand at business and failed. He became a county official with the support of the powerful Democratic Party boss in Missouri, Tom Pendergast. In spite of his association with the corrupt Pendergast machine, Truman was honest and remained free from scandal.

With the help of the Pendergast machine, Truman was elected to the U.S. Senate in 1934 and 1940. He rose to national prominence as the head of a Senate committee that worked to uncover inefficiency and waste in government war spending. The Truman Commission (as it was called) saved the government about $15 billion. He was a compromise candidate for the vice presidency in 1944. In spite of his difficult start, Truman would set American policy that would affect the whole course of the Cold War.

United Nations. Roosevelt had been determined to replace the toothless League of Nations after World War II. Roosevelt had also learned from Wilson's mistakes. The American delegation to negotiate the charter included Senators from both parties and it was not tied to a harsh treaty. The conference to write a charter for the new United Nations opened in San Francisco on April 25, 1945, just two weeks after the death of F.D.R. The charter was written in nine weeks by representatives from about fifty nations. The U.S. Senate approved it in a matter of days.

The United Nations was set up with a general assembly in which all nations have a say and a smaller Security Council that controls major decisions on international disputes. The U.S., U.S.S.R., Britain, France, and China all were given permanent seats on the Security Council. The council must unanimously agree on any decision, which gives any one council member veto power over decisions. The Soviets made regular use of their veto in the early years of the U.N. to block any action they believed was threatening to their power (over 100 times in the first 25 years). This was one factor in the rapid growth of distrust between the allies after the end of World War II.

Post-War Problems. American hopes that the wartime cooperation with the Soviets would continue into the post-war era were quickly dashed. Relations with the Soviets went downhill after the understanding established at Yalta in early 1945. The Soviets quickly established obedient communist governments in Poland, Hungary, Bulgaria, and Romania. Communist governments came to power on their own in Yugoslavia and Albania. The democratic government that took control in Czechoslovakia was overthrown by the communists in 1948. The borders of the U.S.S.R. and its new "satellite" nations were closed to prevent the contamination of communist lies by contact with the truth from the outside world.

Germany and Berlin, its capital, had been divided into four sections occupied by the Soviets, Americans, British, and French. The four sectors were supposed to work together and eventually be reunited under an elected government. From the beginning, the Soviets refused to work with their allies to reunite the nation. They held the agricultural section in the East and refused to ship food to the other areas. They also stripped their section of all valuable industries, transporting whole factories to the U.S.S.R. They refused to sign a treaty with Germany, which would require them to withdraw, and the Soviets set up a communist government in their section.

In the end, the three Western powers worked to unite their sectors as best they could. As the Soviets became more threatening, the Western powers softened their attitude toward Germany, realizing they would need to rebuild the nation to aid in blocking communism. Eventually, two separate nations, communist East Germany and free West Germany would be created out of the defeated Nazi nation.

In 1946, the Soviets refused to remove their troops from Iran, instead using them to aid a separatist movement in the north. The Soviets hoped to gain control over some of the vast oil wealth of the nation. America took the issue to the U.N. and threatened to use force. Stalin backed down as he was not willing to start a war.

American statesmen realized it was only a matter of time until the Soviet Union had its own atomic bomb. These statesmen wanted to avoid a deadly arms race. So, in 1946, when the U.S. was the only nation with the bomb, they proposed giving this technology to the U.N. for international control. The proposal (the Baruch Plan) would have given the U.N. the power to inspect all nuclear sites in the world and insure that the technology was only being used for peaceful purposes. The Soviet Union refused to open its nuclear sites (present or future) to inspectors and used its veto to stop the plan.

Containment. In 1947, the Soviet Union was pressuring Turkey to give them bases and control of the Dardanelles, the straits leading to the Black Sea and the southern Soviet ports. The Soviets were also supporting a communist revolt in Greece. Britain had traditionally been the Western power that handled crises in the Mediterranean. Devastated by the war, Britain

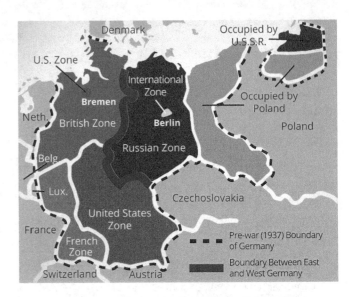

informed the U.S. that they no longer could bear the cost of defending those two nations against Soviet aggression.

Truman faced a key decision. Should the U.S. step in to stop communism in Greece and Turkey, or follow its tradition by not getting involved in Europe? He decided in favor of action. This decision set the course for the U.S. to actively oppose Soviet expansion for the duration of the Cold War.

Truman went before Congress in March of 1947 and asked for $400 million in aid for Greece and Turkey to prevent them from falling to a communist dictatorship. He knew that another war to end communism was out of the question. What he proposed was a policy recommended by an American diplomat, George Kernan. Kernan, who was an expert on the Soviet Union, recommended a steady, patient "containment" of Soviet expansion. If the communists were met with stable, forceful actions that prevented their expansion, they would be forced to calm down or rethink their policies, he believed.

Truman announced that it would be the policy of the U.S. to contain communism where it already existed. America would aid any free nation in the world faced with communist threats. This Containment Policy, or the Truman Doctrine, would be the foundation of all American policy toward

THE IRON CURTAIN

Netherlands

Belgium

German Democratic Republic

Poland

Federal Republic of Germany

U.S.S.R.

France

Czechoslovakia

Neutralized under treaty ending Allied occupation, 1955

Austria

Switzerland

Hungary

Italy

Romania

Yugoslavia

communism during the Cold War. It would have both positive and negative results. American aid would keep many free people from facing the grinding oppression of a communist takeover. However, many petty dictators would receive U.S. aid to enhance their personal power simply because their opponents supported communist ideals or were receiving Soviet aid. It was a good policy in principle, but often unjust in how it was used.

Marshall Plan. Congress, with the support of the American people, approved the aid to Greece and Turkey. Both of these nations overcame their communist threats with the American help. Then, Truman turned his sights on the rest of Europe. The continent was not recovering from the devastation of the war. Communist parties, which were strong in times of economic problems because they promise to control the economy, were threatening to win elections in France and Italy.

George Marshall, who had run the war from Washington, was now Truman's secretary of

state. He invited the nations of Europe to put together a plan for their recovery and the U.S. would supply the funds for it. Western Europe jumped at the offer. A conference in July of 1947 in Paris worked out the European end of the deal. The Soviet Union refused to allow its satellites to participate, calling the plan a capitalist plot. The U.S. Congress was reluctant to approve the Marshall Plan until February of 1948 when the head of the Czech democracy died mysteriously and the communists took over the nation. Congress authorized the funds.

The Marshall Plan was an incredible success. Within a few years, the Western nations were producing as much or more than they had before the war. The communists in France and Italy lost much of their popular support. Trade with Europe helped the American economy return to peacetime production. The Marshall Plan destroyed Soviet hopes of expanding into Western Europe. The strong, healthy Western democracies would not be susceptible to communist pressure, short of war.

Berlin Airlift. The Western powers continued to press forward with reforms in their sectors of Germany. In 1948, over strong Soviet objections, they set up currency reforms to aid the economy. The Soviets retaliated by cutting off all land routes to the American, French, and British sections of Berlin, inside the Soviet sector. The Soviets undoubtedly hoped to drive the democracies out of the city and bring it completely under Soviet control.

The U.S. refused to back down or start a war. Instead, American pilots began to fly supplies into the city. For almost a year, every piece of coal needed for heat, every cup of flour needed for bread, and every drop of medicine needed for the hospitals came in by plane. At the high point of the airlift, "Operation Vittles" landed a plane in Berlin once every three minutes around the clock. If a plane missed its landing on the first pass, it had to return to its home base. There were no openings on the runway for another try. The Soviets dropped the blockade in May of 1949.

NATO. The continuous aggressive action by the Soviets pushed the Western nations of Europe to sign a defensive treaty in 1948. Seeking security for itself and Europe, America was drawn into the alliance. In April of 1949, the United States broke 150 years of tradition when it signed a permanent alliance with eleven other Western democracies. The North Atlantic Treaty Organization (NATO) bound the nations to treat an attack on one nation as an attack on all. It was the first permanent alliance signed by the U.S. since the alliance with France during the Revolution. NATO was an apt symbol of the dramatic change in American thinking. She had now fully replaced Britain as the leader of the Western world.

Iron Curtain. By 1948, it was clear that the world had been divided into two armed camps. America led the free, wealthy Western democracies. They were called the Western Bloc and the Free or First World. The Soviet Union led the Communist nations which were referred to as the Communist or Eastern Bloc and as the Second World. Eventually, the poorer, developing nations of Africa, Asia, and Latin America, which were not clearly allied with either side, would be known as the Third World.

Winston Churchill, Britain's wartime leader, described the situation with his usual eloquence in March of 1946. In a speech at an American university Churchill stated: "an iron curtain has descended across the Continent" of Europe. The term "behind the Iron Curtain" was used throughout the Cold War to refer to the communist nations of Europe.

The United States made one basic assumption about communism during these early years. American leaders assumed that all communist nations and movements were under Soviet control. Many were, but not all. The U.S. was slow to realize that some revolutions that had Soviet support were not under perfect Soviet control. The U.S. also was slow to recognize differences between communist leaders of different nations. This "us against them" mentality limited American diplomatic choices for many years.

✎ **Name the person, treaty, or item.**

1.1 _____ the two systems of government in conflict during
the Cold War

_____

1.2 _____ group that makes the major international decisions
at the U.N.

1.3 _____ basic American policy toward communism

1.4 _____ American reaction to the blockade of Berlin, 1948-49

1.5 _____ America's first permanent alliance since the
Revolution

1.6 _____ President who set the basic American policies for
the Cold War

1.7 _____ aid plan that restored post-war Western Europe

1.8 _____ barrier between the Free and Communist Worlds in
Europe, named by Winston Churchill

1.9 _____ first two nations given U.S. aid to stop communism
after World War II

_____

1.10 _____ international organization created in 1945

1.11 _____ proposal in 1946 to put atomic power under U.N.
control

Complete these items.

1.12 How was Germany administered in the years right after the war?

_____

_____

_____

1.13 How did Germany wind up as two nations for the duration of the Cold War?

_____

_____

_____

1.14 What event in 1948 pushed Congress to approve the Marshall Plan?

_____

1.15 Name the nations of Eastern Europe that became communist after the war.

_____

_____

1.16 Name two Soviet actions in 1946 that pushed the world toward the Cold War.

_____

_____

1.17 Identify each of these groups.

    a. Western Bloc _____

    b. Eastern Bloc _____

    c. Third World _____

1.18 Describe the Truman Doctrine.

_____

_____

1.19 In your own words, describe why the Cold War developed after World War II.

_____

_____

_____

Heating Up, Cooling Down

1949. 1949 was a bad year for the Western Bloc. The Soviet Union exploded its first atomic bomb that year. American experts had been expecting this, but not so soon. The Soviet nuclear program was aided by communist **espionage** in America. The two superpowers immediately began to pour money into bigger and more sophisticated nuclear weapons to make sure their opponents never had an advantage over them. Both sides also realized that a war between the two Blocs now had the potential for destruction beyond anything ever seen before. They would have to make certain that war never started.

Also in 1949, America's ally in China, Chiang Kai-shek, lost in a civil war to the communist forces under Mao Zedong. Chiang's government (Nationalist China) was hopelessly corrupt and never was able to win the support of the huge peasant population, which followed Mao. American policymakers decided there was no way to prevent the loss if Chiang could not get the support of his own people. Chiang and the Nationalists fled to the island of Taiwan to live under American protection. America refused to recognize the new communist government and insisted for years that the Nationalists on Taiwan were the rightful rulers of China.

Mao was a charismatic leader and a different kind of communist than Stalin. Mao saw communism as a continuous revolution to bring his kind of "equality" to all people by force. Stalin was more practical, more interested in simple power than ideas. The Soviets gave the

Chinese communists economic and military aid for years, but the two sides eventually came to distrust each other. In time, communist Russia and communist China would actually fight along their border. However, it was years before the U.S. took advantage of this split.

In the meantime, rabid anti-communists in America demanded to know how we had "lost" China. Some charged that communist spies and sympathizers in the government had blocked the U.S. from giving the Nationalists the support they needed. The intense public reaction to the success of communism in China made future presidents very fearful of "losing" any more countries.

Korean War. The Soviet Union occupied the northern part of the Korean Peninsula after it declared war on Japan in the final days of World War II. The Americans occupied the southern part of the country, below the 38th parallel. Just as in Europe, Stalin set up a communist government in his section while the Americans established a democracy in theirs. The two sides each claimed to be the legitimate government of the whole nation and threatened to attack the other.

The U.S. eventually pulled its soldiers out of Korea and made statements that implied they would not protect the South. On June 25, 1950, the North attacked and quickly drove the smaller Southern army back. It appears, from the murky evidence, that Stalin did not plan the attack, but he did approve it. He probably thought his ally could win a quick, painless victory that the U.S. would be forced to accept as a *fait accompli*. He had not counted on Truman, the U.N., and MacArthur.

Truman was determined to defend his containment policy. If the communists were allowed to succeed with this kind of blatant armed attack in Korea, there was a serious concern they would try it in other places, like Europe. The president appealed to the United Nations. The Soviets were boycotting the Security Council

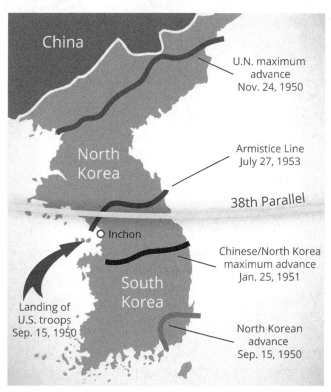

| The Korean War

because the Chinese seat was still held by the Nationalists of Taiwan. Without fear of a Soviet veto, the U.N. condemned the invasion and requested its members send troops to aid South Korea. Truman immediately sent American forces at the command of General Douglas MacArthur. Eventually, sixteen nations would send troops to aid the South, but South Korea and the U.S. would do most of the fighting.

MacArthur and the South Koreans were pushed back until they set up an effective defensive line around the city of Pusan. The Pusan Perimeter barely held the southeast corner of the peninsula. Then, MacArthur launched a brilliant amphibious landing at Inchon, behind the enemy lines, in September of 1950. The Northern lines collapsed and they retreated to their own territory. MacArthur pursued them and pushed north almost to the Chinese border by November.

MacArthur arrogantly dismissed any threat from the communist Chinese as his army came closer to their border. However, the Chinese sent in thousands of "volunteers" who drove the Americans back behind the 38th parallel yet again. Counterattacks stabilized the battle lines near the old border. The two sides remained stalemated there for the rest of the war.

Stung by his defeat, MacArthur wanted to bomb and blockade China, but Truman and his military superiors believed that might start World War III. They were willing to settle for the recovery of South Korea, communism would be contained without a world war. So, once the U.N. forces were back to the 38th parallel, Truman offered to open negotiations.

MacArthur was contemptuous of Truman's approach to the war. The arrogant general wanted a total victory over communism. He made threats against China and sent letters to Congress openly disputing the decisions of his superiors. One of the greatest threats to any democracy is a military that will not obey the elected leaders. MacArthur went too far, and Truman had the courage to fire him for insubordination in April, 1951.

The United States was violently anti-communist in 1951 and MacArthur was incredibly popular. He came home to a hero's welcome in the States. Truman, on the other hand, was so unpopular he could have been impeached easily if some grounds had been found. However, MacArthur's popular support did not survive a Congressional investigation. It quickly became clear that the military leadership in Washington agreed with Truman. None of them wanted to risk a war with China that could easily draw in the Soviet Union, just to the north. General Omar Bradley testified that MacArthur's plan would "involve us in the wrong war, at the wrong place, at the wrong time, and with the wrong enemy."

Peace talks opened in July of 1951 at a village near the 38th parallel. They quickly stuck over the issue of returning prisoners—repatriation.

| Nikita Khrushchev

Many of the prisoners did not want to go home and the U.N. was not willing to force them to do so. The communists insisted that the all prisoners must go home whether they wanted to or not! They did not want the public embarrassment of having many of their soldiers refuse. It would show that their countries were not a paradise as communist propaganda claimed. Over this issue, the talks stalled for two years while men continued to die.

Finally, in March of 1953, Stalin died. The new leadership in the Kremlin, the Soviet capital building, softened its tone somewhat. The newly elected U.S. president, Dwight D. Eisenhower, pushed for peace. As a result, an armistice was finally signed in July of 1953. Repatriation was voluntary, but each nation was allowed to visit the men who refused. About 14,000 Chinese, 7,600 N. Koreans, 325 S. Koreans, 21 Americans, and 1 British refused repatriation. A demilitarized zone was set up along the 38th parallel, but a final peace treaty to end the war was never signed.

Tensions. Tension continued between the two super powers after Korea. America set off a hydrogen bomb (a more powerful atomic weapon) in 1952. The Soviets followed quickly. In 1953, Soviet troops suppressed a rebellion in East Germany. In 1955, the Eastern Bloc created its own "defensive" alliance called the Warsaw Pact to counter NATO. Since communist **ideology** was to take over the world, these incidents kept the U.S. very nervous about Soviet actions and intentions.

For America, the bitterest failure of the Cold War came in Vietnam. Before World War II, part of Indochina (between India and China) had been a French colony. The French unwisely tried to retake it after the war. In Vietnam, they were opposed by Ho Chi Minh, a communist. Minh became very popular in the 1950s as his soldiers fought for the freedom of Vietnam from French domination. Because he was communist, the U.S. provided military aid to the French. In spite of the aid, the communist guerrillas, called Vietminh, continued to defeat the French. In March of 1954, the Vietminh overran a key French fortress called Dien Bien Phu. At that point, the French finally gave up.

An international conference made Laos, Cambodia, and Vietnam independent. Vietnam, however, was divided at the 17th parallel. The communists were given control of the north. The two sides were supposed to be united under free elections within two years. However, the Southern leaders feared the communists would destroy democracy. They, therefore, (with U.S. support) refused to participate. Thus, the U.S. found itself supporting an undemocratic government in the South against a popular leader in the north who had liberated his people from colonial rule. U.S. policy makers saw no alternative if communism was to be contained.

Thaw. Nikita Khrushchev arose as the new leader of the U.S.S.R. in the 1950s. He led the Cold War into its first "thaw," a time when the superpowers negotiated their differences and reduced conflict. In 1955, the Soviet Union finally signed a peace treaty with Austria which had also been split into four occupation zones. The treaty allowed that nation to reunite as a free, neutral country.

Khrushchev continued to soften the communist position. He met with President Eisenhower in Geneva, Switzerland later that same year to discuss issues. In 1956, he called for "peaceful coexistence" with the West, which was a big change from Stalin's position that war between the two sides was inevitable. He also denounced Stalin for his brutal excesses. (Stalin had controlled the U.S.S.R. with an iron hand and killed more people than Hitler.)

However, even with the peaceful words, the communist threat never completely withdrew. The U.S.S.R. continued to encourage and finance communist revolts all over the world. It also kept tight control over its European satellites. In 1956, the people of Hungary revolted against their communist leaders. The Soviet Union quickly sent in an army to overthrow the new government and restore communist rule. The leaders of the revolt were executed and about 200,000 people fled to Western Europe. A similar rebellion and bloody reprisal occurred in Czechoslovakia in 1968.

Middle East. In 1948, the nation of Israel was re-established in the Middle East after 1,878 years. The Arab, Islamic nations nearby immediately attacked and were defeated in a series of wars. The conflict between the Arabs and Israel was drawn into the Cold War, usually with the U.S. supporting Israel and the Soviet Union supporting the more aggressive Arab nations. Both of the superpowers tried to expand their influence in this oil-rich region by the use of financial aid.

Egypt in the mid-1950s came under the control of Gamal Abdel Nasser, an Arab nationalist who wanted to unite all Arabs under Egypt. Nasser needed money to build the massive Aswan Dam on the Nile for irrigation and electrical power. The U.S. and Britain offered to fund the project until Nasser began to make contacts with the Soviets. When the West withdrew its offer of aid, Nasser seized the Suez Canal, which was owned by French and British investors, intending to use the passage fees to build the dam. He closed the canal to Israeli traffic and threatened the supply of oil to Europe, which came through the canal.

Britain and France were irate and worked with Israel who was concerned about the expansion of Egyptian power. The nations attacked together in October of 1956. The French and British seized the canal while the Israelis attacked the Sinai Peninsula. America had not been informed of the assault and Eisenhower was furious with his impetuous allies. Under pressure, the three nations agreed to a cease fire, withdrew their troops and allowed U.N. forces to take over their positions. Eventually, the Soviet Union financed the Aswan Dam for Egypt.

Eisenhower Doctrine. Soviet activities in Egypt alarmed the U.S. In 1957 Congress approved the Eisenhower Doctrine which permitted the president to use armed force to assist any nation in the Middle East that asked for help against aggression from a communist nation. The Doctrine was used to support Lebanon in 1958 after a revolution threw out a pro-Western government in nearby Iraq.

 Choose the correct person. Some will be used more than once.

1.20 _____	leader of Egypt, Arab nationalist	a. Harry S. Truman
1.21 _____	American general in Korea	b. Mao Zedong
1.22 _____	U.S. president at the end of the Korean War	c. Chiang Kai Shek
1.23 _____	Vietnamese communist	d. Douglas MacArthur
1.24 _____	leader of the U.S.S.R. in the 1950s	e. Nikita Khrushchev
1.25 _____	U.S. president, start of the Korean War	f. Dwight D. Eisenhower
1.26 _____	general fired for insubordination	g. Gamal Abdel Nasser
1.27 _____	Communist victor in China, 1949	h. Ho Chi Minh
1.28 _____	leader of the Nationalist Chinese	
1.29 _____	Attacked Stalin for his excesses and called for peaceful coexistence with the West	
1.30 _____	took over the Suez Canal to use the income for the Aswan Dam	
1.31 _____	fought against the French reconquest of Vietnam after World War II	
1.32 _____	President who became very unpopular for a time for firing the U.S. commander in Korea	
1.33 _____	Chinese leader that had the support of the huge peasant population	
1.34 _____	corrupt Chinese leader, driven out to the island of Taiwan	

Give the information requested.

1.35 The two events that made 1949 a bad year for the West

_____

_____

1.36 Why the Soviet Union did not veto the protection of South Korea by the U.N.

_____

1.37 The name of the defensive line that held the southeast corner of Korea after the North

attacked in 1950 _____

1.38 Nation the U.S.S.R. finally allowed to reunite as free country in 1955 _____

1.39 Issue that stalled the Korean peace talks for two years

_____

1.40 The event that finally convinced the French to pull out of Vietnam

_____

1.41 The result of the Hungarian uprising in 1956

_____

_____

1.42 MacArthur's solution for advancing back up the Korean Peninsula in September 1950

_____

1.43 Place where the Korean War stalemated and the demilitarized zone was set up

_____

1.44 Nations that attacked Egypt in 1956 _____

1.45 The reason why Korea was communist in the north and free in the South

_____

_____

1.46 "Defensive" alliance of the Eastern Bloc _____

1.47 The Eisenhower Doctrine and where it was used in 1958

a. _____

_____

b. _____

Technology Race. A race for technology was also part of the Cold War. Both sides particularly worked to develop new ways to control and deliver atomic weapons. One key advance was the ICBM (intercontinental ballistic missile). These rockets were built to deliver atomic bombs to targets half a world away. Over the years of the Cold War, these self-guided bombs became bigger and more accurate. They were also built into special silos that could survive a nuclear attack and return fire. Elaborate precautions were taken to make sure the missiles could not be destroyed by an enemy's first strike.

The Soviets had one unusual advantage in the atomic race, a society that wasn't free. People had very reasonable fears of nuclear weapons. Americans and Europeans in their free societies openly debated whether the weapons should be built and put in place for use. The Soviets encouraged protests in the West against nuclear weapons. They financed elaborate propaganda that aided anti-nuclear groups in the Free World. Sometimes the protests in the West were loud and widespread, but the Western Bloc pressed ahead and refused to let down their guard. On the other hand, behind the Iron Curtain there were no protests as the governments spent money on nuclear weapons and technology. Protests were not allowed.

Sputnik. The Soviet Union shocked the West in October of 1957, by successfully launching the world's first artificial satellite into space, *Sputnik I*. It was followed just a month later by another satellite that carried a small dog. It would be four months after *Sputnik* before the first American satellite, *Explorer I*, was successfully launched into space. The Soviets gloated that their success proved the superiority of their system, as they did every time they beat the West at anything.

Americans were shocked and frightened by the prospect of a Soviet advantage in space and rocketry. The primary fear was that they had also developed more advanced missiles.

President Eisenhower reacted by setting up NASA (the National Aeronautics and Space Administration) to coordinate U.S. space exploration and push the U.S. missile program forward.

NASA was an exceptional success. Although starting behind the Soviet space program, NASA quickly caught up and made America the world leader in space exploration. The Soviets put the first man in space and they were the first to have a man orbit the earth (1961). NASA, however, succeeded in putting the first men on the moon (1969) and developed the first reusable space craft, the Space Shuttle (1981). The moon landing in 1969 was a world-wide event that greatly enhanced American prestige. Millions of people watched on their televisions, as American Astronaut Neil Armstrong took the first human steps on the moon, saying "That's one small step for man. One giant leap for mankind." Thus, much of America's spectacular success in space and satellite technology was a product of the Cold War.

U-2 Affair. As part of the continuing thaw between the U.S. and the U.S.S.R., Eisenhower invited Khrushchev to visit America in 1959. Khrushchev toured the nation amid a great deal of publicity. However, even in this atmosphere of friendship, he harshly predicted to his American listeners that "your grandchildren will live under communism." He and Eisenhower met for talks at Camp David, the presidential retreat. The talks produced little except that Khrushchev withdrew an ultimatum he made that the West had to evacuate West Berlin. Another **summit** was scheduled for Paris in May of 1960, and Eisenhower was invited to visit the U.S.S.R. afterward.

The U.S. had been keeping track of Soviet missile development by the use of spy planes. The planes flew at high altitudes over Soviet territory and took pictures of missile and military sites. Just days before the summit was to begin, the Soviets shot down one of the U-2 spy planes and captured the pilot, Francis Gary

Powers, alive. At first, the U.S. issued bungling denials about the plane's mission. Eventually, Eisenhower admitted the truth and accepted full responsibility. He refused to apologize, however, or stop the flights. Khrushchev stormed out of the Paris meeting and withdrew his invitation for the president to visit Russia.

Cuba. Latin America was suffering from its own woes in the post-war era, mainly from poverty and non-democratic governments. The island of Cuba was an excellent example. From 1933 to 1959 the government was usually under the control of Fulgencio Batista, a dictator. He encouraged American investment in the island, which is only 70 miles south of Florida. As a result, a very wealthy elite of Cubans and Americans ran the nation's economy while most of the people lived in poverty without any political power.

Batista was overthrown in 1959 by a revolutionary named Fidel Castro. At first, the U.S. supported the new regime. However, Castro quickly began to seize American-owned property and relations between the two nations soured. Castro signed a trade agreement with the U.S.S.R. in 1960, so the U.S. stopped buying Cuban sugar. In January, 1961 the U.S. cut off relations with Cuba, by then a communist dictatorship.

Cuba would be a thorn in the side of the U.S. for many years, even after the fall of communism in Russia. The main problem was the threat of a communist nation that close to the American mainland. Also, Castro's economy depended heavily on money and trade concessions from the Soviets. As a result, he was a willing ally for any "wars of liberation" supported by the U.S.S.R. Cuban troops fought in many communist-sponsored revolts in Latin America and Africa, with the Soviets providing the money and the weapons.

| Francis Gary Powers and a U-2 Spy plane

Bay of Pigs. There was strong support in the U.S. government for overthrowing Castro. A group of Cubans who fled the island when he came to power planned to do that in 1961. They were trained by the American CIA (Central Intelligence Agency) with the knowledge and support of Eisenhower. President Kennedy allowed the plan to go as scheduled in April of 1961. However, he did not provide the military aid that had been promised and the people of the island did not support the invasion. As a result, the invasion at the Bay of Pigs in Southern Cuba was a disaster. The invaders were quickly killed or captured and the U.S. suffered a very embarrassing blow to its prestige.

Cuban Missile Crisis. The Cuban Missile Crisis was possibly the most dangerous event of the Cold War. The two superpowers came perilously close to a direct confrontation over this in 1962. It began in October, when spy pictures revealed that the Soviets were in the process of building missile bases in Cuba. Atomic missiles from those bases could have reached most of the continental United States.

Kennedy could not let those missiles be installed, yet he did not want to start a war. Instead, he established a naval blockade around the island to prevent the missiles from being delivered. He demanded the bases be dismantled. However, the seizure of a Soviet ship coming into Cuba would be likely to trigger a war. The question was whether or not the Soviets would challenge the blockade. The world held its breath while Moscow decided. The ships carrying the missiles turned back, rather than challenge the blockade.

Khrushchev offered to remove the missiles in exchange for a U.S. promise never to invade Cuba. He followed that offer with a demand that the U.S. remove the missiles it had in Turkey in return for removing the bases in Cuba. Kennedy accepted the first offer and ignored the second. The Cuban launch sites were dismantled and the U.S. quietly removed its out-of-date missiles in Turkey several months later.

Berlin Wall. Berlin was a sore spot in East-West relations throughout the Cold War. The Western and Eastern sectors had separate governments by 1948, but people could still cross between the two sections freely. Many people fled East Germany by traveling to East Berlin and crossing into the Western sector where they were given asylum.

In the late 1950s and early 60s the Soviets kept threatening to turn over control of Berlin's access routes to the East German government.

| The Berlin Wall before 1989

That would have made Berlin hostage to a communist government which was not bound by the Yalta agreements as the Soviets were. The threat was never carried out, but it raised tensions in Europe. Millions of East Germans fled to the west through Berlin.

The government of East Germany was desperate to stop the outflow of people which reached a height of 1,000 people a day. Many of those leaving were talented young people who saw no future for themselves under communism. Very suddenly, on August 13, 1961, Soviet and East German soldiers sealed the border between East and West Berlin. They immediately began to build a wall to enclose the eastern part of the city. Eventually, the Berlin Wall included tank traps, barbed wire, guard towers, attack dogs, and a high concrete fence which separated the two parts of the city. The West Germans called it **Schandmauer** (wall of shame). It would stand until 1989.

Identify the person, item, or crisis.

1.48 _____ broke up the Paris summit in 1960

1.49 _____ device used by the communists to stop East Germans from defecting to the West through Berlin

1.50 _____ the Soviet ships carrying missiles turned back rather than challenge an American blockade of Cuba

1.51 _____ a U.S. sponsored invasion of Cuba that failed completely

1.52 _____ Soviet satellite, first ever put into orbit

1.53 _____ American space development group founded by Eisenhower

1.54 _____ dictator of Cuba until 1959

1.55 _____ Communist dictator of Cuba after 1959

1.56 _____ rockets designed to carry atomic bombs halfway around the world

1.57 _____ superpower that sent the first animal and man into space

1.58 _____ superpower that put the first man on the moon and developed the first reusable spacecraft

1.59 _____ threatened Americans that "your grandchildren will live under communism"

1.60 _____ this nation's soldiers used Soviet money and weapons to fight for communism all over the world

1.61 _____ American and Soviet leaders who faced off over missile bases in Cuba in 1961

_____

1.62 _____ European city divided into two parts by the Cold War

1.63 _____ Kennedy promised not to do this to end the crisis over missiles in Cuba

Vietnam

The war in Vietnam was a major turning point in the Cold War for American policy and self-confidence. The U.S. backed out of the bitter Vietnamese War, which it could not win, leaving an ally to fall to communism. It was a humiliating failure that still scars American thinking.

Why. The U.S. became deeply involved in Vietnam for several reasons. American policy makers wanted an option between appeasement and nuclear war to prevent the spread of communism. The use of American soldiers to protect non-communist countries in small, "limited" wars seemed to be a good option. There was a substantial fear that if one nation fell to communism, it would naturally export the "disease" to its neighbors. The entire region would fall like dominoes. The "domino theory" made Americans fearful of losing even a small, unimportant nation to communism. Also, since all communist countries were believed to be loyal to Moscow, there was a fear that communist expansion would build an unshakable Soviet world empire. Thus, the U.S. committed its immense power to prevent South Vietnam from falling to communism.

Diem's Failure. The government of South Vietnam had been organized under President Ngo Dinh Diem in 1955, after the Geneva Accords divided the nation in 1954. The U.S. supported Diem when he refused to participate in elections for the entire nation. War began in 1957 when the followers of Ho Chi Minh in South Vietnam began a revolt against Diem's government. The Viet Cong, as they were called, saw this as a continuation of their war for independence. The Viet Cong and the Vietminh (North Vietnamese,) steadily expanded their numbers and attacks in the South. They were kept well-supplied by China and the U.S.S.R. using the Ho Chi Minh trail that ran from North Vietnam through neutral Laos and Cambodia.

| The Vietnam War

The U.S. sent advisors and aid to the Diem's government to protect it from the revolt. Washington initially hoped to support the regime until it could establish a free economy and social justice that would turn the people forever against communism. However, Diem was more interested in his own power than his people. His persecution of Buddhists drew sharp protests from his own people. Finally, Kennedy tacitly approved of a military coup that overthrew Diem, resulting in his death in 1963. By that time, the U.S. had thousands of military and civilian advisors in the South.

The coup destroyed the remaining stability of the South Vietnamese government. Several military governments came to power in the following years. None of them had widespread support among the people. Most were seen as U.S. puppets. In the meantime, the Viet Cong and Vietminh troops took over more and more of the countryside in the South.

Gulf of Tonkin Incident. Two U.S. naval destroyers were allegedly attacked by the North Vietnamese in the Gulf of Tonkin in August of 1964. President Johnson seized on the incident as an excuse to use U.S. troops to turn the tide in South Vietnam. He persuaded Congress to authorize him to take whatever measures the president thought were necessary to protect American forces in Southeast Asia. This sweeping Gulf of Tonkin Resolution was the legal basis for sending in U.S. troops without a declaration of war. It was a blank check for the presidents to do as they pleased. After the 1964 elections were over, Johnson sent the first American troops to fight in Vietnam.

The U.S. strategy was to destroy the communist army in the South. The better organized and better equipped Americans consistently won the battles. For years, the U.S. sent more men, weapons, advisors, and aid, but they could never eliminate the enemy. Men and supplies continued to come from the north. U.S. policy would not permit an advance into North Vietnam because that might trigger a war with Russia or China. Instead, the U.S. only bombed the North. At the high point of American involvement in 1969, over 500,000 American soldiers were fighting in the war, handicapped by their inability to attack the enemy at the source of his strength, North Vietnam.

The Viet Cong favored a strategy of guerrilla warfare. They worked in small groups attacking and retreating. They laid ambushes and traps wherever they went. They often retreated into Laos or Cambodia where U.S. troops could not follow because those were neutral nations. The success of these tactics led to a military stalemate in South Vietnam.

Effect at Home. In the U.S. by the end of the 1960s, a reaction had set in against the war. Television coverage brought the horrors of war into every living room. The increasing number of dead Americans, and the sheer cost of the war made it very unpopular. War spending

| The evacuation of Saigon

caused inflation and forced cutbacks in spending on social programs. Many people began to question whether it was worth the cost and why we were supporting the unpopular, corrupt Southern government. Young people who hated the war, staged huge (and often violent) protests that raged across the nation. Young men fled to Canada to avoid being drafted to serve in the unpopular war. The many men that did serve honorably found themselves hated and scorned by their own countrymen.

Tet Offensive. The U.S. government insisted that it was winning the war. However, in January 1968 the communists launched a major offensive against the Southern cities during the Vietnamese New Year Festival, Tet. The Viet Cong and Vietminh suffered massive casualties as the surprise assault was slowly turned back. However, the attack proved the communists were stronger than the U.S. government had admitted. Americans began to distrust their government even more. As a result, President Johnson cut back the war effort and did not run for re-election in 1968. Peace negotiations were also opened, but they stalled.

U.S. Withdrawal. President Nixon, who was elected in 1968, took the Cold War in a new direction. In Vietnam, he began the process he called "Vietnamization." The goal was for the South Vietnamese to take over the fighting while the U.S. slowly withdrew. He pushed secret peace talks which quickly stalled.

Nixon also freely expanded the war to put pressure on the North to negotiate. In 1970, he authorized an attack on communist supply bases in Cambodia. When the peace talks produced an unacceptable agreement in 1972, he ordered bombing resumed in the north. These produced huge protests in America. The nation wanted out of the pointless, endless war.

North and South Vietnam finally agreed to a "cease fire" in January of 1973. U.S. soldiers left by the end of March. However, the peace treaty did not bring peace. It just created a lull in the fighting that allowed the U.S. to get out of the longest and most controversial war in its history. Nixon called it "peace with honor," but there was no peace and no honor, just a retreat under cover of treaty. North Vietnam kept many of its soldiers in the South, and rapidly began new offensives.

The end for South Vietnam came in April of 1975, when the Northern army captured the Southern capital of Saigon. One of the enduring images of the war was the sight of hundreds of Americans and South Vietnamese officials lined up to take helicopters to safety from the top of the U.S. Embassy as the communist army poured into the city. The U.S. Congress refused to send any aid, washing their hands of the whole situation.

Vietnam was reunited, although under a communist government. Thousands of South Vietnamese were sent to "re-education camps," concentration camps where they were mistreated and forced to learn communist ideology. Thousands more risked death in leaky, overcrowded boats in an attempt to flee. The "boat people" filled refugee camps in the nearby nations. Thousands of American lives and billions of U.S. dollars had not prevented the fall of South Vietnam.

Cambodia. Cambodia, also called Kampuchea, had also been fighting the communists who were using their nation as a base against South Vietnam. In 1975, a Cambodian communist group called the Khmer Rouge took over the nation. Their leader, Pol Pot, was a follower of Mao Zedong and a believer in continuous revolution. He ordered the cities emptied. Educated people were killed. All of the people were forced to work by hand on farms. Over a million people (perhaps as much as one-fifth of the population) died of mistreatment, disease, hunger or murder. The Khmer Rouge was defeated in 1979 by the Vietnamese who invaded and installed a puppet regime there. Laos had fallen to the communists in 1975, thus the U.S. loss was total in French Indochina.

 Complete these sentences.

1.64 Congress authorized the president to conduct the war in Vietnam by passing the

_____ .

1.65 The horrors of war became very real to most Americans because of the

_____ coverage.

1.66 The _____ in January of 1968 proved that the communists were very strong in South Vietnam.

1.67 _____ was the South Vietnamese leader who was overthrown by a military coup in 1963.

1.68 The South Vietnamese communists were called the _____ while those from the North were the _____ .

1.69 Nixon's plan to turn the war over to the South Vietnamese was called _____ _____ .

1.70 _____ was the leader of the Cambodian communists known as the _____ , who killed over a million people in the mid-1970s.

1.71 The idea that if one nation became communist, its neighbors would soon do so also was called the _____ theory.

1.72 The U.S. strategy in the Vietnam War was to _____ _____ in the South without invading _____ .

1.73 The defeat of South Vietnam was completed in 1975 with the fall of the city of _____ _____ .

1.74 The communists in Vietnam used _____ warfare.

1.75 Thousands of South Vietnamese were sent to _____ camps or became _____ attempting to flee after 1975.

1.76 The North and South signed a _____ in 1973 that allowed the U.S. to _____ .

1.77 As the war became unpopular, there were widespread _____ in the U.S. against it.

1.78 Not only Vietnam, but the neighboring nations of _____ and _____ fell to communism in the 1970s.

Review the material in this section in preparation for the Self Test. The Self Test will check your mastery of this particular section. The items missed on this Self Test will indicate specific areas where restudy is needed for mastery.

SELF TEST 1

Choose the correct person for each description (2 points, each answer).

1.01 _____ Leader of Egypt, took over the Suez
        Canal to pay for the Aswan Dam

1.02 _____ Set up containment as U.S. policy

1.03 _____ Created a communist dictatorship in Cuba

1.04 _____ Leader of the U.S.S.R. in the 1950s

1.05 _____ Nationalist Chinese leader, fled to Taiwan

1.06 _____ South Vietnamese leader, refused to allow
        elections with the North, overthrown and
        killed by a military coup

1.07 _____ American commander in Korea, fired
        for insubordination

1.08 _____ Communist victor in China, believed in
        continuous revolution

1.09 _____ Cambodian communist, killed over a million people due to his ideas on revolution

1.010 _____ Pro-American Cuban dictator overthrown by a revolution in 1959

1.011 _____ Communist leader of North Vietnam, fought the French and Americans

a. Harry S. Truman

b. Ho Chi Minh

c. Mao Zedong

d. Chiang Kai Shek

e. Nikita Khrushchev

f. Douglas MacArthur

g. Gamal Abdel Nasser

h. Fidel Castro

i. Fulgencio Batista

j. Ngo Dinh Diem

k. Pol Pot

Answer these questions (each answer, 5 points).

1.012 What was the Cold War and what kept it from becoming "hot?"

_____

_____

_____

1.013 What was the Containment Policy and how was it enforced?

_____

_____

_____

Choose the correct letter (each answer, 2 points).

1.014	_____	American space agency created to catch up with the Soviets in rocketry and space explorations	a. United Nations
1.015	_____	North Vietnamese attack during New Year, showed they were not as weak as U.S. claimed	b. Marshall Plan
1.016	_____	South Vietnamese communists	c. Iron Curtain
1.017	_____	America's first permanent alliance since the 1770s, made to protect against communism	d. Berlin Airlift
1.018	_____	Could deliver nuclear bombs half a world away	e. NATO
1.019	_____	First artificial satellite, Soviet	f. Sputnik
1.020	_____	Failed attempt to overthrow Castro	g. NASA
1.021	_____	New policy of U.S.S.R. toward the U.S. after the death of Stalin	h. peaceful coexistence
1.022	_____	"Defensive" alliance of the communist nations	i. Eisenhower Doctrine
1.023	_____	Name for the Free or First World	j. U-2 Affair
1.024	_____	Dividing line between the free and communist nations of Europe	k. ICBM
1.025	_____	A war fought to stop communism in a specific country that was not allowed to spread	l. Bay of Pigs
1.026	_____	Supplied the divided German capital for a year when the Soviets blockaded it, 1948-49	m. Cuban Missile Crisis
1.027	_____	U.S. blockaded Castro's island to prevent the delivery of Soviet missiles; Soviets backed down	n. Berlin Wall
1.028	_____	U.S. would assist any nation in the Middle East that wanted aid against communist aggression	o. Gulf of Tonkin Resolution
1.029	_____	Aid to Europe that helped it recover from World War II	p. Tet Offensive
1.030	_____	New postwar league of nations which the U.S. quickly joined	q. limited war
1.031	_____	Communist Bloc or the Second World nations	r. Viet Cong
1.032	_____	Congress gave the president uncontrolled freedom to use force in Vietnam	s. Third World
1.033	_____	Undeveloped nations, not closely allied with any side in the Cold War	t. Warsaw Pact
1.034	_____	Way to stop East Germans from escaping to the West through Berlin	u. Eastern Bloc
1.035	_____	An American spy plane was shot down over Russia and the pilot captured; ended plans for a summit and Eisenhower's visit to the U.S.S.R.	v. Western Bloc

Answer these questions (each answer, 5 points).

1.036 What was the course of the fighting in the Korean War?

_____

_____

_____

_____

1.037 What issue held up the peace talks in the Korean War and how was it resolved?

_____

_____

_____

_____

1.038 Why was the war in Vietnam unpopular and how did many Americans react to it?

_____

_____

_____

_____

1.039 What Soviet actions after World War II started the Cold War?

_____

_____

_____

_____

Answer this question (4 points).

1.040 Why was 1949 a bad year for the West?

_____

_____

_____

80 / 100   SCORE _____   TEACHER _____ _____

initials   date

2. BETWEEN WAR AND WATERGATE

America went through many conflicts between World War II, and the scandal called "Watergate" in the 1970s. The era of the Korean War saw the national government torn apart by unjust searches for American communists. Black Americans rose up and organized to demand their rights as citizens. They were violently opposed by some deeply prejudiced white Americans. A president, a famous black leader, and a presidential candidate died by assassination. Young people staged a mass, public rebellion against the values and ideals of American society.

The unpopular Vietnamese War pitted Americans against each other. The Cold War entered a new thaw when the U.S. restored relations with China, and signed several agreements with the U.S.S.R. These, however, did not resolve the fundamental conflict. Finally, a president was forced to resign after a two-year long scandal which dragged his office to its lowest place in generations. In the last section, it was shown that there was trauma abroad. This section will show how the post-war years were very traumatic for America at <u>home</u>.

SECTION OBJECTIVES

Review these objectives. When you have completed this section, you should be able to:

1. Describe the course of the Cold War and the incidents within it.

2. Name the presidents of the Cold War and the events that happened during their administration.

3. Describe the course of the Civil Rights Movement.

4. Describe events in America and changes in American thinking during the Cold War era.

5. Name the important people on both sides of the Cold War.

VOCABULARY

Study these words to enhance your learning success in this section.

censure (sen' chər). A judgment involving condemnation.

conventional (kən vench' nəl). Not making use of nuclear powers.

détente (dā tänt). A relaxation of strained relations or tensions between nations.

inflation (in flā' shən). A substantial and continuing rise in the general level of prices.

poll (pōl). A questioning or canvassing of persons selected at random or by quota to obtain information or opinions to be analyzed.

subpoena (sə pē nə). A writ commanding a person designated in it to appear in court under a penalty for failure.

Truman/Eisenhower

Post-war economy. Truman had to deal with the problems created by the end of World War II as well as the Cold War. After years of crisis (the Great Depression and the war) no one was certain how the American economy would react in the 1940s. The two biggest fears were a depression when war spending stopped, or massive **inflation** as people spent their war savings. There was also a housing shortage because building supplies were not available during the war.

A depression was never a serious threat. During the war, people had earned large amounts of money which they could not spend, because consumer goods were not available. After 1945, the manufacturers quickly retooled to produce those goods, creating jobs. People quickly started buying, keeping the manufacturing going. A boom in construction, especially homes, also created jobs. The G.I. Bill of Rights (passed in 1944) gave veterans loans, grants for college, and other benefits that helped them adjust to civilian life.

Inflation, however, quickly became a problem after the war. Truman wanted to continue the price controls implemented during the war, but the Republican Congress elected in 1946 did not. Price controls were weakened and then eliminated by the end of 1946. Prices continued to rise rapidly, but wages did not go up as fast. The result was widespread labor disputes and strikes.

Truman wanted to continue and expand F.D.R.'s liberal programs. His proposals included a national health care system, civil rights legislation, expansion of Social Security, and laws to protect minorities in employment. The Congress enacted only a fair employment act, giving Truman fodder for the 1948 presidential election. The Republican Congress, however, did pass the Taft-Hartley act that restricted the power of unions, over Truman's veto.

| Truman defeated Dewey in 1948.

Election of 1948. The Democratic Party split three ways in 1948. A group of liberal Democrats formed a new Progressive Party around nominee Henry Wallace favoring a more conciliatory attitude toward the Soviets. Truman was selected as the nominee for the Democratic Party at its convention. However, the party platform called for civil rights legislation to fight discrimination against the black population. Southern Democrats walked out and nominated their own candidate, Strom Thurmond of South Carolina, calling themselves the States' Rights or "Dixiecrat" Party.

The delighted Republicans had every reason to believe they would have an easy victory. They renominated Thomas E. Dewey who had lost to Roosevelt in 1944. Dewey, however, was dangerously overconfident, especially after he established a big lead in the **polls**. He did not establish any clear-cut proposals; in fact, he was deliberately vague about everything.

Truman, on the other hand, surprised everyone. He set out on the road to make a fight of it. He toured the country by train, making speeches at all the stops. He attacked the "do nothing" Congress. He lambasted the Taft-Hartley Act and swung hard at his opponents on every front. His common touch and hard fighting attitude rapidly won support. In the end, he beat out Dewey and both of his quasi-Democratic opponents.

Fair Deal. The Democrats won control of Congress in 1948, which gave Truman high hopes for his legislative program called the "Fair Deal." It was an ambitious expansion of the New Deal. Opposed by conservative Democrats, the program was not very successful. Congress, however, did pass an increase in the minimum wage, an expansion of Social Security, some public works projects, and some low-income housing. Truman's civil rights program, national health insurance, and agricultural reforms, however, all failed.

Bad Deal. The tensions with the U.S.S.R. produced an avalanche of anti-communist sympathy in the U.S. The Cold War crisis made people fearful that they might lose their freedoms to this odious system. Their fears were directed not only against the Soviets, but also against real or imagined communist agents in America. People believed the accusations that communists in the federal government were working to destroy the nation.

These fears were reinforced by two prominent cases. The first case involved Alger Hiss, who had been a prominent official in the State Department. He was credibly accused of having passed secrets to a communist spy. The spy, Whittaker Chambers, changed sides and denounced him in 1948. He produced enough evidence for Hiss to be convicted of perjury for denying the charge under oath. The second case involved Julius and Ethel Rosenberg. They were convicted in 1951 of sending atomic bomb secrets to the Soviet Union. They were executed amidst great controversy in 1953.

In this atmosphere, Truman set up the Federal Employee Loyalty Program, which investigated federal workers. Congress set up its own committees to do the same thing. The committees' investigations resulted in few criminal charges, but also led to a great deal of harassment and intimidation. Hundreds of government, media, and university employees lost their jobs because they favored communism, did not favor strong opposition to communism, had communist/socialist friends or were simply too stubborn to answer questions they felt violated their rights.

Election of 1952. Truman chose not to run in 1952 and gave his support to the Democratic nominee, Adlai Stevenson, governor of Illinois. The Republicans, however, gained the upper hand by nominating the incredibly popular war hero, Dwight (Ike) Eisenhower. Senator Richard M. Nixon from California, a virulent anti-communist, was chosen as his running mate.

The Republican campaign centered on the popularity of their candidate. The campaign slogan said it all: "I Like Ike." Nixon attacked the Democrats as soft on communism, while Ike dramatically promised to personally go to Korea and end that war. During the campaign, it came out that Nixon had access to a secret fund set up in California for his political expenses. Nixon defended himself in an emotional speech and was kept on the ticket by Eisenhower. They won an easy victory and the Republicans gained control of the House and a tie in the Senate.

Dwight D. Eisenhower (1890-1969). Dwight David Eisenhower was very popular and successful, both as a general and as president. He was born in Denison, Texas and grew up in Abilene, Kansas. His father worked in a creamery, and from an early age, Dwight did odd jobs to help support the family. After high school, he worked one year to support a brother in college and, then, secured an appointment to West Point, where he could get a college education paid for by the tax payers.

After graduation in 1915, he served in various posts all over the world. He trained recruits in the U.S. during World War I. Eventually, he impressed his superiors enough that he was given special training for leadership within the army. When World War II came, he was selected to command the U.S. forces for invasion of North Africa and, later, all Allied forces in Europe. He showed considerable skill in making all of the different Allied armies and their opinionated commanders work together. He was eventually promoted to the newly- created rank of five star general. After the war, he served as Army Chief of Staff. He retired briefly to become the president of Columbia University and was recalled to duty to serve as the first commander of NATO. He retired from that to run for the presidency in 1952.

McCarthy. The most famous of the anti-communist Congressmen was Senator Joseph McCarthy of Wisconsin. He became an incredibly powerful person for several years before 1954. His technique was accusing people of being communists in the State Department, or some other organization. He could never prove his charges, but it did not matter. People believed him. He ruined the careers of many honest men by denouncing them as communists on little or no evidence. He did considerable damage to the morale and effectiveness of the government in the early 1950s. People were afraid of him.

McCarthy's witch hunt led him to attack the army in 1954. However, the end of the Korean War in 1953 had eased Cold War tensions and the army fought back. Senate hearings on McCarthy's charges were shown live on television. In the hearings, McCarthy finally came across as a lying bully tossing around unproven charges. He lost public support, was **censured** by the Senate, and faded into obscurity. His excesses made "McCarthyism" a name for an unfair, intrusive investigation based on questionable or made up evidence.

Civil Rights–Background. The Civil War had settled the issue of slavery, but had left black Americans as second-class citizens. They were forced to use segregated, inferior public facilities, and schools. They were often denied the right to vote by special laws or intimidation. They were discriminated against in employment, housing, and services. However, by the 1950s American attitudes were finally beginning to change, and African Americans began an effective campaign to receive equal treatment under the law.

Violent opposition to black equality in the South, and more passive acceptance of white superiority in the North, had kept African Americans from acting sooner. Black leaders of the post-Civil War era faced immense cultural pressure for black people to accept an inferior position. One of the greatest black leaders of the post-Civil War era, Booker T. Washington, was an excellent example of this dilemma.

Washington was born into slavery, but managed by hard work to obtain an education and, eventually, a nationwide reputation as an educator and spokesman for African Americans. He founded and led Tuskegee Institute, which taught black students trades such as carpentry. In order to effectively support black people, especially those who had just recently escaped slavery, and overcome the violent hostility of white people, who held all the political power, Washington argued for a slow approach to black equality. He urged black people to learn a trade and make themselves successful in the American economy. He accepted segregation as a temporary measure to allow black Americans time to build up their wealth and level of education. He stressed the need for black people to get along with the system for now and wait until they became more economically successful before demanding legal equality.

Washington saw his plan as a slow path to equality. Many white people supported it because it had the effect of keeping black Americans "in their place," which aligned with their racist views. Washington's chief opponent was W.E.B. DuBois, a black historian, sociologist, and communist party member. He argued that black people should have the opportunity for higher education and should press for equality now. DuBois was among the founders of the National Association for the Advancement of Colored People (NAACP), which has historically been in the forefront of the battle for civil rights. At that time, there was almost no public support for black equality.

African American soldiers fought bravely in both World Wars in segregated units, although they were often assigned to do manual labor rather than fight. In 1948, Truman used his authority to order the federal bureaucracy and the army to integrate. The integrated units did well in Korea in spite of the dire predictions by white supremacists that they would fail. However, Truman had been unable to get civil rights legislation, and Eisenhower did not make it a priority. Finally, however, the African Americans and the courts stepped in and got the ball rolling.

Civil Rights–Beginnings. The modern movement for civil rights began in December of 1955 in Montgomery, Alabama. It was triggered by a black woman named Rosa Parks who refused, one day, to sit in the back of the bus as segregation laws required. She was arrested and the black people of Montgomery rose to support her. Led by Martin Luther King, Jr., a Baptist pastor, they peacefully boycotted the bus system for a year. With the help of the courts, who sided with the protesters, bus segregation in that city was ended. This incident gave Dr. King a national reputation and set off a mass movement among African Americans to press for full and fair equality.

They were aided in their quest by the federal court system under Earl Warren, Chief Justice of the Supreme Court. The Warren Court moved American law substantially in the direction of individual rights. In 1896 the Supreme Court had ruled in *Plessy v. Ferguson,* that "separate but equal" facilities for black and white people

| Students entering Central High School

were constitutional. The facilities had since then been separate, but <u>never</u> equal. The Court reversed itself in *Brown v. Board of Education of Topeka* in 1954. The Court ruled that segregation in education was "inherently unequal" and ordered schools to integrate with "all deliberate speed."

Following a court order, Central High School in Little Rock, Arkansas prepared to admit nine African American teenagers in 1957. The governor of the state, Orville E. Faubus, mobilized the National Guard and public opinion to stop it. Angry mobs surrounded the school and made it unsafe for the black students to attend. Eisenhower, who had shown little interest in pushing integration, would not let such a challenge to federal authority pass. He sent in armed paratroopers who surrounded the school and escorted the students to class. The image of quiet black students trying to get an education, passing through crowds of jeering, hateful white people began to open the long-closed doors of the American conscience.

In that same year, congress finally passed a new Civil Rights Law (the first since the 1870s). It set up a Civil Rights Commission to investigate violations of the rights of minority groups and authorized some protection of voting rights. It was a start, but it lacked the force needed to be effective.

Second Administration. Eisenhower easily won re-election in 1956 despite the fact of a heart attack in 1955 and an attack of intestinal problems that required surgery in 1956. Besides civil rights legislation, Eisenhower had several successes during his term. He believed in careful control of government finances. He balanced the federal budget three of his eight years by laying off federal workers and eliminating projects. He did, however, approve several expensive projects that benefitted the nation. He supported a plan to invest billions in an interstate highway system and signed a bill setting up the St. Lawrence Seaway that brought ocean traffic into the Great Lakes.

Eisenhower's personal popularity did not extend to the whole Republican Party, however. The Democrats gained control of Congress in 1954 and kept it through the remainder of Ike's term. Nevertheless, he kept the nation on a steady path of increasing prosperity that was only briefly interrupted by a recession in 1957-58. His legacy was a time of stability and growth—a welcome relief after the tempestuous years leading up to the 1950s.

 Name the item, event, or person.

2.1 _____ Truman's legislative program

2.2 _____ Anti-communist senator, censured for his accusations

2.3 _____ Post-Civil War black leader, accepted segregation until black people could gain economic power

2.4 _____ Economic problem right after World War II

2.5 _____ Former State Department official convicted of perjury for lying about passing information to a spy

2.6 _____ First commander of NATO

2.7 _____ The three parties the Democrats split into in 1948
_____
_____

2.8 _____ Anti-union law passed by Republican Congress over Truman's veto

2.9 _____ Set up by Truman to look for government communists
_____

2.10 _____ 1952 Republican presidential slogan

2.11 _____ Black historian/sociologist, helped found NAACP

2.12 _____ Woman whose decision to sit in front triggered the Civil Rights movement

2.13 _____ City that Eisenhower sent paratroopers to escort black teenagers to school

2.14 _____ Gave veterans loans and grants to adjust after the war

2.15 _____ Supreme Court Chief Justice, expanded individual rights

2.16 _____ Expensive transportation plans set up under Eisenhower

_____

2.17 _____ Eisenhower's vice president

2.18 _____ Court decision ordered the end of segregated education

2.19 _____ Black pastor who led the Montgomery bus boycott

2.20 _____ Pair executed for giving atomic secrets to the U.S.S.R.

_____

2.21 _____ Court decision, allowed "separate but equal"

Answer these questions.

2.22 Who was expected to win the presidency in 1948 and why didn't he?

_____

_____

_____

_____

2.23 What legislation did Truman want that never became laws?

_____

_____

Kennedy/Johnson

Election of 1960. The new 22nd Amendment to the Constitution prevented Eisenhower from running in 1960. The Republicans, therefore, nominated Richard Nixon. The Democrats, after a bruising primary fight, selected Senator John F. Kennedy, a Massachusetts millionaire. His closest rival in the party, Senator Lyndon Johnson of Texas, was picked as the vice presidential candidate.

Kennedy was a Roman Catholic and prejudice was still strong enough to be a factor in the campaign. Kennedy won points by facing the issue squarely and assuring Americans that the Pope would not be running the country. Nixon emphasized his own long experience, but the Democrats attacked the easygoing "do nothing" Eisenhower style. The key to the election was probably a series of four televised debates between the candidates (the first in history). The youthful, good-looking Kennedy came across better on TV than Nixon. Kennedy won the election by a thin popular (about 120,000 votes out of 68 million), but comfortable electoral vote (303 to 219). Congress fell to the Democrats by a wide margin.

John F. Kennedy (1917-1963). John F. Kennedy has grown into a legend in U.S. history because of his youth, vigor, and sudden death by assassination. John, or "Jack" as he was also known, was the second of eight children born to Joseph and Rose Kennedy. He was born near Boston in 1917. His father was a self-made millionaire whose family was politically active. Jack attended various schools before graduating from Harvard University in 1939. He turned his senior thesis (why Britain had not been ready for war) into a best-selling book.

Kennedy fought in World War II as the commander of a PT boat in the South Pacific. His boat was cut in half by a Japanese destroyer in 1943. Kennedy, suffering from an injured back, towed another injured man to safety on a nearby island. He spent several days searching

| A Peace Corps Volunteer in Africa

for help. Thanks to his efforts, the survivors were rescued five days later. Kennedy received the Navy and Marine Corps Medal for his leadership and heroism.

Jack's older brother, Joseph, was expected to go into politics, but he died in World War II. So, Jack took up the family passion. He served three terms in the U.S. House, beginning in 1946, and defeated a popular long-term Republican senator in 1952. He wrote a Pulitzer Prize winning book, *Profiles in Courage*, during his first term in the Senate, while recovering from surgery for his old back injury. He was re-elected to the Senate in 1958 and successfully ran for president in 1960. His poise and good looks on television helped overcome a perception that he was too young at 43 to take on the responsibilities of the presidency.

New Frontier. Kennedy brought a new style into the White House. He and his cabinet were younger than any of his predecessors, and far less passive in their politics. Even Kennedy's family was young. He had a 3 year old daughter, Caroline, and a newborn son, John, Jr., when he was inaugurated. He and his stylish wife, Jackie, were widely admired and emulated. Life in Washington was more active and activist than it had been in years. Kennedy challenged Americans to "ask not what your country can do for you: ask what you can do for your country."

Kennedy called his legislative program the "New Frontier." The Democrats controlled Congress, but the Southern Democrats and Republicans worked together to thwart his agenda, as they had the two previous administrations. The president could not get laws to aid education or mass transportation. He also failed to get a medical insurance for the elderly and a new department for housing and cities. However, he did achieve an increase in the minimum wage, expanded presidential power over tariffs, and some aid for depressed areas, but much of his most ambitious plans stayed snarled up in Congressional committees.

Kennedy's greatest success was the Peace Corps. He started it in 1961 by a presidential order. It was a program to send volunteers to Third World nations to help them improve their living conditions. Corps volunteers worked to improve health care, agriculture, transportation, and housing. These volunteers continue to work all over the world bringing their knowledge and their nation's goodwill.

Foreign Affairs. The Cold War pressed hard on the young president. He had to deal with the Bay of Pigs, Soviet threats to give East Germany control of Berlin's supply routes, the Cuban Missile Crisis, and the building of the Berlin Wall during his short administration. Kennedy began a program of aid called the *Alliance for Progress* to promote social reforms in Latin America to reduce the popularity of communism there. He also built up American **conventional** forces to give the U.S. more flexibility than just nuclear weapons. During his term, the U.S. signed a treaty banning atomic bomb testing in the atmosphere, outer space, and under water. This treaty between the U.S., U.S.S.R.,

| Martin Luther King, Jr.

and Britain limited testing to underground, thus eliminating the danger of radioactive fallout. The U.S. and U.S.S.R. also established a "hotline," a direct communications link between the White House and the Kremlin. That gave them immediate access to each other in the event of a crisis. Thus, the trend toward "thaws" continued under Kennedy.

Civil Rights Movement. Following the success of the Montgomery bus boycott, Martin Luther King became the center of a nationwide movement for civil rights. King used non-violent protests to fight the segregation that still dominated the South. His firm commitment to peaceful protest and Christian love won widespread support and sympathy, including white Americans. He rapidly became the most famous and influential African American figure in U.S. history.

The movement took off in the 1960s. Young black students stayed at lunch counters when they were refused service. They just sat there, peacefully, blocking the tables. These "sit-ins" spread all over the South. Other protesters "sat-in" on segregated buses, "waded-in" at segregated beaches, and "prayed-in" at segregated churches. The pressure for change mounted quickly.

In 1963, King and his Southern Christian Leadership Conference organized a series of mass demonstrations and marches in Birmingham, Alabama to protest the heavy segregation there. Birmingham police responded by using fire hoses, attack dogs, and cattle prods against the unarmed, peaceful protesters. The entire travesty was captured on national television. It caused an outcry against segregation and prompted Kennedy to propose a stronger civil rights law.

Later that same year, King organized a massive march in Washington D.C. to push for the Civil Rights Act and draw attention to the need for racial equality. The March on Washington drew over 200,000 people to the Lincoln Memorial in August of 1963. There King gave a memorable, stirring speech that called for a color-blind nation. "I Have a Dream" was a challenge to all Americans to fulfill the promise of freedom.

Kennedy's Death. On November 22, 1963 Kennedy visited Dallas, Texas. While riding in an open car, he was shot in the head with a rifle from a nearby building. He died moments later at a local hospital. Harvey Oswald, a communist sympathizer, was arrested later that day and charged with the crime. Two days later, Oswald was being moved to another jail when another man, Jack Ruby, shot him. The shooting was seen on national television. The entire episode was so bizarre that a special investigation was conducted under Chief Justice Earl Warren. The Warren Commission decided the evidence showed that Oswald acted alone, but many people still believe theories of some sort of conspiracy.

| Johnson and the expansion of the War in Vietnam

Lyndon B. Johnson (1908-1973). Lyndon Baines Johnson was sworn in as the nation's 36th president on an airplane carrying Kennedy's body back to Washington. Johnson was born and raised in central Texas. His parents were teachers who also farmed. He attended local schools and worked his way through Southwest Texas State Teachers College, graduating in 1930. He was successful in debates and school politics in college.

After graduating, Johnson went to Washington as a congressional secretary. In 1935, he was appointed by F.D.R. to run a New Deal administration in Texas. He was elected to the House of Representatives in 1937. During World War II, he served in the navy as a special representative of the president. He was elected to the U.S. Senate in 1948 and 1954, serving as the Democratic majority leader.

Johnson was a remarkable legislator, skilled in the art of passing or preventing laws and getting votes. One of his first acts as president was to push through much of Kennedy's stalled legislation. The Civil Rights Act was passed in 1964. It forbade segregation in public accommodations, barred federal funds for segregated projects, and expanded federal protection of voting rights. He also pushed through a tax cut Kennedy requested and other stalled New Frontier laws.

HISTORY & GEOGRAPHY 809

LIFEPAC TEST

NAME _____

DATE _____

SCORE _____

HISTORY & GEOGRAPHY 809: LIFEPAC TEST

Name the scandal, crisis, war, or event (each answer, 3 points).

1. U.S. aid to Europe to help it recover from World War II

   _____

2. "Defensive alliance" of the Iron Curtain nations

   _____

3. 1990-91 war to drive Saddam Hussein out of Kuwait

   _____

4. Unpopular war that caused protests all over the U.S. in the 1960s and early 70s

   _____

5. Castro was blockaded from receiving Soviet nuclear weapons, 1962

   _____

6. Crisis under Jimmy Carter in which an embassy staff was held for 444 days

   _____

7. Speech given by Martin Luther King during the March on Washington, 1963

   _____

8. Largest economic problem after World War II until the end of the 1970s

   _____

9. Resolution that gave the president wide authority to act in Vietnam

   _____

10. Scandal involving an attempt to "bug" the Democratic National Headquarters

    _____

11. War that included the Pusan Perimeter and the landing at Inchon, peace treaty hung up over
    the return of prisoners _____

12. Scandal under Ronald Reagan, sold weapons to encourage the release of hostages in Beirut,
    used the money for anti-communist rebels in Nicaragua

    _____

13. City divided by the "Wall of Shame" during the Cold War

    _____

14. Volunteers to Third World nations, set up by John Kennedy _____

15. Western Alliance military against communism _____

Define or describe each of these terms (each answer, 4 points).

16. Containment _____

_____

_____

_____

17. Cold War _____

_____

_____

_____

18. Limited War _____

_____

_____

_____

19. *Perestroika* and *glasnost* _____

_____

_____

_____

20. Détente _____

_____

_____

_____

Answer these questions (each answer, 5 points).

21.   What made 1989 a miracle year in the Cold War? _____

       _____

       _____

       _____

22.   What methods were used by the Civil Rights Movement to confront segregation?

       _____

       _____

       _____

23.   What effect did Vietnam have on America? _____

       _____

       _____

       _____

Match these people (each answer, 2 points).

24.   _____   Appointed vice president, pardoned Nixon   a. Harry Truman

25.   _____   Anti-communist senator, led witch hunt   b. Dwight Eisenhower
                  in the government, censured   c. Lyndon Johnson

26.   _____   Bay of Pigs, Alliance for Progress, New Frontier   d. Jimmy Carter

27.   _____   Desert Storm, Invasion of Panama, Savings   e. Richard Nixon
                  and Loan Crisis, Miracle Year in Europe   f. Gerald Ford

28.   _____   Energy Crisis, human rights in foreign policy,   g. Ronald Reagan
                  Camp David Accords   h. Joseph McCarthy

29.   _____   U-2 Affair, end of the Korean War, National Guard   i. John Kennedy
                  escorted black students in Little Rock, Arkansas   j. George H. W. Bush

30.   _____   Passed much of the Civil Rights laws, Great Society,
                  huge build up in Vietnam

31.   _____   Resigned from office, first president to visit Communist China and the U.S.S.R.

32.   _____   Deficits due to tax cuts and increased military spending, invasion of Grenada,
                  the rise of Gorbachev

33.   _____   United Nations, Fair Deal, beginning of Korean War

Election of 1964. Johnson easily won the Democratic nomination in 1964. His liberal program, called the Great Society, called for government spending to end poverty in America. His Republican opponent was Senator Barry Goldwater of Arizona, a strong conservative who wanted to undo much of the New Deal. Goldwater was bluntly honest about his beliefs. The Democrats attacked him as unstable and likely to start World War III. The popularity of Johnson's programs and fears about what Goldwater might do gave Johnson a huge victory. He won 43 million votes to Goldwater's 27 million.

Great Society. The Congress elected in 1964 had a huge Democratic majority and it proceeded to give Johnson anything he wanted. The deficit soared as money was spent on the War on Poverty, aid to education, medical insurance for the elderly (Medicare), and medical care for the poor (Medicaid). Two new cabinet posts were set up for Housing and Urban Development and Transportation.

Johnson was also the president who expanded the U.S. role in Vietnam. He obtained the Gulf of Tonkin Resolution and used it to commit more and more soldiers to the war. As it dragged on, without an end in sight, protests spread all over the country. War costs forced Congress to cut back spending on the Great Society. Johnson became increasingly unpopular as people began to doubt his war strategy and his honesty about the situation. Finally, the Tet Offensive and a stunning showing by a Democratic opponent in the first 1968 primary, convinced Johnson he was finished. He announced he would not run again.

Civil Rights Movement. After the Civil Rights Act, Martin Luther King, Jr. shifted his emphasis to registering black voters. Unjust voting laws and threats kept many black Americans from voting across the South. A drive to register black voters in Mississippi in 1964 was largely unsuccessful due to violence against the organizers. In 1965 King tried again in Selma, Alabama. State police broke up a peaceful march on the capital with tear gas and whips.

Again, the nation was shaken by the violence which was covered by television. Johnson rose to the occasion and quickly passed the Voting Rights Act of 1965 which ended literacy tests (used only to stop black voters) and set up federal registration of voters in several Southern states.

The success of the Civil Rights Movement led to high expectations and anger over slow solutions. Riots broke out in 1965 in Watts, a predominately black section of Los Angeles. Other race riots followed all over the nation in the next few years. Violence against Civil Rights workers continued, and many black people began to believe that King's non-violent approach was inadequate. Anti-white "Black Power" advocates began to call for violence and some occurred. The Civil Rights Movement lost much of its strength and white support. The riots and the violence by more radical black individuals or groups frightened the white majority and took away the movement's high moral standing.

Martin Luther King, Jr. continued to call for peaceful pressure, but in April of 1968 the growing violence of the nation swept over him. He was killed by an assassin's bullet. Riots broke out all over the nation when the news was announced. A white man named James Earl Ray, who was an escaped convict, pled guilty to the shooting and was sentenced to 99 years in jail. As with Kennedy, many people have never accepted the official finding that the assassin acted alone.

The Civil Rights Movement was an amazing success. It forced the end of a hundred years of legal inequality in the "land of the free and the brave." It enabled many talented black artists, teachers, thinkers, and businessmen to fulfill their potential. It promoted black Americans into the halls of power in city, state, and federal governments. Personal prejudice and differences in wealth did and still do exist. The steps taken from 1955 to 1968 were mighty ones, ones that should make all Americans proud of the results and ashamed that it took so long.

🖉 **Locate a copy of Dr. Martin Luther King Jr.'s "I Have a Dream" speech, either online or in a reference book**. Answer these questions about the speech.

2.24 How did Dr. King want his children to be judged?

_____

2.25 What patriotic song did he quote?

_____

2.26 What documents wrote the check Dr. King wanted to cash?

_____

2.27 What did he want the sons of former slave owners and slaves to do?

_____

2.28 What did he caution black Americans not to do?

_____

2.29 What is your personal opinion of the speech?

_____

_____

_____

_____

Complete these sentences.

2.30 President _____ received his college degree from Southwest Texas Teacher's College.

2.31 Kennedy wrote a Pulitzer Prize winning book, _____ , while a senator.

2.32 Kennedy's legislative program was called _____ while Johnson's was _____ .

2.33 Kennedy probably won the 1960 election because he came across well in _____ _____ .

2.34 The unpopularity of the _____ forced Johnson not to run for president in 1968.

2.35 Martin Luther King used _____ protests to push for desegregation.

2.36 _____ was assassinated in April of 1968 by _____

_____ , an escaped convict.

2.37 _____ was assassinated on November 22, 1963 in Dallas, Texas

by _____ .

2.38 The _____ , started by Kennedy, sends volunteers all over the

world to aid developing nations.

2.39 Lyndon Johnson was a very skilled _____ who was able to push

through much of Kennedy's agenda after his death.

2.40 Kennedy's aid program to Latin America was called the _____

_____ .

2.41 King gave his famous _____ speech in Washington

in 1963.

2.42 Kennedy was a decorated war hero as the commander of a _____

in the South Pacific.

2.43 The Civil Rights Act of 1964 was proposed after _____

and passed after the assassination of _____ .

2.44 Kennedy contributed to the Cold War thaw by signing a treaty banning nuclear testing in

_____

and by establishing a communication _____ between

Washington and Moscow.

2.45 At a "sit-in" at a segregated restaurant, Civil Rights protesters would _____

_____ .

2.46 The Republican candidate in 1960 was _____ and in

1964 it was _____ .

2.47 A riot in _____ in 1965 was the first of

many across the nation over the next few years.

Nixon

Election of 1968. The 1968 campaign was marred by the violence of the times. Robert Kennedy, brother of the late president, was assassinated in June while campaigning in California. That took away the leading Democratic anti-war candidate. The eventual nominee, Vice President Hubert Humphrey, fully supported the way Johnson had conducted the war. Frustrated anti-war protesters descended on Chicago for the Democratic convention in August. They clashed with police around the convention hall creating a battle zone that television displayed all over the nation. In the meantime, the Republicans nominated Richard Nixon. George C. Wallace of Alabama ran a third party challenge (American Independent Party). Nixon won by a narrow margin, but Congress remained Democratic.

Richard M. Nixon (1913-1994). Richard Milhous Nixon was the only U.S. president ever to resign from office. Nixon was born and raised in California. His father worked at a variety of jobs as did Richard growing up. He graduated from Whittier College (a Quaker school) in 1934 and obtained a law degree from Duke University in 1937. He practiced law in California after graduating and joined the Board of Trustees at Whittier College. He served in the navy during World War II, and two terms in the U.S. House afterward. He was elected to the Senate in 1950, but he left to become vice president under Eisenhower after the 1952 election.

Social Changes. The 1960s and early '70s were a time of unrest and change in America. Masses of young people rebelled against the morals and traditions of their parents. They protested *en masse* for and against a variety of causes (drugs, feminism, Vietnam, pollution, college courses, etc.). Marriage and traditional families were rejected. Drug use rose. Some people refused to pursue careers, seeking to live without the bonds of the "money-seeking society" they hated. Many dropped out of

| "Hippies"

society forming bands of "hippies" who claimed to practice universal peace and brotherhood, sharing all that they owned with each other.

The rebellion slowly died as the young adults grew up, facing the responsibilities of children, and the necessity of working to survive. However, they sowed rebellion and we still reap the results. The divorce rate in America had been small in the 1950s, but by the 1990s, half of all marriages ended in divorce. Drug use spread from the inner cities to middle class America. Illegitimacy rose and those children were far more likely to live in poverty. Moral standards in America have changed steadily since the 1960s. Many of the changes are apparent in laws and court cases, such as the *Roe v. Wade* case in 1973, which legalized abortion, and state laws that enabled euthanasia. The mass rebellion and change of the 1960s is connected to laws and beliefs of later decades.

Domestic Issues. Nixon's main domestic problems were inflation, the Supreme Court and social unrest. Inflation rose in the 1970s. Prices doubled between 1970 and 1980. Without rapid increases in their wages, people actually earned less as the money they made was worth less! The new president tried to slow down the economy and balance the budget by cutting government spending. This caused unemployment without slowing the inflation at all. (This combination of a stagnant economy and inflation was called "stagflation.") He stopped trying to balance the budget and deficits continued to rise. Nixon did not like price controls, but in 1971, under his New Economic Policy, he instituted some. He began with a three month freeze on all wages and prices. He also established boards to regulate salaries and prices, but the efforts were largely ineffective.

The Supreme Court had been very active under Chief Justice Earl Warren. It had expanded the rights of prisoners, banned prayer in schools, and required equal representation in Congressional districts. The Court was very controversial and Nixon had vowed to tame it. He appointed Warren Burger, a conservative judge, to replace Earl Warren in 1969. He was also able to replace three other justices with more conservative men. The new court did not throw out the Warren Court decisions (as Nixon wanted), but it did modify or soften some of them.

The Burger Court continued to be an activist in some areas including school integration. In the early 1970s, the court ordered "busing" to force racial balance for all schools in a district. For example, if most of the white population in a town was in the East and most of the black population in the West, the Eastern schools would be mainly white and the Western mainly black. Busing required students to be bused to a school across town to obtain the same racial balance in each school. Many people had bought houses near a specific school so their children could go there. Now the children had to ride a bus all the way across town to a different school. Busing was expensive and incredibly unpopular, especially among white Americans. However, it continued in many places until the mid-1980s.

The youthful protesters of the 1960s and early '70s chose the Vietnam War as their favorite cause. These protests reached their height in early '70s as Nixon continued bombing and attacked Cambodia before ending the war. The protests often became violent as students (protests were often at colleges) threw debris, smashed windows, and set fires. At one point, protesters tried to shut down Washington by blocking roads and bridges. One of the worst incidents occurred at Kent State University in May of 1970. National Guardsmen trying to keep order during a protest opened fire on the students. Four people were killed and others wounded.

Vietnam. Nixon's greatest success came in foreign policy. He introduced the one of the last major stages of the Cold War, **détente**. In Vietnam, he quickly began Vietnamization, reducing the number of U.S. troops. He based his actions on what was called the "Nixon Doctrine." The president said that the U.S. would no longer fight in Asia to stop communism. Instead, America would provide supplies and support, but leave the fighting to the nation's army. This was a major modification of the containment policy. Basically, the U.S. had been so hurt by Vietnam that it was no longer willing to fight for containment, only to pay for it. While he was scaling back, Nixon pushed hard for a peace agreement that would allow the Americans to leave entirely. Eventually, Congress also withdrew the Gulf of Tonkin Resolution and passed the War Powers Act that limited how long the president could send out troops without Congressional approval.

Election of 1972. The Democrats nominated Governor George McGovern of Alabama for president in 1972. Nixon easily took the Republican nomination. Vietnam was again a major issue. Nixon had reduced the number of U.S. ground troops, but was still using the president's authority to fight. McGovern called for an immediate withdrawal, regardless of the consequences. He also favored a number of liberal plans that pleased the radicals but not traditional Democrats. He hoped to get the full support of young people who could now vote since the 26th Amendment (1971) lowered the voting age from twenty-one to eighteen, but it did not happen. Right before the election Kissinger announced that "peace was at hand" in the negotiations with North Vietnam. Nixon won by a landslide with over 60% of the votes.

Détente. The break between the U.S.S.R. and China had been obvious for years, but it was Nixon who finally took advantage of it. He and his brilliant foreign policy advisor, later Secretary of State, Henry Kissinger, went back to traditional diplomacy. They treated the U.S.S.R. and China not as two parts of a massive communist alliance, but as rival nations. Nixon made peace overtures toward China, which had had no official contacts with the U.S. since 1949. Nixon's hope was that the Soviet Union would be threatened by a possible American-Chinese friendship. That threat might lead them to make their own offer of friendship with America to avoid being isolated. It was old "balance of power" diplomacy and it worked.

Nixon had made his reputation in politics as an anti-communist. So, when he announced that he would visit China in 1972, it was a national shock. Nixon also allowed China to join the United Nations and replace Taiwan on the Security Council. Taiwan was thrown completely out of the U.N. by the anti-American assembly and has never been allowed back. The China visit in 1972 produced goodwill, images of Nixon walking on the Great Wall and the beginning of direct talks between the two nations.

By the early 1970s, the Soviet Union was firmly under the control of Leonid Brezhnev. The threat of a U.S.-Chinese friendship, as well as the Soviet need for Western technology (the Free World was much better at developing new technology,) pushed Brezhnev to improve relations with the U.S. Nixon became the first U.S. president to visit the Soviet Union when

| President Nixon visits China

he went in 1972 for a summit. The two sides signed SALT (Strategic Arms Limitation Treaty) and agreed not to increase their number of missiles for five years. They also signed agreements for cultural and technical cooperation.

Détente lasted through most of the 1970s, but the Soviet Union never truly wanted peace. It still worked in the Third World to create more communist nations. It used treaties and agreements to improve its weapons and power. It arrested its own citizens who argued for more freedom. Nixon had hoped that détente would open up the Iron Curtain nations to Western ideas and bring the fall of communism. It did not succeed at that time. Relations with China continued to improve even after détente ended in 1979, but that nation remained communist and a major rival power to the U.S. even after the end of the Cold War.

Watergate. Nixon's realistic approach to diplomacy and his moderate success at home would have left him with a fine legacy in history if not for Watergate. Watergate was the name of the scandal that eventually forced Richard Nixon to become the only U.S. president to resign from office. It began in June of 1972 when several men were caught trying to break into the Democratic National Party Headquarters in the Watergate building in Washington. They were carrying electronic equipment to "bug" the office and listen to what went on there. One of the men worked for the Committee for the Re-Election of the President (CRP)! The burglars, a CRP employee, and a White House consultant were eventually convicted for the break-in. Nixon denied any knowledge of the burglary or of a cover-up among his aides to hide their involvement.

After the 1972 election, evidence was found linking several presidential aides to the burglary and a cover-up. An investigation began in May of 1973 when Nixon promised a full inquiry and appointed Archibald Cox as a special prosecutor. Cox and a Senate committee, led by Senator Sam Ervin, conducted a long, public investigation. One White House aide, John Dean, turned on the president, accusing him of covering up his aides' involvement in the burglary and using government agencies to harass his enemies, but there was no evidence to support Dean's story and Nixon denied it.

Then, it was discovered that Nixon had been secretly taping all conversations in his office since 1971. Cox and the committee asked for the tapes of Nixon's conversations with Dean to confirm or deny his version of what happened. Nixon refused, saying it would harm the authority of the president to reveal his private conversations. He offered to give Cox summaries of the tapes in October of 1973. When the prosecutor refused, Nixon ordered the Attorney General to fire him. The Attorney General and his assistant both resigned rather than fire Cox for doing his job. Their replacement finally obeyed the president and fired Cox. This "Saturday night massacre" prompted the House to begin the impeachment process.

In October of 1973, Vice President Spiro Agnew resigned from office because of corruption charges unrelated to Watergate. Nixon appointed Representative Gerald Ford to replace Agnew under the procedure set up in the 25th Amendment. Ford was approved by the Senate and took office in December of 1973 as the nation's first appointed vice president.

Cox was replaced by Leon Jaworski who continued to press the investigation. When Nixon finally bowed to legal pressure and gave some of the tapes to a federal judge in late 1973, several key parts were missing or erased. In April of 1974, Jaworski obtained a **subpoena** for the needed tapes and related documents. In response, the president released over a thousand pages of written transcripts taken from the recordings. Still, Jaworski insisted on getting the tapes and the Supreme Court ruled in his favor in July of 1974. That same month, a House committee asked the whole body to vote on three articles of impeachment against the president for abuse of power and withholding evidence.

The end came in August. Under pressure, Nixon finally released the key missing transcripts which showed he had approved a cover-up just days after the burglary. At that point, Nixon lost all of his support in Congress. Impeachment was certain. He resigned on August 9, 1974 and Gerald Ford became president. Eventually, twenty-nine people went to jail for the burglary or related crimes of trying to hide White House involvement.

Name the item, idea, or person.

2.48 Type of diplomacy used by Nixon and Kissinger with China and the U.S.S.R.

_____

2.49 Cold War thaw of the 1970s _____

2.50 The U.S. would use only money, not soldiers, to pursue containment in Asia

_____

2.51 Soviet leader in the 1970s _____

2.52 Favorite cause of the protesters of the 1960s and 70s _____

2.53 People who clashed with police at the 1968 Democratic convention _____

_____

2.54 The first U.S. president to visit the Soviet Union and Red (Communist) China

_____

2.55 Scandal that ended Nixon's presidency _____

2.56 Combination of a stagnate economy and inflation in the 1970s _____

_____

2.57 First appointed vice president _____

2.58 Place where National Guardsmen opened fire on protesters in May of 1970

_____

2.59 Sending children across town to school to achieve racial balance _____

2.60 Result of the 26th Amendment _____

2.61 What the Watergate burglars were trying to do _____

_____

2.62 Vice president who resigned in 1973 due to corruption charges _____

2.63 Names of the two special prosecutors for Watergate _____

_____

2.64 China replaced this nation at the U.N. _____

2.65 New Supreme Court Chief Justice, 1969 _____

2.66 Law that limits how long the president can send out troops on his own authority

_____

2.67 1968 Democratic candidate _____

2.68 1972 Democratic candidate _____

2.69 Two nuclear weapons agreements signed at 1972 U.S.-U.S.S.R. summit

_____

_____

2.70 White House aide who first accused Nixon of a cover-up _____

2.71 Records kept by Nixon that were eventually used to prove his involvement in the cover-up

_____

2.72 Leading anti-war candidate in 1968, assassinated _____

2.73 Source of many of the social problems of the 1990s _____

_____

2.74 Nixon's brilliant foreign policy advisor/Secretary of State _____

_____

2.75 What did the youth of the 1960s reject? _____

_____

Answer these questions.

2.76 Why was Nixon's visit to China such a shock? _____

_____

2.77 What were two of the social results of the 1960s rebellion? _____

_____

_____

2.78 How did Nixon deal with inflation? _____

_____

_____

2.79 In your opinion, was Richard Nixon a good or bad president? Why? _____

_____

_____

_____

_____

_____

TEACHER CHECK _____ _____
                          initials   date

↺ **Review the material in this section in preparation for the Self Test.** This Self Test will check your mastery of this particular section as well as your knowledge of the previous section.

SELF TEST 2

Match the person with their description (2 points, each answer).

2.01	_____ First appointed vice president	a.	Fidel Castro
2.02	_____ North Vietnamese communist leader	b.	Ho Chi Minh
2.03	_____ Youthful president, assassinated in 1963	c.	Douglas MacArthur
2.04	_____ Civil rights leader, assassinated in 1968	d.	Dwight D. Eisenhower
2.05	_____ Anti-communist who was noted	e.	Richard M. Nixon
	for his false accusations	f.	Gerald Ford
2.06	_____ First commander of NATO, president during	g.	Martin Luther King
	a time of prosperity and stability	h.	Lyndon B. Johnson
2.07	_____ Commander in Korea, fired for insubordination	i.	John F. Kennedy
2.08	_____ President whose Great Society was strangled	j.	Joseph McCarthy
	by increased involvement in the Vietnam War		
2.09	_____ Communist dictator of Cuba		
2.010	_____ First president to visit Red China and the U.S.S.R. and first to resign from office		

Name the item, person, or idea (3 points, each answer).

2.011 America's primary Cold War policy, created by Harry Truman _____

2.012 The incident that began the Civil Rights Movement _____

_____

_____

2.013 Post-Civil War black educator who accepted segregation until black people could build up

their economic power _____

2.014 Martin Luther King's speech at the Lincoln Memorial during the March on Washington

_____

2.015 The biggest problem with the economy between 1945 and 1974 _____

2.016 Kennedy's volunteer organization to aid the Third World _____

2.017 Barrier that divided East and West Berlin _____

2.018 Cold War thaw of the 1970s _____

2.019 President, approved the interstate highway system and the St. Lawrence Seaway

_____

2.020 Congressional resolution that gave the president a free hand in Vietnam

_____

2.021 First artificial satellite in space and the nation that launched it

_____

2.022 Dwight D. Eisenhower's campaign slogan _____

2.023 "Defensive alliance" of the Iron Curtain nations _____

2.024 Kennedy's aid program for Latin America _____

2.025 Harry S. Truman's legislative program _____

Describe each of these incidents or item (5 points, each answer).

2.026 The Cuban Missile Crisis

_____

_____

_____

_____

2.027 The Marshall Plan

_____

_____

_____

_____

2.028 The integration of Central High School in Little Rock, Arkansas, 1957

_____

_____

_____

_____

2.029 Watergate

_____

_____

_____

_____

2.030 How the Civil Rights Movement challenged segregation

_____

_____

_____

_____

2.031 The youth rebellion of the 1960s and early '70s

_____

_____

_____

_____

2.032 The difference between _Plessy v. Ferguson_ and _Brown v. Board of Education_

_____

_____

_____

_____

80 / 100   SCORE _____   TEACHER _____ _____

initials   date

3. UNEXPECTED VICTORY

Vietnam and Watergate shattered American self-confidence. Distrust of the government grew strong and deep. The nation began to doubt that communism could be defeated. America's European allies wanted peace with communism, not antagonism, even when the U.S.S.R. continued its attacks on freedom in the Third World and its own territory. However, an unexpected surprise lay ahead. The U.S.S.R. was about to be broken and the Iron Curtain torn down.

The last presidents of the Cold War had to deal with the aftershocks of Vietnam and Watergate in America. They also had to conduct the Cold War in the new reality that followed those traumatic events. That reality was a nation less willing to follow its leaders, less willing to fight, and suffering from reduced prestige abroad. Détente continued, but its success came under serious question until Soviet aggression ended it in 1979.

By the 1980s America began to heal and regain its composure as a nation. That decade finally saw communism collapse in Europe under the weight of its own stupidity. The world watched breathlessly as the Communist World fell apart and the Soviet Union followed. The Cold War ended with a victory for the Free World, the one side left standing when the dust cleared.

SECTION OBJECTIVES

Review these objectives. When you have completed this section, you should be able to:

1. Describe the course of the Cold War and the incidents within it.

2. Name the presidents of the Cold War and the events that happened during their administration.

4. Describe events in America and changes in American thinking during the Cold War era.

5. Name the important people on both sides of the Cold War.

VOCABULARY

Study these words to enhance your learning success in this section.

fundamentalist (fən də mənt l əst). A movement that stresses strict and literal adherence to a set of beliefs.

infrastructure (in′ frə strək chər). The permanent installations required for military purposes, including: roads, bridges, airports, supply depots, etc.

Aftershocks

Gerald R. Ford (1913-2006). Gerald Ford was the only man to serve as both vice president and president without being elected to either office. He was born in Nebraska and raised in Grand Rapids, Michigan. He was strong and active in sports. He entered the University of Michigan in 1931 and was a valuable member of the school's football team. He graduated from Yale Law School in 1941 and joined the navy soon after the beginning of World War II.

He served on the *U.S.S. Monterey*, which saw considerable action in the Pacific. He returned to his law career and became active in Republican politics after he was discharged. He ran for the U.S. House in 1948 and won. He was re-elected to that office twelve times. In 1973 when Nixon chose him to replace vice president Spiro Agnew, Ford was the minority leader of the House (the highest ranking Republican).

Pardon. Ford was reasonably popular, honest, and easygoing. The nation was disgusted with Watergate and willing to give the new, appointed president a chance. However, one month after he took office, Ford issued a full pardon to Richard Nixon for any crimes he may have committed in office. The pardon severely damaged his popularity and added to the national distrust of the government.

Home Problems. As with Nixon, Ford's greatest problem was inflation. Ford launched an anti-inflation campaign in 1974 called "Whip Inflation Now" or WIN. For a time, the president wore a WIN button everywhere, as he worked to lower spending. The campaign triggered a recession and was quickly abandoned. Stagflation made the economy a difficult problem. Dealing with inflation caused unemployment, and dealing with unemployment caused inflation. It seemed to be a no-win situation.

Congress was controlled by the Democrats during the Ford Administration and little was accomplished. Former New York Governor Nelson Rockefeller (grandson of the Standard Oil Baron) was appointed vice president. Ford also set up an amnesty plan for the over 100,000 men who had avoided the draft or deserted during the Vietnam War. However, the program required the men to do public service work for two years; most refused. Congress also refused to grant Ford's request for more aid to South Vietnam in 1975 when the North launched the offensive that eventually conquered the South. The U.S. was not going to get involved in anything! "No more Vietnams" was a foreign policy law for many years.

Mayaguez. In May of 1975, a month after the fall of Vietnam, the Khmer Rouge in Cambodia seized a U.S. merchant ship, the *Mayaguez*, in international waters. Ford ordered a naval task force with Marine troops to attack. Thirty-eight men were killed, but the crew of the ship was rescued. Some people condemned the raid as too much, but the nation mainly supported Ford. They did not want petty dictators threatening Americans abroad.

Election of 1976. The nation celebrated its Bicentennial and an election in 1976. Ford narrowly won the Republican nomination after a tough primary fight with Governor Ronald Reagan of California. The Democrats nominated Jimmy Carter, Governor of Georgia, who had an excellent record on civil rights and an equally excellent history of honesty. Ford was handicapped by the poor opinion many people had of the government and the pardon, which tied him to the Watergate Scandal. Carter campaigned as an honest outsider who was not smeared by the taint of Washington muck. He won the election by a slim margin.

James E. Carter (1924-). Commonly known as Jimmy, James Earl Carter was the first president to graduate from the U.S. Naval Academy. He was born and raised in Plains, Georgia. His father owned a farm and store in town. He attended public schools and graduated from the Naval Academy in 1946. He served in the navy until 1953, working on the development of the first nuclear powered submarines. In 1953 his father died, and Jimmy left the navy to run the family peanut business. He was an astute manager and the business prospered.

Carter became active in community projects and politics, serving on the local Board of Education, among others. He also opposed segregation, and was one of only a few to vote against banning black Christians in his church. He ran for the state senate in 1962. He won the Democratic nomination only after he successfully charged that his opponent won by violating the voting laws. He then won the election.

He was reelected in 1964, but was defeated in the primary when he ran for governor in 1966. He tried again in 1970 and won. He was unknown outside of Georgia when he decided to run for president in 1976. He built his reputation by campaigning hard and winning early primary elections. He won the nomination against 10 opponents.

Jimmy Carter won the 1976 election as a Washington outsider and that was his undoing. He did not know how to work with the U.S. Congress and had no experience in foreign policy. It showed as he frequently changed positions and failed to establish any clear, achievable goals. His administration quickly began to look confused and naive as it faced stagflation, an energy crisis, the end of détente and a major hostage crisis.

Energy Problems. The nation of Israel had been created by the U.N. in 1948, displacing the Arabs of Palestine. The Arab nations around Israel never accepted it. Israel and its Arab neighbors fought wars in 1948, 1956, and 1967. In October of 1973, a fourth war began when Egypt and Syria attacked Israel on Yom Kippur, the holiest Jewish holiday. As with all the previous wars, Israel won the Yom Kippur War. It was ended by a cease fire due to U.N. and American mediation.

Several of the Arab nations were members of OPEC (Organization of Petroleum Exporting Countries). In 1973 OPEC put an embargo on oil sales to all nations that supported Israel, including the U.S. The embargo held for five months and drove oil prices up dramatically. OPEC used its control over the supply of oil to drive up prices through the 1970s. Oil shortages led to lines at the gas pumps again in 1973 and 1979 as gas stations rationed gas to conserve their supply.

Jimmy Carter pushed hard from the beginning of his administration for the creation of an intelligent energy policy. American's love of the automobile and cheap gas made energy

| The Camp David Accords

controls unpopular. However, a national energy program was passed in 1978 that included a new Department of Energy. The laws taxed cars with poor gas mileage, required businesses to cut petroleum use, and forced higher prices to encourage conservation. These measures drove up the price of oil and added to inflation, hurting Carter's popularity. By the 1980s expanding oil production drove the prices down and ended the "energy crisis" for the time being.

The president appointed Paul Volcker to the Federal Reserve Board in 1979. He began a new policy at the board aimed at controlling inflation by control of the money supply. Using the "Fed's" power to charge interest on money loaned to banks, he forced up the interest rates. The high interest rates caused another recession, but they also tamed inflation which began to slow in the 1980s.

Foreign Policy Successes. Carter had a few successes in foreign policy. His greatest was mediating an agreement between Egypt and Israel. The Egyptian president, Anwar Sadat, had risked his position in the Arab world by visiting Israel and opening negotiations to end the long hostility between the two nations. When negotiations stalled, Jimmy Carter invited the leaders of both nations to America for direct talks. The result was an agreement called the Camp David Accords. Under it, Egypt recognized Israel and Israel returned the Sinai Peninsula, which it had taken in the last war. Sadat and Menachem Begin, Prime Minister of Israel, won the Nobel Peace Prize for their efforts.

Jimmy Carter also completed long standing negotiations with Panama over the fate of the Panama Canal. The two treaties arranged for the canal to be gradually turned over to Panamanian control by the year 2000 and for it to be neutral, open to all shipping. Both treaties were ratified in the Senate by close votes in 1978. The U.S. kept the right to use armed force to protect the canal.

Carter continued the Nixon policy toward China. In 1979 the U.S. and China established formal diplomatic relations and exchanged ambassadors. He developed better relations with the nations of Africa, but he also seemed helpless as the Soviets expanded their influence there.

Death of Détente. Jimmy Carter the idealist, made human rights the centerpiece of his foreign policy. However, it was difficult to press for human rights among sensitive allies like the Philippines and South Korea. The Soviet Union resented Carter's push for them to grant their own people more freedom. They quickly and publicly refused Carter's suggestions for deep cuts in nuclear weapons. Finally, Carter got the SALT talks back on track and got a new treaty limiting weapons expansion. Critics said it favored the Soviets, and SALT II stalled in Congress.

Struggling détente died a sudden death in December of 1979, when the Soviet Union invaded Afghanistan to protect a pro-Soviet government on their southern border. They installed a puppet ruler and quickly became bogged down in a brutal guerrilla war. The Soviets were able to hold the cities, but they could never take the mountainous countryside

| Ayatollah Khomeini

defended by Muslim rebels using U.S. and Chinese weapons. Afghanistan has been called the Soviet Vietnam.

Carter had to react to this blatant aggression. He halted sales of grain and technology to the U.S.S.R. He withdrew SALT II from consideration by the Senate (although both sides honored the limits set in the treaty). He announced that the U.S. would boycott the 1980 Summer Olympics in Moscow (66 other nations also boycotted the games). He also restarted draft registration (cancelled after Vietnam) and increased military spending. Détente was finished and the Cold War continued.

Iran Hostage Crisis. Carter's presidency is remembered most for the crisis in Iran. Shah Mohammad Reza Pahlavi was the ruler of Iran in the 1970s. He was a faithful U.S. ally, but also a ruthless dictator. His attempts to modernize Iran were deeply resented by his conservative Muslim people. With his emphasis on human rights, Carter did not offer the Shah much support as his people began to rebel. In 1979, a Muslim religious leader named Ayatollah Khomeini overthrew the Shah and set up a **fundamentalist** Muslim government very hostile to America.

Later that same year, Carter allowed the exiled Shah to come to the U.S. for medical treatment. Demonstrators outside the U.S. Embassy in Iran attacked the compound in November and took the staff hostage with the tacit support of the government. This was an unbelievable violation of centuries of international law that required nations to protect the embassy staff of foreign countries! The militants holding the hostages demanded the return of the Shah for trial. Carter refused, froze Iranian assets in the U.S. and broke diplomatic relations. After months of fruitless negotiations, Carter authorized a military rescue which ended in a disaster, crashing in the desert without engaging the enemy.

The crisis and the botched rescue damaged U.S. prestige abroad. Americans could not believe that 52 American embassy staff people could be treated this way without any successful U.S. response. Carter's prestige at home fell. Finally, Iran and Iraq got into a destructive war (1980-88) that forced Iran to seek the return of its frozen American assets. The hostages were released after 444 days in captivity, but in a final insult, not until just hours after Carter left office in 1981. They came back to a tumultuous welcome in the U.S. Washington was covered in yellow ribbons, which had become a symbol that the nation was waiting and praying for their safe return.

Election of 1980. By the time of the elections in 1980, Carter's popularity had plummeted very low. He was challenged for the Democratic nomination by Senator Edward Kennedy, another brother of the late president. It was a close contest, but Carter eventually won the nomination due to moral problems in Kennedy's life. The Republicans nominated Governor Ronald Reagan, who chose George Bush for his running mate. Reagan's good looks, poise, and positive outlook for America caught the attention of the voters. He won the election by a substantial majority, leaving Carter to depart, beaten, and bedraggled.

Jimmy Carter, however, was not a man to retire to a rocking chair. He made good use of his prestige as a former president in a number of ways. He became a leading spokesman and worker for Habitat for Humanity, an organization that builds homes for the working poor. He has led numerous efforts to negotiate peace and monitor free elections. He was, for example, instrumental in convincing Haiti's military government to step down before a U.S. invasion in 1994. He has fulfilled the high calling of a statesman with dignity and integrity since leaving the White House.

 Complete these sentences.

3.1 Jimmy Carter emphasized _____ in his foreign policy.

3.2 Détente was ended by the Soviet _____ in 1979.

3.3 Control of the oil supply by _____ caused an energy crisis in the 1970s.

3.4 Ford tried to end inflation with his _____ campaign.

3.5 Carter's presidency is remembered most for the _____

_____ .

3.6 The Federal Reserve Board finally brought inflation under control in the 1980s by controlling

the _____ .

3.7 Carter won the 1976 election by running as an _____

_____ .

3.8 Ford ordered a navy task force to rescue the crew of the _____

in 1975.

3.9 The most controversial action of Ford's administration was when he _____

_____ .

3.10 Jimmy Carter got the Senate to ratify two treaties that gave the _____

to _____ by the year 2000.

3.11 The U.S. established formal relations with _____ in 1979.

3.12 Jimmy Carter mediated between Sadat and Begin to reach the _____

that paved the way for peace between Egypt and Israel.

3.13 Ford's appointed vice president was _____ .

3.14 Jimmy Carter reacted to the invasion of Afghanistan by _____ the

Olympics in Moscow and _____ SALT II.

3.15 Radicals in Iran held _____ American embassy personnel hostage for

_____ days (1979-81).

3.16 _____ was the Muslim religious leader who overthrew

Shah _____ in Iran.

3.17 Iran finally negotiated the release of the hostages when it needed money for its war with

_____ .

3.18 Jimmy Carter defeated _____ to get the 1980

Democratic nomination.

3.19 _____ was elected president in 1980.

Healing and Change

Ronald W. Reagan (1911-2004). Ronald Wilson Reagan was the oldest man ever elected president (69). He was born and raised in Illinois. His father was a shoe salesman. Ronald, nicknamed "Dutch," attended public schools and worked his way through Eureka College, graduating in 1932. He started working as a radio announcer for the Chicago Cubs in Illinois.

He made a screen test for Warner Brothers Studio in 1937, and was hired as an actor. He appeared in over fifty movies between 1937 and 1964. He joined the Air Force during World War II, but poor eyesight forced him to make training films for most of the war. He was elected president of the Screen Actors Guild (the actors union) in 1947, and served in that post for many years.

Reagan became more conservative over time. He cooperated with efforts to remove suspected communists from the movie industry in the 1950s. He joined the Republican Party in 1960. He was elected governor of California in 1966 and reelected in 1970. He was defeated by Gerald Ford for the 1976 Republican presidential nomination, but won it in 1980. He was elected president that year by a large majority.

Terrorism. In the 1980s, unrest in the Middle East caused a wave of terrorism. The U.S. was mainly affected by Arab terrorists who objected to American support for the nation of Israel. The Palestine Liberation Organization (PLO) and radical groups supported by Iran or Libya were among the most active.

Several terrorist attacks killed or endangered Americans during the decade. In 1983 U.S. marines were in Lebanon trying to support a cease fire in a bitter war there. A suicide bomber drove a truck filled with explosives into their barracks. More than 200 men died. In 1985 a TWA jet was seized by terrorists after leaving Italy. One American was killed, but the rest of the passengers were eventually released. Later that same year an Italian cruise ship, the *Achille Lauro,* was hijacked and again one American was killed.

In 1986 terrorists planted a bomb in a German disco used by U.S. soldiers. President Reagan ordered the bombing of terrorist camps in Libya when the evidence connected them to the bombing. That strong reaction caused a decline in Libyan-sponsored terrorism.

Beirut, Lebanon was a center of terrorist activity because a brutal civil war had left it without any effective government. In the 1980s, dozens of American, European, and Israeli citizens were captured and held hostage in the city, some for years. Some died in captivity or were killed. The U.S. had no way to locate or negotiate with those holding the hostages, and it was a frustrating experience.

Reaganomics. Ronald Reagan wanted to reduce the size and influence of the federal government. Reporters called his program *Reaganomics*. He reduced taxes, cut welfare programs, and worked to reduce the power of federal agencies that regulated businesses. Reagan was also a firm believer in a strong military to protect America against communism. He increased military spending significantly. The increased spending and lower taxes caused huge budget deficits. The national debt under Reagan grew from $907.7 billion in 1980 to $2,602.3 billion in 1988.

The economy had gone into a recession after high interest rates were set up to tame inflation in the late 1970s, but by the end of Reagan's first term the recession had ended and a long recovery began. More importantly, inflation did not rise again. Prices rose only slowly as the nation began to prosper again.

Home Notes. Reagan faced a wide variety of problems and events at home in his first term. He was shot in the chest during an assassination attempt in March of 1981. He survived and recovered quickly. He fired many of the nation's air traffic controllers that same year when they disobeyed an order to end a strike. He appointed the first woman to the U.S. Supreme Court, Sandra Day O'Connor. In 1984 the new Space Shuttle Program (begun in 1981) was temporarily halted by an accident. In 1986 the shuttle *Challenger* blew up after takeoff, killing all aboard including a special guest, a school teacher.

Foreign Affairs. Reagan took a very hard line in dealing with the Soviet Union. He was deeply opposed to communism and the expansion of the Soviet "evil empire." He had tremendous faith in the American people and their system of government. His self-confidence was contagious and it made him very popular. He did a great deal to restore American self-confidence after the traumas of the 1970s.

Many Americans also realized that the years of détente had not ended or even slowed Soviet aggression. Reagan, therefore, had public support as he built up military power, invested in more advanced missile technology, challenged Soviet power whenever he could, and tried to revive containment. Vietnam was still enough of an issue that Reagan did not have a free hand to contain communism. However, he often gave support to groups fighting pro-Soviet governments. Two of Reagan's main efforts were in Central America and the Caribbean.

Prior to 1979, the nation of Nicaragua was ruled by a family of dictators named the Somoza. They were overthrown that year by the Sandinista, a communist-style guerrilla group. They set up an oppressive government that received most of its support from Cuba and the Soviet Union. The Sandinistas were also funneling Soviet weapons to rebel groups in nearby Honduras and El Salvador.

Reagan sent U.S. aid to both Honduras and El Salvador. He also sent aid to the *Contras*, a group that was created to fight a guerrilla war against the Sandinista government in Nicaragua. However, evidence of massacres and cruelty by both sides caused many Americans

| Ronald Reagan

to question getting involved. Congress eventually cut off all money for aid to the *Contras* due both to the fear of getting too involved (Vietnam disease) and distaste for the brutal actions of the *Contras*.

The small island nation of Grenada in the Caribbean had also come under the control of a pro-Soviet, communist-style government in 1979. The new regime began to build a massive airstrip that the U.S. feared would be used as a Soviet air base. In October of 1983, a revolution broke out and a communist leader was killed. Many of the other Caribbean nations were very nervous about having a communist government so near. They asked the U.S. to help. Concerned for the many Americans on the island, Reagan agreed. In October of 1983, American and Caribbean soldiers invaded the island, threw out the Cuban "advisors" and set up a democratic government. The action was very popular in the U.S., but was condemned elsewhere.

In 1983, the president proposed a controversial new program to develop a missile defense system for the U.S. that would be set up in orbit above the earth. Called the Strategic Defense Initiative, it was labeled "Star Wars" by its opponents. Many people questioned investing a huge amount of money to expand the Cold War into space. The peace groups opposed it. However, Congress approved some money for the program because there was evidence the U.S.S.R. was already working on its own Star Wars program.

Election of 1984. The economy was in good shape in 1984, and inflation was finally under control. Reagan was very popular and was easily renominated. In fact, many of his opponents called him the "teflon president" because nothing they accused him of stuck! He was opposed by Walter Mondale, who had been Jimmy Carter's vice president. Mondale's running mate was Geraldine Ferraro, a member of the U.S. House and the first woman to run on a major party ticket. Reagan won the election by the largest majority in U.S. history. He was victorious in 49 states and took all but 13 electoral votes.

Changes in the U.S.S.R. In the 1980s, changes began in the Soviet Union that would finally bring the Cold War to a close. The cautious, fearful leaders who had survived under Stalin finally began to die. Brezhnev died in 1982. The next Soviet leader, Yuri Andropov died in 1984. His successor, Konstantin Chernenko died in 1985. At his death, a much younger man, Mikhail Gorbachev, came to power and began astonishing changes.

Gorbachev was one of a group of new party leaders who realized the Soviet Union was in serious trouble. The cost of paying for revolutions all over the world was too much for the U.S.S.R. to continue. Its own economy was in very weak shape. Under communism, people cannot be fired from their jobs and don't receive more pay for better work.

| George H. W. Bush

Thus, most people just do the least they can. Soviet industries were badly out of date because no one had any reason to build new or better equipment. Soviet citizens could not get the goods they wanted and needed. The U.S.S.R. was not developing the new computer technology that was so rapidly changing life in the Free World. In short, Gorbachev and his supporters recognized that things needed to change, immediately!

Gorbachev tried to rearrange the Soviet economy to be more productive. He began a series of reforms called *perestroika* (restructuring). He encouraged more freedom of speech called *glasnost* (openness) to allow new ideas to push changes in the economy. He also tried to improve relations with the Free World to get money, technology, and to reduce the costs of the Cold War. However, his reforms did not change the state control of production and failed to stop the collapse of the Soviet economy. In fact, the new openness would eventually destroy communist control.

American Reaction. Gorbachev quickly became very popular in the West, especially in Western Europe. Reagan, however, did not trust the changes he was seeing in the U.S.S.R. The Soviets had lied too many times in the past about what they were doing. Also, the communist party could easily have decided the reforms were too much and stop them at any time. Many people condemned Reagan for his caution.

The president did agree to meet several times with Gorbachev. He asked the new leader to match his words with deeds. In 1987, Gorbachev began to do so by signing the Intermediate-Range Nuclear Forces Treaty. This treaty committed both sides to <u>destroy</u> an entire group of weapons. It was the first treaty to actually <u>reduce</u>, not limit, the number of nuclear weapons.

Iran-Contra Affair. Reagan was very disturbed by the continued holding of American hostages in Beirut. The terrorists there were supported by Iran which had terrible relations with the U.S. since the taking of the American embassy in 1979. Reagan decided to sell weapons to Iran (which needed them for the war with Iraq) in the hopes of winning freedom for the hostages. This was done in secret because American policy forbade dealing with terrorists. Iran took the weapons, but only three hostages were freed.

Reagan's aides used the profits from the weapon sales to help the *Contras*. This was illegal because Congress had forbidden any U.S. funds to be used for the *Contras*. The activity was exposed in 1987. A Congressional investigation found that several White House aides had acted illegally and blamed Reagan for not controlling his staff better.

Several of Reagan's aides were convicted, but the convictions were overturned on appeal or the men were pardoned by President Bush in 1992. The only thing proven against Reagan was poor management. He left office in 1989, still very popular. In 1994, he announced he had Alzheimer's disease which slowly robbed him of his ability to think and remember. After that, he lived the rest of his life, out of the public eye, under his wife's care.

Election of 1988. George H.W. Bush won the Republican nomination in 1988. He chose Senator Dan Quayle of Indiana as his running mate. The Democrats picked Michael Dukakis (Governor of Mass.), who ran with Senator Lloyd Bentsen of Texas. The Democrats tried to push the Iran-Contra Affair in the election and attacked Reagan's cut backs in welfare services. Bush attacked Dukakis for his lack of experience in foreign policy and accused him of being too easy on criminals. The strong economy, Reagan's popularity and Bush's long experience gave him the presidency by a comfortable margin.

 Complete these items.

3.20 Why did Reagan sell arms to Iran?

_____

_____

3.21 Describe the secret activity of the Iran-Contra Affair.

_____

_____

_____

_____

3.22 List four acts of terrorism in the 1980s.

    a. _____

    b. _____

    c. _____

    d. _____

3.23 Give the Russian name and a description of Gorbachev's two major reforms.

    a. _____

    b. _____

3.24 Why did Reagan oppose the Sandinista government?

_____

_____

3.25 Name four parts of Reaganomics.

    a. _____

    b. _____

    c. _____

    d. _____

3.26 Describe what happened on Grenada in October, 1983.

_____

_____

_____

_____

3.27 What was so important about the Intermediate-Range Nuclear Forces Treaty?

_____

_____

3.28 How many leaders did the Soviet Union have from 1981 to 1986? _____

3.29 List three reasons why the Soviet economy was in trouble in the 1980s.

    a. _____

    b. _____

    c. _____

3.30 What American economic problem of the 1960s and 70s was controlled in the 1980s?

_____

3.31 Name the first woman appointed to the Supreme Court.

_____

3.32 What was "Star Wars?" (Give the real name and a description.) _____

_____

_____

3.33 What group was fired by Reagan for continuing a strike?

_____

Miraculous Victory

George H.W. Bush (1924-2018). George Herbert Walker Bush made his fortune in the oil business before entering government service. He was born to a successful businessman in Massachusetts. His family lived in Connecticut during his childhood, spending their summers in Maine. George attended private schools and entered the navy when he graduated in 1942. He became the navy's youngest pilot in 1943. In 1944 he was shot down during an attack on a Japanese held island. He succeeded in damaging his target before he jumped safely into the ocean. He was rescued by a submarine and received the Distinguished Flying Cross for his valor.

After the war, he entered Yale University, graduating in 1948. Instead of going into business with his father, George moved to Texas and got into the oil business. He worked his way up and earned a fortune on the way. He became interested in politics in the 1950s, working in the local Republican Party. He served in the U.S. House from 1967-1970. He was defeated in a run for the Senate in 1970. He served several appointed positions after that including Ambassador to the U.N., Chairman of the Republican National Committee, U.S. representative to China and Director of the Central Intelligence Agency. He tried for the 1980 Republican nomination for president, but lost to Ronald Reagan, who chose him as a running mate. As Reagan's vice president, Bush was an active member of the president's team. He was kept well informed of the president's decisions and was one of his advisors. He easily won the presidency in 1988.

Savings and Loan Crisis. The biggest domestic problem under Bush was the Savings and Loan Crisis. Lax rules, fraud, and bad debts caused over a thousand Savings and Loans (which are basically banks) to close in the 1980s. Many others were close to bankruptcy. The money people deposited in the S&Ls was insured by the federal government. So, the government had to cover these losses.

President Bush signed legislation in 1989 to deal with the crisis. The shaky S&Ls were taken by the government, depositors were paid, fraud was prosecuted, and the businesses that still had some value were sold to new investors. The total cost to the American taxpayers was estimated to be hundreds of billions of dollars. The legislation also tightened controls to prevent another financial disaster like this one.

Miracle Year. To any person who lived during the Cold War, 1989 was a year of miracles. In 1988 and 1989, the Soviet Union withdrew its troops from Afghanistan. It also reduced the number of soldiers and weapons it kept in the Iron Curtain nations of Europe. Most important of all, Gorbachev made it clear that the Soviet Union <u>would not</u> use force to maintain the communist governments of Eastern Europe! Anyone who believed those communist governments were supported by their people quickly learned otherwise. In the space of one short year, massive street demonstrations behind the Iron Curtain forced communism to disintegrate in Europe.

The speed and scope of the collapse was breathtaking. Hungary made sweeping changes to its constitution in 1989 that allowed non-communist parties to nominate candidates. A reform party won the first free elections that year. Poland had allowed an anti-communist union, Solidarity, for a time in the 1980s. However, the threat of a Soviet invasion led to martial law and the banning of Solidarity. In 1989 it was again allowed and the government held partly free elections. Solidarity candidates won most of the offices. The communist party was dissolved in 1990 and completely free elections were held the next year.

In Czechoslovakia, thousands of people took to the streets demanding reforms. The communist party gave up its hold on power and Václav Havel, an anti-communist playwright became president. Free elections were held in 1990. The change was so smooth that it was called the Velvet Revolution. (The nation divided in 1992 to form the Czech Republic and Slovakia).

Demonstrations in Bulgaria forced the resignation and arrest of the communist leader. Greater freedom was given to the people in 1989 and free elections were held in 1990. In Romania an armed revolt captured and executed the barbaric dictator, Ceausescu, ending communist rule in that nation in 1989. It held free elections the following year.

The most vivid images of change were in Germany which had been divided since World War II, a living symbol of the Cold War. East German citizens not only demonstrated in 1989, they also left. Hungary had opened its borders earlier in the year. So, thousands of East Germans went through Hungary to Austria and then up to West Germany where they were automatically given citizenship.

| Crowds gather as the Berlin Wall comes down

Pressured by demonstrations and the drain on its population, East Germany announced on November 9, 1989 that it was opening its borders with West Germany, including the Berlin Wall. Within hours people were climbing over the wall to join a huge street party on both sides of Berlin. Then, they took sledge hammers and began to tear down the Wall of Shame, the most notorious symbol of the Iron Curtain. The joyful, willful destruction of the Berlin Wall was the most vivid and enduring memory of the Miracle Year. East Germany held free elections and reunited with West Germany in 1990.

Panama. The situation in Panama had become very tense in the 1980s. The government there came under the control of General Manuel Noriega early in the decade. Noriega engaged in election fraud, corruption, and drug trafficking. He was indicted in the U.S. on charges of smuggling drugs into America. The president of Panama dismissed Noriega from his military position, but Noriega forced the president out of office. New elections in 1989 were won by

Guillermo Endara, a political enemy of Noriega. The general invalidated the election. In the unrest that followed, a U.S. soldier in the Canal Zone was killed.

Based on the charges against Noriega, the invalidation of a free election and the threat to U.S. soldiers in the Canal Zone, President Bush ordered the invasion of Panama in December. It was quickly successful and a new civilian government was set up. Noriega surrendered. He was found guilty of drug trafficking and sentenced to 40 years in prison in the U.S.

Domestic Problems. Bush faced a variety of problems at home. He had promised not to raise taxes, but did so in 1990 to cut the deficit. That decision hurt his popularity and was used against him in the 1992 campaign. High rates of crime, drug abuse, and social problems were blamed on the president who could not do much with the still Democratic Congress. In 1989 the oil tanker *Exxon Valdez* hit a reef near Alaska, causing the worst oil spill in U.S. history. The eleven million gallon spill was cleaned up by the military and federal government after the company did not do enough. In 1992 major riots in Los Angeles spread to other cities after white police officers were acquitted of beating a black man, Rodney King, even though the beating had been videotaped. Federal troops were sent in to establish order and Bush released federal funds to help with the clean up afterward.

Persian Gulf War. The Persian Gulf War was George H. W. Bush's greatest success. It also restored the nation's faith in the military that had been so badly damaged in Vietnam. It began in August of 1990 when the dictator of Iraq, Saddam Hussein, invaded the neighboring nation of Kuwait. Hussein was a brutal ruler who had built the fifth largest army in the world with Soviet Cold War support. He conquered Kuwait, a moderate nation with ties to the U.S., to gain control of its oil wealth. He expected the U.S. would not be able to stop him. He was very, very wrong.

George H.W. Bush, who had a long history of diplomatic training, quickly put together a coalition of almost 40 nations under the banner of the United Nations. Led by the U.S., these nations sent troops, tanks, aircraft, bombs, and supplies to neighboring Saudi Arabia to protect it from a possible Iraqi attack and prepare for an invasion of Kuwait. The U.N. gave Hussein until January 15, 1991 to leave Kuwait or the coalition would "use all necessary means" to force him out.

The coalition forces were under the command of American General Norman Schwarzkopf. "Stormin Norman" and his superior, General Colin Powell, Chairman of the Joint Chiefs of Staff, were the first generals to become national heroes since World War II. Also nicknamed "the Bear," Schwarzkopf was a tall, imposing man who dominated the televised press briefings that introduced him to the world. He commanded both "Operation Desert Shield," the protection of Saudi Arabia, and "Operation Desert Storm," the invasion and liberation of Kuwait.

When Hussein failed to meet the January 15 deadline, Operation Desert Storm began on January 16th with the largest air war in history. Using advanced Western technology, "smart bombs" with guidance systems destroyed Iraqi communication, transportation, radar, military, and airport facilities. Then, coalition aircraft began a massive bombing campaign directed against the Iraqi **infrastructure** and the soldiers dug in along the border of Kuwait. The Iraqi air force was quickly eliminated as an effective fighting force. Many of the surviving planes and pilots fled to Iran.

Iraq tried to get Israel into the war by firing "Scud" missiles at Israeli cities, which did limited damage and killed some people. Hussein hoped that if Israel attacked Iraq, the Arab members of the coalition would pull out rather than fight with their most hated enemy. Israel stayed out of the war in spite of the attacks.

Their willingness to let the coalition handle Hussein won international respect.

The intense five week long air war destroyed much of the Iraqi war machine and decimated army morale. Soldiers at the front began to desert in large numbers. As much as half the Iraqi army may have left before the land battle started. Once it did begin, thousands of Iraqi soldiers surrendered without firing a single shot.

The Iraqi commanders were expecting a direct assault on their defenses along the Kuwait border. Also, the U.S. Marines had been very publicly practicing amphibious assaults. So, the defenders prepared extensively for an assault from the Persian Gulf. In fact, no amphibious assault was planned. With all of Hussein's radar and air power destroyed, he was blind. He could only guess where the land assault would come, but with his typical arrogance Hussein promised it would be the "mother of all battles."

Knowing Hussein could not see where the coalition forces were, Schwarzkopf shifted a large portion of his army north, beyond the edge of the Iraqi defenses. On February 24th, the land war began. Coalition forces swept into Iraq behind the Iraqi forces in Kuwait. The army assaulting Kuwait made rapid progress as the Iraqi soldiers surrendered en masse. Hussein ordered a retreat after two days, but it was too late. The army was trapped.

The land war lasted only 100 hours, and destroyed most of the Iraqi army. George H. W. Bush ordered the attack halted after Kuwait was liberated and it was clear that further assaults would just be a massacre. One of the most gruesome sights of the war was the highway from Kuwait City to Iraq. Iraqi soldiers had looted the city, stealing anything they could to take with them as they ran for home. The road was covered with the remains of thousands of vehicles and men, destroyed by allied bombing, caught in the act of mass theft.

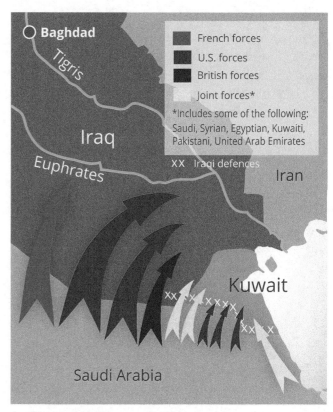

| Operation Desert Storm

Effects of the War. A large rebellion broke out against Saddam Hussein in Iraq after the war, but he was able to quell it. He had ordered his men to set the oil wells of Kuwait on fire as they fled. At the war's end, the air in Kuwait was black from the smoke of over 600 oil fires, the sun invisible. With tremendous innovation and effort the fires were all extinguished within nine months.

America lost only about 150 men in the war and U.S. prestige soared to new heights. The new atmosphere in the Middle East prompted the PLO to open negotiations with Israel to create a homeland for the Palestinian Arabs. Moreover, shortly after the war, the Western hostages held in Lebanon were released.

Cold War Finale. A war like this would not have been possible even a few years earlier. Cold War fears would have stopped it. However, the Soviet Union, needing to keep its goodwill with the West, quietly supported the war.

It appeared as if the Cold War was finally finished, but there was still one danger. Within the Soviet Union were older communist leaders, who still held power and might try to restore the old way. They made their move in August, 1991.

The Union of Soviet Socialist Republics was made up of fifteen "republics" that supposedly were part of the "union." (Many had "joined" the union by force.) In 1989, the U.S.S.R. had its first contested elections. Only communist party members could run, but those that favored reform were elected in large numbers. Boris Yeltsin was elected as president of the largest "republic," Russia.

The new reformers began to demand more self-government for the republics. In August of 1991, Gorbachev was to sign an agreement giving the republics more independence. That was the last straw for the old style communist leadership. They arrested Gorbachev and called in the military to restore the old order. Boris Yeltsin led a dedicated opposition, and within a few days the coup collapsed. Power fell into the hands of the presidents of the republics. They dissolved the U.S.S.R. by the end of the year, creating fifteen new nations. With the enemy gone, the victorious United States was at last miraculously free of the Soviet threat. The Cold War was finally over.

Choose the correct nation.

3.34	_____	Václav Havel, Velvet Revolution	a. Soviet Union
3.35	_____	Destruction of the Berlin Wall after the borders were opened	b. Hungary
3.36	_____	Solidarity temporarily stopped by martial law	c. Germany
3.37	_____	Changed its constitution and held free elections in 1989	d. Romania
3.38	_____	Invaded by the U.S. in 1989	e. Czechoslovakia
3.39	_____	Armed revolt killed Ceausescu	f. Poland
3.40	_____	Conquered by Iraq in 1990	g. Kuwait
3.41	_____	Yeltsin led the successful defense of the reforms against the old communist leaders	h. Panama

Name the item, person, nation, or event.

3.42 Largest domestic crisis of the George H. W. Bush Administration

_____

3.43 Oil tanker that caused the worst oil spill in U.S. history

_____

3.44 Reason for the riots in 1992 in Los Angeles

_____

_____

3.45 Year in which communism collapsed in Europe _____

3.46 Year the Soviet Union was dissolved _____

3.47 War to drive Iraqi army out of Kuwait _____

3.48 U.S. commander of Desert Shield and Desert Storm

_____

3.49 Panamanian strongman, put in U.S. jail for drug trafficking

_____

3.50 Head of the Joint Chiefs of Staff during Desert Shield and Desert Storm

_____

3.51 Dictator of Iraq _____

Answer these questions.

3.52 What was the coalition strategy for the land attack on Kuwait?

_____

_____

_____

3.53 Why were there so many reformers in office in the U.S.S.R. in 1991?

_____

_____

3.54 Why was the Iraqi army blind by the time the land war began in Desert Storm?

_____

_____

3.55 How many new nations were created out of the old Soviet Union? _____

Before you take this last Self Test, you may want to do one or more of these self checks.

1. _____ Read the objectives. See if you can do them.
2. _____ Restudy the material related to any objectives that you cannot do.
3. _____ Use the **SQ3R** study procedure to review the material:

    a. **S**can the sections.
    b. **Q**uestion yourself.
    c. **R**ead to answer your questions.
    d. **R**ecite the answers to yourself.
    e. **R**eview areas you did not understand.

4. _____ Review all vocabulary, activities, and Self Tests, writing a correct answer for every wrong answer.

SELF TEST 3

Name the item, event, or crisis (each numbered answer, 3 points).

3.01   Scandal that forced Richard Nixon to resign _____

3.02   Biggest economic problem of the 1960s and 70s _____

3.03   Crisis that marked Jimmy Carter's presidency, began when the deposed Shah of Iran came

to the U.S. for medical treatment, lasted 444 days _____

3.04   City in the Middle East where Americans were held hostage until after Operation Desert Storm

_____

3.05   Reagan scandal over arms sales with the profits being used to fund a revolt against the

pro-Soviet Sandinistas in Nicaragua _____

3.06   Miraculous event in the Cold War in 1989 _____

_____

3.07   War to drive Iraqi army out of Kuwait, 1990-91 _____

3.08   Action taken by Gerald Ford that made him very unpopular and tied him to the Nixon scandal

_____

3.09   Action by the U.S.S.R. that ended détente in 1979 _____

_____

3.010   Agreement made in the U.S. with the help of Jimmy Carter that allowed for peace between

Egypt and Israel _____

3.011   Incident that began the modern Civil Rights movement in 1955 _____

_____

_____

3.012   Crisis under John Kennedy over nuclear weapons in Cuba _____

_____

3.013   U.S. sponsored plan to rebuild Europe after World War II to prevent communism

_____

3.014 Name the three Blocs of the Cold War era

_____

_____

_____

3.015 The main Cold War policy of the U.S. toward communism, Truman created it

_____

Match the person with the description (each answer, 2 points).

3.016	_____ Dictator of Iraq	a.	Jimmy Carter
3.017	_____ Assassinated, Peace Corps, New Frontier	b.	Gerald Ford
3.018	_____ Escalated U.S. involvement in Vietnam, passed Civil Rights laws	c.	Lyndon Johnson
		d.	Ronald Reagan
3.019	_____ Began *perestroika* and *glasnost* in U.S.S.R.	e.	Martin Luther King
3.020	_____ U.S. war hero, Desert Storm	f.	George H. W. Bush
3.021	_____ Strongman drug trafficker, Panama	g.	Mikhail Gorbachev
3.022	_____ U.S. war hero, World War II and Korea	h.	Boris Yeltsin
3.023	_____ Appointed vice president, became president by Nixon's resignation, *Mayaguez*	i.	Norman Schwarzkopf
		j.	Saddam Hussein
3.024	_____ Dictator of Cuba	k.	Manuel Noriega
3.025	_____ Communist leader of North Vietnam	l.	Douglas MacArthur
3.026	_____ Human rights was the key to his foreign policy	m.	Fidel Castro
3.027	_____ Civil Rights leader, "I Have a Dream"	n.	Ho Chi Minh
3.028	_____ Very anti-communist, tried to reduce the size of the U.S. government	o.	John Kennedy
3.029	_____ Savings and Loan Crisis, formed coalition for Desert Storm		
3.030	_____ President of Russia, led anti-communist reformers when communists tried to retake the U.S.S.R., 1991		

Check the items that were causes of the event (1 point for each letter).

3.031 Fall of communism in Europe and the Soviet Union

a. ☐ Gorbachev came to power

b. ☐ Brezhnev was elected president

c. ☐ Soviet economy was in trouble in the 1980s

d. ☐ Berlin Wall was destroyed

e. ☐ Anti-communist demonstrations

3.032 Civil Rights Reforms

a. ☐ *Brown v. Board of Education*

b. ☐ Work of Booker T. Washington

c. ☐ Warsaw Pact

d. ☐ Lyndon Johnson's legislative skill

e. ☐ Sit-ins

f. ☐ March on Washington

g. ☐ Busing

h. ☐ Gulf of Tonkin Resolution

i. ☐ non-violent protests

j. ☐ Election of Jimmy Carter

3.033 Increased Cold War Tensions

a. ☐ U-2 Affair

b. ☐ Bay of Pigs

c. ☐ NATO

d. ☐ SALT

e. ☐ Détente

f. ☐ Stagflation

g. ☐ Desert Storm

h. ☐ Berlin Wall

i. ☐ Tet Offensive

j. ☐ Iran-Contra Affair

80 / 100   SCORE _____   TEACHER _____ _____
                                              initials   date

Before taking the LIFEPAC Test, you may want to do one or more of these self checks.

1. _____ Read the objectives. See if you can do them.
2. _____ Restudy the material related to any objectives that you cannot do.
3. _____ Use the **SQ3R** study procedure to review the material.
4. _____ Review activities, Self Tests, and LIFEPAC vocabulary words.
5. _____ Restudy areas of weakness indicated by the last Self Test.

HISTORY & GEOGRAPHY 808
A World in Conflict (1915–1945)

LIFEPAC Test is located in the center of the booklet. Please remove before starting the unit.

Author:
Theresa Buskey, B.A., J.D.

Editor:
Alan Christopherson, M.S.

Westover Studios Design Team:
Phillip Pettet, Creative Lead
Teresa Davis, DTP Lead
Nick Castro
Andi Graham
Jerry Wingo

Alpha Omega
PUBLICATIONS

804 N. 2nd Ave. E.
Rock Rapids, IA 51246-1759

A World in Conflict (1915–1945)

Introduction

During the years after the Civil War, America became an industrial power and committed itself to progressive reforms to protect its unique form of government. The strength of both industry and government would be tested by fire between 1915 and 1945. Two world wars and the most devastating depression in American history would tear at the soul of the nation during that scant thirty-year period.

World War I was a very traditional war for power between the nations of Europe. The United States of 1860 would not have dreamt of getting involved, but this was America of 1914. In the early twentieth century, America was a powerful industrial nation with trading ties all over the world. America's biggest trading partner and cultural mother, Britain, was allied with America's European friend, France. Germany, the primary enemy, drew America into the war by destroying American ships and taking American lives.

After the "Great War" (the name for World War I before World War II made the name obsolete), America tried to return to its traditional isolation and enjoy the fruits of its now-massive economy. The "Roaring Twenties" were a time of free credit, heavy spending, social change, and speculation in the stock market. In 1929 the stock market crashed (prices fell rapidly), pulling America into a huge depression. A new Democratic president tried to buy the nation out of the depression through massive government spending, but recovery only came with the tremendous industrial demands of World War II.

The Second World War ended American isolation forever. The U.S. again tried to stay out of the war but was drawn in by a surprise attack on a navy base in Pearl Harbor, Hawaii. America poured its massive human and industrial resources into the war, enabling an Allied victory. The war left Europe in rubble and the U.S. as the leader of the free world for the next half century.

Objectives

Read these objectives. The objectives tell you what you will be able to do when you have successfully completed this LIFEPAC. When you have finished this LIFEPAC, you should be able to:

1. Describe the policies, personalities, and politics of the U.S. presidents from 1915 to 1945.

2. Describe the course of U.S. policy during the early years of World War I and the reasons behind it.

3. Describe the course of World War I.

4. Describe the Fourteen Points, the Treaty of Versailles, the problems negotiating the treaty, and Wilson's efforts to get it accepted in the U.S.

5. Describe the politics, problems, and pastimes of the Roaring Twenties.

6. Describe the course of the Great Depression and the New Deal.

7. Describe the causes and course of World War II.

8. Describe the policy of appeasement and early American neutrality.

9. Name the major U.S. commanders in World War II and their contributions.

10. Describe American involvement in World War II.

11. Name the major leaders of World War II and their nations.

Survey the LIFEPAC. Ask yourself some questions about this study and write your questions here.

1. WORLD WAR I

Relations between the nations of Europe had long been managed by a policy known as "balance of power." Under this theory, every nation used alliances to prevent any one nation from getting too powerful. Ideally, power would be evenly balanced among the competing nations and peace would be maintained.

By 1914 the balance of power was being maintained by two major competing alliances. France, Russia, and Britain formed the *Triple Entente,* while Germany, Austria-Hungary, and Italy formed the *Triple Alliance*. In 1914, rather than maintaining peace, the alliances drew the nations into the bloodiest war in their collective histories. Once the war began, Turkey and Bulgaria joined the Triple Alliance which became known as the Central Powers. The Entente became known as the Allied Powers and were joined by Romania, Serbia, Montenegro, Greece, Japan, Belgium (once it was invaded), Italy (which changed sides), and eventually the United States.

The U.S. followed its longstanding policy of staying out of European affairs in the early years of the war. America remained neutral between 1914 and 1917. During that time, America grew closer to the Allies and came into increasing conflict with Germany. Trade with the Allies, Germany's violations of international law, Allied propaganda, and German submarine attacks on American vessels moved the U.S. slowly away from neutrality. Eventually, President Woodrow Wilson and the majority of the American people felt they could no longer honorably remain neutral. For the first time, America entered a major European war as a European ally.

SECTION OBJECTIVES

Review these objectives. When you have completed this section, you should be able to:

1. Describe the policies, personalities, and politics of the U.S. presidents from 1915 to 1945.

2. Describe the course of U.S. policy during the early years of World War I and the reasons behind it.

3. Describe the course of World War I.

4. Describe the Fourteen Points, the Treaty of Versailles, the problems negotiating the treaty, and Wilson's efforts to get it accepted in the U.S.

VOCABULARY

Study these words to enhance your learning success in this section.

communism (käm' yə niz əm). A totalitarian system of government in which a single authoritarian party controls the state and industry with the official, but never completed, goal of creating a stateless society in which everyone shares equally in work and profits. In the political spectrum, communism is at the far left.

convoy (kän' voi). A protective escort, especially for ships.

mobilize (mō' bə līz). To assemble and make ready for war duty; to prepare for action.

offensive (ə fen' siv). Making attack; of, relating to, or designed for attack.

AMERICA from **1915** to **1945**

Woodrow Wilson
1913-1921
Democratic

Warren G. Harding*
1921-1923
Republican

Calvin Coolidge
1923-1929
Republican

Herbert Hoover
1929-1933
Republican

Franklin D. Roosevelt*
1933-1945
Democratic

Harry S. Truman
1945-1953
Democratic

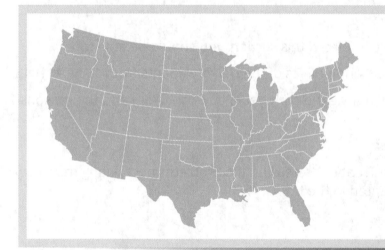

STATES ADMITTED TO THE **UNION**

None

POPULATION of the **United States of America**

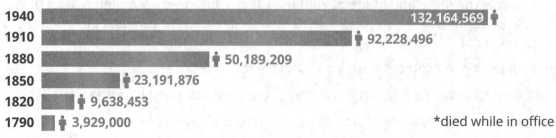

Year	Population
1940	132,164,569
1910	92,228,496
1880	50,189,209
1850	23,191,876
1820	9,638,453
1790	3,929,000

*died while in office

pandemic (pan dem' ik). An outbreak of disease occurring over a wide geographic area and affecting an exceptionally high proportion of the population.

ultimatum (əl tə mā t' əm). A final demand; one whose rejection will end negotiations and cause a resort to force or other direct action.

Note: *All vocabulary words in this LIFEPAC appear in* **boldface** *print the first time they are used. If you are not sure of the meaning when you are reading, study the definitions given.*

Pronunciation Key: hat, āge, cãre, fär; let, ēqual, tėrm; it, īce; hot, ōpen, ôrder; oil; out; cup, pùt, rüle; child; long; thin; /ŦH/ for then; /zh/ for measure; /u/ or /ə/ represents /a/ in about, /e/ in taken, /i/ in pencil, /o/ in lemon, and /u/ in circus.

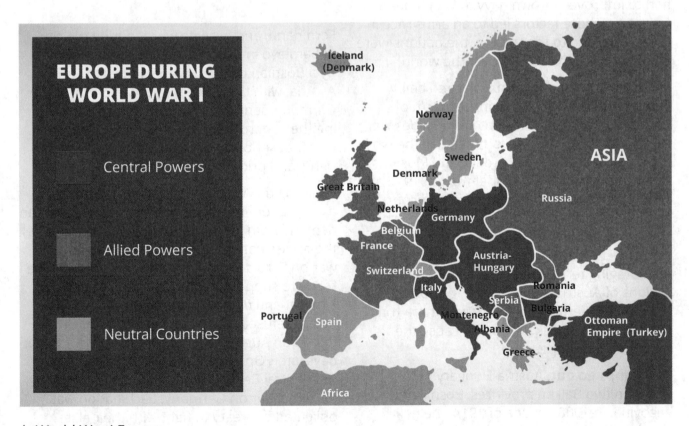

| World War I Europe

Neutral America

Background. In 1914 Europe was a keg of gunpowder waiting for a match. France had been defeated by Germany in the Franco-Prussian War of 1870. She had paid a huge indemnity and gave Germany the border regions of Alsace and Lorraine. The French army had been rebuilt and was eager for revenge.

Germany had been created by the cagey Prussian leader, Otto von Bismarck, from the many small German states after the war with France. Bismarck had defeated France and carefully worked to keep the other nations of Europe from uniting against Germany. In 1890 a new German ruler, Kaiser (Emperor) Wilhelm II threw out Bismarck and his careful policies. Wilhelm II was an unstable man who wanted to make Germany the greatest nation in the world. He began a massive arms buildup, including a huge, modern navy. Their navy threatened the master of the sea. She had to improve her own navy to keep ahead of Germany. These factors led to an arms race in Europe. To add to the tension, the nations were competing for colonies all over the world.

In 1914 the most dangerous place to be in Europe was the Balkan Peninsula north of Greece. Here, many different nationalities were living under the same government, all the while hating each other. Slavs, Croats, and Muslims fought each other in two brief wars in 1912 and 1913 which shifted the borders and encouraged more hatred. The Slavic nation of Serbia in the Balkans was closely allied with Russia, the largest Slavic power in Europe. Serbia was encouraging terrorism in the neighboring Slavic regions of Austria-Hungry, hoping to bring them under Serbian control. It was there that the spark was struck that would cause the explosion in Europe.

The lamps go out. Austria-Hungary had annexed two Balkan provinces, Bosnia and Herzegovina, in 1908. In June of 1914, the heir to the throne of Austria-Hungary, Archduke Franz

| Austria-Hungary's Archduke, Franz Ferdinand

Ferdinand, and his wife were touring the city of Sarajevo in Bosnia. They were assassinated by a Bosnian terrorist who had ties to Serbia. Austria, with the assurance of support from Germany, sent Serbia an **ultimatum** demanding the suppression of Serbian terrorism in a way that seriously violated Serbian national rights and pride.

Realizing this was a serious threat, Serbia sent a conciliatory note that fell short of the Austrian demands. On July 28th, exactly one month after the assassination, Austria-Hungary declared war on Serbia. Russia **mobilized** its army to be ready to support Serbia. Germany saw this as a threat and demanded Russia cease at once. Russia refused. Germany declared war on Russia on August 1st and on its ally, France, two days later. On August 4th, Germany invaded the neutral Belgium and as a result, Britain declared war on Germany. Each nation was obligated by treaty to fight with their allies, bringing on a general war all over Europe.

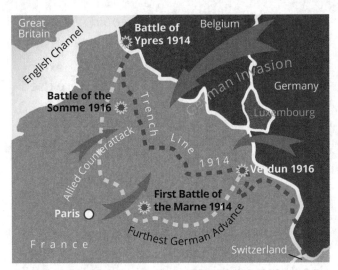

| The Western Front (1914-1916)

National pride, alliances, and an arms race drew Europe into a horrific war. Very few people had the slightest idea how awful the war would be. Sir Edward Grey, the Foreign Secretary of Britain, was one exception. "The lamps are going out all over Europe," he said when Britain declared war. "We shall not see them lit again in our lifetime."

Stalemate. Germany was faced with a two-front war. Its battle plan called for the swift invasion and conquest of France before the huge, but slow, Russian army could be brought into battle. To insure speed on the western front, Germany attacked, not along the protected French-German border, but through neutral Belgium. This was a major mistake. It cast Germany as the aggressor and was a major factor in turning the U.S. toward the Allies.

The well-disciplined, well-equipped Germans made rapid progress, and by September 1914 they were threatening the French capital of Paris. The French and a small British army succeeded in throwing them back at the first Battle of the Marne (September 6-9). Then both sides "raced to the sea" in an effort to go around the enemy army. By November of 1914, a battle line had been established that ran from Switzerland to the North Sea. Both sides dug in and set up defensive positions. Thus began the horrific "trench warfare" of World War I.

Trench warfare was brutal. Each side set up several parallel rows of trenches facing the enemy. These would be 6-8 feet deep and wide enough for two men to pass each other. In between the two armies was "no man's land," bombed-out, open land protected on each side by barbed wire, machine guns, and artillery fire.

Attacks were wholesale slaughters. They began with artillery barrages followed by men "going over the top," out of the trenches into the open across no man's land. They ran unprotected into the machine gun and artillery fire of the enemy who was firing from fortified trenches. Losses were huge and gains were small. For example, close to a million men were wounded, killed, or captured in the battles of Verdun and the Somme in 1916, neither of which accomplished much. Moreover, the generals never learned from the failures. They continued to order attacks in spite of the losses, even when the western front barely moved for three and a half years! The suffering of the men intensified when both sides began to use poison gas that killed and blinded many.

On the eastern front, Germany pushed back the Russian armies that had attacked at the beginning of the war, but Austria-Hungary was less successful. Russia occupied part of their territory until 1915, when a combined German-Austrian army recovered it. Russia

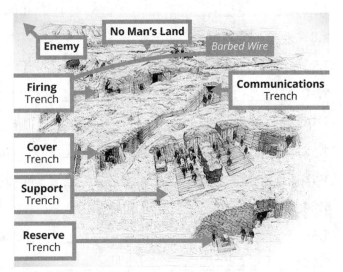

| The Trench Warfare System

and Austria-Hungary battled each other to exhaustion in the years that followed. However, Austria succeeded in its initial goal when it finally occupied Serbia in late 1915.

Because so many nations were involved, battles were fought in many places other than central Europe. There were several clashes between colonial armies in Africa and Asia. Sea battles were fought in all the major oceans. Italy entered the war on the Allied side in the hopes of gaining territory. It fought a bloody but ineffective war against Austria-Hungary along their mountain border. The Allies unsuccessfully tried to capture the Turkish Dardanelles, the straits leading to the Black Sea and Russia's southern ports. This failure meant that the more industrial western Allies could not easily resupply stumbling Russia.

World War I was the first war to see the extensive use of aircraft. Flimsy airplanes were used mainly to observe enemy troops and movements. The Germans used balloon-like airships called *zeppelins* to bomb enemy troops, including targets like London itself. Airplanes would shoot down the zeppelins and enemy observation planes. The often complicated plane-to-plane battles were called *dogfights*. Pilots who shot down five or more enemy ships earned the title of "ace." Eddie Rickenbacker, a professional race car driver before the war, eventually became America's greatest ace with twenty-two airplane and four balloon kills.

Name the correct person or item.

1.1	_____	German Kaiser; World War I
1.2	_____	most dangerous area of 1914 Europe
1.3	_____	nation that wanted revenge for a war in 1870
1.4	_____	weapon that blinded and killed in the trenches
1.5	_____	Austria-Hungarian heir; assassinated to begin the war
1.6	_____	battle which stopped the first German advance on Paris
1.7	_____	pilot with five or more "kills"
1.8	_____	"The lamps are going out all over Europe..."
1.9	_____	French provinces lost to Germany in 1870s
1.10	_____	Prussian leader; united Germany
1.11	_____	neutral nation invaded by Germany
1.12	_____	straits leading to the Black Sea not taken by Allies
1.13	_____	German airships used for bombing
1.14	_____	land between enemy trenches
1.15	_____	America's greatest ace
1.16	_____	European policy of using alliance to prevent any nation from becoming too powerful

Complete the following.

1.17 Give the sequence of events that began the general war in Europe.

   a. Archduke assassinated in _____

   b. _____ sent an ultimatum to _____

   c. _____ declared war on _____ , July 28th

   d. _____ mobilized in support of Serbia

   e. _____ declared war on _____ on August 1st

      and then on _____ on August 3rd

   f. _____ invaded _____ on August 4th

   g. As a result, _____ declared war on _____ .

1.18 What was Germany's basic battle plan?

   _____

   _____

   _____

1.19 What three things drew Europe into this war?

   _____

   _____

   _____

1.20 Why were casualties so heavy during offensives under trench warfare?

   _____

   _____

America's reaction. With the full support of the U.S. public behind him, President Wilson issued a declaration of neutrality as soon as the war began. It was a European war, and most Americans saw it exclusively as a European problem. The Atlantic Ocean would keep America safely away from the battle.

There were several reasons why most Americans (including the president) favored the Allies. First of all, the U.S. had developed very good relations with Britain around the turn of the century. It was the source of American culture, an important business partner, and as many as half of all American citizens could trace their ancestry back to British lands.

Secondly, France was fighting with Britain. France was the nation that had given the U.S. key aid to achieve its own independence. There was a strong pro-French feeling among Americans, especially as France bore the brunt of the warfare in the west. Many Americans served in France as volunteers before America even entered the war.

On top of this, Germany almost worked to make Americans dislike her. Germany had an autocratic and aristocratic society (the type that democratic Americans despised). Wilhelm II was an arrogant man who threatened aggressively and loved military power and display. Moreover, the invasion of Belgium was a brutal violation of international law. Germany itself had signed a treaty in the 1800s guaranteeing Belgian neutrality. The German Chancellor made matters worse by calling that treaty "a scrap of paper." From the beginning, Americans saw Germany as the wrongdoer in the war. However, there were always a few among the anti-British Irish Americans and German Americans who favored the Central Powers throughout the war.

William Jennings Bryan had been rewarded for his years of service to the Democratic Party with the job of Secretary of State under Woodrow Wilson. Bryan was fanatic on the subject of keeping America neutral at all cost. He was

| German Soldiers Marching

an idealist who tried to prevent wars through treaties that required disputes to be arbitrated. At the beginning of the war, Bryan and Wilson were in agreement that America should stay on good terms with both sides and eventually try to mediate a peace.

Neutral trade. The main problem with American neutrality was trade interests. America, and all industrial neutral nations, were willing to sell arms to both sides during a war at an excellent profit. In fact, the war orders from Europe pulled America out of a recession in 1914. Most American trade was with the Allies, which appeared less than neutral to the Germans.

The war trade with Germany quickly declined for a couple of reasons. The main cause was the success of the British blockade of the Central Powers. The British navy, the largest in the world, had cleared German opposition off the oceans by the end of 1914. The British were free to intercept and seize shipments to the Central Powers on the high seas. America resented the capture of American cargoes, but the British paid compensation and did not harm the ships or crew. While infuriating, the British actions were consistent with the Union blockade during the Civil War and did no serious damage to U.S.-British relations.

The second reason for the decline in trade with Germany was that both sides ran out of cash. American bankers were willing to lend money to the Allies and did so throughout the war. Thus, the Allies were able to buy American guns using money from American loans. On the other hand, very few loans were made to the Central Powers who were considered a bad credit risk.

Neutral America rapidly became a munitions and supply factory for the Allies. Germany responded by declaring its own blockade around Britain, hoping to cut off the island nation's vital ocean supply lines. However, Germany had no ships available to enforce a blockade. They resorted to a new technology— submarines called U-boats.

First U-boat crisis. In February of 1915, Germany announced that all *Allied* vessels sailing around Great Britain would be sunk by U-boats without warning. Wilson demanded and received assurances that neutral ships would not be targeted. However, no protection was promised for Americans traveling on Allied vessels. This provoked the first major American-German crisis.

War blockades up until the Great War used battleships to intercept merchant vessels bringing supplies to the enemy. Because most trading ships were unarmed or lightly armed, they quickly surrendered without a fight. The cargo might be seized, but no one died. In the rare instances where the warship sunk the merchant vessel, a warning was always given and arrangements were made for the safety of the crew. This was the accepted international procedure for blockades.

U-boats set up a totally different kind of blockade. They were very vulnerable to any kind of shipboard guns and, therefore attacked without warning. Ships were routinely destroyed with their cargoes and most, if not all, of the crew died! This was a shocking innovation in the history of warfare. This kind of destruction

| The Deadly U-boat

would become normal in Twentieth Century wars, but this was the first time the world had seen it. Americans saw it as an example of German contempt for international law.

On May 7, 1915 a German U-boat sank the unarmed British passenger liner *Lusitania* without warning. The ship sank in less than twenty minutes and 1,198 people died, including 128 Americans. The outcry in America was tremendous. Wilson sent strong notes of protest to Germany. Bryan thought they were worded too strongly and might cause conflict. He resigned rather than sign one of them. The Germans gave some reassurances but did not keep them. After more sinkings, Wilson threatened to break off diplomatic relations (a step toward war) if Germany did not stop sinking unarmed ships without warning. Germany backed down and cut back her submarine operations, ending the crisis.

Election of 1916. Theodore Roosevelt did not want to split the Republican vote again and refused the Progressive Party's nomination in 1916. The Republicans nominated Supreme Court Justice Charles Evans Hughes who had an excellent progressive record as governor of New York. The Democrats naturally chose Wilson who campaigned under the slogan, "He kept us out of war." Hughes failed to make effective use of America's lack of preparation for war by speaking on both sides of the issue. Wilson campaigned on his reform record, prosperity (ironically, due to the war), and American neutrality. He won the election by over a half million out of the 17.5 million votes cast.

War. By the beginning of 1917, Germany was getting desperate. The war was into its third year of stalemate, and Germany was suffering from shortages of all kinds, including food. The high command decided to gamble on a knock-out blow. They announced in January that they would resume submarine warfare and sink *all* ships, including American, in the blockade zone. Germany knew this would bring America into the war, but they believed they could defeat the Allies before the unprepared Americans were ready to fight. They almost succeeded.

Wilson broke diplomatic relations with Germany on February 3rd and began to prepare for war. In early March, an intercepted note from German foreign secretary Zimmermann made the situation worse. In the Zimmermann note, Germany sought an alliance with Mexico, offering them the chance to regain Texas, New Mexico, and Arizona. The offer was never seriously considered, but it did further arouse the American people.

Also in March, a revolution took place in Russia. The long-suffering Russian people rebelled against their autocratic ruler, the czar, and set up a democratic government. The Russian people needed more than just a new form of government. The devastating war was incredibly unpopular, but the new government decided to keep fighting. The **communists** would soon take advantage of that mistake.

Germany ended the last hope for peace when it sank several unarmed American merchant vessels in mid-March. President Wilson's cup of patience was finally drained. Germany was at war with America, but we were not fighting back. On April 2, 1917, Wilson went before a joint session of Congress to ask for a declaration of war. His speech was a masterful presentation of his ideal of a just war. He finished with this statement:

> *It is a fearful thing to lead this great peaceful people into war ... But the right is more precious than peace, and we shall fight for the things which have always carried nearest to our hearts—for democracy, for the right of those who submit to authority to have a voice in their own Governments, for the rights and liberties of small nations, for a universal dominion of right by such a concert of free peoples as shall bring peace and safety to all nations and make the world itself at last free.*

Congress declared war on April 6, 1917.

Answer these questions.

1.21 What were the contents of the Zimmermann note?

_____

_____

_____

1.22 How did U-boats violate established international law and practice?

_____

_____

1.23 What event at the start of the war turned America against Germany?

_____

1.24 What did Secretary of State Bryan want America to do?

_____

1.25 What was Wilson's 1916 campaign slogan, and what later event made it ironic?

_____

_____

_____

1.26 Why did neutral America trade mainly with the Allies?

_____

_____

_____

1.27 When the war began in 1914, what stance did most Americans favor?

_____

1.28 What happened to the _Lusitania,_ and why did the incident cause Bryan to resign?

_____

_____

_____

1.29 What happened to the Russian government in March of 1917?

_____

1.30 What was the primary cause of America's declaration of war against Germany?

_____

The Great War

The Crusade. The American people quickly united in support of the war, with few exceptions, like reformer Robert La Follette who opposed the war to the end. Even William J. Bryan supported the war effort. The peace-loving Woodrow Wilson proved he could lead a war if he had to do it.

Wilson saw the war as a crusade and convinced the American people of his vision. America was not seeking land or money in this war. She was fighting to "make the world safe for democracy." Americans threw themselves into fulfilling that ideal.

The American economy was slowly organized on a war footing. The War Industries Board was set up and given the power to set prices, improve production, and eliminate waste. Railroads and communication were taken over by the federal government for the length of the war. Herbert Hoover, who had run a very successful program to bring food to starving Belgium, was put in charge of the Food Administration. His excellent organizational skills and popular appeals to save food resulted in substantial increases in the amount of food shipped to hungry Allies. Ship production was increased, and the time required to build a ship decreased, although most of the increase in shipping came too late for the war. By the time of the Armistice, Americans were building two ships for every one they lost to the U-boats. (The extended use of **convoys** eventually brought the U-boat menace under control).

One of Wilson's fears about war was that it would arouse hatred among the American people. He was correct. German Americans, who were typically loyal, faced harassment and occasional injury from the aroused public. Orchestras no longer played music by German composers such as Beethoven or Wagner. Sauerkraut was renamed "Liberty Cabbage," and dachshunds became very unpopular. The Socialist Party publicly opposed the war, and its leader was jailed for anti-war speeches. Tolerance has never been a public virtue during a war, and this one was no exception.

"Lafayette, we are here." By 1917 the Allies were in desperate shape. Battle losses were so high that the Allies were literally running out of men. A French **offensive** in the spring had been thrown back with heavy losses. Many of the French troops mutinied in the aftermath of the failure. They had had enough after three years of death and disease. Moreover, the Russian war effort was collapsing under the weak leadership of the new government and the growing communist revolt in the nation. The Allies desperately needed U.S. replacements on the western front.

This was not what the Americans expected. They had not initially planned to raise a huge army and ship it all the way across the Atlantic. In fact, the German high command believed they could not do so even if they tried; but faced with this critical situation, Wilson complied.

Congress reluctantly passed a conscription act a few weeks after the war began. In contrast to the bloody reaction to the Civil War draft, the public responded well to the new law. Eventually, men between the ages of 18 and 45 were required to register for the draft. No one could buy his way out of service, but exceptions were given to people working at jobs critical to the war effort, such as ship building. In the end, over four million men were taken into the armed services to fight the Great War; about half that number served in France.

Still, it took time to organize, equip, train, and ship all of those men. The "Doughboys," as the Americans were called, did not start arriving in France in large numbers until early 1918, almost a year after America entered the war. Recognizing the need to improve Allied morale, a group of soldiers named the American Expeditionary Forces were sent over in June of 1917.

Under the command of General John J. Pershing, the small, inexperienced A.E.F. began to train in quiet sectors of the front. One of Pershing's officers summed up the feelings of many Americans when he said upon arrival, "Lafayette, we are here."

Russian Revolution. The democratic government in Russia was unable to rule that battered land. Germany allowed Lenin, a communist exile, to return to Russia through Germany in 1917 in the hopes of damaging the Russian war effort. Lenin organized a communist revolution which overthrew the Russian government in October of 1917. The Bolsheviks (communists) fought a civil war for control of the country. They could not afford to fight Germany at the same time. In March of 1918, they made an expensive peace with Germany, giving the kaiser a huge chunk of what is now eastern Europe. This freed the Bolsheviks to fight in Russia and the Germans to fight exclusively on the western front.

The End. Germany quickly moved its armies from the east to France for a massive series of offensives beginning in March of 1918. The Americans were just beginning to arrive in strength, and at first the Germans succeeded in pushing forward. The May offensive brought the enemy back to the Marne River. They were again stopped with some American assistance. Newly arrived American troops were thrown into the battle at Château-Thierry near Paris. They held and later cleared the Germans out of the Belleau woods nearby, in spite of high casualty rates.

Pershing insisted that the Americans should be set up as an independent army in charge of one portion of the front. The French and British wanted to use the Americans as replacements for their own battered forces. Pershing lent out units to do just that, but as the number of Americans grew, he continued to insist on a separate command. Gradually, through sheer stubbornness, he got his way. The Americans were given a portion of the front running north from the Swiss border.

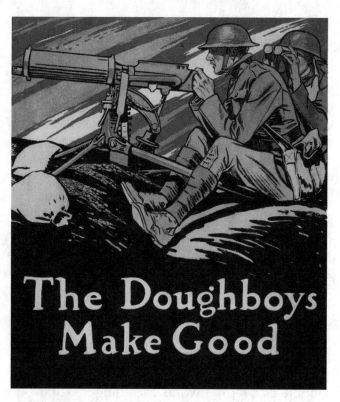

| "Doughboy" War Picture

In September, the Americans were placed in charge of driving the Germans out of the St. Mihiel salient (a bulge in the front). They were aided by a few French divisions. The Germans were quickly overwhelmed and driven back. The Americans immediately moved north and west to join in a major Allied offensive.

The greatest American offensive of the war was in the Meuse-Argonne region. It was an area of dense forest, rugged terrain, and impressive German defenses. More than a million Americans fought in the battle which resulted in over 120,000 casualties. By the end of October, the Germans were steadily pushed back until they lost everything they had gained in their offensives during the spring.

America's greatest hero of the war came out of this grinding battle. Sergeant Alvin York (then a corporal) was a committed Christian from Tennessee. York was a crack shot who suddenly found himself in command when all of the officers and most of the men in his platoon were killed or wounded. York shot more than twenty of the Germans who had tried to finish off the Americans, and he captured 132 others!

By November it was clear that the war was almost over. The German allies had surrendered one by one. Germany itself was now fighting for its life on German soil. Hoping for a reasonable peace, the Germans offered to negotiate a cease fire. Under pressure from the Allies, the kaiser was forced to abdicate and an armistice was signed. The Great War ended on November 11, 1918 at eleven in the morning local time—the 11th hour of the 11th day of the 11th month.

The heavy battle losses of the Great War were augmented by disease, most notably the influenza **pandemic** of 1918-1919. This fierce virus routinely killed healthy young people within hours. The pandemic killed over 20 million people all over the world, including 500,000 Americans. That was <u>four</u> <u>times</u> the number of Americans killed in the war.

The human cost of the Great War was staggering. The number of dead from Russia alone was 1.7 million. Over 1.3 million French and 900,000 from the British Empire died. The American dead from the one year they were in the battle totalled over 100,000. Germany lost 1.7 million and Austria-Hungary 1.2 million. (Figures taken from the *World Book Multimedia Encyclopedia*, 1997). That did not include the men who lost limbs, eyesight, or their health during battle. A whole generation of European men were cut down. The two sides had to succeed in making peace, and that was their greatest failure of all.

Signing of the Armistice in a Railway Carriage

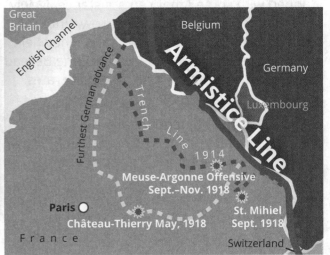

| The First World War's Armistice Line

✎ **Complete these sentences.**

1.31 Led by a man named _____ the _____ overthrew the Russian government in October of 1917.

1.32 America sent a force called the _____ to France under the command of _____ in June of 1917.

1.33 More Americans died in the _____ pandemic of 1917-18 than did in the war.

1.34 According to Woodrow Wilson, America was fighting to "make _____ _____ ."

1.35 Prices and production were under the control of the _____ during the war.

1.36 American soldiers, nicknamed _____ , did not arrive in France in substantial numbers until _____ .

1.37 Newly arrived Americans helped to defend Paris in early 1918 when they held at _____ and then cleared the Germans out of the _____ woods.

1.38 _____ , who killed more than twenty Germans and captured 132 more, was the greatest American hero of the war.

1.39 _____ managed the Belgium famine relief and the wartime Food Administration.

1.40 The greatest American offensive of the war was in the _____ region.

1.41 The Great War ended by an armistice on _____ at _____ local time.

Complete the following.

1.42 What were the terms of the American conscription act?

_____

_____

1.43 How did the communist revolution in Russia help Germany?

_____

_____

_____

1.44 Explain the statement "Lafayette, we are here." (Look up Lafayette, if necessary.)

_____

_____

1.45 How did Pershing want the American forces used in France?

_____

_____

The Peace that Failed

Fourteen Points. Woodrow Wilson was determined that *this* war would end with a just and fair peace. In January of 1918 he outlined Fourteen Points to be used as guidelines for a final treaty of peace. The basic points were:

1. Open negotiations of peace agreements and no secret treaties in the future

2. Freedom of the seas

3. As much free trade as possible

4. Reduction of armaments to the smallest amount necessary for nations to protect themselves

5. Judging of colonial claims in the interest of the people of the colony

6. Removal of German troops from the Russian territory taken by treaty in 1918; Russia to determine its own political future

7. Removal of German troops from Belgium, and the restoration of that nation

8. Removal of German troops from France; the return of Alsace and Lorraine

9. Adjust the borders of Italy based on the nationality of the people

10. Self-government for the different nationalities in Austria-Hungary

11. Removal of German troops from Romania, Serbia and Montenegro with guarantees of their independence; Serbia to get a sea port

12. Independence for Turkey but with self-government for the different nationalities there; Dardanelles open to all shipping

13. Re-establishment of the nation of Poland (It had been divided up among its neighbors in 1795) with access to the sea

14. The creation of an association of nations to protect the smaller nations and preserve peace

These points were hailed all over the world by liberals and the oppressed, but they were quietly reviled by many of the powerful politicians who would have to enact them. The Germans signed the armistice under the belief these would be the basis of the final treaty.

Treaty of Versailles. When the war ended, Wilson announced that he would personally lead the American delegation to the peace conference. It was a bad decision for many reasons. It put him away from Washington for six long months. After the Republicans had gained control of Congress, it made the treaty a personal matter for Wilson and his Republican opponents. He compounded these errors by naming only one unimportant Republican to the peace delegation and no Senators, even though the Senate was required to approve the treaty.

Wilson was given a hero's welcome as he toured the capitals of Europe. His American troops had turned the tide and saved Europe from the "Huns" (Germans). His Fourteen Points held out a hope for a time of lasting peace out of the years of carnage. The crowds that greeted the American president were delirious with joy. From such heights, he fell hard.

In spite of the first of Wilson's points, the Paris treaty negotiations (January 1919) were held in secret. The Germans were not even invited to participate. Most of the decisions were made by the "Big Four": President Woodrow Wilson of the U.S., Prime Minister David Lloyd George of Britain, Premier Georges Clemenceau of France, and Premier Vittorio Orlando of Italy.

Wilson's agenda quickly ran into the hard expectations of his European counterparts. Lloyd George had promised to crush Germany in his election campaign. Clemenceau was determined to protect devastated France from future German militarism at all cost. Italy and

| L to R: David Lloyd George, Italian Foreign Minister Sonnino, Georges Clemenceau, and Woodrow Wilson at the Paris Peace Conference

smaller Allied countries came to collect territory as part of the spoils of war. Italy had actually entered the war because it had been promised territory in a secret treaty with Britain. Wilson was repeatedly forced to compromise on his Fourteen Points.

Wilson concentrated on his last point, the creation of an association of nations to insure peace in the future. He succeeded in making the League of Nations part of the peace treaty itself and personally took charge of writing the League Covenant at the beginning of the conference. He believed the League would be able to rectify any problems created by other areas of the treaty. However, the Senate refused to consider the League without the protection of the Monroe Doctrine, the right of member nations to handle their own immigration and trade as well as the right to withdraw from the League. The European leaders forced Wilson to yield on other key points to get these items added to the League Covenant.

France's primary demands were to make Germany pay for the cost of the war and so cripple that nation that it would never threaten France again. France wanted to take the coal-rich border region of the Saar (as well as Alsace-Lorraine) for itself and also create a buffer state out of the west bank of the Rhine River. This would have placed thousands of Germans under French rule, and Wilson would not allow such a violation of self-determination. In the end, it was agreed that France would occupy the Rhineland for fifteen years, and the Saar region would vote on which nation would rule it after being under League control for that time period.

The Allies demanded that Germany assume full responsibility for starting the war. She was required to pay a huge indemnity to cover the civilian damages during the war, including Allied war pensions. Wilson was forced to agree to this, even though Germany had been stripped of some of its most productive regions, reducing its ability to pay anything. Germany was forced to dismantle most of its army and give the Allies its navy. (German sailors sunk many of their own ships rather than do this.)

Wilson also lost on Italy which took the regions it had been promised by the treaty with Britain, including parts of Austria and the port of Trieste on the Adriatic Sea. Italy demanded the Slavic port of Fiume, which was to be part of the new nation of Yugoslavia. Italy did not get it at the conference, but then forced Yugoslavia to cede the port to Italy in 1924. Japan succeeded in keeping the German colonies it captured in Asia, particularly control over China's Shantung peninsula, which was a gross violation of self-determination. Because of this, China refused to sign the treaty. Other European nations managed to keep control of captured German colonies by taking them as "mandates" under the nominal supervision of the League of Nations.

The map of Europe was redrawn by the Paris Conference. The nation of Poland was recreated from the land given up by Russia when it withdrew from the war, as were Estonia, Latvia,

and Lithuania. Poland was given an outlet to the sea which left part of Germany isolated east of that nation. Austria-Hungary was divided (its emperor abdicated) into Austria and Hungary. Part of its land was given to create the nations of Czechoslovakia and Yugoslavia as well as to expand Romania. The Ottoman Empire was reduced to the nation of Turkey with most of its former territory in the hands of Britain and France.

The Treaty of Versailles came under severe criticism as soon as it became public. France was bitter that its revenge was so limited. Italy was bitter over Fiume. The idealists felt that Wilson had betrayed them. Germany was especially bitter. She had sued for peace, trusting the Fourteen Points. The harsh treaty forced them to accept full responsibility for the war, pay damages, lose a large section of industrial land, and lose their armed forces. Germany had no choice but to sign in June of 1919. However, the terms of the treaty would cause ruin, bitterness, and would build a foundation for the rise of Adolf Hitler and another war twenty years later.

| Post-World War I Europe

Senate battle. Isolationism returned to America with the end of the war. The League of Nations looked suspiciously like an entangling European alliance that the nation had avoided since the time of George Washington. The Senate was especially hostile, fearing the League would interfere with internal decisions. Led by Henry Cabot Lodge, a bitter enemy of Wilson, the Republican senate was in a fighting mood. However, the Senate was unwilling to reject the treaty outright. Instead, it sought to drag out the decision and water it down with amendments. The president refused to consider any amendments or alterations.

Wilson became increasingly frustrated with the Senate. Finally, in September of 1919 he decided to appeal to the American people. He began a speaking tour across the nation in order to build support for the League of Nations which he believed would repair the concessions he was forced to make in the treaty. He traveled 8,000 miles, making 32 speeches in 21 days, against the advice of his doctors. At the end of his tour, he collapsed and suffered a stroke that left him partially paralyzed. He was confined to a sick room during the critical months leading up to the Senate vote, increasingly out of touch and angry. The Senate rejected the treaty and the League of Nations in November of 1919. A serious attempt was made to pass it again in March of 1920 with some reservations written by Lodge. Wilson himself doomed the compromise when he insisted that his supporters should vote against it because of the reservations. America never joined the League of Nations, but it made a separate peace with Germany.

Conclusion. The Great War was supposed to be the "war to end all wars." Instead, it was the precursor to the greatest war yet, World War II. The wanton bloodshed and destruction destroyed ideals as well as nations. When it was over, America wanted to get back to the business of living. Little did they know that the world was changing.

The Great War marked the decline of Europe as the world power. Europe had dominated much of the world by trade and colonization since the 1500–1600s. Bled white by World War I, Europe's power began to decline. A death blow would be delivered by a second great war twenty years later, devastating yet another generation of European manhood. The Great War was pivotal in the transition away from Europe and toward the United States as the leader of the Western world.

Match these items.

1.46 _____ Poland		a. Nation created after the war with a sea outlet through German territory
1.47 _____ Yugoslavia		b. Republican Senate Majority Leader
1.48 _____ Lloyd George		c. Ideals which were supposed to be the basis for the peace treaty
1.49 _____ Henry Cabot Lodge		d. Association of nations created by the Treaty of Versailles
1.50 _____ League of Nations		e. Prime Minister of Great Britain
1.51 _____ Monroe		f. Premier of France
1.52 _____ Fourteen Points		g. Doctrine the Senate wanted protected in the League Covenant
1.53 _____ Czechoslovakia		h. Nation that took over control of Shantung peninsula from the Germans
1.54 _____ Georges Clemenceau		i. New nation built from Serbia, Montenegro, and part of Austria-Hungary
1.55 _____ Vittorio Orlando		j. New nation created within Austria-Hungary
1.56 _____ Japan		k. Premier of Italy

Check the items that were part of the Fourteen Points.

1.57 ☐ recreation of Poland

1.58 ☐ protection of American immigration policy

1.59 ☐ independence for the Rhineland

1.60 ☐ self-determination (their own government) for many of the nationalities of Europe

1.61 ☐ freedom of the seas

1.62 ☐ German responsibility for the war

1.63 ☐ setting up mandates to maintain European control over German colonies

1.64 ☐ an association of nations to keep the peace

1.65 ☐ the right of nations to withdraw from the League of Nations

1.66 ☐ part of Austria being given to Italy

1.67 ☐ payment of a war indemnity by Germany

1.68 ☐ restoration of Belgium

1.69 ☐ open negotiations; no secret treaties

Answer these questions.

1.70 a. How did Wilson counter Senate attempts to stall the treaty?

_____

_____

b. What happened to Wilson personally as a result?

_____

1.71 Why did the Treaty of Versailles lead to World War II?

_____

_____

_____

1.72 What was the goal of France at the negotiations?

_____

_____

_____

1.73 How did America and Germany end the war between their nations?

_____

1.74 What mistakes did Wilson make in setting up the American delegation to the Paris Peace Conference? _____

1.75 What did Wilson believe was the most important part of the Treaty of Versailles?

_____

1.76 Which nations were the "Big Four" at the Paris Peace Conference?

_____

1.77 What did the smaller Allied nations want at the Paris Peace Conference?

_____

1.78 What was the coal-rich section of Germany that France wanted?

_____

1.79 Why would it be difficult for Germany to pay the war indemnity?

_____

1.80 What happened to the world power of Europe because of the Great War?

_____

Review the material in this section in preparation for the Self Test. The Self Test will check your mastery of this particular section. The items missed on this Self Test will indicate specific areas where restudy is needed for mastery.

SELF TEST 1

Match these people (each item, 2 points).

1.01	_____	Wilson's Secretary of State	a. Woodrow Wilson
1.02	_____	Commander of the A.E.F.	b. Wilhelm II
1.03	_____	Russian Bolshevik leader	c. Otto von Bismarck
1.04	_____	Republican Senate Majority Leader	d. Archduke Franz Ferdinand
1.05	_____	Kaiser of Germany	e. William Jennings Bryan
1.06	_____	"He kept us out of war."	f. John J. Pershing
1.07	_____	Prime Minister of Britain	g. Lenin
1.08	_____	Prussian leader who united Germany	h. Lloyd George
1.09	_____	Heir to the throne of Austria	i. Georges Clemenceau
1.010	_____	Premier of France	j. Henry Cabot Lodge

Complete the following (each numbered answer, 3 points).

1.011 What were the three major factors that drew Europe into World War I?

_____

1.012 What triggered the war (place, event, person)?

_____

1.013 Describe why trench warfare offensive was ineffective and devastating.

_____

_____

1.014 What actions by Germany were primarily responsible for drawing America into the war?

_____

1.015 What action by Germany early in the war cast her as the aggressor?

_____

1.016 What event in Russia allowed Germany to move troops away from the eastern front?

_____

1.017 What disease killed more Americans than the war in 1918-19?

_____

1.018 What was the name of Wilson's liberal peace framework?

_____

1.019 What did France primarily want at the Paris Conference?

_____

_____

1.020 Name three nations created by the Treaty of Versailles.

_____

1.021 What was the name of the association of countries created by the Treaty of Versailles?

_____

1.022 What did Wilson do when the Senate stalled over approving the treaty?

_____

_____

1.023 The Great War was the beginning of a change in the leadership of the western world.

The leadership began to switch over to whom? _____

1.024 What were airplanes used for during World War I? _____

1.025 What did Americans want to do about the war when it began? _____

1.026 Why did America wind up trading mainly with the Allies?

_____

_____

1.027 Name the first two nations who were officially at war.

_____

1.028 How did submarine blockades differ from previous war blockades?

_____

_____

1.029 What was the Zimmermann note?

_____

_____

1.030 What was the Allies' greatest need by the time America entered the war? _____

Choose the correct answer (each answer, 2 points).

Alvin York   Eddie Rickenbacker   Meuse-Argonne   St. Mihiel
Lusitania   zeppelins   Dardanelles   War Industries Board
Herbert Hoover   Château-Thierry

1.031 _____ set prices; improved production and eliminated waste

1.032 _____ American troops defended Paris against a German offensive

1.033 _____ airships used for observations and to drop bombs

1.034 _____ America's greatest ace

1.035 _____ Food Administration and Belgium famine relief effort

1.036 _____ greatest American offensive of the war

1.037 _____ salient on the western front; pushed back by the Americans

1.038 _____ straits leading to the Black Sea; supply route to Russia

1.039 _____ American sharpshooter hero; captured 132 Germans

1.040 _____ British passenger liner sunk by German U-boat with the loss of 128 Americans

80 / 100   **SCORE** _____   **TEACHER** _____ _____
initials   date

2. THE GREAT DEPRESSION

After World War I, Americans wanted to return to normalcy. They wanted to make money, buy new "toys," avoid any more crusades, and enjoy life. The 1920s were an era of prosperity and "high living." Profits soared, industrial output grew, and people had money to spend. Under three consecutive Republican presidents, the nation honored its businessmen and "enjoyed the good life."

The wonderful world of American prosperity died in 1929 with the start of the Great Depression. It began with the crash of the stock market in October. It spread into the deepest and longest depression in American history. One-fourth of all Americans lost their jobs.

The traditional faith of the nation in business and private charity was destroyed as the depression and personal desperation grew deeper. A change in outlook was needed, and Franklin Delano Roosevelt brought it.

FDR brought a "New Deal" to the nation. He used the monetary power of the federal government to provide jobs and relief. His new, aggressive policies did not end the depression, but instead gave hope and restored faith in the government. The depression gripped the nation until the demands of World War II pulled it out; however, Roosevelt deserves a great deal of credit for keeping the nation together during those dark years.

SECTION OBJECTIVES

Review these objectives. When you have completed this section, you should be able to:

1. Describe the policies, personalities, and politics of the U.S. presidents from 1915 to 1945.

6. Describe the course of the Great Depression and the New Deal.

VOCABULARY

Study these words to enhance your learning success in this section.

agnostic (ag näs' tik). Person who believes that any understanding or knowledge of God is not possible for man. He also believes reason and science are the only guides for finding truth.

collateral (kə lat' ə rəl). Property pledged to a lender to protect him from loss if the borrower can not pay a loan.

parity (par' ət ē). State of being equal or equivalent.

polio (pō' lē ō). An infectious disease that causes fever, muscle paralysis, and atrophy of muscles often with permanent disability.

quota (kwōt ə). A permitted share or part.

spendthrift (spend' thrift). A person who spends wastefully or without careful thought.

Roaring Twenties

Election of 1920. The Democratic Party nominated James M. Cox, governor of Ohio, for the presidency in 1920. His running mate was a young New Yorker and former assistant secretary of the navy, Franklin Delano Roosevelt. Republicans were at first deadlocked between several leaders. Apparently at a meeting of party bosses in a "smoke-filled back room," they agreed on a compromise candidate, Senator Warren G. Harding of Ohio. Harding was an easygoing man of small intellect, few enemies, and few ideas of his own. Popular Massachusetts governor Calvin Coolidge was chosen as his running mate.

Woodrow Wilson hoped to use the election as a referendum on the now twice-defeated Treaty of Versailles. Cox came out strongly for the treaty and the League of Nations. Harding, who conducted a "back porch" campaign from his home, was vague. He favored some international association, but not necessarily the League of Nations. In the end, it was not a controlling issue. Americans were tired of the war, tired of the crusades, and tired of Woodrow Wilson, whose ideas were running even if he was not. Americans elected the Republican, pro-business candidate who promised a "return to normalcy." Harding won by a commanding popular (60%) and electoral vote (404 to 127) in the first federal election after the 19th Amendment gave women the right to vote.

Warren G. Harding (1865-1923). Warren G. Harding ranks with Ulysses S. Grant among the worst presidents in U.S. history. Harding was born to a farming family in Ohio. He attended various schools and qualified as a teacher in 1882. He did not like teaching and moved into the newspaper business. He purchased the *Marion Star* and built it into a successful paper with the help of his capable wife, Florence. He built a reputation as an editor and Republican speaker. He became active in state politics around the turn of the century, serving as a representative and lieutenant governor. He became a close associate of Harry M. Daugherty, a cagey political insider. Harding successfully ran for the U.S. Senate in 1914 with Daugherty's encouragement. He was a popular senator who introduced no major bills and voted without any independence. Daugherty worked hard to bring him up as the compromise candidate in 1920 for the Republican Party.

Harding's biggest weakness, like Grant before him, was his tendency to blindly trust his friends. He would believe what they told him, support their decisions, take no personal responsibility on the facts, and would not turn them in when betrayal was clear. Harding actually made several good appointments, including Charles Evans Hughes as secretary of state and the efficient Herbert Hoover as secretary of commerce, but these were overshadowed by the "Ohio Gang" which included Secretary of the Interior Albert Fall and Attorney General Harry Daugherty, the political fixer who was responsible for enforcing federal law!

Return to normalcy. A wave of anti-foreign feeling swept the nation in the wake of the war. Fear of the Bolsheviks created a "Red Scare" in 1919–1920 as thousands of immigrants who were suspected of favoring socialism, communism, or other left-wing causes were rounded up and deported. Prosecutions were based on speech rather than actions, a clear violation of American values. The showcase for the fear was the 1921 trial of two Italian immigrants (Nicola Sacco and Bartolomeo Vanzetti) for robbery and murder in Massachusetts. The trial was prejudiced when the jury was told that the men were anarchists. They were condemned to death and hailed as left-wing martyrs when they were finally executed in 1927.

The anti-foreign feeling also led to a resurgence of the Ku Klux Klan in the 1920s. The Klan expanded its original anti-black stand to include hatred of Jews, Catholics, and foreigners. Their ideas were expressed by nighttime attacks and lynchings. The Klan promoted itself as the savior of White Protestant Americans. By the mid-1920s, the Klan had about 5 million members and considerable influence in several state legislatures. The Klan reached its height in 1924 and then declined. American disgust at the Klan's hate-filled techniques and the conviction of a prominent Klan leader for rape and murder led to its decline.

One of the main issues of the Klan and other anti-foreign campaigns was immigration. Many destitute Europeans began the trek to America after the end of World War I, mainly from poorer Catholic countries of the south and east. Americans reacted with fear and Congress reacted with legislation. The previously open door of American immigration was closed with a **quota** system that heavily favored people coming from northern Europe. Japanese immigrants were barred entirely, a distinction that would cause trouble with the racially sensitive and growing power of the Japanese Empire.

Foreign policy could not be completely forgotten as America tried to back away from her World War I intervention. A dangerous naval buildup by Britain and Japan forced Secretary Hughes to call a disarmament conference in 1921-22. It proved impossible to convince France to reduce her land army, but the three leading naval powers (U.S., Britain, and Japan) had some success. They agreed to end their buildup (even scrapping some of their own ships) and maintain their navies on a set plan. The U.S. and Britain were to have **parity** while Japan would have a smaller navy (on a 5 to 3 ratio). Italy and France would have yet a lower limit on their ships. The Five Power Naval Treaty of 1922 limited only the larger battleships. It did not end the naval arms race, but it did diffuse a tense situation for a few more years.

| Members of the Ku Klux Klan

Death and scandal. Harding was saved from public humiliation for the actions of his "friends" when he suddenly died after returning from a trip to Alaska on August 2, 1923. At that time, information was just beginning to be released that would forever condemn his presidency. The stress over the revelations may have contributed to his death. However, he was still very popular and widely mourned at the time of his death because the scandals had not yet been revealed.

Three major scandals were exposed in rapid succession. The first involved Charles Forbes, director of the veteran's bureau. He was selling supplies at cut rates and awarding construction contracts for kickbacks. Harding found out and let him resign rather than face charges. An investigation eventually put him in jail.

The second scandal involved Jesse Smith, a man working under Harry Daugherty at the attorney general's office. He was helping several illegal schemes from that office. Upon the scandalous discovery, he was forced to resign and committed suicide shortly thereafter. Daugherty's involvement was never proven, in spite of a lengthy investigation and two trials.

The Teapot Dome Scandal was the last and biggest of the major scandals. Secretary of the Interior Albert Fall sold oil leases on government property secretly and without any competitive bidding. Years after, Fall was found guilty of taking a bribe for the leases. The wealthy oilmen who gave him the bribes were acquitted, which did not sit well with the American public. These scandals were the only major legacy of the Harding Administration.

Calvin Coolidge (1872-1933). Calvin Coolidge ("Silent Cal") was an unusual figure in the history of the presidency. He had an excellent reputation for honesty and thrift, but is best known for how little he spoke. He rarely smiled or joked. His statements were always short and to the point. One favorite story was about a lady who bet a friend she could get him to say more than two words. When she told the president about the bet, thinking he would comment, he said, "You lose."

| "Silent Cal" Coolidge

Calvin Coolidge was born in Massachusetts in 1875 to a hardworking farmer/storekeeper. His father was active in state politics and passed this interest to his son. Calvin graduated from Amherst College in 1895 and became a member of the Massachusetts bar in 1897. He practiced law and became active in politics in the city of Northampton. He served in various city positions in the state legislature (both houses), as lieutenant governor, and as governor in 1918. He gained nationwide attention for his firm handling of a strike by the Boston police in 1919 when he mobilized the national guard to restore order. (The anti-foreign feeling across the nation included a fear of unions). He was a popular choice to run with Harding in 1920.

Coolidge Administration. Coolidge was visiting his family in Massachusetts when he learned of the president's death. Calvin's father was a notary public and administered the oath of office to his son. On return to Washington, Coolidge continued Harding's pro-business policies. He did some housecleaning in the wake of the scandals,

and his own reputation for honesty kept him clear of scandal. Coolidge supported Secretary of the Treasury Andrew Mellon, one of America's richest men, who cut taxes on the rich and steadily reduced the American war debt. The country was enjoying an era of prosperity, and Coolidge's thrift and support for the businesses creating the booming economy made him popular.

Coolidge faced several foreign problems during his administration. The most critical was the issue of Allied war debts. America had lent billions of dollars to the Allies during the Great War. Now Americans wanted their money back with interest. To President Coolidge and the American people it was simply a matter of paying honest debts. To impoverished Europe, it was not that simple. Most of the loans had been spent in America buying weapons and supplies. America had gained prosperity while Europe, and France in particular, experienced death and destruction. The Europeans felt that some of the debts should be forgiven as America's part of the war effort.

The issue grew very heated as the president insisted that the debts be paid in full. In the end, some concessions were made by the World War Foreign Debt Commission, established in 1922 by Congress. The interest rates were reduced on the loans, the repayment periods were extended and payments were reduced to fit the nation's ability to pay. These agreements were violently unpopular and garnered much ill will in Europe. Americans reacted with disgust and increased their commitment to isolation. The push for repayment also caused the Allies to put more pressure on Germany, already staggering under her reparations payments. The subsequent destruction of the German economy was the primary reason for the rise of Adolf Hitler.

Coolidge had a notable success in foreign policy in Mexico. That nation was trying to reclaim oil leases granted to American companies under a previous administration. As relations deteriorated, Coolidge sent an old friend, Dwight Morrow, to work on the problem. Morrow tactfully found a compromise and restored good relations between the two neighbors.

Another, more dubious success was the Kellogg-Briand Pact that supposedly outlawed war. Created on a tidal wave of public opinion, the signers swore that they would never again use war as an instrument of national policy. Originally created between America and France, it was signed by over sixty nations. However, it had no power to enforce itself and did not outlaw "defensive wars." It won the Nobel Peace Prize for Secretary of State Kellogg, but accomplished little else.

Election of 1924. "Silent Cal" easily took the Republican nomination in 1924. After over a hundred ballots, the hopelessly divided Democrats finally nominated wealthy corporate lawyer John W. Davis. The Progressive Party made its last gasp when it nominated the venerable reformer Robert La Follette of Wisconsin. The two major party candidates were both conservative with pro-business sympathies, so La Follette's traditional progressive agenda created the only debate. The Democrats hammered on the Harding scandals. The Republicans emphasized the prosperous economy, urging voters to "keep cool with Coolidge." Coolidge won both a popular and electoral majority. La Follette had one of the best third-party showings in American history when he won more than half the number of votes cast for the Democratic candidate and 13 electoral votes (from Wisconsin).

✏️ **Choose the best match for each item.**

2.1	_____ thousands of immigrants with leftist ideas were deported	a. Warren G. Harding
2.2	_____ Progressive candidate, 1924	b. Calvin Coolidge
2.3	_____ Democratic candidate, 1920	c. Kellogg-Briand Pact
2.4	_____ peaked in its anti-foreign influence in 1924	d. Teapot Dome Scandal
2.5	_____ "return to normalcy"	e. "Red Scare"
2.6	_____ scandal over government oil leases	f. Ku Klux Klan
2.7	_____ outlawed war	g. Five Power Naval Treaty
2.8	_____ Secretary of the treasury; reduced taxes on the rich and the war debt	h. Nicola Sacco and Bartolomeo Vanzetti
2.9	_____ executed for murder; left-wing martyrs	i. Robert La Follette
2.10	_____ gave U.S. and Britain naval parity; Japan was limited on a 5 to 3 ratio	j. James M. Cox
2.11	_____ famous for how little he talked	k. John W. Davis
2.12	_____ Democratic candidate of 1924; nominated after over 100 ballots	l. Andrew Mellon

Complete these sentences.

2.13 Charles Forbes was accused of getting kickbacks by _____ _____ and _____ .

2.14 Calvin Coolidge gained national attention from his handling of the _____ _____ in Boston (1919).

2.15 Warren G. Harding's biggest weakness was that he _____ _____ .

2.16 Calvin Coolidge's 1924 campaign slogan was _____ _____ .

2.17 Woodrow Wilson wanted the 1920 campaign to be a referendum on the _____ _____ .

2.18 Women first voted in a federal election in _____ thanks to the passage of the _____ Amendment.

2.19 Immigration was controlled in the 1920s by a series of _____ that

favored immigrants from _____ .

2.20 _____ was a political insider who helped

Harding to the presidency and was rewarded with the Attorney General's office.

2.21 a. The American position on Allied war debts was: _____

_____ .

b. The European position on the debts was: _____

_____ .

2.22 Dwight Morrow successfully mediated a dispute with Mexico over _____

_____ to American companies.

Prosperity. After the sacrifice and destruction of the Great War, America was ready to celebrate. The 1920s, also known as the "Roaring Twenties," were a time of prosperity, free spending, illegal drinking, and all kinds of fads. The stark contrast with the Great Depression, which would begin in 1929, makes the decade shine even more brightly as a glittering show in American history.

American business came out of World War I stronger than ever. Treasury Secretary Mellon's policies insured that the rich had money to invest in new factories and businesses. High tariffs insured good prices in the American markets and high profits, but the main reason business flourished was because businesses were producing a wide variety of affordable products for the American public.

The best example of the nation's new prosperity was the automobile. Henry Ford led the way in producing an automobile that was not for the luxury market but for every working American. He created a sturdy, easily repaired car called the Model T that was designed to run on the rutted country roads of the nation. He improved production until he was building one every

ten seconds to sell for $290 (very reasonable in 1924). Americans bought them by the thousands. Other manufacturers followed his lead. By 1930, the nation had one car for every five Americans. Auto purchases drove up production in steel, oil, rubber, and created a demand for better roads. The number of miles of paved road almost doubled during the decade.

Other manufacturers followed the same route, developing new products for all workers.

| A 1920s Model T Ford

Radios, refrigerators, and vacuum cleaners were among the items that began to appear in homes all over the nation. The use of electricity spread so that two-thirds of American homes had it by 1929.

Increased production gave American workers more money to spend, which in turn fed more manufacturing. America was enjoying a time of remarkable prosperity, fueled by the spending of the very workers who were producing the products. Wages were generally good and companies began to include medical, social, and retirement benefits for their employees. People believed that capitalism had finally created permanent prosperity.

Spending habits. America's spending habits changed dramatically in the 1920s. A nation of thrifty savers now became a nation of **spendthrifts**. Advertising was used to create demand for products rather than just telling interested customers about them. People began to buy things just because advertising convinced them it would somehow "improve their quality of life."

More importantly, the 1920s saw the first widespread use of credit to purchase new products. For example, credit allowed a person to buy an automobile by paying only part of the price at the time of purchase, and promising to pay a little each week or month until the entire price, plus interest, had been paid. This allowed people to buy things before they had the money. It was a violation not only of traditional American thinking but of God's laws as well (see Proverbs 22:7, 26).

Credit increased the buying power of the American public and was a major cause of the prosperity of the 1920s. However, credit users had to keep a steady income to meet their payments; otherwise, they lost both the money and the item they bought. This was a dangerous problem which led to the Great Depression.

Prohibition. America had been growing increasingly anti-alcohol in the years leading up to World War I. The war pushed the Temperance Movement into the mainstream of American politics. Under wartime pressure to protect young men from the "demon drink," the 18th Amendment to the Constitution was passed forbidding the manufacture or sale of alcohol in all of the U.S.

However, the free-living post-war generation had no interest in giving up drinking. The "noble experiment" from 1919 to 1932 was a dismal failure. People continued to drink beer, wine, and spirits manufactured or imported illegally. Private saloons called "speakeasies" sprang up behind iron-grilled doors in all major cities. (You got in by speaking and identifying yourself at the door). Liquor was freely available. It was just more expensive, was poor quality, and did not generate government tax money. Probably nothing is a better symbol of the Roaring Twenties than the drinking of illegal alcohol by normally law-abiding people.

The greatest failure of Prohibition was that it directly led to the rise of organized crime. The profits in illegal alcohol were high, but one had to operate a large system of production and distribution outside the law. Well-organized gangs had to arrange to brew the liquor, bottle it, and transport it to the speakeasies. Wholesale bribery kept the police from interfering too much. As profits grew, gangs would fight to control the liquor trade in the cities. Chicago became especially notorious for bloody gang killings under the rule of gangster Al Capone. Federal enforcement was never enough in the light of the widespread violations of the law.

Fads. The free-spending twenties produced a wide variety of fads and fancies that earmarked the colorful decade. The most famous symbol was the "flapper," the emancipated woman of the decade. The traditionally demure American woman appeared to go wild in the personage of the flapper. She bobbed (cut short) her hair, raised her hemlines, wore makeup, enjoyed energetic new dances, drank liquor, and smoked cigarettes in public. These very visible, high-living women did not represent the values of most American women, but they were a public symbol of the era. They were celebrated in movies, advertisements, magazines, and songs.

One of the greatest popular heroes of the decade was airplane pilot Charles Lindbergh. Lindbergh successfully completed a solo flight from New York to Paris in 1927. This remarkable accomplishment captured the imagination of the nation. He was greeted with the largest ticker tape parade in New York City history upon his return and hailed by huge crowds wherever he went.

The nation kept looking for new ways to entertain itself. Sporting events became more popular than ever. George Herman "Babe" Ruth caused a sensation when he hit a record 59 home runs in 1921 and then topped it in 1927 with 60. When the popular boxer Jack Dempsey lost his championship title in 1926, over 100,000 people paid to see the match. Millions more followed it on the radio. Golf, tennis, and bowling expanded across the nation as people looked for ways to use their money and free time.

Forms of entertainment grew, and sometimes fell, in popularity. Crossword puzzles were the rage for a while. People tried to set time records for sitting on top of flag poles. Dance marathons, where the winner was the couple that continued dancing the longest, were another fad. Movies became a regular part of the American entertainment menu, and movie stars like Rudolph Valentino attracted thousands of fans. Entertainment seemed to be the major goal of the decade.

Fundamentalism. Christianity in America was facing conflicts in the 1920s. Many scholars of the era were trying to make Christianity "more modern" by attempting to bring it into step with science. Unfortunately, they did this by assuming science had authority over faith. Miracles cannot be proven by science; therefore, the scholars eliminated them from Christianity. The result was a new religion that was compatible with "modern thinking," one that accepted evolution, denied miracles, and generally treated Christianity as a code of ethics, not a redemptive relationship with Jesus. This "liberal" interpretation of the Bible and Christianity became increasingly popular in the early 1900s and was still held by a large portion of Americans in the late 1900s who called themselves Christians. The liberals or modernists attacked Christians as closed minded and anti-intellectual, charges that are still used against Christians who believe that their God speaks truth through the pages of the Bible.

However, God will always have His faithful defenders. In the 1920s the people who rose to defend the faith were called fundamentalists. The name was taken from a book published in 1910 called *The Fundamentals* which defended traditional Christian doctrine. The basic premise of the fundamentalists was that the Bible taught historical facts and universal truth, not myths and moral guidelines as the liberals proposed. They foresaw very clearly that Christianity without faith is not Christianity at all.

Fundamentalist ideals were put to public ridicule at the Scopes Monkey Trial of 1925. Tennessee had a law that forbade the teaching of evolution in public schools. A biology teacher named John Scopes agreed to challenge the law by teaching this theory in his class. He was arrested and brought to trial in 1925. Nationally renowned lawyer Clarence Darrow, an **agnostic**, stepped forward to lead the defense team. The former Secretary of State William Jennings Bryan, a fundamentalist, came forward to aid the prosecution. Reporters from national newspapers, radio stations, and magazines came to cover the trial. The result was a circus in a courtroom.

The highlight of the trial occurred when Darrow convinced Bryan to take the stand as an expert on the Bible. Darrow then proceeded to ridicule Bryan's belief in the Flood, the swallowing of Jonah, and the day the earth stood still while Joshua fought. He argued that Bryan's Christianity denied the proofs of science. Bryan defended himself ably, but the hostile press generally sided with Darrow.

Scopes was convicted and fined (the decision was later reversed because of a procedural error); however, in the court of public opinion, fundamentalists were labeled as bigoted fanatics who denied clear scientific proof. Darrow and the modernists were portrayed as open-minded, objective, and tolerant. Christ warned us that because men hated Him, they would hate us (John 15:18). Bryan himself died a few days after the trial, ending the career of one of America's most colorful political figures.

Election of 1928. In his usual brief fashion, Calvin Coolidge announced, "I do not choose to run for president in 1928." His logical successor was internationally-known Herbert Hoover, who won the Republican nomination on the first ballot. The divided Democrats chose Al Smith, the governor of New York who was skilled at drawing out the working-class vote.

The liberal Smith proved to be a difficult candidate to sell. He opposed Prohibition when most of the nation still wanted to continue it. He was a Catholic, northeastern city boy when much of the Democratic support was still in the rural, staunchly Protestant former Confederacy. These personal defects were amplified by the fact the nation was rich and having fun under the Republicans. Americans saw no need for change.

| Clarence Darrow talking with William Jennings Bryan during the Scopes Trial

The dignified Hoover provided a sharp contrast to the outgoing, personable Smith. Hoover represented himself as the continuation of Republican prosperity. "A chicken in every pot and a car in every garage" was his campaign slogan. Despite Hoover's attempts to prevent it, mudslingers attacked Smith using nasty anti-Catholic slogans. In the end, Hoover won by the largest popular majority to date, including several of the states in the normally Democratic South. Smith had begun to build an alliance between the urban North and the Democratic South that would be the strength of the party for years to come.

Match these people.

2.23 _____ agnostic defender of John Scopes

2.24 _____ home run champion

2.25 _____ Chicago gangster

2.26 _____ "A chicken in every pot..."

2.27 _____ a fundamentalist, ridiculed on the stand at the Scopes Trial

2.28 _____ flew solo across the Atlantic

2.29 _____ Catholic Democratic candidate in 1928

2.30 _____ designed the Model T for every American

a. Henry Ford

b. Clarence Darrow

c. William Jennings Bryan

d. Herbert Hoover

e. Al Smith

f. Charles Lindbergh

g. Al Capone

h. "Babe" Ruth

Complete these items.

2.31 Define Prohibition.

_____

_____

2.32 Did Prohibition stop drinking? _____

Explain. _____

2.33 What were the major changes in American spending habits in the 1920s?

_____

_____

2.34 What was a "speakeasy?"

_____

2.35 What was a "flapper?"

_____

_____

2.36 List three of the trends, interests, or fads of the 1920s.

_____

_____

2.37 What was the greatest single problem created by Prohibition?

_____

2.38 Describe modernist or liberal Christianity.

_____

_____

2.39 Who were the defenders of traditional Christianity it the 1920s? _____

2.40 What effect did the Scopes Monkey Trial have on public opinion?

_____

_____

2.41 Name three new products that became a regular part of American lives in the 1920s.

_____

_____

2.42 What was the name given to the 1920s? _____

Crash

Herbert Hoover (1874-1964). Herbert Hoover was one of the most hated presidents in American history because he had the misfortune to be in office when the Great Depression began. Hoover was born in Iowa to a blacksmith farmer. Orphaned at the age of nine, he was raised by relatives. He worked his way through Stanford University in California and went to work as a mining engineer. Mainly living abroad, he built a fortune at his chosen profession.

Hoover was in Europe when World War I began. He helped organize the return of Americans trapped by the war, and then was asked to take charge of American aid to the war victims in Belgium. He proved to be a capable administrator. In 1917 President Wilson asked Hoover to head the wartime Food Administration in the U.S. After the war, he again directed famine relief in Europe, gaining an international reputation as a humanitarian and administrator. He showed great skill as a planner and organizer as secretary of commerce under Harding and Coolidge. He also proved to be a mild progressive, favoring some reforms. He was the obvious Republican candidate in 1928, and won the election with ease.

Economic warnings. The booming economy of the 1920s was not as good as it looked. For example, farmers were suffering under terrible conditions. Farm production had been increased rapidly to meet the demands of World War I. Farmers had borrowed heavily to invest in modern equipment and used it to plant more crops. When the war ended, the need for food dropped quickly as European farmers returned to work their fields again. The result was a sharp drop in prices and farm incomes. Many families lost their farms when they could no longer make payments on their debts. Farmers reacted by producing larger crops to increase their income. This only expanded the surplus and drove prices down further.

As traditional Republicans, Harding and Coolidge opposed any aid to the farmers. Hoover, the mildly progressive humanitarian, was willing to at least try something. He signed the Agricultural Marketing Act in 1929. It created a fund to help farmers buy up and store the surplus, which helped prices to rise. The act did not work and it closed in 1933, deeply in debt.

| Images of the Great Depression

Another weakness in the economy was the division of income. Most of the money being made during the 1920s was going to the very wealthy. Rich people bought only a limited number of products for their own use. For the cycle of buying and producing to continue, many ordinary people, not just the rich, needed to have money to spend. Credit had temporarily given people more buying power, but by 1929 that source was running dry as people decided they could not afford more debt.

The straw that broke the camel's back was speculation in the stock market. Since 1927, the stock market had been rising rapidly on a tide of speculation. Prices were rising, not because the stocks were making money, but because people were buying more stocks, hoping to sell later for a better price. As long as prices kept going up, people kept buying, driving prices up even higher. Since the price they paid was much higher than the actual value of the stock, they were, in effect, buying hope. That is called a "speculation bubble." It expands on the hope of rising prices, not on the actual value of what is being bought.

This speculation bubble was even more fragile because so many people bought their stock on *margin* (credit). People would buy the stock using a loan, and would put up the stock itself as **collateral** for the loan. This worked only if the prices kept going up. If the price went down, the stock would be worth less than the amount of the loan. The creditor would demand either his money or more collateral to protect the loan. Most people who purchased on margin did not have enough money to repay the loans. They were simply gambling that the stock prices would go up, they would sell their stock, pay off their loan with interest, and still come out with a handsome profit. It was easy money, and too many people took advantage of it.

Herbert Hoover recognized the dangers of stock market speculation and tried to use the Federal Reserve Board to control it; but it was too little, too late. The market reached its peak in September 1929 and began a steady decline. The first real panic occurred on October 24th when prices fell substantially. People who bought on margin had to sell to pay their loans because they no longer had enough collateral.

As often happened in a stock crash, bankers stepped in and began to buy up stock in an effort to stop the slide. On October 29th, "Black Tuesday," the bankers gave up and everyone sold in a panic. Sixteen million shares of stock were sold that day; however, many of them could not find a buyer at any price. Within ten weeks, the stock market lost half of its value.

The stock market crash had tremendous consequences. The primary effect was a loss of confidence in the economy. Ordinary people did not have much extra money and now they chose to save instead of spend, fearing hard times. When people stopped spending, businesses could not sell their products. They cut back production, firing workers and cutting wages. This reduced the amount of money people had and cut buying power even more. The entire economy was caught in a downward spiral as people and businesses tried to protect themselves. The wide use of credit made things worse as people were unable to pay loans. Banks lost money on loans and lost deposits as people needed their savings to live. Many banks closed and people lost the money they had in savings. The economy slid further and further down.

The statistics were awful. By the depth of the depression in 1933, one out of every four Americans was unemployed (25%). Those who had jobs usually had to take a cut in pay. Between 1930 and 1933, thousands of banks failed. The total amount of goods and services produced in the U.S. was cut almost in half. Spending on new factories and machines stopped.

The human suffering was even worse. Although few people starved to death, hunger and homelessness were common. Thousands of families lost their homes and lived in hand-made shacks called "Hoovervilles" after the man they blamed for their despair. Men took to the road, living in hobo villages, searching for any kind of work. The railroads gave up trying to stop them from traveling (in an endless search for employment,) and let them ride in empty box cars. The streets of the major cities were littered with men earning a few cents shining shoes or selling apples.

The farm situation also grew worse. Farm prices dipped so low that farmers could not afford to ship their goods to market. In the Great Plains, a devastating drought and poor farming methods left the ground dry and unprotected. Winds blew topsoil away, creating huge dust storms and driving farmers off their land. The region, which was once a major producer of grain, became known as the "Dust Bowl." Thousands of displaced farmers took to the road as migrant farm workers, earning pitiful wages. The situation was not corrected until thousands of trees were planted as windbreaks and new techniques for soil conservation were introduced.

This depression was a major threat to U.S. democracy. Millions of people were suffering and desperate. They blamed Hoover, wealthy businessmen (most of whom were still living comfortably), and capitalism. Under these circumstances, people have often turned to dictators who offered them food and security in exchange for their freedom. By God's grace, this did not happen in America.

Hoover's response. Herbert Hoover believed in the soundness of the American business system. The nation had rebounded from every single depression in its history within a few years. At first, there was no reason to believe this would be any different. The main thing the country needed was confidence to spend again. Hoover tried to create this by making positive statements that "things were getting better" or the "worst is over." As the depression got worse, his quotes began to look stupid, naive, and uncaring. His popularity plummeted.

Before the crash, Hoover called a special session of Congress to deal with the agricultural situation. His solution was a new tariff on food that would reduce foreign competition and raise prices. Unfortunately, the pro-tariff Republican Congress saw this as a chance to increase rates and benefit American businesses. The resulting

HISTORY & GEOGRAPHY 808

LIFEPAC TEST

NAME _____

DATE _____

SCORE _____

HISTORY & GEOGRAPHY 808: LIFEPAC TEST

Choose the correct person for each item (each answer, 2 points).

1. _____ became president upon Harding's death; famous for not talking

2. _____ World War I general

3. _____ New Deal; World War II president

4. _____ Secretary of State; Scopes accuser

5. _____ German dictator

6. _____ Russian dictator; U.S. ally

7. _____ "return to normalcy" after World War I; scandal ridden presidency

8. _____ President blamed for the Great Depression

9. _____ World War II general; Philippines; New Guinea; occupation of Japan

10. _____ Supreme Allied commander in Europe; World War II

a. Herbert Hoover

b. Warren G. Harding

c. Joseph Stalin

d. Douglas MacArthur

e. Franklin D. Roosevelt

f. Dwight D. Eisenhower

g. Adolf Hitler

h. Calvin Coolidge

i. John Pershing

j. William J. Bryan

Give the information requested (each answer, 3 points).

11. _____ event that started World War II

12. _____ weapon; ended the war with Japan; World War II

13. _____ reason the U.S. got into World War I

14. _____ Wilson's liberal blueprint for peace; World War I

15. _____ reason Russia withdrew from World War I

16. _____ event that ended the Great Depression

17. _____ percentage of Americans out of work at the height of the Great Depression

18. _____ treaty that ended World War I; set up World War II

19. _____ holiday declared by F.D.R. immediately after he became president

20. _____ Christians who defended the faith in the 1920s

Answer true or false. If the answer is false, change the noun(s) to make it true (each answer, 2 points).

21. _____ Herbert Hoover's campaign slogan in 1916 was "He kept us out of war."

22. _____ The Nazis used surprise, speed, and massive firepower in their *kamikaze* or lightning war.

23. _____ Americans used credit in the 1920s to buy more than they could afford.

24. _____ Mao Tse-tung was the Nationalist Chinese leader who was a U.S. ally during World War II.

25. _____ America was united about fighting to defeat the Axis powers in World War II after the attack on Great Britain.

26. _____ World War I was fought mainly using trench warfare.

27. _____ Midway was the turning point of the Pacific war during World War II.

28. _____ National pride, alliances, and a depression pulled Europe into World War I.

29. _____ Germany's invasion of neutral France in 1914 was condemned in the U.S. and cast her as the aggressor in World War I.

30. _____ The Allied assault on D-Day came at Pas-de-Calais on June 6, 1944.

Answer these questions (each answer, 5 points).

31. Why were Japanese-held islands so difficult to conquer in World War II?

_____

_____

32. What were the FERA, CWA, CCC, NRA, and WPA trying to accomplish as a group?

_____

_____

_____

33. What caused the stock prices to rise so quickly before September 1929?

_____

_____

34. Why is Warren G. Harding considered to be one of America's worst presidents?

_____

_____

35. How were Rommel's forces trapped in North Africa in World War II?

_____

_____

36. What was the Holocaust during World War II?

_____

_____

Hawley-Smoot tariff not only raised rates on farm products, but also raised rates on most goods to the highest level in peacetime history as well. By this time, the depression had begun and economists urged the president not to sign the bill. However, he did sign it, making matters significantly worse. The price of goods in the U.S. rose. Foreign nations raised their own tariff rates, cutting off outlets for U.S. goods abroad. Moreover, the farm tariff did nothing to help farm prices. The tariff spread the depression to Europe where it contributed to the rise of the dictators who would start World War II.

Hoover the humanitarian actually did more than any previous U.S. president had ever done to fight a depression. He secured a large amount of money for government projects to create jobs (called public works projects). He created the Reconstruction Finance Corporation which provided loans to save major businesses such as banks and railroads. This kept businesses afloat. He tried to organize massive, voluntary relief efforts. When those proved hopelessly inadequate, he insisted that aid should come from local and state governments who were closer to the problem. However, hard-pressed cities and states did not have the resources to feed their people. Hoover was not willing to break with his own philosophy and provide federal funds to give people money or food (relief).

Hoover's dwindling popularity suffered yet another blow in 1932. Veterans had been promised a bonus by a generous Congress in 1924 for risking their lives in the Great War. The bonuses were to be paid in 1945, but as the depression grew worse, many began to demand their money immediately. Thousands of veterans and their families marched on Washington in the summer of 1932. Calling themselves the Bonus Expeditionary Force, they built a giant, unsanitary camp ("Hooverville") and pressed their demands. Congress refused to vote for the bonuses and fighting erupted. The army was called in to restore order. The commander, General Douglas

| Bonus Army Veterans at Hooverville

MacArthur, went beyond his orders, driving out the people and burning their shanties. Public sympathy was with the so-called Bonus Army, and it drove the last nail in Hoover's political coffin when he defended the attack.

Election of 1932. By 1932 Hoover and the Republicans were so unpopular that a Democratic pink donkey could have won the election. The Democrats instead chose the dynamic governor of New York, Franklin Delano Roosevelt. Roosevelt had been quick to establish relief programs in New York when the depression began. The people of his state had enough confidence in him to re-elect him in 1930. He accepted the nomination, promising the American people a "New Deal." He was self-confident and willing to experiment—just what the nation wanted.

Hoover was again nominated by the Republicans. He ran on his faith in the American system of business and personal effort to end the depression. Roosevelt attacked the "Hoover Depression" and made vague promises about making things better. He did come out squarely for the end of Prohibition (it was ended in 1932 and the

18th Amendment was repealed in 1933) and, ironically, in favor of a balanced budget. Under Roosevelt, America began to make wide use of debt to pay for programs—deficit spending.

The results were inevitable. Hoover lost by a much wider popular margin than he had won in 1928. He won the electoral votes from only six states. Black people, hurt deeply by the depression and motivated to have a voice for civil rights, turned to the Democratic party for the first time since the Civil War. The new Congress had a Democratic majority in both houses. The people had voted for change, and the president had to deliver.

 Complete the following.

2.43 What event started the Great Depression? _____

2.44 What area of the economy was not booming in the 1920s? _____

2.45 What did FDR promise the people in 1932? _____

2.46 How did Hoover try to help the farmers in 1929? _____

_____

2.47 What was Herbert Hoover's profession? _____

2.48 How did a person in 1928 usually buy stock on margin? _____

_____

2.49 What tariff made the depression worse by raising prices and cutting off trade?

_____

2.50 What did the Bonus Army want and what did they receive?

_____

_____

_____

2.51 Describe the spiral that cut spending and production in 1929.

_____

_____

_____

_____

Check the items that were true of the Great Depression.

2.52	☐ unemployment reached 25%	2.58	☐ thousands starved to death
2.53	☐ thousands of banks failed	2.59	☐ it made Hoover unpopular
2.54	☐ Hoover did nothing	2.60	☐ stock speculation was a cause
2.55	☐ it was a threat to democracy	2.61	☐ homelessness was common
2.56	☐ use of credit made it worse	2.62	☐ Hoover used federal money to feed people
2.57	☐ farm problems got worse		

New Deal

Franklin D. Roosevelt (1882-1945). Franklin Delano Roosevelt (F.D.R.) was the only U.S. president elected to four terms. He was born into privilege in Hyde Park, New York. He was the only child of a wealthy railroad officer. His family impressed upon him the idea that with great wealth came an obligation to serve. He studied under private tutors until he went to preparatory school at the age of 14. He graduated from Harvard in 1903, and after studying at Columbia Law School passed the N.Y. bar exam in 1907. He worked for a short time in law, but quickly turned to politics. He served as a state senator, assistant secretary of the navy under Wilson, and was the Democratic vice presidential candidate in 1920.

In 1921, F.D.R.'s life and outlook was forever changed when he was stricken with **polio**. It left him paralyzed from the waist down, and combating it strengthened his character. He said that after spending two years trying to move his big toe, anything else was easy. He eventually learned to walk using leg braces and crutches. In all his years as president, the press was very respectful of his handicap. They rarely took pictures that showed his legs, taking them instead of his upper body as he spoke from a podium or sat in a chair.

Roosevelt re-entered politics in 1924, giving a convention speech in favor of Al Smith. Smith did not get the presidential nomination in 1924, but he did in 1928. He asked Roosevelt to run for governor of New York that year, and F.D.R. eventually agreed. Smith lost his election, but Roosevelt won the governorship. F.D.R. was a reformer in that office and responded quickly to the Great Depression, using state funds to provide relief. He won the Democratic nomination in 1932 and promised the nation a "New Deal" to meet their needs. On inauguration day in March of 1933, he told the American public that "the only thing we have to fear, is fear itself...."

The Hundred Days. The amazing flurry of action after Roosevelt took office was called the Hundred Days. During that time, Roosevelt proposed dozens of bills aimed at providing relief, helping recovery, and promoting reforms. Congress gave him anything he wanted, often with little or no debate. Many of the bills were only outlines that gave the president power to act in certain areas. F.D.R. quickly became a very powerful president as Congress yielded more and more authority to him.

The first issue Roosevelt addressed was the collapse of the banking system. The president immediately declared a bank holiday, closing every bank in the nation. He announced in a national radio address that federal officials would examine their books and allow only banks that were financially sound to reopen. The president's warm voice, confidence, and quick action convinced the nation. On March 13th, the banks that qualified were reopened and took in more deposits than they had withdrawals. The banking system remained stable through the rest of the depression.

New Deal legislation came quickly in the form of dozens of agencies with different purposes, all known by their initials. The FERA (Federal Emergency Relief Administration) gave money to the states for either relief or job projects. The CWA (Civil Works Administration) provided temporary jobs. The HOLC (Home Owners' Loan Corporation) provided low-interest loans that allowed millions of families to keep their homes. The WPA (Works Progress Administration) provided jobs by building bridges, buildings, and roads. It also made jobs for artists, writers, musicians, and photographers. The NRA (National Recovery Administration) tried to encourage production by setting up codes to control prices, wages, hours, and the rights of workers. The TVA (Tennessee Valley Authority) built dams in that region, providing electricity, housing, and flood control. The AAA (Agricultural Adjustment Administration) paid farmers not to farm part of their land, cutting the farm surplus and raising prices. The CCC (Civilian Conservation Corps) was the most famous of these programs. It housed young men in outdoor camps and put them to work. They planted trees, fought forest fires, drained swamps, and did many other useful conservation jobs. Not all of these agencies were successful, but all this action from the federal government gave Americans hope.

Roosevelt also pursued many other needed reforms. He took the U.S. off the gold standard,

| CCC Workers

which was draining national gold reserves. The Federal Reserve Board was permitted to control the money supply. The Glass-Stengall Banking Reform Act created the Federal Deposit Insurance Corporation (FDIC) which insured bank deposits against loss. The Securities and Exchange Commission (SEC) was set up to monitor the stock market and insure that investors got honest information about stocks. The Public Utility Holding Company Act reformed the corrupt utility companies. The Social Security Act created a system of pensions for retired or disabled workers paid for by taxes on current workers.

Election of 1936. The nation was still in the depression in 1936, but things were better than 1932. Roosevelt was renominated without opposition. The Republicans nominated Alfred Landon, the governor of Kansas. He never had a chance. Running on his achievements, Roosevelt won all but two states.

Court controversy. Flushed with success, F.D.R. unwisely decided to move against the extremely conservative Supreme Court. The nine members of the Court had declared several of the New Deal reforms unconstitutional, angering Roosevelt. In 1937 he proposed to add a new justice for every justice over the age of 70 on the court, up to a total of fifteen. This plan to "pack the court" was widely and quickly denounced. It was an attempt to upset the Constitutional balance of power. Congress, which routinely approved anything Roosevelt wanted, fought his plan. In the end, the Court recognized the threat and began to approve New Deal laws, ending the need for any action. Roosevelt pushed the issue, he lost, and he never regained the control he once had over Congress.

Unions. The business codes created by the NRA specifically guaranteed workers the right to organize unions of their own choosing. This was a long overdue protection for working people. When the NRA was declared unconstitutional, the National Labor Relations (Wagner) Act gave workers the right to unionize and bargain as a group with their employers (collective bargaining). The law created a board that protected unions from unfair management harassment. Union membership flourished under this encouragement, growing substantially in the 1930s. The Congress for Industrial Organizations (CIO), for example, organized unskilled workers in the automobile and steel industries into unions in the 1930s.

Foreign policy. Roosevelt dealt with only a few foreign policy problems in his first two terms. He refused to cooperate with a conference to stabilize currencies in London in 1933, fearing it would interfere with the U.S. recovery. He finally extended official recognition to the communist government in Russia (then called the Soviet Union). International trade got a boost from his efforts to reduce the tariff and sign trade agreements with many other nations.

Roosevelt's main initiative in foreign policy was his "Good Neighbor" policy which promoted better relations with the Caribbean and Latin America. He did this by abandoning many old American controls there. He removed American troops from Haiti and freed Cuba from U.S.

control under the Platt Amendment to their constitution. When controversy arose, he sent diplomats instead of soldiers. The result was a tremendous improvement in relations between the U.S. and its neighbors in the western hemisphere.

The last Depression years. The economy steadily improved from 1933 to 1937, but the nation still could not get out of the depression. In 1937 the stock market crashed again, and the economy got worse (although it never got as bad as the dark days of 1933). The new slide lasted until 1938 when things began to improve again. Roosevelt had cut back spending in the hopes of balancing the budget, but he reversed course. The new Congress was not as cooperative as the earlier Congress of the Hundred Days, and few new programs were initiated. When war began in Europe in 1939, Roosevelt ended the New Deal to concentrate on the war and preparing America for its effects.

Analysis. Franklin Roosevelt did *not* end the Great Depression. In 1939 unemployment was at 17%, a very high number. It was the need for weapons for World War II that finally pulled America out of the depression in 1942. However, F.D.R. *did* have an effect on the depression. He led the nation out of the worst part of it, and convinced the people to trust their system of government. He also preserved our free market economy, even though he added many new controls to it.

On the negative side, Roosevelt standardized the use of deficit spending which has kept the nation in debt for a good number of years since 1932. He also greatly enlarged the size and expense of the U.S. government. Government regulation has expanded constantly since his day and now covers a bewildering variety of items, such as what information must be on food packages or what information people must be given when they take a loan. F.D.R.'s legacy from the Great Depression is mixed and very controversial.

Answer these questions.

2.63 How did F.D.R. respond to the banking problem in 1933?

_____

_____

_____

2.64 What was the plan to "pack the court?" Why was it proposed?

_____

_____

_____

2.65 What were two negative results of the New Deal?

_____

_____

_____

2.66 What was F.D.R.'s policy toward Latin American and the Caribbean called?

_____

_____

2.67 What effect did polio have on Roosevelt?

_____

_____

Match the following.

2.68 _____ insured bank deposits

2.69 _____ pensions for retired or disabled workers

2.70 _____ control the money supply

2.71 _____ public works projects including jobs for artists and writers

2.72 _____ gave money to the states for relief or works projects

2.73 _____ paid farmers to produce less

2.74 _____ provided temporary jobs

2.75 _____ gave workers the right to form unions after NRA declared unconstitutional

2.76 _____ monitor the stock market

2.77 _____ provided low-interest loans for homeowners

2.78 _____ union that organized unskilled steel and auto workers in 1930s

2.79 _____ built dams; provided electricity in Tennessee River Valley

2.80 _____ housed young men in camps and employed them in conservation work

2.81 _____ set prices; wages; hours using codes

2.82 _____ name for Roosevelt's anti-Depression program

a. CIO

b. CCC

c. FERA

d. Wagner Act

e. NRA

f. New Deal

g. TVA

h. Social Security Act

i. WPA

j. HOLC

k. FDIC

l. Federal Reserve Board

m. SEC

n. CWA

o. AAA

Trace the course of the Great Depression.

2.83 The Great Depression began in the year _____ with the crash of the _____ _____ . The economy got worse until it hit bottom in _____ when unemployment was at _____ %. Under F.D.R.'s program, the _____ , the economy improved until there was another drop in _____ and _____ . The depression finally ended in _____ because of the industrial needs for _____ _____ .

⟳ **Review the material in this section in preparation for the Self Test.** This Self Test will check your mastery of this particular section as well as your knowledge of the previous section.

SELF TEST 2

Name the people, event, or item (each answer, 3 points).

2.01 _____ name for the decade of the 1920s

2.02 _____ event that triggered the Great Depression

2.03 _____ defenders of the Christian faith in the 1920s

2.04 _____ experiment to outlaw alcohol in the U.S. failed

2.05 _____ part of the economy that didn't prosper in the 1920s

2.06 _____ German action that got America into World War I

2.07 _____ Veterans who were chased out of Washington by the army; they tried to get money in 1932

2.08 _____ event that finally ended the Great Depression

2.09 _____ name for the first three months of F.D.R.'s term when laws were passed quickly, with little debate

2.010 _____ type of warfare usually used in World War I

Complete these sentences (each sentence, 3 points).

2.011 The Great Depression reached its worst point in the year _____ when _____ % of all Americans were out of work.

2.012 _____ was the commander of the A.E.F. in Europe during World War I.

2.013 Americans were able to buy more than they could pay for in the 1920s by using _____ .

2.014 The press made fun of Christian beliefs at the so-called " _____ Trial" where a Tennessee teacher was fined for teaching evolution in 1925.

2.015 World War I began when _____ was assassinated.

2.016 Right after his inauguration, Roosevelt tackled the banking collapse by declaring a

_____ .

2.017 The greatest failure of the banning of alcohol was the rise of _____

to illegally produce and distribute it.

2.018 After World War I there was a wave of anti-foreign feelings that led to quotas on

_____ .

2.019 The idealistic Kellogg-Briand Pact supposedly outlawed _____ .

2.020 The _____ Scandal involved the Secretary of the Interior taking

bribes to sell government oil leases.

Match the item with the correct president (each answer, 2 points).

2.021 _____ "return to normalcy"   a. Woodrow Wilson

2.022 _____ famous for not talking   b. Warren G. Harding

2.023 _____ suffered a stroke trying to press for   c. Calvin Coolidge
                  acceptance of the League of Nations
                                                           d. Herbert Hoover

2.024 _____ became president when predecessor died   e. Franklin D. Roosevelt

2.025 _____ blamed for the Great Depression

2.026 _____ scandal-ridden administration

2.027 _____ paralyzed by polio

2.028 _____ "We have nothing to fear, but fear itself..."

2.029 _____ Belgium famine relief; World War I Food Administration

2.030 _____ Good Neighbor Policy

Describe the purpose of any five of the following (each answer, 2 points).

2.031 FERA, CWA, HOLC, WPA, NRA, TVA, AAA, CCC, SEC, FDIC

a. _____

b. _____

c. _____

d. _____

e. _____

Answer true or false (each answer, 1 point).

2.032 _____ America declared itself neutral when World War I began.

2.033 _____ Americans enjoyed a decade of prosperity after World War I.

2.034 _____ Charles Lindbergh was a famous home run-hitting baseball player of the 1920s.

2.035 _____ The Treaty of Versailles closely followed Wilson's Fourteen Points.

2.036 _____ Herbert Hoover did nothing to fight the Great Depression.

2.037 _____ Georges Clemenceau of France wanted mainly a just and fair peace after World War I.

2.038 _____ The stock market gains of 1929 were fragile because the rise was based on speculation and many stocks were bought on margin.

2.039 _____ Union membership grew substantially in the 1930s.

2.040 _____ The Ku Klux Klan grew rapidly in the early 1920s.

2.041 _____ The Teapot Dome Scandal involved fraud in the sale of surplus war goods.

80 / 100

SCORE _____   TEACHER _____ _____

initials   date

3. WORLD WAR II

Some historians believe World War II was a continuation of World War I. It is certainly accurate to say that World War I sowed the seeds that grew into the next war. Deprived of much of its productive lands and burdened with war payments due to the Treaty of Versailles, Germany was devastated by the Great Depression. The nation suffered from *hyperinflation*. Prices rose so fast that money became almost worthless. In 1918 a U.S. dollar was worth 4 German marks. In 1923 the same dollar was worth *4 trillion* marks.

Using the financial crisis as a stepping stone, Adolf Hitler and his Nazi Party rose to power in Germany. He blamed the Treaty of Versailles and the Jews for the ills of the nation. Desperate Germans gave him absolute power in exchange for strength, jobs, food, and stability.

Other nations also came under the rule of violent strongmen. Benito Mussolini, leader of the **fascists**, came to power in Italy in 1922. Joseph Stalin became the communist leader of the Soviet Union in late 1920s and kept his power by ruthlessly murdering anyone who might oppose him. In Japan the military came to dominate the civilian government and began a plan of conquest to suit their own desires. By the 1930s, the world had again become a very dangerous place.

SECTION OBJECTIVES

Review these objectives. When you have completed this section, you should be able to:

1. Describe the policies, personalities, and politics of the U.S. presidents from 1915 to 1945.
7. Describe the causes and course of World War II.
8. Describe the policy of appeasement and early American neutrality.
9. Name the major U.S. commanders in World War II and their contributions.
10. Describe American involvement in World War II.
11. Name the major leaders of World War II and their nations.

VOCABULARY

Study these words to enhance your learning success in this section.

amphibious (am fib' ē əs). Executed by coordinated action of land, sea, and air forces organized for an invasion.

atrocity (ə träs' ət ē). An extremely wicked, brutal, or cruel act or situation.

beachhead (bēch' hed). An area on an enemy shore occupied to secure further landing of troops and supplies.

fascism (fash' iz əm). A government system that exalts the nation above the individual and has centralized control by a dictator, heavy controls on society and the economy and allows no freedom to opposing views. On the political spectrum, fascism is on the far right.

genocide (jen' ə sīd). The deliberate and systematic destruction of a racial, political, or cultural group.

ideology (īd äl' ə jē). A group of beliefs.

incendiary (in sen' dē er ē). Relating to missiles that have chemicals which ignite on bursting or contact.

War Returns

American attitude. Preoccupied with the depression, America in the 1930s was extremely isolationist. Popular literature blamed bankers and arms manufacturers for dragging the nation into the First World War. Popular opinion wanted to stay out of all wars. A series of Neutrality Acts passed in that decade forbade the sale of weapons or loaning money to any nation involved in a war. The nation was determined not to be sucked into another war by shipping losses. In effect, America refused to take any leadership or responsibility for the rest of the world.

The first test of the American attitude came in 1936 with the Spanish Civil War. The democratic government of that nation was overthrown in a bloody three-year civil war by General Francisco Franco, a fascist. Franco received arms, men, and weapons from Hitler and Mussolini. The Loyalists (government) received some aid from the Soviet Union, but America refused to help the democratic forces. Spain fell to Franco; democracy was not revived there until his death in 1975. Moreover, the dictators had an excellent chance to test weapons and try out new methods of war.

Appeasement. The democracies of Europe were also desperate to avoid another war. This led to one of the greatest acts of international stupidity and cowardice in world history—appeasement. Basically, as the dictators gained strength they demanded and took territory. Nothing was done to stop them. They were allowed to increase their holdings and resources without any consequences. They were given what they wanted in the vain hope that it would be enough to satisfy them.

Japan began the process in 1931 when it conquered Manchuria in northern China, making it into a puppet state called Manchukuo. The League of Nations protested but took no action, and neither did the United States. Nor was any action taken when Italy invaded Ethiopia in 1935. The Japanese followed up their earlier

| Chamberlain and Hitler at the Munich Conference

successes by occupying much of China's east coast later in the decade without any serious international consequences.

By the mid-1930s, Hitler was rearming Germany in defiance of the Treaty of Versailles. France and Britain, who had the most to lose, refused to act, not wanting to risk another war. In so doing, they let their enemy build its strength for the next conflict. Hitler moved his new army into the Rhineland opposite France in 1936, also in violation of the treaty. In 1938 he marched into Austria, making that German-speaking land part of his "Third Reich." The western leaders hoped that would be enough to satisfy him. At the same time, Hitler was promoting antisemitism (hatred towards Jewish people) and violence, which would be another factor towards the development of war. The Holocaust, the mass killing of Jewish people and other groups, began in 1933 as Hitler was gaining power.

The ultimate appeasement occurred in 1939. Hitler demanded the German-speaking area of Sudetenland in Czechoslovakia. That nation had good defenses along the border and with some support from Britain and France might have been able to defend itself. Instead, Prime Minister Neville Chamberlain flew to Munich to meet with Hitler. He and the French premier agreed to give Hitler what he wanted in exchange for a promise that he would take no more territory in Europe. Chamberlain returned home waving the paper with Hitler's signature, saying that he had achieved "peace in our time."

One man in the British government, Winston Churchill, opposed the agreement. Churchill clearly saw the coming war. He loudly warned his nation that they were giving resources and weapons to a man who would soon try to destroy Britain. He was ridiculed as a warmonger, but he was right. Hitler did not keep his agreement. In 1939 he took the rest of Czechoslovakia to add to his growing industrial and manpower might.

Stalin, in the meantime, realized the west would do nothing to stop Hitler and made a deal with him. In August of 1939, Germany and the Soviet Union signed a non-aggression pact and agreed to divide Poland between themselves. Given the fact that Nazis and communists were sworn enemies, the agreement was an incredibly cold blooded act by men whose ambition was superior to any **ideology**. The agreement left Hitler free from any threat to the east.

World War II. With Czechoslovakia in his pocket and the Soviet Union settled, Hitler began to threaten Poland. Britain and France finally drew a line; if Germany invaded Poland, they would declare war. Germany invaded on September 1, 1939 and World War II began. The U.S. issued a proclamation of neutrality.

Germany attacked Poland with new techniques that prevented the type of trench warfare that had buried German hopes in 1916. The new tactics were called *blitzkrieg*, lightning war. Blitzkrieg used speed, surprise, and massive firepower. Armored guns and tanks were supported by soldiers with cars and motorcycles who could move quickly. Both were given support by airplanes that attacked enemy positions ahead of them. The result was spectacular.

Poland was conquered in three weeks. Stalin quickly moved into the eastern part of the nation to take his share of the spoils.

France and Britain declared war when Poland was invaded, but they did not attack Germany. They just sat behind the heavily fortified Maginot Line that protected France from a German assault. Nothing was done to draw German troops away from Poland. Hitler, by appeasement and by inaction, was allowed to pick up the nations of Europe one at a time, rather than face them all together. Congress yielded to F.D.R.'s urging and allowed sales of arms to Britain and France (the Allies) if they paid cash and transported them on their own ships. Americans favored the Allies but still did not want to get involved.

The "Phony War" continued until April of 1940, with virtually no fighting by either side. Then, Hitler struck again. Without any warning, he attacked and quickly conquered Denmark and Norway. Britain tried to aid Norway, but it was too little, too late. The fiasco forced Chamberlain to resign. Winston Churchill, the clear-sighted realist, became Prime Minister of Britain. The eloquent Churchill told the nation, "I have nothing to offer but blood, toil, tears, and sweat." Again, he foresaw correctly. God had prepared just the man Britain needed to face her darkest hour.

In May, Hitler conquered Belgium and the Netherlands. The swift collapse of the Belgian defenses trapped the British army on the coast of northern France at Dunkirk. Providentially, Hitler did not close in on them immediately. Waiting in orderly lines, over three hundred thousand soldiers were evacuated safely to Britain across the Channel. This "Miracle at Dunkirk" was accomplished by hundreds of boats, including fishing boats and yachts from Britain. Their owners and captains risked death from German planes as they traveled across the English Channel, bringing their army home. The army was saved to fight another day, but most of its weapons and supplies were lost.

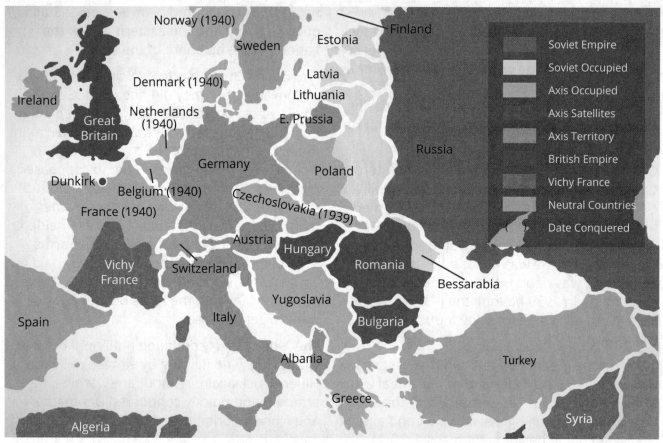

| Europe in 1941

As they did in 1916, the German army again invaded France through Belgium, going around the Maginot Line. The French army collapsed. Paris was occupied on June 14th. On June 21st, France signed a surrender in the same railroad car Germany had signed the armistice in 1918. Hitler had it brought out for the occasion and then danced a joyful jig at his success. Two-thirds of France was given to Germany. The remaining third became a puppet state called Vichy France, named after its capital. Hitler was the master of Europe. Only Britain still stood against him.

Britain alone. Hitler believed Britain would sue for peace after the fall of France. He greatly underestimated Churchill and the British people. The Prime Minister's response was:

> *Even though large tracts of Europe ... have fallen or may fall into the ... odious apparatus of Nazi rule, we shall not flag or fail. We shall go on to the end, we shall fight in France, we shall fight in the seas and oceans, we shall fight with growing confidence and growing strength in the air, we shall defend our island, no matter what the cost may be, we shall fight on the beaches, we shall fight on the landing grounds, we shall fight in the fields and in the streets, we shall fight in the hills; we shall never surrender, and even if ... this island ... were subjugated and starving, then our Empire beyond the seas, armed and guarded by the British fleet, would carry on the struggle, until, in God's good time, the New World, with all its power and might, steps forth to the rescue and liberation of the old.*

Faced with such determination, Hitler began to plan the invasion of Britain, but first he had to destroy the British air force. The Battle of

Britain began in July of 1940 and was entirely an air battle. The Royal Air Force (RAF) won simply because it survived. Germany then tried to force Britain's surrender by bombing her cities. Bombs were dropped almost every night during what was called "the Blitz" through the fall and winter of 1940-41. The British people held firm while their homes were destroyed and their people killed. Finally, in May of 1941, Hitler gave up the idea of invading Britain and turned his attention elsewhere.

Italy and Japan had both formed a loose alliance with Germany by 1940. It was called the Berlin-Rome-Tokyo Axis. Italy had joined the war with the fall of France to collect the spoils. By the end of 1941, the Axis powers controlled the Balkan Peninsula, Hungary, Romania, Crete, and much of North Africa as well, but the hard-pressed British kept Egypt and the vital Suez Canal. Foiled in Britain, Hitler turned and attacked the Soviet Union in June of 1941. Stalin had killed or imprisoned his most capable generals, and the Germans advanced quickly. Britain and the Soviets quickly formed an alliance of necessity. It would last only as long as they had a common enemy to defeat.

 Name the item, land, or person.

3.1 _____ giving the dictators what they wanted, hoping it would satisfy them

3.2 _____ over three hundred thousand soldiers were evacuated across the Channel to Britain on any available ship

3.3 _____ French defenses facing Germany

3.4 _____ fascist dictator of Italy

3.5 _____ name for the German led alliance

3.6 _____ the first part of World War II, from September 1939 to April 1940 when no fighting occurred

3.7 _____ German area of Czechoslovakia given to Hitler at the Munich Conference

3.8 _____ Prime Minister who believed the Munich Conference had established "peace in our time"

3.9 _____ Nazi lightning war

3.10 _____ RAF won this battle by surviving

3.11 _____ war from 1936-39 that allowed Italy and Germany to test weapons and techniques

3.12 _____ Nazi dictator of Germany

3.13 _____ nations defeated by Germany in April of 1940

3.14 _____ laws passed in the U.S. in the 1920s to prevent it being drawn into another war by shipping losses

3.15 _____   "I have nothing to offer but blood, toil, tears, and sweat."

3.16 _____   nations conquered by Germany in May of 1940

3.17 _____   puppet nation made up of one-third of France after its surrender

3.18 _____   daily bombing of British cities in 1940-41

3.19 _____   nation divided between Germany and the Soviet Union by 1939 agreement

3.20 _____   dictator of the Soviet Union

3.21 _____   action that began World War II

3.22 _____   fascist dictator of Spain

3.23 _____   Japanese puppet state in Manchuria

3.24 _____   nation invaded by Italy in 1935

Answer these questions.

3.25 What did Hitler expect Britain to do when France surrendered?

_____

3.26 According to Churchill's speech, where were the British prepared to fight?

_____

_____

_____

3.27 Where was the surrender of France signed?

_____

_____

Arsenal of democracy. The fall of France caused a great deal of alarm in America. Congress quickly approved funds to improve the navy, army, and air force. Roosevelt realized America had to support Britain if it did not want to be left alone to face Germany in the future. However, most Americans still did not want to go to war, and F.D.R. was running for a third term in 1940. Thus, he walked a difficult tightrope, trying to aid Britain without angering the American public.

As things grew worse in Europe, and with Britain fighting alone, America became increasingly less neutral. In September of 1940, Congress passed the nation's first peacetime conscription law. That same month, F.D.R. used his own authority to give Britain fifty old destroyers in exchange for leases on several naval bases. In November, Roosevelt defeated Republican candidate Wendell Willkie, an inexperienced man from Indiana. With the crisis in Europe, Roosevelt's violation of the two-term tradition was not a key issue. The American public trusted F.D.R. and kept him, although by a smaller margin than the first two times.

Britain was rapidly running out of cash to pay for weapons and supplies. In March of 1941, Congress approved Roosevelt's aid plan called Lend-Lease. To protect democracy, America would lend or lease weapons to Britain, who would return them or replace them after the war. Most people realized that little or nothing would be returned. This was a way for America to support Britain by becoming "the arsenal of democracy" without losing American lives. By the war's end, Britain received over $50 billion in Lend-Lease aid. The program was expanded to include the Soviet Union after it was invaded.

Supposedly still neutral, Roosevelt met with Churchill on a warship off the coast of Canada in August of 1941 to discuss strategy for the war. Both sides realized the U.S. was likely to get involved. They agreed to a joint statement called the Atlantic Charter that set goals for the war. Among them were the right of conquered people to self-determination and to choose their own government. It also called for a new organization to protect world peace.

American neutrality continued to slip. In June of 1941, Roosevelt ordered the navy to escort convoys going to Britain as far as Iceland to protect them from German submarines. By September, the escorts were ordered to shoot German subs on sight. In October, American merchant ships were armed in order to defend themselves and were carrying supplies all the way to Britain.

Pearl Harbor. Japan had not been able to subdue China after it attacked in 1937. It was bogged down in a long-term war. The Japanese war machine depended on America for vital supplies such as oil and steel which were unavailable on their resource-poor islands. The U.S. was reluctant to cut off these supplies and provoke the militant Japanese. Finally, by 1941 the U.S. had frozen Japanese funds in America

| The Attack on Pearl Harbor

and cut off her supply of metal and oil. The Japanese had to either withdraw from China as their supplies dwindled or find new sources. The proud military was not willing to consider a humiliating withdrawal. They decided to expand their power into resource-rich Southeast Asia, knowing this would provoke America. Rather than wait for the U.S. to start a war, the Japanese decided to start it themselves by a knockout blow to the U.S. Navy in the Pacific.

On December 7, 1941, with no warning and without declaring war, Japanese bombers from aircraft carriers attacked the American fleet anchored at Pearl Harbor, Hawaii. Over 2,000 Americans were killed, most of them on the *U.S.S. Arizona* which blew up and sank in the harbor. Six battleships were sunk or badly damaged. Almost two hundred planes were destroyed. Providentially, the fleet's three aircraft carriers were out at sea and survived unscathed.

The attack was a complete surprise and a remarkable victory for the Japanese. It was also a major blunder. On December 6th, America was badly divided and undecided about the war. On December 8th, America was united and determined to defeat the Axis, whatever the cost. F.D.R. summed it up in his war message before Congress on December 8th calling the previous day "a day which will live in infamy." Congress voted in favor of war with Japan with only one opposing vote. Germany and Italy declared war on the U.S. immediately after. America was at war again.

Home front. World War II was not an idealistic crusade like World War I. Americans had few illusions about this war. The enemy controlled most of Europe and was rapidly advancing in Asia. The nation pulled together, determined to finish what they knew would be a long, hard, nasty job. The unity among Americans has probably never been greater in all of our history.

As in World War I, America was spared from the worst of the war. American soldiers died, but very few civilians did. Civilian Defense groups in America staged air raid drills and set up stations to watch for enemy planes which never came. Outside of Pearl Harbor and a Japanese landing on the Aleutian Islands, the mainland was spared from direct attack. America suffered shortages and inconvenience, but not wholesale destruction and hunger as had much of Europe.

In fact, the war brought something Americans desperately needed—jobs. Unemployment fell to less than 1% and most of those were just moving between jobs. As the men left for the war, women went to work in record numbers. The image of "Rosie the Riveter" was a popular symbol of the working woman. Wages were good and government controls kept prices from rising too much. Because of war production, there were no new cars, refrigerators, washing machines, or similar goods to buy. All the factories were building weapons. Americans put their money into either war bonds to pay for the conflict or into savings (which would be spent after the war).

Americans contributed to the war on the home front by conserving, making do, and producing what the armed forces needed. Rationing was

| A Victory Garden Poster

established for many key goods, including meat, butter, gasoline, and shoes. Scrap drives gathered up iron pots, aluminum foil, old tires, metal bed frames, and anything else that could be recycled to make weapons or supplies. Americans planted "victory gardens" in every conceivable bare patch of soil to supply their own needs and provide for the Allies and the army.

As in the first Great War, national boards were set up to regulate production. Their most complicated task was to distribute raw materials; for example, who would get a shipment of steel, the tank manufacturers or the airplane industry. Other boards controlled prices and transportation.

Many items were in dangerously short supply. One of the most serious shortages was rubber.

The Japanese captured much of Southeast Asia in their glory days following Pearl Harbor. That was the source of most of the world's natural rubber needed for all cars, ships, and planes. The U.S. created a synthetic rubber industry. This supplied the armed forces with all that they needed.

American industry performed miracles in World War II. Cargo ships were desperately needed to move supplies to Europe. In 1941, such ships required almost a year to build. That was cut to less than two months in 1942. By the war's end they were being built in 12 days using new techniques that prefabricated the pieces and lifted them into place! One cargo ship was built in four days!!

Production of airplanes quadrupled during the war. America's tank production by 1945 had increased to eight times what it had been in 1941. By 1943 the U.S. was producing twice as many weapons as all of the Axis powers combined. By 1945 half of the weapons in the world had been made in the United States! America indeed became the vital "arsenal of democracy."

Japanese internment. Praise for America must be tempered with criticism for the treatment of Japanese Americans on the West Coast. Prejudice against Japanese people and their descendants had long been a problem in California. When the war broke out, people up to and including the governor of the state called for the Japanese to be relocated. The official reason was a fear of sabotage, even though none ever occurred. In what was considered by some as an act of cowardice, F.D.R. signed an order for the Japanese (most of whom were U.S. citizens) to be removed and herded into internment camps in the Midwest and Southwest.

These innocent people lost their jobs, their homes, and their businesses. They were forced to work as farm laborers and live in guarded barbed-wire camps for the length of the war.

In spite of their treatment, many of the men volunteered for the army. A Japanese American unit in Italy became one of the most decorated units of the war. Conditions in the internment camps were not even close to the horrors of the Nazi concentration camps. The American camps had adequate food, shelter, and decent treatment, but this imprisonment was a violation of American and Christian principles. Long after the fact, an apology and some compensation was given to the survivors.

Election of 1944. America continued to have regular elections throughout the war. In 1944 Roosevelt ran for yet another term. He accepted a new vice-president when the Democratic party turned against Henry Wallace who had been elected with him in 1940. The position was awarded to Senator Harry S. Truman of Missouri.

Roosevelt was opposed by Republican Thomas E. Dewey, a liberal governor from New York. By 1944 with the war going well, Americans were not interested in trying out a new leader. With substantial money from the unions to help him, F.D.R. won yet another victory, but his health was declining rapidly. He had a small inaugural ceremony in January of 1945 and died suddenly on April 12, 1945. Vice President Harry S. Truman, who had not even been kept informed of key decisions by F.D.R., was now in command of the American war effort.

✎ **Complete these sentences.**

3.28 America entered World War II after the _____ attacked

_____ on December 7, 1941.

3.29 _____ became president when F.D.R. died in 1945.

3.30 Roosevelt and Churchill agreed on post-war goals in the _____ Charter issued in August of 1941.

3.31 Most of the Americans killed at Pearl Harbor died when the _____ blew up and sank.

3.32 The Republican candidate for president in 1940 was _____ and in 1944 it was _____ .

3.33 F.D.R. called December 7, 1941 "a day _____ ."

Answer these questions.

3.34 What steps were taken that made the U.S. less neutral:

a. in September 1940? _____

_____

b. in March 1941? _____

c. in June of 1941? _____

d. in October of 1941? _____

3.35 Why can Pearl Harbor be described as both a victory and a defeat for Japan?

_____

_____

3.36 What caused the wartime rubber shortage and how was it solved?

_____

_____

_____

3.37 What were four effects of the war on America?

_____ _____

_____ _____

3.38 What happened to Japanese Americans on the West Coast during the war?

_____

_____

War in Europe

Commanders. Churchill and Roosevelt had agreed to defeat Hitler first and then Japan. The U.S. military that tackled this job was led by some remarkable men. General George Marshall was chief of staff for the U.S. Army during the war. He was responsible for training the men, equipping them, planning strategy, and choosing the commanders. His organizational skill was so great that he could not be spared for a command at the front. He stayed in Washington for the entire war doing much work, but winning little glory.

General Dwight D. Eisenhower was selected by Marshall to command the first American offensive of the war, the invasion of North Africa. He eventually became the supreme commander of all Allied forces in Europe. Eisenhower was ideal for that job. He was a superb commander who had the diplomatic skills to get the various Allied generals to work together. He had command of the invasion of France in 1944, which was the largest **amphibious** invasion in history and led the Allied assault on Germany.

General George Patton was a controversial American hero. He loved war and carried a pair of pearl handled pistols into battle. He won numerous battles by attacking recklessly and unpredictably. His reputation earned him the nickname "Old Blood and Guts." He specialized in tank warfare. He almost lost his commission when he slapped two soldiers at a hospital, accusing them of cowardice because they suffered from battle fatigue (a mental collapse in combat).

General Omar Bradley was a calm, steady commander who was a natural opposite of Patton. He rose to command the U.S. Army in the invasion of Europe. He was quiet, competent, and valued the lives of his men with whom he was very popular. He worked close to or at the front lines through the war.

War in Europe

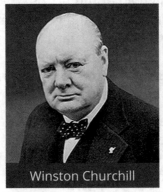
Winston Churchill

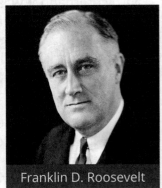
Franklin D. Roosevelt

| War in Europe

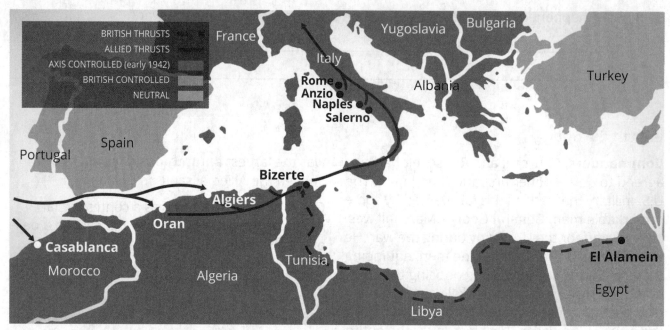

| North African and Italian Campaign

Battle of the Atlantic. If America was to free Europe, it would have to attack from Britain. Therefore, it was essential that the necessary men and supplies get across the Atlantic, past the German submarines. The enemy subs were working in groups called "wolf packs." One sub would locate the convoys of ships, then they would all close in for the kill. The result was devastating. America lost 87 ships along the East Coast in the first four months of the war alone.

The Allies used a variety of ideas to control the shipping problem. They again used convoys to escort valuable cargo and troop ships across the ocean. They assembled ships and planes that acted as sub killers for the convoys. The use of radar and sonar helped Allied sub hunting. Allied intelligence also broke the German navy codes, giving them important information about submarine maneuvers. By 1943 the German navy was losing 80% of the subs it sent out. Moreover, the U.S. was producing cargo ships faster than the Nazis could sink them. The supplies were getting through. The Battle of the Atlantic was a key victory for the Allies.

North Africa. The Soviets were pushing hard for America and Britain to open a second front in Europe. They wanted to take some of the pressure off their troops who were fighting for their lives in Russia. The U.S. leaders wanted to build up for an attack across the English Channel in 1942 or 1943. The British believed that it was too early to attack Hitler in Europe and successfully argued for beginning in North Africa instead. The hope was to open a path to southern Europe across the Mediterranean.

The British had held Egypt against the German army that had taken most of North Africa. The Nazi commander was Erwin Rommel, the "Desert Fox," Germany's most respected general. In October 1942, British General Bernard Montgomery attacked and defeated him at El Alamein. It was the first British victory of the war. Rommel was driven back toward Tunisia.

Then the Allies invaded from Morocco and Algeria in November under the command of General Eisenhower. The Germans were trapped in the middle. French troops in the region, officially German allies from Vichy France, fought the invasion half-heartedly at first, but then joined the Allies under the eventual leadership of Charles de Gaulle. The last Germans surrendered in May 1943 after heavy fighting. The operation, code-named "Torch," was an excellent training ground for the green U.S. troops.

Roosevelt and Churchill held one of several key meetings to discuss strategy in Casablanca, Morocco in January of 1943. They agreed to invade Italy and insisted on the "unconditional surrender' of the Axis powers. This was mainly to reassure the distrustful Soviets that the western powers would not make a separate peace with Germany, leaving Russia to fight alone.

Stalingrad. The Soviets had been badly mauled by the German invasion in 1941, but Hitler made many mistakes and Stalin, in contrast, made some smart moves. Hitler established a policy of terror among the people he conquered in the east. Thus, the people who rejoiced at freedom from communism quickly realized they had a worse master with Hitler. Whole villages were destroyed for minor or imagined offenses. The people of eastern Europe and Russia quickly became hardened to fight this oppressor. Stalin, in the meantime, freed his capable generals and gave them the power they needed to act. He also appealed to the Russian people, not to save communism but to defend "Mother Russia," their homeland. They responded wholeheartedly.

The Russian generals fought a careful war of retreats, trading land for time and waiting for the arrival of their ally, "General Winter." When he arrived in late 1941, it was the coldest winter in over a century. The Russians were prepared for it; however, the Germans were not. Hitler expected the Soviet Union to be conquered before winter. German soldiers did not have warm clothes, and their equipment would not run. The German advance was halted. The Russians moved their factories east and built a tremendous army that held off the Germans through 1941 and 1942.

The turning point in the war in Europe occurred at Stalingrad in the winter of 1942–43. Hitler attacked the city in southern Russia in the summer of 1942. The Soviet Red Army defended it house by house, so the Germans were never able to capture it. One of Stalin's best generals, Zhukov, built up an army nearby and waited for a chance to attack. Once the cruel Russian winter had settled in again, he did so, trapping German General Paulus and all of his men. Hitler refused to allow the men to fight their way to safety. They were ordered to stay and fight. They held out for two-and-a-half months before they ran out of supplies and surrendered in January of 1943. This capture of a German army was the first of many as the war now turned in favor of the Allies.

Italy. The Allies moved from North Africa into Italy, attacking Sicily in July of 1943. George Patton and Bernard Montgomery took the island in a month. The Italians had had enough. Mussolini was removed from power and arrested. Italy surrendered in September. The Germans then moved into Italy, rescued Mussolini, set up a puppet government, and fought ferociously. When the Allies invaded the Italian peninsula in September, they were met by the German army. After the free Italian government declared war on Germany in October, Italian troops were disarmed by the Nazis and imprisoned or used as slave labor in their war machine.

The mountains of Italy were easy to defend, and the Germans did a remarkable job. The Allies moved up the peninsula slowly, suffering heavy casualties in a bitter stalemate. The Americans landed a force at Anzio in central Italy in January of 1944, attempting to get around the German defenses. The men were trapped along the shore for four months before they finally were able to move inland. Rome was not captured until June of 1944. The last German troops in Italy finally surrendered in May of 1945, just before Germany itself surrendered.

D-Day. The Soviets continued to demand a second front in northern Europe. Stalin, Churchill and Roosevelt met at Tehran, Iran in late November of 1943. The meeting was called the Tehran Conference. Roosevelt naively trusted Stalin. Churchill did not, but he needed to keep his wartime ally happy. They agreed on a joint assault in Europe for the spring of 1944. The invasion of France was code-named "Over-lord" and put under the command of Eisen-hower. The Allies were finally poised to attack Hitler's "Fortress Europe."

The invasion force was built up in Britain for months. By June of 1944, there were 1.5 million Americans and 1.75 million men from the British Empire. The Germans expected an attack at the Pas-de-Calais, the narrowest part of the English Channel. Eisenhower, therefore, planned his invasion for Normandy, further west and less fortified. The plan called for 175,000 men and their equipment to go ashore the first day. That would be like moving the population of a fair-sized city and their cars across one of the Great Lakes in one night.

The Allies were by that time in complete control of the skies. The *Luftwaffe* (the German air force) had been badly mauled by air attacks from England. They had few trained pilots and were short of fuel. Allied bombers had been regularly attacking German cities and factories. The bombers also destroyed roads, bridges, and other transport leading into Normandy in the weeks before the assault. They provided observation and support without any serious opposition during the invasion.

June 6, 1944 was D-Day, the day of the invasion. The Allies attacked at five locations code named Utah (U.S.), Omaha (U.S.), Gold (British), Juno (Canadian), and Sword (British). All of the landings succeeded under heavy fighting. The Americans took the worst of it at "Bloody Omaha." High cliffs above the beach gave the Germans an excellent opportunity to cover the beach with artillery and machine gun fire. Some of the first units off the boats suffered 90%

| Troops Approaching Normandy Beach; D-Day

casualty rates, but by the end of the day the Allies had a **beachhead** and were soon bringing in supplies using artificial harbors called "Mulberries."

The invasion stalled for more than a month around Normandy in the hedgerow country where thick natural fences of tall bushes made the land easy to defend. Eventually, the Americans learned to put metal teeth on the front of their tanks and go through the hedges. Patton was returned to a command after sitting out, due to the slapping incident in Italy. He pushed south and west as fast as his tanks could go, only stopping when they ran out of gas. The Allies liberated Paris in August of 1944 and captured the first German city in October of 1944. In the meantime, the Soviets were advancing in the east. Germany was now trapped in the middle of two powerful armies.

Battle of the Bulge. Hitler had insanely refused to allow his generals to retreat and set up strong defenses in Germany. He now foolishly gambled everything on one last offensive. On December 16, 1944 he launched an attack against a weak spot in the American lines in Belgium and Luxembourg. It was a complete surprise. The Allies did not believe Germany had the resources to launch another attack.

The Americans were driven back at first, creating a bulge—hence the name—in the Allied lines. The 101st Airborne Division was rushed in to defend the city of Bastogne and was surrounded. The Germans sent a message demanding the Allies' surrender. General Anthony McAuliffe sent a one word reply, "Nuts!" The 101st held out until clear skies allowed airplanes to drop supplies to them on Christmas Eve. They were rescued a few days later when Patton turned north and drove into the German lines to reach them.

The battle lasted a month. The Americans eventually stopped the German army and drove them back. The Germans began to run out of gasoline as the Americans blocked their way. It was the biggest battle in American history, involving about 600,000 U.S. soldiers. It was Hitler's last gasp. He did not have the men or material for another major attack.

V-E Day. Churchill, Roosevelt, and Stalin met one last time at Yalta on the Black Sea in February 1945. The Soviets promised to enter the war with Japan within three months after the fall of Germany (something America desperately wanted). In exchange, the U.S.S.R. was promised several islands and ports in Asia. The Allies also agreed to divide Germany into four occupation zones (American, British, French, and Soviet). The western powers recognized the Soviet-created government in Poland, and Stalin promised to allow free elections in Eastern Europe (a promise he had no intention of keeping). Stalin also got approval for his plan to take part of eastern Poland and give Poland part of Germany in compensation. Many critics still feel Roosevelt gave Stalin too much at Yalta. The U.S.S.R. would maintain puppet governments in east Europe for forty-five years after the war. They would probably have done it without the agreements at Yalta because the Soviet army controlled that land, and only another war would have driven them out.

Churchill urged Eisenhower to go as far east as he could to prevent the Soviets from taking any more of Europe. Eisenhower kept to military rather than political concerns and stopped his army at the Elbe River, the edge of the American zone, to avoid conflict with the Red Army. He also sent his men south into the Alps to prevent the Nazis from establishing fortified bases there. The Soviets captured Berlin on May 2, 1945 after a terrible battle. It was followed by a wild spree of looting and rape by the victorious Red Army.

Hitler had withdrawn to a bunker in Berlin as his empire crumbled around him. On April 30th, he committed suicide. He named Admiral Karl Doenitz as his successor. Doenitz opened negotiations with the Allies and surrendered to them on May 7, 1945. The following day was declared V-E (Victory in Europe) Day. Wild celebrations occurred in the streets of most of the nations of the western world.

Holocaust. As the Americans and Russians pushed into Germany, they learned the true depth of the Nazi horror. In the concentration camps of Buchenwald, Dachau, Auschwitz, and Bergen-Belsen the Allies found men, women, and children who were little more than walking skeletons. They had been used as slave labor for German war production. Worse still were the emaciated bodies, many stacked up in piles like wood. They found gas chambers where thousands of people, mainly Jewish people had been killed.

Jewish people and enemies of the Reich from all over Europe had been shipped to these camps crammed into cattle cars. Children, old people, and the disabled were killed as soon as they arrived. Healthy young people were forced to work with the goal of working them to death. It is estimated that 6 million Jewish people were killed during the Holocaust, but that does not include all of the other groups (like prisoners of war and people with disabilities). This **genocide** was the worst in history.

Rumors of what was going on in the concentration camps had reached the west during the war, but most people thought they were exaggerations. Even if they did believe, there was little anyone could do except win the war and liberate the camps. That is what Churchill and Roosevelt decided was their only course of action if the reports were to be believed.

When Eisenhower found the camps, he realized it was so awful that many people would not believe it was really true. The general sent for reporters, soldiers, Congressmen, and members of Parliament to tour the camps and see for themselves. He even forced the inhabitants of nearby German towns to come and see the truth, which most of them had carefully avoided during the war. "Blood and Guts" Patton got sick to his stomach on his tour. After the war, twenty-two high-level Nazis were tried at Nuremberg for the **atrocities**. Twelve of them were condemned to death. Trials of less important men continued for years.

| Prisoners in the Dachau Concentration Camp in 1938

| Freedom! 1945

Choose the correct letter for each item. Most will be used more than once.

3.39 _____ turning point of the war in Europe

3.40 _____ D-Day, June 6, 1944

3.41 _____ Hitler's last major attack

3.42 _____ six million Jewish people died

3.43 _____ gave the U.S.S.R. part of Poland and
Poland part of Germany

3.44 _____ meeting between Churchill and F.D.R.

3.45 _____ meeting with Churchill, Stalin, and F.D.R.

3.46 _____ first British victory at El Alamein

3.47 _____ Anthony McAuliffe, "Nuts!" to surrender

3.48 _____ Utah, Omaha, Gold, Sword, and Juno

3.49 _____ Germans took over when the nation surrendered in September of 1943

3.50 _____ had to defeat the "wolf packs"

3.51 _____ operation "Torch"

3.52 _____ trapped General Paulus and his army

3.53 _____ allies landed at Anzio, January 1944

3.54 _____ Germans there surrendered just days before Germany did

3.55 _____ used Mulberries to bring in supplies

3.56 _____ radar, sonar, code breaking, and convoys were all used in the victory

3.57 _____ operation "Overlord"

3.58 _____ fascist leader rescued by Germans

3.59 _____ landings took place at Normandy

3.60 _____ General Zhukov was aided by General Winter

3.61 _____ allies demand "unconditional surrender"

3.62 _____ Vichy France troops join the Allies

3.63 _____ Stalin promised to fight Japan three months after Germany was defeated

3.64 _____ attack stalled in hedgerow country

3.65 _____ Eisenhower insisted that all kinds of people come to see the proof for themselves

3.66 _____ Germany was to be divided into four zones

a. Battle of the Atlantic

b. North Africa

c. Stalingrad

d. Italy

e. Invasion of France

f. Battle of the Bulge

g. Holocaust

h. Yalta Conference

i. Casablanca Conference

3.67 _____ Buchenwald, Auschwitz, Dachau

3.68 _____ key victory before the build up of troops in Europe could occur

3.69 _____ Red Army defended the city house by house; it was never captured

3.70 _____ Germans used the mountains to stage a remarkable defense

3.71 _____ Jewish people and enemies of the Reich died

3.72 _____ Sicily taken in one month

3.73 _____ Hitler attacked, summer of 1942; Germans surrender, January 1943

3.74 _____ weak—killed in gas chambers; strong—worked to death

Name the person.

3.75 _____ "Desert Fox"; respected German general

3.76 _____ British general; El Alamein and Sicily

3.77 _____ free French leader

3.78 _____ U.S. Chief of Staff in Washington

3.79 _____ "Blood and Guts"; slapped two soldiers; tank warrior

3.80 _____ committed suicide in his bunker, April 30, 1945

3.81 _____ allied commander for Overlord and Torch

3.82 _____ one of Stalin's best generals

3.83 _____ Hitler's successor; surrendered to the Allies

3.84 _____ Commander of U.S. army in Europe; quiet and stable

Answer these questions.

3.85 Whose army captured Berlin? _____

3.86 Where did the Allied leaders set the plans for the invasion of France?

_____

3.87 Why did Eisenhower stop American and British troops at the Elbe River?

_____

_____

_____

3.88 Who had control of the skies on D-Day? _____

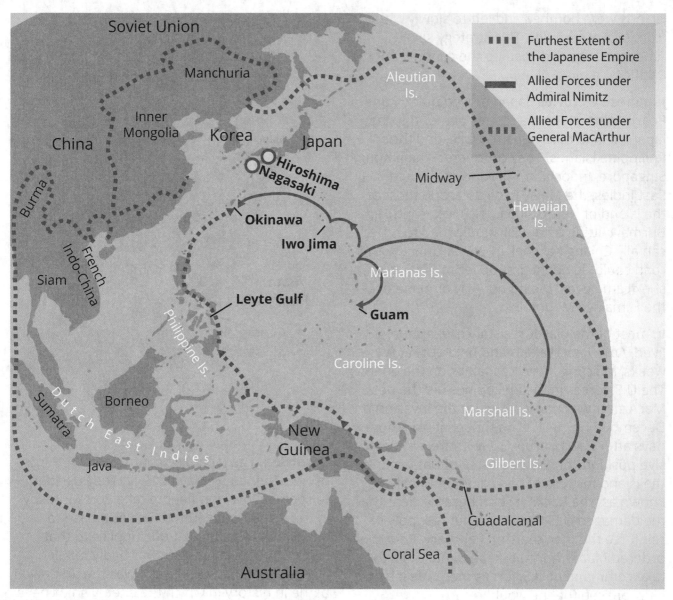

| War In Asia

War in Asia

Commanders. The most famous American commander in Asia was General Douglas MacArthur, who was in command in the Philippines when the war began. Many people believed he should not have been given another command after his poor performance there, but Roosevelt put him in command of the U.S. forces in the South Pacific. He did a remarkable job using his limited manpower during the time America was concentrating on defeating Hitler in Europe.

The U.S. Navy and troops in the central Pacific were under the command of Admiral Chester Nimitz. Nimitz carefully rebuilt the navy after the disaster at Pearl Harbor and insisted on not attacking until he had the ships he needed. His careful approach and confidence restored the badly shaken morale of his men. He formulated much of the American "island hopping" strategy. This strategy avoided the heavily fortified Japanese islands, went around them, and attacked less protected islands. The fortified islands were bombed and left to slowly wither from lack of supplies. This strategy saved American lives and sped up the conquest of the Pacific.

Japanese victories. Japan moved quickly after Pearl Harbor. Within a matter of months, the Japanese had taken Guam, Wake, and the Philippine Islands. They conquered Hong Kong, Singapore, Indochina, Thailand, the Dutch East Indies, the Malay Peninsula, and most of the island of New Guinea. They also captured Burma, cutting off a vital supply road to American ally Chiang Kai-shek in China. Until another road could be opened, supplies to Chiang Kai-shek came over "the hump"—by airplane over the Himalaya Mountains.

In most of the places resistance was short-lived. American Wake Island held out for two weeks, inflicting heavy casualties on the enemy. The U.S. forces in the Philippines did the best. MacArthur was unprepared for the invasion on December 10, 1941, even though it was three days after Pearl Harbor. He withdrew to defensive positions on the peninsula of Bataan and the island fortress of Corregidor in Manila Bay known as "the Rock." It soon became clear that the damaged U.S. fleet could not resupply or reinforce the men there. In February, Roosevelt ordered MacArthur to escape to Australia to take command of U.S. forces there. He left, but he promised that he would return.

The American and Filipino forces on the peninsula fought on until April 6th. By then they were almost out of ammunition and were half starved from lack of food. When they surrendered, the Japanese forced them to march sixty miles to a railroad in what became known as the "Bataan Death March." Men who collapsed along the way were murdered. Thousands died. The last American troops on Corregidor under Gen. Jonathan Wainwright surrendered on May 6, 1942. Thousands of these men later died in the brutal Japanese prison camps.

Coral Sea. The Japanese controlled two-thirds of New Guinea by May of 1942. They decided to send an invasion fleet to take Port Moresby in the Allied-held south to use as a base to attack Australia and cut off supplies to that nation. The invasion fleet was badly mauled at the Battle of the Coral Sea. It was the first naval battle in history in which the enemy ships never saw each other. It was fought completely by planes from the aircraft carriers that had survived the attack on Pearl Harbor. The battle was technically a Japanese victory because the U.S. lost the carrier *Lexington* while Japanese losses were less severe, but the invasion fleet turned back, so the "victory" was meaningless.

Doolittle's Raid. U.S. strategy required the nation to send most of its resources to Europe in 1942, but Americans were clamoring for some action against Japan. Under the command of Col. James Doolittle, sixteen modified B-25 bombers took off from an aircraft carrier on April 18, 1942 on a one-way trip. They dropped bombs on Tokyo and then tried to reach China. Most of the airmen survived crash landings and made it safely back to the U.S. The raid had no strategic value, but it gave American morale a tremendous boost in those dark months. It was also a great shock to the Japanese military who never dreamed the Americans could reach their capital.

Midway. The Japanese sent a large fleet to capture Midway Island in June of 1942. The island north of Hawaii would have given Japan an advance base for attacks on the United States. American intelligence, however, had broken the Japanese code and knew the attack was coming. Nimitz set a trap. The American fleet was outnumbered 48 ships to about 200. Surprise was essential and the Americans got it. They succeeded in attacking the Japanese carriers while their planes were on the decks. The Japanese lost four carriers and more than two hundred planes. The U.S. lost the carrier *Yorktown* and more than 150 planes, but it was a clear American victory. It was also the turning point of the war in Asia. From Midway until the end of the war, the Japanese would experience one defeat after another.

New Guinea. After their failure at the Coral Sea, the Japanese tried to take New Guinea in the summer of 1942 with an attack over the central mountains. They were driven back by November. In the meantime, MacArthur began the reconquest of the island. Using a series of brilliant landings at key points on the coast, he slowly worked his way along the island. Each point he captured was used as a base to attack the next point, a technique that would be used in "island hopping." Fighting continued on the island until the middle of 1944.

Guadalcanal. The Americans began their island campaign with an attack on Guadalcanal in the Solomon Islands southwest of New Guinea on August 7, 1942. They were after a Japanese airbase on the island, which they took quickly. The rest of the island, however, took almost six months to capture. The Americans only won when they finally gained control of the seas around the island and cut off supplies to the Japanese army there. Twenty-five thousand Japanese and fifteen hundred Americans died in the battle.

Island hopping. Guadalcanal gave the Americans a good look at the kind of fighting they would face in the island campaign. The Japanese code of honor required their soldiers to fight to the death. Capture was dishonorable, so very few surrendered. They would dig fortifications all over the islands they held and fight as long as they could. When faced with defeat, they often made suicidal mass charges into enemy fire. Japanese-held islands had to be taken foot by foot, often with hand-to-hand fighting and heavy casualties. The islands were often covered with jungles, giving the Japanese thousands of places to hide and wait for the Americans.

The island attacks would begin with a heavy bombardment from planes and warships. Then an amphibious force (Marines or Army) would "hit the beach." They would slowly drive inland, killing the Japanese since they would not surrender. Right behind them, the navy's Construction Battalion—the Seabees (C.B.'s)—would come in and quickly build an airbase. The new base would be used to bring in supplies and men to bomb the next target, moving ever closer to Japan. As hard as the Japanese fought, they never held any island after the Americans landed. It was always just a matter of time and manpower.

American forces moved steadily north and east from 1942 to 1945. The tiny island of Tarawa, in the Gilbert Islands, was the site of one of the bloodiest fights of the war. The island was taken in four days on November 1943. It cost the lives of almost a thousand U.S. Marines. Out of the 20,000 Japanese soldiers, only 17 surrendered! On islands such as Guam, Tianian, Makin, Peleliu, and Eniwetok, the story was the same—an American victory after a suicidal Japanese defense.

During the June 1944 invasion of Saipan in the Marianas Islands, the American navy was able to corner a large Japanese fleet during the Battle of the Philippine Sea. It became known as the "great Marianas turkey shoot" because a large portion of the fighting strength of the Japanese navy was so easily destroyed. When it was over, Japan had lost three aircraft carriers and almost 500 planes. American losses were minor. Control of the Marianas meant the Americans were within bombing range of Japan. Long-range B-29's would bomb the Japanese cities until the end of the war.

The Americans ran into another horror on Saipan. Japanese civilians who lived on those islands had been told that the Americans were devils who would torture them unmercifully. When it was clear the island was going to be taken, the civilians began to kill themselves. Mothers threw their children off the sea cliffs. Adults blew themselves up with grenades. Hundreds of civilians and soldiers died, including approximately 30,000 soldiers who were defending the island.

Philippines. MacArthur fulfilled his promise when Leyte in the Philippines was invaded, and he followed his men in on October 20, 1944. The Japanese sent most of their remaining ships to oppose the invasion. At the Battle of Leyte Gulf, one of the largest naval battles in history, the Japanese fleet was destroyed as an effective fighting force. It was not a major factor in the fighting for the rest of the war.

However, the Japanese introduced one very damaging weapon at Leyte Gulf—the *kamikaze*. These were suicide planes loaded with explosives that dove into American ships. They were essentially human-guided bombs. They caused tremendous damage to the U.S. fleet, sinking or damaging about 300 ships in the last year of the war; however, it was not enough to save Japan.

The battle for the Philippines was as fierce as previous fights. The Japanese forced the U.S. troops to take the capital of Manila house by

| Island Warfare

house. By the end of the fighting, the city had been reduced to rubble. Over 300,000 Japanese and 14,000 American soldiers died in the Philippines. Some of the Japanese fell back into the jungle and fought until the end of the war. A few were still hiding there as late as the 1970s.

Mainland Asia. The Nationalist Chinese under Chiang Kai-shek were never a match for the Japanese. Moreover, they were often more interested in fighting the Communist Chinese under Mao Tse-tung than the Japanese, but they did keep thousands of Japanese soldiers busy in China. The U.S. helped the Nationalists with supplies and advisors throughout the war.

The British commanded the Allied effort in Southeast Asia. They conducted a successful campaign against the Japanese in Burma during 1943 and 1944. They reopened a badly needed land supply route to China in January of 1945 and captured the Burmese capital that spring.

Closing in. Submarines and airplanes began to put tremendous pressure on Japan by 1945. The submarines sank a heavy percentage of Japanese merchant ships, depriving the island of needed supplies. Bombers engaged in a campaign intended to do nothing less than destroy the Japanese cities. **Incendiary** bombs did incredible damage to the mainly wooden buildings. A large section of Tokyo was destroyed by such a bombing raid in March of 1945.

In February of 1945, the U.S. Marines attacked the island of Iwo Jima between the Marianas and Japan. It was needed as an airbase for fighters to protect the bombers and as an emergency landing field. It was a volcanic island honeycombed with caves, and the Japanese defended almost every one of them. Most of the defenders had to be burned out with flame-throwers one cave at a time. The eight- square-mile island took almost a month to capture, and nearly 7,000 Marines died. Almost 21,000 Japanese died defending Iwo Jima.

On April 1, 1945 the Americans attacked Oki-nawa, an island just 350 miles south of Japan. It had a good harbor and was expected to serve as a base for the invasion of Japan. The enemy defended it fanatically. More than 300,000 Americans participated in the battle, and 49,000 were wounded or killed. Over 110,000 Japanese died. The death toll included many frightened civilians who committed suicide. The navy supported the invasion in spite of heavy damage from kamikaze fighters. The island was secured by June.

Japan was trapped, but there was little hope it would surrender. Experts fully expected the Japanese to defend their homeland even more fanatically than they had their empire. They estimated that the invasion of Japan would cost a million casualties. The new U.S. president, Harry Truman, considered an alternative.

Manhattan Project. Early in the war, America became concerned that Germany would develop an atomic bomb. The Nazi scientists were some of the best in the world, and they were doing the necessary research. Therefore, F.D.R. authorized a top secret program named the Manhattan Project to develop such a bomb for the U.S. Using American industrial power and scientists, many of whom had escaped from Europe, the project successfully exploded

| The Blast that Destroyed Hiroshima

an atomic bomb in the desert of New Mexico on July 16, 1945. Two of the bombs were made and delivered to the U.S. forces in Asia.

President Truman, who was at Potsdam, near Berlin, received word of the successful test. He was attending the last of the major Allied leadership conferences of the war. Stalin was there as was Clement Attlee, who had just been elected Prime Minister of Britain. Little was accomplished. The U.S. was still urging Stalin to declare war on Japan. With the bomb ready, however, Truman issued the Potsdam Declaration, it called for Japan to surrender or face "prompt and utter destruction." Japan refused.

Truman decided to use the bombs on Japan. He hoped it would force a surrender and save thousands, if not millions of lives. On August 6, 1945 the bomber *Enola Gay* dropped an atomic bomb on the city of Hiroshima. Estimates are that between 70,000 and 100,000 people died from the bomb. Some were vaporized instantly, others died later of radiation burns and poisoning. Years later, cancer deaths from the radiation killed even more. On August 8th, the Soviet Union declared war on Japan and swept into northern China. On August 9th another bomb was dropped on the city of Nagasaki. Japan sued for peace on August 10th. The official surrender was signed on September 2, 1945 on board the *U.S.S. Missouri* in Tokyo Bay. Japan was occupied and MacArthur was appointed as military commander of the nation.

Results. An estimated fifty-three million people died in World War II. Germany and Japan were defeated, but those nations were in ruins, their people starving. This war finally surpassed the Civil War for American dead. More than 400,000 died out of more than a million casualties. Europe was devastated. The U.S. was now the most powerful nation on earth, but it had a rival. The Union of Soviet Socialist Republics controlled most of eastern Europe and northern Asia and had no intention of letting them go free. The rivalry between the U.S. and the U.S.S.R. called the Cold War would define the next forty-five years.

 Name the person, battle, or item.

3.89 _____ island in Solomons taken in a six-month battle; 1942–43

3.90 _____ naval battle near the Philippines; one of the largest in history; destroyed the Japanese fleet as an effective fighting force

3.91 _____ American strategy of bypassing fortified islands, using one captured island as a base to attack another nearer to Japan

3.92 _____ trap for the Japanese navy; turning point of Pacific war

3.93 _____ Commander of U.S. fleet in the Pacific; rebuilt it after Pearl Harbor

3.94 _____ Tokyo bombed on April 18, 1942 using a one-way trip

3.95 _____ American ally in China

3.96 _____ volcanic island between Marianas and Japan taken by the U.S. Marines; 8 square miles; took a month to secure

3.97 _____ code name for U.S. effort to produce an atomic bomb

3.98 _____ American commander of the Philippines; the reconquest of New Guinea and the occupation of Japan

3.99 _____ thousands of Americans and Filipinos died after being forced to walk to a railroad after surrendering in April 1942

3.100 _____ after the fall of Burma, U.S. supplies to China came over this "hump"

3.101 _____ date the first atomic bomb was exploded

3.102 _____ the "great Marianas turkey shoot"

3.103 _____ Japanese planes loaded with explosives flown on suicide missions into U.S. ships

3.104 _____ first naval battle in history where the ships did not see each other; Japanese invasion of Port Moresby prevented

3.105 _____ last leadership conference of the war; Stalin, Truman, and Attlee

3.106 _____ islands captured in 1944 which put the U.S. in bomber range of Japan

3.107 _____ cities hit by atomic bombs
_____

3.108 _____ total number of people believed to have died in World War II

3.109 _____ island fortress in Manila Bay; last U.S. troops surrendered there in May 1942

3.110 _____ Navy men who quickly built bases on captured islands

3.111 _____ tiny Gilbert island that took four days and a thousand American lives to capture

3.112 _____ island 350 miles from Japan was to be used as invasion base; 110,000 Japanese dead

Complete these items.

3.113 Name five of the places taken by Japan shortly after Pearl Harbor.

_____

_____

3.114 Why were Japanese-held islands so difficult for Americans to capture?

_____

_____

3.115 What was the horrifying reaction of many Japanese civilians to an American victory?

_____

3.116 How long before the Japanese surrender did the U.S.S.R. declare war on Japan?

_____

Before you take this last Self Test, you may want to do one or more of these self checks.

1. _____ Read the objectives. See if you can do them.

2. _____ Restudy the material related to any objectives that you cannot do.

3. _____ Use the **SQ3R** study procedure to review the material:

    a. **S**can the sections.

    b. **Q**uestion yourself.

    c. **R**ead to answer your questions.

    d. **R**ecite the answers to yourself.

    e. **R**eview areas you did not understand.

4. _____ Review all vocabulary, activities, and Self Tests, writing a correct answer for every wrong answer.

SELF TEST 3

Match these people (each answer, 2 points).

3.01 _____ British general; El Alamein and Sicily

3.02 _____ American general; World War I

3.03 _____ Nationalist Chinese leader

3.04 _____ Soviet dictator

3.05 _____ Admiral of the U.S. Navy in the Pacific

3.06 _____ U.S. general; Philippines; New Guinea; occupation of Japan

3.07 _____ fascist dictator of Italy

3.08 _____ free French leader

3.09 _____ Supreme Allied commander in Europe

3.010 _____ aggressive U.S. tank commander; North Africa and Sicily

a. John Pershing
b. Chester Nimitz
c. Dwight D. Eisenhower
d. Joseph Stalin
e. Bernard Montgomery
f. Douglas MacArthur
g. George Patton
h. Benito Mussolini
i. Charles de Gaulle
j. Chiang Kai-shek

Name the person, battle, nation, or item (each answer, 3 points).

3.011 _____ dictator of Germany during World War II

3.012 _____ President of the U.S. during most of World War II

3.013 _____ Prime Minister of Britain during most of World War II

3.014 _____ attack that brought the U.S. into World War II

3.015 _____ attempt to quiet the dictators' demands by giving them what they wanted, especially at Munich in 1938

3.016 _____ only nation still fighting Germany after the fall of France in 1940

3.017 _____ Americans removed from the west coast and put in internment camps

3.018 _____ Nazi lightning war

3.019 _____ turning point of World War II in Europe

3.020 _____ turning point of World War II in Asia

3.021 _____ main type of warfare in World War I

3.022 _____ American strategy in the Pacific in World War II

3.023 _____ Hitler's last major offensive against the American lines in Belgium and Luxembourg in December 1944

3.024 _____ millions of Jewish people and Nazi enemies died in concentration camps

3.025 _____ one-way bombing raid on Tokyo in April of 1942

Answer these questions (each answer, 3 points).

3.026 What event started the Great Depression? _____

3.027 Why did America get into World War I? _____

3.028 What were the three major WWII invasions by the Americans that freed Europe?

List in chronological order: _____

_____

3.029 What event triggered World War I? _____

_____

3.030 What event began World War II? _____

_____

3.031 Why was America the "arsenal of democracy?" _____

_____

3.032 What were the free-living times of the decade of the 1920s called?

_____

3.033 What happened to Hitler at the end of World War II?

_____

3.034 Who controlled eastern Europe at the end of World War II? _____

3.035 What ended the war with Japan in World War II? _____

_____

Answer true or false (each numbered item, 1 point).

3.036 _____ America was united about getting into World War II after the fall of France.

3.037 _____ Americans got into World War II as an idealist crusade to "make the world safe for democracy."

3.038 _____ Roosevelt's New Deal pulled the U.S. out of the Great Depression.

3.039 _____ The Soviets were aided in stopping the Germans in World War II by the harsh Russian winters.

3.040 _____ German Americans were moved out of the east coast of the U.S. and put in internment camps in California during World War II.

80/100   SCORE _____   TEACHER _____ _____
initials   date

Before taking the LIFEPAC Test, you may want to do one or more of these self checks.

1. _____ Read the objectives. See if you can do them.
2. _____ Restudy the material related to any objectives that you cannot do.
3. _____ Use the **SQ3R** study procedure to review the material.
4. _____ Review activities, Self Tests, and LIFEPAC vocabulary words.
5. _____ Restudy areas of weakness indicated by the last Self Test.

NOTES